SPECIAL INDIAN EDITION

INTRODUCTION TO CHEMICAL ENGINEERING THERMODYNAMICS

SI Units

SEVENTH EDITION

McGraw-Hill Chemical Engineering Series

Coughanowr and LeBlanc: *Process Systems Analysis and Control*
Davis and Davis: *Fundamentals of Chemical Reaction Engineering*
de Nevers: *Air Pollution Control Engineering*
de Nevers: *Fluid Mechanics for Chemical Engineers*
Douglas: *Conceptual Design of Chemical Processes*
Edgar, Himmelblau, and Lasdon: *Optimization of Chemical Processes*
Marlin: Process Control: *Designing Processes and Control Systems for Dynamic Performance*
McCabe, Smith, and Harriott: *Unit Operations of Chemical Engineering*
Perry and Green: *Perry's Chemical Engineers' Handbook*
Peters, Timmerhaus, and West: *Plant Design and Economics for Chemical Engineers*
Smith, Van Ness, and Abbott: *Introduction to Chemical Engineering Thermodynamics*

The Founding of a Discipline: The McGraw-Hill Companies, Inc., Series in Chemical Engineering

Over 80 years ago, fifteen prominent chemical engineers met in New York to plan a continuing literature for their rapidly growing profession. From industry came such pioneer practioners as Leo H. Baekeland, Arthur D. Little, Charles L. Reese, John V. N. Dorr, M. C. Whitaker, and R. S. McBride. From the universities came such eminent educators as William H. Walker, Alfred H. White, D. D. Jackson, J. H. James, Warren K. Lewis, and Harry A. Curtis. H. C. Parmlee, then editor of *Chemical and Metallurgical Engineering,* served as chairman and was joined subsequently by S. D. Kirkpatrick as consulting editor.

After several meetings, this committee submitted its report to the McGraw-Hill Book Company in September 1925. In the report were detailed specifications for a correlated series of more than a dozen texts and reference books which became the McGraw-Hill Series in Chemical Engineering—and in turn became the cornerstone of the chemical engineering curricula.

From this beginning, a series of texts has evolved, surpassing the scope and longevity envisioned by the founding Editorial Board. The McGraw-Hill Series in Chemical Engineering stands as a unique historical record of the development of chemical engineering education and practice. In the series one finds milestones of the subject's evolution: industrial chemistry, stoichiometry, unit operations and processes, thermodynamics, kinetics, and transfer operations.

Textbooks such as McCabe et al, *Unit Operations of Chemical Engineering,* Smith et al, *Introduction to Chemical Engineering Thermodynamics,* and Peters et al, *Plant Design and Economics for Chemical Engineers* have taught generations of students principles that are key to success in chemical engineering. Juan de Pablo, Jay Schieber, and Regina Murphy, McGraw-Hill's next band of classic authors, will lead students worldwide toward the latest developments in chemical engineering.

Chemical engineering is a dynamic profession and its literature continues to grow. McGraw-Hill, with its in-house editors and consulting editors Eduardo Glandt [Dean, Univ. of Pennsylvania], Michael Klein [Dean, Rutgers Univ.], and Thomas Edgar [Professor, Univ. of Texas at Austin] remains committed to a publishing policy that will serve the needs of the global chemical engineering profession throughout the years to come.

INTRODUCTION TO CHEMICAL ENGINEERING THERMODYNAMICS

SI Units

SEVENTH EDITION

J M Smith
Professor Emeritus of Chemical Engineering
University of California,Davis

H C Van Ness
Institute Professor Emeritus of Chemical Engineering
Rensselaer Polytechnic Institute

M M Abbott
Professor of Chemical Engineering
Rensselaer Polytechnic Institute

Adapted by
B I Bhatt
Consulting Engineer
Aavishkar Consultancy Services
Ahmedabad, Gujarat

McGraw Hill Education (India) Private Limited
NEW DELHI

McGraw Hill Education Offices
New Delhi New York St Louis San Francisco Auckland Bogotá Caracas
Kuala Lumpur Lisbon London Madrid Mexico City Milan Montreal
San Juan Santiago Singapore Sydney Tokyo Toronto

McGraw Hill Education (India) Private Limited

Special Indian Edition 2010

Published in India by arrangement with The McGraw-Hill Companies, Inc., New York

Sales territories: India, Pakistan, Nepal, Bangladesh, Sri Lanka and Bhutan

Introduction to Chemical Engineering Thermodynamics (SIE), 7/e

Fourteenth reprint 2014
RAQQCRQUDRCBC

ISBN (13): 978-0-07-014587-0

ISBN (10): 0-07-014587-3

Managing Director: *Kaushik Bellani*
Head—Higher Education (Publishing and Marketing): *Vibha Mahajan*
Manager—Sponsoring: *Shalini Jha*
Editorial Executive: *Surabhi Shukla*
Executive—Editorial Services: *Sohini Mukherjee*
Senior Production Manager: *P L Pandita*
General Manager—Production: *Rajender P Ghansela*

Published by McGraw Hill Education (India) Private Limited, P-24, Green Park Extension, New Delhi 110 016, Typeset at Mukesh Technologies Pvt. Ltd., #10, 100 Feet Road, Ellapillaichavadi, 605 005 and printed at Adarsh Printers, C-50/51, Mohan Park, Naveen, Shahdara, Delhi 110 032

Cover: SDR

Contents

Preface

Thermodynamics, one of the central subjects of science, is based on laws of universal applicability. The justification for presenting the subject from a chemical-engineering viewpoint is our conviction that it is most effectively taught in the context of the discipline of student commitment.

Although *introductory* in nature, the material of this text should not be thought simple. Indeed, there is no way to make it simple, and a student new to the subject will find that a demanding task of discovery lies ahead. New concepts, words, and symbols appear at a bewildering rate, and here memory plays a part. A far greater challenge is the necessity to develop a capacity to reason and to apply thermodynamic principles in the solution of practical problems. While maintaining the rigor characteristic of sound thermodynamic analysis, we have made every effort to avoid unnecessary mathematical complexity. Moreover, we encourage understanding by writing simple active-voice, present-tense sentences. We can hardly supply the required motivation, but our objective, as it has been for all previous editions, is a treatment that may be understood by any student willing to exercise due diligence.

The first two chapters of the book present basic definitions and a development of the first law. Chapters 3 and 4 treat the pressure/volume/temperature behavior of fluids and certain heat effects, allowing early application of the first law to realistic problems. The second law and some of its applications are considered in Chap. 5. A treatment of the thermodynamic properties of pure fluids in Chap. 6 allows general application of the first and second laws, and provides for an expanded treatment of flow processes in Chap. 7. Chapters 8 and 9 deal with power production and refrigeration processes. The remainder of the book, concerned with fluid mixtures, treats topics in the unique domain of chemical-engineering thermodynamics. Chapters 11 and 12 provide a comprehensive exposition of the theory and application of solution thermodynamics. Chemical-reaction equilibrium is covered at length in Chap. 13. Chapter 14 deals with topics in phase equilibria, including an extended treatment of vapor/liquid equilibrium, and adsorption and osmotic equilibria. Chapter 15 treats the thermodynamic analysis of real processes, affording a review of much of the practical subject matter of thermodynamics.

The material of these 15 chapters is more than adequate for an academic-year undergraduate course, and discretion, conditioned by the content of other courses, is required in the choice of what is covered. The first 13 chapters include material thought necessary as part of any chemical engineer's education. Where only a single-semester course in chemical-engineering thermodynamics is provided, these 13 chapters may represent sufficient content.

The laws and principles of classical thermodynamics do not depend on any particular model of the structure of matter; they are free of any molecular considerations. However, the behavior exhibited by matter— gases, liquids, and solids— does depend on its particulate nature, and in Chapter 16 we present an introduction to molecular thermodynamics, to which reference is occasionally made in earlier chapters.

The book is comprehensive enough to make it a useful reference both in graduate courses and for professional practice. However, length considerations make necessary a prudent selectivity. Thus, we do not include certain topics worthy of attention, but of a specialized nature. These include applications to polymers, electrolytes, and biomaterials.

We are indebted to many individuals— students, professors, reviewers— who have contributed in various ways to the quality of this seventh edition, directly and indirectly, through question and comment, praise and criticism, over the 55 years and seven editions of its evolution. To all we extend our thanks.

J M Smith
H C Van Ness
M M Abbott

List of Symbols

A	Area
A	Molar or specific Helmholtz energy $\equiv U - TS$
A	Parameter, empirical equations, e.g., Eq. (4.4), Eq. (6.76), Eq. (12.14)
a	Acceleration
a	Molar area, adsorbed phase
a	Parameter, cubic equations of state
$\bar{a}_i$	Partial parameter, cubic equations of state
B	Second virial coefficient, density expansion
B	Parameter, empirical equations, e.g., Eq. (4.4), Eq. (6.76), Eq. (12.14)
$\hat{B}$	Reduced second-virial coefficient, defined by Eq. (3.62)
B'	Second virial coefficient, pressure expansion
B^0, B^1	Functions, generalized second-virial-coefficient correlation
B_{ij}	Interaction second virial coefficient
b	Parameter, cubic equations of state
$\bar{b}_i$	Partial parameter, cubic equations of state
C	Third virial coefficient, density expansion
C	Parameter, empirical equations, e.g., Eq. (4.4), Eq. (6.76), Eq. (12.14)
$\hat{C}$	Reduced third-virial coefficient, defined on p. 103
C'	Third virial coefficient, pressure expansion
C^0, C^1	Functions, generalized third-virial-coefficient correlation
C_P	Molar or specific heat capacity, constant pressure
C_V	Molar or specific heat capacity, constant volume
C_P°	Standard-state heat capacity, constant pressure
ΔC_P°	Standard heat-capacity change of reaction
$\langle C_P \rangle_H$	Mean heat capacity, enthalpy calculations
$\langle C_P \rangle_S$	Mean heat capacity, entropy calculations
$\langle C_P^\circ \rangle_H$	Mean standard heat capacity, enthalpy calculations
$\langle C_P^\circ \rangle_S$	Mean standard heat capacity, entropy calculations
c	Speed of sound
D	Fourth virial coefficient, density expansion
D	Parameter, empirical equations, e.g., Eq. (4.4), Eq. (6.77)
D'	Fourth virial coefficient, pressure expansion
E_i	Energy level
E_K	Kinetic energy
E_P	Gravitational potential energy
F	Degrees of freedom, phase rule

F	Force
$\mathcal{F}$	Faraday's constant
f_i	Fugacity, pure species i
f_i°	Standard-sate fugacity
$\hat{f}_i$	Fugacity, species i in solution
G	Molar or specific Gibbs energy $\equiv H - TS$
G_i°	Standard-state Gibbs energy, species i
$\bar{G}_i$	Partial Gibbs energy, species i in solution
G^E	Excess Gibbs energy $\equiv G - G^{id}$
G^R	Residual Gibbs energy $\equiv G - G^{ig}$
ΔG	Gibbs-energy change of mixing
ΔG°	Standard Gibbs-energy change of reaction
ΔG_f°	Standard Gibbs-energy change of formation
g	Local acceleration of gravity
g_c	Dimensional constant = 9.806 65 kg m kgf^{-1} s^{-2}
g_i	Degeneracy
H	Molar or specific enthalpy $\equiv U + PV$
$\mathcal{H}_i$	Henry's constant, species i in solution
H_i°	Standard-state enthalpy, pure species i
$\bar{H}_i$	Partial enthalpy, species i in solution
H^E	Excess enthalpy $\equiv H - H^{id}$
H^R	Residual enthalpy $\equiv H - H^{ig}$
$(H^R)^0, (H^R)^1$	Functions, generalized residual-enthalpy correlation
ΔH	Enthalpy change ("heat") of mixing; also, latent heat of phase transition
$\widetilde{\Delta H}$	Heat of solution
ΔH°	Standard enthalpy change of reaction
ΔH_0°	Standard heat of reaction at reference temperature T_0
ΔH_f°	Standard enthalpy change of formation
h	Planck's constant
I	Represents an integral, defined, e.g., by Eqs. (6.65)
I	First ionization potential
K_j	Equilibrium constant, chemical reaction j
K_i	Vapor/liquid equilibrium ratio, species $i \equiv y_i/x_i$
k	Boltzmann's constant
$\mathcal{L}$	Molar fraction of system that is liquid
l	Length
l_{ij}	Equation-of-state interaction parameter, Eq. (14.101)
M	Mach number
M	Molar mass (molecular weight)
M	Molar or specific value, extensive thermodynamic property
$\bar{M}_i$	Partial property, species i in solution
M^E	Excess property $\equiv M - M^{id}$
M^R	Residual property $\equiv M - M^{ig}$
ΔM	Property change of mixing

ΔM°	Standard property change of reaction
ΔM_f°	Standard property change of formation
m	Mass
$\dot{m}$	Mass flowrate
N	Number of chemical species, phase rule
N_A	Avogadro's number
n	Number of moles
$\dot{n}$	Molar flowrate
$\tilde{n}$	Moles of solvent per mole of solute
n_i	Number of moles, species i
P	Absolute pressure
P°	Standard-state pressure
P_c	Critical pressure
P_r	Reduced pressure
P_r^0, P_r^1	Functions, generalized vapor-pressure correlation
P_0	Reference pressure
p_i	Partial pressure, species i
P_i^{sat}	Saturation vapor pressure, species i
Q	Heat
$\dot{Q}$	Rate of heat transfer
q	Volumetric flowrate
q	Parameter, cubic equations of state
q	Electric charge
$\bar{q}_i$	Partial parameter, cubic equations of state
R	Universal gas constant (Table A.2)
r	Compression ratio
r	Intermolecular separation
r	Number of independent chemical reactions, phase rule
S	Molar or specific entropy
$\bar{S}_i$	Partial entropy, species i in solution
S^E	Excess entropy $\equiv S - S^{id}$
S^R	Residual entropy $\equiv S - S^{ig}$
$(S^R)^0$, $(S^R)^1$	Functions, generalized residual-entropy correlation
S_G	Entropy generation per unit amount of fluid
$\dot{S}_G$	Rate of entropy generation
ΔS	Entropy change of mixing
ΔS°	Standard entropy change of reaction
ΔS_f°	Standard entropy change of formation
T	Absolute temperature, kelvins or rankines
T_c	Critical temperature
T_n	Normal-boiling-point temperature
T_r	Reduced temperature
T_0	Reference temperature
T_σ	Absolute temperature of surroundings
T_i^{sat}	Saturation temperature, species i

t	Temperature, °C or (°F)
t	Time
U	Molar or specific internal energy
$\mathcal{U}$	Intermolecular pair-potential function
u	Velocity
V	Molar or specific volume
$\mathcal{V}$	Molar fraction of system that is vapor
$\bar{V}_i$	Partial volume, species i in solution
V_c	Critical volume
V_r	Reduced volume
V^E	Excess volume $\equiv V - V^{id}$
V^R	Residual volume $\equiv V - V^{ig}$
ΔV	Volume change of mixing; also, volume change of phase transition
W	Work
$\dot{W}$	Work rate (power)
W_{ideal}	Ideal work
$\dot{W}_{\text{ideal}}$	Ideal-work rate
W_{lost}	Lost work
$\dot{W}_{\text{lost}}$	Lost-work rate
W_s	Shaft work for flow process
$\dot{W}_s$	Shaft power for flow process
x_i	Mole fraction, species i, liquid phase or general
x^v	Quality (mass fraction vapor in vapor-liquid mixture)
y_i	Mole fraction, species i, vapor phase
Z	Compressibility factor $\equiv PV/RT$
Z_c	Critical compressibility factor $\equiv P_c V_c / RT_c$
Z^0, Z^1	Functions, generalized compressibility-factor correlation
$\mathcal{Z}$	Partition function
z	Adsorbed phase compressibility factor, defined by Eq. (14.108)
z	Elevation above a datum level
z_i	Overall mole fraction or mole fraction in a solid phase

Superscripts

E	Denotes excess thermodynamic property
av	Denotes phase transition from adsorbed phase to vapor
id	Denotes value for an ideal solution
ig	Denotes value for an ideal gas
l	Denotes liquid phase
lv	Denotes phase transition from liquid to vapor
R	Denotes residual thermodynamic property
s	Denotes solid phase
sl	Denotes phase transition from solid to liquid
t	Denotes a total value of an extensive thermodynamic property
v	Denotes vapor phase
∞	Denotes a value at infinite dilution

Greek letters

α	Function, cubic equations of state (Table 3.1, p. 98)
α	Polarizability
α,β	As superscripts, identify phases
$\alpha\beta$	As superscript, denotes phase transition from phase α to phase β
β	Volume expansivity
β	Parameter, cubic equations of state
Γ_i	Integration constant
γ	Ratio of heat capacities C_P/C_V
γ_i	Activity coefficient, species i in solution
δ	Polytropic exponent
ϵ	Constant, cubic equations of state
ϵ	Well depth, intermolecular potential function
ϵ_0	Electric permittivity of vacuum
ε	Reaction coordinate
η	Efficiency
κ	Isothermal compressibility
Π	Spreading pressure, adsorbed phase
Π	Osmotic pressure
π	Number of phases, phase rule
μ	Joule/Thomson coefficient
μ	Dipole moment
μ_i	Chemical potential, species i
ν_i	Stoichiometric number, species i
ρ	Molar or specific density $\equiv 1/V$
ρ_c	Critical density
ρ_r	Reduced density
σ	Constant, cubic equations of state
σ	Molecular collision diameter
τ	Temperature ratio $\equiv T/T_0$ [In Eq. (6.77), $\tau \equiv 1 - T_r$]
Φ_i	Ratio of fugacity coefficients, defined by Eq. (14.2)
ϕ_i	Fugacity coefficient, pure species i
$\hat{\phi}_i$	Fugacity coefficient, species i in solution
ϕ^0, ϕ^1	Functions, generalized fugacity-coefficient correlation
Ψ, Ω	Constants, cubic equations of state
ω	Acentric factor

Notes

cv	As a subscript, denotes a control volume
fs	As a subscript, denotes flowing streams
$\circ$	As a superscript, denotes the standard state
$\bar{}$	Overbar denotes a partial property
$\cdot$	Overdot denotes a time rate
$\hat{}$	Circumflex denotes a property in solution
Δ	Difference operator

Chapter 1

Introduction

1.1 THE SCOPE OF THERMODYNAMICS

The science of thermodynamics was born in the nineteenth century of the need to describe the operation of steam engines and to set forth the limits of what they can accomplish. Thus the name itself denotes power developed from heat, with obvious application to heat engines, of which the steam engine was the initial example. However, the principles observed to be valid for engines are readily generalized, and are known as the first and second laws of thermodynamics. These laws have no proof in the mathematical sense; their validity lies in the absence of contrary experience. Thus thermodynamics shares with mechanics and electromagnetism a basis in primitive laws.

These laws lead through mathematical deduction to a network of equations which find application in all branches of science and engineering. The chemical engineer copes with a particularly wide variety of problems. Among them are calculation of heat and work requirements for physical and chemical processes, and the determination of equilibrium conditions for chemical reactions and for the transfer of chemical species between phases.

Thermodynamic considerations do not establish the *rates* of chemical or physical processes. Rates depend on driving force and resistance. Although driving forces are thermodynamic variables, resistances are not. Neither can thermodynamics, a macroscopic-property formulation, reveal the microscopic (molecular) mechanisms of physical or chemical processes. On the other hand, knowledge of the microscopic behavior of matter can be useful in the calculation of thermodynamic properties.[1] Property values are essential to the practical application of thermodynamics. The chemical engineer deals with many chemical species, and experimental data are often lacking. This has led to development of "generalized correlations" that provide property estimates in the absence of data.

The application of thermodynamics to any real problem starts with the identification of a particular body of matter as the focus of attention. This body of matter is called the *system*, and its thermodynamic state is defined by a few measurable macroscopic properties. These depend on the fundamental *dimensions* of science, of which length, time, mass, temperature, and amount of substance are of interest here.

[1] An elementary treatment is presented in Chap. 16.

1.2 DIMENSIONS AND UNITS

The *fundamental* dimensions are *primitives*, recognized through our sensory perceptions and not definable in terms of anything simpler. Their use, however, requires the definition of arbitrary scales of measure, divided into specific *units* of size. Primary units have been set by international agreement, and are codified as the International System of Units (abbreviated SI, for Système International).

The *second*, symbol s, the SI unit of time, is the duration of 9192 631 770 cycles of radiation associated with a specified transition of the caesium atom. The *meter*, symbol m, is the fundamental unit of length, defined as the distance light travels in a vacuum during 1/299 792 458 of a second. The *kilogram*, symbol kg, is the mass of a platinum/iridium cylinder kept at the International Bureau of Weights and Measures at Sèvres, France. The unit of temperature is the *kelvin*, symbol K, equal to 1/273.16 of the thermodynamic temperature of the triple point of water. A detailed discussion of temperature, the characteristic dimension of thermodynamics, is given in Sec. 1.5. The *mole*, symbol mol, is defined as the amount of substance represented by as many elementary entities (e.g., molecules) as there are atoms in 0.012 kg of carbon-12. This is equivalent to the "gram mole" commonly used by chemists.

Multiples and decimal fractions of SI units are designated by prefixes. Those in common use are listed in Table 1.1. Thus, the centimeter is given as 1 cm = 10^{-2} m, and the kilogram as 1 kg = 10^3 g.

Table 1.1: Prefixes for SI Units

Multiple	Prefix	Symbol	Multiple	Prefix	Symbol
10^{-24}	yocto	y	10^{1}	deca	da
10^{-21}	zepto	z	10^{2}	hecto	h
10^{-18}	atto	a	10^{3}	kilo	k
10^{-15}	femto	f	10^{6}	mega	M
10^{-12}	pico	p	10^{9}	giga	G
10^{-9}	nano	n	10^{12}	tera	T
10^{-6}	micro	μ	10^{15}	peta	P
10^{-3}	milli	m	10^{18}	exa	E
10^{-2}	centi	c	10^{21}	zetta	Z
10^{-1}	deci	d	10^{24}	yotta	Y

Other systems of units, such as the English engineering system, use units that are related to SI units by fixed conversion factors. Thus, the foot (ft) is defined as 0.3048 m, the pound *mass* (lb_m) as 0.453 592 37 kg, and the pound mole (lb mol) as 453.592 37 mol.

1.3 MEASURES OF AMOUNT OR SIZE

Three measures of amount or size are in common use:

- Mass, m
- Number of moles, n
- Total volume, V^t

These measures for a specific system are in direct proportion to one another. Mass, a *primitive* without definition, may be divided by the molar mass M (commonly called the molecular weight by chemists) to yield number of moles:

$$n = \frac{m}{M} \qquad \text{or} \qquad m = Mn$$

Total volume, representing the size of a system, is a defined quantity given as the product of three lengths. It may be divided by the mass or number of moles of the system to yield *specific* or *molar volume*:

- Specific volume: $$V \equiv \frac{V^t}{m} \qquad \text{or} \qquad V^t = mV$$
- Molar volume: $$V \equiv \frac{V^t}{n} \qquad \text{or} \qquad V^t = nV$$

Specific or molar density is defined as the reciprocal of specific or molar volume: $\rho \equiv V^{-1}$.

These quantities (V and ρ) are independent of the size of a system, and are examples of *intensive* thermodynamic variables. They are functions of the temperature, pressure, and composition of a system, additional quantities that are independent of system size.

1.4 FORCE

The SI unit of force is the *newton*, symbol N, derived from Newton's second law, which expresses force F as the product of mass m and acceleration a; thus $F = ma$. The newton is defined as the force which when applied to a mass of 1 kg produces an acceleration of 1 m s^{-2}; thus the newton is a *derived* unit representing 1 kg m s^{-2}.

In the metric engineering system of units, force is treated as an additional independent dimension along with length, time, and mass. The kilogram *force* (kgf) is defined as that force which accelerates 1 kilogram *mass* at 9.806 65 meters per second per second. Newton's law must here include a dimensional proportionality constant if it is to be reconciled with this definition. Thus, we write

$$F = \frac{1}{g_c} ma$$

whence

$$1 \text{ kgf} = \frac{1}{g_c} \times 1 \text{ kg} \times 9.806\ 65 \text{ m s}^{-2}$$

and

$$g_c = 9.806\ 65 \text{ kg m kgf}^{-1} \text{s}^{-2}$$

The kilogram *force* is equivalent to 9.806 65 N.

Since force and mass are different concepts, a kilogram *force* and a kilogram *mass* are different quantities, and their units do not cancel one another. When an equation contains both units, kgf and kg, the dimensional constant g_c must also appear in the equation to make it dimensionally correct.

Weight properly refers to the force of gravity on a body, and is therefore correctly expressed in newtons or in kilograms *force*. Unfortunately, standards of mass are often called "weights", and the use of a balance to compare masses is called "weighing". Thus, one must discern from the context whether force or mass is meant when the word "weight" is used in a casual or informal way.

Example 1.1

An astronaut weighs 730 N in Houston, Texas, where the local acceleration of gravity is $g = 9.792 \text{ m s}^{-2}$. What are the astronaut's mass and weight on the moon, where $g = 1.67 \text{ m s}^{-2}$?

Solution

With $a = g$, Newton's law is: $F = mg$. Whence,

$$m = \frac{F}{g} = \frac{730 \text{ N}}{9.792 \text{ m s}^{-2}} = 74.55 \text{ N m}^{-1} \text{ s}^{2}$$

Because the newton N has the units kg m s^{-2},

$$m = 74.55 \text{ kg}$$

This *mass* of the astronaut is independent of location, but *weight* depends on the local acceleration of gravity. Thus on the moon the astronaut's weight is:

$$F(\text{moon}) = mg(\text{moon}) = 74.55 \text{ kg} \times 1.67 \text{ m s}^{-2}$$

or $$F(\text{moon}) = 124.5 \text{ kg m s}^{-2} = 124.5 \text{ N}$$

1.5 TEMPERATURE

Temperature is commonly measured with liquid-in-glass thermometers, wherein the liquid expands when heated. Thus a uniform tube, partially filled with mercury, alcohol, or some other fluid, can indicate degree of "hotness" simply by the length of the fluid column. However, numerical values are assigned to the various degrees of hotness by arbitrary definition.

For the Celsius[2] scale, the ice point (freezing point of water saturated with air at standard atmospheric pressure) is zero, and the steam point (boiling point of pure water at standard

[2]Anders Celsius, Swedish astronomer (1701–1744).

atmospheric pressure) is 100. A thermometer may be given a numerical scale by immersing it in an ice bath and making a mark for zero at the fluid level, and then immersing it in boiling water and making a mark for 100 at this greater fluid level. The distance between the two marks is divided into 100 equal spaces called *degrees*. Other spaces of equal size may be marked off below zero and above 100 to extend the range of the thermometer.

All thermometers, regardless of fluid, provide the same reading at zero and at 100 if they are calibrated by the method described, but at other points the readings do not usually correspond, because fluids vary in their expansion characteristics. Thus an arbitrary choice of fluid is required, and the temperature scale of the SI system, with its kelvin unit, symbol K, is based on the ideal gas as thermometric fluid. Because the definition of the Kelvin scale depends on the properties of gases, its detailed discussion is delayed until Chap. 3. We note, however, that as an absolute scale, it depends on the concept of a lower limit of temperature.

Kelvin temperatures are given the symbol T; Celsius temperatures, given the symbol t, are defined in relation to Kelvin temperatures:

$$t/°\text{C} = T/\text{K} - 273.15$$

The unit of Celsius temperature is the degree Celsius, °C, equal in size to the kelvin.[3] However, temperatures on the Celsius scale are 273.15 degrees lower than on the Kelvin scale. Thus the lower limit of temperature, called absolute zero on the Kelvin scale, occurs at −273.15°C.

In practice the *International Temperature Scale of 1990* (ITS-90) is used for calibration of scientific and industrial instruments.[4] The ITS-90 scale is defined so that its values differ from ideal-gas temperatures by no more than the accuracy of measurement. It is based on assigned values of temperature for a number of reproducible phase-equilibrium states of pure substances (*fixed points*) and on *standard instruments* calibrated at these temperatures. Interpolation between the fixed-point temperatures is provided by formulas that establish the relation between readings of the standard instruments and values on ITS-90. The platinum-resistance thermometer is an example of a standard instrument; it is used for temperatures from −259.35°C (13.8 K, the triple point of hydrogen) to 961.78°C (1234.93 K, the freezing point of silver).

In addition to the Kelvin and Celsius scales, two others are still used by engineers in the United States: the Rankine scale and the Fahrenheit[5] scale. The Rankine scale is an absolute scale directly related to the Kelvin scale by

$$T(\text{R}) = 1.8\,T\,\text{K}$$

The Fahrenheit scale is related to the Rankine scale by an equation analogous to the relation between the Celsius and Kelvin scales:

$$t(°\text{F}) = T(\text{R}) - 459.67$$

[3]Note that the word *degree* is not used with temperatures in kelvins, and that the word *kelvin* as a unit is not capitalized.

[4]The English-language text describing ITS-90 is given by H. Preston-Thomas, *Metrologia*, vol. 27, pp. 3–10, 1990.

[5]Gabriel Daniel Fahrenheit, German physicist (1686–1736).

Thus the lower limit of temperature on the Fahrenheit scale is −459.67(°F). The relation between the Fahrenheit and Celsius scales is

$$t(°F) = 1.8\, t°C + 32$$

The ice point is therefore 32(°F) and the normal boiling point of water is 212(°F).

The Celsius degree and the kelvin represent the same temperature *interval*, as do the Fahrenheit degree and the rankine. The relationships among the four temperature scales are shown in Fig. 1.1. In thermodynamics, absolute temperature is implied by an unqualified reference to temperature.

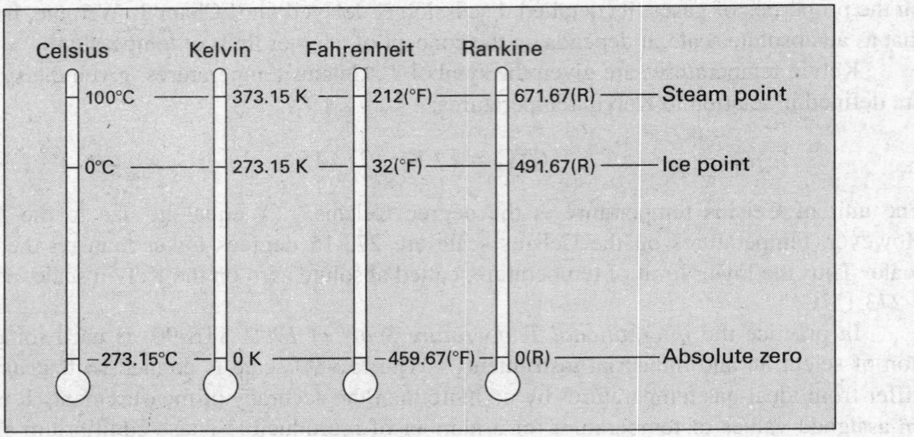

Figure 1.1: Relations among temperature scales (ITS-68 scale)

1.6 PRESSURE

The pressure P exerted by a fluid on a surface is defined as the normal force exerted by the fluid per unit area of the surface. If force is measured in N and area in m^2, the unit is the newton per square meter or N m^{-2}, called the pascal, symbol Pa, the basic SI unit of pressure. In the metric engineering system a common unit is kilogram *force* per square centimeter (kgf cm^{-2}).

The primary standard for pressure measurement is the dead-weight gauge in which a known force is balanced by a fluid pressure acting on a known area; whence $P \equiv F/A$. A simple design is shown in Fig. 1.2. The piston is carefully fitted to the cylinder making the clearance small. Weights are placed on the pan until the pressure of the oil, which tends to make the piston rise, is just balanced by the force of gravity on the piston and all that it supports. With this force given by Newton's law, the pressure of the oil is:

$$P = \frac{F}{A} = \frac{mg}{A}$$

where m is the mass of the piston, pan, and weights; g is the local acceleration of gravity; and A is the cross-sectional area of the piston. Gauges in common use, such as Bourdon gauges, are calibrated by comparison with dead-weight gauges.

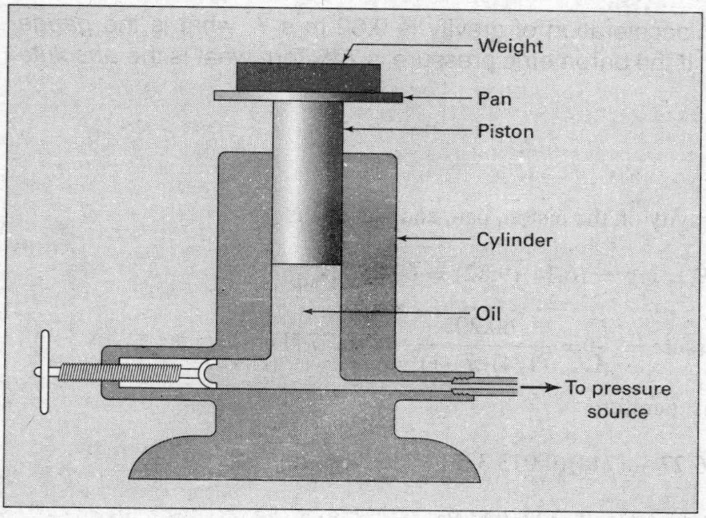

Figure 1.2: Dead-weight gauge

Because a vertical column of a given fluid under the influence of gravity exerts a pressure at its base in direct proportion to its height, pressure is also expressed as the equivalent height of a fluid column. This is the basis for the use of manometers for pressure measurement. Conversion of height to force per unit area follows from Newton's law applied to the force of gravity acting on the mass of fluid in the column. The mass is given by $m = Ah\rho$, where A is the cross-sectional area of the column, h is its height, and ρ is the fluid density. Therefore,

$$P = \frac{F}{A} = \frac{mg}{A} = \frac{Ah\rho g}{A} = h\rho g$$

The pressure to which a fluid height corresponds is determined by the density of the fluid (which depends on its identity and temperature) and the local acceleration of gravity. Thus the (Torr) is the pressure equivalent of 1 millimeter of mercury at 0°C (273.15 K) in a standard gravitational field, and is equal to 133.322 Pa.

Another unit of pressure is the standard atmosphere (atm), the approximate average pressure exerted by the earth's atmosphere at mean sea level, defined as 101 325 Pa, 101.325 kPa, or 0.101 325 MPa. The bar, an SI unit defined as 10^5 Pa, is equal to 0.986 923 atm.

Most pressure gauges give readings which are the difference between the pressure of interest and the pressure of the surrounding atmosphere. These readings are known as *gauge* pressures, and can be converted to *absolute* pressures by addition of the barometric pressure. Absolute pressures must be used in thermodynamic calculations.

Example 1.2

A dead-weight gauge with a 1 cm diameter piston is used to measure pressures very accurately. In a particular instance a mass of 6.14 kg (including piston and pan) brings it into balance. If the local acceleration of gravity is 9.82 m s^{-2}, what is the *gauge* pressure being measured? If the barometric pressure is 748 Torr, what is the *absolute* pressure?

Solution

The force exerted by gravity on the piston, pan, and weights is

$$F = mg = (6.14)(9.82) = 60.295 \text{ N}$$

$$\text{Gauge pressure} = \frac{F}{A} = \frac{60.295}{(1/4)(\pi)(1)^2} = 76.77 \text{ N cm}^{-2}$$

The absolute pressure is therefore

$$P = 76.77 + (748)(0.013\,332) = 86.74 \text{ N cm}^{-2}$$

or

$$P = 867.4 \text{ kPa}$$

Example 1.3

At 27°C (300.15 K) the reading on a manometer filled with mercury is 60.5 cm. The local acceleration of gravity is 9.784 m s^{-2}. To what pressure does this height of mercury correspond?

Solution

Recall the equation in the preceding text, $P = h\rho g$. At 27°C (300.15 K) the density of mercury is 13.53 g cm^{-3}. Then,

$$P = 60.5 \text{ cm} \times 13.53 \text{ g cm}^{-3} \times 9.784 \text{ m s}^{-2} = 8{,}009 \text{ g m s}^{-2} \text{ cm}^{-2}$$

or

$$P = 8.009 \text{ kg m s}^{-2} \text{ cm}^{-2} = 8.009 \text{ N cm}^{-2} \equiv 80.09 \text{ kPa} \equiv 0.8009 \text{ bar}$$

1.7 WORK

Work W is performed whenever a force acts through a distance. By definition, the quantity of work is given by the equation

$$dW = F\,dl \tag{1.1}$$

where F is the component of force acting along the line of the displacement dl. When integrated, this equation yields the work of a finite process. By convention, work is regarded as positive when the displacement is in the same direction as the applied force and negative when they are in opposite directions.

The work which accompanies a change in volume of a fluid is often encountered in thermodynamics. A common example is the compression or expansion of a fluid in a cylinder resulting from the movement of a piston. The force exerted by the piston on the fluid is equal to the product of the piston area and the pressure of the fluid. The displacement of the piston is equal to the total volume change of the fluid divided by the area of the piston. Equation (1.1) therefore becomes

$$dW = -PA\,d\frac{V^t}{A}$$

or, because A is constant,

$$dW = -P\,dV^t \tag{1.2}$$

Integrating,

$$W = -\int_{V_1^t}^{V_2^t} P\,dV^t \tag{1.3}$$

The minus signs in these equations are made necessary by the sign convention adopted for work. When the piston moves into the cylinder so as to compress the fluid, the applied force and its displacement are in the same direction; the work is therefore positive. The minus sign is required because the volume change is negative. For an expansion process, the applied force and its displacement are in opposite directions. The volume change in this case is positive, and the minus sign is required to make the work negative.

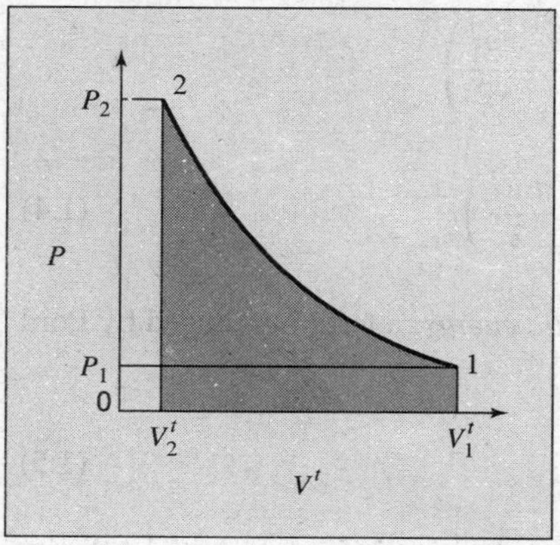

Figure 1.3: Diagram showing a P vs. V^t path

Equation (1.3) expresses the work done by a finite compression or expansion process.[6] Figure 1.3 shows a *path* for compression of a gas from point 1 with initial volume V_1^t at pressure P_1 to point 2 with volume V_2^t at pressure P_2. This path relates the pressure at any point of the process to the volume. The work required is given by Eq. (1.3) and is proportional to the area under the curve of Fig. 1.3. The SI unit of work is the newton-meter or joule, symbol J. In the metric engineering system, the unit often used, is the meter-kilogram force (m kgf).

[6]However, as explained in Sec. 2.8, it may be applied only in special circumstances.

1.8 ENERGY

The general principle of conservation of energy was established in about 1850. The germ of this principle as it applies to mechanics was implicit in the work of Galileo (1564–1642) and Isaac Newton (1642–1726). Indeed, it follows directly from Newton's second law of motion once work is defined as the product of force and displacement.

Kinetic Energy

When a body of mass m, acted upon by a force F, is displaced a distance dl during a differential interval of time dt, the work done is given by Eq. (1.1). In combination with Newton's second law this equation becomes

$$dW = ma\,dl$$

By definition, the acceleration is $a \equiv du/dt$, where u is the velocity of the body. Thus,

$$dW = m\frac{du}{dt}dl = m\frac{dl}{dt}du$$

Because the definition of velocity is $u \equiv dl/dt$, the expression for work becomes

$$dW = mu\,du$$

This equation may now be integrated for a finite change in velocity from u_1 to u_2:

$$W = m\int_{u_1}^{u_2} u\,du = m\left(\frac{u_2^2}{2} - \frac{u_1^2}{2}\right)$$

or

$$W = \frac{mu_2^2}{2} - \frac{mu_1^2}{2} = \Delta\left(\frac{mu^2}{2}\right) \tag{1.4}$$

Each of the quantities $\frac{1}{2}mu^2$ in Eq. (1.4) is a *kinetic energy*, a term introduced by Lord Kelvin[7] in 1856. Thus, by definition,

$$E_K \equiv \frac{1}{2}mu^2 \tag{1.5}$$

Equation (1.4) shows that the work done *on* a body in accelerating it from an initial velocity u_1 to a final velocity u_2 is equal to the change in kinetic energy of the body. Conversely, if a moving body is decelerated by the action of a resisting force, the work done *by* the body is equal to its change in kinetic energy. In the SI system of units with mass in kg and velocity in m s^{-1}, kinetic energy E_K has the units of kg m^2 s^{-2}. Because the newton is the composite unit kg m s^{-2}, E_K is measured in newton-meters or joules. In accord with Eq. (1.4), this is the unit of work.

[7] Lord Kelvin, or William Thomson (1824–1907), was an English physicist who, along with the German physicist Rudolf Clausius (1822–1888), laid the foundations for the modern science of thermodynamics.

In the metric engineering system, kinetic energy is expressed as $\frac{1}{2}mu^2/g_c$, where g_c has the value 9.806 65 and the units kg m kgf^{-1} s^{-2}. Thus the unit of kinetic energy in this system is

$$E_K = \frac{mu^2}{2g_c} = \frac{\text{kg m}^2\ \text{s}^{-2}}{\text{kg m kgf}^{-1}\ \text{s}^{-2}} = \text{m kgf}$$

Dimensional consistency here requires the inclusion of g_c.

Potential Energy

If a body of mass m is raised from an initial elevation z_1 to a final elevation z_2, an upward force at least equal to the weight of the body must be exerted on it, and this force must move through the distance $z_2 - z_1$. Because the weight of the body is the force of gravity on it, the minimum force required is given by Newton's law:

$$F = ma = mg$$

where g is the local acceleration of gravity. The minimum work required to raise the body is the product of this force and the change in elevation:

$$W = F(z_2 - z_1) = mg(z_2 - z_1)$$

or

$$W = mz_2g - mz_1g = \Delta(mzg) \tag{1.6}$$

We see from Eq. (1.6) that work done *on* a body in raising it is equal to the change in the quantity mzg. Conversely, if a body is lowered against a resisting force equal to its weight, the work done *by* the body is equal to the change in the quantity mzg. Each of the quantities mzg in Eq. (1.6) is a *potential energy*.[8] Thus, by definition,

$$E_P \equiv mzg \tag{1.7}$$

In the SI system of units with mass in kg, elevation in m, and the acceleration of gravity in m s^{-2}, potential energy has the units of kg m^2 s^{-2}. This is the newton-meter or joule, the unit of work, in agreement with Eq. (1.6).

In the metric engineering system, potential energy is expressed as mzg/g_c. Thus the unit of potential energy in this system is

$$E_P = \frac{mzg}{g_c} = \frac{\text{kg m}^2\ \text{s}^{-2}}{\text{kg m kgf}^{-1}\ \text{s}^{-2}} = \text{m kgf}$$

Again, g_c must be included for dimensional consistency.

[8]This term was proposed in 1853 by the Scottish engineer William Rankine (1820–1872).

Energy Conservation

In any examination of physical processes, an attempt is made to find or to define quantities which remain constant regardless of the changes which occur. One such quantity, early recognized in the development of mechanics, is mass. The great utility of the law of conservation of mass suggests that other conservation principles could be of comparable value. With respect to energy we observe that Eqs. (1.4) and (1.6) both show that work done on a body is equal to the change in a quantity which describes the condition of the body in relation to its surroundings. In each case the work performed can be recovered by carrying out the reverse process and returning the body to its initial condition. This observation leads naturally to the thought that, if the work done on a body in accelerating it or in elevating it can be subsequently recovered, then the body by virtue of its velocity or elevation contains the ability or capacity to do the work. This concept proved so useful in rigid-body mechanics that the capacity of a body for doing work was given the name *energy*, a word derived from the Greek and meaning "in work." Hence the work of accelerating a body produces a change in its *kinetic energy*:

$$W = \Delta E_K = \Delta\left(\frac{mu^2}{2}\right)$$

And the work done on a body in elevating it produces a change in its *potential energy*:

$$W = E_P = \Delta(mzg)$$

If a body is given energy when it is elevated, then the body conserves or retains this energy until it performs the work of which it is capable. An elevated body, allowed to fall freely, gains in kinetic energy what it loses in potential energy so that its capacity for doing work remains unchanged. For a freely falling body this means that

$$\Delta E_K + \Delta E_P = 0$$

or

$$\frac{mu_2^2}{2} - \frac{mu_1^2}{2} + mz_2g - mz_1g = 0$$

The validity of this equation has been confirmed by countless experiments. Thus the development of the concept of energy led logically to the the principle of energy conservation for all *purely mechanical processes*. Ample experimental evidence to justify this generalization was readily obtained.

Other forms of mechanical energy besides kinetic and gravitational potential energy are possible. The most obvious is potential energy of configuration. When a spring is compressed, work is done by an external force. Because the spring can later perform this work against a resisting force, the spring possesses capacity for doing work. This is potential energy of configuration. Energy of the same form exists in a stretched rubber band or in a bar of metal deformed in the elastic region.

The generality of the principle of conservation of energy in mechanics is increased if we look upon work itself as a form of energy. This is clearly permissible, because both kinetic- and potential-energy changes are equal to the work done in producing them [Eqs. (1.4) and (1.6)]. However, work is energy *in transit* and is never regarded as residing in a body. When work is done and does not appear simultaneously as work elsewhere, it is converted into another form of energy.

The body or assemblage on which attention is focused is called the *system*. All else is called the *surroundings*. When work is done, it is done by the surroundings on the system, or vice versa, and energy is transferred from the surroundings to the system, or the reverse. It is only during this transfer that the form of energy known as work exists. In contrast, kinetic and potential energy reside with the system. Their values, however, are measured with reference to the surroundings; i.e., kinetic energy depends on velocity with respect to the surroundings, and potential energy depends on elevation with respect to a datum level. *Changes* in kinetic and potential energy do not depend on these reference conditions, provided they are fixed.

Example 1.4

An elevator with a mass of 2500 kg rests at a level of 10 m above the base of an elevator shaft. It is raised to 100 m above the base of the shaft, where the cable holding it breaks. The elevator falls freely to the base of the shaft and strikes a strong spring. The spring is designed to bring the elevator to rest and, by means of a catch arrangement, to hold the elevator at the position of maximum spring compression. Assuming the entire process to be frictionless, and taking $g = 9.8$ m s^{-2}, calculate:

(*a*) the potential energy of the elevator in its initial position relative to the base of the shaft

(*b*) the work done in raising the elevator

(*c*) the potential energy of the elevator in its highest position relative to the base of the shaft

(*d*) the velocity and kinetic energy of the elevator just before it strikes the spring

(*e*) the potential energy of the compressed spring

(*f*) the energy of the system consisting of the elevator and spring (1) at the start of the process, (2) when the elevator reaches its maximum height, (3) just before the elevator strikes the spring, and (4) after the elevator has come to rest

Solution

Let subscript 1 designate the initial conditions; subscript 2, conditions when the elevator is at its highest position; and subscript 3, conditions just before the elevator strikes the spring.

(*a*) By Eq. (1.7), $E_{P_1} = mz_1 g = (2500)(10)(9.8) = 245\,000$ J

(*b*) By Eq. (1.1), $W = \int_{z_1}^{z_2} F\,dl = \int_{z_1}^{z_2} mg\,dl = mg(z_2 - z_1)$

whence $W = (2500)(9.8)(100 - 10) = 2205\,000$ J

(*c*) By Eq. (1.7), $E_{P_2} = mz_2 g = (2500)(100)(9.8) = 2450\,000$ J

Note that $W = E_{P_2} - E_{P_1}$.

(*d*) From the principle of conservation of mechanical energy, one may write that the sum of the kinetic- and potential-energy changes during the process from conditions 2 to 3 is zero; that is,

$$\Delta E_{K_{2\to 3}} + \Delta E_{P_{2\to 3}} = 0 \quad \text{or} \quad E_{K_3} - E_{K_2} + E_{P_3} - E_{P_2} = 0$$

However, E_{K_2} and E_{P_3} are zero. Therefore,

$$E_{K_3} = E_{P_2} = 2450\,000 \text{ J}$$

With $E_{K_3} = \frac{1}{2}mu_3^2$, $\quad u_3^2 = \dfrac{2E_{K_3}}{m} = \dfrac{(2)(2450\,000)}{2500}$

Whence, $\quad u_3 = 44.27 \text{ m s}^{-1}$

(*e*) Because the changes in the potential energy of the spring and the kinetic energy of the elevator must sum to zero,

$$\Delta E_P(\text{spring}) + \Delta E_K(\text{elevator}) = 0$$

The initial potential energy of the spring and the final kinetic energy of the elevator are zero; therefore, the final potential energy of the spring must equal the kinetic energy of the elevator just before it strikes the spring. Thus the final potential energy of the spring is 2450 000 J.

(*f*) If the elevator and the spring together are taken as the system, the initial energy of the system is the potential energy of the elevator, or 245 000 J. The total energy of the system can change only if work is transferred between it and the surroundings. As the elevator is raised, work is done on the system by the surroundings in the amount of 2205 000 J. Thus the energy of the system when the elevator reaches its maximum height is 245 000 + 2205 000 = 2450 000 J. Subsequent changes occur entirely within the system, with no work transfer between the system and surroundings. Hence the total energy of the system remains constant at 2450 000 J. It merely changes from potential energy of position (elevation) of the elevator to kinetic energy of the elevator to potential energy of configuration of the spring.

This example illustrates application of the law of conservation of mechanical energy. However, the entire process is assumed to occur without friction; the results obtained are exact only for such an idealized process.

During the period of development of the law of conservation of mechanical energy, heat was not generally recognized as a form of energy, but was considered an indestructible fluid called *caloric*. This concept was firmly entrenched, and for many years no connection was made between heat resulting from friction and the established forms of energy.

The law of conservation of energy was therefore limited in application to frictionless mechanical processes. No such limitation is necessary; heat like work is now regarded as energy in transit, a concept that gained acceptance during the years following 1850, largely on account of the classic experiments of J. P. Joule. These experiments are considered in detail in Chap. 2, but first we examine some of the characteristics of heat.

1.9 HEAT

We know from experience that a hot object brought in contact with a cold object becomes cooler, whereas the cold object becomes warmer. A reasonable view is that something is transferred from the hot object to the cold one, and we call that something heat Q.[9] Thus we say that heat always flows from a higher temperature to a lower one. This leads to the concept of temperature as the driving force for the transfer of energy as heat. More precisely, the rate of heat transfer from one body to another is proportional to the temperature difference between the two bodies; when there is no temperature difference, there is no net transfer of heat. In the thermodynamic sense, heat is never regarded as being stored within a body. Like work, it exists only as energy *in transit* from one body to another; in thermodynamic terminology, between a system and its surroundings. When energy in the form of heat is added to a system, it is stored not as heat but as kinetic and potential energy of the atoms and molecules making up the system.

In spite of the transient nature of heat, it is often viewed in relation to its effect on the body from which it is transferred. As a matter of fact, until about 1930, the definitions of units of heat were based on the temperature changes of a unit mass of water. Thus the *British thermal unit* (commonly known as *thermochemical Btu*) was long defined as 1/180th quantity of heat which when transferred to one pound *mass* of water raised its temperature from ice-point or 32(°F) to steam-point or 212(°F) at standard atmospheric pressure. Likewise the *calorie* (commonly known as *thermochemical calorie*) written as (cal) in the book, was defined as 1/100th quantity of heat which when transferred to one kilogram *mass* of water raised its temperature from 0 to 100°C (273.15 K to 373.15 K) at standard atmospheric pressure. Although these definitions provide a "feel" for the size of heat units, they depend on experiments made with water and are thus subject to change as measurements become more accurate. In order to recognize a common basis for all energy units, *international steam table calorie* is defined in relation to joule, the SI unit of energy, equal to 1 N m. Joule is the mechanical work done when a force of one newton acts through a distance of one meter. By definition, international steam table calorie is equivalent to 4.1868 J (exact) and thermochemical calorie is equivalent to 4.184 J (exact). By arithmetic, using the defined relations of US Customary and SI units, one *international steam table Btu*, written as (Btu) in the book, is equivalent to 1055.056 J as against one thermochemical Btu is equivalent to 1054.35 J. All other energy units are defined as multiples of the joule. The foot-pound *force*, for example, is equivalent to 1.355 8179 J while the meter-kilogram *force* is equivalent to 9.806 65 J. The SI unit of power is the watt, symbol W, defined as energy rate of one joule per second.

Table A.1 of App. A provides an extensive list of conversion factors for energy as well as for other units.

[9] An equally reasonable view would regard "cool" as something transferred from the cold object to the hot one.

PROBLEMS

1.1. What is the value of g_c and what are its units in a system in which the second, the meter, and the kilogram *mass* are defined as in Sec. 1.2, and the unit of force is the kilogram-force, defined as the force required to give kg an acceleration of 1 m s^{-2}?

1.2. *Electric current* is the fundamental SI electrical dimension, with *ampere* (A) as unit. Determine units for the following quantities, as combinations of *fundamental* SI units.

(*a*) Electric power (*b*) Electric charge (*c*) Electric potential difference
(*d*) Electric resistance (*e*) Electric capacitance

1.3. Liquid/vapor saturation pressure P^{sat} is often represented as a function of temperature by an equation of the form

$$\log_{10} P^{\text{sat}}/\text{Torr} = a - \frac{b}{t/°\text{C} + c}$$

Here, parameters a, b, and c are substance-specific constants. Suppose it is required to represent P^{sat} by the equivalent equation:

$$\ln P^{\text{sat}}/\text{kPa} = A - \frac{B}{T/\text{K} + C}$$

Show how the parameters in the two equations are related.

1.4. At what absolute temperature do the Celsius and Fahrenheit temperature scales give the same numerical value? What is the value?

1.5. Pressures up to 3000 bar are measured with a dead-weight gauge. The piston diameter is 4 mm. What is the approximate mass in kg of the weights required?

1.6. Pressures up to 3000 atm are measured with a dead-weight gauge. The piston diameter is 0.432 cm. What is the approximate mass in kg of the weights required?

1.7. The reading on a mercury manometer at 25°C (298.15 K) (open to the atmosphere at one end) is 56.38 cm. The local acceleration of gravity is 9.832 m s^{-2}. Atmospheric pressure is 101.78 kPa. What is the absolute pressure in kPa being measured? The density of mercury at 25°C (298.15 K) is 13.534 g cm^{-3}.

1.8. Liquids that boil at relatively low temperatures are often stored as liquids under their vapor pressures, which at ambient temperature can be quite large. Thus, *n*-butane stored as a liquid/vapor system is at a pressure of 2.581 bar for a temperature of 27°C (300.15 K). Large-scale storage (>50 m^3) of this kind is sometimes done in *spherical* tanks. Suggest two reasons, why.

C.10

1.9. The first accurate measurements of the properties of high-pressure gases were made by E. H. Amagat in France between 1869 and 1893. Before developing the dead-weight gauge, he worked in a mine shaft, and used a mercury manometer for measurements of pressure to more than 400 bar. Estimate the height of manometer required.

1.10. An instrument to measure the acceleration of gravity on Mars is constructed of a spring from which is suspended a mass of 0.40 kg. At a place on earth where the local acceleration of gravity is 9.81 m s^{-2}, the spring extends 1.08 cm. When the instrument package is landed on Mars, it radios the information that the spring is extended 0.40 cm. What is the Martian acceleration of gravity?

1.11. The variation of fluid pressure with height is described by the differential equation:

$$\frac{dP}{dz} = -\rho g$$

Here, ρ is specific density and g is the local acceleration of gravity. For an *ideal gas*, $\rho = \mathcal{M}P/RT$, where $\mathcal{M}$ is molar mass and R is the universal gas constant. Modeling the atmosphere as an isothermal column of ideal gas at 10°C (283.15 K), estimate the ambient pressure in Denver, where $z = 1.6$ km relative to sea level. For air, take $\mathcal{M} = 29$ g mol^{-1}; values of R are given in App. A.

1.12. A group of engineers has landed on the moon, and they wish to determine the mass of some rocks. They have a spring scale calibrated to read kilogram *mass* at a location where the acceleration of gravity is 9.81 m s^{-2}. One of the moon rocks gives a reading of 8.5 on this scale. What is its mass? What is its weight on the moon? Take $g(\text{moon}) = 1.622$ m s^{-2}.

1.13. A 70 W outdoor security light burns, on average, 10 hours a day. A new bulb costs \$ 5.00, and the lifetime is about 1000 hours. If electricity costs \$ 0.10 per kWh, what is the yearly price of "security," per light?

1.14. A gas is confined in a 0.47 m diameter cylinder by a piston, on which rests a weight. The mass of the piston and weight together is 150 kg. The local acceleration of gravity is 9.813 m s^{-2}, and atmospheric pressure is 101.57 kPa.

(*a*) What is the force in newtons exerted on the gas by the atmosphere, the piston, and the weight, assuming no friction between the piston and cylinder?

(*b*) What is the pressure of the gas in kPa?

(*c*) If the gas in the cylinder is heated, it expands, pushing the piston and weight upward. If the piston and weight are raised by 0.83 m, what is the work done by the gas in kJ? What is the change in potential energy of the piston and weight?

1.15. Verify that the SI unit of kinetic and potential energy is the joule.

1.16. An automobile having a mass of 1250 kg is traveling at 40 m s^{-1}. What is its kinetic energy in kJ? How much work must be done to bring it to a stop?

1.17. The turbines in a hydroelectric plant are fed by water falling from a 50 m height. Assuming 91% efficiency for conversion of potential to electrical energy, and 8% loss of the resulting power in transmission, what is the mass flow rate of water required to power a 200 W light bulb?

1.18. Below is a list of approximate conversion factors, useful for "back-of-the-envelope" estimates. None of them is exact, but most are accurate to within about ±10%. Use Table A.1 (App. A) to establish the exact conversions.

- 1 atm ≈ 1 bar
- 1(Btu) ≈ 1 kJ
- 1(hp) ≈ 0.75 kW
- 1(inch) ≈ 2.5 cm
- 1(lb_m) ≈ 0.5 kg
- 1(mile) ≈ 1.6 km
- 1(quart) ≈ 1 liter
- 1(yard) ≈ 1 m

Add your own items to the list. The idea is to keep the conversion factors simple and easy to remember.

1.19. Consider the following proposal for a decimal calendar. The fundamental unit is the decimal year (Yr), equal to the number of conventional (SI) seconds required for the earth to complete a circuit of the sun. Other units are defined in the table below. Develop, where possible, factors for converting decimal calendar units to conventional calendar units. Discuss pros and cons of the proposal.

Decimal Calendar Unit	Symbol	Definition
Second	Sc	10^{-6} Yr
Minute	Mn	10^{-5} Yr
Hour	Hr	10^{-4} Yr
Day	Dy	10^{-3} Yr
Week	Wk	10^{-2} Yr
Month	Mo	10^{-1} Yr
Year	Yr	

1.20. Energy costs vary greatly with energy source: coal @ \$25.00/t, gasoline @ a pump price of \$ 0.53 L^{-1}, and electricity @ \$ 0.1000/kWh. Conventional practice is to put these on a common basis by expressing them in \$ GJ^{-1}. For this purpose, assume gross heating values of 29 MJ kg^{-1} for coal and 37 GJ m^{-3} for gasoline.

(*a*) Rank order the three energy sources with respect to energy cost in \$ GJ^{-1}.

(*b*) Explain the large disparity in the numerical results of Part (*a*). Discuss the advantages and disadvantages of the three energy sources.

1.21. Chemical-plant equipment costs rarely vary in proportion to size. In the simplest case, cost C varies with size S according to the *allometric* equation

$$C = \alpha S^{\beta}$$

The size exponent β is typically between 0 and 1. For a wide varity of equipment types it is approximately 0.6.

(*a*) For $0 < \beta < 1$, show that cost per *unit size* decreases with increasing size. ("Economy of scale.")

(*b*) Consider the case of a spherical storage tank. The size is commonly measured by internal volume V_i^t. Show that $\beta = 2/3$. On what parameters or properties would you expect quantity α to depend?

1.22. A laboratory reports the following vapor-pressure (P^{sat}) data for a particular organic chemical:

t/°C	P^{sat}/kPa	t/°C	P^{sat}/kPa
−18.5	3.18	32.7	41.9
−9.5	5.48	44.4	66.6
0.2	9.45	52.1	89.5
11.8	16.9	63.3	129.
23.1	28.2	75.5	187.

Correlate the data by fitting them to the Antoine equation:

$$\ln P^{\text{sat}}/\text{kPa} = A - \frac{B}{T/\text{K} + C}$$

That is, find numerical values of parameters A, B, and C by an appropriate regression procedure. Discuss the comparison of correlated with experimental values. What is the predicted normal boiling point of this chemical?

1.23. (*a*) In summer 1970, the pump price of gasoline was about \$ 0.092 L^{-1}. Between 1970 and 2000, the average rate of inflation was about 5% per year. What might be the expected pump price in summer 2000? What conclusion might one reach from this calculation?

(*b*) A Ph.D. engineer starting his career in 1970 at a salary of \$ 16 000 y^{-1}, retired in 2000 at a salary of \$ 80 000 y^{-1}. How well did his salary keep up with an inflation rate of 5% per year?

(*c*) Tuition increases at major private universities in the United States have led inflation rates by about 3% per year. Use this observation to suggest strategies for paying the future tuition for a child at a private university. Assume no financial aid, an annual inflation rate of 5% per year, and a current tuition of \$ 25 000 y^{-1}.

Recall the compound interest formula:

$$\frac{C(t_2)}{C(t_1)} = (1+i)^{t_2-t_1}$$

where C can be cost, salary, etc., t_1 and t_2 indicate times, and i is a rate (inflation, interest, etc.), expressed as a decimal.

Chapter 2

The First Law and Other Basic Concepts

2.1 JOULE'S EXPERIMENTS

The modern concept of heat developed following crucial experiments carried out by James P. Joule[1] (1818–1889), in the cellar of his home near Manchester, England, during the decade following 1840.

In their essential elements Joule's experiments were simple enough, but he took elaborate precautions to insure accuracy. In the most famous series of measurements, he placed known amounts of water, oil, and mercury in an insulated container and agitated the fluid with a rotating stirrer. The amounts of work done on the fluid by the stirrer were accurately measured, and the temperature changes of the fluid were carefully noted. He found for each fluid that a fixed amount of work was required per unit mass for every degree of temperature rise caused by the stirring, and that the original temperature of the fluid could be restored by the transfer of heat through simple contact with a cooler object. Thus Joule demonstrated that a quantitative relationship exists between work and heat and, therefore, that heat is a form of energy.

2.2 INTERNAL ENERGY

In experiments like those of Joule, energy added to a fluid as work is later transferred from the fluid as heat. Where is this energy between its addition to and transfer from the fluid? A rational concept is that it is contained within the fluid in another form, called *internal energy*.

The internal energy of a substance does not include energy that it may possess as a result of its macroscopic position or movement. Rather it refers to energy of the molecules internal to the substance. Because of their ceaseless motion, all molecules possess kinetic energy of translation; except for monatomic molecules, they also possess kinetic energy of rotation and of internal vibration. The addition of heat to a substance increases this molecular activity, and

[1]These experiments and their influence on the development of thermodynamics are described by H. J. Steffens, *James Prescott Joule and the Concept of Energy*, Neale Watson Academic Publications, Inc., New York, 1979.

thus causes an increase in its internal energy. Work done on the substance can have the same effect, as was shown by Joule.

The internal energy of a substance also includes the potential energy resulting from intermolecular forces (Sec. 16.1). On a submolecular scale energy is associated with the electrons and nuclei of atoms, and with bond energy resulting from the forces holding atoms together as molecules. This form of energy is named *internal* to distinguish it from the kinetic and potential energy associated with a substance because of its macroscopic position or motion, which can be thought of as *external* forms of energy.

Internal energy has no concise thermodynamic definition. It is a thermodynamic *primitive*. It cannot be directly measured; there are no internal-energy meters. As a result, absolute values are unknown. However, this is not a disadvantage in thermodynamic analysis, because only *changes* in internal energy are required.

2.3 THE FIRST LAW OF THERMODYNAMICS

The recognition of heat and internal energy as forms of energy makes possible a generalization of the law of conservation of mechanical energy (Sec. 1.8) to include heat and internal energy in addition to work and external potential and kinetic energy. Indeed, the generalization can be extended to still other forms, such as surface energy, electrical energy, and magnetic energy. Overwhelming evidence of the validity of this generalization has raised its stature to a law of nature, known as the first law of thermodynamics. One formal statement is the following:

Although energy assumes many forms, the total quantity of energy is constant, and when energy disappears in one form it appears simultaneously in other forms.

In application of this law to a given process, the sphere of influence of the process is divided into two parts, the *system* and its *surroundings*. The region in which the process occurs is set apart as the system; everything with which the system interacts is its surroundings. A system may be of any size; its boundaries may be real or imaginary, rigid or flexible. Frequently a system consists of a single substance; in other cases it may be complex. In any event, the equations of thermodynamics are written with reference to a well-defined system. This focuses attention on the particular process of interest and on the equipment and material directly involved in the process. However, the first law applies to the system *and* its surroundings; not to the system alone. For any process, the first law requires

$$\Delta(\text{Energy of the system}) + \Delta(\text{Energy of surroundings}) = 0 \tag{2.1}$$

where the difference operator "Δ" signifies finite changes in the quantities enclosed in parentheses. The system may change in its internal energy, in its potential or kinetic energy, and in the potential or kinetic energy of its finite parts.

In the context of thermodynamics, heat and work represent energy *in transit across the boundary* dividing the system from its surroundings, and are never *stored* or *contained* in the system. Potential, kinetic, and internal energy on the other hand reside with and are stored with matter. In practice Eq. (2.1) assumes special forms suitable to specific practical applications. The development of these forms and their subsequent application are the subject of the remainder of this chapter.

2.4 ENERGY BALANCE FOR CLOSED SYSTEMS

If the boundary of a system does not permit the transfer of matter between the system and its surroundings, the system is said to be *closed*, and its mass is necessarily constant. The development of basic concepts in thermodynamics is facilitated by a careful examination of closed systems, and for this reason they are treated in detail here. Far more important for industrial practice are processes in which matter crosses the system boundary as streams that enter and leave process equipment. Such systems are said to be *open*, and they are treated later in this chapter, once the necessary foundation material has been presented.

Because no streams enter or leave a closed system, no energy associated with matter is *transported* across the boundary which divides the system from its surroundings. All energy exchange between a closed system and its surroundings then appears as heat and work, and the total energy change of the surroundings equals the net energy transferred to or from it as heat and work. The second term of Eq. (2.1) may therefore be replaced by

$$\Delta(\text{Energy of surroundings}) = \pm Q \pm W$$

Heat Q and work W always refer to the system, and the choice of signs used with these quantities depends on which direction of energy transfer with respect to the system is regarded as positive. The modern sign convention makes the numerical values of both quantities positive for transfer *into* the system from the surroundings. The corresponding quantities taken with reference to the surroundings, Q_{surr} and W_{surr}, have the opposite sign, i.e., $Q_{\text{surr}} = -Q$ and $W_{\text{surr}} = -W$. With this understanding

$$\Delta(\text{Energy of surroundings}) = Q_{\text{surr}} + W_{\text{surr}} = -Q - W$$

Equation (2.1) now becomes[2]

$$\Delta(\text{Energy of the system}) = Q + W \tag{2.2}$$

This equation means that the total energy change of a closed system equals the net energy transferred into it as heat and work.

Closed systems often undergo processes during which only the *internal* energy of the system changes. For such processes, Eq. (2.2) reduces to

$$\boxed{\Delta U^t = Q + W} \tag{2.3}$$

where U^t is the total internal energy of the system. Equation (2.3) applies to processes involving *finite* changes in the internal energy of the system. For *differential* changes

$$\boxed{dU^t = dQ + dW} \tag{2.4}$$

[2]The sign convention used here is recommended by the International Union of Pure and Applied Chemistry. However, the original choice of sign for work and the one used in the first four editions of this text was the opposite, and the right side of Eq. (2.2) was then written $Q - W$.

In Eqs. (2.3) and (2.4) the symbols Q, W, and U^t pertain to the entire system, which may be of any size and must be clearly defined. All terms require expression in the same energy units. In the SI system the unit is the joule.

Total volume V^t and total internal energy U^t depend on the quantity of material in a system, and are called *extensive* properties. In contrast, temperature and pressure, the principal thermodynamic coordinates for pure homogeneous fluids, are independent of the quantity of material, and are known as *intensive* properties. For a homogeneous system, an alternative means of expression for the extensive properties, such as V^t and U^t, is

$$V^t = mV \quad \text{or} \quad V^t = nV \qquad \text{and} \qquad U^t = mU \quad \text{or} \quad U^t = nU$$

where the plain symbols V and U represent the volume and internal energy of a unit amount of material, either a unit mass or a mole. These are respectively *specific* or *molar* properties, and they are *intensive*, independent of the quantity of material actually present.

Although V^t and U^t for a homogeneous system of arbitrary size are extensive properties, specific and molar volume V (or density) and specific and molar internal energy U are intensive.

Note that the intensive coordinates T and P have no extensive counterparts.

For a closed system of n moles Eqs. (2.3) and (2.4) may now be written:

$$\boxed{\Delta(nU) = n\,\Delta U = Q + W} \tag{2.5}$$

$$\boxed{d(nU) = n\,dU = dQ + dW} \tag{2.6}$$

In this form, these equations show explicitly the amount of substance comprising the system.

The equations of thermodynamics are often written for a representative unit amount of material, either a unit mass or a mole. Thus for $n = 1$ Eqs. (2.5) and (2.6) become

$$\Delta U = Q + W \qquad \text{and} \qquad dU = dQ + dW$$

The basis for Q and W is always implied by the mass or number of moles associated with the left side of the energy equation.

Equation (2.6) is the ultimate source of all *property relations* that connect the internal energy to measurable quantities. It does not represent a *definition* of internal energy; there is none. Nor does it lead to *absolute* values for the internal energy. What it provides is the means for calculating *changes* in this property. Without it, the first law of thermodynamics could not be formulated. Indeed, the first law requires prior affirmation of the existence of the internal energy, the essential nature of which is summarized in the following axiom:

There exists a form of energy, known as internal energy U, which is an intrinsic property of a system, functionally related to the measurable coordinates which characterize the system. For a closed system, not in motion, changes in this property are given by Eqs. (2.5) and (2.6).

Example 2.1

Water flows over a waterfall 100 m in height. Take 1 kg of the water as the system, and assume that it does not exchange energy with its surroundings.

(*a*) What is the potential energy of the water at the top of the falls with respect to the base of the falls?

(*b*) What is the kinetic energy of the water just before it strikes bottom?

(*c*) After the 1 kg of water enters the stream below the falls, what change has occurred in its state?

Solution

The 1 kg of water exchanges no energy with the surroundings. Thus, for each part of the process Eq. (2.1) reduces to

$$\Delta(\text{Energy of the system}) = \Delta U + \Delta E_K + \Delta E_P = 0$$

(*a*) From Eq. (1.7), with g equal to its standard value,

$$E_P = mzg = 1 \text{ kg} \times 100 \text{ m} \times 9.8066 \text{ m s}^{-2}$$

$$= 980.66 \frac{\text{kg m}^2}{\text{s}^2} = 980.66 \text{ N m} = 980.66 \text{ J}$$

(*b*) During the free fall of the water no mechanism exists for conversion of potential or kinetic energy into internal energy. Thus ΔU must be zero:

$$\Delta E_K + \Delta E_P = E_{K_2} - E_{K_1} + E_{P_2} - E_{P_1} = 0$$

As an excellent approximation, let $E_{K_1} = E_{P_2} = 0$. Then,

$$E_{K_2} = E_{P_1} = 980.66 \text{ J}$$

(*c*) As the 1 kg of water strikes bottom and mixes with other falling water to form a stream, the resulting turbulence has the effect of converting kinetic energy into internal energy. During this process, ΔE_P is essentially zero, and Eq. (2.1) becomes

$$\Delta U + \Delta E_K = 0 \qquad \text{or} \qquad \Delta U = E_{K_2} - E_{K_3}$$

However, the stream velocity is assumed small, making E_{K_3} negligible. Thus,

$$\Delta U = E_{K_2} = 980.66 \text{ J}$$

The overall result of the process is the conversion of potential energy of the water into internal energy of the water. This change in internal energy is manifested by a temperature rise of the water. Because energy in the amount of 4,184 J kg^{-1} is required for a temperature rise of 1°C in water, the temperature increase is 980.66/4,184 = 0.234°C, assuming no heat transfer with the surroundings.

2.5 THERMODYNAMIC STATE AND STATE FUNCTIONS

The notation of Eqs. (2.3) through (2.6) suggests that the internal-energy terms on the left are different in kind from the quantities on the right. Those on the left reflect *changes* in the *thermodynamic state* of the system as reflected by its *thermodynamic properties*, among which are temperature, pressure, and density. For a homogeneous pure substance we know from experience that fixing two of these properties also fixes all the others, and thus determines its thermodynamic state. For example, nitrogen gas at a temperature of 300 K and a pressure of 10^5 kPa (1 bar) has a fixed specific volume or density and a fixed molar internal energy. Indeed, it has a complete set of intensive thermodynamic properties. If this gas is heated or cooled, compressed or expanded, and then returned to its initial temperature and pressure, its intensive properties are restored to their initial values. They do not depend on the past history of the substance nor on the means by which it reaches a given state. They depend only on present conditions, however reached. Such quantities are known as *state functions*. When two of them are held at fixed values for a homogeneous pure substance,[3] the *thermodynamic state* of the substance is fully determined. This means that a state function, such as specific internal energy, is a property that always has a value; it may therefore be expressed mathematically as a function of such coordinates as temperature and pressure, or temperature and density, and its values may be identified with points on a graph.

On the other hand, the terms on the right sides of Eqs. (2.3) through (2.6), representing heat and work quantities, are not properties; they account for the energy changes that occur in the surroundings. They depend on the nature of the process, and may be associated with areas rather than points on a graph, as suggested by Fig. 1.3. Although time is not a thermodynamic coordinate, the passage of time is inevitable whenever heat is transferred or work is accomplished.

The differential of a state function represents an infinitesimal *change* in its value. Integration of such a differential results in a finite difference between two of its values, e.g.,

$$\int_{P_1}^{P_2} dP = P_2 - P_1 = \Delta P \qquad \text{and} \qquad \int_{V_1}^{V_2} dV = V_2 - V_1 = \Delta V$$

The differentials of heat and work are not *changes*, but are infinitesimal *amounts*. When integrated, these differentials give not finite changes, but finite amounts. Thus,

$$\int dQ = Q \qquad \text{and} \qquad \int dW = W$$

For a closed system undergoing the same change in state by several processes, experiment shows that the amounts of heat and work required differ for different processes, but that *the sum $Q + W$ is the same for all processes*. This is the basis for identification of internal energy as a state function. The same value of ΔU^t is given by Eq. (2.3) regardless of the process, provided only that the change in the system is between the same initial and final states.

[3]For systems more complex than a simple homogeneous pure substance, the number of state functions that must be arbitrarily specified in order to define the state of the system may be different from two. The method of determining this number is the subject of Sec. 2.7.

Example 2.2

A gas is confined in a cylinder by a piston. The initial pressure of the gas is 7 bar, and the volume is 0.10 m^3. The piston is held in place by latches in the cylinder wall. The whole apparatus is placed in a total vacuum. What is the energy change of the apparatus if the restraining latches are removed so that the gas suddenly expands to double its initial volume, the piston striking other latches at the end of the process?

Solution

Because the question concerns the entire apparatus, the system is taken as the gas, piston, and cylinder. No work is done during the process, because no force external to the system moves, and no heat is transferred through the vacuum surrounding the apparatus. Hence Q and W are zero, and the total energy of the system does not change. Without further information we can say nothing about the distribution of energy among the parts of the system. This may well be different than the initial distribution.

Example 2.3

If the process described in Ex. 2.2 is repeated, not in a vacuum but in air at atmospheric pressure of 101.3 kPa, what is the energy change of the apparatus? Assume the rate of heat exchange between the apparatus and the surrounding air is slow compared with the rate at which the process occurs.

Solution

The system is chosen as before, but here work is done by the system in pushing back the atmosphere. It is evaluated as the product of the force of atmospheric pressure on the back side of the piston $F = P_{\text{atm}} A$ and the displacement of the piston $\Delta l = \Delta V^t / A$. Here, A is the area of the piston and ΔV^t is the volume change of the gas. This is work done by the system on the surroundings, and is a negative quantity; thus,

$$W = -F\,\Delta l = -P_{\text{atm}}\,\Delta V^t = -(101.3)(0.2 - 0.1)\text{ kPa m}^3 = -10.13\ \frac{\text{kN}}{\text{m}^2}\ \text{m}^3$$

or

$$W = -10.13\text{ kN m} = -10.13\text{ kJ}$$

Heat transfer between the system and surroundings is also possible in this case, but the problem is worked for the instant after the process has occurred and before appreciable heat transfer has had time to take place. Thus Q is assumed to be zero in Eq. (2.2), giving

$$\Delta(\text{Energy of the system}) = Q + W = 0 - 10.13 = -10.13\text{ kJ}$$

The total energy of the system has *decreased* by an amount equal to the work done on the surroundings.

Example 2.4

When a system is taken from state *a* to state *b* in Fig. 2.1 along path *acb*, 100 J of heat flows into the system and the system does 40 J of work.

(*a*) How much heat flows into the system along path *aeb* if the work done by the system is 20 J?

(*b*) The system returns from *b* to *a* along path *bda*. If the work done on the system is 30 J, does the system absorb or liberate heat? How much?

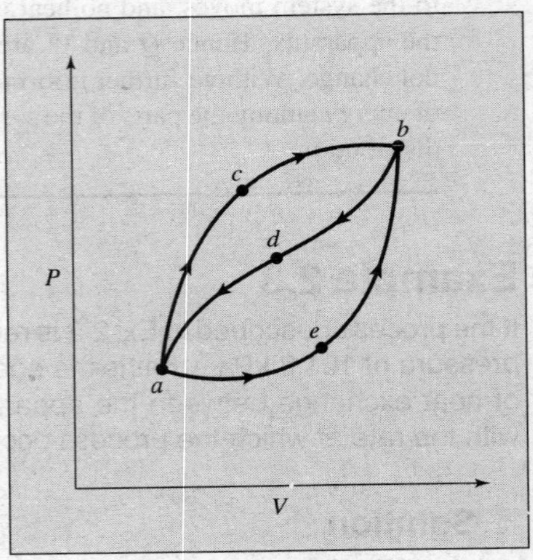

Figure 2.1: Diagram for Ex. 2.4

Solution

Assume that the system changes only in its internal energy and that Eq. (2.3) is applicable. For path *acb*, and thus for *any* path leading from *a* to *b*,

$$\Delta U^t_{ab} = Q_{acb} + W_{acb} = 100 - 40 = 60 \text{ J}$$

(*a*) For path *aeb*,

$$\Delta U^t_{ab} = 60 = Q_{aeb} + W_{aeb} = Q_{aeb} - 20 \qquad \text{whence} \qquad Q_{aeb} = 80 \text{ J}$$

(*b*) For path *bda*,

$$\Delta U^t_{ba} = -\Delta U^t_{ab} = -60 = Q_{bda} + W_{bda} = Q_{bda} + 30$$

and $$Q_{bda} = -60 - 30 = -90 \text{ J}$$

Heat is therefore transferred from the system to the surroundings.

2.6 EQUILIBRIUM

Equilibrium is a word denoting a static condition, the absence of change. In thermodynamics it means not only the absence of change but the absence of any *tendency* toward change on a macroscopic scale. Thus a system at equilibrium exists under conditions such that no change in state can occur. Because any tendency toward change is caused by a driving force of one kind or another, the absence of such a tendency indicates also the absence of any driving force. Hence for a system at equilibrium all forces are in exact balance. Whether a change actually occurs in a system *not* at equilibrium depends on resistance as well as on driving force. In many systems subject to appreciable driving forces change occurs at a negligible rate, because the resistance to change is very large.

Different kinds of driving forces tend to bring about different kinds of change. For example, imbalance of mechanical forces such as pressure on a piston tend to cause energy transfer as work; temperature differences tend to cause the flow of heat; gradients in chemical potential tend to cause substances to be transferred from one phase to another. At equilibrium all such forces are in balance.

In many applications of thermodynamics, chemical reactions are of no concern. For example, a mixture of hydrogen and oxygen at ordinary conditions is not in chemical equilibrium, because of the large driving force for the formation of water. However, if chemical reaction is not initiated, this system can exist in long-term thermal and mechanical equilibrium, and purely physical processes may be analyzed without regard to possible chemical reaction.

2.7 THE PHASE RULE

As indicated earlier, the state of a pure homogeneous fluid is fixed whenever two intensive thermodynamic properties are set at specific values. In contrast, when *two* phases are in equilibrium, the state of the system is fixed when only a single property is specified. For example, a mixture of steam and liquid water in equilibrium at 101.33 kPa can exist only at 100°C (373.15 K). It is impossible to change the temperature without also changing the pressure if vapor/liquid equilibrium is to be maintained.

For multi-phase systems at equilibrium, the number of independent variables that must be arbitrarily fixed to establish its *intensive* state is given by the celebrated phase rule of J. Willard Gibbs,[4] who deduced it by theoretical reasoning in 1875. It is presented here without proof in the form applicable to nonreacting systems:[5]

$$\boxed{F = 2 - \pi + N} \qquad (2.7)$$

where π is the number of phases, N is the number of chemical species, and F is called the *degrees of freedom* of the system.

[4]Josiah Willard Gibbs (1839–1903), American mathematical physicist.

[5]The justification of the phase rule for nonreacting systems is given in Sec. 10.2, and the phase rule for reacting systems is considered in Sec. 13.8.

The intensive state of a system at equilibrium is established when its temperature, pressure, and the compositions of all phases are fixed. These are therefore phase-rule variables, but they are not all independent. The phase rule gives the number of variables from this set which must be arbitrarily specified to fix all remaining phase-rule variables, and thus the intensive state of the system.

A *phase* is a homogeneous region of matter. A gas or a mixture of gases, a liquid or a liquid solution, and a crystalline solid are examples of phases. A phase need not be continuous; examples of discontinuous phases are a gas dispersed as bubbles in a liquid, a liquid dispersed as droplets in another liquid with which it is immiscible, and solid crystals dispersed in either a gas or liquid. In each case a dispersed phase is distributed throughout a continuous phase. An abrupt change in properties always occurs at the boundary between phases. Various phases can coexist, but they *must be in equilibrium* for the phase rule to apply. An example of a three-phase system at equilibrium is a saturated aqueous salt solution at its boiling point with excess salt crystals present. The three phases ($\pi = 3$) are crystalline salt, the saturated aqueous solution, and vapor generated at the boiling point. The two chemical species ($N = 2$) are water and salt. For this system, $F = 1$.

The phase-rule variables are *intensive* properties, independent of the extent of the system and of the individual phases. Thus the phase rule gives the same information for a large system as for a small one and for different relative amounts of the phases. Moreover, only individual-phase compositions are phase-rule variables. Overall or total compositions are not when more than one phase is present.

The minimum number of degrees of freedom for any system is zero. When $F = 0$, the system is *invariant*; Eq. (2.7) becomes $\pi = 2 + N$. This value of π is the maximum number of phases which can coexist at equilibrium for a system containing N chemical species. When $N = 1$, this number is 3, characteristic of a triple point (Sec. 3.1). For example, the triple point of water, where liquid, vapor, and the common form of ice exist together in equilibrium, occurs at 0.01°C (273.16 K) and 0.0061 bar. Any change from these conditions causes at least one phase to disappear.

Example 2.5

How many degrees of freedom has each of the following systems?

(*a*) Liquid water in equilibrium with its vapor

(*b*) Liquid water in equilibrium with a mixture of water vapor and nitrogen

(*c*) A liquid solution of alcohol in water in equilibrium with its vapor

Solution

(*a*) The system contains a single chemical species existing as two phases (one liquid and one vapor). Thus,

$$F = 2 - \pi + N = 2 - 2 + 1 = 1$$

This result is in agreement with the fact that for a given pressure water has but one boiling point. Temperature or pressure, but not both, may be specified for a system comprised of water in equilibrium with its vapor.

(*b*) In this case two chemical species are present. Again there are two phases.

Thus, $$F = 2 - \pi + N = 2 - 2 + 2 = 2$$

The addition of an inert gas to a system of water in equilibrium with its vapor changes the characteristics of the system. Now temperature and pressure may be independently varied, but once they are fixed the system described can exist in equilibrium only at a particular composition of the vapor phase. (If nitrogen is considered negligibly soluble in water, the liquid phase is pure water.)

(*c*) Here $N = 2$, and $\pi = 2$, and

$$F = 2 - \pi + N = 2 - 2 + 2 = 2$$

The phase-rule variables are temperature, pressure, and the phase compositions. The composition variables are either the mass or mole fractions of the species in a phase, and they must sum to unity for each phase. Thus fixing the mole fraction of the water in the liquid phase automatically fixes the mole fraction of the alcohol. These two compositions cannot both be arbitrarily specified.

2.8 THE REVERSIBLE PROCESS

The development of thermodynamics is facilitated by introduction of a special kind of closed-system process characterized as *reversible*:

A process is reversible when its direction can be reversed at any point by an infinitesimal change in external conditions.

Reversible Expansion of a Gas

The nature of reversible processes is illustrated by the example of a simple expansion of gas in a piston/cylinder arrangement. The apparatus shown in Fig. 2.2 is imagined to exist in an evacuated space. The gas trapped inside the cylinder is chosen as the system; all else is the surroundings. Expansion processes result when mass is removed from the piston. For simplicity, assume that the piston slides within the cylinder without friction and that the piston and cylinder neither absorb nor transmit heat. Moreover, because the density of the gas in the cylinder is low and because the mass of gas is small, we ignore the effects of gravity on the contents of the cylinder. This means that gravity-induced pressure gradients in the gas are very small relative to its pressure and that changes in potential energy of the gas are negligible in comparison with the potential-energy changes of the piston assembly.

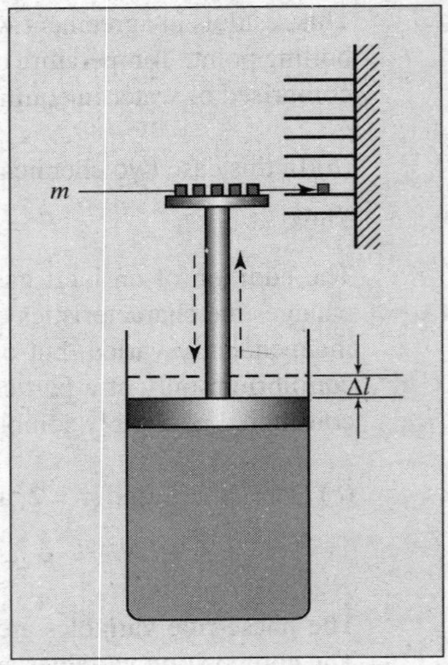

Figure 2.2: Expansion of a gas

The piston in Fig. 2.2 confines the gas at a pressure just sufficient to balance the weight of the piston and all that it supports. This is a condition of equilibrium, for the system has no tendency to change. Mass must be removed from the piston if it is to rise. Imagine first that a mass m is suddenly slid from the piston to a shelf (at the same level). The piston assembly accelerates upward, reaching its maximum velocity at the point where the upward force on the piston just balances its weight. Its momentum then carries it to a higher level, where it reverses direction. If the piston were held in this position of maximum elevation, its potential-energy increase would very nearly equal the work done by the gas during the initial stroke. However, when unconstrained, the piston assembly oscillates, with decreasing amplitude, ultimately coming to rest at a new equilibrium position at a level above its initial position.

The oscillations of the piston assembly are damped out because the viscous nature of the gas gradually converts gross directed motion of the molecules into chaotic molecular motion. This *dissipative* process transforms some of the work initially done by the gas to raise the piston back into internal energy of the gas. Once the process is initiated, no *infinitesimal* change in external conditions can reverse its direction; the process is *irreversible*.

All processes carried out in finite time with real substances are accompanied in some degree by dissipative effects of one kind or another, and all are therefore irreversible. However, one can *imagine* processes that are free of dissipative effects. For the expansion process of Fig. 2.2, such effects have their origin in the sudden removal of a finite mass from the piston. The resulting imbalance of forces acting on the piston causes its acceleration, and leads to its subsequent oscillation. The sudden removal of smaller mass increments reduces but does not eliminate this dissipative effect. Even the removal of an infinitesimal mass leads to piston oscillations of infinitesimal amplitude and a consequent dissipative effect. However, one may *imagine* a process wherein small mass increments are removed one after another at a rate such that the piston's rise is continuous, with minute oscillation only at the end of the process.

The limiting case of removal of a succession of infinitesimal masses from the piston is approximated when the masses m in Fig. 2.2 are replaced by a pile of powder, blown in a very fine stream from the piston. During this process, the piston rises at a uniform but very slow rate, and the powder collects in storage at ever higher levels. The system is never more than differentially displaced from internal equilibrium or from equilibrium with its surroundings. If the removal of powder from the piston is stopped and the direction of transfer of powder is reversed, the process reverses direction and proceeds backwards along its original path. Both the system and its surroundings are ultimately restored to virtually their initial conditions. The original process approaches *reversibility*.

Without the assumption of a frictionless piston, we cannot imagine a reversible process. If the piston sticks because of friction, a finite mass must be removed before the piston breaks free. Thus the equilibrium condition necessary to reversibility is not maintained. Moreover, friction between two sliding parts is a mechanism for the dissipation of mechanical energy into internal energy.

This discussion has centered on a single closed-system process, the expansion of a gas in a cylinder. The opposite process, compression of a gas in a cylinder, can be described in exactly the same way. There are, however, many processes which are driven by the imbalance of forces other than mechanical forces. For example, heat flow occurs when a temperature difference exists, electricity flows under the influence of an electromotive force, and chemical reactions occur because a chemical potential exists. In general, a process is reversible when the net force driving it is only differential in size. Thus heat is transferred reversibly when it flows from a finite object at temperature T to another such object at temperature $T - dT$.

Reversible Chemical Reaction

The concept of a reversible chemical reaction is illustrated by the decomposition of calcium carbonate, which when heated forms calcium oxide and carbon dioxide gas. At equilibrium, this system exerts a specific decomposition pressure of CO_2 for a given temperature. When the pressure falls below this value, $CaCO_3$ decomposes. Assume that a cylinder is fitted with a frictionless piston and contains $CaCO_3$, CaO, and CO_2 in equilibrium. It is immersed in a constant-temperature bath, as shown in Fig. 2.3, and thermal equilibrium assures equality of the system temperature with that of the bath. The temperature is adjusted to a value such that the decomposition pressure is just sufficient to balance the weight on the piston, a condition of mechanical equilibrium. The chemical reaction is held in balance (in equilibrium) by the pressure of the CO_2. Any change of conditions, however slight, upsets the equilibrium and causes the reaction to proceed in one direction or the other.

If the weight is differentially increased, the CO_2 pressure rises differentially, and CO_2 combines with CaO to form $CaCO_3$, allowing the weight to fall slowly. The heat given off by this reaction raises the temperature in the cylinder, and heat flows to the bath. Decreasing the weight differentially sets off the opposite chain of events. The same results are obtained if the temperature of the bath is raised or lowered. If the temperature of the bath is raised differentially, heat flows into the cylinder and calcium carbonate decomposes. The CO_2 generated causes the pressure to rise differentially, which in turn raises the piston and weight. This continues until the $CaCO_3$ is completely decomposed. The process is reversible, for the system is never more than differentially displaced from equilibrium, and only a differential lowering of the temperature of the bath causes the system to return to its initial state.

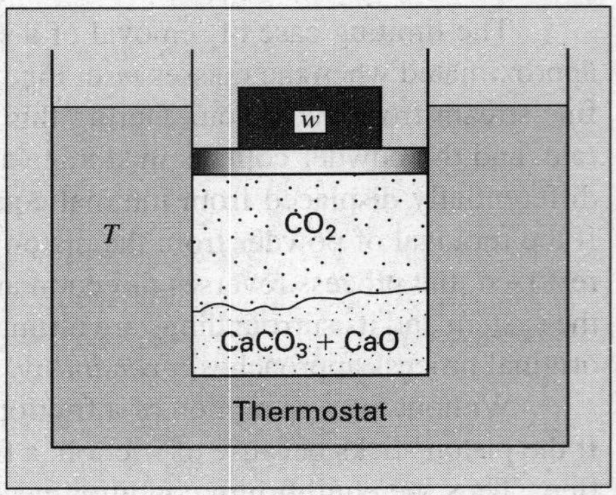

Figure 2.3: Reversibility of a chemical reaction

Some chemical reactions can be carried out in an electrolytic cell, and in this case they may be held in balance by an applied potential difference. If such a cell consists of two electrodes, one of zinc and the other of platinum, immersed in an aqueous solution of hydrochloric acid, the reaction that occurs is

$$Zn + 2HCl \rightleftharpoons H_2 + ZnCl_2$$

The cell is held under fixed conditions of temperature and pressure, and the electrodes are connected externally to a potentiometer. If the electromotive force produced by the cell is exactly balanced by the potential difference of the potentiometer, the reaction is held in equilibrium. The reaction may be made to proceed in the forward direction by a slight decrease in the opposing potential difference, and it may be reversed by a corresponding increase in the potential difference above the emf of the cell.

Summary Remarks on Reversible Processes

A reversible process

- is frictionless
- is never more than differentially removed from equilibrium
- traverses a succession of equilibrium states
- is driven by forces whose imbalance is differential in magnitude
- can be reversed at any point by a differential change in external conditions
- when reversed, retraces its forward path, and restores the initial state of system and surroundings

An equation derived in Sec. 1.7 gives the work of compression or expansion of a gas caused by the differential displacement of a piston in a cylinder:

$$dW = -P\,dV^t \qquad (1.2)$$

The work done on the system is given by this equation only when certain characteristics of the reversible process are realized. The first requirement is that the system be no more than infinitesimally displaced from a state of *internal* equilibrium, characterized by uniformity of temperature and pressure. The system then always has an identifiable set of properties, including pressure P. The second requirement is that the system be no more than infinitesimally displaced from mechanical equilibrium with its surroundings. In this event, the internal pressure P is never more than minutely out of balance with the external force, and we may make the substitution $F = PA$ that transforms Eq. (1.1) into Eq. (1.2). Processes for which these requirements are met are said to be *mechanically reversible*, and Eq. (1.2) may be integrated:

$$W = -\int_{V_1^t}^{V_2^t} P\,dV^t \tag{1.3}$$

The reversible process is ideal in that it produces the best possible result. It represents a limit to the performance of actual processes, but is never fully realized. An initial calculation of work is often made for a reversible process, because the choice is between such a calculation and no calculation at all. The reversible work as the limiting value may be combined with an appropriate *efficiency* to yield a reasonable approximation to the work of an actual process.

Example 2.6

A horizontal piston/cylinder arrangement is placed in a constant-temperature bath. The piston slides in the cylinder with negligible friction, and an external force holds it in place against an initial gas pressure of 14 bar. The initial gas volume is 0.03 m^3. The external force on the piston is reduced gradually, and the gas expands isothermally as its volume doubles. If the volume of the gas is related to its pressure so that the product PV^t is constant, what is the work done by the gas in moving the external force?

How much work would be done if the external force were suddenly reduced to half its initial value instead of being gradually reduced?

Solution

The process, carried out as first described, is mechanically reversible, and Eq. (1.3) is applicable. If $PV^t = k$, then $P = k/V^t$, and

$$W = -\int_{V_1^t}^{V_2^t} P\,dV^t = -k\int_{V_1^t}^{V_2^t} \frac{dV^t}{V^t} = -k \ln \frac{V_2^t}{V_1^t}$$

With $\quad V_1^t = 0.03 \text{ m}^3 \qquad V_2^t = 0.06 \text{ m}^3$

and $\quad k = PV^t = P_1V_1^t = (14 \times 10^5)(0.03) = 42\,000 \text{ J}$

$$W = -42\,000 \ln 2 = -29\,112 \text{ J}$$

The final pressure is

$$P_2 = \frac{k}{V_2^t} = \frac{42\,000}{0.06} = 700\,000 \text{ Pa} \qquad \text{or} \qquad 7 \text{ bar}$$

In the second case, reduction of the initial force by half is followed by sudden expansion of the gas against a constant force equivalent to a pressure of 7 bar. Eventually, heat transfer returns the system to the same final equilibrium state as in the reversible process. Thus ΔV^t is the same as before, but the work accomplished is not given by Eq. (1.3). Rather, the work done against the external force equals the equivalent external pressure times the volume change:

$$W = -(7 \times 10^5)(0.06 - 0.03) = -21\,000 \text{ J}$$

This process is clearly irreversible, and compared with the reversible process is said to have an efficiency of:

$$21\,000/29\,112 = 0.721 \qquad \text{or} \qquad 72.1\%$$

Example 2.7

The piston/cylinder arrangement shown in Fig. 2.4 contains nitrogen gas trapped below the piston at a pressure of 7 bar. The piston is held in place by latches. The space above the piston is evacuated. A pan is attached to the piston rod and a mass m of 45 kg is fastened to the pan. The piston, piston rod, and pan together have a mass of 23 kg.

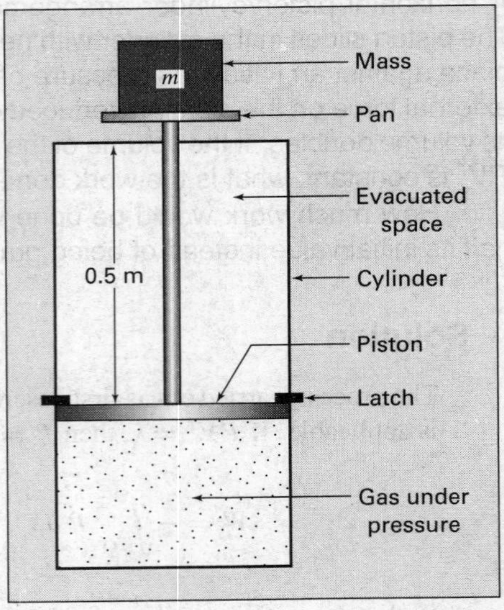

Figure 2.4: Diagram for Ex. 2.7

The latches holding the piston are released, allowing the piston to rise rapidly until it strikes the top of the cylinder. The distance moved by the piston is 0.5 m. The local acceleration of gravity is 9.8 m s^{-2}. Discuss the energy changes that occur because of this process.

Solution

This example illustrates the limited capacity of thermodynamics for analysis of irreversible nonflow processes. Let the gas alone be the system. By its basic definition, work done by the gas on the surroundings equals $\int P' dV^t$, where P' is the pressure exerted by the gas on the piston. Because the expansion is very rapid, pressure gradients exist in the gas, and neither P' nor the integral can be evaluated. However, a return to Eq. (2.1) avoids the calculation of work. The energy change of the system (the gas) is ΔU^t_{sys}. In the surroundings the piston, rod, pan, and mass m change in potential energy and the piston, rod, and cylinder change in internal energy. With $Q = 0$, Eq. (2.1) is written:

$$\Delta U^t_{\text{sys}} + (\Delta U^t_{\text{surr}} + \Delta E_{P\,\text{surr}}) = 0$$

where $$\Delta E_{P\,\text{surr}} = (45 + 23)(9.8)(0.5) = 333.2 \text{ N m}$$

Therefore $$\Delta U^t_{\text{sys}} + \Delta U^t_{\text{surr}} = -333.2 \text{ N m} = -333.2 \text{ J}$$

Values for ΔU^t_{sys} and ΔU^t_{surr} cannot be determined.

2.9 CONSTANT-*V* AND CONSTANT-*P* PROCESSES

For n moles of a homogeneous fluid contained in a closed system the energy balance is:

$$d(nU) = dQ + dW \tag{2.6}$$

where Q and W always represent *total* heat and work, whatever the value of n. The work for a mechanically reversible, closed-system process is given by Eq. (1.2), here written:

$$dW = -P\,d(nV)$$

These two equations combine to form

$$d(nU) = dQ - P\,d(nV) \tag{2.8}$$

This energy balance is general for n moles of homogeneous fluid in a closed system undergoing a mechanically reversible process.

Constant-Volume Process

If the process occurs at constant total volume, the work is zero. Moreover, for closed systems the last term of Eq. (2.8) is also zero, because n and V are both constant. Thus,

$$dQ = d(nU) \qquad (\text{const } V) \tag{2.9}$$

Integration yields $$Q = n\,\Delta U \qquad (\text{const } V) \tag{2.10}$$

Thus the heat transferred in a mechanically reversible, constant-volume, closed-system process equals the internal-energy change of the system.

Constant-Pressure Process

Solved for dQ, Eq. (2.8) becomes

$$dQ = d(nU) + P\,d(nV)$$

For a constant-pressure change of state

$$dQ = d(nU) + d(nPV) = d[n(U + PV)]$$

The appearance of the group $U + PV$, both here and in other applications, suggests the definition for convenience of a new thermodynamic property. Thus, the mathematical (and only) **definition** of enthalpy (en-**thal**′-py)[6] is:

$$\boxed{H \equiv U + PV} \tag{2.11}$$

where H, U, and V are molar or unit-mass values. The preceding energy balance may now be written:

$$dQ = d(nH) \qquad \text{(const } P\text{)} \tag{2.12}$$

Integration yields

$$Q = n\,\Delta H \qquad \text{(const } P\text{)} \tag{2.13}$$

Thus the heat transferred in a mechanically reversible, constant-pressure, closed-system process equals the enthalpy change of the system. Comparison of Eqs. (2.12) and (2.13) with Eqs. (2.9) and (2.10) shows that the enthalpy plays a role in constant-pressure processes analogous to the internal energy in constant-volume processes.

2.10 ENTHALPY

The usefulness of the enthalpy is suggested by Eqs. (2.12) and (2.13). It also appears in energy balances for flow processes as applied to heat exchangers, evaporators, distillation columns, pumps, compressors, turbines, engines, etc., for calculation of heat and work.

The tabulation of values of Q and W for the infinite array of possible processes is impossible. The intensive state functions, however, such as specific volume, specific internal energy, and specific enthalpy, are intrinsic properties of matter. Once determined for a particular substance, their values for liquid nd vapor phases can be tabulated as functions of T and P for future use in the calculation of Q and W for any process involving that substance. The determination of numerical values for these state functions and their correlation and use are treated in later chapters.

All terms of Eq. (2.11) must be expressed in the same units. The product PV has units of energy per mole or per unit mass, as does U; therefore H also has units of energy per mole or per unit mass. In the SI system the basic unit of pressure is the pascal or N m^{-2} and, for molar

[6]A word proposed by H. Kamerlingh Onnes, Dutch physicist who first liquefied helium in 1908, discovered superconductivity in 1911, and won the Nobel prize for physics in 1913. (See: *Communications from the Physical Laboratory of the University of Leiden*, no. 109, p. 3, footnote 2, 1909.)

volume, $m^3\ mol^{-1}$. The PV product then has the units $N\ m\ mol^{-1}$ or $J\ mol^{-1}$. In the metric engineering system a common unit for the PV product is the m kgf kg^{-1}, which arises when pressure is in kgf m^{-2} with volume in $m^3\ kg^{-1}$. This result is usually converted to kcal kg^{-1} through division by 426.935 for use in Eq. (2.11), because the common metric engineering unit for U and H is the kcal kg^{-1}.

Because U, P, and V are all state functions, H as defined by Eq. (2.11) is also a state function. Like U and V, H is an intensive property of matter. The differential form of Eq. (2.11) is:

$$dH = dU + d(PV) \tag{2.14}$$

This equation applies whenever a differential change occurs in the system. Upon integration, it becomes an equation for a finite change in the system:

$$\Delta H = \Delta U + \Delta(PV) \tag{2.15}$$

Equations (2.11), (2.14), and (2.15) apply to a unit mass of substance or to a mole.

Example 2.8

Calculate ΔU and ΔH for 1 kg of water when it is vaporized at the constant temperature of 100°C (373.15 K) and the constant pressure of 101.325 kPa. The specific volumes of liquid and vapor water at these conditions are 0.001 04 and 1.673 $m^3\ kg^{-1}$. For this change, heat in the amount of 2256.9 kJ is added to the water.

Solution

We take the 1 kg of water as the system, because it alone is of interest, and imagine it contained in a cylinder by a frictionless piston which exerts a constant pressure of 101.325 kPa. As heat is added, the water evaporates, expanding from its initial to its final volume. Equation (2.13) as written for the 1-kg system is

$$\Delta H = Q = 2256.9 \text{ kJ}$$

By Eq. (2.15), $\Delta U = \Delta H - \Delta(PV) = \Delta H - P\,\Delta V$

Evaluate the final term:

$$P\,\Delta V = 101.325 \text{ kPa} \times (1.673 - 0.001) \text{ m}^3$$

$$= 169.4 \text{ kPa m}^3 = 169.4 \text{ kN m}^{-2} \text{ m}^3 = 169.4 \text{ kJ}$$

Then $\Delta U = 2256.9 - 169.4 = 2087.5 \text{ kJ}$

2.11 HEAT CAPACITY

The modern view of heat as energy in transit was preceded by the idea that a body has a capacity for heat. The smaller the temperature change in a body caused by the transfer of a given quantity of heat, the greater its capacity. Indeed, a *heat capacity* might be defined as $C \equiv dQ/dT$. The difficulty with this is that it makes C, like Q, a process-dependent quantity rather than a state function. However, it does suggest the definition of two quantities with this outmoded name that are in fact state functions, unambiguously related to other state functions.

Heat Capacity at Constant Volume

The constant-volume heat capacity of a substance is **defined** as

$$C_V \equiv \left(\frac{\partial U}{\partial T}\right)_V \qquad (2.16)$$

This definition accommodates both the molar heat capacity and the specific heat capacity (usually called *specific heat*), depending on whether U is the molar or specific internal energy. Although this definition makes no reference to any process, it relates in an especially simple way to a constant-volume process in a closed system, for which Eq. (2.16) may be written:

$$dU = C_V\, dT \qquad \text{(const } V\text{)} \qquad (2.17)$$

Integration yields: $$\Delta U = \int_{T_1}^{T_2} C_V\, dT \qquad \text{(const } V\text{)} \qquad (2.18)$$

This result with Eq. (2.10) for a mechanically reversible, constant-volume process[7] gives:

$$Q = n\,\Delta U = n\int_{T_1}^{T_2} C_V\, dT \qquad \text{(const } V\text{)} \qquad (2.19)$$

If the volume varies during the process but returns at the end of the process to its initial value, the process cannot rightly be called one of constant volume, even though $V_2 = V_1$ and $\Delta V = 0$. However, changes in state functions are independent of path, and may therefore be calculated by equations for a truly constant-volume process with the same initial and final conditions. Equation (2.18) then gives $\Delta U = \int C_V\, dT$, because U, C_V, and T are all state functions. On the other hand, Q and W depend on path, and Eq. (2.19) is a valid expression for Q, and W is in general zero, only for a *constant-volume* process. This is the reason for the distinction between state functions and Q and W. The principle that state functions are independent of the process is an important and useful concept.

> **For the calculation of property changes, an actual process may be replaced by any other process which accomplishes the same change in state.**

Such an alternative process may be selected, for example, because of its simplicity.

[7]These restrictions serve to rule out work of stirring, which is inherently irreversible.

Heat Capacity at Constant Pressure

The constant-pressure heat capacity is **defined** as

$$C_P \equiv \left(\frac{\partial H}{\partial T}\right)_P \tag{2.20}$$

Again, the definition accommodates both molar and specific heat capacities, depending on whether H is the molar or specific enthalpy. This heat capacity relates in an especially simple way to a constant-pressure, closed-system process, for which Eq. (2.20) is equally well written:

$$dH = C_P\,dT \quad \text{(const } P\text{)} \tag{2.21}$$

whence

$$\Delta H = \int_{T_1}^{T_2} C_P\,dT \quad \text{(const } P\text{)} \tag{2.22}$$

For a mechanically reversible, constant-P process, this result may be combined with Eq. (2.13):

$$Q = n\,\Delta H = n\int_{T_1}^{T_2} C_P\,dT \quad \text{(const } P\text{)} \tag{2.23}$$

Because H, C_P, and T are state functions, Eq. (2.22) applies to any process for which $P_2 = P_1$ whether or not it is actually carried out at constant pressure. However, only for the mechanically reversible, constant-pressure process can heat and work be calculated by the equations $Q = n\,\Delta H$, $Q = n\int C_P\,dT$, and $W = -Pn\,\Delta V$.

Example 2.9

Air at 1 bar and 25°C (298.15 K) is compressed to 5 bar and 25°C (298.15) K by two different mechanically reversible processes:

(*a*) Cooling at constant pressure followed by heating at constant volume

(*b*) Heating at constant volume followed by cooling at constant pressure

Calculate the heat and work requirements and ΔU and ΔH of the air for each path. The following heat capacities for air may be assumed independent of temperature:

$$C_V = 20.78 \quad \text{and} \quad C_P = 29.10 \text{ J mol}^{-1}\text{ K}^{-1}$$

Assume also for air that PV/T is a constant, regardless of the changes it undergoes. At 25°C (298.15 K) and 1 bar the molar volume of air is 0.024 79 m^3 mol^{-1}.

Solution

In each case take the system as 1 mol of air contained in an imaginary piston/cylinder arrangement. Because the processes considered are mechanically reversible, the piston is imagined to move in the cylinder without friction. The final volume is

$$V_2 = V_1 \frac{P_1}{P_2} = 0.024\,79 \left(\frac{1}{5}\right) = 0.004\,958 \text{ m}^3$$

(*a*) During the first step the air is cooled at the constant pressure of 1 bar until the final volume of 0.004 958 m^3 is reached. The temperature of the air at the end of this cooling step is

$$T' = T_1 \frac{V_2}{V_1} = 298.15 \left(\frac{0.004\,958}{0.024\,79}\right) = 59.63 \text{ K}$$

Whence,

$$Q = \Delta H = C_P\, \Delta T = (29.10)(59.63 - 298.15) = -6941 \text{ J}$$

$$\Delta U = \Delta H - \Delta(PV) = \Delta H - P\,\Delta V$$

$$= -6941 - (1 \times 10^5)(0.004\,958 - 0.024\,79) = -4958 \text{ J}$$

During the second step the volume is held constant at V_2 while the air is heated to its final state. By Eq. (2.19),

$$\Delta U = Q = C_V\, \Delta T = (20.78)(298.15 - 59.63) = 4958 \text{ J}$$

The complete process represents the sum of its steps. Hence,

$$Q = -6941 + 4958 = -1983 \text{ J}$$

and

$$\Delta U = -4958 + 4958 = 0$$

Because the first law applies to the entire process, $\Delta U = Q + W$, and therefore,

$$0 = -1983 + W \qquad \text{whence} \qquad W = 1983 \text{ J}$$

Equation (2.15), $\Delta H = \Delta U + \Delta(PV)$, also applies to the entire process. But $T_1 = T_2$, and therefore, $P_1 V_1 = P_2 V_2$. Hence $\Delta(PV) = 0$, and

$$\Delta H = \Delta U = 0$$

(*b*) Two different steps are used in this case to reach the same final state of the air. In the first step the air is heated at a constant volume equal to its initial value until the final pressure of 5 bar is reached. The air temperature at the end of this step is

$$T' = T_1 \frac{P_2}{P_1} = 298.15 \left(\frac{5}{1}\right) = 1490.75 \text{ K}$$

For this step the volume is constant, and

$$Q = \Delta U = C_V \, \Delta T = (20.78)(1490.75 - 298.15) = 24\,788 \text{ J}$$

In the second step the air is cooled at $P = 5$ bar to its final state:

$$\begin{aligned} Q &= \Delta H = C_P \, \Delta T = (29.10)(298.15 - 1490.75) = -34\,703 \text{ J} \\ \Delta U &= \Delta H - \Delta(PV) = \Delta H - P \, \Delta V \\ &= -34\,703 - (5 \times 10^5)(0.004\,958 - 0.024\,79) = -24\,788 \text{ J} \end{aligned}$$

For the two steps combined,

$$\begin{aligned} Q &= 24\,788 - 34\,703 = -9915 \text{ J} \\ \Delta U &= 24\,788 - 24\,788 = 0 \\ W &= \Delta U - Q = 0 - (-9915) = 9915 \text{ J} \end{aligned}$$

and as before $$\Delta H = \Delta U = 0$$

The property changes ΔU and ΔH calculated for the given change in state are the same for both paths. On the other hand the answers to parts (*a*) and (*b*) show that Q and W depend on the path.

Example 2.10

Calculate the internal energy and enthalpy changes that occur when air is changed from an initial state of 277 K and 10 bar, where its molar volume is 2.28 m^3 $kmol^{-1}$ to a final state of 333 K and 1 atm. Assume for air that PV/T is constant and that $C_V =$ 21 and $C_P = 29.3$ kJ $kmol^{-1}K^{-1}$.

Solution

Since property changes are independent of the process that brings them about, we can base calculations on a simple two-step, mechanically reversible process in which 1 kmol of air is (*a*) cooled at constant volume to the final pressure, and (*b*) heated at constant pressure to the final temperature. The absolute temperatures here are on the Kelvin scale:

$$T_1 = 277 \text{ K}$$

$$T_2 = 333 \text{ K}$$

Since $PV = kT$, the ratio T/P is constant for step (*a*). The intermediate temperature between the two steps is therefore

$$T' = (277)(1/10) = 27.7 \text{ K}$$

and the temperature changes for the two steps are

$$\begin{aligned} \Delta T_a &= 27.7 - 277 = -249.3 \text{ K} \\ \Delta T_b &= 333 - 27.7 = 305.3 \text{ K} \end{aligned}$$

For step (a), by Eqs. (2.18) and (2.15)

$$\Delta U_a = C_V\,\Delta T_a$$
$$\Delta U_a = (21)(-249.3) = -5235.3 \text{ kJ kmol}^{-1}$$
$$\Delta H_a = \Delta U_a + V\Delta P_a$$
$$\Delta H_a = -5235.3 + (2.28)(1-10)(10^5)/(10^3) = -7287.3 \text{ kJ kmol}^{-1}$$

The final volume of the air is given by

$$V_2 = V_1\frac{P_1T_2}{P_2T_1} = \frac{(2.28)(10)(333)}{(1)(277)}$$

from which we find that $V_2 = 27.41$ m^3 kmol^{-1}.

For step (b), by Eqs. (2.21) and (2.15)

$$\Delta H_b = C_P\,\Delta T_b$$
$$\Delta H_b = (29.3)(305.3) = 8945.3 \text{ kJ kmol}^{-1}$$
$$\Delta U_b = \Delta H_b - P\Delta V_b$$
$$\Delta U_b = 8945.3 - (1)(27.41 - 2.28)(10^5)/(10^3) = 6432.3 \text{ kJ kmol}^{-1}$$

For the two steps together,

$$\Delta U = -5235.3 + 6432.3 = 1197 \text{ kJ kmol}^{-1}$$
$$\Delta H = -7287.3 + 8945.3 = 1658 \text{ kJ kmol}^{-1}$$

2.12 MASS AND ENERGY BALANCES FOR OPEN SYSTEMS

Although the focus of the preceding sections has been on closed systems, the concepts presented find far more extensive application. The laws of mass and energy conservation apply to *all* processes, to open as well as to closed systems. Indeed, the open system includes the closed system as a special case. The remainder of this chapter is therefore devoted to the treatment of open systems and thus to the development of equations of wide applicability.

Measures of Flow

Open systems are characterized by flowing streams; there are four common measures of flow:

- Mass flowrate, $\dot{m}$
- Molar flowrate, $\dot{n}$
- Volumetric flowrate, q
- Velocity, u

The measures of flow are interrelated:

$$\dot{m} = M\dot{n} \qquad \text{and} \qquad q = uA$$

where M is molar mass. Importantly, mass and molar flowrates relate to velocity:

$\dot{m} = uA\rho$ (2.24a)	$\dot{n} = uA\rho$ (2.24b)

The area for flow A is the cross-sectional area of a conduit, and ρ is specific or molar density. Although velocity is a *vector quantity*, its scalar magnitude u is used here as the average speed of a stream in the direction normal to A. Flowrates $\dot{m}$, $\dot{n}$, and q represent measures of quantity per unit of time. Velocity u is quite different in nature, as it does not suggest the magnitude of flow. Nevertheless, it is an important design parameter.

Example 2.11

Liquid n-hexane flows at a rate of $\dot{m} = 0.75$ kg s^{-1} in a pipe with inside diameter $D = 5$ cm. What are q, $\dot{n}$, and u? What would these quantities be for the same $\dot{m}$ if $D = 2$ cm? Assume for liquid n-hexane that $\rho = 659$ kg m^{-3}.

Solution

We have $q = \dot{m}\rho^{-1}$ and $\dot{n} = \dot{m}M^{-1}$

whence
$$q = \frac{0.75 \text{ kg s}^{-1}}{659 \text{ kg m}^{-3}} = 0.001\,14 \text{ m}^3 \text{ s}^{-1}$$

$$\dot{n} = \frac{(0.75 \text{ kg s}^{-1})(10^3 \text{ g kg}^{-1})}{86.177 \text{ g mol}^{-1}} = 8.703 \text{ mol s}^{-1}$$

Given $\dot{m}$, these quantities are independent of D. The velocity, however, depends on diameter through $u = qA^{-1}$, where, for a circular cross-section, $A = (\pi/4)D^2$. For $D = 5$ cm,

$$A = \frac{\pi}{4}(5 \times 10^{-2} \text{ m})^2 = 0.001\,96 \text{ m}^2$$

whence
$$u = \frac{0.001\,14 \text{ m}^3 \text{ s}^{-1}}{0.001\,96 \text{ m}^2} = 0.582 \text{ m s}^{-1}$$

Similarly, for $D = 2$ cm,

$$A = 0.000\,314 \text{ m}^2 \quad \text{and} \quad u = \frac{0.001\,14}{0.000\,314} = 3.63 \text{ m s}^{-1}$$

Mass Balance for Open Systems

The region of space identified for analysis of open systems is called a *control volume*; it is separated from its surroundings by a *control surface*. The fluid within the control volume

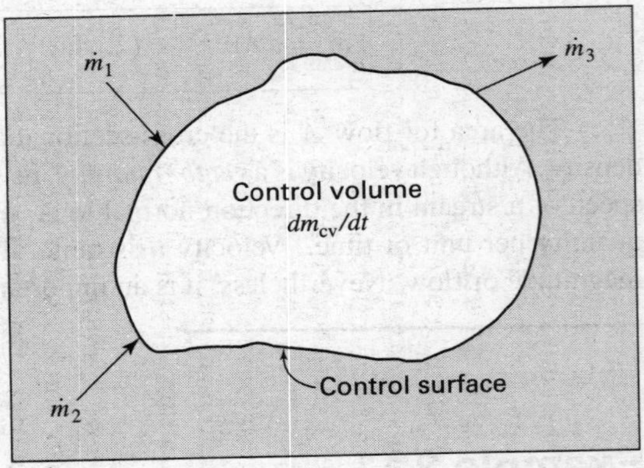

Figure 2.5: Schematic representation of a control volume

is the thermodynamic system for which mass and energy balances are written. The control volume shown schematically in Fig. 2.5 is separated from its surroundings by an extensible control surface. Two streams with flow rates $\dot{m}_1$ and $\dot{m}_2$ are shown directed into the control volume, and one stream with flow rate $\dot{m}_3$ is directed out. Because mass is conserved, the rate of change of mass within the control volume, dm_{cv}/dt, equals the net rate of flow of mass into the control volume. The convention is that flow is positive when directed into the control volume and negative when directed out. The mass balance is expressed mathematically by

$$\boxed{\frac{dm_{cv}}{dt} + \Delta(\dot{m})_{fs} = 0} \tag{2.25}$$

where the second term for the control volume of Fig. 2.5 is

$$\Delta(\dot{m})_{fs} = \dot{m}_3 - \dot{m}_1 - \dot{m}_2$$

The difference operator "Δ" here signifies the difference between exit and entrance flows and the subscript "fs" indicates that the term applies to all flowing streams.

When the mass flowrate $\dot{m}$ is given by Eq. (2.24a), Eq. (2.25) becomes

$$\frac{dm_{cv}}{dt} + \Delta(\rho u A)_{fs} = 0 \tag{2.26}$$

In this form the mass-balance equation is often called the *continuity equation*.

The flow process characterized as *steady state* is an important special case for which conditions within the control volume do not change with time. The control volume then contains a constant mass of fluid, and the first or *accumulation* term of Eq. (2.25) is zero, reducing Eq. (2.26) to

$$\Delta(\rho u A)_{fs} = 0$$

The term "steady state" does not necessarily imply that flowrates are constant, merely that the inflow of mass is exactly matched by the outflow of mass.

When there is but a single entrance and a single exit stream, the mass flowrate $\dot{m}$ is the same for both streams; then,

$$\rho_2 u_2 A_2 - \rho_1 u_1 A_1 = 0$$

or $$\dot{m} = \text{const} = \rho_2 u_2 A_2 = \rho_1 u_1 A_1$$

Because specific volume is the reciprocal of density,

$$\boxed{\dot{m} = \frac{u_1 A_1}{V_1} = \frac{u_2 A_2}{V_2} = \frac{uA}{V}} \tag{2.27}$$

This form of the continuity equation finds frequent use.

The General Energy Balance

Because energy, like mass, is conserved, the rate of change of energy within the control volume equals the net rate of energy transfer into the control volume. Streams flowing into and out of the control volume have associated with them energy in its internal, potential, and kinetic forms, and all contribute to the energy change of the system. Each unit mass of a stream carries with it a total energy $U + \frac{1}{2}u^2 + zg$, where u is the average velocity of the stream, z is its elevation above a datum level, and g is the local acceleration of gravity. Thus, each stream transports energy at the rate $(U + \frac{1}{2}u^2 + zg)\dot{m}$. The net energy transported *into* the system by the flowing streams is therefore $-\Delta\left[\left(U + \frac{1}{2}u^2 + zg\right)\dot{m}\right]_{\text{fs}}$, where the effect of the minus sign with "Δ" is to make the term read *in* − *out*. The rate of energy accumulation within the control volume includes this quantity in addition to the heat transfer rate $\dot{Q}$ and work rate:

$$\frac{d(mU)_{\text{cv}}}{dt} = -\Delta\left[\left(U + \tfrac{1}{2}u^2 + zg\right)\dot{m}\right]_{\text{fs}} + \dot{Q} + \text{work rate}$$

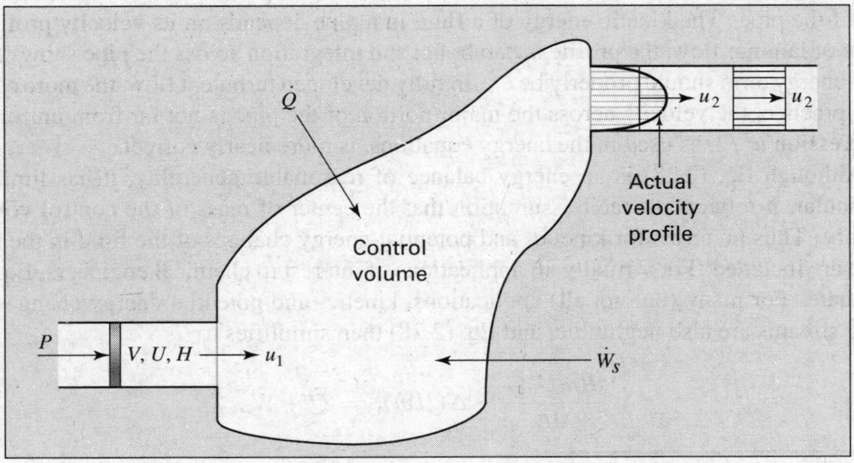

Figure 2.6: Control volume with one entrance and one exit

The work rate may include work of several forms. First, work is associated with moving the flowing streams through entrances and exits. The fluid at any entrance or exit has a set of average properties, P, V, U, H, etc. Imagine that a unit mass of fluid with these properties exists at an entrance or exit, as shown in Fig. 2.6 (at the entrance). This unit mass of fluid is acted upon by additional fluid, here replaced by a piston which exerts the constant pressure P. The work done by this piston in moving the unit mass through the entrance is PV, and the work rate is $(PV)\dot{m}$. Because "Δ" denotes the difference between exit and entrance quantities, the net work done *on* the system when all entrance and exit sections are taken into account is $-\Delta[(PV)\dot{m}]_{\text{fs}}$.

Another form of work is the shaft work indicated in Fig. 2.6 by rate $\dot{W}_s$. In addition work may be associated with expansion or contraction of the control volume and there may be stirring work. These forms of work are all included in a rate term represented by $\dot{W}$. The preceding equation may now be written:

$$\frac{d(mU)_{\text{cv}}}{dt} = -\Delta\left[\left(U + \tfrac{1}{2}u^2 + zg\right)\dot{m}\right]_{\text{fs}} + \dot{Q} - \Delta[(PV)\dot{m}]_{\text{fs}} + \dot{W}$$

Combination of terms in accord with the definition of enthalpy, $H = U + PV$, leads to:

$$\frac{d(mU)_{\text{cv}}}{dt} = -\Delta\left[\left(H + \tfrac{1}{2}u^2 + zg\right)\dot{m}\right]_{\text{fs}} + \dot{Q} + \dot{W}$$

which is usually written:

$$\boxed{\frac{d(mU)_{\text{cv}}}{dt} + \Delta\left[\left(H + \tfrac{1}{2}u^2 + zg\right)\dot{m}\right]_{\text{fs}} = \dot{Q} + \dot{W}} \tag{2.28}$$

The velocity u in the kinetic-energy terms of energy balances is the bulk-mean velocity as defined by the equation, $u = \dot{m}/\rho A$. Fluids flowing in pipes exhibit a velocity profile, as shown in Fig. 2.6, which rises from zero at the wall (the no-slip condition) to a maximum at the center of the pipe. The kinetic energy of a fluid in a pipe depends on its velocity profile. For the case of laminar flow, the profile is parabolic, and integration across the pipe shows that the kinetic-energy term should properly be u^2. In fully developed turbulent flow, the more common case in practice, the velocity across the major portion of the pipe is not far from uniform, and the expression $u^2/2$, as used in the energy equations, is more nearly correct.

Although Eq. (2.28) is an energy balance of reasonable generality, it has limitations. In particular, it reflects the tacit assumption that the center of mass of the control volume is stationary. Thus no terms for kinetic- and potential-energy changes of the fluid in the control volume are included. For virtually all applications of interest to chemical engineers, Eq. (2.28) is adequate. For many (but not all) applications, kinetic- and potential-energy changes in the flowing streams are also negligible, and Eq. (2.28) then simplifies to

$$\frac{d(mU)_{\text{cv}}}{dt} + \Delta(H\dot{m})_{\text{fs}} = \dot{Q} + \dot{W} \tag{2.29}$$

Example 2.12

Show that Eq. (2.29) reduces to Eq. (2.3) for the case of a closed system.

Solution

The second term of Eq. (2.29) is omitted in the absence of flowing streams, and the equation is then multiplied by dt:

$$d(mU)_{\text{cv}} = \dot{Q}\,dt + \dot{W}\,dt$$

Integration over time gives:

$$\Delta(mU)_{\text{cv}} = \int_{t_1}^{t_2} \dot{Q}\,dt + \int_{t_1}^{t_2} \dot{W}\,dt$$

or

$$\Delta U^t = Q + W$$

The Q and W terms are defined by the integrals of the preceding equation.

Equation (2.29) may be applied to a variety of processes of a transient nature, as illustrated in the following examples.

Example 2.13

An evacuated tank is filled with gas from a constant-pressure line. What is the relation between the enthalpy of the gas in the entrance line and the internal energy of the gas in the tank? Neglect heat transfer between the gas and the tank.

Solution

The tank with its single entrance serves as the control volume. Because there is no expansion work, stirring work, or shaft work, $\dot{W} = 0$. If kinetic- and potential-energy changes are negligible, Eq. (2.29) becomes

$$\frac{d(mU)_{\text{tank}}}{dt} - H'\dot{m}' = 0$$

where the prime (′) identifies the entrance stream and the minus sign is required because it *is* an entrance stream. The mass balance is

$$\dot{m}' = \frac{dm_{\text{tank}}}{dt}$$

Combining these two balance equations yields

$$\frac{d(mU)_{\text{tank}}}{dt} - H'\frac{dm_{\text{tank}}}{dt} = 0$$

Multiplying by dt and integrating over time (noting that H' is constant) gives

$$\Delta(mU)_{\text{tank}} - H'\Delta m_{\text{tank}} = 0$$

Whence $$m_2U_2 - m_1U_1 = H'(m_2 - m_1)$$

where subscripts 1 and 2 denote initial and final conditions in the tank.

Because the mass in the tank initially is zero, $m_1 = 0$; then,

$$U_2 = H'$$

a result showing that in the absence of heat transfer, the energy of the gas contained within the tank at the end of the process is equal to the enthalpy of the gas added.

Example 2.14

An insulated, electrically heated tank for hot water contains 190 kg of liquid water at 60°C (333.15 K) when a power outage occurs. If water is withdrawn from the tank at a steady rate of $\dot{m} = 0.2$ kg s^{-1}, how long will it take for the temperature of the water in the tank to drop from 60 to 35°C (333.15 K to 308.15 K)? Assume cold water enters the tank at 10°C (283.15 K), and negligible heat losses from the tank. For liquid water let $C_V = C_P = C$, independent of T and P.

Solution

Here, $\dot{Q} = \dot{W} = 0$. Additionally, assume perfect mixing of the contents of the tank; this implies that the properties of the water leaving the tank are those of the water in the tank. With the mass flowrate into the tank equal to the mass flowrate out, m_{cv} is constant; moreover, the differences between inlet and outlet kinetic and potential energies can be neglected. Equation (2.29) is therefore written as

$$m\frac{dU}{dt} + \dot{m}(H - H_1) = 0$$

where unsubscripted quantities refer to the contents of the tank and H_1 is the specific enthalpy of the water entering the tank. With $C_V = C_P = C$,

$$\frac{dU}{dt} = C\frac{dT}{dt} \qquad \text{and} \qquad H - H_1 = C(T - T_1)$$

The energy balance then becomes, on rearrangement,

$$dt = -\frac{m}{\dot{m}}\frac{dT}{T - T_1}$$

Integration from $t = 0$ (where $T = T_0$) to arbitrary time t yields

$$t = -\frac{m}{\dot{m}}\ln\left(\frac{T - T_1}{T_0 - T_1}\right)$$

Substitution of numerical values into this equation gives, for the conditions of this problem,

$$t = -\frac{190}{0.2} \ln \left(\frac{308.15 - 283.15}{333.15 - 283.15} \right) = 658.5 \text{ s}$$

Thus, it takes about 11 minutes for the water temperature in the tank to drop from 60 to 35°C (333.15 K to 308.15 K).

Energy Balances for Steady-State Flow Processes

Flow processes for which the accumulation term of Eq. (2.28), $d(mU)_{cv}/dt$, is zero are said to occur at *steady state*. As discussed with respect to the mass balance, this means that the mass of the system within the control volume is constant; it also means that no changes occur with time in the properties of the fluid within the control volume nor at its entrances and exits. No expansion of the control volume is possible under these circumstances. The only work of the process is shaft work, and the general energy balance, Eq. (2.28), becomes

$$\Delta\left[\left(H + \tfrac{1}{2}u^2 + zg\right)\dot{m}\right]_{fs} = \dot{Q} + \dot{W}_s \tag{2.30}$$

Although "steady state" does not necessarily imply "steady flow," the usual application of this equation is to steady-state, steady-flow processes, because such processes represent the industrial norm.[8]

A further specialization results when the control volume has but one entrance and one exit. The same mass flowrate $\dot{m}$ then applies to both streams, and Eq. (2.30) reduces to

$$\Delta\left(H + \tfrac{1}{2}u^2 + zg\right)\dot{m} = \dot{Q} + \dot{W}_s \tag{2.31}$$

where subscript "fs" has been omitted in this simple case and "Δ" denotes the change from entrance to exit. Division by $\dot{m}$ gives

$$\Delta\left(H + \tfrac{1}{2}u^2 + zg\right) = \frac{\dot{Q}}{\dot{m}} + \frac{\dot{W}_s}{\dot{m}} = Q + W_s$$

or

$$\Delta H + \frac{\Delta u^2}{2} + g\,\Delta z = Q + W_s \tag{2.32a}$$

This equation is the mathematical expression of the first law for a steady-state, steady-flow process between one entrance and one exit. All terms represent energy per unit mass of fluid.

In all of the energy-balance equations so far written, the energy unit is presumed to be the joule, in accord with the SI system of units. For the metric engineering system of units, the

[8]An example of a steady-state process that is not steady flow is a water heater in which variations in flow rate are exactly compensated by changes in the rate of heat transfer so that temperatures throughout remain constant.

kinetic- and potential-energy terms, wherever they appear, require division by the dimensional constant g_c (Secs. 1.4 and 1.8). In this event Eq. (2.32a), for example, is written

$$\boxed{\Delta H + \frac{\Delta u^2}{2g_c} + \frac{g}{g_c}\Delta z = Q + W_s} \tag{2.32b}$$

Here, the usual unit for ΔH and Q is the kcal; kinetic energy, potential energy, and work are usually expressed as m kgf. Therefore the factor 426.935 m kgf kcal^{-1} must be used with the appropriate terms to put them all in consistent units of either m kgf or kcal.

In many applications, kinetic- and potential-energy terms are omitted, because they are negligible compared with other terms.[9] For such cases, Eqs. (2.32a) and (2.32b) reduce to

$$\Delta H = Q + W_s \tag{2.33}$$

This expression of the first law for a steady-state, steady-flow process is analogous to Eq. (2.3) for a nonflow process. However, enthalpy rather than internal energy is the thermodynamic property of importance.

A Flow Calorimeter for Enthalpy Measurements

The application of Eqs. (2.32) and (2.33) to the solution of practical problems requires enthalpy values. Because H is a state function, its values depend only on point conditions; once determined, they may be tabulated for subsequent use for the same sets of conditions. To this end, Eq. (2.33) may be applied to laboratory processes designed for enthalpy measurements.

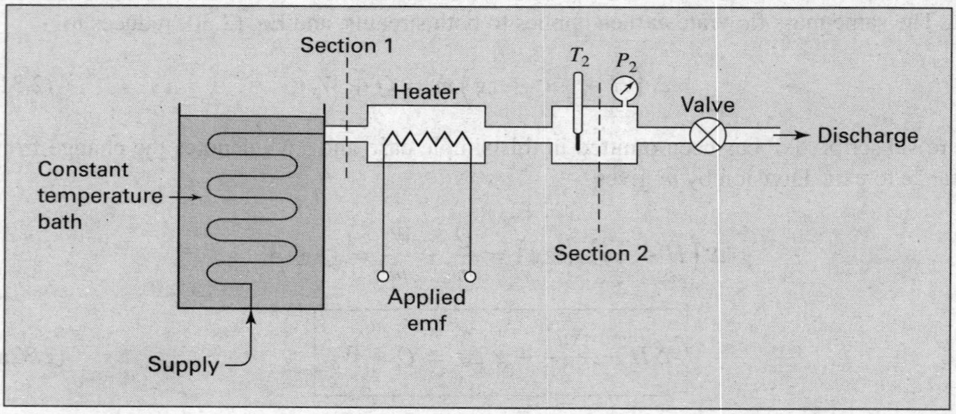

Figure 2.7: Flow calorimeter

A simple flow calorimeter is illustrated schematically in Fig. 2.7. Its essential feature is an electric resistance heater immersed in a flowing fluid. The design provides for minimal

[9] Exceptions are applications to nozzles, metering devices, wind tunnels, and hydroelectric power stations.

velocity and elevation changes from section 1 to section 2, making kinetic- and potential-energy changes of the fluid negligible. With no shaft work entering the system, Eq. (2.33) reduces to $\Delta H = H_2 - H_1 = Q$. The rate of heat transfer to the fluid is determined from the resistance of the heater and the current passing through it. In practice a number of details need attention, but in principle the operation of the flow calorimeter is simple. Measurements of the heat rate and flowrate allow calculation of the change ΔH between sections 1 and 2.

For example, enthalpies of both liquid and vapor H_2O are readily determined. The constant-temperature bath is filled with a mixture of crushed ice and water to maintain a temperature of 0°C (273.15 K). Liquid water is supplied to the apparatus, and the coil that carries it through the constant-temperature bath is long enough to bring it to an exit temperature of essentially 0°C (273.15 K). The temperature and pressure at section 2 are measured by suitable instruments. Values of the enthalpy of H_2O for various conditions at section 2 are given by

$$H_2 = H_1 + Q$$

where Q is the heat added per unit mass of water flowing.

The pressure varies from run to run, but in the range encountered here it has a negligible effect on the enthalpy of the entering water, and for practical purposes H_1 is a constant. Absolute values of enthalpy, like absolute values of internal energy, are unknown. An arbitrary value may therefore be assigned to H_1 as the *basis* for all other enthalpy values. Setting $H_1 = 0$ for liquid water at 0°C (273.15 K) makes

$$H_2 = H_1 + Q = 0 + Q = Q$$

Enthalpy values may be tabulated for the temperatures and pressures existing at section 2 for a large number of runs. In addition, specific-volume measurements made for these same conditions may be added to the table, along with corresponding values of the internal energy calculated by Eq. (2.11), $U = H - PV$. In this way tables of thermodynamic properties are compiled over the entire useful range of conditions. The most widely used such tabulation is for H_2O and is known as the *steam tables*.[10]

The enthalpy may be taken as zero for some other state than liquid at 0°C (273.15 K). The choice is arbitrary. The equations of thermodynamics, such as Eqs. (2.32) and (2.33), apply to *changes* of state, for which the enthalpy *differences* are independent of the location of the zero point. However, once an arbitrary zero point is selected for the enthalpy, an arbitrary choice cannot be made for the internal energy, because the internal energy can be calculated from the enthalpy by Eq. (2.11).

Example 2.15

For the flow calorimeter just discussed, the following data are taken with water as the test fluid:

Flow rate = 4.15 g s^{-1} $t_1/T_1 = 0°C/273.15$ K $t_2/T_2 = 300°C/573.15$ K $P_2 = 3$ bar

[10]Steam tables are given in App. F. Tables for various other substances are found in the literature. A discussion of compilations of thermodynamic properties appears in Chap. 6.

Rate of heat addition from resistance heater = 12 740 W

The water is completely vaporized in the process. Calculate the enthalpy of steam at 300°C (573.15 K) and 3 bar based on $H = 0$ for liquid water at 0°C (273.15 K).

Solution

If Δz and Δu^2 are negligible and if W_s and H_1 are zero, then $H_2 = Q$, and

$$H_2 = \frac{12\,740 \text{ J s}^{-1}}{4.15 \text{ g s}^{-1}} = 3070 \text{ J g}^{-1}$$

Example 2.16

Air at 1 bar and 25°C (298.15 K) enters a compressor at low velocity, discharges at 3 bar, and enters a nozzle in which it expands to a final velocity of 600 m s^{-1} at the initial conditions of pressure and temperature. If the work of compression is 240 kJ per kilogram of air, how much heat must be removed during compression?

Solution

Because the air returns to its initial conditions of T and P, the overall process produces no change in enthalpy of the air. Moreover, the potential-energy change of the air is presumed negligible. Neglecting also the initial kinetic energy of the air, we write Eq. (2.32a) as

$$Q = \frac{u_2^2}{2} - W_s$$

The kinetic-energy term is evaluated as follows:

$$\frac{1}{2}u_2^2 = \frac{1}{2}\left(600\,\frac{\text{m}}{\text{s}}\right)^2 = 180\,000\,\frac{\text{m}^2}{\text{s}^2}$$

$$= 180\,000\,\frac{\text{m}^2}{\text{s}^2}\cdot\frac{\text{kg}}{\text{kg}} = 180\,000 \text{ N m kg}^{-1} = 180 \text{ kJ kg}^{-1}$$

Then $$Q = 180 - 240 = -60 \text{ kJ kg}^{-1}$$

Heat in the amount of 60 kJ must be removed per kilogram of air compressed.

Example 2.17

Water at 93.5°C (366.65 K) is pumped from a storage tank at the rate of 3.15 × 10^{-3} m^3 s^{-1}. The motor for the pump supplies work at the rate of 1.5 kW. The water goes through a heat exchanger, giving up heat at the rate of 700 kW, and is delivered to a second storage tank at an elevation 15 m above the first tank. What is the temperature of the water delivered to the second tank?

Solution

This is a steady-state steady-flow process for which Eq. (2.32b) applies. The initial and final velocities of water in the storage tanks are negligible, and the term $\Delta u^2/2g_c$ may be omitted. The remaining terms are expressed in units of kJ kg^{-1}through use of appropriate conversion factors. At 366.65 K the density of water is 958 kg m^{-3}thus the mass flow rate is

$$(3.15)(10^{-3})(958) = 3.018 \text{ kg s}^{-1}$$

from which we obtain

$$Q = -700/3.018 = -231.9 \text{ kJ kg}^{-1}$$

Since 1 kW is equivalent to 1 kJ s^{-1}, the shaft work is

$$W_s = (1.5)(1)/(3.018) = 0.497 \text{ kJ kg}^{-1}$$

If the local acceleration of gravity is taken as the standard value of 9.807 m s^{-2}, the potential-energy term becomes

$$\frac{g}{g_c}\Delta z = \left(\frac{9.807}{9.807}\right)\frac{(15)(9.807)}{1000} = 0.147 \text{ kJ kg}^{-1}$$

Equation (2.32b) now yields ΔH:

$$\Delta H = Q + W_s - \frac{g}{g_c}\Delta z = -231.9 + 0.497 - 0.147 = -231.55 \text{ kJ kg}^{-1}$$

The enthalpy of saturated water at 93.5°C (366.65 K) is given in the steam tables as 391.6 kJ kg^{-1} Thus

$$\Delta H = H_2 - H_1 = H_2 - 391.6 = -231.55$$

and

$$H_2 = 391.6 - 231.55 = 160.05 \text{ kJ kg}^{-1}$$

The temperature of water having this enthalpy is found from the steam tables to be

$$t = 38.2°\text{C} \quad \text{or} \quad T = 311.35 \text{ K}$$

In this example W_s and $(g/g_c)\Delta z$ are small compared with Q, and for practical purposes they could be neglected.

PROBLEMS

2.1. A nonconducting container filled with 25 kg of water at 20°C (293.15 K) is fitted with a stirrer, which is made to turn by gravity acting on a weight of mass 35 kg. The weight falls slowly through a distance of 5 m in driving the stirrer. Assuming that all work done on the weight is transferred to the water and that the local acceleration of gravity is 9.8 m s^{-2}, determine the

(*a*) amount of work done on the water
(*b*) internal-energy change of the water
(*c*) final temperature of the water, for which $C_P = 4.18$ kJ kg^{-1} $°C^{-1}$
(*d*) amount of heat that must be removed from the water to return it to its initial temperature
(*e*) total energy change of the universe because of (1) the process of lowering the weight, (2) the process of cooling the water back to its initial temperature, and (3) both processes together

2.2. Rework Prob. 2.1 for an insulated container that changes in temperature along with the water and has a heat capacity equivalent to 5 kg of water. Work the problem with

(*a*) the water and container as the system; (*b*) the water alone as the system

2.3. An egg, initially at rest, is dropped onto a concrete surface and breaks. With the egg treated as the system, answer the following:

(*a*) What is the sign of W?
(*b*) What is the sign of ΔE_P?
(*c*) What is ΔE_K?
(*d*) What is ΔU^t?
(*e*) What is the sign of Q?

In modeling this process, assume the passage of sufficient time for the broken egg to return to its initial temperature. What is the origin of the heat transfer of part (*e*)?

2.4. An electric motor under steady load draws 9.7 amperes at 110 volts, delivering 0.93 kW of mechanical energy. What is the rate of heat transfer from the motor, in kW?

2.5. One mole of gas in a closed system undergoes a four step thermodynamic cycle. Use the data given in the following table to determine numerical values for the missing quantities, i.e., "fill in the blanks."

Step	ΔU^t/J	Q/J	W/J
12	−200	?	−6000
23	?	−3800	?
34	?	−800	300
41	4700	?	?
12341	?	?	−1400

2.6. Comment on the feasibility of cooling your kitchen in the summer by opening the door to the electrically powered refrigerator.

2.7. A renowned laboratory reports quadruple-point coordinates of 10.2 Mbar and 24.1°C (297.25 K) for four-phase equilibrium of allotropic solid forms of the exotic chemical β-miasmone. Evaluate the claim.

2.8. A closed, nonreactive system contains species 1 and 2 in vapor/liquid equilibrium. Species 2 is a very light gas, essentially insoluble in the liquid phase. The vapor phase contains both species 1 and 2. Some additional moles of species 2 are added to the system, which is then restored to its initial T and P. As a result of the process, does the total number of moles of liquid increase, decrease, or remain unchanged?

2.9. A system comprised of chloroform, 1,4-dioxane, and ethanol exists as a two-phase vapor/liquid system at 50°C (323.15 K) and 55 kPa. It is found, after the addition of some pure ethanol, that the system can be returned to two-phase equilibrium at the initial T and P. In what respect has the system changed, and in what respect has it not changed?

2.10. For the system described in Pb. 2.9,

(*a*) how many phase-rule variables in addition to T and P must be chosen so as to fix the compositions of both phases?
(*b*) if the temperature and pressure are to remain the same, can the *overall* composition of the system be changed (by adding or removing material) without affecting the compositions of the liquid and vapor phases?

2.11. A tank containing 20 kg of water at 20°C (293.15 K) is fitted with a stirrer that delivers work to the water at the rate of 0.25 kW. How long does it take for the temperature of the water to rise to 30°C (303.15 K) if no heat is lost from the water? For water, $C_P = 4.18$ kJ kg^{-1} °C^{-1}.

2.12. Heat in the amount of 7.5 kJ is added to a closed system while its internal energy decreases by 12 kJ. How much energy is transferred as work? For a process causing the same change of state but for which the work is zero, how much heat is transferred?

2.13. A steel casting weighing 2 kg has an initial temperature of 500°C (773.15 K); 40 kg of water initially at 25°C (298.15 K) is contained in a perfectly insulated steel tank weighing 5 kg. The casting is immersed in the water and the system is allowed to come to equilibrium. What is its final temperature? Ignore effects of expansion or contraction, and assume constant specific heats of 4.18 kJ kg^{-1} K^{-1} for water and 0.50 kJ kg^{-1} K^{-1} for steel.

2.14. An incompressible fluid (ρ = constant) is contained in an insulated cylinder fitted with a frictionless piston. Can energy as work be transferred to the fluid? What is the change in internal energy of the fluid when the pressure is increased from P_1 to P_2?

2.15. One kg of liquid water at 25°C (298.15 K)

(*a*) Experiences a temperature increase of 1°C (1 K). What is ΔU^t, in kJ?
(*b*) Experiences a change in elevation Δz. The change in potential energy ΔE_P is the same as ΔU^t for part (*a*). What is Δz, in meters?
(*c*) Is accelerated from rest to final velocity u. The change in kinetic energy ΔE_K is the same as ΔU^t for part (*a*). What is u, in m s^{-1}?

Compare and discuss the results of the three preceding parts.

2.16. An electric motor runs "hot" under load, owing to internal irreversibilities. It has been suggested that the associated energy loss be minimized by thermally insulating the motor casing. Comment critically on this suggestion.

2.17. A hydroturbine operates with a head of 50 m of water. Inlet and outlet conduits are 2 m in diameter. Estimate the mechanical power developed by the turbine for an outlet velocity of 5 m s^{-1}.

2.18. Liquid water at 180°C (453.15 K) and 1002.7 kPa has an internal energy (on an arbitrary scale) of 762.0 kJ kg^{-1} and a specific volume of 1.128 cm^3 g^{-1}.

(*a*) What is its enthalpy?
(*b*) The water is brought to the vapor state at 300°C (573.15 K) and 1500 kPa, where its internal energy is 2784.4 kJ kg^{-1} and its specific volume is 169.7 cm^3 g^{-1}. Calculate ΔU and ΔH for the process.

2.19. A solid body at initial temperature T_0 is immersed in a bath of water at initial temperature T_{w0}. Heat is transferred from the solid to the water at a rate $\dot{Q} = K \cdot (T_w - T)$, where K is a constant and T_w and T are *instantaneous* values of the temperatures of the water and solid. Develop an expression for T as a function of time τ. Check your result for the limiting cases, $\tau = 0$ and $\tau = \infty$. Ignore effects of expansion or contraction, and assume constant specific heats for both water and solid.

2.20. A list of common unit operations follows

(*a*) Single-pipe heat exchanger; (*b*) Double-pipe heat exchanger; (*c*) Pump;
(*d*) Gas compressor: (*e*) Gas turbine; (*f*) Throttle valve; (*g*) Nozzle

Develop a simplified form of the general steady-state energy balance appropriate for each operation. State carefully, and justify, any assumptions you make.

2.21. The Reynolds number Re is a dimensionless group which characterizes the intensity of a flow. For large Re, a flow is turbulent; for small Re, it is laminar. For pipe flow, $\text{Re} \equiv u\rho D/\mu$, where D is pipe diameter and μ is dynamic viscosity.

(*a*) If D and μ are fixed, what is the effect of increasing mass flowrate $\dot{m}$ on Re?
(*b*) If $\dot{m}$ and μ are fixed, what is the effect of increasing D on Re?

2.22. An incompressible (ρ = constant) liquid flows steadily through a conduit of circular cross-section and increasing diameter. At location 1, the diameter is 2.5 cm and the velocity is 2 m s^{-1}; at location 2, the diameter is 5 cm.

(*a*) What is the velocity at location 2?

(*b*) What is the kinetic-energy change (J kg^{-1}) of the fluid between locations 1 and 2?

2.23. A stream of warm water is produced in a steady-flow mixing process by combining 1.0 kg s^{-1} of cool water at 25°C (298.15 K) with 0.8 kg s^{-1} of hot water at 75°C (348.15 K). During mixing, heat is lost to the surroundings at the rate of 30 kJ s^{-1}. What is the temperature of the warm-water stream? Assume the specific heat of water constant at 4.18 kJ kg^{-1} K^{-1}.

2.24. Gas is bled from a tank. Neglecting heat transfer between the gas and the tank, show that mass and energy balances produce the differential equation:

$$\frac{dU}{H' - U} = \frac{dm}{m}$$

Here, U and m refer to the gas remaining in the tank; H' is the specific enthalpy of the gas leaving the tank. Under what conditions can one assume $H' = H$?

2.25. Water at 28°C (301.15 K) flows in a straight horizontal pipe in which there is no exchange of either heat or work with the surroundings. Its velocity is 14 m s^{-1} in a pipe with an internal diameter of 2.5 cm until it flows into a section where the pipe diameter abruptly increases. What is the temperature change of the water if the downstream diameter is 3.8 cm? If it is 7.5 cm? What is the maximum temperature change for an enlargement in the pipe?

2.26. Fifty kmol per hour of air is compressed from P_1 = 1.2 bar to P_2 = 6.0 bar in a steady-flow compressor. Delivered mechanical power is 98.8 kW. Temperatures and velocities are

$$T_1 = 300 \text{ K} \qquad T_2 = 520 \text{ K}$$
$$u_1 = 10 \text{ m s}^{-1} \qquad u_2 = 3.5 \text{ m s}^{-1}$$

Estimate the rate of heat transfer from the compressor. Assume for air that $C_P = \frac{7}{2}R$ and that enthalpy is independent of pressure.

2.27. Nitrogen flows at steady state through a horizontal, insulated pipe with inside diameter of 38.1 mm. A pressure drop results from flow through a partially opened valve. Just upstream from the valve the pressure is 690 kPa, the temperature is 49°C (322.15 K), and the average velocity is 6.09 m s^{-1}. If the pressure just downstream from the valve is 138 kPa, what is the temperature? Assume for nitrogen that PV/T is constant, $C_V = (5/2)R$, and $C_P = (7/2)R$. (Values for R are given in App. A.)

2.28. Water flows through a horizontal coil heated from the outside by high-temperature flue gases. As it passes through the coil the water changes state from liquid at 200 kPa and 80°C (353.15 K) to vapor at 100 kPa and 125°C (398.15 K). Its entering velocity is 3 m s^{-1} and its exit velocity is 200 m s^{-1}. Determine the heat transferred through the coil per unit mass of water. Enthalpies of the inlet and outlet streams are
Inlet: 334.9 kJ kg^{-1}; Outlet: 2726.5 kJ kg^{-1}

2.29. Steam flows at steady state through a converging, insulated nozzle, 25 cm long and with an inlet diameter of 5 cm. At the nozzle entrance (state 1), the temperature and pressure are 325°C (598.15 K) and 700 kPa, and the velocity is 30 m s^{-1}. At the nozzle exit (state 2), the steam temperature and pressure are 240°C (513.15 K) and 350 kPa. Property values are

$H_1 = 3112.5$ kJ kg^{-1} $\qquad V_1 = 388.61$ cm^3 g^{-1}
$H_2 = 2945.7$ kJ kg^{-1} $\qquad V_2 = 667.75$ cm^3 g^{-1}

What is the velocity of the steam at the nozzle exit, and what is the exit diameter?

2.30. In the following take $C_V = 20.8$ and $C_P = 29.1$ J mol^{-1} $°C^{-1}$ for nitrogen gas:

(*a*) Three moles of nitrogen at 30°C (303.15 K), contained in a rigid vessel, is heated to 250°C (523.15 K). How much heat is required if the vessel has a negligible heat capacity? If the vessel weighs 100 kg and has a heat capacity of 0.5 kJ kg^{-1} $°C^{-1}$, how much heat is required?

(*b*) Four moles of nitrogen at 200°C (473.15 K) is contained in a piston/cylinder arrangement. How much heat must be extracted from this system, which is kept at constant pressure, to cool it to 40°C (313.15 K) if the heat capacity of the piston and cylinder is neglected?

2.31. In the following take $C_V = 21$ and $C_P = 29.3$ kJ $kmol^{-1}K^{-1}$for nitrogen gas:

(*a*) 1.5 kmol of nitrogen at 21°C (294.15 K) contained in a rigid vessel, is heated to 177°C (450.15 K). How much heat is required if the vessel has a negligible heat capacity? If it weighs 90.7 kg and has a heat capacity of 0.5 kJ kg^{-1} K^{-1}, how much heat is required?

(*b*) Two kmol of nitrogen at 174°C (447.15 K) is contained in a piston/cylinder arrangement. How much heat must be extracted from this system, which is kept at constant pressure, to cool it to 65°C (338.15 K) if the heat capacity of the piston and cylinder is neglected?

2.32. Find the equation for the work of a reversible, isothermal compression of 1 mol of gas in a piston/cylinder assembly if the molar volume of the gas is given by

$$V = \frac{RT}{P} + b$$

where b and R are positive constants.

2.33. Steam at 14 bar and 315°C (588.15 K) [state 1] enters a turbine through a 75 mm-diameter pipe with a velocity of 3 m s^{-1}. The exhaust from the turbine is carried through a 250 mm- diameter pipe and is at 0.35 bar and 93°C (366.15 K) [state 2]. What is the power output of the turbine?

$H_1 = 3074.5$ kJ kg^{-1} $\quad V_1 = 0.1909$ m^3 kg^{-1}

$H_2 = 2871.6$ kJ kg^{-1} $\quad V_2 = 4.878$ m^3 kg^{-1}

2.34. Carbon dioxide gas enters a water-cooled compressor at the initial conditions $P_1 = 1.04$ bar and $T_1 = 10°C$ (283.15 K) and is discharged at the final conditions $P_2 = 35.8$ bar and $T_2 = 93°C$ (366.15 K). The entering CO_2 flows through a 100 mm-diameter pipe with a velocity of 6 s m^{-1}, and is discharged through a 25 mm-diameter pipe. The shaft work supplied to the compressor is 12 500 kJ $kmol^{-1}$. What is the heat-transfer rate from the compressor in kW?

$H_1 = 714$ kJ kg^{-1} $\quad V_1 = 0.5774$ m^3 kg^{-1}

$H_2 = 768$ kJ kg^{-1} $\quad V_2 = 0.0175$ m^3 kg^{-1}.

2.35. Show that W and Q for an *arbitrary* mechanically reversible nonflow process are given by

$$W = \int V\,dP - \Delta(PV) \qquad Q = \Delta H - \int V\,dP$$

2.36. One kilogram of air is heated reversibly at constant pressure from an initial state of 300 K and 1 bar until its volume triples. Calculate W, Q, ΔU, and ΔH for the process. Assume for air that $PV/T = 83.14$ bar cm^3 mol^{-1} K^{-1} and $C_P = 29$ J mol^{-1} K^{-1}.

2.37. The conditions of a gas change in a steady-flow process from 20°C (293.15 K) and 1000 kPa to 60°C (333.15 K) and 100 kPa. Devise a reversible nonflow process (any number of steps) for accomplishing this change of state, and calculate ΔU and ΔH for the process on the basis of 1 mol of gas. Assume for the gas that PV/T is constant, $C_V = (5/2)R$, and $C_P = (7/2)R$.

2.38. (*a*) An incompressible fluid (ρ = constant) flows through a pipe of constant cross-sectional area. If the flow is steady, show that velocity u and volumetric flowrate q are constant.

(*b*) A chemically reactive gas stream flows steadily through a pipe of constant cross-sectional area. Temperature and pressure vary with pipe length. Which of the following quantities are necessarily constant: $\dot{m}$, $\dot{n}$, q, u?

2.39. The *mechanical-energy balance* provides a basis for estimating pressure drop owing to friction in fluid flow. For steady flow of an incompressible fluid in a horizontal pipe of constant cross-sectional area, it may be written,

$$\frac{\Delta P}{\Delta L} + \frac{2}{D} f_F \rho u^2 = 0$$

where f_F is the *Fanning friction factor*. Churchill[11] gives the following expression for f_F for turbulent flow:

$$f_F = 0.3305 \left\{ \ln \left[0.27 \frac{\epsilon}{D} + \left(\frac{7}{\text{Re}} \right)^{0.9} \right] \right\}^{-2}$$

Here, Re is the Reynolds number (see Pb. 2.21), and ϵ/D is the dimensionless pipe roughness. Turbulent flow obtains for Re > 3,000.

Consider the flow of liquid water at 25°C (298.15 K). For one of the sets of conditions given below, determine $\dot{m}$ (in kg s^{-1}) and $\Delta P/\Delta L$ (in kPa m^{-1}). Assume $\epsilon/D = 0.0001$. For liquid water at 25°C (298.15 K), $\rho = 996$ kg m^{-3}, and $\mu = 9.0 \times 10^{-4}$ kg m^{-1} s^{-1}. Verify that the flow is turbulent.

(*a*) $D = 2$ cm, $u = 1$ m s^{-1}
(*b*) $D = 5$ cm, $u = 1$ m s^{-1}
(*c*) $D = 2$ cm, $u = 5$ m s^{-1}
(*d*) $D = 5$ cm, $u = 5$ m s^{-1}

2.40. A system of propane and *n*-butane exists in two-phase vapor/liquid equilibrium at 10 bar and 323 K. The mole fraction of propane is about 0.67 in the vapor phase and about 0.40 in the liquid phase. Additional pure propane is added to the system, which is brought again to equilibrium at the same T and P, with both liquid and vapor phases still present. What is the effect of the addition of propane on the mole fractions of propane in the vapor and liquid phases?

2.41. Six chemical species are present in significant amounts in a light-ends petroleum fractionation system: methane, ethane, propane, isobutane, *n*-butane, and *n*-pentane. A mixture of these species exists in vapor/liquid equilibrium in a closed vessel. On how many phase-rule variables in addition to T and P do the compositions of the phases depend?

If T and P are to remain the same, is there any way the composition of the total contents of the vessel can be changed (by adding or removing material) without affecting the compositions of the phases?

2.42. Ethylene enters a turbine at 10 bar and 450 K, and exhausts at 1 atm and 325 K. For $\dot{m} = 4.5$ kg s^{-1}, determine the cost C of the turbine. State any assumptions you make.

Data: $H_1 = 761.1$ $\quad H_2 = 536.9$ kJ kg^{-1} $\quad C/\$ = (15\,200)(|\dot{W}|/\text{kW})^{0.573}$

2.43. The heating of a home to increase its temperaature must be modeled as an open system, because expansion of the household air at constant pressure results in leakage of air to the outdoors. Assuming that the molar properties of air leaving the home are the

[11] *AIChE J.*, vol. 19, pp. 375–376, 1973

same as those of the air in the home, show that eneregy and mole balances yield the following differential equation:

$$\dot{Q} = -PV\frac{dn}{dt} + n\frac{dU}{dt}$$

Here, $\dot{Q}$ is the rate of heat transfer to the air in the home, and t is time. Quantities P, V, n, and U refer to the air in the home.

2.44. (*a*) Water flows through the nozzle of a garden hose. Find an expression for $\dot{m}$ in terms of line pressure P_1, ambient pressure P_2, inside hose diameter D_1, and nozzle outlet diameter D_2. Assume steady flow, and isothermal, adiabatic operation. For liquid water modeled as an incompressible fluid, $H_2 - H_1 = (P_2 - P_1)/\rho$ for constant temperature.

(*b*) In fact, the flow cannot be truly isothermal: we expect $T_2 > T_1$, owing to fluid friction. Hence, $H_2 - H_1 = C(T_2 - T_1) + (P_2 - P_1)/\rho$, where C is the specific heat of water. Directionally, how would inclusion of the temperature change affect the value of $\dot{m}$ as found in Part (*a*)?

Chapter 3

Volumetric Properties of Pure Fluids

The quantities of heat and work necessary to carry out industrial processes are calculated from knowledge of such thermodynamic properties as internal energy and enthalpy. For fluids, these properties are often evaluated from measurements of molar volume as a function of temperature and pressure, yielding pressure/volume/temperature (PVT) relations, which may be expressed mathematically as *equations of state*. The least-complex equation, $PV = RT$, provides the simplest realistic model of fluid behavior. Equations of state serve also for the metering of fluids and the sizing of vessels and pipelines.

In this chapter we first describe the general nature of the PVT behavior of pure fluids. There follows a detailed treatment of the ideal gas. Attention then turns to more realistic equations of state, which provide the foundation for quantitative description of real-fluid behavior. Finally, *generalized correlations* are presented that allow prediction of the PVT behavior of fluids for which experimental data are lacking.

3.1 *PVT* BEHAVIOR OF PURE SUBSTANCES

Lines 1-2 and 2-C of Fig. 3.1 represent for a pure substance conditions of pressure and temperature at which solid and liquid phases exist in equilibrium with a vapor phase. These *vapor pressure* vs. temperature lines characterize solid/vapor (line 1-2) and liquid/vapor (line 2-C) equilibrium relationships. The solid/liquid equilibrium relationship is represented by line 2-3. The three lines display conditions of P and T at which two phases may coexist, and divide the diagram into single-phase regions. Line 1-2, the *sublimation curve*, separates the solid and gas regions; line 2-3, the *fusion curve*, separates the solid and liquid regions; line 2-C, the *vaporization curve*, separates the liquid and gas regions. Point C is known as the *critical point*; its coordinates P_c and T_c are the highest pressure and highest temperature at which a pure chemical species is observed to exist in vapor/liquid equilibrium. The three lines meet at the *triple point*, where the three phases coexist in equilibrium. According to the phase rule, Eq. (2.7), the triple point is invariant ($F = 0$). If the system exists along any of the two-phase lines of Fig. 3.1, it is univariant ($F = 1$), whereas in the single-phase regions it is divariant ($F = 2$).

Changes of state may be represented by lines on the PT diagram: an isothermal change by a vertical line; an isobaric change by a horizontal line. When such a line crosses a phase boundary, an abrupt change in properties of the fluid occurs at constant T and P; e.g., vaporization for the transition from liquid to vapor.

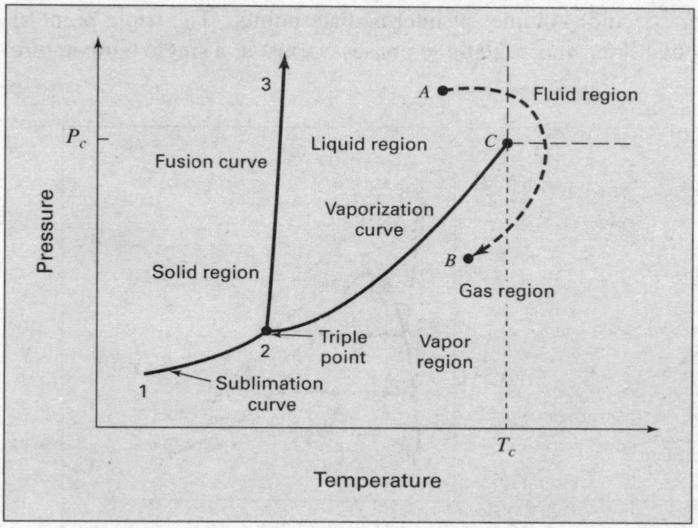

Figure 3.1: PT diagram for a pure substance

Water in an open flask is obviously a liquid in contact through a meniscus with air. If the flask is sealed and the air is pumped out, water vaporizes to replace the air, and H_2O fills the flask. Though the pressure in the flask is much reduced, everything appears unchanged. The liquid water resides at the bottom of the flask because its density is much greater than that of water vapor (steam), and the two phases are in equilibrium at conditions represented by a point on curve 2-C of Fig. 3.1. The properties of liquid and vapor are very different. However, if the temperature is raised so that the equilibrium state progresses upward along curve 2-C, the properties of the two phases become more and more nearly alike; at point C they become identical, and the menniscus disappears. One consequence is that transitions from liquid to vapor may occur along paths that do not cross the vaporization curve 2-C, i.e., from A to B. The transition from liquid to gas is then gradual, and does not include a vaporization step.

The region existing at temperatures and pressures greater than T_c and P_c is marked off by dashed lines in Fig. 3.1; these do not represent phase boundaries, but rather are limits fixed by the meanings accorded the *words* liquid and gas. A phase is generally considered a liquid if vaporization results from pressure reduction at constant temperature. A phase is considered a gas if condensation results from temperature reduction at constant pressure. Since neither process can be initiated in the region beyond the dashed lines, it is called the *fluid region*.

The gas region is sometimes divided into two parts, as indicated by the dotted vertical line of Fig. 3.1. A gas to the left of this line, which can be condensed either by compression at constant temperature or by cooling at constant pressure, is called a vapor. A fluid existing at a temperature greated than T_c is said to be *supercritical*. An example is atmospheric air.

PV Diagram

Figure 3.1 does not provide any information about volume; it merely displays the phase boundaries on a PT diagram. On a PV diagram [Fig. 3.2(a)] these boundaries in turn become *regions* where two phases— solid/liquid, solid/vapor, and liquid/vapor— coexist in equilibrium. These regions are separated by bounding curves that represent single phases, the relative amounts of which determine the molar (or specific) volumes at intermediate points. The triple point of Fig. 3.1 here becomes a horizontal line, where the three phases coexist at a single temperature and pressure.

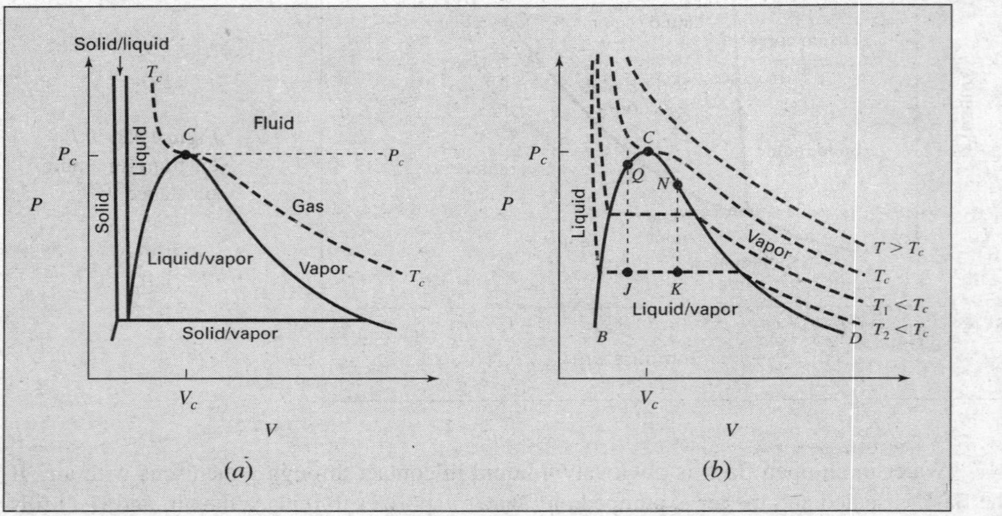

Figure 3.2: PV diagrams for a pure substance: (a) Showing solid, liquid, and gas regions (b) Showing liquid, liquid/vapor, and vapor regions with isotherms

Figure 3.2(b) shows the liquid, liquid/vapor, and vapor regions of the PV diagram, with four isotherms superimposed. Isotherms on Fig. 3.1 are vertical lines, and at temperatures greater than T_c do not cross a phase boundary. On Fig. 3.2(b) the isotherm labeled $T > T_c$ is therefore smooth.

The lines labeled T_1 and T_2 are for subcritical temperatures, and consist of three segments. The horizontal segment of each isotherm represents all possible mixtures of liquid and vapor in equilibrium, ranging from 100% liquid at the left end to 100% vapor at the right end. The locus of these end points is the dome-shaped curve labeled BCD, the left half of which (from B to C) represents single-phase liquids at their vaporization (boiling) temperatures, and the right half (from C to D), single-phase vapors at their condensation temperatures. Liquids and vapors represented by BCD are said to be *saturated*, and coexisting phases are connected by the horizontal segment of the isotherm at the *saturation* pressure specific to the isotherm. Also called the vapor pressure, it is given by a point on Fig. 3.1 where an isotherm (vertical line) crosses the vaporization curve.

The two-phase liquid/vapor region lies under dome BCD; the *subcooled-liquid* region lies to the left of the saturated-liquid curve BC, and the *superheated-vapor* region lies to right of the saturated-vapor curve CD. Subcooled liquid exists at temperatures *below*, and superheated vapor, at temperatures *above* the boiling point for the given pressure. Isotherms in the subcooled-liquid region are very steep, because liquid volumes change little with large changes in pressure.

The horizontal segments of the isotherms in the two-phase region become progressively shorter at higher temperatures, being ultimately reduced to a point at C. Thus, the critical isotherm, labeled T_c, exhibits a horizontal inflection at the critical point C at the top of the dome, where the liquid and vapor phases become indistinguishable.

Critical Behavior

Insight into the nature of the critical point is gained from a description of the changes that occur when a pure substance is heated in a sealed upright tube of constant volume. The dotted vertical lines of Fig. 3.2(*b*) indicate such processes. They may also be traced on the PT diagram of Fig. 3.3, where the solid line is the vaporization curve (Fig. 3.1), and the dashed lines are constant-volume paths in the single-phase regions. If the tube is filled with either liquid or vapor, the heating process produces changes which lie along the dashed lines, e.g., by the change from E to F (subcooled-liquid) and by the change from G to H (superheated-vapor). The corresponding vertical lines on Fig. 3.2(*b*) are not shown, but lie to the left and right of BCD respectively.

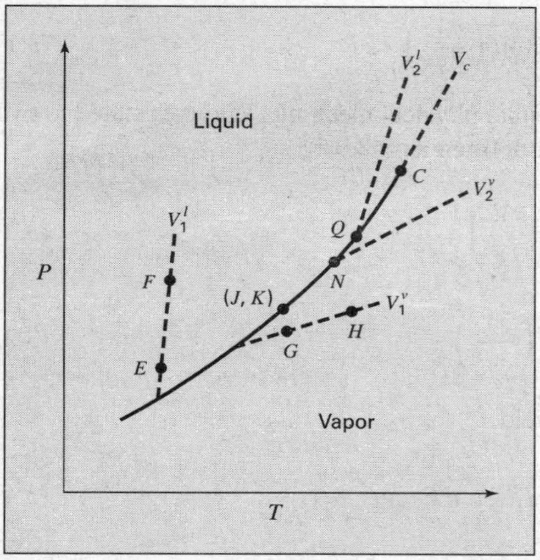

Figure 3.3: PT diagram for a pure fluid showing the vapor-pressure curve and constant-volume lines in the single-phase regions

If the tube is only partially filled with liquid (the remainder being vapor in equilibrium with the liquid), heating at first causes changes described by the vapor-pressure curve (solid line) of Fig. 3.3. For the process indicated by line JQ on Fig. 3.2(*b*), the meniscus is initially near the top of the tube (point J), and the liquid expands sufficiently upon heating to fill the tube (point Q). On Fig. 3.3 the process traces a path from (J, K) to Q, and with further heating departs from the vapor-pressure curve along the line of constant molar volume V_2^l.

The process indicated by line KN on Fig. 3.2(*b*) starts with a lower meniscus level in the tube (point K), and heating vaporizes liquid to the extent that the meniscus recedes to the bottom of the tube (point N). On Fig. 3.3 the process traces a path from (J, K) to N. With further heating the path continues along the line of constant molar volume V_2^v.

For a unique filling of the tube, with a particular intermediate meniscus level, the heating process follows a vertical line on Fig. 3.2(*b*) that passes through the critical point C. Physically, heating does not produce much change in the level of the meniscus. As the critical point is approached, the meniscus becomes indistinct, then hazy, and finally disappears. On Fig. 3.3 the path first follows the vapor-pressure curve, proceeding from point (J, K) to the critical point C, where it enters the single-phase fluid region, and follows V_c, the line of constant molar volume equal to the critical volume of the fluid.

Single-Phase Region

For the regions of the diagram where a single phase exists, Fig. 3.2(*b*) implies a relation connecting P, V, and T. Expressed analytically, as $f(P, V, T) = 0$, such a relation is known as a *PVT equation of state*. It relates pressure, molar or specific volume, and temperature for a pure homogeneous fluid in equilibrium states. The ideal-gas equation of state, $PV = RT$, has approximate validity for the low-pressure gas region of Fig. 3.2(*b*), and is discussed in detail in Sec. 3.3.

An equation of state may be solved for any one of the three quantities P, V, or T as a function of the other two. For example, if V is considered a function of T and P, then $V = V(T, P)$, and

$$dV = \left(\frac{\partial V}{\partial T}\right)_P dT + \left(\frac{\partial V}{\partial P}\right)_T dP \tag{3.1}$$

The partial derivatives in this equation have definite physical meanings, and are related to two properties, commonly tabulated for liquids, and **defined** as follows:

- ***Volume expansivity*** $$\beta \equiv \frac{1}{V}\left(\frac{\partial V}{\partial T}\right)_P \tag{3.2}$$

- ***Isothermal compressibility*** $$\kappa \equiv -\frac{1}{V}\left(\frac{\partial V}{\partial P}\right)_T \tag{3.3}$$

In combination Equations (3.1) through (3.3) yield

$$\frac{dV}{V} = \beta\, dT - \kappa\, dP \tag{3.4}$$

The isotherms for the liquid phase on the left side of Fig. 3.2(*b*) are very steep and closely spaced. Thus both $(\partial V/\partial T)_P$ and $(\partial V/\partial P)_T$ and hence both β and κ are small. This characteristic behavior of liquids (outside the critical region) suggests an idealization, commonly employed in fluid mechanics and known as the *incompressible fluid*, for which both β and κ are zero. No real fluid is truly incompressible, but the idealization is useful, because it provides a sufficiently realistic model of liquid behavior for many practical purposes. No equation of state exists for an incompressible fluid, because V is independent of T and P.

For liquids, β is almost always positive (liquid water between 0°C (273.15 K) and 4°C (277.15 K) is an exception), and κ is necessarily positive. At conditions not close to the critical point, β and κ are weak functions of temperature and pressure. Thus for small changes in T and P little error is introduced if they are assumed constant. Integration of Eq. (3.4) then yields:

$$\ln \frac{V_2}{V_1} = \beta(T_2 - T_1) - \kappa(P_2 - P_1) \tag{3.5}$$

This is a less restrictive approximation than the assumption of an incompressible fluid.

Example 3.1

For liquid acetone at 20°C (293.15 K) and 1 bar,

$$\beta = 1.487 \times 10^{-3}\ °\text{C}^{-1} \qquad \kappa = 62 \times 10^{-6}\ \text{bar}^{-1} \qquad V = 1.287\ \text{cm}^3\ \text{g}^{-1}$$

For acetone, find the

(*a*) value of $(\partial P/\partial T)_V$ at 20°C (293.15 K) and 1 bar

(*b*) pressure generated by heating at constant V from 20°C (293.15 K) and 1 bar to 30°C (303.15 K)

(*c*) change in volume for a change from 20°C (293.15 K) and 1 bar to 0°C (273.15 K) and 10 bar

Solution

(*a*) The derivative $(\partial P/\partial T)_V$ is determined by application of Eq. (3.4) to the case for which V is constant and $dV = 0$:

$$\beta\, dT - \kappa\, dP = 0 \qquad (\text{const } V)$$

or

$$\left(\frac{\partial P}{\partial T}\right)_V = \frac{\beta}{\kappa} = \frac{1.487 \times 10^{-3}}{62 \times 10^{-6}} = 24\ \text{bar}\ °\text{C}^{-1}$$

(*b*) If β and κ are assumed constant in the 10°C (10 K) temperature interval, then the equation derived in (*a*) may be written (V = const):

$$\Delta P = \frac{\beta}{\kappa}\Delta T = (24)(10) = 240\ \text{bar}$$

and

$$P_2 = P_1 + \Delta P = 1 + 240 = 241\ \text{bar}$$

(*c*) Direct substitution into Eq. (3.5) gives:

$$\ln \frac{V_2}{V_1} = (1.487 \times 10^{-3})(-20) - (62 \times 10^{-6})(9) = -0.0303$$

$$\frac{V_2}{V_1} = 0.9702 \qquad \text{and} \qquad V_2 = (0.9702)(1.287) = 1.249\ \text{cm}^3\ \text{g}^{-1}$$

Then, $\Delta V = V_2 - V_1 = 1.249 - 1.287 = -0.038\ \text{cm}^3\ \text{g}^{-1}$

3.2 VIRIAL EQUATIONS OF STATE

Isotherms for gases and vapors, lying above and to the right of CD in Fig. 3.2(b), are relatively simple curves for which V decreases as P increases. Here, the product PV for a given T should be much more nearly constant than either of its members, and hence more easily represented analytically as a function of P. This suggests expressing PV for an isotherm by a power series in P:

$$PV = a + bP + cP^2 + \cdots$$

If $b \equiv aB'$, $c \equiv aC'$, etc., then,

$$PV = a(1 + B'P + C'P^2 + D'P^3 + \cdots) \qquad (3.6)$$

where a, B', C', etc., are constants for a given temperature and a given chemical species.

In principle, the right side of Eq. (3.6) is an infinite series. However, in practice a finite number of terms is used. In fact, PVT data show that at low pressures truncation after two terms often provides satisfactory results.

Ideal-Gas Temperatures; Universal Gas Constant

Parameters B', C', etc., in Eq. (3.6) are species dependent and functions of temperature, but parameter a is found by experiment to be the same function of temperature for all chemical species. This is shown by measurements of volume as a function of P for various gases at constant temperature. Figure 3.4, for example, is a plot of PV vs. P for four gases at the triple-point temperature of water. The limiting value of PV as $P \rightarrow 0$ is the same for all of the gases. In this limit (denoted by the asterisk), Eq. (3.6) becomes

$$(PV)^* = a = f(T)$$

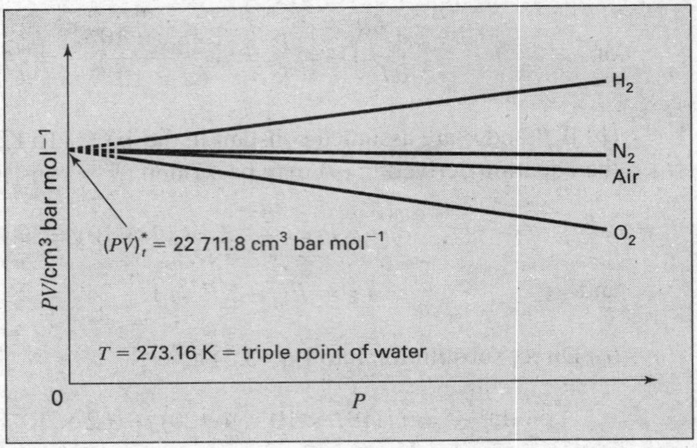

Figure 3.4: $(PV)^*$, the limiting value of PV as $P \rightarrow 0$, is independent of the gas

This property of gases is the basis for establishing an absolute temperature scale. All that is required is the arbitrary assignment of the functional relationship $f(T)$ and the assignment of a specific value to a single point on the scale. The simplest procedure, the one adopted internationally to define the Kelvin scale (Sec. 1.5):

- Makes $(PV)^*$ directly proportional to T, with R as the proportionality constant:

$$(PV)^* = a \equiv RT \tag{3.7}$$

- Assigns the value 273.16 K to the temperature of the triple point of water (denoted by subscript t):

$$(PV)^*_t = R \times 273.16\ \text{K} \tag{3.8}$$

Division of Eq. (3.7) by Eq. (3.8) gives

$$\frac{(PV)^*}{(PV)^*_t} = \frac{T/\text{K}}{273.16\ \text{K}}$$

or

$$\boxed{T/\text{K} = 273.16\frac{(PV)^*}{(PV)^*_t}} \tag{3.9}$$

Equation (3.9) establishes the Kelvin temperature scale throughout the temperature range for which values of $(PV)^*$ are experimentally accessible.

The state of a gas at the limiting condition where $P \to 0$ deserves discussion. The molecules making up a gas become more and more widely separated as pressure is decreased, and the volume of the molecules themselves becomes a smaller and smaller fraction of the total volume occupied by the gas. Furthermore, the forces of attraction between molecules become ever smaller because of the increasing distances between them (Sec. 16.1). In the limit, as $P \to 0$, the molecules are separated by infinite distances. Their volumes become negligible compared with the total volume of the gas, and the intermolecular forces approach zero. These conditions define an *ideal-gas state*, and Eq. (3.9) establishes the *ideal-gas temperature scale*. The proportionality constant R in Eq. (3.7) is called the *universal gas constant*. Its numerical value is determined by means of Eq. (3.8) from experimental PVT data:

$$R = \frac{(PV)^*_t}{273.16\ \text{K}}$$

Because PVT data cannot in fact be taken at zero pressure, data taken at finite pressures are extrapolated to the zero-pressure state. Determined as indicated by Fig. 3.4, the accepted value of $(PV)^*_t$ is 22 711.8 cm^3 bar mol^{-1}, leading to the following value of R:[1]

$$R = \frac{22\,711.8\ \text{cm}^3\ \text{bar mol}^{-1}}{273.16\ \text{K}} = 83.1447\ \text{cm}^3\ \text{bar mol}^{-1}\ \text{K}^{-1}$$

Through the use of conversion factors, R may be expressed in various units. Commonly used values are given in Table A.2 of App. A.

[1] http://physics.nist.gov/constants.

Two Forms of the Virial Equation

A useful auxiliary thermodynamic property is **defined** by the equation:

$$Z \equiv \frac{PV}{RT} \tag{3.10}$$

This dimensionless ratio is called the *compressibility factor*. With this definition and with $a = RT$ [Eq. (3.7)], Eq. (3.6) becomes:

$$Z = 1 + B'P + C'P^2 + D'P^3 + \cdots \tag{3.11}$$

An alternative expression for Z is also in common use:[2]

$$Z = 1 + \frac{B}{V} + \frac{C}{V^2} + \frac{D}{V^3} + \cdots \tag{3.12}$$

Both of these equations are known as *virial expansions*, and the parameters B', C', D', etc., and B, C, D, etc., are called *virial coefficients*. Parameters B' and B are *second* virial coefficients; C' and C are *third* virial coefficients; etc. For a given gas the virial coefficients are functions of temperature only.

The two sets of coefficients in Eqs. (3.11) and (3.12) are related as follows:

$$B' = \frac{B}{RT} \quad (3.13a) \qquad C' = \frac{C - B^2}{(RT)^2} \quad (3.13b) \qquad D' = \frac{D - 3BC + 2B^3}{(RT)^3} \quad (3.13c)$$

To derive these relations, we set $Z = PV/RT$ in Eq. (3.12), and solve for P. This allows elimination of P on the right of Eq. (3.11). The resulting equation reduces to a power series in $1/V$ which may be compared term by term with Eq. (3.12) to yield the given relations. They hold exactly only for the two virial expansions as infinite series, but are acceptable approximations for the truncated forms used in practice.

Many other equations of state have been proposed for gases, but the virial equations are the only ones firmly based on statistical mechanics, which provides physical significance to the virial coefficients. Thus, for the expansion in $1/V$, the term B/V arises on account of interactions between pairs of molecules (Sec. 16.2); the C/V^2 term, on account of three-body interactions; etc. Because two-body interactions are many times more common than three-body interactions, and three-body interactions are many times more numerous than four-body interactions, etc., the contributions to Z of the successively higher-ordered terms decrease rapidly.

[2]Proposed by H. Kamerlingh Onnes, "Expression of the Equation of State of Gases and Liquids by Means of Series," *Communications from the Physical Laboratory of the University of Leiden*, no. 71, 1901.

3.3 THE IDEAL GAS

Because the terms B/V, C/V^2, etc., of the virial expansion [Eq. (3.12)] arise on account of molecular interactions, the virial coefficients B, C, etc., would be zero where no such interactions to exist, and the virial expansion would reduce to

$$Z = 1 \qquad \text{or} \qquad PV = RT$$

Molecular interactions *do* in fact exist, and influence the observed behavior of real gases. As pressure is reduced at constant temperature, V increases and the contributions of the terms, $B/V, C/V^2, D/V^3, \ldots$ in Eq. (3.12), decrease. For $P \to 0$, Z approaches unity, not because of any change in the virial coefficients, but because V becomes infinite. Thus in the limit as $P \to 0$, the equation of state reduces to the same simple form as for the hypothetical case of $B = C = \cdots = 0$; i.e.,

$$Z \to 1 \qquad \text{or} \qquad PV \to RT$$

We know from the phase rule that the internal energy of a real gas is a function of pressure as well as of temperature. This pressure dependency results from forces between the molecules. If such forces did not exist, no energy would be required to alter the average intermolecular distance, and therefore no energy would be required to bring about volume and pressure changes in a gas at constant temperature. We conclude that in the absence of molecular interactions, the internal energy of a gas depends on temperature only. These considerations of the behavior of a hypothetical gas in which no intermolecular forces exist and of a real gas in the limit as pressure approaches zero lead to the definition of an ideal gas as one whose macroscopic behavior is characterized by:

- The equation of state:

$$\boxed{PV = RT} \qquad \textbf{(ideal gas)} \tag{3.14}$$

- An internal energy that is a function of temperature only:

$$\boxed{U = U(T)} \qquad \textbf{(ideal gas)} \tag{3.15}$$

Implied Property Relations for an Ideal Gas

The definition of heat capacity at constant volume, Eq. (2.16), leads for an ideal gas to the conclusion that C_V is a function of temperature only:

$$C_V \equiv \left(\frac{\partial U}{\partial T}\right)_V = \frac{dU(T)}{dT} = C_V(T) \tag{3.16}$$

The defining equation for enthalpy, Eq. (2.11), applied to an ideal gas, leads to the conclusion that H also is a function of temperature only:

$$H \equiv U + PV = U(T) + RT = H(T) \tag{3.17}$$

The heat capacity at constant pressure C_P, defined by Eq. (2.20), like C_V, is a function of temperature only:

$$C_P \equiv \left(\frac{\partial H}{\partial T}\right)_P = \frac{dH(T)}{dT} = C_P(T) \tag{3.18}$$

A useful relation between C_P and C_V for an ideal gas comes from differentiation of Eq. (3.17):

$$C_P = \frac{dH}{dT} = \frac{dU}{dT} + R = C_V + R \tag{3.19}$$

This equation does not imply that C_P and C_V are themselves constant for an ideal gas, but only that they vary with temperature in such a way that their difference is equal to R.

For any change of state of an ideal gas Eqs. (3.16) and (3.18) lead to:

$dU = C_V\,dT$ (3.20a)	$\Delta U = \int C_V\,dT$ (3.20b)
$dH = C_P\,dT$ (3.21a)	$\Delta H = \int C_P\,dT$ (3.21b)

Because both the internal energy and C_V of an ideal gas are functions of temperature only, ΔU for an ideal gas is *always* given by Eq. (3.20b), regardless of the kind of process causing the change. This is demonstrated in Fig. 3.5, which shows a graph of internal energy as a function of molar volume with temperature as parameter. Because U is independent of V, a plot of U vs. V at constant temperature is a horizontal line. For different temperatures, U has different values, with a separate line for each temperature. Two such lines are shown in

Figure 3.5: Internal energy changes for an ideal gas

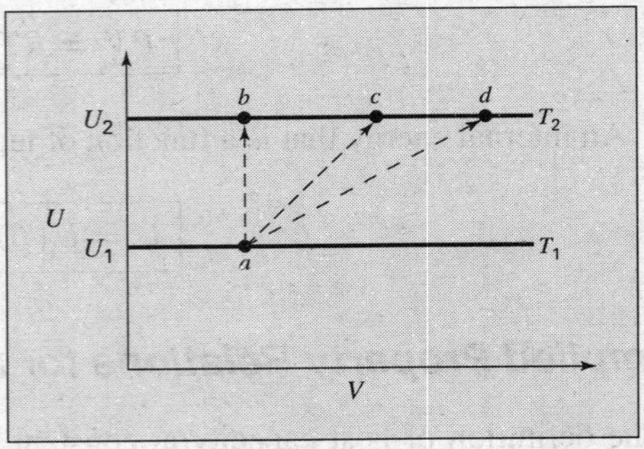

Fig. 3.5, one for temperature T_1 and one for a higher temperature T_2. The dashed line connecting points a and b represents a constant-volume process for which the temperature increases from T_1 to T_2 and the internal energy changes by $\Delta U = U_2 - U_1$. This change in internal energy is given by Eq. (3.20b) as $\Delta U = \int C_V\,dT$. The dashed lines connecting points a and c and points a and d represent other processes not occurring at constant volume but which also lead from an initial temperature T_1 to a final temperature T_2. The graph shows that the change in U for these processes is the same as for the constant-volume process, and it is therefore given by the same equation, namely, $\Delta U = \int C_V\,dT$. However, ΔU is *not* equal to Q for

these processes, because Q depends not only on T_1 and T_2 but also on the path of the process. An entirely analogous discussion applies to the enthalpy H of an ideal gas. (See Sec. 2.11.)

The ideal gas is a model fluid described by simple *property relations*, which are frequently good approximations when applied to actual gases. In *process calculations*, gases at pressures up to a few bars may often be considered ideal, and simple equations then apply.

Equations for Process Calculations for Ideal Gases

Process calculations provide work and heat quantities. The work of a mechanically reversible closed-system process is given by Eq. (1.2), here written for a unit mass or a mole:

$$dW = -P\,dV$$

For an ideal gas in any closed-system process, the first law as given by Eq. (2.6) written for a unit mass or a mole, may be combined with Eq. (3.20a) to give

$$dQ + dW = C_V\,dT$$

Substitution for dW and solution for dQ yields an equation valid for an ideal gas in any mechanically reversible closed-system process:

$$dQ = C_V\,dT + P\,dV$$

This equation contains the variables P, V, and T, only two of which are independent. Working equations for dQ and dW depend on which pair of these variables is selected as independent; i.e., upon which variable is eliminated by Eq. (3.14). With $P = RT/V$,

$$dQ = C_V\,dT + RT\frac{dV}{V} \qquad (3.22)$$

$$dW = -RT\frac{dV}{V} \qquad (3.23)$$

With $V = RT/P$ and with C_V given by Eq. (3.19), the equations for dQ and dW become

$$dQ = C_P\,dT - RT\frac{dP}{P} \qquad (3.24)$$

$$dW = -R\,dT + RT\frac{dP}{P} \qquad (3.25)$$

With $T = PV/R$, the work is simply $dW = -P\,dV$, and with C_V given again by Eq. (3.19),

$$dQ = \frac{C_V}{R}V\,dP + \frac{C_P}{R}P\,dV \qquad (3.26)$$

These equations may be applied for ideal gases to various kinds of processes, as described in what follows. The assumptions implicit in their derivation are that the system is closed and the process is mechanically reversible.

Isothermal Process

By Eqs. (3.20b) and (3.21b), $\Delta U = \Delta H = 0$

By Eqs. (3.22) and (3.24), $Q = RT \ln \frac{V_2}{V_1} = -RT \ln \frac{P_2}{P_1}$

By Eqs. (3.23) and (3.25), $W = -RT \ln \frac{V_2}{V_1} = RT \ln \frac{P_2}{P_1}$

Note that $Q = -W$, a result that also follows from Eq. (2.3). Therefore,

$$Q = -W = RT \ln \frac{V_2}{V_1} = -RT \ln \frac{P_2}{P_1} \qquad (\text{const } T) \tag{3.27}$$

Isobaric Process

By Eqs. (3.20b) and (3.21b),

$$\Delta U = \int C_V \, dT \qquad \text{and} \qquad \Delta H = \int C_P \, dT$$

and by Eqs. (3.24) and (3.25),

$$Q = \int C_P \, dT \qquad \text{and} \qquad W = -R(T_2 - T_1)$$

Note that $Q = \Delta H$, a result also given by Eq. (2.13). Therefore,

$$Q = \Delta H = \int C_P \, dT \qquad (\text{const } P) \tag{3.28}$$

Isochoric (Constant-*V*) Process

Equations (3.20b) and (3.21b) again apply:

$$\Delta U = \int C_V \, dT \qquad \text{and} \qquad \Delta H = \int C_P \, dT$$

By Eq. (3.22) and the basic equation for work,

$$Q = \int C_V \, dT \qquad \text{and} \qquad W = -\int P \, dV = 0$$

Note that $Q = \Delta U$, a result also given by Eq. (2.10). Therefore,

$$Q = \Delta U = \int C_V \, dT \qquad (\text{const } V) \tag{3.29}$$

Adiabatic Process; Constant Heat Capacities

An adiabatic process is one for which there is no heat transfer between the system and its surroundings; i.e., $dQ = 0$. Each of Eqs. (3.22), (3.24), and (3.26) may therefore be set equal to zero. Integration with C_V and C_P constant then yields simple relations among the variables T, P, and V, valid for mechanically reversible adiabatic compression or expansion of ideal gases. For example, Eq. (3.22) becomes

$$\frac{dT}{T} = -\frac{R}{C_V}\frac{dV}{V}$$

Integration with C_V constant gives

$$\frac{T_2}{T_1} = \left(\frac{V_1}{V_2}\right)^{R/C_V}$$

Similarly, Eqs. (3.24) and (3.26) lead to

$$\frac{T_2}{T_1} = \left(\frac{P_2}{P_1}\right)^{R/C_P} \quad \text{and} \quad \frac{P_2}{P_1} = \left(\frac{V_1}{V_2}\right)^{C_P/C_V}$$

These equations may also be expressed as

$TV^{\gamma-1} = \text{const.}$ (3.30a)	$TP^{(1-\gamma)/\gamma} = \text{const.}$ (3.30b)	$PV^{\gamma} = \text{const.}$ (3.30c)

where by **definition,**[3]

$$\gamma \equiv \frac{C_P}{C_V} \tag{3.31}$$

Equations (3.30) are restricted in application to ideal gases with constant heat capacities undergoing mechanically reversible adiabatic expansion or compression.

For ideal gases, the work of *any* adiabatic closed-system process is given by:

$$dW = dU = C_V\, dT$$

For constant C_V,

$$W = \Delta U = C_V\, \Delta T \tag{3.32}$$

Alternative forms of Eq. (3.32) result if C_V is eliminated in favor of the heat-capacity ratio γ:

$$\gamma \equiv \frac{C_P}{C_V} = \frac{C_V + R}{C_V} = 1 + \frac{R}{C_V} \quad \text{or} \quad C_V = \frac{R}{\gamma - 1}$$

[3]If C_V and C_P are constant, γ is necessarily constant. For an ideal gas, the assumption of constant γ is equivalent to the assumption that the heat capacities themselves are constant. This is the only way that the ratio $C_P/C_V \equiv \gamma$ and the difference $C_P - C_V = R$ can *both* be constant. Except for the monotonic gases, both C_P and C_V actually increase with temperature, but the ratio γ is less sensitive to temperature than the heat capacities themselves.

Whence

$$W = C_V \Delta T = \frac{R \Delta T}{\gamma - 1}$$

Because $RT_1 = P_1 V_1$ and $RT_2 = P_2 V_2$, this expression may be written:

$$W = \frac{RT_2 - RT_1}{\gamma - 1} = \frac{P_2 V_2 - P_1 V_1}{\gamma - 1} \qquad (3.33)$$

Equations (3.32) and (3.33) are general for adiabatic compression and expansion processes in a closed system, whether reversible or not, because P, V, and T are state functions, independent of path. However, T_2 and V_2 are usually unknown. Elimination of V_2 from Eq. (3.33) by Eq. (3.30c), valid only for mechanically reversible processes, leads to the expression:

$$W = \frac{P_1 V_1}{\gamma - 1}\left[\left(\frac{P_2}{P_1}\right)^{(\gamma-1)/\gamma} - 1\right] = \frac{RT_1}{\gamma - 1}\left[\left(\frac{P_2}{P_1}\right)^{(\gamma-1)/\gamma} - 1\right] \qquad (3.34)$$

The same result is obtained when the relation between P and V given by Eq. (3.30c) is used for the integration, $W = -\int P\,dV$. Equation (3.34) is valid only for ideal gases with constant heat capacities in adiabatic, mechanically reversible, closed-system processes.

When applied to real gases, Eqs. (3.30) through (3.34) often yield satisfactory approximations, provided the deviations from ideality are relatively small. For monatomic gases, $\gamma = 1.67$; approximate values of γ are 1.4 for diatomic gases and 1.3 for simple polyatomic gases such as CO_2, SO_2, NH_3, and CH_4.

Polytropic Process

Because *polytropic* means "turning many ways," *polytropic process* suggests a model of some versatility. With δ a constant, it is defined as a process represented by the empirical equation:

$$\boxed{PV^{\delta} = \text{constant}} \qquad (3.35a)$$

For an ideal gas equations analogous to Eqs. (3.30a) and (3.30b) are readily derived:

$$\boxed{TV^{\delta-1} = \text{constant} \quad (3.35b) \qquad TP^{(1-\delta)/\delta} = \text{constant} \quad (3.35c)}$$

When the relation between P and V is given by Eq. (3.35a), evaluation of $\int P\,dV$ yields Eq. (3.34) with γ replaced by δ:

$$W = \frac{RT_1}{\delta - 1}\left[\left(\frac{P_2}{P_1}\right)^{(\delta-1)/\delta} - 1\right] \qquad (3.36)$$

Moreover, for constant heat capacities, the first law solved for Q yields

$$Q = \frac{(\delta - \gamma)RT_1}{(\delta - 1)(\gamma - 1)}\left[\left(\frac{P_2}{P_1}\right)^{(\delta-1)/\delta} - 1\right] \qquad (3.37)$$

The processes described in this section correspond to the four paths[4] shown on Fig. 3.6 for specific values of δ:

- Isobaric process: By Eq. (3.35a), $\delta = 0$.
- Isothermal process: By Eq. (3.35b), $\delta = 1$.
- Adiabatic process: $\delta = \gamma$.
- Isochoric process: By Eq. (3.35a), $dV/dP = V/P\delta$; for constant V, $\delta = \pm\infty$.

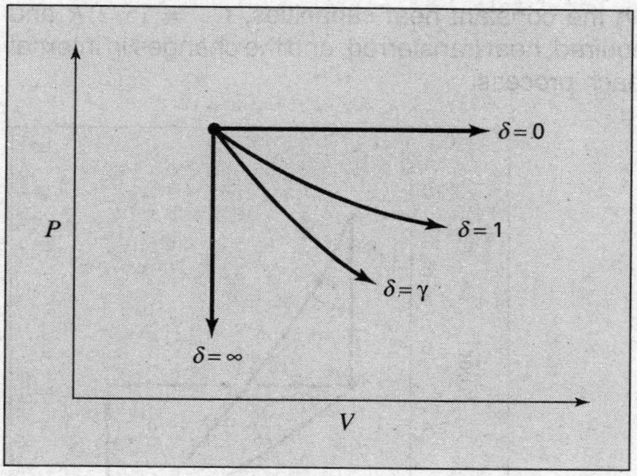

Figure 3.6: Paths of polytropic processes characterized by specific values of δ

Irreversible Process

All equations developed in this section have been *derived* for mechanically reversible, closed-system processes for ideal gases. However, those equations which give *property changes*—$dU, dH, \Delta U$, and ΔH—are valid for ideal gases regardless of the process. They apply equally to reversible and irreversible processes in both closed and open systems, because changes in properties depend only on the initial and final states of the system. On the other hand, an equation for Q or W, unless it is equal to a property change, is subject to the restrictions of derivation.

The work of an *irreversible* process is calculated by a two-step procedure. First, W is determined for a mechanically reversible process that accomplishes the same change of state as the actual irreversible process. Second, this result is multiplied or divided by an efficiency to give the actual work. If the process produces work, the absolute value for the reversible process is too large and must be multiplied by an efficiency. If the process requires work, the value for the reversible process is too small and must be divided by an efficiency.

Applications of the concepts and equations of this section are illustrated in the examples that follow. In particular, the work of irreversible processes is treated in Ex. 3.4.

[4]See Pb. 3.13.

Example 3.2

Air is compressed from an initial state of 1 bar and 25°C (298.15 K) to a final state of 5 bar and 25°C (298.15 K) by three different mechanically reversible processes in a closed system:

(*a*) Heating at constant volume followed by cooling at constant pressure

(*b*) Isothermal compression

(*c*) Adiabatic compression followed by cooling at constant volume.

Assume air to be an ideal gas with the constant heat capacities, $C_V = (5/2)R$ and $C_P = (7/2)R$. Calculate the work required, heat transferred, and the changes in internal energy and enthalpy of the air for each process.

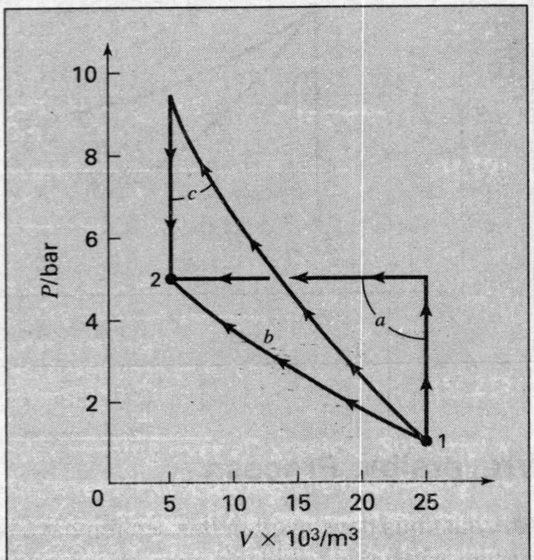

Figure 3.7: Diagram for Ex. 3.2

Solution

Choose the system as 1 mol of air. For $R = 8.314$ J mol^{-1} K^{-1},

$$C_V = 20.785 \qquad C_P = 29.099 \text{ J mol}^{-1}\text{ K}^{-1}$$

The initial and final states of the air are identical with those of Ex. 2.9, where

$$V_1 = 0.024\,79 \qquad V_2 = 0.004\,958 \text{ m}^3$$

Because T is same at the beginning and end of the process, in all cases,

$$\Delta U = \Delta H = 0$$

(*a*) The process here is exactly that of Ex. 2.9(*b*), for which

$$Q = -9915 \text{ J} \qquad \text{and} \qquad W = 9915 \text{ J}$$

(*b*) Equation (3.27) for the isothermal compression of an ideal gas applies

$$Q = -W = RT \ln \frac{P_1}{P_2} = (8.314)(298.15) \ln \frac{1}{5} = -3990 \text{ J}$$

(*c*) The initial step of adiabatic compression takes the air it to its final volume of 0.004 958 m^3. By Eq. (3.30a), the temperature at this point is

$$T' = T_1 \left(\frac{V_1}{V_2}\right)^{\gamma-1} = (298.15)\left(\frac{0.024\,79}{0.004\,958}\right)^{0.4} = 567.57 \text{ K}$$

For this step, $Q = 0$, and by Eq. (3.32), the work of compression is

$$W = C_V \,\Delta T = (20.785)(567.57 - 298.15) = 5600 \text{ J}$$

For the constant-volume step, no work is done; the heat transfer is

$$Q = \Delta U = C_V(T_2 - T') = -5600 \text{ J}$$

Thus for process (*c*),

$$W = 5600 \text{ J} \qquad \text{and} \qquad Q = -5600 \text{ J}$$

Although the property changes ΔU and ΔH are zero for each process, Q and W are path-dependent, but here $Q = -W$. Figure 3.7 shows each process on a PV diagram. Because the work for each of these mechanically reversible processes is given by $W = -\int P\,dV$, the work for each process is proportional to the total area below the paths on the PV diagram from 1 to 2. The relative sizes of these areas correspond to the numerical values of W.

Example 3.3

An ideal gas undergoes the following sequence of mechanically reversible processes in a closed system:

(*a*) From an initial state of 70°C (343.15 K) and 1 bar, it is compressed adiabatically to 150°C (423.15 K).

(*b*) It is then cooled from 150 to 70°C (423.15 K to 343.15 K) at constant pressure.

(*c*) Finally, it is expanded isothermally to its original state.

Calculate W, Q, ΔU, and ΔH for each of the three processes and for the entire cycle. Take $C_V = (3/2)R$ and $C_P = (5/2)R$.

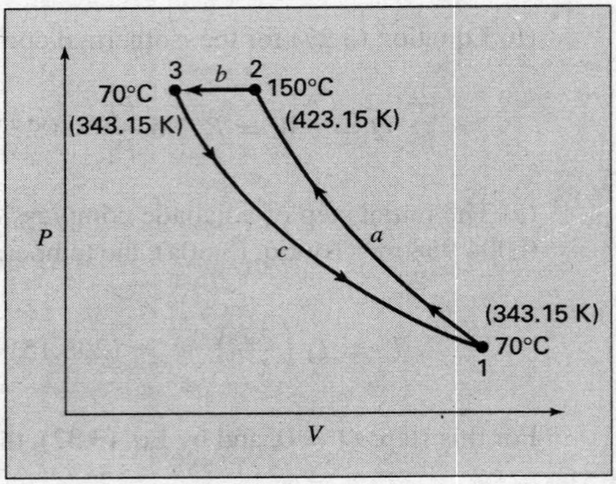

Figure 3.8: Diagram for Ex. 3.3

Solution

For $R = 8.314$ J mol^{-1} K^{-1},

$$C_V = 12.471 \qquad C_P = 20.785 \text{ J mol}^{-1} \text{ K}^{-1}$$

The cycle is shown on a PV diagram in Fig. 3.8. Take as a basis 1 mol of gas.

(*a*) For an ideal gas undergoing adiabatic compression, $Q = 0$; whence

$$\Delta U = W = C_V \,\Delta T = (12.471)(150 - 70) = 998 \text{ J}$$

$$\Delta H = C_P \,\Delta T = (20.785)(150 - 70) = 1663 \text{ J}$$

Pressure P_2 is found from Eq. (3.30b):

$$P_2 = P_1 \left(\frac{T_2}{T_1}\right)^{\gamma/(\gamma-1)} = (1)\left(\frac{423.15}{343.15}\right)^{2.5} = 1.689 \text{ bar}$$

(*b*) For this constant-pressure process,

$$Q = \Delta H = C_P \,\Delta T = (20.785)(70 - 150) = -1663 \text{ J}$$

$$\Delta U = C_V \,\Delta T = (12.471)(70 - 150) = -998 \text{ J}$$

$$W = \Delta U - Q = -998 - (-1663) = 665 \text{ J}$$

(*c*) For ideal gases undergoing an isothermal process, ΔU and ΔH are zero; Eq. (3.27) yields

$$Q = -W = RT \ln \frac{P_3}{P_1} = RT \ln \frac{P_2}{P_1} = (8.314)(343.15) \ln \frac{1.689}{1} = 1495 \text{ J}$$

For the entire cycle,

$$Q = 0 - 1663 + 1495 = -168 \text{ J}$$
$$W = 998 + 665 - 1495 = 168 \text{ J}$$
$$\Delta U = 998 - 998 + 0 = 0$$
$$\Delta H = 1663 - 1663 + 0 = 0$$

The property changes ΔU and ΔH both are zero for the entire cycle, because the initial and final states are identical. Note also that $Q = -W$ for the cycle. This follows from the first law with $\Delta U = 0$.

Example 3.4

If the processes of Ex. 3.3 are carried out *irreversibly* but so as to accomplish exactly the same *changes of state* — the same changes in P, T, U, and H — then different values of Q and W result. Calculate Q and W if each step is carried out with an efficiency of 80%.

Solution

If the same changes of state as in Ex. 3.3 are carried out by irreversible processes, the property changes for the steps are identical with those of Ex. 3.3. However, the values of Q and W change.

(*a*) For mechanically reversible, adiabatic compression, $W = 998$ J. If the process is 80% efficient compared with this, $W = 998/0.80 = 1248$ J. This step cannot here be adiabatic. By the first law,

$$Q = \Delta U - W = 998 - 1248 = -250 \text{ J}$$

(*b*) The work for the mechanically reversible cooling process is 665 J. For the irreversible process, $W = 665/0.80 = 831$ J, and

$$Q = \Delta U - W = -998 - 831 = -1829 \text{ J}$$

(*c*) As work is done *by* the system in this step, the irreversible work in absolute value is less than the reversible work of -1495 J:

$$W = (0.80)(-1495) = -1196 \text{ J}$$

$$Q = \Delta U - W = 0 + 1196 = 1196 \text{ J}$$

For the entire cycle, ΔU and ΔH are zero, with

$$Q = -250 - 1829 + 1196 = -883 \text{ J}$$

$$W = 1248 + 831 - 1196 = 883 \text{ J}$$

A summary of these results and those for Ex. 3.3 is given in the following table; values are in joules.

	Mechanically reversible, Ex. 3.3				Irreversible, Ex. 3.4			
	ΔU	ΔH	Q	W	ΔU	ΔH	Q	W
(*a*)	998	1663	0	998	998	1663	−250	1248
(*b*)	−998	−1663	−1663	665	−998	−1663	−1829	831
(*c*)	0	0	1495	−1495	0	0	1196	−1196
Sum	0	0	−168	168	0	0	−883	883

The cycle is one which requires work and produces an equal amount of heat. The striking feature of the comparison shown in the table is that the total work required when the cycle consists of three irreversible steps is more than five times the total work required when the steps are mechanically reversible, even though each irreversible step is assumed 80% efficient.

Example 3.5

A quantity of nitrogen gas is confined in a vertical cylinder by a frictionless piston. The top of the piston is open to the atmosphere. The weight of the piston makes the pressure of the nitrogen 0.35 bar higher than that of the surrounding atmosphere, which is at 1 bar and 27°C (300.15 K). Thus the nitrogen is initially at a pressure of 1.35 bar, and is in mechanical and thermal equilibrium with its surroundings. The piston is forced into the cylinder so as to compress the nitrogen to a pressure of 2.7 bar. The nitrogen at this pressure is allowed to come to thermal equilibrium with the surrounding atmosphere at 27°C (300.15 K). At this point the piston is locked in place by latches.

The latches are removed, freeing the piston from constraint, and the apparatus in time returns to mechanical and thermal equilibrium with its surroundings. Discuss the application of thermodynamics to this process. Assume nitrogen at these conditions is an ideal gas.

Solution

When the latches holding the frictionless piston are removed, the piston moves rapidly upward, and owing to its inertia goes beyond its equilibrium position. This initial expansion approximates a reversible, adiabatic process, because little turbulence results from a single stroke of the piston and because heat transfer is relatively slow. However, the subsequent oscillation of the piston introduces irreversibility as a result of stirring and turbulence in both the gas and the atmosphere. This process goes on for a considerable time during which heat transfer occurs in an amount sufficient to return the nitrogen to its initial temperature of 27°C (300.15 K) at a pressure of 1.35 bar.

It is not possible to specify the path of an irreversible process, and this makes impossible the calculation of either Q or W. Unlike heat and work, the property changes of the system can be calculated, because they depend solely on the initial and final states, and these are known. Both ΔU and ΔH for the expansion process are zero, because the initial and final temperatures are 27°C (300.15 K). The first law applies to irreversible as well as to reversible processes, and it becomes:

$$\Delta U = Q + W = 0 \qquad \text{whence} \qquad Q = -W$$

Although neither Q nor W can be calculated, their absolute values are the same. The process results in elevation of the piston and the atmosphere, and a compensating decrease in the internal energy of the surrounding atmosphere.

Example 3.6

Air flows at a steady rate through a horizontal pipe to a partly closed valve. The pipe leaving the valve is enough larger than the entrance pipe that the kinetic-energy change of the air as it flows through the valve is negligible. The valve and connecting pipes are well insulated. The conditions of the air upstream from the valve are 20°C (293.15 K) and 6 bar, and the downstream pressure is 3 bar. If air is regarded as an ideal gas, what is the temperature of the air some distance downstream from the valve?

Solution

Flow through a partly closed valve is known as a *throttling process*. The system is insulated, making Q negligible; moreover, the potential-energy and kinetic-energy changes are negligible. Because no shaft work is accomplished, $W_s = 0$. Hence, Eq. (2.32) reduces to: $\Delta H = 0$. Thus, for an ideal gas,

$$\Delta H = \int_{T_1}^{T_2} C_P \, dT = 0 \qquad \text{whence} \qquad T_2 = T_1$$

The result that $\Delta H = 0$ is general for a throttling process, because the assumptions of negligible heat transfer and potential- and kinetic-energy changes are usually valid. If the fluid is an ideal gas, no temperature change occurs. The throttling process is inherently irreversible, but this is immaterial to the calculation, because Eq. (3.21b) is valid for an ideal gas whatever the process.

Example 3.7

If in Ex. 3.6 the flow rate of the air is 1 mol s^{-1} and if both upstream and downstream pipes have an inner diameter of 5 cm, what is the kinetic-energy change of the air and what is its temperature change? For air, $C_P = (7/2)R$ and $M = 29$ g mol^{-1}.

Solution

By Eq. (2.24b), $$u = \frac{\dot{n}}{A\rho} = \frac{\dot{n}V}{A}$$

where $$A = \frac{\pi}{4}D^2 = \left(\frac{\pi}{4}\right)(5 \times 10^{-2})^2 = 1.964 \times 10^{-3}\ \text{m}^2$$

The upstream molar volume as given by the ideal-gas equation is

$$V_1 = \frac{RT_1}{P_1} = \frac{(83.14)(293.15)}{6} \times 10^{-6} = 4.062 \times 10^{-3}\ \text{m}^3\ \text{mol}^{-1}$$

Then, $$u_1 = \frac{(1)(4.062 \times 10^{-3})}{1.964 \times 10^{-3}} = 2.069\ \text{m s}^{-1}$$

If the downstream temperature is little changed from the upstream temperature, then to a good approximation:

$$V_2 = 2V_1 \qquad \text{and} \qquad u_2 = 2u_1 = 4.138\ \text{m s}^{-1}$$

The rate of change in kinetic energy is therefore:

$$\dot{m}\,\Delta(\tfrac{1}{2}u^2) = \dot{n}M\,\Delta(\tfrac{1}{2}u^2)$$
$$= (1 \times 29 \times 10^{-3})\frac{(4.138^2 - 2.069^2)}{2} = 0.186\ \text{J s}^{-1}\ \text{or W}$$

In the absence of heat transfer and work, the energy balance, Eq. (2.31), becomes

$$\Delta(H + \tfrac{1}{2}u^2)\dot{m} = \dot{m}\,\Delta H + \dot{m}\,\Delta(\tfrac{1}{2}u^2) = 0$$
$$\dot{m}\frac{C_P}{M}\Delta T + \dot{m}\,\Delta(\tfrac{1}{2}u^2) = \dot{n}C_P\,\Delta T + \dot{m}\,\Delta(\tfrac{1}{2}u^2) = 0$$

Whence $$(1)(7/2)(8.314)\Delta T = -\dot{m}\,\Delta(\tfrac{1}{2}u^2) = -0.186$$

and $$\Delta T = -0.0064\ \text{K}$$

Clearly, the assumption of negligible temperature change across the valve is justified. Even for an upstream pressure of 10 bar and a downstream pressure of 1 bar and for the same flow rate, the temperature change is only −0.076 K. We conclude that, except for very unusual conditions, $\Delta H = 0$ is a satisfactory energy balance for a throttling process.

3.4 APPLICATION OF THE VIRIAL EQUATIONS

The two forms of the virial expansion given by Eqs. (3.11) and (3.12) are infinite series. For engineering purposes their use is practical only where convergence is very rapid, that is, where two or three terms suffice for reasonably close approximations to the values of the series. This is realized for gases and vapors at low to moderate pressures.

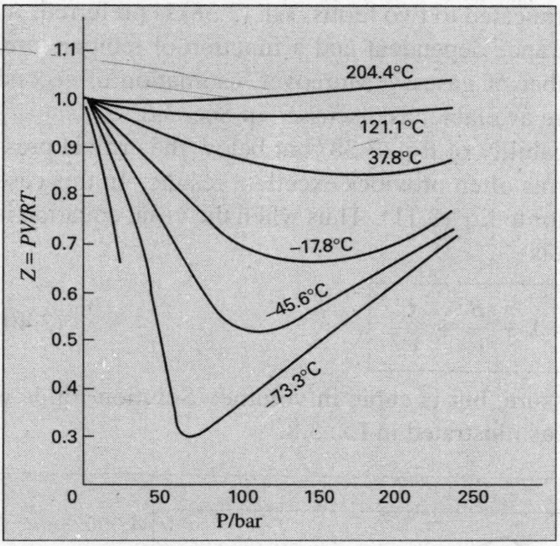

Figure 3.9: Compressibility-factor graph for methane

Figure 3.9 shows a compressibility-factor graph for methane. Values of the compressibility factor Z (as calculated from PVT data for methane by the defining equation $Z = PV/RT$) are plotted vs. pressure for various constant temperatures. The resulting isotherms show graphically what the virial expansion in P is intended to represent analytically. All isotherms originate at the value $Z = 1$ for $P = 0$, and the isotherms are nearly straight lines at low pressures. Thus the tangent to an isotherm at $P = 0$ is a good approximation of the isotherm from $P \to 0$ to some finite pressure. Differentiation of Eq. (3.11) for a given temperature gives

$$\left(\frac{\partial Z}{\partial P}\right)_T = B' + 2C'P + 3D'P^2 + \cdots$$

from which,
$$\left(\frac{\partial Z}{\partial P}\right)_{T;P=0} = B'$$

Thus the equation of the tangent line is $Z = 1 + B'P$, a result also given by truncating Eq. (3.11) to two terms.

A more common form of this equation results from substitution for B' by Eq. (3.13a):

$$\boxed{Z = \frac{PV}{RT} = 1 + \frac{BP}{RT}} \qquad (3.38)$$

This equation expresses a direct proportionality between Z and P, and is often applied to vapors at subcritical temperatures up to their saturation pressures. At higher temperatures it provides a reasonable approximation for gases up to a pressure of several bars, with the pressure range increasing as the temperature increases.

Equation (3.12) as well may be truncated to two terms for application at low pressures:

$$Z = \frac{PV}{RT} = 1 + \frac{B}{V} \tag{3.39}$$

However, Eq. (3.38) is more convenient in application and is normally at least as accurate as Eq. (3.39). Thus when the virial equation is truncated to two terms, Eq. (3.38) is preferred.

The second virial coefficient B is substance dependent and a function of temperature. Experimental values are available for a number of gases.[5] Moreover, estimation of second virial coefficients is possible where no data are available, as discussed in Sec. 3.6.

For pressures above the range of applicability of Eq. (3.38) but below the critical pressure, the virial equation truncated to three terms often provides excellent results. In this case Eq. (3.12), the expansion in $1/V$, is far superior to Eq. (3.11). Thus when the virial equation is truncated to three terms, the appropriate form is

$$Z = \frac{PV}{RT} = 1 + \frac{B}{V} + \frac{C}{V^2} \tag{3.40}$$

This equation can be solved directly for pressure, but is cubic in volume. Solution for V is readily accomplished by an iterative scheme, as illustrated in Ex. 3.8.

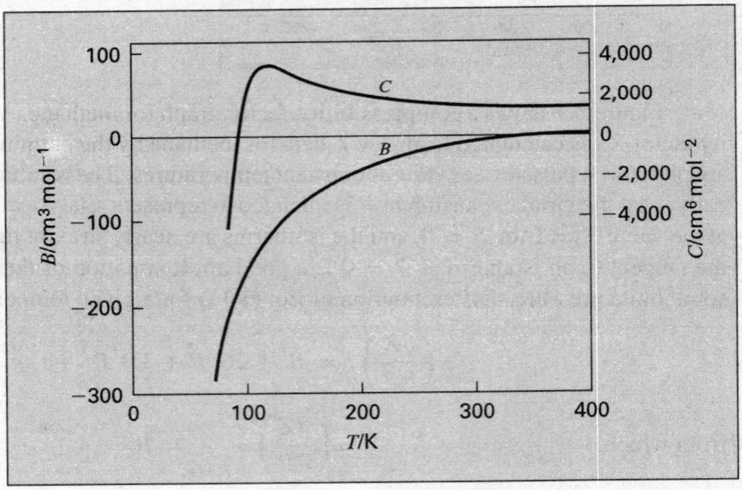

Figure 3.10: Virial coefficients B and C for nitrogen

Values of C, like those of B, depend on the gas and on temperature. However, much less is known about third virial coefficients than about second virial coefficients, though data for a number of gases are found in the literature. Because virial coefficients beyond the third are rarely known and because the virial expansion with more than three terms becomes unwieldy, its use is uncommon.

[5] J. H. Dymond and E. B. Smith, *The Virial Coefficients of Pure Gases and Mixtures*, Clarendon Press, Oxford, 1980.

Figure 3.10 illustrates the effect of temperature on the virial coefficients B and C for nitrogen; although numerical values are different for other gases, the trends are similar. The curve of Fig. 3.10 suggests that B increases monotonically with T; however, at temperatures much higher than shown B reaches a maximum and then slowly decreases. The temperature dependence of C is more difficult to establish experimentally, but its main features are clear: C is negative at low temperatures, passes through a maximum at a temperature near the critical, and thereafter decreases slowly with increasing T.

A class of equations inspired by Eq. (3.12), known as *extended* virial equations, is illustrated by the Benedict/Webb/Rubin equation:[6]

$$P = \frac{RT}{V} + \frac{B_0RT - A_0 - C_0/T^2}{V^2} + \frac{bRT - a}{V^3} + \frac{a\alpha}{V^6} + \frac{c}{V^3T^2}\left(1 + \frac{\gamma}{V^2}\right)\exp\frac{-\gamma}{V^2}$$

where A_0, B_0, C_0, a, b, c, α, and γ are all constant for a given fluid. This equation and its modifications, despite their complexity, are used in the petroleum and natural-gas industries for light hydrocarbons and a few other commonly encountered gases.

Example 3.8

Reported values for the virial coefficients of isopropanol vapor at 200°C (473.15 K) are:

$$B = -388 \text{ cm}^3 \text{ mol}^{-1} \qquad C = -26\,000 \text{ cm}^6 \text{ mol}^{-2}$$

Calculate V and Z for isopropanol vapor at 200°C (473.15 K) and 10 bar by

(*a*) the ideal-gas equation (*b*) Equation (3.38) (*c*) Equation (3.40)

Solution

The absolute temperature is $T = 473.15$ K, and the appropriate value of the gas constant is $R = 83.14$ cm^3 bar mol^{-1} K^{-1}.

(*a*) For an ideal gas, $Z = 1$, and

$$V = \frac{RT}{P} = \frac{(83.14)(473.15)}{10} = 3934 \text{ cm}^3 \text{ mol}^{-1}$$

(*b*) Solving Eq. (3.38) for V gives:

$$V = \frac{RT}{P} + B = 3934 - 388 = 3546 \text{ cm}^3 \text{ mol}^{-1}$$

[6] M. Benedict, G. B. Webb, L. C. Rubin, *J. Chem. Phys.*, vol. 8, pp. 334–345, 1940; vol. 10, pp. 747–758, 1942.

Whence,
$$Z = \frac{PV}{RT} = \frac{V}{RT/P} = \frac{3546}{3934} = 0.9014$$

(*c*) To facilitate iteration, write Eq. (3.40) as

$$V_{i+1} = \frac{RT}{P}\left(1 + \frac{B}{V_i} + \frac{C}{V_i^2}\right)$$

where subscript i denotes the iteration number. For the first iteration, $i = 0$, and

$$V_1 = \frac{RT}{P}\left(1 + \frac{B}{V_0} + \frac{C}{V_0^2}\right)$$

where $V_0 = 3934$, the ideal-gas value. Numerically,

$$V_1 = 3934\left[1 - \frac{388}{3934} - \frac{26\,000}{(3934)^2}\right] = 3539$$

The second iteration depends on this result:

$$V_2 = \frac{RT}{P}\left(1 + \frac{B}{V_1} + \frac{C}{V_1^2}\right) = 3934\left[1 + \frac{388}{3539} - \frac{26\,000}{(3539)^2}\right] = 3495$$

Iteration continues until the difference $V_{i+1} - V_i$ is insignificant, and leads after five iterations to the final value,[7]

$$V = 3488 \text{ cm}^3 \text{ mol}^{-1}$$

from which $Z = 0.8866$. In comparison with this result, the ideal-gas value is 13% too high and Eq. (3.38) gives a value 1.7% too high.

3.5 CUBIC EQUATIONS OF STATE

If an equation of state is to represent the PVT behavior of both liquids and vapors, it must encompass a wide range of temperatures and pressures. Yet it must not be so complex as to present excessive numerical or analytical difficulties in application. Polynomial equations that are cubic in molar volume offer a compromise between generality and simplicity that is suitable to many purposes. Cubic equations are in fact the simplest equations capable of representing both liquid and vapor behavior.

[7] Iteration schemes, incorporated in software packages, accomplish this iteration routinely and unobserved.

The van der Waals Equation of State

The first practical cubic equation of state was proposed by J. D. van der Waals[8] in 1873:

$$\boxed{P = \frac{RT}{V - b} - \frac{a}{V^2}} \tag{3.41}$$

Here, a and b are positive constants; when they are zero, the ideal-gas equation is recovered.

Given values of a and b for a particular fluid, one can calculate P as a function of V for various values of T. Figure 3.11 is a schematic PV diagram showing three such isotherms. Superimposed is the "dome" representing states of saturated liquid and saturated vapor. For the isotherm $T_1 > T_c$, pressure is a monotonically decreasing function with increasing molar volume. The critical isotherm (labeled T_c) contains the horizontal inflection at C characteristic of the critical point. For the isotherm $T_2 < T_c$, the pressure decreases rapidly in the subcooled-liquid region with increasing V; after crossing the saturated-liquid line, it goes through a minimum, rises to a maximum, and then decreases, crossing the saturated-vapor line and continuing downward into the superheated-vapor region.

Experimental isotherms do not exhibit this smooth transition from saturated liquid to saturated vapor; rather, they contain a horizontal segment within the two-phase region where saturated liquid and saturated vapor coexist in varying proportions at the saturation or vapor pressure. This behavior, shown by the dashed line in Fig. 3.11, is nonanalytic, and we accept as inevitable the unrealistic behavior of equations of state in the two-phase region.

Actually, the PV behavior predicted in this region by proper cubic equations of state is not wholly fictitious. If pressure is decreased on a saturated liquid devoid of vapor-nucleation sites in a carefully controlled experiment, vaporization does not occur, and liquid persists alone to pressures well below its vapor pressure. Similarly, raising the pressure on a saturated vapor in a suitable experiment does not cause condensation, and vapor persists alone to pressures well above the vapor pressure. These nonequilibrium or metastable states of superheated liquid and subcooled vapor are approximated by those portions of the PV isotherm which lie in the two-phase region adjacent to the states of saturated liquid and saturated vapor.

Cubic equations of state have three volume roots, of which two may be complex. Physically meaningful values of V are always real, positive, and greater than constant b. For an isotherm at $T > T_c$, reference to Fig. 3.11 shows that solution for V at any positive value of P yields only one such root. For the critical isotherm ($T = T_c$), this is also true, except at the critical pressure, where there are three roots, all equal to V_c. For isotherms at $T < T_c$, the equation may exhibit one or three real roots, depending on the pressure. Although these roots are real and positive, they are not physically stable states for the portion of an isotherm lying between saturated liquid and saturated vapor (under the "dome"). Only for the vapor or *saturation* pressure P^{sat} are the roots, $V^{\text{sat}}(\text{liq})$ and $V^{\text{sat}}(\text{vap})$, stable states, lying at the ends of the horizontal portion of the true isotherm. For other pressures (as indicated by the horizontal lines shown on Fig. 3.11 above and below P^{sat}), the smallest root is a liquid or "liquid-like" volume, and the largest is a vapor or "vapor-like" volume. The third root, lying between the other values, is of no significance.

[8]Johannes Diderik van der Waals (1837–1923), Dutch physicist who won the 1910 Nobel Prize for physics.

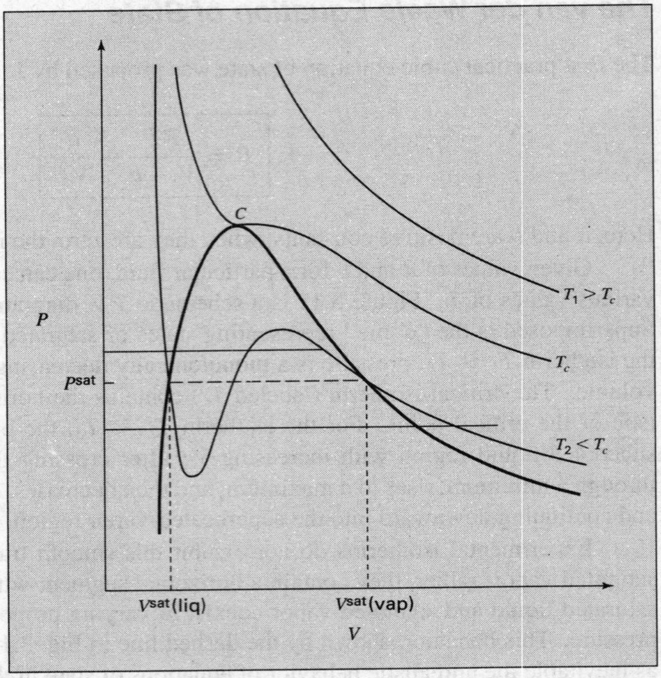

Figure 3.11: Isotherms as given by a cubic equation of state

A Generic Cubic Equation of State

Since the introduction of the van der Waals equation, several hundred cubic equations of state have been proposed[9]. All are special cases of the equation:

$$P = \frac{RT}{V - b} - \frac{\theta(V - \eta)}{(V - b)(V^2 + \kappa V + \lambda)}$$

Here, b, θ, κ, λ, and η are parameters which in general depend on temperature and (for mixtures) composition. Although this equation appears to possess great flexibility, it has inherent limitations because of its cubic form.[10] It reduces to the van der Waals equation when $\eta = b$, $\theta = a$, and $\kappa = \lambda = 0$.

An important class of cubic equations results from the preceding equation with the assignments:

$$\eta = b \qquad \theta = a(T) \qquad \kappa = (\epsilon + \sigma)b \qquad \lambda = \epsilon\sigma b^2$$

It is thus transformed into an expression general enough to serve as a *generic cubic equation of*

[9]For a review, see J. O. Valderrama, *Ind. Eng. Chem. Res.*, vol. 42, pp. 1603–1618, 2003.

[10]M. M. Abbott, *AIChE J.*, vol. 19, pp. 596–601, 1973; *Adv. in Chem. Series 182*, K. C. Chao and R. L. Robinson, Jr., eds., pp. 47–70, Am. Chem. Soc., Washington, D.C., 1979.

state, which reduces to all others of interest here upon assignment of appropriate parameters:

$$P = \frac{RT}{V-b} - \frac{a(T)}{(V+\epsilon b)(V+\sigma b)} \tag{3.42}$$

For a given equation, ϵ and σ are pure numbers, the same for all substances, whereas parameters $a(T)$ and b are substance dependent. The temperature dependence of $a(T)$ is specific to each equation of state. For the van der Waals equation, $a(T) = a$ is a substance-dependent constant, and $\epsilon = \sigma = 0$.

Determination of Equation-of-State Parameters

The constants in an equation of state for a particular substance may be evaluated by a fit to available PVT data. For cubic equations of state, however, suitable estimates are usually found from values for the critical constants T_c and P_c. Because the critical isotherm exhibits a horizontal inflection at the critical point, we may impose the mathematical conditions:

$$\left(\frac{\partial P}{\partial V}\right)_{T;\text{cr}} = 0 \quad (3.43) \qquad \left(\frac{\partial^2 P}{\partial V^2}\right)_{T;\text{cr}} = 0 \quad (3.44)$$

where the subscript "cr" denotes the critical point. Differentiation of Eq. (3.42) yields expressions for both derivatives, which may be equated to zero for $P = P_c$, $T = T_c$, and $V = V_c$. The equation of state may itself be written for the critical conditions. These three equations contain five constants: P_c, V_c, T_c, $a(T_c)$, and b. Of the several ways to treat these equations, the most suitable is elimination of V_c to yield expressions relating $a(T_c)$ and b to P_c and T_c. The reason is that P_c and T_c are usually more accurately known than V_c.

An equivalent, but more straightforward, procedure is illustrated for the van der Waals equation. Because $V = V_c$ for each of the three roots at the critical point,

$$(V - V_c)^3 = 0$$

or

$$V^3 - 3V_cV^2 + 3V_c^2V - V_c^3 = 0 \tag{A}$$

Equation (3.41), written for ($T = T_c$, $P = P_c$) and expanded in polynomial form, becomes:

$$V^3 - \left(b + \frac{RT_c}{P_c}\right)V^2 + \frac{a}{P_c}V - \frac{ab}{P_c} = 0 \tag{B}$$

where parameters a and b are substance dependent, but independent of temperature.

Term-by-term comparison of Eqs. (A) and (B) provides three equations:

$$3V_c = b + \frac{RT_c}{P_c} \quad (C) \qquad 3V_c^2 = \frac{a}{P_c} \quad (D) \qquad V_c^3 = \frac{ab}{P_c} \quad (E)$$

Solving Eq. (D) for a, combining the result with Eq. (E), and solving for b gives

$$a = 3P_cV_c^2 \qquad b = \frac{1}{3}V_c$$

Substitution for b in Eq. (C) allows solution for V_c, which can then be eliminated from the equations for a and b:

$$V_c = \frac{3}{8}\frac{RT_c}{P_c} \qquad a = \frac{27}{64}\frac{R^2T_c^2}{P_c} \qquad b = \frac{1}{8}\frac{RT_c}{P_c}$$

Although these equations may not yield the best possible results, they provide reasonable values which can almost always be determined, because critical temperatures and pressures (in contrast to extensive PVT data) are often known, or can be reliably estimated.

Substitution for V_c in the equation for the critical compressibility factor reduces it immediately to

$$Z_c \equiv \frac{P_cV_c}{RT_c} = \frac{3}{8}$$

A single value for Z_c, applicable alike to all substances, results whenever the parameters of a two-parameter equation of state are found by imposition of the critical constraints. Different values are found for different equations of state, as indicated in Table 3.1, p. 98. Unfortunately, the values so obtained do not in general agree with those calculated from experimental values of T_c, P_c, and V_c; each chemical species in fact has its own value of Z_c. Moreover, the values given in Table B.1 of App. B for various substances are almost all smaller than any of the equation values given in Table 3.1.

An analogous procedure applied to the generic cubic, Eq. (3.42), yields expressions for parameters $a(T_c)$ and b. For the former,

$$a(T_c) = \Psi\frac{R^2T_c^2}{P_c}$$

This result is extended to temperatures other than the critical by introduction of a dimensionless function $\alpha(T_r)$ that becomes unity at the critical temperature. Thus

$$a(T) = \Psi\frac{\alpha(T_r)R^2T_c^2}{P_c} \tag{3.45}$$

Function $\alpha(T_r)$ is an empirical expression, specific to a particular equation of state (Table 3.1). Parameter b is given by

$$b = \Omega\frac{RT_c}{P_c} \tag{3.46}$$

In these equations Ω and Ψ are pure numbers, independent of substance and determined for a particular equation of state from the values assigned to ϵ and σ.

The modern development of cubic equations of state was initiated in 1949 by publication of the Redlich/Kwong (RK) equation:[11]

$$P = \frac{RT}{V-b} - \frac{a(T)}{V(V+b)} \tag{3.47}$$

where $a(T)$ is given by Eq. (3.45) with $\alpha(T_r) = T_r^{-1/2}$.

[11]Otto Redlich and J. N. S. Kwong, *Chem. Rev.*, vol. 44, pp. 233–244, 1949.

Theorem of Corresponding States; Acentric Factor

Experimental observation shows that compressibility factors Z for different fluids exhibit similar behavior when correlated as a function of *reduced temperature* T_r and *reduced pressure* P_r; by **definition**,

$$T_r \equiv \frac{T}{T_c} \qquad \text{and} \qquad P_r \equiv \frac{P}{P_c}$$

These dimensionless thermodynamic coordinates provide the basis for the simplest form of the *theorem of corresponding states*:

> **All fluids, when compared at the same reduced temperature and reduced pressure, have approximately the same compressibility factor, and all deviate from ideal-gas behavior to about the same degree.**

Corresponding-states correlations of Z based on this theorem are called *two-parameter* correlations, because they require use of the two reducing parameters T_c and P_c. Although these correlations are very nearly exact for the *simple fluids* (argon, krypton, and xenon) systematic deviations are observed for more complex fluids. Appreciable improvement results from introduction of a third corresponding-states parameter (in addition to T_c and P_c), characteristic of molecular structure; the most popular such parameter is the *acentric factor* ω, introduced by K. S. Pitzer and coworkers.[12]

The acentric factor for a pure chemical species is defined with reference to its vapor pressure. Because the logarithm of the vapor pressure of a pure fluid is approximately linear in the reciprocal of absolute temperature,

$$\frac{d \log P_r^{\text{sat}}}{d(1/T_r)} = \mathcal{S}$$

where P_r^{sat} is the reduced vapor pressure, T_r is the reduced saturation temperature, and $\mathcal{S}$ is the slope of a plot of $\log P_r^{\text{sat}}$ vs. $1/T_r$. Note that "log" denotes a logarithm to the base 10.

If the two-parameter theorem of corresponding states were generally valid, the slope $\mathcal{S}$ would be the same for all pure fluids. This is observed not to be true; each fluid has its own characteristic value of $\mathcal{S}$, which could in principle serve as a third corresponding-states parameter. However, Pitzer noted that all vapor-pressure data for the simple fluids (Ar, Kr, Xe) lie on the same line when plotted as $\log P_r^{\text{sat}}$ vs. $1/T_r$ and that the line passes through $\log P_r^{\text{sat}} = -1.0$ at $T_r = 0.7$. This is illustrated in Fig. 3.12. Data for other fluids define other lines whose locations can be fixed in relation to the line for the simple fluids (SF) by the difference:

$$\log P_r^{\text{sat}}(\text{SF}) - \log P_r^{\text{sat}}$$

The acentric factor is **defined** as this difference evaluated at $T_r = 0.7$:

$$\boxed{\omega \equiv -1.0 - \log(P_r^{\text{sat}})_{T_r=0.7}} \tag{3.48}$$

Therefore ω can be determined for any fluid from T_c, P_c, and a single vapor-pressure measurement made at $T_r = 0.7$. Values of ω and the critical constants T_c, P_c, and V_c for a number of fluids are listed in App. B.

[12]Fully described in K. S. Pitzer, *Thermodynamics*, 3d ed., App. 3, McGraw-Hill, New York, 1995.

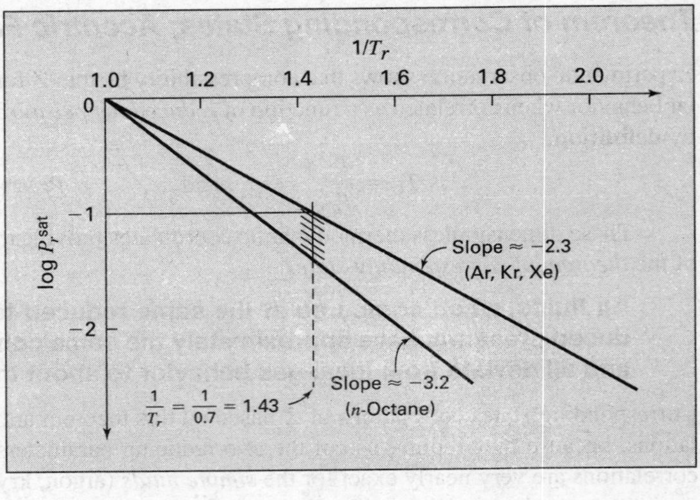

Figure 3.12: Approximate temperature dependence of the reduced vapor pressure

The definition of ω makes its value zero for argon, krypton, and xenon, and experimental data yield compressibility factors for all three fluids that are correlated by the same curves when Z is represented as a function of T_r and P_r. This is the basic premise of the following *three-parameter theorem of corresponding states*:

All fluids having the same value of ω, when compared at the same T_r and P_r, have about the same value of Z, and all deviate from ideal-gas behavior to about the same degree.

Vapor and Vapor-Like Roots of the Generic Cubic Equation of State

Although one may solve explicitly for its three roots, the generic cubic equation of state, Eq. (3.42), is in practice far more commonly solved by iterative procedures.[13] Convergence problems are most likely avoided when the equation is rearranged to a form suited to the solution for a particular root. For the largest root, i.e., a vapor or vapor-like volume, Eq. (3.42) is multiplied through by $(V - b)/RT$. It can then be written:

$$V = \frac{RT}{P} + b - \frac{a(T)}{P} \frac{V - b}{(V + \epsilon b)(V + \sigma b)} \tag{3.49}$$

Solution for V may be by trial, iteration, or with the solve routine of a software package. An initial estimate for V is the ideal-gas value RT/P. For iteration, this value is substituted on the right side of Eq. (3.49). The resulting value of V on the left is then returned to the right side, and the process continues until the change in V is suitably small.

An equation for Z equivalent to Eq. (3.49) is obtained by substituting $V = ZRT/P$. In addition, the definition of two dimensionless quantities leads to simplification. Thus,

[13]Such procedures are built into computer software packages for technical calculations. With these packages one can solve routinely for V in equations such as (3.42) with little thought as to how it is done. However, careful thought should be given to the question of whether the answers are reasonable.

$\beta \equiv \dfrac{bP}{RT}$ (3.50)	$q \equiv \dfrac{a(T)}{bRT}$ (3.51)

With these substitutions Eq. (3.49) becomes:

$$Z = 1 + \beta - q\beta \frac{Z - \beta}{(Z + \epsilon\beta)(Z + \sigma\beta)} \tag{3.52}$$

Equations (3.50) and (3.51) in combination with Eqs. (3.45) and (3.46) yield:

$\beta = \Omega \dfrac{P_r}{T_r}$ (3.53)	$q = \dfrac{\Psi\,\alpha(T_r)}{\Omega\,T_r}$ (3.54)

Iterative solution of Eq. (3.52) starts with the value $Z = 1$ substituted on the right side. The calculated value of Z is returned to the right side and the process continues to convergence. The final value of Z yields the volume root through $V = ZRT/P$.

Liquid and Liquid-Like Roots of the Generic Cubic Equation of State

Equation (3.49) may be solved for the V in the numerator of the final fraction to give

$$V = b + (V + \epsilon b)(V + \sigma b)\left[\frac{RT + bP - VP}{a(T)}\right] \tag{3.55}$$

This equation with a starting value of $V = b$ on the right side converges upon iteration to a liquid or liquid-like root.

An equation for Z equivalent to Eq. (3.55) is obtained when Eq. (3.52) is solved for the Z in the numerator of the final fraction:

$$Z = \beta + (Z + \epsilon\beta)(Z + \sigma\beta)\left(\frac{1 + \beta - Z}{q\beta}\right) \tag{3.56}$$

For iteration a starting value of $Z = \beta$ is substituted on the right side. Once Z is known, the volume root is $V = ZRT/P$.

Equations of state which express Z as a function of T_r and P_r are said to be *generalized*, because of their general applicability to all gases and liquids. Any equation of state can be put into this form to provide a generalized correlation for the properties of fluids. This allows the estimation of property values from very limited information. Equations of state, such as the van der Waals and Redlich/Kwong equations, which express Z as functions of T_r and P_r only, yield two-parameter corresponding states correlations. The Soave/Redlich/Kwong (SRK) equation[14] and the Peng/Robinson (PR) equation,[15] in which the acentric factor enters through function $\alpha(T_r;\omega)$ as an additional parameter, yield three-parameter corresponding-states correlations. The numerical assignments for parameters ϵ, σ, Ω, and Ψ, both for these equations and for the van der Waals and Redlich/Kwong equations, are given in Table 3.1. Expressions are also given for $\alpha(T_r;\omega)$ for the SRK and PR equations.

[14] G. Soave, *Chem. Eng. Sci.*, vol. 27, pp. 1197–1203, 1972.

[15] D.-Y. Peng and D. B. Robinson, *Ind. Eng. Chem. Fundam.*, vol. 15, pp. 59–64, 1976.

Table 3.1: Parameter Assignments for Equations of State

For use with Eqs. (3.49) through (3.56)

Eq. of State	$\alpha(T_r)$	σ	ϵ	Ω	Ψ	Z_c
vdW (1873)	1	0	0	1/8	27/64	3/8
RK (1949)	$T_r^{-1/2}$	1	0	0.086 64	0.427 48	1/3
SRK (1972)	$\alpha_{\text{SRK}}(T_r;\omega)^\dagger$	1	0	0.086 64	0.427 48	1/3
PR (1976)	$\alpha_{\text{PR}}(T_r;\omega)^\ddagger$	$1+\sqrt{2}$	$1-\sqrt{2}$	0.077 80	0.457 24	0.307 40

$$^\dagger\alpha_{\text{SRK}}(T_r;\omega) = \left[1 + (0.480 + 1.574\,\omega - 0.176\,\omega^2)\left(1 - T_r^{1/2}\right)\right]^2$$

$$^\ddagger\alpha_{\text{PR}}(T_r;\omega) = \left[1 + (0.374\,64 + 1.542\,26\,\omega - 0.269\,92\,\omega^2)\left(1 - T_r^{1/2}\right)\right]^2$$

Example 3.9

Given that the vapor pressure of *n*-butane at 350 K is 9.4573 bar, find the molar volumes of (*a*) saturated-vapor and (*b*) saturated-liquid *n*-butane at these conditions as given by the Redlich/Kwong equation.

Solution

Values of T_c and P_c for *n*-butane from App. B yield

$$T_r = \frac{350}{425.1} = 0.8233 \qquad \text{and} \qquad P_r = \frac{9.4573}{37.96} = 0.2491$$

Parameter q is given by Eq. (3.54) with Ω, Ψ, and $\alpha(T_r)$ for the RK equation from Table 3.1:

$$q = \frac{\Psi T_r^{-1/2}}{\Omega T_r} = \frac{\Psi}{\Omega} T_r^{-3/2} = \frac{0.427\,48}{0.086\,64}(0.8233)^{-3/2} = 6.6048$$

Parameter β is found from Eq. (3.53):

$$\beta = \Omega\frac{P_r}{T_r} = \frac{(0.086\,64)(0.2491)}{0.8233} = 0.026\,214$$

(*a*) For the saturated vapor, write the RK form of Eq. (3.52) which results upon substitution of appropriate values for ϵ and σ from Table 3.1:

$$Z = 1 + \beta - q\beta\frac{(Z-\beta)}{Z(Z+\beta)}$$

Iteration with an initial value $Z = 1$ converges on $Z = 0.8305$. Thus,

$$V^v = \frac{ZRT}{P} = \frac{(0.8305)(83.14)(350)}{9.4573} = 2555 \text{ cm}^3 \text{ mol}^{-1}$$

An experimental value is 2482 $\text{cm}^3 \text{ mol}^{-1}$.

(*b*) For the saturated liquid, apply Eq. (3.56) in its RK form:

$$Z = \beta + Z(Z + \beta)\left(\frac{1 + \beta - Z}{q\beta}\right)$$

or

$$Z = 0.026\,214 + Z(Z + 0.026\,214)\frac{(1.026\,214 - Z)}{(6.6048)(0.026\,214)}$$

The initial step is substitution of $Z = \beta$ on the right side of this equation. Iteration leads to convergence on the value $Z = 0.043\,31$. Whence,

$$V^l = \frac{ZRT}{P} = \frac{(0.043\,31)(83.14)(350)}{9.4573} = 133.3 \text{ cm}^3 \text{ mol}^{-1}$$

An experimental value is 115.0 $\text{cm}^3 \text{ mol}^{-1}$.

For comparison, values of V^v and V^l calculated for the conditions of Ex. 3.9 by all four of the cubic equations of state considered here are summarized as follows:

$V^v/\text{cm}^3 \text{ mol}^{-1}$					$V^l/\text{cm}^3 \text{ mol}^{-1}$				
Exp.	vdW	RK	SRK	PR	Exp.	vdW	RK	SRK	PR
2482	2667	2555	2520	2486	115.0	191.0	133.3	127.8	112.6

The Soave/Redlich/Kwong and the Peng/Robinson equations were developed specifically for vapor/liquid equilibrium calculations (Sec. 14.2).

Roots of equations of state are most easily found with a software package such as Mathcad® or Maple®, in which iteration is an integral part of the equation-solving routine. Starting values or bounds may be required, and must be appropriate to the particular root of interest. A Mathcad® program for solving Ex. 3.9 is given in App. D.2.

3.6 GENERALIZED CORRELATIONS FOR GASES

Generalized correlations find widespread use. Most popular are correlations of the kind developed by Pitzer and coworkers for the compressibility factor Z and for the second virial coefficient B.[16]

[16] See Pitzer, *op. cit.*

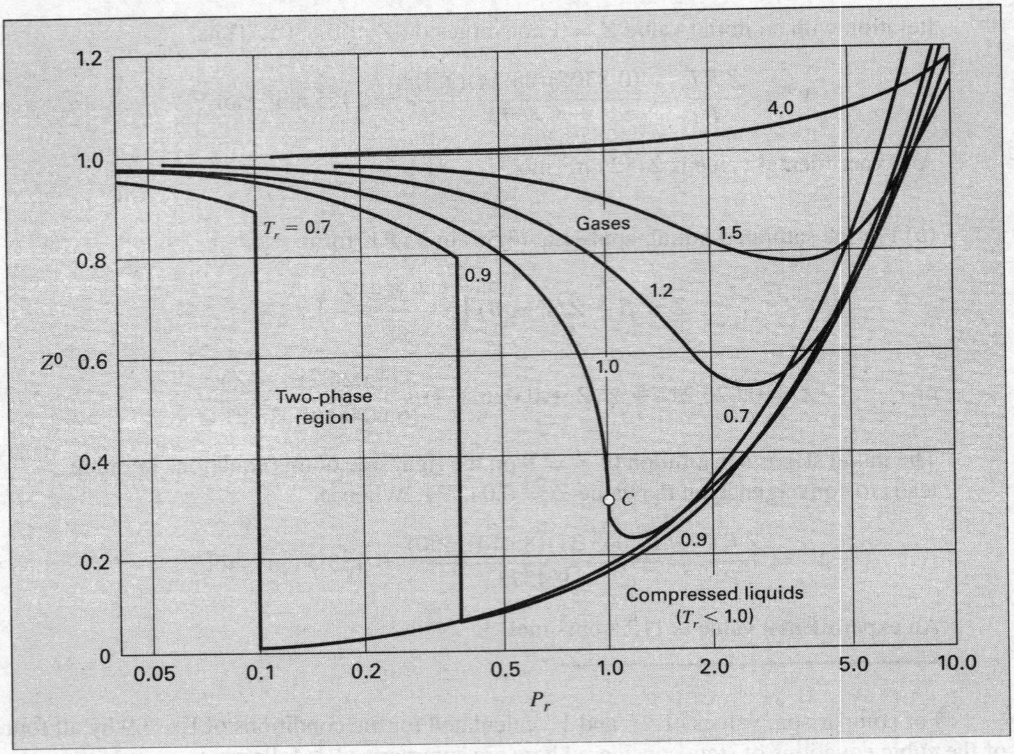

Figure 3.13: The Lee/Kesler correlation for $Z^0 = F^0(T_r, P_r)$

Pitzer Correlations for the Compressibility Factor

The correlation for Z is

$$Z = Z^0 + \omega Z^1 \tag{3.57}$$

where Z^0 and Z^1 are functions of both T_r and P_r. When $\omega = 0$, as is the case for the simple fluids, the second term disappears, and Z^0 becomes identical with Z. Thus a generalized correlation for Z as a function of T_r and P_r based on data for just argon, krypton, and xenon provides the relationship $Z^0 = F^0(T_r, P_r)$. By itself, this represents a *two*-parameter corresponding-states correlation for Z. Because the second term of Eq. (3.57) is a relatively small correction to this correlation, its omission does not introduce large errors, and a correlation for Z^0 may be used alone for quick but less accurate estimates of Z than are obtained from a three-parameter correlation.

Equation (3.57) is a simple linear relation between Z and ω for given values of T_r and P_r. Experimental data for Z for nonsimple fluids plotted vs. ω at constant T_r and P_r do indeed yield approximately straight lines, and their slopes provide values for Z^1 from which the generalized function $Z^1 = F^1(T_r, P_r)$ can be constructed.

Of the Pitzer-type correlations available, the one developed by Lee and Kesler[17] has

[17] B. I. Lee and M. G. Kesler, *AIChE J.*, vol. 21, pp. 510–527, 1975.

found greatest favor. Although its development is based on a modified form of the Benedict/Webb/Rubin equation of state, it takes the form of tables which present values of Z^0 and Z^1 as functions of T_r and P_r. These are given in App. E as Tables E.1 through E.4. Use of these tables often requires interpolation, which is treated at the beginning of App. F. The nature of the correlation is indicated by Fig. 3.13, a plot of Z^0 vs. P_r for six isotherms.

The Lee/Kesler correlation provides reliable results for gases which are nonpolar or only slightly polar; for these, errors of no more than 2 or 3 percent are indicated. When applied to highly polar gases or to gases that associate, larger errors can be expected.

The quantum gases (e.g., hydrogen, helium, and neon) do not conform to the same corresponding-states behavior as do normal fluids. Their treatment by the usual correlations is sometimes accommodated by use of temperature-dependent *effective* critical parameters.[18] For hydrogen, the quantum gas most commonly found in chemical processing, the recommended equations are

$$T_c/\mathrm{K} = \frac{43.6}{1 + \dfrac{21.8}{2.016\,T}} \quad (\text{for } H_2) \tag{3.58}$$

$$P_c/\mathrm{bar} = \frac{20.5}{1 + \dfrac{44.2}{2.016\,T}} \quad (\text{for } H_2) \tag{3.59}$$

$$V_c/\mathrm{cm^3\,mol^{-1}} = \frac{51.5}{1 - \dfrac{9.91}{2.016\,T}} \quad (\text{for } H_2) \tag{3.60}$$

where T is absolute temperature in kelvins. Use of these *effective* critical parameters for hydrogen requires the further specification that $\omega = 0$.

Pitzer Correlations for the Second Virial Coefficient

The tabular nature of the generalized compressibility-factor correlation is a disadvantage, but the complexity of the functions Z^0 and Z^1 precludes their accurate representation by simple equations. However, we can give approximate analytical expression to these functions for a limited range of pressures. The basis for this is Eq. (3.38), the simplest form of the virial equation:

$$Z = 1 + \frac{BP}{RT} = 1 + \hat{B}\frac{P_r}{T_r} \tag{3.61}$$

where $\hat{B}$ is a reduced second virial coefficient, given by

$$\hat{B} = \frac{BP_c}{RT_c} \tag{3.62}$$

[18] J. M. Prausnitz, R. N. Lichtenthaler, and E. G. de Azevedo, *Molecular Thermodynamics of Fluid-Phase Equilibria*, 3d ed., pp. 172–173, Prentice Hall PTR, Upper Saddle River, NJ, 1999.

Thus, Pitzer and coworkers proposed a second correlation, which yields values for $\hat{B}$:

$$\hat{B} = B^0 + \omega B^1 \tag{3.63}$$

Equations (3.61) and (3.63) together become

$$Z = 1 + B^0 \frac{P_r}{T_r} + \omega B^1 \frac{P_r}{T_r}$$

Comparison of this equation with Eq. (3.57) provides the following identifications:

$$Z^0 = 1 + B^0 \frac{P_r}{T_r} \tag{3.64}$$

and

$$Z^1 = B^1 \frac{P_r}{T_r}$$

Second virial coefficients are functions of temperature only, and similarly B^0 and B^1 are functions of reduced temperature only. They are reasonably well represented by the following equations[19]

$$B^0 = 0.083 - \frac{0.422}{T_r^{1.6}} \tag{3.65}$$

$$B^1 = 0.139 - \frac{0.172}{T_r^{4.2}} \tag{3.66}$$

The simplest form of the virial equation has validity only at low to moderate pressures where Z is linear in pressure. The generalized virial-coefficient correlation is therefore useful only where Z^0 and Z^1 are at least approximately linear functions of reduced pressure. Figure 3.14 compares the linear relation of Z^0 to P_r as given by Eqs. (3.64) and (3.65) with values of Z^0 from the Lee/Kesler compressibility-factor correlation, Tables E.1 and E.3. The two correlations differ by less than 2% in the region above the dashed line of the figure. For reduced temperatures greater than $T_r \approx 3$, there appears to be no limitation on the pressure. For lower values of T_r the allowable pressure range decreases with decreasing temperature. A point is reached, however, at $T_r \approx 0.7$ where the pressure range is limited by the saturation pressure.[20] This is indicated by the left-most segment of the dashed line. The minor contributions of Z^1 to the correlations are here neglected. In view of the uncertainty associated with any generalized correlation, deviations of no more than 2% in Z^0 are not significant.

The relative simplicity of the generalized second-virial-coefficient correlation does much to recommend it. Moreover, temperatures and pressures of many chemical-processing operations lie within the region where it does not deviate by a significant amount from the compressibility-factor correlation. Like the parent correlation, it is most accurate for nonpolar species and least accurate for highly polar and associating molecules.

[19] These correlations first appeared in 1975 in the third edition of this book, attributed as a personal communication to M. M. Abbott, who developed them.

[20] Although the Lee/Kesler tables of Appendix E list values for superheated vapor and subcooled liquid, they do not provide values at saturation conditions.

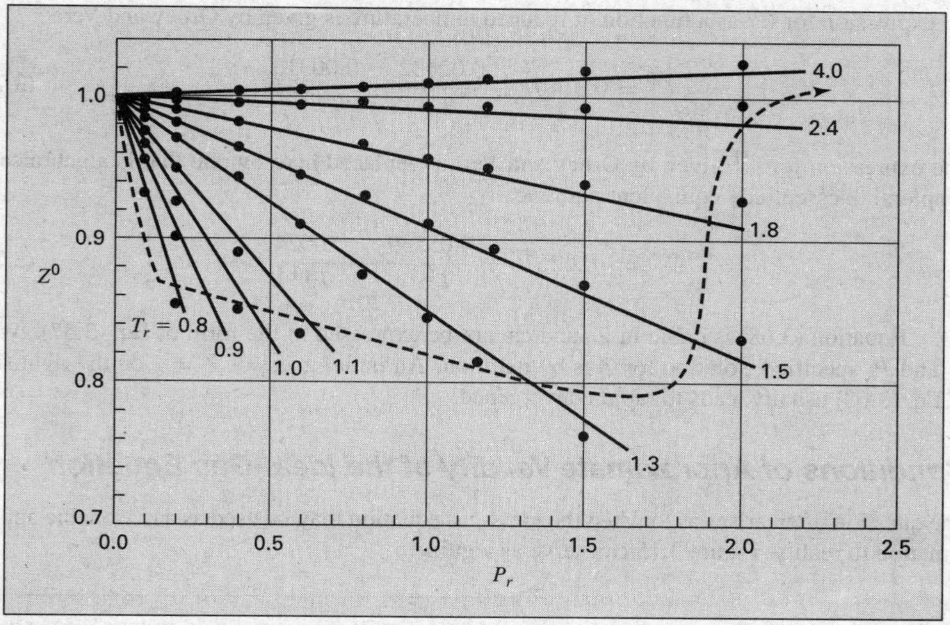

Figure 3.14: Comparison of correlations for Z^0. The virial-coefficient correlation is represented by the straight lines; the Lee/Kesler correlation, by the points. In the region above the dashed line the two correlations differ by less than 2%

Correlations for the Third Virial Coefficient

Accurate data for third virial coefficients are far less common than for second virial coefficients. Nevertheless, generalized correlations for third virial coefficients do appear in the literature.

Equation (3.40) may be written as

$$Z = 1 + B\rho + C\rho^2 \tag{3.67}$$

where $\rho = 1/V$ is molar density. Rewritten in reduced form, this equation becomes

$$Z = 1 + \hat{B}\frac{P_r}{T_r Z} + \hat{C}\left(\frac{P_r}{T_r Z}\right)^2 \tag{3.68}$$

where the reduced second virial coefficient $\hat{B}$ is defined by Eq. (3.62), and the reduced third virial coefficient is defined as

$$\hat{C} \equiv \frac{C P_c^2}{R^2 T_c^2}$$

A Pitzer-type correlation for $\hat{C}$ is written as

$$\hat{C} = C^0 + \omega C^1 \tag{3.69}$$

An expression for C^0 as a function of reduced temperature is given by Orbey and Vera:[21]

$$C^0 = 0.01407 + \frac{0.02432}{T_r} - \frac{0.00313}{T_r^{10.5}} \tag{3.70}$$

The expression for C^1 given by Orbey and Vera is replaced here by one that is algebraically simpler, but essentially equivalent numerically

$$C^1 = -0.02676 + \frac{0.05539}{T_r^{2.7}} - \frac{0.00242}{T_r^{10.5}} \tag{3.71}$$

Equation (3.68) is cubic in Z, and cannot be expressed in the form of Eq. (3.57). With T_r and P_r specified, solution for Z is by iteration. An initial guess of $Z = 1$ on the right side of Eq. (3.68) usually leads to rapid convergence.

Conditions of Approximate Validity of the Ideal-Gas Equation

The question often arises as to when the ideal-gas equation may be used as a reasonable approximation to reality. Figure 3.15 can serve as a guide.

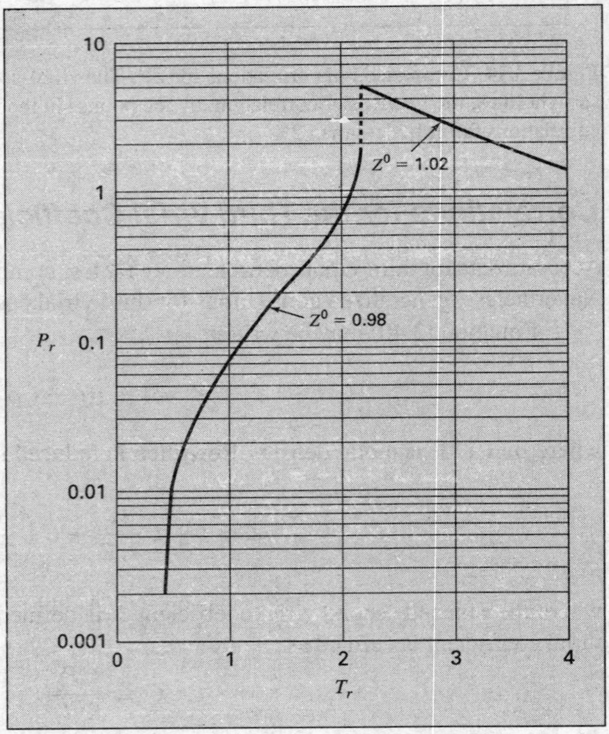

Figure 3.15: Region where Z^0 lies between 0.98 and 1.02, and the ideal-gas equation is a reasonable approximation

[21] H. Orbey and J. H. Vera, *AIChE J.*, vol. 29, pp. 107–113, 1983.

Example 3.10

Determine the molar volume of *n*-butane at 510 K and 25 bar by each of the following:

(*a*) The ideal-gas equation

(*b*) The generalized compressibility-factor correlation

(*c*) Equation (3.61), with the generalized correlation for $\hat{B}$

(*d*) Equation (3.68), with the generalized correlations for $\hat{B}$ and $\hat{C}$

Solution

(*a*) By the ideal-gas equation,

$$V = \frac{RT}{P} = \frac{(83.14)(510)}{25} = 1696.1 \text{ cm}^3 \text{ mol}^{-1}$$

(*b*) From the values of T_c and P_c given in Table B.1 of App. B,

$$T_r = \frac{510}{425.1} = 1.200 \qquad P_r = \frac{25}{37.96} = 0.659$$

Interpolation in Tables E.1 and E.2 then provides:

$$Z^0 = 0.865 \qquad Z^1 = 0.038$$

Thus, by Eq. (3.57) with $\omega = 0.200$,

$$Z = Z^0 + \omega Z^1 = 0.865 + (0.200)(0.038) = 0.873$$

and
$$V = \frac{ZRT}{P} = \frac{(0.873)(83.14)(510)}{25} = 1480.7 \text{ cm}^3 \text{ mol}^{-1}$$

If Z^1, the secondary term, is neglected, $Z = Z^0 = 0.865$. This two-parameter corresponding-states correlation yields $V = 1467.1$ cm^3 mol^{-1}, which is less than 1% lower than the value given by the three-parameter correlation.

(*c*) Values of B^0 and B^1 are given by Eqs. (3.65) and (3.66):

$$B^0 = -0.232 \qquad B^1 = 0.059$$

Equations (3.63) and (3.61) then yield

$$\hat{B} = B^0 + \omega B^1 = -0.232 + (0.200)(0.059) = -0.220$$

$$Z = 1 + (-0.220)\frac{0.659}{1.200} = 0.879$$

from which $V = 1489.1$ cm^3 mol^{-1}, a value less than 1% higher than that given by the compressibility-factor correlation.

(*d*) Values of C^0 and C^1 are given by Eqs. (3.70) and (3.71):

$$C^0 = 0.0339 \qquad C^1 = 0.0067$$

Equation (3.69) then yields

$$\hat{C} = C^0 + \omega C^1 = 0.0339 + (0.200)(0.0067) = 0.0352$$

With this value of $\hat{C}$ and the value of $\hat{B}$ from part (*c*), Eq. (3.68) becomes,

$$Z = 1 + (-0.220)\left(\frac{0.659}{1.200Z}\right) + (0.0352)\left(\frac{0.659}{1.200Z}\right)^2$$

or

$$Z = 1 - \frac{0.121}{Z} + \frac{0.0106}{Z^2}$$

Whence, $Z = 0.876$ and $V = 1485.8 \text{ cm}^3 \text{ mol}^{-1}$

The value of V differs from that of part (*c*) by about 0.2%. An experimental value for V is 1480.7 $\text{cm}^3 \text{ mol}^{-1}$. Significantly, the results of parts (*b*), (*c*), and (*d*) are in excellent agreement. Mutual agreement at these conditions is suggested by Fig. 3.14.

Example 3.11

What pressure is generated when 1 kmol of methane is stored in a volume of 0.125 m^3 at 50°C (323.15 K)? Base calculations on each of the following:

(*a*) The ideal-gas equation

(*b*) The Redlich/Kwong equation

(*c*) A generalized correlation

Solution

(*a*) By the ideal-gas equation,

$$P = \frac{RT}{V} = \frac{(0.083\,14)(323.15)}{0.125} = 214.9 \text{ bar}$$

(*b*) For the Redlich/Kwong equation, values of $a(T)$ and b come from Eqs. (3.42) and Eqs. (3.43):

$$T_r = \frac{T}{T_c} = \frac{323.15}{190.6} = 1.695$$

$$a = \frac{(0.427\,48)(1.695)^{-0.5}(0.083\,14)^2(190.6)^2}{45.99} = 1.7922 \text{ bar m}^6$$

and

$$b = \frac{(0.086\,64)(0.083\,14)(190.6)}{45.99} = 0.029\,85 \text{ m}^3$$

where values of T_c and P_c from App. B. Substitution of known values into Eq. (3.41) now gives

$$P = \frac{(0.083\,14)(323.15)}{(0.125 - 0.029\,85)} - \frac{1.7922}{0.125(0.125 + 0.029\,85)} = 189.65 \text{ bar}$$

(*c*) Since the pressure here is high, the generalized compressibility-factor correlation is the proper choice. In the absence of a known value for P_r, an iterative procedure is based on the following equation:

$$P = \frac{ZRT}{V} = \frac{Z(0.08314)(323.15)}{0.125} = 214.9Z$$

Since $P = P_c P_r = 45.99 P_r$, this equation becomes

$$Z = \frac{45.99 P_r}{214.9} = 0.214 P_r$$

or

$$P_r = \frac{Z}{0.214}$$

One now assumes a starting value for Z, say $Z = 1$. This gives $P_r = 4.673$, and allows a new value of Z to be calculated by Eq. (3.54) from values interpolated in Tables E.3 and E.4 at the reduced temperature of $T_r = 323.15/190.6 = 1.695$. With this new value of Z, a new value of P_r is calculated, and the procedure continues until no significant change occurs from one step to the next. The final value of Z so found is 0.889 at $P_r = 4.14$. This may be confirmed by substitution into Eq. (3.54) of values for Z^0 and Z^1 from Tables E.3 and E.4 interploated at $P_r = 4.14$ and $T_r = 1.695$. Since $\omega = 0.012$, we have

$$Z = Z^0 + \omega Z^1 = 0.887 + (0.012)(0.258) = 0.890$$

and

$$P = \frac{ZRT}{V} = \frac{(0.890)(0.083\,14)(323.15)}{0.125} = 191.3 \text{ bar}$$

Since the acentric factor is small, the two-and three-parameter compressibility-factor correlations are little different. Both the Redlich/Kwong equation and the Generalized compressibility-factor correlation give answers very close to the experimental value of 187.5 bar. The ideal-gas equation yields a result that is high by 14.6 percent.

Example 3.12

A mass of 500 g of gaseous ammonia is contained in a 30 000 cm^3 vessel immersed in a constant-temperature bath at 65°C (338.15 K) . Calculate the pressure of the gas by

(*a*) The ideal-gas equation (*b*) A generalized correlation

Solution

The molar volume of ammonia in the vessel is

$$V = \frac{V^t}{n} = \frac{V^t}{m/M} = \frac{30\,000}{500/17.02} = 1021.2 \text{ cm}^3 \text{ mol}^{-1}$$

(*a*) By the ideal-gas equation,

$$P = \frac{RT}{V} = \frac{(83.14)(65 + 273.15)}{1021.2} = 27.53 \text{ bar}$$

(*b*) Because the reduced pressure is low ($P_r \approx 27.53/112.8 = 0.244$), the generalized virial-coefficient correlation should suffice. Values of B^0 and B^1 are given by Eqs. (3.65) and (3.66), with $T_r = 338.15/405.7 = 0.834$:

$$B^0 = -0.482 \qquad B^1 = -0.232$$

Substitution into Eq. (3.63) with $\omega = 0.253$ yields

$$\hat{B} = -0.482 + (0.253)(-0.232) = -0.541$$

$$B = \frac{\hat{B} R T_c}{P_c} = \frac{-(0.541)(83.14)(405.7)}{112.8} = -161.8 \text{ cm}^3 \text{ mol}^{-1}$$

Solve Eq. (3.38) for P:

$$P = \frac{RT}{V - B} = \frac{(83.14)(338.15)}{1{,}021.2 + 161.8} = 23.76 \text{ bar}$$

An iterative solution is not necessary, because B is independent of pressure. The calculated P corresponds to a reduced pressure of $P_r = 23.76/112.8 = 0.211$. Reference to Fig. 3.14 confirms the suitability of the generalized virial-coefficient correlation.

Experimental data indicate that the pressure is 23.82 bar at the given conditions. Thus the ideal-gas equation yields an answer high by about 15%, whereas the virial-coefficient correlation gives an answer in substantial agreement with experiment, even though ammonia is a polar molecule.

3.7 GENERALIZED CORRELATIONS FOR LIQUIDS

Although the molar volumes of liquids can be calculated by means of generalized cubic equations of state, the results are often not of high accuracy. However, the Lee/Kesler correlation includes data for subcooled liquids, and Fig. 3.13 illustrates curves for both liquids and gases. Values for both phases are provided in Tables E.1 through E.4. Recall, however, that this correlation is most suitable for nonpolar and slightly polar fluids.

In addition, generalized equations are available for the estimation of molar volumes of *saturated* liquids. The simplest equation, proposed by Rackett,[22] is an example:

$$V^{\text{sat}} = V_c Z_c^{(1-T_r)^{2/7}} \tag{3.72}$$

An alternative form of this equation is sometimes useful:

$$Z^{\text{sat}} = \frac{P_r}{T_r} Z_c^{[1+(1-T_r)^{2/7}]} \tag{3.73}$$

The only data required are the critical constants, given in Table B.1. Results are usually accurate to 1 or 2%.

Lydersen, Greenkorn, and Hougen[23] developed a two-parameter corresponding-states correlation for estimation of liquid volumes. It provides a correlation of reduced density ρ_r as a function of reduced temperature and pressure. By definition,

$$\rho_r \equiv \frac{\rho}{\rho_c} = \frac{V_c}{V} \tag{3.74}$$

where ρ_c is the density at the critical point. The generalized correlation is shown by Fig. 3.16. This figure may be used directly with Eq. (3.74) for determination of liquid volumes if the value of the critical volume is known. A better procedure is to make use of a single known liquid volume (state 1) by the identity,

$$V_2 = V_1 \frac{\rho_{r_1}}{\rho_{r_2}} \tag{3.75}$$

where
V_2 = required volume
V_1 = known volume
ρ_{r_1}, ρ_{r_2} = reduced densities read from Fig. 3.16

This method gives good results and requires only experimental data that are usually available. Figure 3.16 makes clear the increasing effects of both temperature and pressure on liquid density as the critical point is approached.

Correlations for the molar densities as functions of temperature are given for many pure liquids by Daubert and coworkers.[24]

[22] H. G. Rackett, *J. Chem. Eng. Data*, vol. 15, pp. 514–517, 1970; see also C. F. Spencer and S. B. Adler, *ibid.*, vol. 23, pp. 82–89, 1978, for a review of available equations.

[23] A. L. Lydersen, R. A. Greenkorn, and O. A. Hougen, "Generalized Thermodynamic Properties of Pure Fluids," *Univ. Wisconsin, Eng. Expt. Sta. Rept. 4*, 1955.

[24] T. E. Daubert, R. P. Danner, H. M. Sibul, and C. C. Stebbins, *Physical and Thermodynamic Properties of Pure Chemicals: Data Compilation*, Taylor & Francis, Bristol, PA, extant 1995.

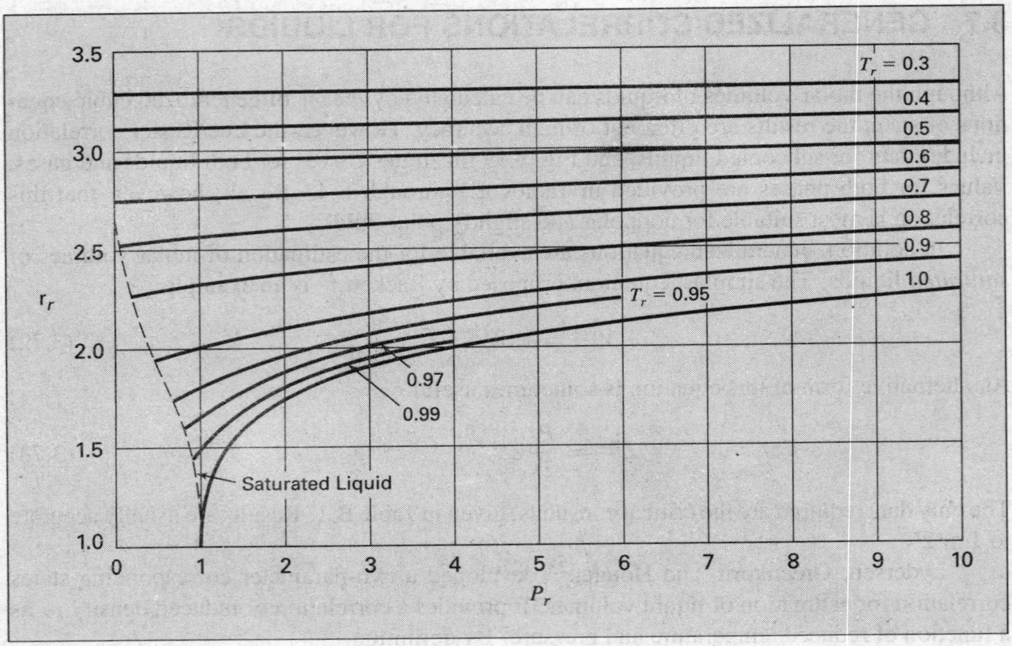

Figure 3.16: Generalized density correlation for liquids

Example 3.13

For ammonia at 310 K, estimate the density of the

(*a*) saturated liquid (*b*) liquid at 100 bar

Solution

(*a*) Apply Eq. (3.72) at the reduced temperature, $T_r = 310/405.7 = 0.7641$. With $V_c = 72.47$ and $Z_c = 0.242$ (from Table B.1),

$$V^{\text{sat}} = V_c Z_c^{(1-T_r)^{2/7}} = (72.47)(0.242)^{(0.2359)^{2/7}} = 28.33 \text{ cm}^3 \text{ mol}^{-1}$$

For comparison, the experimental value is 29.14 cm^3 mol^{-1}, a 2.7% difference.

(*b*) The reduced conditions are

$$T_r = 0.7641 \qquad P_r = \frac{100}{112.8} = 0.887$$

Substituting the value, $\rho_r = 2.38$ (from Fig. 3.16), and V_c into Eq. (3.74) gives

$$V = \frac{V_c}{\rho_r} = \frac{72.47}{2.38} = 30.45 \text{ cm}^3 \text{ mol}^{-1}$$

In comparison with the experimental value of 28.6 $cm^3 mol^{-1}$, this result is higher by 6.5%.

If we start with the experimental value of 29.14 $cm^3 mol^{-1}$ for saturated liquid at 310 K, Eq. (3.75) may be used. For the saturated liquid at $T_r = 0.764$, $\rho_{r_1} = 2.34$ (from Fig. 3.16). Substitution of known values into Eq. (3.75) gives

$$V_2 = V_1 \frac{\rho_{r_1}}{\rho_{r_2}} = (29.14)\left(\frac{2.34}{2.38}\right) = 28.65 \text{ cm}^3 \text{ mol}^{-1}$$

This result is in essential agreement with the experimental value.

Direct application of the Lee/Kesler correlation with values of Z^0 and Z^1 interpolated from Tables E.1 and E.2 leads to a value of 33.87 $cm^3 mol^{-1}$, which is significantly in error, no doubt owing to the highly polar nature of ammonia.

PROBLEMS

3.1. Express the volume expansivity and the isothermal compressibility as functions of density ρ and its partial derivatives. For water at 50°C (323.15 K) and 1 bar, $\kappa = 44.18 \times 10^{-6}$ bar^{-1}. To what pressure must water be compressed at 50°C (323.15 K) to change its density by 1%? Assume that κ is independent of P.

3.2. Generally, volume expansivity β and isothermal compressibility κ depend on T and P. Prove that

$$\left(\frac{\partial \beta}{\partial P}\right)_T = -\left(\frac{\partial \kappa}{\partial T}\right)_P$$

3.3. The Tait equation for liquids is written for an isotherm as

$$V = V_0\left(1 - \frac{AP}{B + P}\right)$$

where V is molar or specific volume, V_0 is the hypothetical molar or specific volume at zero pressure, and A and B are positive constants. Find an expression for the isothermal compressibility consistent with this equation.

3.4. For liquid water the isothermal compressibility is given by

$$\kappa = \frac{c}{V(P + b)}$$

where c and b are functions of temperature only. If 1 kg of water is compressed isothermally and reversibly from 1 to 500 bar at 60°C (333.15 K), how much work is required? At 60°C (333.15 K), $b = 2700$ bar and $c = 0.125$ $cm^3 g^{-1}$.

3.5. Calculate the reversible work done in compressing 0.0283m^3 of mercury at a constant temperature of 0°C (273.15 K) from 1(atm) to 3,000 atm. The isothermal compressibility of mercury at 0°C (273.15 K) is

$$\kappa = 3.9 \times 10^{-6} - 0.1 \times 10^{-9} P$$

where P is in atm and κ is in atm^{-1}.

3.6. Five kilograms of liquid carbon tetrachloride undergo a mechanically reversible, isobaric change of state at 1 bar during which the temperature changes from 0°C to 20°C (273.15 K to 293.15 K). Determine ΔV^t, W, Q, ΔH^t, and ΔU^t. The properties for liquid carbon tetrachloride at 1 bar and 0°C (273.15 K) may be assumed independent of temperature: $\beta = 1.2 \times 10^{-3}\ \text{K}^{-1}$, $C_P = 0.84\ \text{kJ kg}^{-1}\ \text{K}^{-1}$, and $\rho = 1{,}590\ \text{kg m}^{-3}$.

3.7. A substance for which κ is a constant undergoes an isothermal, mechanically reversible process from initial state (P_1, V_1) to final state (P_2, V_2), where V is molar volume.

(*a*) Starting with the definition of κ, show that the path of the process is described by

$$V = A(T) \exp(-\kappa P)$$

(*b*) Determine an exact expression which gives the isothermal work done on 1 mol of this constant-κ substance.

3.8. One mole of an ideal gas with $C_P = (7/2)R$ and $C_V = (5/2)R$ expands from $P_1 =$ 8 bar and $T_1 = 600$ K to $P_2 = 1$ bar by each of the following paths:

(*a*) Constant volume (*b*) Constant temperature (*c*) Adiabatically

Assuming mechanical reversibility, calculate W, Q, ΔU, and ΔH for each process. Sketch each path on a single PV diagram.

3.9. An ideal gas initially at 600 K and 10 bar undergoes a four-step mechanically reversible cycle in a closed system. In step 12, pressure decreases isothermally to 3 bar; in step 23, pressure decreases at constant volume to 2 bar; in step 34, volume decreases at constant pressure; and in step 41, the gas returns adiabatically to its initial state. Take $C_P = (7/2)R$ and $C_V = (5/2)R$.

(*a*) Sketch the cycle on a PV diagram.
(*b*) Determine (where unknown) both T and P for states 1, 2, 3, and 4.
(*c*) Calculate Q, W, ΔU, and ΔH for each step of the cycle.

3.10. An ideal gas, $C_P = (5/2)R$ and $C_V = (3/2)R$, is changed from $P = 1$ bar and $V_1^t = 12\ \text{m}^3$ to $P_2 = 12$ bar and $V_2^t = 1\ \text{m}^3$ by the following mechanically reversible processes:

(*a*) Isothermal compression
(*b*) Adiabatic compression followed by cooling at constant pressure
(*c*) Adiabatic compression followed by cooling at constant volume
(*d*) Heating at constant volume followed by cooling at constant pressure

(*e*) Cooling at constant pressure followed by heating at constant volume.

Calculate Q, W, ΔU^t, and ΔH^t for each of these processes, and sketch the paths of all processes on a single PV diagram.

3.11. The *environmental lapse rate* dT/dz characterizes the local variation of temperature with elevation in the earth's atmosphere. Atmospheric pressure varies with elevation according to the hydrostatic formula,

$$\frac{dP}{dz} = -\mathcal{M}\rho g$$

where $\mathcal{M}$ is molar mass, ρ is molar density, and g is the local acceleration of gravity. Asssume that the atmosphere is an ideal gas, with T related to P by the polytropic formula, Eq. (3.35c). Develop an expression for the environmental lapse rate in relation to $\mathcal{M}$, g, R, and δ.

3.12. An evacuated tank is filled with gas from a constant-pressure line. Develop an expression relating the temperature of the gas in the tank to the temperature T' of the gas in the line. Assume the gas is ideal with constant heat capacities, and ignore heat transfer between the gas and the tank. Mass and energy balances for this problem are treated in Ex. 2.13.

3.13. Show how Eqs. (3.36) and (3.37) reduce to the appropriate expressions for the four particular values of δ listed following Eq. (3.37).

3.14. A tank of 0.1 m^3 volume contains air at 25°C (298.15 K) and 101.33 kPa. The tank is connected to a compressed-air line which supplies air at the constant conditions of 45°C (318.15 K) and 1500 kPa. A valve in the line is cracked so that air flows slowly into the tank until the pressure equals the line pressure. If the process occurs slowly enough that the temperature in the tank remains at 25°C (298.15 K), how much heat is lost from the tank? Assume air to be an ideal gas for which $C_P = (7/2)R$ and $C_V = (5/2)R$.

3.15. Gas at constant T and P is contained in a supply line connected through a valve to a closed tank containing the same gas at a lower pressure. The valve is opened to allow flow of gas into the tank, and then is shut again.

(*a*) Develop a general equation relating n_1 and n_2, the moles (or mass) of gas in the tank at the beginning and end of the process, to the properties U_1 and U_2, the internal energy of the gas in the tank at the beginning and end of the process, and H', the enthalpy of the gas in the supply line, and to Q, the heat transferred to the material in the tank during the process.

(*b*) Reduce the general equation to its simplest form for the special case of an ideal gas with constant heat capacities.

(*c*) Further reduce the equation of (*b*) for the case of $n_1 = 0$.

(*d*) Further reduce the equation of (*c*) for the case in which, in addition, $Q = 0$.

(*e*) Treating nitrogen as an ideal gas for which $C_P = (7/2)R$, apply the appropriate equation to the case in which a steady supply of nitrogen at 25°C (298.15 K) and 3 bar flows into an evacuated tank of 4 m^3 volume, and calculate the moles of nitrogen that flow into the tank to equalize the pressures for two cases:

1. Assume that no heat flows from the gas to the tank or through the tank walls.
2. The tank weighs 400 kg, is perfectly insulated, has an initial temperature of 25°C (298.15 K), has a specific heat of 0.46 kJ kg^{-1} K^{-1}, and is heated by the gas so as always to be at the temperature of the gas in the tank.

3.16. Develop equations which may be solved to give the final temperature of the gas remaining in a tank after the tank has been bled from an initial pressure P_1 to a final pressure P_2. Known quantities are initial temperature, tank volume, heat capacity of the gas, total heat capacity of the containing tank, P_1, and P_2. Assume the tank to be always at the temperature of the gas remaining in the tank, and the tank to be perfectly insulated.

3.17. A rigid, nonconducting tank with a volume of 4 m^3 is divided into two unequal parts by a thin membrane. One side of the membrane, representing 1/3 of the tank, contains nitrogen gas at 6 bar and 100°C (373.15 K), and the other side, representing 2/3 of the tank, is evacuated. The membrane ruptures and the gas fills the tank.

(*a*) What is the final temperature of the gas? How much work is done? Is the process reversible?

(*b*) Describe a reversible process by which the gas can be returned to its initial state. How much work is done?

Assume nitrogen is an ideal gas for which $C_P = (7/2)R$ and $C_V = (5/2)R$.

3.18. An ideal gas, initially at 30°C (303.15 K) and 100 kPa, undergoes the following cyclic processes in a closed system:

(*a*) In mechanically reversible processes, it is first compressed adiabatically to 500 kPa, then cooled at a constant pressure of 500 kPa to 30°C (303.15 K), and finally expanded isothermally to its original state.

(*b*) The cycle traverses exactly the same changes of state, but each step is irreversible with an efficiency of 80% compared with the corresponding mechanically reversible process. *Note*: The initial step can no longer be adiabatic.

Calculate Q, W, ΔU, and ΔH for each step of the process and for the cycle. Take $C_P = (7/2)R$ and $C_V = (5/2)R$.

3.19. One cubic meter of an ideal gas at 600 K and 1000 kPa expands to five times its initial volume as follows:

(*a*) By a mechanically reversible, isothermal process

(*b*) By a mechanically reversible, adiabatic process

(*c*) By an adiabatic, irreversible process in which expansion is against a restraining pressure of 100 kPa

For each case calculate the final temperature, pressure, and the work done by the gas. $C_P = 21$ J mol^{-1} K^{-1}.

3.20. One mole of air, initially at 150°C (423.15 K) and 8 bar, undergoes the following mechanically reversible changes. It expands isothermally to a pressure such that when it is cooled at constant volume to 50°C (323.15 K) its final pressure is 3 bar. Assuming air is an ideal gas for which $C_P = (7/2)R$ and $C_V = (5/2)R$, calculate W, Q, ΔU, and ΔH.

3.21. An ideal gas flows through a horizontal tube at steady state. No heat is added and no shaft work is done. The cross-sectional area of the tube changes with length, and this causes the velocity to change. Derive an equation relating the temperature to the velocity of the gas. If nitrogen at 150°C (423.15 K) flows past one section of the tube at a velocity of 2.5 m s^{-1}, what is its temperature at another section where its velocity is 50 m s^{-1}? Let $C_P = (7/2)R$.

3.22. One mole of an ideal gas, initially at 30°C (303.15 K) and 1 bar, is changed to 130°C (403.15 K) and 10 bar by three different mechanically reversible processes:

- The gas is first heated at constant volume until its temperature is 130°C (403.15 K); then it is compressed isothermally until its pressure is 10 bar
- The gas is first heated at constant pressure until its temperature is 130°C (403.15 K); then it is compressed isothermally to 10 bar
- The gas is first compressed isothermally to 10 bar; then it is heated at constant pressure to 130°C (403.15 K)

Calculate Q, W, ΔU, and ΔH in each case. Take $C_P = (7/2)R$ and $C_V = (5/2)R$. Alternatively, take $C_P = (5/2)R$ and $C_V = (3/2)R$.

3.23. One mole of an ideal gas, initially at 30°C (303.15 K) and 1 bar, undergoes the following mechanically reversible changes. It is compressed isothermally to a point such that when it is heated at constant volume to 120°C (393.15 K) its final pressure is 12 bar. Calculate Q, W, ΔU, and ΔH for the process. Take $C_P = (7/2)R$ and $C_V = (5/2)R$.

3.24. A process consists of two steps: (1) One mole of air at $T = 800$ K and $P = 4$ bar is cooled at constant volume to $T = 350$ K. (2) The air is then heated at constant pressure until its temperature reaches 800 K. If this two-step process is replaced by a single isothermal expansion of the air from 800 K and 4 bar to some final pressure P, what is the value of P that makes the work of the two processes the same? Assume mechanical reversibility and treat air as an ideal gas with $C_P = (7/2)R$ and $C_V = (5/2)R$.

3.25. A scheme for finding the internal volume V_B^t of a gas cylinder consists of the following steps. The cylinder is filled with a gas to a low pressure P_1, and connected through a small line and valve to an evacuated reference tank of known volume V_A^t. The valve is opened, and gas flows through the line into the reference tank. After the system returns to its initial temperature, a sensitive pressure transducer provides a value for the pressure change ΔP in the cylinder. Determine the cylinder volume V_B^t from the following data:

- $V_A^t = 256\ \text{cm}^3$
- $\Delta P/P_1 = -0.0639$

3.26. A closed, nonconducting, horizontal cylinder is fitted with a nonconducting, frictionless, floating piston which divides the cylinder into Sections A and B. The two sections contain equal masses of air, initially at the same conditions, $T_1 = 300$ K and $P_1 = 1$ atm. An electrical heating element in Section A is activated, and the air temperatures slowly increase: T_A in Section A because of heat transfer, and T_B in Section B because of adiabatic compression by the slowly moving piston. Treat air as an ideal gas with $C_P = \frac{7}{2}R$, and let n_A be the number of moles of air in Section A. For the process as described, evaluate one of the following sets of quantities:

(*a*) T_A, T_B, and Q/n_A, if $P(\text{final}) = 1.25$ atm
(*b*) T_B, Q/n_A, and $P(\text{final})$, if $T_A = 425$ K
(*c*) T_A, Q/n_A, and $P(\text{final})$, if $T_B = 325$ K
(*d*) T_A, T_B, and $P(\text{final})$, if $Q/n_A = 3\ \text{kJ mol}^{-1}$

3.27. One mole of an ideal gas with constant heat capacities undergoes an arbitrary mechanically reversible process. Show that

$$\Delta U = \frac{1}{\gamma - 1}\Delta(PV)$$

3.28. Derive an equation for the work of mechanically reversible, isothermal compression of 1 mol of a gas from an initial pressure P_1 to a final pressure P_2 when the equation of state is the virial expansion [Eq. (3.11)] truncated to

$$Z = 1 + B'P$$

How does the result compare with the corresponding equation for an ideal gas?

3.29. A certain gas is described by the equation of state:

$$PV = RT + \left(b - \frac{\theta}{RT}\right)P$$

Here, b is a constant and θ is a function of T only. For this gas, determine expressions for the isothermal compressibility κ and the thermal pressure coefficient $(\partial P/\partial T)_V$. These expressions should contain only T, P, θ, $d\theta/dT$, and constants.

3.30. For methyl chloride at 100°C (373.15 K) the second and third virial coefficients are

$$B = -242.5\ \text{cm}^3\ \text{mol}^{-1} \qquad C = 25\,200\ \text{cm}^6\ \text{mol}^{-2}$$

Calculate the work of mechanically reversible, isothermal compression of 1 mol of methyl chloride from 1 bar to 55 bar at 100°C (373.15 K). Base calculations on the following forms of the virial equation:

(*a*) $$Z = 1 + \frac{B}{V} + \frac{C}{V^2}$$

(*b*) $$Z = 1 + B'P + C'P^2$$

where $$B' = \frac{B}{RT} \qquad \text{and} \qquad C' = \frac{C - B^2}{(RT)^2}$$

Why don't both equations give exactly the same result?

3.31. Any equation of state valid for gases in the zero-pessure limit implies a full set of virial coefficients. Show that the second and third virial coefficients implied by the generic cubic equation of state, Eq. (3.42), are

$$B = b - \frac{a(T)}{RT} \qquad C = b^2 + \frac{(\epsilon + \sigma)ba(T)}{RT}$$

Specialize the result for B to the Redlich/Kwong equation of state, express it in reduced form, and compare it numerically with the generalized correlation for B for simple fluids, Eq. (3.65). Discuss what you find.

3.32. Calculate Z and V for ethylene at 25°C (298.15 K) and 12 bar by the following equations:

(*a*) The truncated virial equation [Eq. (3.40)] with the following experimental values of virial coefficients:

$$B = -140 \text{ cm}^3 \text{ mol}^{-1} \qquad C = 7200 \text{ cm}^6 \text{ mol}^{-2}$$

(*b*) The truncated virial equation [Eq. (3.38)], with a value of B from the generalized Pitzer correlation [Eq. (3.63)]

(*c*) The Redlich/Kwong equation

(*d*) The Soave/Redlich/Kwong equation

(*e*) The Peng/Robinson equation

3.33. Calculate Z and V for ethane at 50°C (323.15 K) and 15 bar by the following equations:

(*a*) The truncated virial equation [Eq. (3.40)] with the following experimental values of virial coefficients:

$$B = -156.7 \text{ cm}^3 \text{ mol}^{-1} \qquad C = 9650 \text{ cm}^6 \text{ mol}^{-2}$$

(*b*) The truncated virial equation [Eq. (3.38)], with a value of B from the generalized Pitzer correlation [Eq. (3.63)]

(*c*) The Redlich/Kwong equation

(*d*) The Soave/Redlich/Kwong equation

(*e*) The Peng/Robinson equation

3.34. Calculate Z and V for sulfur hexafluoride at 75°C (348.15 K) and 15 bar by the following equations:

(*a*) The truncated virial equation [Eq. (3.40)] with the following experimental values of virial coefficients:

$$B = -194 \text{ cm}^3 \text{ mol}^{-1} \qquad C = 15\,300 \text{ cm}^6 \text{ mol}^{-2}$$

(*b*) The truncated virial equation [Eq. (3.38)], with a value of B from the generalized Pitzer correlation [Eq. (3.63)]

(*c*) The Redlich/Kwong equation

(*d*) The Soave/Redlich/Kwong equation

(*e*) The Peng/Robinson equation

For sulfur hexafluoride, $T_c = 318.7$ K, $P_c = 37.6$ bar, $V_c = 198$ cm^3 mol^{-1}, and $\omega = 0.286$.

3.35. Determine Z and V for steam at 250°C (523.15 K) and 1800 kPa by the following:

(*a*) The truncated virial equation [Eq. (3.40)] with the following experimental values of virial coefficients:

$$B = -152.5 \text{ cm}^3 \text{ mol}^{-1} \qquad C = -5800 \text{ cm}^6 \text{ mol}^{-2}$$

(*b*) The truncated virial equation [Eq. (3.38)], with a value of B from the generalized Pitzer correlation [Eq. (3.63)]

(*c*) The steam tables (App. F)

3.36. With respect to the virial expansions, Eqs. (3.11) and (3.12), show that:

$$B' = \left(\frac{\partial Z}{\partial P}\right)_{T,P=0} \qquad \text{and} \qquad B = \left(\frac{\partial Z}{\partial \rho}\right)_{T,\rho=0}$$

where $\rho \equiv 1/V$.

3.37. Equation (3.12) when truncated to *four* terms accurately represents the volumetric data for methane gas at 0°C (273.15 K) with

$$B = -53.4 \text{ cm}^3 \text{ mol}^{-1} \qquad C = 2620 \text{ cm}^6 \text{ mol}^{-2} \qquad D = 5000 \text{ cm}^9 \text{ mol}^{-3}$$

(*a*) Use these data to prepare a plot of Z vs. P for methane at 0°C (273.15 K) from 0 to 200 bar.

(*b*) To what pressures do Eqs. (3.38) and (3.39) provide good approximations?

3.38. Calculate the molar volume of saturated liquid and the molar volume of saturated vapor by the Redlich/Kwong equation for one of the following and compare results with values found by suitable generalized correlations.

(*a*) Propane at 40°C (313.15 K) where $P^{\text{sat}} = 13.71$ bar

(*b*) Propane at 50°C (323.15 K) where P^{sat} = 17.16 bar
(*c*) Propane at 60°C (333.15 K) where P^{sat} = 21.22 bar
(*d*) Propane at 70°C (343.15 K) where P^{sat} = 25.94 bar
(*e*) *n*-Butane at 100°C (373.15 K) where P^{sat} = 15.41 bar
(*f*) *n*-Butane at 110°C (383.15 K) where P^{sat} = 18.66 bar
(*g*) *n*-Butane at 120°C (393.15 K) where P^{sat} = 22.38 bar
(*h*) *n*-Butane at 130°C (403.15 K) where P^{sat} = 26.59 bar
(*i*) Isobutane at 90°C (363.15 K) where P^{sat} = 16.54 bar
(*j*) Isobutane at 100°C (373.15 K) where P^{sat} = 20.03 bar
(*k*) Isobutane at 110°C (383.15 K) where P^{sat} = 24.01 bar
(*l*) Isobutane at 120°C (393.15 K) where P^{sat} = 28.53 bar
(*m*) Chlorine at 60°C (333.15 K) where P^{sat} = 18.21 bar
(*n*) Chlorine at 70°C (343.15 K) where P^{sat} = 22.49 bar
(*o*) Chlorine at 80°C (353.15 K) where P^{sat} = 27.43 bar
(*p*) Chlorine at 90°C (363.15 K) where P^{sat} = 33.08 bar
(*q*) Sulfur dioxide at 80°C (353.15 K) where P^{sat} = 18.66 bar
(*r*) Sulfur dioxide at 90°C (363.15 K) where P^{sat} = 23.31 bar
(*s*) Sulfur dioxide at 100°C (373.15 K) where P^{sat} = 28.74 bar
(*t*) Sulfur dioxide at 110°C (383.15 K) where P^{sat} = 35.01 bar

3.39. Use the Soave/Redlich/Kwong equation to calculate the molar volumes of saturated liquid and saturated vapor for the substance and conditions given by one of the parts of Pb. 3.38 and compare results with values found by suitable generalized correlations.

3.40. Use the Peng/Robinson equation to calculate the molar volumes of saturated liquid and saturated vapor for the substance and conditions given by one of the parts of Pb. 3.38 and compare results with values found by suitable generalized correlations.

3.41. Estimate the following:

(*a*) The volume occupied by 18 kg of ethylene at 55°C (328.15 K) and 35 bar
(*b*) The mass of ethylene contained in a 0.25 m^3 cylinder at 50°C (323.15 K) and 115 bar

3.42. The vapor-phase molar volume of a particular compound is reported as 23 000 $cm^3 \ mol^{-1}$ at 300 K and 1 bar. No other data are available. Without assuming ideal-gas behavior, determine a reasonable estimate of the molar volume of the vapor at 300 K and 5 bar.

3.43. To a good approximation, what is the molar volume of ethanol vapor at 480°C (753.15 K) and 6000 kPa? How does this result compare with the ideal-gas value?

3.44. A 0.35 m^3 vessel is used to store liquid propane at its vapor pressure. Safety considerations dictate that at a temperature of 320 K the liquid must occupy no more than 80% of the total volume of the vessel. For these conditions, determine the mass of vapor and the mass of liquid in the vessel. At 320 K the vapor pressure of propane is 16.0 bar.

3.45. A 30 m^3 tank contains 14 m^3 of liquid *n*-butane in equilibrium with its vapor at 25°C (298.15 K). Estimate the mass of *n*-butane vapor in the tank. The vapor pressure of *n*-butane at the given temperature is 2.43 bar.

3.46. Estimate

(*a*) The mass of ethane contained in a 0.15 m^3 vessel at 60°C (333.15 K) and 14 000 kPa

(*b*) The temperature at which 40 kg of ethane stored in a 0.15 m^3 vessel exerts a pressure 20 000 kPa

3.47. To what pressure does one fill a 0.15 m^3 vessel at 25°C (298.15 K) in order to store 40 kg of ethylene in it?

3.48. If 15 kg of H_2O in a 0.4 m^3 container is heated to 400°C (673.15 K), what pressure is developed?

3.49. A 0.35 m^3 vessel holds ethane vapor at 25°C (298.15 K) and 2200 kPa. If it is heated to 220°C (493.15 K), what pressure is developed?

3.50. What is the pressure in a 0.5 m^3 vessel when it is charged with 10 kg of carbon dioxide at 30°C (303.15 K)?

3.51. A rigid vessel, filled to one-half its volume with liquid nitrogen at its normal boiling point, is allowed to warm to 25°C (298.15 K). What pressure is developed? The molar volume of liquid nitrogen at its normal boiling point is 34.7 $cm^3\ mol^{-1}$.

3.52. The specific volume of isobutane liquid at 300 K and 4 bar is 1.824 $cm^3\ g^{-1}$. Estimate the specific volume at 415 K and 75 bar.

3.53. The density of liquid *n*-pentane is 0.630 g cm^{-3} at 18°C (291.15 K) and 1 bar. Estimate its density at 140°C (413.15 K) and 120 bar.

3.54. Estimate the density of liquid ethanol at 180°C (453.15 K) and 200 bar.

3.55. Estimate the volume change of vaporization for ammonia at 20°C (293.15 K). At this temperature the vapor pressure of ammonia is 857 kPa.

3.56. PVT data may be taken by the following procedure. A mass m of a substance of molar mass M is introduced into a thermostated vessel of known total volume V^t. The system is allowed to equilibrate, and the temperature T and pressure P are measured.

(*a*) Approximately what percentage errors are allowable in the measured variables (m, M, V^t, T and P) if the maximum allowable error in the calculated compressibility factor Z is $\pm 1\%$?

(*b*) Approximately what percentage errors are allowable in the measured variables if the maximum allowable error in calculated values of the second virial coefficient B is $\pm 1\%$? Assume that $Z \simeq 0.9$ and that values of B are calculated by Eq. (3.39).

3.57. For a gas described by the Redlich/Kwong equation and for a temperature greater than T_c, develop expressions for the two limiting slopes,

$$\lim_{P\to 0}\left(\frac{\partial Z}{\partial P}\right)_T \qquad \lim_{P\to \infty}\left(\frac{\partial Z}{\partial P}\right)_T$$

Note that in the limit as $P \to 0$, $V \to \infty$, and that in the limit as $P \to \infty$, $V \to b$.

3.58. If 3.965 m^3 of methane gas at 15.6°C (288.75 K) and 1 atm is equivalent to 3.785 $\times$ 10^{-3} m^3 of gasoline as fuel for an automobile engine, what would be the volume of the tank required to hold methane at 207 bar and 15.6°C (288.75 K) in an amount equivalent to 3.785 $\times$ 10^{-3} m^3 of gasoline?

3.59. Determine a good estimate for the compressibility factor Z of saturated hydrogen vapor at 25 K and 3.213 bar. For comparison, an experimental value is $Z = 0.7757$.

3.60. The *Boyle temperature* is the temperature for which

$$\lim_{P\to 0}\left(\frac{\partial Z}{\partial P}\right)_T = 0$$

(*a*) Show that the second virial coefficient B is zero at the Boyle temperature.
(*b*) Use the generalized correlation for B, Eq. (3.63), to estimate the *reduced* Boyle temperature for simple fluids.

3.61. Natural gas (assume pure methane) is delivered to a city via pipeline at a volumetric rate of 4 normal Mm^3 per day. Average delivery conditions are 10°C (283.15 K) and 20.7 bar. Determine the

(*a*) volumetric delivery rate in *actual* Mm^3 per day
(*b*) molar delivery rate in kmol per hour
(*c*) gas velocity at delivery conditions in m s^{-1}

The pipe is 600 mm heavy duty steel with an inside diameter of 575 mm. Normal conditions are 0°C (273.15 K) and 1 atm.

3.62. Some corresponding-states correlations use the critical compressibility factor Z_c, rather than the acentric factor ω, as a third parameter. The two types of correlation (one based on T_c, P_c, and Z_c, the other on T_c, P_c, and ω) would be equivalent were there a one-to-one correspondence between Z_c and ω. The data of App. B allow a test of this correspondence. Prepare a plot of Z_c vs. ω to see how well Z_c correlates with ω. Develop a linear correlation ($Z_c = a + b\omega$) for nonpolar substances.

3.63. Figure 3.3 suggests that the isochores (paths of constant volume) are approximately straight lines on a PT diagram. Show that the following models imply linear isochores.

(*a*) Constant-β, κ equation for liquids (*b*) Ideal-gas equation (*c*) van der Waals equation

3.64. Shown below is the *Equation of State Decision Tree*. For each item discuss the conditions appropriate to its use.

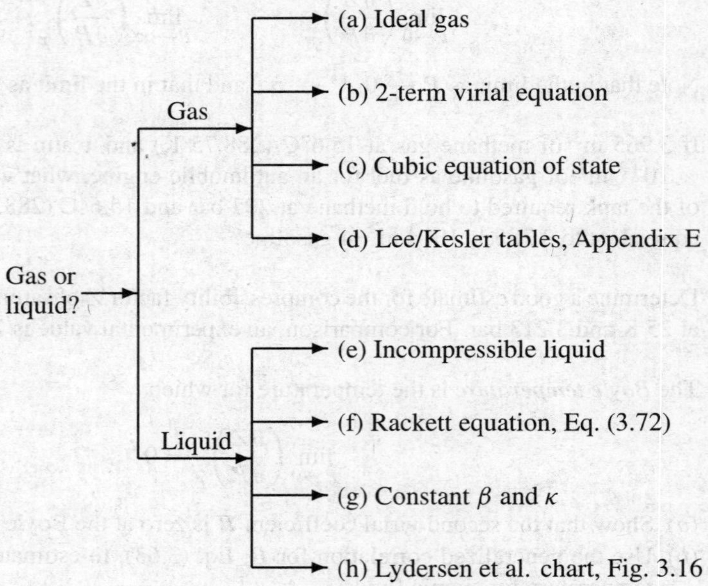

3.65. An ideal gas, initially at 25°C (298.15 K) and 1 bar, undergoes the following cyclic processes in a closed system:

(*a*) In mechanically reversible processes, it is first compressed adiabatically to 5 bar, then cooled at a constant pressure of 5 bar to 25°C (298.15 K), and finally expanded isothermally to its original pressure.

(*b*) The cycle is irreversible and each step has an efficiency of 80% compared with the corresponding mechanically reversible process. The cycle still consists of an adiabatic compression step, an isobaric cooling step, and an isothermal expansion.

Calculate Q, W, ΔU, and ΔH for each step of the process and for the cycle. Take $C_P = (7/2)R$ and $C_V = (5/2)R$.

3.66. Show that the density-series second virial coefficients can be derived from isothermal volumetric data via the expression:

$$B = \lim_{\rho \to 0} (Z - 1)/\rho \qquad \rho \text{ (molar density)} \equiv 1/V$$

3.67. Use the equation of the preceding problem and data from Table F.2 to obtain a value of B for water at one of the following temperatures:

(*a*) 300°C (573.15 K) (*b*) 350°C (623.15 K) (*c*) 400°C (673.15 K)

3.68. Derive the values of Ω, Ψ, and Z_c given in Table 3.1 for the

(*a*) Redlich/Kwong equation of state
(*b*) Soave/Redlich/Kwong equation of state
(*c*) Peng/Robinson equation of state

3.69. Suppose Z vs. P_r data are available at constant T_r. Show that the reduced density-series second virial coefficient can be derived from such data via the expression:

$$\hat{B} = \lim_{P_r \to 0} (Z - 1) Z T_r / P_r$$

Suggestion: Base the development on the full virial expansion in density, Eq. (3.12).

3.70. Use the result of the preceding problem and data from Table E.1 to obtain a value of $\hat{B}$ for simple fluids at $T_r = 1$. Compare the result with the value implied by Eq. (3.65).

3.71. The following conversation was overheard in the corridors of a large engineering firm.

New engineer: "Hi, boss. Why the big smile?"

Old-timer: "I finally won a wager with Harry Carey, from Research. He bet me that I couldn't come up with a quick but accurate estimate for the molar volume of argon at 30°C (303.15 K) and 300 bar. Nothing to it; I used the ideal-gas equation, and got about 83 $cm^3\ mol^{-1}$. Harry shook his head, but paid up. What do you think about that?"

New engineer (consulting his thermo text): "I think you must be living right."

Argon at the stated conditions is **not** an ideal gas. Demonstrate numerically why the old-timer won his wager.

3.72. Five mol of calcium carbide are combined with 10 mol of water in a closed, rigid, high-pressure vessel of 1800 cm^3 internal empty volume. Acetylene gas is produced by the reaction:

$$CaC_2(s) + 2H_2O(l) \rightarrow C_2H_2(g) + Ca(OH)_2(s)$$

The vessel contains packing with a porosity of 40% to prevent explosive decomposition of the acetylene. Initial conditions are 25°C (298.15 K) and 1 bar, and the reaction goes to completion. The reaction is exothermic, but owing to heat transfer, the final temperature is only 125°C (398.15 K). Determine the final pressure in the vessel. *Note*: At 125°C (398.15 K), the molar volume of $Ca(OH)_2$ is 33.0 $cm^3\ mol^{-1}$. Ignore the effects of any gases (e.g., air) initially present in the vessel.

3.73. Storage is required for 35 000 kg of propane, received as a gas at 10°C (283.15 K) and 1 atm. Two proposals have been made:

(*a*) Store it as a gas at 10°C (283.15 K) and 1 atm.
(*b*) Store it as a liquid in equilibrium with its vapor at 10°C (283.15 K) and 6.294 atm. For this mode of storage, 90% of the tank volume is occupied by liquid.

Compare the two proposals, discussing pros and cons of each. Be quantitative where possible.

3.74. The definition of compressibility factor Z, Eq. (3.10), may be written in the more intuitive form:

$$Z \equiv \frac{V}{V\,(\text{ideal gas})}$$

where both volumes are at the same T and P. Recall that an ideal gas is a model substance comprising particles with no intermolecular forces. Use the intuitive definition of Z to argue that

(*a*) Intermolecular attractions promote values of $Z < 1$
(*b*) Intermolecular repulsions promote values of $Z > 1$
(*c*) A balance of attractions and repulsions implies that $Z = 1$ (Note that an ideal gas is a special case for which there are *no* attractions or repulsions.)

3.75. Write the general form of an equation of state as

$$Z = 1 + Z_{\text{rep}}(\rho) - Z_{\text{attr}}(T, \rho)$$

where $Z_{\text{rep}}(\rho)$ represents contributions from repulsions, and $Z_{\text{attr}}(T, \rho)$ represents contributions from attractions. What are the repulsive and attractive contributions to the van der Waals equation of state?

3.76. Given below are four proposed modifications of the van der Waals equation of state. Are any of these modifications *reasonable*? Explain carefully; statements such as, "It isn't cubic in volume." do not qualify.

(*a*) $P = \dfrac{RT}{V-b} - \dfrac{a}{V}$

(*b*) $P = \dfrac{RT}{(V-b)^2} - \dfrac{a}{V}$

(*c*) $P = \dfrac{RT}{V(V-b)} - \dfrac{a}{V^2}$

(*d*) $P = \dfrac{RT}{V} - \dfrac{a}{V^2}$

3.77. With reference to Pb. 2.43, assume air to be an ideal gas, and develop an expression giving the household air temperature as a function of time.

3.78. A garden hose with the water valve shut and the nozzle closed sits in the sun, full of liquid water. Initially, the water is at 10°C (283.15 K) and 6 bar. After some time the temperature of the water rises to 40°C (313.15 K). Owing to the increase in temperature and pressure and the elasticity of the hose, the internal diameter of the hose increases by 0.35%. Estimate the final pressure of the water in the hose.

Data: $\beta(\text{ave}) = 250 \times 10^{-6}\ \text{K}^{-1}$; $\kappa(\text{ave}) = 45 \times 10^{-6}\ \text{bar}^{-1}$

Chapter 4

Heat Effects

Heat transfer is a common operation in the chemical industry. Consider, for example, the manufacture of ethylene glycol (an antifreeze agent) by the oxidation of ethylene to ethylene oxide and its subsequent hydration to glycol. The catalytic oxidation reaction is most effective when carried out at temperatures near 250°C (523.15 K). The reactants, ethylene and air, are therefore heated to this temperature before they enter the reactor. The preheater design depends on the rate of heat transfer. The combustion reactions of ethylene with oxygen in the catalyst bed tend to raise the temperature. However, heat is removed from the reactor, and the temperature does not rise much above 250°C (523.15 K). Higher temperatures promote the production of CO_2, an unwanted product. Design of the reactor requires knowledge of the heat-transfer rate, and this depends on the heat effects associated with the chemical reactions. The ethylene oxide product is hydrated to glycol by absorption in water. Heat is evolved not only because of the phase change and dissolution process but also because of the hydration reaction between the dissolved ethylene oxide and water. Finally, the glycol is recovered from water by distillation, a process of vaporization and condensation, which results in the separation of a solution into its components.

All of the important heat effects are illustrated by this relatively simple chemical-manufacturing process. In contrast to *sensible* heat effects, which are characterized by temperature changes, the heat effects of chemical reaction, phase transition, and the formation and separation of solutions are determined from experimental measurements made at constant temperature. In this chapter we apply thermodynamics to the evaluation of most of the heat effects that accompany physical and chemical operations. However, the heat effects of mixing processes, which depend on the thermodynamic properties of mixtures, are treated in Chap. 12.

4.1 SENSIBLE HEAT EFFECTS

Heat transfer to a system in which there are no phase transitions, no chemical reactions, and no changes in composition causes the temperature of the system to change. We develop here relations between the quantity of heat transferred and the resulting temperature change.

When the system is a homogeneous substance of constant composition, the phase rule indicates that fixing the values of two intensive properties establishes its state. The molar or specific internal energy of a substance may therefore be expressed as a *function of two other state variables*. When these are arbitrarily selected as temperature and molar or specific volume, $U = U(T, V)$. Whence,

$$dU = \left(\frac{\partial U}{\partial T}\right)_V dT + \left(\frac{\partial U}{\partial V}\right)_T dV$$

As a result of Eq. (2.16) this becomes

$$dU = C_V\,dT + \left(\frac{\partial U}{\partial V}\right)_T dV$$

The final term may be set equal to zero in two circumstances:

- For any constant-volume process, regardless of substance.
- Whenever the internal energy is independent of volume, regardless of the process. This is exactly true for ideal gases and incompressible fluids and approximately true for low-pressure gases.

In either case, $$dU = C_V\,dT$$

and $$\Delta U = \int_{T_1}^{T_2} C_V\,dT \tag{4.1}$$

For a mechanically reversible constant-volume process, $Q = \Delta U$, and Eq. (2.19) may be written for a unit mass or a mole:

$$Q = \Delta U = \int_{T_1}^{T_2} C_V\,dT$$

Similarly, the molar or specific enthalpy may be expressed as a function of temperature and pressure. Then $H = H(T, P)$, and

$$dH = \left(\frac{\partial H}{\partial T}\right)_P dT + \left(\frac{\partial H}{\partial P}\right)_T dP$$

As a result of Eq. (2.20) this becomes

$$dH = C_P\,dT + \left(\frac{\partial H}{\partial P}\right)_T dP$$

Again, two circumstances allow the final term to be set equal to zero:

- For any constant-pressure process, regardless of the substance.
- Whenever the enthalpy of the substance is independent of pressure, regardless of the process. This is exactly true for ideal gases and approximately true for low-pressure gases.

In either case,
$$dH = C_P\,dT$$

and
$$\Delta H = \int_{T_1}^{T_2} C_P\,dT \tag{4.2}$$

Moreover, $Q = \Delta H$ for mechanically reversible, constant-pressure, closed-system processes [Eq. (2.23)] and for the transfer of heat in steady-flow exchangers where ΔE_P and ΔE_K are negligible and $W_s = 0$ [Eq. (2.33)]. In either case,

$$Q = \Delta H = \int_{T_1}^{T_2} C_P\,dT \tag{4.3}$$

The common engineering application of this equation is to steady-flow heat transfer.

Temperature Dependence of the Heat Capacity

Evaluation of the integral in Eq. (4.3) requires knowledge of the temperature dependence of the heat capacity. This is usually given by an empirical equation; the two simplest expressions of practical value are

$$\frac{C_P}{R} = \alpha + \beta T + \gamma T^2 \qquad \text{and} \qquad \frac{C_P}{R} = a + bT + cT^{-2}$$

where α, β, and γ and a, b, and c are constants characteristic of the particular substance. With the exception of the last term, these equations are of the same form. We therefore combine them to provide a single expression:

$$\frac{C_P}{R} = A + BT + CT^2 + DT^{-2} \tag{4.4}$$

where either C or D is zero, depending on the substance considered. Because the ratio C_P/R is dimensionless, the units of C_P are governed by the choice of R.

As shown in Chap. 6, for gases the *ideal-gas heat capacity*, rather than the actual heat capacity is used in the evaluation of such thermodynamic properties as the enthalpy. The reason is that thermodynamic-property evaluation is most conveniently accomplished in two steps: first, calculation of values for a hypothetical *ideal-gas state* wherein ideal-gas heat capacities are used; second, correction of the ideal-gas-state values to the real-gas values. A real gas becomes ideal in the limit as $P \to 0$; if it were to remain ideal when compressed to a finite pressure, it would exist in a hypothetical ideal-gas state. In such states gases have properties that reflect their molecular structure just as do real gases. Ideal-gas-state heat capacities (designated by C_P^{ig} and C_V^{ig}) are therefore different for different gases; although functions of temperature, they are independent of pressure.

Ideal-gas heat capacities increase smoothly with increasing temperature toward an upper limit, which is reached when all translational, rotational, and vibrational modes of molecular motion are fully excited [see Eq. (16.18)]. The influence of temperature on C_P^{ig} for argon nitrogen, water, and carbon dioxide is illustrated in Fig. 4.1. Temperature dependence is ex pressed analytically by equations such as Eq. (4.4), here written:

$$\frac{C_P^{ig}}{R} = A + BT + CT^2 + DT^{-2}$$

Values of the parameters are given in Table C.1 of App. C for a number of common organic and inorganic gases. More accurate but more complex equations are found in the literature.[1]

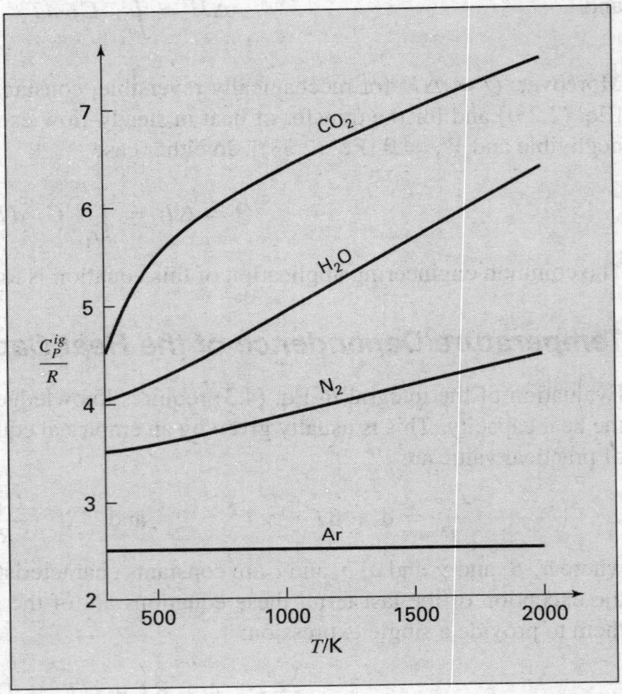

Figure 4.1: Ideal-gas heat capacities of argon, nitrogen, water, and carbon dioxide

As a result of Eq. (3.19), the two ideal-gas heat capacities are related:

$$\frac{C_V^{ig}}{R} = \frac{C_P^{ig}}{R} - 1 \tag{4.5}$$

The temperature dependence of C_V^{ig}/R follows from the temperature dependence of C_P^{ig}/R.

The effects of temperature on C_P^{ig} or C_V^{ig} are determined by experiment, most often from spectroscopic data and knowledge of molecular structure through calculations based on statistical mechanics. Where experimental data are not available, methods of estimation are employed, as described by Reid, Prausnitz, and Poling.[2]

Although ideal-gas heat capacities are exactly correct for real gases only at zero pressure, the departure of real gases from ideality is seldom significant at pressures below several bars, and here C_P^{ig} and C_V^{ig} are usually good approximations to their true heat capacities.

[1]See F. A. Aly and L. L. Lee, *Fluid Phase Equilibria*, vol. 6, pp. 169–179, 1981, and its bibliography; see also T. E. Daubert, R. P. Danner, H. M. Sibul, and C. C. Stebbins, *Physical and Thermodynamic Properties of Pure Chemicals: Data Compilation*, Taylor & Francis, Bristol, PA, extant 1995.

[2]J. M. Prausnitz, B. E. Poling, and J. P. O'Connell, *The Properties of Gases and Liquids*, 5th ed., chap. 3, McGraw-Hill, New York, 2001.

Example 4.1

The parameters listed in Table C.1 require use of Kelvin temperatures in Eq. (4.4). Equation of the same form may also be developed for use with temperatures in °C but the parameter values are different. The molar heat capacity of methane in the ideal-gas state is given as a function of temperature in kelvins by:

$$\frac{C_P^{ig}}{R} = 1.702 + 9.081 \times 10^{-3}T - 2.164 \times 10^{-6}T^2$$

where the parameter values are from Table C.1. Develop an equation for C_P^{ig}/R for temperatures in °C.

Solution

The relation between the two temperature scales is

$$T\ \text{K} = t\,°\text{C} + 273.15$$

Therefore, as a function of t,

$$\frac{C_P^{ig}}{R} = 1.702 + 9.081 \times 10^{-3}(t + 273.15) - 2.164 \times 10^{-6}(t + 273.15)^2$$

or

$$\frac{C_P^{ig}}{R} = 4.021 + 7.899 \times 10^{-3}t - 2.164 \times 10^{-6}t^2$$

Gas mixtures of constant composition behave exactly as do pure gases. In an ideal-gas mixture the molecules have no influence on one another, and each gas exists independent of the others. The ideal-gas heat capacity of a mixture is therefore the mole-fraction-weighted sum of the heat capacities of the individual gases. Thus for gases A, B, and C the molar heat capacity of a mixture in the ideal-gas state is

$$C_{P_{\text{mixture}}}^{ig} = y_A C_{P_A}^{ig} + y_B C_{P_B}^{ig} + y_C C_{P_C}^{ig} \qquad (4.6)$$

where $C_{P_A}^{ig}$, $C_{P_B}^{ig}$, and $C_{P_C}^{ig}$ are the molar heat capacities of pure A, B, and C in the ideal-gas state, and y_A, y_B, and y_C are mole fractions.

As with gases, the heat capacities of solids and liquids are found by experiment. Parameters for the temperature dependence of C_P as expressed by Eq. (4.4) are given for a few solids and liquids in Tables C.2 and C.3 of App. C. Correlations for the heat capacities of many solids and liquids are given by Perry and Green and by Daubert et al.[3]

[3]R. H. Perry and D. Green, *Perry's Chemical Engineers' Handbook*, 7th ed., Sec. 2, McGraw-Hill, New York, 1997; T. E. Daubert et al., *op. cit.*

Evaluation of the Sensible-Heat Integral

Evaluation of the integral $\int C_P\,dT$ is accomplished by substitution for C_P as a function of T, followed by formal integration. For temperature limits of T_0 and T the result is conveniently expressed as

$$\int_{T_0}^{T} \frac{C_P}{R}dT = AT_0(\tau - 1) + \frac{B}{2}T_0^2(\tau^2 - 1) + \frac{C}{3}T_0^3(\tau^3 - 1) + \frac{D}{T_0}\left(\frac{\tau - 1}{\tau}\right) \tag{4.7}$$

where
$$\tau \equiv \frac{T}{T_0}$$

Given T_0 and T, the calculation of Q or ΔH is straightforward. Less direct is the calculation of T, given T_0 and Q or ΔH. Here, an iteration scheme may be useful. Factoring $(\tau - 1)$ from each term on the right-hand side of Eq. (4.7) gives

$$\int_{T_0}^{T} \frac{C_P}{R}dT = \left[AT_0 + \frac{B}{2}T_0^2(\tau + 1) + \frac{C}{3}T_0^3(\tau^2 + \tau + 1) + \frac{D}{\tau T_0}\right](\tau - 1)$$

Because
$$\tau - 1 = \frac{T - T_0}{T_0}$$

this may be written

$$\int_{T_0}^{T} \frac{C_P}{R}dT = \left[A + \frac{B}{2}T_0(\tau + 1) + \frac{C}{3}T_0^2(\tau^2 + \tau + 1) + \frac{D}{\tau T_0^2}\right](T - T_0)$$

We identify the quantity in square brackets as $\langle C_P\rangle_H/R$, where $\langle C_P\rangle_H$ is defined as a *mean heat capacity*:

$$\frac{\langle C_P\rangle_H}{R} = A + \frac{B}{2}T_0(\tau + 1) + \frac{C}{3}T_0^2(\tau^2 + \tau + 1) + \frac{D}{\tau T_0^2} \tag{4.8}$$

Equation (4.2) may therefore be written

$$\Delta H = \langle C_P\rangle_H (T - T_0) \tag{4.9}$$

The angular brackets enclosing C_P identify it as a mean value; subscript "H" denotes a mean value specific to enthalpy calculations, and distinguishes this mean heat capacity from a similar quantity introduced in the next chapter.

Solution of Eq. (4.9) for T gives

$$T = \frac{\Delta H}{\langle C_P\rangle_H} + T_0 \tag{4.10}$$

A starting value for T (and hence for $\tau = T/T_0$) allows evaluation of $\langle C_P\rangle_H$ by Eq. (4.8). Substitution of this value into Eq. (4.10) provides a new value of T from which to reevaluate $\langle C_P\rangle_H$. Iteration continues to convergence on a final value of T.

Example 4.2

Calculate the heat required to raise the temperature of 1 mol of methane from 260 to 600°C (533.15 K to 873.15 K) in a steady-flow process at a pressure sufficiently low that methane may be considered an ideal gas.

Solution

Equation (4.3) in combination with Eq. (4.7) provides the required result. Parameters for C_P^{ig}/R come from Table C.1; temperatures are

$$T_0 = 533.15\text{ K} \qquad T = 873.15\text{ K} \qquad \tau = \frac{873.15}{533.15} = 1.6377$$

Whence,
$$Q = \Delta H = R\int_{533.15}^{873.15} \frac{C_P^{ig}}{R}\,dT$$

$$Q = (8.314)\left[1.702\,T_0(\tau - 1) + \frac{9.081\times10^{-3}}{2}T_0^2(\tau^2 - 1) - \frac{2.164\times10^{-6}}{3}T_0^3(\tau^3 - 1)\right] = 19\,778\text{ J}$$

Use of Defined Functions

The integral $\int(C_P/R)\,dT$ often appears in thermodynamic calculations. As a matter of convenience, we therefore define the right side of Eq. (4.7) as the function, ICPH(T0,T;A,B,C,D), and write a computer routine for its evaluation. Equation (4.7) then becomes

$$\int_{T_0}^{T}\frac{C_P}{R}\,dT \equiv \text{ICPH(T0,T;A,B,C,D)}$$

The function name is ICPH, and the quantities in parentheses are the variables T_0 and T, followed by parameters A, B, C, and D. When these quantities are assigned numerical values, the notation represents a value for the integral. Thus, for the evaluation of Q in Ex. 4.2:

$$Q = 8.314 \times \text{ICPH(533.15,873.15;1.702,9.081E-3,-2.164E-6,0.0)} = 19\,778\text{ J}$$

Representative computer programs for evaluation of the integral are given in App. D. For added flexibility the programs also evaluate the dimensionless quantity $\langle C_P\rangle_H/R$ as given by Eq. (4.8). The right-hand side of this equation is another function, MCPH(T0,T;A,B,C,D). With this definition, Eq. (4.8) becomes

$$\frac{\langle C_P\rangle_H}{R} = \text{MCPH(T0,T;A,B,C,D)}$$

A specific numerical value of this function is

$$\text{MCPH}(533.15,873.15;1.702,9.081\text{E-}3,-2.164\text{E-}6,0.0) = 6.9965$$

representing $\langle C_P \rangle_H / R$ for methane in the calculation of Ex. 4.2. By Eq. (4.9),

$$\Delta H = (8.314)(6.9965)(873.15 - 533.15) = 19\ 778 \text{ J}$$

Example 4.3

What is the final temperature when heat in the amount of 422 MJ is added to 11.3 kmol of ammonia initially at 260°C (533.15 K) in a steady-flow process at approximately 1 atm?

Solution

If ΔH is the enthalpy change for 1 kmol, $Q = n\Delta H$, and

$$\Delta H = \frac{Q}{n} = \frac{422 \times 10^3}{11.3} = 37\ 345 \text{ kJ kmol}^{-1}$$

With

$$T_0 = 533.15 \text{ K}$$

we may evaluate $\langle C_P^{ig} \rangle_H / R$ for any value of T:

$$\text{MCPH}\ (533.15, \text{T};\ 3.578, 3.020\text{E} - 3, 0.0, -0.186\text{E} + 5)$$

Iteration between (A) and Eq. (4.10) starts with a value $T \geq T_0$, and converges on the final value,

$$T = 1250 \text{ K } (977°\text{C})$$

4.2 LATENT HEATS OF PURE SUBSTANCES

When a pure substance is liquefied from the solid state or vaporized from the liquid at constant pressure, no change in temperature occurs; however, the process requires the transfer of a finite amount of heat to the substance. These heat effects are called the latent heat of fusion and the latent heat of vaporization. Similarly, there are heats of transition accompanying the change of a substance from one solid state to another; for example, the heat absorbed when rhombic crystalline sulfur changes to the monoclinic structure at 95°C (368.15 K) and 1 bar is 360 J for each gram-atom.

The characteristic feature of all these processes is the coexistence of two phases. According to the phase rule, a two-phase system consisting of a single species is univariant, and its intensive state is determined by the specification of just one intensive property. Thus the latent heat accompanying a phase change is a function of temperature only, and is related to other system properties by an exact thermodynamic equation:

$$\boxed{\Delta H = T\,\Delta V \frac{dP^{\text{sat}}}{dT}} \qquad (4.11)$$

where for a pure species at temperature T,

ΔH = latent heat
ΔV = volume change accompanying the phase change
P^{sat} = saturation pressure

The derivation of this equation, known as the Clapeyron equation, is given in Chap. 6.

When Eq. (4.11) is applied to the vaporization of a pure liquid, dP^{sat}/dT is the slope of the vapor pressure-vs.-temperature curve at the temperature of interest, ΔV is the difference between molar volumes of saturated vapor and saturated liquid, and ΔH is the latent heat of vaporization. Thus values of ΔH may be calculated from vapor-pressure and volumetric data.

Latent heats may also be measured calorimetrically. Experimental values are available at selected temperatures for many substances.[4] Correlations for the latent heats of many compounds as a function of temperature are given by Daubert et al.[5] Nevertheless, data are not always available at the temperature of interest, and in many cases the data necessary for application of Eq. (4.11) are also not known. In this event approximate methods are used for estimates of the heat effect accompanying a phase change. Because heats of vaporization are by far the most important from a practical point of view, they have received most attention. One procedure is the use of a group-contribution method, known as UNIVAP.[6] Alternative methods serve one of two purposes:

- Prediction of the heat of vaporization at the normal boiling point, i.e., at a pressure of 1 standard atmosphere, defined as 101 325 Pa
- Estimation of the heat of vaporization at any temperature from the known value at a single temperature

Rough estimates of latent heats of vaporization for pure liquids at their normal boiling points are given by *Trouton's rule*:

$$\frac{\Delta H_n}{RT_n} \sim 10$$

where T_n is the absolute temperature of the normal boiling point. The units of ΔH_n, R, and T_n must be chosen so that $\Delta H_n/RT_n$ is dimensionless. Dating from 1884, this rule still provides

[4] V. Majer and V. Svoboda, IUPAC Chemical Data Series No. 32, Blackwell, Oxford, 1985; R. H. Perry and D. Green, *op. cit.*, Sec. 2.

[5] T. E. Daubert et al., *op. cit.*

[6] M. Klüppel, S. Schulz, and P. Ulbig, *Fluid Phase Equilibria*, vol. 102, pp. 1–15, 1994.

a simple check on whether values calculated by other methods are reasonable. Representative experimental values for this ratio are Ar, 8.0; N_2, 8.7; O_2, 9.1; HCl, 10.4; C_6H_6, 10.5; H_2S, 10.6; and H_2O, 13.1.

Of the same nature, but not quite so simple, is the equation proposed by Riedel:[7]

$$\frac{\Delta H_n}{RT_n} = \frac{1.092(\ln P_c - 1.013)}{0.930 - T_{r_n}} \tag{4.12}$$

where P_c is the critical pressure in bars and T_{r_n} is the reduced temperature at T_n. Equation (4.12) is surprisingly accurate for an empirical expression; errors rarely exceed 5 percent. Applied to water it gives

$$\frac{\Delta H_n}{RT_n} = \frac{1.092(\ln 220.55 - 1.013)}{0.930 - 0.577} = 13.56$$

Whence,

$$\Delta H_n = (13.56)(8.314)(373.15) = 42\,065 \text{ J mol}^{-1}$$

This corresponds to 2334 J g^{-1}; the steam-table value of 2257 J g^{-1}, is lower by 3.4 percent.

Estimates of the latent heat of vaporization of a pure liquid at any temperature from the known value at a single temperature may be based on a known experimental value or on a value estimated by Eq. (4.12). The method proposed by Watson[8] has found wide acceptance:

$$\frac{\Delta H_2}{\Delta H_1} = \left(\frac{1 - T_{r_2}}{1 - T_{r_1}}\right)^{0.38} \tag{4.13}$$

This equation is simple and fairly accurate; its use is illustrated in the following example.

Example 4.4

Given that the latent heat of vaporization of water at 100°C (373.15 K) is 2257 J g^{-1}, estimate the latent heat at 300°C (573.15 K).

Solution

Let ΔH_1 = latent heat at 100°C (373.15 K) = 2257 J g^{-1}

ΔH_2 = latent heat at 300°C (573.15 K)

$T_{r_1} = 373.15/647.1 = 0.577$

$T_{r_2} = 573.15/647.1 = 0.886$

Then by Eq. (4.13),

$$\Delta H_2 = (2257)\left(\frac{1 - 0.886}{1 - 0.577}\right)^{0.38} = (2257)(0.270)^{0.38} = 1371 \text{ J g}^{-1}$$

The value given in the steam tables is 1406 J g^{-1}.

[7] L. Riedel, *Chem. Ing. Tech.*, vol. 26, pp. 679–683, 1954.

[8] K. M. Watson, *Ind. Eng. Chem.*, vol. 35, pp. 398–406, 1943.

4.3 STANDARD HEAT OF REACTION

Heat effects discussed so far have been for physical processes. Chemical reactions also are accompanied either by the transfer of heat or by temperature changes during the course of reaction—in some cases by both. These effects are manifestations of the differences in molecular structure, and therefore in energy, of the products and reactants. For example, the reactants in a combustion reaction possess greater energy on account of their structure than do the products, and this energy must either be transferred to the surroundings as heat or produce products at an elevated temperature.

Each of the vast number of possible chemical reactions may be carried out in many different ways, and each reaction carried out in a particular way is accompanied by a particular heat effect. Tabulation of all possible heat effects for all possible reactions is impossible. We therefore *calculate* the heat effects for reactions carried out in diverse ways from data for reactions carried out in a *standard* way. This reduces the required data to a minimum.

The heat associated with a specific chemical reaction depends on the temperatures of both the reactants and products. A consistent (standard) basis for treatment of reaction heat effects results when the products of reaction and the reactants are all at the *same* temperature.

Consider the flow-calorimeter method for measurement of heats of combustion of fuel gases. The fuel is mixed with air at ambient temperature and the mixture flows into a combustion chamber where reaction occurs. The combustion products enter a water-jacketed section in which they are cooled to the temperature of the reactants. Because no shaft work is produced by the process, and the calorimeter is built so that changes in potential and kinetic energy are negligible, the overall energy balance, Eq. (2.32), reduces to

$$Q = \Delta H$$

Thus the heat flowing from the calorimeter and absorbed by the water is equal in magnitude to the enthalpy change caused by the combustion reaction. The enthalpy change of reaction ΔH is called the *heat of reaction*.

For purposes of data tabulation with respect to the reaction,

$$aA + bB \rightarrow lL + mM$$

the *standard* heat of reaction is defined as the enthalpy change when a moles of A and b moles of B in their *standard states at temperature* T react to form l moles of L and m moles of M in their *standard states at the same temperature* T.

A standard state is a particular state of a species at temperature T and at specified conditions of pressure, composition, and physical condition as, e.g., gas, liquid, or solid.

A *standard-state pressure* of 1 standard atmosphere (101 325 Pa) was in use for many years, and older data tabulations are for this pressure. The present standard is 1 bar (10^5 Pa), but for purposes of this chapter, the difference is of negligible consequence. With respect to composition, the standard states used in this chapter are states of the *pure* species. For gases, the physical state is the ideal-gas state and for liquids and solids, the real state at the standard-state pressure and at the system temperature. In summary, the standard states used in this chapter are

- *Gases* The pure substance in the ideal-gas state at 1 bar.

- *Liquids and solids* The real pure liquid or solid at 1 bar.

Property values in the standard state are denoted by the degree symbol. For example, C_P° is the standard-state heat capacity. Because the standard state for gases is the ideal-gas state, C_P° for gases is identical with C_P^{ig}, and the data of Table C.1 apply to the standard state for gases. All conditions for a standard state are fixed except temperature, which is always the temperature of the system. Standard-state properties are therefore functions of temperature only. The standard state chosen for gases is a hypothetical one, for at 1 bar actual gases are not ideal. However, they seldom deviate much from ideality, and in most instances enthalpies for the real-gas state at 1 bar and the ideal-gas state are little different.

When a heat of reaction is given for a particular reaction, it applies for the stoichiometric coefficients as written. If each stoichiometric coefficient is doubled, the heat of reaction is doubled. For example, the ammonia synthesis reaction may be written:

$$\tfrac{1}{2}N_2 + \tfrac{3}{2}H_2 \rightarrow NH_3 \qquad \Delta H_{298}^\circ = -46\,110 \text{ J}$$

or

$$N_2 + 3H_2 \rightarrow 2NH_3 \qquad \Delta H_{298}^\circ = -92\,220 \text{ J}$$

The symbol ΔH_{298}° indicates that the heat of reaction is the *standard* value for a temperature of 25°C (298.15 K).

4.4 STANDARD HEAT OF FORMATION

Tabulation of data for just the *standard* heats of reaction for all of the vast number of possible reactions is impractical. Fortunately, the standard heat of any reaction can be calculated if the *standard heats of formation* of the compounds taking part in the reaction are known. A *formation* reaction is defined as a reaction which forms a single compound *from its constituent elements*. For example, the reaction $C + \tfrac{1}{2}O_2 + 2H_2 \rightarrow CH_3OH$ is the formation reaction for methanol. The reaction $H_2O + SO_3 \rightarrow H_2SO_4$ is *not* a formation reaction, because it forms sulfuric acid not from the elements but from other compounds. Formation reactions are understood to produce 1 mol of product; the heat of formation is therefore based on *1 mol of the compound formed*.

Heats of reaction at any temperature can be calculated from heat-capacity data if the value for one temperature is known; the tabulation of data can therefore be reduced to the compilation of *standard heats of formation at a single temperature*. The usual choice for this temperature is 298.15 K or 25°C. The standard heat of formation of a compound at this temperature is represented by the symbol $\Delta H_{f_{298}}^\circ$. The degree symbol denotes the standard value, subscript f identifies a heat of formation, and the 298 is the approximate absolute temperature in kelvins. Tables of these values for common substances may be found in standard handbooks, but the most extensive compilations available are in specialized reference works.[9] An abridged list of values is given in Table C.4 of App. C.

[9]For example, see *TRC Thermodynamic Tables—Hydrocarbons* and *TRC Thermodynamic Tables—Non-hydrocarbons*, serial publications of the Thermodynamics Research Center, Texas A & M Univ. System, College Station, Texas; "The NBS Tables of Chemical Thermodynamic Properties," *J. Physical and Chemical Reference Data*, vol. 11, supp. 2, 1982. See also, T. E. Daubert et al., *op. cit.* Where data are unavailable, estimates based only on molecular structure may be found by the methods of L. Constantinou and R. Gani, *Fluid Phase Equilibria*, vol. 103, pp. 11–22, 1995.

When chemical equations are combined by addition, the standard heats of reaction may also be added to give the standard heat of the resulting reaction. This is possible because enthalpy is a state function, and its changes for given initial and final states are independent of path. In particular, formation equations and standard heats of formation may always be combined to produce any desired equation (not itself a formation equation) and its accompanying standard heat of reaction. Equations written for this purpose often include an indication of the physical state of each reactant and product, i.e., the letter *g*, *l*, or *s* is placed in parentheses after the chemical formula to show whether it is a gas, a liquid, or a solid. This might seem unnecessary, because a pure chemical species at a particular temperature and 1 bar can usually exist only in one physical state. However, fictitious states are often assumed for convenience.

Consider the reaction $CO_2(g) + H_2(g) \rightarrow CO(g) + H_2O(g)$ at 25°C (298.15 K). This water-gas-shift reaction is commonly encountered in the chemical industry, though it takes place only at temperatures well above 25°C (298.15 K). However, the data used are for 25°C (298.15 K), and the initial step in any calculation of heat effects for this reaction is evaluation the standard heat of reaction at 25°C (298.15 K). The pertinent formation reactions and their heats of formation from Table C.4 are

$$\begin{array}{lll} CO_2(g): & C(s) + O_2(g) \rightarrow CO_2(g) & \Delta H^\circ_{f_{298}} = -393\ 509 \text{ J} \\ H_2(g): & \text{Because hydrogen is an element} & \Delta H^\circ_{f_{298}} = 0 \\ CO(g): & C(s) + \frac{1}{2}O_2(g) \rightarrow CO(g) & \Delta H^\circ_{f_{298}} = -110\ 525 \text{ J} \\ H_2O(g): & H_2(g) + \frac{1}{2}O_2(g) \rightarrow H_2O(g) & \Delta H^\circ_{f_{298}} = -241\ 818 \text{ J} \end{array}$$

Because the reaction is actually carried out entirely in the gas phase at high temperature, convenience dictates that the standard states of all products and reactants at 25°C (298.15 K) be taken as the ideal-gas state at 1 bar, even though water cannot actually exist as a gas at these conditions.

Writing the formation reactions so that their sum yields the desired reaction, requires that the formation reaction for CO_2 be written in reverse; the heat of reaction is then of opposite sign to its standard heat of formation:

$$\begin{array}{rl} CO_2(g) \rightarrow C(s) + O_2(g) & \Delta H^\circ_{298} = 393\ 509 \text{ J} \\ C(s) + \frac{1}{2}O_2(g) \rightarrow CO(g) & \Delta H^\circ_{298} = -110\ 525 \text{ J} \\ H_2(g) + \frac{1}{2}O_2(g) \rightarrow H_2O(g) & \Delta H^\circ_{298} = -241\ 818 \text{ J} \\ \hline CO_2(g) + H_2(g) \rightarrow CO(g) + H_2O(g) & \Delta H^\circ_{298} = 41\ 166 \text{ J} \end{array}$$

The meaning of this result is that the enthalpy of 1 mol of CO plus 1 mol of H_2O is greater than the enthalpy of 1 mol of CO_2 plus 1 mol of H_2 by 41 166 J when each product and reactant is taken as the pure gas at 25°C (298.15 K) in its ideal-gas state at 1 bar.

In this example the standard heat of formation of H_2O is available for its hypothetical ideal-gas standard state at 25°C (298.15 K). One might expect the value of the heat of formation of water to be listed for its actual state as a liquid at 1 bar and 25°C (298.15 K). As a matter of fact, values for both states are given in Table C.4 because they are both frequently used. This is true for many compounds that normally exist as liquids at 25°C (298.15 K) and 1 bar. Cases do arise, however, in which a value is given only for the standard state as a liquid or as an ideal gas when what is needed is the other value. Suppose this were the case for the preceding example, with only the standard heat of formation of liquid H_2O available. We would then include an equation for the physical change that transforms water from its standard state as a liquid into its standard state as an ideal gas. The enthalpy change for this physical process is the difference between the heats of formation of water in its two standard states:

$$-241\ 818 - (-285\ 830) = 44\ 012 \text{ J}$$

This is approximately the latent heat of vaporization of water at 25°C (298.15 K). The sequence of steps is now:

$$\begin{array}{rl} CO_2(g) \rightarrow C(s) + O_2(g) & \Delta H^\circ_{298} = 393\ 509 \text{ J} \\ C(s) + \frac{1}{2}O_2(g) \rightarrow CO(g) & \Delta H^\circ_{298} = -110\ 525 \text{ J} \\ H_2(g) + \frac{1}{2}O_2(g) \rightarrow H_2O(l) & \Delta H^\circ_{298} = -285\ 830 \text{ J} \\ H_2O(l) \rightarrow H_2O(g) & \Delta H^\circ_{298} = 44\ 012 \text{ J} \\ \hline CO_2(g) + H_2(g) \rightarrow CO(g) + H_2O(g) & \Delta H^\circ_{298} = 41\ 166 \text{ J} \end{array}$$

This result is of course in agreement with the original answer.

Example 4.5

Calculate the standard heat at 25°C (298.15 K) for the following reaction:

$$4HCl(g) + O_2(g) \rightarrow 2H_2O(g) + 2Cl_2(g)$$

Solution

Standard heats of formation at 298.15 K from Table C.4 are

$$HCl(g){:}\ -92\ 307 \text{ J} \qquad H_2O(g){:}\ -241\ 818 \text{ J}$$

The following combination gives the desired result:

$$\begin{array}{rl} 4HCl(g) \rightarrow 2H_2(g) + 2Cl_2(g) & \Delta H^\circ_{298} = (4)(92\ 307) \\ 2H_2(g) + O_2(g) \rightarrow 2H_2O(g) & \Delta H^\circ_{298} = (2)(-241\ 818) \\ \hline 4HCl(g) + O_2(g) \rightarrow 2H_2O(g) + 2Cl_2(g) & \Delta H^\circ_{298} = -114\ 408 \text{ J} \end{array}$$

This result is four times the standard heat of combustion of $4HCl(g)$ (see below).

4.5 STANDARD HEAT OF COMBUSTION

Only a few *formation* reactions can actually be carried out at the conditions of interest, and therefore data for these reactions must usually be determined indirectly. One kind of reaction that readily lends itself to experiment is the combustion reaction, and many standard heats of formation come from standard heats of combustion, measured calorimetrically. A combustion reaction is defined as a reaction between an element or compound and oxygen to form specified combustion products. For organic compounds made up of carbon, hydrogen, and oxygen only, the products are carbon dioxide and water, but the state of the water may be either vapor or liquid. Data are always based on *1 mol of the substance burned.*

A reaction such as the formation of *n*-butane:

$$4C(s) + 5H_2(g) \rightarrow C_4H_{10}(g)$$

is not feasible in practice. However, this equation results from combination of the following combustion reactions:

$$4C(s) + 4O_2(g) \rightarrow 4CO_2(g) \qquad \Delta H^\circ_{298} = (4)(-393\,509)$$

$$5H_2(g) + 2\tfrac{1}{2}O_2(g) \rightarrow 5H_2O(l) \qquad \Delta H^\circ_{298} = (5)(-285\,830)$$

$$4CO_2(g) + 5H_2O(l) \rightarrow C_4H_{10}(g) + 6\tfrac{1}{2}O_2(g) \qquad \Delta H^\circ_{298} = 2877\,396$$

$$4C(s) + 5H_2(g) \rightarrow C_4H_{10}(g) \qquad \Delta H^\circ_{298} = -125\,790 \text{ J}$$

This result is the standard heat of formation of *n*-butane listed in Table C.4.

4.6 TEMPERATURE DEPENDENCE OF ΔH°

In the foregoing sections, standard heats of reaction are discussed for a reference temperature of 298.15 K or 25°C. In this section we treat the calculation of standard heats of reaction at other temperatures from knowledge of the value at the reference temperature.

The general chemical reaction may be written:

$$|\nu_1|A_1 + |\nu_2|A_2 + \cdots \rightarrow |\nu_3|A_3 + |\nu_4|A_4 + \cdots$$

where $|\nu_i|$ is a stoichiometric coefficient and A_i stands for a chemical formula. The species on the left are reactants; those on the right, products. The sign convention for ν_i is as follows:

positive (+) *for products* and *negative* (−) *for reactants*

The ν_i with their accompanying signs are called stoichiometric *numbers*. For example, when the ammonia synthesis reaction is written:

$$N_2 + 3H_2 \rightarrow 2NH_3$$

then $$\nu_{N_2} = -1 \qquad \nu_{H_2} = -3 \qquad \nu_{NH_3} = 2$$

This sign convention allows the definition of a standard heat of reaction to be expressed mathematically by the simple equation:

$$\Delta H^\circ \equiv \sum_i \nu_i H_i^\circ \tag{4.14}$$

where H_i° is the enthalpy of species i in its standard state and the summation is over all products and reactants. The standard-state enthalpy of a chemical compound is equal to its heat of formation plus the standard-state enthalpies of its constituent elements. If the standard-state enthalpies of all elements are arbitrarily set equal to zero as the basis of calculation, then the standard-state enthalpy of each compound is its heat of formation. In this event, $H_i^\circ = \Delta H_{f_i}^\circ$ and Eq. (4.14) becomes

$$\Delta H^\circ = \sum_i \nu_i \, \Delta H_{f_i}^\circ \tag{4.15}$$

where the summation is over all products and reactants. This formalizes the procedure described in the preceding section for calculation of standard heats of other reactions from standard heats of formation. Applied to the reaction,

$$4HCl(g) + O_2(g) \rightarrow 2H_2O(g) + 2Cl_2(g)$$

Eq. (4.15) is written:

$$\Delta H^\circ = 2\Delta H_{f_{H_2O}}^\circ - 4\Delta H_{f_{HCl}}^\circ$$

With data from Table C.4 for 298.15 K, this becomes

$$\Delta H_{298}^\circ = (2)(-241\,818) - (4)(-92\,307) = -114\,408 \text{ J}$$

in agreement with the result of Ex. 4.5.

For standard reactions, products and reactants are always at the standard-state pressure of 1 bar. Standard-state enthalpies are therefore functions of temperature only, and by Eq. (2.21),

$$dH_i^\circ = C_{P_i}^\circ \, dT$$

where subscript i identifies a particular product or reactant. Multiplying by ν_i and summing over all products and reactants gives

$$\sum_i \nu_i \, dH_i^\circ = \sum_i \nu_i C_{P_i}^\circ \, dT$$

Because ν_i is a constant, it may be placed inside the differential:

$$\sum_i d(\nu_i H_i^\circ) = \sum_i \nu_i C_{P_i}^\circ \, dT \qquad \text{or} \qquad d\sum_i \nu_i H_i^\circ = \sum_i \nu_i C_{P_i}^\circ \, dT$$

The term $\sum_i \nu_i H_i^\circ$ is the standard heat of reaction, defined by Eq. (4.14) as ΔH°. The standard heat-capacity change of reaction is defined similarly

$$\Delta C_P^\circ \equiv \sum_i \nu_i C_{P_i}^\circ \tag{4.16}$$

As a result of these definitions,

$$\boxed{d\,\Delta H^\circ = \Delta C_P^\circ\, dT} \tag{4.17}$$

This is the fundamental equation relating heats of reaction to temperature.

Upon integration Eq. (4.17) becomes

$$\Delta H^\circ = \Delta H_0^\circ + R\int_{T_0}^{T} \frac{\Delta C_P^\circ}{R}\, dT \tag{4.18}$$

where ΔH° and ΔH_0° are heats of reaction at temperature T and at reference temperature T_0 respectively. If the temperature dependence of the heat capacity of each product and reactant is given by Eq. (4.4), then the integral is given by the analog of Eq. (4.7) ($\tau \equiv T/T_0$):

$$\int_{T_0}^{T} \frac{\Delta C_P^\circ}{R}\, dT = (\Delta A)T_0(\tau - 1) + \frac{\Delta B}{2}T_0^2(\tau^2 - 1) + \frac{\Delta C}{3}T_0^3(\tau^3 - 1) + \frac{\Delta D}{T_0}\left(\frac{\tau - 1}{\tau}\right) \tag{4.19}$$

where by definition, $$\Delta A \equiv \sum_i \nu_i A_i$$

with analogous definitions for ΔB, ΔC, and ΔD.

An alternative formulation results when a mean heat capacity change of reaction is defined in analogy to Eq. (4.8):

$$\frac{\langle \Delta C_P^\circ \rangle_H}{R} = \Delta A + \frac{\Delta B}{2}T_0(\tau + 1) + \frac{\Delta C}{3}T_0^2(\tau^2 + \tau + 1) + \frac{\Delta D}{\tau T_0^2} \tag{4.20}$$

Equation (4.18) then becomes

$$\Delta H^\circ = \Delta H_0^\circ + \langle \Delta C_P^\circ \rangle_H (T - T_0) \tag{4.21}$$

The integral of Eq. (4.19) is of the same form as that of Eq. (4.7), and in analogous fashion may be set equal to a function:

$$\int_{T_0}^{T} \frac{\Delta C_P^\circ}{R}\, dT = \mathsf{IDCPH(T0,T;DA,DB,DC,DD)}$$

where "D" denotes "Δ". The analogy requires simple replacement of C_P by ΔC_P° and of A, etc. by ΔA, etc. The same computer program serves for evaluation of either integral. The only difference is in the function name.

Just as function MCPH is defined to represent $\langle C_P \rangle_H / R$, so function MDCPH by analogy is defined to represent $\langle \Delta C_P^\circ \rangle_H / R$; thus,

$$\frac{\langle \Delta C_P^\circ \rangle_H}{R} = \mathsf{MDCPH(T0,T;DA,DB,DC,DD)}$$

Example 4.6

Calculate the standard heat of the methanol-synthesis reaction at 800°C (1073.15 K):

$$CO(g) + 2H_2(g) \rightarrow CH_3OH(g)$$

Solution

Apply Eq. (4.15) to this reaction for reference temperature $T_0 = 298.15$ K and with heat-of-formation data from Table C.4:

$$\Delta H_0^\circ = \Delta H_{298}^\circ = -200\,660 - (-110\,525) = -90\,135 \text{ J}$$

Evaluation of the parameters in Eq. (4.19) is based on data taken from Table C.1:

i	ν_i	A	$10^3\,B$	$10^6\,C$	$10^{-5}\,D$
CH_3OH	1	2.211	12.216	−3.450	0.000
CO	−1	3.376	0.557	0.000	−0.031
H_2	−2	3.249	0.422	0.000	0.083

From its definition,

$$\Delta A = (1)(2.211) + (-1)(3.376) + (-2)(3.249) = -7.663$$

Similarly,

$$\Delta B = 10.815 \times 10^{-3} \qquad \Delta C = -3.450 \times 10^{-6} \qquad \Delta D = -0.135 \times 10^5$$

The value of the integral of Eq. (4.19) for $T = 1073.15$ K is represented by:

IDCPH(298.15 1073.15;-7.663,10.815E-3,-3.450E-6,-0.135E+5) $= -1615.5$ K

Then by Eq. (4.18),

$$\Delta H^\circ = -90\,135 + 8.314(-1615.5) = -103\,566 \text{ J}$$

4.7 HEAT EFFECTS OF INDUSTRIAL REACTIONS

The preceding sections have dealt with the *standard* heat of reaction. Industrial reactions are rarely carried out under standard-state conditions. Furthermore, in actual reactions the reactants may not be present in stoichiometric proportions, the reaction may not go to completion, and the final temperature may differ from the initial temperature. Moreover, inert species may be present, and several reactions may occur simultaneously. Nevertheless, calculations of the heat effects of actual reactions are based on the principles already considered and are best illustrated by example.

Example 4.7

What is the maximum temperature that can be reached by the combustion of methane with 20% excess air? Both the methane and the air enter the burner at 25°C (298.15 K).

Solution

The reaction is $CH_4 + 2\,O_2 \rightarrow CO_2 + 2H_2O(g)$ for which,

$$\Delta H^\circ_{298} = -393\,509 + (2)(-241\,818) - (-74\,520) = -802\,625 \text{ J}$$

Because the maximum attainable temperature (called the *theoretical flame temperature*) is sought, assume that the combustion reaction goes to completion adiabatically ($Q = 0$). If the kinetic- and potential-energy changes are negligible and if $W_s = 0$, the overall energy balance for the process reduces to $\Delta H = 0$. For purposes of calculation of the final temperature, any convenient path between the initial and final states may be used. The path chosen is indicated in the diagram.

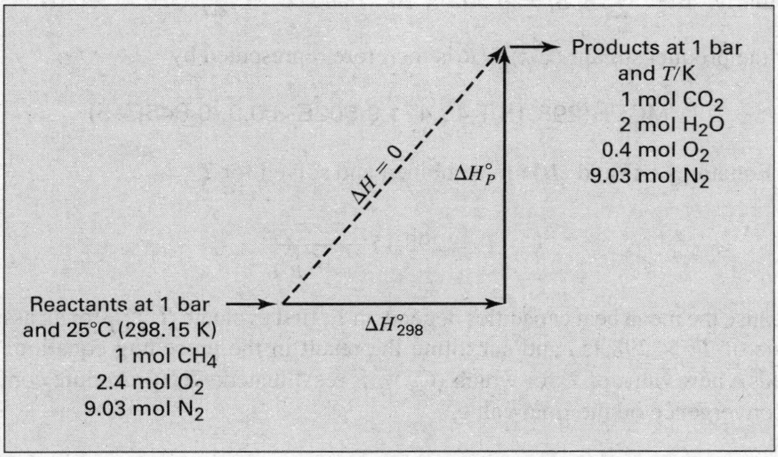

When one mole of methane burned is the basis for all calculations, the following quantities of oxygen and nitrogen are supplied by the entering air:

Moles O_2 required = 2.0
Moles excess O_2 = (0.2)(2.0) = 0.4
Moles N_2 entering = (2.4)(79/21) = 9.03

The gases leaving the burner contain 1 mol CO_2, 2 mol $H_2O(g)$, 0.4 mol O_2, and 9.03 mol N_2. Because the enthalpy change must be independent of path,

$$\Delta H^\circ_{298} + \Delta H^\circ_P = \Delta H = 0 \qquad (A)$$

where all enthalpies are on the basis of 1 mol CH_4 burned. The enthalpy change of the products as they are heated from 298.15 K to T is

$$\Delta H^\circ_P = \langle C^\circ_P \rangle_H (T - 298.15) \qquad (B)$$

where we define $\langle C^\circ_P \rangle_H$ as the mean heat capacity for the *total* product stream:

$$\langle C^\circ_P \rangle_H \equiv \sum_i n_i \langle C^\circ_{P_i} \rangle_H$$

The simplest procedure here is to sum the mean-heat-capacity equations for the products, each multiplied by its appropriate mole number. Because $C = 0$ for each product gas (Table C.1), Eq. (4.8) yields

$$\langle C_P^\circ \rangle_H = \sum_i n_i \langle C_{P_i}^\circ \rangle_H = R\left[\sum_i n_i A_i + \frac{\sum_i n_i B_i}{2} T_0(\tau + 1) + \frac{\sum_i n_i D_i}{\tau T_0^2}\right]$$

Data from Table C.1 are combined as follows:

$$A = \sum_i n_i A_i = (1)(5.457)+(2)(3.470)+(0.4)(3.639)+(9.03)(3.280) = 43.471$$

Similarly, $B = \sum_i n_i B_i = 9.502 \times 10^{-3}$ and $D = \sum_i n_i D_i = -0.645 \times 10^5$.

For the product stream $\langle C_P^\circ \rangle_H / R$ is therefore represented by

MCPH(298.15,T;43.471,9.502E-3,0.0,-0.645E+5)

Equations (A) and (B) are combined and solved for T

$$T = 298.15 - \frac{\Delta H_{298}^\circ}{\langle C_P^\circ \rangle_H}$$

Because the mean heat capacities depend on T, first evaluate $\langle C_P^\circ \rangle_H$ for an assumed value of $T > 298.15$, and substitute the result in the preceding equation. This yields a new value of T for which $\langle C_P^\circ \rangle_H$ is reevaluated. The procedure continues to convergence on the final value,

$$T = 2066 \text{ K} \qquad \text{or} \qquad 1793°\text{C}$$

Example 4.8

One method for the manufacture of "synthesis gas" (a mixture of CO and H_2) is the catalytic reforming of CH_4 with steam at high temperature and atmospheric pressure:

$$CH_4(g) + H_2O(g) \rightarrow CO(g) + 3H_2(g)$$

The only other reaction to be considered is the water-gas-shift reaction:

$$CO(g) + H_2O(g) \rightarrow CO_2(g) + H_2(g)$$

If the reactants are supplied in the ratio, 2 mol steam to 1 mol CH_4, and if heat is supplied to the reactor so that the products reach a temperature of 1300 K, the CH_4 is completely converted and the product stream contains 17.4 mole % CO. Assuming the reactants to be preheated to 600 K, calculate the heat requirement for the reactor.

Solution

The standard heats of reaction at 25°C (298.15 K) for the two reactions are calculated from the data of Table C.4:

$$CH_4(g) + H_2O(g) \rightarrow CO(g) + 3H_2(g) \qquad \Delta H^\circ_{298} = 205\,813 \text{ J}$$

$$CO(g) + H_2O(g) \rightarrow CO_2(g) + H_2(g) \qquad \Delta H^\circ_{298} = -41\,166 \text{ J}$$

These two reactions may be added to give a third reaction:

$$CH_4(g) + 2H_2O(g) \rightarrow CO_2(g) + 4H_2(g) \qquad \Delta H^\circ_{298} = 164\,647 \text{ J}$$

Any pair of the three reactions constitutes an independent set. The third reaction is not independent; it is obtained by combination of the other two. The reactions most convenient to work with here are the first and third:

$$CH_4(g) + H_2O(g) \rightarrow CO(g) + 3H_2(g) \qquad \Delta H^\circ_{298} = 205\,813 \text{ J} \qquad (A)$$

$$CH_4(g) + 2H_2O(g) \rightarrow CO_2(g) + 4H_2(g) \qquad \Delta H^\circ_{298} = 164\,647 \text{ J} \qquad (B)$$

First determine the fraction of CH_4 converted by each of these reactions. As a basis for calculations, let 1 mol CH_4 and 2 mol steam be fed to the reactor. If x mol CH_4 reacts by Eq. (A), then $1 - x$ mol reacts by Eq. (B). On this basis the products of the reaction are

CO:	x
H_2:	$3x + 4(1 - x) = 4 - x$
CO_2:	$1 - x$
H_2O:	$2 - x - 2(1 - x) = x$
Total:	5 mol products

The mole fraction of CO in the product stream is $x/5 = 0.174$; whence $x = 0.870$. Thus, on the basis chosen, 0.870 mol CH_4 reacts by Eq. (A) and 0.130 mol reacts by Eq. (B). Furthermore, the amounts of the species in the product stream are

$$\text{Moles CO} = x = 0.87$$
$$\text{Moles } H_2 = 4 - x = 3.13$$
$$\text{Moles } CO_2 = 1 - x = 0.13$$
$$\text{Moles } H_2O = x = 0.87$$

We now devise a path, for purposes of calculation, to proceed from reactants at 600 K to products at 1300 K. Because data are available for the standard heats of reaction at 25°C (298.15 K), the most convenient path is the one which includes the reactions at 25°C (298.15 K). This is shown schematically in the accompanying diagram. The dashed line represents the actual path for which the enthalpy change is ΔH. Because this enthalpy change is independent of path,

$$\Delta H = \Delta H^\circ_R + \Delta H^\circ_{298} + \Delta H^\circ_P$$

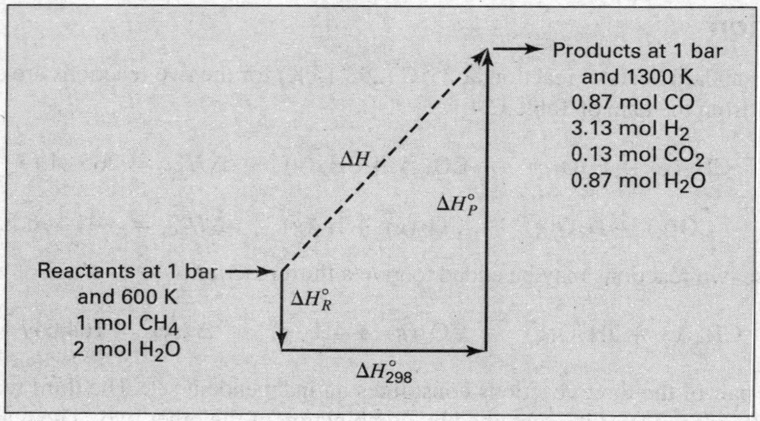

For the calculation of ΔH°_{298}, reactions (A) and (B) must both be taken into account. Because 0.87 mol CH_4 reacts by (A) and 0.13 mol reacts by (B),

$$\Delta H^\circ_{298} = (0.87)(205\ 813) + (0.13)(164\ 647) = 200\ 460 \text{ J}$$

The enthalpy change of the reactants for cooling from 600 K to 298.15 K is

$$\Delta H^\circ_R = \left(\sum_i n_i \langle C^\circ_{P_i} \rangle_H \right) (298.15 - 600)$$

where the values of $\langle C^\circ_{P_i} \rangle_H / R$ are

CH_4: MCPH(298.15,600;1.702,9.081E-3,-2.164E-6,0.0) = 5.3272
H_2O: MCPH(298.15,600;3.470,1.450E-3,0.0,0.121E+5) = 4.1888

Whence,

$$\Delta H^\circ_R = (8.314)[(1)(5.3272) + (2)(4.1888)](298.15 - 600) = -34\ 390 \text{ J}$$

The enthalpy change of the products as they are heated from 298.15 to 1300 K is calculated similarly:

$$\Delta H^\circ_P = \left(\sum_i n_i \langle C^\circ_{P_i} \rangle_H \right) (1300 - 298.15)$$

where $\langle C^\circ_{P_i} \rangle_H / R$ values are

CO: MCPH(298.15,1300;3.376,0.557E-3,0.0,-0.031E+5) = 3.8131
H_2: MCPH(298.15,1300;3.249,0.422E-3,0.0,0.083E+5) = 3.6076
CO_2: MCPH(298.15,1300;5.457,1.045E-3,0.0,-1.157E+5) = 5.9935
H_2O: MCPH(298.15,1300;3.470,1.450E-3,0.0,0.121E+5) = 4.6599

Whence,

$$\begin{aligned}\Delta H_P^\circ &= (8.314)[(0.87)(3.8131) + (3.13)(3.6076) \\ &\quad + (0.13)(5.9935) + (0.87)(4.6599)] \times (1300 - 298.15) \\ &= 161\,940 \text{ J}\end{aligned}$$

Therefore,

$$\Delta H = -34\,390 + 200\,460 + 161\,940 = 328\,010 \text{ J}$$

The process is one of steady flow for which W_s, Δz, and $\Delta u^2/2$ are presumed negligible. Thus,

$$Q = \Delta H = 328\,010 \text{ J}$$

This result is on the basis of 1 mol CH_4 fed to the reactor.

Example 4.9

A boiler is fired with a high-grade fuel oil (consisting only of hydrocarbons) having a standard heat of combustion of $-43\,515$ J g^{-1} at 25°C (298.15 K) with $CO_2(g)$ and $H_2O(l)$ as products. The temperature of the fuel and air entering the combustion chamber is 25°C (298.15 K). The air is assumed dry. The flue gases leave at 300°C (573.15 K), and their average analysis (on a dry basis) is 11.2% CO_2, 0.4% CO, 6.2% O_2, and 82.2% N_2 on volume basis. Calculate the fraction of the heat of combustion of the oil that is transferred as heat to the boiler.

Solution

Take as a basis 100 mol dry flue gases, consisting of

CO_2	11.2 mol
CO	0.4 mol
O_2	6.2 mol
N_2	82.2 mol
Total	100.0 mol

This analysis, on a dry basis, does not take into account the H_2O vapor present in the flue gases. The amount of H_2O formed by the combustion reaction is found from an oxygen balance. The O_2 supplied in the air represents 21 mol-% of the air stream. The remaining 79% is N_2, which goes through the combustion process unchanged. Thus the 82.2 mol N_2 appearing in 100 mol dry flue gases is supplied with the air, and the O_2 accompanying this N_2 is

$$\text{Moles } O_2 \text{ entering in air} = (82.2)(21/79) = 21.85$$

However,

$$\text{Moles } O_2 \text{ in the dry flue gases} = 11.2 + 0.4/2 + 6.2 = 17.60$$

The difference between these figures is the moles of O_2 that react to form H_2O. Therefore on the basis of 100 mol dry flue gases,

$$\text{Moles } H_2O \text{ formed} = (21.85 - 17.60)(2) = 8.50$$

$$\text{Moles } H_2 \text{ in the fuel} = \text{moles of water formed} = 8.50$$

The amount of C in the fuel is given by a carbon balance:

$$\text{Moles C in flue gases} = \text{moles C in fuel} = 11.2 + 0.4 = 11.60$$

These amounts of C and H_2 together give

$$\text{Mass of fuel burned} = (8.50)(2) + (11.6)(12) = 156.2 \text{ g}$$

If this amount of fuel is burned completely to $CO_2(g)$ and $H_2O(l)$ at 25°C (298.15 K), the heat of combustion is

$$\Delta H^\circ_{298} = (-43\,515)(156.2) = -6797\,040 \text{ J}$$

However, the reaction actually occurring does not represent complete combustion, and the H_2O is formed as vapor rather than as liquid. The 156.2 g of fuel, consisting of 11.6 mol of C and 8.5 mol of H_2, is represented by the empirical formula $C_{11.6}H_{17}$. Omit the 6.2 mol O_2 and 82.2 mol N_2 which enter and leave the reactor unchanged, and write the reaction:

$$C_{11.6}H_{17}(l) + 15.65O_2(g) \rightarrow 11.2CO_2(g) + 0.4CO(g) + 8.5H_2O(g)$$

This result is obtained by addition of the following reactions, for each of which the standard heat of reaction at 25°C (298.15 K) is known:

$$C_{11.6}H_{17}(l) + 15.85O_2(g) \rightarrow 11.6CO_2(g) + 8.5H_2O(l)$$

$$8.5H_2O(l) \rightarrow 8.5H_2O(g)$$

$$0.4CO_2(g) \rightarrow 0.4CO(g) + 0.2O_2(g)$$

The sum of these reactions yields the actual reaction, and the sum of the ΔH°_{298} values gives the standard heat of the reaction occurring at 25°C (298.15 K):

$$\Delta H^\circ_{298} = -6797\,040 + (44\,012)(8.5) + (282\,984)(0.4) = -6309\,740 \text{ J}$$

The actual process leading from reactants at 25°C (298.15 K) to products at 300°C (573.15 K) is represented by the dashed line in the accompanying diagram. For purposes of calculating ΔH for this process, we may use any convenient path. The one drawn with solid lines is a logical one: ΔH°_{298} has already been calculated and ΔH°_P is easily evaluated.

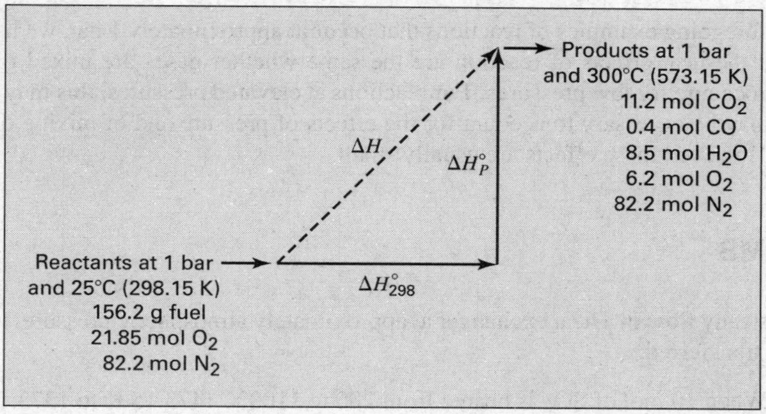

The enthalpy change caused by heating the products of reaction from 25 to 300°C (298.15 K to 573.15 K) is

$$\Delta H_P^\circ = \left(\sum_i n_i \langle C_{P_i}^\circ \rangle_H\right)(573.15 - 298.15)$$

where the $\langle C_{P_i}^\circ \rangle_H / R$ values are

CO_2: MCPH(298.15,573.15;5.457,1.045E-3,0.0,-1.157E+5) = 5.2352
CO: MCPH(298.15,573.15;3.376,0.557E-3,0.0,-0.031E+5) = 3.6005
H_2O: MCPH(298.15,573.15;3.470,1.450E-3,0.0,0.121E+5) = 4.1725
O_2: MCPH(298.15,573.15;3.639,0.506E-3,0.0,-0.227E+5) = 3.7267
N_2: MCPH(298.15,573.15;3.280,0.593E-3,0.0,0.040E+5) = 3.5618

Whence,

$$\begin{aligned}\Delta H_P^\circ &= (8.314)[(11.2)(5.2352) + (0.4)(3.6005) + (8.5)(4.1725) \\ &\quad + (6.2)(3.7267) + (82.2)(3.5618)](573.15 - 298.15) \\ &= 940\,660 \text{ J}\end{aligned}$$

and

$$\Delta H = \Delta H_{298}^\circ + \Delta H_P^\circ = -6309\,740 + 940\,660 = -5369\,080 \text{ J}$$

Since the process is one of steady flow for which the shaft work and kinetic- and potential-energy terms in the energy balance [Eq. (2.32)] are zero or negligible, $\Delta H = Q$. Thus, $Q = -5369.08$ kJ, and this amount of heat is transferred to the boiler for every 100 mol dry flue gases formed. This represents

$$\frac{5369\,080}{6797\,040}(100) = 79.0\%$$

of the heat of combustion of the fuel.

In the foregoing examples of reactions that occur at approximately 1 bar, we have tacitly assumed that the heat effects of reaction are the same whether gases are mixed or pure, an acceptable procedure for low pressures. For reactions at elevated pressures, this may not be the case, and it may be necessary to account for the effects of pressure and of mixing on the heat of reaction. However, these effects are usually small.

PROBLEMS

4.1. For steady flow in a heat exchanger at approximately atmospheric pressure, what is the heat transferred:

(*a*) When 10 mol of SO_2 is heated from 200 to 1100°C (473.15 K to 1373.15 K)?
(*b*) When 12 mol of propane is heated from 250 to 1200°C (523.15 K to 1473.15 K)?

4.2. For steady flow through a heat exchanger at approximately atmospheric pressure, what is the final temperature,

(*a*) When heat in the amount of 800 kJ is added to 10 mol of ethylene initially at 200°C (473.15 K)?
(*b*) When heat in the amount of 2500 kJ is added to 15 mol of 1-butene initially at 260°C (533.15 K)?
(*c*) When heat in the amount of 1055 GJ is added to 18.14 kmol of ethylene initially at 260°C (533.15 K)?

4.3. If 7.08 $m^3\ s^{-1}$ of air at 50°C (323.15 K) and approximately atmospheric pressure is preheated for a combustion process to 500°C (773.15 K), what rate of heat transfer is required?

4.4. How much heat is required when 10 000 kg of $CaCO_3$ is heated at atmospheric pressure from 50°C to 880°C (323.15 K to 1153.15 K)?

4.5. If the heat capacity of a substance is correctly represented by an equation of the form,

$$C_P = A + BT + CT^2$$

show that the error resulting when $\langle C_P \rangle_H$ is assumed equal to C_P evaluated at the arithmetic mean of the initial and final temperatures is $C(T_2 - T_1)^2/12$.

4.6. If the heat capacity of a substance is correctly represented by an equation of the form,

$$C_P = A + BT + DT^{-2}$$

show that the error resulting when $\langle C_P \rangle_H$ is assumed equal to C_P evaluated at the arithmetic mean of the initial and final temperatures is:

$$\frac{D}{T_1 T_2}\left(\frac{T_2 - T_1}{T_2 + T_1}\right)^2$$

4.7. Calculate the heat capacity of a gas sample from the following information: The sample comes to equilibrium in a flask at 25°C (298.15 K) and 121.3 kPa. A stopcock is opened briefly, allowing the pressure to drop to 101.3 kPa. With the stopcock closed, the flask warms, returning to 25°C (298.15 K), and the pressure is measured as 104.0 kPa. Determine C_P in J mol^{-1} K^{-1} assuming the gas to be ideal and the expansion of the gas remaining in the flask to be reversible and adiabatic.

4.8. A process stream is heated as a gas from 25°C to 250°C (298.15 K to 523.15 K) at constant P. A quick estimate of the energy requirement is obtained from Eq. (4.3), with C_P taken as constant and equal to its value at 25°C (298.15 K). Is the estimate of Q likely to be low or high? Why?

4.9. (*a*) For one of the compounds listed in Table B.2 of App. B, evaluate the latent heat of vaporization ΔH_n by Eq. (4.12). How does this result compare with the value listed in Table B.2?

(*b*) Handbook values for the latent heats of vaporization at 25°C (298.15 K) of four compounds are given in the table. For one of these calculate ΔH_n by Eq. (4.13), and compare the result with the value given in Table B.2.

Latent heats of vaporization at 25°C (298.15 K) in J g^{-1}

n-Pentane	366.3	Benzene	433.3
n-Hexane	366.1	Cyclohexane	392.5

4.10. Table 9.1 lists the thermodynamic properties of saturated liquid and vapor tetrafluoroethane. Making use of the vapor pressures as a function of temperature and of the saturated-liquid and saturated-vapor volumes, calculate the latent heat of vaporization by Eq. (4.11) at one of the following temperatures and compare the result with the value calculated from the enthalpy values given in the table.
(*a*) −15°C (258.15 K), (*b*) −1°C (272.15 K), (*c*) 13°C (286.15 K), (*d*) 27°C (300.15 K), (*e*) 40°C (313.15 K)

4.11. Handbook values for the latent heats of vaporization in J g^{-1} are given in the table for several pure liquids at 0°C (273.15 K).

	ΔH at 0°C (273.15 K)
Chloroform	270.9
Methanol	1189.5
Tetrachloromethane	217.8

For one of these substances, calculate the

(*a*) value of the latent heat at T_n by Eq. (4.13), given the value at 0°C (273.15 K)
(*b*) value of the latent heat at T_n by Eq. (4.12)

By what percentages do these results differ from the value listed in Table B.2 of App. B?

4.12. Table B.2 of Appendix B provides parameters for an equation that gives P^{sat} as a function of T for a number of pure compounds. For one of them, determine the heat of vaporization at its normal boiling point by application of Eq. (4.11), the Clapeyron equation. Evaluate dP^{sat}/dT from the given vapor-pressure equation, and use generalized correlations from Chap. 3 to estimate ΔV. Compare the computed value with the value of ΔH_n listed in Table B.2. Note that normal boiling points are listed in the last column of Table B.2.

4.13. A method for determination of the second virial coefficient of a pure gas is based on the Clapeyron equation and measurements of the molar latent heat of vaporization ΔH^{lv}, the molar volume of saturated liquid V^l, and the vapor pressure P^{sat}. Determine B in $cm^3\ mol^{-1}$ for methyl ethyl ketone at 75°C (348.15 K) from the following data at this temperature:

$$\Delta H^{lv} = 31\ 600\ \text{J mol}^{-1} \qquad V^l = 96.49\ \text{cm}^3\ \text{mol}^{-1}$$

$$\ln P^{sat}/\text{kPa} = 48.157\ 543 - 5622.7/T - 4.705\ 04 \ln T \qquad [T = \text{K}]$$

4.14. One hundred kmol per hour of subcooled liquid at 300 K and 3 bar is superheated to 500 K in a steady-flow heat exchanger. Estimate the exchanger duty (in kW) for one of the following:

(*a*) Methanol, for which $T^{sat} = 368.0$ K at 3 bar
(*b*) Benzene, for which $T^{sat} = 392.3$ K at 3 bar
(*c*) Toluene, for which $T^{sat} = 426.9$ K at 3 bar

4.15. Saturated-liquid benzene at pressure $P_1 = 10$ bar ($T_1^{sat} = 451.7$ K) is throttled in a steady-flow process to a pressure $P_2 = 1.2$ bar ($T_2^{sat} = 358.7$ K), where it is a liquid/vapor mixture. Estimate the molar fraction of the exit stream that is vapor. For liquid benzene, $C_P = 162\ \text{J mol}^{-1}\ \text{K}^{-1}$. Ignore the effect of pressure on the enthalpy of liquid benzene.

4.16. Estimate $\Delta H^\circ_{f_{298}}$ for one of the following compounds as a *liquid* at 25°C (298.15 K).

(*a*) Acetylene (*b*) 1,3-Butadiene (*c*) Ethylbenzene (*d*) *n*-Hexane (*e*) Styrene

4.17. A reversible compression of 1 mol of an ideal gas in a piston/cylinder device results in a pressure increase from 1 bar to P_2 and a temperature increase from 400 K to 950 K. The path followed by the gas during compression is given by $PV^{1.55} = \text{const}$, and the molar heat capacity of the gas is given by

$$C_P/R = 3.85 + 0.57 \times 10^{-3}T \qquad [T/\text{K}]$$

Determine the heat transferred during the process and the final pressure.

4.18. Hydrocarbon fuels can be produced from methanol by reactions such as the following, which yields 1-hexene:

$$6CH_3OH(g) \rightarrow C_6H_{12}(g) + 6H_2O(g)$$

Compare the standard heat of combustion at 25°C (298.15 K) of $6CH_3OH(g)$ with the standard heat of combustion at 25°C (298.15 K of $C_6H_{12}(g)$ for reaction products $CO_2(g)$ and $H_2O(g)$.

4.19. Calculate the theoretical flame temperature when ethylene at 25°C (298.15 K) is burned with:

(*a*) The theoretical amount of air at 25°C (298.15 K)
(*b*) 25% excess air at 25°C (298.15 K)
(*c*) 50% excess air at 25°C (298.15 K)
(*d*) 100% excess air at 25°C (298.15 K)
(*e*) 50% excess air preheated to 500°C (773.15 K)

4.20. What is the standard heat of combustion of *n*-pentane gas at 25°C (298.15 K) if the combustion products are $H_2O(l)$ and $CO_2(g)$?

4.21. Determine the standard heat of each of the following reactions at 25°C (298.15 K):

(*a*) $N_2(g) + 3H_2(g) \rightarrow 2NH_3(g)$
(*b*) $4NH_3(g) + 5O_2(g) \rightarrow 4NO(g) + 6H_2O(g)$
(*c*) $3NO_2(g) + H_2O(l) \rightarrow 2HNO_3(l) + NO(g)$
(*d*) $CaC_2(s) + H_2O(l) \rightarrow C_2H_2(g) + CaO(s)$
(*e*) $2Na(s) + 2H_2O(g) \rightarrow 2NaOH(s) + H_2(g)$
(*f*) $6NO_2(g) + 8NH_3(g) \rightarrow 7N_2(g) + 12H_2O(g)$
(*g*) $C_2H_4(g) + \frac{1}{2}O_2(g) \rightarrow \langle(CH_2)_2\rangle O(g)$
(*h*) $C_2H_2(g) + H_2O(g) \rightarrow \langle(CH_2)_2\rangle O(g)$
(*i*) $CH_4(g) + 2H_2O(g) \rightarrow CO_2(g) + 4H_2(g)$
(*j*) $CO_2(g) + 3H_2(g) \rightarrow CH_3OH(g) + H_2O(g)$
(*k*) $CH_3OH(g) + \frac{1}{2}O_2(g) \rightarrow HCHO(g) + H_2O(g)$
(*l*) $2H_2S(g) + 3O_2(g) \rightarrow 2H_2O(g) + 2SO_2(g)$
(*m*) $H_2S(g) + 2H_2O(g) \rightarrow 3H_2(g) + SO_2(g)$
(*n*) $N_2(g) + O_2(g) \rightarrow 2NO(g)$
(*o*) $CaCO_3(s) \rightarrow CaO(s) + CO_2(g)$
(*p*) $SO_3(g) + H_2O(l) \rightarrow H_2SO_4(l)$
(*q*) $C_2H_4(g) + H_2O(l) \rightarrow C_2H_5OH(l)$
(*r*) $CH_3CHO(g) + H_2(g) \rightarrow C_2H_5OH(g)$
(*s*) $C_2H_5OH(l) + O_2(g) \rightarrow CH_3COOH(l) + H_2O(l)$
(*t*) $C_2H_5CH{:}CH_2(g) \rightarrow CH_2{:}CHCH{:}CH_2(g) + H_2(g)$
(*u*) $C_4H_{10}(g) \rightarrow CH_2{:}CHCH{:}CH_2(g) + 2H_2(g)$
(*v*) $C_2H_5CH{:}CH_2(g) + \frac{1}{2}O_2(g) \rightarrow CH_2{:}CHCH{:}CH_2(g) + H_2O(g)$

(*w*) $4NH_3(g) + 6NO(g) \rightarrow 6H_2O(g) + 5N_2(g)$
(*x*) $N_2(g) + C_2H_2(g) \rightarrow 2HCN(g)$
(*y*) $C_6H_5.C_2H_5(g) \rightarrow C_6H_5CH{:}CH_2(g) + H_2(g)$
(*z*) $C(s) + H_2O(l) \rightarrow H_2(g) + CO(g)$

4.22. Determine the standard heat for one of the reactions of Pb. 4.21: Part (*a*) at 600°C (873.15 K), Part (*b*) at 500°C (773.15 K), Part (*f*) at 650°C (923.15 K), Part (*i*) at 700°C (973.15 K), Part (*j*) at 310°C (583.15 K), Part (*l*) at 410°C (683.15 K), Part (*m*) at 850 K, Part (*n*) at 1300 K, Part (*o*) at 800°C (1073.15 K), Part (*r*) at 450°C (723.15 K), Part (*t*) at 460°C (733.15 K), Part (*u*) at 750 K, Part (*v*) at 900 K, Part (*w*) at 400°C (673.15 K), Part (*x*) at 375°C (648.15 K), Part (*y*) at 810°C (1083.15 K).

4.23. Develop a general equation for the standard heat of reaction as a function of temperature for one of the reactions given in parts (*a*), (*b*), (*e*), (*f*), (*g*), (*h*), (*j*), (*k*), (*l*), (*m*), (*n*), (*o*), (*r*), (*t*), (*u*), (*v*), (*w*), (*x*), (*y*), and (*z*) of Pb. 4.21.

4.24. Natural gas (assume pure methane) is delivered to a city via pipeline at a volumetric rate of 4.0 mega normal m^3 per day. If the selling price of the gas is $5.00 per GJ of higher heating value, what is the expected revenue in dollars per day? Normal conditions are 0°C (273.15 K) and 1 atm.

4.25. Natural gases are rarely pure methane; they usually also contain other light hydrocarbons and nitrogen. Determine an expression for the standard heat of combustion as a function of composition for a natural gas containing methane, ethane, propane, and nitrogen. Assume liquid water as a product of combustion. Which of the following natural gases has the highest heat of combustion?

(*a*) $y_{CH_4} = 0.95,\ y_{C_2H_6} = 0.02,\ y_{C_3H_8} = 0.02,\ y_{N_2} = 0.01.$
(*b*) $y_{CH_4} = 0.90,\ y_{C_2H_6} = 0.05,\ y_{C_3H_8} = 0.03,\ y_{N_2} = 0.02.$
(*c*) $y_{CH_4} = 0.85,\ y_{C_2H_6} = 0.07,\ y_{C_3H_8} = 0.03,\ y_{N_2} = 0.05.$

4.26. If the heat of combustion of urea, $(NH_2)_2CO(s)$, at 25°C (298.15 K) is 631 660 J mol^{-1} when the products are $CO_2(g)$, $H_2O(l)$, and $N_2(g)$, what is $\Delta H^\circ_{f_{298}}$ for urea?

4.27. The *higher heating value* (HHV) of a fuel is its standard heat of combustion at 25°C (298.15 K) with liquid water as a product; the *lower heating value* (LHV) is for water vapor as product.

(*a*) Explain the origins of these terms.
(*b*) Determine the HHV and the LHV for natural gas, modeled as pure methane.
(*c*) Determine the HHV and the LHV for a home-heating oil, modeled as pure liquid *n*-decane. For *n*-decane as a liquid $\Delta H^\circ_{f_{298}} = -249\,700$ J mol^{-1}.

4.28. A light fuel oil with an average chemical composition of $C_{10}H_{18}$ is burned with oxygen in a bomb calorimeter. The heat evolved is measured as 43 960 J g^{-1} for the reaction at 25°C (298.15 K). Calculate the standard heat of combustion of the fuel oil at 25°C

(298.15 K) with $H_2O(g)$ and $CO_2(g)$ as products. Note that the reaction in the bomb occurs at constant volume, produces liquid water as a product, and goes to completion.

4.29. Methane gas is burned completely with 30% excess air at approximately atmospheric pressure. Both the methane and the air enter the furnace at 30°C (303.15 K) saturated with water vapor, and the flue gases leave the furnace at 1500°C (1773.15 K). The flue gases then pass through a heat exchanger from which they emerge at 50°C (323.15 K). Per mole of methane, how much heat is lost from the furnace, and how much heat is transferred in the heat exchanger?

4.30. Ammonia gas enters the reactor of a nitric acid plant mixed with 30% more dry air than is required for the complete conversion of the ammonia to nitric oxide and water vapor. If the gases enter the reactor at 75°C (348.15 K), if conversion is 80%, if no side reactions occur, and if the reactor operates adiabatically, what is the temperature of the gases leaving the reactor? Assume ideal gases.

4.31. Ethylene gas and steam at 320°C (593.15 K) and atmospheric pressure are fed to a reaction process as an equimolar mixture. The process produces ethanol by the reaction:

$$C_2H_4(g) + H_2O(g) \rightarrow C_2H_5OH(l)$$

The liquid ethanol exits the process at 25°C (298.15 K). What is the heat transfer associated with this overall process per mole of ethanol produced?

4.32. A gas mixture of methane and steam at atmospheric pressure and 500°C (773.15 K) is fed to a reactor, where the following reactions occur:

$$CH_4 + H_2O \rightarrow CO + 3H_2 \qquad \text{and} \qquad CO + H_2O \rightarrow CO_2 + H_2$$

The product stream leaves the reactor at 850°C. Its composition (mole fractions) is

$$y_{CO_2} = 0.0275 \qquad y_{CO} = 0.1725 \qquad y_{H_2O} = 0.1725 \qquad y_{H_2} = 0.6275$$

Determine the quantity of heat added to the reactor per mole of product gas.

4.33. A fuel consisting of 75 mole % methane and 25 mole % ethane enters a furnace with 80% excess air at 30°C (303.15 K). If 8×10^5 kJ per kmol of fuel is transferred as heat to boiler tubes, at what temperature does the flue gas leave the furnace? Assume complete combustion of the fuel.

4.34. The gas stream from a sulfur burner consists of 15 mole % SO_2, 20 mole % O_2, and 65 mole % N_2. The gas stream at atmospheric pressure and 400°C (673.15 K) enters a catalytic converter where 86% of the SO_2 is further oxidized to SO_3. On the basis of 1 mol of gas entering, how much heat must be removed from the converter so that the product gases leave at 500°C (773.15 K)?

4.35. Hydrogen is produced by the reaction: $CO(g) + H_2O(g) \rightarrow CO_2(g) + H_2(g)$. The feed stream to the reactor is an equimolar mixture of carbon monoxide and steam, and it enters the reactor at 125°C (398.15 K) and atmospheric pressure. If 60% of the H_2O is converted to H_2 and if the product stream leaves the reactor at 425°C (698.15 K), how much heat must be transferred from the reactor?

4.36. A direct-fired dryer burns a fuel oil with a net heating value of 44 200 kJ kg^{-1}. [The *net* heating value is obtained when the products of combustion are $CO_2(g)$ and $H_2O(g)$.] The composition of the oil is 85% carbon, 12% hydrogen, 2% nitrogen, and 1% water by mass. The flue gases leave the dryer at 204°C (477.15 K), and a partial analysis shows that they contain 3 mole % CO_2 and 11.8 mole % CO on a dry basis. The fuel, air, and material being dried enter the dryer at 25°C (298.15 K). If the entering air is saturated with water and if 30% of the net heating value of the oil is allowed for heat losses (including the sensible heat carried out with the dried product), how much water is evaporated in the dryer per kg of oil burned?

4.37. An equimolar mixture of nitrogen and acetylene enters a steady-flow reactor at 25°C (298.15 K) and atmospheric pressure. The only reaction occurring is: $N_2(g) + C_2H_2(g) \rightarrow 2HCN(g)$. The product gases leave the reactor at 600°C (873.15 K) and contain 24.2 mole % HCN. How much heat is supplied to the reactor per mole of product gas?

4.38. Chlorine is produced by the reaction: $4HCl(g) + O_2(g) \rightarrow 2H_2O(g) + 2Cl_2(g)$. The feed stream to the reactor consists of 60 mole % HCl, 36 mole % O_2, and 4 mole % N_2, and it enters the reactor at 550°C (823.15 K). If the conversion of HCl is 75% and if the process is isothermal, how much heat must be transferred from the reactor per mole of the entering gas mixture?

4.39. A gas consisting only of CO and N_2 is made by passing a mixture of flue gas and air through a bed of incandescent coke (assume pure carbon). The two reactions that occur both go to completion:

$$CO_2 + C \rightarrow 2CO \qquad \text{and} \qquad 2C + O_2 \rightarrow 2CO$$

They yield a flue gas of composition: 12.8 mole % CO, 3.7 mole % CO_2, 5.4 mole % O_2, and 78.1 mole % N_2. The flue gas/air mixture is so proportioned that the heats of the two reactions cancel, and the temperature of the coke bed is therefore constant. If this temperature is 875°C (1148.15 K), if the feed stream is preheated to 875°C (1148.15 K), and if the process is adiabatic, what ratio of moles of flue gas to moles of air is required, and what is the composition of the gas produced?

4.40. A fuel gas consisting of 94 mole % methane and 6 mole % nitrogen is burned with 35% excess air in a continuous water heater. Both fuel gas and air enter dry at 25°C (298.15 K). Water is heated at a rate of 34.0 kg s^{-1} from 25 to 95°C (298.15 K to 368.15 K). The flue gases leave the heater at 210°C (483.15 K). Of the entering methane, 70% burns to carbon dioxide and 30% burns to carbon monoxide. What volumetric flow rate of fuel gas is required if there are no heat losses to the surroundings?

4.41. A process for the production of 1,3-butadiene results from the catalytic dehydrogenation at atmospheric pressure of 1-butene according to the reaction:

$$C_4H_8(g) \rightarrow C_4H_6(g) + H_2(g)$$

To suppress side reactions, the 1-butene feed stream is diluted with steam in the ratio of 10 moles of steam per mole of 1-butene. The reaction is carried out *isothermally* at 525°C (798.15 K), and at this temperature 33% of the 1-butene is converted to 1,3-butadiene. How much heat is transferred to the reactor per mole of entering 1-butene?

4.42. An air-cooled condenser transfers heat at the rate of 12 kJ s^{-1} to ambient air at 24°C (297.15 K). If the air temperature is raised by 13°C (13 K), what is the required volumetric flowrate of the air?

4.43. An air-conditioning unit cools 1.5 m^3 s^{-1} of air at 35°C (308.15 K) to 25°C (298.15 K). What is the required heat transfer rate in kJ s^{-1} (or kW)?

4.44. A propane-fired water heater delivers 80% of the standard heat of combustion of the propane [at 25°C (298.15 K) with $CO_2(g)$ and $H_2O(g)$ as products] to the water. If the price of propane is $0.58 per liter as measured at 25°C (298.15 K), what is the heating cost in $ per MJ?

4.45. Determine the heat transfer (J mol^{-1}) when one of the gases identified below is heated in a steady-flow process from 25 to 500°C (298.15 K to 773.15 K) at atmospheric pressure.

(*a*) Acetylene (*b*) Ammonia (*c*) *n*-Butane (*d*) Carbon dioxide
(*e*) Carbon monoxide (*f*) Ethane (*g*) Hydrogen (*h*) Hydrogen chloride
(*i*) Methane (*j*) Nitric oxide (*k*) Nitrogen (*l*) Nitrogen dioxide
(*m*) Nitrous oxide (*n*) Oxygen (*o*) Propylene

4.46. Determine the final temperature for one of the gases of the preceding problem if heat in the amount of 30 000 J mol^{-1} is transferred to the gas, initially at 25°C (298.15 K), in a steady-flow process at atmospheric pressure.

4.47. Quantitative thermal analysis has been suggested as a technique for monitoring the composition of a binary gas stream. To illustrate the principle, do one of the following problems.

(*a*) A methane/ethane gas mixture is heated from 25 to 250°C (298.15 K to 523.15 K) at 1 atm in a steady-flow process. If $Q = 11\ 500$ J mol^{-1}, what is the composition of the mixture?

(*b*) A benzene/cyclohexane gas mixture is heated from 100 to 400°C (373.15 K to 673.15 K) at 1 atm in a steady-flow process. If $Q = 54\ 000$ J mol^{-1}, what is the composition of the mixture?

(*c*) A toluene/ethylbenzene gas mixture is heated from 150 to 250°C (423.15 K to 523.15 K) at 1 atm in a steady-flow process. If $Q = 17\ 500$ J mol^{-1}, what is the composition of the mixture?

4.48. Saturated steam at 1 atm and 100°C (373.15 K) is continuously generated from liquid water at 1 atm and 25°C (298.15 K) by thermal contact with hot air in a counterflow heat exchanger. The air flows steadily at 1 atm. Determine values for $\dot{m}(\text{steam})/\dot{n}(\text{air})$ for two cases:

(*a*) Air enters the exchanger at 1000°C (1273.15 K).

(*b*) Air enters the exchanger at 500°C (773.15 K).

For both cases, assume a minimum approach ΔT for heat exchange of 10°C (10 K).

4.49. Saturated water vapor, i.e., *steam*, is commonly used as a heat source in heat-exchanger applications. Why *saturated* vapor? Why saturated *water* vapor? In a plant of any reasonable size, several varieties of saturated steam are commonly available; for example, saturated steam at 4.5, 9, 17, and 33 bar. But the higher the pressure the lower the useful energy content (why?), and the greater the unit cost. Why then is higher-pressure steam used?

4.50. The oxidation of glucose provides the principal source of energy for animal cells. Assume the reactants are glucose [$C_6H_{12}O_6(s)$] and oxygen [$O_2(g)$]. The products are $CO_2(g)$ and $H_2O(l)$.

(*a*) Write a balanced equation for glucose oxidation, and determine the standard heat of reaction at 298.15 K.

(*b*) During a day an average person consumes about 150 kJ of energy per kg of body mass. Assuming glucose the sole source of energy, estimate the mass (grams) of glucose required daily to sustain a person of 57 kg.

(*c*) For a population of 275 million persons, what mass of CO_2 (a greenhouse gas). is produced daily by mere respiration.

Data: For glucose, $\Delta H^\circ_{f_{298}} = -1274.4$ kJ mol^{-1}. Ignore the effect of temperature on the heat of reaction.

4.51. A natural-gas fuel contains 85 mole % methane, 10 mole % ethane, and 5 mole % nitrogen.

(*a*) What is the standard heat of combustion (kJ mol^{-1}) of the fuel at 25°C (298.15 K) with $H_2O(g)$ as a product?

(*b*) The fuel is supplied to a furnace with 50% excess air, both entering at 25°C (298.15 K). The products leave at 600°C (873.15 K). If combustion is complete and if no side reactions occur, how much heat (kJ mol^{-1} of fuel) is transferred in the furnace?

Chapter 5

The Second Law of Thermodynamics

Thermodynamics is concerned with transformations of energy, and the laws of thermodynamics describe the bounds within which these transformations are observed to occur. The first law reflects the observation that energy is conserved, but it imposes no restriction on the process direction. Yet, all experience indicates the existence of such a restriction, the concise statement of which constitutes the *second* law.

The differences between the two forms of energy, heat and work, provide some insight into the second law. In an energy balance, both work and heat are included as simple additive terms, implying that one unit of heat, a joule, is equivalent to the same unit of work. Although this is true with respect to an energy balance, experience teaches that there is a difference of kind between heat and work. This experience is summarized by the following facts.

Work is readily transformed into other forms of energy: for example, into potential energy by elevation of a weight, into kinetic energy by acceleration of a mass, into electrical energy by operation of a generator. These processes can be made to approach a conversion efficiency of 100% by elimination of friction, a dissipative process that transforms work into heat. Indeed, work is readily transformed completely into heat, as demonstrated by Joule's experiments.

On the other hand, all efforts to devise a process for the continuous conversion of heat completely into work or into mechanical or electrical energy have failed. Regardless of improvements to the devices employed, conversion efficiencies do not exceed about 40%. Evidently, heat is a form of energy intrinsically less useful and hence less valuable than an equal quantity of work or mechanical or electrical energy.

Drawing further on our experience, we know that the flow of heat between two bodies always takes place from the hotter to the cooler body, and never in the reverse direction (Sec 1.9). This fact is of such significance that its restatement serves as an acceptable expression of the second law.

5.1 STATEMENTS OF THE SECOND LAW

The observations just described suggest a general restriction on processes beyond that imposed by the first law. The second law is equally well expressed in two statements that describe this restriction:

- **Statement 1** No apparatus can operate in such a way that its *only effect* (in system and surroundings) is to convert heat absorbed by a system *completely* into work done by the system.

- **Statement 2** No process is possible which consists *solely* in the transfer of heat from one temperature level to a higher one.

Statement 1 does not say that heat cannot be converted into work; only that the process cannot leave both the system and its surroundings unchanged. If an ideal gas in a piston/cylinder assembly expands reversibly and isothermally to a lower pressure, Eq. (2.3) requires that $\Delta U^t = Q + W$. For an ideal gas, $\Delta U^t = 0$, and therefore, $Q = -W$. The heat absorbed by the gas from the surroundings is equal to the work transferred to the surroundings by the reversible expansion of the gas. This might seem a contradiction of statement 1, because in the surroundings the result is the complete conversion of heat into work. However, this statement requires in addition no change in the system, a requirement that is not met owing to the change in pressure.

This process is limited in another way, because the pressure of the gas ultimately reaches that of the surroundings, and expansion ceases. Therefore, the continuous production of work from heat by this method is impossible. If the original state of the system is restored so as to comply with the requirements of statement 1, energy from the surroundings in the form of work is needed to compress the gas back to its original pressure. At the same time energy as heat is transferred to the surroundings to maintain constant temperature. This reverse process requires at least the amount of work gained from the expansion; hence no net work is produced. Evidently, statement 1 may be expressed in an alternative way, *viz*.:

- **Statement 1a** It is impossible by a cyclic process to convert the heat absorbed by a system completely into work done by the system.

The word *cyclic* requires that the system be restored periodically to its original state. In the case of a gas in a piston/cylinder assembly, an initial expansion may be followed by steps that restore the original state, thus producing a complete cycle. If the process is repeated, it becomes a cyclic process. The restriction to a *cyclic* process in statement 1a amounts to the same limitation as that introduced by the words *only effect* in statement 1.

The second law does not prohibit the production of work from heat, but it does place a limit on how much of the heat directed into a cyclic process can be converted into work done by the process. With the exception of water and wind power, the partial conversion of heat into work is the basis for nearly all commercial production of power. The development of a quantitative expression for the efficiency of this conversion is the next step in the treatment of the second law.

5.2 HEAT ENGINES

The classical approach to the second law is based on a *macroscopic* viewpoint of properties, independent of any knowledge of the structure of matter or behavior of molecules. It arose from the study of *heat engines*, devices or machines that produce work from heat in a cyclic process. An example is a steam power plant in which the working fluid (H_2O) periodically returns to its original state. This cycle (in its simplest form) consists of the following steps:

- Liquid water from a condenser is pumped into a boiler at elevated pressure.
- Heat from a fuel (heat of combustion of a fossil fuel or heat from a nuclear reaction) is transferred in the boiler to the water, converting it to high-temperature steam at the boiler pressure.
- Energy is transferred as shaft work from the steam to the surroundings by a device such as a turbine, in which the steam expands to reduced pressure and temperature.
- Exhaust steam from the turbine is condensed by transfer of heat to the surroundings, producing liquid water for return to the boiler, thus completing the cycle.

Essential to all heat-engine cycles are absorption of heat into the system at a high temperature, rejection of heat to the surroundings at a lower temperature, and production of work. In the theoretical treatment of heat engines, the two temperature levels which characterize their operation are maintained by *heat reservoirs*, bodies imagined capable of absorbing or rejecting unlimited quantities of heat without temperature change[1]. In operation, the working fluid of a heat engine absorbs heat $|Q_H|$ from a hot reservoir, produces a net amount of work $|W|$, discards heat $|Q_C|$ to a cold reservoir, and returns to its initial state. The first law therefore reduces to:

$$|W| = |Q_H| - |Q_C| \tag{5.1}$$

The *thermal efficiency* of the engine is defined as: $\eta \equiv$ net work output/heat absorbed. With Eq. (5.1) this becomes

$$\eta \equiv \frac{|W|}{|Q_H|} = \frac{|Q_H| - |Q_C|}{|Q_H|} = 1 - \frac{|Q_C|}{|Q_H|} \tag{5.2}$$

Absolute-value signs are used to make the equations independent of the sign conventions for Q and W. For η to be unity (100% thermal efficiency), $|Q_C|$ must be zero. No engine has ever been built that approaches this result; heat is always rejected to the cold reservoir. This observation from engineering experience is the basis for statements 1 and 1*a* of the second law.

If a thermal efficiency of 100% is not possible for heat engines, what then determines the upper limit? One would certainly expect the thermal efficiency of a heat engine to depend on the degree of reversibility of its operation. Indeed, a heat engine operating in a completely reversible manner is very special, and is called a *Carnot engine*. The characteristics of such an ideal engine were first described by N. L. S. Carnot[2] in 1824. The four steps that make up a *Carnot cycle* are performed in the following order:

[1] The firebox of a furnace is in effect a hot reservoir, and the surrounding atmosphere, a cold reservoir.

[2] Nicolas Leonard Sadi Carnot (1796–1832), a French engineer.

- **Step 1** A system at an initial temperature of a cold reservoir at T_C undergoes a *reversible* adiabatic process that causes its temperature to rise to that of a hot reservoir at T_H.

- **Step 2** The system maintains contact with the hot reservoir at T_H, and undergoes a *reversible* isothermal process during which heat $|Q_H|$ is absorbed from the hot reservoir.

- **Step 3** The system undergoes a *reversible* adiabatic process in the opposite direction of step 1 that brings its temperature back to that of the cold reservoir at T_C.

- **Step 4** The system maintains contact with the reservoir at T_C, and undergoes a *reversible* isothermal process in the opposite direction of step 2 that returns it to its initial state with rejection of heat $|Q_C|$ to the cold reservoir.

This set of processes can in principle be performed on any kind of system, but only a few, to be described later, are of practical interest. Regardless of the system, the energy balance of Eq. (5.1) requires that $|W| = |Q_H| - |Q_C|$.

A Carnot engine operates between two heat reservoirs in such a way that all heat absorbed is transferred at the constant temperature of the hot reservoir and all heat rejected is transferred at the constant temperature of the cold reservoir. Any *reversible* engine operating between two heat reservoirs is a Carnot engine; an engine operating on a different cycle must necessarily transfer heat across finite temperature differences and therefore cannot be reversible.

Carnot's Theorem

Statement 2 of the second law is the basis for *Carnot's theorem*:

> **For two given heat reservoirs no engine can have a thermal efficiency higher than that of a Carnot engine.**

The proof is based on the premise that an engine E exists with a thermal efficiency *greater than* that of a Carnot engine operating between the same two heat reservoirs. Let the Carnot engine absorb heat $|Q_H|$ from the hot reservoir, produce work $|W|$, and discard heat $|Q_H|-|W|$ to the cold reservoir. Engine E absorbs heat $|Q'_H|$ from the hot reservoir, produces the same work $|W|$, and discards heat $|Q'_H| - |W|$ to the cold reservoir. If engine E has the greater efficiency,

$$\frac{|W|}{|Q'_H|} > \frac{|W|}{|Q_H|} \qquad \text{and} \qquad |Q_H| > |Q'_H|$$

Because a Carnot engine is reversible, it may be operated in reverse; the Carnot cycle is then traversed in the opposite direction, and it becomes a reversible refrigeration cycle for which the quantities $|Q_H|$, $|Q_C|$, and $|W|$ are the same as for the engine cycle but are reversed in direction. Let engine E drive the Carnot engine backward as a Carnot refrigerator, as shown schematically in Fig. 5.1. For the engine/refrigerator combination, the net heat extracted from the cold reservoir is

$$|Q_H| - |W| - \left(|Q'_H| - |W|\right) = |Q_H| - |Q'_H|$$

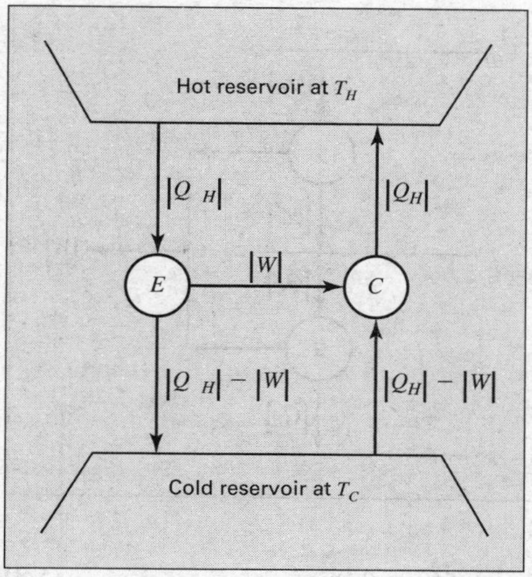

Figure 5.1: Engine E operating a Carnot refrigerator C

The net heat delivered to the hot reservoir is also $|Q_H| - |Q'_H|$. Thus, the sole result of the engine/refrigerator combination is the transfer of heat from temperature T_C to the higher temperature T_H. Because this is in violation of statement 2 of the second law, the original premise that engine E has a greater thermal efficiency than the Carnot engine is false, and Carnot's theorem is proved.

In similar fashion, one can prove that all Carnot engines operating between heat reservoirs at the same two temperatures have the same thermal efficiency. Thus a *corollary to Carnot's theorem* states:

The thermal efficiency of a Carnot engine depends only on the temperature levels and not upon the working substance of the engine.

5.3 THERMODYNAMIC TEMPERATURE SCALES

In the preceding discussion we identified temperature levels by the Kelvin scale, established with ideal-gas thermometry. This does not preclude taking advantage of the opportunity provided by the Carnot engine to establish a *thermodynamic* temperature scale that is truly independent of any material properties. Let θ represent temperature on some empirical scale that unequivocally identifies temperature levels. Consider two Carnot engines, one operating between a hot reservoir at temperature θ_H and a cold reservoir at temperature θ_C, and a second operating between the reservoir at θ_C and a still colder reservoir at θ_F, as shown in Fig. 5.2. The heat rejected by the first engine $|Q_C|$ is absorbed by the second; therefore the two engines working together constitute a third Carnot engine absorbing heat $|Q_H|$ from the reservoir at θ_H and rejecting heat $|Q_F|$ to the reservoir at θ_F. The corollary to Carnot's theorem indicates that the thermal efficiency of the first engine is a function of θ_H and θ_C:

$$\eta = 1 - \frac{|Q_C|}{|Q_H|} = \phi(\theta_H, \theta_C)$$

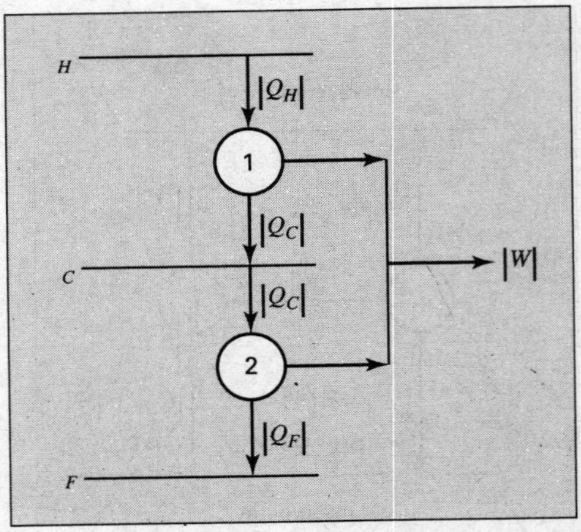

Figure 5.2: Carnot engines 1 and 2 constitute a third Carnot engine

Rearrangement gives
$$\frac{|Q_H|}{|Q_C|} = \frac{1}{1 - \phi(\theta_H, \theta_C)} = f(\theta_H, \theta_C) \tag{5.3}$$

where f is an unknown function.

For the second and third engines, equations of the same functional form apply:

$$\frac{|Q_C|}{|Q_F|} = f(\theta_C, \theta_F) \quad \text{and} \quad \frac{|Q_H|}{|Q_F|} = f(\theta_H, \theta_F)$$

Division of the second of these equations by the first gives

$$\frac{|Q_H|}{|Q_C|} = \frac{f(\theta_H, \theta_F)}{f(\theta_C, \theta_F)}$$

Comparison of this equation with Eq. (5.3) shows that the arbitrary temperature θ_F must cancel from the ratio on the right:

$$\frac{|Q_H|}{|Q_C|} = \frac{\psi(\theta_H)}{\psi(\theta_C)} \tag{5.4}$$

where ψ is another unknown function.

We see from Eq. (5.4) that the ψs evaluated at two thermodynamic temperatures (θ) are in the same ratio as the absolute values of heat absorbed and heat rejected by a Carnot engine operating between these two temperature levels, quite independent of the properties of any substance. Because the choice of scale is arbitrary, we may set θ equal to the Kelvin temperature T; Eq. (5.4) then becomes

$$\frac{|Q_H|}{|Q_C|} = \frac{\psi(T_H)}{\psi(T_C)} \tag{5.5}$$

This leaves the function ψ to be determined.

Ideal-Gas Temperature Scale; Carnot's Equations

The cycle traversed by an ideal gas serving as the working fluid in a Carnot engine is shown by a PV diagram in Fig. 5.3. It consists of four *reversible* processes corresponding to Steps 1 through 4 of the general Carnot cycle described in the preceding section:

- $a \to b$ Adiabatic compression until the temperature rises from T_C to T_H.
- $b \to c$ Isothermal expansion to arbitrary point c with absorption of heat $|Q_H|$.
- $c \to d$ Adiabatic expansion until the temperature decreases to T_C.
- $d \to a$ Isothermal compression to the initial state with rejection of heat $|Q_C|$.

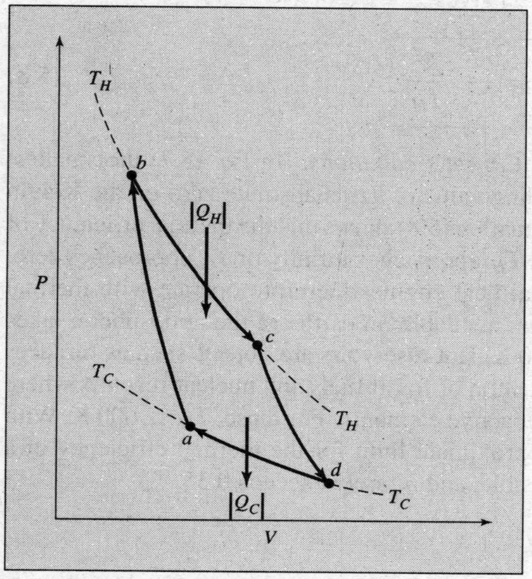

Figure 5.3: PV diagram showing Carnot cycle for an ideal gas

For the isothermal steps $b \to c$ and $d \to a$, Eq. (3.27) yields

$$|Q_H| = RT_H \ln \frac{V_c}{V_b} \qquad \text{and} \qquad |Q_C| = RT_C \ln \frac{V_d}{V_a}$$

Therefore,

$$\frac{|Q_H|}{|Q_C|} = \frac{T_H}{T_C} \frac{\ln(V_c/V_b)}{\ln(V_d/V_a)} \tag{5.6}$$

For an adiabatic process Eq. (3.22) with $dQ = 0$ becomes,

$$-\frac{C_V}{R}\frac{dT}{T} = \frac{dV}{V}$$

For step $a \to b$ and $c \to d$, integration gives

$$\int_{T_C}^{T_H} \frac{C_V}{R}\frac{dT}{T} = \ln \frac{V_a}{V_b} \qquad \text{and} \qquad \int_{T_C}^{T_H} \frac{C_V}{R}\frac{dT}{T} = \ln \frac{V_d}{V_c}$$

Because the left sides of these two equations are the same,

$$\ln \frac{V_a}{V_b} = \ln \frac{V_d}{V_c} \qquad \text{or} \qquad \ln \frac{V_c}{V_b} = \ln \frac{V_d}{V_a}$$

Equation (5.6) now becomes

$$\boxed{\frac{|Q_H|}{|Q_C|} = \frac{T_H}{T_C}} \tag{5.7}$$

Comparison of this result with Eq. (5.5) yields the simplest possible functional relation for ψ, namely, $\psi(T) = T$. We conclude that the Kelvin temperature scale, based on the properties of ideal gases, is in fact a thermodynamic scale, independent of the characteristics of any particular substance. Substitution of Eq. (5.7) into Eq. (5.2) gives

$$\boxed{\eta \equiv \frac{|W|}{|Q_H|} = 1 - \frac{T_C}{T_H}} \tag{5.8}$$

Equations (5.7) and (5.8) are known as *Carnot's equations*. In Eq. (5.7) the smallest possible value of $|Q_C|$ is zero; the corresponding value of T_C is absolute zero on the Kelvin scale (i.e. 0 K), which occurs at −273.15°C. Equation (5.8) shows that the thermal efficiency of a Carnot engine can approach unity only when T_H approaches infinity or T_C approaches zero. Neither condition exists on earth; all terrestrial heat engines therefore operate with thermal efficiencies less than unity. The cold reservoirs available on earth are the atmosphere, lakes and rivers, and the oceans, for which $T_C \simeq 300$ K. Hot reservoirs are objects such as furnaces where the temperature is maintained by combustion of fossil fuels and nuclear reactors where the temperature is maintained by fission of radioactive elements. For these, $T_H \simeq 600$ K. With these values, $\eta = 1 - 300/600 = 0.5$, an approximate limit for the thermal efficiency of a Carnot engine. Actual heat engines are irreversible, and η rarely exceeds 0.35.

Example 5.1

A central power plant, rated at 800 000 kW, generates steam at 585 K and discards heat to a river at 295 K. If the thermal efficiency of the plant is 70% of the maximum possible value, how much heat is discarded to the river at rated power?

Solution

The maximum possible thermal efficiency is given by Eq. (5.8). With T_H as the steam-generation temperature and T_C as the river temperature,

$$\eta_{\max} = 1 - \frac{295}{585} = 0.4957 \qquad \text{and} \qquad \eta = (0.7)(0.4957) = 0.3470$$

where η is the actual thermal efficiency. Equations (5.1) and (5.2) may be combined to eliminate $|Q_H|$; solution for $|Q_C|$ then yields

$$|Q_C| = \left(\frac{1-\eta}{\eta}\right)|W| = \left(\frac{1-0.347}{0.347}\right)(800\,000) = 1505\,500 \text{ kW}$$

This heat rate of 1505 500 kJ s^{-1} would cause a temperature rise of several °C in a modest river.

5.4 ENTROPY

Equation (5.7) for a Carnot engine may be written as

$$\frac{|Q_H|}{T_H} = \frac{|Q_C|}{T_C}$$

If the heat quantities refer to the working fluid of the engine (rather than to the heat reservoirs), the numerical value of Q_H is positive and that of Q_C is negative. The equivalent equation written without absolute-value signs is therefore

$$\frac{Q_H}{T_H} = \frac{-Q_C}{T_C}$$

or

$$\frac{Q_H}{T_H} + \frac{Q_C}{T_C} = 0 \tag{5.9}$$

Thus for a complete cycle of a Carnot engine, the two quantities Q/T associated with the absorption and rejection of heat by the working fluid of the engine sum to zero. The working fluid of a cyclic engine periodically returns to its initial state, and its properties, e.g., temperature, pressure, and internal energy, return to their initial values. Indeed, a primary characteristic of a property is that the sum of its changes is zero for any complete cycle. Thus for a Carnot cycle Eq. (5.9) suggests the existence of a property whose changes are given by the quantities Q/T.

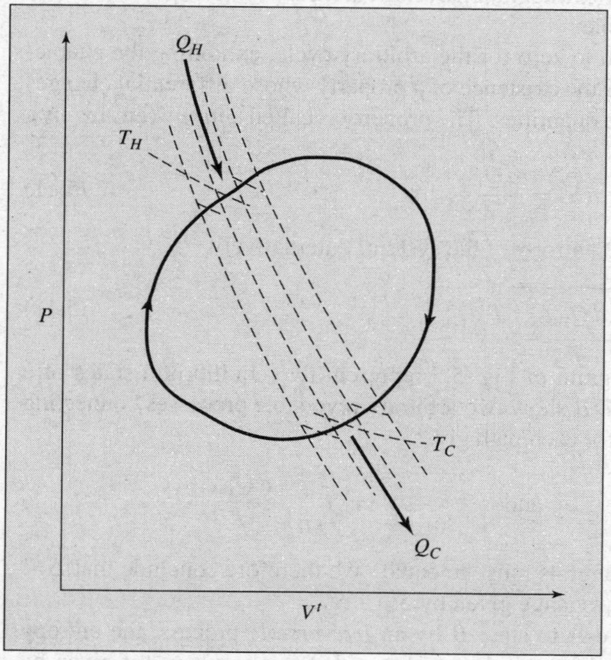

Figure 5.4: An arbitrary reversible cyclic process drawn on a PV^t diagram

Our purpose now is to show that Eq. (5.9) for a reversible Carnot cycle also applies to other reversible cycles. The closed curve on the PV^t diagram of Fig. 5.4 represents an arbitrary reversible cycle traversed by an arbitrary fluid. Divide the enclosed area by a series of reversible adiabatic curves; because such curves cannot intersect (Pb. 5.1), they may be drawn arbitrarily close to one another. Several such curves are shown on the figure as long dashed lines. Connect adjacent adiabatic curves by two short reversible isotherms which approximate the curve of the arbitrary cycle as closely as possible. The approximation clearly improves as the adiabatic curves are more closely spaced. When the separation becomes arbitrarily small, the original cycle is faithfully represented. Each pair of adjacent adiabatic curves and their isothermal connecting curves represent a Carnot cycle for which Eq. (5.9) applies.

Each Carnot cycle has its own pair of isotherms T_H and T_C and associated heat quantities Q_H and Q_C. These are indicated on Fig. 5.4 for a representative cycle. When the adiabatic curves are so closely spaced that the isothermal steps are infinitesimal, the heat quantities become dQ_H and dQ_C, and Eq. (5.9) for each Carnot cycle is written:

$$\frac{dQ_H}{T_H} + \frac{dQ_C}{T_C} = 0$$

In this equation T_H and T_C, absolute temperatures of the working fluid of the Carnot engines, are also the temperatures traversed by the working fluid of the arbitrary cycle. Summation of all quantities dQ/T for the Carnot engines leads to the integral

$$\oint \frac{dQ_{\text{rev}}}{T} = 0 \tag{5.10}$$

where the circle in the integral sign signifies integration over the arbitrary cycle, and the subscript "rev" indicates that the cycle is reversible.

Thus the quantities dQ_{rev}/T sum to zero for the arbitrary cycle, exhibiting the characteristic of a property. We therefore infer the existence of a property whose differential changes for the arbitrary cycle are given by these quantities. The property is called *entropy* (**en**′-tro-py), and its differential changes are

$$dS^t = \frac{dQ_{\text{rev}}}{T} \tag{5.11}$$

where S^t is the total (rather than molar) entropy of the system. Alternatively,

$$\boxed{dQ_{\text{rev}} = T\,dS^t} \tag{5.12}$$

Points A and B on the PV^t diagram of Fig. 5.5 represent two equilibrium states of a particular fluid, and paths ACB and ADB show two arbitrary reversible processes connecting these points. Integration of Eq. (5.11) for each path gives:

$$\Delta S^t = \int_{ACB} \frac{dQ_{\text{rev}}}{T} \qquad \text{and} \qquad \Delta S^t = \int_{ADB} \frac{dQ_{\text{rev}}}{T}$$

where in view of Eq. (5.10) the two integrals must be equal. We therefore conclude that ΔS^t is independent of path and is a property change given by $S^t_B - S^t_A$.

If the fluid is changed from state A to state B by an *irreversible* process, the entropy change must still be $\Delta S^t = S^t_B - S^t_A$, but experiment shows that this result is *not* given by $\int dQ/T$ evaluated for the irreversible process itself, because the calculation of entropy changes by this integral must in general be along reversible paths.

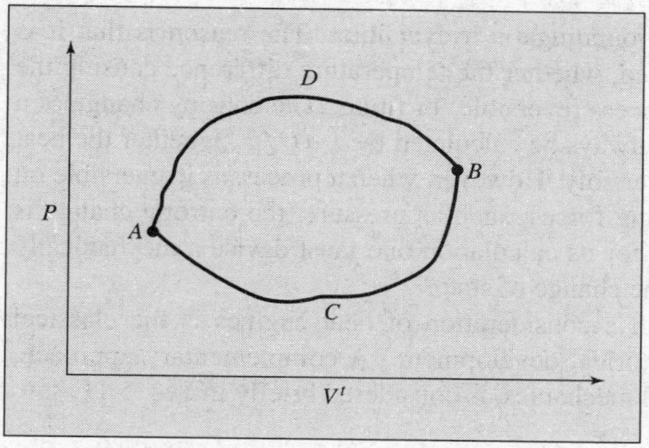

Figure 5.5: Two reversible paths joining equilibrium states A and B

The entropy change of a *heat reservoir*, however, is always given by Q/T, where Q is the quantity of heat transferred to or from the reservoir at temperature T, whether the transfer is reversible or irreversible. The reason is that the effect of heat transfer on a heat reservoir is the same regardless of the temperature of the source or sink of the heat.

If a process is reversible and adiabatic, $dQ_{\text{rev}} = 0$; then by Eq. (5.11), $dS^t = 0$. Thus the entropy of a system is constant during a reversible adiabatic process, and the process is said to be *isentropic*.

This discussion of entropy can be summarized as follows:

- Entropy owes its existence to the second law, from which it arises in much the same way as internal energy does from the first law. Equation (5.11) is the ultimate source of all equations that relate the entropy to measurable quantities. It does not represent a definition of entropy; there is none in the context of classical thermodynamics. What it provides is the means for calculating *changes* in this property. Its essential nature is summarized by the following axiom:

  There exists a property called entropy S, which is an intrinsic property of a system, functionally related to the measurable coordinates which characterize the system. For a reversible process, changes in this property are given by Eq. (5.11).

- The change in entropy of any system undergoing a finite *reversible* process is

$$\Delta S^t = \int \frac{dQ_{\text{rev}}}{T} \tag{5.13}$$

- When a system undergoes an *irreversible* process between two equilibrium states, the entropy change of the system ΔS^t is evaluated by application of Eq. (5.13) to *an arbitrarily chosen reversible process* that accomplishes the same change of state as the actual process. Integration is *not* carried out for the irreversible path. Because entropy is a state function, the entropy changes of the irreversible and reversible processes are identical.

In the special case of a *mechanically reversible* process (Sec. 2.8), the entropy change of the system is correctly evaluated from $\int dQ/T$ applied to the actual process, even though the *heat transfer* between system and surroundings is irreversible. The reason is that it is immaterial, as far as the system is concerned, whether the temperature difference causing the heat transfer is differential (making the process reversible) or finite. The entropy change of a system *caused by the transfer of heat* can always be calculated by $\int dQ/T$, whether the heat transfer is accomplished reversibly or irreversibly. However, when a process is irreversible on account of finite differences in other driving forces, such as pressure, the entropy change is not caused solely by the heat transfer, and for its calculation one must devise a mechanically reversible means of accomplishing the same change of state.

This introduction to entropy through a consideration of heat engines is the classical approach, closely following its actual historical development. A complementary approach, based on molecular concepts and statistical mechanics, is considered briefly in Sec. 5.11.

5.5 ENTROPY CHANGES OF AN IDEAL GAS

For one mole or a unit mass of fluid undergoing a mechanically reversible process in a closed system, the first law, Eq. (2.8), becomes

$$dU = dQ_{\text{rev}} - P\,dV$$

Differentiation of the defining equation for enthalpy, $H = U + PV$, yields

$$dH = dU + P\,dV + V\,dP$$

Eliminating dU gives: $$dH = dQ_{\text{rev}} - P\,dV + P\,dV + V\,dP$$

or $$dQ_{\text{rev}} = dH - V\,dP$$

For an ideal gas, $dH = C_P^{ig}dT$ and $V = RT/P$. With these substitutions and division by T,

$$\frac{dQ_{\text{rev}}}{T} = C_P^{ig}\frac{dT}{T} - R\frac{dP}{P}$$

As a result of Eq. (5.11), this becomes

$$dS = C_P^{ig}\frac{dT}{T} - R\frac{dP}{P} \qquad \text{or} \qquad \frac{dS}{R} = \frac{C_P^{ig}}{R}\frac{dT}{T} - d\ln P$$

where S is the molar entropy of an ideal gas. Integration from an initial state at conditions T_0 and P_0 to a final state at conditions T and P gives

$$\boxed{\frac{\Delta S}{R} = \int_{T_0}^{T}\frac{C_P^{ig}}{R}\frac{dT}{T} - \ln\frac{P}{P_0}} \tag{5.14}$$

Although *derived* for a mechanically reversible process, this equation relates properties only, and is independent of the process causing the change of state. It is therefore a general equation for the calculation of entropy changes of an ideal gas.

Example 5.2

For an ideal gas with constant heat capacities undergoing a reversible adiabatic (and therefore isentropic) process, Eq. (3.30b) can be written as

$$\frac{T_2}{T_1} = \left(\frac{P_2}{P_1}\right)^{(\gamma-1)/\gamma}$$

Show that this same equation results from application of Eq. (5.14) with $\Delta S = 0$.

Solution

Because C_P^{ig} is constant, Eq. (5.14) can be written as

$$0 = \ln\frac{T_2}{T_1} - \frac{R}{C_P^{ig}}\ln\frac{P_2}{P_1}$$

By Eq. (3.19) for an ideal gas, with $\gamma = C_P^{ig}/C_V^{ig}$:

$$C_P^{ig} = C_V^{ig} + R \qquad \text{or} \qquad \frac{R}{C_P^{ig}} = \frac{\gamma - 1}{\gamma}$$

Whence,

$$\ln\frac{T_2}{T_1} = \frac{\gamma - 1}{\gamma}\ln\frac{P_2}{P_1}$$

This result is readily rearranged into the given equation.

Equation (4.4) for the temperature dependence of the molar heat capacity C_P^{ig} allows integration of the first term on the right of Eq. (5.14). The result is conveniently expressed as

$$\int_{T_0}^{T}\frac{C_P^{ig}}{R}\frac{dT}{T} = A\ln\tau + \left[BT_0 + \left(CT_0^2 + \frac{D}{\tau^2 T_0^2}\right)\left(\frac{\tau+1}{2}\right)\right](\tau - 1) \tag{5.15}$$

where $\tau \equiv T/T_0$. Because this integral must often be evaluated, we include in App. D representative computer programs for its evaluation. For computational purposes the right side of Eq. (5.15) is defined as the function, ICPS(T0,T;A,B,C,D). Equation (5.15) then becomes

$$\int_{T_0}^{T}\frac{C_P^{ig}}{R}\frac{dT}{T} = \text{ICPS(T0,T;A,B,C,D)}$$

The computer programs also calculate a mean heat capacity defined as

$$\langle C_P^{ig}\rangle_S = \frac{\int_{T_0}^{T} C_P^{ig}\, dT/T}{\ln(T/T_0)} \tag{5.16}$$

Here, the subscript "S" denotes a mean value specific to entropy calculations. Division of Eq. (5.15) by $\ln(T/T_0)$ or $\ln \tau$ therefore yields

$$\frac{\langle C_P^{ig} \rangle_S}{R} = A + \left[BT_0 + \left(CT_0^2 + \frac{D}{\tau^2 T_0^2} \right) \left(\frac{\tau + 1}{2} \right) \right] \left(\frac{\tau - 1}{\ln \tau} \right) \tag{5.17}$$

The right side of this equation is defined as another function, MCPS(T0,T;A,B,C,D). Equation (5.17) then becomes

$$\frac{\langle C_P^{ig} \rangle_S}{R} = \text{MCPS(T0,T;A,B,C,D)}$$

Solving for the integral in Eq. (5.16) gives

$$\int_{T_0}^{T} C_P^{ig} \frac{dT}{T} = \langle C_P^{ig} \rangle_S \ln \frac{T}{T_0}$$

and Eq. (5.14) becomes

$$\boxed{\frac{\Delta S}{R} = \frac{\langle C_P^{ig} \rangle_S}{R} \ln \frac{T}{T_0} - \ln \frac{P}{P_0}} \tag{5.18}$$

This form of the equation for entropy changes of an ideal gas may be useful when iterative calculations are required.

Example 5.3

Methane gas at 550 K and 5 bar undergoes a reversible adiabatic expansion to 1 bar. Assuming methane to be an ideal gas at these conditions, find its final temperature.

Solution

For this process $\Delta S = 0$, and Eq. (5.18) becomes

$$\frac{\langle C_P^{ig} \rangle_S}{R} \ln \frac{T_2}{T_1} = \ln \frac{P_2}{P_1} = \ln \frac{1}{5} = -1.6094$$

Because $\langle C_P^{ig} \rangle_S$ depends on T_2, we rearrange this equation for iterative solution:

$$\ln \frac{T_2}{T_1} = \frac{-1.6094}{\langle C_P^{ig} \rangle_S / R} \quad \text{or} \quad T_2 = T_1 \exp\left(\frac{-1.6094}{\langle C_P^{ig} \rangle_S / R} \right)$$

With constants from Table C.1, $\langle C_P^{ig} \rangle_S / R$ is evaluated by Eq. (5.17) written in its functional form:

$$\frac{\langle C_P^{ig} \rangle_S}{R} = \text{MCPS(550,T2;1.702,9.081E-3,-2.164E-6,0.0)}$$

For an initial value of $T_2 < 550$, compute a value of $\langle C_P^{ig} \rangle_S / R$ for substitution into the equation for T_2. This new value of T_2 allows recalculation of $\langle C_P^{ig} \rangle_S / R$, and the process continues to convergence on a final value of $T_2 = 411.34$ K (138.19°C).

5.6 MATHEMATICAL STATEMENT OF THE SECOND LAW

Consider two heat reservoirs, one at temperature T_H and a second at the lower temperature T_C. Let a quantity of heat $|Q|$ be transferred from the hotter to the cooler reservoir. The entropy changes of the reservoirs at T_H and at T_C are

$$\Delta S_H^t = \frac{-|Q|}{T_H} \quad \text{and} \quad \Delta S_C^t = \frac{|Q|}{T_C}$$

These two entropy changes are added to give

$$\Delta S_{\text{total}} = \Delta S_H^t + \Delta S_C^t = \frac{-|Q|}{T_H} + \frac{|Q|}{T_C} = |Q| \left(\frac{T_H - T_C}{T_H T_C} \right)$$

Because $T_H > T_C$, the *total* entropy change as a result of this irreversible process is positive. Also, ΔS_{total} becomes smaller as the difference $T_H - T_C$ gets smaller. When T_H is only infinitesimally higher than T_C, the heat transfer is reversible, and ΔS_{total} approaches zero. Thus for the process of irreversible heat transfer, ΔS_{total} is always positive, approaching zero as the process becomes reversible.

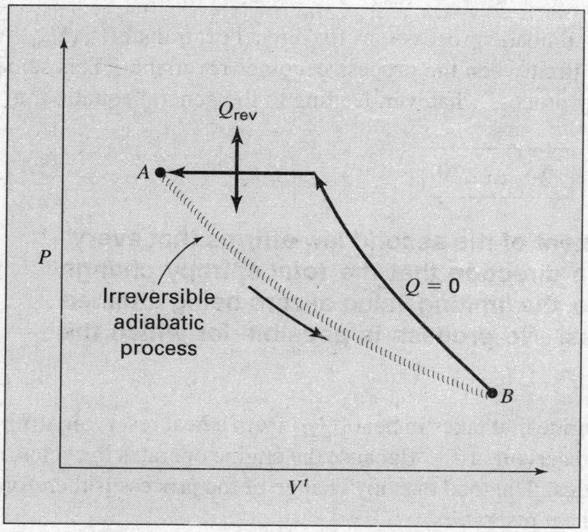

Figure 5.6: Cycle containing an irreversible adiabatic process A to B

Consider now an *irreversible* process in a closed system wherein no heat transfer occurs. Such a process is represented on the PV^t diagram of Fig. 5.6, which shows an *irreversible*, adiabatic expansion of 1 mol of fluid from an initial equilibrium state at point A to a final equilibrium state at point B. Now suppose the fluid is restored to its initial state by a *reversible* process consisting of two steps: first, the reversible, adiabatic (constant-entropy) compression of the fluid to the initial pressure, and second, a reversible, constant-pressure step that restores the initial volume. If the initial process results in an entropy change of the fluid, then there must be heat transfer during the reversible, constant-P second step such that

$$\Delta S^t = S_A^t - S_B^t = \int_B^A \frac{dQ_{\text{rev}}}{T}$$

The original irreversible process and the reversible restoration process constitute a cycle for which $\Delta U = 0$ and for which the work is therefore

$$-W = Q_{\text{rev}} = \int_B^A dQ_{\text{rev}}$$

However, according to statement 1a of the second law, Q_{rev} cannot be directed *into* the system, for the cycle would then be a process for the complete conversion into work of the heat absorbed. Thus, $\int dQ_{\text{rev}}$ is negative, and it follows that $S_A^t - S_B^t$ is also negative; whence $S_B^t > S_A^t$. Because the original irreversible process is adiabatic ($\Delta S_{\text{surr}} = 0$), the total entropy change of the system and surroundings as a result of the process is $\Delta S_{\text{total}} = S_B^t - S_A^t > 0$.

In arriving at this result, our presumption is that the original irreversible process results in an entropy change of the fluid. If the original process is in fact isentropic, then the system can be restored to its initial state by a simple reversible adiabatic process. This cycle is accomplished with no heat transfer and therefore with no net work. Thus the system is restored without leaving any change elsewhere, and this implies that the original process is reversible rather than irreversible.

Thus the same result is found for adiabatic processes as for direct heat transfer: ΔS_{total} is always positive, approaching zero as a limit when the process becomes reversible. This same conclusion can be demonstrated for any process whatever, leading to the general equation:

$$\boxed{\Delta S_{\text{total}} \geq 0} \tag{5.19}$$

This mathematical statement of the second law affirms that every process proceeds in such a direction that the *total* entropy change associated with it is positive, the limiting value of zero being attained only by a reversible process. No process is possible for which the total entropy decreases.

We return now to a cyclic heat engine that takes in heat $|Q_H|$ from a heat reservoir at T_H, and discards heat $|Q_C|$ to another heat reservoir at T_C. Because the engine operates in cycles, it undergoes no net changes in its properties. The total entropy change of the process is therefore the sum of the entropy changes of the heat reservoirs:

$$\Delta S_{\text{total}} = \frac{-|Q_H|}{T_H} + \frac{|Q_C|}{T_C}$$

The work produced by the engine as given by Eq. (5.1) is $|W| = |Q_H| - |Q_C|$. Elimination of $|Q_C|$ between these two equations and solution for $|W|$ gives

$$|W| = -T_C\,\Delta S_{\text{total}} + |Q_H|\left(1 - \frac{T_C}{T_H}\right)$$

This is the general equation for work of a heat engine for temperature levels T_C and T_H. The minimum work output is zero, resulting when the engine is completely inefficient and the process degenerates into simple irreversible heat transfer between the two heat reservoirs. In this case solution for ΔS_{total} yields the equation obtained at the beginning of this section. The maximum work is obtained when the engine is reversible, in which case $\Delta S_{\text{total}} = 0$, and the equation reduces to the second term on the right, the work of a Carnot engine.

Example 5.4

A 40-kg steel casting (C_P = 0.5 kJ kg^{-1} K^{-1}) at a temperature of 450°C (723.15 K) is quenched in 150 kg of oil (C_P = 2.5 kJ kg^{-1} K^{-1}) at 25°C (298.15 K). If there are no heat losses, what is the change in entropy of (*a*) the casting, (*b*) the oil, and (*c*) both considered together?

Solution

The final temperature t of the oil and the steel casting is found by an energy balance. Because the change in energy of the oil and steel together must be zero,

$$(40)(0.5)(t - 450) + (150)(2.5)(t - 25) = 0$$

Solution yields $t = 46.52$°C or T = 319.67 K

(*a*) Change in entropy of the casting:

$$\Delta S^t = m\int \frac{C_P\,dT}{T} = mC_P \ln\frac{T_2}{T_1}$$

$$= (40)(0.5)\ln\frac{273.15 + 46.52}{273.15 + 450} = -16.33 \text{ kJ K}^{-1}$$

(*b*) Change in entropy of the oil:

$$\Delta S^t = (150)(2.5)\ln\frac{273.15 + 46.52}{273.15 + 25} = 26.13 \text{ kJ K}^{-1}$$

(*c*) Total entropy change:

$$\Delta S_{\text{total}} = -16.33 + 26.13 = 9.80 \text{ kJ K}^{-1}$$

Note that although the total entropy change is positive, the entropy of the casting has decreased.

5.7 ENTROPY BALANCE FOR OPEN SYSTEMS

Just as an energy balance can be written for processes in which fluid enters, exits, or flows through a control volume (Sec. 2.12), so too can an entropy balance be written. There is, however, an important difference: *Entropy is not conserved.* The second law states that the *total* entropy change associated with any process must be positive, with a limiting value of zero for a reversible process. This requirement is taken into account by writing the entropy balance for both the system and its surroundings, considered together, and by including an *entropy-generation* term to account for the irreversibilities of the process. This term is the sum of three others: one for the difference in entropy between exit and entrance streams, one for entropy change within the control volume, and one for entropy change in the surroundings. If the process is reversible, these three terms sum to zero, making $\Delta S_{\text{total}} = 0$. If the process is irreversible, they sum to a positive quantity, the entropy-generation term.

The statement of balance, expressed as rates, is therefore:

$$\left\{\begin{array}{c}\text{Net rate of}\\ \text{change in}\\ \text{entropy of}\\ \text{flowing streams}\end{array}\right\} + \left\{\begin{array}{c}\text{Time rate of}\\ \text{change of}\\ \text{entropy}\\ \text{in control}\\ \text{volume}\end{array}\right\} + \left\{\begin{array}{c}\text{Time rate of}\\ \text{change of}\\ \text{entropy in}\\ \text{surroundings}\end{array}\right\} = \left\{\begin{array}{c}\text{Total rate}\\ \text{of entropy}\\ \text{generation}\end{array}\right\}$$

The equivalent *equation of entropy balance* is

$$\Delta(S\dot{m})_{\text{fs}} + \frac{d(mS)_{\text{cv}}}{dt} + \frac{dS^t_{\text{surr}}}{dt} = \dot{S}_G \geq 0 \qquad (5.20)$$

where $\dot{S}_G$ is the rate of entropy generation. This equation is the general *rate* form of the entropy balance, applicable at any instant. Each term can vary with time. The first term is simply the net rate of gain in entropy of the flowing streams, i.e., the difference between the total entropy transported out by exit streams and the total entropy transported in by entrance streams. The second term is the time rate of change of the total entropy of the fluid contained within the control volume. The third term is the time rate of change of the entropy of the surroundings, resulting from heat transfer between system and surroundings.

Let rate of heat transfer $\dot{Q}_j$ with respect to a particular part of the control surface be associated with $T_{\sigma,j}$ where subscript σ, j denotes a temperature in the surroundings. The rate of entropy change in the surroundings as a result of this transfer is then $-\dot{Q}_j/T_{\sigma,j}$. The minus sign converts $\dot{Q}_j$, defined with respect to the system, to a heat rate with respect to the surroundings. The third term in Eq. (5.20) is therefore the sum of all such quantities:

$$\frac{dS^t_{\text{surr}}}{dt} = -\sum_j \frac{\dot{Q}_j}{T_{\sigma,j}}$$

Equation (5.20) is now written:

$$\boxed{\Delta(S\dot{m})_{\text{fs}} + \frac{d(mS)_{\text{cv}}}{dt} - \sum_j \frac{\dot{Q}_j}{T_{\sigma,j}} = \dot{S}_G \geq 0} \qquad (5.21)$$

The final term, representing the *rate of entropy generation* $\dot{S}_G$, reflects the second-law requirement that it be positive for irreversible processes. There are two sources of irreversibility: (*a*) those *within* the control volume, i.e., *internal* irreversibilities, and (*b*) those resulting from heat transfer across finite temperature differences between system and surroundings, i.e., *external* thermal irreversibilities. In the limiting case where $\dot{S}_G = 0$, the process must be *completely reversible*, implying the following:

- The process is internally reversible within the control volume.
- Heat transfer between the control volume and its surroundings is reversible.

The second item means either that heat reservoirs are included in the surroundings with temperatures equal to those of the control surface or that Carnot engines are interposed in the surroundings between the control-surface temperatures and the heat-reservoir temperatures.

For a steady-state flow process the mass and entropy of the fluid in the control volume are constant, and $d(mS)_{cv}/dt$ is zero. Equation (5.21) then becomes

$$\Delta(S\dot{m})_{fs} - \sum_j \frac{\dot{Q}_j}{T_{\sigma,j}} = \dot{S}_G \geq 0 \qquad (5.22)$$

If in addition there is but one entrance and one exit, with $\dot{m}$ the same for both streams, dividing through by $\dot{m}$ yields

$$\Delta S - \sum_j \frac{Q_j}{T_{\sigma,j}} = S_G \geq 0 \qquad (5.23)$$

Each term in Eq. (5.23) is based on a unit amount of fluid flowing through the control volume.

Example 5.5

In a steady-state flow process, 1 mol s^{-1} of air at 600 K (326.85°C) and 1 atm is continuously mixed with 2 mol s^{-1} of air at 450 K (176.85°C) and 1 atm. The product stream is at 400 K (126.85°C) and 1 atm. A schematic representation of the process is shown in Fig. 5.7. Determine the rate of heat transfer and the rate of entropy generation for the process. Assume that air is an ideal gas with $C_P = (7/2)R$, that the surroundings are at 300 K (26.85°C), and that kinetic- and potential-energy changes are negligible.

Solution

By Eq. (2.30), with $\dot{m}$ replaced by $\dot{n}$,

$$\dot{Q} = \dot{n}H - \dot{n}_A H_A - \dot{n}_B H_B = \dot{n}_A(H - H_A) + \dot{n}_B(H - H_B)$$

$$= \dot{n}_A C_P(T - T_A) + \dot{n}_B C_P(T - T_B) = C_P\,[\dot{n}_A(T - T_A) + \dot{n}_B(T - T_B)]$$

$$= (7/2)(8.314)\,[(1)(400 - 600) + (2)(400 - 450)] = -8729.7 \text{ J s}^{-1}$$

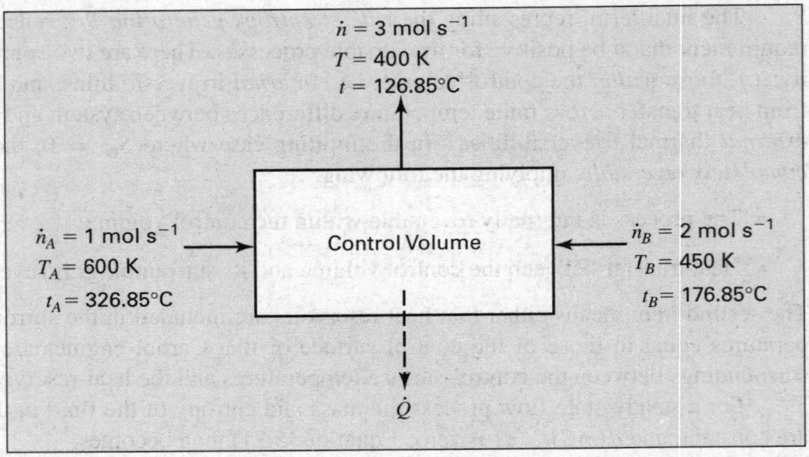

Figure 5.7: Process described in Ex. 5.5

By Eq. (5.22), again with $\dot{m}$ replaced by $\dot{n}$,

$$\dot{S}_G = \dot{n}S - \dot{n}_A S_A - \dot{n}_B S_B - \frac{\dot{Q}}{T_\sigma} = \dot{n}_A(S - S_A) + \dot{n}_B(S - S_B) - \frac{\dot{Q}}{T_\sigma}$$

$$= \dot{n}_A C_P \ln \frac{T}{T_A} + \dot{n}_B C_P \ln \frac{T}{T_B} - \frac{\dot{Q}}{T_\sigma} = C_P \left(\dot{n}_A \ln \frac{T}{T_A} + \dot{n}_B \ln \frac{T}{T_B} \right) - \frac{\dot{Q}}{T_\sigma}$$

$$= (7/2)(8.314) \left[(1) \ln \frac{400}{600} + (2) \ln \frac{400}{450} \right] + \frac{8729.7}{300} = 10.446 \text{ J K}^{-1} \text{ s}^{-1}$$

The rate of entropy generation is positive, as it must be for any real process.

Example 5.6

An inventor claims to have devised a process which takes in only saturated steam at 100°C (373.15 K) and which by a complicated series of steps makes heat continuously available at a temperature level of 200°C (473.15 K), where 2000 kJ of energy as heat is liberated for every kilogram of steam taken into the process. Show whether or not this process is possible. To give this process the most favorable conditions, assume cooling water available in unlimited quantity at a temperature of 0°C (273.15 K).

Solution

For any process to be even theoretically possible, it must meet the requirements of the first and second laws of thermodynamics. The detailed mechanism need not be known to determine whether this is the case; only the overall result is required. If the claims of the inventor satisfy the laws of thermodynamics, means for realizing the claims are theoretically possible. The determination of a mechanism is then a

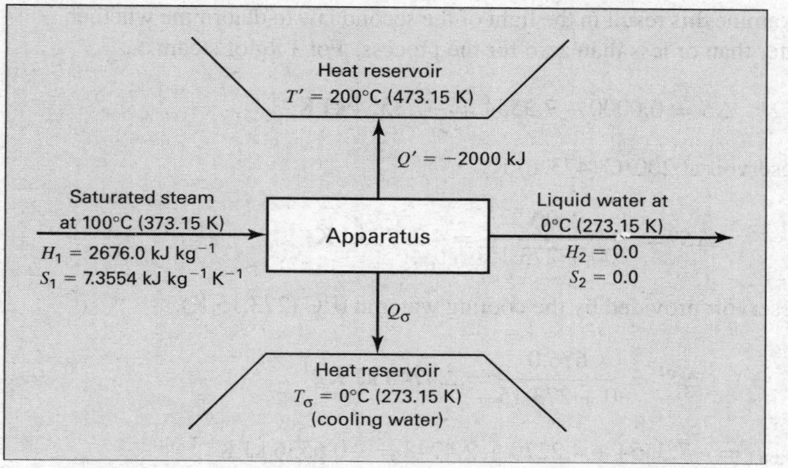

Figure 5.8: Process described in Ex. 5.6

matter of ingenuity. Otherwise, the process is impossible, and no mechanism for carrying it out can be devised.

In the present instance, a continuous process takes in saturated steam, and heat is made continuously available at a temperature level $t'/T' = 200°C/473.15$ K. Because cooling water is available at $t_a/T_a = 0°C/273.15$ K, maximum use is made of the steam if it leaves the process at this temperature. Assume therefore that the steam is condensed, cooled, and discharged from the process at 0°C (273.15 K) and at atmospheric pressure. *All* the heat liberated in this operation cannot be made available at temperature level $t'/T' = 200°C$ (473.15 K), because this would violate statement 2 of the second law. We must suppose that some heat Q_σ is transferred to the cooling water at $t_a/T_a = 0°C$ (273.15 K). Moreover, the process must satisfy the first law; thus by Eq. (2.33):

$$\Delta H = Q + W_s$$

where ΔH is the enthalpy change of the steam as it flows through the apparatus and Q is the *total* heat transfer between the apparatus and its surroundings. Because no shaft work accompanies the process, $W_s = 0$. The surroundings consist of cooling water, which acts as a heat reservoir at the constant temperature of $t_a/T_a = 0°C$ (273.15 K), and a heat reservoir at $t'/T' = 200°C/473.15$ K to which heat in the amount of 2000 kJ is transferred for each kilogram of steam entering the apparatus. The diagram of Fig. 5.8 indicates the overall results of the process.

The values of H and S for saturated steam at 100°C (373.15 K) and for liquid water at 0°C (273.15 K) are taken from the steam tables (App. F). The total heat transfer is

$$Q = Q' + Q_\sigma = -2000 + Q_\sigma$$

Thus on the basis of 1 kg of entering steam, the first law becomes

$$\Delta H = 0.0 - 2676.0 = -2000 + Q_\sigma \qquad \text{and} \qquad Q_\sigma = -676.0 \text{ kJ}$$

We now examine this result in the light of the second law to determine whether ΔS_{total} is greater than or less than zero for the process. For 1 kg of steam,

$$\Delta S = 0.0000 - 7.3554 = -7.3554 \text{ kJ K}^{-1}$$

For the heat reservoir at 200°C (473.15 K),

$$\Delta S^t = \frac{2000}{200 + 273.15} = 4.2270 \text{ kJ K}^{-1}$$

For the heat reservoir provided by the cooling water at 0°C (273.15 K),

$$\Delta S^t = \frac{676.0}{0 + 273.15} = 2.4748 \text{ kJ K}^{-1}$$

Thus, $$\Delta S_{\text{total}} = -7.3554 + 4.2270 + 2.4748 = -0.6536 \text{ kJ K}^{-1}$$

This result means that the process as described is impossible, because Eq. (5.19) requires $\Delta S_{\text{total}} \geq 0$.

This does not mean that all processes of this general nature are impossible, but only that the inventor has claimed too much. Indeed, the maximum amount of heat which can be transferred to the heat reservoir at 200°C (473.15 K) is readily calculated. The energy balance is

$$Q' + Q_\sigma = \Delta H \qquad (A)$$

Similarly, the entropy balance of Eq. (5.23) is

$$\Delta S = \frac{Q'}{T'} + \frac{Q_\sigma}{T_\sigma} + S_G$$

The maximum heat rejection to the hot reservoir occurs when the process is completely reversible, in which case $S_G = 0$, and

$$\frac{Q'}{T'} + \frac{Q_\sigma}{T_\sigma} = \Delta S \qquad (B)$$

Combination of Eqs. (*A*) and (*B*) and solution for Q' yields

$$Q' = \frac{T'}{T' - T_\sigma}(\Delta H - T_\sigma \, \Delta S)$$

With $T_\sigma = 273.15$ K and $T' = 473.15$ K, this becomes

$$Q' = \frac{473.15}{200}(-2676.0 + 273.15 \times 7.3554) = -1577.7 \text{ kJ kg}^{-1}$$

This value of Q' is *smaller* in magnitude than the -2000 kJ kg^{-1} claimed. One also notes that the inventor's claim implies a negative rate of entropy generation.

5.8 CALCULATION OF IDEAL WORK

In any steady-state flow process requiring work, there is an absolute minimum amount which must be expended to accomplish the desired change of state of the fluid flowing through the control volume. In a process producing work, there is an absolute maximum amount which may be accomplished as the result of a given change of state of the fluid flowing through the control volume. In either case, the limiting value obtains when the change of state associated with the process is accomplished *completely reversibly*. For such a process, the entropy generation is zero, and Eq. (5.22), written for the uniform surroundings temperature T_σ, becomes

$$\Delta(S\dot{m})_{\text{fs}} - \frac{\dot{Q}}{T_\sigma} = 0 \qquad \text{or} \qquad \dot{Q} = T_\sigma\,\Delta(S\dot{m})_{\text{fs}}$$

Substitute this expression for $\dot{Q}$ in the energy balance, Eq. (2.30):

$$\Delta\left[\left(H + \tfrac{1}{2}u^2 + zg\right)\dot{m}\right]_{\text{fs}} = T_\sigma\,\Delta(S\dot{m})_{\text{fs}} + \dot{W}_s(\text{rev})$$

The shaft work, $\dot{W}_s(\text{rev})$, is here the work of a completely reversible process. If $\dot{W}_s(\text{rev})$ is given the name *ideal work*, $\dot{W}_{\text{ideal}}$, the preceding equation may be rewritten:

$$\dot{W}_{\text{ideal}} = \Delta\left[\left(H + \tfrac{1}{2}u^2 + zg\right)\dot{m}\right]_{\text{fs}} - T_\sigma\,\Delta(S\dot{m})_{\text{fs}} \tag{5.24}$$

In most applications to chemical processes, the kinetic- and potential-energy terms are negligible compared with the others; in this event Eq. (5.24) reduces to

$$\boxed{\dot{W}_{\text{ideal}} = \Delta(H\dot{m})_{\text{fs}} - T_\sigma\,\Delta(S\dot{m})_{\text{fs}}} \tag{5.25}$$

For the special case of a single stream flowing through the control volume, the terms of Eq. (5.25) may be expressed as rates or upon division by $\dot{m}$ on the basis of a unit amount of fluid flowing through the control volume. Thus,

$$\dot{W}_{\text{ideal}} = \dot{m}(\Delta H - T_\sigma\,\Delta S) \quad (5.26) \qquad W_{\text{ideal}} = \Delta H - T_\sigma\,\Delta S \quad (5.27)$$

A completely reversible process is hypothetical, devised solely for determination of the ideal work associated with a given change of state.

The only connection between the hypothetical reversible process and the actual process is that both are associated with the same change of state.

Our objective is to compare the actual work of a process with the work of the hypothetical reversible process. No description is ever required of hypothetical processes devised for the calculation of ideal work. One need only realize that such processes may always be imagined. Nevertheless, an illustration of a hypothetical reversible process is given in Ex. 5.7.

Equations (5.24) through (5.27) give the work of a completely reversible process associated with given property changes in the flowing streams. When the same property changes occur in an actual process, the actual work $\dot{W}_s$ (or W_s) as given by an energy balance, can be compared with the ideal work. When $\dot{W}_{\text{ideal}}$ (or W_{ideal}) is positive, it is the *minimum work required* to bring about a given change in the properties of the flowing streams, and is smaller than $\dot{W}_s$. In this case a thermodynamic efficiency η_t is defined as the ratio of the ideal work to the actual work:

$$\eta_t(\text{work required}) = \frac{\dot{W}_{\text{ideal}}}{\dot{W}_s} \tag{5.28}$$

When $\dot{W}_{\text{ideal}}$ (or W_{ideal}) is negative, $|\dot{W}_{\text{ideal}}|$ is the *maximum work obtainable* from a given change in the properties of the flowing streams, and is larger than $|\dot{W}_s|$. In this case, the thermodynamic efficiency is defined as the ratio of the actual work to the ideal work:

$$\eta_t(\text{work produced}) = \frac{\dot{W}_s}{\dot{W}_{\text{ideal}}} \tag{5.29}$$

Example 5.7

What is the maximum work that can be obtained in a steady-state flow process from 1 mol of nitrogen (assumed an ideal gas) at 800 K and 50 bar? Take the temperature and pressure of the surroundings as 300 K and 1.0133 bar.

Solution

The maximum possible work is obtained from any completely reversible process that reduces the nitrogen to the temperature and pressure of the surroundings, i.e., to 300 K (26.85°C) and 1.0133 bar. (Any gain in work done by the nitrogen because of a final temperature or pressure below that of the surroundings would be at least equaled by the work required to produce the final condition.) What is required here is the calculation of W_{ideal} by Eq. (5.27), in which ΔS and ΔH are the molar entropy and enthalpy changes of the nitrogen as its state changes from 800 K (526.85°C) and 50 bar to 300 K (26.85°C) and 1.0133 bar. For an ideal gas, enthalpy is independent of pressure, and its change is given by

$$\Delta H = \int_{T_1}^{T_2} C_P^{ig}\, dT$$

The value of this integral is found from Eq. (4.7), and is represented by

$$8.314 \times \text{ICPH(800,300;3.280,0.593E-3,0.0,0.040E+5)} = -15\,060 \text{ J mol}^{-1}$$

The parameters in the heat-capacity equation for nitrogen come from Table C.1.

Similarly, the entropy change is found from Eq. (5.14), here written:

$$\Delta S = \int_{T_1}^{T_2} C_P^{ig} \frac{dT}{T} - R \ln \frac{P_2}{P_1}$$

The value of the integral, found from Eq. (5.15), is represented by

$$8.314 \times \text{ICPS(800,300;3.280,0.593E-3,0.0,0.040E+5)}$$

$$= -29.373 \text{ J mol}^{-1} \text{ K}^{-1}$$

Whence, $\Delta S = -29.373 - 8.314 \ln \dfrac{1.0133}{50} = 3.042 \text{ J mol}^{-1} \text{ K}^{-1}$

With these values of ΔH and ΔS, Eq. (5.27) becomes

$$W_{\text{ideal}} = -15\,060 - (300)(3.042) = -15\,973 \text{ J mol}^{-1}$$

The significance of this simple calculation becomes evident from examination of the steps of a specific reversible process designed to bring about the given change of state. Suppose the nitrogen is continuously changed to its final state at 1.0133 bar and $T_2 = T_\sigma = 300$ K (26.85°C) by the following two-step process:

- **Step 1** Reversible, adiabatic expansion (as in a turbine) from initial state P_1, T_1, H_1 to 1.0133 bar. Let T' denote the discharge temperature.
- **Step 2** Cooling (or heating, if T' is less than T_2) to the final temperature T_2 at a constant pressure of 1.0133 bar.

For step 1, a steady-state flow process, the energy balance is $Q + W_s = \Delta H$. Because the process is adiabatic, this reduces to

$$W_s = \Delta H = (H' - H_1)$$

where H' is the enthalpy at the intermediate state of T' and 1.0133 bar.

For maximum work production, step 2 must also be reversible, with heat transferred reversibly to the surroundings at T_σ. These requirements are met by use of Carnot engines which receive heat from the nitrogen, produce work W_{Carnot}, and reject heat to the surroundings at T_σ. Because the temperature of the heat source, the nitrogen, decreases from T' to T_2, Eq. (5.8) for the work of a Carnot engine is written in differential form:

$$dW_{\text{Carnot}} = \left(1 - \frac{T_\sigma}{T}\right) dQ$$

Here dQ refers to the nitrogen, which is taken as the system. Integration yields

$$W_{\text{Carnot}} = Q - T_\sigma \int_{T'}^{T_2} \frac{dQ}{T}$$

The first term on the right is the heat transferred with respect to the nitrogen, given by $Q = H_2 - H'$. The integral is the change in entropy of the nitrogen as it is cooled by the Carnot engines. Because step 1 occurs at constant entropy, the integral also represents ΔS for both steps. Hence,

$$W_{\text{Carnot}} = (H_2 - H') - T_\sigma \, \Delta S$$

The sum of W_s and W_{Carnot} gives the ideal work; thus,

$$W_{\text{ideal}} = (H' - H_1) + (H_2 - H') - T_\sigma\,\Delta S = (H_2 - H_1) - T_\sigma\,\Delta S$$

or

$$W_{\text{ideal}} = \Delta H - T_\sigma\,\Delta S$$

which is the same as Eq. (5.27).

This derivation makes clear the difference between W_s, the ideal (reversible adiabatic) shaft work of the turbine, and W_{ideal}. The ideal work includes not only the ideal shaft work, but also all work obtainable by the operation of heat engines for the reversible transfer of heat to the surroundings at T_σ.

Example 5.8

Rework Ex. 5.6, making use of the equation for ideal work.

Solution

The procedure here is to calculate the maximum possible work W_{ideal} which can be obtained from 1 kg of steam in a flow process as it undergoes a change in state from saturated steam at 100°C (373.15 K) to liquid water at 0°C (273.15 K). Now the problem reduces to the question of whether this amount of work is sufficient to operate a Carnot refrigerator rejecting 2000 kJ as heat at 200°C (473.15 K) and taking heat from the unlimited supply of cooling water at 0°C (273.15 K).

For the steam,

$$\Delta H = 0 - 2676.0 = -2676.0 \qquad \Delta S = 0 - 7.3554 = -7.3554$$

With negligible kinetic- and potential-energy terms, Eq. (5.27) yields:

$$W_{\text{ideal}} = \Delta H - T_\sigma\,\Delta S = -2676.0 - (273.15)(-7.3554) = -666.9 \text{ kJ kg}^{-1}$$

If this amount of work, numerically the maximum obtainable from the steam, is used to drive the Carnot refrigerator operating between the temperatures of 0°C (273.15 K) and 200°C (473.15 K), the heat rejected is found from Eq. (5.8), solved for $|Q|$:

$$|Q| = |W|\frac{T}{T_\sigma - T} = (666.9)\left(\frac{200 + 273.15}{200 - 0}\right) = 1577.7 \text{ kJ}$$

This is the maximum possible heat release at 200°C (473.15 K); it is less than the claimed value of 2000 kJ. As in Ex. 5.6, we conclude that the process described is not possible.

5.9 LOST WORK

Work that is wasted as the result of irreversibilities in a process is called *lost work*, W_{lost}, and is defined as the difference between the actual work of a process and the ideal work for the process. Thus by definition,

$$W_{\text{lost}} \equiv W_s - W_{\text{ideal}} \tag{5.30}$$

In terms of rates,

$$\dot{W}_{\text{lost}} \equiv \dot{W}_s - \dot{W}_{\text{ideal}} \tag{5.31}$$

The actual work rate comes from Eq. (2.30), and the ideal work rate is given by Eq. (5.24):

$$\dot{W}_s = \Delta\left[\left(H + \tfrac{1}{2}u^2 + zg\right)\dot{m}\right]_{\text{fs}} - \dot{Q}$$

$$\dot{W}_{\text{ideal}} = \Delta\left[\left(H + \tfrac{1}{2}u^2 + zg\right)\dot{m}\right]_{\text{fs}} - T_\sigma\,\Delta(S\dot{m})_{\text{fs}}$$

Substituting these expressions for $\dot{W}_s$ and $\dot{W}_{\text{ideal}}$ in Eq. (5.31) yields

$$\boxed{\dot{W}_{\text{lost}} = T_\sigma\,\Delta(S\dot{m})_{\text{fs}} - \dot{Q}} \tag{5.32}$$

For the case of a single surroundings temperature T_σ, Eq. (5.22) becomes

$$\dot{S}_G = \Delta(S\dot{m})_{\text{fs}} - \frac{\dot{Q}}{T_\sigma} \tag{5.33}$$

Multiplication by T_σ gives:

$$T_\sigma\,\dot{S}_G = T_\sigma\,\Delta(S\dot{m})_{\text{fs}} - \dot{Q}$$

The right sides of this equation and Eq. (5.32) are identical; therefore,

$$\boxed{\dot{W}_{\text{lost}} = T_\sigma\,\dot{S}_G} \tag{5.34}$$

As a consequence of the second law, $\dot{S}_G \geq 0$; it follows that $\dot{W}_{\text{lost}} \geq 0$. When a process is completely reversible, the equality holds, and $\dot{W}_{\text{lost}} = 0$. For irreversible processes the inequality holds, and $\dot{W}_{\text{lost}}$, i.e., the energy that becomes unavailable for work, is positive.

The engineering significance of this result is clear: The greater the irreversibility of a process, the greater the rate of entropy production and the greater the amount of energy that becomes unavailable for work. Thus every irreversibility carries with it a price.

For the special case of a single stream flowing through the control volume, $\dot{m}$ factors, and becomes a multiplier of the entropy difference in Eqs. (5.32) and (5.33). Then, division by $\dot{m}$, converts all terms to the basis of a unit amount of fluid flowing through the control volume. Thus,

$\dot{W}_{\text{lost}} = \dot{m}T_\sigma\,\Delta S - \dot{Q}$ (5.35)	$W_{\text{lost}} = T_\sigma\,\Delta S - Q$ (5.36)
$\dot{S}_G = \dot{m}\,\Delta S - \dfrac{\dot{Q}}{T_\sigma}$ (5.37)	$S_G = \Delta S - \dfrac{Q}{T_\sigma}$ (5.38)

Equations (5.36) and (5.38) combine for a unit amount of fluid to give

$$W_{\text{lost}} = T_\sigma S_G \tag{5.39}$$

Again, because $S_G \geq 0$, it follows that $W_{\text{lost}} \geq 0$.

Example 5.9

The two basic types of steady-flow heat exchanger are characterized by their flow patterns: *cocurrent* and *countercurrent*. The two types are indicated in Fig. 5.9. In cocurrent flow, heat is transferred from a hot stream, flowing from left to right, to a cold stream flowing in the same direction, as indicated by arrows. In countercurrent flow, the cold stream, again flowing from left to right, receives heat from the hot stream flowing in the opposite direction.

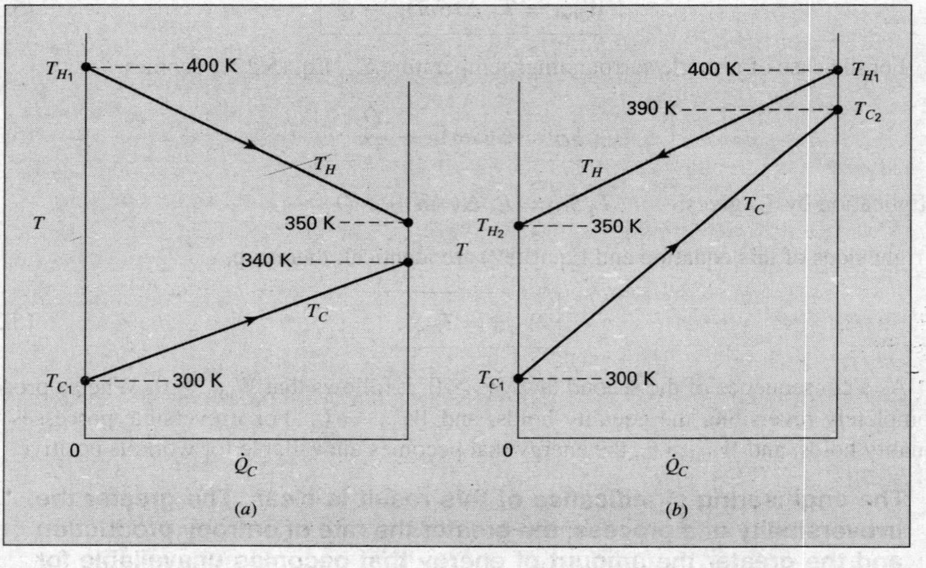

Figure 5.9: Heat exchangers. (*a*) Case I, cocurrent. (*b*) Case II, countercurrent.

The lines relate the temperatures of the hot and cold streams, T_H and T_C respectively, to $\dot{Q}_C$, the accumulated rate of heat addition to the cold stream as it progresses through the exchanger from the left end to an arbitrary downstream location. Consider the two cases, for each of which the following specifications apply:

$$T_{H_1} = 400 \text{ K} \qquad T_{H_2} = 350 \text{ K} \qquad T_{C_1} = 300 \text{ K} \qquad \dot{n}_H = 1 \text{ mol s}^{-1}$$

The minimum temperature difference between the flowing streams is 10 K. Assume that both streams are ideal gases with $C_P = (7/2)R$. Find the lost work for both cases. Take $T_\sigma = 300$ K.

Solution

The following equations apply to both cases. Assume negligible kinetic- and potential-energy changes. Also $\dot{W}_s = 0$, and therefore by Eq. (2.30):

$$\dot{n}_H(\Delta H)_H + \dot{n}_C(\Delta H)_C = 0$$

or in view of Eq. (3.28),

$$\dot{n}_H C_P(T_{H_2} - T_{H_1}) + \dot{n}_C C_P(T_{C_2} - T_{C_1}) = 0 \qquad (A)$$

The total rate of entropy change for the flowing streams is

$$\Delta(S\dot{n})_{\text{fs}} = \dot{n}_H(\Delta S)_H + \dot{n}_C(\Delta S)_C$$

By Eq. (5.14), with the assumption of negligible pressure change in the flowing streams, this becomes,

$$\Delta(S\dot{n})_{\text{fs}} = \dot{n}_H C_P\left(\ln\frac{T_{H_2}}{T_{H_1}} + \frac{\dot{n}_C}{\dot{n}_H}\ln\frac{T_{C_2}}{T_{C_1}}\right) \qquad (B)$$

Finally, by Eq. (5.32), with negligible heat transfer to the surroundings,

$$\dot{W}_{\text{lost}} = T_\sigma\,\Delta(S\dot{n})_{\text{fs}} \qquad (C)$$

- **Case I** Cocurrent flow. By Eqs. (*A*), (*B*), and (*C*),

$$\frac{\dot{n}_C}{\dot{n}_H} = \frac{400 - 350}{340 - 300} = 1.25$$

$$\Delta(S\dot{n})_{\text{fs}} = (1)(7/2)(8.314)\left(\ln\frac{350}{400} + 1.25\ln\frac{340}{300}\right) = 0.667 \text{ J K}^{-1}\text{ s}^{-1}$$

$$\dot{W}_{\text{lost}} = (300)(0.667) = 200.1 \text{ J s}^{-1} \text{ or } 200.1 \text{ W}$$

- **Case II** Countercurrent flow. By Eqs. (*A*), (*B*), and (*C*),

$$\frac{\dot{n}_C}{\dot{n}_H} = \frac{400 - 350}{390 - 300} = 0.5556$$

$$\Delta(S\dot{n})_{\text{fs}} = (1)(7/2)(8.314)\left(\ln\frac{350}{400} + 0.5556\ln\frac{390}{300}\right) = 0.356 \text{ J K}^{-1}\text{ s}^{-1}$$

$$\dot{W}_{\text{lost}} = (300)(0.356) = 106.7 \text{ J s}^{-1} \text{ or } 106.7 \text{ W}$$

Although the total rate of heat transfer is the same for both exchangers, the temperature rise of the cold stream in countercurrent flow is more than twice that for cocurrent flow. On the other hand, the flow rate of the heated gas in the former is less than half that of the latter. From the thermodynamic point of view, the countercurrent case is much more efficient. Because $\Delta(S\dot{n})_{\text{fs}} = \dot{S}_G$, both the rate of entropy generation and the lost work for the cocurrent case are nearly twice the values for the countercurrent case.

5.10 THE THIRD LAW OF THERMODYNAMICS

Measurements of heat capacities at very low temperatures provide data for the calculation from Eq. (5.13) of entropy changes down to 0 K. When these calculations are made for different crystalline forms of the same chemical species, the entropy at 0 K appears to be the same for all forms. When the form is noncrystalline, e.g., amorphous or glassy, calculations show that the entropy of the more random form is greater than that of the crystalline form. Such calculations, which are summarized elsewhere,[3] lead to the postulate that *the absolute entropy is zero for all perfect crystalline substances at absolute zero temperature.* While the essential ideas were advanced by Nernst and Planck at the beginning of the twentieth century, more recent studies at very low temperatures have increased confidence in this postulate, which is now accepted as the third law.

If the entropy is zero at $T = 0$ K, then Eq. (5.13) lends itself to the calculation of absolute entropies. With $T = 0$ as the lower limit of integration, the absolute entropy of a gas at temperature T based on calorimetric data is

$$S = \int_0^{T_f} \frac{(C_P)_s}{T} dT + \frac{\Delta H_f}{T_f} + \int_{T_f}^{T_v} \frac{(C_P)_l}{T} dT + \frac{\Delta H_v}{T_v} + \int_{T_v}^{T} \frac{(C_P)_g}{T} dT \tag{5.40}$$

This equation[4] is based on the supposition that no solid-state transitions take place and thus no heats of transition need appear. The only constant-temperature heat effects are those of fusion at T_f and vaporization at T_v. When a solid-phase transition occurs, a term $\Delta H_t/T_t$ is added.

5.11 ENTROPY FROM THE MICROSCOPIC VIEWPOINT

Because the molecules of an ideal gas do not interact, its internal energy resides with individual molecules. This is not true of the entropy. The microscopic interpretation of entropy is based on an entirely different concept, as suggested by the following example.

Suppose an insulated container, partitioned into two equal volumes, contains Avogadro's number N_A of ideal-gas molecules in one section and no molecules in the other. When the partition is withdrawn, the molecules quickly distribute themselves uniformly throughout the total volume. The process is an adiabatic expansion that accomplishes no work. Therefore,

$$\Delta U = C_V \Delta T = 0$$

and the temperature does not change. However, the pressure of the gas decreases by half, and the entropy change as given by Eq. (5.14) is:

$$\Delta S = -R \ln \frac{P_2}{P_1} = R \ln 2$$

[3] K. S. Pitzer, *Thermodynamics*, 3d ed., chap. 6, McGraw-Hill, New York, 1995.

[4] Evaluation of the first term on the right is not a problem for crystalline substances, because C_P/T remains finite as $T \to 0$.

Because this is the total entropy change, the process is clearly irreversible.

At the instant when the partition is removed the molecules occupy only half the space available to them. In this momentary initial state the molecules are not randomly distributed over the total volume to which they have access, but are crowded into just half the total volume. In this sense they are more ordered than they are in the final state of uniform distribution throughout the entire volume. Thus, the final state can be regarded as a more random, or more disordered, state than the initial state. Generalizing from this example, one is led to the notion that increasing disorder (or decreasing structure) on the molecular level corresponds to increasing entropy.

The means for expressing disorder in a quantitative way was developed by L. Boltzmann and J. W. Gibbs through a quantity Ω, defined as the *number of different ways* that microscopic particles can be distributed among the "states" accessible to them. It is given by the general formula

$$\Omega = \frac{N!}{(N_1!)(N_2!)(N_3!)\cdots} \tag{5.41}$$

where N is the total number of particles, and N_1, N_2, N_3, etc., represent the numbers of particles in "states" 1, 2, 3, etc. The term "state" denotes the condition of the microscopic particles, and the quotation marks distinguish this idea of state from the usual thermodynamic meaning as applied to a macroscopic system.

With respect to our example there are but two "states," representing location in one half or the other of the container. The total number of particles is N_A molecules, and initially they are all in a single "state." Thus

$$\Omega_1 = \frac{N_A!}{(N_A!)(0!)} = 1$$

This result confirms that initially the molecules can be distributed between the two accessible "states" in just one way. They are all in a given "state," all in just one half of the container. For an assumed final condition of uniform distribution of the molecules between the two halves of the container, $n_1 = n_2 = N_A/2$, and

$$\Omega_2 = \frac{N_A!}{[(N_A/2)!]^2}$$

This expression gives a very large number for Ω_2, indicating that the molecules can be distributed uniformly between the two "states" in many different ways. Many other values of Ω_2 are possible, each one of which is associated with a particular *nonuniform* distribution of the molecules between the two halves of the container. The ratio of a particular Ω_2 to the sum of all possible values is the probability of that particular distribution.

The connection established by Boltzmann between entropy S and Ω is given by the equation

$$S = k \ln \Omega \tag{5.42}$$

Boltzmann's constant k equals R/N_A. The entropy difference between states 1 and 2 is

$$S_2 - S_1 = k \ln \frac{\Omega_2}{\Omega_1}$$

Substituting values for Ω_1 and Ω_2 from our example into this expression gives

$$S_2 - S_1 = k \ln \frac{N_A!}{[(N_A/2)!]^2} = k[\ln N_A! - 2\ln(N_A/2)!]$$

Because N_A is very large, we take advantage of Stirling's formula for the logarithms of factorials of large numbers:

$$\ln X! = X \ln X - X$$

Whence,
$$S_2 - S_1 = k\left[N_A \ln N_A - N_A - 2\left(\frac{N_A}{2}\ln\frac{N_A}{2} - \frac{N_A}{2}\right)\right]$$

$$= kN_A \ln \frac{N_A}{N_A/2} = kN_A \ln 2 = R \ln 2$$

This value for the entropy change of the expansion process is the same as that given by Eq. (5.14), the classical thermodynamic formula for ideal gases.

Equations (5.41) and (5.42) are the basis for relating thermodynamic properties to statistical mechanics (Sec. 16.4).

PROBLEMS

5.1. Prove that it is impossible for two lines representing reversible, adiabatic processes on a PV diagram to intersect. (*Hint*: Assume that they do intersect, and complete the cycle with a line representing a reversible, isothermal process. Show that performance of this cycle violates the second law.)

5.2. A Carnot engine receives 250 kJ s^{-1} of heat from a heat-source reservoir at 525°C (798.15 K) and rejects heat to a heat-sink reservoir at 50°C (323.15 K). What are the power developed and the heat rejected?

5.3. The following heat engines produce power of 95 000 kW. Determine in each case the rates at which heat is absorbed from the hot reservoir and discarded to the cold reservoir.

(*a*) A Carnot engine operates between heat reservoirs at 750 K and 300 K.

(*b*) A practical engine operates between the same heat reservoirs but with a thermal efficiency $\eta = 0.35$.

5.4. A particular power plant operates with a heat-source reservoir at 350°C (623.15 K) and a heat-sink reservoir at 30°C (303.15 K). It has a thermal efficiency equal to 55% of the Carnot-engine thermal efficiency for the same temperatures.

(*a*) What is the thermal efficiency of the plant?

(*b*) To what temperature must the heat-source reservoir be raised to increase the thermal efficiency of the plant to 35%? Again η is 55% of the Carnot-engine value.

5.5. An egg, initially at rest, is dropped onto a concrete surface; it breaks. Prove that the process is irreversible. In modeling this process treat the egg as the system, and assume the passage of sufficient time for the egg to return to its initial temperature.

5.6. Which is the more effective way to increase the thermal efficiency of a Carnot engine: to increase T_H with T_C constant, or to decrease T_C with T_H constant? For a real engine, which would be the more *practical* way?

5.7. Large quantities of liquefied natural gas (LNG) are shipped by ocean tankers. At the unloading port provision is made for vaporization of the LNG so that it may be delivered to pipelines as gas. The LNG arrives in the tanker at atmospheric pressure and 113.7 K (−159.45°C), and represents a possible heat sink for use as the cold reservoir of a heat engine. For unloading of LNG as a vapor at the rate of 9000 m^3 s^{-1}, as measured at 25°C (298.15 K) and 1.0133 bar, and assuming the availability of an adequate heat source at 30°C (303.15 K), what is the maximum possible power obtainable and what is the rate of heat transfer from the heat source? Assume that LNG at 25°C (298.15 K) and 1.0133 bar is an ideal gas with the molar mass of 17. Also assume that the LNG vaporizes only, absorbing only its latent heat of 512 kJ kg^{-1} at 113.7 K (−159.45°C).

5.8. With respect to 1 kg of liquid water:

(*a*) Initially at 0°C (273.15 K), it is heated to 100°C (373.15 K) by contact with a heat reservoir at 100°C (373.15 K). What is the entropy change of the water? Of the heat reservoir? What is ΔS_{total}?

(*b*) Initially at 0°C (273.15 K), it is first heated to 50°C (323.15 K) by contact with a heat reservoir at 50°C (373.15 K) and then to 100°C (373.15 K) by contact with a reservoir at 100°C (373.15 K). What is ΔS_{total}?

(*c*) Explain how the water might be heated from 0°C to 100°C (273.15 K to 373.15 K) so that $\Delta S_{\text{total}} = 0$.

5.9. A rigid vessel of 0.06 m^3 volume contains an ideal gas, $C_V = (5/2)R$, at 500 K and 1 bar.

(*a*) If heat in the amount of 15 000 J is transferred to the gas, determine its entropy change.

(*b*) If the vessel is fitted with a stirrer that is rotated by a shaft so that work in the amount of 15 000 J is done on the gas, what is the entropy change of the gas if the process is adiabatic? What is ΔS_{total}? What is the irreversible feature of the process?

5.10. An ideal gas, $C_P = (7/2)R$, is heated in a steady-flow heat exchanger from 70°C (343.15 K) to 190°C (463.15 K) by another stream of the same ideal gas which enters at 320°C (593.15 K). The flow rates of the two streams are the same, and heat losses from the exchanger are negligible.

(*a*) Calculate the molar entropy changes of the two gas streams for both parallel and countercurrent flow in the exchanger.

(*b*) What is ΔS_{total} in each case?

(*c*) Repeat parts (*a*) and (*b*) for countercurrent flow if the heating stream enters at 200°C (473.15 K).

5.11. For an ideal gas with constant heat capacities, show that

(*a*) for a temperature change from T_1 to T_2, ΔS of the gas is greater when the change occurs at constant pressure than when it occurs at constant volume

(*b*) for a pressure change from P_1 to P_2, the sign of ΔS for an isothermal change is opposite that for a constant-volume change

5.12. For an ideal gas prove that

$$\frac{\Delta S}{R} = \int_{T_0}^{T} \frac{C_V^{ig}}{R} \frac{dT}{T} + \ln \frac{V}{V_0}$$

5.13. A Carnot engine operates between two *finite* heat reservoirs of total heat capacity C_H^t and C_C^t.

(*a*) Develop an expression relating T_C to T_H at any time.

(*b*) Determine an expression for the work obtained as a function of C_H^t, C_C^t, T_H, and the initial temperatures T_{H_0} and T_{C_0}.

(*c*) What is the *maximum* work obtainable? This corresponds to infinite time, when the reservoirs attain the same temperature.

In approaching this problem, use the differential form of Carnot's equation,

$$\frac{dQ_H}{dQ_C} = -\frac{T_H}{T_C}$$

and a differential energy balance for the engine,

$$dW - dQ_C - dQ_H = 0$$

Here, Q_C and Q_H refer to the *reservoirs*.

5.14. A Carnot engine operates between an infinite hot reservoir and a *finite* cold reservoir of total heat capacity C_C^t.

(*a*) Determine an expression for the work obtained as a function of C_C^t, T_H (= constant), T_C, and the initial cold-reservoir temperature T_{C_0}.

(*b*) What is the *maximum* work obtainable? This corresponds to infinite time, when T_C becomes equal to T_H.

The approach to this problem is the same as for Pb. 5.13.

5.15. A heat engine operating in outer space may be assumed equivalent to a Carnot engine operating between reservoirs at temperatures T_H and T_C. The only way heat can be discarded from the engine is by radiation, the rate of which is given (approximately) by:

$$|\dot{Q}_C| = kAT_C^4$$

where k is a constant and A is the area of the radiator. Prove that, for fixed power output $|\dot{W}|$ and for fixed temperature T_H, the radiator area A is a minimum when the temperature ratio T_C/T_H is 0.75.

5.16. Imagine that a stream of fluid in steady-state flow serves as a heat source for an infinite set of Carnot engines, each of which absorbs a differential amount of heat from the fluid, causing its temperature to decrease by a differential amount, and each of which rejects a differential amount of heat to a heat reservoir at temperature T_σ. As a result of the operation of the Carnot engines, the temperature of the fluid decreases from T_1 to T_2. Equation (5.8) applies here in differential form, wherein η is defined as

$$\eta \equiv dW/dQ$$

where Q is heat transfer with respect to the flowing fluid. Show that the total work of the Carnot engines is given by

$$W = Q - T_\sigma \Delta S$$

where ΔS and Q both refer to the fluid. In a particular case the fluid is an ideal gas, $C_P = (7/2)R$, for which $T_1 = 600$ K and $T_2 = 400$ K. If $T_\sigma = 300$ K, what is the value of W in J mol^{-1}? How much heat is discarded to the heat reservoir at T_σ? What is the entropy change of the heat reservoir? What is ΔS_{total}?

5.17. A Carnot engine operates between temperature levels of 600 K and 300 K. It drives a Carnot refrigerator, which provides cooling at 250 K and discards heat at 300 K. Determine a numerical value for the ratio of heat extracted by the refrigerator ("cooling load") to the heat delivered to the engine ("heating load").

5.18. An ideal gas with constant heat capacities undergoes a change of state from conditions T_1, P_1 to conditions T_2, P_2. Determine ΔH (J mol^{-1}) and ΔS (J mol^{-1} K^{-1}) for one of the following cases.

(*a*) $T_1 = 300$ K, $P_1 = 1.2$ bar, $T_2 = 450$ K, $P_2 = 6$ bar, $C_P/R = 7/2$.
(*b*) $T_1 = 300$ K, $P_1 = 1.2$ bar, $T_2 = 500$ K, $P_2 = 6$ bar, $C_P/R = 7/2$.
(*c*) $T_1 = 450$ K, $P_1 = 10$ bar, $T_2 = 300$ K, $P_2 = 2$ bar, $C_P/R = 5/2$.
(*d*) $T_1 = 400$ K, $P_1 = 6$ bar, $T_2 = 300$ K, $P_2 = 1.2$ bar, $C_P/R = 9/2$.
(*e*) $T_1 = 500$ K, $P_1 = 6$ bar, $T_2 = 300$ K, $P_2 = 1.2$ bar, $C_P/R = 4$.

5.19. An ideal gas, $C_P = (7/2)R$ and $C_V = (5/2)R$, undergoes a cycle consisting of the following mechanically reversible steps:

- An adiabatic compression from P_1, V_1, T_1 to P_2, V_2, T_2
- An isobaric expansion from P_2, V_2, T_2 to $P_3 = P_2, V_3, T_3$

- An adiabatic expansion from P_3, V_3, T_3 to P_4, V_4, T_4
- A constant-volume process from P_4, V_4, T_4 to $P_1, V_1 = V_4, T_1$

Sketch this cycle on a PV diagram and determine its thermal efficiency if $T_1 = 200°\text{C}$ (473.15 K), $T_2 = 1000°\text{C}$ (1273.15 K), and $T_3 = 1700°\text{C}$ (1973.15 K).

5.20. The infinite heat reservoir is an abstraction, often approximated in engineering applications by large bodies of air or water. Apply the closed-system form of the energy balance [Eq. (2.3)] to such a reservoir, treating it as a constant-volume system. How is it that heat transfer to or from the reservoir can be nonzero, yet the temperature of the reservoir remains constant?

5.21. One mole of an ideal gas, $C_P = (7/2)R$ and $C_V = (5/2)R$, is compressed adiabatically in a piston/cylinder device from 2 bar and 25°C (298.15 K) to 7 bar. The process is irreversible and requires 35% more work than a reversible, adiabatic compression from the same initial state to the same final pressure. What is the entropy change of the gas?

5.22. A mass m of liquid water at temperature T_1 is mixed adiabatically and isobarically with an equal mass of liquid water at temperature T_2. Assuming constant C_P, show

$$\Delta S^t = \Delta S_{\text{total}} = S_G = 2mC_P \ln \frac{(T_1 + T_2)/2}{(T_1 T_2)^{1/2}}$$

and prove that this is positive. What would be the result if the masses of the water were *different*, say, m_1 and m_2?

5.23. Reversible adiabatic processes are *isentropic*. Are isentropic processes necessarily reversible and adiabatic? If so, explain why; if not, give an illustrative example.

5.24. Prove that the mean heat capacities $\langle C_P \rangle_H$ and $\langle C_P \rangle_S$ are inherently *positive*, whether $T > T_0$ or $T < T_0$. Explain why they are well defined for $T = T_0$.

5.25. A reversible cycle executed by 1 mol of an ideal gas for which $C_P = (5/2)R$ and $C_V = (3/2)R$ consists of the following:

- Starting at $T_1 = 700$ K and $P_1 = 1.5$ bar, the gas is cooled at constant pressure to $T_2 = 350$ K.
- From 350 K and 1.5 bar, the gas is compressed isothermally to pressure P_2.
- The gas returns to its initial state along a path for which $PT = \text{constant}$.

What is the thermal efficiency of the cycle?

5.26. One mole of an ideal gas is compressed isothermally but irreversibly at 130°C (403.15 K) from 2.5 bar to 6.5 bar in a piston/cylinder device. The work required is 30% greater than the work of reversible, isothermal compression. The heat transferred from the gas during compression flows to a heat reservoir at 25°C (298.15 K). Calculate the entropy changes of the gas, the heat reservoir, and ΔS_{total}.

5.27. For a steady-flow process at approximately atmospheric pressure, what is the entropy change of the gas

(*a*) When 10 mol of SO_2 is heated from 200 to 1100°C (473.15 K to 1373.15 K)?
(*b*) When 12 mol of propane is heated from 250 to 1200°C (523.15 K to 1473.15 K)?

5.28. What is the entropy change of the gas, heated in a steady-flow process at approximately atmospheric pressure,

(*a*) When 800 kJ is added to 10 mol of ethylene initially at 200°C (473.15 K)?
(*b*) When 2500 kJ is added to 15 mol of 1-butene initially at 260°C (533.15 K)?
(*c*) When 1.055 GJ is added to 18.14 kmol of ethylene initially at 260°C (533.15 K)?

5.29. A device with no moving parts provides a steady stream of chilled air at −25°C (248.15 K) and 1 bar. The feed to the device is compressed air at 25°C (298.15 K) and 5 bar. In addition to the stream of chilled air, a second stream of warm air flows from the device at 75°C (348.15 K) and 1 bar. Assuming adiabatic operation, what is the ratio of chilled air to warm air that the device produces? Assume that air is an ideal gas for which $C_P = (7/2)R$.

5.30. An inventor has devised a complicated nonflow process in which 1 mol of air is the working fluid. The net effects of the process are claimed to be

- A change in state of the air from 250°C (523.15 K) and 3 bar to 80°C (353.15 K) and 1 bar
- The production of 1800 J of work
- The transfer of an undisclosed amount of heat to a heat reservoir at 30°C (303.15 K)

Determine whether the claimed performance of the process is consistent with the second law. Assume that air is an ideal gas for which $C_P = (7/2)R$.

5.31. Consider the heating of a house by a furnace, which serves as a heat-source reservoir at a high temperature T_F. The house acts as a heat-sink reservoir at temperature T, and heat $|Q|$ must be added to the house during a particular time interval to maintain this temperature. Heat $|Q|$ can of course be transferred directly from the furnace to the house, as is the usual practice. However, a third heat reservoir is readily available, namely, the surroundings at temperature T_σ, which can serve as another heat source, thus reducing the amount of heat required from the furnace. Given that $T_F = 810$ K, $T = 295$ K, $T_\sigma = 265$ K, and $|Q| = 1000$ kJ, determine the minimum amount of heat $|Q_F|$ which must be extracted from the heat-source reservoir (furnace) at T_F. No other sources of energy are available.

5.32. Consider the air conditioning of a house through use of solar energy. At a particular location experiment has shown that solar radiation allows a large tank of pressurized water to be maintained at 175°C (448.15 K). During a particular time interval, heat in the amount of 1500 kJ must be extracted from the house to maintain its temperature at 24°C (299.15 K) when the surroundings temperature is 33°C (306.15 K). Treating the tank of water, the house, and the surroundings as heat reservoirs, determine the minimum amount of heat that must be extracted from the tank of water by any device built to accomplish the required cooling of the house. No other sources of energy are available.

5.33. A refrigeration system cools a brine from 25°C (298.15 K) to −15°C (258.15 K) at the rate 20 kg s^{-1}. Heat is discarded to the atmosphere at a temperature of 30°C (303.15 K). What is the power requirement if the thermodynamic efficiency of the system is 0.27? The specific heat of the brine is 3.5 kJ kg^{-1} °C^{-1}.

5.34. An electric motor under steady load draws 9.7 amperes at 110 volts; it delivers 0.93 kW of mechanical energy. The temperature of the surroundings is 300 K. What is the total rate of entropy generation in W K^{-1}?

5.35. A 25 ohm resistor at steady state draws a current of 10 amperes. Its temperature is 310 K; the temperature of the surroundings is 300 K. What is the total rate of entropy generation $\dot{S}_G$? What is its origin?

5.36. Show how the general rate form of the entropy balance, Eq. (5.21), reduces to Eq. (5.19) for the case of a closed system.

5.37. A list of common unit operations follows:

(*a*) Single-pipe heat exchanger (*b*) Double-pipe heat exchanger (*c*) Pump
(*d*) Gas compressor (*e*) Gas turbine (expander) (*f*) Throttle valve (*g*) Nozzle

Develop a simplified form of the general steady-state entropy balance appropriate to each operation. State carefully, and justify, any assumptions you make.

5.38. Ten kmol per hour of air is throttled from upstream conditions of 25°C (298.15 K) and 10 bar to a downstream pressure of 1.2 bar. Assume air to be an ideal gas with $C_P = (7/2)R$.

(*a*) What is the downstream temperature?
(*b*) What is the entropy change of the air in J mol^{-1} K^{-1}?
(*c*) What is the rate of entropy generation in W K^{-1}?
(*d*) If the surroundings are at 20°C (293.15 K), what is the lost work?

5.39. A steady-flow adiabatic turbine (expander) accepts gas at conditions T_1, P_1, and discharges at conditions T_2, P_2. Assuming ideal gases, determine (per mole of gas) W, W_{ideal}, W_{lost}, and S_G for one of the following cases. Take $T_\sigma = 300$ K.

(*a*) $T_1 = 500$ K, $P_1 = 6$ bar, $T_2 = 371$ K, $P_2 = 1.2$ bar, $C_P/R = 7/2$.
(*b*) $T_1 = 450$ K, $P_1 = 5$ bar, $T_2 = 376$ K, $P_2 = 2$ bar, $C_P/R = 4$.
(*c*) $T_1 = 525$ K, $P_1 = 10$ bar, $T_2 = 458$ K, $P_2 = 3$ bar, $C_P/R = 11/2$.
(*d*) $T_1 = 475$ K, $P_1 = 7$ bar, $T_2 = 372$ K, $P_2 = 1.5$ bar, $C_P/R = 9/2$.
(*e*) $T_1 = 550$ K, $P_1 = 4$ bar, $T_2 = 403$ K, $P_2 = 1.2$ bar, $C_P/R = 5/2$.

5.40. Consider the direct heat transfer from a heat reservoir at T_1 to another heat reservoir at temperature T_2, where $T_1 > T_2 > T_\sigma$. It is not obvious why the lost work of this process should depend on T_σ, the temperature of the surroundings, because the surroundings are not involved in the actual heat-transfer process. Through appropriate use of the Carnot-engine formula, show for the transfer of an amount of heat equal to $|Q|$ that

$$W_{\text{lost}} = T_\sigma |Q| \frac{T_1 - T_2}{T_1 T_2} = T_\sigma S_G$$

5.41. An ideal gas at 2500 kPa is throttled adiabatically to 150 kPa at the rate of 20 mol s^{-1}. Determine $\dot{S}_G$ and $\dot{W}_{\text{lost}}$ if $T_\sigma = 300$ K.

5.42. An inventor claims to have devised a cyclic engine which exchanges heat with reservoirs at 25°C (298.15 K) and 250°C (523.15 K), and which produces 0.45 kJ of work for each kJ of heat extracted from the hot reservoir. Is the clain believable?

5.43. Heat in the amount of 150 kJ is transferred directly from a hot reservoir at T_H= 550 K to two cooler reservoirs at T_1 = 350 K and T_2 = 250 K. The surroundings temperatrue is T_σ= 300 K. If the heat transferred to the reservoir at T_1 is half that transferred to the reservior at T_2, calculate the

(*a*) entropy generation in kJ K^{-1}

(*b*) lost work

How could the process be made reversible?

5.44. A nuclear power plant generates 750 MW; the reactor temperature is 315°C (588.15 K) and a river with water temperature of 20°C (293.15 K) is available.

(*a*) What is the maximum possible thermal efficiency of the plant, and what is the minimum rate at which heat must be discarded to the river?

(*b*) If the actual thermal efficiency of the plant is 60% of the maximum, at what rate must heat be discarded to the river, and what is the temperature rise of the river if it has a flowrate of 165 m^3 s^{-1}?

5.45. A single gas stream enters a process at conditions T_1, P_1, and leaves at pressure P_2. The process is adiabatic. Prove that the outlet temperature T_2 for the actual (irreversible) adiabatic process is greater than that for a *reversible* adiabatic process. Assume the gas is ideal with constant heat capacities.

5.46. A Hilsch vortex tube operates with no moving mechanical parts, and splits a gas stream into two streams: one warmer and the other cooler than the entering stream. One such tube is reported to operate with air entering at 5 bar and 20°C (293.15 K), and air streams leaving at 27°C (300.15 K) and −22°C (251.15 K), both at 1 atm. The mass flowrate of warm air leaving is 6 times that of the cool air. Are these results possible? Assume air to be an ideal gas at the conditions given.

5.47. Air at 25°C (298.15 K) and 1 atm is cooled at the rate of 3000 $m^3\ h^{-1}$ to −8°C (265.15 K) by refrigeration. For a surroundings temperature of 25°C (298.15 K), what is the minimum power requirement in kW?

5.48. A flue gas is cooled from 1100 to 150°C (1373.15 K to 423.15 K), and the heat is used to generate saturated steam at 100°C (373.15 K) in a boiler. The flue gas has a heat capacity given by:

$$\frac{C_P}{R} = 3.83 + 0.000\,551\,T/\text{K}$$

Water enters the boiler at 100°C (373.15 K), and is vaporized at this temperature; its latent heat of vaporization is 2256.9 kJ kg^{-1}.

(*a*) With reference to a surroundings temperature of 25°C (298.15 K), what is the lost work of this process in kJ mol^{-1} of flue gas?
(*b*) With reference to a surroundings temperature of 25°C (298.15 K), what is the maximum work in kJ mol^{-1} of flue gas that can be accomplished by the saturated steam at 100°C (373.15 K) if it condenses only, and does not subcool?
(*c*) How does the answer to Part (*b*) compare with the maximum work theoretically obtainable from the flue gas itself as it is cooled from 1100 to 150°C (1373.15 K to 423.15 K)?

5.49. Ethylene vapor is cooled at atmospheric pressure from 830 to 35°C (1103.15 K to 308.15 K) by direct heat transfer to the surroundings at a temperature of 25°C (298.15 K). With respect to this surroundings temperature, what is the lost work of the process in kJ mol^{-1}? Show that the same result is obtained as the work which can be derived from reversible heat engines operating with the ethylene vapor as heat source and the surroundings as sink. The heat capacity of ethylene is given in Table C.1 of App. C.

Chapter 6

Thermodynamic Properties of Fluids

The phase rule (Sec. 2.7) tells us that specification of a certain number of intensive properties of a system also fixes the values of all other intensive properties. However, the phase rule provides no information about how values for these other properties may be obtained.

Numerical values for thermodynamic properties are essential to the calculation of heat and work quantities for industrial processes. Consider, for example, the work requirement of a steady-state compressor designed to operate adiabatically and to raise the pressure of a gas from P_1 to P_2. This work is given by Eq. (2.33), wherein the small kinetic- and potential-energy changes of the gas are neglected:

$$W_s = \Delta H = H_2 - H_1$$

Thus, the shaft work is simply ΔH, the difference between initial and final enthalpy values of the gas.

Our initial purpose in this chapter is to develop from the first and second laws the fundamental property relations which underlie the mathematical structure of thermodynamics. From these, we derive equations which allow calculation of enthalpy and entropy values from PVT and heat-capacity data. We then discuss the diagrams and tables by which property values are presented for convenient use. Finally, we develop generalized correlations which provide estimates of property values in the absence of complete experimental information.

6.1 PROPERTY RELATIONS FOR HOMOGENEOUS PHASES

Equation (2.6), the first law for a closed system of n moles, may be written for the special case of a reversible process:

$$d(nU) = dQ_{\text{rev}} + dW_{\text{rev}}$$

Equations (1.2) and (5.12) as applied to this process are

$$dW_{\text{rev}} = -P\,d(nV) \qquad\qquad dQ_{\text{rev}} = T\,d(nS)$$

Together these three equations give:

$$\boxed{d(nU) = T\,d(nS) - P\,d(nV)} \tag{6.1}$$

where U, S, and V are molar values of the internal energy, entropy, and volume.

This equation, combining the first and second laws, is *derived* for the special case of a reversible process. However, it contains only *properties* of the system. Properties depend on state alone, and not on the kind of process that leads to the state. Therefore, Eq. (6.1) is not restricted in *application* to reversible processes. However, the restrictions placed on the *nature of the system* cannot be relaxed. Thus Eq. (6.1) applies to *any* process in a system of *constant mass* that results in a differential change from one *equilibrium* state to another. The system may consist of a single phase (a homogeneous system), or it may be made up of several phases (a heterogeneous system); it may be chemically inert, or it may undergo chemical reaction.

The only requirements are that the system be closed and that the change occurs between equilibrium states.

All of the *primary* thermodynamic properties— P, V, T, U, and S— are included in Eq. (6.1). Additional thermodynamic properties arise only by **definition** in relation to these primary properties. The enthalpy, defined In Chap. 2 as a matter of convenience, is:

$$\boxed{H \equiv U + PV} \tag{2.11}$$

Two additional properties, also defined for convenience, are the *Helmholtz energy* and the *Gibbs energy*:

$$\boxed{A \equiv U - TS} \tag{6.2}$$

$$\boxed{G \equiv H - TS} \tag{6.3}$$

Each of these defined properties leads directly to an equation like Eq. (6.1). Upon multiplication by n, Eq. (2.11) may be differentiated to yield

$$d(nH) = d(nU) + P\,d(nV) + (nV)dP$$

When $d(nU)$ is replaced by Eq. (6.1), this reduces to

$$\boxed{d(nH) = T\,d(nS) + (nV)dP} \tag{6.4}$$

Similarly, Eq. (6.2) may be multiplied by n, differentiated, and combined with Eq. (6.1):

$$\boxed{d(nA) = -P\,d(nV) - (nS)dT} \tag{6.5}$$

In analogous fashion, Eqs. (6.3) and (6.4) combine to yield

$$\boxed{d(nG) = (nV)dP - (nS)dT} \tag{6.6}$$

Equations (6.4) through (6.6) are subject to the same restrictions as Eq. (6.1). All are written for the entire mass of any closed system.

Our immediate application of these equations is to one mole (or to a unit mass) of a homogeneous fluid of constant composition. For this case, they simplify to

$dU = T\,dS - P\,dV$ (6.7)	$dH = T\,dS + V\,dP$ (6.8)
$dA = -P\,dV - S\,dT$ (6.9)	$dG = V\,dP - S\,dT$ (6.10)

These *fundamental property relations* are general equations for a homogeneous fluid of constant composition.

Another set of equations follows from Eqs. (6.7) through (6.10) by application of the criterion of exactness for a differential expression. If $F = F(x, y)$, then the total differential of F is defined as

$$dF \equiv \left(\frac{\partial F}{\partial x}\right)_y dx + \left(\frac{\partial F}{\partial y}\right)_x dy$$

or

$$dF = M\,dx + N\,dy \tag{6.11}$$

where $$M \equiv \left(\frac{\partial F}{\partial x}\right)_y \qquad N \equiv \left(\frac{\partial F}{\partial y}\right)_x$$

Then $$\left(\frac{\partial M}{\partial y}\right)_x = \frac{\partial^2 F}{\partial y\,\partial x} \qquad \left(\frac{\partial N}{\partial x}\right)_y = \frac{\partial^2 F}{\partial x\,\partial y}$$

The order of differentiation in mixed second derivatives is immaterial, and these equations combine to give:

$$\left(\frac{\partial M}{\partial y}\right)_x = \left(\frac{\partial N}{\partial x}\right)_y \tag{6.12}$$

When F is a function of x and y, the right side of Eq. (6.11) is an *exact differential expression*; because Eq. (6.12) must then be satisfied, it serves as the criterion of exactness.

The thermodynamic properties U, H, A, and G are *known* to be functions of the variables on the right sides of Eqs. (6.7) through (6.10); we may therefore write the relationship expressed by Eq. (6.12) for each of these equations. They are known as *Maxwell's equations*.[1]

$\left(\frac{\partial T}{\partial V}\right)_S = -\left(\frac{\partial P}{\partial S}\right)_V$ (6.13)	$\left(\frac{\partial T}{\partial P}\right)_S = \left(\frac{\partial V}{\partial S}\right)_P$ (6.14)
$\left(\frac{\partial P}{\partial T}\right)_V = \left(\frac{\partial S}{\partial V}\right)_T$ (6.15)	$\left(\frac{\partial V}{\partial T}\right)_P = -\left(\frac{\partial S}{\partial P}\right)_T$ (6.16)

Equations (6.7) through (6.10) are the basis not only for derivation of Maxwell's equations but also of a large number of other equations relating thermodynamic properties. We develop here only a few expressions useful for evaluation of thermodynamic properties from experimental data. Their derivation requires application of Eqs. (6.7), (6.8), (6.15), and (6.16).

[1]After James Clerk Maxwell (1831–1879), Scottish physicist.

Enthalpy and Entropy as Functions of T and P

The most useful property relations for the enthalpy and entropy of a homogeneous phase result when these properties are expressed as functions of T and P. What we need to know is how H and S vary with temperature and pressure. This information is contained in the derivatives $(\partial H/\partial T)_P$, $(\partial S/\partial T)_P$, $(\partial H/\partial P)_T$, and $(\partial S/\partial P)_T$.

Consider first the temperature derivatives. Equation (2.20) defines the heat capacity at constant pressure:

$$\left(\frac{\partial H}{\partial T}\right)_P = C_P \tag{2.20}$$

Another expression for this quantity is obtained by division of Eq. (6.8) by dT and restriction of the result to constant P:

$$\left(\frac{\partial H}{\partial T}\right)_P = T\left(\frac{\partial S}{\partial T}\right)_P$$

Combination of this equation with Eq. (2.20) gives

$$\left(\frac{\partial S}{\partial T}\right)_P = \frac{C_P}{T} \tag{6.17}$$

The pressure derivative of the entropy results directly from Eq. (6.16):

$$\left(\frac{\partial S}{\partial P}\right)_T = -\left(\frac{\partial V}{\partial T}\right)_P \tag{6.18}$$

The corresponding derivative for the enthalpy is found by division of Eq. (6.8) by dP and restriction to constant T:

$$\left(\frac{\partial H}{\partial P}\right)_T = T\left(\frac{\partial S}{\partial P}\right)_T + V$$

As a result of Eq. (6.18) this becomes

$$\left(\frac{\partial H}{\partial P}\right)_T = V - T\left(\frac{\partial V}{\partial T}\right)_P \tag{6.19}$$

The functional relations chosen here for H and S are $H = H(T, P)$ and $S = S(T, P)$. Whence,

$$dH = \left(\frac{\partial H}{\partial T}\right)_P dT + \left(\frac{\partial H}{\partial P}\right)_T dP \qquad dS = \left(\frac{\partial S}{\partial T}\right)_P dT + \left(\frac{\partial S}{\partial P}\right)_T dP$$

The partial derivatives are given by Eqs. (2.20) and (6.17) through (6.19):

$$\boxed{dH = C_P\, dT + \left[V - T\left(\frac{\partial V}{\partial T}\right)_P\right] dP} \tag{6.20}$$

$$\boxed{dS = C_P \frac{dT}{T} - \left(\frac{\partial V}{\partial T}\right)_P dP} \tag{6.21}$$

These are general equations relating the enthalpy and entropy of homogeneous fluids of constant composition to temperature and pressure.

Internal Energy as a Function of P

Internal energy is given by Eq. (2.11) as $U = H - PV$. Differentiation yields

$$\left(\frac{\partial U}{\partial P}\right)_T = \left(\frac{\partial H}{\partial P}\right)_T - P\left(\frac{\partial V}{\partial P}\right)_T - V$$

Then by Eq. (6.19),

$$\left(\frac{\partial U}{\partial P}\right)_T = -T\left(\frac{\partial V}{\partial T}\right)_P - P\left(\frac{\partial V}{\partial P}\right)_T \qquad (6.22)$$

The Ideal-Gas State

The coefficients of dT and dP in Eqs. (6.20) and (6.21) are evaluated from heat-capacity and PVT data. The ideal-gas state provides an example of PVT behavior:

$$PV^{ig} = RT \qquad \left(\frac{\partial V^{ig}}{\partial T}\right)_P = \frac{R}{P}$$

Substituting these equations into Eqs. (6.20) and (6.21) reduces them to

$$dH^{ig} = C_P^{ig}\, dT \qquad (6.23) \qquad dS^{ig} = C_P^{ig}\frac{dT}{T} - R\frac{dP}{P} \qquad (6.24)$$

where superscript "ig" denotes an ideal-gas value. These are merely restatements of equations for ideal gases presented in Secs. 3.3 and 5.5.

Alternative Forms for Liquids

Alternative forms of Eqs. (6.18) and (6.19) result when $(\partial V/\partial T)_P$ is replaced by βV [Eq. (3.2)]:

$$\left(\frac{\partial S}{\partial P}\right)_T = -\beta V \qquad (6.25) \qquad \left(\frac{\partial H}{\partial P}\right)_T = (1-\beta T)V \qquad (6.26)$$

An alternative form of Eq. (6.22) results if, in addition, $(\partial V/\partial P)_T$ is replaced by $-\kappa V$ [Eq. (3.3)]:

$$\left(\frac{\partial U}{\partial P}\right)_T = (\kappa P - \beta T)V \qquad (6.27)$$

These equations, incorporating β and κ, although general, are usually applied only to liquids. However, for liquids not near the critical point, the volume itself is small, as are β and κ. Thus at most conditions, pressure has little effect on the properties of liquids. The important special case of an *incompressible fluid* (Sec. 3.1) is considered in Ex. 6.2.

Replacing $(\partial V/\partial T)_P$ in Eqs. (6.20) and (6.21) by βV [see Eq. (3.2)] yields

$$dH = C_P\, dT + (1-\beta T)V\, dP \qquad (6.28) \qquad dS = C_P\frac{dT}{T} - \beta V\, dP \qquad (6.29)$$

Because β and V are weak functions of pressure for liquids, they are usually assumed constant at appropriate average values for integration of the final terms of Eqs. (6.28) and (6.29).

Example 6.1

Determine the enthalpy and entropy changes of liquid water for a change of state from 1 bar and 25°C (298.15 K) to 1000 bar and 50°C (323.15 K). Data for water are given in the following table.

t/°C	T/K	P/bar	C_P/J mol^{-1} K^{-1}	V/cm^3 mol^{-1}	β/K^{-1}
25	298.15	1	75.305	18.071	256×10^{-6}
25	298.15	1000	......	18.012	366×10^{-6}
50	323.15	1	75.314	18.234	458×10^{-6}
50	323.15	1000	......	18.174	568×10^{-6}

Solution

For application to the change of state described, Eqs. (6.28) and (6.29) require integration. Enthalpy and entropy are state functions, and the path of integration is arbitrary; the path most suited to the given data is shown in Fig. 6.1. Because the data indicate that C_P is a weak function of T and that both V and β are weak functions of P, integration with arithmetic means is satisfactory. The integrated forms of Eqs. (6.28) and (6.29) that result are

$$\Delta H = \langle C_P\rangle(T_2 - T_1) + (1 - \langle\beta\rangle\, T_2)\langle V\rangle(P_2 - P_1)$$

$$\Delta S = \langle C_P\rangle \ln\frac{T_2}{T_1} - \langle\beta\rangle\langle V\rangle(P_2 - P_1)$$

For $P = 1$ bar,

$$\langle C_P\rangle = \frac{75.305 + 75.314}{2} = 75.310 \text{ J mol}^{-1}\text{ K}^{-1}$$

and for $t = 50$°C or $T = 323.15$ K,

$$\langle V\rangle = \frac{18.234 + 18.174}{2} = 18.204 \text{ cm}^3\text{ mol}^{-1}$$

$$\langle\beta\rangle = \frac{458 + 568}{2} \times 10^{-6} = 513 \times 10^{-6}\text{ K}^{-1}$$

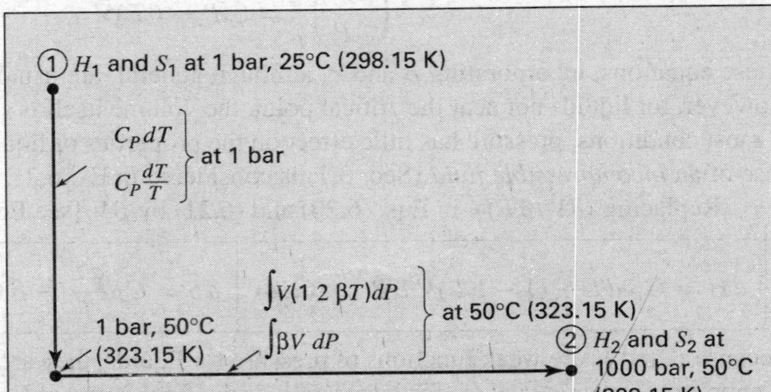

Figure 6.1: Calculational path for Ex. 6.1

Substitution of these numerical values into the equation for ΔH gives

$$\Delta H = 75.310(323.15 - 298.15) + \frac{[1 - (513 \times 10^{-6})(323.15)](18.204)(1000 - 1)}{10 \text{ cm}^3 \text{ bar J}^{-1}}$$

$$= 1883 + 1517 = 3400 \text{ J mol}^{-1}$$

Similarly for ΔS,

$$\Delta S = 75.310 \ln \frac{323.15}{298.15} - \frac{(513 \times 10^{-6})(18.204)(1000 - 1)}{10 \text{ cm}^3 \text{ bar J}^{-1}}$$

$$= 6.06 - 0.93 = 5.13 \text{ J mol}^{-1} \text{ K}^{-1}$$

Note that the effect of a pressure change of almost 1000 bar on the enthalpy and entropy of liquid water is less than that of a temperature change of only 25°C (298.15 K).

Internal Energy and Entropy as Functions of T and V

Temperature and volume often serve as more convenient independent variables than do temperature and pressure. The most useful property relations are then for internal energy and entropy. Required here are the derivatives $(\partial U/\partial T)_V$, $(\partial U/\partial V)_T$, $(\partial S/\partial T)_V$, and $(\partial S/\partial V)_T$. The first two of these follow directly from Eq. (6.7):

$$\left(\frac{\partial U}{\partial T}\right)_V = T\left(\frac{\partial S}{\partial T}\right)_V \qquad \left(\frac{\partial U}{\partial V}\right)_T = T\left(\frac{\partial S}{\partial V}\right)_T - P$$

Combining the first of these with Eq. (2.16) and the second with Eq. (6.15), we get

$$\left(\frac{\partial S}{\partial T}\right)_V = \frac{C_V}{T} \quad (6.30) \qquad \left(\frac{\partial U}{\partial V}\right)_T = T\left(\frac{\partial P}{\partial T}\right)_V - P \quad (6.31)$$

The chosen functional relations here are $U = U(T, V)$ and $S = S(T, V)$. Whence,

$$dU = \left(\frac{\partial U}{\partial T}\right)_V dT + \left(\frac{\partial U}{\partial V}\right)_T dV \qquad dS = \left(\frac{\partial S}{\partial T}\right)_V dT + \left(\frac{\partial S}{\partial V}\right)_T dV$$

The partial derivatives are given by Eqs. (2.16), (6.31), (6.30), and (6.15):

$$dU = C_V\, dT + \left[T\left(\frac{\partial P}{\partial T}\right)_V - P\right] dV \tag{6.32}$$

$$dS = C_V \frac{dT}{T} + \left(\frac{\partial P}{\partial T}\right)_V dV \tag{6.33}$$

These are general equations relating the internal energy and entropy of homogeneous fluids of constant composition to temperature and volume.

Equation (3.4) applied to a change of state at constant volume becomes

$$\left(\frac{\partial P}{\partial T}\right)_V = \frac{\beta}{\kappa} \tag{6.34}$$

Alternative forms of Eqs. (6.32) and (6.33) are therefore

$dU = C_V\,dT + \left(\frac{\beta}{\kappa}T - P\right)dV$ (6.35)	$dS = \frac{C_V}{T}dT + \frac{\beta}{\kappa}dV$ (6.36)

Example 6.2

Develop the property relations appropriate to the *incompressible fluid*, a model fluid for which both β and κ are zero (Sec. 3.1). This is an idealization often employed in fluid mechanics.

Solution

Equations (6.28) and (6.29) written for an incompressible fluid become

$$dH = C_P\,dT + V\,dP \tag{A}$$

$$dS = C_P\frac{dT}{T}$$

The enthalpy of an incompressible fluid is therefore a function of both temperature and pressure, whereas the entropy is a function of temperature only, independent of P. With $\kappa = \beta = 0$, Eq. (6.27) shows that the internal energy is also a function of temperature only, and is therefore given by the equation, $dU = C_V\,dT$. Equation (6.12), the criterion of exactness, applied to Eq. (A), yields:

$$\left(\frac{\partial C_P}{\partial P}\right)_T = \left(\frac{\partial V}{\partial T}\right)_P$$

However, the definition of β, given by Eq. (3.2), shows that the derivative on the right equals βV, which is zero for an incompressible fluid. This means that C_P is a function of temperature only, independent of P.

The relation of C_P to C_V for an incompressible fluid is of interest. For a given change of state, Eqs. (6.29) and (6.36) must give the same value for dS; they are therefore equated. The resulting expression, after rearrangement, is

$$(C_P - C_V)dT = \beta TV\,dP + \frac{\beta T}{\kappa}dV$$

Upon restriction to constant V, this reduces to

$$C_P - C_V = \beta T V \left(\frac{\partial P}{\partial T}\right)_V$$

Elimination of the derivative by Eq. (6.34) yields

$$C_P - C_V = \beta T V \left(\frac{\beta}{\kappa}\right) \tag{B}$$

Because $\beta = 0$, the right side of this equation is zero, provided that the indeterminate ratio β/κ is finite. This ratio is indeed finite for real fluids, and a contrary presumption for the *model* fluid would be irrational. Thus the definition of the incompressible fluid presumes that this ratio is finite, and we conclude for such a fluid that the heat capacities at constant V and at constant P are identical:

$$C_P = C_V = C$$

The Gibbs Energy as a Generating Function

The fundamental property relations for homogeneous fluids of constant composition given by Eqs. (6.7) through (6.10) show that each of the thermodynamic properties U, H, A, and G is functionally related to a special pair of variables. In particular,

$$dG = V\,dP - S\,dT \tag{6.10}$$

expresses the functional relation $G = G(P, T)$. Thus the special, or *canonical*,[2] variables for the Gibbs energy are temperature and pressure. Because these variables can be directly measured and controlled, the Gibbs energy is a property of great potential utility.

An alternative form of Eq. (6.10), a fundamental property relation, follows from the mathematical identity:

$$d\left(\frac{G}{RT}\right) \equiv \frac{1}{RT}dG - \frac{G}{RT^2}dT$$

Substitution for dG by Eq. (6.10) and for G by Eq. (6.3) gives, after algebraic reduction:

$$\boxed{d\left(\frac{G}{RT}\right) = \frac{V}{RT}dP - \frac{H}{RT^2}dT} \tag{6.37}$$

The advantage of this equation is that all terms are dimensionless; moreover, in contrast to Eq. (6.10), the enthalpy rather than the entropy appears on the right side.

Equations such as Eqs. (6.10) and (6.37) are too general for direct practical application, but they are readily applied in restricted form. Thus, from Eq. (6.37),

[2] *Canonical* here means that the variables conform to a general rule that is both simple and clear.

$$\frac{V}{RT} = \left[\frac{\partial(G/RT)}{\partial P}\right]_T \quad (6.38) \qquad \frac{H}{RT} = -T\left[\frac{\partial(G/RT)}{\partial T}\right]_P \quad (6.39)$$

When G/RT is known as a function of T and P, V/RT and H/RT follow by simple differentiation. The remaining properties are given by defining equations. In particular,

$$\frac{S}{R} = \frac{H}{RT} - \frac{G}{RT} \qquad \frac{U}{RT} = \frac{H}{RT} - \frac{PV}{RT}$$

Thus, when we know how G/RT (or G) is related to its canonical variables, T and P, i.e., when we are given $G/RT = g(T, P)$, we can evaluate all other thermodynamic properties by simple mathematical operations.

The Gibbs energy when given as a function of T and P serves as a *generating function* for the other thermodynamic properties, and implicitly represents *complete* property information.

Just as Eq. (6.10) leads to expressions for all thermodynamic properties, so Eq. (6.9) leads to the equations connecting thermodynamic properties to statistical mechanics (Sec. 16.4).

6.2 RESIDUAL PROPERTIES

Unfortunately, no experimental method for the measurement of numerical values of G or G/RT is known, and the equations which relate other properties to the Gibbs energy are of little direct practical use. However, the concept of the Gibbs energy as a generating function for other thermodynamic properties carries over to a closely related property for which numerical values *are* readily obtained. Thus, by **definition** the *residual* Gibbs energy is $G^R \equiv G - G^{ig}$, where G and G^{ig} are the actual and the ideal-gas values of the Gibbs energy at the same temperature and pressure. Other residual properties are defined in an analogous way. The residual volume, for example, is:

$$V^R \equiv V - V^{ig} = V - \frac{RT}{P}$$

Because $V = ZRT/P$, the residual volume and the compressibility factor are related:

$$V^R = \frac{RT}{P}(Z - 1) \tag{6.40}$$

The definition for the generic residual property is

$$\boxed{M^R \equiv M - M^{ig}} \tag{6.41}$$

where M is the molar value of any extensive thermodynamic property, e.g., V, U, H, S, or G. Note that M and M^{ig}, the actual and ideal-gas properties, are at the same T and P.

Equation (6.37), written for the special case of an ideal gas, becomes

$$d\left(\frac{G^{ig}}{RT}\right) = \frac{V^{ig}}{RT}dP - \frac{H^{ig}}{RT^2}dT$$

Subtracting this equation from Eq. (6.37) itself gives

$$\boxed{d\left(\frac{G^R}{RT}\right) = \frac{V^R}{RT}dP - \frac{H^R}{RT^2}dT} \qquad (6.42)$$

This *fundamental residual-property relation* applies to fluids of constant composition. Useful restricted forms are

$$\frac{V^R}{RT} = \left[\frac{\partial(G^R/RT)}{\partial P}\right]_T \qquad (6.43) \qquad\qquad \frac{H^R}{RT} = -T\left[\frac{\partial(G^R/RT)}{\partial T}\right]_P \qquad (6.44)$$

The residual Gibbs energy, a generating function for the other residual properties, has a direct link with experiment. It is provided by Eq. (6.43), written as

$$d\left(\frac{G^R}{RT}\right) = \frac{V^R}{RT}dP \qquad \text{(const } T\text{)}$$

Integration from zero pressure to arbitrary pressure P yields

$$\frac{G^R}{RT} = \left(\frac{G^R}{RT}\right)_{P=0} + \int_0^P \frac{V^R}{RT}dP \qquad \text{(const } T\text{)}$$

For convenience, define $\left(\dfrac{G^R}{RT}\right)_{P=0} \equiv J$

As explained in the subsection that follows, J is a *constant*, independent of T. In view of Eq. (6.40),

$$\frac{G^R}{RT} = J + \int_0^P (Z-1)\frac{dP}{P} \qquad \text{(const } T\text{)} \qquad (6.45)$$

The derivative of this equation in combination with Eq. (6.44) gives

$$\boxed{\frac{H^R}{RT} = -T\int_0^P \left(\frac{\partial Z}{\partial T}\right)_P \frac{dP}{P} \qquad \text{(const } T\text{)}} \qquad (6.46)$$

The defining equation for the Gibbs energy, $G = H - TS$, may also be written for the special case of an ideal gas, $G^{ig} = H^{ig} - TS^{ig}$; by difference, $G^R = H^R - TS^R$, and

$$\frac{S^R}{R} = \frac{H^R}{RT} - \frac{G^R}{RT} \qquad (6.47)$$

Combining this equation with Eqs. (6.45) and (6.46) gives

$$\frac{S^R}{R} = -T\int_0^P \left(\frac{\partial Z}{\partial T}\right)_P \frac{dP}{P} - J - \int_0^P (Z-1)\frac{dP}{P} \qquad \text{(const } T\text{)}$$

In application the need is always for entropy *differences*. Eq. (6.41), written for the entropy and rearranged as $S = S^{ig} + S^R$, may be written for two different states. By difference

$$\Delta S \equiv S_2 - S_1 = (S_2^{ig} - S_1^{ig}) + (S_2^R - S_1^R)$$

Because J is a constant, it cancels out of the residual-entropy difference in this equation. Hence its value is of no consequence, and J may be arbitrarily set equal to zero. The working equation for S^R is then written as

$$\boxed{\frac{S^R}{R} = -T\int_0^P \left(\frac{\partial Z}{\partial T}\right)_P \frac{dP}{P} - \int_0^P (Z-1)\frac{dP}{P} \qquad \text{(const } T\text{)}} \tag{6.48}$$

Equation (6.45) for G^R/RT becomes

$$\boxed{\frac{G^R}{RT} = \int_0^P (Z-1)\frac{dP}{P} \qquad \text{(const } T\text{)}} \tag{6.49}$$

The compressibility factor is defined as $Z = PV/RT$; values of Z and of $(\partial Z/\partial T)_P$ may be calculated from experimental PVT data, with the two integrals in Eqs. (6.46), (6.48), and (6.49) evaluated by numerical or graphical methods. Alternatively, the two integrals may be evaluated analytically when Z is expressed as a function of T and P by a volume-explicit equation of state. This direct connection with experiment allows evaluation of the residual properties H^R and S^R, which are essential to the practical application of thermodynamics.

Residual Properties in the Zero-Presure Limit

The constant J, omitted from Eqs. (6.46), (6.48), and (6.49), is the value of G^R/RT in the limit as $P \to 0$. Its origin becomes clear from a general treatment of residual properties in this limit. Because a gas becomes ideal as $P \to 0$ (in the sense that $Z \to 1$), one might suppose that in this limit all residual properties are zero. This is not in general true, as is easily demonstrated through consideration of the residual volume.

Written for V^R in the limit of zero pressure Eq. (6.41) becomes,

$$\lim_{P\to 0} V^R = \lim_{P\to 0} V - \lim_{P\to 0} V^{ig}$$

Both terms on the right are infinite, and their difference is indeterminate. Experimental insight is provided by Eq. (6.40):

$$\lim_{P\to 0} V^R = RT \lim_{P\to 0}\left(\frac{Z-1}{P}\right) = RT \lim_{P\to 0}\left(\frac{\partial Z}{\partial P}\right)_T$$

Thus, V^R/RT in the limit as $P \to 0$ at a given T equals the slope of the Z vs. P isotherm at $P = 0$. Figure 3.9 shows clearly that these values are finite, and not in general zero.

For the internal energy, $U^R \equiv U - U^{ig}$. Because U^{ig} is a function of T only, a plot of U^{ig} vs. P for a given T is a horizontal line extending to $P = 0$. For a real gas with finite intermolecular forces, an isothermal expansion to $P \to 0$ results in an increase in U, because the molecules move apart against the forces of intermolecular attraction. Expansion to $P = 0$ ($V = \infty$) reduces these forces to zero, exactly as in an ideal gas, and therefore at all temperatures,

$$\lim_{P\to 0} U = U^{ig} \qquad \text{and} \qquad \lim_{P\to 0} U^R = 0$$

From the definition of enthalpy,

$$\lim_{P\to 0} H^R = \lim_{P\to 0} U^R + \lim_{P\to 0} (PV^R)$$

Because both terms on the right are zero, $\lim_{P\to 0} H^R = 0$ for all temperatures.

For the Gibbs energy, by Eq. (6.37):

$$d\left(\frac{G}{RT}\right) = \frac{V}{RT} dP \qquad \text{(const } T\text{)}$$

For an ideal gas, $V = V^{ig} = RT/P$, and this becomes

$$d\left(\frac{G^{ig}}{RT}\right) = \frac{dP}{P} \qquad \text{(const } T\text{)}$$

Integration from $P = 0$ to pressure P yields

$$\frac{G^{ig}}{RT} = \left(\frac{G^{ig}}{RT}\right)_{P=0} + \int_0^P \frac{dP}{P} = \left(\frac{G^{ig}}{RT}\right)_{P=0} + \ln P + \infty \qquad \text{(const } T\text{)}$$

For finite values of G^{ig}/RT at $P > 0$, we must have $\lim_{P\to 0} (G^{ig}/RT) = -\infty$. Because this is true for G as well, we conclude that

$$\lim_{P\to 0} \frac{G^R}{RT} = \lim_{P\to 0} \frac{G}{RT} - \lim_{P\to 0} \frac{G^{ig}}{RT} = \infty - \infty$$

Thus G^R/RT (and of course G^R) is, like V^R, indeterminate in the limit as $P \to 0$. In this case however, no experimental means exists for finding the limiting value. However, we have no reason to presume it is zero, and therefore regard it like $\lim_{P\to 0} V^R$ as finite, and not in general zero.

Equation (6.44) provides an opportunity for further analysis. We write it for the limiting case of $P = 0$:

$$\left(\frac{H^R}{RT^2}\right)_{P=0} = -\left[\frac{\partial (G^R/RT)}{\partial T}\right]_{P=0}$$

As already shown, $H^R(P = 0) = 0$, and therefore the preceding derivative is zero. As a result,

$$\left(\frac{G^R}{RT}\right)_{P=0} = J$$

where J is a constant, independent of T.

Enthalpy and Entropy from Residual Properties

Applied to the enthalpy and entropy, Eq. (6.41) is written as

$$H = H^{ig} + H^R \qquad\qquad S = S^{ig} + S^R$$

Thus, H and S follow from ideal-gas and residual properties by simple addition. General expressions for H^{ig} and S^{ig} are found by integration of Eqs. (6.23) and (6.24) from an ideal-gas state at reference conditions T_0 and P_0 to the ideal-gas state at T and P:[3]

$$H^{ig} = H_0^{ig} + \int_{T_0}^{T} C_P^{ig}\, dT \qquad\qquad S^{ig} = S_0^{ig} + \int_{T_0}^{T} C_P^{ig} \frac{dT}{T} - R \ln \frac{P}{P_0}$$

Substitution into the preceding equations gives

$$H = H_0^{ig} + \int_{T_0}^{T} C_P^{ig}\, dT + H^R \tag{6.50}$$

$$S = S_0^{ig} + \int_{T_0}^{T} C_P^{ig} \frac{dT}{T} - R \ln \frac{P}{P_0} + S^R \tag{6.51}$$

Recall (Secs. 4.1 and 5.5) that for purposes of computation the integrals in Eqs. (6.50) and (6.51) are represented by

$$\int_{T_0}^{T} C_P^{ig}\, dT = R \times \text{ICPH(T0,T;A,B,C,D)}$$

$$\int_{T_0}^{T} C_P^{ig} \frac{dT}{T} = R \times \text{ICPS(T0,T;A,B,C,D)}$$

Equations (6.50) and (6.51) have alternative forms when the integrals are replaced by equivalent terms that include the mean heat capacities introduced in Secs. 4.1 and 5.5:

$$H = H_0^{ig} + \langle C_P^{ig} \rangle_H (T - T_0) + H^R \tag{6.52}$$

$$S = S_0^{ig} + \langle C_P^{ig} \rangle_S \ln \frac{T}{T_0} - R \ln \frac{P}{P_0} + S^R \tag{6.53}$$

In Eqs. (6.50) through (6.53), H^R and S^R are given by Eqs. (6.46) and (6.48). Again, for computational purposes, the mean heat capacities are represented by

$$\langle C_P^{ig} \rangle_H = R \times \text{MCPH(T0,T;A,B,C,D)}$$

$$\langle C_P^{ig} \rangle_S = R \times \text{MCPS(T0,T;A,B,C,D)}$$

Applications of thermodynamics require only *differences* in enthalpy and entropy. The reference-state conditions T_0 and P_0 are therefore selected for convenience, and values are assigned to H_0^{ig} and S_0^{ig} arbitrarily. The only data needed for application of Eqs. (6.52) and (6.53) are ideal-gas heat capacities and PVT data. Once V, H, and S are known at given conditions of T and P, the other thermodynamic properties follow from defining equations.

[3]Thermodynamic properties for organic compounds in the ideal-gas state are given by M. Frenkel, G. J. Kabo, K. N. Marsh, G. N. Roganov, and R. C. Wilhoit, *Thermodynamics of Organic Compounds in the Gas State*, Thermodynamics Research Center, Texas A & M Univ. System, College Station, Texas, 1994.

The true worth of the equations for ideal gases is now evident. They are important because they provide a convenient base for the calculation of real-gas properties.

Residual properties have validity for both gases and liquids. However, the advantage of Eqs. (6.50) and (6.51) in application to gases is that H^R and S^R, the terms which contain all the complex calculations, are *residuals* that are usually small. They act as corrections to the major terms, H^{ig} and S^{ig}. For liquids, this advantage is largely lost, because H^R and S^R must include the large enthalpy and entropy changes of vaporization. Property changes of liquids are usually calculated by integrated forms of Eqs. (6.28) and (6.29), as illustrated in Ex. 6.1.

Example 6.3

Calculate the enthalpy and entropy of saturated isobutane vapor at 360 K from the following information:

1. Table 6.1 gives compressibility-factor data (values of Z) for isobutane vapor.

2. The vapor pressure of isobutane at 360 K is 15.41 bar.

3. Set H_0^{ig} = 18 115.0 J mol^{-1} and S_0^{ig} = 295.976 J mol^{-1} K^{-1} for the ideal-gas reference state at 300 K and 1 bar. [These values are in accord with the bases adopted by R. D. Goodwin and W. M. Haynes, Nat. Bur. Stand. (U.S.), Tech. Note 1051, 1982.]

4. The ideal-gas heat capacity of isobutane vapor at temperatures of interest is

$$C_P^{ig}/R = 1.7765 + 33.037 \times 10^{-3} T \qquad (T/\text{ K})$$

Table 6.1: Compressibility Factors Z for Isobutane

P/bar	340 K	350 K	360 K	370 K	380 K
0.10	0.997 00	0.997 19	0.997 37	0.997 53	0.997 67
0.50	0.987 45	0.988 30	0.989 07	0.989 77	0.990 40
2	0.958 95	0.962 06	0.964 83	0.967 30	0.969 53
4	0.924 22	0.930 69	0.936 35	0.941 32	0.945 74
6	0.887 42	0.898 16	0.907 34	0.915 29	0.922 23
8	0.845 75	0.862 18	0.875 86	0.887 45	0.897 43
10	0.796 59	0.821 17	0.840 77	0.856 95	0.870 61
12	......	0.773 10	0.801 03	0.823 15	0.841 34
14	......	......	0.755 06	0.785 31	0.809 23
15.41	......	......	0.717 27		

Solution

Calculation of H^R and S^R at 360 K and 15.41 bar by application of Eqs. (6.46) and (6.48) requires evaluation of two integrals:

$$\int_0^P \left(\frac{\partial Z}{\partial T}\right)_P \frac{dP}{P} \qquad \int_0^P (Z-1)\frac{dP}{P}$$

Graphical integration requires simple plots of $(\partial Z/\partial T)_P/P$ and $(Z-1)/P$ vs. P. Values of $(Z-1)/P$ are found from the compressibility-factor data at 360 K. The quantity $(\partial Z/\partial T)_P/P$ requires evaluation of the partial derivative $(\partial Z/\partial T)_P$, given by the slope of a plot of Z vs. T at constant pressure. For this purpose, separate plots are made of Z vs. T for each pressure at which compressibility-factor data are given, and a slope is determined at 360 K for each curve (for example, by construction of a tangent line at 360 K). Data for the required plots are shown in Table 6.2.

Table 6.2: Values of the Integrands Required in Ex. 6.3
Values in parentheses are by extrapolation.

P/bar	$[(\partial Z/\partial T)_P/P] \times 10^4$/K^{-1} bar^{-1}	$[-(Z-1)/P] \times 10^2$/bar^{-1}
0	(1.780)	(2.590)
0.10	1.700	2.470
0.50	1.514	2.186
2	1.293	1.759
4	1.290	1.591
6	1.395	1.544
8	1.560	1.552
10	1.777	1.592
12	2.073	1.658
14	2.432	1.750
15.41	(2.720)	(1.835)

The values of the two integrals are

$$\int_0^P \left(\frac{\partial Z}{\partial T}\right)_P \frac{dP}{P} = 26.37 \times 10^{-4}\ \mathrm{K}^{-1} \qquad \int_0^P (Z-1)\frac{dP}{P} = -0.2596$$

By Eq. (6.46), $$\frac{H^R}{RT} = -(360)(26.37 \times 10^{-4}) = -0.9493$$

By Eq. (6.48), $$\frac{S^R}{R} = -0.9493 - (-0.2596) = -0.6897$$

For $R = 8.314$ J mol^{-1} K^{-1},

$$H^R = (-0.9493)(8.314)(360) = -2841.3 \text{ J mol}^{-1}$$

$$S^R = (-0.6897)(8.314) = -5.734 \text{ J mol}^{-1} \text{ K}^{-1}$$

Values of the integrals in Eqs. (6.50) and (6.51) are

$$8.314 \times \text{ICPH}(300,360;1.7765,33.037\text{E-}3,0.0,0.0) = 6324.8 \text{ J mol}^{-1}$$

$$8.314 \times \text{ICPS}(300,360;1.7765,33.037\text{E-}3,0.0,0.0) = 19.174 \text{ J mol}^{-1} \text{ K}^{-1}$$

Substitution of numerical values into Eqs. (6.50) and (6.51) yields:

$$H = 18\,115.0 + 6324.8 - 2841.3 = 21\,598.5 \text{ J mol}^{-1}$$

$$S = 295.976 + 19.174 - 8.314 \ln 15.41 - 5.734 = 286.676 \text{ J mol}^{-1} \text{ K}^{-1}$$

Although calculations are here carried out for just one state, enthalpies and entropies can be evaluated for any number of states, given adequate data. After having completed a set of calculations, one is not irrevocably committed to the particular values of H_0^{ig} and S_0^{ig} initially assigned. The scale of values for either the enthalpy or the entropy can be shifted by addition of a constant to all values. In this way one can give arbitrary values to H and S for some particular state so as to make the scales convenient for one purpose or another.

The calculation of thermodynamic properties is an exacting task, seldom required of an engineer. However, engineers do make practical use of thermodynamic properties, and an understanding of calculational methods should suggest that some uncertainty is associated with every property value. Inaccuracy derives partly from experimental error in the data; they are also frequently incomplete and must be extended by interpolation and extrapolation. Moreover, even with reliable PVT data, a loss of accuracy occurs in the differentiation process required in the calculation of derived properties. Thus data of a high order of accuracy are required to produce enthalpy and entropy values suitable for engineering calculations.

6.3 RESIDUAL PROPERTIES BY EQUATIONS OF STATE

An attractive alternative to the numerical evaluation of integrals in Eqs. (6.46) and (6.48) is their analytical evaluation by equations of state. This requires an equation which can be directly solved for Z (or V) as a function of P at constant T. Such an equation of state is said to be *volume explicit*, and the only example presented in Chap. 3 is the virial expansion in P. The other equations of state are *pressure explicit*; i.e., they can be solved for Z (or P) as functions of V at constant T. They are not suitable for direct use with Eqs. (6.46) and (6.48). The virial expansion in V and all cubic equations of state are pressure explicit,[4] and their use for evaluation of residual properties requires the reformulation of Eqs. (6.46), (6.48), and (6.49). In what

[4]The ideal-gas equation is both pressure and volume explicit.

follows, we treat the calculation of residual properties for gases and vapors through use of the virial equations and cubic equations of state.

Residual Properties from the Virial Equations of State

Equation (3.38), the two-term virial equation, gives $Z-1 = BP/RT$. Substitution in Eq. (6.49) reduces it to

$$\frac{G^R}{RT} = \frac{BP}{RT} \tag{6.54}$$

By Eq. (6.44),
$$\frac{H^R}{RT} = -T\left[\frac{\partial(G^R/RT)}{\partial T}\right]_{P,x} = -T\left(\frac{P}{R}\right)\left(\frac{1}{T}\frac{dB}{dT} - \frac{B}{T^2}\right)$$

or
$$\frac{H^R}{RT} = \frac{P}{R}\left(\frac{B}{T} - \frac{dB}{dT}\right) \tag{6.55}$$

Substitution of Eqs. (6.54) and (6.55) into Eq. (6.47) yields:

$$\frac{S^R}{R} = -\frac{P}{R}\frac{dB}{dT} \tag{6.56}$$

Evaluation of residual enthalpies and residual entropies by Eqs. (6.55) and (6.56) is straightforward for given values of T, P, and composition, provided one has sufficient data to evaluate B and dB/dT. The range of applicability of these equations is the same as for Eq. (3.38), as discussed in Sec. 3.4.

Equations (6.46), (6.48), and (6.49) are incompatible with pressure-explicit equations of state, and must be transformed to make V (or molar density ρ) the variable of integration. In application ρ is a more convenient variable than V, and the equation, $PV = ZRT$, is written in the alternative form,

$$P = Z\rho RT \tag{6.57}$$

Differentiation gives: $dP = RT(Z\,d\rho + \rho\,dZ)$ (const T)

In combination with Eq. (6.57), this equation is recast as

$$\frac{dP}{P} = \frac{d\rho}{\rho} + \frac{dZ}{Z} \qquad \text{(const } T\text{)}$$

Upon substitution for dP/P, Eq. (6.49) becomes

$$\boxed{\frac{G^R}{RT} = \int_0^{\rho}(Z-1)\frac{d\rho}{\rho} + Z - 1 - \ln Z} \tag{6.58}$$

where the integral is evaluated at constant T. Note also that $\rho \to 0$ when $P \to 0$.

Solving Eq. (6.42) for its final term and substituting for V^R by Eq. (6.40) yields

$$\frac{H^R}{RT^2}dT = (Z-1)\frac{dP}{P} - d\left(\frac{G^R}{RT}\right)$$

Division by dT and restriction to constant ρ gives

$$\frac{H^R}{RT^2} = \frac{Z-1}{P}\left(\frac{\partial P}{\partial T}\right)_\rho - \left[\frac{\partial(G^R/RT)}{\partial T}\right]_\rho$$

Differentiation of Eq. (6.57) provides the first derivative on the right, and differentiation of Eq. (6.58) provides the second. Substitution leads to

$$\boxed{\frac{H^R}{RT} = -T\int_0^\rho \left(\frac{\partial Z}{\partial T}\right)_\rho \frac{d\rho}{\rho} + Z - 1} \tag{6.59}$$

The residual entropy is found from Eq. (6.47):

$$\boxed{\frac{S^R}{R} = \ln Z - T\int_0^\rho \left(\frac{\partial Z}{\partial T}\right)_\rho \frac{d\rho}{\rho} - \int_0^\rho (Z-1)\frac{d\rho}{\rho}} \tag{6.60}$$

The three-term virial equation is the simplest pressure-explicit equation of state:

$$Z - 1 = B\rho + C\rho^2 \tag{3.40}$$

Substitution into Eqs. (6.58) through (6.60) leads to

$$\frac{G^R}{RT} = 2B\rho + \frac{3}{2}C\rho^2 - \ln Z \tag{6.61}$$

$$\frac{H^R}{RT} = T\left[\left(\frac{B}{T} - \frac{dB}{dT}\right)\rho + \left(\frac{C}{T} - \frac{1}{2}\frac{dC}{dT}\right)\rho^2\right] \tag{6.62}$$

$$\frac{S^R}{R} = \ln Z - T\left[\left(\frac{B}{T} + \frac{dB}{dT}\right)\rho + \frac{1}{2}\left(\frac{C}{T} + \frac{dC}{dT}\right)\rho^2\right] \tag{6.63}$$

Application of these equations, useful for gases up to moderate pressures, requires data for both the second and third virial coefficients.

Residual Properties by Cubic Equations of State

Results of some generality follow from application of the generic cubic equation of state:

$$P = \frac{RT}{V-b} - \frac{a(T)}{(V+\epsilon b)(V+\sigma b)} \tag{3.42}$$

Derivations with this equation are much more convenient when it is recast to yield Z with density ρ as the independent variable. We therefore divide Eq. (3.42) through by ρRT and substitute $V = 1/\rho$. With q given by Eq. (3.51), the result after some alegbraic reduction is

$$Z = \frac{1}{1-\rho b} - q\frac{\rho b}{(1+\epsilon\rho b)(1+\sigma\rho b)}$$

The two quantities needed for evaluation of the integrals in Eqs. (6.58) through (6.60), $Z - 1$ and $(\partial Z/\partial T)_\rho$, are readily found from this equation:

$$Z - 1 = \frac{\rho b}{1 - \rho b} - q\frac{\rho b}{(1 + \epsilon\rho b)(1 + \sigma\rho b)} \tag{6.64}$$

$$\left(\frac{\partial Z}{\partial T}\right)_\rho = -\left(\frac{dq}{dT}\right)\frac{\rho b}{(1 + \epsilon\rho b)(1 + \sigma\rho b)}$$

The integrals of Eqs. (6.58) through (6.60) are now evaluated as follows:

$$\int_0^\rho (Z - 1)\frac{d\rho}{\rho} = \int_0^\rho \frac{\rho b}{1 - \rho b}\frac{d(\rho b)}{\rho b} - q\int_0^\rho \frac{d(\rho b)}{(1 + \epsilon\rho b)(1 + \sigma\rho b)}$$

$$\int_0^\rho \left(\frac{\partial Z}{\partial T}\right)_\rho \frac{d\rho}{\rho} = -\frac{dq}{dT}\int_0^\rho \frac{d(\rho b)}{(1 + \epsilon\rho b)(1 + \sigma\rho b)}$$

These two equations simplify to

$$\int_0^\rho (Z - 1)\frac{d\rho}{\rho} = -\ln(1 - \rho b) - qI \qquad \int_0^\rho \left(\frac{\partial Z}{\partial T}\right)_\rho \frac{d\rho}{\rho} = -\frac{dq}{dT}I$$

where by definition, $$I \equiv \int_0^\rho \frac{d(\rho b)}{(1 + \epsilon\rho b)(1 + \sigma\rho b)} \qquad \text{(const } T\text{)}$$

The generic equation of state presents two cases for the evaluation of this integral:

Case I $\epsilon \neq \sigma$ $$I = \frac{1}{\sigma - \epsilon}\ln\left(\frac{1 + \sigma\rho b}{1 + \epsilon\rho b}\right) \tag{6.65a}$$

Application of this and subsequent equations is simpler when ρ is eliminated in favor of Z. By Eq. (3.50) and the definition of Z,

$$\beta \equiv \frac{bP}{RT} \qquad Z \equiv \frac{P}{\rho RT} \qquad \text{whence} \qquad \frac{\beta}{Z} = \rho b$$

$$I = \frac{1}{\sigma - \epsilon}\ln\left(\frac{Z + \sigma\beta}{Z + \epsilon\beta}\right) \tag{6.65b}$$

Case II $\epsilon = \sigma$ $$I = \frac{\rho b}{1 + \epsilon\rho b} = \frac{\beta}{Z + \epsilon\beta}$$

The van der Waals equation is the only one considered here to which Case II applies, and this equation then reduces to $I = \beta/Z$.

With evaluation of the integrals, Eqs. (6.58) through (6.60) reduce to

$$\frac{G^R}{RT} = Z - 1 - \ln(1 - \rho b)Z - qI \tag{6.66a}$$

or

$$\boxed{\frac{G^R}{RT} = Z - 1 - \ln(Z - \beta) - qI} \tag{6.66b}$$

$$\frac{H^R}{RT} = Z - 1 + T\left(\frac{dq}{dT}\right)I = Z - 1 + T_r\left(\frac{dq}{dT_r}\right)I$$

and

$$\frac{S^R}{R} = \ln(Z - \beta) + \left(q + T_r\frac{dq}{dT_r}\right)I$$

The quantity $T_r(dq/dT_r)$ is readily found from Eq. (3.54):

$$T_r\frac{dq}{dT_r} = \left[\frac{d\ln\alpha(T_r)}{d\ln T_r} - 1\right]q$$

Substitution for this quantity in the preceding two equations yields:

$$\boxed{\frac{H^R}{RT} = Z - 1 + \left[\frac{d\ln\alpha(T_r)}{d\ln T_r} - 1\right]qI} \tag{6.67}$$

$$\boxed{\frac{S^R}{R} = \ln(Z - \beta) + \frac{d\ln\alpha(T_r)}{d\ln T_r}qI} \tag{6.68}$$

Preliminary to application of these equations one must find Z by solution of Eq. (3.52) for a vapor phase or Eq. (3.56) for a liquid phase.

Example 6.4

Find values for the residual enthalpy H^R and the residual entropy S^R for n-butane gas at 500 K and 50 bar as given by the Redlich/Kwong equation.

Solution

For the given conditions,

$$T_r = \frac{500}{425.1} = 1.176 \qquad P_r = \frac{50}{37.96} = 1.317$$

By Eq. (3.53), with Ω for the Redlich/Kwong equation from Table 3.1, p. 98,

$$\beta = \Omega\frac{P_r}{T_r} = \frac{(0.086\,64)(1.317)}{1.176} = 0.097\,03$$

With values for Ψ and Ω, and with the expression $\alpha(T_r) = T_r^{-1/2}$ from Table 3.1. Eq. (3.54) yields

$$q = \frac{\Psi\,\alpha(T_r)}{\Omega\,T_r} = \frac{0.427\,48}{(0.086\,64)(1.176)^{1.5}} = 3.8689$$

Substitution of β, q, $\epsilon = 0$, and $\sigma = 1$ into Eq. (3.52) reduces it to

$$Z = 1 + 0.097\,03 - (3.8689)(0.097\,03)\frac{Z - 0.097\,03}{Z(Z + 0.097\,03)}$$

Solution of this equation yields $Z = 0.6850$. Then

$$I = \ln\frac{Z + \beta}{Z} = 0.132\,47$$

With $\ln\alpha(T_r) = -\frac{1}{2}\ln T_r$, $d\ln\alpha(T_r)/d\ln T_r = -\frac{1}{2}$. Then Eqs. (6.67) and (6.68) become

$$\frac{H^R}{RT} = 0.6850 - 1 + (-0.5 - 1)(3.8689)(0.132\,47) = -1.0838$$

$$\frac{S^R}{R} = \ln(0.6850 - 0.097\,03) - (0.5)(3.8689)(0.132\,47) = -0.787\,35$$

Whence, $H^R = (8.314)(500)(-1.0838) = -4505 \text{ J mol}^{-1}$

$$S^R = (8.314)(-0.78735) = -6.546 \text{ J mol}^{-1}\text{ K}^{-1}$$

These results are compared with those of other calculations in Table 6.3.

Table 6.3: Values for Z, H^R, and S^R for *n*-Butane at 500 K and 50 bar

Method	Z	H^R/J mol^{-1}	S^R/J mol^{-1} K^{-1}
vdW Eqn.	0.6608	−3937	−5.424
RK Eqn.	0.6850	−4505	−6.546
SRK Eqn.	0.7222	−4824	−7.413
PR Eqn.	0.6907	−4988	−7.426
Lee/Kesler†	0.6988	−4966	−7.632
Handbook‡	0.7060	−4760	−7.170

† Described in Sec. 6.7.
‡ Values derived from numbers in Table 2–240, p. 2–223, *Chemical Engineers' Handbook*, 7th ed., Don Green (ed.), McGraw-Hill, New York, 1997.

6.4 TWO-PHASE SYSTEMS

The curves shown on the PT diagram of Fig. 3.1 represent phase boundaries for a pure substance. A phase transition at constant temperature and pressure occurs whenever one of these curves is crossed, and as a result the molar or specific values of the extensive thermodynamic properties change abruptly. Thus the molar or specific volume of a saturated liquid is very different from the molar or specific volume of saturated vapor at the same T and P. This is true as well for internal energy, enthalpy, and entropy. The exception is the molar or specific Gibbs energy, which for a pure species does not change during a phase transition such as melting, vaporization, or sublimation. Consider a pure liquid in equilibrium with its vapor in a piston/cylinder arrangement at temperature T and the corresponding vapor pressure P^{sat}. When a differential amount of liquid is caused to evaporate at constant T and P, Eq. (6.6) applied to the process reduces to $d(nG) = 0$. Because the number of moles n is constant, $dG = 0$, and this requires the molar (or specific) Gibbs energy of the vapor to be identical with that of the liquid. More generally, for two phases α and β of a pure species coexisting at equilibrium,

$$G^\alpha = G^\beta \tag{6.69}$$

where G^α and G^β are the molar or specific Gibbs energies of the individual phases.

The Clapeyron equation, first introduced in Sec. 4.2, follows from this equality. If the temperature of a two-phase system is changed, then the pressure must also change in accord with the relation between vapor pressure and temperature if the two phases continue to coexist in equilibrium. Because Eq. (6.69) applies throughout this change,

$$dG^\alpha = dG^\beta$$

Substituting expressions for dG^α and dG^β as given by Eq. (6.10) yields:

$$V^\alpha \, dP^{\text{sat}} - S^\alpha \, dT = V^\beta \, dP^{\text{sat}} - S^\beta \, dT$$

which upon rearrangement becomes

$$\frac{dP^{\text{sat}}}{dT} = \frac{S^\beta - S^\alpha}{V^\beta - V^\alpha} = \frac{\Delta S^{\alpha\beta}}{\Delta V^{\alpha\beta}}$$

The entropy change $\Delta S^{\alpha\beta}$ and the volume change $\Delta V^{\alpha\beta}$ are changes which occur when a unit amount of a pure chemical species is transferred from phase α to phase β at the equilibrium T and P. Integration of Eq. (6.8) for this change yields the latent heat of phase transition:

$$\Delta H^{\alpha\beta} = T \Delta S^{\alpha\beta} \tag{6.70}$$

Thus, $\Delta S^{\alpha\beta} = \Delta H^{\alpha\beta}/T$, and substitution in the preceding equation gives

$$\frac{dP^{\text{sat}}}{dT} = \frac{\Delta H^{\alpha\beta}}{T \Delta V^{\alpha\beta}} \tag{6.71}$$

which is the Clapeyron equation.

For the particularly important case of phase transition from liquid l to vapor v, Eq. (6.71) is written as

$$\frac{dP^{\text{sat}}}{dT} = \frac{\Delta H^{lv}}{T \Delta V^{lv}} \tag{6.72}$$

But $$\Delta V^{lv} = \frac{RT}{P^{\text{sat}}} \Delta Z^{lv}$$

where ΔZ^{lv} is the compressibility-factor change of vaporization. Combination of the last two equations gives, on rearrangement:

$$\frac{d \ln P^{\text{sat}}}{dT} = \frac{\Delta H^{lv}}{RT^2 \Delta Z^{lv}} \tag{6.73}$$

or $$\frac{d \ln P^{\text{sat}}}{d(1/T)} = -\frac{\Delta H^{lv}}{R \Delta Z^{lv}} \tag{6.74}$$

Equations (6.72) through (6.74) are equivalent, exact forms of the Clapeyron equation for pure-species vaporization.

Example 6.5

The Clapeyron equation for vaporization may be simplified by introduction of reasonable approximations, namely, that the vapor phase is an ideal gas and that the molar volume of the liquid is negligible compared with the molar volume of the vapor. How do these assumptions alter the Clapeyron equation?

Solution

The assumptions made are expressed by:

$$\Delta V^{lv} = V^v = \frac{RT}{P^{\text{sat}}} \qquad \text{or} \qquad \Delta Z^{lv} = 1$$

Equation (6.74) yields: $$\Delta H^{lv} = -R \frac{d \ln P^{\text{sat}}}{d(1/T)}$$

This approximate equation, known as the Clausius/Clapeyron equation, relates the latent heat of vaporization directly to the vapor-pressure curve. Specifically, it shows that ΔH^{lv} is proportional to the slope of a plot of $\ln P^{\text{sat}}$ vs. $1/T$. Such plots of experimental data produce lines for many substances that are nearly straight. According to the Clausius/Clapeyron equation, this implies that ΔH^{lv} is almost constant, virtually independent of T. This is not true; ΔH^{lv} decreases monotonically with increasing temperature from the triple point to the critical point, where it becomes zero. The assumptions on which the Clausius/Clapeyron equation are based have approximate validity only at low pressures.

Temperature Dependence of the Vapor Pressure of Liquids

The Clapeyron equation is an exact thermodynamic relation, providing a vital connection between the properties of different phases. When applied to the calculation of latent heats of vaporization, its use presupposes knowledge of the vapor pressure-vs.-temperature relation. Because thermodynamics imposes no model of material behavior, either in general or for particular species, such relations are empirical. As noted in Ex. 6.5, a plot of $\ln P^{\text{sat}}$ vs. $1/T$ generally yields a line that is nearly straight:

$$\ln P^{\text{sat}} = A - \frac{B}{T} \tag{6.75}$$

where A and B are constants for a given species. This equation gives a rough approximation of the vapor-pressure relation for the entire temperature range from the triple point to the critical point. Moreover, it provides an excellent basis for interpolation between reasonably spaced values of T.

The Antoine equation, which is more satisfactory for general use, has the form

$$\ln P^{\text{sat}} = A - \frac{B}{T + C} \tag{6.76}$$

A principal advantage of this equation is that values of the constants A, B, and C are readily available for a large number of species.[5] Each set of constants is valid for a specified temperature range, and should not be used much outside of that range. Values of Antoine constants for selected substances are given in Table B.2 of App. B.

The accurate representation of vapor-pressure data over a wide temperature range requires an equation of greater complexity. The Wagner equation is one of the best available; it expresses the reduced vapor pressure as a function of reduced temperature:

$$\ln P_r^{\text{sat}} = \frac{A\tau + B\tau^{1.5} + C\tau^3 + D\tau^6}{1 - \tau} \tag{6.77}$$

where

$$\tau \equiv 1 - T_r$$

and A, B, C, and D are constants. Values of the constants either for this equation or for Eq. (6.76) are given by Reid, Prausnitz, and Poling[6] for many species.

Corresponding-States Correlations for Vapor Pressure

A number of corresponding-states correlations are available for the vapor pressure of non-polar, non-associating liquids. One of the simplest is that of Lee and Kesler.[7] It is a Pitzer-type correlation, of the form

$$\ln P_r^{\text{sat}}(T_r) = \ln P_r^0(T_r) + \omega \ln P_r^1(T_r) \tag{6.78}$$

[5] S. Ohe, *Computer Aided Data Book of Vapor Pressure*, Data Book Publishing Co.,Tokyo, 1976; T. Boublik, V. Fried, and E. Hala, *The Vapor Pressures of Pure Substances*, Elsevier, Amsterdam, 1984.

[6] R. C. Reid, J. M. Prausnitz, and B. E. Poling, *The Properties of Gases and Liquids*, 4th ed., App. A, McGraw-Hill, 1987.

[7] B. I. Lee and M. G. Kesler, *AIChE J.*, vol. 21, pp. 510—527, 1975.

where $$\ln P_r^0(T_r) = 5.927\,14 - \frac{6.096\,48}{T_r} - 1.288\,62 \ln T_r + 0.169\,347 T_r^6 \tag{6.79}$$

$$\ln P_r^1(T_r) = 15.2518 - \frac{15.6875}{T_r} - 13.4721 \ln T_r + 0.435\,77 T_r^6 \tag{6.80}$$

Lee and Kesler recommend that the value of ω used with Eq. (6.78) be found *from the correlation* by requiring that it reproduce the normal boiling point. In other words, ω for a particular substance is determined from:

$$\omega = \frac{\ln P_{r_n}^{\,sat} - \ln P_r^0(T_{r_n})}{\ln P_r^1(T_{r_n})} \tag{6.81}$$

where T_{r_n} is the reduced normal boiling point and $P_{r_n}^{\,sat}$ is the reduced vapor pressure corresponding to 1 standard atmosphere (1.013 25 bar).

Example 6.6

Determine the vapor pressure (in kPa) for liquid n-hexane at 0, 30, 60, and 90°C (273.15 K, 303.15 K, 333.15 K and 363.15 K):

(*a*) With constants from App. B.2 (*b*) From the Lee/Kesler correlation for $P_r^{\,sat}$

Solution

(*a*) With constants from App. B.2, the Antoine equation for n-hexane is:

$$\ln P^{\,sat}/\text{kPa} = 13.8193 - \frac{2696.04}{t/°\text{C} + 224.317}$$

Substitution of temperatures yields the values of $P^{\,sat}$ under the heading "Antoine" in the table below. We take these to be equivalent to good experimental values.

(*b*) We first determine ω from the Lee/Kesler correlation. At the normal boiling point of n-hexane (Table B.1),

$$T_{r_n} = \frac{341.9}{507.6} = 0.6736 \qquad \text{and} \qquad P_{r_n}^{\,sat} = \frac{1.01325}{30.25} = 0.033\,50$$

Application of Eq. (6.81) then gives the value of ω for use with the Lee/Kesler correlation: $\omega = 0.298$. With this value, the correlation produces the $P^{\,sat}$ values shown in the table. The average difference from the Antoine values is about 1.5%.

t/°C	T/K	$P^{\,sat}$/kPa (Antoine)	$P^{\,sat}$/kPa (Lee/Kesler)	t/°C	T/K	$P^{\,sat}$/kPa (Antoine)	$P^{\,sat}$/kPa (Lee/Kesler)
0	273.15	6.052	5.835	30	333.15	24.98	24.49
60	333.15	76.46	76.12	90	363.15	189.0	190.0

Two-Phase Liquid/Vapor Systems

When a system consists of saturated-liquid and saturated-vapor phases coexisting in equilibrium, the total value of any extensive property of the two-phase system is the sum of the total properties of the phases. Written for the volume, this relation is

$$nV = n^l V^l + n^v V^v$$

where V is the molar volume for a system containing a total number of moles $n = n^l + n^v$. Division by n gives

$$V = x^l V^l + x^v V^v$$

where x^l and x^v represent the mole fractions of the total system that are liquid and vapor. With $x^l = 1 - x^v$,

$$V = (1 - x^v)V^l + x^v V^v$$

In this equation the properties V, V^l, and V^v may be either molar or unit-mass values. The mass or molar fraction of the system that is vapor x^v is called the *quality*. Analogous equations can be written for the other extensive thermodynamic properties. All of these relations are represented by the generic equation

$$M = (1 - x^v)M^l + x^v M^v \tag{6.82a}$$

where M represents V, U, H, S, etc. An alternative form is sometimes useful:

$$M = M^l + x^v \Delta M^{lv} \tag{6.82b}$$

6.5 THERMODYNAMIC DIAGRAMS

A thermodynamic diagram is a graph showing for a particular substance a set of properties, e.g., T, P, V, H, and S. The most common diagrams are: TS, PH (usually $\ln P$ vs. H), and HS (called a *Mollier* diagram). The designations refer to the variables chosen for the coordinates. Other diagrams are possible, but are seldom used.

Figures 6.2 through 6.4 show the general features of these diagrams. Though based on data for water, their general character is similar for all substances. The two-phase states, represented by lines on the PT diagram of Fig. 3.1, lie over *areas* in these diagrams, and the triple point of Fig. 3.1 becomes a *line*. Lines of constant quality in a liquid/vapor region, provide directly two-phase property values. The critical point is identified by the letter C, and the solid curve passing through it represents states of saturated liquid (to the left of C) and of saturated vapor (to the right of C). The Mollier diagram (Fig. 6.4) does not usually include volume data. In the vapor or gas region, lines for constant temperature and constant *superheat* appear. Superheat is a term denoting the difference between the actual temperature and the saturation temperature at the same pressure. Thermodynamic diagrams included in this book are the PH diagrams for methane and tetrafluoroethane in App. G, and the Mollier diagram for steam on the inside of the back cover.

Paths of processes are easily traced on a thermodynamic diagram. For example, the boiler of a steam power plant has liquid water as feed at a temperature below its boiling point,

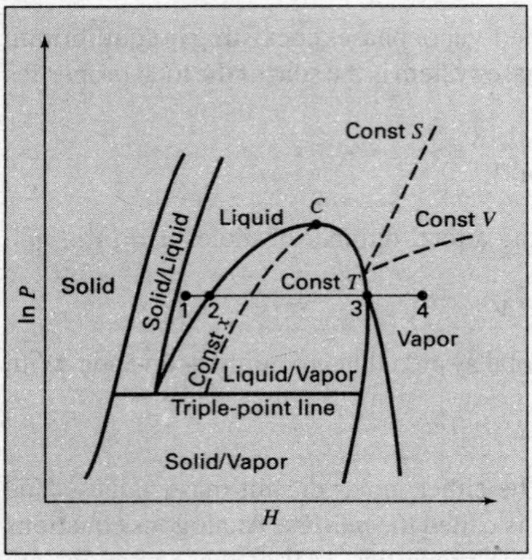

Figure 6.2: PH diagram

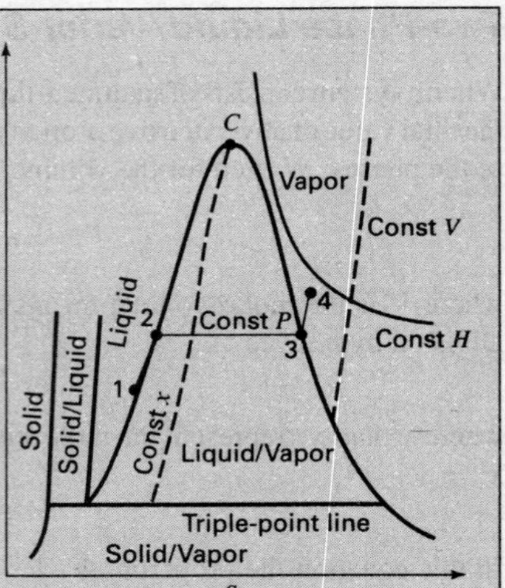

Figure 6.3: TS diagram

and superheated steam as product. Thus, water is heated at constant P to its saturation temperature (line 1–2 in Figs. 6.2 and 6.3), vaporized at constant T and P (line 2–3), and superheated at constant P (line 3–4). On a PH diagram (Fig. 6.2) the whole process is represented by a horizontal line corresponding to the boiler pressure. The same proess is shown on the TS diagram of Fig. 6.3. The compressibility of a liquid is small for temperatures well below T_c, and liquid-phase properties change very slowly with pressure. The constant-P lines on this diagram for the liquid region therefore lie very close together, and line 1–2 nearly coincides with the saturated-liquid curve. The isentropic path of the fluid in a reversible adiabatic turbine or compressor is represented on both the TS and HS (Mollier) diagrams by a vertical line from the initial to the final pressure.

6.6 TABLES OF THERMODYNAMIC PROPERTIES

In many instances thermodynamic properties are tabulated. This has the advantage that data can be presented more precisely than in diagrams, but the need for interpolation is introduced.

Thermodynamic tables for saturated steam from its normal freezing point to the critical point and for superheated steam over a substantial pressure range, in SI units, appear in App. F. Values are given at intervals close enough that linear interpolation is satisfactory.[8] The first table for each system of units shows the equilibrium properties of saturated liquid and saturated vapor at even increments of temperature. The enthalpy and entropy are arbitrarily assigned values of zero for water the saturated-liquid state at the triple point. The second table is for the gas region, and gives properties of superheated steam at temperatures higher

[8]Procedures for linear interpolation are shown at the beginning of App. F.

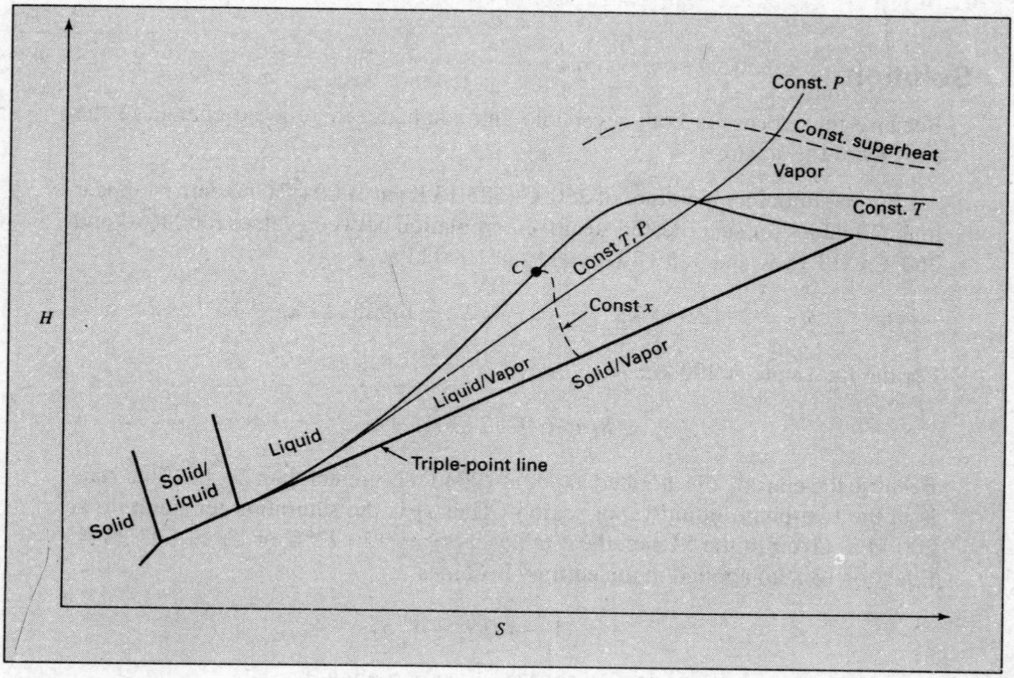

Figure 6.4: Mollier diagram

than the saturation temperature for a given pressure. Volume (V), internal energy (U), enthalpy (H), and entropy (S) are tabulated as functions of pressure at various temperatures. The steam tables are the most thorough compilation of properties for any single material. However, tables are available for a number of other substances.[9]

Example 6.7

Superheated steam originally at P_1 and T_1 expands through a nozzle to an exhaust pressure P_2. Assuming the process is reversible and adiabatic, determine the downstream state of the steam and ΔH for the following conditions:

$$P_1 = 1000 \text{ kPa}, \; t_1 = 250°\text{C (523.15 K), and } P_2 = 200 \text{ kPa}.$$

[9]Data for many common chemicals are given by R. H. Perry and D. Green, *Perry's Chemical Engineers' Handbook*, 7th ed., Sec. 2, McGraw-Hill, New York, 1996. See also N. B. Vargaftik, *Handbook of Physical Properties of Liquids and Gases*, 2d ed., Hemisphere Publishing Corp., Washington, DC, 1975. Data for refrigerants appear in the *ASHRAE Handbook: Fundamentals* (SI Edition), American Society of Heating, Refrigerating, and Air-Conditioning Engineers, Inc., Atlanta, 2005.

Solution

Because the process is both reversible and adiabatic, there is no change in the entropy of the steam.

For the initial temperature of 250°C (523.15 K) at 1000 kPa, no entries appear in the SI tables for superheated steam. Interpolation between values for 240°C and 260°C (513.15 K and 523.15 K) yields, at 1000 kPa:

$$H_1 = 2942.9 \text{ kJ kg}^{-1} \qquad S_1 = 6.9252 \text{ kJ kg}^{-1} \text{ K}^{-1}$$

For the final state at 200 kPa,

$$S_2 = S_1 = 6.9252 \text{ kJ kg}^{-1} \text{ K}^{-1}$$

Because the entropy of saturated vapor at 200 kPa is greater than S_2, the final state is in the two-phase liquid/vapor region. Thus t_2 is the saturation temperature at 200 kPa, given in the SI superheat tables as $t_2 = 120.23°\text{C}$ or $T_2 = 393.38$ K. Equation (6.82a) applied to the entropy becomes

$$S_2 = (1 - x_2^v)S_2^l + x_2^v S_2^v$$

Whence, $$6.9252 = 1.5301(1 - x_2^v) + 7.1268x_2^v$$

where the values 1.5301 and 7.1268 are entropies of saturated liquid and saturated vapor at 200 kPa. Solving,

$$x_2^v = 0.9640 \text{ (also known as dryness fraction)}$$

On a mass basis, the mixture is 96.40% vapor and 3.60% liquid. Its enthalpy is obtained by further application of Eq. (6.82a):

$$H_2 = (0.0360)(504.7) + (0.9640)(2706.3) = 2627.0 \text{ kJ kg}^{-1}$$

Finally, $$\Delta H = H_2 - H_1 = 2627.0 - 2942.9 = -315.9 \text{ kJ kg}^{-1}$$

For a nozzle, under the stated assumptions the steady-flow energy balance, Eq. (2.32a), becomes:

$$\Delta H + \frac{1}{2}\Delta u^2 = 0$$

Thus the decrease in enthalpy is exactly compensated by an increase in kinetic energy of the fluid. In other words, the velocity of a fluid increases as it flows through a nozzle, which is its usual purpose. Nozzles are treated in some detail in Sec. 7.1.

Example 6.8

A 1.5 m^3 tank contains 500 kg of liquid water in equilibrium with pure water vapor, which fills the remainder of the tank. The temperature and pressure are 100°C (373.15 K) and 101.33 kPa. From a water line at a constant temperature of 70°C (343.15 K) and a constant pressure somewhat above 101.33 kPa, 750 kg of liquid is bled into the tank. If the temperature and pressure in the tank are not to change as a result of the process, how much energy as heat must be transferred to the tank?

Solution

Choose the tank as the control volume. There is no work, and kinetic- and potential-energy changes are assumed negligible. Equation (2.29) therefore is written as

$$\frac{d(mU)_{\text{tank}}}{dt} - H'\dot{m}' = \dot{Q}$$

where the prime denotes the state of the inlet stream. The mass balance, $\dot{m}' = dm_{\text{tank}}/dt$, may be combined with the energy balance to yield:

$$\frac{d(mU)_{\text{tank}}}{dt} - H'\frac{dm_{\text{tank}}}{dt} = \dot{Q}$$

Multiplication by dt and integration over time (with H' constant) gives

$$Q = \Delta(mU)_{\text{tank}} - H'\Delta m_{\text{tank}}$$

The definition of enthalpy may be applied to the entire contents of the tank to give

$$\Delta(mU)_{\text{tank}} = \Delta(mH)_{\text{tank}} - \Delta(PmV)_{\text{tank}}$$

Because total tank volume mV and P are constant, $\Delta(PmV)_{\text{tank}} = 0$. Then, with $\Delta(mH)_{\text{tank}} = (m_2H_2)_{\text{tank}} - (m_1H_1)_{\text{tank}}$, the two preceding equations combine to yield

$$Q = (m_2H_2)_{\text{tank}} - (m_1H_1)_{\text{tank}} - H'\Delta m_{\text{tank}} \qquad (A)$$

where Δm_{tank} is the 750 kg of water bled into the tank, and subscripts 1 and 2 refer to conditions in the tank at the beginning and end of the process. At the end of the process the tank still contains saturated liquid and saturated vapor in equilibrium at 100°C (373.15 K) and 101.33 kPa. Hence m_1H_1 and m_2H_2 each consist of two terms, one for the liquid phase and one for the vapor phase.

The numerical solution makes use of the following enthalpies taken from the steam tables:

$$H' = 293.0 \text{ kJ kg}^{-1}; \text{ saturated liquid at 70°C (343.15 K)}$$
$$H^l_{\text{tank}} = 419.1 \text{ kJ kg}^{-1}; \text{ saturated liquid at 100°C (373.15 K)}$$
$$H^v_{\text{tank}} = 2676.0 \text{ kJ kg}^{-1}; \text{ saturated vapor at 100°C (373.15 K)}$$

The volume of vapor in the tank initially is 1.5 m^3 minus the volume occupied by the 500 kg of liquid water. Thus,

$$m_1^v = \frac{1.5 - (500)(0.001\,044)}{1.673} = 0.772 \text{ kg}$$

where 0.001 044 and 1.673 m^3 kg^{-1} are the specific volumes of saturated liquid and saturated vapor at 100°C from the steam tables. Then,

$$(m_1 H_1)_{\text{tank}} = m_1^l H_1^l + m_1^v H_1^v = 500(419.1) + 0.772(2676.0) = 211\,616 \text{ kJ}$$

At the end of the process, the masses of liquid and vapor are determined by a mass balance and by the fact that the tank volume is still 1.5 m^3:

$$m_2 = 500 + 0.772 + 750 = m_2^v + m_2^l$$

$$1.5 = 1.673 m_2^v + 0.001\,044 m_2^l$$

Whence, $m_2^l = 1250.65$ kg and $m_2^v = 0.116$ kg

Then, with $H_2^l = H_1^l$ and $H_2^v = H_1^v$,

$$(m_2 H_2)_{\text{tank}} = (1250.65)(419.1) + (0.116)(2676.0) = 524\,458 \text{ kJ}$$

Substitution of appropriate values into Eq. (A) gives:

$$Q = 524\,458 - 211\,616 - (750)(293.0) = 93\,092 \text{ kJ}$$

6.7 GENERALIZED PROPERTY CORRELATIONS FOR GASES

Of the two kinds of data needed for evaluation of thermodynamic properties, heat capacities and PVT data, the latter are most frequently missing. Fortunately, the generalized methods developed in Sec. 3.6 for the compressibility factor are also applicable to residual properties.

Equations (6.46) and (6.48) are put into generalized form by substitution of the relations:

$$P = P_c P_r \qquad T = T_c T_r$$

$$dP = P_c \, dP_r \qquad dT = T_c \, dT_r$$

The resulting equations [analogous to Equations (6.59) and (6.60)] are:

$$\frac{H^R}{RT_c} = -T_r^2 \int_0^{P_r} \left(\frac{\partial Z}{\partial T_r} \right)_{P_r} \frac{dP_r}{P_r} \tag{6.83}$$

$$\frac{S^R}{R} = -T_r \int_0^{P_r} \left(\frac{\partial Z}{\partial T_r} \right)_{P_r} \frac{dP_r}{P_r} - \int_0^{P_r} (Z - 1) \frac{dP_r}{P_r} \tag{6.84}$$

The terms on the right sides of these equations depend only on the upper limit P_r of the integrals and on the reduced temperature at which they are evaluated. Thus, values of H^R/RT_c and S^R/R may be determined once and for all at any reduced temperature and pressure from generalized compressibility-factor data.

The correlation for Z is based on Eq. (3.57):

$$Z = Z^0 + \omega Z^1$$

Differentiation yields $$\left(\frac{\partial Z}{\partial T_r}\right)_{P_r} = \left(\frac{\partial Z^0}{\partial T_r}\right)_{P_r} + \omega \left(\frac{\partial Z^1}{\partial T_r}\right)_{P_r}$$

Substitution for Z and $(\partial Z/\partial T_r)_{P_r}$ in Eqs. (6.83) and (6.84) gives

$$\frac{H^R}{RT_c} = -T_r^2 \int_0^{P_r} \left(\frac{\partial Z^0}{\partial T_r}\right)_{P_r} \frac{dP_r}{P_r} - \omega T_r^2 \int_0^{P_r} \left(\frac{\partial Z^1}{\partial T_r}\right)_{P_r} \frac{dP_r}{P_r}$$

$$\frac{S^R}{R} = -\int_0^{P_r} \left[T_r \left(\frac{\partial Z^1}{\partial T_r}\right)_{P_r} + Z^0 - 1\right] \frac{dP_r}{P_r} - \omega \int_0^{P_r} \left[T_r \left(\frac{\partial Z^1}{\partial T_r}\right)_{P_r} + Z^1\right] \frac{dP_r}{P_r}$$

The first integrals on the right sides of these two equations may be evaluated numerically or graphically for various values of T_r and P_r from the data for Z^0 given in Tables E.1 and E.3, and the integrals which follow ω in each equation may be similarly evaluated from the data for Z^1 given in Tables E.2 and E.4. Alternatively, their evaluation may be based on an equation of state (Sec. 6.3); Lee and Kesler used a modified form of the Benedict/Webb/Rubin equation of state to extend their generalized correlation to residual properties.

If the first terms on the right sides of the preceding equations (including the minus signs) are represented by $(H^R)^0/RT_c$ and $(S^R)^0/R$ and if the terms which follow ω, together with the preceding minus signs, are represented by $(H^R)^1/RT_c$ and $(S^R)^1/R$, then

$$\frac{H^R}{RT_c} = \frac{(H^R)^0}{RT_c} + \omega \frac{(H^R)^1}{RT_c} \qquad (6.85)$$	$$\frac{S^R}{R} = \frac{(S^R)^0}{R} + \omega \frac{(S^R)^1}{R} \qquad (6.86)$$

Calculated values of the quantities $(H^R)^0/RT_c$, $(H^R)^1/RT_c$, $(S^R)^0/R$, and $(S^R)^1/R$ as determined by Lee and Kesler are given as functions of T_r and P_r in Tables E.5 through E.12. These values, together with Eqs. (6.85) and (6.86), allow estimation of residual enthalpies and entropies on the basis of the three-parameter corresponding-states principle as developed by Lee and Kesler (Sec. 3.6). Calculated values of Z, H^R, and S^R for *n*-butane at 500 K and 50 bar based on the Lee/Kesler correlations are included in Table 6.3.

Tables E.5 and E.6 for $(H^R)^0/RT_c$ and Tables E.9 and E.10 for $(S^R)^0/R$, used alone, provide two-parameter corresponding-states correlations that quickly yield coarse estimates of the residual properties. The nature of these correlations is indicated by Fig. 6.5, which shows a plot of $(H^R)^0/RT_c$ vs. P_r for six isotherms.

As with the generalized compressibility-factor correlation, the complexity of the functions $(H^R)^0/RT_c$, $(H^R)^1/RT_c$, $(S^R)^0/R$, and $(S^R)^1/R$ precludes their general representation by simple equations. However, the generalized second-virial-coefficient correlation forms the

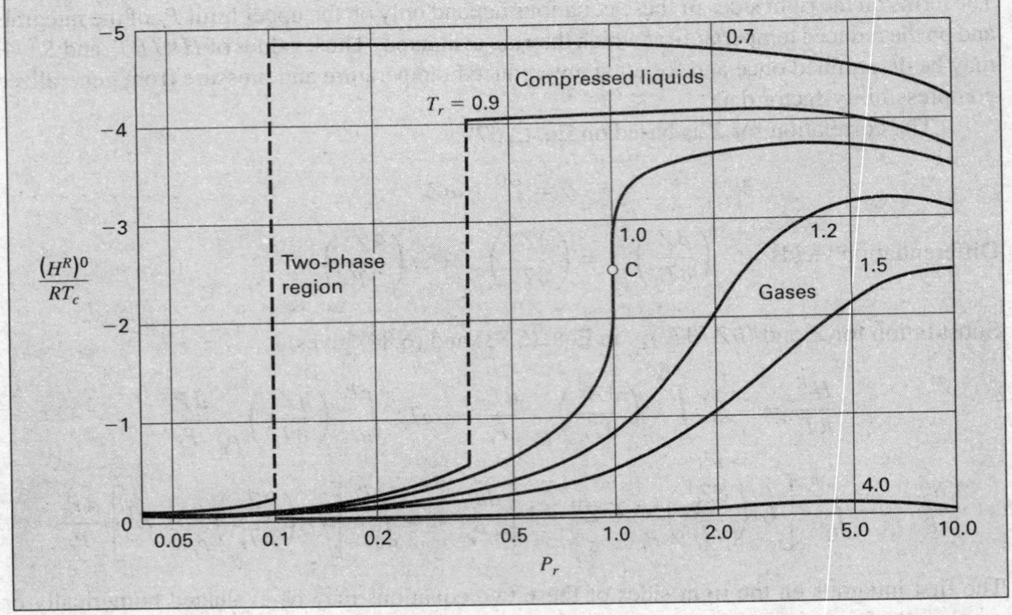

Figure 6.5: The Lee/Kesler correlation for $(H^R)^0/RT_c$ as a function of T_r and P_r.

basis for analytical correlations of the residual properties at low pressures. Recall Eqs. (3.62) and (3.63):

$$\hat{B} = \frac{BP_c}{RT_c} = B^0 + \omega B^1$$

Quantities $\hat{B}$, B^0, and B^1 are functions of T_r only. Hence,

$$\frac{d\hat{B}}{dT_r} = \frac{dB^0}{dT_r} + \omega\frac{dB^1}{dT_r}$$

Equations (6.55) and (6.56) may be written as

$$\frac{H^R}{RT_c} = P_r\left(\hat{B} - T_r\frac{d\hat{B}}{dT_r}\right) \qquad \frac{S^R}{R} = -P_r\frac{d\hat{B}}{dT_r}$$

Combining each of these equations with the previous two equations yields:

$$\frac{H^R}{RT_c} = P_r\left[B^0 - T_r\frac{dB^0}{dT_r} + \omega\left(B^1 - T_r\frac{dB^1}{dT_r}\right)\right] \tag{6.87}$$

$$\frac{S^R}{R} = -P_r\left(\frac{dB^0}{dT_r} + \omega\frac{dB^1}{dT_r}\right) \tag{6.88}$$

The dependence of B^0 and B^1 on reduced temperature is given by Eqs. (3.65) and (3.66). Differentiation of these equations provides expressions for dB^0/dT_r and dB^1/dT_r. Thus the equations required for application of Eqs. (6.87) and (6.88) are

$B^0 = 0.083 - \dfrac{0.422}{T_r^{1.6}}$ (3.65)	$B^1 = 0.139 - \dfrac{0.172}{T_r^{4.2}}$ (3.66)
$\dfrac{dB^0}{dT_r} = \dfrac{0.675}{T_r^{2.6}}$ (6.89)	$\dfrac{dB^1}{dT_r} = \dfrac{0.722}{T_r^{5.2}}$ (6.90)

Figure 3.14, drawn specifically for the compressibility-factor correlation, is also used as a guide to the reliability of the correlations of residual properties based on generalized second virial coefficients. However, all residual-property correlations are less accurate than the compressibility-factor correlations on which they are based and are, of course, least reliable for strongly polar and associating molecules.

The generalized correlations for H^R and S^R, together with ideal-gas heat capacities, allow calculation of enthalpy and entropy values of gases at any temperature and pressure by Eqs. (6.50) and (6.51). For a change from state 1 to state 2, write Eq. (6.50) for both states:

$$H_2 = H_0^{ig} + \int_{T_0}^{T_2} C_P^{ig}\, dT + H_2^R \qquad\qquad H_1 = H_0^{ig} + \int_{T_0}^{T_1} C_P^{ig}\, dT + H_1^R$$

The enthalpy change for the process, $\Delta H = H_2 - H_1$, is the difference between these two equations:

$$\Delta H = \int_{T_1}^{T_2} C_P^{ig}\, dT + H_2^R - H_1^R \tag{6.91}$$

Similarly, by Eq. (6.51),

$$\Delta S = \int_{T_1}^{T_2} C_P^{ig} \frac{dT}{T} - R \ln \frac{P_2}{P_1} + S_2^R - S_1^R \tag{6.92}$$

Written in alternative forms, these equations become

$$\Delta H = \langle C_P^{ig} \rangle_H (T_2 - T_1) + H_2^R - H_1^R \tag{6.93}$$

$$\Delta S = \langle C_P^{ig} \rangle_S \ln \frac{T_2}{T_1} - R \ln \frac{P_2}{P_1} + S_2^R - S_1^R \tag{6.94}$$

Just as we have given names to functions used in evaluation of the integrals in Eqs. (6.91) and (6.92) and the mean heat capacities in Eqs. (6.93) and (6.94), so also do we name functions useful for evaluation of H^R and S^R. Equations (6.87), (3.65), (6.89), (3.66), and (6.90) together provide a function for the evaluation of H^R/RT_c, named HRB(TR,PR,OMEGA):

$$\frac{H^R}{RT_c} = \text{HRB(TR,PR,OMEGA)}$$

A numerical value of H^R is therefore represented by

$$RT_c \times \text{HRB(TR,PR,OMEGA)}$$

Similarly, Eqs. (6.88) through (6.90) provide a function for the evaluation of S^R/R, named SRB(TR,PR,OMEGA):

$$\frac{S^R}{R} = \text{SRB(TR,PR,OMEGA)}$$

A numerical value of S^R is therefore represented by

$$R \times \text{SRB(TR,PR,OMEGA)}$$

Computer programs for evaluating these functions are given in App. D.

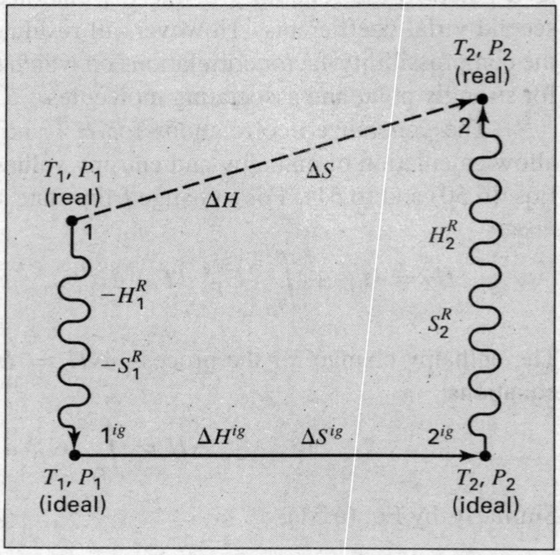

Figure 6.6: Calculational path for property changes ΔH and ΔS.

The terms on the right sides of Eqs. (6.91) through (6.94) are readily associated with steps in a *calculational path* leading from an initial to a final state of a system. Thus, in Fig. 6.6, the actual path from state 1 to state 2 (dashed line) is replaced by a three-step calculational path:

- **Step** $1 \to 1^{ig}$ A hypothetical process that transforms a real gas into an ideal gas at T_1 and P_1. The enthalpy and entropy changes for this process are

$$H_1^{ig} - H_1 = -H_1^R \qquad\qquad S_1^{ig} - S_1 = -S_1^R$$

- **Step** $1^{ig} \to 2^{ig}$ Changes in the ideal-gas state from (T_1, P_1) to (T_2, P_2). For this process,

$$\Delta H^{ig} = H_2^{ig} - H_1^{ig} = \int_{T_1}^{T_2} C_P^{ig}\, dT \tag{6.95}$$

$$\Delta S^{ig} = S_2^{ig} - S_1^{ig} = \int_{T_1}^{T_2} C_P^{ig} \frac{dT}{T} - R \ln \frac{P_2}{P_1} \tag{6.96}$$

- **Step** $2^{ig} \to 2$ Another hypothetical process that transforms the ideal gas back into a real gas at T_2 and P_2. Here,

$$H_2 - H_2^{ig} = H_2^R \qquad\qquad S_2 - S_2^{ig} = S_2^R$$

Equations (6.91) and (6.92) result from addition of the enthalpy and entropy changes for the three steps.

Example 6.9

Estimate V, U, H, and S for 1-butene vapor at 200°C (473.15 K) and 70 bar if H and S are set equal to zero for saturated liquid at 0°C (273.15 K). Assume that the only data available are

$$T_c = 420.0 \text{ K} \qquad P_c = 40.43 \text{ bar} \qquad \omega = 0.191$$

$$T_n = 266.9 \text{ K} \qquad \text{(normal boiling point)}$$

$$C_P^{ig}/R = 1.967 + 31.630 \times 10^{-3}T - 9.837 \times 10^{-6}T^2 \qquad (T/\text{K})$$

Solution

The volume of 1-butene vapor at 200°C (473.15 K) and 70 bar is calculated directly from the equation $V = ZRT/P$, where Z is given by Eq. (3.57) with values of Z^0 and Z^1 interpolated in Tables E.3 and E.4. For the reduced conditions,

$$T_r = \frac{200 + 273.15}{420.0} = 1.127 \qquad P_r = \frac{70}{40.43} = 1.731$$

the compressibility factor and molar volume are

$$Z = Z^0 + \omega Z^1 = 0.485 + (0.191)(0.142) = 0.512$$

$$V = \frac{ZRT}{P} = \frac{(0.512)(83.14)(473.15)}{70} = 287.8 \text{ cm}^3 \text{ mol}^{-1}$$

For H and S, use a calculational path like that of Fig. 6.6, leading from an initial state of saturated liquid 1-butene at 0°C (273.15 K), where H and S are zero, to the final state of interest. In this case, an initial vaporization step is required, leading to the four-step path shown by Fig. 6.7. The steps are

(*a*) Vaporization at T_1 and $P_1 = P^{sat}$

(*b*) Transition to the ideal-gas state at (T_1, P_1)

(*c*) Change to (T_2, P_2) in the ideal-gas state

(*d*) Transition to the actual final state at (T_2, P_2)

- **Step (*a*)** Vaporization of saturated liquid 1-butene at 0°C (273.15 K). The vapor pressure must be estimated, as it is not given. One method is based on the equation

$$\ln P^{sat} = A - \frac{B}{T} \qquad (6.75)$$

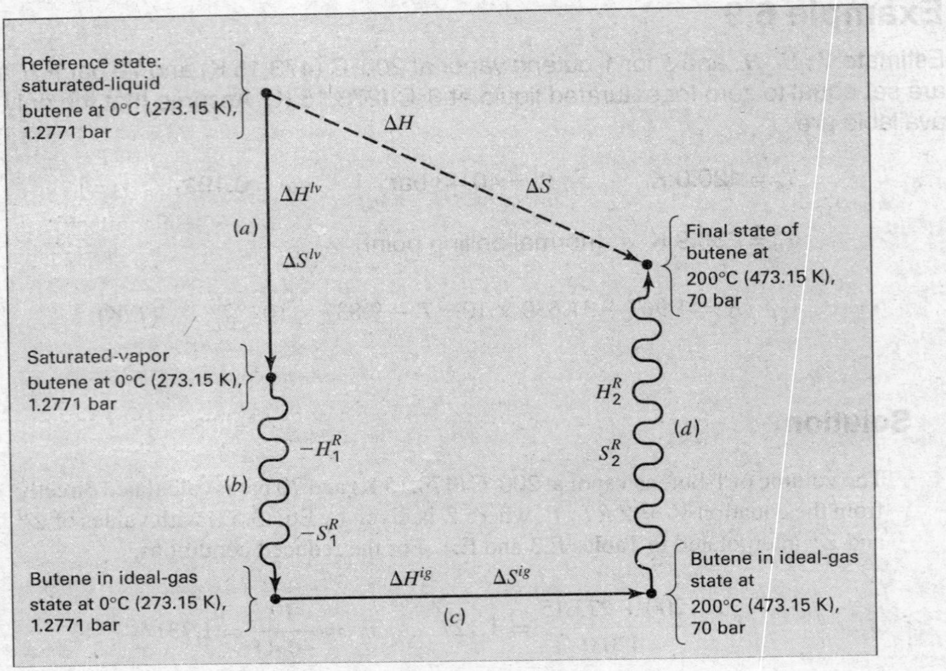

Figure 6.7: Calculational path for Ex. 6.9

The vapor-pressure curve contains both the normal boiling point, for which $P^{sat} = 1.0133$ bar at 266.9 K, and the critical point, for which $P^{sat} = 40.43$ bar at 420.0 K. For these two points,

$$\ln 1.0133 = A - \frac{B}{266.9} \qquad \ln 40.43 = A - \frac{B}{420.0}$$

Whence, $\quad A = 10.1260 \qquad B = 2699.11$

For 0°C (273.15 K), $P^{sat} = 1.2771$ bar, a result used in steps (b) and (c). Here, the latent heat of vaporization is required. Equation (4.12) provides an estimate at the normal boiling point, where $T_{r_n} = 266.9/420.0 = 0.636$:

$$\frac{\Delta H_n^{lv}}{RT_n} = \frac{1.092(\ln P_c - 1.013)}{0.930 - T_{r_n}} = \frac{1.092(\ln 40.43 - 1.013)}{0.930 - 0.636} = 9.979$$

Whence, $\quad \Delta H_n^{lv} = (9.979)(8.314)(266.9) = 22\,137 \text{ J mol}^{-1}$

The latent heat at 273.15 K, or $T_r = 273.15/420.0 = 0.650$, is given by Eq. (4.13):

$$\frac{\Delta H^{lv}}{\Delta H_n^{lv}} = \left(\frac{1 - T_r}{1 - T_{r_n}}\right)^{0.38}$$

or $\quad \Delta H^{lv} = (22\,137)(0.350/0.364)^{0.38} = 21\,810 \text{ J mol}^{-1}$

By Eq. (6.70),

$$\Delta S^{lv} = \Delta H^{lv}/T = 21\,810/273.15 = 79.84 \text{ J mol}^{-1} \text{ K}^{-1}$$

- **Step (*b*)** Transformation of saturated-vapor 1-butene into an ideal gas at the initial conditions (T_1, P_1). Because the pressure is relatively low, the values of H_1^R and S_1^R are estimated by Eqs. (6.87) and (6.88) for the reduced conditions, $T_r = 0.650$ and $P_r = 1.2771/40.43 = 0.0316$. The computational procedure is represented by

$$\text{HRB}(0.650,0.0316,0.191) = -0.0985$$

$$\text{SRB}(0.650,0.0316,0.191) = -0.1063$$

Whence, $H_1^R = (-0.0985)(8.314)(420.0) = -344 \text{ J mol}^{-1}$

$$S_1^R = (-0.1063)(8.314) = -0.88 \text{ J mol}^{-1} \text{ K}^{-1}$$

As indicated in Fig. 6.7, the property changes for this step are $-H_1^R$ and $-S_1^R$, because the change is from the real to the ideal-gas state.

- **Step (*c*)** Changes in the ideal-gas state from (273.15 K, 1.2771 bar) to (473.15 K, 70 bar). Here, ΔH^{ig} and ΔS^{ig} are given by Eqs. (6.95) and (6.96), for which (Secs. 4.1 and 5.5):

8.314 × ICPH(273.15,473.15;1.967,31.630E-3,-9.837E-6,0.0)

$$= 20\,564 \text{ J mol}^{-1}$$

8.314 × ICPS(273.15,473.15;1.967,31.630E-3,-9.837E-6,0.0)

$$= 55.474 \text{ J mol}^{-1} \text{ K}^{-1}$$

Thus, Eqs. (6.95) and (6.96) yield

$$\Delta H^{ig} = 20\,564 \text{ J mol}^{-1}$$

$$\Delta S^{ig} = 55.474 - 8.314 \ln \frac{70}{1.2771} = 22.18 \text{ J mol}^{-1} \text{ K}^{-1}$$

- **Step (*d*)** Transformation of 1-butene from the ideal-gas state to the real-gas state at T_2 and P_2. The final reduced conditions are

$$T_r = 1.127 \qquad P_r = 1.731$$

At the higher pressure of this step, H_2^R and S_2^R are found by Eqs. (6.85) and (6.86), together with the Lee/Kesler correlation. With interpolated values from Tables E.7, E.8, E.11, and E.12, these equations give

$$\frac{H_2^R}{RT_c} = -2.294 + (0.191)(-0.713) = -2.430$$

$$\frac{S_2^R}{R} = -1.566 + (0.191)(-0.726) = -1.705$$

$$\text{Whence,} \quad H_2^R = (-2.430)(8.314)(420.0) = -8485 \text{ J mol}^{-1}$$

$$S_2^R = (-1.705)(8.314) = -14.18 \text{ J mol}^{-1} \text{ K}^{-1}$$

The sums of the enthalpy and entropy changes for the four steps give the total changes for the process leading from the initial reference state (where H and S are set equal to zero) to the final state:

$$H = \Delta H = 21\,810 - (-344) + 20\,564 - 8485 = 34\,233 \text{ J mol}^{-1}$$

$$S = \Delta S = 79.84 - (-0.88) + 22.18 - 14.18 = 88.72 \text{ J mol}^{-1} \text{ K}^{-1}$$

The internal energy is:

$$U = H - PV = 34\,233 - \frac{(70)(287.8)}{10 \text{ cm}^3 \text{ bar J}^{-1}} = 32\,218 \text{ J mol}^{-1}$$

These results are in far better agreement with experimental values than would have been the case had we assumed 1-butene vapor an ideal gas.

Extension to Gas Mixtures

Although no theoretical basis exists for extension of generalized correlations to mixtures, approximate results for mixtures can often be obtained with *pseudocritical parameters* resulting from simple linear mixing rules according to the definitions:

$\omega \equiv \sum_i y_i \omega_i$ (6.97)	$T_{pc} \equiv \sum_i y_i T_{c_i}$ (6.98)	$P_{pc} \equiv \sum_i y_i P_{c_i}$ (6.99)

For quantum gases (e.g., hydrogen, helium and neon), use temperature-dependent effective critical parameters [similar to equations (3.58) and (3.59)] in equations (6.98) and (6.99) with $\omega_i = 0$.

The values so obtained are the mixture ω and pseudocritical temperature and pressure, T_{pc} and P_{pc}, which replace T_c and P_c to define *pseudoreduced parameters*:

$T_{pr} = \dfrac{T}{T_{pc}}$ (6.100)	$P_{pr} = \dfrac{P}{P_{pc}}$ (6.101)

These replace T_r and P_r for reading entries from the tables of App. E, and lead to values of Z by Eq. (3.57), H^R/RT_{pc} by Eq. (6.85), and S^R/R by Eq. (6.86).

Example 6.10

Estimate V, H^R, and S^R for an equimolar mixture of carbon dioxide(1) and propane(2) at 450 K and 140 bar by the Lee/Kesler correlations.

Solution

The pseudocritical parameters are found by Eqs. (6.97) through (6.99) with critical constants from Table B.1 of App. B:

$$\omega = y_1\omega_1 + y_2\omega_2 = (0.5)(0.224) + (0.5)(0.152) = 0.188$$

$$T_{pc} = y_1 T_{c_1} + y_2 T_{c_2} = (0.5)(304.2) + (0.5)(369.8) = 337.0 \text{ K}$$

$$P_{pc} = y_1 P_{c_1} + y_2 P_{c_2} = (0.5)(73.83) + (0.5)(42.48) = 58.15 \text{ bar}$$

Whence, $$T_{pr} = \frac{450}{337.0} = 1.335 \qquad P_{pr} = \frac{140}{58.15} = 2.41$$

Values of Z^0 and Z^1 from Tables E.3 and E.4 at these reduced conditions are

$$Z^0 = 0.697 \qquad \text{and} \qquad Z^1 = 0.205$$

By Eq. (3.57), $$Z = Z^0 + \omega Z^1 = 0.697 + (0.188)(0.205) = 0.736$$

Whence, $$V = \frac{ZRT}{P} = \frac{(0.736)(83.14)(450)}{140} = 196.7 \text{ cm}^3 \text{ mol}^{-1}$$

Similarly, from Tables E.7 and E.8, with substitution into Eq. (6.85):

$$\left(\frac{H^R}{RT_{pc}}\right)^0 = -1.730 \qquad \left(\frac{H^R}{RT_{pc}}\right)^1 = -0.169$$

$$\frac{H^R}{RT_{pc}} = -1.730 + (0.188)(-0.169) = -1.762$$

Whence, $$H^R = (8.314)(337.0)(-1.762) = -4937 \text{ J mol}^{-1}$$

From Tables E.11 and E.12 and substitution into Eq. (6.86),

$$\frac{S^R}{R} = -0.967 + (0.188)(-0.330) = -1.029$$

Whence, $$S^R = (8.314)(-1.029) = -8.56 \text{ J mol}^{-1} \text{ K}^{-1}$$

PROBLEMS

6.1. Starting with Eq. (6.8), show that isobars in the vapor region of a Mollier (HS) diagram must have positive slope and positive curvature.

6.2. (*a*) Making use of the fact that Eq. (6.20) is an exact differential expression, show that:

$$(\partial C_P/\partial P)_T = -T(\partial^2 V/\partial T^2)_P$$

What is the result of application of this equation to an ideal gas?

(*b*) Heat capacities C_V and C_P are defined as temperature derivatives respectively of U and H. Because these properties are related, one expects the heat capacities also to be related. Show that the general expression connecting C_P to C_V is

$$C_P = C_V + T\left(\frac{\partial P}{\partial T}\right)_V\left(\frac{\partial V}{\partial T}\right)_P$$

Show that Eq. (*B*) of Ex. 6.2 is another form of this expression.

6.3. If U is considered a function of T and P, the "natural" heat capacity is neither C_V nor C_P, but rather the derivative $(\partial U/\partial T)_P$. Develop the following connections between $(\partial U/\partial T)_P$, C_P, and C_V:

$$\left(\frac{\partial U}{\partial T}\right)_P = C_P - P\left(\frac{\partial V}{\partial T}\right)_P = C_P - \beta P V$$

$$= C_V + \left[T\left(\frac{\partial P}{\partial T}\right)_V - P\right]\left(\frac{\partial V}{\partial T}\right)_P = C_V + \frac{\beta}{\kappa}(\beta T - \kappa P)V$$

To what do these equations reduce for an ideal gas? For an incompressible liquid?

6.4. The PVT behavior of a certain gas is described by the equation of state:

$$P(V-b) = RT$$

where b is a constant. If in addition C_V is constant, show that

(*a*) U is a function of T only

(*b*) $\gamma = \text{const.}$

(*c*) For a mechanically reversible process, $P(V-b)^\gamma = \text{const.}$

6.5. A pure fluid is described by the *canonical equation of state*: $G = \Gamma(T) + RT \ln P$, where $\Gamma(T)$ is a substance-specific function of temperature. Determine for such a fluid expressions for V, S, H, U, C_P, and C_V. These results are consistent with those for an important model of gas-phase behavior. What is the model?

6.6. A pure fluid, described by the *canonical equation of state*: $G = F(T) + KP$, where $F(T)$ is a substance-specific function of temperature and K is a substance-specific constant. Determine for such a fluid expressions for V, S, H, U, C_P, and C_V. These results are consistent with those for an important model of liquid-phase behavior. What is the model?

6.7. Estimate the change in enthalpy and entropy when liquid ammonia at 270 K is compressed from its saturation pressure of 381 kPa to 1200 kPa. For saturated liquid ammonia at 270 K, $V^l = 1.551 \times 10^{-3}$ m^3 kg^{-1}, and $\beta = 2.095 \times 10^{-3}$ K^{-1}.

6.8. Liquid isobutane is throttled through a valve from an initial state of 360 K and 4000 kPa to a final pressure of 2000 kPa. Estimate the temperature change and the entropy change of the isobutane. The specific heat of liquid isobutane at 360 K is 2.78 J g^{-1} °C^{-1}. Estimates of V and β may be found from Eq. (3.72).

6.9. One kilogram of water (V_1 = 1003 cm^3 kg^{-1}) in a piston/cylinder device at 25°C (298.15 K) and 1 bar is compressed in a mechanically reversible, isothermal process to 1500 bar. Determine $Q, W, \Delta U, \Delta H$, and ΔS given that $\beta = 250 \times 10^{-6}$ K^{-1} and $\kappa = 45 \times 10^{-6}$ bar^{-1}. A satisfactory assumption is that V is constant at its arithmetic average value.

6.10. Liquid water at 25°C (298.15 K) and 1 bar fills a rigid vessel. If heat is added to the water until its temperature reaches 50°C (323.15 K), what pressure is developed? The average value of β between 25 and 50°C (298.15 K and 323.15 K) is 36.2×10^{-5} K^{-1}. The value of κ at 1 bar and 50°C (323.15 K) is 4.42×10^{-5} bar^{-1}, and may be assumed independent of P. The specific volume of liquid water at 25°C (298.15 K) is 1.0030 cm^3 g^{-1}.

6.11. Determine expressions for G^R, H^R, and S^R implied by the three-term virial equation in volume, Eq. (3.40).

6.12. Determine expressions for G^R, H^R, and S^R implied by the van der Waals equation of state, Eq. (3.41).

6.13. Determine expressions for G^R, H^R, and S^R implied by the Dieterici equation:

$$P = \frac{RT}{V - b} \exp\left(-\frac{a}{VRT}\right)$$

Here, parameters a and b are functions of composition only.

6.14. Calculate Z, H^R, and S^R by the Redlich/Kwong equation for one of the following, and compare results with values found from suitable generalized correlations:

(*a*) Acetylene at 300 K and 40 bar
(*b*) Argon at 175 K and 75 bar
(*c*) Benzene at 575 K and 30 bar
(*d*) *n*-Butane at 500 K and 50 bar
(*e*) Carbon dioxide at 325 K and 60 bar
(*f*) Carbon monoxide at 175 K and 60 bar
(*g*) Carbon tetrachloride at 575 K and 35 bar
(*h*) Cyclohexane at 650 K and 50 bar
(*i*) Ethylene at 300 K and 35 bar
(*j*) Hydrogen sulfide at 400 K and 70 bar
(*k*) Nitrogen at 150 K and 50 bar
(*l*) *n*-Octane at 575 K and 15 bar
(*m*) Propane at 375 K and 25 bar
(*n*) Propylene at 475 K and 75 bar

6.15. Calculate Z, H^R, and S^R by the Soave/Redlich/Kwong equation for the substance and conditions given by one of the parts of Pb. 6.14, and compare results with values found from suitable generalized correlations.

6.16. Calculate Z, H^R, and S^R by the Peng/Robinson equation for the substance and conditions given by one of the parts of Pb. 6.14, and compare results with values found from suitable generalized correlations.

6.17. Estimate the entropy change of vaporization of benzene at 50°C (323.15 K). The vapor pressure of benzene is given by the equation

$$\ln P^{\text{sat}}/\text{kPa} = 13.8858 - \frac{2788.51}{t/°\text{C} + 220.79}$$

(*a*) Use Eq. (6.72) with an estimated value of ΔV^{lv}.
(*b*) Use the Clausius/Clapeyron equation of Ex. 6.5.

6.18. Let P_1^{sat} and P_2^{sat} be values of the saturation vapor pressure of a pure liquid at absolute temperatures T_1 and T_2. Justify the following interpolation formula for estimation of the vapor pressure P^{sat} at intermediate temperature T:

$$\ln P^{\text{sat}} = \ln P_1^{\text{sat}} + \frac{T_2(T - T_1)}{T(T_2 - T_1)} \ln \frac{P_2^{\text{sat}}}{P_1^{\text{sat}}}$$

6.19. Assuming the validity of Eq. (6.75), derive *Edmister's formula* for estimation of the acentric factor:

$$\omega = \frac{3}{7}\left(\frac{\theta}{1-\theta}\right) \log P_c - 1$$

where $\theta \equiv T_n/T_c$, T_n is the normal boiling point, and P_c is in atm.

6.20. Very pure liquid water can be subcooled at atmospheric pressure to temperatures well below 0°C (273.15 K). Assume that 1 kg has been cooled as a liquid to −6°C (267.15 K). A small ice crystal (of negligible mass) is added to "seed" the subcooled liquid. If the subsequent change occurs adiabatically at atmospheric pressure, what fraction of the system freezes and what is the final temperature? What is ΔS_{total} for the process, and what is its irreversible feature? The latent heat of fusion of water at 0°C (273.15 K) is 333.4 J g^{-1}, and the specific heat of subcooled liquid water is 4.226 J g^{-1} °C^{-1}.

6.21. The state of 1 kg of steam is changed from saturated vapor at 1.38 bar to superheated vapor at 15 bar and 538°C (811.15 K). What are the enthalpy and entropy changes of the steam? What would the enthalpy and entropy changes be if steam were an ideal gas?

6.22. A two-phase system of liquid water and water vapor in equilibrium at 8000 kPa consists of equal volumes of liquid and vapor. If the total volume $V^t = 0.15$ m^3, what is the total enthalpy H^t and what is the total entropy S^t?

6.23. A vessel contains 1 kg of H_2O as liquid and vapor in equilibrium at 1000 kPa. If the vapor occupies 70% of the volume of the vessel, determine H and S for the 1 kg of H_2O.

6.24. A pressure vessel contains liquid water and water vapor in equilibrium at 177°C (450.15 K). The total mass of liquid and vapor is 1.36 kg. If the volume of vapor is 50 times the volume of liquid, what is the total enthalpy of the contents of the vessel?

6.25. Wet steam at 230°C (503.15 K) has a density of 0.025 g cm^{-3}. Determine x, H, and S.

6.26. A vessel of 0.15 m^3 volume containing saturated-vapor steam at 150°C (423.15 K) is cooled to 30°C (303.15 K). Determine the final volume and mass of *liquid* water in the vessel.

6.27. Wet steam at 1100 kPa expands at constant enthalpy (as in a throttling process) to 101.33 kPa, where its temperature is 105°C (378.15 K). What is the quality of the steam in its initial state?

6.28. Steam at 2100 kPa and 260°C (533.15 K) expands at constant enthalpy (as in a throttling process) to 125 kPa. What is the temperature of the steam in its final state and what is its entropy change? What would be the final temperature and entropy change for an ideal gas?

6.29. Steam at 20.7 bar and 260°C (533.15 K) expands at constant enthalpy (as in a throttling process) to 1.38 bar. What is the temperature of the steam in its final state and what is its entropy change? If steam were an ideal gas, what would be its final temperature and its entropy change?

6.30. Superheated steam at 500 kPa and 300°C (573.15 K) expands isentropically to 50 kPa. What is its final enthalpy?

6.31. What is the mole fraction of water vapor in air that is saturated with water at 25°C (298.15 K) and 101.33 kPa? At 50°C (323.15 K) and 101.33 kPa?

6.32. A rigid vessel contains 0.014 m^3 of saturated vapor steam in equilibrium with 0.021 m^3 of saturated-liquid water at 100°C (373.15 K). Heat is transferred to the vessel until one phase just disappears, and a single phase remains. Which phase (liquid or vapor) remains, and what are its temperature and pressure? How much heat is transferred in the process?

6.33. A vessel of 0.25 m^3 capacity is filled with saturated steam at 1500 kPa. If the vessel is cooled until 25 percent of the steam has condensed, how much heat is transferred and what is the final pressure?

6.34. A vessel of 2 m^3 capacity contains 0.02 m^3 of liquid water and 1.98 m^3 of water vapor at 101.33 kPa. How much heat must be added to the contents of the vessel so that the liquid water is just evaporated?

6.35. A rigid vessel of 0.4 m^3 volume is filled with steam at 800 kPa and 350°C (623.15 K). How much heat must be transferred from the steam to bring its temperature to 200°C (473.15 K)?

6.36. One kilogram of steam is contained in a piston/cylinder device at 800 kPa and 200°C (473.15 K).

(*a*) If it undergoes a mechanically reversible, isothermal expansion to 150 kPa, how much heat does it absorb?

(*b*) If it undergoes a reversible, adiabatic expansion to 150 kPa, what is its final temperature and how much work is done?

6.37. Steam at 2000 kPa containing 6% moisture is heated at constant pressure to 575°C (848.15 K). How much heat is required per kilogram?

6.38. Steam at 2700 kPa and with a quality of 0.90 undergoes a reversible, adiabatic expansion in a nonflow process to 400 kPa. It is then heated at constant volume until it is saturated vapor. Determine Q and W for the process.

6.39. Four kilograms of steam in a piston/cylinder device at 400 kPa and 175°C (448.15 K) undergoes a mechanically reversible, isothermal compression to a final pressure such that the steam is just saturated. Determine Q and W for the process.

6.40. Steam undergoes a change from an initial state of 450°C (723.15 K) and 3000 kPa to a final state of 140°C (413.15 K) and 235 kPa. Determine ΔH and ΔS:

(*a*) From steam-table data.

(*b*) By equations for an ideal gas.

(*c*) By appropriate generalized correlations.

6.41. A piston/cylinder device operating in a cycle with steam as the working fluid executes the following steps:

- Steam at 550 kPa and 200°C (473.15 K) is heated at constant volume to a pressure of 800 kPa.
- It then expands, reversibly and adiabatically, to the initial temperature of 200°C (473.15 K).

- Finally, the steam is compressed in a mechanically reversible, isothermal process to the initial pressure of 550 kPa.

What is the thermal efficiency of the cycle?

6.42. A piston/cylinder device operating in a cycle with steam as the working fluid executes the following steps:

- Saturated vapor steam at 20.7 bar is heated at constant pressure to 482°C (755.15 K).
- The steam then expands, reversibly and adiabatically, to the initial temperature of 214°C (487.15 K).
- Finally, the steam is compressed in a mechanically reversible, isothermal process to the initial state.

What is the thermal efficiency of the cycle?

6.43. Steam entering a turbine at 4000 kPa and 400°C (673.15 K) expands reversibly and adiabatically.

(*a*) For what discharge pressure is the exit stream a saturated vapor?
(*b*) For what discharge pressure is the exit stream a wet vapor with quality of 0.95?

6.44. A steam turbine, operating reversibly and adiabatically, takes in superheated steam at 2000 kPa and discharges at 50 kPa.

(*a*) What is the minimum superheat required so that the exhaust contains no moisture?
(*b*) What is the power output of the turbine if it operates under these conditions and the steam rate is 5 kg s^{-1}?

6.45. An operating test of a steam turbine produces the following results. With steam supplied to the turbine at 1350 kPa and 375°C (648.15 K), the exhaust from the turbine at 10 kPa is saturated vapor. Assuming adiabatic operation and negligible changes in kinetic and potential energies, determine the turbine efficiency, i.e., the ratio of actual work of the turbine to the work of a turbine operating isentropically from the same initial conditions to the same exhaust pressure.

6.46. A steam turbine operates adiabatically with a steam rate of 25 kg s^{-1}. The steam is supplied at 1300 kPa and 400°C (673.15 K) and discharges at 40 kPa and 100°C (373.15 K). Determine the power output of the turbine and the efficiency of its operation in comparison with a turbine that operates *reversibly* and adiabatically from the same initial conditions to the same final pressure.

6.47. From steam-table data, estimate values for the residual properties V^R, H^R, and S^R for steam at 225°C (498.15 K) and 1600 kPa, and compare with values found by a suitable generalized correlation.

6.48. From data in the steam tables:

(*a*) Determine values for G^l and G^v for saturated liquid and vapor at 1000 kPa. Should these be the same?

(*b*) Determine values for $\Delta H^{lv}/T$ and ΔS^{lv} at 1000 kPa. Should these be the same?

(*c*) Find values for V^R, H^R, and S^R for saturated vapor at 1000 kPa.

(*d*) Estimate a value for dP^{sat}/dT at 1000 kPa and apply the Clapeyron equation to evaluate ΔS^{lv} at 1000 kPa. Does this result agree with the steam-table value?

Apply appropriate generalized correlations for evaluation of V^R, H^R, and S^R for saturated vapor at 1000 kPa. Do these results agree with the values found in (*c*)?

6.49. From data in the steam tables:

(*a*) Determine numerical values of G^l and G^v for saturated liquid and vapor at 10.3 bar. Should these be the same?

(*b*) Determine numerical values of $\Delta H^{lv}/T$ and ΔS^{lv} at 10.3 bar. Should these be the same?

(*c*) Find numerical values of V^R, H^R, and S^R for saturated vapor at 10.3 bar.

(*d*) Estimate a value for dP^{sat}/dT at 10.3 bar and apply the Clapeyron equation to evaluate ΔS^{lv} at 10.3 bar. How well does this result agree with the steamtable value?

Apply appropriate generalized correlations for evaluation of V^R, H^R, and S^R for saturated vapor at 10.3 bar. How well do these results compare with the values found in (*c*)?

6.50. Propane gas at 1 bar and 35°C (308.15 K) is compressed to a final state of 135 bar and 195°C (468.15 K). Estimate the molar volume of the propane in the final state and the enthalpy and entropy changes for the process. In its initial state, propane may be assumed an ideal gas.

6.51. Propane at 70°C (343.15 K) and 101.33 kPa is compressed isothermally to 1500 kPa. Estimate ΔH and ΔS for the process by suitable generalized correlations.

6.52. A stream of propane gas is partially liquefied by throttling from 200 bar and 370 K to 1 bar. What fraction of the gas is liquefied in this process? The vapor pressure of propane is given by Eq. (6.77) with parameters: $A = -6.722\,19$, $B = 1.332\,36$, $C = -2.138\,68$, $D = -1.385\,51$.

6.53. Estimate the molar volume, enthalpy, and entropy for 1,3-butadiene as a saturated vapor and as a saturated liquid at 380 K. The enthalpy and entropy are set equal to zero for the ideal-gas state at 101.33 kPa and 0°C (273.15 K). The vapor pressure of 1,3-butadiene at 380 K is 1919.4 kPa.

6.54. Estimate the molar volume, enthalpy, and entropy for *n*-butane as a saturated vapor and as a saturated liquid at 370 K. The enthalpy and entropy are set equal to zero for the ideal-gas state at 101.33 kPa and 0°C (273.15 K). The vapor pressure of *n*-butane at 370 K is 1435 kPa.

6.55. The *total* steam demand of a plant over the period of an hour is 6000 kg, but instantaneous demand fluctuates from 4000 to 10000 kg hr^{-1}. Steady boiler operation at 6000 kg $hr^{-1}$is accommodated by inclusion of an *accumulator*, essentially a tank containing mostly saturated liquid water that "floats on the line" between the boiler and the plant. The boiler produces saturated steam at 1000 kPa, and the plant operates with steam at 700 kPa. A control valve regulates the steam pressure upstream from the accumulator and a second control valve regulates the pressure downstream from the accumulator. When steam demand is less than boiler output, steam flows into and is largely condensed by liquid residing in the accumulator, in the process increasing the pressure to values greater than 700 kPa. When steam demand is greater than boiler output, water in the accumulator vaporizes and steam flows out, thus reducing the pressure to values less than 1000 kPa. What accumulator volume is required for this service if no more that 95% of its volume should be occupied by liquid?

6.56. Propylene gas at 127°C (400.15 K) and 38 bar is throttled in a steady-state flow process to 1 bar, where it may be assumed to be an ideal gas. Estimate the final temperature of the propylene and its entropy change.

6.57. Propane gas at 22 bar and 423 K is throttled in a steady-state flow process to 1 bar. Estimate the entropy change of the propane caused by this process. In its final state, propane may be assumed to be an ideal gas.

6.58. Propane gas at 100°C (373.15 K) is compressed isothermally from an initial pressure of 1 bar to a final pressure of 10 bar. Estimate ΔH and ΔS.

6.59. Hydrogen sulfide gas is compressed from an initial state of 400 K and 5 bar to a final state of 600 K and 25 bar. Estimate ΔH and ΔS.

6.60. Carbon dioxide expands at constant enthalpy (as in a throttling process) from 1600 kPa and 45°C (318.15 K) to 101.33 kPa. Estimate ΔS for the process.

6.61. A stream of ethylene gas at 250°C (523.15 K) and 3800 kPa expands isentropically in a turbine to 120 kPa. Determine the temperature of the expanded gas and the work produced if the properties of ethylene are calculated by

(*a*) Equations for an ideal gas (*b*) Appropriate generalized correlations

6.62. A stream of ethane gas at 220°C (493.15 K) and 30 bar expands isentropically in a turbine to 2.6 bar. Determine the temperature of the expanded gas and the work produced if the properties of ethane are calculated by

(*a*) Equations for an ideal gas (*b*) Appropriate generalized correlations

6.63. Estimate the final temperature and the work required when 1 mol of *n*-butane is compressed isentropically in a steady-flow process from 1 bar and 50°C (323.15 K) to 7.8 bar.

6.64. Determine the maximum amount of work obtainable in a flow process from 1 kg of steam at 3000 kPa and 450°C (723.15 K) for surrounding conditions of 300 K and 101.33 kPa.

6.65. Liquid water at 325 K and 8000 kPa flows into a boiler at the rate of 10 kg s^{-1} and is vaporized, producing saturated vapor at 8000 kPa. What is the maximum fraction of the heat added to the water in the boiler that can be converted into work in a process whose product is water at initial conditions, if $T_\sigma = 300$ K? What happens to the rest of the heat? What is the rate of entropy change in the surroundings as a result of the work-producing process? In the system? Total?

6.66. Suppose the heat added to the water in the boiler in the preceding problem comes from a furnace at a temperature of 600°C (873.15 K). What is the total rate of entropy generation as a result of the heating process? What is W_{lost}?

6.67. An ice plant produces 0.5 kg s^{-1} of flake ice at 0°C (273.15 K) from water at 20°C (T_σ= 293.15 K) in a continuous process. If the latent heat of fusion of water is 333.4 kJ kg^{-1} and if the thermodynamic efficiency of the process is 32%, what is the power requirement of the plant?

6.68. An inventor has developed a complicated process for making heat continuously available at an elevated temperature. Saturated steam at 100°C (373.15 K) is the only source of energy. Assuming that there is plenty of cooling water available at 0°C (273.15 K), what is the maximum temperature level at which heat in the amount of 2000 kJ can be made available for each kilogram of steam flowing through the process?

6.69. Two boilers, both operating at 13.8 bar a discharge equal amounts of steam into the same steam main. Steam from the first boiler is superheated at 215°C (488.15 K) and steam from the second is wet with a quality of 96%. Assuming adiabatic mixing and negligible changes in potential and kinetic energies, what is the equilibrium condition after mixing and what is S_G for each kg of discharge steam?

6.70. A rigid tank of 2.265 m^3 capacity contains 1896 kg of saturated liquid water at 221°C (494.15 K). This amount of liquid almost completely fills the tank, the small remaining volume being occupied by saturated-vapor steam. Since a bit more vapor space in the tank is wanted, a valve at the top of the tank is opened, and saturated-vapor steam is vented to the atmosphere until the temperature in the tank falls to 215°C (488.15 K). Assuming no heat transfer to the contents of the tank, determine the mass of steam vented.

6.71. A tank of 50 m^3 capacity contains steam at 4500 kPa and 400°C (673.15 K). Steam is vented from the tank through a relief valve to the atmosphere until the pressure in the tank falls to 3500 kPa. If the venting process is adiabatic, estimate the final temperature of the steam in the tank and the mass of steam vented.

6.72. A tank of 4 m^3 capacity contains 1500 kg of liquid water at 250°C (523.15 K) in equilibrium with its vapor, which fills the rest of the tank. A quantity of 1000 kg of water at 50°C (323.15 K) is pumped into the tank. How much heat must be added during this process if the temperature in the tank is not to change?

6.73. Liquid nitrogen is stored in 0.5 m^3 metal tanks that are thoroughly insulated. Consider the process of filling an evacuated tank, initially at 295 K. It is attached to a line containing liquid nitrogen at its normal boiling point of 77.3 K and at a pressure of several bars. At this condition, its enthalpy is -120.8 kJ kg^{-1}. When a valve in the line is opened, the nitrogen flowing into the tank at first evaporates in the process of cooling the tank. If the tank has a mass of 30 kg and the metal has a specific heat capacity of 0.43 kJ kg^{-1} K^{-1}, what mass of nitrogen must flow into the tank just to cool it to a temperature such that *liquid* nitrogen begins to accumulate in the tank? Assume that the nitrogen and the tank are always at the same temperature. The properties of saturated nitrogen vapor at several temperatures are given as follows:

T/K	P/bar	V^v/m^3 kg^{-1}	H^v/kJ kg^{-1}
80	1.396	0.164 0	78.9
85	2.287	0.101 7	82.3
90	3.600	0.066 28	85.0
95	5.398	0.044 87	86.8
100	7.775	0.031 26	87.7
105	10.83	0.022 23	87.4
110	14.67	0.015 98	85.6

6.74. A well insulated tank of 50 m^3 volume initially contains 16 000 kg of water distributed between liquid and vapor phases at 25°C (298.15 K). Saturated steam at 1500 kPa is admitted to the tank until the pressure reaches 800 kPa. What mass of steam is added?

6.75. An insulated evacuated tank of 1.75 m^3 volume is attached to a line containing steam at 400 kPa and 240°C (513.15 K). Steam flows into the tank until the pressure in the tank reaches 400 kPa. Assuming no heat flow from the steam to the tank, prepare graphs showing the mass of steam in the tank and its temperature as a function of pressure in the tank.

6.76. A 2 m^3 tank initially contains a mixture of saturated-vapor steam and saturated-liquid water at 3000 kPa. Of the total mass, 10% is vapor. Saturated-liquid water is bled from the tank through a valve until the total mass in the tank is 40% of the initial total mass. If during the process the temperature of the contents of the tank is kept constant, how much heat is transferred?

6.77. A stream of water at 85°C (358.15 K), flowing at the rate of 5 kg s^{-1} is formed by mixing water at 24°C (297.15 K) with saturated steam at 400 kPa. Assuming adiabatic operation, at what rates are the steam and water fed to the mixer?

6.78. In a desuperheater, liquid water at 3100 kPa and 50°C (298.15 K) is sprayed into a stream of superheated steam at 3000 kPa and 375°C (648.15 K) in an amount such that a single stream of saturated-vapor steam at 2900 kPa flows from the desuperheater at the rate of 15 kg s^{-1}. Assuming adiabatic operation, what is the mass flowrate of the water? What is $\dot{S}_G$ for the process? What is the irreversible feature of the process?

6.79. Superheated steam at 700 kPa and 280°C (553.15 K) flowing at the rate of 50 kg s^{-1} is mixed with liquid water at 40°C (313.15 K) to produce steam at 700 kPa and 200°C (473.15 K). Assuming adiabatic operation, at what rate is water supplied to the mixer? What is $\dot{S}_G$ for the process? What is the irreversible feature of the process?

6.80. A stream of air at 12 bar and 900 K is mixed with another stream of air at 2 bar and 400 K with 2.5 times the mass flowrate. If this process were accomplished reversibly and adiabatically, what would be the temperature and pressure of the resulting air stream? Assume air to be an ideal gas for which $C_P = (7/2)R$.

6.81. Hot nitrogen gas at 400°C (673.15 K) and atmospheric pressure flows into a waste-heat boiler at the rate of 20 kg s^{-1}, and transfers heat to water boiling at 101.33 kPa. The water feed to the boiler is saturated liquid at 101.33 kPa, and it leaves the boiler as superheated steam at 101.33 kPa and 150°C (423.15 K). If the nitrogen is cooled to 170°C (443.15 K) and if heat is lost to the surroundings at a rate of 80 kJ for each kilogram of steam generated, what is the steam-generation rate? If the surroundings are at 25°C (298.15 K), what is $\dot{S}_G$ for the process? Assume nitrogen to be an ideal gas for which $C_P = (7/2)R$.

6.82. Show that isobars and isochores have positive slopes in the single-phase regions of a TS diagram. Suppose that $C_P = a + bT$, where a and b are positive constants. Show that the curvature of an isobar is also positive. For specified T and S, which is steeper: an isobar or an isochore? Why? Note that $C_P > C_V$.

6.83. Starting with Eq. (6.8), show that isotherms in the vapor region of a Mollier (HS) diagram have slopes and curvatures given by:

$$\left(\frac{\partial H}{\partial S}\right)_T = \frac{1}{\beta}(\beta T - 1) \qquad \left(\frac{\partial^2 H}{\partial S^2}\right)_T = -\frac{1}{\beta^3 V}\left(\frac{\partial \beta}{\partial P}\right)_T$$

Here, β is volume expansivity. If the vapor is described by the two-term virial equation in P, Eq. (3.38), what can be said about the *signs* of these derivatives? Assume that, for normal temperatures, B is negative and dB/dT is positive.

6.84. The temperature dependence of the second virial coefficient B is shown for nitrogen on Fig. 3.10. Qualitatively, the shape of $B(T)$ is the same for all gases; quantitatively, the temperature for which $B = 0$ corresponds to a reduced temperature of about $T_r = 2.7$

for many gases. Use these observations to show by Eqs. (6.54) through (6.56) that the residual properties G^R, H^R, and S^R are *negative* for most gases at modest pressures and normal temperatures. What can you say about the signs of V^R and C_P^R?

6.85. An equimolar mixture of methane and propane is discharged from a compressor at 5500 kPa and 90°C (363.15 K) at the rate of 1.4 kg s^{-1}. If the velocity in the discharge line is not to exceed 30 m s^{-1}, what is the minimum diameter of the discharge line?

6.86. Estimate V^R, H^R, and S^R for one of the following by appropriate generalized correlations:

(*a*) 1,3-Butadiene at 500 K and 20 bar
(*b*) Carbon dioxide at 400 K and 200 bar
(*c*) Carbon disulfide at 450 K and 60 bar
(*d*) *n*-Decane at 600 K and 20 bar
(*e*) Ethylbenzene at 620 K and 20 bar
(*f*) Methane at 250 K and 90 bar
(*g*) Oxygen at 150 K and 20 bar
(*h*) *n*-Pentane at 500 K and 10 bar
(*i*) Sulfur dioxide at 450 K and 35 bar
(*j*) Tetrafluoroethane at 400 K and 15 bar

6.87. Estimate Z, H^R, and S^R for one of the following *equimolar* mixtures by the Lee/Kesler correlations:

(*a*) Benzene/cyclohexane at 650 K and 60 bar
(*b*) Carbon dioxide/carbon monoxide at 300 K and 100 bar
(*c*) Carbon dioxide/*n*-octane at 600 K and 100 bar
(*d*) Ethane/ethylene at 350 K and 75 bar
(*e*) Hydrogen sulfide/methane at 400 K and 150 bar
(*f*) Methane/nitrogen at 200 K and 75 bar
(*g*) Methane/*n*-pentane at 450 K and 80 bar
(*h*) Nitrogen/oxygen at 250 K and 100 bar

6.88. For the reversible isothermal compression of a liquid for which β and κ may be assumed independent of pressure, show that

(*a*) $W = P_1V_1 - P_2V_2 - \dfrac{V_2 - V_1}{\kappa}$

(*b*) $\Delta S = \dfrac{\beta}{\kappa}(V_2 - V_1)$

(*c*) $\Delta H = \dfrac{1 - \beta T}{\kappa}(V_2 - V_1)$

Do not assume that V is constant at an average value, but use Eq. (3.5) for its P dependence (with V_2 replaced by V). Apply these equations to the conditions stated in Pb. 6.9. What do the results suggest with respect to use of an average value for V?

6.89. In general, for an arbitrary thermodynamic property of a pure substance, $M = M(T, P)$; whence

$$dM = \left(\frac{\partial M}{\partial T}\right)_P dT + \left(\frac{\partial M}{\partial P}\right)_T dP$$

For what *two* distinct conditions is the following equation true?

$$\Delta M = \int_{T_1}^{T_2} \left(\frac{\partial M}{\partial T}\right)_P dT$$

6.90. The enthalpy of a pure ideal gas depends on temperature only. Hence, H^{ig} is often said to be "independent of pressure," and one writes $(\partial H^{ig}/\partial P)_T = 0$. Determine expressions for $(\partial H^{ig}/\partial P)_V$ and $(\partial H^{ig}/\partial P)_S$. Why are these quantities not zero?

6.91. Prove that
$$dS = \frac{C_V}{T}\left(\frac{\partial T}{\partial P}\right)_V dP + \frac{C_P}{T}\left(\frac{\partial T}{\partial V}\right)_P dV$$

For an ideal gas with constant heat capacities, use this result to derive Eq. (3.30c).

6.92. The derivative $(\partial U/\partial V)_T$ is sometimes called the *internal pressure*, and the product $T(\partial P/\partial T)_V$, the *thermal pressure*. Find equations for their evaluation for

(*a*) An ideal gas (*b*) A van der Waals fluid (*c*) A Redlich/Kwong fluid

6.93. (*a*) A pure substance is described by an expression for $G(T, P)$. Show how to determine Z, U, and C_V, in relation to G, T, and P and/or derivatives of G with respect to T and P.

(*b*) A pure substance is described by an expression for $A(T, V)$. Show how to determine Z, H, and C_P, in relation to A, T, and V and/or derivatives of A with respect to T and V.

6.94. Use steam tables to estimate a value of the acentric factor ω for water. Compare the result with the value given in Table B.1.

6.95. The critical coordinates for tetrafluoroethane (refrigerant HFC-134a) are given in Table B.1, and Table 9.1 (p. 319) shows saturation properties for the same refrigerant. From these data determine the acentric factor ω for HFC-134a, and compare it with the value given in Table B.1.

6.96. As noted in Ex. 6.5, ΔH^{lv} is not independent of T; in fact, it becomes zero at the critical point. Not may saturated vapors *in general* be considered ideal gases. Why is it then that Eq. (6.75) provides a reasonable approximation to vapor-pressure behavior over the entire liquid range?

6.97. Rationalize the following approximate expressions for solid/liquid saturation pressures:

(*a*) $P_{sl}^{\text{sat}} = A + BT$; (*b*) $P_{sl}^{\text{sat}} = A + B \ln T$

6.98. As suggested by Fig. 3.1, the slope of the sublimation curve at the triple point is generally greater than that of the vaporization curve at the same state. Rationalize this observation. Note that triple-point pressures are usually low; hence assume for this exercise that $\Delta Z^{sv} \approx \Delta Z^{lv} \approx 1$.

6.99. Show that the Clapeyron equation for liquid/vapor equilibrium may be written in the reduced form:

$$\frac{d \ln P_r^{\text{sat}}}{dT_r} = \frac{\widehat{\Delta H}^{lv}}{T_r^2 \Delta Z^{lv}} \qquad \text{where} \qquad \widehat{\Delta H}^{lv} \equiv \frac{\Delta H^{lv}}{RT_c}$$

6.100. Use the result of the preceding problem to estimate the heat of vaporization at the normal boiling point for one of the substances listed below. Compare the result with the value given in Table B.2 of App. B.

Ground rules: Represent P_r^{sat} with Eqs. (6.78), (6.79), and (6.80), with ω given by Eq. (6.81). Use Eqs. (3.61), (3.62), (3.63), (3.65), and (3.66) for Z^v, and Eq. (3.73) for Z^l. Critical properties and and normal boiling points are given in Table B.1.

(*a*) Benzene; (*b*) *iso*-Butane; (*c*) Carbon tetrachloride; (*d*) Cyclohexane; (*e*) *n*-Decane; (*f*) *n*-Hexane; (*g*) *n*-Octane; (*h*) Toluene; (*i*) *o*-Xylene

6.101. Riedel proposed a third corresponding-states parameter α_c, related to the vapor-pressure curve by:

$$\alpha_c \equiv \left[\frac{d \ln P^{\text{sat}}}{d \ln T}\right]_{T=T_c}$$

For simple fluids, experiment shows that $\alpha_c \approx 5.8$; for non-simple fluids, α_c increases with increasing molecular complexity. How well does the Lee/Kesler correlation for P_r^{sat} accommodate these observations?

6.102. Triple-point coordinates for carbon dioxide are $T_t = 216.55$ K and $P_t = 5.170$ bar. Hence, CO_2 has no normal boiling point. (Why?) Nevertheless, one can define a *hypothetical* normal boiling point by extrapolation of the vapor-pressure curve.

(*a*) Use the Lee/Kesler correlation for P_r^{sat} in conjunction with the triple-point coordinates to estimate ω for CO_2. Compare it with the value in Table B.1

(*b*) Use the Lee/Kesler correlation to estimate the hypothetical normal boiling point for CO_2. Comment on the likely reasonableness of this result.

Chapter 7

Applications of Thermodynamics to Flow Processes

The thermodynamics of flow is based on mass, energy, and entropy balances, which have been developed in Chaps. 2 and 5. The application of these balances to specific processes is considered in this chapter. The discipline underlying the study of flow is fluid mechanics,[1] which encompasses not only the balances of thermodynamics but also the linear-momentum principle (Newton's second law). This makes fluid mechanics a broader field of study. The distinction between *thermodynamics problems* and *fluid-mechanics problems* depends on whether this principle is required for solution. Those problems whose solutions depend only on mass conservation and on the laws of thermodynamics are commonly set apart from the study of fluid mechanics and are treated in courses on thermodynamics. Fluid mechanics then deals with the broad spectrum of problems which *require* application of the momentum principle. This division is arbitrary, but it is traditional and convenient.

Consider for example the flow of gas through a pipeline. If the states and thermodynamic properties of the gas entering and leaving the pipeline are known, then application of the first law establishes the magnitude of the energy exchange with the surroundings of the pipeline. The mechanism of the process, the details of flow, and the state path actually followed by the fluid between entrance and exit are not pertinent to this calculation. On the other hand, if one has only incomplete knowledge of the initial or final state of the gas, then more detailed information about the process is needed before any calculations are made. For example, the exit pressure of the gas may not be specified. In this case, one must apply the momentum principle of fluid mechanics, and this requires an empirical or theoretical expression for the shear stress at the pipe wall.

[1] Noel de Nevers, *Fluid Mechanics for Chemical Engineers*, 3rd ed., McGraw-Hill, New York, 2005. Fluid mechanics is treated as an integral part of transport processes by R. B. Bird, W. E. Stewart, and E. N. Lightfoot in *Transport Phenomena*, 2nd ed., John Wiley, New York, 2001; by C. O. Bennett and J. E. Myers in *Momentum, Heat, and Mass Transfer*, 2nd ed., McGraw-Hill, New York, 1982; by J. L. Plawsky in *Transport Phenomena Fundamentals*, Marcel Dekker, New York, 2001; by D. P. Kessler and R. A. Greenkorn in *Momentum, Heat, and Mass Transfer Fundamentals*, Marcel Dekker, New York, 1999; and by D. E. Rosner in *Transport Processes in Chemically Reacting Systems*, Butterworths, Boston, 1986, and DOVER, Mineola, New York, 2000.

Flow processes inevitably result from pressure gradients within the fluid. Moreover, temperature, velocity, and even concentration gradients may exist within the flowing fluid. This contrasts with the uniform conditions that prevail at equilibrium in closed systems. The distribution of conditions in flow systems requires that properties be attributed to point masses of fluid. Thus we assume that intensive properties, such as density, specific enthalpy, specific entropy, etc., at a point are determined solely by the temperature, pressure, and composition at the point, uninfluenced by gradients that may exist at the point. Moreover, we assume that the fluid exhibits the same set of intensive properties at the point as though it existed at equilibrium at the same temperature, pressure, and composition. The implication is that an equation of state applies locally and instantaneously at any point in a fluid system, and that one may invoke a concept of *local state*, independent of the concept of equilibrium. Experience shows that this leads for practical purposes to results in accord with observation.

The equations of balance for open systems from Chaps. 2 and 5 are summarized here in Table 7.1 for easy reference. Included are Eqs. (7.1) and (7.2), restricted forms of the mass balance. These equations are the basis for the thermodynamic analysis of *processes* in this and the next two chapters. When combined with thermodynamic *property* statements, they allow calculation of process rates and system states.

7.1 DUCT FLOW OF COMPRESSIBLE FLUIDS

Such problems as the sizing of pipes and the shaping of nozzles require application of the momentum principle of fluid mechanics, [2] and therefore do not lie within the province of thermodynamics. However, thermodynamics does provide equations that interrelate the changes occurring in pressure, velocity, cross-sectional area, enthalpy, entropy, and specific volume of a flowing stream. We consider here the adiabatic, steady-state, one-dimensional flow of a compressible fluid in the absence of shaft work and of changes in potential energy. The pertinent thermodynamic equations are first derived; they are then applied to flow in pipes and nozzles.

The appropriate energy balance is Eq. (2.32). With Q, W_s and Δz all set equal to zero,

$$\Delta H + \frac{\Delta u^2}{2} = 0$$

In differential form,

$$dH = -u\,du \tag{7.3}$$

The continuity equation, Eq. (2.27), is also applicable. Because $\dot{m}$ is constant, its differential form is

$$d(uA/V) = 0$$

or

$$\frac{dV}{V} - \frac{du}{u} - \frac{dA}{A} = 0 \tag{7.4}$$

[2]See W. L. McCabe, J. C. Smith, and P. Harriott, *Unit Operations of Chemical Engineering*, 7th ed., Sec. 2, McGraw-Hill, New York, 2006; R. H. Perry and D. Green, *Perry's Chemical Engineers' Handbook*, 7th ed., Sec. 6, McGraw-Hill, New York, 1997.

Table 7.1: Equations of Balance

General Equations of Balance	Balance Equations for Steady-Flow Processes	Balance Equations for Single-Stream Steady-Flow Processes
$\frac{dm_{cv}}{dt} + \Delta(\dot{m})_{fs} = 0$ (2.25)	$\Delta(\dot{m})_{fs} = 0$ (7.1)	$\dot{m}_1 = \dot{m}_2 = \dot{m}$ (7.2)
$\frac{d(mU)_{cv}}{dt} + \Delta\left[\left(H + \frac{1}{2}u^2 + zg\right)\dot{m}\right]_{fs} = \dot{Q} + \dot{W}$ (2.28)	$\Delta\left[\left(H + \frac{1}{2}u^2 + zg\right)\dot{m}\right]_{fs} = \dot{Q} + \dot{W}_s$ (2.30)	$\Delta H + \frac{\Delta u^2}{2} + g\Delta z = Q + W_s$ (2.32a)
$\frac{d(mS)_{cv}}{dt} + \Delta(S\dot{m})_{fs} - \sum_j \frac{\dot{Q}_j}{T_{\sigma,j}} = \dot{S}_G \geq 0$ (5.21)	$\Delta(S\dot{m})_{fs} - \sum_j \frac{\dot{Q}_j}{T_{\sigma,j}} = \dot{S}_G \geq 0$ (5.22)	$\Delta S - \sum_j \frac{Q_j}{T_{\sigma,j}} = S_G \geq 0$ (5.23)

The fundamental property relation appropriate to this application is

$$dH = T\,dS + V\,dP \tag{6.8}$$

In addition, the specific volume of the fluid may be considered a function of its entropy and pressure: $V = V(S, P)$. Then,

$$dV = \left(\frac{\partial V}{\partial S}\right)_P dS + \left(\frac{\partial V}{\partial P}\right)_S dP$$

This equation is put into more convenient form through the mathematical identity:

$$\left(\frac{\partial V}{\partial S}\right)_P = \left(\frac{\partial V}{\partial T}\right)_P \left(\frac{\partial T}{\partial S}\right)_P$$

Substituting for the two partial derivatives on the right by Eqs. (3.2) and (6.17) gives

$$\left(\frac{\partial V}{\partial S}\right)_P = \frac{\beta V T}{C_P}$$

where β is the volume expansivity. The equation derived in physics for the speed of sound c in a fluid is

$$c^2 = -V^2 \left(\frac{\partial P}{\partial V}\right)_S \qquad \text{or} \qquad \left(\frac{\partial V}{\partial P}\right)_S = -\frac{V^2}{c^2}$$

Substituting for the two partial derivatives in the equation for dV now yields:

$$\frac{dV}{V} = \frac{\beta T}{C_P} dS - \frac{V}{c^2} dP \tag{7.5}$$

Equations (7.3), (7.4), (6.8), and (7.5) relate the six differentials—$dH, du, dV, dA, dS,$ and dP. With but four equations, we treat dS and dA as independent, and develop equations that express the remaining differentials as functions of these two. First, Eqs. (7.3) and (6.8) are combined:

$$T\,dS + V\,dP = -u\,du \tag{7.6}$$

Eliminating dV and du from Eq. (7.4) by Eqs. (7.5) and (7.6) gives upon rearrangement:

$$(1 - \mathbf{M}^2) V\,dP + \left(1 + \frac{\beta u^2}{C_P}\right) T\,dS - \frac{u^2}{A} dA = 0 \tag{7.7}$$

where $\mathbf{M}$ is the Mach number, defined as the ratio of the speed of the fluid in the duct to the speed of sound in the fluid, u/c. Equation (7.7) relates dP to dS and dA.

Equations (7.6) and (7.7) are combined to eliminate $V\,dP$:

$$u\,du - \left(\frac{\dfrac{\beta u^2}{C_P} + \mathbf{M}^2}{1 - \mathbf{M}^2}\right) T\,dS + \left(\frac{1}{1 - \mathbf{M}^2}\right) \frac{u^2}{A} dA = 0 \tag{7.8}$$

This equation relates du to dS and dA. Combined with Eq. (7.3) it relates dH to dS and dA, and combined with (7.4) it relates dV to these same independent variables.

The differentials in the preceding equations represent changes in the fluid as it traverses a differential length of its path. If this length is dx, then each of the equations of flow may be divided through by dx. Equations (7.7) and (7.8) then become

$$V(1-\mathbf{M}^2)\frac{dP}{dx}+T\left(1+\frac{\beta u^2}{C_P}\right)\frac{dS}{dx}-\frac{u^2}{A}\frac{dA}{dx}=0 \tag{7.9}$$

$$u\frac{du}{dx}-T\left(\frac{\frac{\beta u^2}{C_P}+\mathbf{M}^2}{1-\mathbf{M}^2}\right)\frac{dS}{dx}+\left(\frac{1}{1-\mathbf{M}^2}\right)\frac{u^2}{A}\frac{dA}{dx}=0 \tag{7.10}$$

According to the second law, the irreversibilities due to fluid friction in adiabatic flow cause an entropy increase in the fluid in the direction of flow. In the limit as the flow approaches reversibility, this increase approaches zero. In general, then,

$$\frac{dS}{dx}\geq 0$$

Pipe Flow

For the case of steady-state adiabatic flow of compressible fluids in a horizontal pipe of constant cross-sectional area, $dA/dx=0$, and Eqs. (7.9) and (7.10) reduce to:

$$\frac{dP}{dx}=-\frac{T}{V}\left(\frac{1+\frac{\beta u^2}{C_P}}{1-\mathbf{M}^2}\right)\frac{dS}{dx} \qquad u\frac{du}{dx}=T\left(\frac{\frac{\beta u^2}{C_P}+\mathbf{M}^2}{1-\mathbf{M}^2}\right)\frac{dS}{dx}$$

For subsonic flow, $\mathbf{M}^2<1$; all terms on the right sides of these equations are then positive, and

$$\frac{dP}{dx}<0 \qquad \text{and} \qquad \frac{du}{dx}>0$$

Thus the pressure decreases and the velocity increases in the direction of flow. However, the velocity cannot increase indefinitely. If the velocity were to exceed the sonic value, then the above inequalities would reverse. Such a transition is not possible in a pipe of constant cross-sectional area. For subsonic flow, the maximum fluid velocity obtainable in a pipe of constant cross section is the speed of sound, and this value is reached at the *exit* of the pipe. At this point dS/dx reaches its limiting value of zero. Given a discharge pressure low enough for the flow to become sonic, lengthening the pipe does not alter this result; the mass rate of flow decreases so that the sonic velocity is still obtained at the outlet of the lengthened pipe.

The equations for pipe flow indicate that when flow is supersonic the pressure increases and the velocity decreases in the direction of flow. However, such a flow regime is unstable, and when a supersonic stream enters a pipe of constant cross section, a compression shock occurs, the result of which is an abrupt and finite increase in pressure and decrease in velocity to a subsonic value.

Example 7.1

Consider the steady-state, adiabatic, irreversible flow of an *incompressible* liquid in a horizontal pipe of constant cross-sectional area. Show that the

(*a*) velocity is constant

(*b*) temperature increases in the direction of flow

(*c*) pressure decreases in the direction of flow

Solution

(*a*) The control volume here is simply a finite length of horizontal pipe, with entrance and exit sections identified as 1 and 2. By the continuity equation, Eq. (2.27),

$$\frac{u_2 A_2}{V_2} = \frac{u_1 A_1}{V_1}$$

However, $A_2 = A_1$ (constant cross-sectional area) and $V_2 = V_1$ (incompressible fluid). Hence, $u_2 = u_1$.

(*b*) The entropy balance of Eq. (5.23) here becomes simply $S_G = S_2 - S_1$. For an incompressible liquid with heat capacity C (see Ex. 6.2, pp. 203–204),

$$S_G = S_2 - S_1 = \int_{T_1}^{T_2} C \frac{dT}{T}$$

But S_G is positive (flow is irreversible) and hence, by the last equation, $T_2 > T_1$, and temperature increases in the direction of flow.

(*c*) As shown in (*a*), $u_2 = u_1$, and therefore the energy balance, Eq. (2.32), reduces for the stated conditions to $H_2 - H_1 = 0$. Combining this with the integrated form of Eq. (*A*) of Ex. 6.2 applied to an incompressible liquid yields

$$H_2 - H_1 = \int_{T_1}^{T_2} C\,dT + V(P_2 - P_1) = 0$$

Whence, $$V(P_2 - P_1) = -\int_{T_1}^{T_2} C\,dT$$

As shown in (*b*), $T_2 > T_1$; thus by the last equation, $P_2 < P_1$, and pressure decreases in the direction of flow.

Repeating this example for the case of *reversible* adiabatic flow is instructive. In this case $u_2 = u_1$ as before, but $S_G = 0$. The entropy balance then shows that $T_2 = T_1$, in which case the energy balance yields $P_2 = P_1$. We conclude that the temperature increase of (*b*) and the pressure decrease of (*c*) *originate* from flow irreversibilities, specifically from the irreversibilities associated with fluid friction.

Nozzles

The limitations observed for flow of compressible fluids in pipes do not extend to properly designed nozzles, which bring about the interchange of internal and kinetic energy of a fluid as the result of a changing cross-sectional area available for flow. The relation between nozzle length and cross-sectional area is not susceptible to thermodynamic analysis, but is a problem in fluid mechanics. In a properly designed nozzle the area changes with length in such a way as to make the flow nearly frictionless. In the limit of reversible flow, the rate of entropy increase approaches zero, and $dS/dx = 0$. In this event Eqs. (7.9) and (7.10) become

$$\frac{dP}{dx} = \frac{u^2}{VA}\left(\frac{1}{1-\mathbf{M}^2}\right)\frac{dA}{dx} \qquad \frac{du}{dx} = -\frac{u}{A}\left(\frac{1}{1-\mathbf{M}^2}\right)\frac{dA}{dx}$$

The characteristics of flow depend on whether the flow is subsonic ($\mathbf{M} < 1$) or supersonic ($\mathbf{M} > 1$). The various cases are summarized in Table 7.2.

Table 7.2: Characteristics of Flow for a Nozzle

	Subsonic: $\mathbf{M} < 1$		Supersonic: $\mathbf{M} > 1$	
	Converging	Diverging	Converging	Diverging
$\frac{dA}{dx}$	−	+	−	+
$\frac{dP}{dx}$	−	+	+	−
$\frac{du}{dx}$	+	−	−	+

Thus, for subsonic flow in a converging nozzle, the velocity increases and the pressure decreases as the cross-sectional area diminishes. The maximum obtainable fluid velocity is the speed of sound, reached at the exit. Because of this, a converging subsonic nozzle can be used to deliver a constant flowrate into a region of variable pressure. Suppose a compressible fluid enters a converging nozzle at pressure P_1 and discharges from the nozzle into a chamber of variable pressure P_2. As this discharge pressure decreases below P_1, the flowrate and velocity increase. Ultimately, the pressure ratio P_2/P_1 reaches a critical value at which the velocity at the nozzle exit is sonic. Further reduction in P_2 has no effect on the conditions in the nozzle. The flow remains constant, and the velocity at the nozzle exit is sonic, regardless of the value of P_2/P_1, provided it is always less than the critical value. For steam, the critical value of this ratio is about 0.55 at moderate temperatures and pressures.

Supersonic velocities are readily attained in the diverging section of a properly designed converging/diverging nozzle (Fig. 7.1). With sonic velocity reached at the throat, a further increase in velocity and decrease in pressure requires an increase in cross-sectional area, a diverging section to accommodate increasing volume of flow. The transition occurs at the throat, where $dA/dx = 0$. The relationships between velocity, area, and pressure in a converging/diverging nozzle are illustrated numerically in Ex. 7.2.

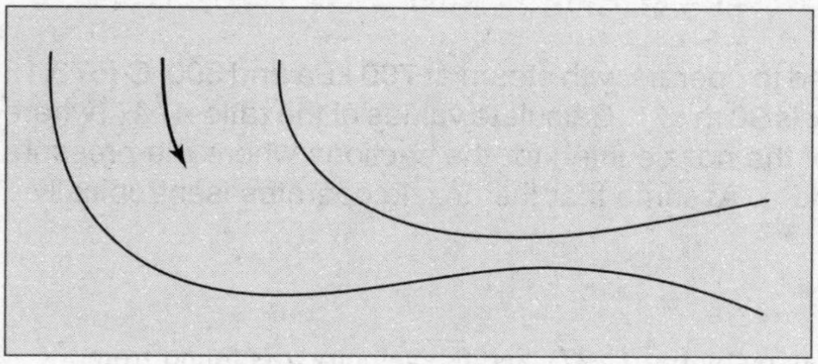

Figure 7.1: Converging/diverging nozzle

The speed of sound is attained at the throat of a converging/diverging nozzle only when the pressure at the throat is low enough that the critical value of P_2/P_1 is reached. If insufficient pressure drop is available in the nozzle for the velocity to become sonic, the diverging section of the nozzle acts as a diffuser. That is, after the throat is reached the pressure rises and the velocity decreases; this is the conventional behavior for subsonic flow in diverging sections.

The relation of velocity to pressure in an isentropic nozzle can be expressed analytically if the fluid behaves as an ideal gas with constant heat capacities. Combination of Eqs. (6.8) and (7.3) for isentropic flow gives

$$u\,du = -V\,dP$$

Integration, with nozzle entrance and exit conditions denoted by 1 and 2, yields

$$u_2^2 - u_1^2 = -2\int_{P_1}^{P_2} V\,dP = \frac{2\gamma P_1 V_1}{\gamma - 1}\left[1 - \left(\frac{P_2}{P_1}\right)^{(\gamma-1)/\gamma}\right] \tag{7.11}$$

where the final term is obtained upon elimination of V by Eq. (3.30c), $PV^\gamma = \text{const}$.

Equation (7.11) may be solved for the pressure ratio P_2/P_1 for which u_2 reaches the speed of sound, i.e., where

$$u_2^2 = c^2 = -V^2\left(\frac{\partial P}{\partial V}\right)_S$$

The derivative is found by differentiation with respect to V of $PV^\gamma = \text{const.}$:

$$\left(\frac{\partial P}{\partial V}\right)_S = -\frac{\gamma P}{V}$$

Substitution then yields $$u_2^2 = \gamma P_2 V_2$$

With this value for u_2^2 in Eq. (7.11) and with $u_1 = 0$, solution for the pressure ratio at the throat gives

$$\frac{P_2}{P_1} = \left(\frac{2}{\gamma + 1}\right)^{\gamma/(\gamma-1)} \tag{7.12}$$

Example 7.2

A high-velocity nozzle is designed to operate with steam at 700 kPa and 300°C (573.15 K). At the nozzle inlet the velocity is 30 m s^{-1}. Calculate values of the ratio A/A_1 (where A_1 is the cross-sectional area of the nozzle inlet) for the sections where the pressure is 600, 500, 400, 300, and 200 kPa. Assume that the nozzle operates isentropically.

Solution

The required area ratios are given by Eq. (2.27), and the velocity u is found from the integrated form of Eq. (7.3):

$$\frac{A}{A_1} = \frac{u_1 V}{V_1 u} \quad \text{and} \quad u^2 = u_1^2 - 2(H - H_1)$$

For velocity units of m s^{-1}, u^2 has the units, m^2 s^{-2}. Units of J kg^{-1} for H are consistent with these, because 1 J = 1 kg m^2 s^{-2}, whence 1 J kg^{-1} = 1 m^2 s^{-2}.

Initial values for entropy, enthalpy, and specific volume from the steam tables:

$$S_1 = 7.2997 \text{ kJ kg}^{-1} \text{ K}^{-1} \quad H_1 = 3059.8 \times 10^3 \text{ J kg}^{-1} \quad V_1 = 371.39 \text{ cm}^3 \text{ g}^{-1}$$

Thus,

$$\frac{A}{A_1} = \left(\frac{30}{371.39}\right)\frac{V}{u} \qquad (A)$$

and

$$u^2 = 900 - 2(H - 3059.8 \times 10^3) \qquad (B)$$

Because the expansion is isentropic, $S = S_1$; steam-table values at 600 kPa are

$$S = 7.2997 \text{ kJ kg}^{-1} \text{ K}^{-1} \quad H = 3020.4 \times 10^3 \text{ J kg}^{-1} \quad V = 418.25 \text{ cm}^3 \text{ g}^{-1}$$

From Eq. (B),

$$u = 282.3 \text{ m s}^{-1}$$

By Eq. (A),

$$\frac{A}{A_1} = \left(\frac{30}{371.39}\right)\left(\frac{418.25}{282.3}\right) = 0.120$$

Area ratios for other pressures are evaluated the same way, and the results are summarized in the following table.

P/kPa	V/cm^3 g^{-1}	u/m s^{-1}	A/A_1	P/kPa	V/cm^3 g^{-1}	u/m s^{-1}	A/A_1
700	371.39	30	1.0	400	571.23	523.0	0.088
600	418.25	282.3	0.120	300	711.93	633.0	0.091
500	481.26	411.2	0.095	200	970.04	752.2	0.104

The pressure at the throat of the nozzle is about 380 kPa. At lower pressures, the nozzle clearly diverges.

Example 7.3

Consider again the nozzle of Ex. 7.2, assuming now that steam behaves as an ideal gas. Calculate the

(*a*) critical pressure ratio and the velocity at the throat

(*b*) discharge pressure for a Mach number of 2.0 at the nozzle exhaust

Solution

(*a*) The ratio of specific heats for steam is about 1.3. Substituting in Eq. (7.12),

$$\frac{P_2}{P_1} = \left(\frac{2}{1.3+1}\right)^{1.3/(1.3-1)} = 0.55$$

The velocity at the throat, equal to the speed of sound, is found from Eq. (7.11), which contains the product $P_1 V_1$. For steam as an ideal gas,

$$P_1 V_1 = \frac{RT_1}{M} = \frac{(8314)(573.15)}{18.015} = 264\,511 \text{ m}^2 \text{ s}^{-2}$$

In this equation R/M has the units

$$\frac{\text{J}}{\text{kg K}} = \frac{\text{N m}}{\text{kg K}} = \frac{\text{kg m s}^{-2} \text{ m}}{\text{kg K}} = \frac{\text{m}^2 \text{ s}^{-2}}{\text{K}}$$

Thus RT/M, and hence $P_1 V_1$, is in $\text{m}^2 \text{ s}^{-2}$, the units of velocity squared. Substitution in Eq. (7.11) gives

$$u^2_{\text{throat}} = (30)^2 + \frac{(2)(1.3)(264\,511)}{1.3-1}\left[1 - (0.55)^{(1.3-1)/1.3}\right] = 296\,322$$

$$u_{\text{throat}} = 544.35 \text{ m s}^{-1}$$

This result is in good agreement with the value obtained in Ex. 7.2, because steam at these conditions closely approximates an ideal gas.

(*b*) For a Mach number of 2.0 (based on the velocity of sound at the nozzle throat) the discharge velocity is

$$2u_{\text{throat}} = (2)(544.35) = 1088.7 \text{ m s}^{-1}$$

Substitution of this value in Eq. (7.11) allows calculation of the pressure ratio:

$$(1088.7)^2 - (30)^2 = \frac{(2)(1.3)(264\,511)}{1.3-1}\left[1 - \left(\frac{P_2}{P_1}\right)^{(1.3-1)/1.3}\right]$$

Thus, $\left(\frac{P_2}{P_1}\right)^{(1.3-1)/1.3} = 0.4834$ and $P_2 = (0.0428)(700) = 30.0$ kPa

Throttling Process

When a fluid flows through a restriction, such as an orifice, a partly closed valve, or a porous plug, without any appreciable change in kinetic or potential energy, the primary result of the process is a pressure drop in the fluid. Such a *throttling process* produces no shaft work, and in the absence of heat transfer, Eq. (2.32) reduces to

$$\Delta H = 0 \qquad \text{or} \qquad H_2 = H_1$$

The process therefore occurs at constant enthalpy.

Because the enthalpy of an ideal gas depends on temperature only, a throttling process does not change the temperature of an ideal gas. For most real gases at moderate conditions of temperature and pressure, a reduction in pressure at constant enthalpy results in a decrease in temperature. For example, if steam at 1000 kPa and 300°C (573.15 K) is throttled to 101.325 kPa (atmospheric pressure),

$$H_2 = H_1 = 3052.1 \text{ kJ kg}^{-1}$$

Interpolation in the steam tables at this enthalpy and at a pressure of 101.325 kPa indicates a downstream temperature of 288.8°C (561.95 K). The temperature has decreased, but the effect is small.

Throttling of *wet* steam to sufficiently low pressure may cause the liquid to evaporate and the vapor to become superheated. Thus if wet steam at 1000 kPa (t^{sat}/T^{sat} = 179.88°C/ 453.03 K) with a quality of 0.96 is throttled to 101.325 kPa,

$$H_2 = H_1 = (0.04)(762.6) + (0.96)(2776.2) = 2695.7 \text{ kJ kg}^{-1}$$

At 101.325 kPa steam with this enthalpy has a temperature of 109.8°C (382.95 K); it is therefore superheated (t^{sat}/T^{sat} = 100°C/373.15 K). The considerable temperature drop here results from evaporation of liquid.

If a saturated liquid is throttled to a lower pressure, some of the liquid vaporizes or *flashes*, producing a mixture of saturated liquid and saturated vapor at the lower pressure. Thus if saturated liquid water at 1000 kPa (t^{sat}/T^{sat} = 179.88°C/453.03 K) is flashed to 101.325 kPa (t^{sat}/T^{sat} = 100°C/373.15 K),

$$H_2 = H_1 = 762.6 \text{ kJ kg}^{-1}$$

At 101.325 kPa the quantity of the resulting steam is found from Eq. (6.73a) with $M = H$:

$$762.6 = (1 - x)(419.1) + x(2676.0)$$

$$= 419.1 + x(2676.0 - 419.1)$$

Hence $$x = 0.152 \text{ kg per kg saturated liquid}$$

Thus 15.2% of the original liquid vaporizes in the process. Again, the large temperature drop results from evaporation of liquid. Throttling processes find frequent application in refrigeration (Chap. 9).

The following example illustrates use of generalized correlations in calculations for a throttling process.

Example 7.4

Propane gas at 20 bar and 400 K is throttled in a steady-state flow process to 1 bar. Estimate the final temperature of the propane and its entropy change. Properties of propane can be found from suitable generalized correlations.

Solution

Apply Eq. (6.93) to this constant-enthalpy process:

$$\Delta H = \langle C_P^{ig} \rangle_H (T_2 - T_1) + H_2^R - H_1^R = 0$$

If propane in its final state at 1 bar is assumed to be an ideal gas, then $H_2^R = 0$, and the preceding equation, solved for T_2, becomes

$$T_2 = \frac{H_1^R}{\langle C_P^{ig} \rangle_H} + T_1 \qquad (A)$$

For propane, $T_c = 369.8$ K $\quad P_c = 42.48$ bar $\quad \omega = 0.152$

Thus for the initial state,

$$T_{r_1} = \frac{400}{369.8} = 1.082 \qquad P_{r_1} = \frac{20}{42.48} = 0.471$$

At these conditions the generalized correlation based on second virial coefficients is satisfactory (Fig. 3.14), and calculation of H_1^R by Eqs. (6.87), (3.65), (6.89), (3.66), and (6.90) is represented by (Sec. 6.7):

$$\frac{H_1^R}{RT_c} = \text{HRB}(1.082{,}0.471{,}0.152) = -0.452$$

Whence, $\quad H_1^R = (8.314)(369.8)(-0.452) = -1390 \text{ J mol}^{-1}$

The only remaining quantity in Eq. (*A*) to be evaluated is $\langle C_P^{ig} \rangle_H$. Data for propane from Table C.1 provide the heat-capacity equation:

$$\frac{C_P^{ig}}{R} = 1.213 + 28.785 \times 10^{-3} T - 8.824 \times 10^{-6} T^2$$

For an initial calculation, assume that $\langle C_P^{ig} \rangle_H$ equals the value of C_P^{ig} at the initial temperature of 400 K, i.e., $\langle C_P^{ig} \rangle_H = 94.07 \text{ J mol}^{-1} \text{ K}^{-1}$.

From Eq. (*A*), $\quad T_2 = \dfrac{-1390}{94.07} + 400 = 385.2 \text{ K}$

Clearly, the temperature change is small, and $\langle C_P^{ig} \rangle_H$ is reevaluated to an excellent approximation as C_P^{ig} at the arithmetic mean temperature,

$$T_{\text{am}} = \frac{400 + 385.2}{2} = 392.6 \text{ K}$$

This gives $$\langle C_P^{ig} \rangle_H = 92.73 \text{ J mol}^{-1} \text{ K}^{-1}$$

and recalculation of T_2 by Eq. (A) yields the final value: $T_2 = 385.0$ K.

The entropy change of the propane is given by Eq. (6.94), which here becomes:

$$\Delta S = \langle C_P^{ig} \rangle_S \ln \frac{T_2}{T_1} - R \ln \frac{P_2}{P_1} - S_1^R$$

Because the temperature change is so small, to an excellent approximation,

$$\langle C_P^{ig} \rangle_S = \langle C_P^{ig} \rangle_H = 92.73 \text{ J mol}^{-1} \text{ K}^{-1}$$

Calculation of S_1^R by Eqs. (6.88) through (6.90) is represented by

$$\frac{S_1^R}{R} = \text{SRB}(1.082, 0.471, 0.152) = -0.2934$$

Whence, $$S_1^R = (8.314)(-0.2934) = -2.439 \text{ J mol}^{-1} \text{ K}^{-1}$$

and $$\Delta S = 92.73 \ln \frac{385.0}{400} - 8.314 \ln \frac{1}{20} + 2.439 = 23.80 \text{ J mol}^{-1} \text{ K}^{-1}$$

The positive value reflects the irreversibility of throttling processes.

Example 7.5

Throttling a real gas from conditions of moderate temperature and pressure usually results in a temperature decrease. Under what conditions would an *increase* in temperature be expected?

Solution

The sign of the temperature change is determined by the sign of the derivative $(\partial T/\partial P)_H$, called the *Joule/Thomson coefficient* μ:

$$\mu \equiv \left(\frac{\partial T}{\partial P}\right)_H$$

When μ is positive, throttling results in a temperature decrease; when negative, in a temperature increase.

Because $H = f(T, P)$, the following equation relates the Joule/Thomson coefficient to other thermodynamic properties:[3]

$$\left(\frac{\partial T}{\partial P}\right)_H = -\left(\frac{\partial T}{\partial H}\right)_P \left(\frac{\partial H}{\partial P}\right)_T = -\left(\frac{\partial H}{\partial T}\right)_P^{-1} \left(\frac{\partial H}{\partial P}\right)_T$$

[3] Recall the general equation from differential calculus,

$$\left(\frac{\partial x}{\partial y}\right)_z = -\left(\frac{\partial x}{\partial z}\right)_y \left(\frac{\partial z}{\partial y}\right)_x$$

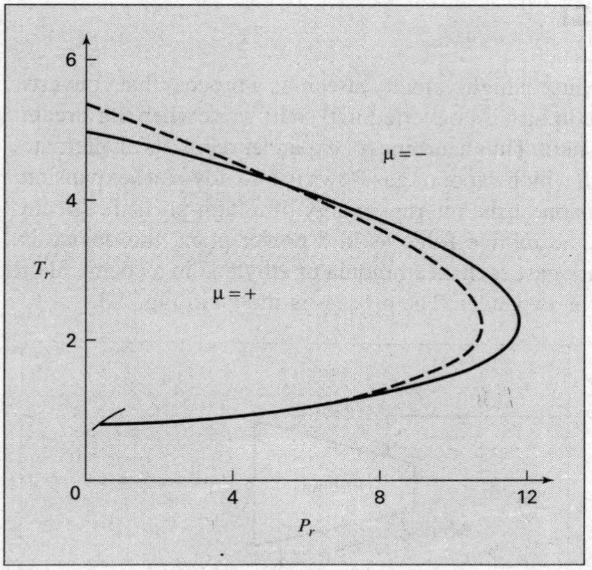

Figure 7.2: Inversion curves for reduced coordinates. Each line represents a locus of points for which $\mu = 0$. Solid curve is from a data correlation; dashed curve, from the Redlich/Kwong equation. A temperature increase results from throttling in the region where μ is negative.

Whence, by Eq. (2.20),
$$\mu = -\frac{1}{C_P}\left(\frac{\partial H}{\partial P}\right)_T \qquad (A)$$

Because C_P is necessarily positive, the sign of μ is determined by the sign of $(\partial H/\partial P)_T$, which in turn is related to PVT behavior:
$$\left(\frac{\partial H}{\partial P}\right)_T = V - T\left(\frac{\partial V}{\partial T}\right)_P \qquad (6.19)$$

Because $V = ZRT/P$, this equation may be written more concisely as
$$\left(\frac{\partial H}{\partial P}\right)_T = -\frac{RT^2}{P}\left(\frac{\partial Z}{\partial T}\right)_P$$

where Z is the compressibility factor. Substitution into Eq. (A) gives
$$\mu = \frac{RT^2}{C_P P}\left(\frac{\partial Z}{\partial T}\right)_P$$

Thus, $(\partial Z/\partial T)_P$ and μ have the same sign. When $(\partial Z/\partial T)_P$ is zero, as for an ideal gas, then $\mu = 0$, and no temperature change accompanies throttling.

The condition $(\partial Z/\partial T)_P = 0$ may obtain locally for *real* gases. Such points define the Joule/Thomson *inversion curve*, which separates the region of positive μ from that of negative μ. Figure 7.2 shows *reduced* inversion curves giving the relation between T_r and P_r for which $\mu = 0$. The solid line correlates data for Ar, CH_4, N_2, CO, C_2H_4, C_3H_8, CO_2, and NH_3.[4] The dashed line is calculated from the condition $(\partial Z/\partial T_r)_{P_r} = 0$ applied to the Redlich/Kwong equation of state.

[4]D. G. Miller, *Ind. Eng. Chem. Fundam.*, vol. 9, pp. 585–589, 1970.

7.2 TURBINES (EXPANDERS)

The expansion of a gas in a nozzle to produce a high-velocity stream is a process that converts internal energy into kinetic energy, which in turn is converted into shaft work when the stream impinges on blades attached to a rotating shaft. Thus a turbine (or expander) consists of alternate sets of nozzles and rotating blades through which vapor or gas flows in a steady-state expansion process. The overall result is the conversion of the internal energy of a high-pressure stream into shaft work. When steam provides the motive force as in a power plant, the device is called a turbine; when it is a high-pressure gas, such as ammonia or ethylene in a chemical or petrochemical plant, the device is called an expander. The process is shown in Fig. 7.3.

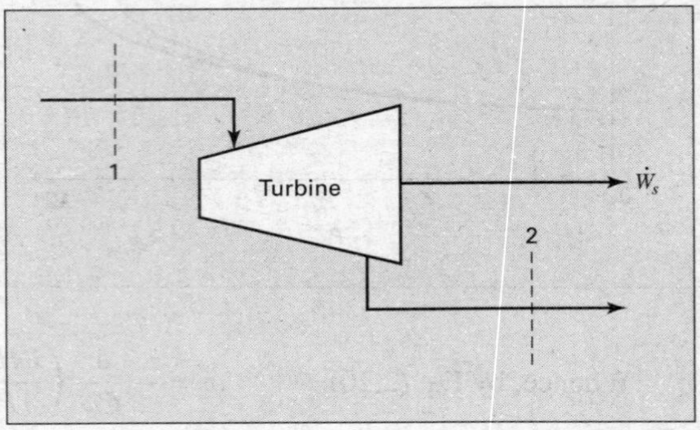

Figure 7.3: Steady-state flow through a turbine or expander

Equations (2.31) and (2.32) are appropriate energy relations. However, the potential-energy term can be omitted, because there is little change in elevation. Moreover, in any properly designed turbine, heat transfer is negligible and the inlet and exit pipes are sized to make fluid velocities roughly equal. Equations (2.31) and (2.32) therefore reduce to

$$\dot{W}_s = \dot{m}\,\Delta H = \dot{m}(H_2 - H_1) \qquad (7.13)$$

$$W_s = \Delta H = H_2 - H_1 \qquad (7.14)$$

Usually, the inlet conditions T_1 and P_1 and the discharge pressure P_2 are fixed. Thus in Eq. (7.14) only H_1 is known; both H_2 and W_s are unknown, and the energy equation alone does not allow their calculation. However, if the fluid in the turbine expands *reversibly and adiabatically*, the process is isentropic, and $S_2 = S_1$. This second equation fixes the final state of the fluid and determines H_2. For this special case, W_s is given by Eq. (7.14), written as

$$W_s(\text{isentropic}) = (\Delta H)_S \qquad (7.15)$$

The shaft work $|W_s|$(isentropic) is the *maximum* that can be obtained from an adiabatic turbine with given inlet conditions and given discharge pressure. Actual turbines produce less work, because the actual expansion process is irreversible; we define a *turbine efficiency* as

$$\eta \equiv \frac{W_s}{W_s(\text{isentropic})}$$

where W_s is the actual shaft work. By Eqs. (7.14) and (7.15),

$$\eta = \frac{\Delta H}{(\Delta H)_S} \qquad (7.16)$$

Values of η usually range from 0.7 to 0.8. The HS diagram of Fig. 7.4 shows an actual expansion in a turbine and a reversible expansion for the same intake conditions and the same discharge pressure. The reversible path is the dashed vertical (constant-entropy) line from point 1 at intake pressure P_1 to point $2'$ at discharge pressure P_2. The solid line, showing the actual irreversible path, starts at point 1 and terminates at point 2 on the isobar for P_2. Because the process is adiabatic, irreversibilities cause an increase in entropy of the fluid, and the path is directed toward increasing entropy. The more irreversible the process, the further point 2 lies to the right on the P_2 isobar, and the lower the efficiency η of the process.

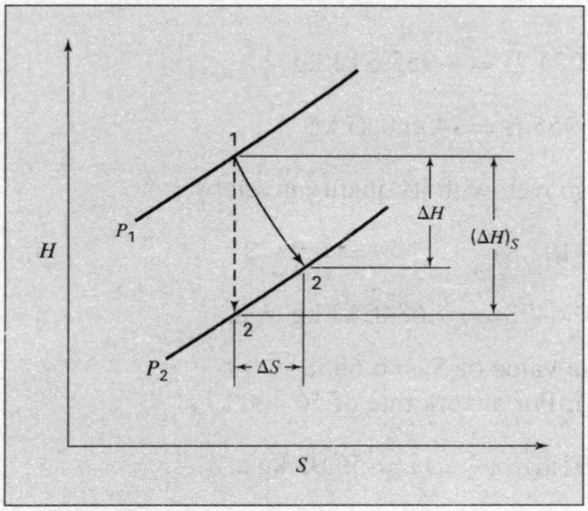

Figure 7.4: Adiabatic expansion process in a turbine or expander

Example 7.6

A steam turbine with rated capacity of 56 400 kW (56 400 kJ s^{-1}) operates with steam at inlet conditions of 8600 kPa and 500°C (773.15 K), and discharges into a condenser at a pressure of 10 kPa. Assuming a turbine efficiency of 0.75, determine the state of the steam at discharge and the mass rate of flow of the steam.

Solution

At the inlet conditions of 8600 kPa and 500°C (773.15 K), the steam tables provide:

$$H_1 = 3391.6 \text{ kJ kg}^{-1} \qquad S_1 = 6.6858 \text{ kJ kg}^{-1} \text{ K}^{-1}$$

If the expansion to 10 kPa is isentropic, then, $S_2' = S_1 = 6.6858$. Steam with this entropy at 10 kPa is wet, and Eq. (6.82b), with $M = S$ and $x^v = x_2'$, yields

$$S_2' = S_2^l + x_2'(S_2^v - S_2^l)$$

Then, $\quad 6.6858 = 0.6493 + x_2'(8.1511 - 0.6493) \qquad x_2' = 0.8047$

This is the quality (fraction vapor) of the discharge stream at point 2′. The enthalpy H_2' is also given by Eq. (6.82b), written as

$$H_2' = H_2^l + x_2'(H_2^v - H_2^l)$$

Thus, $H_2' = 191.8 + (0.8047)(2584.8 - 191.8) = 2117.4 \text{ kJ kg}^{-1}$

$$(\Delta H)_S = H_2' - H_1 = 2117.4 - 3391.6 = -1274.2 \text{ kJ kg}^{-1}$$

and by Eq. (7.16),

$$\Delta H = \eta(\Delta H)_S = (0.75)(-1274.2) = -955.6 \text{ kJ kg}^{-1}$$

Whence, $H_2 = H_1 + \Delta H = 3391.6 - 955.6 = 2436.0 \text{ kJ kg}^{-1}$

Thus the steam in its actual final state is also wet, with its quality given by

$$2436.0 = 191.8 + x_2(2584.8 - 191.8) \qquad x_2 = 0.9378$$

Then $S_2 = 0.6493 + (0.9378)(8.1511 - 0.6493) = 7.6846 \text{ kJ kg}^{-1} \text{ K}^{-1}$

This value may be compared with the initial value of $S_1 = 6.6858$.

The steam rate $\dot{m}$ is given by Eq. (7.13). For a work rate of 56 400 kJ s^{-1},

$$\dot{W}_s = -56{,}400 = \dot{m}(2436.0 - 3391.6) \qquad \dot{m} = 59.02 \text{ kg s}^{-1}$$

Example 7.6 is solved with data from the steam tables. When a comparable set of tables is not available for the working fluid, the generalized correlations of Sec. 6.7 may be used in conjunction with Eqs. (6.93) and (6.94), as illustrated in the following example.

Example 7.7

A stream of ethylene gas at 300°C (573.15 K) and 45 bar is expanded adiabatically in a turbine to 2 bar. Calculate the isentropic work produced. Find the properties of ethylene by

(*a*) Equations for an ideal gas (*b*) Appropriate generalized correlations

Solution

The enthalpy and entropy changes for the process are:

$$\Delta H = \langle C_P^{ig} \rangle_H (T_2 - T_1) + H_2^R - H_1^R \qquad (6.93)$$

$$\Delta S = \langle C_P^{ig} \rangle_S \ln \frac{T_2}{T_1} - R \ln \frac{P_2}{P_1} + S_2^R - S_1^R \qquad (6.94)$$

Given values are $P_1 = 45$ bar, $P_2 = 2$ bar, and $T_1 = 300 + 273.15 = 573.15$ K.

(*a*) If ethylene is assumed an ideal gas, then all residual properties are zero, and the preceding equations reduce to

$$\Delta H = \langle C_P^{ig} \rangle_H (T_2 - T_1) \qquad \Delta S = \langle C_P^{ig} \rangle_S \ln \frac{T_2}{T_1} - R \ln \frac{P_2}{P_1}$$

For an isentropic process, $\Delta S = 0$, and the second equation becomes

$$\frac{\langle C_P^{ig} \rangle_S}{R} \ln \frac{T_2}{T_1} = \ln \frac{P_2}{P_1} = \ln \frac{2}{45} = -3.1135$$

or

$$\ln T_2 = \frac{-3.1135}{\langle C_P^{ig} \rangle_S / R} + \ln 573.15$$

Then,

$$T_2 = \exp\left(\frac{-3.1135}{\langle C_P^{ig} \rangle_S / R} + 6.3511 \right) \qquad (A)$$

Equation (5.17) provides an expression for $\langle C_P^{ig} \rangle_S / R$, which for computational purposes is represented by

$$\frac{\langle C_P^{ig} \rangle_S}{R} = \text{MCPS(573.15,T2;1.424,14.394E-3,-4.392E-6,0.0)}$$

where the constants for ethylene come from Table C.1. Temperature T_2 is found by iteration. Assume an initial value for evaluation of $\langle C_P^{ig} \rangle_S / R$. Equation ($A$) then provides a new value of T_2 from which to recompute $\langle C_P^{ig} \rangle_S / R$, and the procedure continues to convergence on the final value: $T_2 = 370.8$ K. The value of $\langle C_P^{ig} \rangle_H / R$, given by Eq. (4.8), is for computational purposes represented by

$$\frac{\langle C_P^{ig} \rangle_H}{R} = \text{MCPH(573.15,370.8;1.424,14.394E-3,-4.392E-6,0.0)} = 7.224$$

Then

$$W_s(\text{isentropic}) = (\Delta H)_S = \langle C_P^{ig} \rangle_H (T_2 - T_1)$$

$$W_s(\text{isentropic}) = (7.224)(8.314)(370.8 - 573.15) = -12\,153 \text{ J mol}^{-1}$$

(*b*) For ethylene,

$$T_c = 282.3 \text{ K} \qquad P_c = 50.4 \text{ bar} \qquad \omega = 0.087$$

At the initial state,

$$T_{r_1} = \frac{573.15}{282.3} = 2.030 \qquad P_{r_1} = \frac{45}{50.4} = 0.893$$

According to Fig. 3.14, the generalized correlations based on second virial coefficients should be satisfactory. The computational procedures of Eqs. (6.87), (6.88), (3.65), (3.66), (6.89) and (6.90) are represented by

$$\frac{H_1^R}{RT_c} = \text{HRB(2.030,0.893,0.087)} = -0.234$$

$$\frac{S_1^R}{R} = \text{SRB}(2.030,0.893,0.087) = -0.097$$

Then, $$H_1^R = (-0.234)(8.314)(282.3) = -549 \text{ J mol}^{-1}$$

$$S_1^R = (-0.097)(8.314) = -0.806 \text{ J mol}^{-1} \text{ K}^{-1}$$

For an initial estimate of S_2^R, assume that $T_2 = 370.8$ K, the value determined in part (*a*). Then,

$$T_{r_2} = \frac{370.8}{282.3} = 1.314 \qquad P_{r_2} = \frac{2}{50.4} = 0.040$$

Whence, $$\frac{S_2^R}{R} = \text{SRB}(1.314,0.040,0.087) = -0.0139$$

and $$S_2^R = (-0.0139)(8.314) = -0.116 \text{ J mol}^{-1} \text{ K}^{-1}$$

If the expansion process is isentropic, Eq. (6.94) becomes

$$0 = \langle C_P^{ig} \rangle_S \ln \frac{T_2}{573.15} - 8.314 \ln \frac{2}{45} - 0.116 + 0.806$$

Whence, $$\ln \frac{T_2}{573.15} = \frac{-26.576}{\langle C_P^{ig} \rangle_S}$$

or $$T_2 = \exp\left(\frac{-26.576}{\langle C_P^{ig} \rangle_S} + 6.3511\right)$$

An iteration process exactly like that of part (*a*) yields the results

$$T_2 = 365.8 \text{ K} \qquad \text{and} \qquad T_{r_2} = 1.296$$

With this value of T_{r_2} and with $P_{r_2} = 0.040$,

$$\frac{S_2^R}{R} = \text{SRB}(1.296,0.040,0.087) = -0.0144$$

and $$S_2^R = (-0.0144)(8.314) = -0.120 \text{ J mol}^{-1} \text{ K}^{-1}$$

This result is so little changed from the initial estimate that another recalculation of T_2 is unnecessary, and H_2^R is evaluated at the reduced conditions just established:

$$\frac{H_2^R}{RT_c} = \text{HRB}(1.296,0.040,0.087) = -0.0262$$

$$H_2^R = (-0.0262)(8.314)(282.3) = -61 \text{ J mol}^{-1}$$

By Eq. (6.93), $$(\Delta H)_S = \langle C_P^{ig} \rangle_H (365.8 - 573.15) - 61 + 549$$

Evaluation of $\langle C_P^{ig} \rangle_H$ as in part (*a*) with $T_2 = 365.8$ K gives

$$\langle C_P^{ig} \rangle_H = 59.843 \text{ J mol}^{-1} \text{ K}^{-1}$$

Whence, $$(\Delta H)_S = -11\,920 \text{ J mol}^{-1}$$

and $$W_s(\text{isentropic}) = (\Delta H)_S = -11\,920 \text{ J mol}^{-1}$$

This differs from the ideal-gas value by less than 2%.

7.3 COMPRESSION PROCESSES

Just as expansion processes result in pressure reductions in a flowing fluid, so compression processes bring about pressure increases. Compressors, pumps, fans, blowers, and vacuum pumps are all devices designed for this purpose. They are vital for the transport of fluids, for fluidization of particulate solids, for bringing fluids to the proper pressure for reaction or processing, etc. We are concerned here not with the design of such devices, but with specification of energy requirements for steady-state compression causing an increase in fluid pressure.

Compressors

The compression of gases may be accomplished in equipment with rotating blades (like a turbine operating in reverse) or in cylinders with reciprocating pistons. Rotary equipment is used for high-volume flow where the discharge pressure is not too high. For high pressures, reciprocating compressors are generally preferred. The energy equations are independent of the type of equipment; indeed, they are the same as for turbines or expanders, because here too potential- and kinetic-energy changes are presumed negligible. Thus, Eqs. (7.13) through (7.15) apply to adiabatic compression, a process represented by Fig. 7.5.

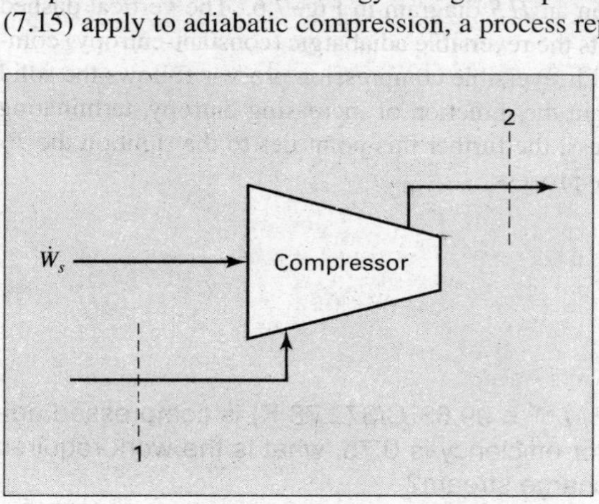

Figure 7.5: Steady-state compression process

In a compression process, the isentropic work, as given by Eq. (7.15), is the *minimum* shaft work required for compression of a gas from a given initial state to a given discharge pressure. Thus we define a compressor efficiency as

$$\eta \equiv \frac{W_s(\text{isentropic})}{W_s}$$

In view of Eqs. (7.14) and (7.15), this is also given by

$$\eta \equiv \frac{(\Delta H)_S}{\Delta H} \tag{7.17}$$

Compressor efficiencies are usually in the range of 0.7 to 0.8.

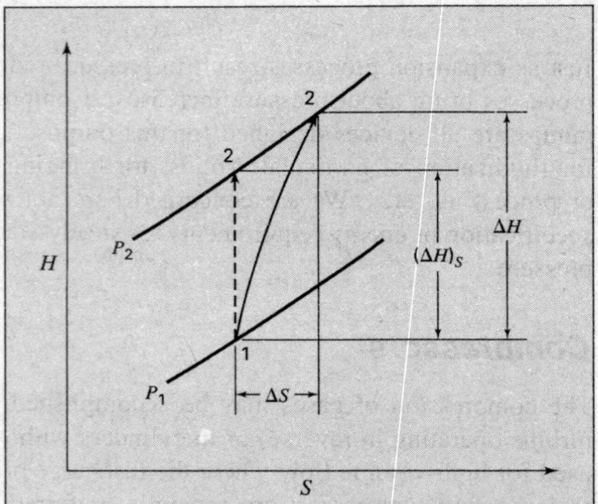

Figure 7.6: Adiabatic compression process

The compression process is shown on an HS diagram in Fig. 7.6. The vertical dashed line rising from point 1 to point 2′ represents the reversible adiabatgic (constant-entropy) compression process from P_1 to P_2. The actual irreversible compression process follows the solid line from point 1 upward and to the right in the direction of increasing entropy, terminating at point 2. The more irreversible the process, the further this point lies to the right on the P_2 isobar, and the lower the efficiency η of the process.

Example 7.8

Saturated-vapor steam at 100 kPa ($t^{\text{sat}}/T^{\text{sat}}$ = 99.63°C/372.78 K) is compressed adiabatically to 300 kPa. If the compressor efficiency is 0.75, what is the work required and what are the properties of the discharge stream?

Solution

For saturated steam at 100 kPa,

$$S_1 = 7.3598 \text{ kJ kg}^{-1} \text{ K}^{-1} \qquad H_1 = 2675.4 \text{ kJ kg}^{-1}$$

For isentropic compression to 300 kPa, $S_2' = S_1 = 7.3598$ kJ kg^{-1} K^{-1}. Interpolation in the tables for superheated steam at 300 kPa shows that steam with this entropy has the enthalpy: $H_2' = 2888.8$ kJ kg^{-1}.

Thus, $$(\Delta H)_S = 2888.8 - 2675.4 = 213.4 \text{ kJ kg}^{-1}$$

By Eq. (7.17), $$\Delta H = \frac{(\Delta H)_S}{\eta} = \frac{213.4}{0.75} = 284.5 \text{ kJ kg}^{-1}$$

Whence, $$H_2 = H_1 + \Delta H = 2675.4 + 284.5 = 2959.9 \text{ kJ kg}^{-1}$$

For superheated steam with this enthalpy, interpolation yields:

$$t_2/T_2 = 246.1°\text{C}/519.25 \text{ K} \qquad S_2 = 7.5019 \text{ kJ kg}^{-1} \text{ K}^{-1}$$

Moreover, by Eq. (7.14), the work required is

$$W_s = \Delta H = 284.5 \text{ kJ kg}^{-1}$$

The direct application of Eqs. (7.13) through (7.15) presumes the availability of tables of data or an equivalent thermodynamic diagram for the fluid being compressed. Where such information is not available, the generalized correlations of Sec. 6.7 may be used in conjunction with Eqs. (6.93) and (6.94), exactly as illustrated in Ex. 7.7 for an expansion process.

The assumption of ideal gases leads to equations of relative simplicity. By Eq. (5.18) for an ideal gas:

$$\Delta S = \langle C_P \rangle_S \ln \frac{T_2}{T_1} - R \ln \frac{P_2}{P_1}$$

where for simplicity the superscript "ig" has been omitted from the mean heat capacity. If the compression is isentropic, $\Delta S = 0$, and this equation becomes

$$T_2' = T_1 \left(\frac{P_2}{P_1} \right)^{R/\langle C_P' \rangle_S} \tag{7.18}$$

where T_2' is the temperature that results when compression from T_1 and P_1 to P_2 is *isentropic* and where $\langle C_P' \rangle_S$ is the mean heat-capacity for the temperature range from T_1 to T_2'.

Applied to isentropic compression, Eq. (4.9) here becomes

$$(\Delta H)_S = \langle C_P' \rangle_H (T_2' - T_1)$$

In accord with Eq. (7.15), $$W_s(\text{isentropic}) = \langle C_P' \rangle_H (T_2' - T_1) \tag{7.19}$$

This result may be combined with the compressor efficiency to give

$$W_s = \frac{W_s(\text{isentropic})}{\eta} \tag{7.20}$$

The *actual* discharge temperature T_2 resulting from compression is also found from Eq. (4.9), rewritten as

$$\Delta H = \langle C_P \rangle_H (T_2 - T_1)$$

Whence,
$$T_2 = T_1 + \frac{\Delta H}{\langle C_P \rangle_H} \tag{7.21}$$

where by Eq. (7.14) $\Delta H = W_s$. Here $\langle C_P \rangle_H$ is the mean heat-capacity for the temperature range from T_1 to T_2.

For the special case of an ideal gas with constant heat capacities,

$$\langle C'_P \rangle_H = \langle C_P \rangle_H = \langle C'_P \rangle_S = C_P$$

Equations (7.18) and (7.19) therefore become

$$T'_2 = T_1 \left(\frac{P_2}{P_1} \right)^{R/C_P} \qquad \text{and} \qquad W_s(\text{isentropic}) = C_P (T'_2 - T_1)$$

Combining these equations gives[5]

$$W_s(\text{isentropic}) = C_P T_1 \left[\left(\frac{P_2}{P_1} \right)^{R/C_P} - 1 \right] \tag{7.22}$$

For monatomic gases, such as argon and helium, $R/C_P = 2/5 = 0.4$. For such diatomic gases as oxygen, nitrogen, and air at moderate temperatures, $R/C_P \approx 2/7 = 0.2857$. For gases of greater molecular complexity the ideal-gas heat capacity depends more strongly on temperature, and Eq. (7.22) is less likely to be suitable. One can easily show that the assumption of constant heat capacities also leads to the result:

$$T_2 = T_1 + \frac{T'_2 - T_1}{\eta} \tag{7.23}$$

Example 7.9

If methane (assumed to be an ideal gas) is compressed adiabatically from 20°C (293.15 K) and 140 kPa to 560 kPa, estimate the work requirement and the discharge temperature of the methane. The compressor efficiency is 0.75.

[5]Because $R = C_P - C_V$ for an ideal gas: $\dfrac{R}{C_P} = \dfrac{C_P - C_V}{C_P} = \dfrac{\gamma - 1}{\gamma}$. An alternative form of Eq. (7.22) is therefore: $W_s(\text{isentropic}) = \dfrac{\gamma R T_1}{\gamma - 1} \left[\left(\dfrac{P_2}{P_1} \right)^{(\gamma-1)/\gamma} - 1 \right]$. Although this is the form commonly encountered, Eq. (7.22) is simpler and more easily applied.

Solution

Application of Eq. (7.18) requires evaluation of the exponent $R/\langle C'_P\rangle_S$. This is provided Eq. (5.17), which for the present computation is represented by

$$\frac{\langle C'_P\rangle_S}{R} = \mathrm{MCPS(293.15,T2;1.702,9.081E\text{-}3,\text{-}2.164E\text{-}6,0.0)}$$

where the constants for methane are from Table C.1. Choose a value for T'_2 somewhat higher than the initial temperature $T_1 = 293.15$ K. The exponent in Eq. (7.18) is the reciprocal of $\langle C'_P\rangle_S/R$. With $P_2/P_1 = 560/140 = 4.0$ and $T_1 = 293.15$ K, find a new value of T'_2. The procedure is repeated until no further significant change occurs in the value of T'_2. This process produces the values

$$\frac{\langle C'_P\rangle_S}{R} = 4.5574 \qquad \text{and} \qquad T'_2 = 397.37\ \text{K} \quad \text{or} \quad t'_2 = 124.22°\text{C}$$

For the same T_1 and T'_2, evaluate $\langle C'_P\rangle_H/R$ by Eq. (4.8):

$$\frac{\langle C'_P\rangle_H}{R} = \mathrm{MCPH(293.15,397.37;1.702,9.081E\text{-}3,\text{-}2.164E\text{-}6,0.0)} = 4.5774$$

Whence. $\langle C'_P\rangle_H = (4.5774)(8.314) = 38.056\ \text{J mol}^{-1}\ \text{K}^{-1}$

Then by Eq. (7.19),

$$W_s(\text{isentropic}) = (38.056)(397.37 - 293.15) = 3966.2\ \text{J mol}^{-1}$$

The actual work is found from Eq. (7.20):

$$W_s = \frac{3966.2}{0.75} = 5288.3\ \text{J mol}^{-1}$$

Application of Eq. (7.21) for the calculation of T_2 gives

$$T_2 = 293.15 + \frac{5288.3}{\langle C_P\rangle_H}$$

Because $\langle C_P\rangle_H$ depends on T_2, we again iterate. With T'_2 as a starting value, this leads to the results

$$T_2 = 428.65\ \text{K} \qquad \text{or} \qquad t_2 = 155.5°\text{C}$$

and $\langle C_P\rangle_H = 39.027\ \text{J mol}^{-1}\ \text{K}^{-1}$

Pumps

Liquids are usually moved by pumps, generally rotating equipment. The same equations apply to adiabatic pumps as to adiabatic compressors. Thus, Eqs. (7.13) through (7.15) and Eq. (7.17) are valid. However, application of Eq. (7.14) for the calculation of $W_s = \Delta H$ requires values of the enthalpy of compressed (subcooled) liquids, and these are seldom available. The fundamental property relation, Eq. (6.8), provides an alternative. For an isentropic process,

$$dH = V\,dP \qquad \text{(const } S\text{)}$$

Combining this with Eq. (7.15) yields

$$W_s(\text{isentropic}) = (\Delta H)_S = \int_{P_1}^{P_2} V\,dP$$

The usual assumption for liquids (at conditions well removed from the critical point) is that V is independent of P. Integration then gives

$$W_s(\text{isentropic}) = (\Delta H)_S = V(P_2 - P_1) \tag{7.24}$$

Also useful are the following equations from Chap. 6:

$dH = C_P\,dT + V(1-\beta T)\,dP \quad (6.28)$	$dS = C_P \dfrac{dT}{T} - \beta V\,dP \quad (6.29)$

where the volume expansivity β is defined by Eq. (3.2). Because temperature changes in the pumped fluid are very small and because the properties of liquids are insensitive to pressure (again at conditions not close to the critical point), these equations are usually integrated on the assumption that C_P, V, and β are constant, usually at initial values. Thus, to a good approximation

$\Delta H = C_P\,dT + V(1-\beta T)\,\Delta P \quad (7.25)$	$\Delta S = C_P \dfrac{T_2}{T_1} - \beta V\,\Delta P \quad (7.26)$

Example 7.10

Water at 45°C (318.15 K) and 10 kPa enters an adiabatic pump and is discharged at a pressure of 8600 kPa. Assume the pump efficiency to be 0.75. Calculate the work of the pump, the temperature change of the water, and the entropy change of the water.

Solution

The following are properties for saturated liquid water at 45°C (318.15 K):

$$V = 1010\ \text{cm}^3\ \text{kg}^{-1} \qquad \beta = 425 \times 10^{-6}\ \text{K}^{-1} \qquad C_P = 4.178\ \text{kJ kg}^{-1}\ \text{K}^{-1}$$

By Eq. (7.24),

$$W_s(\text{isentropic}) = (\Delta H)_S = (1010)(8600 - 10) = 8.676 \times 10^6 \text{ kPa cm}^3 \text{ kg}^{-1}$$

Because 1 kJ = 10^6 kPa cm^3,

$$W_s(\text{isentropic}) = (\Delta H)_S = 8.676 \text{ kJ kg}^{-1}$$

By Eq. (7.17), $$\Delta H = \frac{(\Delta H)_S}{\eta} = \frac{8.676}{0.75} = 11.57 \text{ kJ kg}^{-1}$$

and $$W_s = \Delta H = 11.57 \text{ kJ kg}^{-1}$$

The temperature change of the water during pumping, from Eq. (7.25):

$$11.57 = 4.178\,\Delta T + 1010\left[1 - (425 \times 10^{-6})(318.15)\right]\frac{8590}{10^6}$$

Solution for ΔT gives

$$\Delta T = 0.97 \text{ K} \quad \text{or} \quad 0.97°\text{C}$$

The entropy change of the water is given by Eq. (7.26):

$$\Delta S = 4.178 \ln \frac{319.12}{318.15} - (425 \times 10^{-6})(1010)\frac{8590}{10^6} = 0.0090 \text{ kJ kg}^{-1} \text{ K}^{-1}$$

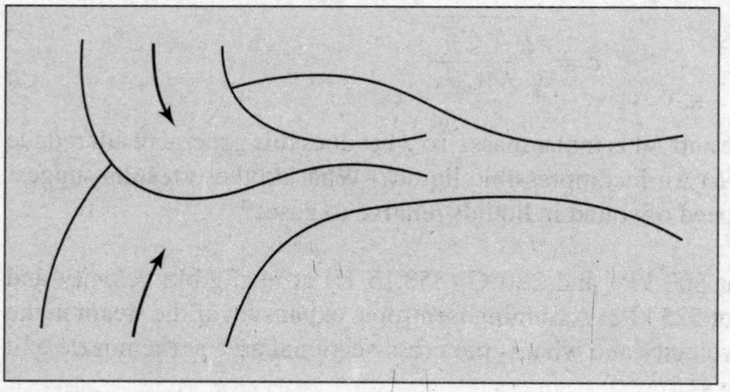

Figure 7.7: Single-stage ejector

Ejectors

Ejectors remove gases or vapors from an evacuated space and compress them for discharge at a higher pressure. Where mixing of the gases or vapors with the driving fluid is allowable, ejectors are usually lower in first cost and maintenance costs than other types of vacuum pumps. As illustrated in Fig. 7.7 an ejector consists of an inner converging/diverging nozzle through which the driving fluid (commonly steam) is fed, and an outer, larger nozzle through which both the extracted gases or vapors and the driving fluid pass. The momentum of the high-speed fluid leaving the driving nozzle is partly transferred to the extracted gases or vapors, and the mixture velocity is therefore less than that of the driving fluid leaving the smaller nozzle. It is nevertheless higher than the speed of sound, and the larger nozzle therefore acts as a converging/diverging *diffuser* in which the pressure rises and the velocity decreases, passing through the speed of sound at the throat. Although the usual energy equations for nozzles apply, the mixing process is complex, and as a result ejector design is largely empirical.[6]

PROBLEMS

7.1. Air expands adiabatically through a nozzle from a negligible initial velocity to a final velocity of 325 m s^{-1}. What is the temperature drop of the air, if air is assumed to be an ideal gas for which $C_P = (7/2)R$?

7.2. In Ex. 7.5 an expression is found for the Joule/Thomson coeficient, $\mu = (\partial T/\partial P)_H$, that relates it to a heat capacity and equation-of-state information. Develop similar expressions for the derivatives:

(*a*) $(\partial T/\partial P)_S$ (*b*) $(\partial T/\partial V)_U$

What can you say about the *signs* of these derivatives? For what types of processes might these derivatives be important characterizing quantities?

7.3. The thermodynamic sound speed c is defined in Sec. 7.1. Prove that

$$c = \sqrt{\frac{VC_P}{\mathcal{M}C_V\kappa}}$$

where V is *molar* volume and $\mathcal{M}$ is molar mass. To what does this general result reduce for: (*a*) An ideal gas? (*b*) An incompressible liquid? What do these results suggest qualitatively about the speed of sound in liquids relative to gases?

7.4. Steam enters a nozzle at 800 kPa and 280°C (553.15 K) at negligible velocity and discharges at a pressure of 525 kPa. Assuming isentropic expansion of the steam in the nozzle, what is the exit velocity and what is the cross-sectional area at the nozzle exit for a flow rate of 0.75 kg s^{-1}?

7.5. Steam enters a converging nozzle at 800 kPa and 280°C (553.15 K) with negligible velocity. If expansion is isentropic, what is the minimum pressure that can be reached in such a nozzle and what is the cross-sectional area at the nozzle throat at this pressure for a flow rate of 0.75 kg s^{-1}?

[6] R. H. Perry and D. Green, *Perry's Chemical Engineers' Handbook*, 7th ed., pp. 10-56–10-57, McGraw-Hill, New York, 1997.

7.6. A gas enters a converging nozzle at pressure P_1 with negligible velocity, expands isentropically in the nozzle, and discharges into a chamber at pressure P_2. Sketch graphs showing the velocity at the throat and the mass flowrate as functions of the pressure ratio P_2/P_1.

7.7. For isentropic expansion in a converging/diverging nozzle with negligible entrance velocity, sketch graphs of mass flowrate $\dot{m}$, velocity u, and area ratio A/A_1 vs. the pressure ratio P/P_1. Here, A is the cross-sectional area of the nozzle at the point in the nozzle where the pressure is P, and subscript 1 denotes the nozzle entrance.

7.8. An ideal gas with constant heat capacities enters a converging/diverging nozzle with negligible velocity. If it expands isentropically within the nozzle, show that the throat velocity is given by

$$u_{\text{throat}}^2 = \frac{\gamma R T_1}{M}\left(\frac{2}{\gamma + 1}\right)$$

where T_1 is the temperature of the gas entering the nozzle, M is the molar mass, and R is the molar gas constant.

7.9. Steam expands isentropically in a converging/diverging nozzle from inlet conditions of 1400 kPa, 325°C (598.15 K), and negligible velocity to a discharge pressure of 140 kPa. At the throat the cross-sectional area is 6 cm^2. Determine the mass flowrate of the steam and the state of the steam at the exit of the nozzle.

7.10. Steam expands adiabatically in a nozzle from inlet conditions of 9 bar, 215°C (488.15 K), and a velocity of 70 m s^{-1} to a discharge pressure of 2.4 bar where its velocity is 609.6 m s^{-1}. What is the state of the steam at the nozzle exit, and what is $\dot{S}_G$ for the process?

7.11. Air discharges from an adiabatic nozzle at 15°C (288.15 K) with a velocity of 580 m s^{-1}. What is the temperature at the entrance of the nozzle if the entrance velocity is negligible? Assume air to be an ideal gas for which $C_P = (7/2)R$.

7.12. Cool water at 15°C (288.15 K) is throttled from 5 atm to 1 atm, as in a kitchen faucet. What is the temperature change of the water? What is the lost work per kilogram of water for this everyday household happening? At 15°C (288.15 K) and 1 atm, the volume expansivity β for liquid water is about 1.5×10^{-4} K^{-1}. The surroundings temperature T_σ is 20°C (293.15 K). State carefully any assumptions you make. The steam tables are a source of data.

7.13. A gas at upstream conditions (T_1, P_1) is throttled to a downstream pressure of 1.2 bar. Use the Redlich/Kwong equation to estimate the downstream temperature and ΔS of the gas for one of the following:

(*a*) Carbon dioxide, with $T_1 = 350$ K and $P_1 = 80$ bar
(*b*) Ethylene, with $T_1 = 350$ K and $P_1 = 60$ bar
(*c*) Nitrogen, with $T_1 = 250$ K and $P_1 = 60$ bar
(*d*) Propane, with $T_1 = 400$ K and $P_1 = 20$ bar

7.14. A gas at upstream conditions given by one of the parts of Pb. 7.13 is throttled to a pressure of 1.2 bar. Use the Soave/Redlich/Kwong equation to estimate the downstream temperature and ΔS of the gas.

7.15. A gas at upstream conditions given by one of the parts of Pb. 7.13 is throttled to a pressure of 1.2 bar. Use the Peng/Robinson equation to estimate the downstream temperature and ΔS of the gas.

7.16. For a pressure-explicit equation of state, prove that the Joule/Thompson inversion curve is the locus of states for which

$$T\left(\frac{\partial Z}{\partial T}\right)_\rho = \rho\left(\frac{\partial Z}{\partial \rho}\right)_T$$

Apply this equation to (*a*) the van der Waals equation; (*b*) the Redlich/Kwong equation. Discuss the results.

7.17. Two nonconducting tanks of negligible heat capacity and of equal volume initially contain equal quantities of the same ideal gas at the same T and P. Tank A discharges to the atmosphere through a small turbine in which the gas expands isentropically; tank B discharges to the atmosphere through a porous plug. Both devices operate until discharge ceases.

(*a*) When discharge ceases, is the temperature in tank A less than, equal to, or greater than the temperature in tank B?

(*b*) When the pressures in both tanks have fallen to half the initial pressure, is the temperature of the gas discharging from the turbine less than, equal to, or greater than the temperature of the gas discharging from the porous plug?

(*c*) During the discharge process, is the temperature of the gas leaving the turbine less than, equal to, or greater than the temperature of the gas leaving tank A at the same instant?

(*d*) During the discharge process, is the temperature of the gas leaving the porous plug less than, equal to, or greater than the temperature of the gas leaving tank B at the same instant?

(*e*) When discharge ceases, is the mass of gas remaining in tank A less than, equal to, or greater than the mass of gas remaining in tank B?

7.18. A steam turbine operates adiabatically at a power level of 3500 kW. Steam enters the turbine at 2400 kPa and 500°C (773.15 K) and exhausts from the turbine as saturated vapor at 20 kPa. What is the steam rate through the turbine, and what is the turbine efficiency?

7.19. A turbine operates adiabatically with superheated steam entering at T_1 and P_1 with a mass flowrate $\dot{m}$. The exhaust pressure is P_2 and the turbine efficiency is η. For one of the following sets of operating conditions, determine the power output of the turbine and the enthalpy and entropy of the exhaust steam.

(*a*) $t_1/T_1 = 450°\text{C}/723.15\ \text{K}$, $P_1 = 8000\ \text{kPa}$, $\dot{m} = 80\ \text{kg s}^{-1}$, $P_2 = 30\ \text{kPa}$, $\eta = 0.80$.
(*b*) $t_1/T_1 = 550°\text{C}/823.15\ \text{K}$, $P_1 = 9000\ \text{kPa}$, $\dot{m} = 90\ \text{kg s}^{-1}$, $P_2 = 20\ \text{kPa}$, $\eta = 0.77$.
(*c*) $t_1/T_1 = 600°\text{C}/873.15\ \text{K}$, $P_1 = 8600\ \text{kPa}$, $\dot{m} = 70\ \text{kg s}^{-1}$, $P_2 = 10\ \text{kPa}$, $\eta = 0.82$.
(*d*) $t_1/T_1 = 400°\text{C}/673.15\ \text{K}$, $P_1 = 7000\ \text{kPa}$, $\dot{m} = 65\ \text{kg s}^{-1}$, $P_2 = 50\ \text{kPa}$, $\eta = 0.75$.
(*e*) $t_1/T_1 = 200°\text{C}/473.15\ \text{K}$, $P_1 = 1400\ \text{kPa}$, $\dot{m} = 50\ \text{kg s}^{-1}$, $P_2 = 200\ \text{kPa}$, $\eta = 0.75$.
(*f*) $t_1/T_1 = 482°\text{C}/755.15\ \text{K}$, $P_1 = 75.8\ \text{bar}$, $\dot{m} = 68\ \text{kg s}^{-1}$, $P_2 = 0.14\ \text{bar}$, $\eta = 0.80$.
(*g*) $t_1/T_1 = 427°\text{C}/700.15\ \text{K}$, $P_1 = 69\ \text{bar}$, $\dot{m} = 45.4\ \text{kg s}^{-1}$, $P_2 = 0.28\ \text{bar}$, $\eta = 0.75$.

7.20. Nitrogen gas initially at 8.5 bar expands isentropically to 1 bar and 150°C (423.15 K). Assuming nitrogen to be an ideal gas, calculate the *initial* temperature and the work produced per mole of nitrogen.

7.21. Combustion products from a burner enter a gas turbine at 10 bar and 950°C (1223.15 K) and discharge at 1.5 bar. The turbine operates adiabatically with an efficiency of 77%. Assuming the combustion products to be an ideal-gas mixture with a heat capacity of 32 J mol^{-1} K^{-1}, what is the work output of the turbine per mole of gas, and what is the temperature of the gases discharging from the turbine?

7.22. Isobutane expands adiabatically in a turbine from 5000 kPa and 250°C (523.15 K) to 500 kPa at the rate of 0.7 kmol s^{-1}. If the turbine efficiency is 0.80, what is the power output of the turbine and what is the temperature of the isobutane leaving the turbine?

7.23. The steam rate to a turbine for variable output is controlled by a throttle valve in the inlet line. Steam is supplied to the throttle valve at 1700 kPa and 225°C (498.15 K). During a test run, the pressure at the turbine inlet is 1000 kPa, the exhaust steam at 10 kPa has a quality of 0.95, the steam flow rate is 0.5 kg s^{-1}, and the power output of the turbine is 180 kW.

(*a*) What are the heat losses from the turbine?

(*b*) What would be the power output if the steam supplied to the throttle valve were expanded isentropically to the final pressure?

7.24. Carbon dioxide gas enters an adiabatic expander at 8 bar and 400°C (673.15 K) and discharges at 1 bar. If the turbine efficiency is 0.75, what is the discharge temperature and what is the work output per mole of CO_2? Assume CO_2 to be an ideal gas at these conditions.

7.25. Tests on an adiabatic gas turbine (expander) yield values for inlet conditions (T_1, P_1) and outlet conditions (T_2, P_2). Assuming ideal gases with constant heat capacities, determine the turbine efficiency for one of the following:

(*a*) $T_1 = 500$ K, $P_1 = 6$ bar, $T_2 = 371$ K, $P_2 = 1.2$ bar, $C_P/R = 7/2$.
(*b*) $T_1 = 450$ K, $P_1 = 5$ bar, $T_2 = 376$ K, $P_2 = 2$ bar, $C_P/R = 4$.
(*c*) $T_1 = 525$ K, $P_1 = 10$ bar, $T_2 = 458$ K, $P_2 = 3$ bar, $C_P/R = 11/2$.
(*d*) $T_1 = 475$ K, $P_1 = 7$ bar, $T_2 = 372$ K, $P_2 = 1.5$ bar, $C_P/R = 9/2$.
(*e*) $T_1 = 550$ K, $P_1 = 4$ bar, $T_2 = 403$ K, $P_2 = 1.2$ bar, $C_P/R = 5/2$.

7.26. The efficiency of a particular series of adiabatic gas turbines (expanders) correlates with power output according to the empirical expression: $\eta = 0.065 + 0.080 \ln |\dot{W}|$. Here, $|\dot{W}|$ is the absolute value of the *actual* power output in kW. Nitrogen gas is to be expanded from inlet conditions of 550 K and 6 bar to an outlet pressure of 1.2 bar. For a molar flowrate of 175 mol s^{-1}, what is the delivered power in kW? What is the efficiency of the turbine? What is the rate of entropy generation $\dot{S}_G$? Assume nitrogen to be an ideal gas with $C_P = (7/2)R$.

7.27. A turbine operates adiabatically with superheated steam entering at 45 bar and 400°C (673.15 K). If the exhaust steam must be "dry," what is the minimum allowable exhaust pressure for a turbine efficiency, $\eta = 0.75$? Suppose the efficiency were 0.80. Would the minimum exhaust pressure be lower or higher? Why?

7.28. Turbines can be used to recover energy from high-pressure liquid streams. However, they are not used when the high-pressure stream is a *saturated* liquid. Why? Illustrate by determining the downstream state for isentropic expansion of saturated liquid water at 5 bar to a final pressure of 1 bar.

7.29. Liquid water enters an adiabatic hydroturbine at 5 atm and 15°C (288.15 K), and exhausts at 1(atm). Estimate the power output of the turbine in J kg^{-1} of water if its efficiency is $\eta = 0.55$. What is the outlet temperature of the water? Assume water to be an incompressible liquid.

7.30. An expander operates adiabatically with nitrogen entering at T_1 and P_1 with a molar flow rate $\dot{n}$. The exhaust pressure is P_2, and the expander efficiency is η. Estimate the power output of the expander and the temperature of the exhaust stream for one of the following sets of operating conditions.

(*a*) $t_1/T_1 = 480°\text{C}/753.15$ K, $P_1 = 6$ bar, $\dot{n} = 200$ mol s^{-1}, $P_2 = 1$ bar, $\eta = 0.80$.
(*b*) $t_1/T_1 = 400°\text{C}/673.15$ K, $P_1 = 5$ bar, $\dot{n} = 150$ mol s^{-1}, $P_2 = 1$ bar, $\eta = 0.75$.
(*c*) $t_1/T_1 = 500°\text{C}/773.15$ K, $P_1 = 7$ bar, $\dot{n} = 175$ mol s^{-1}, $P_2 = 1$ bar, $\eta = 0.78$.
(*d*) $t_1/T_1 = 450°\text{C}/723.15$ K, $P_1 = 8$ bar, $\dot{n} = 100$ mol s^{-1}, $P_2 = 2$ bar, $\eta = 0.85$.
(*e*) $t_1/T_1 = 482°\text{C}/755.15$ K, $P_1 = 6.55$ bar, $\dot{n} = 230$ mol s^{-1}, $P_2 = 1.03$ bar, $\eta = 0.80$.

7.31. What is the ideal-work rate for the expansion process of Ex. 7.6? What is the thermodynamic efficiency of the process? What is the rate of entropy generation $\dot{S}_G$? What is $\dot{W}_{\text{lost}}$? Take $T_\sigma = 300$ K.

7.32. Exhaust gas at 400°C (673.15 K) and 1 bar from internal-combustion engines flows at the rate of 125 mol s^{-1} into a waste-heat boiler where saturated steam is generated at a pressure of 1200 kPa. Water enters the boiler at 20°C (293.15 K) (T_σ), and the exhaust gases are cooled to within 10°C (10 K) of the steam temperature. The heat capacity of the exhaust gases is $C_P/R = 3.34 + 1.12 \times 10^{-3} T/\text{K}$. The steam flows into an adiabatic turbine and exhausts at a pressure of 25 kPa. If the turbine efficiency η is 72%,

(*a*) What is $\dot{W}_s$, the power output of the turbine?
(*b*) What is the thermodynamic efficiency of the boiler/turbine combination?
(*c*) Determine $\dot{S}_G$ for the boiler and for the turbine.
(*d*) Express $\dot{W}_{\text{lost}}$(boiler) and $\dot{W}_{\text{lost}}$(turbine) as fractions of $|\dot{W}_{\text{ideal}}|$, the ideal work of the process.

7.33. A small adiabatic air compressor is used to pump air into a 20 m^3 insulated tank. The tank initially contains air at 25°C (298.15 K) and 101.33 kPa, exactly the conditions at which air enters the compressor. The pumping process continues until the pressure in the tank reaches 1000 kPa. If the process is adiabatic and if compression is isentropic, what is the shaft work of the compressor? Assume air to be an ideal gas for which $C_P = (7/2)R$ and $C_V = (5/2)R$.

7.34. Saturated steam at 125 kPa is compressed adiabatically in a centrifugal compressor to 700 kPa at the rate of 2.5 kg s^{-1}. The compressor efficiency is 78%. What is the power requirement of the compressor and what are the enthalpy and entropy of the steam in its final state?

7.35. A compressor operates adiabatically with air entering at T_1 and P_1 with a molar flow rate $\dot{n}$. The discharge pressure is P_2 and the compressor efficiency is η. Estimate the power requirement of the compressor and the temperature of the discharge stream for one of the following sets of operating conditions.

(*a*) $t_1/T_1 = 25°\text{C}/298.15$ K, $P_1 = 101.33$ kPa, $\dot{n} = 100$ mol s^{-1}, $P_2 = 375$ kPa, $\eta = 0.75$.
(*b*) $t_1/T_1 = 80°\text{C}/353.15$ K, $P_1 = 375$ kPa, $\dot{n} = 100$ mol s^{-1}, $P_2 = 1000$ kPa, $\eta = 0.70$.
(*c*) $t_1/T_1 = 30°\text{C}/303.15$ K, $P_1 = 100$ kPa, $\dot{n} = 150$ mol s^{-1}, $P_2 = 500$ kPa, $\eta = 0.80$.
(*d*) $t_1/T_1 = 100°\text{C}/373.15$ K, $P_1 = 500$ kPa, $\dot{n} = 50$ mol s^{-1}, $P_2 = 1300$ kPa, $\eta = 0.75$.
(*e*) $t_1/T_1 = 27°\text{C}/300.15$ K, $P_1 = 1.01$ bar, $\dot{n} = 230$ mol s^{-1}, $P_2 = 3.8$ bar, $\eta = 0.75$.
(*f*) $t_1/T_1 = 66°\text{C}/339.15$ K, $P_1 = 3.8$ bar, $\dot{n} = 230$ mol s^{-1}, $P_2 = 9.3$ bar, $\eta = 0.70$.

7.36. Ammonia gas is compressed from 21°C (294.15 K) and 200 kPa to 1000 kPa in an adiabatic compressor with an efficiency of 0.82. Estimate the final temperature, the work required, and the entropy change of the ammonia.

7.37. Propylene is compressed adiabatically from 11.5 bar and 30°C (303.15 K) to 18 bar at the rate of 1 kmol s^{-1}. If the compressor efficiency is 0.8, what is the power requirement of the compressor and what is the discharge temperature of the propylene?

7.38. Methane is compressed adiabatically in a pipeline pumping station from 3500 kPa and 35°C (308.15 K) to 5500 kPa at the rate of 1.5 kmol s^{-1}. If the compressor efficiency is 0.78, what is the power requirement of the compressor and what is the discharge temperature of the methane?

7.39. What is the ideal work for the compression process of Ex. 7.9? What is the thermodynamic efficiency of the process? What are S_G and W_{lost}? Take $T_\sigma = 293.15$ K.

7.40. A *fan* is (in effect) a gas compressor which moves large volumes of air at low pressure across small (1 to 15 kPa) pressure differences. The usual design equation is

$$\dot{W} = \dot{n}\frac{RT_1}{\eta P_1}\Delta P$$

where subscript 1 denotes inlet conditions and η is the efficiency with respect to isentropic operation. Develop this equation. Show also how it follows from the usual equation for compression of an ideal gas with constant heat capacities.

7.41. For an adiabatic gas compressor, the efficiency with respect to isentropic operation η is a measure of internal irreversibilities; so is the dimensionless rate of entropy generation $S_G/R \equiv \dot{S}_G/\dot{n}R$. Assuming that the gas is ideal with constant heat capacities, show that η and S_G/R are related through the expression:

$$\frac{S_G}{R} = \frac{C_P}{R}\ln\left(\frac{\eta + \pi - 1}{\eta\pi}\right)$$

where $\pi \equiv (P_2/P_1)^{R/C_P}$

7.42. Air at 1 atm and 35°C (308.15 K) is compressed in a staged reciprocating compressor (with intercooling) to a final pressure of 50 atm. For each stage, the inlet gas temperature is 35°C (308.15 K) and the maximum allowable outlet temperature is 200°C (473.15 K). Mechanical power is the same for all stages, and isentropic efficiency is 65% for each stage. The volumetric flowrate of air is 0.5 m^3 s^{-1} at the inlet to the first stage.

(*a*) How many stages are required?
(*b*) What is the mechanical-power requirement per stage?
(*c*) What is the heat duty for each intercooler?
(*d*) Water is the coolant for the intercoolers. It enters at 25°C (298.15 K) and leaves at 45°C (318.15 K). What is the cooling-water rate per intercooler?

Assume air is an ideal gas with $C_P = (7/2)R$.

7.43. Demonstrate that the power requirement for compressing a gas is smaller, the more complex the gas. Assume fixed values of $\dot{n}$, η, T_1, P_1, and P_2, and that the gas is ideal with constant heat capacities.

7.44. Tests on an adiabatic gas compressor yield values for inlet conditions (T_1, P_1) and outlet conditions (T_2, P_2). Assuming ideal gases with constant heat capacities, determine the compressor efficiency for one of the following:

(*a*) $T_1 = 300$ K, $P_1 = 2$ bar, $T_2 = 464$ K, $P_2 = 6$ bar, $C_P/R = 7/2$.
(*b*) $T_1 = 290$ K, $P_1 = 1.5$ bar, $T_2 = 547$ K, $P_2 = 5$ bar, $C_P/R = 5/2$.
(*c*) $T_1 = 295$ K, $P_1 = 1.2$ bar, $T_2 = 455$ K, $P_2 = 6$ bar, $C_P/R = 9/2$.
(*d*) $T_1 = 300$ K, $P_1 = 1.1$ bar, $T_2 = 505$ K, $P_2 = 8$ bar, $C_P/R = 11/2$.
(*e*) $T_1 = 305$ K, $P_1 = 1.5$ bar, $T_2 = 496$ K, $P_2 = 7$ bar, $C_P/R = 4$.

7.45. Air is compressed in a steady-flow compressor, entering at 1.2 bar and 300 K and leaving at 5 bar and 500 K. Operation is *non*adiabatic, with heat transfer to the surroundings at 295 K. For the same change in state of the air, is the mechanical-power requirement per mole of air greater or less for nonadiabatic than for adiabatic operation? Why?

7.46. A boiler house produces a large excess of low-pressure [3.45 bar g, 3°C (3 K) superheat] steam. An upgrade is proposed that would first run the low-pressure steam through an adiabatic steady-flow compressor, producing medium-pressure [10.35 bar g] steam. A young engineer expresses concern that compression could result in the formation of liquid water, damaging the compressor. Is there cause for concern? *Suggestion*: Refer to the Mollier diagram of Fig. 6.4.

7.47. A pump operates adiabatically with liquid water entering at T_1 and P_1 with a mass flowrate $\dot{m}$. The discharge pressure is P_2, and the pump efficiency is η. For one of the following sets of operating conditions, determine the power requirement of the pump and the temperature of the water discharged from the pump.

(*a*) $t_1/T_1 = 25°\text{C}/298.15$ K, $P_1 = 100$ kPa, $\dot{m} = 20\ \text{kg s}^{-1}$, $P_2 = 2000$ kPa, $\eta = 0.75$, $\beta = 257.2 \times 10^{-6}\ \text{K}^{-1}$.
(*b*) $t_1/T_1 = 90°\text{C}/363.15$ K, $P_1 = 200$ kPa, $\dot{m} = 30\ \text{kg s}^{-1}$, $P_2 = 5000$ kPa, $\eta = 0.70$, $\beta = 696.2 \times 10^{-6}\ \text{K}^{-1}$.
(*c*) $t_1/T_1 = 60°\text{C}/333.15$ K, $P_1 = 20$ kPa, $\dot{m} = 15\ \text{kg s}^{-1}$, $P_2 = 5000$ kPa, $\eta = 0.75$, $\beta = 523.1 \times 10^{-6}\ \text{K}^{-1}$.
(*d*) $t_1/T_1 = 21°\text{C}/294.15$ K, $P_1 = 1$ atm, $\dot{m} = 22.7\ \text{kg s}^{-1}$, $P_2 = 20$ atm, $\eta = 0.70$, $\beta = 217.3 \times 10^{-6}\ \text{K}^{-1}$.
(*e*) $t_1/T_1 = 93°\text{C}/366.15$ K, $P_1 = 1.03$ bar, $\dot{m} = 36.3\ \text{kg s}^{-1}$, $P_2 = 103.4$ bar, $\eta = 0.75$, $\beta = 714.3 \times 10^{-6}\ \text{K}^{-1}$.

7.48. What is the ideal work for the pumping process of Ex. 7.10? What is the thermodynamic efficiency of the process? What is S_G? What is W_{lost}? Take $T_\sigma = 300$ K.

7.49. Show that the points on the Joule/Thomson inversion curve [for which $\mu = (\partial T/\partial P)_H = 0$] are also characterized by each of the following:

$$(a)\ \left(\frac{\partial Z}{\partial T}\right)_P = 0; \quad (b)\ \left(\frac{\partial H}{\partial P}\right)_T = 0; \quad (c)\ \left(\frac{\partial V}{\partial T}\right)_P = \frac{V}{T}; \quad (d)\ \left(\frac{\partial Z}{\partial V}\right)_P = 0;$$

$$(e)\ V\left(\frac{\partial P}{\partial V}\right)_T + T\left(\frac{\partial P}{\partial T}\right)_V = 0$$

7.50. According to Pb. 7.3, the thermodynamic sound speed c depends on the PVT equation of state. Show how isothermal sound-speed measurements can be used to estimate the second virial coefficient B of a gas. Assume that Eq. (3.38) applies, and that the ratio C_P/C_V is given by its ideal-gas value.

7.51. Real-gas behavior for turbomachinery is sometimes empirically accommodated through the expression $\dot{W} = \langle Z \rangle \dot{W}^{ig}$, where $\dot{W}^{ig}$ is the ideal-gas mechanical power and $\langle Z \rangle$ is some suitably defined average value of the compressibility factor.

(*a*) Rationalize this expression.

(*b*) Devise a turbine example incorporating real-gas behavior via residual properties, and determine a numerical value of $\langle Z \rangle$ for the example.

7.52. Operating data are taken on an air turbine. For a particular run, $P_1 = 8$ bar, $T_1 = 600$ K, and $P_2 = 1.2$ bar. However, the recorded outlet temperature is only partially legible; it could be $T_2 = 318$, 348, or 398 K. Which must it be? For the given conditions, assume air to be an ideal gas with constant $C_P = (7/2)R$.

7.53. Liquid benzene at 25°C (298.15 K) and 1.2 bar is converted to vapor at 200°C (473.15 K) and 5 bar in a two-step steady-flow process: compression by a pump to 5 bar, followed by vaporization in a counter-flow heat exchanger. Determine the power requirement of the pump and the duty of the exchanger in kJ mol^{-1}. Assume a pump efficiency of 70%, and treat benzene vapor as as an ideal gas with constant $C_P = 105$ J mol^{-1} K^{-1}.

7.54. Liquid benzene at 25°C (298.15 K) and 1.2 bar is converted to vapor at 200°C (473.15 K) and 5 bar in a two-step steady-flow process: vaporization in a counter-flow heat exchanger at 1.2 bar, followed by compression as a gas to 5 bar. Determine the duty of the exchanger and the power requirement of the compressor in kJ mol^{-1}. Assume a compressor efficiency of 75%, and treat benzene vapor as as an ideal gas with constant $C_P = 105$ J mol^{-1} K^{-1}.

7.55. Of the processes proposed in Pbs. 7.53 and 7.54, which would you recommend? Why?

7.56. Liquids (identified below) at 25°C (298.15 K) are completely vaporized at 1 atm in a counter-current heat exchanger. Saturated steam is the heating medium, available at four pressures: 4.5, 9, 17, and 33 bar. Which variety of steam is most appropriate for each case? Assume a minimum approach ΔT of 10°C (10 K) for heat exchange.

(*a*) Benzene; (*b*) *n*-Decane; (*c*) Ethylene glycol; (*d*) *o*-Xylene

7.57. One hundred kmol h^{-1} of ethylene is compressed from 1.2 bar and 300 K to 6 bar by an electric-motor-driven compressor. Determine the capital cost C of the unit. Treat ethylene as an ideal gas with constant $C_P = 50.6$ J mol^{-1} K^{-1}.

Data: η (compressor) = 0.70

$C(\text{compressor})/\$ = 3{,}040(\dot{W}_S/\text{kW})^{0.952}$

where $\dot{W}_S \equiv$ *isentropic* power requirement for the compressor

$C(\text{motor})/\$ = 380(|\dot{W}_e|/\text{kW})^{0.855}$

where $\dot{W}_e \equiv$ *delivered* shaft power of motor

7.58. Four different types of drivers for gas compressors are: electric motors, gas expanders, steam turbines, and internal-combustion engines. Suggest when each might be appropriate. How would you estimate operating costs for each of these drivers? Ignore such add-ons as maintenance, operating labor, and overhead.

7.59. Two schemes are proposed for the reduction in pressure of ethylene gas at 375 K and 18 bar to 1.2 bar in a steady-flow process:

(*a*) Pass it through a throttle valve.
(*b*) Send it through an adiabatic expander of 70% efficiency.

For each proposal, determiine the downstream temperature, and the rate of entropy generation in J mol^{-1} K^{-1}. What is the power output for proposal (*b*) in kJ mol^{-1}? Discuss the pros and cons of the two proposals. Do not assume ideal gases.

7.60. A stream of hydrocarbon gas at 500°C (773.15 K) is cooled by continuously combining it with a stream of light oil in an adiabatic tower. The light oil enters as a liquid at 25°C (298.15 K); the combined stream leaves as a gas at 200°C (473.15 K).

(*a*) Draw a carefully labeled flow diagram for the process.
(*b*) Let F and D denote respectively the molar mass of hot hydrocarbon gas and light oil. Use data given below to determine a numerical value for the oil-to-gas ratio D/F. Explain your analysis.
(*c*) What is the advantage to quenching the hydrocarbon gas with a ***liquid*** rather than with another (cooler) gas? Explain.

Data: $C_P^v(\text{ave}) = 150$ J mol^{-1} K^{-1} for the hydrocarbon gas.

$C_P^v(\text{ave}) = 200$ J mol^{-1} K^{-1} for the oil vapor.

$\Delta H^{lv}(\text{oil}) = 35\,000$ J mol^{-1} at 25°C (298.15 K).

Chapter 8

Production of Power from Heat

Except for nuclear power, the sun is the ultimate source of all the mechanical energy used by mankind. The total rate at which energy reaches the earth from the sun is staggering, but the rate at which it falls on a square meter of surface is small. Energy gathered over a large area is required to make practical its use in any large-scale production of work. Nevertheless, solar photovoltaic cells are used for electric power in small-scale special applications. Solar radiation also finds direct application for heating water and buildings, for generation of high temperatures in metallurgical applications (solar furnaces), and for evaporating water in the production of salt.

The kinetic energy associated with atmospheric winds is increasingly used in favorable locations to produce power by large windmills. The potential energy of tides is another possible source of power, but production from these sources remains small in comparison with world demands for energy. Eventually, such alternatives will become essential.

Significant hydroelectric power is generated by conversion of the potential energy of water into work, a process that can in principle be accomplished with an efficiency of 100%. However, by far the most important sources of power are the chemical (molecular) energy of fuels and nuclear energy. *Large-scale* installations for this purpose depend on the evolution of heat and its subsequent partial conversion into work. Despite improvements in equipment design, the efficiency of conversion does not approach 100%. This is a consequence of the second law. The efficiency of conventional fossil-fuel steam-power plants rarely exceeds 35%. However, efficiencies greater than 50% can be realized in combined-cycle plants with dual power generation:

- From advanced-technology gas turbines

- From steam-power cycles operating on heat recovered from hot turbine exhaust gases

A common device for the direct conversion of chemical energy into electrical energy, without the intermediate generation of heat, is the electrochemical cell, e.g., a battery. A related device is the *fuel cell*, in which reactants are supplied continuously to the electrodes. The prototype is a cell in which hydrogen reacts with oxygen to produce water through electrochemical conversion. The resulting efficiency can be as great as 85%, a considerable improvement over processes that first convert chemical energy into heat. This technology has potential application in transportation, and may well find other uses. Its theoretical basis is considered in Sec. 13.10.

In a conventional power plant the molecular energy of fuel is released by a combustion process. The function of the work-producing device is to convert part of the heat of combustion into mechanical energy. In a nuclear power plant the fission process releases energy of the nucleus of the atom as heat, which is then partially converted into work. Thus, the thermodynamic analysis of heat engines, as presented in this chapter, applies equally well to conventional (fossil-fuel) and nuclear power plants.

The steam power plant is a large-scale heat engine in which the working fluid (H_2O) is in steady-state flow successively through a pump, a boiler, a turbine, and a condenser in a cyclic process (Sec. 5.2). The working fluid is separated from the heat source, and heat is transferred across a physical boundary. In a fossil-fuel-fired plant the combustion gases are separated from the steam by boiler-tube walls.

The *internal*-combustion engine is another form of heat engine, wherein high temperatures are attained by conversion of the chemical energy of a fuel directly into internal energy within the work-producing device. Examples are Otto and Diesel engines and the gas turbine.[1]

This chapter is devoted to the analysis of several common heat-engine cycles.

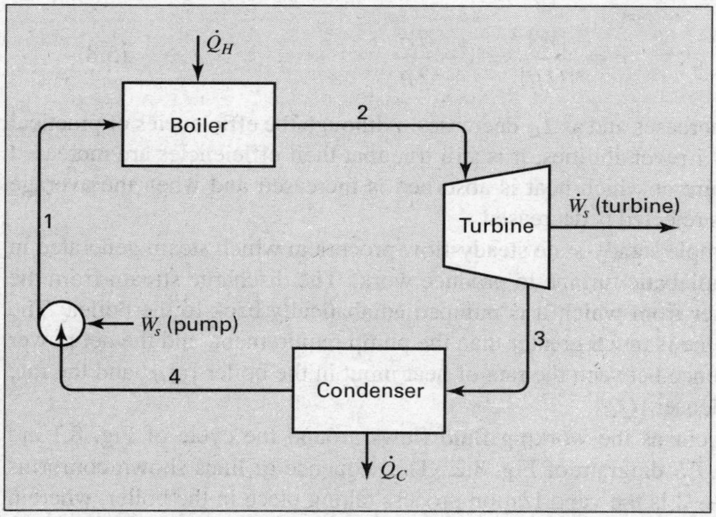

Figure 8.1: Simple steam power plant.

8.1 THE STEAM POWER PLANT

The Carnot-engine cycle, described in Sec. 5.2, operates reversibly and consists of two isothermal steps connected by two adiabatic steps. In the isothermal step at higher temperature T_H, heat $|Q_H|$ is absorbed by the working fluid of the engine, and in the isothermal step at lower

[1]Details of steam power plants and internal-combustion engines can be found in E. B. Woodruff, H. B. Lammers, and T. S. Lammers, *Steam Plant Operation*, 6th ed., McGraw-Hill, New York, 1992; and C. F. Taylor, *The Internal Combustion Engine in Theory and Practice: Thermodynamics, Fluid Flow, Performance*, MIT Press, Boston, 1984.

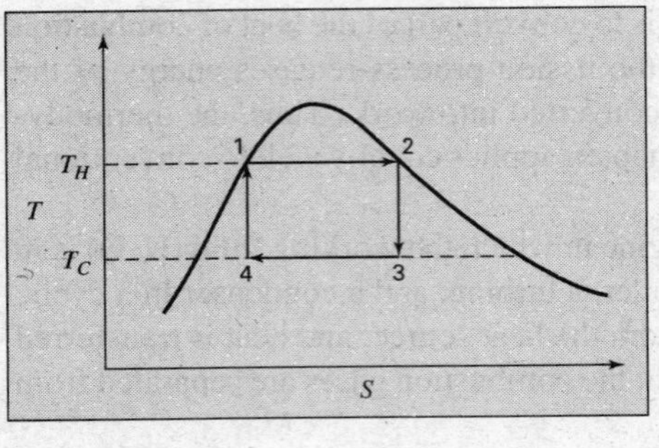

Figure 8.2: Carnot cycle on a TS diagram

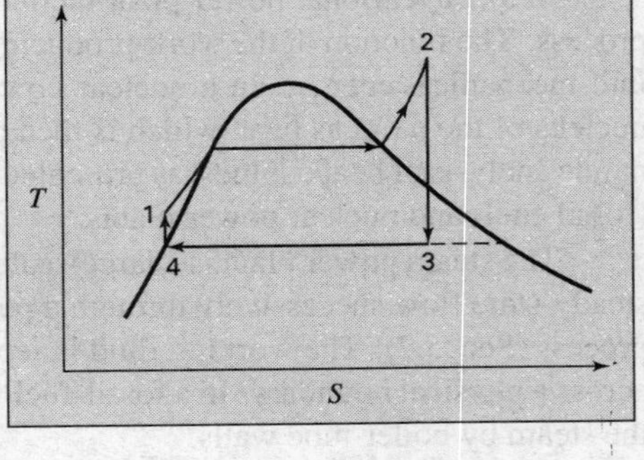

Figure 8.3: The Rankine cycle

temperature T_C, heat $|Q_C|$ is discarded by the fluid. The work produced is $|W| = |Q_H| - |Q_C|$, and the thermal efficiency of the Carnot engine is:

$$\eta \equiv \frac{|W|}{|Q_H|} = 1 - \frac{T_C}{T_H} \tag{5.8}$$

Clearly, η increases as T_H increases and as T_C decreases. Although the efficiencies of practical heat engines are lowered by irreversibilities, it is still true that their efficiencies are increased when the average temperature at which heat is absorbed is increased and when the average temperature at which heat is rejected is decreased.

Figure 8.1 shows a simple steady-state steady-flow process in which steam generated in a boiler is expanded in an adiabatic turbine to produce work. The discharge stream from the turbine passes to a condenser from which it is pumped adiabatically back to the boiler. The power produced by the turbine is much greater than the pump requirement, and the net power output is equal to the difference between the rate of heat input in the boiler $|\dot{Q}_H|$ and the rate of heat rejection in the condenser $|\dot{Q}_C|$.

The processes that occur as the working fluid flows around the cycle of Fig. 8.1 are represented by lines on the TS diagram of Fig. 8.2. The sequence of lines shown conforms to a *Carnot* cycle. Step 1 → 2 is the vaporization process taking place in the boiler, wherein saturated liquid water absorbs heat at the constant temperature T_H, and produces saturated vapor. Step 2 → 3 is a reversible, adiabatic expansion of saturated vapor into the two-phase region to produce a mixture of saturated liquid and vapor at T_C. This isentropic expansion is represented by a vertical line. Step 3 → 4 is a partial condensation process wherein heat is rejected at T_C. Step 4 → 1 takes the cycle back to its origin, producing saturated-liquid water at point 1. It is an isentropic compression process represented by a vertical line.

The Rankine Cycle

The thermal efficiency of the Carnot cycle just described is given by Eq. (5.8). As a reversible cycle, it could serve as a standard of comparison for actual steam power plants. However, severe practical difficulties attend the operation of equipment intended to carry out steps 2 → 3 and 4 → 1. Turbines that take in saturated steam produce an exhaust with high liquid content, which causes severe erosion problems.[2] Even more difficult is the design of a pump that takes in a mixture of liquid and vapor (point 4) and discharges a saturated liquid (point 1). For these reasons, an alternative model cycle is taken as the standard, at least for fossil-fuel-burning power plants. It is called the *Rankine cycle*, and differs from the cycle of Fig. 8.2 in two major respects. First, the heating step $1 \rightarrow 2$ is carried well beyond vaporization, so as to produce a superheated vapor, and second, the cooling step $3 \rightarrow 4$ brings about complete condensation, yielding saturated liquid to be pumped to the boiler. The Rankine cycle therefore consists of the four steps shown by Fig. 8.3, and described as follows:

- $1 \rightarrow 2$ A constant-pressure heating process in a boiler. The step lies along an isobar (the pressure of the boiler), and consists of three sections: heating of subcooled liquid water to its saturation temperature, vaporization at constant temperature and pressure, and superheating of the vapor to a temperature well above its saturation temperature.
- $2 \rightarrow 3$ Reversible, adiabatic (isentropic) expansion of vapor in a turbine to the pressure of the condenser. The step normally crosses the saturation curve, producing a wet exhaust. However, the superheating accomplished in step $1 \rightarrow 2$ shifts the vertical line far enough to the right on Fig. 8.3 that the moisture content is not too large.
- $3 \rightarrow 4$ A constant-pressure, constant-temperature process in a condenser to produce saturated liquid at point 4.
- $4 \rightarrow 1$ Reversible, adiabatic (isentropic) pumping of the saturated liquid to the pressure of the boiler, producing compressed (subcooled) liquid. The vertical line (whose length is exaggerated in Fig. 8.3) is very short, because the temperature rise associated with compression of a liquid is small.

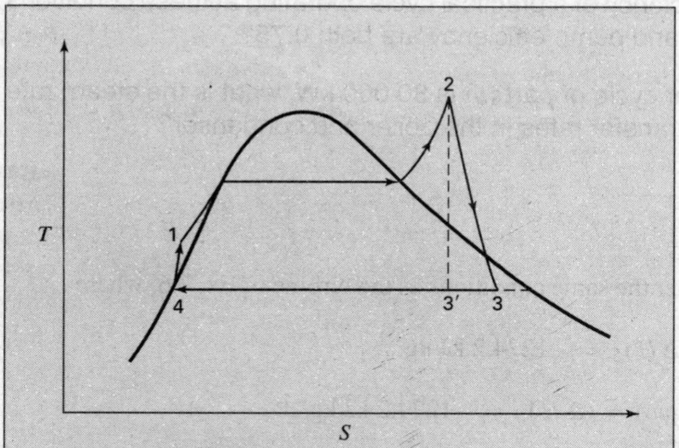

Figure 8.4: Simple practical power cycle

Power plants can be built to operate on a cycle that departs from the Rankine cycle solely because of the irreversibilities of the work-producing and work-requiring steps. Figure 8.4

[2]Nevertheless, present-day nuclear power plants generate saturated steam and operate with turbines designed to eject liquid at various stages of expansion.

illustrates the effects of these irreversibilities on steps 2 → 3 and 4 → 1. The lines are no longer vertical, but tend in the direction of increasing entropy. The turbine exhaust is normally still wet, but as long as the moisture content is less than about 10%, erosion problems are not serious. Slight subcooling of the condensate in the condenser may occur, but the effect is inconsequential.

The boiler serves to transfer heat from a burning fuel (or from a nuclear reactor) to the cycle, and the condenser transfers heat from the cycle to the surroundings. Neglecting kinetic- and potential-energy changes reduces the energy relations, Eqs. (2.31) and (2.32), in either case to:

$$\dot{Q} = \dot{m}\,\Delta H \qquad (8.1) \qquad\qquad Q = \Delta H \qquad (8.2)$$

Turbine and pump calculations are treated in detail in Secs. 7.2 and 7.3.

Example 8.1

Steam generated in a power plant at a pressure of 8600 kPa and a temperature of 500°C (773.15 K) is fed to a turbine. Exhaust from the turbine enters a condenser at 10 kPa, where it is condensed to saturated liquid, which is then pumped to the boiler.

(*a*) What is the thermal efficiency of a Rankine cycle operating at these conditions?

(*b*) What is the thermal efficiency of a practical cycle operating at these conditions if the turbine efficiency and pump efficiency are both 0.75?

(*c*) If the rating of the power cycle of part (*b*) is 80 000 kW, what is the steam rate and what are the heat-transfer rates in the boiler and condenser?

Solution

(*a*) The turbine operates under the same conditions as the turbine of Ex. 7.6, where

$$(\Delta H)_S = -1274.2 \text{ kJ kg}^{-1}$$

Thus $\qquad W_s(\text{isentropic}) = (\Delta H)_S = -1274.2 \text{ kJ kg}^{-1}$

Moreover, the enthalpy at the end of isentropic expansion, H_2' in Ex. 7.6, is here:

$$H_3' = 2117.4 \text{ kJ kg}^{-1}$$

The enthalpy of saturated liquid at 10 kPa (and $t^{\text{sat}}/T^{\text{sat}} = 45.83°\text{C}/318.98$ K) is

$$H_4 = 191.8 \text{ kJ kg}^{-1}$$

Thus by Eq. (8.2) applied to the condenser,

$$Q(\text{condenser}) = H_4 - H_3' = 191.8 - 2117.4 = -1925.6 \text{ kJ kg}^{-1}$$

where the minus sign signifies that heat flows out of the system.

The pump operates under essentially the same conditions as the pump of Ex. 7.10, where

$$W_s(\text{isentropic}) = (\Delta H)_S = 8.7 \text{ kJ kg}^{-1}$$

Whence, $H_1 = H_4 + (\Delta H)_S = 191.8 + 8.7 = 200.5 \text{ kJ kg}^{-1}$

The enthalpy of superheated steam at 8600 kPa and 500°C (773.15 K) is

$$H_2 = 3391.6 \text{ kJ kg}^{-1}$$

By Eq. (8.2) applied to the boiler,

$$Q(\text{boiler}) = H_2 - H_1 = 3391.6 - 200.5 = 3191.1 \text{ kJ kg}^{-1}$$

The net work of the Rankine cycle is the sum of the turbine work and the pump work:

$$W_s(\text{Rankine}) = -1274.2 + 8.7 = -1265.5 \text{ kJ kg}^{-1}$$

This result is of course also

$$W_s(\text{Rankine}) = -Q(\text{boiler}) - Q(\text{condenser})$$

$$= -3191.1 + 1925.6 = -1265.5 \text{ kJ kg}^{-1}$$

The thermal efficiency of the cycle is

$$\eta = \frac{|W_s(\text{Rankine})|}{Q(\text{boiler})} = \frac{1265.5}{3191.1} = 0.3966$$

(*b*) With a turbine efficiency of 0.75, then also from Ex. 7.6:

$$W_s(\text{turbine}) = \Delta H = -955.6 \text{ kJ kg}^{-1}$$

Whence $H_3 = H_2 + \Delta H = 3391.6 - 955.6 = 2436.0 \text{ kJ kg}^{-1}$

For the condenser,

$$Q(\text{condenser}) = H_4 - H_3 = 191.8 - 2436.0 = -2244.2 \text{ kJ kg}^{-1}$$

By Ex. 7.10 for the pump,

$$W_s(\text{pump}) = \Delta H = 11.6 \text{ kJ kg}^{-1}$$

The net work of the cycle is therefore

$$\dot{W}_s(\text{net}) = -955.6 + 11.6 = -944.0 \text{ kJ kg}^{-1}$$

and $$H_1 = H_4 + \Delta H = 191.8 + 11.6 = 203.4 \text{ kJ kg}^{-1}$$

Then $$Q(\text{boiler}) = H_2 - H_1 = 3391.6 - 203.4 = 3188.2 \text{ kJ kg}^{-1}$$

The thermal efficiency of the cycle is therefore:

$$\eta = \frac{|W_s(\text{net})|}{Q(\text{boiler})} = \frac{944.0}{3188.2} = 0.2961$$

which may be compared with the result of part (*a*).

(*c*) For a power rating of 80 000 kW,

$$\dot{W}_s(\text{net}) = \dot{m} W_s(\text{net})$$

or $$\dot{m} = \frac{\dot{W}_s(\text{net})}{W_s(\text{net})} = \frac{-80\,000 \text{ kJ s}^{-1}}{-944.0 \text{ kJ kg}^{-1}} = 84.75 \text{ kg s}^{-1}$$

Then by Eq. (8.1),

$$\dot{Q}(\text{boiler}) = (84.75)(3188.2) = 270.2 \times 10^3 \text{ kJ s}^{-1}$$

$$\dot{Q}(\text{condenser}) = (84.75)(-2244.2) = -190.2 \times 10^3 \text{ kJ s}^{-1}$$

Note that $$\dot{Q}(\text{boiler}) + \dot{Q}(\text{condenser}) = -\dot{W}_s(\text{net})$$

The Regenerative Cycle

The thermal efficiency of a steam power cycle is increased when the pressure and hence the vaporization temperature in the boiler is raised. It is also increased by increased superheating in the boiler. Thus, high boiler pressures and temperatures favor high efficiencies. However, these same conditions increase the capital investment in the plant, because they require heavier construction and more expensive materials of construction. Moreover, these costs increase even more rapidly as more severe conditions are imposed. Thus, in practice power plants seldom operate at pressures much above 10 000 kPa or temperatures much above 600°C (873.15 K). The thermal efficiency of a power plant increases as the pressure (and hence the temperature) in the condenser is reduced. However, the condensation temperature must be higher than the temperature of the cooling medium, usually water, and this is controlled by local conditions of climate and geography. Power plants universally operate with condenser pressures as low as practical.

Most modern power plants operate on a modification of the Rankine cycle that incorporates feedwater heaters. Water from the condenser, rather than being pumped directly back to the boiler, is first heated by steam extracted from the turbine. This is normally done in several stages, with steam taken from the turbine at several intermediate states of expansion. An arrangement with four feedwater heaters is shown in Fig. 8.5. The operating conditions indicated on this figure and described in the following paragraphs are typical, and are the basis for the illustrative calculations of Ex. 8.2.

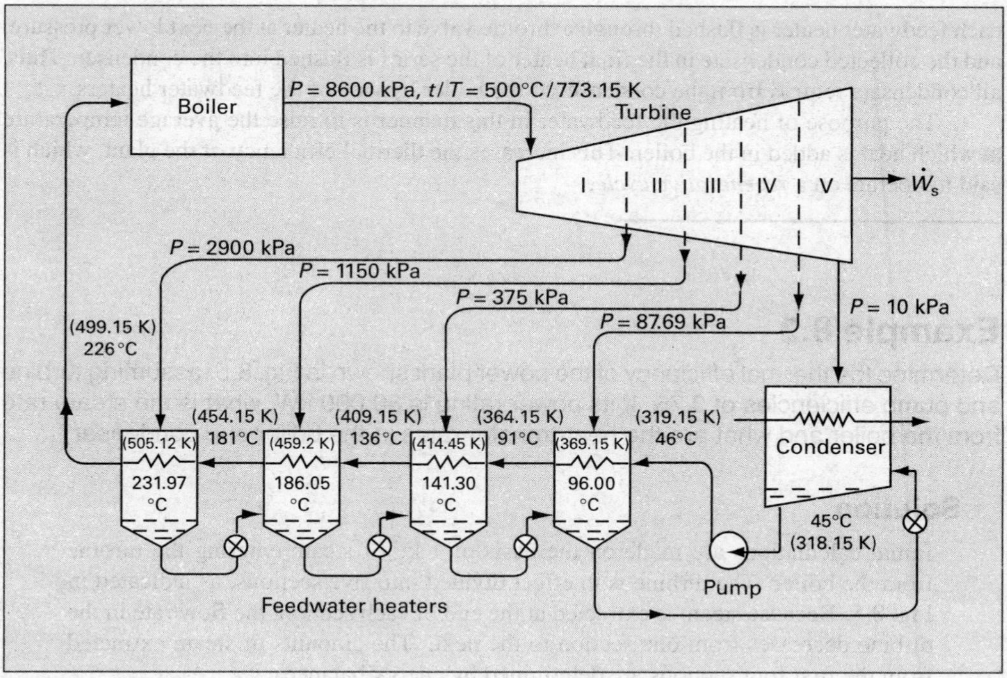

Figure 8.5: Steam power plant with feedwater heating

The conditions of steam generation in the boiler are the same as in Ex. 8.1: 8600 kPa and 500°C (773.15 K). The exhaust pressure of the turbine, 10 kPa, is also the same. The saturation temperature of the exhaust steam is therefore 45.83°C (318.98 K). Allowing for slight subcooling of the condensate, we fix the temperature of the liquid water from the condenser at 45°C (318.15 K). The feedwater pump, which operates under exactly the conditions of the pump in Ex. 7.10, causes a temperature rise of about 1°C (1 K), making the temperature of the feedwater entering the series of heaters equal to 46°C (319.15 K).

The saturation temperature of steam at the boiler pressure of 8600 kPa is 300.06°C (573.21 K), and the temperature to which the feedwater can be raised in the heaters is certainly less. This temperature is a design variable, which is ultimately fixed by economic considerations. However, a value must be chosen before any thermodynamic calculations can be made. We have therefore arbitrarily specified a temperature of 226°C (499.15 K) for the feedwater stream entering the boiler. We have also specified that all four feedwater heaters accomplish the same temperature rise. Thus, the total temperature rise of 226 − 46 = 180°C (499.15 K − 319.15 K = 180 K) is divided into four 45°C (45 K) increments. This establishes all intermediate feedwater temperatures at the values shown on Fig. 8.5.

The steam supplied to a given feedwater heater must be at a pressure high enough that its saturation temperature is above that of the feedwater stream leaving the heater. We have here presumed a minimum temperature difference for heat transfer of no less than 5°C (5 K), and have chosen extraction steam pressures such that the t^{sat} values shown in the feedwater heaters are at least 5°C (5 K) greater than the exit temperatures of the feedwater streams. The condensate from each feedwater heater is flashed through a throttle valve to the heater at the next lower pressure, and the collected condensate in the final heater of the series is flashed into the condenser. Thus, all condensate returns from the condenser to the boiler by way of the feedwater heaters.

The purpose of heating the feedwater in this manner is to raise the average temperature at which heat is added in the boiler. This increases the thermal efficiency of the plant, which is said to operate on a *regenerative cycle*.

Example 8.2

Determine the thermal efficiency of the power plant shown in Fig. 8.5, assuming turbine and pump efficiencies of 0.75. If its power rating is 80 000 kW, what is the steam rate from the boiler and what are the heat-transfer rates in the boiler and condenser?

Solution

Initial calculations are made on the basis of 1 kg of steam entering the turbine from the boiler. The turbine is in effect divided into five sections, as indicated in Fig. 8.5. Because steam is extracted at the end of each section, the flow rate in the turbine decreases from one section to the next. The amounts of steam extracted from the first four sections are determined by energy balances.

This requires enthalpies of the compressed feedwater streams. The effect of pressure at constant temperature on a liquid is given by Eq. (7.25):

$$\Delta H = V(1 - \beta T)\Delta P \qquad (\text{const } T)$$

For saturated liquid water at 226°C (499.15 K), the steam tables provide

$$P^{\text{sat}} = 2598.2 \text{ kPa} \qquad H = 971.5 \text{ kJ kg}^{-1} \qquad V = 1201 \text{ cm}^3 \text{ kg}^{-1}$$

In addition, at this temperature,

$$\beta = 1.582 \times 10^{-3} \text{ K}^{-1}$$

Thus, for a pressure change from the saturation pressure to 8600 kPa:

$$\Delta H = 1201[1 - (1.528 \times 10^{-3})(499.15)]\frac{(8600 - 2598.2)}{10^6} = 1.5 \text{ kJ kg}^{-1}$$

and $\quad H = H(\text{sat. liq.}) + \Delta H = 971.5 + 1.5 = 973.0 \text{ kJ kg}^{-1}$

Similar calculations yield the enthalpies of the feedwater at other temperatures. All pertinent values are given in the following table.

$t^{\text{sat}}/T^{\text{sat}}$	226/499.15	181/454.15	136/409.15	91/364.15	46/319.15
H/kJ kg^{-1} for water at t/T and P = 8600 kPa	973.0	771.3	577.4	387.5	200.0

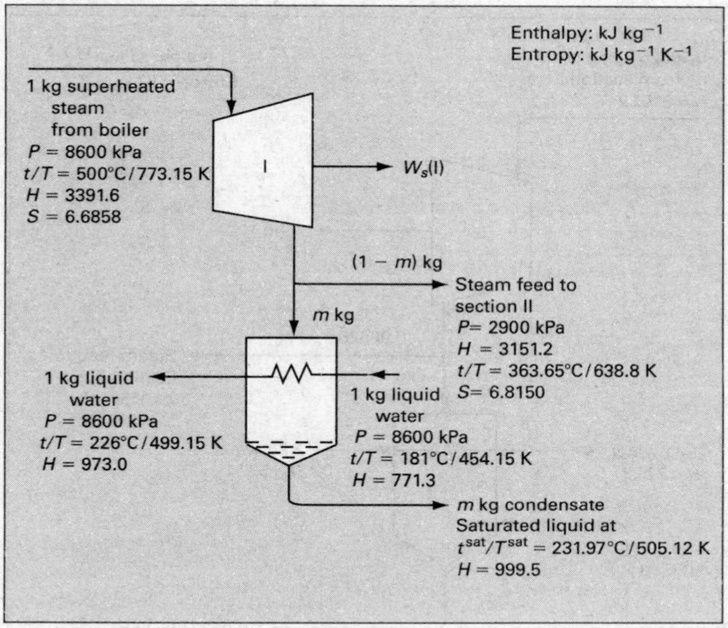

Figure 8.6: Section I of turbine and first feedwater heater

Consider the first section of the turbine and the first feedwater heater, as shown by Fig. 8.6. The enthalpy and entropy of the steam entering the turbine are found from the tables for superheated steam. The assumption of isentropic expansion of steam in section I of the turbine to 2900 kPa leads to the result:

$$(\Delta H)_S = -320.5 \text{ kJ kg}^{-1}$$

If we assume that the turbine efficiency is independent of the pressure to which the steam expands, then Eq. (7.16) gives

$$\Delta H = \eta(\Delta H)_S = (0.75)(-320.5) = -240.4 \text{ kJ kg}^{-1}$$

By Eq. (7.14), $\quad W_s(\text{I}) = \Delta H = -240.4 \text{ kJ}$

In addition, the enthalpy of steam discharged from this section of the turbine is

$$H = 3391.6 - 240.4 = 3151.2 \text{ kJ kg}^{-1}$$

A simple energy balance on the feedwater heater results from the assumption that kinetic- and potential-energy changes are negligible and from the assignments, $\dot{Q} = -\dot{W}_s = 0$. Equation (2.30) then reduces to

$$\Delta(\dot{m}H)_{\text{fs}} = 0$$

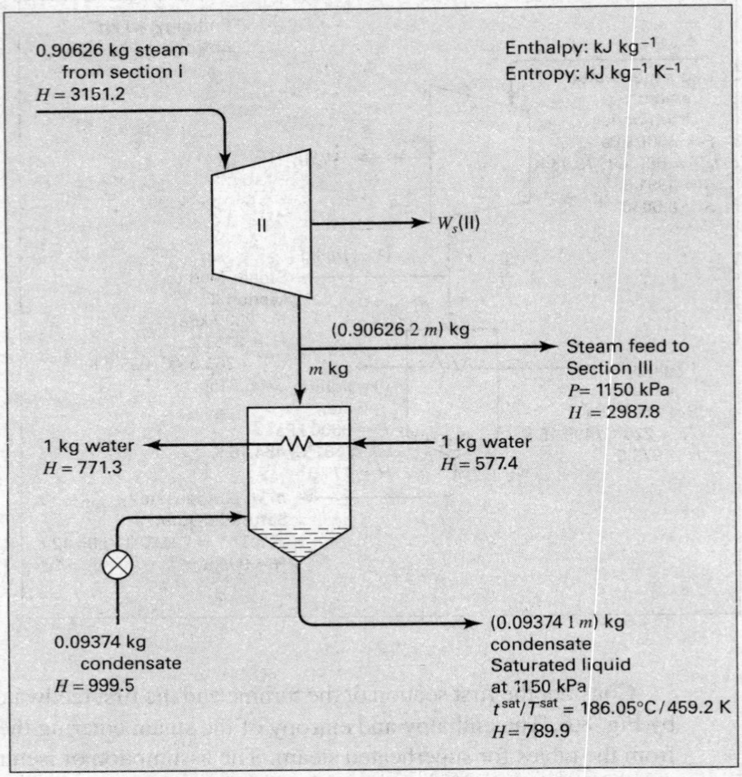

Figure 8.7: Section II of turbine and second feedwater heater

This equation gives mathematical expression to the requirement that the total enthalpy change for the process be zero. Thus on the basis of 1 kg of steam entering the turbine (Fig. 8.6):

$$m(999.5 - 3151.2) + (1)(973.0 - 771.3) = 0$$

Whence, $\quad m = 0.093\ 74$ kg $\quad$ and $\quad 1 - m = 0.906\ 26$ kg

On the basis of 1 kg of steam entering the turbine, $1 - m$ is the mass of steam flowing into section II of the turbine.

Section II of the turbine and the second feedwater heater are shown in Fig. 8.7. In doing the same calculations as for section I, we assume that each kilogram of steam leaving section II expands from its state *at the turbine entrance* to the exit of section II with an efficiency of 0.75 compared with isentropic expansion. The enthalpy of the steam leaving section II found in this way is

$$H = 2987.8 \text{ kJ kg}^{-1}$$

Then on the basis of 1 kg of steam entering the turbine,

$$W_s(\text{II}) = (2987.8 - 3151.2)(0.906\ 26) = -148.08 \text{ kJ}$$

An energy balance on the feedwater heater (Fig. 8.7) gives

$$(0.093\,74 + m)(789.9) - (0.093\,74)(999.5) - m(2987.8) + (1)(771.3 - 577.4) = 0$$

Whence, $$m = 0.079\,71 \text{ kg}$$

Note that throttling the condensate stream does not change its enthalpy.

These results and those of similar calculations for the remaining sections of the turbine are listed in the accompanying table. From the results shown,

$$\sum W_s = -804.0 \text{ kJ} \qquad \text{and} \qquad \sum m = 0.3055 \text{ kg}$$

	H/kJ kg^{-1} at section exit	W_s/kJ for section	t°C/T K at section exit	State	m/kg of steam extracted
Sec. I	3151.2	−240.40	363.65 (636.8)	Superheated vapor	0.093 74
Sec. II	2987.8	−148.08	272.48 (545.63)	Superheated vapor	0.079 28
Sec. III	2827.4	−132.65	183.84 (456.99)	Superheated vapor	0.069 93
Sec. IV	2651.3	−133.32	96.00 (369.15)	Wet vapor $x = 0.9919$	0.062 57
Sec. V	2435.9	−149.59	45.83 (319.98)	Wet vapor $x = 0.9378$	

Thus for every kilogram of steam entering the turbine, the work produced is 804.0 kJ, and 0.3055 kg of steam is extracted from the turbine for the feedwater heaters. The work required by the pump is exactly the work calculated for the pump in Ex. 7.10, that is, 11.6 kJ. The net work of the cycle on the basis of 1 kg of steam generated in the boiler is therefore

$$W_s(\text{net}) = -804.0 + 11.6 = -792.4 \text{ kJ}$$

On the same basis, the heat added in the boiler is:

$$Q(\text{boiler}) = \Delta H = 3391.6 - 973.0 = 2418.6 \text{ kJ}$$

The thermal efficiency of the cycle is therefore

$$\eta = \frac{|W_s(\text{net})|}{Q(\text{boiler})} = \frac{792.4}{2418.6} = 0.3276$$

This is a significant improvement (10.6%) over the value 0.2961 of Ex. 8.1.

Because $\dot{W}_s(\text{net}) = -80\,000 \text{ kJ s}^{-1}$,

$$\dot{m} = \frac{\dot{W}_s(\text{net})}{W_s(\text{net})} = \frac{-80\,000}{-792.4} = 100.96 \text{ kg s}^{-1}$$

This is the steam rate to the turbine, used to calculate the heat-transfer rate in the boiler:

$$\dot{Q}(\text{boiler}) = \dot{m}\,\Delta H = (100.96)(2418.6) = 244.2 \times 10^3 \text{ kJ s}^{-1}$$

The heat-transfer rate to the cooling water in the condenser is:

$$\begin{aligned}\dot{Q}(\text{condenser}) &= -\dot{Q}(\text{boiler}) - \dot{W}_s(\text{net}) \\ &= -244.2 \times 10^3 - (-80.0 \times 10^3) = -164.2 \times 10^3 \text{ kJ s}^{-1}\end{aligned}$$

Although the steam generation rate is higher than was found in Ex. 8.1, the heat-transfer rates in the boiler and condenser are appreciably less, (9.62% and 13.67%, respectively), because their functions are partly taken over by the feedwater heaters.

8.2 INTERNAL-COMBUSTION ENGINES

In a steam power plant, the steam is an inert medium to which heat is transferred from a burning fuel or from a nuclear reactor. It is therefore characterized by large heat-transfer surfaces: (1) for the absorption of heat by the steam at a high temperature in the boiler, and (2) for the rejection of heat from the steam at a relatively low temperature in the condenser. The disadvantage is that when heat must be transferred through walls (as through the metal walls of boiler tubes) the ability of the walls to withstand high temperatures and pressures imposes a limit on the temperature of heat absorption. In an internal-combustion engine, on the other hand, a fuel is burned within the engine itself, and the combustion products serve as the working medium, acting for example on a piston in a cylinder. High temperatures are internal, and do not involve heat-transfer surfaces.

Burning of fuel within the internal-combustion engine complicates thermodynamic analysis. Moreover, fuel and air flow steadily into an internal-combustion engine and combustion products flow steadily out of it; no working medium undergoes a cyclic process, as does steam in a steam power plant. However, for making simple analyses, one imagines cyclic engines with air as the working fluid that are equivalent in performance to actual internal-combustion engines. In addition, the combustion step is replaced by the addition to the air of an equivalent amount of heat. In what follows, each internal-combustion engine is introduced by a qualitative description. This is followed by a quantitative analysis of an ideal cycle in which air, treated as an ideal gas with constant heat capacities, is the working medium.

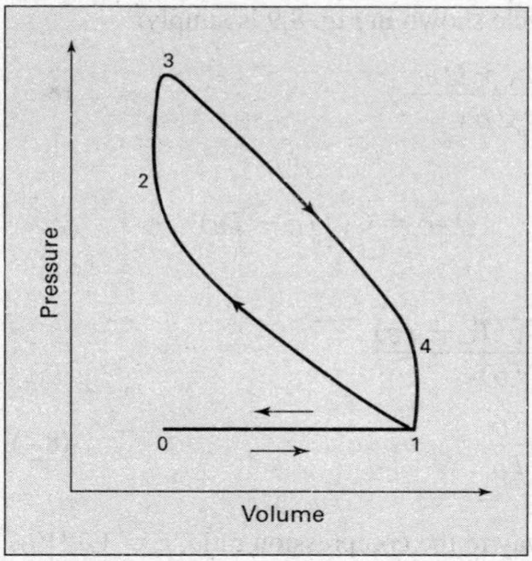

Figure 8.8: Otto engine cycle

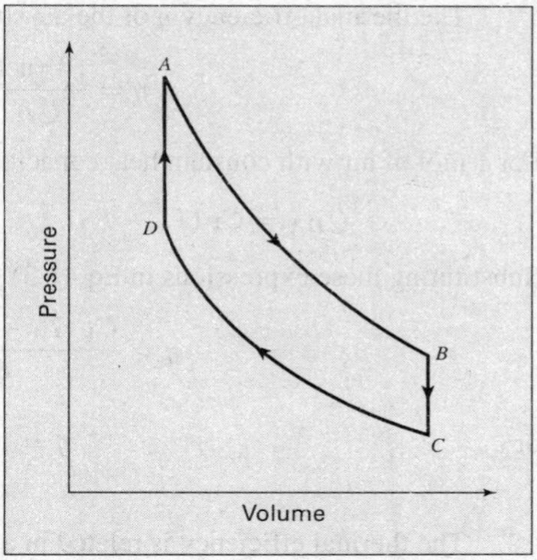

Figure 8.9: Air-standard Otto cycle

The Otto Engine

The most common internal-combustion engine, because of its use in automobiles, is the Otto engine. Its cycle consists of four strokes, and starts with an intake stroke at essentially constant pressure, during which a piston moving outward draws a fuel/air mixture into a cylinder. This is represented by line $0 \rightarrow 1$ in Fig. 8.8. During the second stroke ($1 \rightarrow 2 \rightarrow 3$), all valves are closed, and the fuel/air mixture is compressed, approximately adiabatically along line segment $1 \rightarrow 2$; the mixture is then ignited, and combustion occurs so rapidly that the volume remains nearly constant while the pressure rises along line segment $2 \rightarrow 3$. It is during the third stroke ($3 \rightarrow 4 \rightarrow 1$) that work is produced. The high-temperature, high-pressure products of combustion expand, approximately adiabatically along line segment $3 \rightarrow 4$; the exhaust valve then opens and the pressure falls rapidly at nearly constant volume along line segment $4 \rightarrow 1$. During the fourth or exhaust stroke (line $1 \rightarrow 0$), the piston pushes the remaining combustion gases (except for the contents of the clearance volume) from the cylinder. The volume plotted in Fig. 8.8 is the total volume of gas contained in the engine between the piston and the cylinder head.

The effect of increasing the compression ratio, i.e., the ratio of the volumes at the beginning and end of compression from point 1 to point 2, is to increase the efficiency of the engine, i.e., to increase the work produced per unit quantity of fuel. We demonstrate this for an idealized cycle, called the air-standard Otto cycle, shown in Fig. 8.9. It consists of two adiabatic and two constant-volume steps, which comprise a heat-engine cycle for which the working fluid is air, considered an ideal gas with constant heat capacities. Step CD, a reversible adiabatic compression, is followed by step DA, in which sufficient heat is absorbed by the air at constant volume to raise its temperature and pressure to the values resulting from combustion in an actual Otto engine. Then the air is expanded adiabatically and reversibly (step AB), and cooled at constant volume (step BC) to the initial state at C.

The thermal efficiency η of the air-standard cycle shown in Fig. 8.9 is simply:

$$\eta = \frac{|W(\text{net})|}{Q_{DA}} = \frac{Q_{DA} + Q_{BC}}{Q_{DA}} \tag{8.3}$$

For 1 mol of air with constant heat capacities,

$$Q_{DA} = C_V(T_A - T_D) \qquad \text{and} \qquad Q_{BC} = C_V(T_C - T_B)$$

Substituting these expressions in Eq. (8.3) gives

$$\eta = \frac{C_V(T_A - T_D) + C_V(T_C - T_B)}{C_V(T_A - T_D)}$$

or

$$\eta = 1 - \frac{T_B - T_C}{T_A - T_D} \tag{8.4}$$

The thermal efficiency is related in a simple way to the compression ratio, $r \equiv V_C / V_D$. Each temperature in Eq. (8.4) is replaced by an appropriate group PV/R, in accord with the ideal-gas equation. Thus,

$$T_B = \frac{P_B V_B}{R} = \frac{P_B V_C}{R} \qquad T_C = \frac{P_C V_C}{R}$$

$$T_A = \frac{P_A V_A}{R} = \frac{P_A V_D}{R} \qquad T_D = \frac{P_D V_D}{R}$$

Substituting into Eq. (8.4) leads to

$$\eta = 1 - \frac{V_C}{V_D}\left(\frac{P_B - P_C}{P_A - P_D}\right) = 1 - r\left(\frac{P_B - P_C}{P_A - P_D}\right) \tag{8.5}$$

For the two adiabatic, reversible steps, $PV^\gamma = \text{const.}$ Hence

$$P_A V_D^\gamma = P_B V_C^\gamma \qquad \text{(because } V_D = V_A \text{ and } V_C = V_B\text{)}$$

$$P_C V_C^\gamma = P_D V_D^\gamma$$

These expressions are combined to eliminate the volumes:

$$\frac{P_B}{P_C} = \frac{P_A}{P_D} \qquad \text{whence} \qquad \frac{P_B}{P_C} - 1 = \frac{P_A}{P_D} - 1 \qquad \text{or} \qquad \frac{P_B - P_C}{P_C} = \frac{P_A - P_D}{P_D}$$

Thus,

$$\frac{P_B - P_C}{P_A - P_D} = \frac{P_C}{P_D} = \left(\frac{V_D}{V_C}\right)^\gamma = \left(\frac{1}{r}\right)^\gamma$$

where we have used the relation $P_C V_C^\gamma = P_D V_D^\gamma$. Equation (8.5) now becomes

$$\eta = 1 - r\left(\frac{1}{r}\right)^\gamma = 1 - \left(\frac{1}{r}\right)^{\gamma - 1} \tag{8.6}$$

This equation shows that the thermal efficiency increases rapidly with the compression ratio r at low values of r, but more slowly at high compression ratios. This agrees with the results of actual tests on Otto engines.

The Diesel Engine

The fundamental difference between the Otto cycle and the Diesel cycle is that in the Diesel cycle the temperature at the end of compression is sufficiently high that combustion is initiated spontaneously. This higher temperature results because of a higher compression ratio that carries the compression step to a higher pressure. The fuel is not injected until the end of the compression step, and then is added slowly enough that the combustion process occurs at approximately constant pressure.

For the same compression ratio, the Otto engine has a higher efficiency than the Diesel engine. Because preignition limits the compression ratio attainable in the Otto engine, the Diesel engine operates at higher compression ratios, and consequently at higher efficiencies.

Example 8.3

Sketch the air-standard Diesel cycle on a PV diagram, and derive an equation giving the thermal efficiency of this cycle in relation to the compression ratio r (ratio of volumes at the beginning and end of the compression step) and the expansion ratio r_e (ratio of volumes at the end and beginning of the adiabatic expansion step).

Solution

The air-standard Diesel cycle is the same as the air-standard Otto cycle, except that the heat-absorption step (corresponding to the combustion process in the actual engine) is at constant pressure, as indicated by line DA in Fig. 8.10.

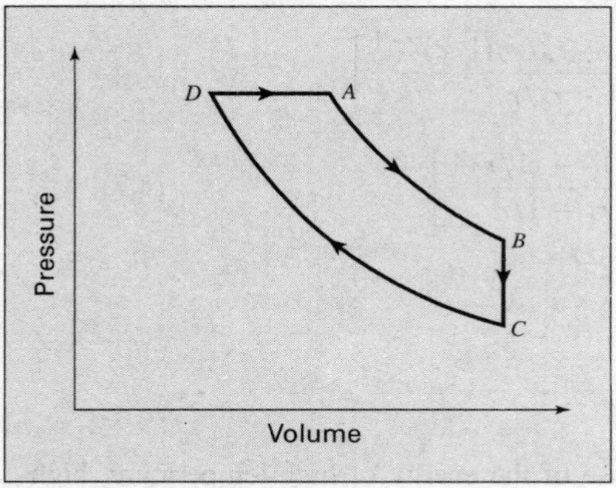

Figure 8.10: Air-standard Diesel cycle

On the basis of 1 mol of air, considered to be an ideal gas with constant heat capacities, the heat quantities absorbed in step DA and rejected in step BC are

$$Q_{DA} = C_P(T_A - T_D) \qquad \text{and} \qquad Q_{BC} = C_V(T_C - T_B)$$

The thermal efficiency, Eq. (8.3), is

$$\eta = 1 + \frac{Q_{BC}}{Q_{DA}} = 1 + \frac{C_V(T_C - T_B)}{C_P(T_A - T_D)} = 1 - \frac{1}{\gamma}\left(\frac{T_B - T_C}{T_A - T_D}\right) \qquad (A)$$

For reversible, adiabatic expansion (step AB) and reversible, adiabatic compression (step CD), Eq. (3.30a) applies:

$$T_A V_A^{\gamma-1} = T_B V_B^{\gamma-1} \qquad \text{and} \qquad T_D V_D^{\gamma-1} = T_C V_C^{\gamma-1}$$

By definition, the compression ratio is $r \equiv V_C/V_D$; in addition the expansion ratio is defined as $r_e \equiv V_B/V_A$. Thus,

$$T_B = T_A\left(\frac{1}{r_e}\right)^{\gamma-1} \qquad T_C = T_D\left(\frac{1}{r}\right)^{\gamma-1}$$

Substituting these equations into Eq. (A) gives:

$$\eta = 1 - \frac{1}{\gamma}\left[\frac{T_A(1/r_e)^{\gamma-1} - T_D(1/r)^{\gamma-1}}{T_A - T_D}\right] \qquad (B)$$

Also $P_A = P_D$, and from the ideal-gas equation,

$$P_D V_D = RT_D \qquad \text{and} \qquad P_A V_A = RT_A$$

Moreover, $V_C = V_B$, and therefore:

$$\frac{T_D}{T_A} = \frac{V_D}{V_A} = \frac{V_D/V_C}{V_A/V_B} = \frac{r_e}{r}$$

This relation combines with Eq. (B):

$$\eta = 1 - \frac{1}{\gamma}\left[\frac{(1/r_e)^{\gamma-1} - (r_e/r)(1/r)^{\gamma-1}}{1 - r_e/r}\right]$$

or

$$\eta = 1 - \frac{1}{\gamma}\left[\frac{(1/r_e)^{\gamma} - (1/r)^{\gamma}}{1/r_e - 1/r}\right] \qquad (8.7)$$

The Gas-Turbine Engine

The Otto and Diesel engines exemplify direct use of the energy of high-temperature, high-pressure gases acting on a piston within a cylinder; no heat transfer with an external source is required. However, turbines are more efficient than reciprocating engines, and the advantages of internal combustion are combined with those of the turbine in the gas-turbine engine.

The gas turbine is driven by high-temperature gases from a combustion chamber, as indicated in Fig. 8.11. The entering air is compressed (supercharged) to a pressure of several bars before combustion. The centrifugal compressor operates on the same shaft as the turbine, and part of the work of the turbine serves to drive the compressor. The higher the temperature of the

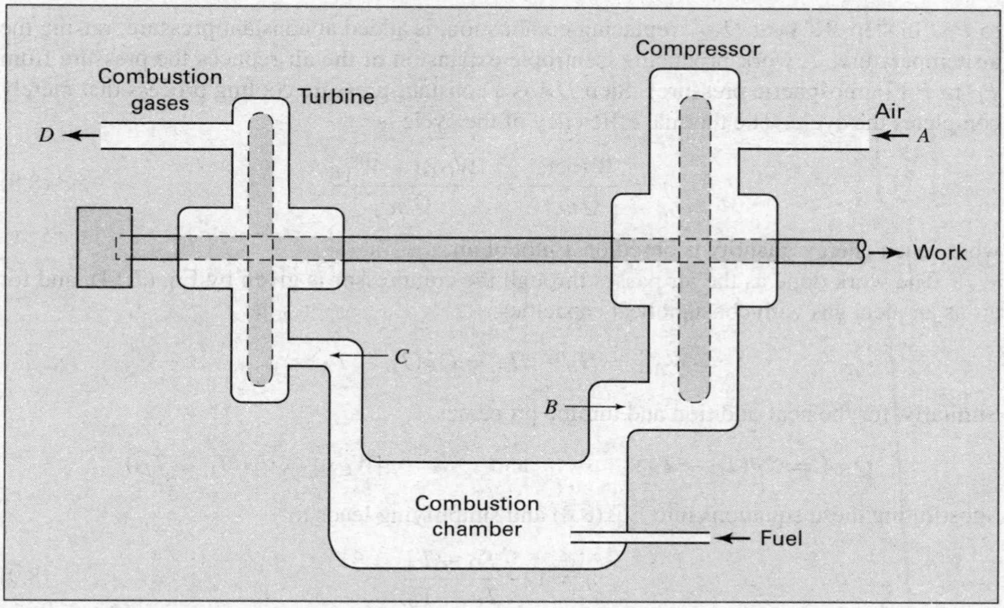

Figure 8.11: Gas-turbine engine

combustion gases entering the turbine, the higher the efficiency of the unit, i.e., the greater the work produced per unit of fuel burned. The limiting temperature is determined by the strength of the metal turbine blades, and is much lower than the theoretical flame temperature (Ex. 4.7) of the fuel. Sufficient excess air must be supplied to keep the combustion temperature at a safe level.

The idealization of the gas-turbine engine, called the Brayton cycle, is shown on a PV diagram in Fig. 8.12. The working fluid is taken as air, considered an ideal gas with constant heat capacities. Step AB is a reversible adiabatic compression from P_A (atmospheric pressure)

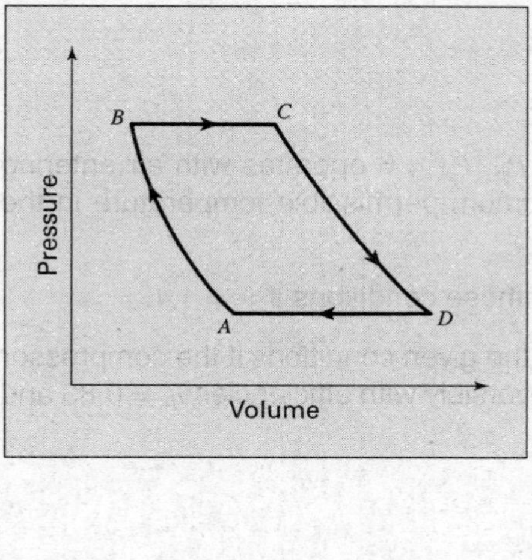

Figure 8.12: Ideal cycle for gas-turbine engine; i.e., the Brayton cycle

to P_B. In step BC heat Q_{BC}, replacing combustion, is added at constant pressure, raising the air temperature. A work-producing isentropic expansion of the air reduces the pressure from P_C to P_D (atmospheric pressure). Step DA is a constant-pressure cooling process that merely completes the cycle. The thermal efficiency of the cycle is

$$\eta = \frac{|W(\text{net})|}{Q_{BC}} = \frac{|W_{CD}| - W_{AB}}{Q_{BC}} \tag{8.8}$$

where each energy quantity is based on 1 mol of air.

The work done as the air passes through the compressor is given by Eq. (7.14), and for air as an ideal gas with constant heat capacities:

$$W_{AB} = H_B - H_A = C_P(T_B - T_A)$$

Similarly, for the heat-addition and turbine processes,

$$Q_{BC} = C_P(T_C - T_B) \qquad \text{and} \qquad |W_{CD}| = C_P(T_C - T_D)$$

Substituting these equations into Eq. (8.8) and simplifying leads to

$$\eta = 1 - \frac{T_D - T_A}{T_C - T_B} \tag{8.9}$$

Because processes AB and CD are isentropic, the temperatures and pressures are related by Eq. (3.30b):

$$\frac{T_B}{T_A} = \left(\frac{P_B}{P_A}\right)^{(\gamma-1)/\gamma} \tag{8.10}$$

and

$$\frac{T_D}{T_C} = \left(\frac{P_D}{P_C}\right)^{(\gamma-1)/\gamma} = \left(\frac{P_A}{P_B}\right)^{(\gamma-1)/\gamma} \tag{8.11}$$

With these equations T_A and T_D may be eliminated to give

$$\eta = 1 - \left(\frac{P_A}{P_B}\right)^{(\gamma-1)/\gamma} \tag{8.12}$$

Example 8.4

A gas-turbine engine with a compression ratio $P_B/P_A = 6$ operates with air entering the compressor at 25°C (298.15 K). If the maximum permissible temperature in the turbine is 760°C (1033.15 K), determine:

(*a*) The efficiency η of the ideal air cycle for these conditions if $\gamma = 1.4$.

(*b*) The thermal efficiency of an air cycle for the given conditions if the compressor and turbine operate adiabatically but irreversibly with efficiencies $\eta_c = 0.83$ and $\eta_t = 0.86$.

Solution

(*a*) Direct substitution in Eq. (8.12) gives the ideal-cycle efficiency:

$$\eta = 1 - (1/6)^{(1.4-1)/1.4} = 1 - 0.60 = 0.40$$

(*b*) Irreversibilities in both the compressor and turbine reduce the thermal efficiency of the engine, because the net work is the difference between the work required by the compressor and the work produced by the turbine. The temperature of the air entering the compressor T_A and the temperature of the air entering the turbine, the specified maximum for T_C, are the same as for the ideal cycle. However, the temperature after irreversible compression in the compressor T_B is higher than the temperature after *isentropic* compression T'_B, and the temperature after irreversible expansion in the turbine T_D is higher than the temperature after *isentropic* expansion T'_D.

The thermal efficiency of the engine is given by

$$\eta = \frac{|W(\text{turb})| - W(\text{comp})}{Q}$$

The two work terms are found from the expressions for isentropic work:

$$|W(\text{turb})| = \eta_t C_P (T_C - T'_D)$$

$$W(\text{comp}) = \frac{C_P(T'_B - T_A)}{\eta_c} \qquad (A)$$

The heat absorbed to simulate combustion is

$$Q = C_P(T_C - T_B)$$

These equations combine to yield

$$\eta = \frac{\eta_t(T_C - T'_D) - (1/\eta_c)(T'_B - T_A)}{T_C - T_B}$$

An alternative expression for the compression work is

$$W(\text{comp}) = C_P(T_B - T_A) \qquad (B)$$

Combining Eqs. (*A*) and (*B*) and using the result to eliminate T_B from the equation for η gives after simplification:

$$\eta = \frac{\eta_t\eta_c(T_C/T_A - T'_D/T_A) - (T'_B/T_A - 1)}{\eta_c(T_C/T_A - 1) - (T'_B/T_A - 1)} \qquad (C)$$

The ratio T_C/T_A depends on given conditions. The ratio T'_B/T_A is related to the pressure ratio by Eq. (8.10). In view of Eq. (8.11), the ratio T'_D/T_A can be expressed as

$$\frac{T'_D}{T_A} = \frac{T_C T'_D}{T_A T_C} = \frac{T_C}{T_A}\left(\frac{P_A}{P_B}\right)^{(\gamma-1)/\gamma}$$

Substituting these expressions in Eq. (C) yields

$$\eta = \frac{\eta_t \eta_c (T_C/T_A)(1 - 1/\alpha) - (\alpha - 1)}{\eta_c (T_C/T_A - 1) - (\alpha - 1)} \tag{8.13}$$

where $$\alpha = \left(\frac{P_B}{P_A}\right)^{(\gamma-1)/\gamma}$$

One can show by Eq. (8.13) that the thermal efficiency of the gas-turbine engine increases as the temperature of the air entering the turbine (T_C) increases, and as the compressor and turbine efficiencies η_c and η_t increase.

The given efficiency values are here:

$$\eta_t = 0.86 \quad \text{and} \quad \eta_c = 0.83$$

Other given data provide

$$\frac{T_C}{T_A} = \frac{760 + 273.15}{25 + 273.15} = 3.47$$

and $$\alpha = (6)^{(1.4-1)/1.4} = 1.67$$

Substituting these quantities in Eq. (8.13) gives

$$\eta = \frac{(0.86)(0.83)(3.47)(1 - 1/1.67) - (1.67 - 1)}{(0.83)(3.47 - 1) - (1.67 - 1)} = 0.235$$

This analysis shows that, even with a compressor and turbine of rather high efficiencies, the thermal efficiency (23.5%) is considerably reduced from the ideal-cycle value of 40%.

8.3 JET ENGINES; ROCKET ENGINES

In the power cycles so far considered the high-temperature, high-pressure gas expands in a turbine (steam power plant, gas turbine) or in the cylinders of an Otto or Diesel engine with reciprocating pistons. In either case, the power becomes available through a rotating shaft. Another device for expanding the hot gases is a nozzle. Here the power is available as kinetic energy in the jet of exhaust gases leaving the nozzle. The entire power plant, consisting of a compression device and a combustion chamber, as well as a nozzle, is known as a jet engine. Because the kinetic energy of the exhaust gases is directly available for propelling the engine and its attachments, jet engines are most commonly used to power aircraft. There are several types of jet-propulsion engines based on different ways of accomplishing the compression and expansion processes. Because the air striking the engine has kinetic energy (with respect to the engine), its pressure may be increased in a diffuser.

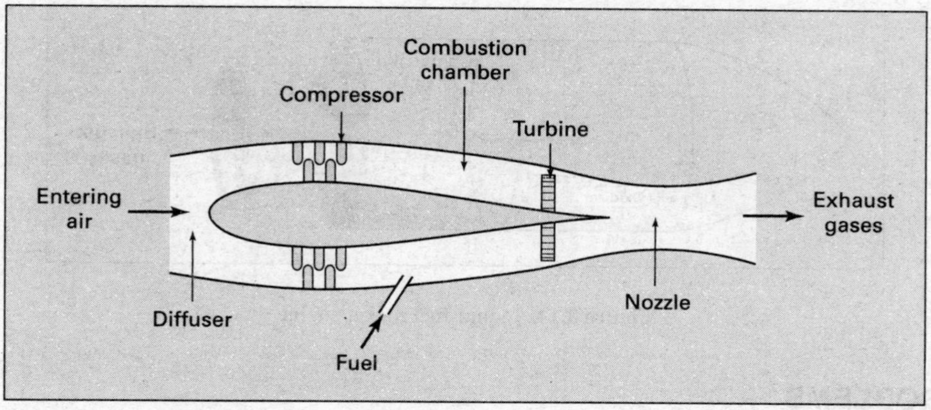

Figure 8.13: The turbojet power plant

The turbojet engine (usually called simply a jet engine) illustrated in Fig. 8.13 takes advantage of a diffuser to reduce the work of compression. The axial-flow compressor completes the job of compression, and then the fuel is injected and burned in the combustion chamber. The hot combustion-product gases first pass through a turbine where the expansion provides just enough power to drive the compressor. The remainder of the expansion to the exhaust pressure is accomplished in the nozzle. Here, the velocity of the gases with respect to the engine is increased to a level above that of the entering air. This increase in velocity provides a thrust (force) on the engine in the forward direction. If the compression and expansion processes are adiabatic and reversible, the turbojet-engine cycle is identical to the ideal gas turbine cycle shown in Fig. 8.12. The only differences are that, physically, the compression and expansion steps are carried out in devices of different types.

A rocket engine differs from a jet engine in that the oxidizing agent is carried with the engine. Instead of depending on the surrounding air for burning the fuel, the rocket is self-contained. This means that the rocket can operate in a vacuum such as in outer space. In fact, the performance is better in a vacuum, because none of the thrust is required to overcome friction forces.

In rockets burning liquid fuels the oxidizing agent (e.g., liquid oxygen) is pumped from tanks into the combustion chamber. Simultaneously, fuel (e.g., hydrogen, kerosene) is pumped into the chamber and burned. The combustion takes place at a constant high pressure and produces high-temperature product gases that are expanded in a nozzle, as indicated in Fig. 8.14.

In rockets burning solid fuels the fuel (organic polymers) and oxidizer (e.g., ammonium perchlorate) are contained together in a solid matrix and stored at the forward end of the combustion chamber.

In an ideal rocket, the combustion and expansion steps are the same as those for an ideal jet engine (Fig. 8.12). A solid-fuel rocket requires no compression work, and in a liquid-fuel rocket the compression energy is small, because the fuel and oxidizer are pumped as liquids.

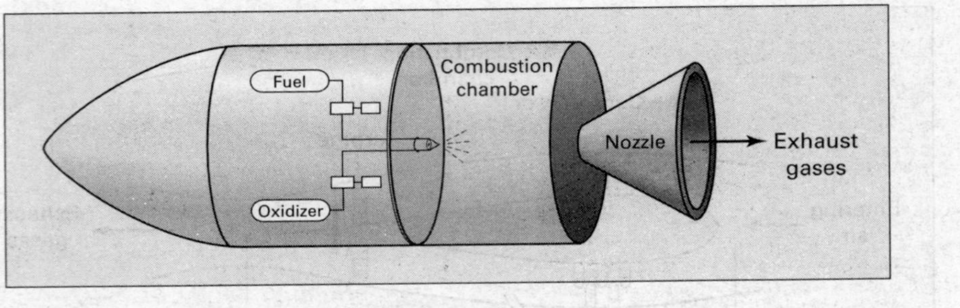

Figure 8.14: Liquid-fuel rocket engine

PROBLEMS

8.1. The basic cycle for a steam power plant is shown by Fig. 8.1. The turbine operates adiabatically with inlet steam at 6800 kPa and 550°C (823.15 K) and the exhaust steam enters the condenser at 50°C (323.15 K) with a quality of 0.96. Saturated liquid water leaves the condenser, and is pumped to the boiler. Neglecting pump work and kinetic- and potential-energy changes, determine the thermal efficiency of the cycle and the turbine efficiency.

8.2. A Carnot engine with H_2O as the working fluid operates on the cycle shown in Fig. 8.2. The H_2O circulation rate is 1 kg s^{-1}. For $T_H = 475$ K and $T_C = 300$ K, determine the

(*a*) pressures at states 1, 2, 3, and 4
(*b*) quality x^v at states 3 and 4
(*c*) rate of heat addition
(*d*) rate of heat rejection
(*e*) mechanical power for each of the four steps
(*f*) thermal efficiency η of the cycle

8.3. A steam power plant operates on the cycle of Fig. 8.4. For one of the following sets of operating conditions, determine the steam rate, the heat-transfer rates in the boiler and condenser, and the thermal efficiency of the plant.

(*a*) $P_1 = P_2 = 10\,000$ kPa; $t_2/T_2 = 600°\text{C}/873.15$ K; $P_3 = P_4 = 10$ kPa; $\eta(\text{turbine}) = 0.80$; $\eta(\text{pump}) = 0.75$; power rating = 80 000 kW
(*b*) $P_1 = P_2 = 7000$ kPa; $t_2/T_2 = 550°\text{C}/823.15$ K; $P_3 = P_4 = 20$ kPa; $\eta(\text{turbine}) = 0.75$; $\eta(\text{pump}) = 0.75$; power rating = 100 000 kW
(*c*) $P_1 = P_2 = 8500$ kPa; $t_2/T_2 = 600°\text{C}/873.15$ K; $P_3 = P_4 = 10$ kPa; $\eta(\text{turbine}) = 0.80$; $\eta(\text{pump}) = 0.80$; power rating = 70 000 kW
(*d*) $P_1 = P_2 = 6500$ kPa; $t_2/T_2 = 525°\text{C}/798.15$ K; $P_3 = P_4 = 101.33$ kPa; $\eta(\text{turbine}) = 0.78$; $\eta(\text{pump}) = 0.75$; power rating = 50 000 kW
(*e*) $P_1 = P_2 = 7760$ kPa; $t_2/T_2 = 593°\text{C}/866.15$ K; $P_3 = P_4 = 7$ kPa; $\eta(\text{turbine}) = 0.80$; $\eta(\text{pump}) = 0.75$; power rating = 80 000 kW

8.4. Steam enters the turbine of a power plant operating on the Rankine cycle (Fig. 8.3) at 3300 kPa and exhausts at 50 kPa. To show the effect of superheating on the performance of the cycle, calculate the thermal efficiency of the cycle and the quality of the exhaust steam from the turbine for turbine-inlet steam temperatures of 450, 550, and 650°C (723.15 K, 823.15 K and 923.15 K).

8.5. Steam enters the turbine of a power plant operating on the Rankine cycle (Fig. 8.3) at 600°C (873.15 K) and exhausts at 30 kPa. To show the effect of boiler pressure on the performance of the cycle, calculate the thermal efficiency of the cycle and the quality of the exhaust steam from the turbine for boiler pressures of of 5000, 7500, and 10 000 kPa.

8.6. A steam power plant employs two adiabatic turbines in series. Steam enters the first turbine at 650°C (923.15 K) and 7000 kPa and discharges from the second turbine at 20 kPa. The system is designed for equal power outputs from the two turbines, based on a turbine efficiency of 78% for *each* turbine. Determine the temperature and pressure of the steam in its intermediate state between the two turbines. What is the overall efficiency of the two turbines together with respect to isentropic expansion of the steam from the initial to the final state?

8.7. A steam power plant operating on a regenerative cycle, as illustrated in Fig. 8.5, includes just one feedwater heater. Steam enters the turbine at 4500 kPa and 500°C (773.15 K) and exhausts at 20 kPa. Steam for the feedwater heater is extracted from the turbine at 350 kPa, and in condensing raises the temperature of the feedwater to within 6°C (6 K) of its condensation temperature at 350 kPa. If the turbine and pump efficiencies are both 0.78, what is the thermal efficiency of the cycle and what fraction of the steam entering the turbine is extracted for the feedwater heater?

8.8. A steam power plant operating on a regenerative cycle, as illustrated in Fig. 8.5, includes two feedwater heaters. Steam enters the turbine at 6500 kPa and 600°C (873.15 K) and exhausts at 6.9 kPa. Steam for the feedwater heaters is extracted from the turbine at 3.45 bar pressures and in condensing raises the temperature of the feedwater to within of its condensation temperature at 3.45 bar a 6 K (6°C) approaches to the steam-condensation temperature. If the turbine and pump efficiencies are both 0.78, what is the thermal efficiency of the cycle and what fraction of the steam entering the turbine is extracted for each feedwater heater?

8.9. A steam power plant operating on a regenerative cycle, as illustrated in Fig. 8.5, includes two feedwater heaters. Steam enters the turbine at 6500 kPa and 600°C (873.15 K) and exhausts at 20 kPa. Steam for the feedwater heaters is extracted from the turbine at pressures such that the feedwater is heated to 190°C (463.15 K) in two equal increments of temperature rise, with 5°C (5 K) approaches to the steam-condensation temperature in each feedwater heater. If the turbine and pump efficiencies are both 0.80, what is the thermal efficiency of the cycle and what fraction of the steam entering the turbine is extracted for each feedwater heater?

8.10. A power plant operating on heat recovered from the exhaust gases of internal combustion engines uses isobutane as the working medium in a modified Rankine cycle in which the upper pressure level is above the critical pressure of isobutane. Thus the isobutane does not undergo a change of phase as it absorbs heat prior to its entry into the turbine. Isobutane vapor is heated at 4800 kPa to 260°C (533.15 K), and enters the turbine as a supercritical fluid at these conditions. Isentropic expansion in the turbine produces a superheated vapor at 450 kPa, which is cooled and condensed at constant pressure. The resulting saturated liquid enters the pump for return to the heater. If the power output of the modified Rankine cycle is 1000 kW, what is the isobutane flow rate, the heat-transfer rates in the heater and condenser, and the thermal efficiency of the cycle? The vapor pressure of isobutane is given in Table B.2 of App. B.

8.11. A power plant operating on heat from a geothermal source uses isobutane as the working medium in a Rankine cycle (Fig. 8.3). Isobutane is heated at 3400 kPa (a pressure just a little below its critical pressure) to a temperature of 140°C (413.15 K), at which conditions it enters the turbine. Isentropic expansion in the turbine produces superheated vapor at 450 kPa, which is cooled and condensed to saturated liquid and pumped to the heater/boiler. If the flowrate of isobutane is 75 kg s^{-1}, what is the power output of the Rankine cycle and what are the heat-transfer rates in the heater/boiler and cooler/condenser? What is the thermal efficiency of the cycle? The vapor pressure of isobutane is given in Table B.2 of App. B.Repeat these calculations for a cycle in which the turbine and pump each have an efficiency of 80%.

8.12. For comparison of Diesel- and Otto-engine cycles:

(*a*) Show that the thermal efficiency of the air-standard Diesel cycle can be expressed as

$$\eta = 1 - \left(\frac{1}{r}\right)^{\gamma-1} \frac{r_c^\gamma - 1}{\gamma(r_c - 1)}$$

where r is the compression ratio and r_c is the *cutoff ratio*, defined as $r_c = V_A/V_D$. (See Fig. 8.10.)

(*b*) Show that for the same compression ratio the thermal efficiency of the air-standard Otto engine is greater than the thermal efficiency of the air-standard Diesel cycle. *Hint*: Show that the fraction which multiplies $(1/r)^{\gamma-1}$ in the above equation for η is greater than unity by expanding r_c^γ in a Taylor series with the remainder taken to the first derivative.

(*c*) If $\gamma = 1.4$, how does the thermal efficiency of an air-standard Otto cycle with a compression ratio of 8 compare with the thermal efficiency of an air-standard Diesel cycle with the same compression ratio and a cutoff ratio of 2? How is the comparison changed if the cutoff ratio is 3?

8.13. An air-standard Diesel cycle absorbs 1500 J mol^{-1} of heat (step DA of Fig. 8.10, which simulates combustion). The pressure and temperature at the beginning of the compression step are 1 bar and 20°C (293.15 K), and the pressure at the end of the compression step is 4 bar. Assuming air to be an ideal gas for which $C_P = (7/2)R$ and $C_V = (5/2)R$, what are the compression ratio and the expansion ratio of the cycle?

8.14. Calculate the efficiency for an air-standard gas-turbine cycle (the Brayton cycle) operating with a pressure ratio of 3. Repeat for pressure ratios of 5, 7, and 9. Take $\gamma = 1.35$.

8.15. An air-standard gas-turbine cycle is modified by installation of a regenerative heat exchanger to transfer energy from the air leaving the turbine to the air leaving the compressor. In an optimum countercurrent exchanger, the temperature of the air leaving the compressor is raised to that of point D in Fig. 8.12, and the temperature of the gas leaving the turbine is cooled to that of point B in Fig. 8.12. Show that the thermal efficiency of this cycle is given by

$$\eta = 1 - \frac{T_A}{T_C}\left(\frac{P_B}{P_A}\right)^{(\gamma-1)/\gamma}$$

8.16. Consider an air-standard cycle for the turbojet power plant shown in Fig. 8.13. The temperature and pressure of the air entering the compressor are 1 bar and 30°C (303.15 K). The pressure ratio in the compressor is 6.5, and the temperature at the turbine inlet is 1100°C (1373.15 K). If expansion in the nozzle is isentropic and if the nozzle exhausts at 1 bar, what is the pressure at the nozzle inlet (turbine exhaust) and what is the velocity of the air leaving the nozzle?

8.17. Air enters a gas-turbine engine (see Fig. 8.11) at 305 K and 1.05 bar, and is compressed to 7.5 bar. The fuel is methane at 300 K and 7.5 bar; compressor and turbine efficiencies are each 80%. For one of the turbine inlet temperatures T_C given below, determine: the molar fuel-to-air ratio, the *net* mechanical power delivered per mole of fuel, and the turbine exhaust temperature T_D. Assume complete combustion of the methane, and expansion in the turbine to 1 atm.

(*a*) $T_C = 1000$ K; (*b*) $T_C = 1250$ K; (*c*) $T_C = 1500$ K

8.18. Most electrical energy in the United States is generated in large-scale power cycles through conversion of thermal energy to mechanical energy, which is then converted to electrical energy. Assume a thermal efficiency of 0.35 for conversion of thermal to mechanical energy, and an efficiency of 0.95 for conversion of mechanical to electrical energy. Line losses in the distribution system amount to 20%. If the cost of fuel for the power cycle is \$4.00 GJ^{-1}, estimate the cost of electricity delivered to the customer in \$ per kWh. Ignore operating costs, profits, and taxes. Compare this number with that found on a typical electric bill.

8.19. Liquefied natural gas (LNG) is transported in very large tankers, stored as liquid in equilibrium with its vapor at approximately atmospheric pressure. If LNG is essentially pure methane, the storage temperature then is about 111.4 K, the normal boiling point of methane. The enormous amount of cold liquid can in principle serve as a heat sink for an on-board heat engine. Energy discarded to the LNG serves for its vaporization. If the heat source is ambient air at 300 K, and if the efficiency of a heat engine is 60% of its Carnot value, estimate the vaporization rate, in moles vaporizsed per kJ of power output. For methane, $\Delta H_n^{lv} = 8.206$ kJ mol^{-1}.

8.20. The oceans in the tropics have substantial surface-to-deep-water temperature gradients. Depending on location, relatively constant temperature differences of 15 to 25°C (288.15 K to 298.15 K) can be obtained for depths of 500 to 1000 m. This provides the opportunity for using cold (deep) water as a heat sink and warm (surface) water as a heat source for a power cycle. The technology is known as "OTEC" (Ocean Thermal Energy Conversion).

(*a*) Consider a location where the surface temperature is 27°C (300.15 K) and the temperature at a depth of 750 m is 6°C (279.15 K). What is the efficiency of a Carnot engine operating between these temperature levels?

(*b*) Part of the output of a power cycle must be used to pump the cold water to the surface, where the cycle hardware resides. If the inherent efficiency of a real cycle is 0.6 of the Carnot value, and if 1/3 of the generated power is used for moving cold water to the surface, what is the actual efficiency of the cycle?

(*c*) The choice of working fluid for the cycle is critical. Suggest some possibilities. Here, you may want to consult a handbook, such as *Perry's Chemical Engineers' Handbook*.

8.21. Air-standard power cycles are conventionally displayed on PV diagrams. An alternative is the PT diagram. Sketch air-standard cycles on PT diagrams for the following:

(*a*) Carnot cycle; (*b*) Otto cycle; (*c*) Diesel cycle; (*d*) Brayton cycle.

Why would a PT diagram not be helpful for depicting power cycles involving liquid/vapor phase changes?

8.22. A steam plant operates on the cycle of Fig. 8.4. The pressure levels are 10 kPa and 6000 kPa, and steam leaves the turbine as saturated vapor. The pump efficiency is 0.70, and the turbine efficiency is 0.75. Determine the thermal efficiency of the plant.

8.23. Devise a general scheme for analyzing four-step air-standard power cycles. Model each step of the cycle as a polytropic process described by Eq. (3.35c) with a specified value of δ. Decide which states to fix, partially or completely, by values of T and/or P. Analysis here means determination of: T and P for initial and final states of each step; Q and W for each step; and the thermal efficiency of the cycle. The analysis should also include a sketch of the cycle on a PT diagram.

Chapter 9

Refrigeration and Liquefaction

Refrigeration is best known for its use in the air conditioning of buildings and in the treatment, transportation, and preservation of foods and beverages. It also finds large-scale industrial application, for example, in the manufacture of ice and the dehydration of gases. Applications in the petroleum industry include lubricating-oil purification, low-temperature reactions, and separation of volatile hydrocarbons. A closely related process is gas liquefaction, which has important commercial applications.

The purpose of this chapter is to present a thermodynamic analysis of refrigeration and liquefaction processes. However, the details of equipment design are left to specialized books.[1]

The word *refrigeration* implies the maintenance of a temperature below that of the surroundings. This requires continuous absorption of heat at a low temperature level, usually accomplished by evaporation of a liquid in a steady-state flow process. The vapor formed may be returned to its original liquid state for reevaporation in either of two ways. Most commonly, it is simply compressed and then condensed. Alternatively, it may be absorbed by a liquid of low volatility, from which it is subsequently evaporated at higher pressure. Before treating these practical refrigeration cycles, we consider the Carnot refrigerator, which provides a standard of comparison.

9.1 THE CARNOT REFRIGERATOR

In a continuous refrigeration process, the heat absorbed at a low temperature is continuously rejected to the surroundings at a higher temperature. Basically, a refrigeration cycle is a reversed heat-engine cycle. Heat is transferred from a low temperature level to a higher one; according to the second law, this requires an external source of energy. The ideal refrigerator, like the ideal heat engine (Sec. 5.2), operates on a Carnot cycle, consisting in this case of two isothermal steps in which heat $|Q_C|$ is absorbed at the lower temperature T_C and heat $|Q_H|$ is rejected at the higher temperature T_H, and two adiabatic steps. The cycle requires the addition

[1]*ASHRAE Handbook: Refrigeration*, 1994; *Fundamentals*, 1993; *HVAC Systems and Equipment*, 1992; *HVAC Applications*, 1991; American Society of Heating, Refrigerating and Air-Conditioning Engineers, Inc., Atlanta; Shan K. Wang, *Handbook of Air Conditioning and Refrigeration*, McGraw-Hill, New York, 1993.

of net work W to the system. Because ΔU of the working fluid is zero for the cycle, the first law is written as

$$W = |Q_H| - |Q_C| \tag{9.1}$$

The measure of the effectiveness of a refrigerator is its *coefficient of performance* ω, defined as

$$\omega \equiv \frac{\text{heat absorbed at the lower temperature}}{\text{net work}} = \frac{|Q_C|}{W} \tag{9.2}$$

Equation (9.1) may be divided by $|Q_C|$ and then combined with Eq. (5.7):

$$\frac{W}{|Q_C|} = \frac{|Q_H|}{|Q_C|} - 1 \qquad\qquad \frac{W}{|Q_C|} = \frac{T_H}{T_C} - 1 = \frac{T_H - T_C}{T_C}$$

Equation (9.2) becomes

$$\boxed{\omega = \frac{T_C}{T_H - T_C}} \tag{9.3}$$

This equation applies only to a refrigerator operating on a Carnot cycle, and it gives the maximum possible value of ω for any refrigerator operating between given values of T_H and T_C. It shows clearly that the refrigeration effect per unit of work decreases as the temperature of heat absorption T_C decreases and as the temperature of heat rejection T_H increases. For refrigeration at a temperature level of 5°C (278.15 K) in a surroundings at 30°C (303.15 K), the value of ω for a Carnot refrigerator is:

$$\omega = \frac{5 + 273.15}{(30 + 273.15) - (5 + 273.15)} = 11.13$$

9.2 THE VAPOR-COMPRESSION CYCLE

The vapor-compression refrigeration cycle is represented in Fig. 9.1. Shown on the TS diagram are the four steps of the process. A liquid evaporating at constant pressure (line $1 \rightarrow 2$) provides a means for heat absorption at a low constant temperature. The vapor produced is compressed to a higher pressure, and is then cooled and condensed with rejection of heat at a higher temperature level. Liquid from the condenser returns to its original pressure by an expansion process. In principle, this can be carried out in an expander from which work is obtained, but for practical reasons is usually accomplished by throttling through a partly open valve. The pressure drop in this irreversible process results from fluid friction in the valve. As shown in Sec. 7.1, the throttling process occurs at constant enthalpy. In Fig. 9.1 line $4 \rightarrow 1$ represents this throttling process. The dashed line $2 \rightarrow 3'$ is the path of isentropic compression (Fig. 7.6). Line $2 \rightarrow 3$, representing the actual compression process, slopes in the direction of increasing entropy, reflecting inherent irreversibilities.

On the basis of a unit mass of fluid, the equations for the heat absorbed in the evaporator and the heat rejected in the condenser are

$$|Q_C| = H_2 - H_1 \qquad \text{and} \qquad |Q_H| = H_3 - H_4$$

These equations follow from Eq. (2.32) when the small changes in potential and kinetic energy are neglected. The work of compression is simply: $W = H_3 - H_2$, and by Eq. (9.2), the

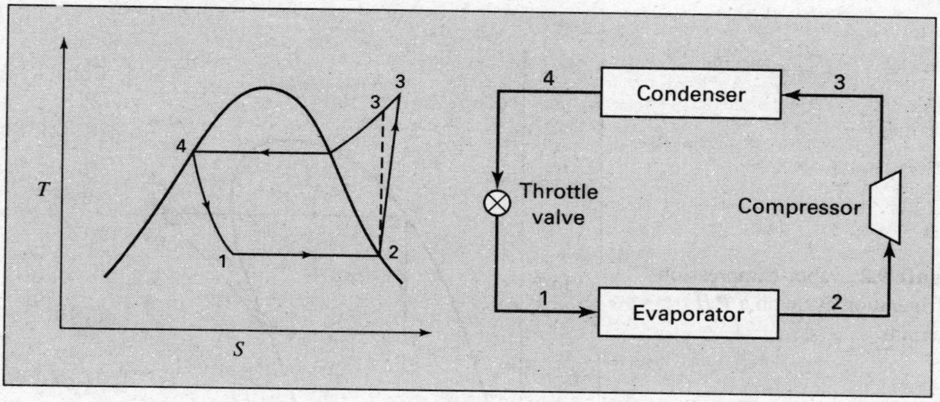

Figure 9.1: Vapor-compression refrigeration cycle

coefficient of performance is

$$\omega = \frac{H_2 - H_1}{H_3 - H_2} \tag{9.4}$$

To design the evaporator, compressor, condenser, and auxiliary equipment one must know the rate of circulation of refrigerant $\dot{m}$. This is determined from the rate of heat absorption in the evaporator[2] by the equation:

$$\dot{m} = \frac{|\dot{Q}_C|}{H_2 - H_1} \tag{9.5}$$

The vapor-compression cycle of Fig. 9.1 is shown on a PH diagram in Fig. 9.2. Such diagrams are more commonly used in the description of refrigeration processes than TS diagrams, because they show directly the required enthalpies. Although the evaporation and condensation processes are represented by constant-pressure paths, small pressure drops do occur because of fluid friction.

For given values of T_C and T_H, the highest possible value of ω is attained for Carnot-cycle refrigeration. The lower values for the vapor-compression cycle result from irreversible expansion in a throttle valve and irreversible compression. The following example provides an indication of typical values for coefficients of performance.

Example 9.1

A refrigerated space is maintained at −12°C (261.15 K), and cooling water is available at 21°C (294.15 K). Refrigeration capacity is 35.2 kW. The evaporator and condenser

[2]In the United States refrigeration equipment is commonly rated in *tons of refrigeration*; a ton of refrigeration is defined as heat absorption at the rate of 12 000 Btu h^{-1} or 12 652.2 kJ h^{-1}. This corresponds approximately to the rate of heat removal required to freeze 1 short ton [or 2000 (lb)] of water initially at 32(°F) per day or remove 3.5145 kW at 0°C (273.15 K).

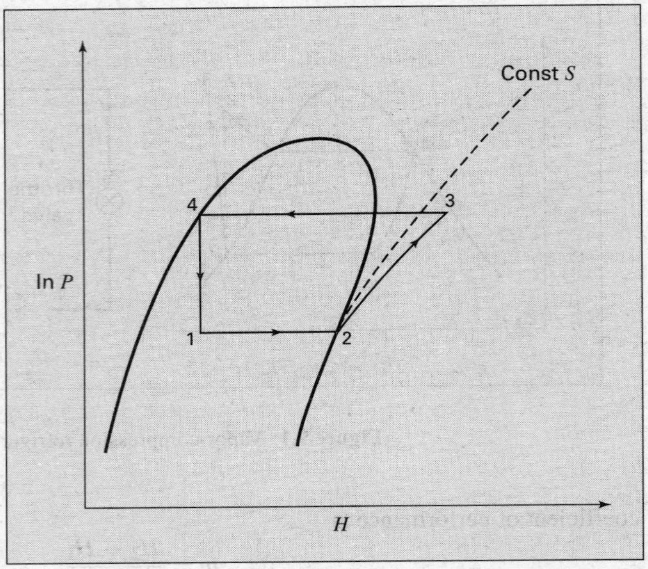

Figure 9.2: Vapor-compression refrigeration cycle on a PH diagram

are of sufficient size that a 5.6°C (5.6 K) minimum temperature difference for heat transfer can be realized in each. The refrigerant is tetrafluoroethane (HFC-134a), for which data are given in Table 9.1 and Fig. G.2 (App. G).

(*a*) What is the value of ω for a Carnot refrigerator?

(*b*) Calculate ω and $\dot{m}$ for the vapor-compression cycle of Fig. 9.1 if the compressor efficiency is 0.80.

Solution

(*a*) By Eq. (9.3) for a Carnot refrigerator,

$$\omega = \frac{(261.15 - 5.6)}{(294.15 + 5.6) - (261.15 - 5.6)} = 5.78$$

(*b*) Because HFC-134a is the refrigerant, the enthalpies for states 2 and 4 of Figs. 9.1 and 9.2 are read directly from Table 9.1. The entry at 261.15 − 5.6 = 255.55 K indicates that HFC-134a vaporizes in the evaporator at a pressure of 0.1471 MPa (1.471 bar). Its properties as a saturated vapor at these conditions are

$$H_2 = 388.03 \text{ kJ kg}^{-1} \qquad S_2 = 1.7392 \text{ kJ kg}^{-1} \text{ K}^{-1}$$

The entry at 294.15 + 5.6 = 299.75 K (26.6°C) in Table 9.1 shows that HFC-134a condenses at 0.6977 MPa (6.977 bar); its enthalpy as a saturated liquid at these conditions is

$$H_4 = 236.83 \text{ kJ kg}^{-1}$$

If the compression step is reversible and adiabatic (isentropic) from saturated vapor at state 2 to superheated vapor at state 3′,

$$S_3' = S_2 = 1.7392 \text{ kJ kg}^{-1} \text{ K}^{-1}$$

The enthalpy from Fig. G.2 at this entropy and at a pressure of 6.977 bar is about:

$$H_3' = 420.33 \text{ kJ kg}^{-1}$$

and the enthalpy change is:

$$(\Delta H)_S = H_3' - H_2 = 420.33 - 388.03 = 32.3 \text{ kJ kg}^{-1}$$

By Eq. (7.17) for a compressor efficiency of 0.80, the actual enthalpy change for step 2 → 3 is:

$$H_3 - H_2 = \frac{(\Delta H)_S}{\eta} = \frac{32.3}{0.80} = 40.38$$

Because the throttling process of step 1 → 4 is isenthalpic, $H_1 = H_4$. The coefficient of performance as given by Eq. (9.4) therefore becomes:

$$\omega = \frac{H_2 - H_4}{H_3 - H_2} = \frac{388.03 - 236.83}{40.38} = 3.74$$

and the HFC-134a circulation rate as given by Eq. (9.5) is:

$$\dot{m} = \frac{|\dot{Q}_C|}{H_2 - H_4} = \frac{35.2}{388.05 - 236.83} = 0.2328 \text{ kg s}^{-1}$$

9.3 THE CHOICE OF REFRIGERANT

As shown in Sec. 5.2, the efficiency of a Carnot heat engine is independent of the working medium of the engine. Similarly, the coefficient of performance of a Carnot refrigerator is independent of the refrigerant. However, the irreversibilities inherent in the vapor-compression cycle cause the coefficient of performance of practical refrigerators to depend to some extent on the refrigerant. Nevertheless, such characteristics as its toxicity, flammability, cost, corrosion properties, and vapor pressure in relation to temperature are of greater importance in the choice of refrigerant. So that air cannot leak into the refrigeration system, the vapor pressure of the refrigerant at the evaporator temperature should be greater than atmospheric pressure. On the other hand, the vapor pressure at the condenser temperature should not be unduly high, because of the initial cost and operating expense of high-pressure equipment. These two requirements limit the choice of refrigerant to relatively a few fluids. The final selection then depends on the other characteristics mentioned.

Table 9.1: Thermodynamic Properties of Saturated 1,1,1,2-Tetrafluoroethane (HFC-134a)[1]

Temperature		Saturation pressure	Specific Volume		Specific Enthalpy		Specific Entropy	
°C	K	MPa	m^{-3} kg^{-1}		kJ kg^{-1}		kJ $kg^{-1}K^{-1}$	
t	T	P	V^l	V^g	H^l	H^g	S^l	S^g
−40	233.15	0.05121	0.000705	0.36108	148.14	374.00	0.7956	1.7643
−35	238.15	0.06614	0.000713	0.28402	154.44	377.17	0.8223	1.7575
−30	243.15	0.08438	0.000720	0.22594	160.79	380.32	0.8486	1.7515
−26.07	**247.076***	**0.10133**	**0.000726**	**0.19018**	**165.81**	**382.78**	**0.8691**	**1.7472**
−25	248.15	0.10640	0.000728	0.18162	167.19	383.45	0.8746	1.7461
−20	253.15	0.13273	0.000736	0.14739	173.64	386.55	0.9003	1.7413
−15	258.15	0.16394	0.000745	0.12067	180.14	389.63	0.9256	1.7371
−10	263.15	0.20060	0.000754	0.099590	186.70	392.66	0.9507	1.7334
−5	268.15	0.24334	0.000763	0.082801	193.32	395.66	0.9754	1.7300
0	273.15	0.29280	0.000772	0.069309	200.00	398.60	1.0000	1.7271
5	278.15	0.34966	0.000782	0.058374	206.75	401.49	1.0243	1.7245
10	283.15	0.41461	0.000793	0.049442	213.58	404.32	1.0485	1.7221
15	288.15	0.48837	0.000804	0.042090	220.48	407.07	1.0724	1.7200
20	293.15	0.57171	0.000816	0.035997	227.47	409.75	1.0962	1.7180
25	298.15	0.66538	0.000829	0.030912	234.55	412.33	1.1199	1.7162
30	303.15	0.77020	0.000842	0.026642	241.72	414.82	1.1435	1.7145
35	308.15	0.88698	0.000857	0.023033	249.01	417.19	1.1670	1.7128
40	313.15	1.0166	0.000872	0.019966	256.41	419.43	1.1905	1.7111
45	318.15	1.1599	0.000889	0.017344	263.94	421.52	1.2139	1.7092
50	323.15	1.3179	0.000907	0.015089	271.62	423.44	1.2375	1.7072
55	328.15	1.4915	0.000927	0.013140	279.47	425.15	1.2611	1.7050
60	333.15	1.6818	0.000950	0.011444	287.50	426.63	1.2848	1.7024
65	338.15	1.8898	0.000975	0.009960	295.76	427.82	1.3088	1.6993
70	343.15	2.1168	0.00100	0.008653	304.28	428.65	1.3332	1.6956
75	348.15	2.3641	0.00104	0.007491	313.13	429.03	1.3580	1.6909
80	353.15	2.6332	0.00108	0.006448	322.39	428.81	1.3836	1.6850
85	358.15	2.9258	0.00113	0.005499	332.22	427.76	1.4104	1.6771
90	363.15	3.2442	0.00119	0.004613	342.93	425.42	1.4390	1.6662
95	368.15	3.5912	0.00129	0.003743	355.25	420.67	1.4715	1.6492
100	373.15	3.9724	0.00154	0.002681	373.30	407.68	1.5188	1.6109

*normal boiling point

[1] NIST Standard Reference Data Base 23, (REFPROP) Version 8, 2007

Ammonia, methyl chloride, carbon dioxide, propane and other hydrocarbons can serve as refrigerants. Halogenated hydrocarbons came into common use as refrigerants in the 1930s. Most common were the fully halogenated chlorofluorocarbons, CCl_3F (trichlorofluoromethane or CFC-11)[3] and CCl_2F_2 (dichlorodifluoromethane or CFC-12). These stable molecules persist in the atmosphere for hundreds of years, causing severe ozone depletion. Their production has mostly ended. Replacements are certain hydrochlorofluorocarbons, less than fully halogenated hydrocarbons which cause relatively little ozone depletion, and hydrofluorocarbons, which contain no chlorine and cause no ozone depletion. Examples are $CHCl_2CF_3$ (dichlorotrifluoroethane or HCFC-123), CF_3CH_2F (1,1,1,2-tetrafluoroethane or HFC-134a), and CHF_2CF_3 (pentafluoroethane or HFC-125). A pressure/enthalpy diagram for tetrafluoroethane (HFC-134a) is shown in Fig. G.2; Table 9.1 provides saturation data for the same refrigerant. Tables and diagrams for a variety of other refrigerants are readily available.[4]

Limits placed on the operating pressures of the evaporator and condenser of a refrigeration system also limit the temperature difference $T_H - T_C$ over which a simple vapor-compression cycle can operate. With T_H fixed by the temperature of the cooling medium for condenser, a lower limit is placed on the temperature level of refrigeration. This can be overcome by the operation of two or more refrigeration cycles employing different refrigerants in a *cascade*. A two-stage cascade is shown in Fig. 9.3.

Here, the two cycles operate so that the heat absorbed in the interchanger by the refrigerant of the higher-temperature cycle 2 serves to condense the refrigerant in the lower-temperature cycle 1. The two refrigerants are so chosen that at the required temperature levels each cycle operates at reasonable pressures. For example, assume the following operating temperatures (Fig. 9.3):

$$T_H = 303 \text{ K} \qquad T'_C = 255 \text{ K} \qquad T'_H = 261 \text{ K} \qquad T_C = 227 \text{ K}$$

If tetrafluoroethane (HFC-134a) is the refrigerant in cycle 2, then the intake and discharge pressures for the compressor are about 1.45 bar and 7.72 bar, and the pressure ratio is about 5.32. If propylene is the refrigerant in cycle 1, these pressures are about 1.1 bar and 4 bar, and the pressure ratio is about 3.64. These are all reasonable values. On the other hand, for a single cycle operating between 227 K and 303 K with HFC-134a as refrigerant, the intake pressure to the condenser is about 0.4 bar, well below atmospheric pressure. Moreover, for a discharge pressure of about 7.72 bar the pressure ratio is 19.3, too high a value for a single-stage compressor.

9.4 ABSORPTION REFRIGERATION

In vapor-compression refrigeration the work of compression is usually supplied by an electric motor. But the source of the electric energy for the motor is probably a heat engine (central

[3] The abbreviated designation is nomenclature of the American Society of Heating, Refrigerating, and Air-Conditioning Engineers.

[4] *ASHRAE Handbook: Fundamentals*, Chap. 17, 1989; R. H. Perry and D. Green, *Perry's Chemical Engineers' Handbook*, 7th ed., Sec. 2, 1997; NIST Standard Reference Data Base 23, REFPROP, Ver. 8, 2007. Extensive data for ammonia are given by L. Haar and J. S. Gallagher, *J. Phys. Chem. Ref. Data*, vol. 7, pp. 635–792, 1978.

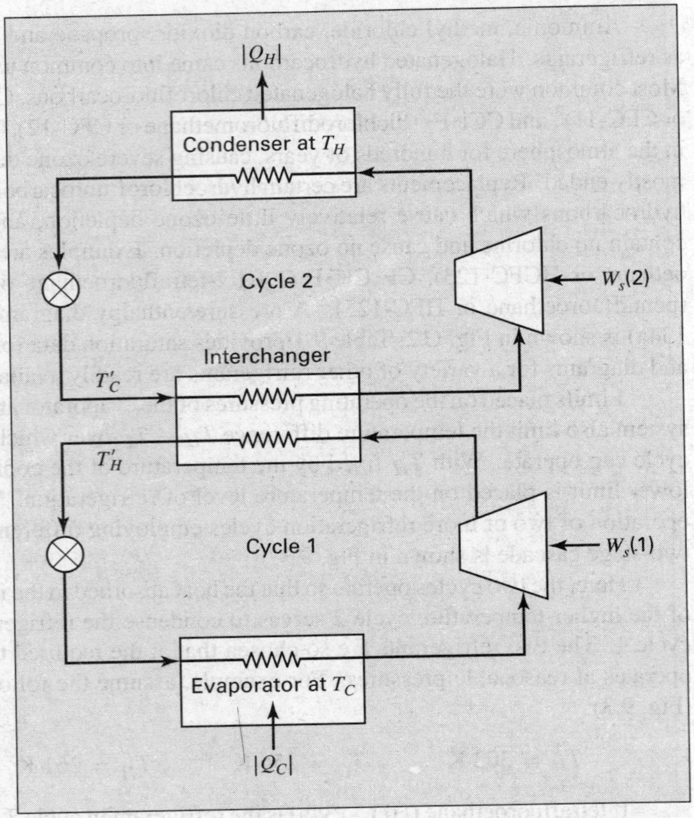

Figure 9.3: A two-stage cascade refrigeration system

power plant) used to drive a generator. Thus the work for refrigeration comes ultimately from heat at a high temperature level. This suggests the direct use of heat as the energy source for refrigeration. The absorption-refrigeration machine is based on this idea.

The work required by a Carnot refrigerator absorbing heat at temperature T_C and rejecting heat at the temperature of the surroundings, here designated T_S, follows from Eqs. (9.2) and (9.3):

$$W = \frac{T_S - T_C}{T_C}|Q_C|$$

where $|Q_C|$ is the heat absorbed. If a source of heat is available at a temperature above that of the surroundings, say at T_H, then work can be obtained from a Carnot engine operating between this temperature and the surroundings temperature T_S. The heat required $|Q_H|$ for the production of work $|W|$ is found from Eq. (5.8):

$$\eta = \frac{|W|}{|Q_H|} = 1 - \frac{T_S}{T_H} \quad \text{and} \quad |Q_H| = |W|\frac{T_H}{T_H - T_S}$$

Elimination of $|W|$ gives

$$|Q_H| = |Q_C|\frac{T_H}{T_H - T_S}\frac{T_S - T_C}{T_C} \tag{9.6}$$

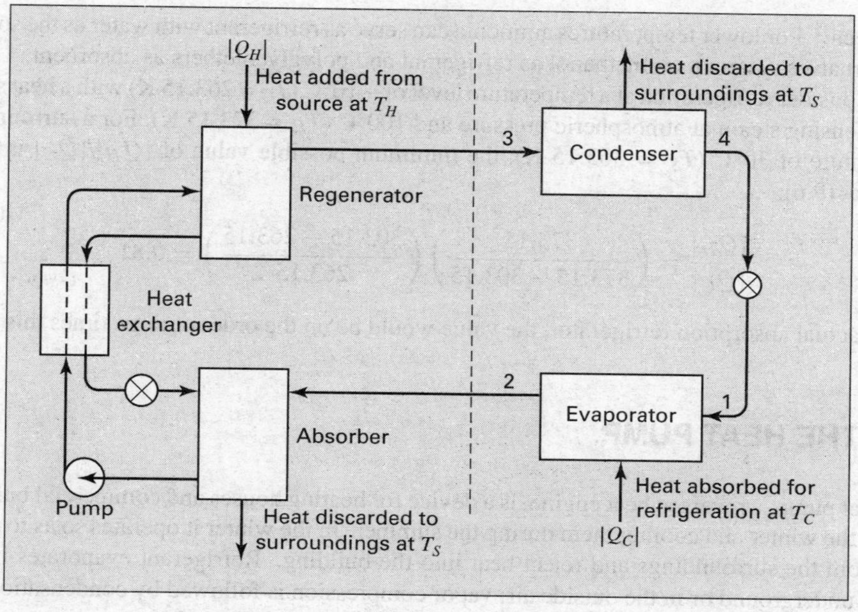

Figure 9.4: Schematic diagram of an absorption-refrigeration unit

The value of $|Q_H|/|Q_C|$ given by this equation is of course a minimum, because Carnot cycles cannot be achieved in practice.

A schematic diagram for a typical absorption refrigerator is shown in Fig. 9.4. The essential difference between a vapor-compression and an absorption refrigerator is in the different means employed for compression. The section of the absorption unit to the right of the dashed line in Fig. 9.4 is the same as in a vapor-compression refrigerator, but the section to the left accomplishes compression by what amounts to a heat engine. Refrigerant as vapor from the evaporator is absorbed in a relatively nonvolatile liquid solvent at the pressure of the evaporator and at relatively low temperature. The heat given off in the process is discarded to the surroundings at T_S. This is the lower temperature level of the heat engine. The liquid solution from the absorber, which contains a relatively high concentration of refrigerant, passes to a pump, which raises the pressure of the liquid to that of the condenser. Heat from the higher temperature source at T_H is transferred to the compressed liquid solution, raising its temperature and evaporating the refrigerant from the solvent. Vapor passes from the regenerator to the condenser, and solvent, which now contains a relatively low concentration of refrigerant, returns to the absorber by way of a heat exchanger, which serves to conserve energy and adjust stream temperatures toward optimum values. Low-pressure steam is the usual source of heat for the regenerator.

The most commonly used absorption-refrigeration system operates with water as the refrigerant and a lithium bromide solution as the absorbent. This system is obviously limited to refrigeration temperatures above the freezing point of water. It is treated in detail by Perry and Green.[5] For lower temperatures ammonia can serve as refrigerant with water as the solvent. An alternative system uses methanol as refrigerant and polyglycolethers as absorbent.

Consider refrigeration at a temperature level of -10°C ($T_C = 263.15$ K) with a heat source of condensing steam at atmospheric pressure and 100°C ($T_H = 373.15$ K). For a surroundings temperature of 30°C ($T_S = 303.15$ K), the minimum possible value of $|Q_H|/|Q_C|$ is found from Eq. (9.6):

$$\frac{|Q_H|}{|Q_C|} = \left(\frac{373.15}{373.15 - 303.15}\right)\left(\frac{303.15 - 263.15}{263.15}\right) = 0.81$$

For an actual absorption refrigerator, the value would be on the order of three times this result.

9.5 THE HEAT PUMP

The heat pump, a reversed heat engine, is a device for heating houses and commercial buildings during the winter and cooling them during the summer. In the winter it operates so as to absorb heat from the surroundings and reject heat into the building. Refrigerant evaporates in coils placed underground or in the outside air; vapor compression is followed by condensation, heat being transferred to air or water, which is used to heat the building. Compression must be to a pressure such that the condensation temperature of the refrigerant is higher than the required temperature level of the building. The operating cost of the installation is the cost of electric power to run the compressor. If the unit has a coefficient of performance, $|Q_C|/W = 4$, the heat available to heat the house $|Q_H|$ is equal to five times the energy input to the compressor. Any economic advantage of the heat pump as a heating device depends on the cost of electricity in comparison with the cost of fuels such as oil and natural gas.

The heat pump also serves for air conditioning during the summer. The flow of refrigerant is simply reversed, and heat is absorbed from the building and rejected through underground coils or to the outside air.

Example 9.2

A house has a winter heating requirement of 30 kJ s^{-1} and a summer cooling requirement of 60 kJ s^{-1}. Consider a heat-pump installation to maintain the house temperature at 20°C (293.15 K) in winter and 25°C (298.15 K) in summer. This requires circulation of the refrigerant through interior exchanger coils at 30°C (303.15 K) in winter and 5°C (278.15 K) in summer. Underground coils provide the heat source in winter and the heat sink in summer. For a year-round ground temperature of 15°C (288.15 K), the heat-transfer characteristics of the coils necessitate refrigerant temperatures of 10°C (283.15 K) in winter and 25°C (298.15 K) in summer. What are the minimum power requirements for winter heating and summer cooling?

[5] R. H. Perry and D. Green, *op. cit.*, pp. 11-88–11-89.

Solution

The minimum power requirements are provided by a Carnot heat pump. For winter heating, the house coils are at the higher temperature level T_H, and the heat requirement is $|Q_H| = 30$ kJ s^{-1}. Application of Eq. (5.7) gives

$$|Q_C| = |Q_H|\frac{T_C}{T_H} = 30\left(\frac{10 + 273.15}{30 + 273.15}\right) = 28.02 \text{ kJ s}^{-1}$$

This is the heat absorbed in the ground coils. By Eq. (9.1),

$$W = |Q_H| - |Q_C| = 30 - 28.02 = 1.98 \text{ kJ s}^{-1}$$

Thus the power requirement is 1.98 kW.

For summer cooling, $|Q_C| = 60$ kJ s^{-1}, and the house coils are at the lower-temperature level T_C. Combine Eqs. (9.2) and (9.3) and solve for W:

$$W = |Q_C|\frac{T_H - T_C}{T_C} = 60\left(\frac{298.15 - 278.15}{5 + 273.15}\right) = 4.31 \text{ kJ s}^{-1}$$

The power requirement here is therefore 4.31 kW.

9.6 LIQUEFACTION PROCESSES

Liquefied gases are used for a variety of purposes. For example, liquid propane in cylinders serves as a domestic fuel, liquid oxygen is carried in rockets, natural gas is liquefied for ocean transport, and liquid nitrogen provides low-temperature refrigeration. Gas mixtures (e.g., air) are liquefied for separation into their component species by distillation.

Liquefaction results when a gas is cooled to a temperature in the two-phase region. This may be accomplished in several ways:

1. By heat exchange at constant pressure
2. By an expansion process from which work is obtained
3. By a throttling process

The first method requires a heat sink at a temperature lower than that to which the gas is cooled, and is most commonly used to precool a gas prior to its liquefaction by the other two methods. An external refrigerator is required for a gas temperature below that of the surroundings.

The three methods are illustrated in Fig. 9.5. The constant-pressure process (1) approaches the two-phase region (and liquefaction) most closely for a given drop in temperature. The throttling process (3) does not result in liquefaction unless the initial state is at a low

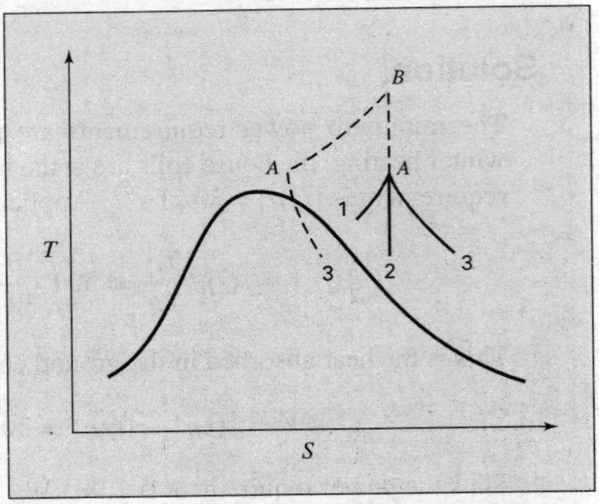

Figure 9.5: Cooling processes on a TS diagram

enough temperature and high enough pressure for the constant-enthalpy process to cut into the two-phase region. This is indeed the situation for an initial state at A', but not at A, where the temperature is the same but the pressure is lower than at A. The change of state from A to A' may be accomplished by compression of the gas to the pressure at B, and constant-pressure cooling to A'. Reference to a TS diagram for air[6] shows that at a temperature of 167 K the pressure must be greater than about 90 atm for any liquefaction to occur along a path of constant enthalpy. Thus, if air is compressed to at least 90 atm and cooled below 167 K, it is partially liquefied by throttling. An efficient process for cooling the gas is by countercurrent heat exchange with that portion of the gas which does not liquefy in the throttling process.

Liquefaction by isentropic expansion along process (2) occurs from lower pressures (for given temperature) than by throttling. For example, continuation of process (2) from initial state A ultimately results in liquefaction.

The throttling process (3) is commonly employed in small-scale commercial liquefaction plants. The temperature of the gas must decrease during expansion, and this indeed occurs with most gases at usual conditions of temperature and pressure. The exceptions are hydrogen and helium, which increase in temperature upon throttling unless the initial temperature is below about 100 K for hydrogen and 20 K for helium. Liquefaction of these gases by throttling requires initial cooling to temperatures lower than obtained by method 1 or 2.

The Linde liquefaction process, which depends solely on throttling expansion, is shown in Fig. 9.6. After compression, the gas is precooled to ambient temperature. It may be even further cooled by refrigeration. The lower the temperature of the gas entering the throttle valve, the greater the fraction of gas that is liquefied. For example, a refrigerant evaporating in the cooler at −40°C (233.15 K) provides a lower temperature at the valve than if water at 21°C (294.15 K) is the cooling medium.

A more efficient liquefaction process would replace the throttle valve by an expander, but operating such a device into the two-phase region is impractical. However, the Claude process, shown in Fig. 9.7, is based in part on this idea. Gas at an intermediate temperature is extracted from the heat-exchange system and passed through an expander from which it

[6]R. H. Perry and D. Green, *op. cit.*, Fig. 2-5, p. 2-213.

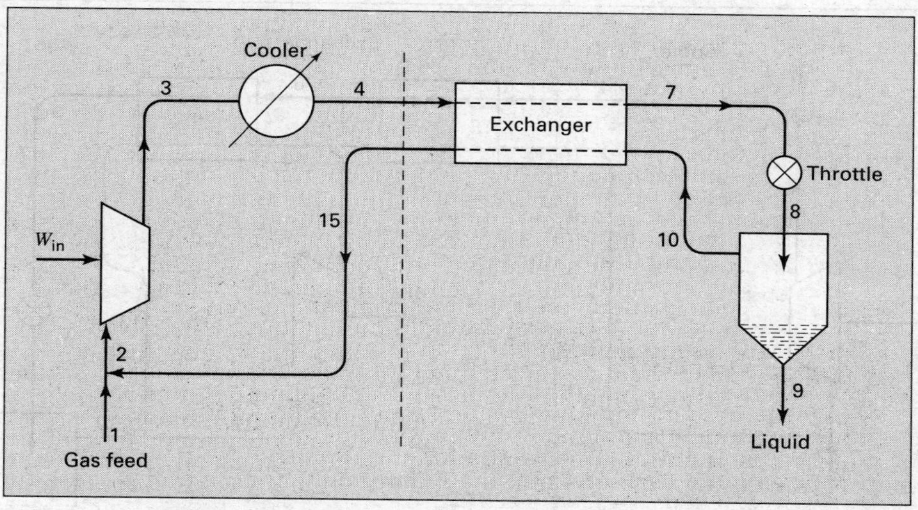

Figure 9.6: Linde liquefaction process

exhausts as a saturated or slightly superheated vapor. The remaining gas is further cooled and throttled through a valve to produce liquefaction as in the Linde process. The unliquefied portion, which is saturated vapor, mixes with the expander exhaust and returns for recycle through the heat-exchanger system.

An energy balance, Eq. (2.30), applied to that part of the process lying to the right of the dashed vertical line yields

$$\dot{m}_9 H_9 + \dot{m}_{15} H_{15} - \dot{m}_4 H_4 = \dot{W}_{\text{out}}$$

If the expander operates adiabatically, $\dot{W}_{\text{out}}$ as given by Eq. (7.13), is

$$\dot{W}_{\text{out}} = \dot{m}_{12}(H_{12} - H_5)$$

Moreover, by a mass balance, $\dot{m}_{15} = \dot{m}_4 - \dot{m}_9$. The energy balance, after division by $\dot{m}_4$, therefore becomes

$$\frac{\dot{m}_9}{\dot{m}_4} H_9 + \frac{\dot{m}_4 - \dot{m}_9}{\dot{m}_4} H_{15} - H_4 = \frac{\dot{m}_{12}}{\dot{m}_4}(H_{12} - H_5)$$

With the definitions, $z \equiv \dot{m}_9/\dot{m}_4$ and $x \equiv \dot{m}_{12}/\dot{m}_4$, solution of this equation for z yields

$$z = \frac{x(H_{12} - H_5) + H_4 - H_{15}}{H_9 - H_{15}} \tag{9.7}$$

In this equation z is the fraction of the stream entering the heat-exchanger system that is liquefied, and x is the fraction of this stream that is drawn off between the heat exchangers and passed through the expander. This latter quantity (x) is a design variable, and must be specified before Eq. (9.7) can be solved for z. Note that the Linde process results when $x = 0$, and in this event Eq. (9.7) reduces to

$$z = \frac{H_4 - H_{15}}{H_9 - H_{15}} \tag{9.8}$$

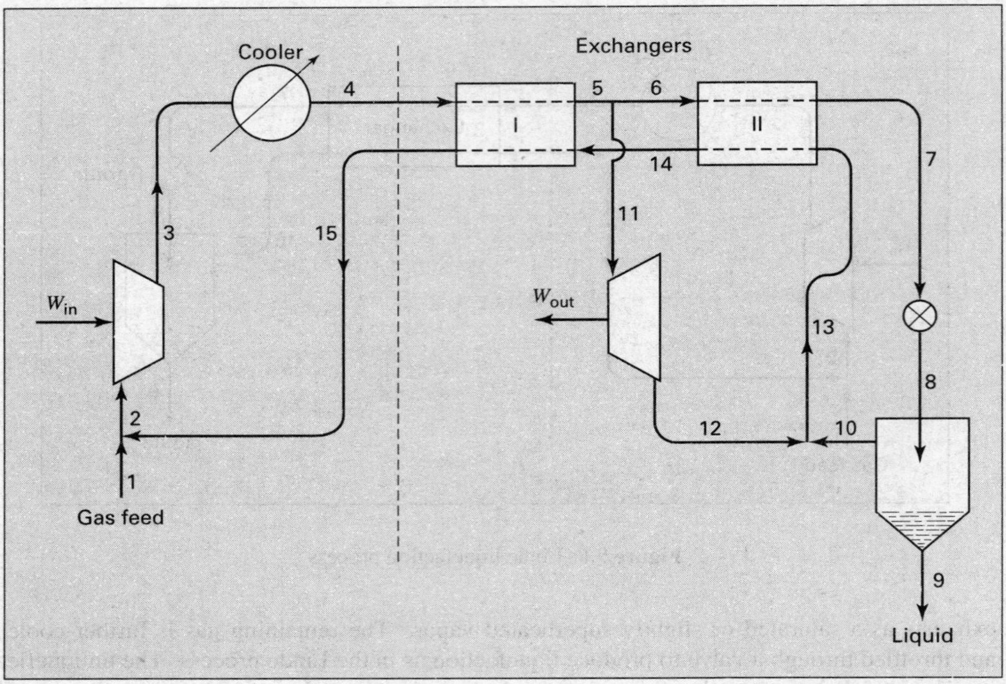

Figure 9.7: Claude liquefaction process

Thus the Linde process is a limiting case of the Claude process, obtained when none of the high-pressure gas stream is sent to an expander.

Equations (9.7) and (9.8) suppose that no heat flows into the system from the surroundings. This can never be exactly true, and heat leakage may be significant when temperatures are very low, even with well-insulated equipment.

Example 9.3

Natural gas, assumed here to be pure methane, is liquefied in a Claude process. Compression is to 60 bar and precooling is to 300 K. The expander and throttle exhaust to a pressure of 1 bar. Recycle methane at this pressure leaves the exchanger system (point 15, Fig. 9.7) at 295 K. Assume no heat leaks into the system from the surroundings, an expander efficiency of 75%, and an expander exhaust of saturated vapor. For a draw-off to the expander of 25% of the methane entering the exchanger system ($x = 0.25$), what fraction z of the methane is liquefied, and what is the temperature of the high-pressure stream entering the throttle valve?

Solution

Data for methane are given by Perry and Green.[7] By linear interpolation in the table of properties for superheated methane:

$$H_4 = 1140.0 \text{ kJ kg}^{-1} \qquad \text{(at 300 K and 60 bar)}$$

$$H_{15} = 1188.9 \text{ kJ kg}^{-1} \qquad \text{(at 295 K and 1 bar)}$$

By interpolation based on ln P in the table of properties for saturated liquid and vapor, we find for a pressure of 1 bar that:

$$T^{\text{sat}} = 111.5 \text{ K}$$

$$H_9 = 285.4 \text{ kJ kg}^{-1} \qquad \text{(saturated liquid)}$$

$$H_{12} = 796.9 \text{ kJ kg}^{-1} \qquad \text{(saturated vapor)}$$

$$S_{12} = 9.521 \text{ kJ kg}^{-1} \text{ K}^{-1} \qquad \text{(saturated vapor)}$$

The enthalpy at the draw-off point between exchangers I and II, H_5, is required for solution of Eq. (9.7). The expander efficiency η is known, as is H_{12}, the enthalpy of the expander exhaust. The calculation of H_5 $(= H_{11})$, the expander inlet enthalpy, is less straightforward than the usual calculation of the exhaust enthalpy from the entrance enthalpy. The equation defining expander efficiency can be written as

$$\Delta H = H_{12} - H_5 = \eta(\Delta H)_S = \eta(H'_{12} - H_5)$$

Solution for H_{12} yields

$$H_{12} = H_5 + \eta(H'_{12} - H_5) \qquad (A)$$

where H'_{12} is the enthalpy at 1 bar as the result of *isentropic* expansion from point 5. This enthalpy is readily found once the conditions at point 5 are known. Thus a trial calculation is indicated, wherein the first step is to assume temperature T_5. This leads to values for H_5 and S_5, from which H'_{12} can be found. All quantities in Eq. (A) are then known, and their substitution into this equation shows whether or not it is satisfied. If not, a new value is chosen for T_5, and the process continues until Eq. (A) is satisfied. This procedure leads to the values:

$$T_5 = 253.6 \text{ K} \qquad H_5 = 1009.8 \text{ kJ kg}^{-1} \qquad \text{(at 60 bar)}$$

Substitution of values into Eq. (9.7) now yields

$$z = \frac{0.25(796.9 - 1009.8) + 1140.0 - 1188.9}{285.4 - 1188.9} = 0.1130$$

Thus 11.3% of the methane entering the exchanger system is liquefied.

[7] R. H. Perry and D. Green, *op. cit.*, Table 2-281, p. 2-251; Table 2-282, p. 2-253.

The temperature at point 7 depends on its enthalpy, which is found from energy balances on the exchanger system. Thus, for exchanger I,

$$\dot{m}_4(H_5 - H_4) + \dot{m}_{15}(H_{15} - H_{14}) = 0$$

With $\dot{m}_{15} = \dot{m}_4 - \dot{m}_9$ and $\dot{m}_9/\dot{m}_4 = z$, this equation may be rearranged to give

$$H_{14} = \frac{H_5 - H_4}{1 - z} + H_{15} = \frac{1009.8 - 1140.0}{1 - 0.1130} + 1188.9$$

Whence,

$$H_{14} = 1042.1 \text{ kJ kg}^{-1} \qquad T_{14} = 227.2 \text{ K} \qquad \text{(at 1 bar)}$$

where T_{14} is found by interpolation in the tables for superheated methane at 60 bar.

For exchanger II,

$$\dot{m}_7(H_7 - H_5) + \dot{m}_{14}(H_{14} - H_{12}) = 0$$

With $\dot{m}_7 = \dot{m}_4 - \dot{m}_{12}$ and $\dot{m}_{14} = \dot{m}_4 - \dot{m}_9$ and with the definitions of z and x, this equation upon rearrangement becomes

$$H_7 = H_5 - \frac{1-z}{1-x}(H_{14} - H_{12}) = 1009.8 - \frac{1 - 0.1130}{1 - 0.25}(1042.1 - 796.9)$$

Whence,

$$H_7 = 719.8 \text{ kJ kg}^{-1} \qquad T_7 = 197.6 \text{ K} \qquad \text{(at 60 bar)}$$

As the value of x increases, T_7 decreases, eventually approaching the saturation temperature in the separator, and requiring an exchanger II of infinite area. Thus x is limited on the high side by the cost of the exchanger system.

The other limit is for $x = 0$, the Linde system, for which by Eq. (9.8),

$$z = \frac{1140.0 - 1188.9}{285.4 - 1188.9} = 0.0541$$

In this case only 5.41% of the gas entering the throttle valve emerges as liquid. The temperature of the gas at point 7 is again found from its enthalpy, calculated by the energy balance

$$H_7 = H_4 - (1 - z)(H_{15} - H_{10})$$

Substitution of known values yields

$$H_7 = 1140.0 - (1 - 0.0541)(1188.9 - 796.9) = 769.2 \text{ kJ kg}^{-1}$$

The corresponding temperature of the methane entering the throttle valve is $T_7 = 206.6$ K.

PROBLEMS

9.1. An easy way to rationalize definitions of cycle performance is to think of them as:

$$\text{Measure of performance} = \frac{\text{What you get}}{\text{What you pay for}}$$

Thus, for an engine, thermal efficiency is $\eta = |W|/|Q_H|$; for a refrigerator, the coefficient of performance is $\omega = |Q_C|/|W|$. Define a coefficient of performance ϕ for a heat pump. What is ϕ for a *Carnot* heat pump?

9.2. The contents of the freezer in a home refrigerator are maintained at −20°C (253.15 K). The kitchen temperature is 20°C (293.15 K). If heat leaks amount to 125 000 kJ per day, and if electricity costs \$0.08/kWh, estimate the yearly cost of running the refrigerator. Assume a coefficient of performance equal to 60% of the Carnot value.

9.3. Consider the startup of a refrigerator. Initially, the contents are at the same temperature as the surroundings: $T_{C_0} = T_H$, where T_H is the (constant) surroundings temperature. With the passage of time, owing to work input, the contents temperature is reduced from T_{C_0} to its design value T_C. Modeling the process as a Carnot refrigerator operating between an infinite hot reservoir and a *finite* cold reservoir of total heat capacity C^t, determine an expression for the minimum work required to decrease the contents temperature from T_{C_0} to T_C.

9.4. A Carnot refrigerator has tetrafluoroethane as the working fluid. The cycle is the same as that shown by Fig. 8.2, except the directions are reversed. For $T_C = -12$°C (261.15 K) and $T_H = 38$°C (311.15 K), determine the

(*a*) pressures at states 1, 2, 3, and 4
(*b*) quality x^v at states 3 and 4
(*c*) heat addition per kg of fluid
(*d*) heat rejection per kg of fluid
(*e*) mechanical power per kg of fluid for each of the four steps
(*f*) coefficient of performance ω for the cycle

9.5. Which is the more effective way to increase the coefficient of performance of a Carnot refrigerator: to increase T_C with T_H constant, or to decrease T_H with T_C constant? For a real refrigerator, does either of these strategies make sense?

9.6. In comparing the performance of a real cycle with that of a Carnot cycle, one has in principle a choice of temperatures to use for the Carnot calculation. Consider a vapor-compression refrigeration cycle in which the average fluid temperatures in the condenser and evaporator are T_H and T_C, respectively. Corresponding to T_H and T_C, the heat transfer occurs with respect to surroundings at temperature T_{σ_H} and T_{σ_C}. Which provides the more conservative estimate of ω(Carnot): a calculation based on T_H and T_C, or one based on T_{σ_H} and T_{σ_C}?

9.7. A Carnot engine is coupled to a Carnot refrigerator so that all of the work produced by the engine is used by the refrigerator in extraction of heat from a heat reservoir at 0°C (273.15 K) at the rate of 35 kJ s^{-1}. The source of energy for the Carnot engine is a heat reservoir at 250°C (523.15 K). If both devices discard heat to the surroundings at 25°C (298.15 K), how much heat does the engine absorb from its heat-source reservoir?

If the actual coefficient of performance of the refrigerator is $\omega = 0.6\,\omega_{\text{Carnot}}$ and if the thermal efficiency of the engine is $\eta = 0.6\,\eta_{\text{Carnot}}$, how much heat does the engine absorb from its heat-source reservoir?

9.8. A refrigeration system requires 1.5 kW of power for a refrigeration rate of 4 kJ s^{-1}.

(*a*) What is the coefficient of performance?
(*b*) How much heat is rejected in the condenser?
(*c*) If heat rejection is at 40°C, what is the lowest temperature the system can possibly maintain?

9.9. A vapor-compression refrigeration system operates on the cycle of Fig. 9.1. The refrigerant is tetrafluoroethane (Table 9.1, Fig. G.2). For one of the following sets of operating conditions, determine the circulation rate of the refrigerant, the heat-transfer rate in the condenser, the power requirement, the coefficient of performance of the cycle, and the coefficient of performance of a Carnot refrigeration cycle operating between the same temperature levels.

(*a*) Evaporation T/t = 272.15 K/−1°C; condensation T/t = 300.15 K/27°C; η(compressor) = 0.79; refrigeration rate = 633 kW
(*b*) Evaporation T/t = 266.15 K/−7°C; condensation T/t = 300.15 K/27°C η(compressor) = 0.78; refrigeration rate = 527.5 kW
(*c*) Evaporation T/t = 261.15 K/−12°C; condensation T/t = 300.15 K/27°C η(compressor) = 0.77; refrigeration rate = 422 kW
(*d*) Evaporation T/t = 255.15 K/−18°C; condensation T/t = 300.15 K/27°C; η(compressor) = 0.76; refrigeration rate = 316.5 kW
(*e*) Evaporation T/t =250.15 K/−23°C; condensation T/t = 300.15 K/27°C; η(compressor) = 0.75; refrigeration rate = 211 kW

9.10. A vapor-compression refrigeration system operates on the cycle of Fig. 9.1. The refrigerant is water. Given that the evaporation $t(T)$ = 4°C (277.15 K), the condensation $t(T)$ = 34°C (307.15 K), η(compressor) = 0.76, and the refrigeration rate = 1200 kJ s^{-1}, determine the circulation rate of the refrigerant, the heat-transfer rate in the condenser, the power requirement, the coefficient of performance of the cycle, and the coefficient of performance of a Carnot refrigeration cycle operating between the same temperature levels.

9.11. A refrigerator with tetrafluoroethane (Table 9.1, Fig. G.2) as refrigerant operates with an evaporation temperature of −26°C (247.15 K) and a condensation temperature of 27°C (300.15 K). Saturated liquid refrigerant from the condenser flows through an expansion valve into the evaporator, from which it emerges as saturated vapor.

(*a*) For a cooling rate of 5.275 kW, what is the circulation rate of the refrigerant?

(*b*) By how much would the circulation rate be reduced if the throttle valve were replaced by a turbine in which the refrigerant expands isentropically?

(*c*) Suppose the cycle of (*a*) is modified by the inclusion of a countercurrent heat exchanger between the condenser and the throttle valve in which heat is transferred to vapor returning from the evaporator. If liquid from the condenser enters the exchanger at 27°C (300.15 K) and if vapor from the evaporator enters the exchanger at −26°C (247.15 K) and leaves at 21°C (294.15 K), what is the circulation rate of the refrigerant?

(*d*) For each of (*a*), (*b*), and (*c*), determine the coefficient of performance for isentropic compression of the vapor.

9.12. A vapor-compression refrigeration system is conventional except that a countercurrent heat exchanger is installed to subcool the liquid from the condenser by heat exchange with the vapor stream from the evaporator. The minimum temperature difference for heat transfer is 5.6°C (5.6 K). Tetrafluoroethane is the refrigerant (Table 9.1, Fig. G.2), evaporating at −7°C (266.15 K) and condensing at 27°C (300.15 K). The heat load on the evaporator is 2110 kW. If the compressor efficiency is 75%, what is the power requirement?

How does this result compare with the power required by the compressor if the system operates without the heat exchanger? How do the refrigerant circulation rates compare for the two cases?

9.13. Consider the vapor-compression refrigeration cycle of Fig. 9.1 with tetrafluoroethane as refrigerant (Table 9.1, Fig. G.2). If the evaporation temperature is −12°C (261.15 K), show the effect of condensation temperature on the coefficient of performance by making calculations for condensation temperatures of 38°C (311.15 K) and 27°C (300.15 K).

(*a*) Assume isentropic compression of the vapor.

(*b*) Assume a compressor efficiency of 75%.

9.14. A heat pump is used to heat a house in the winter and to cool it in the summer. During the winter, the outside air serves as a low-temperature heat source; during the summer, it acts as a high-temperature heat sink. The heat-transfer rate through the walls and roof of the house is 0.75 kJ s^{-1} for each °C of temperature difference between the inside and outside of the house, summer and winter. The heat-pump motor is rated at 1.5 kW. Determine the minimum outside temperature for which the house can be maintained at 20°C (293.15 K) during the winter and the maximum outside temperature for which the house can be maintained at 25°C (298.15 K) during the summer.

9.15. Dry methane is supplied by a compressor and precooling system to the cooler of a Linde liquid-methane system (Fig. 9.6) at 180 bar and 300 K. The low-pressure methane leaves the cooler at a temperature 6°C (6 K) lower than the temperature of the incoming high-pressure methane. The separator operates at 1 bar, and the product is saturated liquid at this pressure. What is the maximum fraction of the methane entering the cooler that can be liquefied? *Perry's Chemical Engineers' Handbook* (footnote 7) is a source of data for methane.

9.16. Rework the preceding problem for methane entering at 200 bar, and precooled to 240 K by external refrigeration.

9.17. An advertisement is noted in a rural newspaper for a dairy-barn unit that combines a milk cooler with a water heater. Milk must, of course, be refrigerated, and hot water is required for washing purposes. The usual barn is equipped with a conventional air-cooled electric refrigerator and an electric-resistance water heater. The new unit is said to provide both the necessary refrigeration and the required hot water at a cost for electricity about the same as the cost of running just the refrigerator in the usual installation. To assess this claim, compare two refrigeration units: The advertised unit takes 14.65 kW from a milk cooler at −1°C (272.15 K), and discards heat through a condenser at 66°C (338.15 K) to raise the temperature of water from 13°C (286.15 K) to 63°C (336.15 K). The conventional unit takes the same amount of heat from the same milk cooler at −1°C (272.15 K) and discards heat through an air-cooled condenser at 13°C (286.15 K); in addition, the same amount of water is heated electrically from 13°C (286.15 K) to 63°C (336.15 K). Estimate the *total* electric power requirements for the two cases, assuming that the actual work in both is 50% greater than required by Carnot refrigerators operating between the given temperatures.

9.18. A two-stage cascade refrigeration system (see Fig. 9.3) operates between $T_C = 210$ K and $T_H = 305$ K. Intermediate temperatures are $T'_C = 255$ K and $T'_H = 260$ K. Coefficients of performance ω of each stage are 65% of the corresponding values for a Carnot refrigerator. Determine ω for the real cascade, and compare it with that for a Carnot refrigerator operating between T_C and T_H.

9.19. Do a parametric study for the Claude liquefaction process treated in Sec. 9.6 and Ex. 9.3. In particular, show numerically the effect of changing the draw-off ratio x on other process variables. *Perry's Chemical Engineers' Handbook* (footnote 7) is a source of data for methane.

9.20. The condenser of a home refrigerator is commonly underneath the appliance; thus, the condensing refrigerant exchanges heat with household air, which has an average temperature of about 21°C (294.15 K). It is proposed to reconfigure a refrigerator so that the condenser is *outside* the home, where the average yearly temperature is about 10°C (283.15 K). Discuss the pros and cons of this proposal. Assume a freezer temperature of −18°C (255.15 K), and an actual coefficient of performance 60% that of a Carnot refrigerator.

9.21. A common misconception is that the coefficient of performance of a refrigerator must be less than unity. In fact, this is rarely the case. To see why, consider a real refrigerator for which $\omega = 0.6\omega_{\text{Carnot}}$. What condition must be satisfied in order that $\omega < 1$? Assume that T_H is fixed.

9.22. A furnace fails in a home in the winter. Mercifully, the electric power remains on. The resident engineer tells her spouse not to worry; they'll move into the kitchen, where the heat discarded from the refrigerator may provide for a temporarily comfortable living space. However (the engineer is reminded), the kitchen loses heat to the outdoors. Use the following data to determine the allowable rate of heat loss (kW) from the kitchen for the engineer's proposal to make sense.

Data: Desired kitchen temperature = 290 K
Refrigerator freezer temperature = 250 K
Average mechanical power input to refrigerator = 0.40 kW
Performance: Actual ω = 65% of Carnot ω

9.23. Fifty kmol h^{-1} of liquid toluene at 1.2 bar is cooled from 100 to 20°C (373.15 K to 293.15 K). A vapor-compression refrigeration cycle is used for the purpose. Ammonia is the working fluid. Condensation in the cycle is effected by an air-cooled fin/fan heat exchanger for which the air temperature may be assumed essentially constant at 20°C (293.15 K). Determine:

(*a*) The low and high pressure levels (bar) in the refrigeration cycle.
(*b*) The circulation rate of ammonia (mol s^{-1}).

Assume 10°C (10 K) minimum approach ΔTs for heat exchange. Data for ammonia:

$$\Delta H_n^{lv} = 23.34 \text{ kJ mol}^{-1}$$

$$\ln P^{\text{sat}} = 45.327 - \frac{4104.67}{T} - 5.146 \ln T + 615.0 \frac{P^{\text{sat}}}{T^2}$$

where P^{sat} is in bars and T is in kelvins.

Chapter 10

Vapor/Liquid Equilibrium: Introduction

Preceding chapters have dealt largely with pure substances or with constant-composition mixtures. e.g., air. However, composition changes are the desired outcome, not only of chemical reactions, but of a number of industrially important mass-transfer operations. Thus composition becomes a primary variable in the remaining chapters of this text. Processes such as distillation, absorption, and extraction bring phases of different composition into contact, and when the phases are not in equilibrium, mass transfer between the phases alters their compositions. Both the extent of change and the rate of transfer depend on the departure of the system from equilibrium. Thus, for quantitative treatment of mass transfer the equilibrium T, P, and phase compositions must be known.

The most commonly encountered coexisting phases in industrial practice are vapor and liquid, although liquid/liquid, vapor/solid, and liquid/solid systems are also found. In this chapter we first discuss the nature of equilibrium, and then consider two rules that give the number of independent variables required to determine equilibrium states. There follows in Sec. 10.3 a qualitative discussion of vapor/liquid phase behavior. In Sec. 10.4 we introduce the two simplest formulations that allow calculation of temperatures, pressures, and phase compositions for systems in vapor/liquid equilibrium. The first, known as Raoult's law, is valid only for systems at low to moderate pressures and in general only for systems comprised of chemically similar species. The second, known as Henry's law, is valid for any species present at low concentration, but as presented here is also limited to systems at low to moderate pressures. A modification of Raoult's law that removes the restriction to chemically similar species is treated in Sec. 10.5. Finally in Sec. 10.6 calculations based on equilibrium ratios or K-values are considered. The treatment of vapor/liquid equilibrium is developed further in Chaps. 12 and 14.

10.1 THE NATURE OF EQUILIBRIUM

Equilibrium is a static condition in which no changes occur in the macroscopic properties of a system with time. This implies a balance of all potentials that may cause change. In engineering practice, the assumption of equilibrium is justified when it leads to results of satisfactory accuracy. For example, in the reboiler for a distillation column, equilibrium between vapor and liquid phases is commonly assumed. For finite vaporization rates this is an approximation, but it does not introduce significant error into engineering calculations.

An isolated system consisting of liquid and vapor phases in intimate contact eventually reaches a final state wherein no tendency exists for change to occur within the system. The temperature, pressure, and phase compositions reach final values which thereafter remain fixed. The system is in equilibrium. Nevertheless, at the microscopic level, conditions are not static. The molecules comprising a phase at a given instant are not the same molecules that later occupy the same phase. Molecules with sufficiently high velocities near the interface overcome surface forces and pass into the other phase. However, the average rate of passage of molecules is the same in both directions, and no net interphase transfer of material occurs.

Measures of Composition

The three most common measures of composition are mass fraction, mole fraction, and molar concentration. Mass or mole fraction is defined as the ratio of the mass or number of moles of a particular chemical species in a mixture or solution to the total mass or number of moles of mixture or solution:

$$x_i \equiv \frac{m_i}{m} = \frac{\dot{m}_i}{\dot{m}} \qquad \text{or} \qquad x_i \equiv \frac{n_i}{n} = \frac{\dot{n}_i}{\dot{n}}$$

Molar concentration is defined as the ratio of the mole fraction of a particular chemical species in a mixture or solution to the molar volume of the mixture or solution:

$$C_i \equiv \frac{x_i}{V}$$

This quantity has units of moles of i per unit volume. For flow processes convenience suggests its expression as a ratio of rates. Multiplying and dividing by molar flow rate $\dot{n}$ gives

$$C_i = \frac{\dot{n}_i}{q}$$

where $\dot{n}_i$ is molar flow rate of species i, and q is volumetric flow rate.

The molar mass of a mixture or solution is, by definition, the mole-fraction-weighted sum of the molar masses of all species present:

$$M \equiv \sum_i x_i M_i$$

10.2 THE PHASE RULE; DUHEM'S THEOREM

The phase rule for nonreacting systems, presented without proof in Sec. 2.7, results from application of a rule of algebra. Thus, the number of variables that may be independently fixed in a system at equilibrium is the difference between the total number of variables that characterize the intensive state of the system and the number of independent equations that can be written connecting the variables.

The *intensive* state of a PVT system containing N chemical species and π phases in equilibrium is characterized by the intensive variables, temperature T, pressure P, and $N - 1$ mole fractions[1] for each phase. The number of these phase-rule variables is $2 + (N - 1)(\pi)$. The masses of the phases are not phase-rule variables, because they have no influence on the intensive state of the system.

As will become clear later in this chapter, an independent phase-equilibrium equation may be written connecting intensive variables for each of the N species for each pair of phases present. Thus, the number of independent phase-equilibrium equations is $(\pi - 1)(N)$. The difference between the number of phase-rule variables and the number of independent equations connecting them is the number of variables that may be independently fixed. Called the degrees of freedom of the system F, the number is

$$F = 2 + (N - 1)(\pi) - (\pi - 1)(N)$$

Upon reduction, this becomes the phase rule:

$$\boxed{F = 2 - \pi + N} \qquad (2.7)$$

Duhem's theorem is another rule, similar to the phase rule, but less celebrated. It applies to closed systems at equilibrium for which the extensive state as well as the intensive state of the system is fixed. The state of such a system is said to be *completely determined*, and is characterized not only by the $2 + (N - 1)\pi$ intensive phase-rule variables but also by the π extensive variables represented by the masses (or mole numbers) of the phases. Thus the total number of variables is:

$$2 + (N - 1)\pi + \pi = 2 + N\pi$$

For a closed system formed from specified amounts of the chemical species present, a material-balance equation can be written for each of the N chemical species. These in addition to the $(\pi - 1)N$ phase-equilibrium equations represent a number of independent equations equal to:

$$(\pi - 1)N + N = \pi N$$

The difference between the number of variables and the number of equations is therefore:

$$2 + N\pi - \pi N = 2$$

On the basis of this result, Duhem's theorem is stated as follows:

For any closed system formed initially from given masses of prescribed chemical species, the equilibrium state is completely determined when any two independent variables are fixed.

The two independent variables subject to specification may in general be either intensive or extensive. However, the number of *independent intensive* variables is given by the phase rule. Thus when $F = 1$, at least one of the two variables must be extensive, and when $F = 0$, both must be extensive.

[1]Only $N - 1$ mole fractions are required, because $\sum_i x_i = 1$.

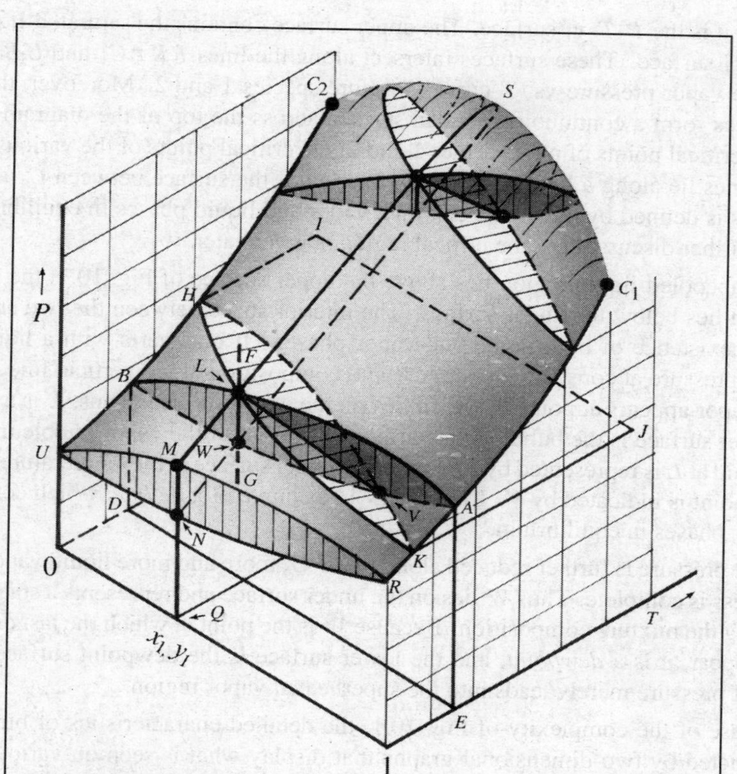

Figure 10.1: *PTxy* diagram for vapor/liquid equilibrium

10.3 VLE: QUALITATIVE BEHAVIOR

Vapor/liquid equilibrium (VLE) is the state of coexistence of liquid and vapor phases. In this qualitative discussion, we limit consideration to systems comprised of two chemical species, because systems of greater complexity cannot be adequately represented graphically.

When $N = 2$, the phase rule becomes $F = 4 - \pi$. Because there must be at least one phase ($\pi = 1$), the maximum number of phase-rule variables which must be specified to fix the intensive state of the system is *three*: namely, P, T, and one mole (or mass) fraction. All equilibrium states of the system can therefore be represented in three-dimensional P-T-composition space. Within this space, the states of *pairs* of phases coexisting at equilibrium ($F = 4 - 2 = 2$) define surfaces. A schematic three-dimensional diagram illustrating these surfaces for VLE is shown in Fig. 10.1.

This figure shows schematically the P-T-composition surfaces which contain the equilibrium states of saturated vapor and saturated liquid for species 1 and 2 of a binary system. Here, species 1 is the "lighter" or more volatile. The under surface contains the saturated-vapor states; it is the P-T-y_1 surface. The upper surface contains the saturated-liquid states; it is the P-T-x_1 surface. These surfaces intersect along the lines $RKAC_1$ and $UBHC_2$, which represent the vapor pressure-vs.-T curves for pure species 1 and 2. Moreover, the under and upper surfaces form a continuous rounded surface across the top of the diagram between C_1 and C_2, the critical points of pure species 1 and 2; the critical points of the various mixtures of the two species lie along a line on the rounded edge of the surface between C_1 and C_2. This critical locus is defined by the points at which vapor and liquid phases in equilibrium become identical. Further discussion of the critical region is given later.

The subcooled-liquid region lies above the upper surface of Fig. 10.1; the superheated-vapor region lies below the under surface. The interior space between the two surfaces is the region of coexistence of both liquid and vapor phases. If one starts with a liquid at F and reduces the pressure at constant temperature and composition along vertical line FG, the first bubble of vapor appears at point L, which lies on the upper surface. Thus, L is a *bubblepoint*, and the upper surface is the bubblepoint surface. The state of the vapor bubble in equilibrium with the liquid at L is represented by a point on the under surface at the temperature and pressure of L. This point is indicated by V. Line LV is an example of a *tie line*, which connects points representing phases in equilibrium.

As the pressure is further reduced along line FG, more and more liquid vaporizes until at W the process is complete. Thus W lies on the under surface and represents a state of saturated vapor having the mixture composition. Because W is the point at which the last drops of liquid (dew) disappear, it is a *dewpoint*, and the lower surface is the dewpoint surface. Continued reduction of pressure merely leads into the superheated vapor region.

Because of the complexity of Fig. 10.1, the detailed characteristics of binary VLE are usually depicted by two-dimensional graphs that display what is seen on various planes that cut the three-dimensional diagram. The three principal planes, each perpendicular to one of the coordinate axes, are illustrated in Fig. 10.1. Thus a vertical plane perpendicular to the temperature axis is outlined as $AEDBLA$. The lines on this plane form a P-x_1-y_1 phase diagram at constant T. If the lines from several such planes are projected on a single parallel plane, a diagram like Fig. 10.2(a) is obtained. It shows P-x_1-y_1 plots for three different temperatures. The one for T_a represents the section of Fig. 10.1 indicated by $AEDBLA$. The horizontal lines are tie lines connecting the compositions of phases in equilibrium. The temperatures T_b and T_d lie between the two pure-species critical temperatures identified by C_1 and C_2 in Fig. 10.1. The curves for these two temperatures therefore do not extend all the way across the diagram. The mixture critical points are denoted by the letter C. Each is a tangent point at which a horizontal line touches the curve. This is so because all tie lines connecting phases in equilibrium are horizontal, and the tie line connecting *identical* phases (the definition of a critical point) must therefore be the last such line to cut the diagram.

A horizontal plane passed through Fig. 10.1 perpendicular to the P axis is identified by $KJIHLK$. Viewed from the top, the lines on this plane represent a T-x_1-y_1 diagram. When lines for several pressures are projected on a parallel plane, the resulting diagram appears as in Fig. 10.2(b). This figure is analogous to Fig. 10.2(a), except that it represents phase behavior for three constant pressures, P_a, P_b, and P_d. The one for P_a represents the section of Fig. 10.1 indicated by $KJIHLK$. Pressure P_b lies between the critical pressures of the two pure species at points C_1 and C_2. Pressure P_d is above the critical pressures of *both* pure species; therefore, the T-x_1-y_1 diagram appears as an "island." Similar P-x_1-y_1 behavior [Fig. 10.2(a)] is unusual.

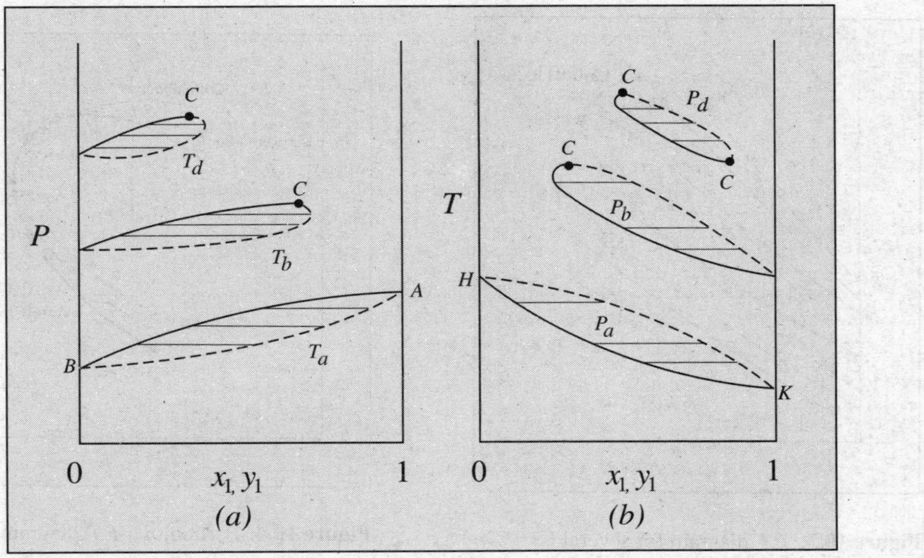

Figure 10.2: (*a*) *Pxy* diagram for three temperatures (*b*) *Txy* diagram for three pressures
—— Saturated liquid (bubble line); - - - Saturated vapor (dew line)

Other possible plots are vapor mole fraction y_1 vs. liquid mole fraction x_1 for either the constant-T conditions of Fig. 10.2(*a*) or the constant-P conditions of Fig. 10.2(*b*).

The third plane identified in Fig. 10.1, vertical and perpendicular to the composition axis, passes through points $SLMN$ and Q. When projected on a parallel plane, the lines from several planes form a diagram such as shown by Fig. 10.3. This is the P-T diagram; lines UC_2 and RC_1 are vapor-pressure curves for the pure species, identified by the same letters as in Fig. 10.1. Each interior loop represents the P-T behavior of saturated liquid and of saturated vapor for a *mixture of fixed composition*; the different loops are for different compositions. Clearly, the P-T relation for saturated liquid is different from that for saturated vapor of the same composition. This is in contrast with the behavior of a pure species, for which the bubble and dew lines coincide. At points A and B in Fig. 10.3 saturated-liquid and saturated-vapor lines intersect. At such points a saturated liquid of one composition and a saturated vapor of another composition have the same T and P, and the two phases are therefore in equilibrium. The tie lines connecting the coinciding points at A and at B are perpendicular to the P-T plane, as illustrated by the tie line LV in Fig. 10.1.

The critical point of a binary mixture occurs where the nose of a loop in Fig. 10.3 is tangent to the envelope curve. Put another way, the envelope curve is the critical locus. One can verify this by considering two closely adjacent loops and noting what happens to the point of intersection as their separation becomes infinitesimal. Figure 10.3 shows that the location of the critical point on the nose of the loop varies with composition. For a pure species the critical point is the highest temperature and highest pressure at which vapor and liquid phases can coexist, but for a mixture it is in general neither. Therefore under certain conditions a condensation process occurs as the result of a *reduction* in pressure.

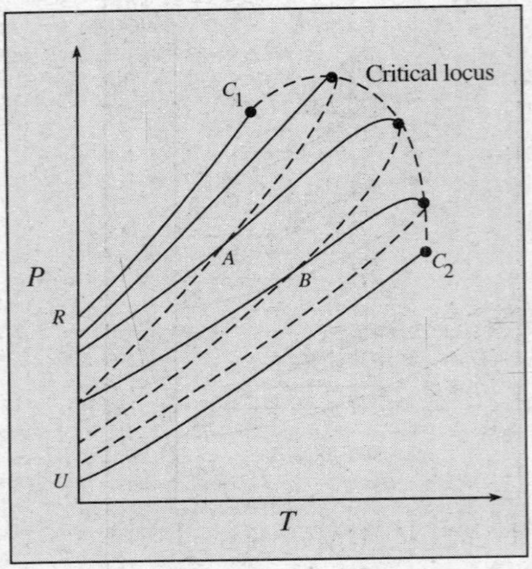

Figure 10.3: PT diagram for several compositions
—— Saturated liquid (bubble line)
– – – Saturated vapor (dew line)

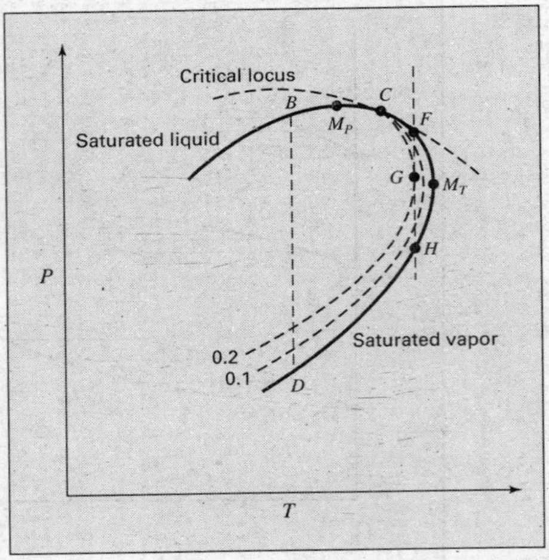

Figure 10.4: Portion of a PT diagram in the critical region

Consider the enlarged nose section of a single P-T loop shown in Fig.10.4. The critical point is at C. The points of maximum pressure and maximum temperature are identified as M_P and M_T. The interior dashed curves indicate the fraction of the overall system that is liquid in a two-phase mixture of liquid and vapor. To the left of the critical point C a reduction in pressure along a line such as BD is accompanied by vaporization of liquid from bubblepoint to dewpoint, as would be expected. However, if the original condition corresponds to point F, a state of saturated *vapor*, liquefaction occurs upon reduction of the pressure and reaches a maximum at point G, after which vaporization takes place until the dewpoint is reached at point H. This phenomenon is called *retrograde condensation*. It can be important in the operation of deep natural-gas wells where the pressure and temperature in the underground formation may be at conditions represented by point F. If the pressure at the wellhead is that of point G, the product stream from the well is an equilibrium mixture of liquid and vapor. Because the less-volatile species are concentrated in the liquid phase, significant separation is accomplished. Within the underground formation itself, the pressure tends to drop as the gas supply is depleted. If not prevented, this leads to the formation of a liquid phase and a consequent reduction in the production of the well. Repressuring is therefore a common practice; i.e., lean gas (gas from which the less-volatile species have been removed) is returned to the underground reservoir to maintain an elevated pressure.

A P-T diagram for the ethane(1)/n-heptane(2) system is shown in Fig. 10.5, and a y_1-x_1 diagram for several pressures for the same system appears in Fig. 10.6. According to convention, one plots as y_1 and x_1 the mole fractions of the more volatile species in the mixture. The maximum and minimum concentrations of the more volatile species obtainable by distillation at a given pressure are indicated by the points of intersection of the appropriate y_1-x_1 curve

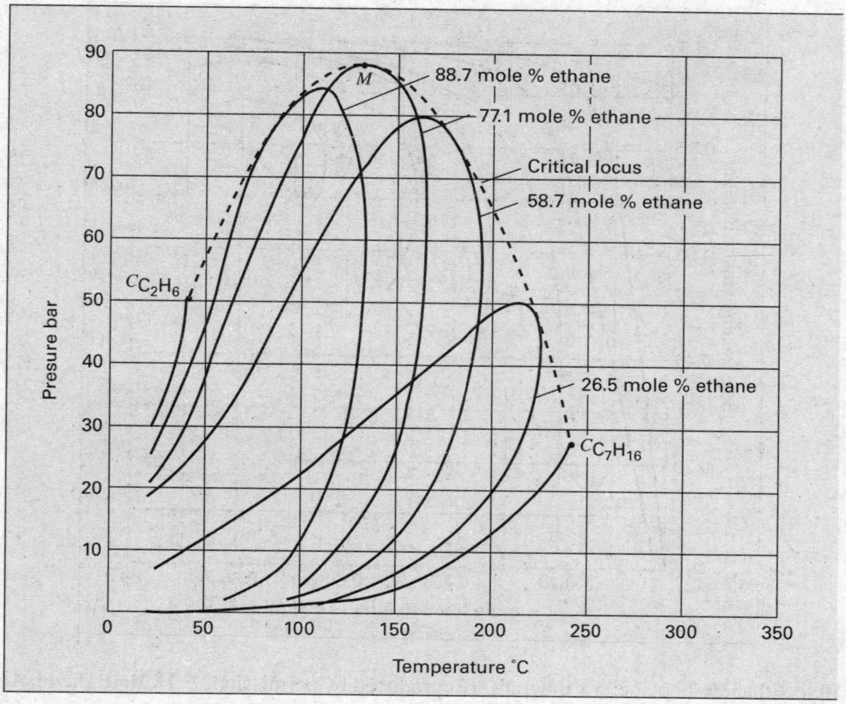

Figure 10.5: Ethane/*n*-heptane: *PT* diagram. (Reproduced by permission. F. H. Barr-David, *AIChE J.*, vol. 2, pp. 426–427, 1956.)

with the diagonal, for at these points the vapor and liquid have the same composition. They are in fact mixture critical points, unless $y_1 = x_1 = 0$ or $y_1 = x_1 = 1$. Point *A* in Fig. 10.6 represents the composition of the vapor and liquid phases at the maximum pressure at which the phases can coexist in the ethane/*n*-heptane system. The composition is about 77 mol-% ethane and the pressure is about 87.1 bar. The corresponding point on Fig. 10.5 is labeled *M*. A complete set of consistent phase diagrams for this system has been prepared by Barr-David.[2]

The *P*-*T* diagram of Fig. 10.5 is typical for mixtures of nonpolar substances such as hydrocarbons. A *P*-*T* diagram for a very different kind of system, methanol(1)/benzene(2), is shown in Fig. 10.7. The nature of the curves in this figure suggests how difficult it can be to predict phase behavior for species so dissimilar as methanol and benzene.

Although VLE in the critical region is of considerable importance in the petroleum and natural-gas industries, most chemical processing is accomplished at much lower pressures. Figures 10.8 and 10.9 display common types of *P*-*x*-*y* and *t*-*x*-*y* behavior at conditions well removed from the critical region.

Figure 10.8(*a*) shows data for tetrahydrofuran(1)/carbon tetrachloride(2) at 30°C (303.15 K). Here, the P-x_1 or bubblepoint curve on a P-x_1-y_1 diagram lies below the linear P-x_1 relation characteristic of Raoult's-law behavior, as described in the following section. When such

[2]F. H. Barr-David, *AIChE J.*, vol. 2, p. 426, 1956.

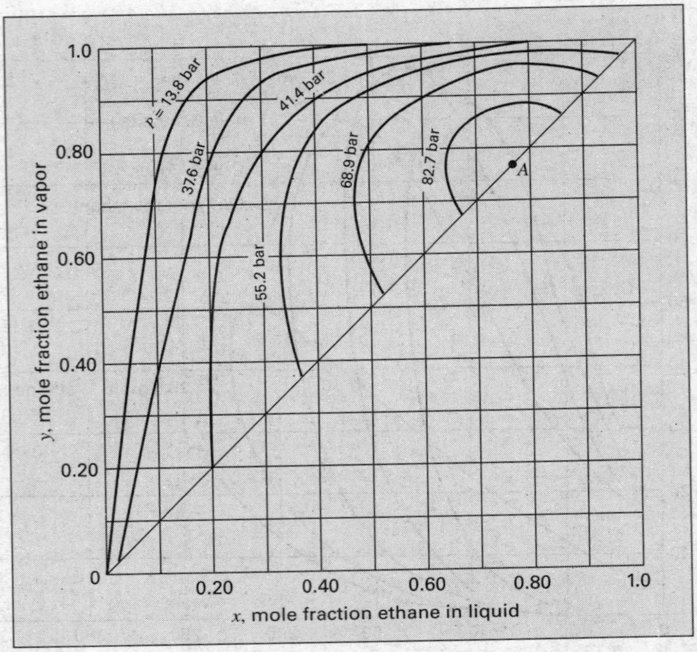

Figure 10.6: Ethane/*n*-heptane: *yx* diagram. (Reproduced by permission. F. H. Barr-David, *AIChE J.*, vol. 2, p. 426–427, 1956.)

negative departures from linearity become sufficiently large relative to the difference between the two pure-species vapor pressures, the P-x curve exhibits a minimum, as illustrated in Fig. 10.8(*b*) for the chloroform(1)/tetrahydrofuran(2) system at 30°C (303.15 K). This figure shows that the P-y_1 curve also has a minimum at the same point. Thus at this point where $x_1 = y_1$ the dewpoint and bubblepoint curves are tangent to the same horizontal line. A boiling liquid of this composition produces a vapor of exactly the same composition, and the liquid therefore does not change in composition as it evaporates. No separation of such a constant-boiling solution is possible by distillation. The term *azeotrope* is used to describe this state.[3]

The data for furan(1)/carbon tetrachloride(2) at 30°C (303.15 K) shown by Fig. 10.8(*c*) provide an example of a system for which the P-x_1 curve lies above the linear P-x_1 relation. The system shown in Fig. 10.8(*d*) for ethanol(1)/toluene(2) at 65°C (338.15 K) exhibits positive departures from linearity sufficiently large to cause a *maximum* in the P-x_1 curve. This state is a maximum-pressure azeotrope. Just as for the minimum-pressure azeotrope the vapor and liquid phases in equilibrium have the identical composition.

Appreciable negative departures from P-x_1 linearity reflect stronger liquid-phase intermolecular attractions between unlike than between like pairs of molecules. Conversely, appreciable positive departures result for solutions for which liquid-phase intermolecular forces between like molecules are stronger than between unlike. In this latter case the forces between

[3]A compilation of data for such states is given by J. Gmehling, *Azeotropic Data*, John Wiley & Sons, Inc., New York, 1994.

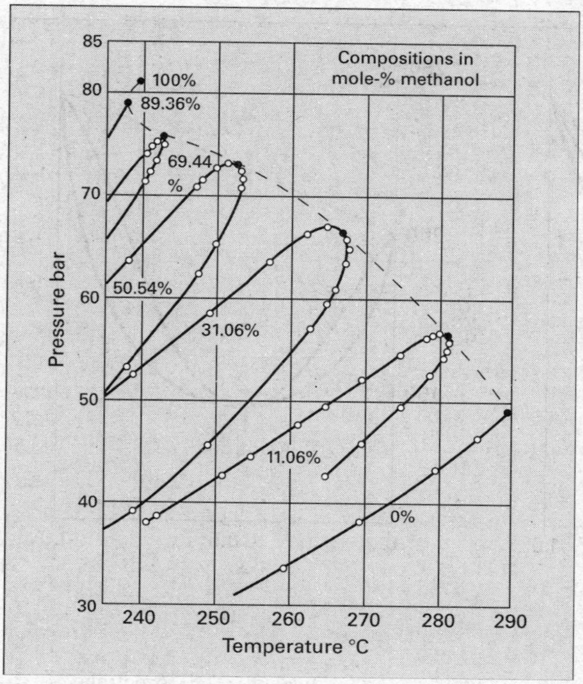

Figure 10.7: *PT* diagram for methanol/benzene (redrawn from *Chem. Eng. Sci.*, vol. 19, J. M. Skaates and W. B. Kay, "The phase relations of binary systems that form azeotropes," pp. 431–444, copyright 1964, with permission from Elsevier Science Ltd., Pergamon Imprint, The Boulevard, Langford Lane, Kidlington OX5 1GB, UK)

like molecules may be so strong as to prevent complete miscibility, and the system then forms two separate liquid phases over a range of compositions, as described in Sec. 14.4.

Because distillation processes are carried out more nearly at constant pressure than at constant temperature, t-x_1-y_1 diagrams of data at constant P are of practical interest. The four such diagrams corresponding to those of Fig. 10.8 are shown for atmospheric pressure in Fig. 10.9. Note that the dewpoint (t-y_1) curves lie above the bubblepoint (t-x_1) curves. Moreover, the minimum-pressure azeotrope of Fig. 10.8(b) appears as a maximum-temperature (or maximum-boiling) azeotrope on Fig. 10.9(b). An analogous correspondence exists between Figs. 10.8(d) and 10.9(d). The y_1-x_1 diagrams at constant P for the same four systems are shown in Fig. 10.10. The point at which a curve crosses the diagonal line of the diagram represents an azeotrope, for at such a point $y_1 = x_1$.

10.4 SIMPLE MODELS FOR VAPOR/LIQUID EQUILIBRIUM

The preceding section describes what is observed through experiment. When thermodynamics is applied to vapor/liquid equilibrium, the goal is to find by calculation the temperatures, pressures, and compositions of phases in equilibrium. Indeed, thermodynamics provides the mathematical framework for the systematic correlation, extension, generalization, evaluation, and interpretation of data. Moreover, it is the means by which the predictions of various theories of molecular physics and statistical mechanics may be applied to practical purposes. None of this can be accomplished without *models* for the behavior of systems in vapor/liquid equilibrium. The two simplest are Raoult's law and Henry's law.

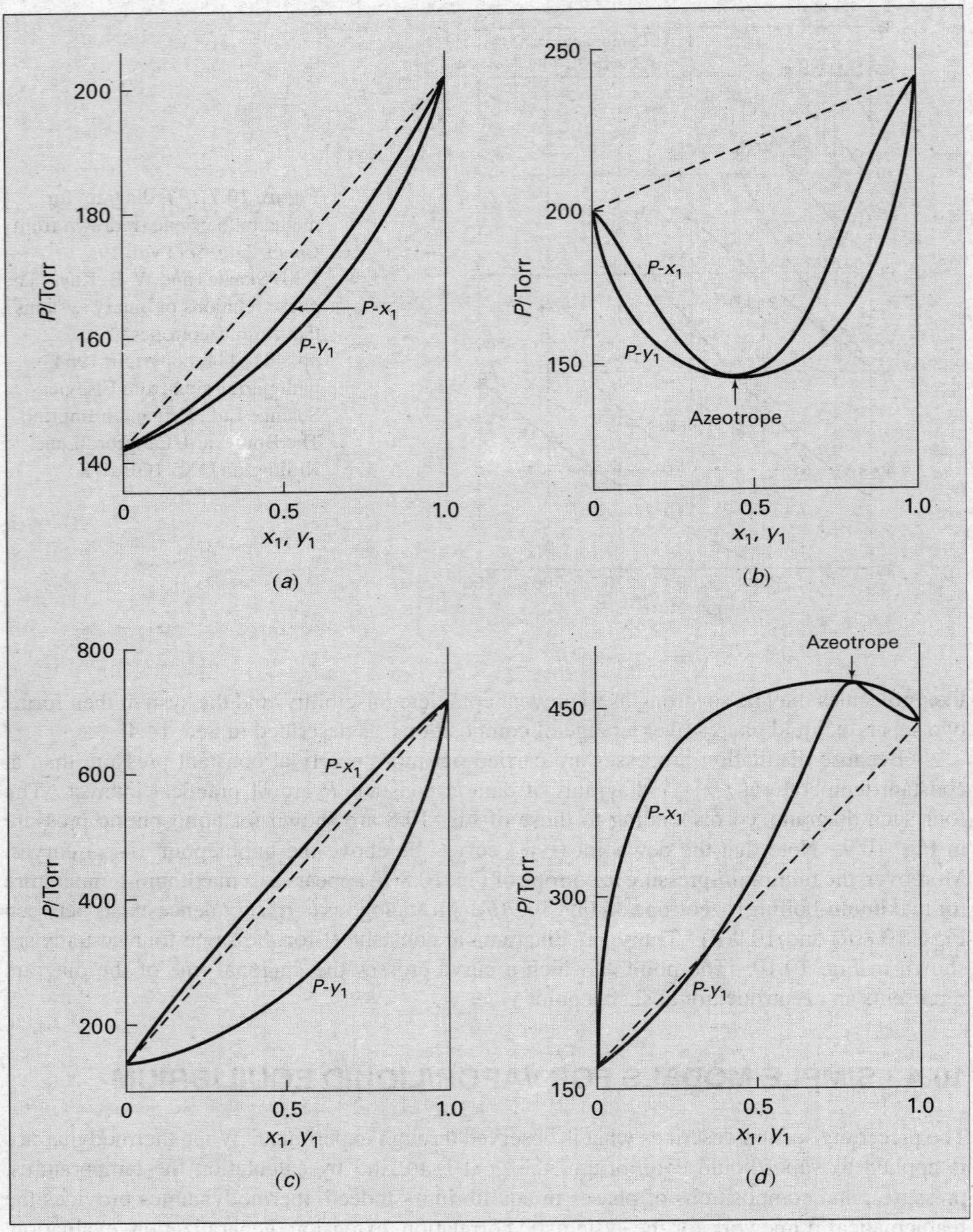

Figure 10.8: Pxy diagrams at constant T: (*a*) tetrahydrofuran(1)/carbon tetrachloride(2) at 30°C (303.15 K); (*b*) chloroform(1)/tetrahydrofuran(2) at 30°C (303.15 K); (*c*) furan(1)/carbon tetrachloride(2) at 30°C (303.15 K); (*d*) ethanol(1)/toluene(2) at 65°C (338.15 K). Dashed lines: Px relation for Raoult's law

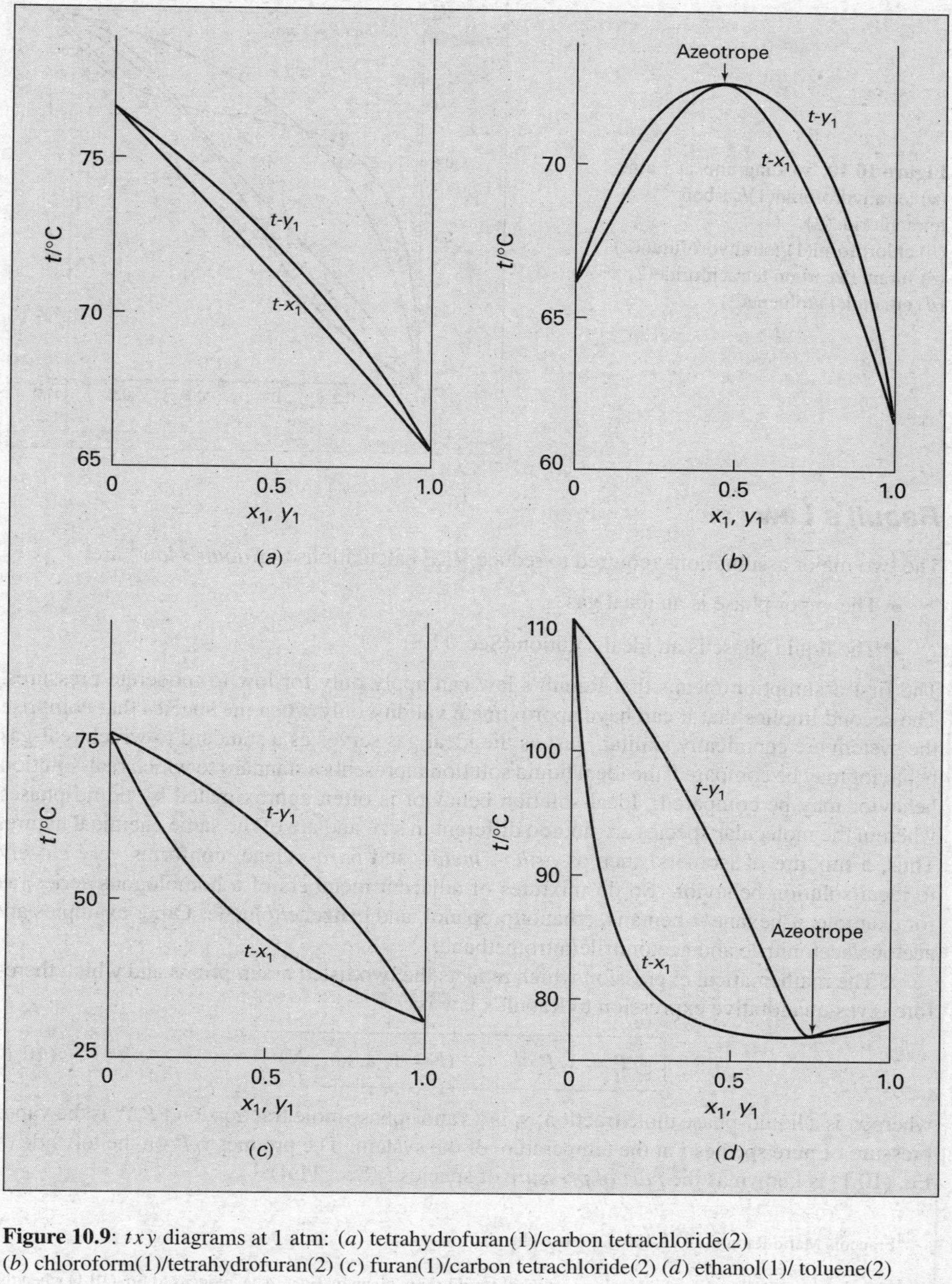

Figure 10.9: txy diagrams at 1 atm: (*a*) tetrahydrofuran(1)/carbon tetrachloride(2) (*b*) chloroform(1)/tetrahydrofuran(2) (*c*) furan(1)/carbon tetrachloride(2) (*d*) ethanol(1)/ toluene(2)

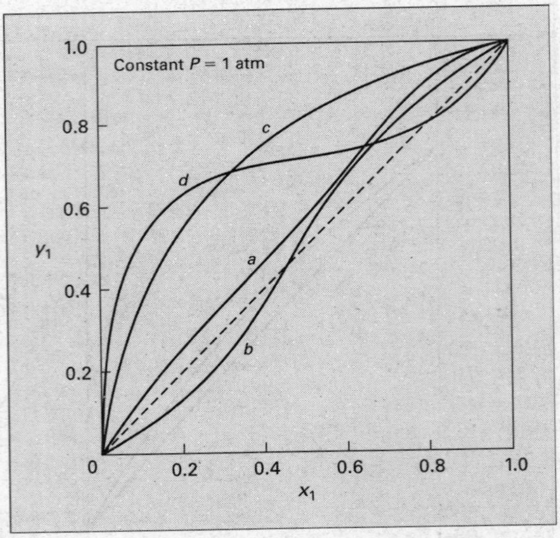

Figure 10.10: yx diagrams at 1 atm:
(*a*) tetrahydrofuran(1)/carbon tetrachloride(2)
(*b*) chloroform(1)/tetrahydrofuran(2)
(*c*) furan(1)/carbon tetrachloride(2)
(*d*) ethanol(1)/toluene(2)

Raoult's Law

The two major assumptions required to reduce VLE calculations to *Raoult's law*[4] are

- The vapor phase is an ideal gas
- The liquid phase is an ideal solution (Sec. 11.8)

The first assumption means that Raoult's law can apply only for low to moderate pressures. The second implies that it can have approximate validity only when the species that comprise the system are chemically similar. Just as the ideal gas serves as a standard to which real-gas behavior may be compared, the ideal liquid solution represents a standard to which real-solution behavior may be compared. Ideal-solution behavior is often approximated by liquid phases wherein the molecular species are not too different in size and are of the same chemical nature. Thus, a mixture of isomers, such as *ortho*-, *meta*-, and *para*-xylene, conforms very closely to ideal-solution behavior. So do mixtures of adjacent members of a homologous series, as for example, n-hexane/n-heptane, ethanol/propanol, and benzene/toluene. Other examples are acetone/acetonitrile and acetonitrile/nitromethane.

The mathematical expression which reflects the two listed assumptions and which therefore gives quantitative expression to Raoult's law is[5]

$$\boxed{y_i P = x_i P_i^{sat} \qquad (i = 1, 2, \ldots, N)} \tag{10.1}$$

where x_i is a liquid-phase mole fraction, y_i is a vapor-phase mole fraction, and P_i^{sat} is the vapor pressure of pure species i at the temperature of the system. The product $y_i P$ on the left side of Eq. (10.1) is known as the *partial pressure* of species i (Sec. 11.4).

[4]Francois Marie Raoult (1830–1901), French chemist.

[5]The rigorous equation for subcritical vapor/liquid equilibrium, given by Eq. (14.1), reduces to Eq. (10.1) when the two listed assumptions are imposed.

The simple model for VLE represented by Eq. (10.1) provides a realistic description of actual behavior for a relatively small class of systems. Nevertheless, it is useful for displaying VLE calculations in their simplest form, and it also serves as a standard of comparison for more complex systems. A limitation of Raoult's law is that it can be applied only to species of known vapor pressure, and this requires the species to be "subcritical," i.e., to be at a temperature below its critical temperature.

An important and useful feature of Raoult's law is that it is valid for *any species* present at a mole fraction approaching unity, provided only that the vapor phase is an ideal gas. Chemical similarity of the constituent species is not here a requirement.

Dewpoint and Bubblepoint Calculations with Raoult's Law

Although VLE problems with other combinations of variables are possible, engineering interest centers on dewpoint and bubblepoint calculations; there are four classes:

BUBL P:	Calculate $\{y_i\}$ and P, given $\{x_i\}$ and T
DEW P:	Calculate $\{x_i\}$ and P, given $\{y_i\}$ and T
BUBL T:	Calculate $\{y_i\}$ and T, given $\{x_i\}$ and P
DEW T:	Calculate $\{x_i\}$ and T, given $\{y_i\}$ and P

In each case the name indicates the quantities to be calculated: either a *BUBL* (vapor) or a *DEW* (liquid) composition *and* either P or T. Thus, one must specify either the liquid-phase or the vapor-phase composition *and* either P or T, thus fixing $1 + (N - 1)$ or N phase-rule variables, exactly the number of degrees of freedom F required by the phase rule [Eq. (2.7)] for vapor/liquid equilibrium. The rigorous solution of VLE problems is provided by equations with complex functionality, and their use to determine bubblepoints and dewpoints requires iterative calculations (Secs. 14.1 and 14.2). In the following sections calculations are made for conditions where simplifying assumptions prevail. The general procedures for solution of VLE problems thus become evident through calculations of relative simplicity. We focus first on the application of Raoult's law.

Because $\sum_i y_i = 1$, Eq. (10.1) may be summed over all species to yield

$$P = \sum_i x_i P_i^{sat} \tag{10.2}$$

This equation finds application in bubblepoint calculations, where the vapor-phase composition is unknown. For a binary system with $x_2 = 1 - x_1$,

$$P = P_2^{sat} + (P_1^{sat} - P_2^{sat})x_1$$

and a plot of P vs. x_1 at constant temperature is a straight line connecting P_2^{sat} at $x_1 = 0$ with P_1^{sat} at $x_1 = 1$. The P-x-y diagrams of Fig. 10.8 show this linear relation.

Equation (10.1) may also be solved for x_i and summed over all species. With $\sum_i x_i = 1$, this yields

$$P = \frac{1}{\sum_i y_i / P_i^{sat}} \tag{10.3}$$

an equation applied in dewpoint calculations, where liquid-phase compositions are not known.

Example 10.1

Binary system acetonitrile(1)/nitromethane(2) conforms closely to Raoult's law. Vapor pressures for the pure species are given by the following Antoine equations:

$$\ln P_1^{sat}/\text{kPa} = 14.2724 - \frac{2945.47}{T - 49.15}$$

$$\ln P_2^{sat}/\text{kPa} = 14.2043 - \frac{2972.64}{T - 64.15}$$

(*a*) Prepare a graph showing P vs. x_1 and P vs. y_1 for a temperature of 75°C (348.15 K).

(*b*) Prepare a graph showing t vs. x_1 and t vs. y_1 for a pressure of 70 kPa.

Solution

(*a*) *BUBL P* calculations are required. The basis is the binary-system form of Eq. (10.2), repeated here as:

$$P = P_2^{sat} + (P_1^{sat} - P_2^{sat})x_1 \qquad (A)$$

At 348.15 K (75°C), by the Antoine equations,

$$P_1^{sat} = 83.21 \qquad \text{and} \qquad P_2^{sat} = 41.98 \text{ kPa}$$

Calculations are here very simple, as illustrated for $x_1 = 0.6$:

$$P = 41.98 + (83.21 - 41.98)(0.6) = 66.72 \text{ kPa}$$

The corresponding value of y_1 is then found from Eq. (10.1):

$$y_1 = \frac{x_1 P_1^{sat}}{P} = \frac{(0.6)(83.21)}{66.72} = 0.7483$$

These results mean that at 75°C (348.15 K) a liquid mixture of 60 mole % acetonitrile and 40 mole % nitromethane is in equilibrium with a vapor containing 74.83 mole % acetonitrile at a pressure of 66.72 kPa. The results of calculations for 75°C (348.15 K) at a number of values of x_1 are tabulated as follows:

x_1	y_1	P/kPa	x_1	y_1	P/kPa
0.0	0.0000	41.98	0.6	0.7483	66.72
0.2	0.3313	50.23	0.8	0.8880	74.96
0.4	0.5692	58.47	1.0	1.0000	83.21

These same results are shown by the P-x_1-y_1 diagram of Fig. 10.11. This figure is a phase diagram on which the straight line labeled P-x_1 represents states of saturated liquid; the subcooled-liquid region lies above this line. The curve

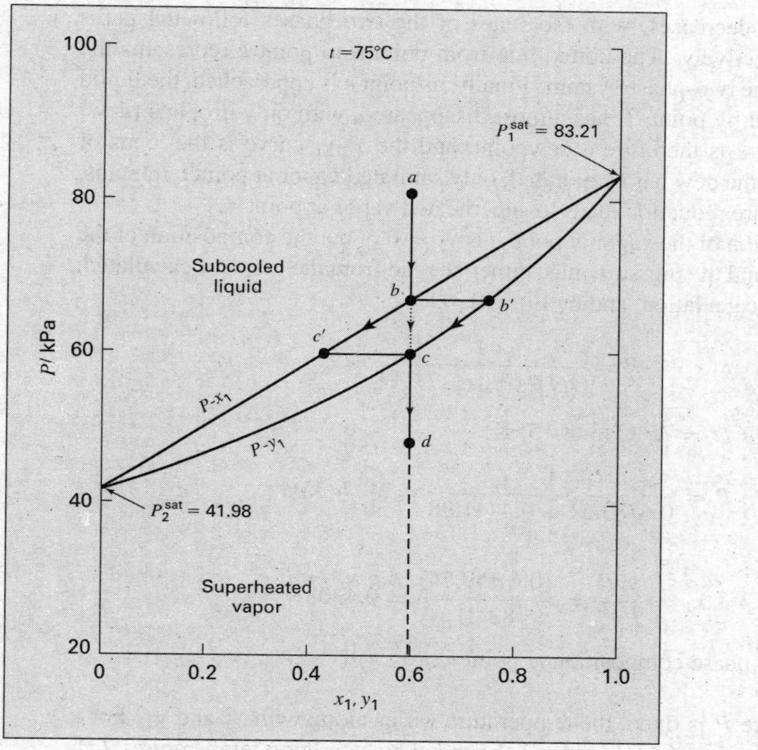

Figure 10.11: Pxy diagram for acetonitrile(1)/nitromethane(2) at 75°C (348.15 K) as given by Raoult's law

labeled P-y_1 represents states of saturated vapor; the superheated-vapor region lies below this curve. Points lying between the saturated-liquid and saturated-vapor lines are in the two-phase region, where saturated liquid and saturated vapor coexist in equilibrium. The P-x_1 and P-y_1 lines meet at the edges of the diagram, where saturated liquid and saturated vapor of the pure species coexist at the vapor pressures P_1^{sat} and P_2^{sat}.

To illustrate the nature of phase behavior in this binary system we follow the course of a constant-temperature process on the P-x_1-y_1 diagram. Imagine a subcooled liquid mixture of 60 mole % acetonitrile and 40 mole % nitromethane existing in a piston/cylinder arrangement at 75°C (348.15 K). Its state is represented by point a in Fig. 10.11. Withdrawing the piston slowly enough reduces the pressure while maintaining the system at equilibrium at 75°C (348.15 K). Since the system is closed, the overall composition remains constant during the process, and the states of the system *as a whole* fall on the vertical line descending from point a. When the pressure reaches the value at point b, the system is saturated liquid on the verge of vaporizing. A minuscule further decrease in pressure produces a bubble of vapor, represented by point b'. The two points b and b' ($x_1 = 0.6$, $P = 66.72$ kPa, and $y_1 = 0.7483$) together represent the state determined by earlier calculations. Point b is a bubblepoint, and the P-x_1 line is the locus of bubblepoints.

As the pressure is further reduced, the amount of vapor increases and the amount of liquid decreases, with the states of the two phases following paths $b'c$ and bc', respectively. The dotted line from point b to point c represents the *overall* states of the two-phase system. Finally, as point c is approached, the liquid phase, represented by point c', has almost disappeared, with only droplets (dew) remaining. Point c is therefore a dewpoint, and the P-y_1 curve is the locus of dewpoints. Once the dew has evaporated, only saturated vapor at point c remains, and further pressure reduction leads to superheated vapor at point d.

The composition of the vapor at point c is $y_1 = 0.6$, but the composition of the liquid at point c' and the pressure must either be read from the graph or calculated. This is a *DEW P* calculation, and by Eq. (10.3),

$$P = \frac{1}{y_1/P_1^{sat} + y_2/P_2^{sat}}$$

For $y_1 = 0.6$ and $T/t = 75°C$ (348.15) K,

$$P = \frac{1}{0.6/83.21 + 0.4/41.98} = 59.74 \text{ kPa}$$

By Eq. (10.1),

$$x_1 = \frac{y_1 P}{P_1^{sat}} = \frac{(0.6)(59.74)}{83.21} = 0.4308$$

This is the liquid-phase composition at point c'.

(*b*) When pressure P is fixed, the temperature varies along with x_1 and y_1. For a given pressure, the temperature range is bounded by saturation temperatures T_1^{sat} and T_2^{sat}, the temperatures at which the pure species exert vapor pressures equal to P. For the present system, these temperatures are calculated from the Antoine equations:

$$T_i^{sat} = \frac{B_i}{A_i - \ln P} - C_i$$

For $P = 70$ kPa, $T_1^{sat}/t_1^{sat} = 342.99$ K/69.84°C and $T_1^{sat}/t_2^{sat} = 362.73$ K/89.58°C. The simplest way to prepare a T-x_1-y_1 diagram is to select values of T between these two temperatures, calculate P_1^{sat} and P_2^{sat} for these temperatures, and evaluate x_1 by Eq. (A), written as

$$x_1 = \frac{P - P_2^{sat}}{P_1^{sat} - P_2^{sat}}$$

For example, at 78°C (351.15 K), $P_1^{sat} = 91.76$ kPa, $P_2^{sat} = 46.84$ kPa, and

$$x_1 = \frac{70 - 46.84}{91.76 - 46.84} = 0.5156$$

By Eq. (10.1),

$$y_1 = \frac{x_1 P_1^{sat}}{P} = \frac{(0.5156)(91.76)}{70} = 0.6759$$

The results of this and similar calculations for $P = 70$ kPa are as follows:

x_1	y_1	$T/t(K/°C)$	x_1	y_1	$T/t(K/°C)$
0.0000	0.0000	362.73 (89.58) T_2^{sat} (t_2^{sat})	0.5156	0.6759	351.15 (78)
0.1424	0.2401	359.15 (86)	0.7378	0.8484	347.15 (74)
0.3184	0.4742	355.15 (82)	1.0000	1.0000	342.99 (69.84) T_1^{sat} (t_1^{sat})

Figure 10.12 is the t-x_1-y_1 diagram showing these results. On this phase diagram, drawn for a constant pressure of 70 kPa, the t-y_1 curve represents states of saturated vapor, with states of superheated vapor lying above it. The t-x_1 curve represents states of saturated liquid, with states of subcooled liquid lying below it. The two-phase region lies between these curves.

With reference to Fig. 10.12, consider a constant-pressure heating process leading from a state of subcooled liquid at point a to a state of superheated vapor at point d. The path shown on the figure is for a constant overall composition of 60 mole % acetonitrile. The temperature of the liquid increases as the result of heating from point a to point b, where the first bubble of vapor appears. Thus point b is a bubblepoint, and the t-x_1 curve is the locus of bubblepoints.

For $x_1 = 0.6$ and $P = 70$ kPa, T/t is determined by a *BUBL T* calculation, which requires iteration. Equation (10.2) is here written as

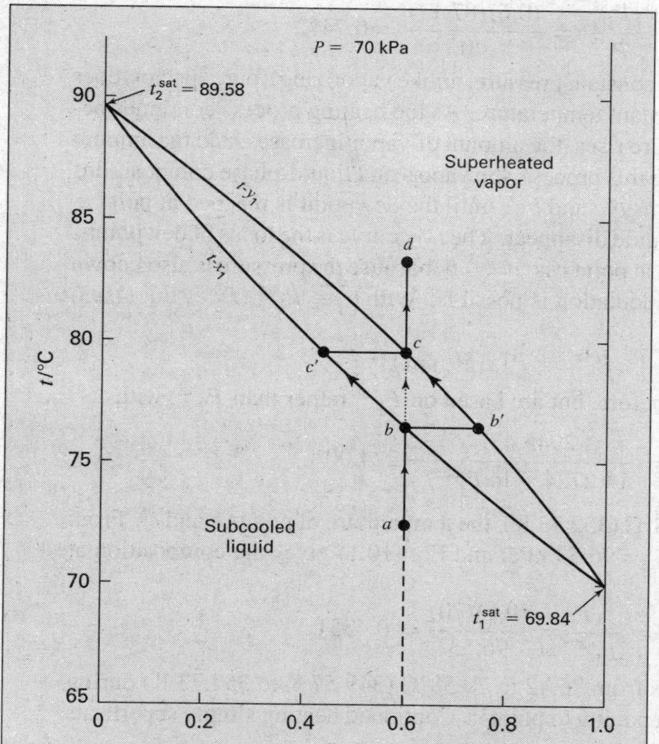

Figure 10.12: txy diagram for acetonitrile(1)/nitromethane(2) at 70 kPa as given by Raoult's law

$$P_2^{sat} = \frac{P}{x_1\alpha + x_2} \tag{B}$$

where $\alpha \equiv P_1^{sat}/P_2^{sat}$. Subtracting $\ln P_2^{sat}$ from $\ln P_1^{sat}$ as given by the Antoine equations yields

$$\ln \alpha = 0.0681 - \frac{2945.47}{t + 224.00} + \frac{2972.64}{t + 209.00} \tag{C}$$

The reason for introducing α is that as the controlling variable it is far less sensitive to t than an individual vapor pressure. An initial value of α is found for an arbitrary intermediate temperature. Iteration is then as follows:

- With the current value of α, calculate P_2^{sat} by Eq. (B).
- Calculate t from the Antoine equation for species 2:

$$t = \frac{2972.64}{14.2043 - \ln P_2^{sat}} - 209.00$$

- Find a new value of α by Eq. (C).
- Return to the initial step and iterate to convergence for a final value of t.

The result is $t = 76.42$°C (349.57 K), the temperature of points b and b'. From the Antoine equation, $P_1^{sat} = 87.17$ kPa, and by Eq. (10.1) the composition at point b' is

$$y_1 = \frac{x_1 P_1^{sat}}{P} = \frac{(0.6)(87.17)}{70} = 0.7472$$

Vaporizing a mixture at constant pressure, unlike vaporizing a pure species, does not in general occur at constant temperature. As the heating process continues beyond point b, the temperature rises, the amount of vapor increases, and the amount of liquid decreases. During this process, the vapor- and liquid-phase compositions change as indicated by paths $b'c$ and bc', until the dewpoint is reached at point c, where the last droplets of liquid disappear. The t-y_1 curve is the locus of dewpoints.

The vapor composition at point c is $y = 0.6$; because the pressure is also known ($P = 70$ kPa), a *DEW T* calculation is possible. With $\alpha \equiv P_1^{sat}/P_2^{sat}$, Eq. (10.3) is written as

$$P_1^{sat} = P(y_1 + y_2\alpha)$$

The iteration steps are as before, but are based on P_1^{sat} rather than P_2^{sat}, with

$$t = \frac{2945.47}{14.2724 - \ln P_1^{sat}} - 224.00$$

The result here is $t = 79.58$°C (352.73 K), the temperature of points c and c'. From the Antoine equation, $P_1^{sat} = 96.53$ kPa, and Eq. (10.1) gives the composition at point c':

$$x_1 = \frac{y_1 P}{P_1^{sat}} = \frac{(0.6)(70)}{96.53} = 0.4351$$

Thus the temperature rises from 76.42 to 79.58°C (349.57 K to 352.73 K) during the vaporization step from point b to point c. Continued heating simply superheats the vapor to point d.

Table 10.1: Henry's Constants for Gases Dissolved in Water at 25°C (298.15 K)

Gas	$\mathcal{H}$/bar	Gas	$\mathcal{H}$/bar
Acetylene	1 350	Helium	126 600
Air	72 950	Hydrogen	71 600
Carbon dioxide	1 670	Hydrogen sulfide	550
Carbon monoxide	54 600	Methane	41 850
Ethane	30 600	Nitrogen	87 650
Ethylene	11 550	Oxygen	44 380

Henry's Law

Application of Raoult's law to species i requires a value for P_i^{sat} at the temperature of application, and thus is not appropriate for a species whose critical temperature is less than the temperature of application. If a system of air in contact with liquid water is presumed at equilibrium, then the air is saturated with water. The mole fraction of water vapor in the air is usually found from Raoult's law applied to the water with the assumption that no air dissolves in the liquid phase. Thus, the liquid water is regarded as pure and Raoult's law for the water (species 2) becomes $y_2 P = P_2^{sat}$. At 25°C (298.15 K) and atmospheric pressure, this equation yields:

$$y_2 = \frac{P_2^{sat}}{P} = \frac{3.166}{101.33} = 0.0312$$

where the pressures are in kPa, and P_2^{sat} comes from the steam tables.

If one wishes to calculate the mole fraction of air dissolved in the water, then Raoult's law cannot be applied, because the critical temperature of air is much lower than 25°C (298.15 K). This problem can be solved by Henry's law, applied here for pressures low enough that the vapor phase may be assumed an ideal gas. For a species present as a very dilute solute in the liquid phase, **Henry's law then states that the partial pressure of the species in the vapor phase is directly proportional to its liquid-phase mole fraction. Thus,**

$$\boxed{y_i P = x_i \mathcal{H}_i} \tag{10.4}$$

where $\mathcal{H}_i$ is *Henry's constant*. Values of $\mathcal{H}_i$ come from experiment, and Table 10.1 lists values at 25°C (298.15 K) for a few gases dissolved in water. For the air/water system at 25°C (298.15 K) and atmospheric pressure, Henry's law applied to the air (species 1) with $y_1 = 1 - 0.0312 = 0.9688$ yields:

$$x_1 = \frac{y_1 P}{\mathcal{H}_1} = \frac{(0.9688)(101.33)}{72\,950} = 1.35 \times 10^{-5}$$

This result justifies the assumption made in application of Raoult's law to the water.

Example 10.2

Assuming that carbonated water contains only $CO_2(1)$ and $H_2O(2)$, determine the compositions of the vapor and liquid phases in a sealed can of "soda" and the pressure exerted on the can at 10°C (283.15 K). Henry's constant for CO_2 in water at 10°C (283.15 K) is about 990 bar.

Solution

As a matter of course, one should always heed whatever insight the phase rule may provide with respect to the solution of an equilibrium problem. Application of the phase rule to this 2-phase, 2-species system yields $F = 2$. However, only the temperature is given in the problem statement, and a further intensive variable must be specified if the problem is to have a unique solution. The liquid-phase mole fraction of CO_2 is an appropriate additional variable, and for a particular value of x_1 the problem has a particular solution. We illustrate with $x_1 = 0.01$.

Henry's law for species 1 and Raoult's law for species 2 are written:

$$y_1 P = x_1 \mathcal{H}_1 \qquad y_2 P = x_2 P_2^{sat}$$

These equations sum to give

$$P = x_1 \mathcal{H}_1 + x_2 P_2^{sat}$$

With $\mathcal{H}_1 = 990$ bar and $P_2^{sat} = 0.012\,27$ bar (from the steam tables at 10°C on 283.15 K),

$$P = (0.01)(990) + (0.99)(0.012\,27) = 9.912 \text{ bar}$$

Then by Raoult's law, Eq. (10.1) written for species 2:

$$y_2 = \frac{x_2 P_2^{sat}}{P} = \frac{(0.99)(0.012\,27)}{9.912} = 0.0012$$

Whence $y_1 = 1 - y_2 = 1 - 0.0012 = 0.9988$, and the vapor phase is nearly pure CO_2, as one might expect.

10.5 VLE BY MODIFIED RAOULT'S LAW

For low to moderate pressures a much more realistic equation for VLE results when the second major Raoult's-law assumption is abandoned, and account is taken of deviations from solution ideality in the liquid phase. Modified Raoult's law results when γ_i, an *activity coefficient*, is inserted into Raoult's law:

$$\boxed{y_i P = x_i \gamma_i P_i^{sat} \qquad (i = 1, 2, \ldots, N)} \tag{10.5}$$

Bubblepoint and dewpoint calculations made with this equation are only a bit more complex than the same calculations made with Raoult's law. Activity coefficients are functions of temperature and liquid-phase composition, and ultimately are based on experiment (Sec. 12.1). For present purposes, the necessary values are assumed known.[6]

Because $\sum_i y_i = 1$, Eq. (10.5) may be summed over all species to yield

$$P = \sum_i x_i \gamma_i P_i^{\text{sat}} \tag{10.6}$$

Alternatively, Eq. (10.5) may be solved for x_i, in which case summing over all species yields

$$P = \frac{1}{\sum_i y_i / \gamma_i P_i^{\text{sat}}} \tag{10.7}$$

Example 10.3

For the system methanol(1)/methyl acetate(2), the following equations provide a reasonable correlation for the activity coefficients:

$$\ln \gamma_1 = A x_2^2 \qquad \ln \gamma_2 = A x_1^2 \qquad \text{where} \qquad A = 2.771 - 0.005\,23\,T$$

In addition, the following Antoine equations provide vapor pressures:

$$\ln P_1^{\text{sat}} = 16.591\,58 - \frac{3643.31}{T - 33.424} \qquad \ln P_2^{\text{sat}} = 14.253\,26 - \frac{2665.54}{T - 53.424}$$

where T is in kelvins and the vapor pressures are in kPa. Assuming the validity of Eq. (10.5), calculate

(*a*) P and $\{y_i\}$, for t/T = 45°C/318.15 K and x_1 = 0.25

(*b*) P and $\{x_i\}$, for t/T = 45°C/318.15 K and y_1 = 0.60

(*c*) T and $\{y_i\}$, for P = 101.33 kPa and x_1 = 0.85

(*d*) T and $\{x_i\}$, for P = 101.33 kPa and y_1 = 0.40

(*e*) The azeotropic pressure, and the azeotropic composition, for t/T = 45°C/318.15 K

[6]The correlation of activity-coefficient data is treated in Secs. 12.1 and 12.2.

Solution

(*a*) A *BUBL P* calculation. For $T = 318.15$ K, the Antoine equations yield

$$P_1^{\text{sat}} = 44.51 \text{ kPa} \qquad P_2^{\text{sat}} = 65.64 \text{ kPa}$$

Activity coefficients are calculated from the correlating equations:

$$A = 2.771 - (0.005\,23)(318.15) = 1.107$$

$$\gamma_1 = \exp(Ax_2^2) = \exp\left[(1.107)(0.75)^2\right] = 1.864$$

$$\gamma_2 = \exp(Ax_1^2) = \exp\left[(1.107)(0.25)^2\right] = 1.072$$

The pressure is given by Eq. (10.6):

$$P = (0.25)(1.864)(44.51) + (0.75)(1.072)(65.64) = 73.50 \text{ kPa}$$

By Eq. (10.5) written, $y_i = x_i \gamma_i P_i^{\text{sat}}/P$,

$$y_1 = 0.282 \qquad y_2 = 0.718$$

(*b*) A *DEW P* calculation. With T unchanged from part (*a*), the values of P_1^{sat}, P_2^{sat}, and A are unchanged. However, the liquid-phase composition is here unknown, but is required in the calculation of activity coefficients. An iterative procedure is indicated; initial values are provided by Raoult's law, for which $\gamma_1 = \gamma_2 = 1.0$. The required steps, with current values of γ_1 and γ_2, are:

- Calculate P by Eq. (10.7), written

$$P = \frac{1}{y_1/\gamma_1 P_1^{\text{sat}} + y_2/\gamma_2 P_2^{\text{sat}}}$$

- Calculate x_1 by Eq. (10.5):

$$x_1 = \frac{y_1 P}{\gamma_1 P_1^{\text{sat}}} \qquad \text{then} \qquad x_2 = 1 - x_1$$

- Evaluate activity coefficients; return to the first step.

Iteration to convergence on a value for P leads to final values:

$$P = 62.89 \text{ kPa} \qquad x_1 = 0.8169 \qquad \gamma_1 = 1.0378 \qquad \gamma_2 = 2.0935$$

(*c*) A *BUBL T* calculation. An initial value for the unknown temperature is found from the saturation temperatures of the pure species at the known pressure. The Antoine equation, solved for T, becomes:

$$T_i^{\text{sat}} = \frac{B_i}{A_i - \ln P} - C_i$$

Application for $P = 101.33$ kPa leads to

$$T_1^{sat} = 337.71 \text{ K} \qquad T_2^{sat} = 330.08 \text{ K}$$

A mole-fraction-weighted average of these values then provides an initial T:

$$T = (0.85)(337.71) + (0.15)(330.08) = 336.57 \text{ K}$$

An iterative procedure consists of the steps:

- For the current value of T calculate values for A, γ_1, γ_2, and $\alpha \equiv P_1^{sat}/P_2^{sat}$ from the given equations.
- Find a new value for P_1^{sat} from Eq. (10.6) written:

$$P_1^{sat} = \frac{P}{x_1\gamma_1 + x_2\gamma_2/\alpha}$$

- Find a new value for T from the Antoine equation written for species 1:

$$T = \frac{B_1}{A_1 - \ln P_1^{sat}} - C_1$$

- Return to the initial step.

Iteration to convergence on a value for T yields final values:

$T = 331.20$ K or $t = 58.05$°C $\qquad P_1^{sat} = 95.24$ kPa $\qquad P_2^{sat} = 48.73$ kPa

$A = 1.0388 \qquad \gamma_1 = 1.0236 \qquad \gamma_2 = 2.1182$

The vapor-phase mole fractions are given by

$$y_1 = \frac{x_1\gamma_1 P_1^{sat}}{P} = 0.670 \qquad \text{and} \qquad y_2 = 1 - y_1 = 0.330$$

(*d*) A *DEW T* calculation. Because $P = 101.33$ kPa, the saturation temperatures are the same as those of part (*c*), and an initial value for the unknown temperature is found as a mole-fraction weighted average of these values:

$$T = (0.40)(337.71) + (0.60)(330.08) = 333.13 \text{ K or } t = 59.98°\text{C}$$

Because the liquid-phase composition is not known, the activity coefficients are initialized as $\gamma_1 = \gamma_2 = 1$. As in part (*c*) an iterative procedure is indicated:

- Evaluate A, P_1^{sat}, P_2^{sat}, and $\alpha \equiv P_1^{sat}/P_2^{sat}$ at the current value of T from the Antoine equations.
- Calculate x_1 by Eq. (10.5):

$$x_1 = \frac{y_1 P}{\gamma_1 P_1^{sat}} \qquad \text{then} \qquad x_2 = 1 - x_1$$

- Calculate values of γ_1 and γ_2 from the correlating equations.
- Find a new value for P_1^{sat} from Eq. (10.7) written:

$$P_1^{sat} = P\left(\frac{y_1}{\gamma_1} + \frac{y_2}{\gamma_2}\alpha\right)$$

- Find a new value for T from the Antoine equation written for species 1:

$$T = \frac{B_1}{A_1 - \ln P_1^{sat}} - C_1$$

- Return to the initial step and iterate with the current values of γ_1 and γ_2 until the process converges on a value of T.

The process yields the final values

$T = 326.70$ K or $t = 53.55$°C $P_1^{sat} = 64.63$ kPa $P_2^{sat} = 90.89$ kPa

$A = 1.0624$ $\gamma_1 = 1.3629$ $\gamma_2 = 1.2523$

$x_1 = 0.4602$ $x_2 = 0.5398$

(*e*) First determine whether or not an azeotrope exists at the given temperature. This calculation is facilitated by the definition of a quantity called the *relative volatility*:

$$\boxed{\alpha_{12} \equiv \frac{y_1/x_1}{y_2/x_2}} \tag{10.8}$$

At an azeotrope $y_1 = x_1$, $y_2 = x_2$, and $\alpha_{12} = 1$. In general, by Eq. (10.5),

$$\frac{y_i}{x_i} = \frac{\gamma_i P_i^{sat}}{P}$$

Therefore,

$$\alpha_{12} = \frac{\gamma_1 P_1^{sat}}{\gamma_2 P_2^{sat}} \tag{10.9}$$

The correlating equations for the activity coefficients show that when $x_1 = 0$, $\gamma_2 = 1$, and $\gamma_1 = \exp(A)$; when $x_1 = 1$, $\gamma_1 = 1$ and $\gamma_2 = \exp(A)$. Therefore in these limits,

$$(\alpha_{12})_{x_1=0} = \frac{P_1^{sat}\exp(A)}{P_2^{sat}} \qquad \text{and} \qquad (\alpha_{12})_{x_1=1} = \frac{P_1^{sat}}{P_2^{sat}\exp(A)}$$

Values of P_1^{sat}, P_2^{sat}, and A are given in part (*a*) for the temperature of interest. The limiting values of α_{12} are therefore

$$(\alpha_{12})_{x_1=0} = \frac{(44.51)\exp(1.107)}{65.64} = 2.052$$

$$(\alpha_{12})_{x_1=1} = \frac{44.51}{(65.64)\exp(1.107)} = 0.224$$

Because the value at one limit is greater than 1, whereas the value at the other limit is less than 1, an azeotrope does exist, because α_{12} is a continuous function of x_1 and must pass through the value of 1.0 at some intermediate composition.

For the azeotrope, $\alpha_{12} = 1$, and Eq. (10.9) becomes

$$\frac{\gamma_1^{\text{az}}}{\gamma_2^{\text{az}}} = \frac{P_2^{\text{sat}}}{P_1^{\text{sat}}} = \frac{65.64}{44.51} = 1.4747$$

The difference between the correlating equations for $\ln \gamma_1$ and $\ln \gamma_2$ provides the general relation:

$$\ln \frac{\gamma_1}{\gamma_2} = Ax_2^2 - Ax_1^2 = A(x_2 - x_1)(x_2 + x_1) = A(x_2 - x_1) = A(1 - 2x_1)$$

Thus the azeotropic occurs at the value of x_1 for which this equation is satisfied when the activity-coefficient ratio has its azeotrope value of 1.4747; i.e., when

$$\ln \frac{\gamma_1}{\gamma_2} = \ln 1.4747 = 0.388$$

Solution gives $x_1^{\text{az}} = 0.325$. For this value of x_1, $\gamma_1^{\text{az}} = 1.657$. With $x_1^{\text{az}} = y_1^{\text{az}}$, Eq. (10.5) becomes

$$P^{\text{az}} = \gamma_1^{\text{az}} P_1^{\text{sat}} = (1.657)(44.51)$$

Thus, $\quad P^{\text{az}} = 73.76 \text{ kPa} \qquad x_1^{\text{az}} = y_1^{\text{az}} = 0.325$

Dewpoint and bubblepoint calculations are readily made with software packages such as Mathcad® and Maple®, in which iteration is an integral part of an equation-solving routine. Mathcad programs for solution of Ex. 10.3, parts (*a*) through (*d*), are given in App. D.2.

Calculations for multicomponent systems made without simplifying assumptions are readily carried out in like manner by computer. The procedures are presented in Sec. 14.1.

10.6 VLE FROM *K*-VALUE CORRELATIONS

A convenient measure of the tendency of a given chemical species to partition itself preferentially between liquid and vapor phases is the equilibrium ratio K_i, defined as

$$\boxed{K_i \equiv \frac{y_i}{x_i}} \tag{10.10}$$

This quantity is usually called simply a *K-value*. Although it adds nothing to thermodynamic knowledge of VLE, it does serve as a measure of the "lightness" of a constituent species, i.e., of its tendency to favor the vapor phase. When K_i is greater than unity, species i exhibits a higher concentration in the vapor phase; when less, a higher concentration in the liquid phase, and is considered a "heavy" constituent. Moreover, the use of K-values makes for computational convenience, allowing elimination of one set of mole fractions $\{y_i\}$ or $\{x_i\}$ in favor of the other.

Reference to Eq. (10.1) shows that the K-value for Raoult's law is

$$K_i = \frac{P_i^{\text{sat}}}{P} \tag{10.11}$$

and reference to Eq. (10.5) shows that for modified Raoult's law it is

$$K_i = \frac{\gamma_i P_i^{\text{sat}}}{P} \tag{10.12}$$

According to Eq. (10.10), $y_i = K_i x_i$. Summation with $\sum_i y_i = 1$ yields

$$\sum_i K_i x_i = 1 \tag{10.13}$$

Thus for bubblepoint calculations, where the x_i are known, the problem is to find the set of K-values that satisfies Eq. (10.13). Alternatively, Eq. (10.10) can be written, $x_i = y_i/K_i$. Summation with $\sum_i x_i = 1$ yields

$$\sum_i \frac{y_i}{K_i} = 1 \tag{10.14}$$

Thus for dewpoint calculations, where the y_i are known, the problem is to find the set of K-values that satisfies Eq. (10.14).

Equations (10.11) and (10.12) together with Eq. (10.10) represent alternative forms of Raoult's law and modified Raoult's law. The great attraction of Raoult's law is that it expresses K-values as functions of just T and P, independent of the compositions of the liquid and vapor phases. Where the assumptions which underlie Raoult's law are appropriate, this allows K-values to be calculated and correlated as functions of T and P. For mixtures of light hydrocarbons and other simple molecules, in which the molecular force fields are relatively uncomplicated, correlations of this kind have approximate validity. Figures 10.13 and 10.14, show nomographs for the K-values of light hydrocarbons as functions of T and P, prepared by Dadyburjor.[7] They do allow for an *average* effect of composition, but the essential basis is Raoult's law.

Example 10.4

For a mixture of 10 mole % methane, 20 mole % ethane, and 70 mole % propane at 10°C (283.15 K), determine the

(*a*) the dewpoint pressure

(*b*) the bubblepoint pressure

The K-values are given by Fig. 10.13.

[7] D. B. Dadyburjor, *Chem. Eng. Progr.*, vol. 74(4), pp. 85–86, April, 1978.

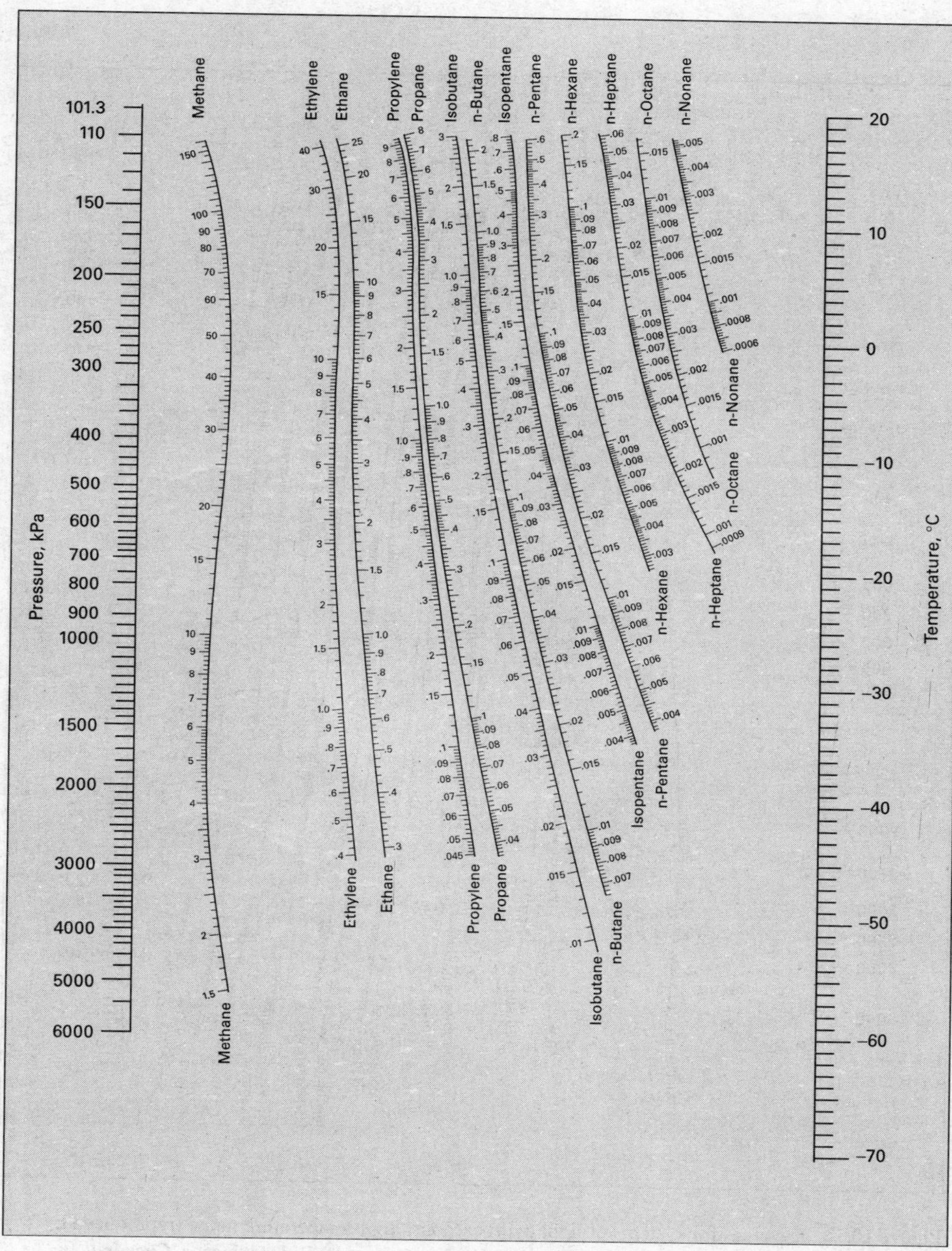

Figure 10.13: *K*-values for systems of light hydrocarbons, low-temperature range (reproduced by permission of the American Institute of Chemical Engineers from D. B. Dadyburjor, *Chemical Engineering Progress*, vol. 74, No. 4, p. 85, 1978)

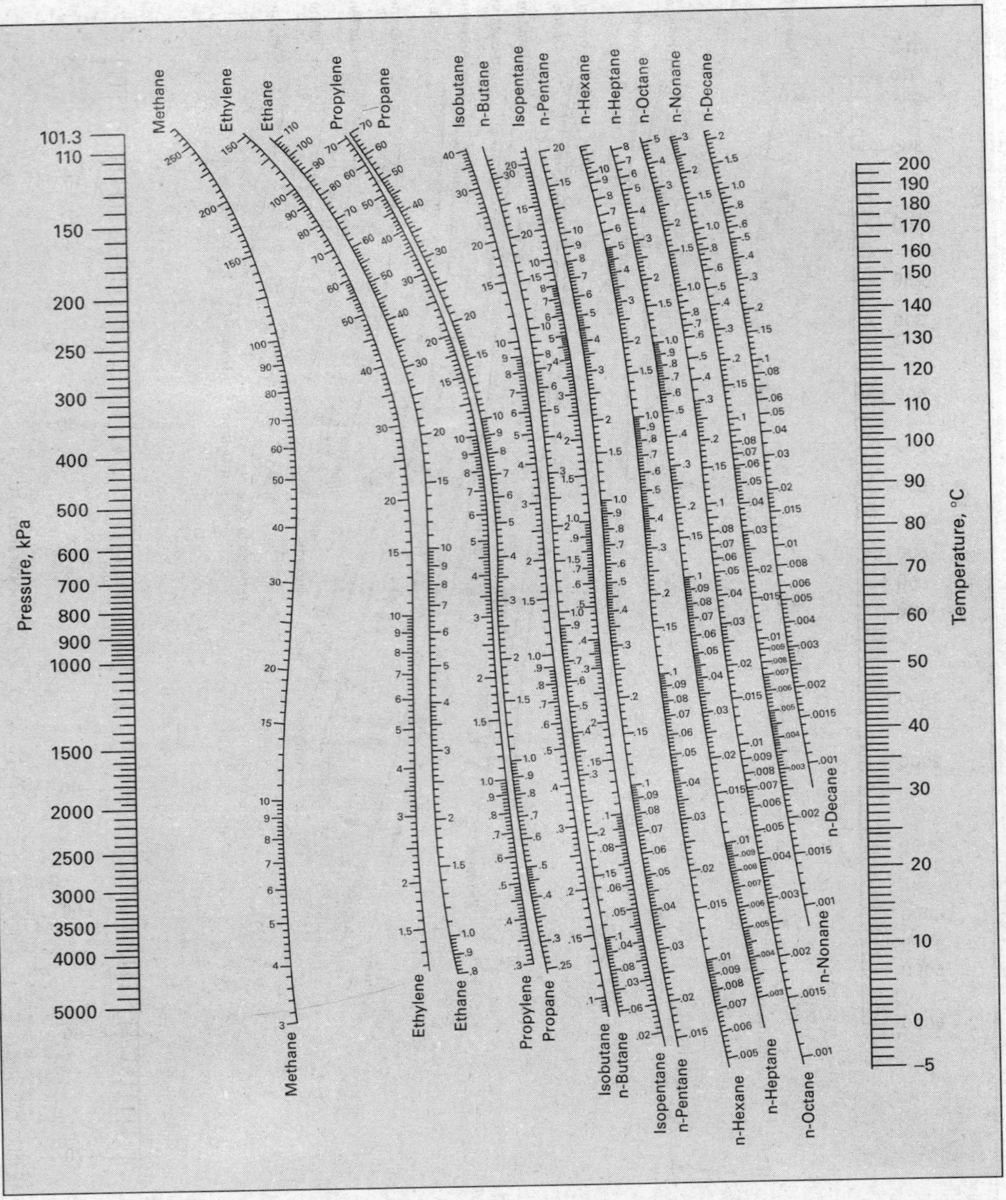

Figure 10.14: K-values for systems of light hydrocarbons, high-temperature range (reproduced by permission of the American Institute of Chemical Engineers from D. B. Dadyburjor, *Chemical Engineering Progress*, vol. 74, No. 4, p. 86, 1978)

Solution

(*a*) When the system is at its dewpoint, only an insignificant amount of liquid is present, and the given mole fractions are values of y_i. For the given temperature, the K-values depend on the choice of P, and by trial we find the value for which Eq. (10.14) is satisfied. Results for several values of P are given as follows:

		P = 6.9 bar		P = 10.34 bar		P = 8.7 bar	
Species	y_i	K_i	y_i/K_i	K_i	y_i/K_i	K_i	y_i/K_i
Methane	0.10	20.0	0.005	13.2	0.008	16.0	0.006
Ethane	0.20	3.25	0.062	2.25	0.089	2.65	0.075
Propane	0.70	0.92	0.761	0.65	1.077	0.762	0.919
		$\Sigma(y_i/K_i) = 0.828$		$\Sigma(y_i/K_i) = 1.174$		$\Sigma(y_i/K_i) = 1.000$	

The results given in the last two columns show that Eq. (10.14) is satisfied when $P = 8.7$ bar. This is the dewpoint pressure, and the composition of the dew is given by the values of $x_i = y_i/K_i$ listed in the last column of the table.

(*b*) When the system is almost completely condensed, it is at its bubblepoint, and the given mole fractions become values of x_i. In this case we find by trial the value of P for which the K-values satisfy Eq. (10.13). Results for several values of P are given in the following table:

		P = 26.2 bar		P = 27.6 bar		P = 26.54 bar	
Species	x_i	K_i	$K_i x_i$	K_i	$K_i x_i$	K_i	$K_i x_i$
Methane	0.10	5.60	0.560	5.25	0.525	5.49	0.549
Ethane	0.20	1.11	0.222	1.07	0.214	1.10	0.220
Propane	0.70	0.335	0.235	0.32	0.224	0.33	0.231
		$\Sigma K_i x_i = 1.017$		$\Sigma K_i x_i = 0.963$		$\Sigma K_i x_i = 1.000$	

Equation (10.13) is satisfied when $P = 26.54$ bar. This is the bubblepoint pressure. The composition of the bubble of vapor is given by $y_i = K_i x_i$, as shown in the last column.

Flash Calculations

An important application of VLE is the *flash calculation*. The name originates from the fact that a liquid at a pressure equal to or greater than its bubblepoint pressure "flashes" or partially evaporates when the pressure is reduced, producing a two-phase system of vapor and liquid in equilibrium. We consider here only the P, T-flash, which refers to any calculation of the quantities and compositions of the vapor and liquid phases making up a two-phase system in equilibrium at known T, P, and *overall* composition. This poses a problem known to be determinate on the basis of Duhem's theorem, because two independent variables (T and P) are specified for a system of fixed overall composition, that is, a system formed from given masses of nonreacting chemical species.

Consider a system containing one mole of nonreacting chemical species with an *overall* composition represented by the set of mole fractions $\{z_i\}$. Let $\mathcal{L}$ be the moles of liquid, with mole fractions $\{x_i\}$, and let $\mathcal{V}$ be the moles of vapor, with mole fractions $\{y_i\}$. The material-balance equations are:

$$\mathcal{L} + \mathcal{V} = 1$$

$$z_i = x_i\mathcal{L} + y_i\mathcal{V} \qquad (i = 1, 2, \ldots, N)$$

Combining these equations to eliminate $\mathcal{L}$ gives:

$$z_i = x_i(1 - \mathcal{V}) + y_i\mathcal{V} \qquad (i = 1, 2, \ldots, N) \tag{10.15}$$

Substituting $x_i = y_i/K_i$, and solving for y_i yields:

$$y_i = \frac{z_i K_i}{1 + \mathcal{V}(K_i - 1)} \qquad (i = 1, 2, \ldots, N) \tag{10.16}$$

Because $\sum_i y_i = 1$, Eq. (10.16) is summed over all species:

$$\sum_i \frac{z_i K_i}{1 + \mathcal{V}(K_i - 1)} = 1 \tag{10.17}$$

The initial step in solving a P, T-flash problem is to find the value of $\mathcal{V}$ which satisfies this equation. Note that $\mathcal{V} = 1$ is always a trivial solution.

Example 10.5

The system acetone(1)/acetonitrile(2)/nitromethane(3) at 80°C (353.15 K) and 110 kPa has the overall composition, $z_1 = 0.45$, $z_2 = 0.35$, $z_3 = 0.20$. Assuming that Raoult's law is appropriate to this system, determine $\mathcal{L}$, $\mathcal{V}$, $\{x_i\}$, and $\{y_i\}$. The vapor pressures of the pure species at 80°C (353.15 K) are:

$$P_1^{sat} = 195.75 \qquad P_2^{sat} = 97.84 \qquad P_3^{sat} = 50.32 \text{ kPa}$$

Solution

First, do a *BUBL P* calculation with $\{z_i\} = \{x_i\}$ to determine P_{bubl}. By Eq. (10.2),

$$P_{\text{bubl}} = x_1 P_1^{sat} + x_2 P_2^{sat} + x_3 P_3^{sat}$$

$$= (0.45)(195.75) + (0.35)(97.84) + (0.20)(50.32) = 132.40 \text{ kPa}$$

Second, do a *DEW P* calculation with $\{z_i\} = \{y_i\}$ to find P_{dew}. By Eq. (10.3),

$$P_{\text{dew}} = \frac{1}{y_1/P_1^{\text{sat}} + y_2/P_2^{\text{sat}} + y_3/P_3^{\text{sat}}} = 101.52 \text{ kPa}$$

Because the given pressure lies between P_{bubl} and P_{dew}, the system is in the two-phase region, and a flash calculation can be made.

By Eq. (10.11), $K_i = P_i^{\text{sat}}/P$; whence,

$$K_1 = 1.7795 \qquad K_2 = 0.8895 \qquad K_3 = 0.4575$$

Substitute known values into Eq. (10.17):

$$\frac{(0.45)(1.7795)}{1 + 0.7795\mathcal{V}} + \frac{(0.35)(0.8895)}{1 - 0.1105\mathcal{V}} + \frac{(0.20)(0.4575)}{1 - 0.5425\mathcal{V}} = 1 \qquad (A)$$

Solution for $\mathcal{V}$ by trial yields or by Mathcad

$$\mathcal{V} = 0.7364 \text{ mol}$$

Whence, $\qquad \mathcal{L} = 1 - \mathcal{V} = 0.2636 \text{ mol}$

Equation (10.16) shows that each term on the left side of Eq. (*A*) is an expression for y_i. Evaluation of these terms gives

$$y_1 = 0.5087 \qquad y_2 = 0.3389 \qquad y_3 = 0.1524$$

Then by Eq. (10.10), $x_i = y_i/K_i$; whence,

$$x_1 = 0.2859 \qquad x_2 = 0.3810 \qquad x_3 = 0.3331$$

Obviously, $\sum_i y_i = \sum_i x_i = 1$. The procedure of this example is valid regardless of the number of species present.

Flash calculations can also be made for light hydrocarbons with the data of Figs. 10.13 and 10.14. The procedure here is exactly as described in Ex. 10.5, where Raoult's law applied. With T and P specified, the K-values for light hydrocarbons as given by Figs. 10.13 and 10.14 are known, and $\mathcal{V}$, the only unknown in Eq. (10.17), is found by trial.

Example 10.6

For the system described in Ex. 10.4, what fraction of the system is vapor when the pressure is 13.8 bar and what are the compositions of the equilibrium vapor and liquid phases?

Solution

The given pressure lies between the dewpoint and bubblepoint pressures established for this system in Ex. 10.4. The system therefore consists of two phases. With K-values from Fig. 10.13, the procedure is to find by trial that value of $\mathcal{V}$ for which Eq. (10.17) is satisfied. The results of several trials are shown in the accompanying table. The columns headed y_i give values of the terms in the sum of Eq. (10.17), because each such term is in fact a y_i value.

Species	z_i	K_i	y_i for $\mathcal{V} = 0.35$	y_i for $\mathcal{V} = 0.25$	y_i for $\mathcal{V} = 0.273$	$x_i = y_i/K_i$ for $\mathcal{V} = 0.273$
Methane	0.10	10.0	0.241	0.308	0.289	0.029
Ethane	0.20	1.76	0.278	0.296	0.292	0.166
Propane	0.70	0.52	0.438	0.414	0.419	0.805
			$\Sigma y_i = 0.957$	$\Sigma y_i = 1.018$	$\Sigma y_i = 1.000$	$\Sigma x_i = 1.000$

Thus Eq. (10.17) is satisfied when $\mathcal{V} = 0.273$. The phase compositions are given in the last two columns of the table.

PROBLEMS

Solutions to some of the problems of this chapter require vapor pressures as a function of temperature for species which constitute systems in VLE. Table B.2, Appendix B, lists parameter values for the Antoine equation,

$$\ln P^{\text{sat}}/\text{kPa} = A - \frac{B}{T/\text{K} + C}$$

10.1. Assuming the validity of Raoult's law, do the following calculations for the benzene(1)/toluene(2) system:

(*a*) Given $x_1 = 0.33$ and $T = 100°\text{C}$ (373.15 K), find y_1 and P

(*b*) Given $y_1 = 0.33$ and $T = 100°\text{C}$ (373.15 K), find x_1 and P

(*c*) Given $x_1 = 0.33$ and $P = 120$ kPa, find y_1 and T

(*d*) Given $y_1 = 0.33$ and $P = 120$ kPa, find x_1 and T

(*e*) Given $T = 105°\text{C}$ (378.15 K) and $P = 120$ kPa, find x_1 and y_1

(*f*) For part (*e*), if the *overall* mole fraction of benzene is $z_1 = 0.33$, what molar fraction of the two-phase system is vapor?

(*g*) Why is Raoult's law likely to be an excellent VLE model for this system at the stated (or computed) conditions?

10.2. Assuming Raoult's law to be valid, prepare a P-x-y diagram for a temperature of 90°C (363.15 K) and a t-x-y diagram for a pressure of 90 kPa for one of the following systems:

(*a*) Benzene(1)/ethylbenzene(2) (*b*) 1-Chlorobutane(1)/chlorobenzene(2)

10.3. Assuming Raoult's law to apply to the system n-pentane(1)/n-heptane(2),

(*a*) What are the values of x_1 and y_1 at $t/T = 55°\text{C}$ (328.15 K) and $P = \frac{1}{2}(P_1^{\text{sat}} + P_2^{\text{sat}})$? For these conditions plot the fraction of system that is vapor $\mathcal{V}$ vs. overall composition z_1.

(*b*) For $t/T = 55°\text{C}/328.15$ K and $z_1 = 0.5$, plot P, x_1, and y_1 vs. $\mathcal{V}$.

10.4. Rework Pb. 10.3 for one of the following:

(*a*) $t/T = 65°\text{C}/338.15$ K; (*b*) $t/T = 75°\text{C}/348.15$ K; (*c*) $t/T = 85°\text{C}/358.15$ K; (*d*) $t/T = 95°\text{C}/368.15$ K.

10.5. Prove: An equilibrium liquid/vapor system described by Raoult's law cannot exhibit an azeotrope.

10.6. Of the binary liquid/vapor systems following, which can be approximately modeled by Raoult's law? For those which cannot, why? Table B.1 (App. B) may be useful.

(*a*) Benzene/toluene at 1 atm
(*b*) n-Hexane/n-heptane at 25 bar
(*c*) Hydrogen/propane at 200 K
(*d*) Isooctane/n-octane at 100°C (373.15 K)
(*e*) Water/n-decane at 1 bar

10.7. A single-stage liquid/vapor separation for the benzene(1)/ethylbenzene(2) system must produce phases of the following equilibrium compositions. For one of these sets, determine the T and P in the separator. What additional information is needed to compute the relative amounts of liquid and vapor leaving the separator? Assume that Raoult's law applies.

(*a*) $x_1 = 0.35$, $y_1 = 0.70$
(*b*) $x_1 = 0.35$, $y_1 = 0.725$
(*c*) $x_1 = 0.35$, $y_1 = 0.75$
(*d*) $x_1 = 0.35$, $y_1 = 0.775$

10.8. Do all four parts of Pb. 10.7, and compare the results. The required temperatures and pressures vary significantly. Discuss possible processing implications of the various temperature and pressure levels.

10.9. A mixture containing equimolar amounts of benzene(1), toluene(2), and ethylbenzene(3) is flashed to conditions T and P. For one of the conditions following determine the equilibrium mole fractions $\{x_i\}$ and $\{y_i\}$ of the liquid and vapor phases formed and the molar fraction $\mathcal{V}$ of the vapor formed. Assume that Raoult's law applies.

(*a*) $t/T = 110°C/383.15$ K, $P = 90$ kPa
(*b*) $t/T = 110°C/383.15$ K, $P = 100$ kPa
(*c*) $t/T = 110°C/383.15$ K, $P = 110$ kPa
(*d*) $t/T = 110°C/383.15$ K, $P = 120$ kPa

10.10. Do all four parts of Pb. 10.9, and compare the results. Discuss any trends that appear.

10.11. A binary mixture of mole fraction z_1 is flashed to conditions T and P. For one of the following determine: the equilibrium mole fractions x_1 and y_1 of the liquid and vapor phases formed, the molar fraction $\mathcal{V}$ of the vapor formed, and the fractional recovery $\mathcal{R}$ of species 1 in the vapor phase (defined as the ratio for species 1 of moles in the vapor to moles in the feed). Assume that Raoult's law applies.

(*a*) Acetone(1)/acetonitrile(2), $z_1 = 0.75$, $T = 340$ K, $P = 115$ kPa
(*b*) Benzene(1)/ethylbenzene(2), $z_1 = 0.50$, $T = 100°C$ (373.15 K), $P = 0.75$ atm
(*c*) Ethanol(1)/1-propanol(2), $z_1 = 0.25$, $T = 360$ K, $P = 0.80$ atm
(*d*) 1-Chlorobutane(1)/chlorobenzene(2), $z_1 = 0.50$, $T = 125°C$ (398.15 K), $P = 1.75$ bar

10.12. Humidity, relating to the quantity of moisture in atmospheric air, is accurately given by equations derived from the ideal-gas law and Raoult's law for H_2O.

(*a*) The *absolute humidity h* is defined as the mass of water vapor in a unit mass of dry air. Show that it is given by

$$h = \frac{\mathcal{M}_{H_2O}}{\mathcal{M}_{air}} \frac{p_{H_2O}}{P - p_{H_2O}}$$

where $\mathcal{M}$ represents a molar mass and p_{H_2O} is the partial pressure of the water vapor, i.e., $p_{H_2O} = y_{H_2O}P$.

(*b*) The *saturation humidity* h^{sat} is defined as the value of h when air is in equilibrium with a large body of pure water. Show that it is given by

$$h^{sat} = \frac{\mathcal{M}_{H_2O}}{\mathcal{M}_{air}} \frac{P^{sat}_{H_2O}}{P - P^{sat}_{H_2O}}$$

where $P^{sat}_{H_2O}$ is the vapor pressure of water at the ambient temperature.

(*c*) The *percentage humidity* is defined as the ratio of h to its saturation value, expressed as a percentage. On the other hand, the *relative humidity* is defined as the ratio of the partial pressure of water vapor in air to its vapor pressure, expressed as a percentage. What is the relation between these two quantities?

10.13. A concentrated binary solution containing mostly species 2 (but $x_2 \neq 1$) is in equilibrium with a vapor phase containing both species 1 and 2. The pressure of this two-phase system is 1 bar; the temperature is 25°C (298.15 K). Determine from the following data good estimates of x_1 and y_1.

$$\mathcal{H}_1 = 200 \text{ bar} \qquad P_2^{sat} = 0.10 \text{ bar}$$

State and justify all assumptions.

10.14. Air, even more so than carbon dioxide, is inexpensive and nontoxic. Why is it not the gas of choice for making soda water and (cheap) champagne effervescent? Table 10.1 may provide useful data.

10.15. Helium-laced gases are used as breathing media for deep-sea divers. Why? Table 10.1 may provide useful data.

10.16. A binary system of species 1 and 2 consists of vapor and liquid phases in equilibrium at temperature T. The *overall* mole fraction of species 1 in the system is $z_1 = 0.65$. At temperature T,

- $\ln \gamma_1 = 0.67x_2^2$ $\qquad \ln \gamma_2 = 0.67x_1^2$.
- $P_1^{\text{sat}} = 32.27$ kPa $\qquad P_2^{\text{sat}} = 73.14$ kPa.

Assuming the validity of Eq. (10.5),

(*a*) Over what range of pressures can this system exist as two phases at given T and z_1?

(*b*) For a liquid-phase mole fraction $x_1 = 0.75$, what is the pressure P and what molar fraction $\mathcal{V}$ of the system is vapor?

(*c*) Show whether or not the system exhibits an azeotrope.

10.17. For the system ethyl ethanoate(1)/*n*-heptane(2) at 70°C (343.15 K),

- $\ln \gamma_1 = 0.95x_2^2$ $\qquad \ln \gamma_2 = 0.95x_1^2$.
- $P_1^{\text{sat}} = 79.80$ kPa $\qquad P_2^{\text{sat}} = 40.50$ kPa.

Assuming the validity of Eq. (10.5),

(*a*) Make a *BUBL P* calculation for $t/T = 70°\text{C}/343.15$ K, $x_1 = 0.05$.

(*b*) Make a *DEW P* calculation for $t/T = 70°\text{C}/343.15$ K, $y_1 = 0.05$.

(*c*) What is the azeotrope composition and pressure at $t/T = 70°\text{C}/343.15$ K?

10.18. A liquid mixture of cyclohexanone(1)/phenol(2) for which $x_1 = 0.6$ is in equilibrium with its vapor at 144°C (417.15 K). Determine the equilibrium pressure P and vapor composition y_1 from the following information:

- $\ln \gamma_1 = Ax_2^2$ $\qquad \ln \gamma_2 = Ax_1^2$.
- At 144°C (417.15 K), $P_1^{\text{sat}} = 75.20$ and $P_2^{\text{sat}} = 31.66$ kPa.
- The system forms an azeotrope at 144°C (417.15 K) for which $x_1^{\text{az}} = y_1^{\text{az}} = 0.294$.

10.19. A binary system of species 1 and 2 consists of vapor and liquid phases in equilibrium at temperature T, for which

- $\ln \gamma_1 = 1.8x_2^2$ $\qquad \ln \gamma_2 = 1.8x_1^2$.
- $P_1^{\text{sat}} = 1.24$ bar $\qquad P_2^{\text{sat}} = 0.89$ bar.

Assuming the validity of Eq. (10.5),

(*a*) For what range of values of the *overall* mole fraction z_1 can this two-phase system exist with a *liquid* mole fraction $x_1 = 0.65$?

(*b*) What is the pressure P and vapor mole fraction y_1 within this range?

(*c*) What are the pressure and composition of the azeotrope at temperature T?

10.20. For the acetone(1)/methanol(2) system a vapor mixture for which $z_1 = 0.25$ and $z_2 = 0.75$ is cooled to temperature T in the two-phase region and flows into a separation chamber at a pressure of 1 bar. If the composition of the liquid product is to be $x_1 = 0.175$, what is the required value of T, and what is the value of y_1? For liquid mixtures of this system to a good approximation:

$$\ln \gamma_1 = 0.64x_2^2 \qquad \ln \gamma_2 = 0.64x_1^2$$

10.21. The following is a rule of thumb: For a binary system in VLE at low pressure, the equilibrium vapor-phase mole fraction y_1 corresponding to an equimolar liquid mixture is approximately

$$y_1 = \frac{P_1^{\text{sat}}}{P_1^{\text{sat}} + P_2^{\text{sat}}}$$

where P_i^{sat} is a pure-species vapor pressure. Clearly, this equation is valid if Raoult's law applies. Prove that it is also valid for VLE described by Eq. (10.5), with:

$$\ln \gamma_1 = Ax_2^2 \qquad \ln \gamma_2 = Ax_1^2$$

10.22. A process stream contains light species 1 and heavy species 2. A relatively pure liquid stream containing mostly 2 is desired, obtained by a single-stage liquid/vapor separation. Specifications on the equilibrium composition are: $x_1 = 0.002$ and $y_1 = 0.950$. Use data given below to determine T(K) and P(bar) for the separator. Assume that Eq. (10.5) applies; the calculated P should validate this assumption. Data:

For the liquid phase, $\ln \gamma_1 = 0.93x_2^2 \qquad \ln \gamma_2 = 0.93x_1^2$

$$\ln P_i^{\text{sat}}/\text{bar} = A_i - \frac{B_i}{T/\text{K}}$$

$$A_1 = 10.08,\ B_1 = 2572.0,\ A_2 = 11.63,\ B_2 = 6254.0$$

10.23. If a system exhibits VLE, at least one of the K-values must be greater than 1.0 and at least one must be less than 1.0. Offer a proof of this observation.

10.24. Flash calculations are simpler for binary systems than for the general multicomponent case, because the equilibrium compositions for a binary are independent of the overall composition. Show that, for a binary system in VLE,

$$x_1 = \frac{1 - K_2}{K_1 - K_2} \qquad y_1 = \frac{K_1(1 - K_2)}{K_1 - K_2}$$

$$\mathcal{V} = \frac{z_1(K_1 - K_2) - (1 - K_2)}{(K_1 - 1)(1 - K_2)}$$

10.25. Assuming the validity of the Dadyburjor charts (Fig 10.13 and 10.14), make the following VLE calculations for the methane(1)/ethylene(2)/ethane(3) system:

(*a*) *BUBL P*, given $x_1 = 0.10$, $x_2 = 0.50$, and $t/T = -51°C/222.15$ K
(*b*) *DEW P*, given $y_1 = 0.50$, $y_2 = 0.25$, and $t/T = -51°C/222.15$ K
(*c*) *BUBL T*, given $x_1 = 0.12$, $x_2 = 0.40$, and $P = 17.24$ bar
(*d*) *DEW T*, given $y_1 = 0.43$, $y_2 = 0.36$, and $P = 17.24$ bar

10.26. Assuming the validity of the De Priester charts, make the following VLE calculations for the ethane(1)/propane(2)/isobutane(3)/isopentane(4) system:

(*a*) *BUBL P*, given $x_1 = 0.10$, $x_2 = 0.20$, $x_3 = 0.30$, and $t/T = 60°C/333.15$ K
(*b*) *DEW P*, given $y_1 = 0.48$, $y_2 = 0.25$, $y_3 = 0.15$, and $t/T = 60°C/333.15$ K
(*c*) *BUBL T*, $x_1 = 0.14$, $x_2 = 0.13$, $x_3 = 0.25$, and $P = 15$ bar
(*d*) *DEW T*, given $y_1 = 0.42$, $y_2 = 0.30$, $y_3 = 0.15$, and $P = 15$ bar

10.27. The stream from a gas well is a mixture containing 50 mole % methane, 10 mole % ethane, 20 mole % propane, and 20 mole % *n*-butane. This stream is fed into a partial condenser maintained at a pressure of 17.24 bar, where its temperature is brought to 27°C (300.15 K). Determine the molar fraction of the gas that condenses and the compositions of the liquid and vapor phases leaving the condenser.

10.28. An equimolar mixture of *n*-butane and *n*-hexane at pressure P is brought to a temperature of 95°C (368.15 K), where it exists as a vapor/liquid mixture in equilibrium. If the mole fraction of *n*-hexane in the liquid phase is 0.75, what is pressure P (in bar), what is the molar fraction of the system that is liquid, and what is the composition of the vapor phase?

10.29. A mixture— 25 mole % *n*-pentane, 45 mole % *n*-hexane, and 30 mole % *n*-heptane— is brought to a condition of 93°C (366.15 K) and 2 atm. What molar fraction of the system is liquid, and what are the phase compositions?

10.30. A mixture containing 15 mole % ethane, 35 mole % propane, and 50 mole % *n*-butane is brought to a condition of 40°C (313.15 K) at pressure P. If the molar fraction of liquid in the system is 0.40, what is pressure P (in bar) and what are the compositions of the liquid and vapor phases?

10.31. A mixture consisting of 1 mole % ethane, 5 mole % propane, 44 mole % *n*-butane, and 50 mole % isobutane is brought to a condition of 21°C (294.15 K) at pressure P. If the molar fraction of the system that is vapor is 0.2, what is pressure P (in bar), and what are the compositions of the vapor and liquid phases?

10.32. A mixture comprised of 30 mole % methane, 10 mole % ethane, 30 mole % propane, and 30 mole % *n*-butane is brought to a condition of −15°C (258.15 K) at pressure P, where it exists as a vapor/liquid mixture in equilibrium. If the mole fraction of the methane in the vapor phase is 0.80, what is pressure P (in bar)?

10.33. The top tray of a distillation column and the condenser are at a pressure of 1.38 bar. The liquid on the top tray is an equimolar mixture of *n*-butane and *n*-pentane. The vapor from the top tray, assumed to be in equilibrium with the liquid, goes to the condenser where 50 mole % of the vapor is condensed. What is the temperature on the top tray? What are the temperature and composition of the vapor leaving the condenser?

10.34. *n*-Butane is separated from an equimolar methane/*n*-butane gas mixture by compression of the gas to pressure P at 40°C (313.15 K). If 40% of the feed on a mole basis is condensed, what is pressure P (in bar) and what are the compositions of the resulting vapor and liquid phases?

10.35. The NIST Chemistry WebBook repoets critically evaluated Henry's constants for selected chemicals in water at 25°C (298.15 K). Henry's constants from this source, denoted here ky k_i, appear in the VLE equation written for the solute in the form:

$$k_i y_i P = \mathcal{M}_i$$

where $\mathcal{M}_i$ is the liquid-phase molality of solute species i, expressed as mol i/kg solvent.

(*a*) Determine an algebraic relation connecting k_i to $\mathcal{H}_i$, Henry's constant in Eq. (10.4). Assune that x_i is "small."

(*b*) The NIST Chemistry WebBook provides a value of 0.034 mol kg^{-1} bar^{-1} for k_i of CO_2 in H_2O at 25°C (298.15 K). What is the implied value of $\mathcal{H}_i$ in bar? Compare this with the value given in Table 10.1, which came from a different source.

10.36. (*a*) A feed containing equimolar amounts of acetone(1) and acetonitrile(2) is throttled to pressure P and temperature T. For what pressure range (atm) will two phases (liquid and vapor) be formed for T = 50°C (323.15 K)? Assume that Raoult's law applies.

(*b*) A feed containing equimolar amounts of acetone(1) and acetonitrile(2) is throttled to pressure P and temperature T. For what temperature range (°C) will two phases (liquid and vapor) be formed for P = 0.5 atm? Assume that Raoult's law applies.

10.37. A binary mixture of benzene(1) and toluene(2) is flashed to 75 kPa and 90°C (363.15 K). Analysis of the effluent liquid and vapor streams from the separator yields: $x_1 = 0.1604$ and $y_1 = 0.2919$.

An operator remarks that the product streams are "off-spec," and you are asked to diagnose the problem.

(*a*) Verify that the exiting streams are not in binary equilibrium.

(*b*) Verify that an air leak into the separator could be the cause.

10.38. Ten kmol h^{-1} of cool flue gas at 100°C (373.15 K) is further cooled to 25°C (298.15 K). Pressure is constant at 1 atm. What is the rate of heat transfer for the process? Initial composition of the flue gas: $y_{O_2} = 0.0387$, $y_{N_2} = 0.7288$, $y_{CO_2} = 0.0775$, $y_{H_2O} = 0.1550$.

10.39. A light hydrocarbon mixture containing 5 mole % propane, 85 mole % *n*-butane, and 10 mole % *n*-pentane is stored as a liquid under its vapor pressure in a refrigerated tank. Available refrigertion keeps the contents of the tank at 4.5°C (277.65 K). Although the tank contains ample vapor space, it is essentially full of liquid on a *molar* basis. What is the storage pressure?

10.40. Ten kmol h^{-1} of hydrogen sulfide gas is burned with the stoichiometric amount of pure oxygen in a special unit. Reactants enter as gases at 25°C (298.15 K) and 1 atm. Products leave as two streams in equilibrium at 70°C (343.15 K) and 1 atm: a phase of pure liquid water, and a saturated vapor stream containing H_2O and SO_2.

(*a*) What is the composition (mole fractions) of the product vapor stream?
(*b*) What are the rates (kmol h^{-1}) of the two product streams?

10.41. Physiological studies show the neutral comfort level (NCL) of moist air to correspond to an absolute humidity of about 0.01 kg H_2O per kg of dry air.

(*a*) What is the vapor-phase mole fraction of H_2O at the NCL?
(*b*) What is the partial pressure of H_2O at the NCL? Here, and in part (*c*), take $P =$ 1.01325 bar, i.e. 1 standard atmosphere.
(*c*) What is the dewpoint temperature at the NCL?

10.42. An industrial dehumidifier accepts 50 kmol h^{-1} of moist air with a dewpoint of 20°C (293.15 K). Conditioned air leaving the dehumidifier has a dewpoint temperature of 10°C (283.15 K). At what rate (kg h^{-1}) is liquid water removed in this steady-flow process? Assune P is constantr at 1 atm.

10.43. Vapor/liquid-equilibrium azeotropy is impossible for binary systems rigorously described by Raoult's law (Pb. 10.5). For *real* systems (those with $\gamma_i \neq 1$), azeotropy is inevitable at temperatures where the P_i^{sat} are equal. Such a temperature is called a *Bancroft point*. Not all binary systems exhibit such a point. With Table B.2 of App. B as a resource, identify three binary systems with Bancroft points, and determine the T and P coordinates.

Ground rule: A Bancroft point must lie in the temperture ranges of validity of the Antoine equarions.

Chapter 11

Solution Thermodynamics: Theory

Our purpose in this chapter is to lay the theoretical foundation for applications of thermodynamics to gas mixtures and liquid solutions. In the chemical, petroleum, and pharmaceutical industries multicomponent gases and liquids commonly undergo composition changes brought about by mixing and separation processes, the transfer of species from one phase to another, and chemical reaction. Thus compositions become essential variables, along with temperature and pressure, the variables considered in detail in Chapt. 6.

We first develop a *fundamental property relation* more comprehensive than Eq. (6.10) in that its scope extends to open phases of variable composition. Convenience here prompts definition of the *chemical potential*, a fundamental new property which facilitates treatment of phase and chemical-reaction equilibria. This prompts introduction of an entire class of thermodynamic properties known as *partial properties*, defined mathematically so as to suggest interpretation as properties of individual species as they exist in solution. They are composition-dependent, and distinct from the molar properties of pure species.

Property relations for mixtures of ideal gases provide the basis for treatment of real-gas mixtures. Important here is the definition of yet another useful property, the *fugacity*. Related to the chemical potential, it lends itself to mathematical formulation of both phase- and chemical-reaction-equilibrium problems.

Another useful class of solution properties, known as *excess properties*, is introduced in conjunction with an idealization of solution behavior called the *ideal solution*. Its role is like that of the ideal gas in that it serves as a reference, in this case for real-solution behavior. Of particular interest is the excess Gibbs energy, a property which underlies the activity coefficient, introduced from a practical point of view in the preceding chapter.

11.1 FUNDAMENTAL PROPERTY RELATION

Equation (6.6) relates the total Gibbs energy of any closed system to its *canonical* variables, temperature and pressure:

$$d(nG) = (nV)dP - (nS)dT \tag{6.6}$$

where n is the total number of moles of the system. An appropriate application is to a single-phase fluid in a closed system wherein no chemical reactions occur. For such a system the composition is necessarily constant, and therefore

$$\left[\frac{\partial(nG)}{\partial P}\right]_{T,n} = nV \qquad \text{and} \qquad \left[\frac{\partial(nG)}{\partial T}\right]_{P,n} = -nS$$

The subscript n indicates that the numbers of moles of *all* chemical species are held constant.

For the more general case of a single-phase, *open* system, material may pass into and out of the system, and nG becomes a function of the numbers of moles of the chemical species present. Presumably, it is still a function of T and P, and we rationalize the functional relation:

$$nG = g(P, T, n_1, n_2, \ldots, n_i, \ldots)$$

where n_i is the number of moles of species i. The total differential of nG is then:

$$d(nG) = \left[\frac{\partial(nG)}{\partial P}\right]_{T,n} dP + \left[\frac{\partial(nG)}{\partial T}\right]_{P,n} dT + \sum_i \left[\frac{\partial(nG)}{\partial n_i}\right]_{P,T,n_j} dn_i$$

The summation is over all species present, and subscript n_j indicates that all mole numbers except the ith are held constant. The derivative in the final term is given its own symbol and name. Thus, by **definition** the *chemical potential* of species i in the mixture is

$$\mu_i \equiv \left[\frac{\partial(nG)}{\partial n_i}\right]_{P,T,n_j} \tag{11.1}$$

With this definition and with the first two partial derivatives replaced by (nV) and $-(nS)$, the preceding equation becomes

$$d(nG) = (nV)dP - (nS)dT + \sum_i \mu_i\, dn_i \tag{11.2}$$

Equation (11.2) is the fundamental property relation for single-phase fluid systems of variable mass and composition. It is the foundation upon which the structure of solution thermodynamics is built. For the special case of one mole of solution, $n = 1$ and $n_i = x_i$:

$$dG = V\,dP - S\,dT + \sum_i \mu_i\, dx_i \tag{11.3}$$

Implicit in this equation is the functional relationship of the molar Gibbs energy to its *canonical* variables, here: T, P, and $\{x_i\}$:

$$G = G(T, P, x_1, x_2, \ldots, x_i, \ldots)$$

Equation (6.10) for a constant-composition solution is a special case of Eq. (11.3). Although the mole numbers n_i of Eq. (11.2) are independent variables, the mole fractions x_i in Eq. (11.3) are not, because $\sum_i x_i = 1$. This precludes certain mathematical operations which depend upon independence of the variables. Nevertheless, Eq. (11.3) does imply

$$V = \left(\frac{\partial G}{\partial P}\right)_{T,x} \quad (11.4) \qquad S = -\left(\frac{\partial G}{\partial T}\right)_{P,x} \quad (11.5)$$

Other solution properties come from definitions; e.g., the enthalpy, from $H = G + TS$. Thus, by Eq, (11.5),

$$H = G - T\left(\frac{\partial G}{\partial T}\right)_{P,x}$$

When the Gibbs energy is expressed as a function of its canonical variables, it plays the role of a *generating function*, providing the means for calculation of all other thermodynamic properties by simple mathematical operations (differentiation and elementary algebra), and implicitly represents *complete* property information.

11.2 THE CHEMICAL POTENTIAL AND PHASE EQUILIBRIA

For a *closed* system consisting of two phases in equilibrium, each individual phase is *open* to the other, and mass transfer between phases may occur. Equation (11.2) applies separately to each phase:

$$d(nG)^\alpha = (nV)^\alpha dP - (nS)^\alpha dT + \sum_i \mu_i^\alpha \, dn_i^\alpha$$

$$d(nG)^\beta = (nV)^\beta dP - (nS)^\beta dT + \sum_i \mu_i^\beta \, dn_i^\beta$$

where superscripts α and β identify the phases. The presumption here is that *equilibrium* implies uniformity of T and P throughout the entire system.

The change in the total Gibbs energy of the two-phase system is the sum of these equations. When each total-system property is expressed by an equation of the form,

$$nM = (nM)^\alpha + (nM)^\beta$$

the sum is
$$d(nG) = (nV)dP - (nS)dT + \sum_i \mu_i^\alpha \, dn_i^\alpha + \sum_i \mu_i^\beta \, dn_i^\beta$$

Because the two-phase system is closed, Eq. (6.6) is also valid. Comparison of the two equations shows that at equilibrium,

$$\sum_i \mu_i^\alpha \, dn_i^\alpha + \sum_i \mu_i^\beta \, dn_i^\beta = 0$$

The changes dn_i^α and dn_i^β result from mass transfer between the phases; mass conservation therefore requires

$$dn_i^\alpha = -dn_i^\beta \qquad \text{and} \qquad \sum_i (\mu_i^\alpha - \mu_i^\beta) dn_i^\alpha = 0$$

Quantities dn_i^α are independent and arbitrary; therefore the only way the left side of the second equation can in general be zero is for each term in parentheses separately to be zero. Hence,

$$\mu_i^\alpha = \mu_i^\beta \qquad (i = 1, 2, \ldots, N)$$

where N is the number of species present in the system. Successive application of this result to pairs of phases permits its generalization to multiple phases; for π phases:

$$\boxed{\mu_i^\alpha = \mu_i^\beta = \cdots = \mu_i^\pi} \qquad (i = 1, 2, \ldots, N) \tag{11.6}$$

A similar but more comprehensive derivation shows (as we have supposed) that for equilibrium T and P must be the same in all phases.

Thus, multiple phases at the same *T* and *P* are in equilibrium when the chemical potential of each species is the same in all phases.

The application of Eq. (11.6) in later chapters to specific phase-equilibrium problems requires use of *models* of solution behavior, which provide expressions for G and μ_i as functions of temperature, pressure, and composition. The simplest of these, the ideal-gas mixture and the ideal solution, are treated in Secs. 11.4 and 11.8.

11.3 PARTIAL PROPERTIES

The definition of the chemical potential by Eq. (11.1) as the mole-number derivative of nG suggests that other derivatives of this kind should prove useful in solution thermodynamics. Thus, we **define** partial molar property $\bar{M}_i$ of species i in solution as

$$\boxed{\bar{M}_i \equiv \left[\frac{\partial(nM)}{\partial n_i}\right]_{P,T,n_j}} \tag{11.7}$$

It is a *response function*, i.e., a *measure* of the response of total property nM to the addition at constant T and P of a differential amount of species i to a finite amount of solution.

The generic symbols M and $\bar{M}_i$ may express solution properties on a unit-mass basis as well as on a mole basis. Equation (11.7) retains the same form, with n, the number of moles, replaced by m, representing mass, and yielding partial *specific* properties rather than partial *molar* properties. To accommodate either, one may speak simply of partial properties.

Interest here centers on solutions; their molar (or unit-mass) properties are therefore represented by the plain symbol M. Partial properties are denoted by an overbar, with a subscript to identify the species; the symbol is therefore $\bar{M}_i$. In addition, properties of the individual species as they exist in the *pure state at the T and P of the solution* are identified by only a subscript, and the symbol is M_i. In summary, the three kinds of properties used in solution thermodynamics are distinguished by the following symbolism:

Solution properties	M,	for example: V, U, H, S, G
Partial properties	$\bar{M}_i$,	for example: $\bar{V}_i, \bar{U}_i, \bar{H}_i, \bar{S}_i, \bar{G}_i$
Pure-species properties	M_i,	for example: V_i, U_i, H_i, S_i, G_i

Comparison of Eq. (11.1) with Eq. (11.7) written for the Gibbs energy shows that the chemical potential and the partial molar Gibbs energy are identical; i.e.,

$$\mu_i \equiv \bar{G}_i \tag{11.8}$$

Example 11.1

The partial molar volume is defined as

$$\bar{V}_i \equiv \left[\frac{\partial(nV)}{\partial n_i}\right]_{P,T,n_j} \tag{A}$$

What physical interpretation can be given to this equation?

Solution

An open beaker containing an equimolar mixture of alcohol and water occupies a total volume nV at room temperature T and atmospheric pressure P. Add to this solution a drop of pure water, also at T and P, containing Δn_w moles, and mix it thoroughly into the solution, allowing sufficient time for heat exchange to return the contents of the beaker to the initial temperature. One might suppose that the volume of solution increases by an amount equal to the volume of the water added, i.e., by $V_w \, \Delta n_w$, where V_w is the molar volume of pure water at T and P. If this were true, the total volume change would be

$$\Delta(nV) = V_w \, \Delta n_w$$

However, experiment shows that the actual volume change is somewhat less. Evidently, the *effective* molar volume of water in the final solution is less than the molar volume of pure water at the same T and P. We may therefore write

$$\Delta(nV) = \widetilde{V}_w \, \Delta n_w \tag{B}$$

where $\widetilde{V}_w$ represents the effective molar volume of water in the final solution. Its experimental value is therefore given by

$$\widetilde{V}_w = \frac{\Delta(nV)}{\Delta n_w} \tag{C}$$

In the process described a drop of water is mixed with a substantial amount of solution, and the result is a small but measurable change in composition of the solution. For the effective molar volume of the water to be considered a property of the original equimolar solution, the process must be taken to the limit of an infinitesimal drop. Whence, $\Delta n_w \to 0$, and Eq. (C) becomes

$$\widetilde{V}_w = \lim_{\Delta n_w \to 0} \frac{\Delta(nV)}{\Delta n_w} = \frac{d(nV)}{dn_w}$$

Because T, P, and n_a (the number of moles of alcohol) are constant, this equation is more appropriately written as

$$\widetilde{V}_w = \left[\frac{\partial(nV)}{\partial n_w}\right]_{P,T,n_a}$$

Comparison with Eq. (A) shows that in this limit $\widetilde{V}_w$ is the partial molar volume $\bar{V}_w$ of the water in the equimolar solution, i.e., the rate of change of the total solution volume with n_w at constant T, P, and n_a for a specific composition. Written for the addition of dn_w moles of water to the solution, Eq. (B) is then

$$d(nV) = \bar{V}_w \, dn_w \qquad (D)$$

When $\bar{V}_w$ is considered the molar property of water as it exists in solution, the total volume change $d(nV)$ is merely this molar property multiplied by the number of moles dn_w of water added.

If dn_w moles of water is added to a volume of *pure* water, then we have every reason to expect the volume change of the system to be

$$d(nV) = V_w \, dn_w \qquad (E)$$

where V_w is the molar volume of pure water at T and P. Comparison of Eqs. (D) and (E) indicates that $\bar{V}_w = V_w$ when the "solution" is pure water.

Equations Relating Molar and Partial Molar Properties

The definition of a partial molar property, Eq. (11.7), provides the means for calculation of partial properties from solution-property data. Implicit in this definition is another, equally important, equation that allows the reverse, i.e., calculation of solution properties from knowledge of the partial properties. The derivation of this equation starts with the observation that the total thermodynamic properties of a homogeneous phase are functions of T, P, and the numbers of moles of the individual species which comprise the phase.[1] Thus for property M:

$$nM = \mathcal{M}(T, P, n_1, n_2, \ldots, n_i, \ldots)$$

The total differential of nM is

$$d(nM) = \left[\frac{\partial(nM)}{\partial P}\right]_{T,n} dP + \left[\frac{\partial(nM)}{\partial T}\right]_{P,n} dT + \sum_i \left[\frac{\partial(nM)}{\partial n_i}\right]_{P,T,n_j} dn_i$$

where subscript n indicates that *all* mole numbers are held constant, and subscript n_j that all mole numbers *except* n_i are held constant. Because the first two partial derivatives on the right are evaluated at constant n and because the partial derivative of the last term is given by Eq. (11.7), this equation has the simpler form:

$$d(nM) = n\left(\frac{\partial M}{\partial P}\right)_{T,x} dP + n\left(\frac{\partial M}{\partial T}\right)_{P,x} dT + \sum_i \bar{M}_i \, dn_i \qquad (11.9)$$

where subscript x denotes differentiation at constant composition. Because $n_i = x_i n$,

$$dn_i = x_i \, dn + n \, dx_i$$

Moreover,

$$d(nM) \equiv n \, dM + M \, dn$$

[1]Mere functionality does not make a set of variables into *canonical* variables. These are the canonical variables only for G.

When dn_i and $d(nM)$ are replaced in Eq. (11.9), it becomes

$$n\,dM + M\,dn = n\left(\frac{\partial M}{\partial P}\right)_{T,x} dP + n\left(\frac{\partial M}{\partial T}\right)_{P,x} dT + \sum_i \bar{M}_i(x_i\,dn + n\,dx_i)$$

The terms containing n are collected and separated from those containing dn to yield

$$\left[dM - \left(\frac{\partial M}{\partial P}\right)_{T,x} dP - \left(\frac{\partial M}{\partial T}\right)_{P,x} dT - \sum_i \bar{M}_i\,dx_i\right] n + \left[M - \sum_i x_i \bar{M}_i\right] dn = 0$$

In application, one is free to choose a system of any size, as represented by n, and to choose any variation in its size, as represented by dn. Thus n and dn are independent and arbitrary. The only way that the left side of this equation can then, in general, be zero is for *each* term in brackets to be zero. Therefore,

$$dM = \left(\frac{\partial M}{\partial P}\right)_{T,x} dP + \left(\frac{\partial M}{\partial T}\right)_{P,x} dT + \sum_i \bar{M}_i\,dx_i \tag{11.10}$$

and

$$M = \sum_i x_i \bar{M}_i \tag{11.11}$$

Multiplication of Eq. (11.11) by n yields the alternative expression:

$$nM = \sum_i n_i \bar{M}_i \tag{11.12}$$

Equation (11.10) is in fact just a special case of Eq. (11.9), obtained by setting $n = 1$, which also makes $n_i = x_i$. Equations (11.11) and (11.12) on the other hand are new and vital. Known as *summability relations*, they allow calculation of mixture properties from partial properties, playing a role opposite to that of Eq. (11.7), which provides for the calculation of partial properties from mixture properties.

One further important equation follows directly from Eqs. (11.10) and (11.11). With Eq. (11.11) a general expression for M, its differentiation yields a general expression for dM:

$$dM = \sum_i x_i\,d\bar{M}_i + \sum_i \bar{M}_i\,dx_i$$

Comparison of this equation with Eq. (11.10), another general equation for dM, yields the *Gibbs/Duhem*[2] *equation*:

$$\left(\frac{\partial M}{\partial P}\right)_{T,x} dP + \left(\frac{\partial M}{\partial T}\right)_{P,x} dT - \sum_i x_i\,d\bar{M}_i = 0 \tag{11.13}$$

[2]Pierre-Maurice-Marie Duhem (1861–1916), French physicist.

This equation must be satisfied for all changes in P, T, and the $\bar{M}_i$ caused by changes of state in a homogeneous phase. For the important special case of changes at constant T and P, it simplifies to:

$$\boxed{\sum_i x_i \, d\bar{M}_i = 0} \qquad \text{(const } T, P) \tag{11.14}$$

A Rationale for Partial Properties

Central to applied solution thermodynamics, the partial-property concept implies that a solution property represents a "whole," i.e., the sum of its parts as represented by partial properties $\bar{M}_i$ of the constituent species. This is the implication of Eq. (11.11), and is a proper interpretation provided one understands that the defining equation for $\bar{M}_i$, Eq. (11.7), is an apportioning formula which *arbitrarily* assigns to each species i its share of the solution property.[3]

The constituents of a solution are in fact intimately intermixed, and owing to molecular interactions cannot have private properties of their own. Nevertheless, partial properties, as defined by Eq. (11.7), have all the characteristics of properties of the individual species as they exist in solution. Thus for practical purposes they may be *assigned* as property values to the individual species.

Partial properties, like solution properties, are functions of composition. In the limit as a solution becomes pure in species i, both M and $\bar{M}_i$ approach the pure-species property M_i. Mathematically,

$$\lim_{x_i \to 1} M = \lim_{x_i \to 1} \bar{M}_i = M_i$$

For a species that approaches its infinite-dilution limit, i.e., the value as its mole fraction approaches zero, we can make no general statements. Values come from experiment or from models of solution behavior. Because it is an important quantity, we do give it a symbol, and by definition write:

$$\lim_{x_i \to 0} \bar{M}_i \equiv \bar{M}_i^{\infty}$$

The essential equations of this section are summarized as follows:

Definition
$$\bar{M}_i \equiv \left[\frac{\partial(nM)}{\partial n_i}\right]_{P,T,n_j} \tag{11.7}$$

which yields partial properties from total properties.

Summability
$$M = \sum_i x_i \bar{M}_i \tag{11.11}$$

which yields total properties from partial properties.

Gibbs/Duhem
$$\sum_i x_i \, d\bar{M}_i = \left(\frac{\partial M}{\partial P}\right)_{T,x} dP + \left(\frac{\partial M}{\partial T}\right)_{P,x} dT \tag{11.13}$$

which shows that the partial properties of species making up a solution are *not* independent of one another.

[3]Other apportioning equations, which make different allocations of the solution property, are possible and are equally valid.

Partial Properties in Binary Solutions

An equation for a partial property as a function of composition can always be derived from an equation for the solution property by direct application of Eq. (11.7). For binary systems, however, an alternative procedure may be more convenient. Written for a binary solution, the summability relation, Eq. (11.11), becomes

$$M = x_1 \bar{M}_1 + x_2 \bar{M}_2 \tag{A}$$

Whence,

$$dM = x_1\, d\bar{M}_1 + \bar{M}_1\, dx_1 + x_2\, d\bar{M}_2 + \bar{M}_2\, dx_2 \tag{B}$$

When M is known as a function of x_1 at constant T and P, the appropriate form of the Gibbs/Duhem equation is Eq. (11.14), expressed here as

$$x_1\, d\bar{M}_1 + x_2\, d\bar{M}_2 = 0 \tag{C}$$

Because $x_1 + x_2 = 1$, it follows that $dx_1 = -dx_2$. Eliminating dx_2 in favor of dx_1 in Eq. (B) and combining the result with Eq. (C) gives

$$\frac{dM}{dx_1} = \bar{M}_1 - \bar{M}_2 \tag{D}$$

Two equivalent forms of Eq. (A) result from elimination separately of x_1 and x_2:

$$M = \bar{M}_1 - x_2(\bar{M}_1 - \bar{M}_2) \qquad \text{and} \qquad M = x_1(\bar{M}_1 - \bar{M}_2) + \bar{M}_2$$

In combination with Eq. (D) these become

$$\bar{M}_1 = M + x_2 \frac{dM}{dx_1} \quad (11.15) \qquad \bar{M}_2 = M - x_1 \frac{dM}{dx_1} \quad (11.16)$$

Thus for binary systems, the partial properties are readily calculated directly from an expression for the solution property as a function of composition at constant T and P. The corresponding equations for multicomponent systems are much more complex, and are given in detail by Van Ness and Abbott.[4]

Equation (C), the Gibbs/Duhem equation, may be written in derivative forms:

$$x_1 \frac{d\bar{M}_1}{dx_1} + x_2 \frac{d\bar{M}_2}{dx_1} = 0 \quad (E) \qquad \frac{d\bar{M}_1}{dx_1} = -\frac{x_2}{x_1}\frac{d\bar{M}_2}{dx_1} \quad (F)$$

Clearly, when $\bar{M}_1$ and $\bar{M}_2$ are plotted vs. x_1, the slopes must be of opposite sign. Moreover,

$$\lim_{x_1 \to 1} \frac{d\bar{M}_1}{dx_1} = 0 \qquad \left(\text{Provided } \lim_{x_1 \to 1} \frac{d\bar{M}_2}{dx_1} \text{ is finite}\right)$$

Similarly,

$$\lim_{x_2 \to 1} \frac{d\bar{M}_2}{dx_1} = 0 \qquad \left(\text{Provided } \lim_{x_2 \to 1} \frac{d\bar{M}_1}{dx_1} \text{ is finite}\right)$$

[4] H. C. Van Ness and M. M. Abbott, *Classical Thermodynamics of Nonelectrolyte Solutions: With Applications to Phase Equilibria*, pp. 46–54, McGraw-Hill, New York, 1982.

Thus, plots of $\bar{M}_1$ and $\bar{M}_2$ vs. x_1 become horizontal as each species approaches purity.

Finally, given an expression for $\bar{M}_1(x_1)$, integration of Eq. (E) or Eq. (F) yields an expression for $\bar{M}_2(x_1)$ that satisfies the Gibbs/Duhem equation. This means that expressions cannot be specified arbitrarily for both $\bar{M}_1(x_1)$ and $\bar{M}_2(x_1)$.

Example 11.2

Describe a graphical interpretation of Eqs. (11.15) and (11.16).

Solution

Figure 11.1(a) shows a representative plot of M vs. x_1 for a binary system. The tangent line shown extends across the figure, intersecting the edges (at $x_1 = 1$ and $x_1 = 0$) at points labeled I_1 and I_2. As is evident from the figure, two equivalent expressions can be written for the slope of this tangent line:

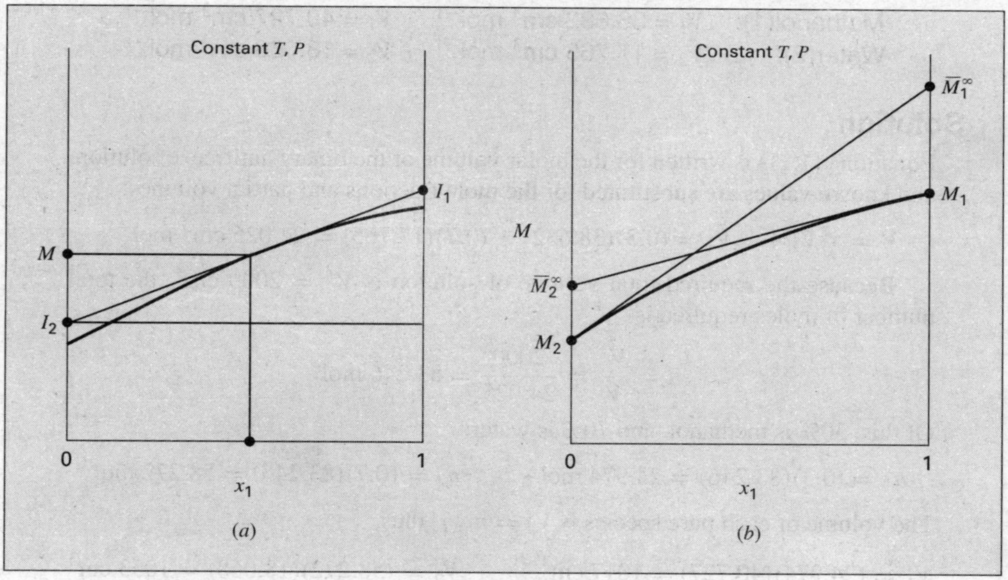

Figure 11.1: (a) Graphical construction of Example 11.2 (b) Infinite-dilution values of partial properties

$$\frac{dM}{dx_1} = \frac{M - I_2}{x_1} \quad \text{and} \quad \frac{dM}{dx_1} = I_1 - I_2$$

The first equation is solved for I_2; it combines with the second to give I_1:

$$I_2 = M - x_1\frac{dM}{dx_1} \quad \text{and} \quad I_1 = M + (1 - x_1)\frac{dM}{dx_1}$$

Comparisons of these expressions with Eqs. (11.16) and (11.15) show that

$$I_1 = \bar{M}_1 \qquad \text{and} \qquad I_2 = \bar{M}_2$$

Thus, the tangent intercepts give directly the values of the two partial properties. These intercepts of course shift as the point of tangency moves along the curve, and the limiting values are indicated by the constructions shown in Fig. 11.1(*b*). For the tangent line drawn at $x_1 = 0$ (pure species 2), $\bar{M}_2 = M_2$, and at the opposite intercept, $\bar{M}_1 = \bar{M}_1^{\infty}$. Similar comments apply to the tangent drawn at $x_1 = 1$ (pure species 1). In this case $\bar{M}_1 = M_1$ and $\bar{M}_2 = \bar{M}_2^{\infty}$.

Example 11.3

The need arises in a laboratory for 2000 cm^3 of an antifreeze solution consisting of 30 mole % methanol in water. What volumes of pure methanol and of pure water at 25°C (298.15 K) must be mixed to form the 2000 cm^3 of antifreeze, also at 25°C (298.15 K)? Partial molar volumes for methanol and water in a 30 mole % methanol solution and their pure-species molar volumes, both at 25°C (298.15 K), are

Methanol(1):	$\bar{V}_1 = 38.632$ cm^3 mol^{-1}	$V_1 = 40.727$ cm^3 mol^{-1}
Water(2):	$\bar{V}_2 = 17.765$ cm^3 mol^{-1}	$V_2 = 18.068$ cm^3 mol^{-1}

Solution

Equation (11.11) is written for the molar volume of the binary antifreeze solution, and known values are substituted for the mole fractions and partial volumes:

$$V = x_1\bar{V}_1 + x_2\bar{V}_2 = (0.3)(38.632) + (0.7)(17.765) = 24.025 \text{ cm}^3 \text{ mol}^{-1}$$

Because the required total volume of solution is $V^t = 2000$ cm^3, the total number of moles required is

$$n = \frac{V^t}{V} = \frac{2000}{24.025} = 83.246 \text{ mol}$$

Of this, 30% is methanol, and 70% is water:

$$n_1 = (0.3)(83.246) = 24.974 \text{ mol} \qquad n_2 = (0.7)(83.246) = 58.272 \text{ mol}$$

The volume of each pure species is $V_i^t = n_i V_i$; thus,

$$V_1^t = (24.974)(40.727) = 1017 \text{ cm}^3 \qquad V_2^t = (58.272)(18.068) = 1053 \text{ cm}^3$$

Values of $\bar{V}_1$, $\bar{V}_2$, and V for the binary solution methanol(1)/water(2) at 25°C (298.15 K) are plotted in Fig. 11.2 as functions of x_1. The line drawn tangent to the V-vs.-x_1 curve at $x_1 = 0.3$ illustrates the graphical procedure by which values of $\bar{V}_1$ and $\bar{V}_2$ may be obtained. Note that in conformance with the Gibbs/Duhem equation the slopes of the lines for $\bar{V}_1$ and $\bar{V}_2$ are everywhere of opposite sign, and that $\bar{V}_1$ becomes horizontal ($d\bar{V}_1/dx_1 = 0$) at $x_1 = 1$ and the curve for $\bar{V}_2$ becomes horizontal at $x_1 = 0$ or $x_2 = 1$. The curves for $\bar{V}_1$ and $\bar{V}_2$ in Fig. 11.2 appear to be horizontal at *both* ends; this is a peculiarity of the system considered.

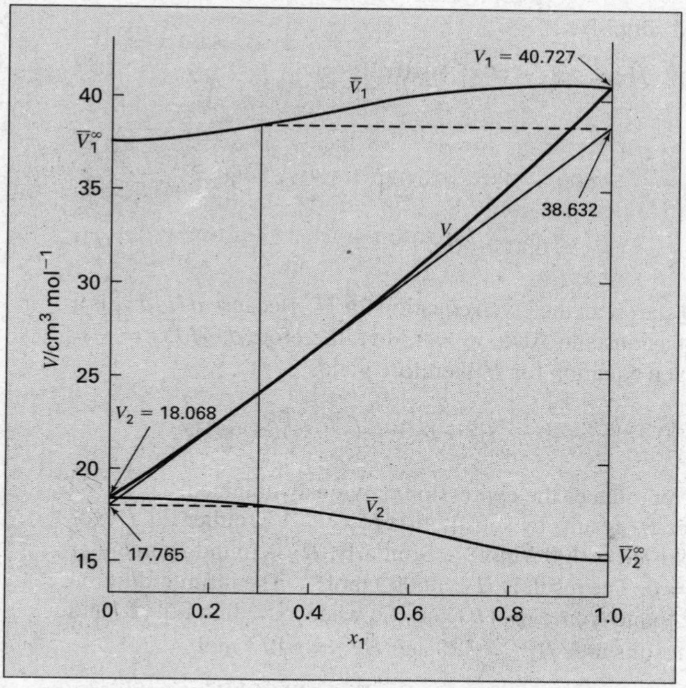

Figure 11.2: Molar volumes for methanol(1)/water(2) at 25°C and 1(atm). Numerical values relate to Ex. 11.3

Example 11.4

The enthalpy of a binary liquid system of species 1 and 2 at fixed T and P is represented by the equation

$$H = 400x_1 + 600x_2 + x_1x_2(40x_1 + 20x_2)$$

where H is in J mol^{-1}. Determine expressions for $\bar{H}_1$ and $\bar{H}_2$ as functions of x_1, numerical values for the pure-species enthalpies H_1 and H_2, and numerical values for the partial enthalpies at infinite dilution $\bar{H}_1^\infty$ and $\bar{H}_2^\infty$.

Solution

Replace x_2 by $1 - x_1$ in the given equation for H and simplify:

$$H = 600 - 180x_1 - 20x_1^3 \qquad (A)$$

Whence,
$$\frac{dH}{dx_1} = -180 - 60x_1^2$$

By Eq. (11.15),
$$\bar{H}_1 = H + x_2\frac{dH}{dx_1}$$

Then,
$$\bar{H}_1 = 600 - 180x_1 - 20x_1^3 - 180x_2 - 60x_1^2x_2$$

Replace x_2 by $1 - x_1$ and simplify:

$$\bar{H}_1 = 420 - 60x_1^2 + 40x_1^3 \qquad (B)$$

By Eq. (11.16),

$$\bar{H}_2 = H - x_1 \frac{dH}{dx_1} = 600 - 180x_1 - 20x_1^3 + 180x_1 + 60x_1^3$$

or

$$\bar{H}_2 = 600 + 40x_1^3 \qquad (C)$$

One can equally well start with the given equation for H. Because dH/dx_1 is a *total* derivative, x_2 is not a constant. Also, $x_2 = 1 - x_1$; therefore $dx_2/dx_1 = -1$. Differentiation of the given equation for H therefore yields

$$\frac{dH}{dx_1} = 400 - 600 + x_1 x_2(40 - 20) + (40x_1 + 20x_2)(-x_1 + x_2)$$

Replacing x_2 by $1 - x_1$ reproduces the expression previously obtained.

A numerical value for H_1 results by substitution of $x_1 = 1$ in either Eq. (A) or (B). Both equations yield $H_1 = 400 \text{ J mol}^{-1}$. Similarly, H_2 is found from either Eq. (A) or (C) when $x_1 = 0$. The result is $H_2 = 600 \text{ J mol}^{-1}$. The infinite-dilution values $\bar{H}_1^\infty$ and $\bar{H}_2^\infty$ are found from Eqs. (B) and (C) when $x_1 = 0$ in Eq. (B) and $x_1 = 1$ in Eq. (C). The results are: $\bar{H}_1^\infty = 420$ and $\bar{H}_2^\infty = 640 \text{ J mol}^{-1}$

Exercise: Show that the partial properties as given by Eqs. (B) and (C) combine by summability to give Eq. (A), and conform to all requirements of the Gibbs/Duhem equation.

Relations among Partial Properties

We show now how partial properties are related to one another. By Eq. (11.8), $\mu_i \equiv \bar{G}_i$, and Eq. (11.2) may be written as

$$d(nG) = (nV)dP - (nS)dT + \sum_i \bar{G}_i \, dn_i \qquad (11.17)$$

Application of the criterion of exactness, Eq. (6.12), yields the Maxwell relation,

$$\left(\frac{\partial V}{\partial T}\right)_{P,n} = -\left(\frac{\partial S}{\partial P}\right)_{T,n} \qquad (6.16)$$

plus the two additional equations:

$$\left(\frac{\partial \bar{G}_i}{\partial P}\right)_{T,n} = \left[\frac{\partial (nV)}{\partial n_i}\right]_{P,T,n_j} \qquad \left(\frac{\partial \bar{G}_i}{\partial T}\right)_{P,n} = -\left[\frac{\partial (nS)}{\partial n_i}\right]_{P,T,n_j}$$

where subscript n indicates constancy of all n_i, and therefore of composition, and subscript n_j indicates that all mole numbers except the ith are held constant. In view of Eq. (11.7), the last two equations are most simply expressed:

$$\left(\frac{\partial \bar{G}_i}{\partial P}\right)_{T,x} = \bar{V}_i \qquad (11.18)$$	$$\left(\frac{\partial \bar{G}_i}{\partial T}\right)_{P,x} = -\bar{S}_i \qquad (11.19)$$

These equations allow calculation of the effects of P and T on the partial Gibbs energy (or chemical potential). They are the partial-property analogs of Eqs. (11.4) and (11.5).

Every equation that provides a *linear* relation among thermodynamic properties of a *constant-composition* solution has as its counterpart an equation connecting the corresponding partial properties of each species in the solution.

An example is based on the equation that defines enthalpy: $H = U + PV$. For n moles,

$$nH = nU + P(nV)$$

Differentiation with respect to n_i at constant T, P, and n_j yields

$$\left[\frac{\partial(nH)}{\partial n_i}\right]_{P,T,n_j} = \left[\frac{\partial(nU)}{\partial n_i}\right]_{P,T,n_j} + P\left[\frac{\partial(nV)}{\partial n_i}\right]_{P,T,n_j}$$

By Eq. (11.7) this becomes $\qquad \bar{H}_i = \bar{U}_i + P\bar{V}_i$

which is the partial-property analog of Eq. (2.11).

In a constant-composition solution, $\bar{G}_i$ is a function of P and T, and therefore:

$$d\bar{G}_i = \left(\frac{\partial \bar{G}_i}{\partial P}\right)_{T,x} dP + \left(\frac{\partial \bar{G}_i}{\partial T}\right)_{P,x} dT$$

By Eqs. (11.18) and (11.19), $\qquad d\bar{G}_i = \bar{V}_i\, dP - \bar{S}_i\, dT$

This may be compared with Eq. (6.10). These examples illustrate the parallelism that exists between equations for a constant-composition solution and the corresponding equations for the partial properties of the species in solution. We can therefore write simply by analogy many equations that relate partial properties.

11.4 THE IDEAL-GAS MIXTURE MODEL

Despite its limited ability to describe actual mixture behavior, the ideal-gas mixture model provides a conceptual basis upon which to build the structure of solution thermodynamics. It is a useful property model because it

- has a molecular basis
- approximates reality in the well-defined limit of zero pressure
- is analytically simple

At the molecular level, an ideal gas is a collection of particles with no intermolecular forces and negligible particle volume (compared with the molar volume). However, the particles themselves have *structure*, and differences in molecular structure give rise to differences in ideal-gas heat capacities (Sec. 4.1).

The molar volume of an ideal gas is $V = RT/P$ [Eq. (3.14)] regardless of the nature of the gas. Thus all ideal gases, whether pure or mixed, have the same molar volume at the same T and P. The partial molar volume of species i in an ideal-gas mixture is found from Eq. (11.7) applied to the volume; superscript ig denotes the ideal-gas state:

$$\bar{V}_i^{ig} = \left[\frac{\partial(nV^{ig})}{\partial n_i}\right]_{T,P,n_j} = \left[\frac{\partial(nRT/P)}{\partial n_i}\right]_{T,P,n_j} = \frac{RT}{P}\left(\frac{\partial n}{\partial n_i}\right)_{n_j} = \frac{RT}{P}$$

where the final equality depends on the equation $n = n_i + \sum_j n_j$. This result means that for ideal gases at given T and P the partial molar volume, the pure-species molar volume, and the mixture molar volume are identical:

$$\bar{V}_i^{ig} = V_i^{ig} = V^{ig} = \frac{RT}{P} \tag{11.20}$$

We **define** the *partial pressure* of species i in an ideal-gas mixture as the pressure that species i would exert if it alone occupied the molar volume of the mixture. Thus,[5]

$$p_i = \frac{y_i RT}{V^{ig}} = y_i P \qquad (i = 1, 2, \ldots, N)$$

where y_i is the mole fraction of species i. The partial pressures obviously sum to the total pressure.

Because the ideal-gas mixture model presumes molecules of zero volume that do not interact, the thermodynamic properties (other than molar volume) of the constituent species are independent of one another, and each species has its own set of private properties. This is the basis for the following statement of *Gibbs's theorem*:

A partial molar property (other than volume) of a constituent species in an ideal-gas mixture is equal to the corresponding molar property of the species as a pure ideal gas at the mixture temperature but at a pressure equal to its partial pressure in the mixture.

This is expressed mathematically for generic partial property $\bar{M}_i^{ig} \neq \bar{V}_i^{ig}$ by the equation:

$$\bar{M}_i^{ig}(T, P) = M_i^{ig}(T, p_i) \tag{11.21}$$

The enthalpy of an ideal gas is independent of pressure; therefore

$$\bar{H}_i^{ig}(T, P) = H_i^{ig}(T, p_i) = H_i^{ig}(T, P)$$

More simply,

$$\bar{H}_i^{ig} = H_i^{ig} \tag{11.22}$$

[5]This definition does *not* make the partial pressure a partial molar property.

where H_i^{ig} is the pure-species value at the *mixture* T and P. An analogous equation applies for U^{ig} and other properties that are *independent of pressure.*

The entropy of an ideal gas *does* depend on pressure, and by Eq. (6.24),

$$dS_i^{ig} = -R\,d\ln P \qquad \text{(const } T)$$

Integration from p_i to P gives

$$S_i^{ig}(T,P) - S_i^{ig}(T,p_i) = -R\ln\frac{P}{p_i} = -R\ln\frac{P}{y_i P} = R\ln y_i$$

Whence,

$$S_i^{ig}(T,p_i) = S_i^{ig}(T,P) - R\ln y_i$$

Substituting this result into Eq. (11.21) written for the entropy yields

$$\bar{S}_i^{ig}(T,P) = S_i^{ig}(T,P) - R\ln y_i$$

or

$$\bar{S}_i^{ig} = S_i^{ig} - R\ln y_i \tag{11.23}$$

where S_i^{ig} is the pure-species value at the mixture T and P.

For the Gibbs energy of an ideal-gas mixture, $G^{ig} = H^{ig} - TS^{ig}$; the parallel relation for partial properties is

$$\bar{G}_i^{ig} = \bar{H}_i^{ig} - T\bar{S}_i^{ig}$$

In combination with Eqs. (11.22) and (11.23) this becomes

$$\bar{G}_i^{ig} = H_i^{ig} - TS_i^{ig} + RT\ln y_i$$

or

$$\mu_i^{ig} \equiv \bar{G}_i^{ig} = G_i^{ig} + RT\ln y_i \tag{11.24}$$

Differentiation of this equation in accord with Eqs. (11.18) and (11.19) confirms the results expressed by Eqs. (11.20) and (11.23).

The summability relation, Eq. (11.11), with Eqs. (11.22), (11.23), and (11.24) yields

$$H^{ig} = \sum_i y_i H_i^{ig} \tag{11.25}$$

$$S^{ig} = \sum_i y_i S_i^{ig} - R\sum_i y_i \ln y_i \tag{11.26}$$

$$G^{ig} = \sum_i y_i G_i^{ig} + RT\sum_i y_i \ln y_i \tag{11.27}$$

Equations analogous to Eq. (11.25) may be written for both C_P^{ig} and V^{ig}. The former appears as Eq. (4.6), but the latter reduces to an identity because of Eq. (11.20).

When Eq. (11.25) is written,

$$H^{ig} - \sum_i y_i H_i^{ig} = 0$$

the difference on the left is the enthalpy change associated with a process in which appropriate amounts of the pure species at T and P are mixed to form one mole of mixture at the same T and P. For ideal gases, this *enthalpy change of mixing* (Sec. 12.3) is zero.

When Eq. (11.26) is rearranged as

$$S^{ig} - \sum_i y_i S_i^{ig} = R \sum_i y_i \ln \frac{1}{y_i}$$

the left side is the *entropy change of mixing* for ideal gases. Because $1/y_i > 1$, this quantity is always positive, in agreement with the second law. The mixing process is inherently irreversible, and for ideal gases mixing at constant T and P is not accompanied by heat transfer [Eq. (11.25)].

An alternative expression for the chemical potential μ_i^{ig} results when G_i^{ig} in Eq. (11.24) is replaced by an expression giving its T and P dependence. This comes from Eq. (6.10) written for an ideal gas:

$$dG_i^{ig} = V_i^{ig} dP = \frac{RT}{P} dP = RT\, d\ln P \qquad \text{(const } T\text{)}$$

Integration gives

$$G_i^{ig} = \Gamma_i(T) + RT \ln P \tag{11.28}$$

where $\Gamma_i(T)$, the integration constant at constant T, is a species-dependent function of temperature only.[6] Equation (11.24) is now written as

$$\boxed{\mu_i^{ig} \equiv \bar{G}_i^{ig} = \Gamma_i(T) + RT \ln(y_i P)} \tag{11.29}$$

where the argument of the logarithm is the partial pressure. Application of the summability relation, Eq. (11.11), produces an expression for the Gibbs energy of an ideal-gas mixture:

$$\boxed{G^{ig} = \sum_i y_i \Gamma_i(T) + RT \sum_i y_i \ln(y_i P)} \tag{11.30}$$

These equations, remarkable in their simplicity, provide a full description of ideal-gas behavior. Because T, P, and $\{y_i\}$ are the canonical variables for the Gibbs energy, all other equations for the ideal-gas model can be generated from them.

11.5 FUGACITY AND FUGACITY COEFFICIENT: PURE SPECIES

As evident from Eq. (11.6), the chemical potential μ_i provides the fundamental criterion for phase equilibria. This is true as well for chemical-reaction equilibria. However, it exhibits

[6] A dimensional ambiguity is evident with Eq. (11.28) and with analogous equations to follow in that P has units, whereas $\ln P$ must be dimensionless. This difficulty is more apparent than real, because the Gibbs energy is always expressed on a relative scale, absolute values being unknown. Thus in application only *differences* in Gibbs energy appear, leading to *ratios* of quantities with units of pressure in the argument of the logarithm. The only requirement is that consistency of pressure units be maintained.

characteristics which discourage its use. The Gibbs energy, and hence μ_i, is defined in relation to the internal energy and entropy. Because absolute values of internal energy are unknown, the same is true for μ_i. Moreover, Eq. (11.29) shows that μ_i^{ig} approaches negative infinity when either P or y_i approaches zero. This is true not just for an ideal gas but for any gas. Although these characteristics do not preclude the use of chemical potentials, the application of equilibrium criteria is facilitated by introduction of the *fugacity*,[7] a property that takes the place of μ_i but which does not exhibit its less desirable characteristics.

The origin of the fugacity concept resides in Eq. (11.28), valid only for pure species i in the ideal-gas state. For a real fluid, we write an analogous equation that **defines** f_i, the *fugacity* of pure species i:

$$G_i \equiv \Gamma_i(T) + RT \ln f_i \tag{11.31}$$

This new property f_i, with units of pressure, replaces P in Eq. (11.28). Clearly, if Eq. (11.28) is a special case of Eq. (11.31), then:

$$f_i^{ig} = P \tag{11.32}$$

and the fugacity of pure species i as an ideal gas is necessarily equal to its pressure. Subtraction of Eq. (11.28) from Eq. (11.31), both written for the same T and P, gives

$$G_i - G_i^{ig} = RT \ln \frac{f_i}{P}$$

By the definition of Eq. (6.41), $G_i - G_i^{ig}$ is the *residual Gibbs energy*, G_i^R; thus,

$$\boxed{G_i^R = RT \ln \phi_i} \tag{11.33}$$

where the dimensionless ratio f_i/P has been **defined** as another new property, the *fugacity coefficient*, given by symbol ϕ_i:

$$\boxed{\phi_i \equiv \frac{f_i}{P}} \tag{11.34}$$

These equations apply to pure species i in any phase at any condition. However, as a special case they must be valid for ideal gases, for which $G_i^R = 0$, $\phi_i = 1$, and Eq. (11.28) is recovered from Eq. (11.31). Moreover, we may write Eq. (11.33) for $P = 0$, and combine it with Eq. (6.45):

$$\lim_{P\to 0}\left(\frac{G_i^R}{RT}\right) = \lim_{P\to 0} \ln \phi_i = J$$

As explained in connection with Eq. (6.48), the value of J is immaterial, and is set equal to zero. Whence,

$$\lim_{P\to 0} \ln \phi_i = \lim_{P\to 0} \ln\left(\frac{f_i}{P}\right) = 0$$

[7]This quantity originated with Gilbert Newton Lewis (1875–1946), American physical chemist, who also developed the concepts of the partial property and the ideal solution.

and
$$\lim_{P\to 0}\phi_i = \lim_{P\to 0}\frac{f_i}{P} = 1$$

The identification of $\ln\phi_i$ with G_i^R/RT by Eq. (11.33) permits its evaluation by the integral of Eq. (6.49):

$$\boxed{\ln\phi_i = \int_0^P (Z_i - 1)\frac{dP}{P}} \qquad \text{(const } T\text{)} \tag{11.35}$$

Fugacity coefficients (and therefore fugacities) for pure gases are evaluated by this equation from PVT data or from a volume-explicit equation of state.

For example, when the compressibility factor is given by Eq. (3.38),

$$Z_i - 1 = \frac{B_{ii}P}{RT}$$

Because the second virial coefficient B_{ii} is a function of temperature only for a pure species, substitution into Eq. (11.35) gives

$$\ln\phi_i = \frac{B_{ii}}{RT}\int_0^P dP \qquad \text{(const } T\text{)}$$

Whence,
$$\ln\phi_i = \frac{B_{ii}P}{RT} \tag{11.36}$$

Fugacity Coefficients from the Generic Cubic Equation of State

Evaluation of fugacity coefficients through cubic equations of state (e.g., the van der Waals, Redlich/Kwong, Soave/Redlich/Kwong, and Peng/Robinson equations) follows directly from combination of Eqs. (11.33) and (6.66b):

$$\boxed{\ln\phi_i = Z_i - 1 - \ln(Z_i - \beta_i) - q_i I_i} \tag{11.37}$$

where β_i is given by Eq. (3.50); q_i, by Eq. (3.51); and I_i, by Eq. (6.65b), all written for pure species i [for the van der Waals equation, $I_i = \beta_i/Z_i$]. Application of Eq. (11.37) at a given T and P requires prior solution of an equation of state for Z_i by Eq. (3.52) for a vapor phase or Eq. (3.56) for a liquid phase.

Vapor/Liquid Equilibrium for Pure Species

Equation (11.31), which defines the fugacity of pure species i, may be written for species i as a saturated vapor and as a saturated liquid at the same temperature:

$$G_i^v = \Gamma_i(T) + RT\ln f_i^v \tag{11.38a}$$

$$G_i^l = \Gamma_i(T) + RT\ln f_i^l \tag{11.38b}$$

By difference,

$$G_i^v - G_i^l = RT \ln \frac{f_i^v}{f_i^l}$$

This equation applies to the change of state from saturated liquid to saturated vapor, both at temperature T and at the vapor pressure P_i^{sat}. According to Eq. (6.69), $G_i^v - G_i^l = 0$; therefore:

$$f_i^v = f_i^l = f_i^{\text{sat}} \tag{11.39}$$

where f_i^{sat} indicates the value for either saturated liquid or saturated vapor. Coexisting phases of saturated liquid and saturated vapor are in equilibrium; Eq. (11.39) therefore expresses a fundamental principle:

For a pure species coexisting liquid and vapor phases are in equilibrium when they have the same temperature, pressure, and fugacity.[8]

An alternative formulation is based on the corresponding fugacity coefficients:

$$\phi_i^{\text{sat}} = \frac{f_i^{\text{sat}}}{P_i^{\text{sat}}} \tag{11.40}$$

Whence,

$$\phi_i^v = \phi_i^l = \phi_i^{\text{sat}} \tag{11.41}$$

This equation, expressing equality of fugacity coefficients, is an equally valid criterion of vapor/liquid equilibrium for pure species.

Fugacity of a Pure Liquid

The fugacity of pure species i as a compressed liquid may be calculated from the product of easily evaluated ratios:

$$f_i^l(P) = \underbrace{\frac{f_i^v(P_i^{\text{sat}})}{P_i^{\text{sat}}}}_{(A)} \underbrace{\frac{f_i^l(P_i^{\text{sat}})}{f_i^v(P_i^{\text{sat}})}}_{(B)} \underbrace{\frac{f_i^l(P)}{f_i^l(P_i^{\text{sat}})}}_{(C)} P_i^{\text{sat}}$$

All terms are at the temperature of interest. Inspection reveals that cancelation of numerators and denominators produces a mathematical identity.

Ratio (A) is the vapor-phase fugacity coefficient of pure vapor i at its vapor/liquid saturation pressure, designated ϕ_i^{sat}. It is given by Eq. (11.35), written,

$$\ln \phi_i^{\text{sat}} = \int_0^{P_i^{\text{sat}}} (Z_i^v - 1)\frac{dP}{P} \qquad \text{(const } T\text{)} \tag{11.42}$$

In accord with Eq. (11.39) ratio (B) is unity. Ratio (C) reflects the effect of pressure on the fugacity of pure liquid i. The basis for its calculation is Eq. (6.10), integrated at constant T to

[8]The word *fugacity* is based on a Latin root meaning to flee or escape, also the basis for the word *fugitive*. Thus fugacity has been interpreted to mean "escaping tendency." When the escaping tendency is the same for the two phases, they are in equilibrium.

give

$$G_i - G_i^{\text{sat}} = \int_{P_i^{\text{sat}}}^{P} V_i^l \, dP$$

Another expression for this difference results when Eq. (11.31) is written for both G_i and G_i^{sat}; subtraction then yields

$$G_i - G_i^{\text{sat}} = RT \ln \frac{f_i}{f_i^{\text{sat}}}$$

The two expressions for $G_i - G_i^{\text{sat}}$ are set equal:

$$\ln \frac{f_i}{f_i^{\text{sat}}} = \frac{1}{RT} \int_{P_i^{\text{sat}}}^{P} V_i^l \, dP$$

Ratio (C) is then

$$\frac{f_i^l(P)}{f_i^l(P_i^{\text{sat}})} = \exp \frac{1}{RT} \int_{P_i^{\text{sat}}}^{P} V_i^l \, dP$$

Substituting for the three ratios in the initial equation yields

$$f_i = \phi_i^{\text{sat}} P_i^{\text{sat}} \exp \frac{1}{RT} \int_{P_i^{\text{sat}}}^{P} V_i^l \, dP \qquad (11.43)$$

Because V_i^l, the liquid-phase molar volume, is a very weak function of P at temperatures well below T_c, an excellent approximation is often obtained when V_i^l is assumed constant at the value for saturated liquid. In this case,

$$f_i = \phi_i^{\text{sat}} P_i^{\text{sat}} \exp \frac{V_i^l (P - P_i^{\text{sat}})}{RT} \qquad (11.44)$$

The exponential is known as a Poynting[9] factor. Data required for application of this equation:

- Values of Z_i^v for calculation of ϕ_i^{sat} by Eq. (11.42). These may come from an equation of state, from experiment, or from a generalized correlation.
- The liquid-phase molar volume V_i^l, usually the value for saturated liquid.
- A value for P_i^{sat}.

If Z_i^v is given by Eq. (3.38), the simplest form of the virial equation, then

$$Z_i^v - 1 = \frac{B_{ii} P}{RT} \qquad \text{and} \qquad \phi_i^{\text{sat}} = \exp \frac{B_{ii} P_i^{\text{sat}}}{RT}$$

and Eq. (11.44) becomes

$$f_i = P_i^{\text{sat}} \exp \frac{B_{ii} P_i^{\text{sat}} + V_i^l (P - P_i^{\text{sat}})}{RT} \qquad (11.45)$$

In the following example data from the steam tables form the basis for calculation of the fugacity and fugacity coefficient of both vapor and liquid water as a function of pressure.

[9] John Henry Poynting (1852–1914), British physicist.

Example 11.5

For H_2O at a temperature of 300°C (573.15 K) and for pressures up to 10 000 kPa (100 bar) calculate values of f_i and ϕ_i from data in the steam tables and plot them vs. P.

Solution

Equation (11.31) is written twice: first, for a state at pressure P; second, for a low-pressure reference state, denoted by *, both for temperature T:

$$G_i = \Gamma_i(T) + RT \ln f_i \qquad \text{and} \qquad G_i^* = \Gamma_i(T) + RT \ln f_i^*$$

Subtraction eliminates $\Gamma_i(T)$, and yields

$$\ln \frac{f_i}{f_i^*} = \frac{1}{RT}(G_i - G_i^*)$$

By definition $G_i = H_i - TS_i$ and $G_i^* = H_i^* - TS_i^*$; substitution gives

$$\ln \frac{f_i}{f_i^*} = \frac{1}{R}\left[\frac{H_i - H_i^*}{T} - (S_i - S_i^*)\right] \qquad (A)$$

The lowest pressure for which data at 300°C (573.15 K) are given in the steam tables is 1 kPa. Steam at these conditions is for practical purposes an ideal gas, for which $f_i^* = P^* = 1$ kPa. Data for this state provide the following reference values:

$$H_i^* = 3076.8 \text{ J g}^{-1} \qquad S_i^* = 10.3450 \text{ J g}^{-1}\text{ K}^{-1}$$

Equation (A) may now be applied to states of superheated steam at 300°C (573.15 K) for various values of P from 1 kPa to the saturation pressure of 8592.7 kPa. For example, at $P = 4000$ kPa and 300°C (573.15 K):

$$H_i = 2962.0 \text{ J g}^{-1} \qquad S_i = 6.3642 \text{ J g}^{-1}\text{ K}^{-1}$$

Values of H and S must be multiplied by the molar mass of water (18.015) to put them on a molar basis for substitution into Eq. (A):

$$\ln \frac{f_i}{f^*} = \frac{18.015}{8.314}\left[\frac{2962.0 - 3076.8}{573.15} - (6.3642 - 10.3450)\right] = 8.1917$$

Whence,
$$f_i/f^* = 3611.0$$

$$f_i = (3611.0)(f^*) = (3611.0)(1 \text{ kPa}) = 3611.0 \text{ kPa}$$

Thus the fugacity coefficient at 4000 kPa is

$$\phi_i = \frac{f_i}{P} = \frac{3611.0}{4000} = 0.9028$$

Similar calculations at other pressures lead to the values plotted in Fig. 11.3 at pressures up to the saturation pressure $P_i^{sat} = 8592.7$ kPa. At this pressure,

$$\phi_i^{sat} = 0.7843 \qquad \text{and} \qquad f_i^{sat} = 6738.9 \text{ kPa}$$

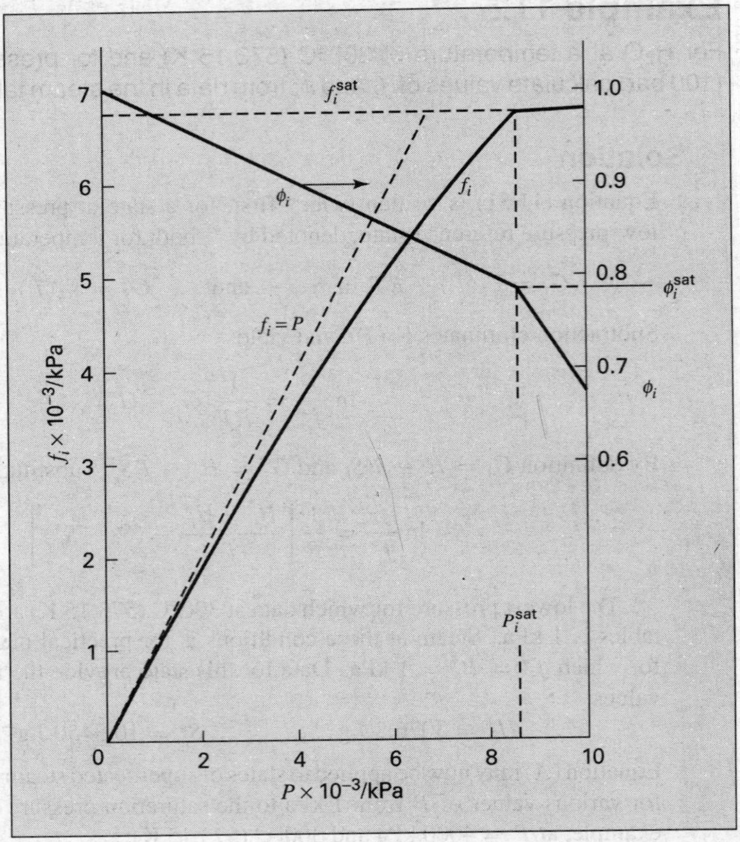

Figure 11.3: Fugacity and fugacity coefficient of steam at 300°C (573.15 K)

According to Eqs. (11.39) and (11.41), the saturation values are unchanged by condensation. Although the plots are therefore continuous, they do show discontinuities in slope. Values of f_i and ϕ_i for liquid water at higher pressures are found by application of Eq. (11.44), with V_i^l equal to the molar volume of saturated liquid water at 300°C:

$$V_i^l = (1.403)(18.015) = 25.28 \text{ cm}^3 \text{ mol}^{-1}$$

At 10 000 kPa, for example, Eq. (11.44) becomes

$$f_i = (0.7843)(8592.7) \exp \frac{(25.28)(10\,000 - 8592.7)}{(8{,}314)(573.15)} = 6789.8 \text{ kPa}$$

The fugacity coefficient of liquid water at these conditions is

$$\phi_i = f_i/P = 6789.8/10\,000 = 0.6790$$

Such calculations allow completion of Fig. 11.3, where the solid lines show how f_i and ϕ_i vary with pressure.

The curve for f_i starts at the origin, and deviates increasingly from the dashed line for an ideal gas ($f_i = P$) as the pressure rises. At P_i^{sat} there is a discontinuity in slope, and the curve then rises very slowly with increasing pressure, indicating that the fugacity of liquid water at 300°C (573.15 K) is a weak function of pressure. This behavior is characteristic of liquids at temperatures well below the critical temperature. The fugacity coefficient ϕ_i decreases steadily from its zero-pressure value of unity as the pressure rises. Its rapid decrease in the liquid region is a consequence of the near-constancy of the fugacity itself.

11.6 FUGACITY AND FUGACITY COEFFICIENT: SPECIES IN SOLUTION

The definition of the fugacity of a species in solution is parallel to the definition of the pure-species fugacity. For species i in a mixture of real gases or in a solution of liquids, the equation analogous to Eq. (11.29), the ideal-gas expression, is

$$\mu_i \equiv \Gamma_i(T) + RT \ln \hat{f}_i \qquad (11.46)$$

where $\hat{f}_i$ is the fugacity of species i in solution, replacing the partial pressure $y_i P$. This definition of $\hat{f}_i$ does not make it a partial molar property, and it is therefore identified by a circumflex rather than by an overbar.

A direct application of this definition indicates its potential utility. Equation (11.6) is the fundamental criterion for phase equilibrium. Because all phases in equilibrium are at the same temperature, an alternative and equally general criterion follows immediately from Eq. (11.46):

$$\boxed{\hat{f}_i^\alpha = \hat{f}_i^\beta = \cdots = \hat{f}_i^\pi} \qquad (i = 1, 2, \ldots, N) \qquad (11.47)$$

Thus, multiple phases at the same *T* and *P* are in equilibrium when the fugacity of each constituent species is the same in all phases.

This criterion of equilibrium is the one usually applied by chemical engineers in the solution of phase-equilibrium problems.

For the specific case of multicomponent vapor/liquid equilibrium, Eq. (11.47) becomes:

$$\hat{f}_i^v = \hat{f}_i^l \qquad (i = 1, 2, \ldots, N) \qquad (11.48)$$

Equation (11.39) results as a special case when this relation is applied to the vapor/liquid equilibrium of *pure* species i.

The definition of a residual property is given in Sec. 6.2:

$$M^R \equiv M - M^{ig} \qquad (6.41)$$

where M is the molar (or unit-mass) value of a thermodynamic property and M^{ig} is the value that the property would have for an ideal gas of the same composition at the same T and P. The defining equation for a *partial residual property* $\bar{M}_i^R$ follows from this equation. Multiplied by n mol of mixture, it becomes

$$nM^R = nM - nM^{ig}$$

Differentiation with respect to n_i at constant T, P, and n_j gives

$$\left[\frac{\partial(nM^R)}{\partial n_i}\right]_{P,T,n_j} = \left[\frac{\partial(nM)}{\partial n_i}\right]_{P,T,n_j} - \left[\frac{\partial(nM^{ig})}{\partial n_i}\right]_{P,T,n_j}$$

Reference to Eq. (11.7) shows that each term has the form of a partial molar property. Thus,

$$\bar{M}_i^R = \bar{M}_i - \bar{M}_i^{ig} \tag{11.49}$$

Because residual properties measure departures§ from ideal-gas values, their most logical use is as gas-phase properties, but in fact they also find use as liquid-phase properties.

Written for the residual Gibbs energy, Eq. (11.49) becomes

$$\boxed{\bar{G}_i^R = \bar{G}_i - \bar{G}_i^{ig}} \tag{11.50}$$

an equation which defines the *partial residual Gibbs energy.*

Subtracting Eq. (11.29) from Eq. (11.46), both written for the same T and P, yields

$$\mu_i - \mu_i^{ig} = RT \ln \frac{\hat{f}_i}{y_i P}$$

This result combined with Eq. (11.50) and the identity $\mu_i \equiv \bar{G}_i$ gives

$$\boxed{\bar{G}_i^R = RT \ln \hat{\phi}_i} \tag{11.51}$$

where by **definition**,

$$\boxed{\hat{\phi}_i \equiv \frac{\hat{f}_i}{y_i P}} \tag{11.52}$$

The dimensionless ratio $\hat{\phi}_i$ is called the *fugacity coefficient of species i in solution*. Although most commonly applied to gases, the fugacity coefficient may also be used for liquids, and in this case mole fraction y_i is replaced by x_i. Because Eq. (11.29) for an ideal gas is a special case of the Eq. (11.46), then

$$\hat{f}_i^{ig} = y_i P \tag{11.53}$$

Thus the fugacity of species i in an ideal-gas mixture is equal to its partial pressure. Moreover, $\hat{\phi}_i^{ig} = 1$, and for an ideal gas $\bar{G}_i^R = 0$.

The Fundamental Residual-Property Relation

The fundamental property relation given by Eq. (11.2) is put into an alternative form through the mathematical identity (also used in Sec. 6.1):

$$d\left(\frac{nG}{RT}\right) \equiv \frac{1}{RT}d(nG) - \frac{nG}{RT^2}dT$$

In this equation $d(nG)$ is eliminated by Eq. (11.2) and G is replaced by its definition, $H - TS$. The result, after algebraic reduction, is

$$d\left(\frac{nG}{RT}\right) = \frac{nV}{RT}dP - \frac{nH}{RT^2}dT + \sum_i \frac{\bar{G}_i}{RT}dn_i \tag{11.54}$$

All terms in Eq. (11.54) have the units of moles; moreover, in contrast to Eq. (11.2), the enthalpy rather than the entropy appears on the right side. Equation (11.54) is a general relation expressing nG/RT as a function of *all* of its canonical variables, T, P, and the mole numbers. It reduces to Eq. (6.37) for the special case of 1 mol of a constant-composition phase. Equations (6.38) and (6.39) follow from either equation, and equations for the other thermodynamic properties then come from appropriate defining equations. Knowledge of G/RT as a function of its canonical variables allows evaluation of all other thermodynamic properties, and therefore implicitly contains complete property information. Unfortunately, we do not have the experimental means by which to exploit this characteristic. However, an analogous equation relating residual properties proves useful.

Because Eq. (11.54) is general, it may be written for the special case of an ideal gas:

$$d\left(\frac{nG^{ig}}{RT}\right) = \frac{nV^{ig}}{RT}dP - \frac{nH^{ig}}{RT^2}dT + \sum_i \frac{\bar{G}_i^{ig}}{RT}dn_i$$

In view of Eqs. (6.41) and (11.50), subtracting this equation from Eq. (11.54) gives

$$d\left(\frac{nG^R}{RT}\right) = \frac{nV^R}{RT}dP - \frac{nH^R}{RT^2}dT + \sum_i \frac{\bar{G}_i^R}{RT}dn_i \tag{11.55}$$

Equation (11.55) is the *fundamental residual-property relation.* Its derivation from Eq. (11.2) parallels the derivation in Chap. 6 that led from Eq. (6.10) to Eq. (6.42). Indeed, Eqs. (6.10) and (6.42) are special cases of Eqs. (11.2) and (11.55), valid for 1 mol of a constant-composition fluid. An alternative form of Eq. (11.55) follows by introduction of the fugacity coefficient as given by Eq. (11.51)

$$d\left(\frac{nG^R}{RT}\right) = \frac{nV^R}{RT}dP - \frac{nH^R}{RT^2}dT + \sum_i \ln\hat{\phi}_i\, dn_i \tag{11.56}$$

Equations so general as Eqs. (11.55) and (11.56) are useful for practical application only in restricted forms. Division of Eqs. (11.55) and (11.56), first, by dP with restriction to constant T and composition, and second, by dT and restriction to constant P and composition leads to

$$\frac{V^R}{RT} = \left[\frac{\partial(G^R/RT)}{\partial P}\right]_{T,x} \qquad (11.57) \qquad \frac{H^R}{RT} = -T\left[\frac{\partial(G^R/RT)}{\partial T}\right]_{P,x} \qquad (11.58)$$

These equations are restatements of Eqs. (6.43) and (6.44) wherein the restriction of the derivatives to constant composition is shown explicitly. They lead to Eqs. (6.46), (6.48), and (6.49) for the calculation of residual properties from volumetric data. Moreover, Eq. (11.57) is the basis for the direct derivation of Eq. (11.35), which yields fugacity coefficients from volumetric data. It is through the residual properties that this kind of experimental information enters into the practical application of thermodynamics.

In addition, from Eq. (11.56),

$$\ln \hat{\phi}_i = \left[\frac{\partial(nG^R/RT)}{\partial n_i}\right]_{P,T,n_j} \qquad (11.59)$$

This equation demonstrates that $\ln \hat{\phi}_i$ is a partial property with respect to G^R/RT.

Example 11.6

Develop a general equation to calculate $\ln \hat{\phi}_i$ values from compressibility-factor data.

Solution

For n mol of a constant-composition mixture, Eq. (6.49) becomes

$$\frac{nG^R}{RT} = \int_0^P (nZ - n)\frac{dP}{P}$$

In accord with Eq. (11.59) this equation may be differentiated with respect to n_i at constant T, P, and n_j to yield

$$\ln \hat{\phi}_i = \int_0^P \left[\frac{\partial(nZ - n)}{\partial n_i}\right]_{P,T,n_j} \frac{dP}{P}$$

Because $\partial(nZ)/\partial n_i = \bar{Z}_i$ and $\partial n/\partial n_i = 1$, this reduces to

$$\ln \hat{\phi}_i = \int_0^P (\bar{Z}_i - 1)\frac{dP}{P} \qquad (11.60)$$

where integration is at constant temperature and composition. This equation is the partial-property analog of Eq. (11.35). It allows the calculation of $\hat{\phi}_i$ values from PVT data.

Fugacity Coefficients from the Virial Equation of State

Values of $\hat{\phi}_i$ for species i in solution are readily found from equations of state. The simplest form of the virial equation provides a useful example. Written for a gas mixture it is exactly the same as for a pure species:

$$Z = 1 + \frac{BP}{RT} \tag{3.38}$$

The mixture second virial coefficient B is a function of temperature and composition. Its *exact* composition dependence is given by statistical mechanics, and this makes the virial equation preeminent among equations of state where it is applicable, i.e., to gases at low to moderate pressures. The equation giving this composition dependence is

$$\boxed{B = \sum_i \sum_j y_i y_j B_{ij}} \tag{11.61}$$

where y represents mole fractions in a gas mixture. The indices i and j identify species, and both run over all species present in the mixture. The virial coefficient B_{ij} characterizes a bimolecular interaction between molecule i and molecule j, and therefore $B_{ij} = B_{ji}$. The summations account for all possible bimolecular interactions.

For a binary mixture $i = 1, 2$ and $j = 1, 2$; the expansion of Eq. (11.61) then gives

$$B = y_1 y_1 B_{11} + y_1 y_2 B_{12} + y_2 y_1 B_{21} + y_2 y_2 B_{22}$$

or

$$B = y_1^2 B_{11} + 2 y_1 y_2 B_{12} + y_2^2 B_{22} \tag{11.62}$$

Two types of virial coefficients have appeared: B_{11} and B_{22}, for which the successive subscripts are the same, and B_{12}, for which the two subscripts are different. The first type is a pure-species virial coefficient; the second is a mixture property, known as a *cross coefficient*. Both are functions of temperature only. Expressions such as Eqs. (11.61) and (11.62) relate mixture coefficients to pure-species and cross coefficients. They are called *mixing rules*.

Equation (11.62) allows derivation of expressions for $\ln \hat{\phi}_1$ and $\ln \hat{\phi}_2$ for a binary gas mixture that obeys Eq. (3.38). Written for n mol of gas mixture, it becomes:

$$nZ = n + \frac{nBP}{RT}$$

Differentiation with respect to n_1 gives

$$\bar{Z}_1 \equiv \left[\frac{\partial(nZ)}{\partial n_1}\right]_{P,T,n_2} = 1 + \frac{P}{RT}\left[\frac{\partial(nB)}{\partial n_1}\right]_{T,n_2}$$

Substitution for $\bar{Z}_1$ in Eq. (11.60) yields

$$\ln \hat{\phi}_1 = \frac{1}{RT}\int_0^P \left[\frac{\partial(nB)}{\partial n_1}\right]_{T,n_2} dP = \frac{P}{RT}\left[\frac{\partial(nB)}{\partial n_1}\right]_{T,n_2}$$

where the integration is elementary, because B is not a function of pressure. All that remains is evaluation of the derivative.

Equation (11.62) for the second virial coefficient may be written:

$$\begin{aligned} B &= y_1(1-y_2)B_{11} + 2y_1y_2B_{12} + y_2(1-y_1)B_{22} \\ &= y_1B_{11} - y_1y_2B_{11} + 2y_1y_2B_{12} + y_2B_{22} - y_1y_2B_{22} \end{aligned}$$

or $$B = y_1B_{11} + y_2B_{22} + y_1y_2\delta_{12} \qquad \text{with} \qquad \delta_{12} \equiv 2B_{12} - B_{11} - B_{22}$$

Multiplying by n and substituting $y_i = n_i/n$ gives,

$$nB = n_1B_{11} + n_2B_{22} + \frac{n_1n_2}{n}\delta_{12}$$

By differentiation,

$$\begin{aligned} \left[\frac{\partial(nB)}{\partial n_1}\right]_{T,n_2} &= B_{11} + \left(\frac{1}{n} - \frac{n_1}{n^2}\right)n_2\delta_{12} \\ &= B_{11} + (1-y_1)y_2\delta_{12} = B_{11} + y_2^2\delta_{12} \end{aligned}$$

Therefore, $$\ln\hat{\phi}_1 = \frac{P}{RT}(B_{11} + y_2^2\delta_{12}) \tag{11.63a}$$

Similarly, $$\ln\hat{\phi}_2 = \frac{P}{RT}(B_{22} + y_1^2\delta_{12}) \tag{11.63b}$$

Equations (11.63) are readily extended for application to multicomponent gas mixtures; the general equation is[10]

$$\ln\hat{\phi}_k = \frac{P}{RT}\left[B_{kk} + \frac{1}{2}\sum_i\sum_j y_iy_j(2\delta_{ik} - \delta_{ij})\right] \tag{11.64}$$

where the dummy indices i and j run over all species, and

$$\delta_{ik} \equiv 2B_{ik} - B_{ii} - B_{kk} \qquad \delta_{ij} \equiv 2B_{ij} - B_{ii} - B_{jj}$$

with $\delta_{ii} = 0,\ \delta_{kk} = 0$, etc., and $\delta_{ki} = \delta_{ik}$, etc.

Example 11.7

Determine the fugacity coefficients as given by Eqs. (11.63) for nitrogen and methane in a $N_2(1)/CH_4(2)$ mixture at 200 K and 30 bar if the mixture contains 40 mole % N_2. Experimental virial-coefficient data are as follows:

$$B_{11} = -35.2 \qquad B_{22} = -105.0 \qquad B_{12} = -59.8 \text{ cm}^3 \text{ mol}^{-1}$$

[10] H. C. Van Ness and M. M. Abbott, *Classical Thermodynamics of Nonelectrolyte Solutions: With Applications to Phase Equilibria*, pp. 135–140, McGraw-Hill, New York, 1982.

Solution

By definition, $\delta_{12} = 2B_{12} - B_{11} - B_{22}$. Whence,

$$\delta_{12} = 2(-59.8) + 35.2 + 105.0 = 20.6 \text{ cm}^3 \text{ mol}^{-1}$$

Substitution of numerical values in Eqs. (11.63) yields

$$\ln \hat{\phi}_1 = \frac{30}{(83.14)(200)}\left[-35.2 + (0.6)^2(20.6)\right] = -0.0501$$

$$\ln \hat{\phi}_2 = \frac{30}{(83.14)(200)}\left[-105.0 + (0.4)^2(20.6)\right] = -0.1835$$

Whence, $\hat{\phi}_1 = 0.9511$ and $\hat{\phi}_2 = 0.8324$

Note that the second virial coefficient of the mixture as given by Eq. (11.62) is $B = -72.14 \text{ cm}^3 \text{ mol}^{-1}$, and that substitution in Eq. (3.38) yields a mixture compressibility factor, $Z = 0.870$.

11.7 GENERALIZED CORRELATIONS FOR THE FUGACITY COEFFICIENT

The generalized methods developed in Sec. 3.6 for the compressibility factor Z and in Sec. 6.7 for the residual enthalpy and entropy of pure gases are applied here to the fugacity coefficient. Equation (11.35) is put into generalized form by substitution of the relations,

$$P = P_c P_r \qquad dP = P_c \, dP_r$$

Hence,

$$\ln \phi_i = \int_0^{P_r} (Z_i - 1)\frac{dP_r}{P_r} \tag{11.65}$$

where integration is at constant T_r. Substitution for Z_i by Eq. (3.57) yields

$$\ln \phi = \int_0^{P_r} (Z^0 - 1)\frac{dP_r}{P_r} + \omega \int_0^{P_r} Z^1 \frac{dP_r}{P_r}$$

where for simplicity subscript i is omitted. This equation may be written in alternative form:

$$\ln \phi = \ln \phi^0 + \omega \ln \phi^1 \tag{11.66}$$

where $\ln \phi^0 \equiv \int_0^{P_r} (Z^0 - 1)\frac{dP_r}{P_r}$ and $\ln \phi^1 \equiv \int_0^{P_r} Z^1 \frac{dP_r}{P_r}$

The integrals in these equations may be evaluated numerically or graphically for various values of T_r and P_r from the data for Z^0 and Z^1 given in Tables E.1 through E.4 (App. E). Another method, and the one adopted by Lee and Kesler to extend their correlation to fugacity coefficients, is based on an equation of state.

Equation (11.66) may also be written,

$$\phi = (\phi^0)(\phi^1)^{\omega} \tag{11.67}$$

and we have the option of providing correlations for ϕ^0 and ϕ^1 rather than for their logarithms. This is the choice made here, and Tables E.13 through E.16 present values for these quantities as derived from the Lee/Kesler correlation as functions of T_r and P_r, thus providing a three-parameter generalized correlation for fugacity coefficients. Tables E.13 and E.15 for ϕ^0 can be used alone as a two-parameter correlation which does not incorporate the refinement introduced by the acentric factor.

Example 11.8

Estimate from Eq. (11.67) a value for the fugacity of 1-butene vapor at 200°C (473.15 K) and 70 bar.

Solution

These are the same conditions given in Example 6.9:

$$T_r = 1.127 \qquad P_r = 1.731 \qquad \omega = 0.191$$

By interpolation in Tables E.15 and E.16 at these conditions,

$$\phi^0 = 0.627 \qquad \text{and} \qquad \phi^1 = 1.096$$

Equation (11.67) then gives

$$\phi = (0.627)(1.096)^{0.191} = 0.638$$

and

$$f = \phi P = (0.638)(70) = 44.7 \text{ bar}$$

A useful generalized correlation for $\ln \phi$ results when the simplest form of the virial equation is valid. Equations (3.61) and (3.63) combine to give

$$Z - 1 = \frac{P_r}{T_r}(B^0 + \omega B^1)$$

Substitution in Eq. (11.65) and integration yield

$$\ln \phi = \frac{P_r}{T_r}(B^0 + \omega B^1)$$

or

$$\phi = \exp\left[\frac{P_r}{T_r}(B^0 + \omega B^1)\right] \tag{11.68}$$

This equation, used in conjunction with Eqs. (3.65) and (3.66), provides reliable values of ϕ for any nonpolar or slightly polar gas when applied at conditions where Z is approximately linear in pressure. Figure 3.14 again serves as a guide to its suitability.

Named functions, HRB(TR,PR,OMEGA) and SRB(TR,PR,OMEGA), for evaluation of H^R/RT_c and S^R/R by the generalized virial-coefficient correlation were described in Sec. 6.7. Similarly, we introduce here a function named PHIB(TR,PR,OMEGA) for evaluation of ϕ:

$$\phi = \text{PHIB(TR,PR,OMEGA)}$$

It combines Eq. (11.68) with Eqs. (3.65) and (3.66), as indicated in the representative computer programs given in App. D. For example, the value of ϕ for 1-butene vapor at the conditions of Example 6.9, Step (*b*), is:

$$\text{PHIB}(0.650,0.0316,0.191) = 0.956$$

Extension to Mixtures

The generalized correlation just described is for *pure* gases only. The remainder of this section shows how the virial equation may be generalized to allow calculation of fugacity coefficients $\hat{\phi}_i$ for species in gas *mixtures*.

The general expression for calculation of $\ln \hat{\phi}_k$ from second-virial-coefficient data is given by Eq. (11.64). Values of the pure-species virial coefficients B_{kk}, B_{ii}, etc., are found from the generalized correlation represented by Eqs. (3.62), (3.63), (3.65), and (3.66). The cross coefficients B_{ik}, B_{ij}, etc., are found from an extension of the same correlation. For this purpose, Eq. (3.63) is rewritten in the more general form[11]

$$\hat{B}_{ij} = B^0 + \omega_{ij} B^1 \tag{11.69a}$$

where

$$\hat{B}_{ij} \equiv \frac{B_{ij} P_{cij}}{RT_{cij}} \tag{11.69b}$$

and B^0 and B^1 are the same functions of T_r as given by Eqs. (3.65) and (3.66). The combining rules proposed by Prausnitz et al. for calculation of ω_{ij}, T_{cij}, and P_{cij} are

$$\omega_{ij} = \frac{\omega_i + \omega_j}{2} \tag{11.70}$$

$$T_{cij} = (T_{ci} T_{cj})^{1/2}(1 - k_{ij}) \tag{11.71}$$

$$P_{cij} = \frac{Z_{cij} RT_{cij}}{V_{cij}} \tag{11.72}$$

$$Z_{cij} = \frac{Z_{ci} + Z_{cj}}{2} \tag{11.73}$$

[11] J. M. Prausnitz, R. N. Lichtenthaler, and E. G. de Azevedo, *Molecular Thermodynamics of Fluid-Phase Equilibria*, 2d ed., pp. 132 and 162, Prentice-Hall, Englewood Cliffs, NJ, 1986.

$$V_{cij} = \left(\frac{V_{ci}^{1/3} + V_{cj}^{1/3}}{2} \right)^3 \tag{11.74}$$

In Eq. (11.71), k_{ij} is an empirical interaction parameter specific to an i-j molecular pair. When $i = j$ and for chemically similar species, $k_{ij} = 0$. Otherwise, it is a small positive number evaluated from minimal PVT data or in the absence of data set equal to zero. When $i = j$, all equations reduce to the appropriate values for a pure species. When $i \neq j$, these equations define a set of interaction parameters having no physical significance. Reduced temperature is given for each ij pair by $T_{rij} \equiv T/T_{cij}$. For a mixture, values of B_{ij} from Eq. (11.69b) substituted into Eq. (11.61) yield the mixture second virial coefficient B, and substituted into Eq. (11.64) [Eqs. (11.63) for a binary] they yield values of $\ln \hat{\phi}_i$.

The primary virtue of the generalized correlation for second virial coefficients presented here is simplicity; more accurate, but more complex, correlations appear in the literature.[12]

Example 11.9

Estimate $\hat{\phi}_1$ and $\hat{\phi}_2$ by Eqs. (11.63) for an equimolar mixture of methyl ethyl ketone(1)/toluene(2) at 50°C (323.15 K) and 25 kPa. Set all $k_{ij} = 0$.

Solution

The required data are as follows:

ij	T_{cij}/K	P_{cij}/bar	V_{cij}/cm^3 mol^{-1}	Z_{cij}	ω_{ij}
11	535.5	41.5	267.	0.249	0.323
22	591.8	41.1	316.	0.264	0.262
12	563.0	41.3	291.	0.256	0.293

where values in the last row have been calculated by Eqs. (11.70) through (11.74). The values of T_{rij}, together with B^0, B^1, and B_{ij} calculated for each ij pair by Eqs. (3.65), (3.66), and (11.69), are as follows:

ij	T_{rij}	B^0	B^1	B_{ij}/cm^3 mol^{-1}
11	0.603	−0.865	−1.300	−1,387.
22	0.546	−1.028	−2.045	−1,860.
12	0.574	−0.943	−1.632	−1,611.

[12] C. Tsonopoulos, *AIChE J.*, vol. 20, pp. 263–272, 1974, vol. 21, pp. 827–829, 1975, vol. 24, pp. 1112–1115, 1978.; C. Tsonopoulos, *Adv. in Chemistry Series 182*, pp. 143–162, 1979; J. G. Hayden and J. P. O'Connell, *Ind. Eng. Chem. Proc. Des. Dev.*, vol. 14, pp. 209–216, 1975; D. W. McCann and R. P. Danner, *Ibid.*, vol. 23, pp. 529–533, 1984; J. A. Abusleme and J. H. Vera, *AIChE J.*, vol. 35, pp. 481–489, 1989.

Calculating δ_{12} according to its definition gives:

$$\delta_{12} = 2B_{12} - B_{11} - B_{22} = (2)(-1611) + 1387 + 1860 = 25 \text{ cm}^3 \text{ mol}^{-1}$$

Equations (11.63) then yield:

$$\ln \hat{\phi}_1 = \frac{P}{RT}(B_{11} + y_2^2 \delta_{12}) = \frac{25}{(8314)(323.15)}[-1387 + (0.5)^2(25)] = -0.0128$$

$$\ln \hat{\phi}_2 = \frac{P}{RT}(B_{22} + y_1^2 \delta_{12}) = \frac{25}{(8314)(323.15)}[-1860 + (0.5)^2(25)] = -0.0172$$

Whence, $\hat{\phi}_1 = 0.987$ and $\hat{\phi}_2 = 0.983$

These results are representative of values obtained for vapor phases at typical conditions of low-pressure vapor/liquid equilibrium.

11.8 THE IDEAL-SOLUTION MODEL

The chemical potential as given by the ideal-gas mixture model,

$$\mu_i^{ig} \equiv \bar{G}_i^{ig} = G_i^{ig}(T, P) + RT \ln y_i \tag{11.24}$$

contains a final term that gives it the simplest possible composition dependence; indeed, one that could reasonably serve for dense gases and liquids. However, the pure-species behavior implied by the term $G_i^{ig}(T, P)$ is unrealistic except for ideal gases. A natural extension of Eq. (11.24) therefore replaces $G_i^{ig}(T, P)$ by $G_i(T, P)$, the Gibbs energy of pure i in its *real physical state* of gas, liquid, or even solid. Thus, we **define** an *ideal* solution as one for which

$$\boxed{\mu_i^{id} \equiv \bar{G}_i^{id} = G_i(T, P) + RT \ln x_i} \tag{11.75}$$

where superscript *id* denotes an ideal-solution property. Mole fraction is here represented by x_i to reflect the fact that application is most often to liquids. However, a consequence of this definition is that an ideal-gas mixture is a special case, namely, an ideal solution of ideal gases, for which x_i in Eq. (11.75) is replaced by y_i.

All other thermodynamic properties for an ideal solution follow from Eq. (11.75). The partial volume results from differentiation with respect to pressure at constant temperature and composition in accord with Eq. (11.18):

$$\bar{V}_i^{id} = \left(\frac{\partial \bar{G}_i^{id}}{\partial P}\right)_{T,x} = \left(\frac{\partial G_i}{\partial P}\right)_T$$

By Eq. (11.4), $(\partial G_i/\partial P)_T = V_i$; whence,

$$\boxed{\bar{V}_i^{id} = V_i} \tag{11.76}$$

Similarly, as a result of Eq. (11.19),

$$\bar{S}_i^{id} = -\left(\frac{\partial \bar{G}_i^{id}}{\partial T}\right)_{P,x} = -\left(\frac{\partial G_i}{\partial T}\right)_P - R \ln x_i$$

By Eq. (11.5),

$$\boxed{\bar{S}_i^{id} = S_i - R \ln x_i} \tag{11.77}$$

Because $\bar{H}_i^{id} = \bar{G}_i^{id} + T\bar{S}_i^{id}$, substitutions by Eqs. (11.75) and (11.77) yield

$$\bar{H}_i^{id} = G_i + RT \ln x_i + TS_i - RT \ln x_i$$

or

$$\boxed{\bar{H}_i^{id} = H_i} \tag{11.78}$$

The summability relation, Eq. (11.11), applied to the special case of an ideal solution, is written:

$$M^{id} = \sum_i x_i \bar{M}_i^{id}$$

Application to Eqs. (11.75) through (11.78) yields

$G^{id} = \sum_i x_i G_i + RT \sum_i x_i \ln x_i$ (11.79)	$S^{id} = \sum_i x_i S_i - R \sum_i x_i \ln x_i$ (11.80)

$V^{id} = \sum_i x_i V_i$ (11.81)	$H^{id} = \sum_i x_i H_i$ (11.82)

If in Example 11.3 the solution formed by mixing methanol(1) and water(2) were assumed ideal, the final volume would be given by Eq. (11.81), and the V-vs.-x_1 relation would be a straight line connecting the pure-species volumes, V_2 at $x_1 = 0$ with V_1 at $x_1 = 1$. For the specific calculation at $x_1 = 0.3$, use of V_1 and V_2 in place of partial volumes yields:

$$V_1^t = 983 \text{ cm}^3 \qquad V_2^t = 1017 \text{ cm}^3$$

Both values are about 3.4% low.

The Lewis/Randall Rule

The composition dependence of the fugacity of a species in an ideal solution is particularly simple. Recall Eqs. (11.46) and (11.31):

$\mu_i \equiv \Gamma_i(T) + RT \ln \hat{f}_i$ (11.46)	$G_i \equiv \Gamma_i(T) + RT \ln f_i$ (11.31)

Subtraction yields the *general* equation:

$$\mu_i = G_i + RT \ln(\hat{f}_i / f_i)$$

For the special case of an ideal solution,

$$\mu_i^{id} \equiv \bar{G}_i^{id} = G_i + RT \ln(\hat{f}_i^{id} / f_i)$$

Comparison with Eq. (11.75) gives:

$$\boxed{\hat{f}_i^{id} = x_i f_i} \qquad (11.83)$$

This equation, known as the *Lewis/Randall rule*, applies to each species in an ideal solution at all conditions of temperature, pressure, and composition. It shows that the fugacity of each species in an ideal solution is proportional to its mole fraction; the proportionality constant is the fugacity of *pure* species i in the same physical state as the solution and at the same T and P. Division of both sides of Eq. (11.83) by Px_i and substitution of $\hat{\phi}_i^{id}$ for $\hat{f}_i^{id}/x_i P$ [Eq. (11.52)] and of ϕ_i for f_i/P [Eq. (11.34)] gives an alternative form:

$$\hat{\phi}_i^{id} = \phi_i \qquad (11.84)$$

Thus the fugacity coefficient of species i in an ideal solution is equal to the fugacity coefficient of *pure* species i in the same physical state as the solution and at the same T and P. Because Raoult's law is based on the assumption of ideal-solution behavior for the liquid phase, the same systems that obey Raoult's law form ideal solutions. Recall that phases comprised of liquids whose molecules are of similar size and which are of similar chemical nature approximate ideal solutions. Mixtures of isomers closely conform to these conditions. Mixtures of adjacent members of homologous series are also examples.

11.9 EXCESS PROPERTIES

The residual Gibbs energy and the fugacity coefficient are directly related to experimental PVT data by Eqs. (6.49), (11.35), and (11.60). Where such data can be adequately correlated by equations of state, thermodynamic-property information is advantageously provided by residual properties. Indeed, if convenient treatment of all fluids by means of equations of state were possible, the thermodynamic-property relations already presented would suffice. However, *liquid* solutions are often more easily dealt with through properties that measure their departures, not from ideal-gas behavior, but from ideal-solution behavior. Thus the mathematical formalism of *excess* properties is analogous to that of the residual properties.

If M represents the molar (or unit-mass) value of any extensive thermodynamic property (e.g., V, U, H, S, G, etc.), then an excess property M^E is **defined** as the difference between the actual property value of a solution and the value it would have as an ideal solution at the same temperature, pressure, and composition. Thus,

$$\boxed{M^E \equiv M - M^{id}} \qquad (11.85)$$

For example,

$$G^E \equiv G - G^{id} \qquad H^E \equiv H - H^{id} \qquad S^E \equiv S - S^{id}$$

Moreover,
$$G^E = H^E - TS^E \tag{11.86}$$

which follows from Eq. (11.85) and Eq. (6.3), the definition of G.

The definition of M^E is analogous to the definition of a residual property as given by Eq. (6.41). Indeed, excess properties have a simple relation to residual properties, found by subtracting Eq. (6.41) from Eq. (11.85):

$$M^E - M^R = -(M^{id} - M^{ig})$$

As already noted, an ideal-gas mixture is an ideal solution of ideal gases. Equations (11.79) through (11.82) therefore become expressions for M^{ig} when M_i is replaced by M_i^{ig}. Equation (11.82) becomes Eq. (11.25), Eq. (11.80) becomes Eq. (11.26), and Eq. (11.79) becomes Eq. (11.27). The two sets of equations, for M^{id} and M^{ig}, therefore provide a general relation for the difference:

$$M^{id} - M^{ig} = \sum_i x_i M_i - \sum_i x_i M_i^{ig} = \sum_i x_i M_i^R$$

wherein the summation terms with logarithms have canceled. This leads immediately to

$$M^E = M^R - \sum_i x_i M_i^R \tag{11.87}$$

Note that excess properties have no meaning for pure species, whereas residual properties exist for pure species as well as for mixtures.

The partial-property relation analogous to Eq. (11.49) is

$$\bar{M}_i^E = \bar{M}_i - \bar{M}_i^{id} \tag{11.88}$$

where $\bar{M}_i^E$ is a partial excess property. The fundamental excess-property relation is derived in exactly the same way as the fundamental residual-property relation and leads to analogous results. Equation (11.54), written for the special case of an ideal solution, is subtracted from Eq. (11.54) itself, yielding:

$$d\left(\frac{nG^E}{RT}\right) = \frac{nV^E}{RT}dP - \frac{nH^E}{RT^2}dT + \sum_i \frac{\bar{G}_i^E}{RT}dn_i \tag{11.89}$$

This is the *fundamental excess-property relation*, analogous to Eq. (11.55), the fundamental residual-property relation.

The exact analogy that exists between properties M, residual properties M^R, and excess properties M^E is indicated by Table 11.1. All of the equations that appear are basic property relations, although only Eqs. (11.4) and (11.5) have been shown explicitly before.

Table 11.1: Summary of Equations for the Gibbs Energy and Related Properties

M in Relation to G	M^R in Relation to G^R	M^E in Relation to G^E
$V = (\partial G/\partial P)_{T,x}$ (11.4)	$V^R = (\partial G^R/\partial P)_{T,x}$	$V^E = (\partial G^E/\partial P)_{T,x}$
$S = -(\partial G/\partial T)_{P,x}$ (11.5)	$S^R = -(\partial G^R/\partial T)_{P,x}$	$S^E = -(\partial G^E/\partial T)_{P,x}$
$H = G + TS$ $= G - T(\partial G/\partial T)_{P,x}$ $= -RT^2\left[\frac{\partial(G/RT)}{\partial T}\right]_{P,x}$	$H^R = G^R + TS^R$ $= G^R - T(\partial G^R/\partial T)_{P,x}$ $= -RT^2\left[\frac{\partial(G^R/RT)}{\partial T}\right]_{P,x}$	$H^E = G^E + TS^E$ $= G^E - T(\partial G^E/\partial T)_{P,x}$ $= -RT^2\left[\frac{\partial(G^E/RT)}{\partial T}\right]_{P,x}$
$C_P = (\partial H/\partial T)_{P,x}$ $= -T(\partial^2 G/\partial T^2)_{P,x}$	$C_P^R = (\partial H^R/\partial T)_{P,x}$ $= -T(\partial^2 G^R/\partial T^2)_{P,x}$	$C_P^E = (\partial H^E/\partial T)_{P,x}$ $= -T(\partial^2 G^E/\partial T^2)_{P,x}$

Example 11.10

(*a*) If C_P^E is a constant, independent of T, find expressions for G^E, S^E, and H^E as functions of T.

(*b*) From the equations developed in Part (*a*), find values for G^E, S^E, and H^E for an equimolar solution of benzene(1)/ *n*-hexane(2) at 50°C (323.15 K), given the following excess-property values for an equimolar solution at 25°C (298.15 K):

$$C_P^E = -2.86 \text{ J mol}^{-1} \text{ K}^{-1} \qquad H^E = 897.9 \text{ J mol}^{-1} \qquad G^E = 384.5 \text{ J mol}^{-1}$$

Solution

(*a*) Let $C_P^E = a$, where a is a constant. From the last column of Table 11.1:

$$C_P^E = -T\left(\frac{\partial^2 G^E}{\partial T^2}\right)_{P,x} \qquad \text{whence} \qquad \left(\frac{\partial^2 G^E}{\partial T^2}\right)_{P,x} = -\frac{a}{T}$$

Integration yields:
$$\left(\frac{\partial G^E}{\partial T}\right)_{P,x} = -a \ln T + b$$

where b is a constant of integration. A second integration gives

$$G^E = -a(T \ln T - T) + bT + c \qquad (A)$$

where c is another integration constant. With $S^E = -(\partial G^E/\partial T)_{P,x}$ (Table 11.1),

$$S^E = a \ln T - b \qquad (B)$$

Because $H^E = G^E + TS^E$, combination of Eqs. (A) and (B) yields

$$H^E = aT + c \qquad (C)$$

(*b*) Let $C_{P_0}^E$, H_0^E, and G_0^E represent the given values at $T_0 = 298.15$ K. But C_P^E is constant, and therefore $a = C_{P_0}^E = -2.86$.

By Eq. (A),
$$c = H_0^E - aT_0 = 1750.6$$

By Eq. (C),
$$b = \frac{G_0^E + a(T_0 \ln T_0 - T_0) - c}{T_0} = -18.0171$$

Substitution of known values into Eqs. (A), (B), and (C) for $T = 323.15$ yields

$$G^E = 344.4 \text{ J mol}^{-1} \qquad S^E = 1.492 \text{ J mol}^{-1} \text{ K}^{-1} \qquad H^E = 826.4 \text{ J mol}^{-1}$$

The Excess Gibbs Energy and the Activity Coefficient

The excess Gibbs energy is of particular interest. Equation (11.46) may be written as

$$\bar{G}_i = \Gamma_i(T) + RT \ln \hat{f}_i$$

In accord with Eq. (11.83) for an ideal solution, this becomes

$$\bar{G}_i^{id} = \Gamma_i(T) + RT \ln x_i f_i$$

By difference, $$\bar{G}_i - \bar{G}_i^{id} = RT \ln \frac{\hat{f}_i}{x_i f_i}$$

The left side of this equation is the partial excess Gibbs energy $\bar{G}_i^E$; the dimensionless ratio $\hat{f}_i / x_i f_i$ appearing on the right is the *activity coefficient* of species i in solution, symbol γ_i. Thus, by **definition**,

$$\boxed{\gamma_i \equiv \frac{\hat{f}_i}{x_i f_i}} \tag{11.90}$$

Whence, $$\boxed{\bar{G}_i^E = RT \ln \gamma_i} \tag{11.91}$$

These equations establish a thermodynamic foundation for the activity coefficient, which appeared in Sec. 10.5 as a factor introduced into Raoult's law to account for liquid-phase non-idealities. Comparison with Eq. (11.51) shows that Eq. (11.91) relates γ_i to $\bar{G}_i^E$ exactly as Eq. (11.51) relates $\hat{\phi}_i$ to $\bar{G}_i^R$. For an ideal solution, $\bar{G}_i^E = 0$, and therefore $\gamma_i = 1$.

A further relation of interest results from the combination of Eq. (11.91) with Eq. (11.88) written for the excess Gibbs energy:

$$RT \ln \gamma_i = \bar{G}_i - \bar{G}_i^{id}$$

Elimination of the final term by Eq. (11.75) and rearrangement gives

$$\bar{G}_i \equiv \mu_i = G_i + RT \ln \gamma_i x_i \tag{11.92}$$

One could in fact use this equation as an alternative definition of the activity coefficient.

The conceptual development leading to Eq. (11.92) is evident in the following set of equations:

$$\mu_i^{ig} = G_i^{ig} + RT \ln y_i \tag{11.24}$$

$$\mu_i^{id} = G_i + RT \ln x_i \tag{11.75}$$

$$\mu_i = G_i + RT \ln \gamma_i x_i \tag{11.92}$$

The first of these equations reveals the significance of the ideal-gas mixture model. The second equation, for the ideal-solution model, preserves the term giving composition dependence, but includes a pure-species term of physical reality. The third equation, through inclusion of a composition-dependent activity coefficient, has the capability to represent fully the actual behavior of soultions.

Excess-Property Relations

An alternative form of Eq. (11.89) follows by introduction of the activity coefficient through Eq. (11.91):

$$d\left(\frac{nG^E}{RT}\right) = \frac{nV^E}{RT}dP - \frac{nH^E}{RT^2}dT + \sum_i \ln\gamma_i\, dn_i \tag{11.93}$$

The generality of these equations precludes their direct practical application. Rather, use is made of restricted forms, which are written by inspection:

$$\frac{V^E}{RT} = \left[\frac{\partial(G^E/RT)}{\partial P}\right]_{T,x} \tag{11.94}$$

$$\frac{H^E}{RT} = -T\left[\frac{\partial(G^E/RT)}{\partial T}\right]_{P,x} \tag{11.95}$$

$$\ln\gamma_i = \left[\frac{\partial(nG^E/RT)}{\partial n_i}\right]_{P,T,n_j} \tag{11.96}$$

Equations (11.93) through (11.96) are analogs of Eqs. (11.56) through (11.59) for residual properties. Whereas the fundamental *residual*-property relation derives its usefulness from its direct relation to experimental PVT data and equations of state, the fundamental *excess*-property relation is useful because V^E, H^E, and γ_i are all experimentally accessible. Activity coefficients are found from vapor/liquid equilibrium data, and V^E and H^E values come from mixing experiments, topics treated in the following chapter.

Equation (11.96) demonstrates that $\ln\gamma_i$ is a partial property with respect to G^E/RT. It is the analog of Eq. (11.59), which shows the same relation of $\ln\hat{\phi}_i$ to G^R/RT. The partial-property analogs of Eqs. (11.94) and (11.95) are

$$\left(\frac{\partial \ln\gamma_i}{\partial P}\right)_{T,x} = \frac{\bar{V}_i^E}{RT} \tag{11.97}$$

$$\left(\frac{\partial \ln\gamma_i}{\partial T}\right)_{P,x} = -\frac{\bar{H}_i^E}{RT^2} \tag{11.98}$$

These equations allow calculation of the effect of pressure and temperature on the activity coefficient.

The following forms of the summability and Gibbs/Duhem equations result from the fact that $\ln\gamma_i$ is a partial property with respect to G^E/RT:

$$\frac{G^E}{RT} = \sum_i x_i \ln\gamma_i \tag{11.99}$$

$$\sum_i x_i\, d\ln\gamma_i = 0 \qquad \text{(const } T, P) \tag{11.100}$$

These equations find important applications in phase-equilibrium thermodynamics.

Equations (11.94) and (11.95) allow direct calculation of the effects of pressure and temperature on the excess Gibbs energy. For example, an equimolar mixture of benzene and cyclohexane at 25°C (298.15 K) and 1 bar has an excess volume of about 0.65 cm^3 mol^{-1} and an excess enthalpy of about 800 J mol^{-1}. Thus at these conditions,

$$\left[\frac{\partial(G^E/RT)}{\partial P}\right]_{T,x} = \frac{0.65}{(83.14)(298.15)} = 2.62 \times 10^{-5} \text{ bar}^{-1}$$

$$\left[\frac{\partial(G^E/RT)}{\partial T}\right]_{P,x} = \frac{-800}{(8.314)(298.15)^2} = -1.08 \times 10^{-3} \text{ K}^{-1}$$

The most striking observation about these results is that it takes a pressure change of more than 40 bar to have an effect on the excess Gibbs energy equivalent to that of a temperature change of 1°C (1 K). Similar calculations based on Eqs. (11.97) and (11.98) produce similar results. This is the reason that for liquids at low pressures the effect of pressure on the excess Gibbs energy and on the activity coefficients is usually neglected.

Just as the fundamental property relation of Eq. (11.54) provides complete property information from a canonical equation of state expressing G/RT as a function of T, P, and composition, so the fundamental *residual*-property relation, Eq. (11.55) or (11.56), provides complete *residual*-property information from a PVT equation of state, from PVT data, or from generalized PVT correlations. However, for complete *property* information, one needs in addition to PVT data the ideal-gas-state heat capacities of the species that comprise the system. In complete analogy, the fundamental *excess*-property relation, Eq. (11.89) or (11.93), provides complete *excess*-property information, given an equation for G^E/RT as a function of its canonical variables, T, P, and composition, However, this formulation represents less-complete property information than does the residual-property formulation, because it tells us nothing about the properties of the pure constituent chemical species.

The Nature of Excess Properties

Peculiarities of liquid-mixture behavior are dramatically revealed in the excess properties. Those of primary interest are G^E, H^E, and S^E. The excess Gibbs energy comes from experiment through reduction of vapor/liquid equilibrium data, and H^E is determined by mixing experiments (Chap. 12). The excess entropy is not measured directly, but is found from Eq. (11.86), written as

$$S^E = \frac{H^E - G^E}{T}$$

Excess properties are often strong functions of temperature, but at normal temperatures are not strongly influenced by pressure. Their composition dependence is illustrated in Fig. 11.4 for six binary liquid mixtures at 50°C (323.15 K) and approximately atmospheric pressure. For consistency with Eq. (11.86), the product TS^E is shown rather than S^E itself. Although the systems exhibit a diversity of behavior, they have common features:

1. All excess properties become zero as either species approaches purity.
2. Although G^E vs. x_1 is approximately parabolic in shape, both H^E and TS^E exhibit individualistic composition dependencies.
3. When an excess property M^E has a single sign (as does G^E in all six cases), the extreme value of M^E (maximum or minimum) often occurs near the equimolar composition.

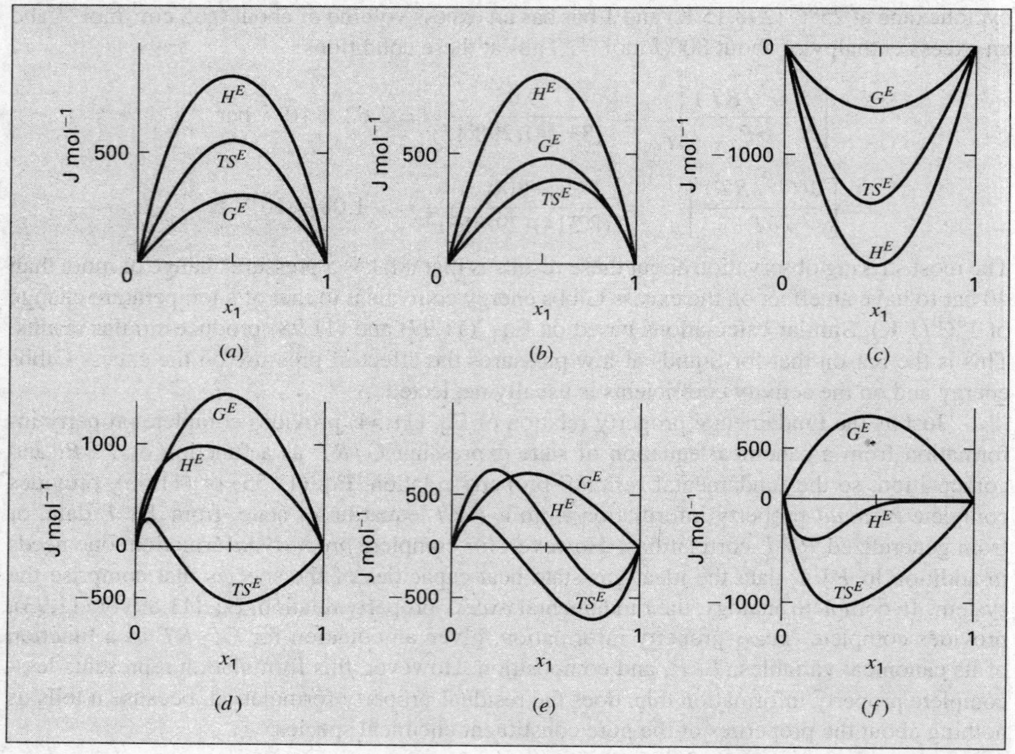

Figure 11.4: Excess properties at 50°C (323.15 K) for six binary liquid systems: (*a*) chloroform(1)/*n*-heptane(2) (*b*) acetone(1)/methanol(2) (*c*) acetone(1)/chloroform(2) (*d*) ethanol(1)/*n*-heptane(2) (*e*) ethanol(1)/chloroform(2) (*f*) ethanol(1)/water(2)

Feature 1 is a consequence of the definition of an excess property, Eq. (11.85); as any x_i approaches unity, both M and M^{id} approach M_i, the corresponding property of pure species i. Features 2 and 3 are generalizations based on observation, and admit exceptions (note, e.g., the behavior of H^E for the ethanol/water system).

A detailed discussion of excess-property behavior is given in Sec. 16.6.

PROBLEMS

11.1. What is the change in entropy when 0.7 m^3 of CO_2 and 0.3 m^3 of N_2, each at 1 bar and 25°C (298.15 K) blend to form a gas mixture at the same conditions? Assume ideal gases.

11.2. A vessel, divided into two parts by a partition, contains 4 mol of nitrogen gas at 75°C (348.15 K) and 30 bar on one side and 2.5 mol of argon gas at 130°C (403.15 K) and 20 bar on the other. If the partition is removed and the gases mix adiabatically and completely, what is the change in entropy? Assume nitrogen to be an ideal gas with $C_V = (5/2)R$ and argon to be an ideal gas with $C_V = (3/2)R$.

11.3. A stream of nitrogen flowing at the rate of 2 kg s^{-1} and a stream of hydrogen flowing at the rate of 0.5 kg s^{-1} mix adiabatically in a steady-flow process. If the gases are assumed ideal, what is the rate of entropy increase as a result of the process?

11.4. What is the ideal work for the separation of an equimolar mixture of methane and ethane at 175°C (448.15 K) and 3 bar in a steady-flow process into product streams of the pure gases at 35°C (308.15 K) and 1 bar if $T_\sigma = 300$ K?

11.5. What is the work required for the separation of air (21 mole % oxygen and 79 mole % nitrogen) at 25°C (298.15 K) and 1 bar in a steady-flow process into product streams of pure oxygen and nitrogen, also at 25°C (298.15 K) and 1 bar, if the thermodynamic efficiency of the process is 5% and if $T_\sigma = 300$ K?

11.6. What is the partial molar temperature? What is the partial molar pressure? Express results in relation to the T and P of the mixture.

11.7. Show that

(*a*) The "partial molar mass" of a species in solution is equal to its molar mass.

(*b*) A partial *specific* property of a species in solution is obtained by division of the partial *molar* property by the molar mass of the species.

11.8. If the molar density of a binary mixture is given by the empirical expression

$$\rho = a_0 + a_1 x_1 + a_2 x_1^2$$

find the corresponding expressions for $\bar{V}_1$ and $\bar{V}_2$.

11.9. For a ternary solution at constant T and P, the composition dependence of molar property M is given by

$$M = x_1 M_1 + x_2 M_2 + x_3 M_3 + x_1 x_2 x_3 C$$

where M_1, M_2, and M_3 are the values of M for pure species 1, 2, and 3, and C is a parameter independent of composition. Determine expressions for $\bar{M}_1$, $\bar{M}_2$, and $\bar{M}_3$ by application of Eq. (11.7). As a partial check on your results, verify that they satisfy the summability relation, Eq. (11.11). For this correlating equation, what are the $\bar{M}_i$ at infinite dilution?

11.10. A *pure-component pressure* p_i for species i in a gas mixture may be defined as the pressure that species i would exert if it alone occupied the mixture volume. Thus,

$$p_i \equiv \frac{y_i Z_i RT}{V}$$

where y_i is the mole fraction of species i in the gas mixture, Z_i is evaluated at p_i and T, and V is the molar volume of the gas mixture. Note that p_i as defined here is not a partial pressure $y_i P$, except for an ideal gas. Dalton's "law" of additive pressures states that the total pressure exerted by a gas mixture is equal to the sum of the pure-component pressures of its constituent species: $P = \sum_i p_i$. Show that Dalton's "law" implies that $Z = \sum_i y_i Z_i$, where Z_i is the compressibility factor of pure species i evaluated at the mixture temperature but at its pure-component pressure.

11.11. If for a binary solution one starts with an expression for M (or M^R or M^E) as a function of x_1 and applies Eqs. (11.15) and (11.16) to find $\bar{M}_1$ and $\bar{M}_2$ (or $\bar{M}_1^R$ and $\bar{M}_2^R$ or $\bar{M}_1^E$ and $\bar{M}_2^E$) and then combines these expressions by Eq. (11.11), the initial expression for M is regenerated. On the other hand, if one starts with expressions for $\bar{M}_1$ and $\bar{M}_2$, combines them in accord with Eq. (11.11), and then applies Eqs. (11.15) and (11.16), the initial expressions for $\bar{M}_1$ and $\bar{M}_2$ are regenerated if and only if the initial expressions for these quantities meet a specific condition. What is the condition?

11.12. With reference to Ex. 11.4,

(*a*) Apply Eq. (11.7) to Eq. (*A*) to verify Eqs. (*B*) and (*C*).
(*b*) Show that Eqs. (*B*) and (*C*) combine in accord with Eq. (11.11) to regenerate Eq. (*A*).
(*c*) Show that Eqs. (*B*) and (*C*) satisfy Eq. (11.14), the Gibbs/Duhem equation.
(*d*) Show that at constant T and P,

$$(d\bar{H}_1/dx_1)_{x_1=1} = (d\bar{H}_2/dx_1)_{x_1=0} = 0$$

(*e*) Plot values of H, $\bar{H}_1$, and $\bar{H}_2$, calculated by Eqs. (*A*), (*B*), and (*C*), vs. x_1. Label points H_1, H_2, $\bar{H}_1^\infty$, and $\bar{H}_2^\infty$, and show their values.

11.13. The molar volume (cm^3 mol^{-1}) of a binary liquid mixture at T and P is given by

$$V = 120x_1 + 70x_2 + (15x_1 + 8x_2)x_1x_2$$

(*a*) Find expressions for the partial molar volumes of species 1 and 2 at T and P.
(*b*) Show that when these expressions are combined in accord with Eq. (11.11) the given equation for V is recovered.
(*c*) Show that these expressions satisfy Eq. (11.14), the Gibbs/Duhem equation.
(*d*) Show that $(d\bar{V}_1/dx_1)_{x_1=1} = (d\bar{V}_2/dx_1)_{x_1=0} = 0$.
(*e*) Plot values of V, $\bar{V}_1$, and $\bar{V}_2$ calculated by the given equation for V and by the equations developed in (*a*) vs. x_1. Label points V_1, V_2, $\bar{V}_1^\infty$, and $\bar{V}_2^\infty$, and show their values.

11.14. For a particular binary liquid solution at constant T and P, the molar enthalpies of mixtures are represented by the equation

$$H = x_1(a_1 + b_1x_1) + x_2(a_2 + b_2x_2)$$

where the a_i and b_i are constants. Because the equation has the form of Eq. (11.11), it might be that $\bar{H}_i = a_i + b_ix_i$. Show whether this is true.

11.15. Analogous to the conventional partial property $\bar{M}_i$, one can define a constant-T,V partial property $\widetilde{M}_i$:

$$\widetilde{M}_i \equiv \left[\frac{\partial(nM)}{\partial n_i}\right]_{T,V,n_j}$$

Show that $\widetilde{M}_i$ and $\bar{M}_i$ are related by the equation

$$\widetilde{M}_i = \bar{M}_i + (V - \bar{V}_i)\left(\frac{\partial M}{\partial V}\right)_{T,x}$$

Demonstrate that the $\widetilde{M}_i$ satisfy a summability relation, $M = \sum_i x_i \widetilde{M}_i$.

11.16. From the following compressibility-factor data for CO_2 at 150°C (423.15 K) prepare plots of the fugacity and fugacity coefficient of CO_2 vs. P for pressures up to 500 bar. Compare results with those found from the generalized correlation represented by Eq. (11.68).

P/bar	Z	P/bar	Z
10	0.985	100	0.869
20	0.970	200	0.765
40	0.942	300	0.762
60	0.913	400	0.824
80	0.885	500	0.910

11.17. For SO_2 at 600 K and 300 bar, determine good estimates of the fugacity and of G^R/RT.

11.18. Estimate the fugacity of isobutylene as a gas:

(*a*) At 280°C (553.15 K) and 20 bar (*b*) At 280°C (553.15 K) and 100 bar

11.19. Estimate the fugacity of one of the following:

(*a*) Cyclopentane at 110°C (383.15 K) and 275 bar. At 110°C (383.15 K) the vapor pressure of cyclopentane is 5.267 bar.

(*b*) 1-Butene at 120°C (393.15 K) and 34 bar. At 120°C (393.15 K) the vapor pressure of 1-butene is 25.83 bar.

11.20. Justify the following equations:

$$\left(\frac{\partial \ln \hat{\phi}_i}{\partial P}\right)_{T,x} = \frac{\bar{V}_i^R}{RT} \qquad \left(\frac{\partial \ln \hat{\phi}_i}{\partial T}\right)_{P,x} = -\frac{\bar{H}_i^R}{RT^2}$$

$$\frac{G^R}{RT} = \sum_i x_i \ln \hat{\phi}_i \qquad \sum_i x_i \, d\ln \hat{\phi}_i = 0 \quad (\text{const } T,\, P)$$

11.21. From data in the steam tables, determine a good estimate for f/f^{sat} for liquid water at 150°C (423.15 K) and 150 bar, where f^{sat} is the fugacity of saturated liquid at 150°C (423.15 K).

11.22. For one of the following, determine the ratio of the fugacity in the final state to that in the initial state for steam undergoing the isothermal change of state:

(*a*) From 9000 kPa and 400°C (673.15 K) to 300 kPa
(*b*) From 7000 kPa and 700 K to 345 kPa.

11.23. Estimate the fugacity of one of the following liquids at its normal boiling point temperature and 200 bar:

(*a*) *n*-Pentane (*b*) Isobutylene (*c*) 1-Butene

11.24. Assuming that Eq. (11.68) is valid for the vapor phase and that the molar volume of saturated liquid is given by Eq. (3.72), prepare plots of f vs. P and of ϕ vs. P for one of the following:

(*a*) Chloroform at 200°C (473.15 K) for the pressure range from 0 to 40 bar. At 200°C (473.15 K) the vapor pressure of chloroform is 22.27 bar
(*b*) Isobutane at 40°C (313.15 K) for the pressure range from 0 to 10 bar. At 40°C (313.15 K) the vapor pressure of isobutane is 5.28 bar

11.25. For the system ethylene(1)/propylene(2) as a gas, estimate $\hat{f}_1$, $\hat{f}_2$, $\hat{\phi}_1$, and $\hat{\phi}_2$ at $t/T = 150$°C/423.15 K, $P = 30$ bar, and $y_1 = 0.35$:

(*a*) Through application of Eqs. (11.63)
(*b*) Assuming that the mixture is an ideal solution.

11.26. Rationalize the following expression, valid at sufficiently low pressures, for estimating the fugacity coefficient: $\ln \phi \approx Z - 1$.

11.27. For the system methane(1)/ethane(2)/propane(3) as a gas, estimate $\hat{f}_1$, $\hat{f}_2$, $\hat{f}_3$, $\hat{\phi}_1$, $\hat{\phi}_2$, and $\hat{\phi}_3$ at $t/T = 100$°C/373.15 K, $P = 35$ bar, $y_1 = 0.21$, and $y_2 = 0.43$:

(*a*) Through application of Eq. (11.64)
(*b*) Assuming that the mixture is an ideal solution

11.28. The excess Gibbs energy of a binary liquid mixture at T and P is given by

$$G^E/RT = (-2.6x_1 - 1.8x_2)x_1x_2$$

(*a*) Find expressions for $\ln \gamma_1$ and $\ln \gamma_2$ at T and P.
(*b*) Show that when these expressions are combined in accord with Eq. (11.99) the given equation for G^E/RT is recovered.
(*c*) Show that these expressions satisfy Eq. (11.100), the Gibbs/Duhem equation.
(*d*) Show that $(d \ln \gamma_1/dx_1)_{x_1=1} = (d \ln \gamma_2/dx_1)_{x_1=0} = 0$.
(*e*) Plot G^E/RT, $\ln \gamma_1$, and $\ln \gamma_2$ as calculated by the given equation for G^E/RT and by the equations developed in (*a*) vs. x_1. Label points $\ln \gamma_1^\infty$ and $\ln \gamma_2^\infty$ and show their values.

11.29. Show that $\gamma_i = \hat{\phi}_i / \phi_i$.

11.30. Given below are values of G^E/J mol^{-1}, H^E/J mol^{-1}, and C_P^E/J mol^{-1} K^{-1} for some equimolar binary liquid mixtures at 298.15 K. Estimate values of G^E, H^E, and S^E at 328.15 K for one of the equimolar mixtures by two procedures: (I) Use all the data; (II) Assume $C_P^E = 0$. Compare and discuss your results for the two procedures.

(*a*) Acetone/chloroform: $G^E = -622$, $H^E = -1920$, $C_P^E = 4.2$
(*b*) Acetone/*n*-hexane: $G^E = 1095$, $H^E = 1595$, $C_P^E = 3.3$
(*c*) Benzene/isooctane: $G^E = 407$, $H^E = 984$, $C_P^E = -2.7$
(*d*) Chloroform/ethanol: $G^E = 632$, $H^E = -208$, $C_P^E = 23.0$
(*e*) Ethanol/*n*-heptane: $G^E = 1445$, $H^E = 605$, $C_P^E = 11.0$
(*f*) Ethanol/water: $G^E = 734$, $H^E = -416$, $C_P^E = 11.0$
(*g*) Ethyl acetate/*n*-heptane: $G^E = 759$, $H^E = 1465$, $C_P^E = -8.0$

11.31. The excess Gibbs energy of a particular ternary liquid mixture is represented by the empirical expression, with parameters A_{12}, A_{13}, and A_{23} functions of T and P only:

$$G^E/RT = A_{12}x_1x_2 + A_{13}x_1x_3 + A_{23}x_2x_3$$

(*a*) Determine the implied expressions for $\ln \gamma_1$, $\ln \gamma_2$, and $\ln \gamma_3$.
(*b*) Verify that your results for part (*a*) satisfy the summability relation, Eq. (11.99).
(*c*) For species 1 determine expressions (or values) for $\ln \gamma_1$ for the limiting cases: $x_1 = 0$, $x_1 = 1$, $x_2 = 0$, and $x_3 = 0$. What do these limiting cases represent?

11.32. The data in Table 11.2 are experimental values of V^E for binary liquid mixtures of 1,3-dioxolane(1) and isooctane(2) at 298.15 K and 1 atm.

Table 11.2: Excess Volumes for 1,3-Dioxane(1)/Isooctane(2) at 25°C (298.15 K)
R. Francesconi et al., *Int. DATA Ser., Ser. A*, vol. 25, no. 3, p. 229, 1997.

x_1	$V^E/10^{-3}$ cm^3 mol^{-1}	x_1	$V^E/10^{-3}$ cm^3 mol^{-1}
0.027 15	87.5	0.699 84	276.4
0.093 29	265.6	0.727 92	252.9
0.174 90	417.4	0.775 14	190.7
0.327 60	534.5	0.792 43	178.1
0.402 44	531.7	0.829 54	138.4
0.566 89	421.1	0.868 35	98.4
0.631 28	347.1	0.932 87	37.6
0.662 33	321.7	0.982 33	10.0

(*a*) Determine from the data numerical values of parameters a, b, and c in the correlating equation

$$V^E = x_1x_2(a + bx_1 + cx_1^2)$$

(*b*) Determine from the results of part (*a*) the maximum value of V^E. At what value of x_1 does this occur?

(*c*) Determine from the results of part (*a*) expressions for $\bar{V}_1^E$ and $\bar{V}_2^E$. Prepare a plot of these quantities vs. x_1, and discuss its features.

11.33. For an equimolar vapor mixture of propane(1) and *n*-pentane(2) at 75°C (348.15 K) and 2 bar, estimate Z, H^R, and S^R. Second virial coefficients, in cm^3 mol^{-1}:

t/T, °C/K	B_{11}	B_{22}	B_{12}
50°C/323.15 K	−331	−980	−558
75°C/348.15 K	−276	−809	−466
100°C/373.15 K	−235	−684	−399

Equations (3.38), (6.55), (6.56), and (11.62) are pertinent.

11.34. Use the data of Pb.11.33 to determine $\hat{\phi}_1$ and $\hat{\phi}_2$ as functions of composition for binary vapor mixtures of propane(1) and *n*-pentane(2) at 75°C (348.15 K) and 2 bar. Plot the results on a single graph. Discuss the features of this plot.

11.35. For a binary gas mixture described by Eqs. (3.38) and (11.62), prove that

$$G^E = \delta_{12} P y_1 y_2 \qquad S^E = -\frac{d\delta_{12}}{dT} P y_1 y_2$$

$$H^E = \left(\delta_{12} - T\frac{d\delta_{12}}{dT}\right) P y_1 y_2 \qquad C_P^E = -T\frac{d^2\delta_{12}}{dT^2} P y_1 y_2$$

See also Eq. (11.87), and note that $\delta_{12} = 2B_{12} - B_{11} - B_{22}$.

11.36. The data in Table 11.3 are experimental values of H^E for binary liquid mixtures of 1,2-dichloroethane(1) and dimethyl carbonate(2) at 40°C (313.15 K) and 1 atm.

Table 11.3: H^E Values for 1,2-Dichloroethane(1)/Dimethyl Carbonate(2) at 40°C (313.15 K)

R. Francesconi et al., *Int. DATA Ser., Ser. A*, vol. 25, no. 3, p. 225, 1997.

x_1	H^E/J mol^{-1}	x_1	H^E/J mol^{-1}
0.0426	−23.3	0.5163	−204.2
0.0817	−45.7	0.6156	−191.7
0.1177	−66.5	0.6810	−174.1
0.1510	−86.6	0.7621	−141.0
0.2107	−118.2	0.8181	−116.8
0.2624	−144.6	0.8650	−85.6
0.3472	−176.6	0.9276	−43.5
0.4158	−195.7	0.9624	−22.6

(*a*) Determine from the data numerical values of parameters a, b, and c in the correlating equation:

$$H^E = x_1 x_2 (a + b x_1 + c x_1^2)$$

(*b*) Determine from the results of part (*a*) the minimum value of H^E. At what value of x_1 does this occur?

(*c*) Determine from the results of part (*a*) expressions for $\bar{H}_1^E$ and $\bar{H}_2^E$. Prepare a plot of these quantities vs. x_1, and discuss its features.

11.37. Make use of Eqs. (3.38), (3.65), (3.66), (6.54), (6.55), (6.56), (6.89), (6.90), (11.62), and (11.69)–(11.74), to estimate V, H^R, S^R, and G^R for one of the following binary vapor mixtures:

(*a*) Acetone(1)/1,3-butadiene(2) with mole fractions $y_1 = 0.28$ and $y_2 = 0.72$ at $t/T = 60°C/333.15$ K and $P = 170$ kPa

(*b*) Acetonitrile(1)/diethyl ether(2) with mole fractions $y_1 = 0.37$ and $y_2 = 0.63$ at $t/T = 50°C/323.15$ K and $P = 120$ kPa

(*c*) Methyl chloride(1)/ethyl chloride(2) with mole fractions $y_1 = 0.45$ and $y_2 = 0.55$ at $t/T = 25°C/298.15$ K and $P = 100$ kPa

(*d*) Nitrogen(1)/ammonia(2) with mole fractions $y_1 = 0.83$ and $y_2 = 0.17$ at $t/T = 20°C/293.15$ K and $P = 300$ kPa

(*e*) Sulfur dioxide(1)/ethylene(2) with mole fractions $y_1 = 0.32$ and $y_2 = 0.68$ at $t/T = 25°C/298.15$ K and $P = 420$ kPa

Note: Set $k_{ij} = 0$ in Eq. (11.71).

11.38. Calculate ϕ and f by the Redlich/Kwong equation of state for one of the following, and compare results with values taken from a suitable generalized correlation:

(*a*) Acetylene at 325 K and 15 bar
(*b*) Argon at 200 K and 100 bar
(*c*) Benzene at 575 K and 40 bar
(*d*) Carbon dioxide at 350 K and 35 bar
(*e*) Ethylene at 300 K and 50 bar
(*f*) *n*-Hexane at 525 K and 10 bar
(*g*) Methane at 225 K and 25 bar
(*h*) Nitrogen at 200 K and 75 bar

11.39. Calculate ϕ and f by the Soave/Redlich/Kwong equation of state for the substance and conditions given by one of the parts of Pb. 11.38, and compare results with values taken from a suitable generalized correlation.

11.40. Calculate ϕ and f by the Peng/Robinson equation of state for the substance and conditions given by one of the parts of Pb. 11.38, and compare results with values taken from a suitable generalized correlation.

11.41. Laboratory A reports the following results for equimolar values of G^E for liquid mixtures of benzene(1) with 1-hexanol(2):

$$G^E = 805 \text{ J mol}^{-1} \text{ at } T = 298 \text{ K} \qquad G^E = 785 \text{ J mol}^{-1} \text{ at } T = 323 \text{ K}$$

Laboratory B reports the following result for the equimolar value of H^E for the same system:

$$H^E = 1060 \text{ J mol}^{-1} \text{ at } T = 313 \text{ K}$$

Are the results from the two laboratories thermodynamically consistent with one another? Explain.

11.42. The following expressions have been proposed for the partial molar properties of a particular binary mixture:

$$\bar{M}_1 = M_1 + Ax_2 \qquad \bar{M}_2 = M_2 + Ax_1$$

Here, parameter A is a constant. Can these expressions possibly be correct? Explain.

11.43. Two kmol h^{-1} of liquid *n*-octane (species 1) are continuously mixed with four kmol h^{-1} of liquid *iso*-octane (species 2). The mixing process occurs at constant T and P; mechanical power requirements are negligible.

(*a*) Use an energy balance to determine the rate of heat transfer.

(*b*) Use an entropy balance to determine the rate of entropy generation (W K^{-1}).

State and justify all assumptions.

11.44. Fifty mol s^{-1} of enriched air (50 mole % N_2, 50 mole % O_2) are produced by continuously combining air (79 mole % N_2, 21 mole % O_2) with a stream of pure oxygen. All streams are at the constant conditions $t/T = 25°\text{C}/298.15$ K and $P = 1.2$ atm. There are no moving parts.

(*a*) Determine the rates of air and oxygen (mol s^{-1}).

(*b*) What is the rate of heat transfer for the process?

(*c*) What is the rate of entropy generation $\dot{S}_G$ (W K^{-1})?

State all assumptions.

Suggestion: Treat the overall process as a combination of demixing and mixing steps.

11.45. A simple expression for M^E of a *symmetrical* binary system is $M^E = Ax_1x_2$. However, countless other empirical expressions can be proposed which exhibit symmetry. How suitable would the two following expressions be for general application?

(*a*) $M^E = Ax_1^2x_2^2$; (*b*) $M^E = A\sin(\pi x_1)$

Suggestion: Look at the implied partial properties $\bar{M}_1^E$ and $\bar{M}_2^E$.

11.46. For a multicomponent mixture containing any number of species, prove that

$$\bar{M}_i = M + \left(\frac{\partial M}{\partial x_i}\right)_{T,P} - \sum_k x_k \left(\frac{\partial M}{\partial x_k}\right)_{T,P}$$

where the summation is over *all* species. Show that for a binary mixture this result reduces to Eqs. (11.15) and (11.16).

11.47. The following empirical two-parameter expression has been proposed for correlation of excess properties of symmetrical liquid mixtures:

$$M^E = Ax_1x_2\left(\frac{1}{x_1 + Bx_2} + \frac{1}{x_2 + Bx_1}\right)$$

Here, quantities A and B are parameters that depend at most on T.

(*a*) Determine from the given equation the implied expressions for $\bar{M}_1^E$ and $\bar{M}_2^E$.
(*b*) Show that the results of part (*a*) satisfy **all** necessary constraints for partial excess properties.
(*c*) Determine from the results of part (*a*) expressions for $(\bar{M}_1^E)^\infty$ and $(\bar{M}_2^E)^\infty$

11.48. Commonly, if M^E for a binary system has a single sign, then the partial properties $\bar{M}_1^E$ and $\bar{M}_2^E$ have the same sign as M^E over the entire composition range. There are occasions, however, where the $\bar{M}_i^E$ may change sign even though M^E has a single sign. In fact, it is the *shape* of the M^E vs. x_1 curve that determines whether the $\bar{M}_i^E$ change sign. Show that a sufficient condition for $\bar{M}_1^E$ and $\bar{M}_2^E$ to have single signs is that the *curvature* of M^E vs. x_1 have a single sign over the entire composition range.

11.49. An engineer claims that the volume expansivity of an ideal solution is given by

$$\beta^{id} = \sum_i x_i \beta_i$$

Is this claim valid? If so, show why. If not, find a correct expression for β^{id}.

11.50. Given below are data for G^E and H^E (both in J mol^{-1}) for equimolar mixtures of the same organic liquids. Use *all* of the data to estimate values of G^E, H^E, and TS^E for the equimolar mixture at 25°C.

- At t/T = 10°C/283.15 K $G^E = 544.0$, $H^E = 932.1$
- At t/T = 30°C/303.15 K $G^E = 513.2$, $H^E = 893.4$
- At t/T = 50°C/323.15 K $G^E = 494.2$, $H^E = 845.9$

Suggestion: Assume C_P^E constant and use material developed in Example 11.10.

Chapter 12

Solution Thermodynamics: Applications

All of the fundamental equations and necessary definitions of solution thermodynamics are given in the preceding chapter. In this chapter we examine what can be learned from experiment. Considered first are measurements of vapor/liquid equilibrium (VLE) data, from which activity-coefficient correlations are derived. Second, we treat mixing experiments, which provide data for property changes of mixing. In particular, practical applications of the enthalpy change of mixing, called the heat of mixing, are presented in detail in Sec. 12.4.

12.1 LIQUID-PHASE PROPERTIES FROM VLE DATA

Figure 12.1 shows a vessel in which a vapor mixture and a liquid solution coexist in vapor/liquid equilibrium. The temperature T and pressure P are uniform throughout the vessel, and can be measured with appropriate instruments. Vapor and liquid samples may be withdrawn for analysis, and this provides experimental values for mole fractions in the vapor $\{y_i\}$ and mole fractions in the liquid $\{x_i\}$.

Fugacity

For species i in the vapor mixture, Eq. (11.52) is written as

$$\hat{f}_i^v = y_i \hat{\phi}_i^v P$$

The criterion of vapor/liquid equilibrium, as given by Eq. (11.48), is that $\hat{f}_i^l = \hat{f}_i^v$. Therefore,

$$\hat{f}_i^l = y_i \hat{\phi}_i^v P$$

Although values for vapor-phase fugacity coefficient $\hat{\phi}_i^v$ are easily calculated (Secs. 11.6 and 11.7), VLE measurements are very often made at pressures low enough ($P \leq 1$ bar) that the vapor phase may be assumed an ideal gas. In this case $\hat{\phi}_i^v = 1$, and the two preceding equations reduce to

$$\hat{f}_i^l = \hat{f}_i^v = y_i P$$

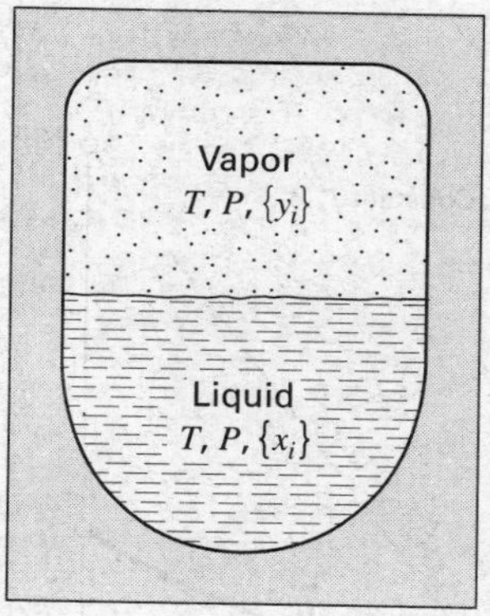

Figure 12.1: Schematic representation of VLE

Thus, the fugacity of species i (in both the liquid and vapor phases) is equal to the partial pressure of species i in the vapor phase. Its value increases from zero at infinite dilution ($x_i = y_i \rightarrow 0$) to P_i^{sat} for pure species i. This is illustrated by the data of Table 12.1 for the methyl ethyl ketone(1)/toluene(2) system at 50°C (323.15 K).[1] The first three columns list a set of experimental P-x_1-y_1 data and columns 4 and 5 show

$$\hat{f}_1 = y_1 P \qquad \text{and} \qquad \hat{f}_2 = y_2 P$$

Table 12.1: VLE Data for Methyl Ethyl Ketone(1)/Toluene(2) at 50°C (323.15 K)

P/kPa	x_1	y_1	$\hat{f}_1 = y_1 P$	$\hat{f}_2 = y_2 P$	γ_1	γ_2
12.30(P_2^{sat})	0.0000	0.0000	0.000	12.300		1.000
15.51	0.0895	0.2716	4.212	11.298	1.304	1.009
18.61	0.1981	0.4565	8.496	10.114	1.188	1.026
21.63	0.3193	0.5934	12.835	8.795	1.114	1.050
24.01	0.4232	0.6815	16.363	7.697	1.071	1.078
25.92	0.5119	0.7440	19.284	6.636	1.044	1.105
27.96	0.6096	0.8050	22.508	5.542	1.023	1.135
30.12	0.7135	0.8639	26.021	4.099	1.010	1.163
31.75	0.7934	0.9048	28.727	3.023	1.003	1.189
34.15	0.9102	0.9590	32.750	1.400	0.997	1.268
36.09(P_1^{sat})	1.0000	1.0000	36.090	0.000	1.000	

The fugacities are plotted in Fig. 12.2 as solid lines. The straight dashed lines represent Eq. (11.83), the Lewis/Randall rule, which expresses the composition dependence of the constituent fugacities in an ideal solution:

$$\hat{f}_i^{id} = x_i f_i \tag{11.83}$$

[1] M. Diaz Peña, A. Crespo Colin, and A. Compostizo, *J. Chem. Thermodyn.*, vol. 10, pp. 337–341, 1978.

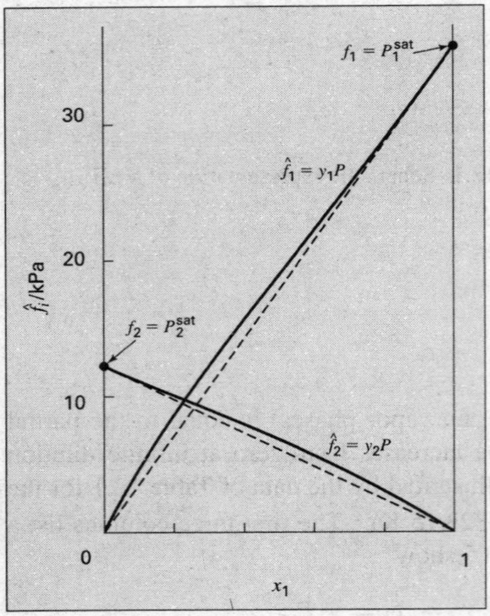

Figure 12.2: Fugacities for methyl ethyl ketone(1)/toluene(2) at 50°C (323.15 K). The dashed lines represent the Lewis/Randall rule

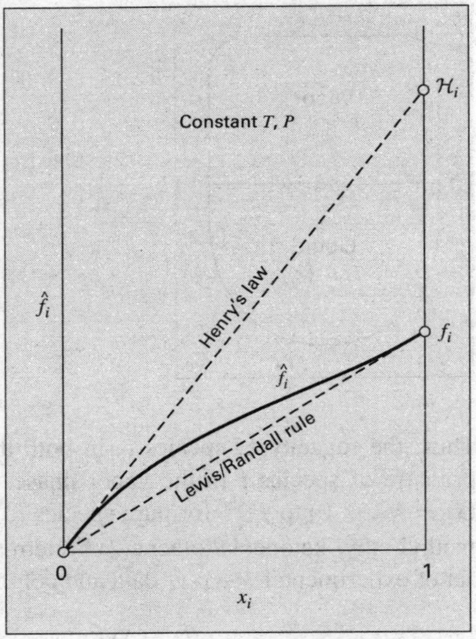

Figure 12.3: Composition dependence of liquid-phase fugacities for species i in a binary solution

Although derived from a particular set of data, Fig. 12.2 illustrates the general nature of the $\hat{f}_1$ and $\hat{f}_2$ vs. x_1 relationships for a binary liquid solution at constant T. The equilibrium pressure P varies with composition, but its influence on the liquid-phase values of $\hat{f}_1$ and $\hat{f}_2$ is negligible. Thus a plc⁺ at constant T *and* P would look the same, as indicated in Fig. 12.3 for species i ($i = 1, 2$) in a binary solution at constant T and P.

Activity Coefficient

The lower dashed line in Fig. 12.3, representing the Lewis/Randall rule, is characteristic of ideal-solution behavior. It provides the simplest possible model for the composition dependence of $\hat{f}_i$, representing a standard to which actual behavior may be compared. Indeed, the activity coefficient as defined by Eq. (11.90) formalizes this comparison:

$$\gamma_i \equiv \frac{\hat{f}_i}{x_i f_i} = \frac{\hat{f}_i}{\hat{f}_i^{id}}$$

Thus the activity coefficient of a species in solution is the ratio of its actual fugacity to the value given by the Lewis/Randall rule at the same T, P, and composition. For the calculation of experimental values, both $\hat{f}_i$ and $\hat{f}_i^{id}$ are eliminated in favor of measurable quantities[2]

$$\gamma_i = \frac{y_i P}{x_i f_i} = \frac{y_i P}{x_i P_i^{\text{sat}}} \qquad (i = 1, 2, \ldots, N) \tag{12.1}$$

This is a restatement of Eq. (10.5), modified Raoult's law, and is adequate for present purposes, allowing easy calculation of activity coefficients from experimental low-pressure VLE data. Values from this equation appear in the last two columns of Table 12.1.

The solid lines in both Figs. 12.2 and 12.3, representing experimental values of $\hat{f}_i$, become tangent to the Lewis/Randall-rule lines at $x_i = 1$. This is a consequence of the Gibbs/Duhem equation, as is shown later. In the other limit, $x_i \to 0$, $\hat{f}_i$ becomes zero. Thus, the ratio $\hat{f}_i/x_i$ is indeterminate in this limit, and application of l'Hôpital's rule yields

$$\lim_{x_i \to 0} \frac{\hat{f}_i}{x_i} = \left(\frac{d\hat{f}_i}{dx_i} \right)_{x_i = 0} \equiv \mathcal{H}_i \tag{12.2}$$

Equation (12.2) defines *Henry's constant* $\mathcal{H}_i$ as the limiting slope of the $\hat{f}_i$-vs.-x_i curve at $x_i = 0$. As shown by Fig. 12.3, this is the slope of a line drawn tangent to the curve at $x_i = 0$. The equation of this tangent line expresses *Henry's law*:

$$\boxed{\hat{f}_i = x_i \mathcal{H}_i} \tag{12.3}$$

Applicable in the limit as $x_i \to 0$, it is also of approximate validity for small values of x_i. Henry's law as given by Eq. (10.4) follows immediately from this equation when $\hat{f}_i = y_i P$, i.e., when $\hat{f}_i$ has its ideal-gas value.

Henry's law is related to the Lewis/Randall rule through the Gibbs/Duhem equation. Writing Eq. (11.14) for a binary solution and replacing $\bar{M}_i$ by $\bar{G}_i = \mu_i$ gives

$$x_1\, d\mu_1 + x_2\, d\mu_2 = 0 \qquad (\text{const } T, P)$$

Differentiation of Eq. (11.46) at constant T and P yields: $d\mu_i = RT\, d\ln \hat{f}_i$; whence,

$$x_1\, d\ln \hat{f}_1 + x_2\, d\ln \hat{f}_2 = 0 \qquad (\text{const } T, P)$$

Upon division by dx_1 this becomes

$$\boxed{x_1 \frac{d\ln \hat{f}_1}{dx_1} + x_2 \frac{d\ln \hat{f}_2}{dx_1} = 0 \qquad (\text{const } T, P)} \tag{12.4}$$

This is a special form of the Gibbs/Duhem equation. Substitution of $-dx_2$ for dx_1 in the second term produces

$$x_1 \frac{d\ln \hat{f}_1}{dx_1} = x_2 \frac{d\ln \hat{f}_2}{dx_2} \qquad \text{or} \qquad \frac{d\hat{f}_1/dx_1}{\hat{f}_1/x_1} = \frac{d\hat{f}_2/dx_2}{\hat{f}_2/x_2}$$

[2]In a more rigorous treatment (Sec. 14.1), $\hat{f}_i$ is given by Eq. (11.52), in which case,

$$\gamma_i = \frac{y_i \hat{\phi}_i P}{x_i P_i^{\text{sat}}} \qquad \text{with } \hat{\phi}_i \text{ evaluated by Eqs. (11.63) or by Eq. (11.64).}$$

In the limit as $x_1 \to 1$ and $x_2 \to 0$,

$$\lim_{x_1 \to 1} \frac{d\hat{f}_1/dx_1}{\hat{f}_1/x_1} = \lim_{x_2 \to 0} \frac{d\hat{f}_2/dx_2}{\hat{f}_2/x_2}$$

Because $\hat{f}_1 = f_1$ when $x_1 = 1$, this may be rewritten as

$$\frac{1}{f_1}\left(\frac{d\hat{f}_1}{dx_1}\right)_{x_1=1} = \frac{(d\hat{f}_2/dx_2)_{x_2=0}}{\lim\limits_{x_2 \to 0} (\hat{f}_2/x_2)}$$

According to Eq. (12.2), the numerator and denominator on the right side of this equation are equal, and therefore:

$$\left(\frac{d\hat{f}_1}{dx_1}\right)_{x_1=1} = f_1 \qquad (12.5)$$

This equation is the exact expression of the Lewis/Randall rule as applied to real solutions. It also implies that Eq. (11.83) provides approximately correct values of $\hat{f}_i$ when $x_i \approx 1$: $\hat{f}_i \approx \hat{f}_i^{id} = x_i f_i$.

Henry's law applies to a species as it approaches infinite dilution in a binary solution, and the Gibbs/Duhem equation insures validity of the Lewis/Randall rule for the other species as it approaches purity.

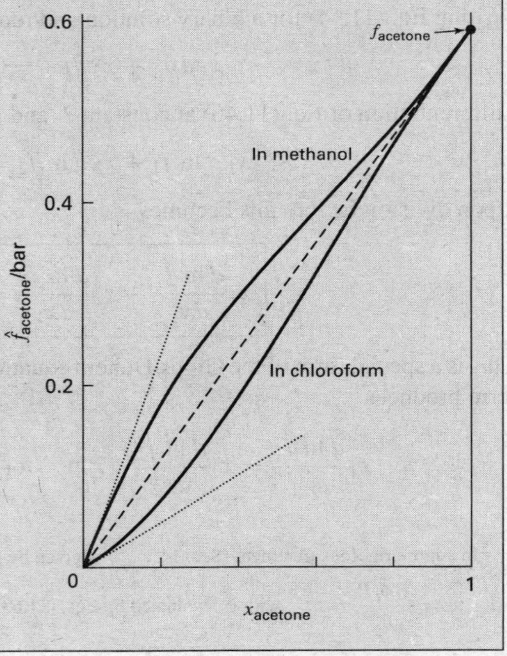

Figure 12.4: Composition dependence of the fugacity of acetone in two binary liquid solutions at 50°C (323.15 K)

The fugacity shown by Fig. 12.3 is for a species with positive deviations from ideality in the sense of the Lewis/Randall rule. Negative deviations are less common, but are also observed; the $\hat{f}_i$-vs.-x_i curve then lies below the Lewis/Randall line. In Fig. 12.4 the fugacity of acetone is shown as a function of composition for two different binary liquid solutions at 50°C (323.15 K). When the second species is methanol, acetone exhibits positive deviations from ideality. When the second species is chloroform, the deviations are negative. The fugacity of pure acetone f_{acetone} is of course the same regardless of the identity of the second species. However, Henry's constants, represented by slopes of the two dotted lines, are very different for the two cases.

Excess Gibbs Energy

In Table 12.2 the first three columns repeat the P-x_1-y_1 data of Table 12.1 for the system methyl ethyl ketone(1)/toluene(2). These data points are also shown as circles on Fig. 12.5(a). Values of $\ln \gamma_1$ and $\ln \gamma_2$ are listed in columns 4 and 5, and are shown by the open squares and triangles of Fig. 12.5(b). They are combined for a binary system in accord with Eq. (11.99):

$$\boxed{\frac{G^E}{RT} = x_1 \ln \gamma_1 + x_2 \ln \gamma_2} \tag{12.6}$$

The values of G^E/RT so calculated are then divided by $x_1 x_2$ to provide values of $G^E/x_1 x_2 RT$; the two sets of numbers are listed in columns 6 and 7 of Table 12.2, and appear as solid circles on Fig. 12.5(b).

Table 12.2: VLE Data for Methyl Ethyl Ketone(1)/Toluene(2) at 50°C (323.15 K)

P/kPa	x_1	y_1	$\ln \gamma_1$	$\ln \gamma_2$	G^E/RT	$G^E/x_1 x_2 RT$
12.30(P_2^{sat})	0.0000	0.0000		0.000	0.000	
15.51	0.0895	0.2716	0.266	0.009	0.032	0.389
18.61	0.1981	0.4565	0.172	0.025	0.054	0.342
21.63	0.3193	0.5934	0.108	0.049	0.068	0.312
24.01	0.4232	0.6815	0.069	0.075	0.072	0.297
25.92	0.5119	0.7440	0.043	0.100	0.071	0.283
27.96	0.6096	0.8050	0.023	0.127	0.063	0.267
30.12	0.7135	0.8639	0.010	0.151	0.051	0.248
31.75	0.7934	0.9048	0.003	0.173	0.038	0.234
34.15	0.9102	0.9590	−0.003	0.237	0.019	0.227
36.09(P_1^{sat})	1.0000	1.0000	0.000		0.000	

The four thermodynamic functions, $\ln \gamma_1$, $\ln \gamma_2$, G^E/RT, and $G^E/x_1 x_2 RT$, are properties of the liquid phase. Figure 12.5(b) shows how their experimental values vary with composition for a particular binary system at a specified temperature. This figure is characteristic of systems for which

$$\gamma_i \geq 1 \qquad \text{and} \qquad \ln \gamma_i \geq 0 \qquad (i = 1, 2)$$

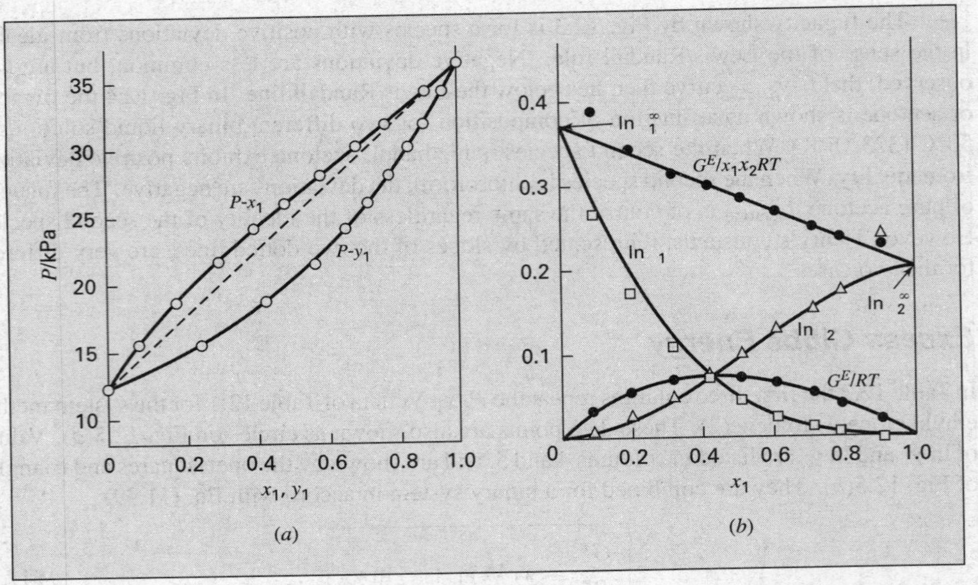

Figure 12.5: The methyl ethyl ketone(1)/toluene(2) system at 50°C (323.15 K) (*a*) Pxy data and their correlation (*b*) Liquid-phase properties and their correlation

In such cases the liquid phase shows *positive deviations* from Raoult's-law behavior. This is seen also in Fig. 12.5(*a*), where the P-x_1 data points all lie above the dashed straight line, which represents Raoult's law.

Because the activity coefficient of a species in solution becomes unity as the species becomes pure, each $\ln \gamma_i$ $(i = 1, 2)$ tends to zero as $x_i \to 1$. This is evident in Fig. 12.5(*b*). At the other limit, where $x_i \to 0$ and species i becomes infinitely dilute, $\ln \gamma_i$ approaches a finite limit, namely, $\ln \gamma_i^\infty$. In the limit as $x_1 \to 0$, the dimensionless excess Gibbs energy G^E/RT as given by Eq. (12.6) becomes

$$\lim_{x_1 \to 0} \frac{G^E}{RT} = (0) \ln \gamma_1^\infty + (1)(0) = 0$$

The same result is obtained for $x_2 \to 0$ $(x_1 \to 1)$. The value of G^E/RT (and G^E) is therefore zero at both $x_1 = 0$ and $x_1 = 1$.

The quantity G^E/x_1x_2RT becomes indeterminate both at $x_1 = 0$ and $x_1 = 1$, because G^E is zero in both limits, as is the product x_1x_2. Thus for $x_1 \to 0$, l'Hôpital's rule yields

$$\lim_{x_1 \to 0} \frac{G^E}{x_1x_2RT} = \lim_{x_1 \to 0} \frac{G^E/RT}{x_1} = \lim_{x_1 \to 0} \frac{d(G^E/RT)}{dx_1} \tag{A}$$

Differentiation of Eq. (12.6) with respect to x_1 provides the derivative of the final member:

$$\frac{d(G^E/RT)}{dx_1} = x_1 \frac{d \ln \gamma_1}{dx_1} + \ln \gamma_1 + x_2 \frac{d \ln \gamma_2}{dx_1} - \ln \gamma_2 \tag{B}$$

The minus sign preceding the last term comes from $dx_2/dx_1 = -1$, a consequence of the equation, $x_1 + x_2 = 1$. The Gibbs/Duhem equation, Eq. (11.100), written for a binary system, is divided by dx_1 to give

$$x_1 \frac{d \ln \gamma_1}{dx_1} + x_2 \frac{d \ln \gamma_2}{dx_1} = 0 \qquad \text{(const } T, P) \tag{12.7}$$

Substitution into Eq. (B) reduces it to

$$\frac{d(G^E/RT)}{dx_1} = \ln \frac{\gamma_1}{\gamma_2} \tag{12.8}$$

Applied to the composition limit at $x_1 = 0$, this equation yields

$$\lim_{x_1 \to 0} \frac{d(G^E/RT)}{dx_1} = \lim_{x_1 \to 0} \ln \frac{\gamma_1}{\gamma_2} = \ln \gamma_1^\infty$$

By Eq. (A), $\displaystyle \lim_{x_1 \to 0} \frac{G^E}{x_1 x_2 RT} = \ln \gamma_1^\infty$ Similarly, $\displaystyle \lim_{x_1 \to 1} \frac{G^E}{x_1 x_2 RT} = \ln \gamma_2^\infty$

Thus the limiting values of $G^E/x_1 x_2 RT$ are equal to the infinite-dilution limits of $\ln \gamma_1$ and $\ln \gamma_2$. This result is illustrated in Fig. 12.5(b).

These results depend on Eq. (12.7), which is valid for constant T and P. Although the data of Table 12.2 are for constant T, but variable P, negligible error is introduced through Eq. (12.7), because liquid-phase activity coefficients are very nearly independent of P for systems at low to moderate pressures.

Equation (12.7) has further influence on the nature of Fig. 12.5(b). Rewritten as,

$$\frac{d \ln \gamma_1}{dx_1} = -\frac{x_2}{x_1} \frac{d \ln \gamma_2}{dx_1}$$

it requires the slope of the $\ln \gamma_1$ curve to be everywhere of opposite sign to the slope of the $\ln \gamma_2$ curve. Furthermore, when $x_2 \to 0$ (and $x_1 \to 1$), the slope of the $\ln \gamma_1$ curve is zero. Similarly, when $x_1 \to 0$, the slope of the $\ln \gamma_2$ curve is zero. Thus, each $\ln \gamma_i$ ($i = 1, 2$) curve terminates at zero with zero slope at $x_i = 1$.

Data Reduction

Of the sets of points shown in Fig. 12.5(b), those for $G^E/x_1 x_2 RT$ most closely conform to a simple mathematical relation. Thus a straight line provides a reasonable approximation to this set of points, and mathematical expression is given to this linear relation by the equation:

$$\frac{G^E}{x_1 x_2 RT} = A_{21} x_1 + A_{12} x_2 \tag{12.9a}$$

where A_{21} and A_{12} are constants in any particular application. Alternatively,

$$\frac{G^E}{RT} = (A_{21} x_1 + A_{12} x_2) x_1 x_2 \tag{12.9b}$$

Expressions for $\ln \gamma_1$ and $\ln \gamma_2$ are derived from Eq. (12.9b) by application of Eq. (11.96). Because this requires differentiation of nG^E/RT with respect to a mole number, Eq. (12.9b) is multiplied by n and all mole fractions are converted to mole numbers. Thus on the right side x_1 is replaced by $n_1/(n_1 + n_2)$, and x_2, by $n_2/(n_1 + n_2)$. Because $n \equiv n_1 + n_2$, this gives

$$\frac{nG^E}{RT} = (A_{21}n_1 + A_{12}n_2)\frac{n_1 n_2}{(n_1 + n_2)^2}$$

Differentiating with respect to n_1 in accord with Eq. (11.96) yields

$$\ln \gamma_1 = \left[\frac{\partial(nG^E/RT)}{\partial n_1}\right]_{P,T,n_2}$$

$$= n_2\left[(A_{21}n_1 + A_{12}n_2)\left(\frac{1}{(n_1 + n_2)^2} - \frac{2n_1}{(n_1 + n_2)^3}\right) + \frac{n_1 A_{21}}{(n_1 + n_2)^2}\right]$$

Reconversion of the n_i to x_i ($n_i = nx_i$) gives

$$\ln \gamma_1 = x_2\left[(A_{21}x_1 + A_{12}x_2)(1 - 2x_1) + A_{21}x_1\right]$$

Further reduction, noting that $x_2 = 1 - x_1$, leads to

$$\boxed{\ln \gamma_1 = x_2^2[A_{12} + 2(A_{21} - A_{12})x_1]} \qquad (12.10a)$$

Similarly, multiplication of Eq. (12.9b) by n and differentiation with respect to n_2 yields

$$\boxed{\ln \gamma_2 = x_1^2[A_{21} + 2(A_{12} - A_{21})x_2]} \qquad (12.10b)$$

These are the *Margules*[3] *equations*, and they represent a commonly used empirical model of solution behavior. For the limiting conditions of infinite dilution, they become

$$\ln \gamma_1^\infty = A_{12} \quad (x_1 = 0) \qquad \text{and} \qquad \ln \gamma_2^\infty = A_{21} \quad (x_2 = 0)$$

For the methyl ethyl ketone/toluene system considered here, the curves of Fig. 12.5(*b*) for G^E/RT, $\ln \gamma_1$, and $\ln \gamma_2$ represent Eqs. (12.9b) and (12.10) with

$$A_{12} = 0.372 \qquad \text{and} \qquad A_{21} = 0.198$$

These are values of the intercepts at $x_1 = 0$ and $x_1 = 1$ of the straight line drawn to represent the G^E/x_1x_2RT data points.

A set of VLE data has here been *reduced* to a simple mathematical equation for the dimensionless excess Gibbs energy:

$$\frac{G^E}{RT} = (0.198x_1 + 0.372x_2)x_1x_2$$

[3]Max Margules (1856–1920), Austrian meteorologist and physicist.

This equation concisely stores the information of the data set. Indeed, the Margules equations for $\ln \gamma_1$ and $\ln \gamma_2$ allow construction of a correlation of the original P-x_1-y_1 data set. Equation (12.1) is rearranged and written for species 1 and 2 of a binary system as

$$y_1 P = x_1 \gamma_1 P_1^{\text{sat}} \qquad \text{and} \qquad y_2 P = x_2 \gamma_2 P_2^{\text{sat}}$$

Addition gives,

$$\boxed{P = x_1 \gamma_1 P_1^{\text{sat}} + x_2 \gamma_2 P_2^{\text{sat}}} \tag{12.11}$$

Whence,

$$\boxed{y_1 = \frac{x_1 \gamma_1 P_1^{\text{sat}}}{x_1 \gamma_1 P_1^{\text{sat}} + x_2 \gamma_2 P_2^{\text{sat}}}} \tag{12.12}$$

Values of γ_1 and γ_2 from Eqs. (12.10) with A_{12} and A_{21} as determined for the methyl ethyl ketone(1)/toluene(2) system are combined with the experimental values of P_1^{sat} and P_2^{sat} to calculate P and y_1 by Eqs. (12.11) and (12.12) at various values of x_1. The results are shown by the solid lines of Fig. 12.5(a), which represent the calculated P-x_1 and P-y_1 relations. They clearly provide an adequate correlation of the experimental data points.

Table 12.3: VLE Data for Chloroform(1)/1,4-Dioxane(2) at 50°C (323.15 K)

P/kPa	x_1	y_1	$\ln \gamma_1$	$\ln \gamma_2$	G^E/RT	G^E/x_1x_2RT
15.79(P_2^{sat})	0.0000	0.0000		0.000	0.000	
17.51	0.0932	0.1794	−0.722	0.004	−0.064	−0.758
18.15	0.1248	0.2383	−0.694	−0.000	−0.086	−0.790
19.30	0.1757	0.3302	−0.648	−0.007	−0.120	−0.825
19.89	0.2000	0.3691	−0.636	−0.007	−0.133	−0.828
21.37	0.2626	0.4628	−0.611	−0.014	−0.171	−0.882
24.95	0.3615	0.6184	−0.486	−0.057	−0.212	−0.919
29.82	0.4750	0.7552	−0.380	−0.127	−0.248	−0.992
34.80	0.5555	0.8378	−0.279	−0.218	−0.252	−1.019
42.10	0.6718	0.9137	−0.192	−0.355	−0.245	−1.113
60.38	0.8780	0.9860	−0.023	−0.824	−0.120	−1.124
65.39	0.9398	0.9945	−0.002	−0.972	−0.061	−1.074
69.36(P_1^{sat})	1.0000	1.0000	0.000		0.000	

A second set of P-x_1-y_1 data, for chloroform(1)/1,4-dioxane(2) at 50°C (323.15 K),[4] is given in Table 12.3, along with values of pertinent thermodynamic functions. Figures 12.6(a) and 12.6(b) display as points all of the experimental values. This system shows *negative* deviations from Raoult's-law behavior; because γ_1 and γ_2 are less than unity, values of $\ln \gamma_1$, $\ln \gamma_2$, G^E/RT, and G^E/x_1x_2RT are negative. Moreover, the P-x_1 data points in Fig. 12.6(a) all lie

[4]M. L. McGlashan and R. P. Rastogi, *Trans. Faraday Soc.*, vol. 54, p. 496, 1958.

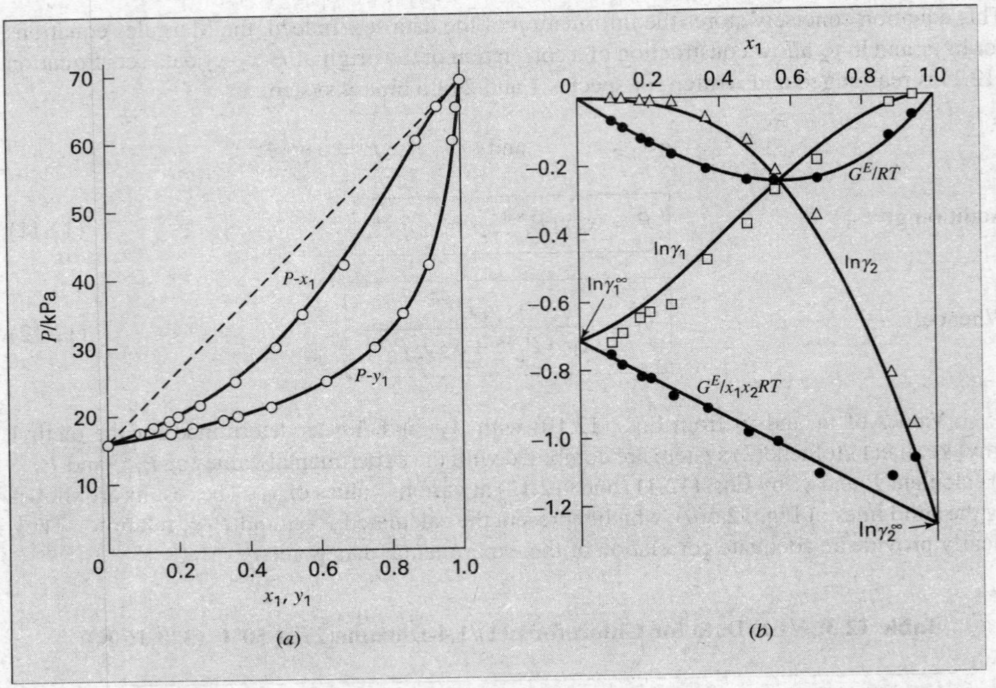

Figure 12.6: The chloroform(1)/1,4-dioxane(2) system at 50°C (323.15 K) (a) Pxy data and their correlation (b) Liquid-phase properties and their correlation

below the dashed line representing Raoult's-law behavior. Again the data points for G^E/x_1x_2RT are reasonably well correlated by Eq. (12.9a), and the Margules equations [Eqs. (12.10)] again apply, here with parameters:

$$A_{12} = -0.72 \qquad \text{and} \qquad A_{21} = -1.27$$

Values of G^E/RT, $\ln \gamma_1$, $\ln \gamma_2$, P, and y_1 calculated by Eqs. (12.9b), (12.10), (12.11), and (12.12) provide the curves shown for these quantities in Figs. 12.6(a) and 12.6(b). Again, the experimental P-x_1-y_1 data are adequately correlated.

Although the correlations provided by the Margules equations for the two sets of VLE data presented here are satisfactory, they are not perfect. The two possible reasons are, first, that the Margules equations are not precisely suited to the data set; second, that the P-x_1-y_1 data themselves are systematically in error such that they do not conform to the requirements of the Gibbs/Duhem equation.

We have presumed in applying the Margules equations that the deviations of the experimental points for G^E/x_1x_2RT from the straight lines drawn to represent them result from random error in the data. Indeed, the straight lines do provide excellent correlations of all but a few data points. Only toward edges of a diagram are there significant deviations, and these have been discounted, because the error bounds widen rapidly as the edges of a diagram are approached. In the limits as $x_1 \to 0$ and $x_1 \to 1$, G^E/x_1x_2RT becomes indeterminate;

experimentally this means that the values are subject to unlimited error and are not measurable. However, the possibility exists that the correlation would be improved were the G^E/x_1x_2RT points represented by an appropriate *curve*. Finding the correlation that best represents the data is a trial procedure.

Thermodynamic Consistency

The Gibbs/Duhem equation imposes a constraint on activity coefficients that may not be satisfied by a set of experimental values derived from P-x_1-y_1 data. The *experimental* values of $\ln \gamma_1$ and $\ln \gamma_2$ combine by Eq. (12.6) to give values of G^E/RT. This addition process is independent of the Gibbs/Duhem equation. On the other hand, the Gibbs/Duhem equation is implicit in Eq. (11.96), and activity coefficients derived from this equation necessarily obey the Gibbs/Duhem equation. These *derived* activity coefficients cannot possibly be consistent with the *experimental* values unless the experimental values also satisfy the Gibbs/Duhem equation. Nor can a P-x_1-y_1 correlation calculated by Eqs. (12.11) and (12.12) be consistent with experimental values. If the experimental data are *inconsistent* with the Gibbs/Duhem equation, they are necessarily incorrect as the result of systematic error in the data. Because correlating equations for G^E/RT impose consistency on derived activity coefficients, no such correlation exists that can precisely reproduce P-x_1-y_1 data that are inconsistent.

Our purpose now is to develop a simple test for the *consistency* with respect to the Gibbs/Duhem equation of a P-x_1-y_1 data set. Equation (12.6) is written with *experimental* values, calculated by (Eq. 12.1), and denoted by an asterisk:

$$\left(\frac{G^E}{RT}\right)^* = x_1 \ln \gamma_1^* + x_2 \ln \gamma_2^*$$

Differentiation gives

$$\frac{d(G^E/RT)^*}{dx_1} = x_1 \frac{d \ln \gamma_1^*}{dx_1} + \ln \gamma_1^* + x_2 \frac{d \ln \gamma_2^*}{dx_1} - \ln \gamma_2^*$$

or

$$\frac{d(G^E/RT)^*}{dx_1} = \ln \frac{\gamma_1^*}{\gamma_2^*} + x_1 \frac{d \ln \gamma_1^*}{dx_1} + x_2 \frac{d \ln \gamma_2^*}{dx_1}$$

This equation is subtracted from Eq. (12.8), written for *derived* property values, i.e., those given by a correlation, such as the Margules equations:

$$\frac{d(G^E/RT)}{dx_1} - \frac{d(G^E/RT)^*}{dx_1} = \ln \frac{\gamma_1}{\gamma_2} - \ln \frac{\gamma_1^*}{\gamma_2^*} - \left(x_1 \frac{d \ln \gamma_1^*}{dx_1} + x_2 \frac{d \ln \gamma_2^*}{dx_1} \right)$$

The differences between like terms are *residuals*, which may be represented by a δ notation. The preceding equation then becomes

$$\frac{d\,\delta(G^E/RT)}{dx_1} = \delta \ln \frac{\gamma_1}{\gamma_2} - \left(x_1 \frac{d \ln \gamma_1^*}{dx_1} + x_2 \frac{d \ln \gamma_2^*}{dx_1} \right)$$

If a data set is reduced so as to make the residuals in G^E/RT scatter about zero, then the derivative $d\,\delta(G^E/RT)/dx_1$ is effectively zero, reducing the preceding equation to

$$\boxed{\delta \ln \frac{\gamma_1}{\gamma_2} = x_1 \frac{d \ln \gamma_1^*}{dx_1} + x_2 \frac{d \ln \gamma_2^*}{dx_1}} \tag{12.13}$$

The right side of this equation is exactly the quantity that Eq. (12.7), the Gibbs/Duhem equation, requires to be zero for consistent data. The residual on the left therefore provides a direct measure of deviation from the Gibbs/Duhem equation. The extent to which a data set departs from consistency is measured by the degree to which these residuals fail to scatter about zero.[5]

Table 12.4: VLE Data for Diethyl Ketone(1)/*n*-Hexane(2) at 65°C (338.15 K)

P/kPa	x_1	y_1	$\ln \gamma_1^*$	$\ln \gamma_2^*$	$\left(\frac{G^E}{x_1 x_2 RT}\right)^*$
90.15(P_2^{sat})	0.000	0.000		0.000	
91.78	0.063	0.049	0.901	0.033	1.481
88.01	0.248	0.131	0.472	0.121	1.114
81.67	0.372	0.182	0.321	0.166	0.955
78.89	0.443	0.215	0.278	0.210	0.972
76.82	0.508	0.248	0.257	0.264	1.043
73.39	0.561	0.268	0.190	0.306	0.977
66.45	0.640	0.316	0.123	0.337	0.869
62.95	0.702	0.368	0.129	0.393	0.993
57.70	0.763	0.412	0.072	0.462	0.909
50.16	0.834	0.490	0.016	0.536	0.740
45.70	0.874	0.570	0.027	0.548	0.844
29.00(P_1^{sat})	1.000	1.000	0.000		

Example 12.1

VLE data for diethyl ketone(1)/*n*-hexane(2) at 65°C (338.15 K) as reported by Maripuri and Ratcliff,[6] are given in the first three columns of Table 12.4. Reduce this set of data.

[5] This test and other aspects of VLE data reduction are treated by H. C. Van Ness, *J. Chem. Thermodyn.*, vol. 27, pp. 113–134, 1995; *Pure & Appl. Chem.*, vol. 67, pp. 859–872, 1995. See also, P. T. Eubank, B. G. Lamonte, and J. F. Javier Alvarado, *J. Chem. Eng. Data*, vol. 45, pp. 1040–1048, 2000.

[6] V. C. Maripuri and G. A. Ratcliff, *J. Appl. Chem. Biotechnol.*, vol. 22, pp. 899–903, 1972.

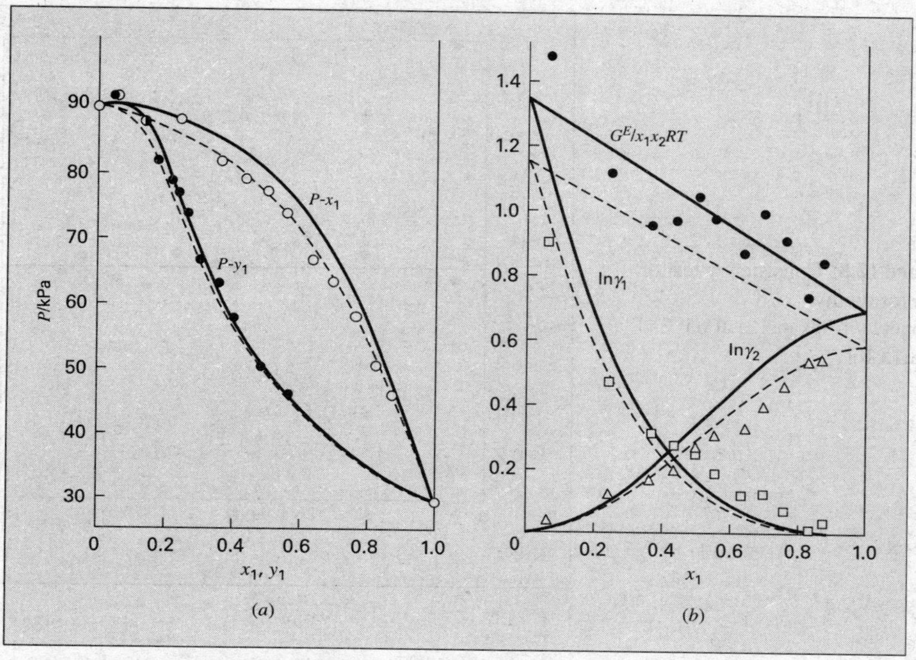

Figure 12.7: The diethyl ketone(1)/*n*-hexane(2) system at 65°C (338.15 K) (a) Pxy data and their correlations (b) Liquid-phase properties and their correlation

Solution

The last three columns of Table 12.4 present the *experimental* values, $\ln\gamma_1^*$, $\ln\gamma_2^*$, and $(G^E/x_1x_2RT)^*$, calculated from the data by Eqs. (12.1) and (12.6). All values are shown as points on Figs. 12.7(a) and 12.7(b). The object here is to find an equation for G^E/RT that provides a suitable correlation of the data. Although the data points of Fig. 12.7(b) for $(G^E/x_1x_2RT)^*$ show scatter, they are adequate to define a straight line, drawn here by eye and represented by the equation

$$\frac{G^E}{x_1x_2RT} = 0.70x_1 + 1.35x_2$$

This is Eq. (12.9a) with $A_{21} = 0.70$ and $A_{12} = 1.35$. Values of $\ln\gamma_1$ and $\ln\gamma_2$ at the given values of x_1, *derived* from this equation, are calculated by Eqs. (12.10), and *derived* values of P and y_1 at the same values of x_1 come from Eqs. (12.11) and (12.12). These results are plotted as the solid lines of Figs. 12.7(a) and 12.7(b). They clearly do not represent a good correlation of the data.

The difficulty is that the data are not *consistent* with the Gibbs/Duhem equation. That is, the sets of *experimental* values, $\ln\gamma_1^*$ and $\ln\gamma_2^*$, shown in Table 12.4 are not in accord with Eq. (12.7). However, the values of $\ln\gamma_1$ and $\ln\gamma_2$ *derived*

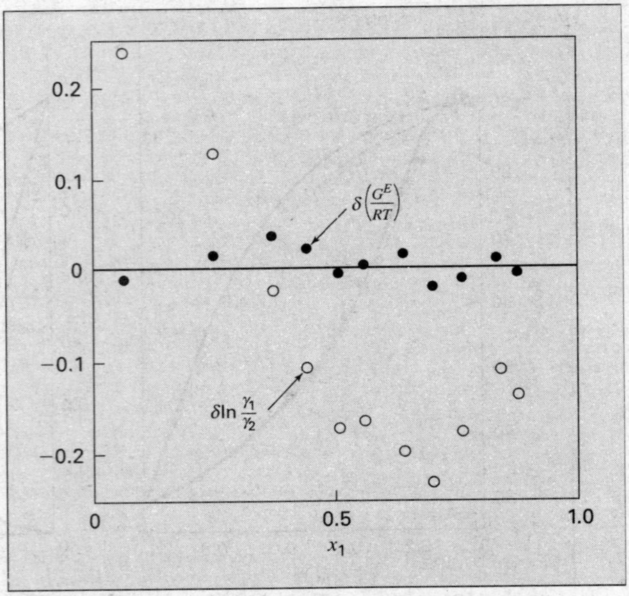

Figure 12.8: Consistency test of data for diethyl ketone(1)/n-hexane(2) at 65°C (338.15 K)

from the correlation necessarily obey this equation; the experimental and derived values therefore cannot possibly agree, and the resulting correlation cannot provide a precise representation of the complete set of P-x_1-y_1 data.

Application of the test for consistency represented by Eq. (12.13) requires calculation of the residuals $\delta(G^E/RT)$ and $\delta \ln(\gamma_1/\gamma_2)$, values of which are plotted vs. x_1 in Fig. 12.8. The residuals $\delta(G^E/RT)$ distribute themselves about zero,[7] as is required by the test, but the residuals $\delta \ln(\gamma_1/\gamma_2)$, which show the extent to which the data fail to satisfy the Gibbs/Duhem equation, clearly do not. Average absolute values of this residual less than 0.03 indicate data of a high degree of consistency; average absolute values of less than 0.10 are probably acceptable. The data set considered here shows an average absolute deviation of about 0.15, and must therefore contain significant error. Although one cannot be certain where the error lies, the values of y_1 are usually most suspect.

The method just described produces a correlation that is unnecessarily divergent from the experimental values. An alternative is to process just the P-x_1 data; this is possible because the P-x_1-y_1 data set includes more information than necessary. The procedure requires a computer, but in principle is simple enough. Assuming that the Margules equation is appropriate to the data, one merely searches for values of the parameters A_{12} and A_{21} that yield pressures by Eq. (12.11) that are as close as possible to the measured values. The method is applicable

[7]The simple procedure used here to find a correlation for G^E/RT would no doubt be improved by a regression procedure that determines the values of A_{21} and A_{12} that minimize the sum of squares of the residuals $\delta(G^E/RT)$.

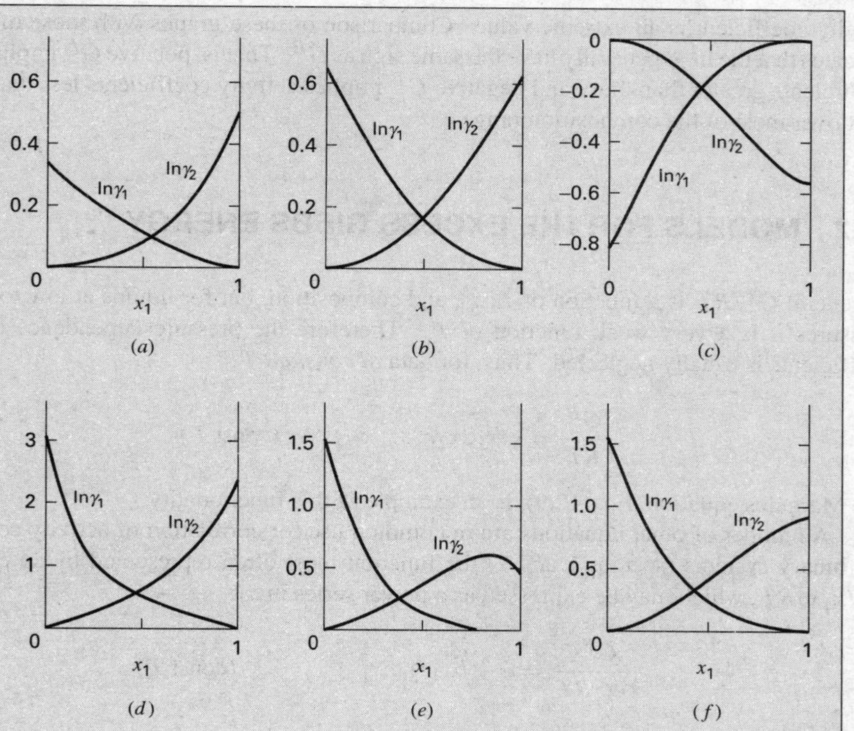

Figure 12.9: Logarithms of the activity coefficients at 50°C (323.15 K) for six binary liquid systems: (*a*) chloroform(1)/*n*-heptane(2) (*b*) acetone(1)/methanol(2) (*c*) acetone(1)/chloroform(2) (*d*) ethanol(1)/*n*-heptane(2) (*e*) ethanol(1)/chloroform(2) (*f*) ethanol(1)/water(2)

regardless of the correlating equation assumed, and is known as *Barker's method*.[8] Applied to the present data set, it yields the parameters:

$$A_{21} = 0.596 \qquad \text{and} \qquad A_{12} = 1.153$$

Use of these parameters in Eqs. (12.9a), (12.10), (12.11), and (12.12) produces the results described by the dashed lines of Figs. 12.7(*a*) and 12.7(*b*). The correlation cannot be precise, but it clearly provides a better overall representation of the experimental P-x_1-y_1 data.

Figure 12.9 shows plots of $\ln \gamma_i$ based on experimental measurements for six binary systems at 50°C (323.15 K), illustrating the variety of behavior that is observed. Note in every case that as $x_i \to 1$, $\ln \gamma_i \to 0$ with zero slope. Usually (but not always) the infinite-dilution

[8] J. A. Barker, *Austral. J. Chem.*, vol. 6, pp. 207–210, 1953.

activity coefficient is an extreme value. Comparison of these graphs with those of Fig. 11.4 indicates that the $\ln \gamma_i$ generally have the same sign as G^E. That is, positive G^E implies activity coefficients greater than unity and negative G^E implies activity coefficients less than unity, at least over most of the composition range.

12.2 MODELS FOR THE EXCESS GIBBS ENERGY

In general G^E/RT is a function of T, P, and composition, but for liquids at low to moderate pressures it is a very weak function of P. Therefore the pressure dependence of activity coefficients is usually neglected. Thus, for data *at constant T*:

$$\frac{G^E}{RT} = g(x_1, x_2, \ldots, x_N) \qquad \text{(const } T\text{)}$$

The Margules equation, Eq. (12.9), is an example of this functionality.

A number of other equations are in common use for correlation of activity coefficients. For binary systems (species 1 and 2) the function most often represented by an equation is G^E/x_1x_2RT, which may be expressed as a power series in x_1:

$$\frac{G^E}{x_1x_2RT} = a + bx_1 + cx_1^2 + \cdots \qquad \text{(const } T\text{)}$$

Because $x_2 = 1 - x_1$, mole fraction x_1 serves as the single independent variable. An equivalent power series with certain advantages is known as the Redlich/Kister expansion[9]

$$\frac{G^E}{x_1x_2RT} = A + B(x_1 - x_2) + C(x_1 - x_2)^2 + \cdots \qquad (12.14)$$

In application, different truncations of this series are appropriate, and in each case specific expressions for $\ln \gamma_1$ and $\ln \gamma_2$ are generated from Eq. (11.96).

When $A = B = C = \cdots = 0$, $G^E/RT = 0$, $\ln \gamma_1 = 0$, $\ln \gamma_2 = 0$, $\gamma_1 = \gamma_2 = 1$, and the solution is ideal.

If $B = C = \cdots = 0$, then

$$\frac{G^E}{x_1x_2RT} = A$$

where A is a constant for a given temperature. Corresponding equations for $\ln \gamma_1$ and $\ln \gamma_2$ are:

$\ln \gamma_1 = Ax_2^2$ (12.15a)	$\ln \gamma_2 = Ax_1^2$ (12.15b)

The symmetrical nature of these relations is evident. Infinite-dilution values of the activity coefficients are $\ln \gamma_1^\infty = \ln \gamma_2^\infty = A$.

[9] O. Redlich, A. T. Kister, and C. E. Turnquist, *Chem. Eng. Progr. Symp. Ser. No. 2*, vol. 48, pp. 49–61, 1952.

If $C = \cdots = 0$, then

$$\frac{G^E}{x_1 x_2 RT} = A + B(x_1 - x_2) = A + B(2x_1 - 1)$$

In this case G^E/x_1x_2RT is linear in x_1. If we define $A + B = A_{21}$ and $A - B = A_{12}$, the Margules equation is obtained:

$$\frac{G^E}{x_1 x_2 RT} = A_{21}x_1 + A_{12}x_2 \tag{12.9a}$$

Another well-known equation results when the reciprocal expression x_1x_2RT/G^E is expressed as a linear function of x_1:

$$\frac{x_1 x_2}{G^E/RT} = A' + B'(x_1 - x_2) = A' + B'(2x_1 - 1)$$

This may also be written as

$$\frac{x_1 x_2}{G^E/RT} = A'(x_1 + x_2) + B'(x_1 - x_2) = (A' + B')x_1 + (A' - B')x_2$$

When new parameters are defined by the equations, $A' + B' = 1/A'_{21}$ and $A' - B' = 1/A'_{12}$, an equivalent form is obtained:

$$\frac{x_1 x_2}{G^E/RT} = \frac{x_1}{A'_{21}} + \frac{x_2}{A'_{12}} = \frac{A'_{12}x_1 + A'_{21}x_2}{A'_{12}A'_{21}}$$

or

$$\frac{G^E}{x_1 x_2 RT} = \frac{A'_{12}A'_{21}}{A'_{12}x_1 + A'_{21}x_2} \tag{12.16}$$

The activity coefficients implied by this equation are

$$\ln \gamma_1 = A'_{12}\left(1 + \frac{A'_{12}x_1}{A'_{21}x_2}\right)^{-2} \tag{12.17a}$$

$$\ln \gamma_2 = A'_{21}\left(1 + \frac{A'_{21}x_2}{A'_{12}x_1}\right)^{-2} \tag{12.17b}$$

These are known as the van Laar[10] equations. When $x_1 = 0$, $\ln \gamma_1^\infty = A'_{12}$; when $x_2 = 0$, $\ln \gamma_2^\infty = A'_{21}$.

The Redlich/Kister expansion, the Margules equations, and the van Laar equations are all special cases of a general treatment based on rational functions, i.e., on equations for G^E/x_1x_2RT given by ratios of polynomials.[11] They provide great flexibility in the fitting of VLE data for binary systems. However, they have scant theoretical foundation, and therefore fail to admit a rational basis for extension to multicomponent systems. Moreover, they do not incorporate an explicit temperature dependence for the parameters, though this can be supplied on an *ad hoc* basis.

[10] Johannes Jacobus van Laar (1860–1938), Dutch physical chemist.

[11] H. C. Van Ness and M. M. Abbott, *Classical Thermodynamics of Nonelectrolyte Solutions: With Applications to Phase Equilibria*, Sec. 5-7, McGraw-Hill, New York, 1982.

Local-Composition Models

Theoretical developments in the molecular thermodynamics of liquid-solution behavior are often based on the concept of *local composition*. Within a liquid solution, local compositions, different from the overall mixture composition, are presumed to account for the short-range order and nonrandom molecular orientations that result from differences in molecular size and intermolecular forces. The concept was introduced by G. M. Wilson in 1964 with the publication of a model of solution behavior since known as the Wilson equation.[12] The success of this equation in the correlation of VLE data prompted the development of alternative local-composition models, most notably the NRTL (**N**on-**R**andom-**T**wo-**L**iquid) equation of Renon and Prausnitz[13] and the UNIQUAC (**UNI**versal **QUA**si-**C**hemical) equation of Abrams and Prausnitz.[14] A further significant development, based on the UNIQUAC equation, is the UNIFAC method,[15] in which activity coefficients are calculated from contributions of the various groups making up the molecules of a solution.

The Wilson equation, like the Margules and van Laar equations, contains just two parameters for a binary system (Λ_{12} and Λ_{21}), and is written as

$$\frac{G^E}{RT} = -x_1 \ln(x_1 + x_2\Lambda_{12}) - x_2 \ln(x_2 + x_1\Lambda_{21}) \tag{12.18}$$

$$\ln \gamma_1 = -\ln(x_1 + x_2\Lambda_{12}) + x_2 \left(\frac{\Lambda_{12}}{x_1 + x_2\Lambda_{12}} - \frac{\Lambda_{21}}{x_2 + x_1\Lambda_{21}} \right) \tag{12.19a}$$

$$\ln \gamma_2 = -\ln(x_2 + x_1\Lambda_{21}) - x_1 \left(\frac{\Lambda_{12}}{x_1 + x_2\Lambda_{12}} - \frac{\Lambda_{21}}{x_2 + x_1\Lambda_{21}} \right) \tag{12.19b}$$

For infinite dilution, these equations become:

$$\ln \gamma_1^\infty = -\ln \Lambda_{12} + 1 - \Lambda_{21} \qquad \text{and} \qquad \ln \gamma_2^\infty = -\ln \Lambda_{21} + 1 - \Lambda_{12}$$

Note that Λ_{12} and Λ_{21} must always be positive numbers.

The NRTL equation, containing three parameters for a binary system, is

$$\frac{G^E}{x_1 x_2 RT} = \frac{G_{21}\tau_{21}}{x_1 + x_2 G_{21}} + \frac{G_{12}\tau_{12}}{x_2 + x_1 G_{12}} \tag{12.20}$$

$$\ln \gamma_1 = x_2^2 \left[\tau_{21} \left(\frac{G_{21}}{x_1 + x_2 G_{21}} \right)^2 + \frac{G_{12}\tau_{12}}{(x_2 + x_1 G_{12})^2} \right] \tag{12.21a}$$

[12] G. M. Wilson, *J. Am. Chem. Soc.*, vol. 86, pp. 127–130, 1964.

[13] H. Renon and J. M. Prausnitz, *AIChE J.*, vol. 14, p. 135–144, 1968.

[14] D. S. Abrams and J. M. Prausnitz, *AIChE J.*, vol. 21, p. 116–128, 1975.

[15] **UNI**QUAC **F**unctional-group **A**ctivity **C**oefficients; proposed by Aa. Fredenslund, R. L. Jones, and J. M. Prausnitz, *AIChE J.*, vol. 21, p. 1086–1099, 1975; given detailed treatment in the monograph: Aa. Fredenslund, J. Gmehling, and P. Rasmussen, *Vapor-Liquid Equilibrium using UNIFAC*, Elsevier, Amsterdam, 1977.

$$\ln \gamma_2 = x_1^2 \left[\tau_{12} \left(\frac{G_{12}}{x_2 + x_1 G_{12}} \right)^2 + \frac{G_{21}\tau_{21}}{(x_1 + x_2 G_{21})^2} \right] \tag{12.21b}$$

Here, $\quad G_{12} = \exp(-\alpha\tau_{12}) \qquad G_{21} = \exp(-\alpha\tau_{21})$

and $\quad \tau_{12} = \dfrac{b_{12}}{RT} \qquad \tau_{21} = \dfrac{b_{21}}{RT}$

where α, b_{12}, and b_{21}, parameters specific to a particular pair of species, are independent of composition and temperature. The infinite-dilution values of the activity coefficients are given by the equations:

$$\ln \gamma_1^\infty = \tau_{21} + \tau_{12} \exp(-\alpha\tau_{12}) \qquad \text{and} \qquad \ln \gamma_2^\infty = \tau_{12} + \tau_{21} \exp(-\alpha\tau_{21})$$

The UNIQUAC equation and the UNIFAC method are models of greater complexity and are treated in App. H.

The local-composition models have limited flexibility in the fitting of data, but they are adequate for most engineering purposes. Moreover, they are implicitly generalizable to multicomponent systems without the introduction of any parameters beyond those required to describe the constituent binary systems. For example, the Wilson equation for multicomponent systems is:

$$\frac{G^E}{RT} = -\sum_i x_i \ln \left(\sum_j x_j \Lambda_{ij} \right) \tag{12.22}$$

$$\ln \gamma_i = 1 - \ln \left(\sum_j x_j \Lambda_{ij} \right) - \sum_k \frac{x_k \Lambda_{ki}}{\sum_j x_j \Lambda_{kj}} \tag{12.23}$$

where $\Lambda_{ij} = 1$ for $i = j$, etc. All indices refer to the same species, and summations are over *all* species. For each ij pair there are two parameters, because $\Lambda_{ij} \neq \Lambda_{ji}$. For a ternary system the three ij pairs are associated with the parameters Λ_{12}, Λ_{21}; Λ_{13}, Λ_{31}; and Λ_{23}, Λ_{32}.

The temperature dependence of the parameters is given by:

$$\Lambda_{ij} = \frac{V_j}{V_i} \exp \frac{-a_{ij}}{RT} \qquad (i \neq j) \tag{12.24}$$

where V_j and V_i are the molar volumes at temperature T of pure liquids j and i, and a_{ij} is a constant independent of composition and temperature. Thus the Wilson equation, like all other local-composition models, has built into it an *approximate* temperature dependence for the parameters. Moreover, all parameters are found from data for binary (in contrast to multicomponent) systems. This makes parameter determination for the local-composition models a task of manageable proportions.

12.3 PROPERTY CHANGES OF MIXING

Equations (11.79) through (11.82) are expressions for the properties of *ideal solutions*. Each may be combined with the defining equation for an excess property, Eq. (11.85), to yield:

$$G^E = G - \sum_i x_i G_i - RT \sum_i x_i \ln x_i \tag{12.25}$$

$$S^E = S - \sum_i x_i S_i + R \sum_i x_i \ln x_i \tag{12.26}$$

$$V^E = V - \sum_i x_i V_i \tag{12.27}$$

$$H^E = H - \sum_i x_i H_i \tag{12.28}$$

The first two terms on the right side of each equation express a difference having the form, $M - \sum_i x_i M_i$. These quantities are *property changes of mixing*, symbol ΔM. By definition,

$$\Delta M \equiv M - \sum_i x_i M_i \tag{12.29}$$

where M is a molar (or unit-mass) solution property and M_i is a molar (or unit-mass) pure-species property, all at the same T and P. Now Eqs. (12.25) through (12.28) can be written:

$$G^E = \Delta G - RT \sum_i x_i \ln x_i \tag{12.30}$$

$$S^E = \Delta S + R \sum_i x_i \ln x_i \tag{12.31}$$

$$V^E = \Delta V \tag{12.32}$$

$$H^E = \Delta H \tag{12.33}$$

where ΔG, ΔS, ΔV, and ΔH are the Gibbs energy change of mixing, the entropy change of mixing, the volume change of mixing, and the enthalpy change of mixing. For an ideal solution, each excess property is zero, and for this special case these equations become

$$\Delta G^{id} = RT \sum_i x_i \ln x_i \tag{12.34}$$

$$\Delta S^{id} = -R \sum_i x_i \ln x_i \tag{12.35}$$

$$\Delta V^{id} = 0 \tag{12.36}$$

$$\Delta H^{id} = 0 \tag{12.37}$$

These equations are alternative forms of Eqs. (11.79) through (11.82). As written here they apply to ideal-gas mixtures as well as to ideal solutions.

Equation (12.29) may be written for an ideal solution:

$$\Delta M^{id} = M^{id} - \sum_i x_i M_i$$

Subtracting this equation from Eq. (12.29) gives

$$\Delta M - \Delta M^{id} = M - M^{id}$$

In combination with Eq. (11.85) this becomes

$$M^E = \Delta M - \Delta M^{id} \tag{12.38}$$

Equations (12.30) through (12.33) show that excess properties and property changes of mixing are readily calculated one from the other. Although historically property changes of mixing were introduced first, because of their direct relation to experiment, excess properties fit more readily into the theoretical framework of solution thermodynamics. Because of their direct measurability, ΔV and ΔH are the property changes of mixing of major interest. Moreover, they are identical with the corresponding excess properties.

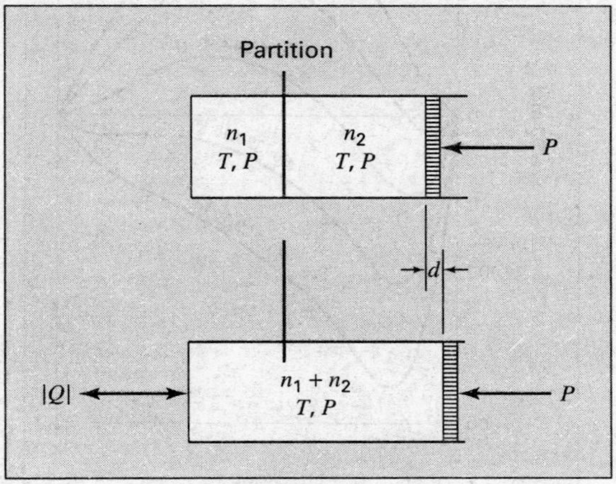

Figure 12.10: Schematic diagram of experimental mixing process

An experimental mixing process for a binary system is represented schematically in Fig. 12.10. The two pure species, both at T and P, are initially separated by a partition, withdrawal of which allows mixing. As mixing occurs, expansion or contraction of the system is accompanied by movement of the piston so that the pressure is constant. In addition, heat is added or extracted to maintain a constant temperature. When mixing is complete, the total volume change of the system (as measured by piston displacement d) is

$$\Delta V^t = (n_1 + n_2)V - n_1 V_1 - n_2 V_2$$

Because the process occurs at constant pressure, the total heat transfer Q is equal to the total enthalpy change of the system:

$$Q = \Delta H^t = (n_1 + n_2)H - n_1 H_1 - n_2 H_2$$

Division of these equations by $n_1 + n_2$ gives

$$\Delta V \equiv V - x_1 V_1 - x_2 V_2 = \frac{\Delta V^t}{n_1 + n_2}$$

and

$$\Delta H \equiv H - x_1 H_1 - x_2 H_2 = \frac{Q}{n_1 + n_2}$$

Thus the *volume change of mixing* ΔV and the *enthalpy change of mixing* ΔH are found from the measured quantities ΔV^t and Q. Because of its association with Q, ΔH is usually called the *heat of mixing*.

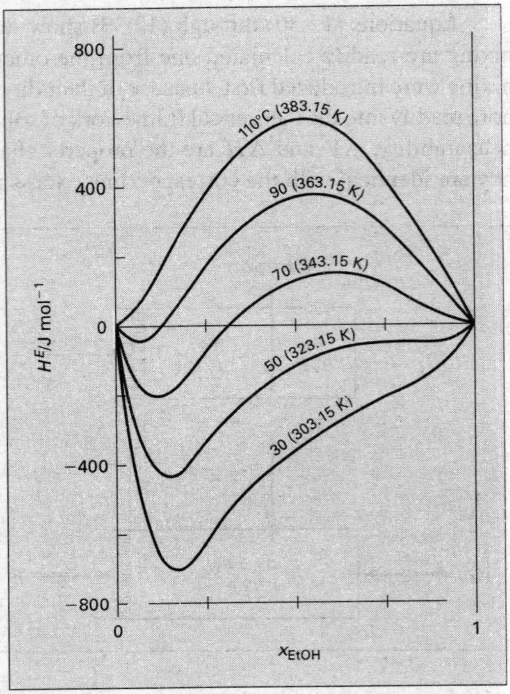

Figure 12.11: Excess enthalpies for ethanol/water

Figure 12.11 shows experimental heats of mixing ΔH (or excess enthalpies H^E) for the ethanol/water system as a function of composition for several temperatures between 30 and 110°C (303.15 K and 383.15 K). This figure illustrates much of the variety of behavior found for $H^E = \Delta H$ and $V^E = \Delta V$ data for binary liquid systems. Such data are also often represented by equations similar to those used for G^E data, in particular by the Redlich/Kister expansion.

Example 12.2

The excess enthalpy (heat of mixing) for a liquid mixture of species 1 and 2 at fixed T and P is represented by the equation

$$H^E = x_1 x_2 (40x_1 + 20x_2)$$

where H^E is in J mol^{-1}. Determine expressions for $\bar{H}_1^E$ and $\bar{H}_2^E$ as functions of x_1.

Solution

The partial properties are found by application of Eqs. (11.15) and (11.16) with $M = H^E$. Thus,

$\bar{H}_1^E = H^E + (1 - x_1)\dfrac{dH^E}{dx_1}$ (A)	$\bar{H}_2^E = H^E - x_1\dfrac{dH^E}{dx_1}$ (B)

Elimination of x_2 in favor of x_1 in the given equation for H^E and differentiation of the result yields

$H^E = 20x_1 - 20x_1^3$ (C)	$\dfrac{dH^E}{dx_1} = 20 - 60x_1^2$ (D)

Substitution of Eqs. (C) and (D) into both Eqs. (A) and (B) leads to:

$$\bar{H}_1^E = 20 - 60x_1^2 + 40x_1^3 \qquad \text{and} \qquad \bar{H}_2^E = 40x_1^3$$

These equations contain much the same information as those of Ex. 11.4, where the last term of the equation for H is identical to the expression given here for H^E. Therefore,

$$H = 400x_1 + 600x_2 + H^E$$

Clearly, $H_1 = 400$ J mol^{-1} and $H_2 = 600$ J mol^{-1}. The partial properties of Ex. 11.4 are related to $\bar{H}_1^E$ and $\bar{H}_2^E$ by the equations:

$$\bar{H}_1 = \bar{H}_1^E + \bar{H}_1^{id} = \bar{H}_1^E + H_1 = \bar{H}_1^E + 400$$

and
$$\bar{H}_2 = \bar{H}_2^E + \bar{H}_2^{id} = \bar{H}_2^E + H_2 = \bar{H}_2^E + 600$$

These two equations follow from combination of Eqs. (11.78) and (11.88).

Excess volumes (volume changes of mixing) for the methanol(1)/water(2) system at 25°C (298.15 K) can be calculated from the volumetric data of Fig. 11.2. By Eq. (11.88),

$$\bar{V}_i^E = \bar{V}_i - \bar{V}_i^{id}$$

According to Eq. (11.76), $\bar{V}_i^{id} = V_i$. Therefore,

$$\bar{V}_1^E = \bar{V}_1 - V_1 \qquad \text{and} \qquad \bar{V}_2^E = \bar{V}_2 - V_2$$

Equation (11.11) may be written for the excess volume of a binary system:

$$V^E = x_1\bar{V}_1^E + x_2\bar{V}_2^E$$

Results are shown in Fig. 12.12. Values on the figure for $x_1 = 0.3$ come from Ex. 11.3. Thus,

$$\bar{V}_1^E = 38.632 - 40.727 = -2.095 \text{ cm}^3 \text{ mol}^{-1}$$

$$\bar{V}_2^E = 17.765 - 18.068 = -0.303 \text{ cm}^3 \text{ mol}^{-1}$$

and
$$V^E = (0.3)(-2.095) + (0.7)(-0.303) = -0.841 \text{ cm}^3 \text{ mol}^{-1}$$

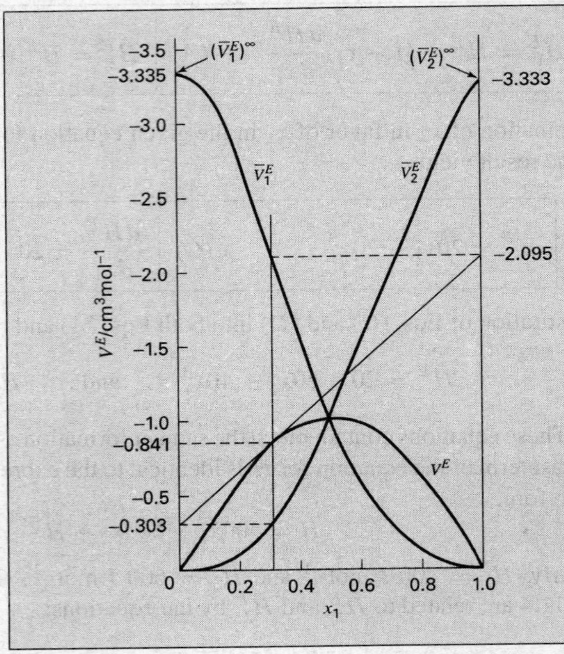

Figure 12.12: Excess volumes: methanol(1)/water(2) at 25°C (298.15).

The tangent line drawn at $x_1 = 0.3$ illustrates the determination of partial excess volumes by the method of tangent intercepts. Whereas the values of V in Fig. 11.2 range from 18.068 to 40.727 cm^3 mol^{-1}, the values of $V^E = \Delta V$ go from zero at both $x_1 = 0$ and $x_1 = 1$ to a value of about -1 cm^3 mol^{-1} at a mole fraction of about 0.5. The curves showing $\bar{V}_1^E$ and $\bar{V}_2^E$ are nearly symmetrical for the methanol/water system, but this is by no means so for all systems.

Figure 12.13 illustrates the composition dependence of ΔG, ΔH, and $T\,\Delta S$ for six binary liquid systems at 50°C (323.15 K) and approximately 1 atm. The related quantities G^E, H^E, and TS^E are shown for the same systems in Fig. 11.4. As with excess properties, property changes of mixing exhibit diverse behavior, but again all systems have common features:

1. Each ΔM is zero for a pure species.
2. The Gibbs energy change of mixing ΔG is always negative.
3. The entropy change of mixing ΔS is positive.

Feature 1 follows from Eq. (12.29). Feature 2 is a consequence of the requirement that the Gibbs energy be a minimum for equilibrium states at specified T and P (Sec. 14.3). Feature 3 reflects the fact that negative entropy changes of mixing are *unusual*; it is *not* a consequence of the second law of thermodynamics, which merely forbids negative entropy changes of mixing for systems *isolated* from their surroundings. For constant T and P, ΔS is observed to be negative for certain special classes of mixtures, none of which is represented in Fig. 12.13. A discussion of the molecular basis of mixture properties is given in Secs. 16.6 and 16.7.

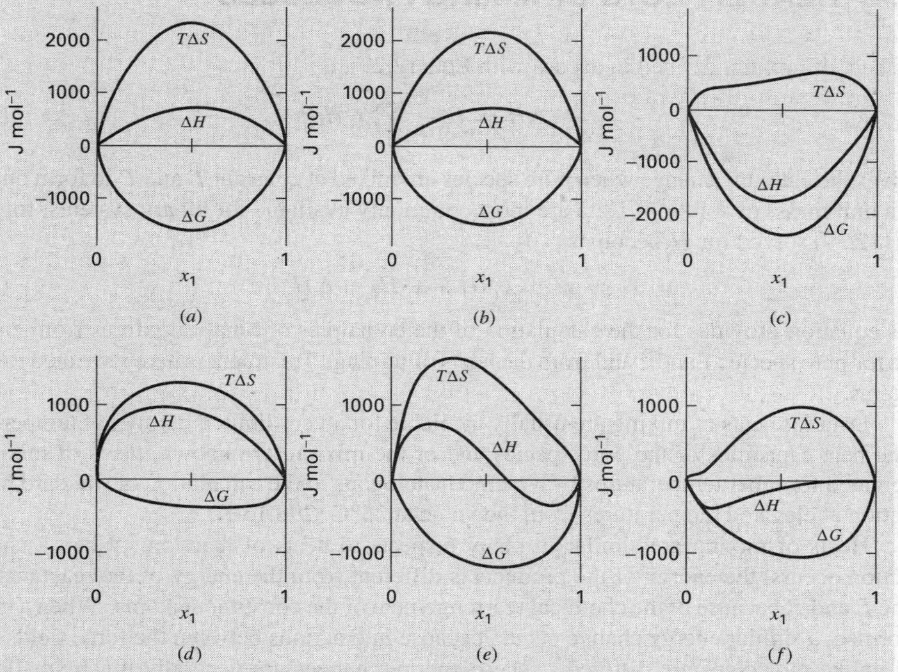

Figure 12.13: Property changes of mixing at 50°C (323.15 K) for six binary liquid systems: (*a*) chloroform(1)/*n*-heptane(2); (*b*) acetone(1)/methanol(2); (*c*) acetone(1)/chloroform(2); (*d*) ethanol(1)/*n*-heptane(2); (*e*) ethanol(1)/chloroform(2); (*f*) ethanol(1)/water(2).

Example 12.3

Property changes of mixing and excess properties are related. Show how Figs. 11.4 and 12.13 are generated from correlated data for $\Delta H(x)$ and $G^E(x)$.

Solution

With $\Delta H(x)$ and $G^E(x)$ given, Eqs. (12.33) and (11.86) provide

$$H^E = \Delta H \qquad \text{and} \qquad S^E = \frac{H^E - G^E}{T}$$

These allow completion of Fig. 11.4. Property changes of mixing ΔG and ΔS follow from G^E and S^E by application of Eqs. (12.30) and (12.31):

$$\Delta G = G^E + RT\sum_i x_i \ln x_i \qquad \Delta S = S^E - R\sum_i x_i \ln x_i$$

These permit completion of Fig. 12.13.

12.4 HEAT EFFECTS OF MIXING PROCESSES

The heat of mixing, defined in accord with Eq. (12.29), is

$$\Delta H = H - \sum_i x_i H_i \tag{12.39}$$

It gives the enthalpy change when pure species are mixed at constant T and P to form one mole (or a unit mass) of solution. Data are most commonly available for binary systems, for which Eq. (12.39) solved for H becomes

$$H = x_1 H_1 + x_2 H_2 + \Delta H \tag{12.40}$$

This equation provides for the calculation of the enthalpies of binary mixtures from enthalpy data for pure species 1 and 2 and from the heats of mixing. Treatment is here restricted to binary systems.

Data for heats of mixing are usually available for a very limited number of temperatures. If the heat capacities of the pure species and of the mixture are known, heats of mixing are calculated for other temperatures by a method analogous to the calculation of standard heats of reaction at elevated temperatures from the value at 25°C (298.15 K).

Heats of mixing are similar in many respects to heats of reaction. When a chemical reaction occurs, the energy of the products is different from the energy of the reactants at the same T and P because of the chemical rearrangement of the constituent atoms. When a mixture is formed, a similar energy change occurs because interactions between the force fields of like and unlike molecules are different. These energy changes are generally much smaller than those associated with chemical bonds; thus heats of mixing are generally much smaller than heats of reaction.

Heats of Solution

When solids or gases are dissolved in liquids, the heat effect is called a *heat of solution*, and is based on the dissolution of *1 mol of solute*. If species 1 is the solute, then x_1 is the moles of solute per mole of solution. Because ΔH is the heat effect per mole of solution, $\Delta H/x_1$ is the heat effect per mole of solute. Thus,

$$\widetilde{\Delta H} = \frac{\Delta H}{x_1}$$

where $\widetilde{\Delta H}$ is the heat of solution on the basis of a mole of *solute*.

Solution processes are conveniently represented by *physical-change* equations analogous to chemical-reaction equations. When 1 mol of LiCl(s) is mixed with 12 mol of H_2O, the process is represented by

$$\text{LiCl}(s) + 12\text{H}_2\text{O}(l) \rightarrow \text{LiCl}(12\text{H}_2\text{O})$$

The designation LiCl($12H_2O$) represents a solution of 1 mol of LiCl dissolved in 12 mol of H_2O. The heat of solution for this process at 25°C (298.15 K) and 1 bar is $\widetilde{\Delta H} = -33\,614$ J. This means that the enthalpy of 1 mol of LiCl in 12 mol of H_2O is 33 614 J less than the combined enthalpies of 1 mol of pure LiCl(s) and 12 mol of pure H_2O(l). Equations for physical changes such as this are readily combined with equations for chemical reactions. This is illustrated in the following example, which incorporates the dissolution process just described.

Example 12.4

Calculate the heat of formation of LiCl in 12 mol of H_2O at 25°C (298.15 K).

Solution

The process implied by the problem statement results in the formation from its constituent elements of 1 mol of LiCl *in solution* in 12 mol of H_2O. The equation representing this process is obtained as follows:

$$\mathrm{Li} + \tfrac{1}{2}\mathrm{Cl_2} \rightarrow \mathrm{LiCl}(s) \qquad \Delta H^\circ_{298} = -408\,610\ \mathrm{J}$$

$$\mathrm{LiCl}(s) + 12\mathrm{H_2O}(l) \rightarrow \mathrm{LiCl}(12\mathrm{H_2O}) \qquad \widetilde{\Delta H}_{298} = -33\,614\ \mathrm{J}$$

$$\mathrm{Li} + \tfrac{1}{2}\mathrm{Cl_2} + 12\mathrm{H_2O}(l) \rightarrow \mathrm{LiCl}(12\mathrm{H_2O}) \qquad \Delta H^\circ_{298} = -442\,224\ \mathrm{J}$$

The first reaction describes a chemical change resulting in the formation of LiCl(s) from its elements, and the enthalpy change accompanying this reaction is the standard heat of formation of LiCl(s) at 25°C (298.15 K). The second reaction represents the physical change resulting in the dissolution of 1 mol of LiCl(s) in 12 mol of $H_2O(l)$, and the enthalpy change is a heat of solution. The overall enthalpy change, −442 224 J, is the heat of formation of LiCl *in* 12 mol of H_2O. This figure does *not* include the heat of formation of the H_2O.

Often heats of solution are not reported directly but must be determined from heats of formation by the reverse of the calculation just illustrated. Typical are data for the heats of formation of 1 mol of LiCl:[16]

LiCl(s)	−408 610 J
LiCl·H_2O(s)	−712 580 J
LiCl·2H_2O(s)	−1,012 650 J
LiCl·3H_2O(s)	−1,311 300 J
LiCl in 3 mol H_2O	−429 366 J
LiCl in 5 mol H_2O	−436 805 J
LiCl in 8 mol H_2O	−440 529 J
LiCl in 10 mol H_2O	−441 579 J
LiCl in 12 mol H_2O	−442 224 J
LiCl in 15 mol H_2O	−442 835 J

Heats of solution are readily calculated from these data. The reaction representing the dissolution of 1 mol of LiCl(s) in 5 mol of $H_2O(l)$ is obtained as follows:

$$\mathrm{Li} + \tfrac{1}{2}\mathrm{Cl_2} + 5\mathrm{H_2O}(l) \rightarrow \mathrm{LiCl}(5\mathrm{H_2O}) \qquad \Delta H^\circ_{298} = -436\,805\ \mathrm{J}$$

$$\mathrm{LiCl}(s) \rightarrow \mathrm{Li} + \tfrac{1}{2}\mathrm{Cl_2} \qquad \Delta H^\circ_{298} = 408\,610\ \mathrm{J}$$

$$\mathrm{LiCl}(s) + 5\mathrm{H_2O}(l) \rightarrow \mathrm{LiCl}(5\mathrm{H_2O}) \qquad \widetilde{\Delta H}_{298} = -28\,195\ \mathrm{J}$$

[16] "The NBS Tables of Chemical Thermodynamic Properties," *J. Phys. Chem. Ref. Data*, vol. 11, suppl. 2, pp. 2-291 and 2-292, 1982.

This calculation can be carried out for each quantity of H_2O for which data are given. The results are then conveniently represented graphically by a plot of $\widetilde{\Delta H}$, the heat of solution per mole of solute, vs. $\tilde{n}$, the moles of solvent per mole of solute. The composition variable, $\tilde{n} \equiv n_2/n_1$, is related to x_1:

$$\tilde{n} = \frac{x_2(n_1 + n_2)}{x_1(n_1 + n_2)} = \frac{1 - x_1}{x_1} \qquad \text{whence} \qquad x_1 = \frac{1}{1 + \tilde{n}}$$

The following equations therefore relate ΔH, the heat of mixing based on 1 mol of solution, and $\widetilde{\Delta H}$, the heat of solution based on 1 mol of solute:

$$\widetilde{\Delta H} = \frac{\Delta H}{x_1} = \Delta H(1 + \tilde{n}) \qquad \text{or} \qquad \Delta H = \frac{\widetilde{\Delta H}}{1 + \tilde{n}}$$

Figure 12.14 shows plots of $\widetilde{\Delta H}$ vs. $\tilde{n}$ for LiCl(s) and HCl(g) dissolved in water at 25°C (298.15 K). Data in this form are readily applied to the solution of practical problems.

Because water of hydration in solids is an integral part of a chemical compound, the heat of formation of a hydrated salt includes the heat of formation of the water of hydration. The dissolution of 1 mol of LiCl·2H$_2$O(s) in 8 mol of H_2O produces a solution containing 1 mol LiCl in 10 mol of H_2O, represented by LiCl(10H$_2$O). The equations which sum to give this process are

$$\mathrm{Li} + \tfrac{1}{2}\mathrm{Cl_2} + 10\mathrm{H_2O}(l) \rightarrow \mathrm{LiCl(10H_2O)} \qquad \Delta H^\circ_{298} = -441\,579 \text{ J}$$

$$\mathrm{LiCl{\cdot}2H_2O}(s) \rightarrow \mathrm{Li} + \tfrac{1}{2}\mathrm{Cl_2} + 2\mathrm{H_2} + \mathrm{O_2} \qquad \Delta H^\circ_{298} = 1012\,650 \text{ J}$$

$$2\mathrm{H_2} + \mathrm{O_2} \rightarrow 2\mathrm{H_2O}(l) \qquad \Delta H^\circ_{298} = (2)(-285\,830) \text{ J}$$

$$\mathrm{LiCl{\cdot}2H_2O}(s) + 8\mathrm{H_2O}(l) \rightarrow \mathrm{LiCl(10H_2O)} \qquad \widetilde{\Delta H}_{298} = -589 \text{ J}$$

Example 12.5

A single-effect evaporator operating at atmospheric pressure concentrates a 15% (by mass) LiCl solution to 40%. The feed enters the evaporator at the rate of 2 kg s^{-1} at 25°C (298.15 K). The normal boiling point of a 40% LiCl solution is about 132°C (402.15 K), and its specific heat is estimated as 2.72 kJ kg^{-1} °C^{-1}. What is the heat-transfer rate in the evaporator?

Solution

The 2 kg of 15% LiCl solution entering the evaporator each second consists of 0.30 kg LiCl and 1.70 kg H_2O. A material balance shows that 1.25 kg of H_2O is evaporated and that 0.75 kg of 40% LiCl solution is produced. The process is represented by Fig. 12.15.

The energy balance for this flow process is $\Delta H^t = Q$, where ΔH^t is the total enthalpy of the product streams minus the total enthalpy of the feed stream. Thus

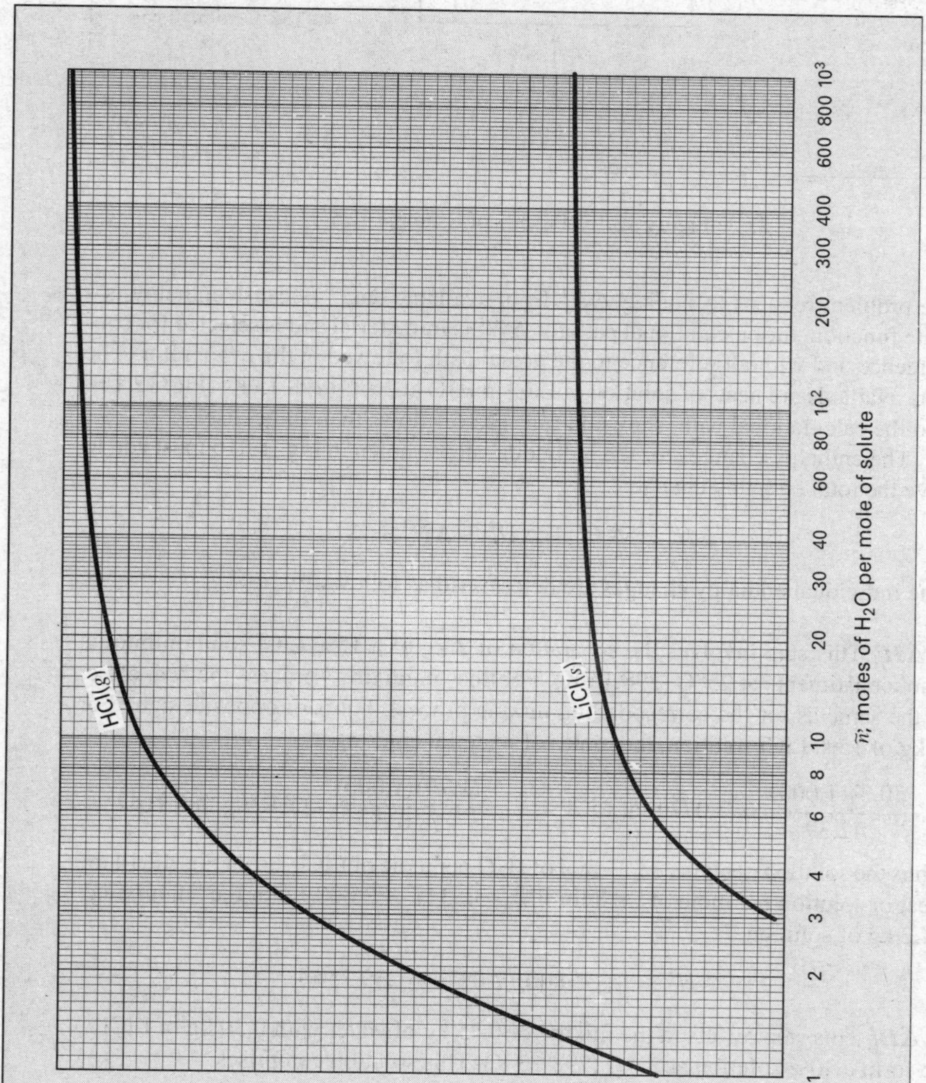

Figure 12.14: Heats of solution at 25°C (298.15 K) (based on data from "The NBS Tables of Chemical Thermodynamic Properties," *J. Phys. Chem. Ref. Data*, vol. 11, suppl. 2, 1982)

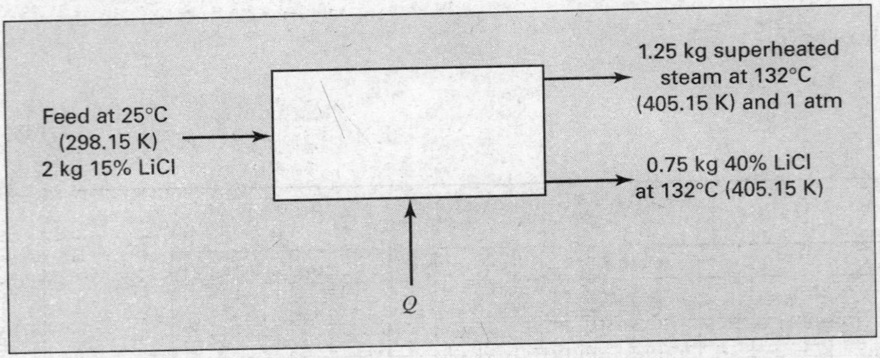

Figure 12.15: Process of Example 12.5

the problem reduces to finding ΔH^t from available data. Because enthalpy is a state function, the calculational path for ΔH^t is immaterial and is selected for convenience and without reference to the actual path followed in the evaporator. The data available are heats of solution of LiCl in H_2O at 25°C (298.15 K) (Fig. 12.14), and the calculational path, shown in Fig. 12.16, allows their direct use.

The enthalpy changes for the individual steps shown in Fig. 12.16 must add to give the total enthalpy change:

$$\Delta H^t = \Delta H_a^t + \Delta H_b^t + \Delta H_c^t + \Delta H_d^t$$

The individual enthalpy changes are determined as follows.

- $\boldsymbol{\Delta H_a^t}$ This step involves the separation of 2 kg of a 15% LiCl solution into its pure constituents at 25°C (298.15 K). For this "unmixing" process the heat effect is the same as for the corresponding mixing process, but is of opposite sign. For 2 kg of 15% LiCl solution, the moles of material entering are

$$\frac{(0.3)(1{,}000)}{42.39} = 7.077 \text{ mol LiCl} \qquad \frac{(1.70)(1{,}000)}{18.015} = 94.366 \text{ mol } H_2O$$

Thus the solution contains 13.33 mol of H_2O per mole of LiCl. From Fig. 12.14 the heat of solution per mole of LiCl for $\tilde{n} = 13.33$ is −33 800 J. For the "unmixing" of 2 kg of solution,

$$\Delta H_a^t = (+33\ 800)(7.077) = 239\ 250 \text{ J}$$

- $\boldsymbol{\Delta H_b^t}$ This step results in the mixing of 0.45 kg of water with 0.30 kg of LiCl(s) to form a 40% solution at 25°C (298.15 K). This solution comprises

$$0.30 \text{ kg} \rightarrow 7.077 \text{ mol LiCl} \qquad \text{and} \qquad 0.45 \text{ kg} \rightarrow 24.979 \text{ mol } H_2O$$

Thus the final solution contains 3.53 mol of H_2O per mole of LiCl. From Fig. 12.14 the heat of solution per mole of LiCl at this value of $\tilde{n}$ is −23 260 J. Therefore,

$$\Delta H_b^t = (-23\ 260)(7.077) = -164\ 630 \text{ J}$$

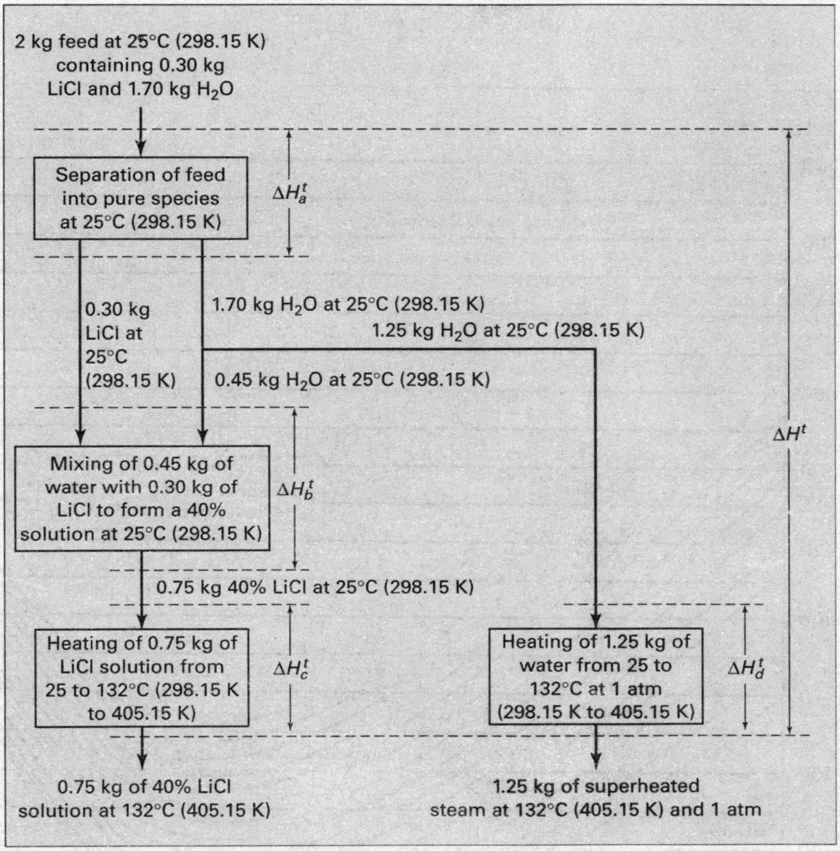

Figure 12.16: Calculational path for process of Example 12.5

• $\boldsymbol{\Delta H_c^t}$ For this step 0.75 kg of 40% LiCl solution is heated from 25 to 132°C (298.15 K to 405.15 K). Because $\Delta H_c^t = mC_P\,\Delta T$,

$$\Delta H_c^t = (0.75)(2.72)(132 - 25) = 218.28 \text{ kJ} \rightarrow 218\,280 \text{ J}$$

• $\boldsymbol{\Delta H_d^t}$ In this step liquid water is vaporized and heated to 132°C (405.15 K). The enthalpy change is obtained from the steam tables:

$$\Delta H_d^t = (1.25)(2740.3 - 104.8) = 3294.4 \text{ kJ} \rightarrow 3294\,400 \text{ J}$$

Adding the individual enthalpy changes gives

$$\begin{aligned}\Delta H &= \Delta H_a^t + \Delta H_b^t + \Delta H_c^t + \Delta H_d^t \\ &= 239\,250 - 164\,630 + 218\,280 + 3294\,400 = 3587\,300 \text{ J}\end{aligned}$$

The required heat-transfer rate is therefore 3587.3 kJ s^{-1} or kW.

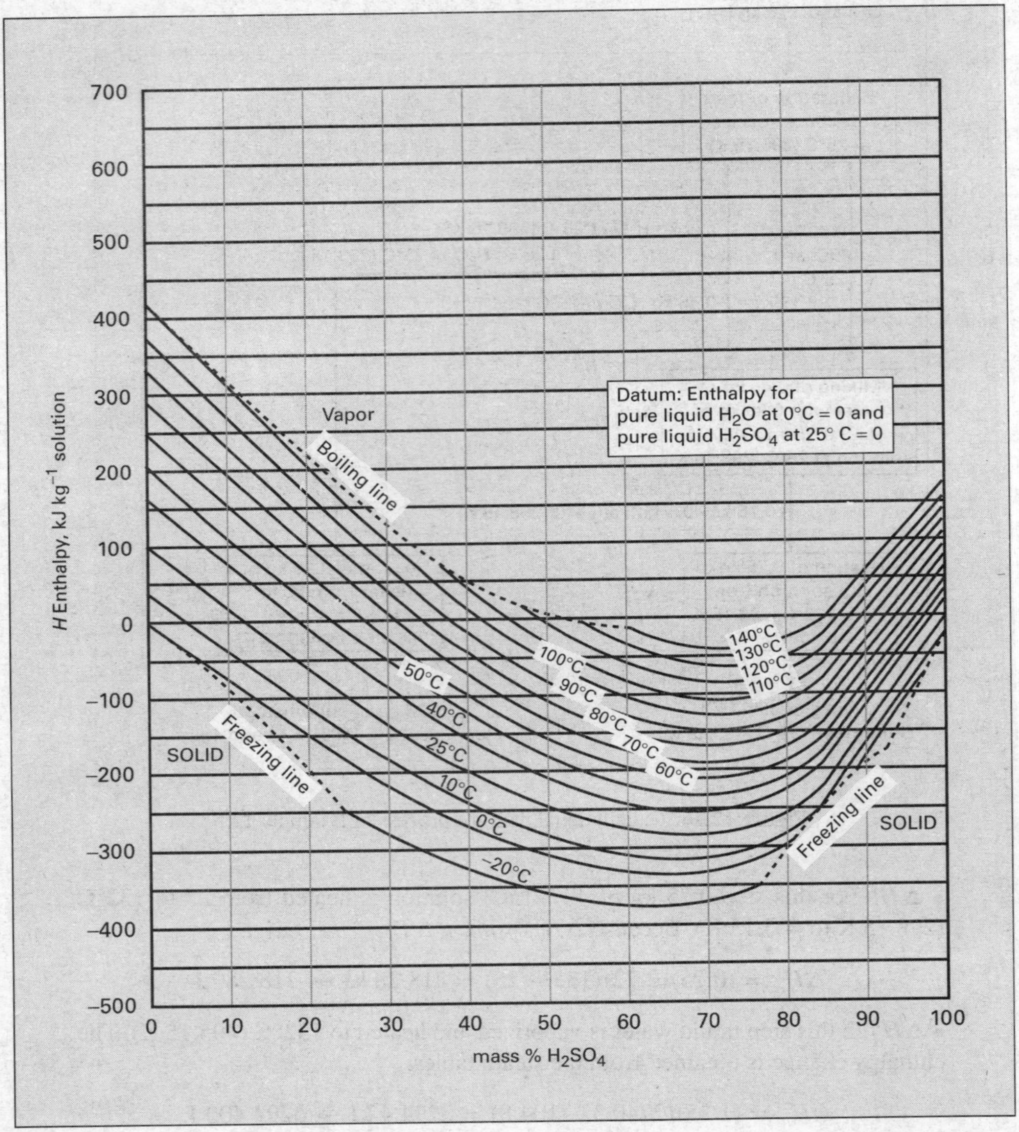

Figure 12.17: *Hx* diagram for H_2SO_4/H_2O (redrawn from data of The NBS Tables of Chemical Thermodynamic Properties, *J. Phy. Chem. Ref. Data*, vol. 11, suppl. 2, pp. 2–58 and 2–59, 1982, T. R. Bump and W. L. Sibbitt, *Ind. Eng. Chem.*, vol. 47, pp. 1665-1670, 1955; and C. M. Gable, H. F. Betz and S. H. Maron, *J. Am. Chem. Soc.*, vol. 72, pp. 1445–1448, 1950, by permissions)

Enthalpy/Concentration Diagrams

The *enthalpy/concentration* (Hx) *diagram* is a useful way to represent enthalpy data for binary solutions. It plots enthalpy as a function of composition (mole fraction or mass fraction of one species) with temperature as parameter. The pressure is a constant and is usually 1 atm. Figure 12.17 shows a partial diagram for the H_2SO_4/H_2O system, where enthalpy values here are for a unit mass of *solution*. Equation (12.40) is therefore directly applicable:

$$H = x_1 H_1 + x_2 H_2 + \Delta H \tag{12.40}$$

Values of H for the solution depend not only on heats of mixing, but also on enthalpies H_1 and H_2 of the pure species. Once these are known for a given T and P, H is fixed for all solutions at the same T and P, because ΔH has a unique and measurable value for each composition. Absolute enthalpies are unknown, and arbitrary zero points are chosen for the enthalpies of the pure species. Thus, the *basis* of an enthalpy/concentration diagram is $H_1 = 0$ for some specified state of species 1 and $H_2 = 0$ for some specified state of species 2. The same temperature need not be selected for these states for both species.

In the case of the H_2SO_4(1)/H_2O(2) diagram shown in Fig. 12.17, $H_2 = 0$ for pure liquid H_2O at the triple point [0.01°C (273.16 K)], and $H_1 = 0$ for pure liquid H_2SO_4 at 25°C [77(°F)]. In this case the 0°C (273.15 K) isotherm terminates at $H = 0$ at the pure-H_2O edge of the diagram, and the 25°C (298.15 K) isotherm terminates at $H = 0$ at the pure-H_2SO_4 edge of the diagram. The advantage of taking $H = 0$ for pure liquid water at its triple point is that this is the base of the steam tables. Enthalpy values from the steam tables can then be used in conjunction with values taken from the enthalpy/concentration diagram. Were some other base used for the diagram, one would have to apply a correction to the steam-table values to put them on the same basis as the diagram.

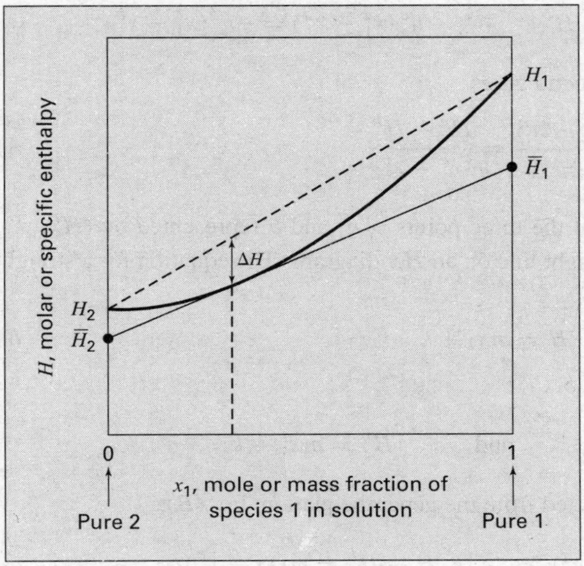

Figure 12.18: Graphical constructions on an Hx diagram

For an *ideal solution*, isotherms on an enthalpy/concentration diagram are straight lines connecting the enthalpy of pure species 2 at $x_1 = 0$ with the enthalpy of pure species 1 at $x_1 = 1$, as illustrated for a single isotherm in Fig. 12.18 by the dashed line. The solid curve represents an isotherm for a real solution. Also shown is a tangent line from which partial enthalpies may be determined in accord with Eqs. (11.15) and (11.16). Equations (11.82) and (12.40) combine to give $\Delta H = H - H^{id}$; ΔH is therefore the vertical distance between the curve and the dashed line of Fig. 12.18. Here, the actual isotherm lies below the ideal-solution isotherm, and ΔH is everywhere negative. This means that heat is evolved whenever the pure species at the given temperature are mixed to form a solution at the same temperature. Such a system is *exothermic*. The H_2SO_4/H_2O system is an example. An *endothermic* system is one for which the heats of solution are positive; in this case heat is absorbed to keep the temperature constant. An example is the methanol/benzene system.

One useful feature of an enthalpy/concentration diagram is that all solutions formed by adiabatic mixing of two other solutions are represented by points lying on a straight line connecting the points that represent the initial solutions. This is shown as follows.

Let the superscripts a and b denote two initial binary solutions, consisting of n^a and n^b moles respectively. Let superscript c denote the final solution obtained by simple mixing of solutions a and b in an adiabatic process, either batch mixing at constant P or steady-flow mixing with no shaft work or change in potential or kinetic energy. In either case, $\Delta H^t = Q = 0$, and the total energy balance is

$$(n^a + n^b)H^c = n^a H^a + n^b H^b$$

In addition, we may write a material balance for species 1:

$$(n^a + n^b)x_1^c = n^a x_1^a + n^b x_1^b$$

These two equations may be rearranged as

$$n^a(H^c - H^a) = -n^b(H^c - H^b) \qquad n^a(x_1^c - x_1^a) = -n^b(x_1^c - x_1^b)$$

Division of the first equation by the second gives

$$\frac{H^c - H^a}{x_1^c - x_1^a} = \frac{H^c - H^b}{x_1^c - x_1^b} \tag{A}$$

Our purpose now is to show that the three points c, a, and b represented by (H^c, x_1^c), (H^a, x_1^a), and (H^b, x_1^b) lie along a straight line on an Hx diagram. The equation for a straight line in these coordinates is

$$H = mx_1 + k \tag{B}$$

If this line passes through points a and b,

$$H^a = mx_1^a + k \qquad \text{and} \qquad H^b = mx_1^b + k$$

Each of these equations may be subtracted from the general equation, Eq. (B):

$$H - H^a = m(x_1 - x_1^a) \qquad H - H^b = m(x_1 - x_1^b)$$

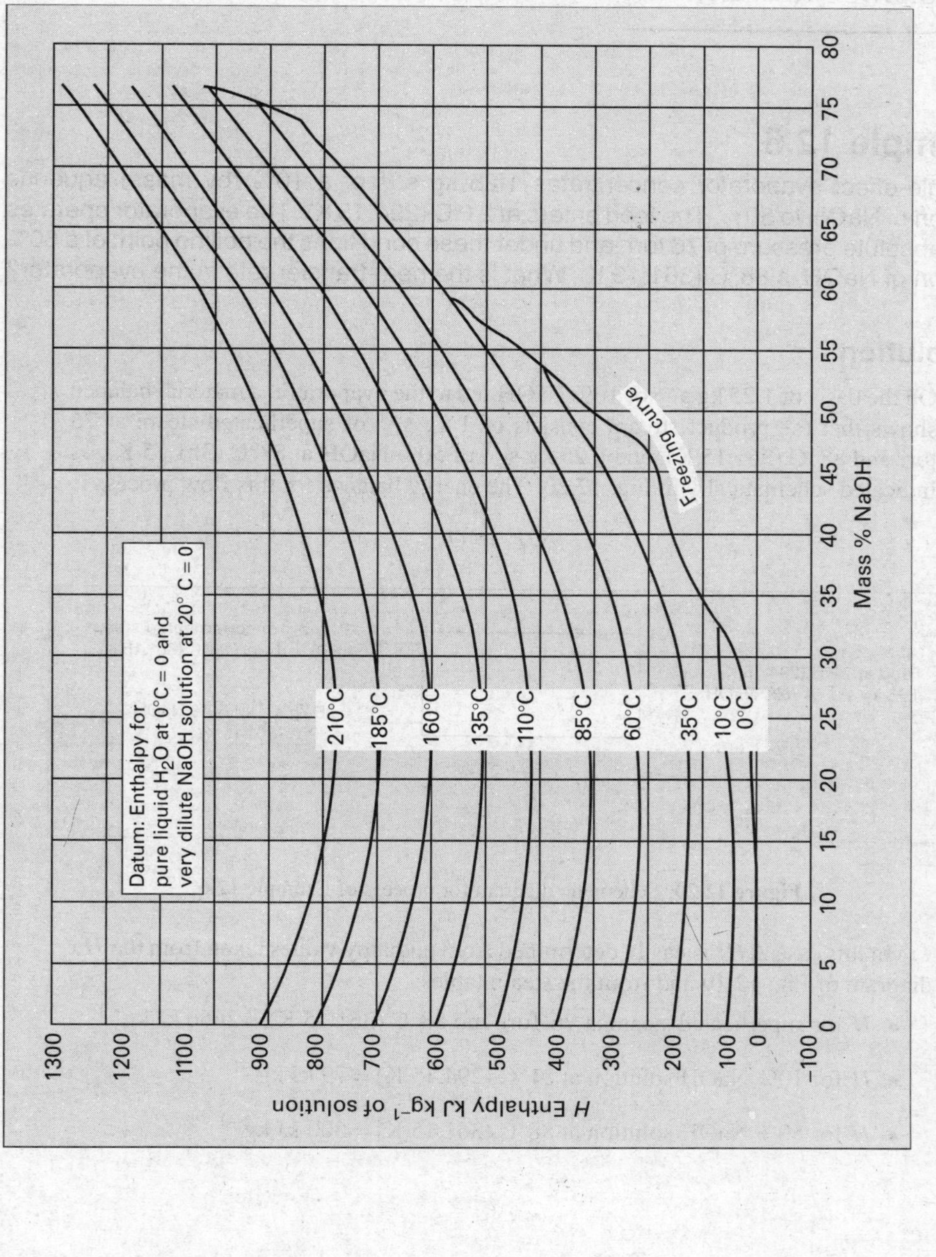

Figure 12.19: Hx diagram for NaOH/H_2O (reproduced by permission of John Wiley & Sons, Inc., USA from J.I. Kroschwitz (Ed.), *Kirk-Othmer Encyclopedia of Chemical Technology*, IV Ed., Vol. 1, pp. 1005, 1991)

Dividing the first of these by the second yields

$$\frac{H - H^a}{H - H^b} = \frac{x_1 - x_1^a}{x_1 - x_1^b} \qquad \text{or} \qquad \frac{H - H^a}{x_1 - x_1^a} = \frac{H - H^b}{x_1 - x_1^b}$$

Any point with the coordinates (H, x_1) which satisfies the last equation lies on the straight line that contains points a and b. Equation (A) shows that (H^c, x_1^c) is such a point.

The use of enthalpy/concentration diagrams is illustrated in the following examples for the NaOH/H_2O system; an Hx diagram is shown in Fig. 12.19.

Example 12.6

A single-effect evaporator concentrates 1.25 kg s^{-1} of a 10% (by mass) aqueous solution of NaOH to 50%. The feed enters at 21°C (294.15 K). The evaporator operates at an absolute pressure of 76 torr, and under these conditions the boiling point of a 50% solution of NaOH is 88°C (361.15 K). What is the heat-transfer rate in the evaporator?

Solution

On the basis of 1.25 kg s^{-1} of 10% NaOH fed to the evaporator, a material balance shows that the product stream consists of 1 kg s^{-1} of superheated steam at 76 torr and 88°C (361.15 K), and 0.25 kg s^{-1} of 50% NaOH at 88°C (361.15 K), as indicated schematically in Fig. 12.20. The energy balance for this flow process is

$$\Delta H^t = Q$$

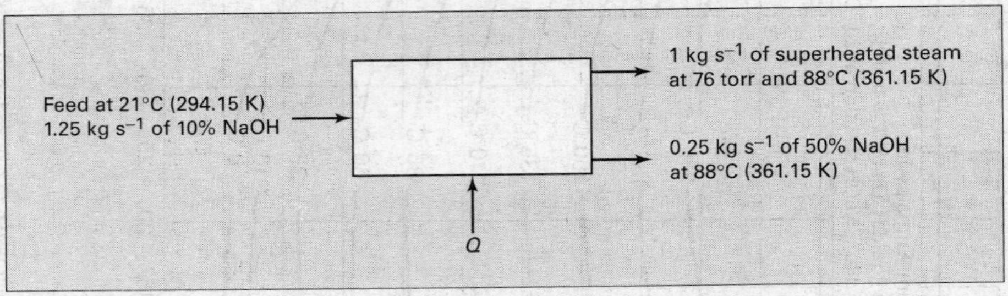

Figure 12.20: Schematic diagram for process of Example 12.6

In this case ΔH^t is easily determined from enthalpy values taken from the Hx diagram of Fig. 12.19 and from the steam tables:

- H for superheated steam at 76 Torr and 88°C (361.15 K) = 2666 kJ kg^{-1}
- H for 10% NaOH solution at 21°C (294.15 K) = 79 kJ kg^{-1}
- H for 50% NaOH solution at 88°C (361.15 K) = 500 kJ kg^{-1}

Thus,

$$Q = \Delta H^t = (1)(2666) + (0.25)(500) - (1.25)(79)$$
$$= 2692.25 \text{ kJ s}^{-1} \text{ or kW}$$

A comparison of this example with Example 12.5 shows the simplification introduced by use of an enthalpy/concentration diagram.

Example 12.7

A 10% aqueous NaOH solution at 21°C (294.15 K) is mixed with a 70% aqueous NaOH solution at 93°C (366.15 K) to form a solution containing 40% NaOH.

(*a*) If the mixing is done adiabatically, what is the final temperature of the solution?

(*b*) If the final temperature is brought to 21°C (294.15 K), how much heat must be removed during the process?

Solution

(*a*) A straight line drawn on Fig. 12.19 connecting the points representing the two initial solutions must contain the point representing the final solution. The particular solution represented by a point on this line at a concentration of 40% NaOH has an enthalpy of 447 kJ kg^{-1}. Moreover, the isotherm for 104°C (377.15 K) passes through this point. Thus the final temperature, obtained graphically, is 104°C (377.15 K).

(*b*) The total process cannot be represented by a single straight line on Fig. 12.19. However, any convenient path may be selected for calculating ΔH of the process. The energy balance then gives $Q = \Delta H$. Thus the process may be considered as occurring in two steps: adiabatic mixing, followed by simple cooling of the resulting solution to the final temperature. The first step is considered in part (*a*). It results in a solution at 104°C (377.15 K) with an enthalpy of 447 kJ kg^{-1}. When this solution is cooled to 21°C (294.15 K), the resulting enthalpy from Fig. 12.19 is 163 kJ kg^{-1}. Therefore,

$$Q = \Delta H = 70 - 192 = -122 \text{ kJ kg}^{-1}$$

and 284 kJ is *evolved* for each kg of solution formed

Example 12.8

Determine the enthalpy of solid NaOH at 20°C (293.15 K) on the basis used for the $NaOH/H_2O$ enthalpy/concentration diagram of Fig. 12.19.

Solution

The isotherms on an Hx diagram for a system such as $NaOH/H_2O$ terminate at points where the limit of solubility of the solid in water is reached. Thus the isotherms in Fig. 12.19 do not extend to a mass fraction representing pure NaOH. How, then, is the basis of the diagram with respect to NaOH selected? In the case of the water the basis is $H_{H_2O} = 0$ for liquid water at 0°C (273.15 K), consistent with the base of the steam tables. For NaOH the basis is $\bar{H}_{NaOH} = 0$ for NaOH in an infinitely dilute solution at 20°C (293.15 K).

This means that the partial specific enthalpy of NaOH at infinite dilution (i.e., at $x_{NaOH} \to 0$) is arbitrarily set equal to zero at 20°C (293.15 K). The graphical interpretation is that the diagram is constructed in such a way that a tangent drawn to the 20°C (293.15 K) isotherm at $x_{NaOH} = 0$ intersects the $x_{NaOH} = 1$ ordinate (not shown) at an enthalpy of zero. The selection of $\bar{H}^{\infty}_{NaOH}$ as zero at 20°C (293.15 K) automatically fixes the values of the enthalpy of NaOH in all other states.

In particular, the enthalpy of solid NaOH at 20°C (293.15 K) can be calculated for the basis selected. If 1 kg of solid NaOH at 20°C (293.15 K) is dissolved in an infinite amount of water at 20°C (293.15 K), and if the temperature is held constant by extraction of the heat of solution, the result is an infinitely dilute solution at 20°C (293.15 K). Since the water is pure in both the initial and final states, its enthalpy does not change. The heat of solution at 20°C (293.15 K) is:

$$\widetilde{\Delta H}^{\infty}_{NaOH} = \bar{H}^{\infty}_{NaOH} - H_{NaOH}$$

However, $\bar{H}^{\infty}_{NaOH} = 0$ at 20°C (293.15 K). Therefore,

$$\widetilde{\Delta H}^{\infty}_{NaOH} = -H_{NaOH} \qquad [20°\text{C (293.15K)}]$$

The enthalpy of solid NaOH at 20°C (293.15 K), H_{NaOH}, is therefore equal to the negative of the heat of solution of NaOH in an infinite amount of water at 20°C (293.15 K). A literature value[17] for this heat of solution at 25°C (298.15 K) on the basis of 1mol of NaOH is:

$$\widetilde{\Delta H}^{\infty}_{NaOH} = -10.637 \text{ kcal} \qquad [25°\text{C (298.15 K)}]$$

If the difference in temperature between [25°C (298.15 K)] and 20°C (293.15 K) is neglected, the enthalpy of solid NaOH at 20°C (293.15 K) is:

$$H_{NaOH} = -\widetilde{\Delta H}^{\infty}_{NaOH} = \frac{-(-10.637)(4.1868)(1000)}{40.00} = 1113 \text{ kJ kg}^{-1}$$

This figure represents the enthalpy of solid NaOH at 20°C (293.15 K) on the same basis as was selected for the $NaOH/H_2O$ enthalpy/concentration diagram of Fig. 12.19.

[17] M. W. Chase, Jr., et al., "JANAF Thermochemical Tables," 3d ed., *J. Phys. Chem. Ref. Data*, vol. 14, suppl. 1, p. 1243, 1985.

Example 12.9

Solid NaOH at 21°C(294.15 K) is mixed with H_2O at 21°C(294.15 K) to produce a solution containing 45% NaOH at 21°C(294.15 K). How much heat must be transferred per pound *mass* of solution formed?

Solution

On the basis of kg of 45% NaOH solution, 0.45 kg of solid NaOH must be dissolved in 0.55 kg of H_2O. The energy balance is $\Delta H = Q$. The enthalpy of H_2O at 21°C(294.15 K) may be taken from the steam tables, or it may be read from Fig. 12.19 at $x_1 = 0$. In either case, $H_{H_2O} = 88$ kJ kg^{-1}. The enthalpy of 45% NaOH at 21°C (294.15 K) is read from Fig. 12.19 as $H = 216$ kJ kg^{-1}. We assume that the enthalpy of solid NaOH at 21°C (294.15 K) is essentially the same as the value calculated in the preceding example for 21°C(294.15 K): $H_{\text{NaOH}} = 1113$ kJ kg^{-1}. Therefore, the heat *evolved* for each pound *mass* of solution formed is:

$$Q = \Delta H = (1)(216) - (0.55)(88) - (0.45)(1113) = -333 \text{ kJ kg}^{-1}$$

PROBLEMS

12.1. The following is a set of VLE data for the system methanol(1)/water(2) at 60°C (333.15 K) (extracted from K. Kurihara et al., *J. Chem. Eng. Data*, vol. 40, pp. 679–684, 1995)

P/kPa	x_1	y_1	P/kPa	x_1	y_1
19.953	0.0000	0.0000	60.614	0.5282	0.8085
39.223	0.1686	0.5714	63.998	0.6044	0.8383
42.984	0.2167	0.6268	67.924	0.6804	0.8733
48.852	0.3039	0.6943	70.229	0.7255	0.8922
52.784	0.3681	0.7345	72.832	0.7776	0.9141
56.652	0.4461	0.7742	84.562	1.0000	1.0000

(*a*) Basing calculations on Eq. (12.1), find parameter values for the Margules equation that provide the best fit of G^E/RT to the data, and prepare a Pxy diagram that compares the experimental points with curves determined from the correlation.

(*b*) Repeat (*a*) for the van Laar equation.

(*c*) Repeat (*a*) for the Wilson equation.

(*d*) Using Barker's method, find parameter values for the Margules equation that provide the best fit of the P-x_1 data. Prepare a diagram showing the residuals δP and δy_1 plotted vs. x_1.

(*e*) Repeat (*d*) for the van Laar equation.
(*f*) Repeat (*d*) for the Wilson equation.

12.2. If Eq. (12.1) is valid for isothermal VLE in a binary system, show that

$$\left(\frac{dP}{dx_1}\right)_{x_1=0} \geq -P_2^{sat} \qquad \left(\frac{dP}{dx_1}\right)_{x_1=1} \leq P_1^{sat}$$

12.3. The following is a set of VLE data for the system acetone(1)/methanol(2) at 55°C (328.15 K) (extracted from D. C. Freshwater and K. A. Pike, *J. Chem. Eng. Data*, vol. 12, pp. 179–183, 1967):

P/kPa	x_1	y_1	P/kPa	x_1	y_1
68.728	0.0000	0.0000	97.646	0.5052	0.5844
72.278	0.0287	0.0647	98.462	0.5432	0.6174
75.279	0.0570	0.1295	99.811	0.6332	0.6772
77.524	0.0858	0.1848	99.950	0.6605	0.6926
78.951	0.1046	0.2190	100.278	0.6945	0.7124
82.528	0.1452	0.2694	100.467	0.7327	0.7383
86.762	0.2173	0.3633	100.999	0.7752	0.7729
90.088	0.2787	0.4184	101.059	0.7922	0.7876
93.206	0.3579	0.4779	99.877	0.9080	0.8959
95.017	0.4050	0.5135	99.799	0.9448	0.9336
96.365	0.4480	0.5512	96.885	1.0000	1.0000

(*a*) Basing calculations on Eq. (12.1), find parameter values for the Margules equation that provide the best fit of G^E/RT to the data, and prepare a P-x-y diagram that compares the experimental points with curves determined from the correlation.
(*b*) Repeat (*a*) for the van Laar equation.
(*c*) Repeat (*a*) for the Wilson equation.
(*d*) Using Barker's method, find parameter values for the Margules equation that provide the best fit of the P-x_1 data. Prepare a diagram showing the residuals δP and δy_1 plotted vs. x_1.
(*e*) Repeat (*d*) for the van Laar equation.
(*f*) Repeat (*d*) for the Wilson equation.

12.4. The excess Gibbs energy for binary systems consisting of liquids not too dissimilar in chemical nature is represented to a reasonable approximation by the equation

$$G^E/RT = Ax_1x_2$$

where A is a function of temperature only. For such systems, it is often observed that the ratio of the vapor pressures of the pure species is nearly constant over a considerable temperature range. Let this ratio be r, and determine the range of values of A, expressed as a function of r, for which no azeotrope can exist. Assume the vapor phase to be an ideal gas.

12.5. For the ethanol(1)/chloroform(2) system at 50°C, the activity coefficients show interior extrema with respect to composition [see Fig. 12.9(*e*)].

(*a*) Prove that the van Laar equation cannot represent such behavior.

(*b*) The two-parameter Margules equation can represent this behavior, but only for particular ranges of the ratio A_{21}/A_{12}. What are they?

12.6. VLE data for methyl *tert*-butyl ether(1)/dichloromethane(2) at 35°C (308.15 K) (extracted from F. A. Mato, C. Berro, and A. Péneloux, *J. Chem. Eng. Data*, vol. 36, pp. 259–262, 1991) are as follows:

P/kPa	x_1	y_1	P/kPa	x_1	y_1
85.265	0.0000	0.0000	59.651	0.5036	0.3686
83.402	0.0330	0.0141	56.833	0.5749	0.4564
82.202	0.0579	0.0253	53.689	0.6736	0.5882
80.481	0.0924	0.0416	51.620	0.7676	0.7176
76.719	0.1665	0.0804	50.455	0.8476	0.8238
72.422	0.2482	0.1314	49.926	0.9093	0.9002
68.005	0.3322	0.1975	49.720	0.9529	0.9502
65.096	0.3880	0.2457	49.624	1.0000	1.0000

The data are well correlated by the three-parameter Margules equation [an extension of Eq. (12.9)]:

$$\frac{G^E}{RT} = (A_{21}x_1 + A_{12}x_2 - Cx_1x_2)x_1x_2$$

Implied by this equation are the expressions:

$$\ln \gamma_1 = x_2^2[A_{12} + 2(A_{21} - A_{12} - C)x_1 + 3Cx_1^2]$$

$$\ln \gamma_2 = x_1^2[A_{21} + 2(A_{12} - A_{21} - C)x_2 + 3Cx_2^2]$$

(*a*) Basing calculations on Eq. (12.1), find the values of parameters A_{12}, A_{21}, and C that provide the best fit of G^E/RT to the data.

(*b*) Prepare a plot of $\ln \gamma_1$, $\ln \gamma_2$, and G^E/x_1x_2RT vs. x_1 showing both the correlation and experimental values.

(*c*) Prepare a P-x-y diagram [see Fig. 12.7(*a*)] that compares the experimental data with the correlation determined in (*a*).

(*d*) Prepare a consistency-test diagram like Fig. 12.8.

(*e*) Using Barker's method, find the values of parameters A_{12}, A_{21}, and C that provide the best fit of the P-x_1 data. Prepare a diagram showing the residuals δP and δy_1 plotted vs. x_1.

12.7. Equations analogous to Eqs. (11.15) and (11.16) apply for excess properties. Because $\ln \gamma_i$ is a partial property with respect to G^E/RT, these analogous equations can be written for $\ln \gamma_1$ and $\ln \gamma_2$ in a binary system.

(*a*) Write these equations, and apply them to Eq. (12.16) to show that Eqs. (12.17) are indeed obtained.

(*b*) The alternative procedure is to apply Eq. (11.96). Proceeding in the manner that led to Eqs. (12.10), show that Eqs. (12.17) are again reproduced.

12.8. The following is a set of activity-coefficient data for a binary liquid system as determined from VLE data:

x_1	γ_1	γ_2	x_1	γ_1	γ_2
0.0523	1.202	1.002	0.5637	1.120	1.102
0.1299	1.307	1.004	0.6469	1.076	1.170
0.2233	1.295	1.006	0.7832	1.032	1.298
0.2764	1.228	1.024	0.8576	1.016	1.393
0.3482	1.234	1.022	0.9388	1.001	1.600
0.4187	1.180	1.049	0.9813	1.003	1.404
0.5001	1.129	1.092			

Inspection of these experimental values suggests that they are *noisy*, but the question is whether they are *consistent*, and therefore possibly on average correct.

(*a*) Find experimental values for G^E/RT and plot them along with the experimental values of $\ln \gamma_1$ and $\ln \gamma_2$ on a single graph.

(*b*) Develop a valid correlation for the composition dependence of G^E/RT and show lines on the graph of part (*a*) that represent this correlation for all three of the quantities plotted there.

(*c*) Apply the consistency test described in Ex. 12.1 to these data, and draw a conclusion with respect to this test.

12.9. Following are VLE data for the system acetonitrile(1)/benzene(2) at 45°C (318.15 K) (extracted from I. Brown and F. Smith, *Austral. J. Chem.*, vol. 8, p. 62, 1955):

P/kPa	x_1	y_1	P/kPa	x_1	y_1
29.819	0.0000	0.0000	36.978	0.5458	0.5098
31.957	0.0455	0.1056	36.778	0.5946	0.5375
33.553	0.0940	0.1818	35.792	0.7206	0.6157
35.285	0.1829	0.2783	34.372	0.8145	0.6913
36.457	0.2909	0.3607	32.331	0.8972	0.7869
36.996	0.3980	0.4274	30.038	0.9573	0.8916
37.068	0.5069	0.4885	27.778	1.0000	1.0000

The data are well correlated by the three-parameter Margules equation (see Pb. 12.6).

(*a*) Basing calculations on Eq. (12.1), find the values of parameters A_{12}, A_{21}, and C that provide the best fit of G^E/RT to the data.

(*b*) Prepare a plot of $\ln \gamma_1$, $\ln \gamma_2$, and G^E/x_1x_2RT vs. x_1 showing both the correlation and experimental values.

(*c*) Prepare a P-x-y diagram [see Fig. 12.7(*a*)] that compares the experimental data with the correlation determined in (*a*).

(*d*) Prepare a consistency-test diagram like Fig. 12.8.

(*e*) Using Barker's method, find the values of parameters A_{12}, A_{21}, and C that provide the best fit of the P-x_1 data. Prepare a diagram showing the residuals δP and δy_1 plotted vs. x_1.

12.10. An unusual type of low-pressure VLE behavior is that of *double azeotropy*, in which the dew and bubble curves are S-shaped, thus yielding at different compositions both a minimum-pressure and a maximum-pressure azeotrope. Assuming that Eq. (12.11) applies, determine under what circumstances double azeotropy is likely to occur.

12.11. Rationalize the following rule of thumb, appropriate for an *equimolar* binary liquid mixture:

$$\frac{G^E}{RT}(\text{equimolar}) \approx \frac{1}{8}\ln(\gamma_1^\infty \gamma_2^\infty)$$

Problems 12.12 through 12.23 require parameter values for the Wilson or NRTL equation for liquid-phase activity coefficients. Table 12.5 gives parameter values for both equations. Antoine equations for vapor pressure are given in Table B.2, Appendix B.

12.12. For one of the binary systems listed in the preceding table, based on Eq. (10.5) and the Wilson equation prepare a P-x-y diagram for $t/T = 60°\text{C}/333.15$ K.

12.13. For one of the binary systems listed in the preceding table, based on Eq. (10.5) and the Wilson equation prepare a t-x-y diagram for $P = 101.33$ kPa.

12.14. For one of the binary systems listed in the preceding table, based on Eq. (10.5) and the NRTL equation prepare a P-x-y diagram for $t/T = 60°\text{C}/333.15$ K.

12.15. For one of the binary systems listed in the preceding table, based on Eq. (10.5) and the NRTL equation prepare a t-x-y diagram for $P = 101.33$ kPa.

12.16. For one of the binary systems listed in the preceding table, based on Eq. (10.5) and the Wilson equation make the following calculations:

(*a*) *BUBL P*: $t = 60°\text{C}$ $t/T = 60°\text{C}/333.15$ K, $x_1 = 0.3$

(*b*) *DEW P*: $t = 60°\text{C}$ $t/T = 60°\text{C}/333.15$ K, $y_1 = 0.3$

(*c*) P, T-flash: $t = 60°\text{C}$ $t/T = 60°\text{C}/333.15$ K, $P = \frac{1}{2}(P_{\text{bubble}} + P_{\text{dew}})$, $z_1 = 0.3$

(*d*) If an azeotrope exists at $t = 60°\text{C}$ $t/T = 60°\text{C}/333.15$ K, find P^{az} and $x_1^{\text{az}} = y_1^{\text{az}}$

12.17. Work the preceding problem for the NRTL equation.

Table 12.5: Parameter Values for the Wilson and NRTL Equations.

Parameters a_{12}, a_{21}, b_{12}, and b_{21} have units of cal mol^{-1}, and V_1 and V_2 have units of $cm^3\ mol^{-1}$. Values are those recommended by Gmehling et al. *Vapor-Liquid Equilibrium Data Collection*, Chemistry Data Series, vol. I, parts 1a, 1b, 2c and 2e, DECHEMA, Frankfurt/Main, 1981–1988.

System	V_1 / V_2	Wilson equation a_{12}	a_{21}	NRTL equation b_{12}	b_{21}	α
Acetone(1)	74.05	291.27	1,448.01	631.05	1,197.41	0.5343
Water(2)	18.07					
Methanol(1)	40.73	107.38	469.55	−253.88	845.21	0.2994
Water(2)	18.07					
1-Propanol(1)	75.14	775.48	1,351.90	500.40	1,636.57	0.5081
Water(2)	18.07					
Water(1)	18.07	1,696.98	−219.39	715.96	548.90	0.2920
1,4-Dioxane(2)	85.71					
Methanol(1)	40.73	504.31	196.75	343.70	314.59	0.2981
Acetonitrile(2)	66.30					
Acetone(1)	74.05	−161.88	583.11	184.70	222.64	0.3084
Methanol(2)	40.73					
Methyl acetate(1)	79.84	−31.19	813.18	381.46	346.54	0.2965
Methanol(2)	40.73					
Methanol(1)	40.73	1,734.42	183.04	730.09	1,175.41	0.4743
Benzene(2)	89.41					
Ethanol(1)	58.68	1,556.45	210.52	713.57	1,147.86	0.5292
Toluene(2)	106.85					

12.18. For one of the binary systems listed in the preceding table, based on Eq. (10.5) and the Wilson equation make the following calculations:

(*a*) *BUBL T*: $P = 101.33$ kPa, $x_1 = 0.3$

(*b*) *DEW T*: $P = 101.33$ kPa, $y_1 = 0.3$

(*c*) P, T-flash: $P = 101.33$ kPa, $T = \frac{1}{2}(T_{\text{bubble}} + T_{\text{dew}})$, $z_1 = 0.3$

(*d*) If an azeotrope exists at $P = 101.33$ kPa, find T^{az} and $x_1^{az} = y_1^{az}$

12.19. Work the preceding problem for the NRTL equation.

12.20. For the acetone(1)/methanol(2)/water(3) system, based on Eq. (10.5) and the Wilson equation make the following calculations:

(*a*) *BUBL P*: $t/T = 65°C/338.15$ K, $x_1 = 0.3$, $x_2 = 0.4$

(*b*) *DEW P*: $t/T = 65°\text{C}/338.15$ K, $y_1 = 0.3$, $y_2 = 0.4$
(*c*) P, T-flash: $t/T = 65°\text{C}/338.15$ K, $P = \frac{1}{2}(P_{\text{bubble}} + P_{\text{dew}})$, $z_1 = 0.3$, $z_2 = 0.4$

12.21. Work the preceding problem for the NRTL equation.

12.22. For the acetone(1)/methanol(2)/water(3) system, based on Eq. (10.5) and the Wilson equation make the following calculations:

(*a*) *BUBL T*: $P = 101.33$ kPa, $x_1 = 0.3$, $x_2 = 0.4$
(*b*) *DEW T*: $P = 101.33$ kPa, $y_1 = 0.3$, $y_2 = 0.4$
(*c*) P, T-flash: $P = 101.33$ kPa, $T = \frac{1}{2}(T_{\text{bubble}} + T_{\text{dew}})$, $z_1 = 0.3$, $z_2 = 0.2$

12.23. Work the preceding problem for the NRTL equation.

12.24. The following expressions have been reported for the activity coefficients of species 1 and 2 in a binary liquid mixture at given T and P:

$$\ln \gamma_1 = x_2^2(0.273 + 0.096\,x_1) \qquad \ln \gamma_2 = x_1^2(0.273 - 0.096\,x_2)$$

(*a*) Determine the implied expression for G^E/RT.
(*b*) *Generate* expressions for $\ln \gamma_1$ and $\ln \gamma_2$ from the result of (*a*).
(*c*) Compare the results of (*b*) with the reported expressions for $\ln \gamma_1$ and $\ln \gamma_2$. Discuss any discrepancy. Can the reported expressions possibly be correct?

12.25. Possible correlating equations for $\ln \gamma_1$ in a binary liquid system are given following. For one of these cases determine by integration of the Gibbs/Duhem equation [Eq. (11.100)] the corresponding equation for $\ln \gamma_2$. What is the corresponding equation for G^E/RT? Note that by its definition, $\gamma_i = 1$ for $x_i = 1$.

(*a*) $\ln \gamma_1 = Ax_2^2$; (*b*) $\ln \gamma_1 = x_2^2(A + Bx_2)$; (*c*) $\ln \gamma_1 = x_2^2(A + Bx_2 + Cx_2^2)$.

12.26. At 25°C (298.15 K) and atmospheric pressure the volume change of mixing of binary liquid mixtures of species 1 and 2 is given by the equation

$$\Delta V = x_1 x_2(45x_1 + 25x_2)$$

where ΔV is in cm^3 mol^{-1}. At these conditions, $V_1 = 110$ and $V_2 = 90$ cm^3 mol^{-1}. Determine the partial molar volumes $\bar{V}_1$ and $\bar{V}_2$ in a mixture containing 40 mole % of species 1 at the given conditions.

12.27. The volume change of mixing (cm^3 mol^{-1}) for the system ethanol(1)/methyl butyl ether(2) at 25°C (298.15 K) is given by the equation

$$\Delta V = x_1 x_2[-1.026 + 0.220(x_1 - x_2)]$$

Given that $V_1 = 58.63$ and $V_2 = 118.46$ cm^3 mol^{-1}, what volume of mixture is formed when 750 cm^3 of pure species 1 is mixed with 1500 cm^3 of species 2 at 25°C (298.15 K)? What would be the volume if an ideal solution were formed?

12.28. If $LiCl{\cdot}2H_2O(s)$ and $H_2O(l)$ are mixed isothermally at 25°C (298.15 K) to form a solution containing 10 mol of water for each mole of LiCl, what is the heat effect per mole of solution?

12.29. If a liquid solution of HCl in water, containing 1 mol of HCl and 4.5 mol of H_2O, absorbs an additional 1 mol of HCl(*g*) at the constant temperature of 25°C (298.15 K), what is the heat effect? Heat of solution of HCl(*g*) is given in Fig. 12.14.

12.30. What is the heat effect when 20 kg of LiCl(*s*) is added to 125 kg of an aqueous solution containing 10 mass % LiCl in an isothermal process at 25°C (298.15 K)?

12.31. An LiCl/H_2O solution at 25°C (298.15 K) is made by *adiabatically* mixing cool water at 10°C (283.15 K) with a 20 mole % LiCl/H_2O solution at 25°C (298.15 K). What is the composition of the solution formed?

12.32. A 20 mole % LiCl/H_2O solution at 25°C (298.15 K) is made by mixing a 25 mole % LiCl/H_2O solution at 25°C (298.15 K) with chilled water at 5°C (278.15 K). What is the heat effect in joules per mole of final solution?

12.33. A 20 mole % LiCl/H_2O solution is made by six different mixing processes:

(*a*) Mix LiCl(*s*) with $H_2O(l)$
(*b*) Mix $H_2O(l)$with a 25 mole % LiCl/H_2O solution
(*c*) Mix $LiCl{\cdot}H_2O(s)$ with $H_2O(l)$
(*d*) Mix LiCl(*s*) with a 10 mole % LiCl/H_2O solution.
(*e*) Mix a 25-mol-% LiCl/H_2O solution with a 10 mole % LiCl/H_2O solution
(*f*) Mix $LiCl{\cdot}H_2O(s)$ with a 10 mole % LiCl/H_2O solution.

Mixing in all cases is isothermal, at 25°C (298.15 K). For each part determine the heat effect in J $mol^{-1}$of final solution.

12.34. A mass of 12 kg s^{-1} of $Cu(NO_3)_2{\cdot}6H_2O$ along with 15 kg s^{-1} of water, both at 25°C (298.15 K), are fed to a tank where mixing takes place. The resulting solution passes through a heat exchanger which adjusts its temperature to 25°C (298.15 K). What is the rate of heat transfer in the exchanger?

- For $Cu(NO_3)_2$, $\Delta H^\circ_{f_{298}} = -302.9$ kJ
- For $Cu(NO_3)_2{\cdot}6H_2O$, $\Delta H^\circ_{f_{298}} = -2110.8$ kJ
- The heat of solution of 1 mol of $Cu(NO_3)_2$ in water at 25°C (298.15 K) is −47.84 kJ, independent of $\tilde{n}$ for values of interest here.

12.35. A liquid solution of LiCl in water at 25°C (298.15 K) contains 1 mol of LiCl and 7 mol of water. If 1 mol of $LiCl{\cdot}3H_2O(s)$ is dissolved isothermally in this solution, what is the heat effect?

12.36. It is required to produce an aqueous LiCl solution by mixing $LiCl{\cdot}2H_2O(s)$ with water. The mixing occurs *both* adiabatically and without change in temperature at 25°C (298.15 K). Determine the mole fraction of LiCl in the final solution.

12.37. Data from the Bureau of Standards (*J. Phys. Chem. Ref. Data*, vol. 11, suppl. 2, pp. 2–267, 1982) include the following heats of formation for 1 mol of $CaCl_2$ in water at 25°C (298.15 K):

$CaCl_2$ in 10 mol H_2O	−862.74 kJ
$CaCl_2$ in 15 mol H_2O	−867.85 kJ
$CaCl_2$ in 20 mol H_2O	−870.06 kJ
$CaCl_2$ in 25 mol H_2O	−871.07 kJ
$CaCl_2$ in 50 mol H_2O	−872.91 kJ
$CaCl_2$ in 100 mol H_2O	−873.82 kJ
$CaCl_2$ in 300 mol H_2O	−874.79 kJ
$CaCl_2$ in 500 mol H_2O	−875.13 kJ
$CaCl_2$ in 1000 mol H_2O	−875.54 kJ

From these data prepare a plot of $\widetilde{\Delta H}$, the heat of solution at 25°C (298.15 K) of $CaCl_2$ in water, vs. $\tilde{n}$, the mole ratio of water to $CaCl_2$.

12.38. A liquid solution contains 1 mol of $CaCl_2$ and 25 mol of water. Using data from Pb. 12.37, determine the heat effect when an additional 1 mol of $CaCl_2$ is dissolved isothermally in this solution.

12.39. Solid $CaCl_2{\cdot}6H_2O$ and liquid water at 25°C (298.15 K) are mixed *adiabatically* in a continuous process to form a brine of 15 mass % $CaCl_2$. Using data from Pb. 12.37, determine the temperature of the brine solution formed. The specific heat of a 15 mass % aqueous $CaCl_2$ solution at 25°C (298.15 K) is 3.28 kJ kg^{-1} °C^{-1}.

$$\text{For } CaCl_2{\cdot}6H_2O, \quad \Delta H^\circ_{f298} = -2607.9 \text{ kJ}$$

12.40. Consider a plot of $\widetilde{\Delta H}$, the heat of solution based on 1 mol of solute (species 1), vs. $\tilde{n}$, the moles of solvent per mole of solute, at constant T and P. Figure 12.14 is an example of such a plot, except that the plot considered here has a linear rather than logarithmic scale along the abscissa. Let a tangent drawn to the $\widetilde{\Delta H}$ vs. $\tilde{n}$ curve intercept the ordinate at point I.

(*a*) Prove that the slope of the tangent at a particular point is equal to the partial excess enthalpy of the solvent in a solution with the composition represented by $\tilde{n}$; i.e., prove that

$$\frac{d\widetilde{\Delta H}}{d\tilde{n}} = \bar{H}_2^E$$

(*b*) Prove that the intercept I equals the partial excess enthalpy of the solute in the same solution; i.e., prove that

$$I = \bar{H}_1^E$$

12.41. Suppose that ΔH for a particular solute(1)/solvent(2) system is represented by the equation:

$$\Delta H = x_1 x_2 (A_{21} x_1 + A_{12} x_2) \qquad (A)$$

Relate the behavior of a plot of $\widetilde{\Delta H}$ vs. $\tilde{n}$ to the features of this equation. Specifically, rewrite Eq. (*A*) in the form $\widetilde{\Delta H}(\tilde{n})$, and then show that

(*a*) $\lim_{\tilde{n}\to 0} \widetilde{\Delta H} = 0$

(*b*) $\lim_{\tilde{n}\to \infty} \widetilde{\Delta H} = A_{12}$

(*c*) $\lim_{\tilde{n}\to 0} d\widetilde{\Delta H}/d\tilde{n} = A_{21}$

12.42. If the heat of mixing at temperature t_0 is ΔH_0 and if the heat of mixing of the same solution at temperature t is ΔH, show that the two heats of mixing are related by

$$\Delta H = \Delta H_0 + \int_{t_0}^{t} \Delta C_P \, dt$$

where ΔC_P is the heat-capacity change of mixing, defined by Eq. (12.29).

12.43. What is the heat effect when 68 kg of H_2SO_4 is mixed with 159 kg of an aqueous solution containing 25 mass % H_2SO_4 in an isothermal process at 38°C (311.15 K)?

12.44. For a 50 mass % aqueous solution of H_2SO_4 at 60°C (333.15 K), what is the excess enthalpy H^E in kJ kg^{-1}?

12.45. A mass of 180 kg of 10 mass % aqueous NaOH solution at 54°C (327.15 K) is mixed with 79 kg of 10 mass % solution at 93°C (366.15 K).

(*a*) What is the heat effect if the final temperature is 27°C (300.15 K)?

(*b*) If the mixing is adiabatic, what is the final temperature?

12.46. A single-effect evaporator concentrates a 20 mass % aqueous solution of H_2SO_4 to 70%. The feed rate is 11.3 kg s^{-1}, and the feed temperature is 27°C (300.15 K). The evaporator is maintained at an absolute pressure of 0.1 bar, at which pressure the boiling point of 70% H_2SO_4 is 103°C (376.15 K). What is the heat-transfer rate in the evaporator?

12.47. What temperature results when sufficient NaOH(*s*) at 20°C (293.15 K) is dissolved adiabatically in a 10 mass % aqueous NaOH solution, originally at 27°C (300.15 K), to bring the concentration up to 35%?

12.48. What is the heat effect when sufficient $SO_3(l)$ at 25°C (298.15 K) is reacted with H_2O at 25°C (298.15 K) to give a 50 mass % H_2SO_4 solution at 60°C (333.15 K)?

12.49. A mass of 63.5 kg of 15 mass % solution of H_2SO_4 in water at 71°C (344.15 K) is mixed at atmospheric pressure with 104.3 kg of 80 mass % H_2SO_4 at 38°C (311.15 K). During the process heat in the amount of 21 000 kJ is transferred from the system. Determine the temperature of the product solution.

12.50. An insulated tank, open to the atmosphere, contains 680 kg of 40 mass % sulfuric acid at 20°C (293.15 K). It is heated to 82°C (355.15 K) by injection of live saturated steam at 1 atm, which fully condenses in the process. How much steam is required, and what is the final concentration of H_2SO_4 in the tank?

12.51. Saturated steam at 2.75 bar is throttled to 1 atm and mixed adiabatically (and condensed) with 45 mass % sulfuric acid at 27°C (300.15 K) in a flow process that raises the temperature of the acid to 71°C (344.15 K). How much steam is required for each kilogram *mass* of entering acid, and what is the concentration of the hot acid?

12.52. A batch of 40 mass % NaOH solution in water at atmospheric pressure and 27°C (300.15 K) is heated in an insulated tank by injection of live steam drawn through a valve from a line containing saturated steam at 2.4 bar. The process is stopped when the NaOH solution reaches a concentration of 38 mass %. At what temperature does this occur?

12.53. For a 35 mass % aqueous solution of H_2SO_4 at 38°C (311.15 K), what is the heat of mixing ΔH in kJ kg^{-1}?

12.54. If pure liquid H_2SO_4 at 27°C (300.15 K) is added adiabatically to pure liquid water at 27°C (300.15 K) to form a 40 mass % solution, what is the final temperature of the solution?

12.55. A liquid solution containing 0.9 kmol H_2SO_4 and 6.8 kmol H_2O at 38°C (311.15 K) absorbs 0.45 kmol of $SO_3(g)$, also at 38°C (311.15 K), forming a more concentrated sulfuric acid solution. If the process occurs isothermally, determine the heat transferred.

12.56. Determine the heat of mixing ΔH of sulfuric acid in water and the partial specific enthalpies of H_2SO_4 and H_2O for a solution containing 65 mass % H_2SO_4 at 25°C (298.15 K).

12.57. It is proposed to cool a stream of 75 mass % sulfuric acid solution at 60°C (333.15 K) by diluting it with chilled water at 4°C (277.15 K). Determine the amount of water that must be added to 0.45 kg of 75% acid before cooling below 60°C (333.15 K) actually occurs.

12.58. The following liquids, all at atmospheric pressure and 49°C (322.15 K), are mixed: 11.3 kg of pure water, 40 kg of pure sulfuric acid, and 34 kg of 25 mass % sulfuric acid.

(*a*) How much heat is liberated if mixing is isothermal at 49°C (322.15 K)?

(*b*) The mixing process is carried out in two steps: First, the pure sulfuric acid and the 25 mass % solution are mixed, and the total heat of part (*a*) is extracted; second, the pure water is added adiabatically. What is the temperature of the intermediate solution formed in the first step?

12.59. A large quantity of very dilute aqueous NaOH solution is neutralized by addition of the stoichiometric amount of a 10 mole % aqueous HCl solution. Estimate the heat effect per mole of NaOH neutralized if the tank is maintained at 25°C (298.15 K) and 1 atm and the neutralization reaction goes to completion. Data:

- For NaCl, $\lim_{\tilde{n}\to\infty} \widetilde{\Delta H} = 3.88$ kJ mol^{-1}
- For NaOH, $\lim_{\tilde{n}\to\infty} \widetilde{\Delta H} = -44.50$ kJ mol^{-1}

12.60. A large quantity of very dilute aqueous HCl solution is neutralized by addition of the stoichiometric amount of a 10 mole % aqueous NaOH solution. Estimate the heat effect per mole of HCl neutralized if the tank is maintained at 25°C (298.15 K) and 1 atm and the neutralization reaction goes to completion.

- For NaCl, $\lim_{\tilde{n}\to\infty} \widetilde{\Delta H} = 3.88$ kJ mol^{-1}

12.61. (*a*) Making use of Eqs. (11.15) and (11.16), written for excess properties, show for a binary system that

$$\bar{M}_1^E = x_2^2\left(\mathcal{M} + x_1\frac{d\mathcal{M}}{dx_1}\right) \quad \text{and} \quad \bar{M}_2^E = x_1^2\left(\mathcal{M} - x_2\frac{d\mathcal{M}}{dx_1}\right)$$

where

$$\mathcal{M} \equiv \frac{M^E}{x_1x_2}$$

(*b*) Plot on a single graph the values of H^E/x_1x_2, $\bar{H}_1^E$, and $\bar{H}_2^E$ determined from the following heat-of-mixing data for the H_2SO_4(1)/H_2O(2) system at 25°C (298.15 K):

x_1	$-\Delta H$/kJ kg^{-1}	x_1	$-\Delta H$/kJ kg^{-1}
0.10	73.27	0.70	320.98
0.20	144.21	0.80	279.58
0.30	208.64	0.85	237.25
0.40	262.83	0.90	178.87
0.50	302 84	0.95	100.71
0.60	323.31		

x_1 = mass fraction H_2SO_4

Explain with reference to these plots why sulfuric acid is diluted by adding acid to water rather than water to acid.

12.62. A 90 mass % aqueous H_2SO_4 solution at 25°C (298.15 K) is added over a period of 6 hours to a tank containing 4000 kg of pure water also at 25°C (298.15 K). The final concentration of acid in the tank is 50 mass %. The contents of the tank are cooled continuously to maintain a constant temperature of 25°C (298.15 K). Because the cooling system is designed for a constant rate of heat transfer, this requires the addition of acid at a variable rate. Determine the instantaneous 90 mass % acid rate as a function of time, and plot this rate (kg s^{-1}) vs. time. The data of the preceding problem may be fit to a cubic equation expressing H^E/x_1x_2 as a function of x_1, and the equations of the preceding problem then provide expressions for $\bar{H}_1^E$ and $\bar{H}_2^E$.

12.63. Develop Eq. (12.35) for ΔS^{id} by appropriate application of Eqs. (5.41) and (5.42) to a mixing process.

12.64. Nine thousand kg h^{-1} of an 80 mass % H_2SO_4 solution in water at 50°C (323.15 K) is continuously diluted with chilled water at 5°C (278.15 K) to yield a stream containing 50 mass % H_2SO_4 at 60°C (333.15 K).

(*a*) What is the mass flowrate of chilled water in kg h^{-1}?

(*b*) What is the rate of heat transfer in kJ s^{-1} for the mixing process? Is heat added or removed?

(*c*) If the mixing occurred *adiabatically*, what would be the temperature of the product stream? Assume here the same inlet conditions and the same product composition as for part (*b*).

12.65. A storage tank contains a heavy organic liquid. Chemical analysis shows the liquid to contain 600 ppm (molar basis) of water. It is proposed to reduce the water concentration to 50 ppm by boiling the contents of the tank at constant atmospheric pressure. Because the water is lighter than the organic, the vapor will be rich in water; continuous removal of the vapor serves to reduce the water content of the system. Estimate the percentage loss of organic (molar basis) in the boil-off process. Comment on the reasonableness of the proposal.

Suggestion: Designate the system water(1)/organic(2) and do unsteady-state molar balances for water and for water + organic. State all assumptions.

Data: T_{n_2} = normal boiling point of organic = 130°C (403.15 K).

$\gamma_1^\infty = 5.8$ for water in the liquid phase at 130°C (403.15 K).

12.66. Binary VLE data are commonly measured at constant T or at constant P. Isothermal data are *much* preferred for determination of a correlation for G^E for the liquid phase. Why?

12.67. Consider the following model for G^E/RT:

$$\frac{G^E}{x_1 x_2 RT} = \left(x_1 A_{21}^k + x_2 A_{12}^k\right)^{1/k}$$

This equation in fact represents a *family* of two-parameter expressions for G^E/RT; specification of k leaves A_{12} and A_{21} as the free parameters.

(*a*) Find general expressions for $\ln \gamma_1$ and $\ln \gamma_2$, for any k.
(*b*) Show that $\ln \gamma_1^\infty = A_{12}$ and $\ln \gamma_2^\infty = A_{21}$, for any k.
(*c*) Specialize the model to the cases where k equals $-\infty$, -1, 0, +1, and $+\infty$. Two of the cases should generate familiar results. What are they?

12.68. A breathalyzer measures volume % ethanol in gases exhaled from the lungs. Calibration relates it to volume % ethanol in the bloodstream. Use VLE concepts to develop an approximate relation between the two quantities. Numerous assumptions are required; state and justify them where possible.

12.69. The table on p. 474 gives values of parameters for the Wilson equation for the acetone(1)/methanol(2) system. Estimate values of $\ln \gamma_1^\infty$ and $\ln \gamma_2^\infty$ at 50°C (323.15 K). Compare with the values suggested by Fig. 12.9(*b*). Repeat the exercise with the NRTL equation.

12.70. For a binary system derive the expression for H^E implied by the Wilson equation for G^E/RT. Show that the implied excess heat capacity C_P^E is necessarily *positive*. Recall that the Wilson parameters depend on T, in accord with Eq. (12.24).

12.71. A single P-x_1-y_1 data point is available for a binary system at 25°C (298.15 K). Estimate from the data

(*a*) the total pressure and vapor-phase composition at 25°C (298.15 K) for an equimolar liquid mixture.
(*b*) whether azeotropy is likely at 25°C (298.15 K).

Data: At 25°C (298.15 K), $P_1^{sat} = 183.4$ kPa and $P_2^{sat} = 96.7$ kPa
For $x_1 = 0.253$, $y_1 = 0.456$ and $P = 139.1$ kPa

12.72. A single P-x_1 data point is available for a binary system at 35°C (308.15 K). Estimate from the data

(*a*) the corresponding value of y_1
(*b*) the total pressure at 35°C (308.15 K) for an equimolar liquid mixture
(*c*) whether azeotropy is likely at 35°C (308.15 K)

Data: At 35°C (308.15 K), $P_1^{sat} = 120.2$ kPa and $P_2^{sat} = 73.9$ kPa
For $x_1 = 0.389$, $P = 108.6$ kPa

Chapter 13

Chemical-Reaction Equilibria

The transformation of raw materials into products of greater value by means of chemical reaction is a major industry, and a vast array of commercial products is obtained by chemical synthesis. Sulfuric acid, ammonia, ethylene, propylene, phosphoric acid, chlorine, nitric acid, urea, benzene, methanol, ethanol, and ethylene glycol are examples of chemicals produced in the United States in billions of kilograms each year. These in turn are used in the large-scale manufacture of fibers, paints, detergents, plastics, rubber, paper, fertilizers, insecticides, etc. Clearly, the chemical engineer must be familiar with chemical-reactor design and operation.

Both the rate and the equilibrium conversion of a chemical reaction depend on the temperature, pressure, and composition of reactants. Often, a reasonable reaction rate is achieved only with a suitable catalyst. For example, the rate of oxidation of sulfur dioxide to sulfur trioxide, carried out with a vanadium pentoxide catalyst, becomes appreciable at about 300°C (573.15 K) and increases at higher temperatures. On the basis of rate alone, one would operate the reactor at the highest practical temperature. However, the equilibrium conversion to sulfur trioxide falls as temperature rises, decreasing from about 90% at 520°C (793.15 K) to 50% at about 680°C (953.15 K). These values represent maximum possible conversions regardless of catalyst or reaction rate. The evident conclusion is that both equilibrium and rate must be considered in the exploitation of chemical reactions for commercial purposes. Although reaction *rates* are not susceptible to thermodynamic treatment, equilibrium conversions are. Therefore, the purpose of this chapter is to determine the effect of temperature, pressure, and initial composition on the equilibrium conversions of chemical reactions.

Many industrial reactions are not carried to equilibrium; reactor design is then based primarily on reaction rate. However, the choice of operating conditions may still be influenced by equilibrium considerations. Moreover, the equilibrium conversion of a reaction provides a goal by which to measure improvements in a process. Similarly, it may determine whether or not an experimental investigation of a new process is worthwhile. For example, if thermodynamic analysis indicates that a yield of only 20% is possible at equilibrium and if a 50% yield is necessary for the process to be economically attractive, there is no purpose to an experimental study. On the other hand, if the equilibrium yield is 80%, an experimental program to determine the reaction rate for various conditions of operation (catalyst, temperature, pressure, etc.) may be warranted.

Reaction stoichiometry is treated in Sec. 13.1, and reaction equilibrium, in Sec. 13.2. The equilibrium constant is introduced in Sec. 13.3, and its temperature dependence and evaluation are considered in Secs. 13.4 and 13.5. The connection between the equilibrium constant and composition is developed in Sec. 13.6. The calculation of equilibrium conversions for single reactions is taken up in Sec. 13.7. In Sec. 13.8, the phase rule is reconsidered; multireaction equilibrium is treated in Sec. 13.9;[1] finally, in Sec. 13.10 the fuel cell is given an introductory treatment.

13.1 THE REACTION COORDINATE

The general chemical reaction as written in Sec. 4.6 is

$$|\nu_1|A_1 + |\nu_2|A_2 + \cdots \to |\nu_3|A_3 + |\nu_4|A_4 + \cdots \tag{13.1}$$

where $|\nu_i|$ is a stoichiometric coefficient and A_i stands for a chemical formula. The symbol ν_i itself is called a stoichiometric *number*, and by the sign convention of Sec. 4.6 it is

positive (+) *for a product* and *negative* (−) *for a reactant*

Thus for the reaction, $CH_4 + H_2O \to CO + 3H_2$
the stoichiometric numbers are

$$\nu_{CH_4} = -1 \qquad \nu_{H_2O} = -1 \qquad \nu_{CO} = 1 \qquad \nu_{H_2} = 3$$

The stoichiometric number for an inert species is zero.

As the reaction represented by Eq. (13.1) progresses, the *changes* in the numbers of moles of species present are in direct proportion to the stoichiometric numbers. Thus for the preceding reaction, if 0.5 mol of CH_4 disappears by reaction, 0.5 mol of H_2O also disappears; simultaneously 0.5 mol of CO and 1.5 mol of H_2 are formed. Applied to a differential amount of reaction, this principle provides the equations:

$$\frac{dn_2}{\nu_2} = \frac{dn_1}{\nu_1} \qquad \frac{dn_3}{\nu_3} = \frac{dn_1}{\nu_1} \qquad \text{etc.}$$

The list continues to include all species. Comparison of these equations yields

$$\frac{dn_1}{\nu_1} = \frac{dn_2}{\nu_2} = \frac{dn_3}{\nu_3} = \frac{dn_4}{\nu_4} = \cdots$$

All terms being equal, they can be identified collectively by a single quantity representing an amount of reaction. Thus a **definition** of $d\varepsilon$ is given by the equation:

$$\boxed{\frac{dn_1}{\nu_1} = \frac{dn_2}{\nu_2} = \frac{dn_3}{\nu_3} = \frac{dn_4}{\nu_4} = \cdots \equiv d\varepsilon} \tag{13.2}$$

[1]For a comprehensive treatment of chemical-reaction equilibria, see W. R. Smith and R. W. Missen, *Chemical Reaction Equilibrium Analysis*, John Wiley & Sons, New York, 1982.

The general relation connecting the differential change dn_i with $d\varepsilon$ is therefore

$$\boxed{dn_i = \nu_i \, d\varepsilon \qquad (i = 1, 2, \ldots, N)} \tag{13.3}$$

This new variable ε, called the *reaction coordinate*, characterizes the extent or degree to which a reaction has taken place.[2] Only *changes* in ε with respect to changes in a mole number are defined by Eq. (13.3). The definition of ε itself depends for a specific application on setting it equal to *zero* for the initial state of the system prior to reaction. Thus, integration of Eq. (13.3) from an initial unreacted state where $\varepsilon = 0$ and $n_i = n_{i_0}$ to a state reached after an arbitrary amount of reaction gives

$$\int_{n_{i_0}}^{n_i} dn_i = \nu_i \int_0^{\varepsilon} d\varepsilon$$

or

$$n_i = n_{i_0} + \nu_i \varepsilon \qquad (i = 1, 2, \ldots, N) \tag{13.4}$$

Summation over all species yields

$$n = \sum_i n_i = \sum_i n_{i_0} + \varepsilon \sum_i \nu_i$$

or

$$n = n_0 + \nu \varepsilon$$

where

$$n \equiv \sum_i n_i \qquad n_0 \equiv \sum_i n_{i_0} \qquad \nu \equiv \sum_i \nu_i$$

Thus the mole fractions y_i of the species present are related to ε by

$$\boxed{y_i = \frac{n_i}{n} = \frac{n_{i_0} + \nu_i \varepsilon}{n_0 + \nu \varepsilon}} \tag{13.5}$$

Application of this equation is illustrated in the following examples.

Example 13.1

For a system in which the following reaction occurs,

$$CH_4 + H_2O \rightarrow CO + 3H_2$$

assume there are present initially 2 mol CH_4, 1 mol H_2O, 1 mol CO, and 4 mol H_2. Determine expressions for the mole fractions y_i as functions of ε.

[2]The reaction coordinate ε has been given various names, such as: degree of advancement, degree of reaction, extent of reaction, and progress variable.

Solution

For the reaction, $\nu = \sum_i \nu_i = -1 - 1 + 1 + 3 = 2$

For the given numbers of moles of species initially present,

$$n_0 = \sum_i n_{i_0} = 2 + 1 + 1 + 4 = 8$$

Equation (13.5) now yields

$$y_{CH_4} = \frac{2-\varepsilon}{8+2\varepsilon} \qquad y_{H_2O} = \frac{1-\varepsilon}{8+2\varepsilon}$$

$$y_{CO} = \frac{1+\varepsilon}{8+2\varepsilon} \qquad y_{H_2} = \frac{4+3\varepsilon}{8+2\varepsilon}$$

The mole fractions of the species in the reacting mixture are seen to be functions of the single variable ε.

Example 13.2

Consider a vessel which initially contains only n_0 mol of water vapor. If decomposition occurs according to the reaction,

$$H_2O \rightarrow H_2 + \tfrac{1}{2}O_2$$

find expressions which relate the number of moles and the mole fraction of each chemical species to the reaction coordinate ε.

Solution

For the given reaction, $\nu = -1 + 1 + \frac{1}{2} = \frac{1}{2}$. Application of Eqs. (13.4) and (13.5) yields

$$n_{H_2O} = n_0 - \varepsilon \qquad y_{H_2O} = \frac{n_0 - \varepsilon}{n_0 + \frac{1}{2}\varepsilon}$$

$$n_{H_2} = \varepsilon \qquad y_{H_2} = \frac{\varepsilon}{n_0 + \frac{1}{2}\varepsilon}$$

$$n_{O_2} = \tfrac{1}{2}\varepsilon \qquad y_{O_2} = \frac{\frac{1}{2}\varepsilon}{n_0 + \frac{1}{2}\varepsilon}$$

The fractional decomposition of water vapor is

$$\frac{n_0 - n_{H_2O}}{n_0} = \frac{n_0 - (n_0 - \varepsilon)}{n_0} = \frac{\varepsilon}{n_0}$$

Thus when $n_0 = 1$, ε is directly related to the fractional decomposition of the water vapor.

The ν_i are pure numbers without units; Eq. (13.3) therefore requires ε to be expressed in moles. This leads to the concept of a *mole of reaction*, meaning a change in ε of one mole. When $\Delta\varepsilon = 1$ mol, the reaction proceeds to such an extent that the change in mole number of each reactant and product is equal to its stoichiometric number.

Multireaction Stoichiometry

When two or more independent reactions proceed simultaneously, subscript j serves as the reaction index. A separate reaction coordinate ε_j then applies to each reaction. The stoichiometric numbers are doubly subscripted to identify their association with both a species and a reaction. Thus $\nu_{i,j}$ designates the stoichiometric number of species i in reaction j. Because the number of moles of a species n_i may change because of several reactions, the general equation analogous to Eq. (13.3) includes a sum:

$$dn_i = \sum_j \nu_{i,j}\, d\varepsilon_j \qquad (i = 1, 2, \ldots, N)$$

Integration from $n_i = n_{i_0}$ and $\varepsilon_j = 0$ to arbitrary n_i and ε_j gives

$$n_i = n_{i_0} + \sum_j \nu_{i,j}\varepsilon_j \qquad (i = 1, 2, \ldots, N) \tag{13.6}$$

Summing over all species yields

$$n = \sum_i n_{i_0} + \sum_i \sum_j \nu_{i,j}\varepsilon_j = n_0 + \sum_j \left(\sum_i \nu_{i,j} \right) \varepsilon_j$$

The definition of a total stoichiometric number ν $(\equiv \sum_i \nu_i)$ for a single reaction has its counterpart here in the definition:

$$\nu_j \equiv \sum_i \nu_{i,j} \qquad \text{whence} \qquad n = n_0 + \sum_j \nu_j \varepsilon_j$$

Combination of this last equation with Eq. (13.6) gives the mole fraction

$$\boxed{y_i = \frac{n_{i_0} + \sum_j \nu_{i,j}\varepsilon_j}{n_0 + \sum_j \nu_j \varepsilon_j} \qquad (i = 1, 2, \ldots, N)} \tag{13.7}$$

Example 13.3

Consider a system in which the following reactions occur:

$$CH_4 + H_2O \rightarrow CO + 3H_2 \quad (1)$$

$$CH_4 + 2H_2O \rightarrow CO_2 + 4H_2 \quad (2)$$

where the numbers (1) and (2) indicate the value of j, the reaction index. If there are present initially 2 mol CH_4 and 3 mol H_2O, determine expressions for the y_i as functions of ε_1 and ε_2.

Solution

The stoichiometric numbers $\nu_{i,j}$ can be arrayed as follows:

$i =$	CH_4	H_2O	CO	CO_2	H_2	
j						ν_j
1	−1	−1	1	0	3	2
2	−1	−2	0	1	4	2

Application of Eq. (13.7) now gives

$$y_{CH_4} = \frac{2 - \varepsilon_1 - \varepsilon_2}{5 + 2\varepsilon_1 + 2\varepsilon_2} \qquad y_{CO} = \frac{\varepsilon_1}{5 + 2\varepsilon_1 + 2\varepsilon_2}$$

$$y_{H_2O} = \frac{3 - \varepsilon_1 - 2\varepsilon_2}{5 + 2\varepsilon_1 + 2\varepsilon_2} \qquad y_{CO_2} = \frac{\varepsilon_2}{5 + 2\varepsilon_1 + 2\varepsilon_2}$$

$$y_{H_2} = \frac{3\varepsilon_1 + 4\varepsilon_2}{5 + 2\varepsilon_1 + 2\varepsilon_2}$$

The composition of the system is a function of independent variables ε_1 and ε_2.

13.2 APPLICATION OF EQUILIBRIUM CRITERIA TO CHEMICAL REACTIONS

In Sec. 14.3 it is shown that the total Gibbs energy of a closed system at constant T and P must decrease during an irreversible process and that the condition for equilibrium is reached when G^t attains its minimum value. At this equilibrium state,

$$(dG^t)_{T,P} = 0 \tag{14.68}$$

Thus if a mixture of chemical species is not in chemical equilibrium, any reaction that occurs at constant T and P must lead to a decrease in the total Gibbs energy of the system. The significance of this for a single chemical reaction is seen in Fig. 13.1, which shows a schematic diagram of G^t vs. ε, the reaction coordinate. Because ε is the single variable that characterizes the progress of the reaction, and therefore the composition of the system, the total Gibbs energy at constant T and P is determined by ε. The arrows along the curve in Fig. 13.1 indicate the directions of changes in $(G^t)_{T,P}$ that are possible on account of reaction. The reaction coordinate has its equilibrium value ε_e at the minimum of the curve. The meaning of Eq. (14.68) is that differential displacements of the chemical reaction can occur at the equilibrium state without causing changes in the total Gibbs energy of the system.

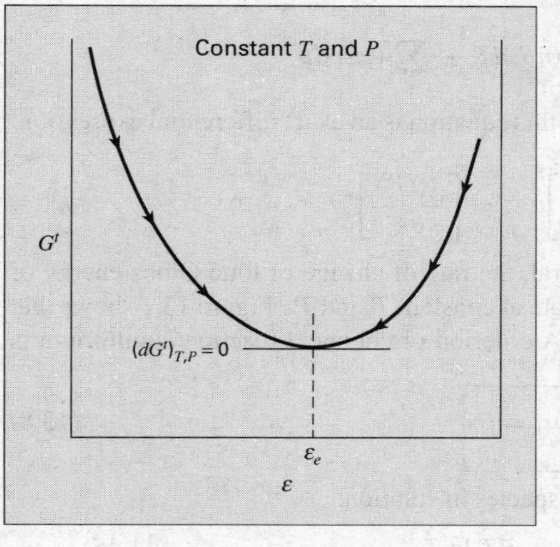

Figure 13.1: The total Gibbs energy in relation to the reaction coordinate

Figure 13.1 indicates the two distinctive features of the equilibrium state for given temperature and pressure:

- The total Gibbs energy G^t is a minimum.
- Its differential is zero.

Each of these may serve as a criterion of equilibrium. Thus, we may write an expression for G^t as a function of ε and seek the value of ε which minimizes G^t, or we may differentiate the expression, equate it to zero, and solve for ε. The latter procedure is almost always used for single reactions (Fig. 13.1), and leads to the method of equilibrium constants, as described in the following sections. It may also be extended to multiple reactions, but in this case the direct minimization of G^t is often more convenient, and is considered in Sec. 13.9.

Although the equilibrium expressions are *developed* for closed systems at constant T and P, they are not restricted in *application* to systems that are actually closed and reach equilibrium states along paths of constant T and P. Once an equilibrium state is reached, no further changes occur, and the system continues to exist in this state at fixed T and P. How this state was *actually* attained does not matter. Once it is known that an equilibrium state exists at given T and P, the criteria apply.

13.3 THE STANDARD GIBBS-ENERGY CHANGE AND THE EQUILIBRIUM CONSTANT

Equation (11.2), the fundamental property relation for single-phase systems, provides an expression for the total differential of the Gibbs energy:

$$d(nG) = (nV)dP - (nS)dT + \sum_i \mu_i \, dn_i \qquad (11.2)$$

If changes in the mole numbers n_i occur as the result of a single chemical reaction in a closed system, then by Eq. (13.3) each dn_i may be replaced by the product $\nu_i \, d\varepsilon$. Equation (11.2) then becomes

$$d(nG) = (nV)dP - (nS)dT + \sum_i \nu_i \mu_i \, d\varepsilon$$

Because nG is a state function, the right side of this equation is an exact differential expression; whence,

$$\sum_i \nu_i \mu_i = \left[\frac{\partial(nG)}{\partial \varepsilon}\right]_{T,P} = \left[\frac{\partial(G^t)}{\partial \varepsilon}\right]_{T,P}$$

Thus the quantity $\sum_i \nu_i \mu_i$ represents, in general, the rate of change of total Gibbs energy of the system with respect to the reaction coordinate at constant T and P. Figure 13.1 shows that this quantity is zero at the equilibrium state. A criterion of chemical-reaction equilibrium is therefore

$$\boxed{\sum_i \nu_i \mu_i = 0} \qquad (13.8)$$

Recall the definition of the fugacity of a species in solution:

$$\mu_i = \Gamma_i(T) + RT \ln \hat{f}_i \qquad (11.46)$$

In addition, Eq. (11.31) may be written for pure species i in its *standard state*[3] at the same temperature:

$$G_i^\circ = \Gamma_i(T) + RT \ln f_i^\circ$$

The difference between these two equations is

$$\mu_i - G_i^\circ = RT \ln \frac{\hat{f}_i}{f_i^\circ} \qquad (13.9)$$

Combining Eq. (13.8) with Eq. (13.9) to eliminate μ_i gives for the equilibrium state of a chemical reaction:

$$\sum_i \nu_i [G_i^\circ + RT \ln(\hat{f}_i / f_i^\circ)] = 0$$

or

$$\sum_i \nu_i G_i^\circ + RT \sum_i \ln(\hat{f}_i / f_i^\circ)^{\nu_i} = 0$$

or

$$\ln \prod_i (\hat{f}_i / f_i^\circ)^{\nu_i} = \frac{-\sum_i \nu_i G_i^\circ}{RT}$$

where $\prod_i$ signifies the product over all species i. In exponential form, this equation becomes

$$\boxed{\prod_i (\hat{f}_i / f_i^\circ)^{\nu_i} = K} \qquad (13.10)$$

where the **definition** of K and its logarithm are given by

$$K \equiv \exp\left(\frac{-\Delta G^\circ}{RT}\right) \quad (13.11a) \qquad \ln K = \frac{-\Delta G^\circ}{RT} \quad (13.11b)$$

[3]Standard states are introduced and discussed in Sec. 4.3.

Also by **definition**,

$$\Delta G^\circ \equiv \sum_i \nu_i G_i^\circ \tag{13.12}$$

Because G_i° is a property of pure species i in its standard state at fixed pressure, it depends only on temperature. By Eq. (13.12) it follows that ΔG° and hence K, are also functions of temperature only.

> **In spite of its dependence on temperature, K is called the equilibrium *constant* for the reaction; $\sum_i \nu_i G_i^\circ$, represented by ΔG°, is called *the standard Gibbs-energy change of reaction*.**

The fugacity ratios in Eq. (13.10) provide the connection between the *equilibrium* state of interest and the *standard* states of the individual species, for which data are presumed available, as discussed in Sec. 13.5. The standard states are arbitrary, but must always be at the equilibrium temperature T. The standard states selected need not be the same for all species taking part in a reaction. However, for a *particular* species the standard state represented by G_i° must be the same state as for the fugacity f_i°.

The function $\Delta G^\circ \equiv \sum_i \nu_i G_i^\circ$ in Eq. (13.12) is the difference between the Gibbs energies of the products and reactants (weighted by their stoichiometric coefficients) when each is in its standard state as a pure substance at the standard-state pressure, but at the *system* temperature. Thus the value of ΔG° is fixed for a given reaction once the temperature is established, and is independent of the equilibrium pressure and composition. Other *standard property changes of reaction* are similarly defined. Thus, for the general property M:

$$\Delta M^\circ \equiv \sum_i \nu_i M_i^\circ$$

In accord with this, ΔH° is defined by Eq. (4.14) and ΔC_P° by Eq. (4.16). These quantities are functions of temperature only for a given reaction, and are related to one another by equations analogous to property relations for pure species.

For example, the relation between the standard heat of reaction and the standard Gibbs-energy change of reaction may be developed from Eq. (6.39) written for species i in its standard state:

$$H_i^\circ = -RT^2 \frac{d(G_i^\circ/RT)}{dT}$$

Total derivatives are appropriate here because the properties in the standard state are functions of temperature only. Multiplication of both sides of this equation by ν_i and summation over all species gives

$$\sum_i \nu_i H_i^\circ = -RT^2 \frac{d(\sum_i \nu_i G_i^\circ/RT)}{dT}$$

In view of the definitions of Eqs. (4.14) and (13.12), this may be written as

$$\Delta H^\circ = -RT^2 \frac{d(\Delta G^\circ/RT)}{dT} \tag{13.13}$$

13.4 EFFECT OF TEMPERATURE ON THE EQUILIBRIUM CONSTANT

Because the standard-state temperature is that of the equilibrium mixture, the standard property changes of reaction, such as ΔG° and ΔH°, vary with the equilibrium temperature. The dependence of ΔG° on T is given by Eq. (13.13), which may be rewritten as

$$\frac{d(\Delta G^\circ/RT)}{dT} = \frac{-\Delta H^\circ}{RT^2}$$

In view of Eq. (13.11b), this becomes

$$\boxed{\frac{d \ln K}{dT} = \frac{\Delta H^\circ}{RT^2}} \tag{13.14}$$

Equation (13.14) gives the effect of temperature on the equilibrium constant, and hence on the equilibrium conversion. If ΔH° is negative, i.e., if the reaction is exothermic, the equilibrium constant decreases as the temperature increases. Conversely, K increases with T for an endothermic reaction.

If ΔH°, the standard enthalpy change (heat) of reaction, is assumed independent of T, integration of Eq. (13.14) from a particular temperature T' to an arbitrary temperature T leads to the simple result:

$$\ln \frac{K}{K'} = -\frac{\Delta H^\circ}{R}\left(\frac{1}{T} - \frac{1}{T'}\right) \tag{13.15}$$

This approximate equation implies that a plot of ln K vs. the reciprocal of absolute temperature is a straight line. Figure 13.2, a plot of ln K vs. $1/T$ for a number of common reactions, illustrates this near linearity. Thus, Eq. (13.15) provides a reasonably accurate relation for the interpolation and extrapolation of equilibrium-constant data.

The *rigorous* development of the effect of temperature on the equilibrium constant is based on the definition of the Gibbs energy, written for a chemical species in its standard state:

$$G_i^\circ = H_i^\circ - TS_i^\circ$$

Multiplication by ν_i and summation over all species gives

$$\sum_i \nu_i G_i^\circ = \sum_i \nu_i H_i^\circ - T \sum_i \nu_i S_i^\circ$$

As a result of the definition of a standard property change of reaction, this reduces to

$$\Delta G^\circ = \Delta H^\circ - T\Delta S^\circ \tag{13.16}$$

The standard heat of reaction is related to temperature:

$$\Delta H^\circ = \Delta H_0^\circ + R \int_{T_0}^{T} \frac{\Delta C_P^\circ}{R} dT \tag{4.18}$$

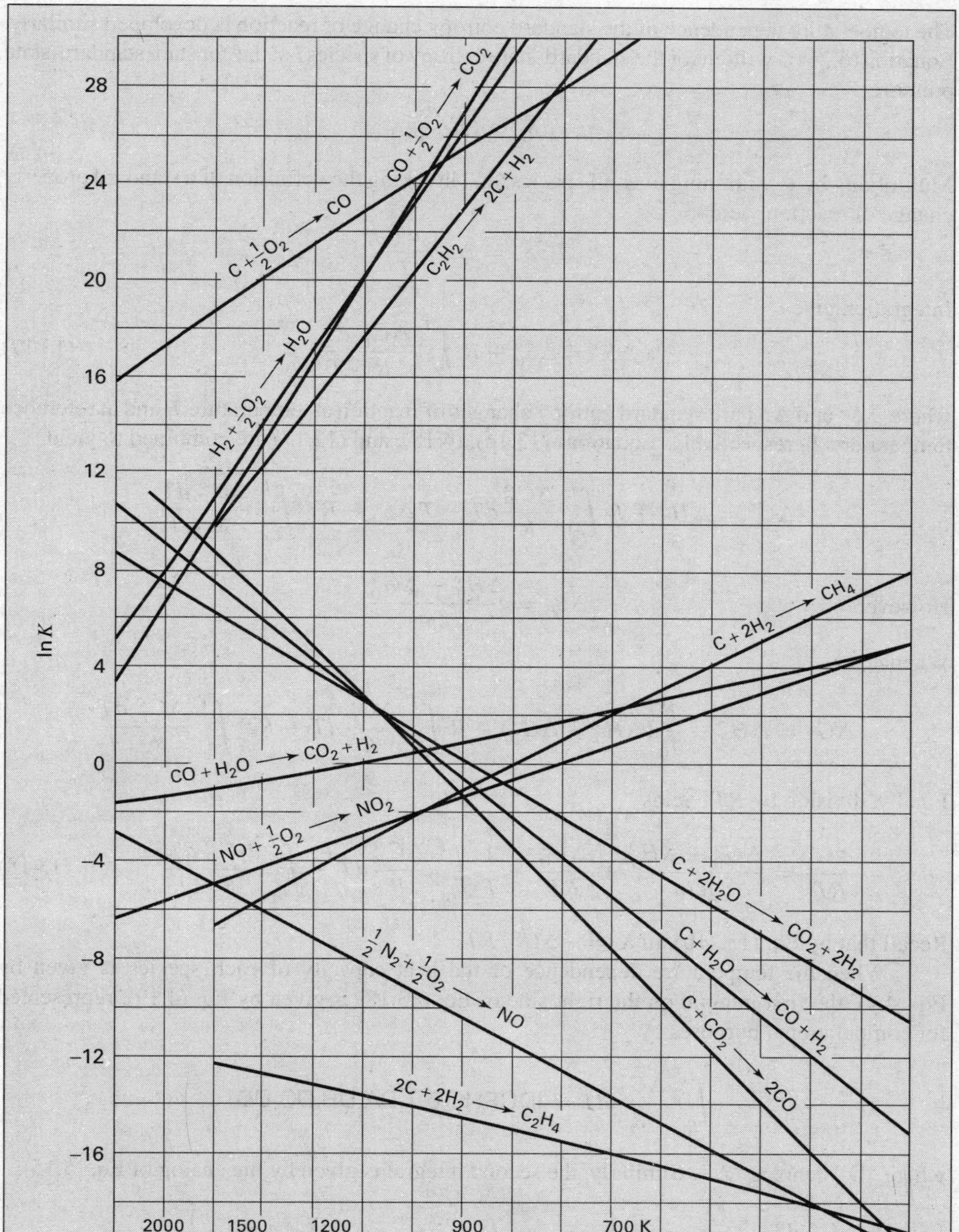

Figure 13.2: Equilibrium constants as a function of temperature

The temperature dependence of the standard entropy change of reaction is developed similarly. Equation (6.21) is written for the standard-state entropy of species i at the constant standard-state pressure P°:

$$dS_i^\circ = C_{P_i}^\circ \frac{dT}{T}$$

Multiplying by ν_i, summing over all species, and invoking the definition of a standard property change of reaction yields

$$d\Delta S^\circ = \Delta C_P^\circ \frac{dT}{T}$$

Integration gives

$$\Delta S^\circ = \Delta S_0^\circ + R \int_{T_0}^{T} \frac{\Delta C_P^\circ}{R} \frac{dT}{T} \tag{13.17}$$

where ΔS° and ΔS_0° are standard entropy changes of reaction at temperature T and at reference temperature T_0 respectively. Equations (13.16), (4.18), and (13.17) are combined to yield

$$\Delta G^\circ = \Delta H_0^\circ + R \int_{T_0}^{T} \frac{\Delta C_P^\circ}{R} dT - T \Delta S_0^\circ - RT \int_{T_0}^{T} \frac{\Delta C_P^\circ}{R} \frac{dT}{T}$$

However,

$$\Delta S_0^\circ = \frac{\Delta H_0^\circ - \Delta G_0^\circ}{T_0}$$

Whence,

$$\Delta G^\circ = \Delta H_0^\circ - \frac{T}{T_0}(\Delta H_0^\circ - \Delta G_0^\circ) + R \int_{T_0}^{T} \frac{\Delta C_P^\circ}{R} dT - RT \int_{T_0}^{T} \frac{\Delta C_P^\circ}{R} \frac{dT}{T}$$

Finally, division by RT yields

$$\frac{\Delta G^\circ}{RT} = \frac{\Delta G_0^\circ - \Delta H_0^\circ}{RT_0} + \frac{\Delta H_0^\circ}{RT} + \frac{1}{T} \int_{T_0}^{T} \frac{\Delta C_P^\circ}{R} dT - \int_{T_0}^{T} \frac{\Delta C_P^\circ}{R} \frac{dT}{T} \tag{13.18}$$

Recall that by Eq. (13.11b), $\ln K = -\Delta G^\circ / RT$.

When the temperature dependence of the heat capacity of each species is given by Eq. (4.4), the first integral on the right side of Eq. (13.18) is given by Eq. (4.19), represented for computational purposes by

$$\int_{T_0}^{T} \frac{\Delta C_P^\circ}{R} dT = \mathsf{IDCPH(T0,T;DA,DB,DC,DD)}$$

where "D" denotes "Δ". Similarly, the second integral is given by the analog of Eq. (5.15):

$$\int_{T_0}^{T} \frac{\Delta C_P^\circ}{R} \frac{dT}{T} = \Delta A \ln \tau + \left[\Delta B\, T_0 + \left(\Delta C\, T_0^2 + \frac{\Delta D}{\tau^2 T_0^2} \right) \left(\frac{\tau + 1}{2} \right) \right] (\tau - 1) \tag{13.19}$$

where

$$\tau \equiv \frac{T}{T_0}$$

The integral is evaluated by a function of exactly the same form as given by Eq. (5.15), and the same computer program therefore serves for evaluation of either integral. The only difference is in the name of the function, here: IDCPS(T0,T;DA,DB,DC,DD). By definition,

$$\int_{T_0}^{T} \frac{\Delta C_P^\circ}{R} \frac{dT}{T} = \text{IDCPS(T0,T;DA,DB,DC,DD)}$$

Thus $\Delta G^\circ/RT (= -\ln K)$ as given by Eq. (13.18) is readily calculated at any temperature from the standard heat of reaction and the standard Gibbs-energy change of reaction at a reference temperature (usually 298.15 K), and from two functions which can be evaluated by standard computational procedures.

The preceeding equations may be reorganized so as to factor K into three terms, each representing a basic contribution to its value:

$$K = K_0 K_1 K_2 \tag{13.20}$$

The first factor K_0 represents the equilibrium constant at reference temperature T_0:

$$K_0 \equiv \exp\left(\frac{-\Delta G_0^\circ}{RT_0}\right) \tag{13.21}$$

The second factor K_1 is a multiplier that supplies the major effect of temperature, such that the product $K_0 K_1$ is the equilibrium constant at temperature T when the heat of reaction is assumed independent of temperature:

$$K_1 \equiv \exp\left[\frac{\Delta H_0^\circ}{RT_0}\left(1 - \frac{T_0}{T}\right)\right] \tag{13.22}$$

The third factor K_2 accounts for the much smaller temperature influence resulting from the change of ΔH° with temperature:

$$K_2 \equiv \exp\left(-\frac{1}{T}\int_{T_0}^{T} \frac{\Delta C_P^\circ}{R} dT + \int_{T_0}^{T} \frac{\Delta C_P^\circ}{R} \frac{dT}{T}\right) \tag{13.23}$$

With heat capacities given by Eq. (4.4), the expression for K_2 becomes

$$K_2 = \exp\left\{\Delta A\left[\ln\tau - \left(\frac{\tau - 1}{\tau}\right)\right] + \frac{1}{2}\Delta B T_0 \frac{(\tau - 1)^2}{\tau} + \frac{1}{6}\Delta C T_0^2 \frac{(\tau - 1)^2(\tau + 2)}{\tau} + \frac{1}{2}\frac{\Delta D}{T_0^2}\frac{(\tau - 1)^2}{\tau^2}\right\} \tag{13.24}$$

13.5 EVALUATION OF EQUILIBRIUM CONSTANTS

Values of ΔG° for many *formation reactions* are tabulated in standard references.[4] The reported values of ΔG°_f are not measured experimentally, but are calculated by Eq. (13.16). The determination of ΔS°_f may be based on the third law of thermodynamics, discussed in Sec. 5.10. Combination of values from Eq. (5.40) for the absolute entropies of the species taking part in the reaction gives the value of ΔS°_f. Entropies (and heat capacities) are also commonly determined from statistical calculations based on spectroscopic data.[5]

Values of $\Delta G^\circ_{f_{298}}$ for a limited number of chemical compounds are listed in Table C.4 of App. C. These are for a temperature of 298.15 K, as are the values of $\Delta H^\circ_{f_{298}}$ listed in the same table. Values of ΔG° for other reactions are calculated from formation-reaction values in exactly the same way that ΔH° values for other reactions are determined from formation-reaction values (Sec. 4.4). In more extensive compilations of data, values of ΔG°_f and ΔH°_f are given for a wide range of temperatures, rather than just at 298.15 K. Where data are lacking, methods of estimation are available; these are reviewed by Poling, Prausnitz, and O'Connell.[6]

Example 13.4

Calculate the equilibrium constant for the vapor-phase hydration of ethylene at 145°C (418.15 K) and at 320°C (593.15 K) from data given in App. C.

Solution

First determine values for ΔA, ΔB, ΔC, and ΔD for the reaction

$$C_2H_4(g) + H_2O(g) \rightarrow C_2H_5OH(g)$$

The meaning of Δ is indicated by: $\Delta = (C_2H_5OH) - (C_2H_4) - (H_2O)$. Thus, from the heat-capacity data of Table C.1:

$$\Delta A = 3.518 - 1.424 - 3.470 = -1.376$$

$$\Delta B = (20.001 - 14.394 - 1.450) \times 10^{-3} = 4.157 \times 10^{-3}$$

$$\Delta C = (-6.002 + 4.392 - 0.000) \times 10^{-6} = -1.610 \times 10^{-6}$$

$$\Delta D = (-0.000 - 0.000 - 0.121) \times 10^{5} = -0.121 \times 10^{5}$$

[4]For example, "TRC Thermodynamic Tables–Hydrocarbons" and "TRC Thermodynamic Tables–Non-hydrocarbons," serial publications of the Thermodynamics Research Center, Texas A & M Univ. System, College Station, Texas; "The NBS Tables of Chemical Thermodynamic Properties," *J. Physical and Chemical Reference Data*, vol. 11, supp. 2, 1982.

[5]K. S. Pitzer, *Thermodynamics*, 3d ed., chap. 5, McGraw-Hill, New York, 1995.

[6]B. E. Poling, J. M. Prausnitz, and J. P. O'Connell, *The Properties of Gases and Liquids*, 5th ed., chap. 3, McGraw-Hill, New York, 2001.

Values of ΔH°_{298} and ΔG°_{298} at 25°C (298.15 K) for the hydration reaction are found from the heat-of-formation and Gibbs-energy-of-formation data of Table C.4:

$$\Delta H^\circ_{298} = -235\,100 - 52\,510 - (-241\,818) = -45\,792 \text{ J mol}^{-1}$$

$$\Delta G^\circ_{298} = -168\,490 - 68\,460 - (-228\,572) = -8378 \text{ J mol}^{-1}$$

For $T = 418.15$ K, values of the integrals in Eq. (13.18) are

$$\text{IDCPH(298.15,418.15;-1.376,4.157E-3,-1.610E-6,-0.121E+5)} = -23.121$$

$$\text{IDCPS(298.15,418.15;-1.376,4.157E-3,-1.610E-6,-0.121E+5)} = -0.0692$$

Substitution of values into Eq. (13.18) for a reference temperature of 298.15 gives:

$$\frac{\Delta G^\circ_{418}}{RT} = \frac{-8378 + 45\,792}{(8.314)(298.15)} + \frac{-45\,792}{(8.314)(418.15)} + \frac{-23.121}{418.15} + 0.0692 = 1.9356$$

For $T = 593.15$ K,

$$\text{IDCPH(298.15,593.15;-1.376,4.157E-3,-1.610E-6,-0.121E+5)} = 22.632$$

$$\text{IDCPS(298.15,593.15;-1.376,4.157E-3,-1.610E-6,-0.121E+5)} = 0.0173$$

Whence,

$$\frac{\Delta G^\circ_{593}}{RT} = \frac{-8378 + 45\,792}{(8.314)(298.15)} + \frac{-45\,792}{(8.314)(593.15)} + \frac{22.632}{593.15} - 0.0173 = 5.8286$$

Finally,

$$@\ 418.15 \text{ K:}\quad \ln K = -1.9356 \quad \text{and} \quad K = 1.443 \times 10^{-1}$$

$$@\ 593.15 \text{ K:}\quad \ln K = -5.8286 \quad \text{and} \quad K = 2.942 \times 10^{-3}$$

Application of Eqs. (13.21), (13.22), and (13.24) provides an alternative solution to this example. By Eq. (13.21),

$$K_0 = \exp\frac{8378}{(8.314)(298.15)} = 29.366$$

Moreover, $$\frac{\Delta H^\circ_0}{RT_0} = \frac{-45\,792}{(8.314)(298.15)} = -18.473$$

With these values, the following results are readily obtained:

t/°C	T/K	τ	K_0	K_1	K_2	K
25	298.15	1	29.366	1	1	29.366
145	418.15	1.4025	29.366	4.985×10^{-3}	0.9860	1.443×10^{-1}
320	593.15	1.9894	29.366	1.023×10^{-4}	0.9794	2.942×10^{-3}

Clearly, the influence of K_1 is far greater than that of K_2. This is a typical result, and accounts for the fact that the lines on Fig. 13.2 are nearly linear.

13.6 RELATION OF EQUILIBRIUM CONSTANTS TO COMPOSITION

Gas-Phase Reactions

The standard state for a gas is the ideal-gas state of the pure gas at the standard-state pressure P° of 1 bar. Because the fugacity of an ideal gas is equal to its pressure, $f_i^\circ = P^\circ$ for each species i. Thus for gas-phase reactions $\hat{f}_i / f_i^\circ = \hat{f}_i / P^\circ$, and Eq. (13.10) becomes

$$\prod_i \left(\frac{\hat{f}_i}{P^\circ} \right)^{\nu_i} = K \tag{13.25}$$

The equilibrium constant K is a function of temperature only. However, Eq. (13.25) relates K to fugacities of the reacting species as they exist in the real equilibrium mixture. These fugacities reflect the nonidealities of the equilibrium mixture and are functions of temperature, pressure, and composition. This means that for a fixed temperature the composition at equilibrium must change with pressure in such a way that $\prod_i (\hat{f}_i / P^\circ)^{\nu_i}$ remains constant.

The fugacity is related to the fugacity coefficient by Eq. (11.52):

$$\hat{f}_i = \hat{\phi}_i y_i P$$

Substitution of this equation into Eq. (13.25) provides an equilibrium expression displaying the pressure and the composition:

$$\boxed{\prod_i (y_i \hat{\phi}_i)^{\nu_i} = \left(\frac{P}{P^\circ} \right)^{-\nu} K} \tag{13.26}$$

where $\nu \equiv \sum_i \nu_i$ and P° is the standard-state pressure of 1 bar, *expressed in the same units used for* P. The y_i's may be eliminated in favor of the equilibrium value of the reaction coordinate ε_e. Then, for a fixed temperature Eq. (13.26) relates ε_e to P. In principle, specification of the pressure allows solution for ε_e. However, the problem may be complicated by the dependence of $\hat{\phi}_i$ on composition, i.e., on ε_e. The methods of Secs. 11.6 and 11.7 can be applied to the calculation of $\hat{\phi}_i$ values, for example, by Eq. (11.64). Because of the complexity of the calculations, an iterative procedure, initiated by setting $\hat{\phi}_i = 1$ and formulated for computer solution, is indicated. Once the initial set $\{y_i\}$ is calculated, $\{\hat{\phi}_i\}$ is determined, and the procedure is repeated to convergence.

If the assumption that the equilibrium mixture is an *ideal solution* is justified, then each $\hat{\phi}_i$ becomes ϕ_i, the fugacity coefficient of pure species i at T and P [Eq. (11.84)]. In this case, Eq. (13.26) becomes

$$\boxed{\prod_i (y_i \phi_i)^{\nu_i} = \left(\frac{P}{P^\circ} \right)^{-\nu} K} \tag{13.27}$$

Each ϕ_i for a pure species can be evaluated from a generalized correlation once the equilibrium T and P are specified.

For pressures sufficiently low or temperatures sufficiently high, the equilibrium mixture behaves essentially as an ideal gas. In this event, each $\hat{\phi}_i = 1$, and Eq. (13.26) reduces to:

$$\prod_i (y_i)^{\nu_i} = \left(\frac{P}{P^\circ}\right)^{-\nu} K \tag{13.28}$$

In this equation the temperature-, pressure-, and composition-dependent terms are distinct and separate, and solution for any one of ε_e, T, or P, given the other two, is straightforward.

Although Eq. (13.28) holds only for an ideal-gas reaction, we can base some conclusions on it that are true in general:

- According to Eq. (13.14), the effect of temperature on the equilibrium constant K is determined by the sign of ΔH°. Thus when ΔH° is positive, i.e., when the standard reaction is *endothermic*, an increase in T results in an increase in K. Equation (13.28) shows that an increase in K at constant P results in an increase in $\prod_i (y_i)^{\nu_i}$; this implies a shift of the reaction to the right and an increase in ε_e. Conversely, when ΔH° is negative, i.e., when the standard reaction is *exothermic*, an increase in T causes a decrease in K and a decrease in $\prod_i (y_i)^{\nu_i}$ at constant P. This implies a shift of the reaction to the left and a decrease in ε_e.

- If the total stoichiometric number ν ($\equiv \sum_i \nu_i$) is negative, Eq. (13.28) shows that an increase in P at constant T causes an increase in $\prod_i (y_i)^{\nu_i}$, implying a shift of the reaction to the right and an increase in ε_e. If ν is positive, an increase in P at constant T causes a decrease in $\prod_i (y_i)^{\nu_i}$, a shift of the reaction to the left, and a decrease in ε_e.

Liquid-Phase Reactions

For a reaction occurring in the liquid phase, we return to

$$\prod_i (\hat{f}_i / f_i^\circ)^{\nu_i} = K \tag{13.10}$$

For the usual standard state for liquids f_i° is the fugacity of pure liquid i at the temperature of the system and at 1 bar.

According to Eq. (11.90), which defines the activity coefficient,

$$\hat{f}_i = \gamma_i x_i f_i$$

where f_i is the fugacity of pure liquid i at the temperature *and pressure* of the equilibrium mixture. The fugacity ratio can now be expressed as

$$\frac{\hat{f}_i}{f_i^\circ} = \frac{\gamma_i x_i f_i}{f_i^\circ} = \gamma_i x_i \left(\frac{f_i}{f_i^\circ}\right) \tag{13.29}$$

Because the fugacities of liquids are weak functions of pressure, the ratio f_i / f_i° is often taken as unity. However, it is readily evaluated. For pure liquid i Eq. (11.31) is written twice, first for temperature T and pressure P, and second for the same temperature T but for the standard-state pressure of $P°$. The difference between these two equations is

$$G_i - G_i^\circ = RT \ln \frac{f_i}{f_i^\circ}$$

Integration of Eq. (6.10) at constant temperature T for the change of state of pure liquid i from $P°$ to P yields

$$G_i - G_i^\circ = \int_{P^\circ}^{P} V_i \, dP$$

As a result, $$RT \ln \frac{f_i}{f_i^\circ} = \int_{P^\circ}^{P} V_i \, dP$$

Because V_i changes little with pressure for liquids (and solids), integration from $P°$ to P gives to an excellent approximation:

$$\ln \frac{f_i}{f_i^\circ} = \frac{V_i(P - P^\circ)}{RT} \qquad (13.30)$$

With Eqs. (13.29) and (13.30), Eq. (13.10) may now be written as

$$\boxed{\prod_i (x_i \gamma_i)^{\nu_i} = K \exp\left[\frac{(P^\circ - P)}{RT} \sum_i (\nu_i V_i)\right]} \qquad (13.31)$$

Except for high pressures, the exponential term is close to unity and may be omitted. Then,

$$\prod_i (x_i \gamma_i)^{\nu_i} = K \qquad (13.32)$$

and the only problem is determination of the activity coefficients. One may apply an equation such as the Wilson equation [Eq. (12.19)], or the UNIFAC method [App. H], and the compositions can be found from Eq. (13.32) by a complex iterative computer program. However, the relative ease of experimental investigation for liquid mixtures has worked against the application of Eq. (13.32).

If the equilibrium mixture is an ideal solution, then γ_i is unity, and Eq. (13.32) becomes:

$$\prod_i (x_i)^{\nu_i} = K \qquad (13.33)$$

This simple relation is known as the *law of mass action*. Because liquids often form nonideal solutions, Eq. (13.33) can be expected in many instances to yield poor results.

For species known to be present in high concentration, the equation $\hat{f}_i / f_i = x_i$ is usually nearly correct. The reason, as discussed in Sec. 12.1, is that the Lewis/Randall rule [Eq. (11.83)] always becomes valid for a species as its concentration approaches $x_i = 1$. For species at low concentration in aqueous solution, a different procedure has been widely adopted, because in this case the equality of $\hat{f}_i / f_i$ and x_i is usually far from correct. The method is based on use of a fictitious or hypothetical standard state for the solute, taken as the state that would exist if the solute obeyed Henry's law up to a *molality m* of unity.[7] In this application, Henry's law is expressed as

$$\hat{f}_i = k_i m_i \tag{13.34}$$

and it is always valid for a species whose concentration approaches zero. This hypothetical state is illustrated in Fig. 13.3. The dashed line drawn tangent to the curve at the origin represents Henry's law, and is valid in the case shown to a molality much less than unity. However, one can calculate the properties the solute would have if it obeyed Henry's law to a concentration of 1 molal, and this hypothetical state often serves as a convenient standard state for solutes.

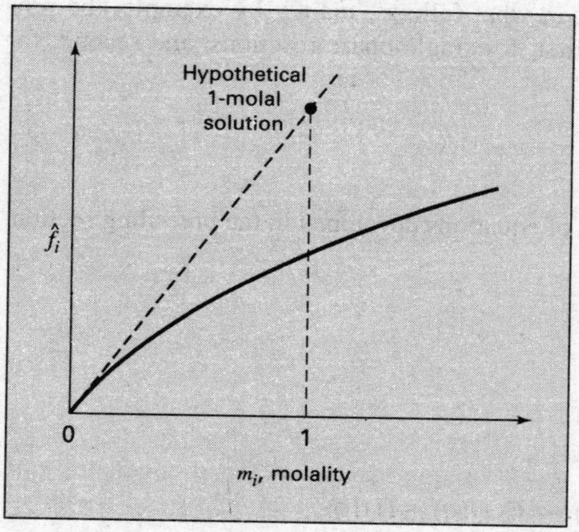

Figure 13.3: Standard state for dilute aqueous solutions

The standard-state fugacity is

$$\hat{f}_i^\circ = k_i m_i^\circ = k_i \times 1 = k_i$$

Hence, for any species at a concentration low enough for Henry's law to hold,

$$\hat{f}_i = k_i m_i = \hat{f}_i^\circ m_i$$

and

$$\frac{\hat{f}_i}{\hat{f}_i^\circ} = m_i \tag{13.35}$$

The advantage of this standard state is that it provides a very simple relation between fugacity and concentration for cases in which Henry's law is at least approximately valid. Its range does not commonly extend to a concentration of 1 molal. In the rare case where it does, the standard state is a real state of the solute. This standard state is useful only where ΔG° data are available for the standard state of a 1-molal solution, for otherwise the equilibrium constant cannot be evaluated by Eq. (13.11).

[7]Molality is a measure of solute concentration, expressed as moles of solute per kilogram of solvent.

13.7 EQUILIBRIUM CONVERSIONS FOR SINGLE REACTIONS

Suppose a single reaction occurs in a *homogeneous* system, and suppose the equilibrium constant is known. In this event, the calculation of the phase composition at equilibrium is straightforward if the phase is assumed an ideal gas [Eq. (13.28)] or an ideal solution [Eq. (13.27) or (13.33)]. When an assumption of ideality is not reasonable, the problem is still tractable for gas-phase reactions through application of an equation of state and solution by computer. For *heterogeneous* systems, where more than one phase is present, the problem is more complicated and requires the superposition of the criterion for phase equilibrium developed in Sec. 11.6. At equilibrium, there can be no tendency for change to occur, either by mass transfer between phases or by chemical reaction. We present in what follows, mainly by example, the procedures in use for equilibrium calculations, first, for single-phase reactions, and second, for heterogeneous reactions.

Single-Phase Reactions

The following examples illustrate application of equations developed in the preceding section.

Example 13.5

The water-gas-shift reaction,

$$CO(g) + H_2O(g) \rightarrow CO_2(g) + H_2(g)$$

is carried out under the different sets of conditions described below. Calculate the fraction of steam reacted in each case. Assume the mixture behaves as an ideal gas.

(*a*) The reactants consist of 1 mol of H_2O vapor and 1 mol of CO. The temperature is 1100 K and the pressure is 1 bar.

(*b*) Same as (*a*) except that the pressure is 10 bar.

(*c*) Same as (*a*) except that 2 mol of N_2 is included in the reactants.

(*d*) The reactants are 2 mol of H_2O and 1 mol of CO. Other conditions are the same as in (*a*).

(*e*) The reactants are 1 mol of H_2O and 2 mol of CO. Other conditions are the same as in (*a*).

(*f*) The initial mixture consists of 1 mol of H_2O, 1 mol of CO, and 1 mol of CO_2. Other conditions are the same as in (*a*).

(*g*) Same as (*a*) except that the temperature is 1650 K.

Solution

(*a*) For the given reaction at 1100 K, $10^4/T = 9.05$, and from Fig. 13.2, $\ln K = 0$ and $K = 1$. For this reaction $\nu = \sum_i \nu_i = 1 + 1 - 1 - 1 = 0$. Because the reaction mixture is an ideal gas, Eq. (13.28) applies, and here becomes

$$\frac{y_{H_2} y_{CO_2}}{y_{CO} y_{H_2O}} = K = 1 \qquad (A)$$

By Eq. (13.5),

$$y_{CO} = \frac{1-\varepsilon_e}{2} \qquad y_{H_2O} = \frac{1-\varepsilon_e}{2} \qquad y_{CO_2} = \frac{\varepsilon_e}{2} \qquad y_{H_2} = \frac{\varepsilon_e}{2}$$

Substitution of these values into Eq. (A) gives

$$\frac{\varepsilon_e^2}{(1-\varepsilon_e)^2} = 1 \qquad \text{or} \qquad \varepsilon_e = 0.5$$

Therefore the fraction of the steam that reacts is 0.5.

(*b*) Because $\nu = 0$, the increase in pressure has no effect on the ideal-gas reaction, and ε_e is still 0.5.

(*c*) The N_2 does not take part in the reaction, and serves only as a diluent. It does increase the initial number of moles n_0 from 2 to 4, and the mole fractions are all reduced by a factor of 2. However, Eq. (A) is unchanged and reduces to the same expression as before. Therefore, ε_e is again 0.5.

(*d*) In this case the mole fractions at equilibrium are

$$y_{CO} = \frac{1-\varepsilon_e}{3} \qquad y_{H_2O} = \frac{2-\varepsilon_e}{3} \qquad y_{CO_2} = \frac{\varepsilon_e}{3} \qquad y_{H_2} = \frac{\varepsilon_e}{3}$$

and Eq. (A) becomes

$$\frac{\varepsilon_e^2}{(1-\varepsilon_e)(2-\varepsilon_e)} = 1 \qquad \text{or} \qquad \varepsilon_e = 0.667$$

The fraction of steam that reacts is then 0.667/2 = 0.333.

(*e*) Here the expressions for y_{CO} and y_{H_2O} are interchanged, but this leaves the equilibrium equation the same as in (*d*). Therefore $\varepsilon_e = 0.667$, and the fraction of steam that reacts is 0.667.

(*f*) In this case Eq. (A) becomes

$$\frac{\varepsilon_e(1+\varepsilon_e)}{(1-\varepsilon_e)^2} = 1 \qquad \text{or} \qquad \varepsilon_e = 0.333$$

The fraction of steam reacted is 0.333.

(*g*) At 1650 K, $10^4/T = 6.06$, and from Fig. 13.2, $\ln K = -1.15$ or $K = 0.316$. Therefore Eq. (*A*) becomes

$$\frac{\varepsilon_e^2}{(1-\varepsilon_e)^2} = 0.316 \qquad \text{or} \qquad \varepsilon_e = 0.36$$

The reaction is exothermic, and conversion decreases with increasing temperature.

Example 13.6

Estimate the maximum conversion of ethylene to ethanol by vapor-phase hydration at 250°C (523.15 K) and 35 bars for an initial steam-to-ethylene ratio of 5.

Solution

The calculation of K for this reaction is treated in Ex. 13.4. For a temperature of 250°C or 523.15 K the calculation yields

$$K = 10.02 \times 10^{-3}$$

The appropriate equilibrium expression is Eq. (13.26). This equation requires evaluation of the fugacity coefficients of the species present in the equilibrium mixture. This may be accomplished with Eq. (11.64). However, the calculations involve iteration, because the fugacity coefficients are functions of composition. For purposes of illustration, we carry out only the first iteration, based on the assumption that the reaction mixture is an ideal solution. In this case Eq. (13.26) reduces to Eq. (13.27), which requires fugacity coefficients of the *pure* gases of the reacting mixture at the equilibrium T and P. Because $\nu = \sum_i \nu_i = -1$, this equation becomes

$$\frac{y_{\text{EtOH}}\phi_{\text{EtOH}}}{y_{C_2H_4}\phi_{C_2H_4}\, y_{H_2O}\phi_{H_2O}} = \left(\frac{P}{P^\circ}\right)(10.02 \times 10^{-3}) \qquad (A)$$

Computations based on Eq. (11.68) in conjunction with Eqs. (3.65) and (3.66) provide values represented by

$$\text{PHIB(TR,PR,OMEGA)} = \phi_i$$

The results of these calculations are summarized in the following table:

	T_c/K	P_c/bar	ω_i	T_{r_i}	P_{r_i}	B^0	B^1	ϕ_i
C_2H_4	282.3	50.40	0.087	1.853	0.694	−0.074	0.126	0.977
H_2O	647.1	220.55	0.345	0.808	0.159	−0.511	−0.281	0.887
EtOH	513.9	61.48	0.645	1.018	0.569	−0.327	−0.021	0.827

The critical data and values of ω_i are from App. B. The temperature and pressure in all cases are 523.15 K and 35 bar. Substitution of values for ϕ_i and for $(P/P°)$ into Eq. (A) gives:

$$\frac{y_{EtOH}}{y_{C_2H_4}y_{H_2O}} = \frac{(0.977)(0.887)}{(0.827)}(35)(10.02\times 10^{-3}) = 0.367 \qquad (B)$$

By Eq. (13.5),

$$y_{C_2H_4} = \frac{1-\varepsilon_e}{6-\varepsilon_e} \qquad y_{H_2O} = \frac{5-\varepsilon_e}{6-\varepsilon_e} \qquad y_{EtOH} = \frac{\varepsilon_e}{6-\varepsilon_e}$$

Substituting these into Eq. (B) yields:

$$\frac{\varepsilon_e(6-\varepsilon_e)}{(5-\varepsilon_e)(1-\varepsilon_e)} = 0.367 \qquad \text{or} \qquad \varepsilon_e^2 - 6.000\varepsilon_e + 1.342 = 0$$

The solution to this quadratic equation for the smaller root is $\varepsilon_e = 0.233$. Because the larger root is greater than unity, it does not represent a physically possible result. The maximum conversion of ethylene to ethanol under the stated conditions is therefore 23.3%.

In this reaction, increasing the temperature decreases K and hence the conversion. Increasing the pressure increases the conversion. Equilibrium considerations therefore suggest that the operating pressure be as high as possible (limited by condensation), and the temperature as low as possible. However, even with the best catalyst known, the minimum temperature for a reasonable reaction rate is about 150°C (423.15 K). This is an instance where both equilibrium and reaction rate influence the commercializing of a reaction process.

The equilibrium conversion is a function of temperature, pressure, and the steam-to-ethylene ratio in the feed. The effects of all three variables are shown in Fig. 13.4. The curves in this figure come from calculations just like those illustrated in this example, except that a less precise relation for K as a function of T was used.

Example 13.7

In a laboratory investigation, acetylene is catalytically hydrogenated to ethylene at 1120°C (1393.15 K) and 1 bar. If the feed is an equimolar mixture of acetylene and hydrogen, what is the composition of the product stream at equilibrium?

Solution

The required reaction is obtained by addition of the two formation reactions written as follows:

$$C_2H_2 \rightarrow 2C + H_2 \quad (I)$$

$$2C + 2H_2 \rightarrow C_2H_4 \qquad (II)$$

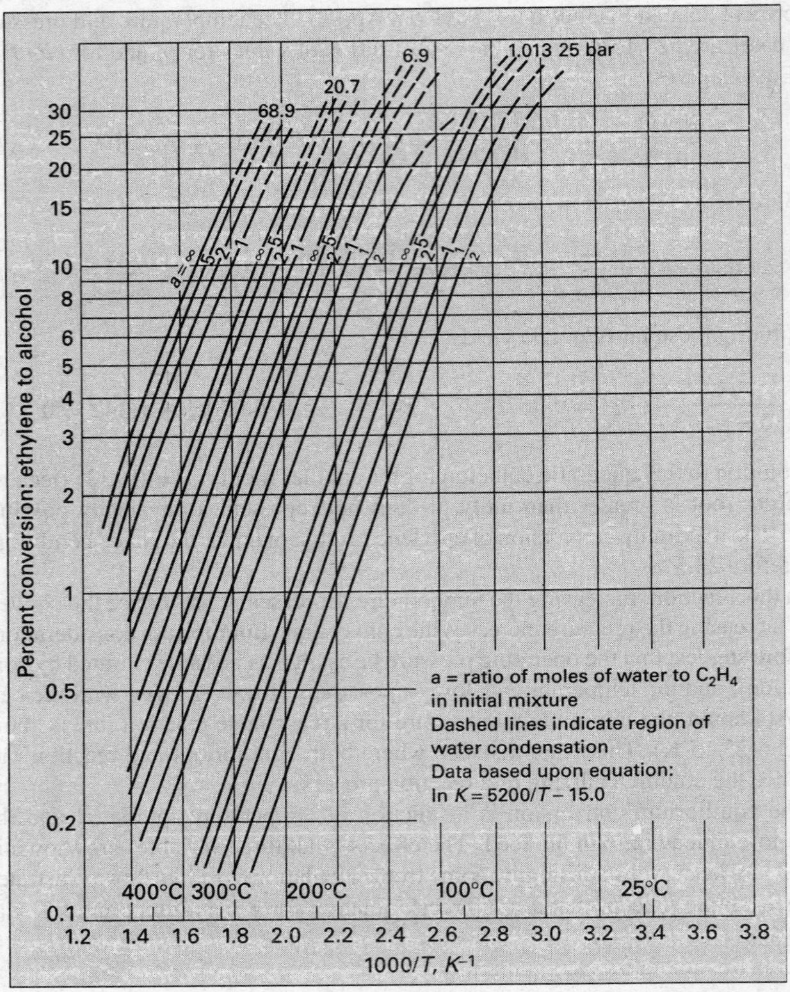

Figure 13.4: Equilibrium conversion of ethylene to ethyl alcohol in the vapor phase

The sum of reactions (I) and (II) is the hydrogenation reaction:

$$C_2H_2 + H_2 \rightarrow C_2H_4$$

Also,

$$\Delta G^\circ = \Delta G_{\mathrm{I}}^\circ + \Delta G_{\mathrm{II}}^\circ$$

By Eq. (13.11b),

$$-RT \ln K = -RT \ln K_{\mathrm{I}} - RT \ln K_{\mathrm{II}} \qquad \text{or} \qquad K = K_{\mathrm{I}} K_{\mathrm{II}}$$

Data for both reactions (I) and (II) are given by Fig. 13.2. For 1120°C (1393.15 K), $10^4/T = 7.18$, the following values are read from the graph:

$$\ln K_{\mathrm{I}} = 12.9 \qquad K_{\mathrm{I}} = 4.0 \times 10^5$$

$$\ln K_{\mathrm{II}} = -12.9 \qquad K_{\mathrm{II}} = 2.5 \times 10^{-6}$$

Therefore, $K = K_{\text{I}} K_{\text{II}} = 1.0$

At this elevated temperature and for a pressure of 1 bar, we can safely assume ideal gases. Application of Eq. (13.28) leads to the expression:

$$\frac{y_{C_2H_4}}{y_{H_2} y_{C_2H_2}} = 1$$

On the basis of one mole initially of each reactant, Eq. (13.5) gives

$$y_{H_2} = y_{C_2H_2} = \frac{1 - \varepsilon_e}{2 - \varepsilon_e} \qquad \text{and} \qquad y_{C_2H_4} = \frac{\varepsilon_e}{2 - \varepsilon_e}$$

Therefore,
$$\frac{\varepsilon_e(2 - \varepsilon_e)}{(1 - \varepsilon_e)^2} = 1$$

The smaller root of this quadratic expression (the larger is > 1) is: $\varepsilon_e = 0.293$. The equilibrium composition of the product gas is then

$$y_{H_2} = y_{C_2H_2} = \frac{1 - 0.293}{2 - 0.293} = 0.414 \qquad y_{C_2H_4} = \frac{0.293}{2 - 0.293} = 0.172$$

Example 13.8

Acetic acid is esterified in the liquid phase with ethanol at 100°C (373.15 K) and atmospheric pressure to produce ethyl acetate and water according to the reaction:

$$CH_3COOH(l) + C_2H_5OH(l) \rightarrow CH_3COOC_2H_5(l) + H_2O(l)$$

If initially there is one mole each of acetic acid and ethanol, estimate the mole fraction of ethyl acetate in the reacting mixture at equilibrium.

Solution

Data for $\Delta H^\circ_{f_{298}}$ and $\Delta G^\circ_{f_{298}}$ are given for liquid acetic acid, ethanol, and water in Table C.4. For liquid ethyl acetate, the corresponding values are

$$\Delta H^\circ_{f_{298}} = -480\,000 \text{ J} \qquad \text{and} \qquad \Delta G^\circ_{f_{298}} = -332\,200 \text{ J}$$

The values of ΔH°_{298} and ΔG°_{298} for the reaction are therefore:

$$\Delta H^\circ_{298} = -480\,000 - 285\,830 + 484\,500 + 277\,690 = -3640 \text{ J}$$

$$\Delta G^\circ_{298} = -332\,200 - 237\,130 + 389\,900 + 174\,780 = -4650 \text{ J}$$

By Eq. (13.11b),

$$\ln K_{298} = \frac{-\Delta G^\circ_{298}}{RT} = \frac{4650}{(8.314)(298.15)} = 1.8759 \qquad \text{or} \qquad K_{298} = 6.5266$$

For the small temperature change from 298.15 to 373.15 K, Eq. (13.15) is adequate for estimation of K. Thus,

$$\ln \frac{K_{373}}{K_{298}} = \frac{-\Delta H^\circ_{298}}{R}\left(\frac{1}{373.15} - \frac{1}{298.15}\right)$$

or
$$\ln \frac{K_{373}}{6.5266} = \frac{3640}{8.314}\left(\frac{1}{373.15} - \frac{1}{298.15}\right) = -0.2951$$

and
$$K_{373} = (6.5266)(0.7444) = 4.8586$$

For the given reaction, Eq. (13.5), with x replacing y, yields

$$x_{\text{AcH}} = x_{\text{EtOH}} = \frac{1-\varepsilon_e}{2} \qquad x_{\text{EtAc}} = x_{\text{H}_2\text{O}} = \frac{\varepsilon_e}{2}$$

Because the pressure is low, Eq. (13.32) is applicable. In the absence of data for the activity coefficients in this complex system, we assume that the reacting species form an ideal solution. In this case Eq. (13.33) is employed, giving

$$K = \frac{x_{\text{EtAc}}x_{\text{H}_2\text{O}}}{x_{\text{AcH}}x_{\text{EtOH}}}$$

Thus,
$$4.8586 = \left(\frac{\varepsilon_e}{1-\varepsilon_e}\right)^2$$

Solution yields:

$$\varepsilon_e = 0.6879 \qquad \text{and} \qquad x_{\text{EtAc}} = 0.6879/2 = 0.344$$

This result is in good agreement with experiment, even though the assumption of ideal solutions may be unrealistic. Carried out in the laboratory, the reaction yields a measured mole fraction of ethyl acetate at equilibrium of about 0.33.

Example 13.9

The gas-phase oxidation of SO_2 to SO_3 is carried out at a pressure of 1 bar with 20% excess air in an adiabatic reactor. Assuming that the reactants enter at 25°C (298.15 K) and that equilibrium is attained at the exit, determine the composition and temperature of the product stream from the reactor.

Solution

The reaction is
$$SO_2 + \tfrac{1}{2}O_2 \rightarrow SO_3$$

for which, $\Delta H^\circ_{298} = -98\,890 \qquad \Delta G^\circ_{298} = -70\,866\ \text{J mol}^{-1}$

On the basis of one mole of SO_2 entering the reactor,

Moles O_2 entering = (0.5)(1.2) = 0.6
Moles N_2 entering = (0.6)(79/21) = 2.257

Application of Eq. (13.4) yields the amounts of the species in the product stream:

$$\begin{aligned}\text{Moles } SO_2 &= 1 - \varepsilon_e\\ \text{Moles } O_2 &= 0.6 - 0.5\varepsilon_e\\ \text{Moles } SO_3 &= \varepsilon_e\\ \text{Moles } N_2 &= 2.257\\ \text{Total moles} &= 3.857 - 0.5\varepsilon_e\end{aligned}$$

Two equations must be written if we are to solve for both ε_e and the temperature. They are an energy balance and an equilibrium equation. For the energy balance, we proceed as in Ex. 4.7:

$$\Delta H^\circ_{298}\,\varepsilon_e + \Delta H^\circ_P = \Delta H = 0 \qquad (A)$$

where all enthalpies are on the basis of 1 mol SO_2 entering the reactor. The enthalpy change of the products as they are heated from 298.15 K to T is

$$\Delta H^\circ_P = \langle C^\circ_P\rangle_H (T - 298.15) \qquad (B)$$

where $\langle C^\circ_P\rangle_H$ is defined as the *total* heat capacity of the product stream:

$$\langle C^\circ_P\rangle_H \equiv \sum_i n_i \langle C^\circ_{P_i}\rangle_H$$

Data from Table C.1 provide $\langle C^\circ_{P_i}\rangle_H/R$ values:

SO_2: MCPH(298.15,T;5.699,0.801E-3,0.0,-1.015E+5)
O_2: MCPH(298.15,T;3.639,0.506E-3,0.0,-0.227E+5)
SO_3: MCPH(298.15,T;8.060,1.056E-3,0.0,-2.028E+5)
N_2: MCPH(298.15,T;3.280,0.593E-3,0.0,0.040E+5)

Equations (A) and (B) combine to yield

$$\Delta H^\circ_{298}\,\varepsilon_e + \langle C^\circ_P\rangle_H (T - 298.15) = 0$$

Solution for T gives

$$T = \frac{-\Delta H^\circ_{298}\,\varepsilon_e}{\langle C^\circ_P\rangle_H} + 298.15 \qquad (C)$$

At the conditions of temperature and pressure of the equilibrium state, the assumption of ideal gases is fully justified, and the equilibrium constant is therefore given by Eq. (13.28), which here becomes

$$K = \left(\frac{\varepsilon_e}{1-\varepsilon_e}\right)\left(\frac{3.857 - 0.5\varepsilon_e}{0.6 - 0.5\varepsilon_e}\right)^{0.5} \qquad (D)$$

Because $-\ln K = \Delta G^\circ/RT$, Eq. (13.18) can be written as

$$-\ln K = \frac{\Delta G^\circ_0 - \Delta H^\circ_0}{RT_0} + \frac{\Delta H^\circ_0}{RT} + \frac{1}{T}\int_{T_0}^{T}\frac{\Delta C^\circ_P}{R}\,dT - \int_{T_0}^{T}\frac{\Delta C^\circ_P}{R}\frac{dT}{T}$$

Substitution of numerical values yields:

$$\ln K = -11.3054 + \frac{11\,894.4}{T} - \frac{1}{T}\,(\text{IDCPH}) + \text{IDCPS} \qquad (E)$$

IDCPH = IDCPH(298.15,T;0.5415,0.002E-3,0.0,-0.8995E+5)

IDCPS = IDCPS(298.15,T;0.5415,0.002E-3,0.0,-0.8995E+5)

These expressions for the computed values of the integrals show parameters ΔA, ΔB, ΔC, and ΔD as evaluated from data of Table C.1.

An iteration scheme for solution of these equations for ε_e and T that converges fairly rapidly is as follows:

1. Assume a starting value for T.
2. Evaluate IDCPH and IDCPS at this value of T.
3. Solve Eq. (E) for K and Eq. (D) for ε_e, probably by trial.
4. Evaluate $\langle C_P^\circ \rangle_H$ and solve Eq. (C) for T.
5. Find a new value of T as the arithmetic mean of the value just calculated and the initial value; return to step 2.

This scheme converges on the values $\varepsilon_e = 0.77$ and $T = 855.7$ K. For the product,

$$y_{SO_2} = \frac{1 - 0.77}{3.857 - (0.5)(0.77)} = \frac{0.23}{3.472} = 0.0662$$

$$y_{O_2} = \frac{0.6 - (0.5)(0.77)}{3.472} = \frac{0.215}{3.472} = 0.0619$$

$$y_{SO_3} = \frac{0.77}{3.472} = 0.2218 \qquad y_{N_2} = \frac{2.257}{3.472} = 0.6501$$

Reactions in Heterogeneous Systems

When liquid and gas phases are both present in an equilibrium mixture of reacting species, Eq. (11.48), a criterion of vapor/liquid equilibrium, must be satisfied along with the equation of chemical-reaction equilibrium. Suppose, for example, that gas A reacts with liquid water B to form an aqueous solution C. Several methods of treatment exist. The reaction may be considered to occur in the gas phase with transfer of material between phases to maintain phase equilibrium. In this case, the equilibrium constant is evaluated from ΔG° data based on standard states for the species as gases, i.e., the ideal-gas states at 1 bar and the reaction temperature. Alternatively, the reaction may be considered to occur in the liquid phase, in which case ΔG° is based on standard states for the species as liquids. Finally, the reaction may be written:

$$A(g) + B(l) \rightarrow C(aq)$$

in which case the ΔG° value is for mixed standard states: C as a solute in an ideal 1-molal aqueous solution, B as a pure liquid at 1 bar, and A as a pure ideal gas at 1 bar. For this choice of standard states, the equilibrium constant as given by Eq. (13.10) becomes:

$$\frac{\hat{f}_C/f_C^\circ}{(\hat{f}_B/f_B^\circ)(\hat{f}_A/f_A^\circ)} = \frac{m_C}{(\gamma_B x_B)(\hat{f}_A/P^\circ)} = K$$

The second term arises from Eq. (13.35) applied to species C, Eq. (13.29) applied to B with $f_B/f_B^\circ = 1$, and the fact that $f_A^\circ = P^\circ$ for species A in the gas phase. Because K depends on the standard states, this value of K is not the same as one obtains when the standard states are chosen differently. However, all methods theoretically lead to the same equilibrium composition, provided Henry's law as applied to species C in solution is valid. In practice, a particular choice of standard states may simplify calculations or yield more accurate results, because it makes better use of available data. The nature of the calculations required for heterogeneous reactions is illustrated in the following example.

Example 13.10

Estimate the compositions of the liquid and vapor phases when ethylene reacts with water to form ethanol at 200°C (473.15 K) and 34.5 bar, conditions which assure the presence of both liquid and vapor phases. The reaction vessel is maintained at 34.5 bar by connection to a source of ethylene at this pressure. Assume no other reactions.

Solution

According to the phase rule (Sec. 13.8), the system has two degrees of freedom. Specification of both T and P therefore fixes the intensive state of the system, independent of the initial amounts of reactants. Material-balance equations are irrelevant, and we can make no use of equations that relate compositions to the reaction coordinate. Instead, phase-equilibrium relations must provide a sufficient number of equations to allow solution for the unknown compositions.

The most convenient approach to this problem is to regard the chemical reaction as occurring in the vapor phase. Thus,

$$C_2H_4(g) + H_2O(g) \rightarrow C_2H_5OH(g)$$

and the standard states are those of the pure ideal gases at 1 bar. For these standard states, the equilibrium expression is Eq. (13.25), which in this case becomes

$$K = \frac{\hat{f}_{EtOH}}{\hat{f}_{C_2H_4}\hat{f}_{H_2O}} P^\circ \qquad (A)$$

where the standard-state pressure P° is 1 bar (expressed in appropriate units). A general expression for $\ln K$ as a function of T is provided by the results of Ex. 13.4. For 200°C (473.15 K), this equation yields

$$\ln K = -3.473 \qquad K = 0.0310$$

The task now is to incorporate the phase-equilibrium equations, $\hat{f}_i^v = \hat{f}_i^l$, into Eq. ($A$) and to relate the fugacities to the compositions in such a way that the equations can be readily solved. Equation (A) may be written as

$$K = \frac{\hat{f}^v_{\text{EtOH}}}{\hat{f}^v_{C_2H_4}\hat{f}^v_{H_2O}} P^\circ = \frac{\hat{f}^l_{\text{EtOH}}}{\hat{f}^v_{C_2H_4}\hat{f}^l_{H_2O}} P^\circ \qquad (B)$$

The liquid-phase fugacities are related to activity coefficients by Eq. (11.90), and the vapor-phase fugacities are related to fugacity coefficients by Eq. (11.52):

$$\hat{f}_i^l = x_i \gamma_i f_i^l \qquad (C) \qquad\qquad \hat{f}_i^v = y_i \hat{\phi}_i P \qquad (D)$$

Elimination of the fugacities in Eq. (B) by Eqs. (C) and (D) gives

$$K = \frac{x_{\text{EtOH}}\gamma_{\text{EtOH}} f^l_{\text{EtOH}} P^\circ}{(y_{C_2H_4}\hat{\phi}_{C_2H_4} P)(x_{H_2O}\gamma_{H_2O} f^l_{H_2O})} \qquad (E)$$

The fugacity f_i^l is for pure liquid i at the temperature and pressure of the system. However, pressure has small effect on the fugacity of a liquid, and to a good approximation, $f_i^l = f_i^{\text{sat}}$; whence by Eq. (11.40),

$$f_i^l = \phi_i^{\text{sat}} P_i^{\text{sat}} \qquad (F)$$

In this equation ϕ_i^{sat} is the fugacity coefficient of pure saturated liquid or vapor evaluated at T of the system and at P_i^{sat}, the vapor pressure of pure species i. The assumption that the vapor phase is an ideal solution allows substitution of $\phi_{C_2H_4}$ for $\hat{\phi}_{C_2H_4}$, where $\phi_{C_2H_4}$ is the fugacity coefficient of pure ethylene at the system T and P. With this substitution and that of Eq. (F), Eq. (E) becomes

$$K = \frac{x_{\text{EtOH}}\gamma_{\text{EtOH}}\phi^{\text{sat}}_{\text{EtOH}} P^{\text{sat}}_{\text{EtOH}} P^\circ}{(y_{C_2H_4}\phi_{C_2H_4} P)(x_{H_2O}\gamma_{H_2O}\phi^{\text{sat}}_{H_2O} P^{\text{sat}}_{H_2O})} \qquad (G)$$

where the standard-state pressure P° is 1 bar, expressed in the units of P.

In addition to Eq. (G) the following expressions apply. Because $\sum_i y_i = 1$,

$$y_{C_2H_4} = 1 - y_{\text{EtOH}} - y_{H_2O} \qquad (H)$$

Eliminate y_{EtOH} and y_{H_2O} from Eq. (H) in favor of x_{EtOH} and x_{H_2O} by the vapor/liquid equilibrium relation, $\hat{f}_i^v = \hat{f}_i^l$. Combination with Eqs. (C), (D), and (F) then gives

$$y_i = \frac{\gamma_i x_i \phi_i^{\text{sat}} P_i^{\text{sat}}}{\phi_i P} \qquad (I)$$

where ϕ_i replaces $\hat{\phi}_i$ because of the assumption that the vapor phase is an ideal solution. Equations (H) and (I) yield

$$y_{C_2H_4} = 1 - \frac{x_{\text{EtOH}}\gamma_{\text{EtOH}}\phi^{\text{sat}}_{\text{EtOH}} P^{\text{sat}}_{\text{EtOH}}}{\phi_{\text{EtOH}} P} - \frac{x_{H_2O}\gamma_{H_2O}\phi^{\text{sat}}_{H_2O} P^{\text{sat}}_{H_2O}}{\phi_{H_2O} P} \qquad (J)$$

Because ethylene is far more volatile than ethanol or water, let $x_{C_2H_4} = 0$. Then,

$$x_{H_2O} = 1 - x_{EtOH} \qquad (K)$$

Equations (G), (J), and (K) are the basis for solution of the problem. The primary variables in these equations are: x_{H_2O}, x_{EtOH}, and $y_{C_2H_4}$. Other quantities are either given or determined from correlations of data. The values of P_i^{sat} are

$$P_{H_2O}^{sat} = 15.55 \qquad P_{EtOH}^{sat} = 30.22 \text{ bar}$$

The quantities ϕ_i^{sat} and ϕ_i are found from the generalized correlation represented by Eq. (11.68) with B^0 and B^1 given by Eqs. (3.65) and (3.66). Computed results are represented by PHIB(TR,PR,OMEGA). With $T = 473.15$ K, $P = 34.5$ bar, and critical data and acentric factors from App. B, computations provide

	T_c/K	P_c/bar	ω_i	T_{r_i}	P_{r_i}	$P_{r_i}^{sat}$	B^0	B^1	ϕ_i	ϕ_i^{sat}
EtOH	513.9	61.48	0.645	0.921	0.561	0.492	−0.399	−0.104	0.753	0.780
H_2O	647.1	220.55	0.345	0.731	0.156	0.071	−0.613	−0.502	0.846	0.926
C_2H_4	282.3	50.40	0.087	1.676	0.685	···	−0.102	0.119	0.963	···

Substitution of values so far determined into Eqs. (G), (J), and (K) reduces these three equations to the following:

$$K = \frac{0.0493 x_{EtOH} \gamma_{EtOH}}{y_{C_2H_4} x_{H_2O} \gamma_{H_2O}} \qquad (L)$$

$$y_{C_2H_4} = 1 - 0.907 x_{EtOH} \gamma_{EtOH} - 0.493 x_{H_2O} \gamma_{H_2O} \qquad (M)$$

$$x_{H_2O} = 1 - x_{EtOH} \qquad (K)$$

The only remaining undetermined thermodynamic properties are γ_{H_2O} and γ_{EtOH}. Because of the highly nonideal behavior of a liquid solution of ethanol and water, these must be determined from experimental data. The required data, found from VLE measurements, are given by Otsuki and Williams.[8] From their results for the ethanol/water system one can estimate values of γ_{H_2O} and γ_{EtOH} at 200°C (473.15 K). (Pressure has little effect on the activity coefficients of liquids.)

A procedure for solution of the foregoing three equations is as follows.

1. Assume a value for x_{EtOH} and calculate x_{H_2O} by Eq. (K).
2. Determine γ_{H_2O} and γ_{EtOH} from data in the reference cited.
3. Calculate $y_{C_2H_4}$ by Eq. (M).
4. Calculate K by Eq. (L) and compare with the value of 0.0310 determined from standard-reaction data.
5. If the two values agree, the assumed value of x_{EtOH} is correct. If they do not agree, assume a new value of x_{EtOH} and repeat the procedure.

[8] H. Otsuki and F. C. Williams, *Chem. Engr. Progr. Symp. Series No. 6*, vol. 49, pp. 55–67, 1953.

If $x_{\mathrm{EtOH}} = 0.06$, then by Eq. (K), $x_{\mathrm{H_2O}} = 0.94$, and from the reference cited,

$$\gamma_{\mathrm{EtOH}} = 3.34 \qquad \text{and} \qquad \gamma_{\mathrm{H_2O}} = 1.00$$

By Eq. (M),

$$y_{\mathrm{C_2H_4}} = 1 - (0.907)(3.34)(0.06) - (0.493)(1.00)(0.94) = 0.355$$

The value of K given by Eq. (L) is then:

$$K = \frac{(0.0493)(0.06)(3.34)}{(0.355)(0.94)(1.00)} = 0.0296$$

This result is in close enough agreement with the value, 0.0310, found from standard-reaction data to make further calculations pointless, and the liquid-phase composition is essentially as assumed ($x_{\mathrm{EtOH}} = 0.06$, $x_{\mathrm{H_2O}} = 0.94$). The remaining vapor-phase compositions ($y_{\mathrm{C_2H_4}}$ has already been determined as 0.356) are found by solution of Eq. (I) for $y_{\mathrm{H_2O}}$ or y_{EtOH}. All results are summarized in the following table.

	x_i	y_i
EtOH	0.060	0.180
H_2O	0.940	0.464
C_2H_4	0.000	0.356
	$\sum_i x_i = 1.000$	$\sum_i y_i = 1.000$

These results are probably reasonable estimates of actual values, provided no other reactions take place.

13.8 PHASE RULE AND DUHEM'S THEOREM FOR REACTING SYSTEMS

The phase rule (applicable to intensive properties) as discussed in Secs. 2.7 and 10.2 for non-reacting systems of π phases and N chemical species is:

$$F = 2 - \pi + N$$

It must be modified for application to systems in which chemical reactions occur. The phase-rule variables are unchanged: temperature, pressure, and $N - 1$ mole fractions in each phase. The total number of these variables is $2 + (N - 1)(\pi)$. The same phase-equilibrium equations apply as before, and they number $(\pi - 1)(N)$. However, Eq. (13.8) provides for each independent reaction an additional relation that must be satisfied at equilibrium. Because the μ_i's are functions of temperature, pressure, and the phase compositions, Eq. (13.8) represents a relation connecting phase-rule variables. If there are r independent chemical reactions at equilibrium within the system, then there is a total of $(\pi - 1)(N) + r$ independent equations relating the phase-rule variables. Taking the difference between the number of variables and the number of equations gives:

$$F = [2 + (N - 1)(\pi)] - [(\pi - 1)(N) + r]$$

or

$$\boxed{F = 2 - \pi + N - r} \tag{13.36}$$

This is the phase rule for reacting systems.

The only remaining problem for application is to determine the number of independent chemical reactions. This can be done systematically as follows:

- Write chemical equations for the formation, from the *constituent elements*, of each chemical compound considered present in the system.
- Combine these equations so as to eliminate from them all elements not considered present *as elements* in the system. A systematic procedure is to select one equation and combine it with each of the others of the set to eliminate a particular element. Then the process is repeated to eliminate another element from the new set of equations. This is done for each element eliminated [see Ex. 13.11(d)], and usually reduces the set by one equation for each element eliminated. However, the simultaneous elimination of two or more elements may occur.

The set of r equations resulting from this reduction procedure is a complete set of independent reactions for the N species considered present in the system. However, more than one such set is possible, depending on how the reduction procedure is carried out, but all sets number r and are equivalent. The reduction procedure also ensures the following relation:

$r \geq$ number of compounds present in the system
$-$ number of constituent elements *not* present *as elements*

The phase-equilibrium and chemical-reaction-equilibrium equations are the only ones considered in the foregoing treatment as interrelating the phase-rule variables. However, in certain situations *special constraints* may be placed on the system that allow additional equations to be written over and above those considered in the development of Eq. (13.36). If the number of equations resulting from special constraints is s, then Eq. (13.36) must be modified to take account of these s additional equations. The still more general form of the phase rule that results is

$$\boxed{F = 2 - \pi + N - r - s} \tag{13.37}$$

Example 13.11 shows how Eqs. (13.36) and (13.37) may be applied to specific systems.

Example 13.11

Determine the number of degrees of freedom F for each of the following systems.

(*a*) A system of two miscible nonreacting species which exists as an azeotrope in vapor/liquid equilibrium.

(*b*) A system prepared by partially decomposing $CaCO_3$ into an evacuated space.

(*c*) A system prepared by partially decomposing NH_4Cl into an evacuated space.

(*d*) A system consisting of the gases CO, CO_2, H_2, H_2O, and CH_4 in chemical equilibrium.

Solution

(*a*) The system consists of two nonreacting species in two phases. If there were no azeotrope, Eq. (13.36) would apply:

$$F = 2 - \pi + N - r = 2 - 2 + 2 - 0 = 2$$

This is the usual result for binary VLE. However, a special constraint is imposed on the system; it is an azeotrope. This provides an equation, $x_1 = y_1$, not considered in the development of Eq. (13.36). Thus, Eq. (13.37) with $s = 1$ yields $F = 1$. If the system is an azeotrope, then just one phase-rule variable— T, P, or x_1 $(= y_1)$— may be arbitrarily specified.

(*b*) Here, a single chemical reaction occurs:

$$CaCO_3(s) \rightarrow CaO(s) + CO_2(g)$$

and $r = 1$. Three chemical species are present, and three phases— solid $CaCO_3$, solid CaO, and gaseous CO_2. One might think a special constraint has been imposed by the requirement that the system be prepared in a special way— by decomposing $CaCO_3$. This is not the case, because no equation connecting the phase-rule variables can be written as a result of this requirement. Therefore,

$$F = 2 - \pi + N - r - s = 2 - 3 + 3 - 1 - 0 = 1$$

and there is a single degree of freedom. This is the reason that $CaCO_3$ exerts a fixed decomposition pressure at fixed T.

(*c*) The chemical reaction here is

$$NH_4Cl(s) \rightarrow NH_3(g) + HCl(g)$$

Three species, but only two phases, are present in this case: solid NH_4Cl and a gas mixture of NH_3 and HCl. In addition, a special constraint is imposed by the requirement that the system be formed by the decomposition of NH_4Cl. This means that the gas phase is equimolar in NH_3 and HCl. Thus a special equation, $y_{NH_3} = y_{HCl}$ $(= 0.5)$, connecting the phase-rule variables can be written. Application of Eq. (13.37) gives

$$F = 2 - \pi + N - r - s = 2 - 2 + 3 - 1 - 1 = 1$$

and the system has but one degree of freedom. This result is the same as that for part (*b*), and it is a matter of experience that NH_4Cl has a given decomposition pressure at a given temperature. This conclusion is reached quite differently in the two cases.

(*d*) This system contains five species, all in a single gas phase. There are no special constraints. Only r remains to be determined. The formation reactions for the compounds present are:

$C + \frac{1}{2}O_2 \rightarrow CO$ $\quad (A)$	$C + O_2 \rightarrow CO_2$ $\quad (B)$
$H_2 + \frac{1}{2}O_2 \rightarrow H_2O$ $\quad (C)$	$C + 2H_2 \rightarrow CH_4$ $\quad (D)$

Systematic elimination of C and O_2, the elements not present in the system, leads to two equations. One such pair of equations is obtained in the following way. Eliminate C from the set of equations by combining Eq. (*B*), first with Eq. (*A*) and then with Eq. (*D*). The two resulting reactions are

$$\text{From } (B) \text{ and } (A)\text{:} \quad CO + \tfrac{1}{2}O_2 \rightarrow CO_2 \qquad (E)$$

$$\text{From } (B) \text{ and } (D)\text{:} \quad CH_4 + O_2 \rightarrow 2H_2 + CO_2 \qquad (F)$$

Equations (*C*), (*E*), and (*F*) are the new set, and we now eliminate O_2 by combining Eq. (*C*), first with Eq. (*E*) and then with Eq. (*F*). This gives

$$\text{From } (C) \text{ and } (E)\text{:} \quad CO_2 + H_2 \rightarrow CO + H_2O \qquad (G)$$

$$\text{From } (C) \text{ and } (F)\text{:} \quad CH_4 + 2H_2O \rightarrow CO_2 + 4H_2 \qquad (H)$$

Equations (*G*) and (*H*) are an independent set and indicate that $r = 2$. The use of different elimination procedures produces other pairs of equations, but always just two equations.

Application of Eq. (13.37) yields

$$F = 2 - \pi + N - r - s = 2 - 1 + 5 - 2 - 0 = 4$$

This result means that one is free to specify four phase-rule variables, for example, T, P, and two mole fractions, in an equilibrium mixture of these five chemical species, provided that nothing else is arbitrarily set. In other words, there can be no special constraints, such as the specification that the system be prepared from given amounts of CH_4 and H_2O. This imposes special constraints through material balances that reduce the degrees of freedom to two. (Duhem's theorem; see the following paragraphs.)

Duhem's theorem for nonreacting systems was developed in Sec. 10.2. It states that for any closed system formed initially from given masses of particular chemical species, the equilibrium state is *completely determined* (extensive as well as intensive properties) by specification of any two independent variables. This theorem gives the difference between the number of independent variables that completely determine the state of the system and the number of independent equations that can be written connecting these variables:

$$[2 + (N - 1)(\pi) + \pi] - [(\pi - 1)(N) + N] = 2$$

When chemical reactions occur, a new variable ε_j is introduced into the material-balance equations for each independent reaction. Furthermore, a new equilibrium relation [Eq. (13.8)] can be written for each independent reaction. Therefore, when chemical-reaction equilibrium is superimposed on phase equilibrium, r new variables appear and r new equations can be written. The difference between the number of variables and number of equations therefore is unchanged, and Duhem's theorem as originally stated holds for reacting systems as well as for nonreacting systems.

Most chemical-reaction equilibrium problems are so posed that it is Duhem's theorem that makes them determinate. The usual problem is to find the composition of a system that reaches equilibrium from an initial state of *fixed amounts of of reacting species* when the *two* variables T and P are specified.

13.9 MULTIREACTION EQUILIBRIA

When the equilibrium state in a reacting system depends on two or more independent chemical reactions, the equilibrium composition can be found by a direct extension of the methods developed for single reactions. One first determines a set of independent reactions as discussed in Sec. 13.8. With each independent reaction there is associated a reaction coordinate in accord with the treatment of Sec. 13.1. In addition, a separate equilibrium constant is evaluated for each reaction j, and Eq. (13.10) becomes

$$\prod_i \left(\frac{\hat{f}_i}{f_i^\circ}\right)^{\nu_{i,j}} = K_j \tag{13.38}$$

with $$K_j \equiv \exp\left(\frac{-\Delta G_j^\circ}{RT}\right) \qquad (j = 1, 2, \ldots, r)$$

For a gas-phase reaction Eq. (13.38) takes the form

$$\prod_i \left(\frac{\hat{f}_i}{P^\circ}\right)^{\nu_{i,j}} = K_j \tag{13.39}$$

If the equilibrium mixture is an ideal gas,

$$\prod_i (y_i)^{\nu_{i,j}} = \left(\frac{P}{P^\circ}\right)^{-\nu_j} K_j \tag{13.40}$$

For r independent reactions there are r separate equations of this kind, and the y_i's can be eliminated by Eq. (13.7) in favor of the r reaction coordinates ε_j. The set of equations is then solved simultaneously for the r reaction coordinates, as illustrated in the following examples.

Example 13.12

A feed stock of pure *n*-butane is cracked at 750 K and 1.2 bar to produce olefins. Only two reactions have favorable equilibrium conversions at these conditions:

$$C_4H_{10} \rightarrow C_2H_4 + C_2H_6 \quad (I)$$

$$C_4H_{10} \rightarrow C_3H_6 + CH_4 \quad (II)$$

If these reactions reach equilibrium, what is the product composition?

With data from App. C and procedures illustrated in Ex. 13.4, the equilibrium constants at 750 K are found to be

$$K_I = 3.856 \quad \text{and} \quad K_{II} = 268.4$$

Solution

Equations relating the product composition to the reaction coordinates are develped as in Ex. 13.3. With a basis of 1 mol of *n*-butane feed, they here become

$$y_{C_4H_{10}} = \frac{1 - \varepsilon_I - \varepsilon_{II}}{1 + \varepsilon_I + \varepsilon_{II}}$$

$$y_{C_2H_4} = y_{C_2H_6} = \frac{\varepsilon_I}{1 + \varepsilon_I + \varepsilon_{II}} \qquad y_{C_3H_6} = y_{CH_4} = \frac{\varepsilon_{II}}{1 + \varepsilon_I + \varepsilon_{II}}$$

The equilibrium relations, by Eq. (13.40), are

$$\frac{y_{C_2H_4}\, y_{C_2H_6}}{y_{C_4H_{10}}} = \left(\frac{P}{P^\circ}\right)^{-1} K_I \qquad \frac{y_{C_3H_6}\, y_{CH_4}}{y_{C_4H_{10}}} = \left(\frac{P}{P^\circ}\right)^{-1} K_{II}$$

Combine these equilibrium equations with the mole-fraction equations:

$$\frac{\varepsilon_I^{\,2}}{(1 - \varepsilon_I - \varepsilon_{II})(1 + \varepsilon_I + \varepsilon_{II})} = \left(\frac{P}{P^\circ}\right)^{-1} K_I \qquad (A)$$

$$\frac{\varepsilon_{II}^{\,2}}{(1 - \varepsilon_I - \varepsilon_{II})(1 + \varepsilon_I + \varepsilon_{II})} = \left(\frac{P}{P^\circ}\right)^{-1} K_{II} \qquad (B)$$

Divide Eq. (*B*) by Eq. (*A*) and solve for ε_{II}:

$$\varepsilon_{II} = \kappa \varepsilon_I \qquad (C)$$

where

$$\kappa \equiv \left(\frac{K_{II}}{K_I}\right)^{1/2} \qquad (D)$$

Combine Eqs. (*A*) and (*C*). After some reduction, solution for ε_I gives

$$\varepsilon_I = \left[\frac{K_I(P^\circ/P)}{1 + K_I(P^\circ/P)(\kappa + 1)^2}\right]^{1/2} \qquad (E)$$

Substitution of numerical values in Eqs. (D), (E), and (C) yields

$$\kappa = \left(\frac{268.4}{3.856}\right)^{1/2} = 8.343$$

$$\varepsilon_{\mathrm{I}} = \left[\frac{(3.856)(1/1.2)}{1 + (3.856)(1/1.2)(9.343)^2}\right]^{1/2} = 0.1068$$

$$\varepsilon_{\mathrm{II}} = (8.343)(0.1068) = 0.8914$$

The product-gas composition is then:

$$y_{C_4H_{10}} = 0.0010 \qquad y_{C_2H_4} = y_{C_2H_6} = 0.0534 \qquad y_{C_3H_6} = y_{CH_4} = 0.4461$$

For this simple reaction scheme, analytical solution is possible. More often, solution of multireaction-equilibrium problems requires numerical techniques.

Example 13.13

A bed of coal (assume pure carbon) in a coal gasifier is fed with steam and air, and produces a gas stream containing H_2, CO, O_2, H_2O, CO_2, and N_2. If the feed to the gasifier consists of 1 mol of steam and 2.38 mol of air, calculate the equilibrium composition of the gas stream at $P = 20$ bar for temperatures of 1000, 1100, 1200, 1300, 1400, and 1500 K. Available data are listed in the following table.

	ΔG°_f/J mol^{-1}		
T/K	H_2O	CO	CO_2
1000	−192 420	−200 240	−395 790
1100	−187 000	−209 110	−395 960
1200	−181 380	−217 830	−396 020
1300	−175 720	−226 530	−396 080
1400	−170 020	−235 130	−396 130
1500	−164 310	−243 740	−396 160

Solution

The feed stream to the coal bed consists of 1 mol of steam and 2.38 mol of air, containing:

$$O_2 : (0.21)(2.38) = 0.5 \text{ mol} \qquad N_2 : (0.79)(2.38) = 1.88 \text{ mol}$$

The species present at equilibrium are C, H_2, CO, O_2, H_2O, CO_2, and N_2. The formation reactions for the compounds present are:

$$H_2 + \tfrac{1}{2}O_2 \rightarrow H_2O \quad \text{(I)}$$

$$C + \tfrac{1}{2}O_2 \rightarrow CO \quad \text{(II)}$$

$$C + O_2 \rightarrow CO_2 \quad \text{(III)}$$

Because elements hydrogen, oxygen, and carbon are themselves presumed present in the system, this set of three independent reactions is a complete set.

All species are present as gases except carbon, which is a pure solid phase. In the equilibrium expression, Eq. (13.38), the fugacity ratio of the pure carbon is $\hat{f}_C/f_C^\circ = f_C/f_C^\circ$, the fugacity of carbon at 20 bar divided by the fugacity of carbon at 1 bar. Because the effect of pressure on the fugacity of a solid is very small, negligible error is introduced by the assumption that this ratio is unity. The fugacity ratio for carbon is then $\hat{f}_C/f_C^\circ = 1$, and it may be omitted from the equilibrium expression. With the assumption that the remaining species are ideal gases, Eq. (13.40) is written for the gas phase only, and it provides the following equilibrium expressions for reactions (I) through (III):

$$K_I = \frac{y_{H_2O}}{y_{O_2}^{1/2}\, y_{H_2}}\left(\frac{P}{P^\circ}\right)^{-1/2} \qquad K_{II} = \frac{y_{CO}}{y_{O_2}^{1/2}}\left(\frac{P}{P^\circ}\right)^{1/2} \qquad K_{III} = \frac{y_{CO_2}}{y_{O_2}}$$

The reaction coordinates for the three reactions are designated ε_I, ε_{II}, and ε_{III}, and they are here the equilibrium values. For the initial state,

$$n_{H_2} = n_{CO} = n_{CO_2} = 0 \qquad n_{H_2O} = 1 \qquad n_{O_2} = 0.5 \qquad n_{N_2} = 1.88$$

Moreover, because only the gas-phase species are considered,

$$\nu_I = -\frac{1}{2} \qquad \nu_{II} = \frac{1}{2} \qquad \nu_{III} = 0$$

Applying Eq. (13.7) to each species gives

$$y_{H_2} = \frac{-\varepsilon_I}{3.38 + (\varepsilon_{II} - \varepsilon_I)/2} \qquad y_{CO} = \frac{\varepsilon_{II}}{3.38 + (\varepsilon_{II} - \varepsilon_I)/2}$$

$$y_{O_2} = \frac{\frac{1}{2}(1 - \varepsilon_I - \varepsilon_{II}) - \varepsilon_{III}}{3.38 + (\varepsilon_{II} - \varepsilon_I)/2} \qquad y_{H_2O} = \frac{1 + \varepsilon_I}{3.38 + (\varepsilon_{II} - \varepsilon_I)/2}$$

$$y_{CO_2} = \frac{\varepsilon_{III}}{3.38 + (\varepsilon_{II} - \varepsilon_I)/2} \qquad y_{N_2} = \frac{1.88}{3.38 + (\varepsilon_{II} - \varepsilon_I)/2}$$

Substitution of these expressions for y_i into the equilibrium equations yields

$$K_I = \frac{(1 + \varepsilon_I)(2n)^{1/2}(P/P^\circ)^{-1/2}}{(1 - \varepsilon_I - \varepsilon_{II} - 2\varepsilon_{III})^{1/2}(-\varepsilon_I)}$$

$$K_{II} = \frac{\sqrt{2}\varepsilon_{II}(P/P^\circ)^{1/2}}{(1 - \varepsilon_I - \varepsilon_{II} - 2\varepsilon_{III})^{1/2} n^{1/2}}$$

$$K_{III} = \frac{2\varepsilon_{III}}{(1 - \varepsilon_I - \varepsilon_{II} - 2\varepsilon_{III})}$$

where
$$n \equiv 3.38 + \frac{\varepsilon_{II} - \varepsilon_I}{2}$$

Numerical values for the K_j calculated by Eq. (13.11) are found to be very large. For example, at 1500 K,

$$\ln K_I = \frac{-\Delta G^\circ_I}{RT} = \frac{164\,310}{(8.314)(1500)} = 13.2 \qquad K_I \sim 10^6$$

$$\ln K_{II} = \frac{-\Delta G^\circ_{II}}{RT} = \frac{243\,740}{(8.314)(1500)} = 19.6 \qquad K_{II} \sim 10^8$$

$$\ln K_{III} = \frac{-\Delta G^\circ_{III}}{RT} = \frac{396\,160}{(8.314)(1500)} = 31.8 \qquad K_{III} \sim 10^{14}$$

With each K_j so large, the quantity $1 - \varepsilon_I - \varepsilon_{II} - 2\varepsilon_{III}$ in the denominator of each equilibrium equation must be nearly zero. This means that the mole fraction of oxygen in the equilibrium mixture is very small. For practical purposes, no oxygen is present.

We therefore reformulate the problem by eliminating O_2 from the formation reactions. For this, Eq. (I) is combined, first with Eq. (II), and then with Eq. (III). This provides two equations:

$$C + CO_2 \rightarrow 2CO \qquad (a)$$

$$H_2O + C \rightarrow H_2 + CO \quad (b)$$

The corresponding equilibrium equations are

$$K_a = \frac{y_{CO}^2}{y_{CO_2}}\left(\frac{P}{P^\circ}\right) \qquad K_b = \frac{y_{H_2}\,y_{CO}}{y_{H_2O}}\left(\frac{P}{P^\circ}\right)$$

The input stream is specified to contain 1 mol H_2, 0.5 mol O_2, and 1.88 mol N_2. Because O_2 has been eliminated from the set of reaction equations, we replace the 0.5 mol of O_2 in the feed by 0.5 mol of CO_2. The presumption is that this amount of CO_2 has been formed by prior reaction of the 0.5 mol O_2 with carbon. Thus the equivalent feed stream contains 1 mol H_2, 0.5 mol CO_2, and 1.88 mol N_2, and application of Eq. (13.7) to Eqs. (a) and (b) gives

$$y_{H_2} = \frac{\varepsilon_b}{3.38 + \varepsilon_a + \varepsilon_b} \qquad y_{CO} = \frac{2\varepsilon_a + \varepsilon_b}{3.38 + \varepsilon_a + \varepsilon_b}$$

$$y_{H_2O} = \frac{1 - \varepsilon_b}{3.38 + \varepsilon_a + \varepsilon_b} \qquad y_{CO_2} = \frac{0.5 - \varepsilon_a}{3.38 + \varepsilon_a + \varepsilon_b}$$

$$y_{N_2} = \frac{1.88}{3.38 + \varepsilon_a + \varepsilon_b}$$

Because values of y_i must lie between zero and unity, the two expressions on the left and the two on the right show that

$$0 \le \varepsilon_b \le 1 \qquad -0.5 \le \varepsilon_a \le 0.5$$

Combining the expressions for the y_i with the equilibrium equations gives:

$$K_a = \frac{(2\varepsilon_a + \varepsilon_b)^2}{(0.5 - \varepsilon_a)(3.38 + \varepsilon_a + \varepsilon_b)}\left(\frac{P}{P^\circ}\right) \qquad (A)$$

$$K_b = \frac{\varepsilon_b(2\varepsilon_a + \varepsilon_b)}{(1 - \varepsilon_b)(3.38 + \varepsilon_a + \varepsilon_b)}\left(\frac{P}{P^\circ}\right) \qquad (B)$$

For reaction (*a*) at 1000 K,

$$\Delta G^\circ_{1000} = 2(-200\,240) - (-395\,790) = -4690$$

and by Eq. (13.11),

$$\ln K_a = \frac{4690}{(8.314)(1000)} = 0.5641 \qquad K_a = 1.758$$

Similarly, for reaction (*b*),

$$\Delta G^\circ_{1000} = (-200\,240) - (-192\,420) = -7820$$

and $$\ln K_b = \frac{7820}{(8.314)(1000)} = 0.9406 \qquad K_b = 2.561$$

Equations (*A*) and (*B*) with these values for K_a and K_b and with $(P/P^\circ) = 20$ constitute two nonlinear equations in unknowns ε_a and ε_b. An *ad hoc* iteration scheme can be devised for their solution, but Newton's method for solving an array of nonlinear algebraic equations is attractive. It is described and applied to this example in App. I. Moreover, the Mathcad® program for solving these equations is included in App. D.2. The results of calculations for all temperatures are shown in the following table.

T/K	K_a	K_b	ε_a	ε_b
1000	1.758	2.561	−0.0506	0.5336
1100	11.405	11.219	0.1210	0.7124
1200	53.155	38.609	0.3168	0.8551
1300	194.430	110.064	0.4301	0.9357
1400	584.85	268.76	0.4739	0.9713
1500	1514.12	583.58	0.4896	0.9863

Values for the mole fractions y_i of the species in the equilibrium mixture are calculated by the equations already given. The results of all such calculations appear in the following table and are shown graphically in Fig. 13.5.

T/K	y_{H_2}	y_{CO}	y_{H_2O}	y_{CO_2}	y_{N_2}
1000	0.138	0.112	0.121	0.143	0.486
1100	0.169	0.226	0.068	0.090	0.447
1200	0.188	0.327	0.032	0.040	0.413
1300	0.197	0.378	0.014	0.015	0.396
1400	0.201	0.398	0.006	0.005	0.390
1500	0.203	0.405	0.003	0.002	0.387

At the higher temperatures the values of ε_a and ε_b are approaching their upper limiting values of 0.5 and 1.0, indicating that reactions (a) and (b) are proceeding nearly to completion. In this limit, which is approached even more closely at still higher temperatures, the mole fractions of CO_2 and H_2O approach zero, and for the product species,

$$y_{H_2} = \frac{1}{3.38 + 0.5 + 1.0} = 0.205$$

$$y_{CO} = \frac{1 + 1}{3.38 + 0.5 + 1.0} = 0.410$$

$$y_{N_2} = \frac{1.88}{3.38 + 0.5 + 1.0} = 0.385$$

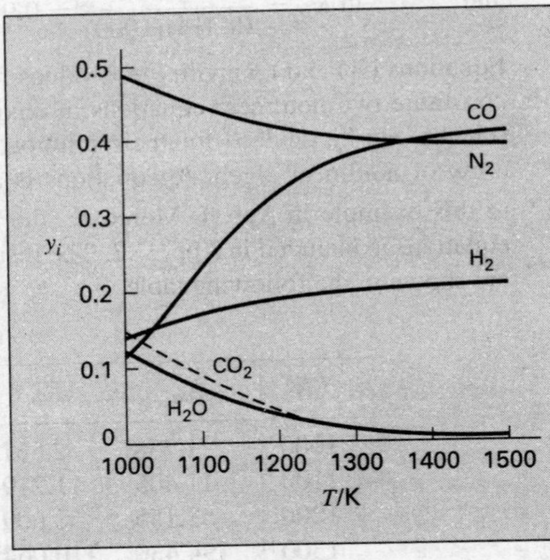

Figure 13.5: Equilibrium compositions of the product gases in Ex. 13.13

We have here assumed a sufficient depth of coal so that the gases reach equilibrium while in contact with incandescent carbon. This need not be the case; if oxygen and steam are supplied at too high a rate, the reactions may not attain equilibrium or may reach equilibrium after they have left the coal bed. In this event, carbon is not present at equilibrium, and the problem must again be reformulated.

Although the Eqs. (*A*) and (*B*) of the preceding example are readily solved, the method of equilibrium constants does not lend itself to standardization so as to allow a *general* program to be written for computer solution. An alternative criterion of equilibrium, mentioned in Sec. 13.2, is based on the fact that at equilibrium the total Gibbs energy of the system has its minimum value, as illustrated for a single reaction in Fig. 13.1. Applied to multiple reactions, this criterion is the basis for a general scheme of computer solution.

The total Gibbs energy of a single-phase system as given by Eq. (11.2) shows that:

$$(G^t)_{T,P} = g(n_1, n_2, n_3, \ldots, n_N)$$

The problem is to find the set $\{n_i\}$ which minimizes G^t for specified T and P, subject to the constraints of the material balances. The standard solution to this problem is based on the method of Lagrange's undetermined multipliers. The procedure for gas-phase reactions is described as follows.

1. The first step is to formulate the constraining equations, i.e., the material balances. Although reacting molecular species are not conserved in a closed system, the total number of atoms of each *element* is constant. Let subscript k identify a particular atom. Then define A_k as the total number of atomic masses of the kth element in the system, as determined by the initial constitution of the system. Further, let a_{ik} be the number of atoms of the kth element present in each molecule of chemical species i. The material balance on each element k may then be written:

$$\boxed{\sum_i n_i a_{ik} = A_k \qquad (k = 1, 2, \ldots, w)} \tag{13.41}$$

or

$$\sum_i n_i a_{ik} - A_k = 0 \qquad (k = 1, 2, \ldots, w)$$

where w is the total number of elements comprising the system.

2. Next, we introduce the Lagrange multipliers λ_k, one for each element, by multiplying each element balance by its λ_k:

$$\lambda_k \left(\sum_i n_i a_{ik} - A_k \right) = 0 \qquad (k = 1, 2, \ldots, w)$$

These equations are summed over k, giving

$$\sum_k \lambda_k \left(\sum_i n_i a_{ik} - A_k \right) = 0$$

3. Then a new function F is formed by addition of this last sum to G^t. Thus,

$$F = G^t + \sum_k \lambda_k \left(\sum_i n_i a_{ik} - A_k \right)$$

This new function is identical with G^t, because the summation term is zero. However, the partial derivatives of F and G^t with respect to n_i are different, because the function F incorporates the constraints of the material balances.

4. The minimum value F (and G^t) occurs when all of the partial derivatives $(\partial F/\partial n_i)_{T,P,n_j}$ are zero. We therefore differentiate the preceding equation, and set the resulting derivative equal to zero:

$$\left(\frac{\partial F}{\partial n_i}\right)_{T,P,n_j} = \left(\frac{\partial G^t}{\partial n_i}\right)_{T,P,n_j} + \sum_k \lambda_k a_{ik} = 0 \qquad (i = 1, 2, \ldots, N)$$

Because the first term on the right is the definition of the chemical potential [see Eq. (11.1)], this equation can be written as

$$\mu_i + \sum_k \lambda_k a_{ik} = 0 \qquad (i = 1, 2, \ldots, N) \tag{13.42}$$

However, the chemical potential is given by Eq. (13.9):

$$\mu_i = G_i^\circ + RT \ln(\hat{f}_i / f_i^\circ)$$

For gas-phase reactions and standard states as the pure ideal gases at 1 bar [or 1(atm)]:

$$\mu_i = G_i^\circ + RT \ln(\hat{f}_i / P^\circ)$$

If G_i° is arbitrarily set equal to zero for all *elements* in their standard states, then for compounds $G_i^\circ = \Delta G_{f_i}^\circ$, the standard Gibbs-energy change of formation for species i. In addition, the fugacity is eliminated in favor of the fugacity coefficient by Eq. (11.52), $\hat{f}_i = y_i \hat{\phi}_i P$. With these substitutions, the equation for μ_i becomes

$$\mu_i = \Delta G_{f_i}^\circ + RT \ln(y_i \hat{\phi}_i P / P^\circ)$$

Combination with Eq. (13.42) gives:

$$\boxed{\Delta G_{f_i}^\circ + RT \ln(y_i \hat{\phi}_i P / P^\circ) + \sum_k \lambda_k a_{ik} = 0 \qquad (i = 1, 2, \ldots, N)} \tag{13.43}$$

Note that P° is 1 bar, expressed in the units used for pressure. If species i is an element, $\Delta G_{f_i}^\circ$ is zero.

Equation (13.43) represents N equilibrium equations, one for each chemical species, and Eq. (13.41) represents w material-balance equations, one for each element— a total of $N + w$ equations. The unknowns are the n_i (note that $y_i = n_i / \sum_i n_i$), of which there are N, and the λ_k's, of which there are w— a total of $N + w$ unknowns. Thus the number of equations is sufficient for the determination of all unknowns.

The foregoing discussion has presumed that each $\hat{\phi}_i$ is known. If the phase is an ideal gas, then for each species $\hat{\phi}_i = 1$. If the phase is an ideal solution, $\hat{\phi}_i = \phi_i$, and values can at least be estimated. For real gases, $\hat{\phi}_i$ is a function of the set $\{y_i\}$, which is being calculated. Thus an iterative procedure is indicated. The calculations are initiated with $\hat{\phi}_i = 1$ for all i. Solution of the equations then provides a preliminary set of $\{y_i\}$. For low pressures or high temperatures this result is usually adequate. Where it is not satisfactory, an equation of state is used together with the calculated $\{y_i\}$ to give a new and more nearly correct set $\{\hat{\phi}_i\}$ for use in Eq. (13.43). Then a new set $\{y_i\}$ is determined. The process is repeated until successive iterations produce no significant change in $\{y_i\}$. All calculations are well suited to computer solution, including the calculation of $\{\hat{\phi}_i\}$ by equations such as Eq. (11.64).

In the procedure just described, the question of what chemical reactions are involved never enters directly into any of the equations. However, the choice of a set of species is entirely equivalent to the choice of a set of independent reactions among the species. In any event, a set of species or an equivalent set of independent reactions must always be assumed, and different assumptions produce different results.

Example 13.14

Calculate the equilibrium compositions at 1000 K and 1 bar of a gas-phase system containing the species CH_4, H_2O, CO, CO_2, and H_2. In the initial unreacted state there are present 2 mol of CH_4 and 3 mol of H_2O. Values of $\Delta G^\circ_{f_i}$ at 1000 K are

$$\Delta G^\circ_{f_{CH_4}} = 19\,720 \text{ J mol}^{-1} \qquad \Delta G^\circ_{f_{H_2O}} = -192\,420 \text{ J mol}^{-1}$$

$$\Delta G^\circ_{f_{CO}} = -200\,240 \text{ J mol}^{-1} \qquad \Delta G^\circ_{f_{CO_2}} = -395\,790 \text{ J mol}^{-1}$$

Solution

The required values of A_k are determined from the initial numbers of moles, and the values of a_{ik} come directly from the chemical formulas of the species. These are shown in the following table.

	Element k		
	Carbon	Oxygen	Hydrogen
	A_k = no. of atomic masses of k in the system		
	$A_C = 2$	$A_O = 3$	$A_H = 14$
Species i	a_{ik} = no. of atoms of k per molecule of i		
CH_4	$a_{CH_4,C} = 1$	$a_{CH_4,O} = 0$	$a_{CH_4,H} = 4$
H_2O	$a_{H_2O,C} = 0$	$a_{H_2O,O} = 1$	$a_{H_2O,H} = 2$
CO	$a_{CO,C} = 1$	$a_{CO,O} = 1$	$a_{CO,H} = 0$
CO_2	$a_{CO_2,C} = 1$	$a_{CO_2,O} = 2$	$a_{CO_2,H} = 0$
H_2	$a_{H_2,C} = 0$	$a_{H_2,O} = 0$	$a_{H_2,H} = 2$

At 1 bar and 1000 K the assumption of ideal gases is justified, and each $\hat{\phi}_i$ is unity. Because $P = 1$ bar, $P/P^\circ = 1$, and Eq. (13.43) is written as

$$\frac{\Delta G^\circ_{f_i}}{RT} + \ln \frac{n_i}{\sum_i n_i} + \sum_k \frac{\lambda_k}{RT} a_{ik} = 0$$

The five equations for the five species then become

$$\mathrm{CH_4}: \quad \frac{19\,720}{RT} + \ln\frac{n_{\mathrm{CH_4}}}{\sum_i n_i} + \frac{\lambda_{\mathrm{C}}}{RT} + \frac{4\lambda_{\mathrm{H}}}{RT} = 0$$

$$\mathrm{H_2O}: \quad \frac{-192\,420}{RT} + \ln\frac{n_{\mathrm{H_2O}}}{\sum_i n_i} + \frac{2\lambda_{\mathrm{H}}}{RT} + \frac{\lambda_{\mathrm{O}}}{RT} = 0$$

$$\mathrm{CO}: \quad \frac{-200\,240}{RT} + \ln\frac{n_{\mathrm{CO}}}{\sum_i n_i} + \frac{\lambda_{\mathrm{C}}}{RT} + \frac{\lambda_{\mathrm{O}}}{RT} = 0$$

$$\mathrm{CO_2}: \quad \frac{-395\,790}{RT} + \ln\frac{n_{\mathrm{CO_2}}}{\sum_i n_i} + \frac{\lambda_{\mathrm{C}}}{RT} + \frac{2\lambda_{\mathrm{O}}}{RT} = 0$$

$$\mathrm{H_2}: \quad \ln\frac{n_{\mathrm{H_2}}}{\sum_i n_i} + \frac{2\lambda_{\mathrm{H}}}{RT} = 0$$

The three atom-balance equations [Eq. (13.41)] and the equation for $\sum_i n_i$ are

$$\mathrm{C}: \quad n_{\mathrm{CH_4}} + n_{\mathrm{CO}} + n_{\mathrm{CO_2}} = 2$$

$$\mathrm{H}: \quad 4n_{\mathrm{CH_4}} + 2n_{\mathrm{H_2O}} + 2n_{\mathrm{H_2}} = 14$$

$$\mathrm{O}: \quad n_{\mathrm{H_2O}} + n_{\mathrm{CO}} + 2n_{\mathrm{CO_2}} = 3$$

$$\sum_i n_i = n_{\mathrm{CH_4}} + n_{\mathrm{H_2O}} + n_{\mathrm{CO}} + n_{\mathrm{CO_2}} + n_{\mathrm{H_2}}$$

With $RT = 8314\ \mathrm{J\ mol^{-1}}$, simultaneous computer solution of these nine equations[9] produces the following results ($y_i = n_i / \sum_i n_i$):

$$y_{\mathrm{CH_4}} = 0.0196 \qquad \frac{\lambda_{\mathrm{C}}}{RT} = 0.7635$$

$$y_{\mathrm{H_2O}} = 0.0980$$

$$y_{\mathrm{CO}} = 0.1743 \qquad \frac{\lambda_{\mathrm{O}}}{RT} = 25.068$$

$$y_{\mathrm{CO_2}} = 0.0371$$

$$y_{\mathrm{H_2}} = 0.6710 \qquad \frac{\lambda_{\mathrm{H}}}{RT} = 0.1994$$

$$\sum_i y_i = 1.0000$$

The values of λ_k / RT are of no significance, but are included for completeness.

---

[9]The Mathcad® formulation of this problem is given in App. D.2.

13.10 FUEL CELLS

A fuel cell, similar in some respects to an electrolytic cell or battery, is a device in which a fuel is oxidized electrochemically to produce electric power. It has the characteristics of a battery in that it consists of two electrodes, separated by an electrolyte. However, the reactants are not stored in the cell, but are fed to it continuously, and the products of reaction are continuously withdrawn. The fuel cell is thus not given an initial electric charge, and in operation it does not lose electric charge. It operates as a continuous-flow system as long as fuel and oxygen are supplied, and produces a steady electric current.

A fuel, e.g., hydrogen, methane, butane, methanol, etc., makes intimate contact with an anode or fuel electrode, and oxygen (usually in air) makes intimate contact with a cathode or oxygen electrode. Half-cell reactions occur at each electrode, and their sum is the overall reaction. Several types of fuel cell exist, each characterized by a particular type of electrolyte.[10]

Cells operating with hydrogen as the fuel are the simplest such devices, and serve to illustrate basic principles. Schematic diagrams of hydrogen/oxygen cells appear in Fig. 13.6. When the electrolyte is acidic [Fig. 13.6(*a*)], the half-cell reaction occurring at the hydrogen electrode (anode) is

$$\mathrm{H_2} \rightarrow 2\,\mathrm{H^+} + 2e^-$$

and that at the oxygen electrode (cathode) is

$$\tfrac{1}{2}\mathrm{O_2} + 2e^- + 2\,\mathrm{H^+} \rightarrow \mathrm{H_2O}(g)$$

When the electrolyte is alkaline [Fig. 13.6(*b*)], the half-cell reaction at the anode is

$$\mathrm{H_2} + 2\,\mathrm{OH^-} \rightarrow 2\,\mathrm{H_2O}(g) + 2e^-$$

and at the cathode:

$$\tfrac{1}{2}\mathrm{O_2} + 2e^- + \mathrm{H_2O}(g) \rightarrow 2\,\mathrm{OH^-}$$

In either case, the sum of the half-cell reactions is the overall reaction of the cell:

$$\mathrm{H_2} + \tfrac{1}{2}\mathrm{O_2} \rightarrow \mathrm{H_2O}(g)$$

This of course is the *combustion reaction* of hydrogen, but combustion in the sense of burning does not occur in the cell.

In both cells electrons with negative charge (e^-) are released at the anode, produce an electric current in an external circuit, and are taken up by the reaction occurring at the cathode. The electrolyte does not allow passage of electrons, but provides a path for migration of an ion from one electrode to the other. With an acid electrolyte cation $\mathrm{H^+}$ migrates from anode to cathode, whereas with an alkaline electrolyte anion $\mathrm{OH^-}$ migrates from cathode to anode.

For many practical applications the most satisfactory hydrogen/oxygen fuel cell is built around a solid polymer that serves as an acid electrolyte. Because it is very thin and conducts $\mathrm{H^+}$ ions or protons, it is known as a proton-exchange membrane. Each side of the membrane is bonded to a porous carbon electrode impregnated with finely divided platinum which serves

[10]Construction details of the various types of fuel cells and extensive explanations of their operation are given by J. Larminie and A. Dicks, *Fuel Cell Systems Explained*, John Wiley & Sons, Ltd., Chichester, England, 2000.

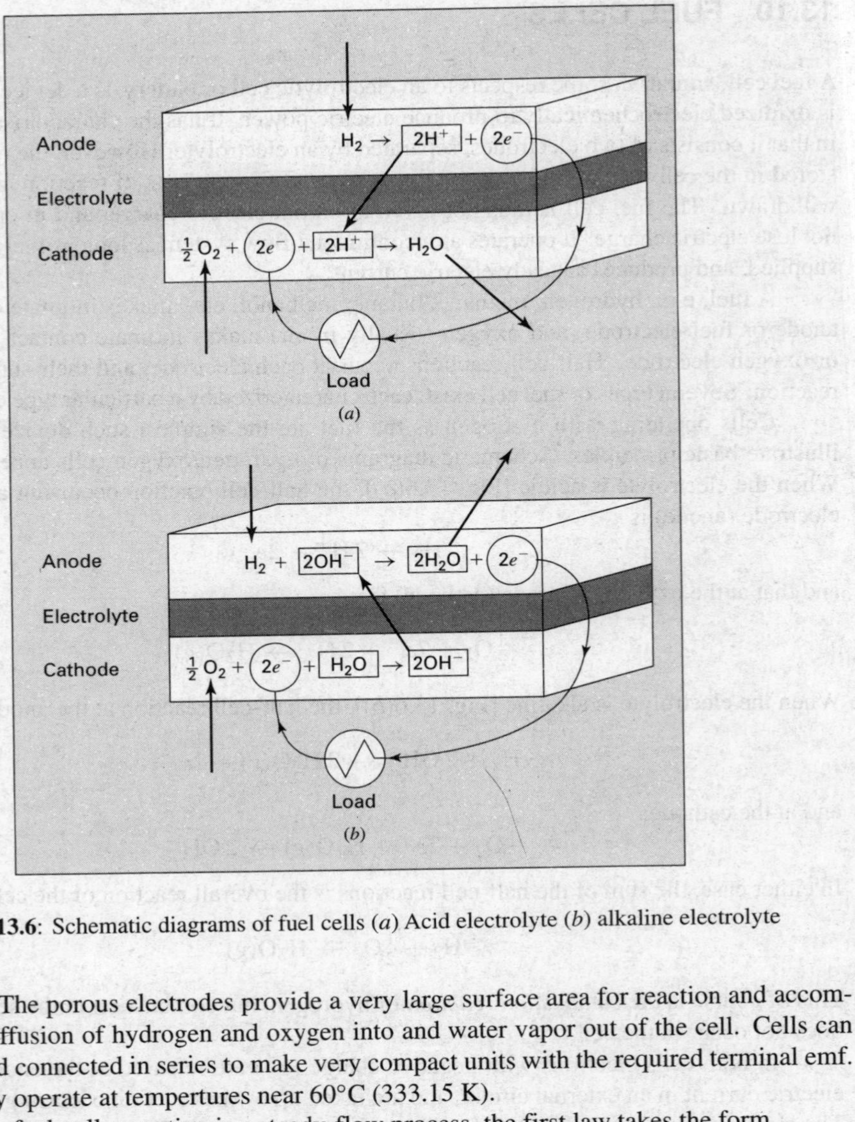

Figure 13.6: Schematic diagrams of fuel cells (*a*) Acid electrolyte (*b*) alkaline electrolyte

as a catalyst. The porous electrodes provide a very large surface area for reaction and accommodate the diffusion of hydrogen and oxygen into and water vapor out of the cell. Cells can be stacked and connected in series to make very compact units with the required terminal emf. They typically operate at tempertures near 60°C (333.15 K).

Because fuel-cell operation is a steady-flow process, the first law takes the form

$$\Delta H = Q + W_{\text{elect}}$$

where potential- and kinetic-energy terms are omitted as negligible and shaft work has been replaced by electrical work. If the cell operates *reversibly and isothermally*,

$$Q = T\,\Delta S \qquad \text{and} \qquad \Delta H = T\,\Delta S + W_{\text{elect}}$$

The electrical work of a reversible cell is therefore

$$W_{\text{elect}} = \Delta H - T\,\Delta S = \Delta G \tag{13.44}$$

where Δ denotes a property change of reaction. The heat transfer to the surroundings required for isothermal operation is

$$Q = \Delta H - \Delta G \tag{13.45}$$

With reference to Fig. 13.6(*a*), we note that for each molecule of hydrogen consumed, 2 electrons pass to the external circuit. On the basis of 1 mol of H_2, the charge (q) transferred between electrodes is

$$q = 2N_A(-e) \text{ coulomb}$$

where $-e$ is the charge on each electron and N_A is Avogadro's number. Because the product $N_A e$ is Faraday's constant $\mathcal{F}$, $q = -2\mathcal{F}$.[11] The electrical work is then the product of the charge transferred and the emf (E volt) of the cell:

$$W_{\text{elect}} = -2\mathcal{F}E \text{ joule}$$

The emf of a reversible cell is therefore

$$E = \frac{-W_{\text{elect}}}{2\mathcal{F}} = \frac{-\Delta G}{2\mathcal{F}} \tag{13.46}$$

These equations may be applied to a hydrogen/oxygen fuel cell operating at 25°C (298.15 K) and 1 bar with pure H_2 and pure O_2 as reactants and pure H_2O vapor as product. If these species are assumed ideal gases, then the reaction occurring is the standard formation reaction for $H_2O(g)$ at 298.15 K, for which values from Table C.4 are

$$\Delta H = \Delta H^\circ_{f_{298}} = -241\,818 \text{ J mol}^{-1} \qquad \text{and} \qquad \Delta G = \Delta G^\circ_{f_{298}} = -228\,572 \text{ J mol}^{-1}$$

Equations (13.44) through (13.46) then yield

$$W_{\text{elect}} = -228\,572 \text{ J mol}^{-1} \qquad Q = -13\,246 \text{ J mol}^{-1} \qquad E = 1.184 \text{ volts}$$

If, as is more commonly the case, air is the source of oxygen, the cell receives O_2 at its partial pressure in air. Because the enthalpy of ideal gases is independent of pressure, the enthalpy change of reaction for the cell is unchanged. However, the Gibbs-energy change of reaction is affected. By Eq. (11.24),

$$G_i^{ig} - \bar{G}_i^{ig} = -RT \ln y_i$$

Therefore, on the basis of 1 mol of H_2O formed,

$$\begin{aligned}\Delta G &= \Delta G^\circ_{f_{298}} + (0.5)(G^{ig}_{O_2} - \bar{G}^{ig}_{O_2}) \\ &= \Delta G^\circ_{f_{298}} - 0.5RT \ln y_{O_2} \\ &= -228\,572 - (0.5)(8.314)(298.15)(\ln 0.21) = -226\,638\end{aligned}$$

Equations (13.44) through (13.46) now yield

$$W_{\text{elect}} = -226\,638 \text{ J mol}^{-1} \qquad Q = -15\,180 \text{ J mol}^{-1} \qquad E = 1.174 \text{ volts}$$

[11] Faraday's constant is equal to 96 485 coulomb mol^{-1}.

The use of air rather than pure oxygen does not significantly reduce the emf and work output of a reversible cell.

The enthalpy and Gibbs-energy changes of reaction are given as functions of temperature by Eqs. (4.18) and (13.18). For a cell temperature of 60°C (333.15 K), the integrals in these equations are evaluated as

$$\int_{298.15}^{333.15} \frac{\Delta C_P^\circ}{R} dT = \text{IDCPH(298.15,333.15;-1.5985,0.775E-3,0.0,0.1515E+5)}$$

$$= -42.0472$$

$$\int_{298.15}^{333.15} \frac{\Delta C_P^\circ}{R} \frac{dT}{T} = \text{IDCPS(298.15,333.15;-1.5985,0.775E-3,0.0,0.1515E+5)}$$

$$= -0.13334$$

Equations (4.18) and (13.18) then yield

$$\Delta H_{f_{333}}^\circ = -242\ 168 \text{ J mol}^{-1} \qquad \text{and} \qquad \Delta G_{f_{333}}^\circ = -226\ 997 \text{ J mol}^{-1}$$

With cell operation at 1 bar and oxygen extracted from air, $\Delta H = \Delta H_{f_{333}}^\circ$, and

$$\Delta G = -226\ 997 - (0.5)(8.314)(333.15)(\ln 0.21) = -224\ 836 \text{ J mol}^{-1}$$

Equations (13.44) through (13.46) now yield

$$W_{\text{elect}} = -224\ 836 \text{ J mol}^{-1} \qquad Q = -17\ 332 \text{ J mol}^{-1} \qquad E = 1.165 \text{ volts}$$

Thus cell operation at 60°C (333.15 K) rather than at 25°C (298.15 K) reduces the voltage and work output of a reversible cell by only a small amount.

These calculations for a reversible cell show that the electrical work output is more than 90% of the heat that would be released (ΔH) by actual combustion of the fuel. Were this heat supplied to a Carnot engine operating at practical temperature levels, a much smaller fraction would be converted into work. The reversible operation of a fuel cell implies that a potentiometer exactly balances its emf, with the result that its current output is negligible. In actual operation under reasonable load, internal irreversibilities inevitably reduce the emf of the cell and decrease its production of electrical work, while increasing the amount of heat transfer to the surroundings. The operating emf of hydrogen/oxygen fuel cells is 0.6–0.7 volts, and its work output is closer to 50% of the heating value of the fuel. Nevertheless, the irreversibilities of a fuel cell are far less than those inherent in combustion of the fuel. It has the additional advantages of simplicity, of clean and quiet operation, and of directly producing electrical energy. Fuels other than hydrogen may well be appropriate for fuel-cell use, but require development of effective catalysts. Methanol, for example, reacts at the anode of a proton-exchange membrane fuel cell according to the equation

$$CH_3OH + H_2O \rightarrow 6H^+ + 6e^- + CO_2$$

The usual reaction of oxygen to form water vapor occurs at the cathode.

PROBLEMS

13.1. Develop expressions for the mole fractions of reacting species as functions of the reaction coordinate for

(*a*) A system initially containing 2 mol NH_3 and 5 mol O_2 and undergoing the reaction

$$4NH_3(g) + 5O_2(g) \rightarrow 4NO(g) + 6H_2O(g)$$

(*b*) A system initially containing 3 mol H_2S and 5 mol O_2 and undergoing the reaction

$$2H_2S(g) + 3O_2(g) \rightarrow 2H_2O(g) + 2SO_2(g)$$

(*c*) A system initially containing 3 mol NO_2, 4 mol NH_3, and 1 mol N_2 and undergoing the reaction

$$6NO_2(g) + 8NH_3(g) \rightarrow 7N_2(g) + 12H_2O(g)$$

13.2. A system initially containing 2 mol C_2H_4 and 3 mol O_2 undergoes the reactions

$$C_2H_4(g) + \tfrac{1}{2}O_2(g) \rightarrow \langle(CH_2)_2\rangle O(g)$$

$$C_2H_4(g) + 3O_2(g) \rightarrow 2CO_2(g) + 2H_2O(g)$$

Develop expressions for the mole fractions of the reacting species as functions of the reaction coordinates for the two reactions.

13.3. A system formed initially of 2 mol CO_2, 5 mol H_2, and 1 mol CO undergoes the reactions

$$CO_2(g) + 3H_2(g) \rightarrow CH_3OH(g) + H_2O(g)$$

$$CO_2(g) + H_2(g) \rightarrow CO(g) + H_2O(g)$$

Develop expressions for the mole fractions of the reacting species as functions of the reaction coordinates for the two reactions.

13.4. Consider the water-gas-shift reaction:

$$H_2(g) + CO_2(g) \rightarrow H_2O(g) + CO(g)$$

At high temperatures and low to moderate pressures the reacting species form an ideal-gas mixture. By Eq. (11.27)

$$G = \sum_i y_i G_i + RT \sum_i y_i \ln y_i$$

When the Gibbs energies of the elements in their standard states are set equal to zero, $G_i = \Delta G^\circ_{f_i}$ for each species, and then

$$G = \sum_i y_i \, \Delta G^\circ_{f_i} + RT \sum_i y_i \ln y_i \qquad (A)$$

At the beginning of Sec. 13.2 we noted that Eq. (14.68) is a criterion of equilibrium. Applied to the water-gas-shift reaction with the understanding that T and P are constant, this equation becomes

$$dG^t = d(nG) = n\,dG + G\,dn = 0 \qquad n\frac{dG}{d\varepsilon} + G\frac{dn}{d\varepsilon} = 0$$

Here, however, $dn/d\varepsilon = 0$. The equilibrium criterion therefore becomes

$$\frac{dG}{d\varepsilon} = 0 \tag{B}$$

Once the y_i are eliminated in favor of ε, Eq. (A) relates G to ε. Data for $\Delta G^\circ_{f_i}$ for the compounds of interest are given with Ex. 13.13. For a temperature of 1000 K (the reaction is unaffected by P) and for a feed of 1 mol H_2 and 1 mol CO_2:

(a) Determine the equilibrium value of ε by application of Eq. (B).

(b) Plot G vs. ε, indicating the location of the equilibrium value of ε determined in (a).

13.5. Rework Pb. 13.4 for a temperature of

(a) 1100 K (b) 1200 K (c) 1300 K

13.6. Use the method of equilibrium constants to verify the value of ε found as an answer in one of the following:

(a) Pb. 13.4 (b) Pb. 13.5(a) (c) Pb. 13.5(b) (d) Pb. 13.5(c)

13.7. Develop a general equation for the standard Gibbs-energy change of reaction ΔG° as a function of temperature for one of the reactions given in parts (a), (f), (i), (n), (r), (t), (u), (x), and (y) of Pb. 4.21.

13.8. For ideal gases, exact mathematical expressions can be developed for the effect of T and P on ε_e. For conciseness, let $\prod_i (y_i)^{\nu_i} \equiv K_y$. Then

$$\left(\frac{\partial \varepsilon_e}{\partial T}\right)_P = \left(\frac{\partial K_y}{\partial T}\right)_P \frac{d\varepsilon_e}{dK_y} \quad \text{and} \quad \left(\frac{\partial \varepsilon_e}{\partial P}\right)_T = \left(\frac{\partial K_y}{\partial P}\right)_T \frac{d\varepsilon_e}{dK_y}$$

Use Eqs. (13.28) and (13.14), to show that

(a) $$\left(\frac{\partial \varepsilon_e}{\partial T}\right)_P = \frac{K_y}{RT^2}\frac{d\varepsilon_e}{dK_y}\Delta H^\circ$$

(b) $$\left(\frac{\partial \varepsilon_e}{\partial P}\right)_T = \frac{K_y}{P}\frac{d\varepsilon_e}{dK_y}(-\nu)$$

(c) $d\varepsilon_e/dK_y$ is always positive. (*Note*: It is equally valid and perhaps easier to show that the reciprocal is positive.)

13.9. For the ammonia synthesis reaction written as

$$\tfrac{1}{2}N_2(g) + \tfrac{3}{2}H_2(g) \rightarrow NH_3(g)$$

with 0.5 mol N_2 and 1.5 mol H_2 as the initial amounts of reactants and with the assumption that the equilibrium mixture is an ideal gas, show that

$$\varepsilon_e = 1 - \left(1 + 1.299K\frac{P}{P^\circ}\right)^{-1/2}$$

13.10. Peter, Paul, and Mary, members of a thermodynamics class, are asked to find the equilibrium composition at a particular T and P and for given initial amounts of reactants for the following gas-phase reaction:

$$2NH_3 + 3NO \rightarrow 3H_2O + \tfrac{5}{2}N_2 \qquad (A)$$

Each solves the problem correctly in a different way. Mary bases her solution on reaction (A) as written. Paul, who prefers whole numbers, multiplies reaction (A) by 2:

$$4NH_3 + 6NO \rightarrow 6H_2O + 5N_2 \qquad (B)$$

Peter, who usually does things backward, deals with the reaction

$$3H_2O + \tfrac{5}{2}N_2 \rightarrow 2NH_3 + 3NO \qquad (C)$$

Write the chemical-equilibrium equations for the three reactions, indicate how the equilibrium constants are related, and show why Peter, Paul, and Mary all obtain the same result.

13.11. The following reaction reaches equilibrium at 500°C (773.15 K) and 2 bar:

$$4HCl(g) + O_2(g) \rightarrow 2H_2O(g) + 2Cl_2(g)$$

If the system initially contains 5 mol HCl for each mole of oxygen, what is the composition of the system at equilibrium? Assume ideal gases.

13.12. The following reaction reaches equilibrium at 650°C (923.15 K) and atmospheric pressure:

$$N_2(g) + C_2H_2(g) \rightarrow 2HCN(g)$$

If the system initially is an equimolar mixture of nitrogen and acetylene, what is the composition of the system at equilibrium? What would be the effect of doubling the pressure? Assume ideal gases.

13.13. The following reaction reaches equilibrium at 350°C (623.15 K) and 3 bar:

$$CH_3CHO(g) + H_2(g) \rightarrow C_2H_5OH(g)$$

If the system initially contains 1.5 mol H_2 for each mole of acetaldehyde, what is the composition of the system at equilibrium? What would be the effect of reducing the pressure to 1 bar? Assume ideal gases.

13.14. The following reaction reaches equilibrium at 650°C (923.15 K) and atmospheric pressure:

$$C_6H_5CH{:}CH_2(g) + H_2(g) \rightarrow C_6H_5.C_2H_5(g)$$

If the system initially contains 1.5 mol H_2 for each mole of styrene, what is the composition of the system at equilibrium? Assume ideal gases.

13.15. The gas stream from a sulfur burner is composed of 15 mole % SO_2, 20 mole % O_2, and 65 mole % N_2. This gas stream at 1 bar and 480°C (753.15 K) enters a catalytic converter, where the SO_2 is further oxidized to SO_3. Assuming that the reaction reaches equilibrium, how much heat must be removed from the converter to maintain isothermal conditions? Base your answer on 1 mol of entering gas.

13.16. For the cracking reaction,

$$C_3H_8(g) \rightarrow C_2H_4(g) + CH_4(g)$$

the equilibrium conversion is negligible at 300 K, but becomes appreciable at temperatures above 500 K. For a pressure of 1 bar, determine the

(*a*) fractional conversion of propane at 625 K
(*b*) temperature at which the fractional conversion is 85%

13.17. Ethylene is produced by the dehydrogenation of ethane. If the feed includes 0.5 mol of steam (an inert diluent) per mole of ethane and if the reaction reaches equilibrium at 1100 K and 1 bar, what is the composition of the product gas on a water-free basis?

13.18. The production of 1,3-butadiene can be carried out by the dehydrogenation of 1-butene:

$$C_2H_5CH{:}CH_2(g) \rightarrow CH_2{:}CHCH{:}CH_2(g) + H_2(g)$$

Side reactions are suppressed by the introduction of steam. If equilibrium is attained at 950 K and 1 bar and if the reactor product contains 10 mole % 1,3-butadiene, find the

(*a*) mole fractions of the other species in the product gas
(*b*) mole fraction of steam required in the feed

13.19. The production of 1,3-butadiene can be carried out by the dehydrogenation of *n*-butane:

$$C_4H_{10}(g) \rightarrow CH_2{:}CHCH{:}CH_2(g) + 2H_2(g)$$

Side reactions are suppressed by the introduction of steam. If equilibrium is attained at 925 K and 1 bar and if the reactor product contains 12 mole % 1,3-butadiene, find the

(*a*) mole fractions of the other species in the product gas
(*b*) mole fraction of steam required in the feed

13.20. For the ammonia synthesis reaction,

$$\tfrac{1}{2}N_2(g) + \tfrac{3}{2}H_2(g) \rightarrow NH_3(g)$$

the equilibrium conversion to ammonia is large at 300 K, but decreases rapidly with increasing T. However, reaction rates become appreciable only at higher temperatures. For a feed mixture of hydrogen and nitrogen in the stoichiometric proportions,

(*a*) What is the equilibrium mole fraction of ammonia at 1 bar and 300 K?
(*b*) At what temperature does the equilibrium mole fraction of ammonia equal 0.50 for a pressure of 1 bar?
(*c*) At what temperature does the equilibrium mole fraction of ammonia equal 0.50 for a pressure of 100 bar, assuming the equilibrium mixture is an ideal gas?
(*d*) At what temperature does the equilibrium mole fraction of ammonia equal 0.50 for a pressure of 100 bar, assuming the equilibrium mixture is an ideal solution of gases?

13.21. For the methanol synthesis reaction,

$$CO(g) + 2H_2(g) \rightarrow CH_3OH(g)$$

the equilibrium conversion to methanol is large at 300 K, but decreases rapidly with increasing T. However, reaction rates become appreciable only at higher temperatures. For a feed mixture of carbon monoxide and hydrogen in the stoichiometric proportions,

(*a*) What is the equilibrium mole fraction of methanol at 1 bar and 300 K.
(*b*) At what temperature does the equilibrium mole fraction of methanol equal 0.50 for a pressure of 1 bar?
(*c*) At what temperature does the equilibrium mole fraction of methanol equal 0.50 for a pressure of 100 bar, assuming the equilibrium mixture is an ideal gas?
(*d*) At what temperature does the equilibrium mole fraction of methanol equal 0.50 for a pressure of 100 bar, assuming the equilibrium mixture is an ideal solution of gases?

13.22. Limestone ($CaCO_3$) decomposes upon heating to yield quicklime (CaO) and carbon dioxide. At what temperature is the decomposition pressure of limestone 1 atm?

13.23. Ammonium chloride [$NH_4Cl(s)$] decomposes upon heating to yield a gas mixture of ammonia and hydrochloric acid. At what temperature does ammonium chloride exert a decomposition pressure of 1.5 bar? For $NH_4Cl(s)$, $\Delta H^\circ_{f_{298}} = -314\ 430$ J and $\Delta G^\circ_{f_{298}} = -202\ 870$ J.

13.24. A chemically reactive system contains the following species in the gas phase: NH_3, NO, NO_2, O_2, and H_2O. Determine a complete set of independent reactions for this system. How many degrees of freedom does the system have?

13.25. The relative compositions of the pollutants NO and NO_2 in air are governed by the reaction,

$$NO + \frac{1}{2}O_2 \rightarrow NO_2$$

For air containing 21 mole % O_2 at 25°C (298.15 K) and 1.0133 bar, what is the concentration of NO in parts per million if the total concentration of the two nitrogen oxides is 5 ppm?

13.26. Consider the gas-phase oxidation of ethylene to ethylene oxide at a pressure of 1 bar with 25% excess air. If the reactants enter the process at 25°C (298.15 K), if the reaction proceeds adiabatically to equilibrium, and if there are no side reactions, determine the composition and temperature of the product stream from the reactor.

13.27. Carbon black is produced by the decomposition of methane:

$$CH_4(g) \rightarrow C(s) + 2H_2(g)$$

For equilibrium at 650°C (923.15 K) and 1 bar,

(*a*) What is the gas-phase composition if pure methane enters the reactor, and what fraction of the methane decomposes?

(*b*) Repeat part (*a*) if the feed is an equimolar mixture of methane and nitrogen.

13.28. Consider the reactions,

$$\frac{1}{2}N_2(g) + \frac{1}{2}O_2(g) \rightarrow NO(g)$$

$$\frac{1}{2}N_2(g) + O_2(g) \rightarrow NO_2(g)$$

If these reactions come to equilibrium after combustion in an internal-combustion engine at 2000 K and 200 bar, estimate the mole fractions of NO and NO_2 present for mole fractions of nitrogen and oxygen in the combustion products of 0.70 and 0.05.

13.29. Oil refineries frequently have both H_2S and SO_2 to dispose of. The following reaction suggests a means of getting rid of both at once:

$$2H_2S(g) + SO_2(g) \rightarrow 3S(s) + 2H_2O(g)$$

For reactants in the stoichiometric proportion, estimate the percent conversion of each reactant if the reaction comes to equilibrium at 450°C (723.15 K) and 8 bar.

13.30. Species N_2O_4 and NO_2 as gases come to equilibrium by the reaction: $N_2O_4 \rightarrow 2NO_2$.

(*a*) For $T = 350$ K and $P = 5$ bar, calculate the mole fractions of these species in the equilibrium mixture. Assume ideal gases.

(*b*) If an equilibrium mixture of N_2O_4 and NO_2 at conditions of part (*a*) flows through a throttle valve to a pressure of 1 bar and through a heat exchanger that restores its initial temperature, how much heat is exchanged, assuming chemical equilibrium is again attained in the final state? Base the answer on an amount of mixture equivalent to 1 mol of N_2O_4, i.e., as though the NO_2 were present as N_2O_4.

13.31. The following isomerization reaction occurs in the *liquid* phase: A → B, where A and B are miscible liquids for which: $G^E/RT = 0.1\,x_A x_B$. If $\Delta G^\circ_{298} = -1000$ J, what is the equilibrium composition of the mixture at 25°C (298.15 K)? How much error is introduced if one assumes that *A* and *B* form an ideal solution?

13.32. Hydrogen gas is produced by the reaction of steam with "water gas," an equimolar mixture of H_2 and CO obtained by the reaction of steam with coal. A stream of "water gas" mixed with steam is passed over a catalyst to convert CO to CO_2 by the reaction:

$$H_2O(g) + CO(g) \rightarrow H_2(g) + CO_2(g)$$

Subsequently, unreacted water is condensed and carbon dioxide is absorbed, leaving a product that is mostly hydrogen. The equilibrium conditions are 1 bar and 800 K.

(*a*) Is any advantage gained by carrying out the reaction at pressures above 1 bar?
(*b*) Would increasing the equilibrium temperature increase the conversion of CO?
(*c*) For the given equilibrium conditions, determine the molar ratio of steam to "water gas" (H_2 + CO) required to produce a *product* gas containing only 2 mole % CO after cooling to 20°C (293.15 K), where the unreacted H_2O has been virtually all condensed.
(*d*) Is there any danger that solid carbon will form at the equilibrium conditions by the reaction

$$2CO(g) \rightarrow CO_2(g) + C(s)$$

13.33. The feed gas to a methanol synthesis reactor is composed of 75 mole % H_2, 15 mole % CO, 5 mole % CO_2, and 5 mole % N_2. The system comes to equilibrium at 550 K and 100 bar with respect to the reactions:

$$2H_2(g) + CO(g) \rightarrow CH_3OH(g) \qquad H_2(g) + CO_2(g) \rightarrow CO(g) + H_2O(g)$$

Assuming ideal gases, determine the composition of the equilibrium mixture.

13.34. "Synthesis gas" may be produced by the catalytic reforming of methane with steam. The reactions are

$$CH_4(g) + H_2O(g) \rightarrow CO(g) + 3H_2(g) \qquad CO(g) + H_2O(g) \rightarrow CO_2(g) + H_2(g)$$

Assume equilibrium is attained for both reactions at 1 bar and 1300 K.

(*a*) Would it be better to carry out the reaction at pressures above 1 bar?
(*b*) Would it be better to carry out the reaction at temperatures below 1300 K?
(*c*) Estimate the molar ratio of hydrogen to carbon monoxide in the synthesis gas if the feed consists of an equimolar mixture of steam and methane.
(*d*) Repeat part (*c*) for a steam to methane mole ratio in the feed of 2.
(*e*) How could the feed composition be altered to yield a lower ratio of hydrogen to carbon monoxide in the synthesis gas than is obtained in part (*c*)?
(*f*) Is there any danger that carbon will deposit by the reaction 2CO → C+CO_2 under conditions of part (*c*)? Part (d)? If so, how could the feed be altered to prevent carbon deposition?

13.35. Consider the gas-phase isomerization reaction: A→B.

(*a*) Assuming ideal gases, develop from Eq. (13.28) the chemical-reaction equilibrium equation for the system.

(*b*) The result of part (*a*) should suggest that there is *one* degree of freedom for the equilibrium state. Upon verifying that the phase rule indicates *two* degrees of freedom, explain the discrepancy.

13.36. A low-pressure, gas-phase isomerization reaction, A→B, occurs at conditions such that vapor and liquid phases are present.

(*a*) Prove that the equilibrium state is univariant.

(*b*) Suppose T is specified. Show how to calculate x_A, y_A, and P. State carefully, and justify, any assumptions.

13.37. Set up the equations required for solution of Ex. 13.14 by the method of equilibrium constants. Verify that your equations yield the same equilibrium compositions as given in the example.

13.38. Reaction-equilibrium calculations may be useful for estimation of the compositions of hydrocarbon feedstocks. A particular feedstock, available as a low-pressure gas at 500 K, is identified as "aromatic C8." It could in principle contain the C_8H_{10} isomers: *o*-xylene (OX), *m*-xylene (MX), *p*-xylene (PX), and ethylbenzene (EB). Estimate how much of each species is present, assuming the gas mixture has come to equilibrium at 500 K and low pressure. The following is a set of independent reactions (why?):

OX → MX (I)	OX → PX (II)	OX → EB (III)

(*a*) Write reaction-equilibrium equations for each equation of the set. State clearly any assumptions.

(*b*) Solve the set of equations to obtain algebraic expressions for the equilibrium vapor-phase mole fractions of the four species in relation to the equilibrium constants, K_{I}, K_{II}, K_{III}.

(*c*) Use the data below to determine numerical values for the equilibrium constants at 500 K. State clearly any assumptions.

(*d*) Determine numerical values for the mole fractions of the four species.

Species	$\Delta H^\circ_{f_{298}}$/J mol^{-1}	$\Delta G^\circ_{f_{298}}$/J mol^{-1}
OX(g)	19 000	122 200
MX(g)	17 250	118 900
PX(g)	17 960	121 200
EB(g)	29 920	130 890

13.39. Ethylene oxide as a vapor and water as liquid, both at 25°C (298.15 K) and 101.33 kPa, react to form a liquid solution containing ethylene glycol (1,2-ethanediol) at the same conditions:

$$\langle (CH_2)_2 \rangle O + H_2O \rightarrow CH_2OH.CH_2OH$$

If the initial molar ratio of ethylene oxide to water is 3.0, estimate the equilibrium conversion of ethylene oxide to ethylene glycol.

At equilibrium the system consists of liquid and vapor in equilibrium, and the intensive state of the system is fixed by the specification of T and P. Therefore, one must first determine the phase compositions, independent of the ratio of reactants. These results may then be applied in the material-balance equations to find the equilibrium conversion.

Choose as standard states for water and ethylene glycol the pure liquids at 1 bar and for ethylene oxide the pure ideal gas at 1 bar. Assume any water present in the liquid phase has an activity coefficient of unity and that the vapor phase is an ideal gas. The partial pressure of ethylene oxide over the liquid phase is given by:

$$p_i/\text{kPa} = 415\, x_i$$

The vapor pressure of ethylene glycol at 25°C (298.15 K) is so low that its concentration in the vapor phase is negligible.

13.40. In chemical-reaction engineering special measures of product distribution are sometimes used when multiple reactions occur. Two of these are *yield* Y_j and *selectivity* $S_{j/k}$. We adopt the following definitions[12]:

$$Y_j \equiv \frac{\text{moles formed of desired product } j}{\text{moles of } j \text{ that would be formed with no side reactions and with complete consumption of the limiting reactant species}}$$

$$S_{j/k} \equiv \frac{\text{moles formed of desired product } j}{\text{moles formed of undesired product } k}$$

For any particular application yield and selectivity can be related to component rates and reaction coordinates. For two-reaction schemes the two reaction coordinates can be found from Y_j and $S_{j/k}$, allowing the usual material-balance equations to be written.

Consider the gas-phase reactions:

$$A + B \longrightarrow C \qquad \text{(I)} \qquad\qquad A + C \longrightarrow D \qquad \text{(II)}$$

Here, C is the desired product, and D is the undesired byproduct. If the feed to a steady-flow reactor contains 10 kmol hr^{-1}of A and 15 kmol h^{-1}of B, and if $Y_C = 0.40$ and $S_{C/D} = 2.0$, determine complete product rates and the product composition (mole fractions), using reaction coordinates.

[12] R. M. Felder and R. W. Rousseau, *Elementary Principles of Chemical Processes*, 3rd ed., Sec. 4.6d, Wiley, New York, 2000.

13.41. The following problems involving chemical-reaction stoichiometry are to be solved through use of reaction coordinates.

(*a*) Feed to a gas-phase reactor comprises 50 kmol h^{-1} of species A, and 50 kmol h^{-1} of species B. Two independent reactions occur:

$$A + B \longrightarrow C \quad (I) \qquad A + C \longrightarrow D \quad (II)$$

Analysis of the gaseous effluent shows mole fractions: $y_A = 0.05$ and $y_B = 0.10$.

(i) What is the reactor effluent rate in kmol h^{-1}?

(ii) What are the mole fractions y_C and y_D in the effluent?

(*b*) Feed to a gas-phase reactor comprises 40 kmol h^{-1} of species A, and 40 kmol h^{-1} of species B. Two independent reactions occur:

$$A + B \longrightarrow C \quad (I) \qquad A + 2B \longrightarrow D \quad (II)$$

Analysis of the gaseous effluent shows mole fractions: $y_C = 0.52$ and $y_D = 0.04$. Determine the rates (kmol h^{-1}) of all species in the effluent stream.

(*c*) Feed to a gas-phase reactor is 100 kmol h^{-1} of pure species A. Two independent reactions occur:

$$A \longrightarrow B + C \quad (I) \qquad A + B \longrightarrow D \quad (II)$$

Reaction (I) produces valuable species C and coproduct B. The side reaction (II) produces byproduct D. Analysis of the gaseous effluent shows mole fractions: $y_C = 0.30$ and $y_D = 0.10$. Determine the rates (kmol h^{-1}) of all species in the effluent stream.

(*d*) The feed to a gas-phase reactor is 100 kmol h^{-1}, containing 40 mole % species A and 60 mole % species B. Two independent reactions occur:

$$A + B \longrightarrow C \quad (I) \qquad A + B \longrightarrow D + E \quad (II)$$

Analysis of the gaseous effluent shows mole fractions: $y_C = 0.25$ and $y_D = 0.20$. Determine:

(i) Rates in kmol h^{-1} of all species in the effluent stream.

(ii) Mole fractions of all species in the effluent stream.

13.42. The following is an industrial-safety rule-of-thumb: Compounds with large positive ΔG°_f must be handled and stored carefully. Explain.

13.43. Two important classes of reactions are *oxidation* reactions and *cracking* reactions. One class is invariably endothermic; the other, exothermic. Which is which? For which class of reactions (oxidation or cracking) does equilibrium conversion increase with increasing T?

13.44. The standard heat of reaction ΔH° for gas-phase reactions is independent of the choice of standard-state pressure P°. (Why?) However, the numerical value of ΔG° for such reactions does depend on P°. Two choices of P° are conventional: 1 bar (the basis adopted in this text), and 1.013 25 bar. Show how to convert ΔG° for gas-phase reactions from values based on $P^\circ = 1$ bar to those based on $P^\circ = 1.013\,25$ bar.

13.45. Ethanol is produced from ethylene via the gas-phase reaction:

$$C_2H_4(g) + H_2O(g) \longrightarrow C_2H_5OH(g)$$

Reaction conditions are 400 K and 2 bar.

(*a*) Determine a numerical value for the equilibrium constant K for this reaction at 25°C (298.15 K).
(*b*) Determine a numerical value for K for this reaction at 400 K.
(*c*) Determine the composition of the *equilibrium* gas mixture for an equimolar feed containing only ethylene and H_2O. State all assumptions.
(*d*) For the same feed as in part (*c*), but for $P = 1$ bar, would the equilibrium mole fraction of ethanol be higher or lower? Explain.

13.46. A good source for formation data for compounds is the NIST Chemistry WebBook site. Values of ΔH_f°, but not of ΔG_f°, are reported. Instead, values of absolute standard entropies S° are listed for compounds and elements. To illustrate the use of NIST data, let H_2O_2 be the compound of interest. Values provided by the Chemistry WebBook:

- $\Delta H_f^\circ[H_2O_2(g)] = -136\,1064$ kJ mol^{-1}
- $S^\circ[H_2O_2(g)] = 232\,95$ J mol^{-1} K^{-1}
- $S^\circ[H_2(g)] = 130\,680$ J mol^{-1} K^{-1}
- $S^\circ[O_2(g)] = 205\,152$ J mol^{-1} K^{-1}

All data are for the ideal-gas state at 25°C (298.15 K) and 1 bar. Determine a value for $\Delta G_{f_{298}}^\circ$ for $H_2O_2(g)$.

13.47. Reagent-grade, liquid-phase chemicals often contain isomers as impurities of the nominal compound, with a consequent effect on the vapor pressure. This can be quantified by phase-equilibrium/reaction-equilibrium analysis. Consider a system containing isomers A and B in vapor/liquid equilibrium, and also in equilibrium with respect to the reaction A → B at relatively low pressure.

(*a*) For the reaction in the liquid phase, determine an expression for P (the "mixture vapor pressure") in terms of P_A^{sat}, P_B^{sat}, and K^l, the reaction equilibrium constant. Check the result for the limits $K^l = 0$ and $K^l = \infty$.
(*b*) For the reaction in the vapor phase, repeat part (*a*). Here, the relevant reaction equilibrium constant is K^v.

(*c*) If equilibrium prevails, it doesn't matter whether the reaction is assumed to occur in one phase or the other. Thus the results for parts (*a*) and (*b*) must be equivalent. Use this idea to show the connection between K^l and K^v through the pure-species vapor pressures.

(*d*) Why is the assumption of ideal gases and ideal solutions both reasonable and prudent?

(*e*) Results for parts (*a*) and (*b*) should suggest that P depends on T only. Show that this is in accord with the phase rule.

13.48. Cracking propane is a route to light olefin production. Suppose that *two* cracking reactions occur in a steady-flow reactor:

$$C_3H_8(g) \longrightarrow C_3H_6(g) + H_2(g) \qquad \text{(I)}$$

$$C_3H_8(g) \longrightarrow C_2H_4(g) + CH_4(g) \qquad \text{(II)}$$

Calculate the product composition if both reactions go to equilibrium at 1.2 bar and

(*a*) 750 K (*b*) 1000 K (*c*) 1250 K

13.49. Equilibrium at 425 K and 15 bar is established for the gas-phase isomerization reaction:

$$n\text{-}C_4H_{10}(g) \longrightarrow iso\text{-}C_4H_{10}(g)$$

Estimate the composaition of the equilibrium mixture by two procedures:

(*a*) Assume an ideal-gas mixture.

(*b*) Assume an ideal solution with the equation of state given by Eq. (3.38).

Compare and discuss the results.

Data: For *iso*-butane, $\Delta H^\circ_{f_{298}} = -134\ 180\ \text{J mol}^{-1}$; $\Delta G^\circ_{f_{298}} = -20\ 760\ \text{J mol}^{-1}$

Chapter 14

Topics in Phase Equilibria

The simplest models for vapor/liquid equilibrium, based on Raoult's law and Henry's law, are presented in Chap. 10, largely from an empirical point of view. The calculations by modified Raoult's law, described in Sec. 10.5, are adequate for many purposes, but are limited to low pressures. The initial sections of this chapter therefore present two general calculational procedures for VLE, the first by an extension of modified Raoult's law and the second by equations of state. The theoretical foundation for both procedures is presented in Chap. 11. The remainder of this chapter deals more generally with phase equilibria, with consideration given in separate sections to liquid/liquid, vapor/liquid/liquid, solid/liquid, solid/vapor, adsorption, and osmotic equilibria.

14.1 THE GAMMA/PHI FORMULATION OF VLE

Modified Raoult's law includes the activity coefficient to account for liquid-phase nonidealities, but is limited by the assumption of vapor-phase ideality. This is overcome by introduction of the vapor-phase fugacity coefficient. For species i in a vapor mixture, Eq. (11.52) is written as

$$\hat{f}_i^v = y_i \hat{\phi}_i P$$

For species i in the liquid phase, Eq. (11.90) becomes

$$\hat{f}_i^l = x_i \gamma_i f_i$$

Equation (11.48) requires these two expressions to be equal; whence,

$$y_i \hat{\phi}_i P = x_i \gamma_i f_i \qquad (i = 1, 2, \ldots, N)$$

Superscripts v and l are not used here because of a presumption that $\hat{\phi}_i$ refers to the vapor phase and that γ_i and f_i are liquid-phase properties. Substituting for f_i by Eq. (11.44) gives

$$\boxed{y_i \Phi_i P = x_i \gamma_i P_i^{\text{sat}} \qquad (i = 1, 2, \ldots, N)} \tag{14.1}$$

where $$\Phi_i \equiv \frac{\hat{\phi}_i}{\phi_i^{sat}} \exp\left[-\frac{V_i^l(P - P_i^{sat})}{RT}\right]$$

Because the Poynting factor (represented by the exponential) at low to moderate pressures differs from unity by only a few parts per thousand, its omission introduces negligible error, and this equation is often simplified:

$$\Phi_i = \frac{\hat{\phi}_i}{\phi_i^{sat}} \tag{14.2}$$

Equation (14.1), called the gamma/phi formulation of VLE, reduces to Raoult's law when $\Phi_i = \gamma_i = 1$, and to modified Raoult's law when $\Phi_i = 1$.

Systematic application of Eqs. (14.1) and (14.2) depends on the availability of correlations of data from which values may be obtained for P_i^{sat}, Φ_i, and γ_i. The vapor pressure of a pure species is most commonly given by the Antoine equation, Eq. (6.76):

$$\ln P_i^{sat} = A_i - \frac{B_i}{T + C_i} \tag{14.3}$$

At moderate pressures Eq. (3.38), the two-term virial expansion in P, is usually adequate for property calculations, and the fugacity coefficients of Eq. (14.2) are then given by Eq. (11.64), here written as

$$\hat{\phi}_i = \exp \frac{P}{RT}\left[B_{ii} + \frac{1}{2}\sum_j \sum_k y_j y_k (2\delta_{ji} - \delta_{jk})\right] \tag{14.4}$$

where $$\delta_{ji} \equiv 2B_{ji} - B_{jj} - B_{ii} \qquad \delta_{jk} \equiv 2B_{jk} - B_{jj} - B_{kk}$$

with $\delta_{ii} = 0$, $\delta_{jj} = 0$, etc., and $\delta_{ij} = \delta_{ji}$, etc. Values of the virial coefficients come from a generalized correlation, as represented for example by Eqs. (11.69) through (11.74). The fugacity coefficient for pure i as a saturated vapor ϕ_i^{sat} is obtained from Eq. (14.4) with δ_{ji} and δ_{jk} set equal to zero:

$$\phi_i^{sat} = \exp \frac{B_{ii} P_i^{sat}}{RT} \tag{14.5}$$

Combination of Eqs. (14.2), (14.4), and (14.5) gives

$$\Phi_i = \exp \frac{B_{ii}(P - P_i^{sat}) + \frac{1}{2} P \sum_j \sum_k y_j y_k (2\delta_{ji} - \delta_{jk})}{RT} \tag{14.6}$$

For a binary system comprised of species 1 and 2, this becomes

$$\Phi_1 = \exp \frac{B_{11}(P - P_1^{sat}) + P y_2^2 \delta_{12}}{RT} \tag{14.7a}$$

$$\Phi_2 = \exp \frac{B_{22}(P - P_2^{sat}) + P y_1^2 \delta_{12}}{RT} \tag{14.7b}$$

Activity coefficients [γ_i in Eq. (14.1)] are evaluated from models for G^E as discussed in Sec. 12.2. Thus for data *at constant* T we presume the availability of a correlation giving

$$\frac{G^E}{RT} = g(x_1, x_2, \ldots, x_{N-1}) \qquad \text{(const } T\text{)}$$

Dewpoint and Bubblepoint Calculations

The nature of dewpoint and bubblepoint calculations is evident from the examples of Secs. 10.4 and 10.5 for Raoult's law and modified Raoult's law. All such calculations made by the gamma/phi formulation require iteration because of its complex functionality:

$$\Phi_i = \Phi(T, P, y_1, y_2, \ldots, y_{N-1})$$
$$\gamma_i = \gamma(T, x_1, x_2, \ldots, x_{N-1})$$
$$P_i^{\text{sat}} = f(T)$$

At the moderate pressures where the gamma/phi approach to VLE is appropriate, activity coefficients are assumed independent of pressure. The need for iteration is evident. For example, a *BUBL P* calculation to yield $\{y_i\}$ and P requires values of Φ_i, which depend on P and $\{y_i\}$, the quantities being found. Simple iterative procedures, described in the following paragraphs, apply to *BUBL P*, *DEW P*, *BUBL T*, and *DEW T* calculations.

Equation (14.1) may be solved for either y_i or x_i:

$$y_i = \frac{x_i \gamma_i P_i^{\text{sat}}}{\Phi_i P} \quad (14.8) \qquad x_i = \frac{y_i \Phi_i P}{\gamma_i P_i^{\text{sat}}} \quad (14.9)$$

Because $\sum_i y_i = 1$ and $\sum_i x_i = 1$, these equations may be summed to give

$$1 = \sum_i \frac{x_i \gamma_i P_i^{\text{sat}}}{\Phi_i P} \qquad 1 = \sum_i \frac{y_i \Phi_i P}{\gamma_i P_i^{\text{sat}}}$$

Solved for P, they become

$$P = \sum_i \frac{x_i \gamma_i P_i^{\text{sat}}}{\Phi_i} \quad (14.10) \qquad P = \frac{1}{\sum_i y_i \Phi_i / \gamma_i P_i^{\text{sat}}} \quad (14.11)$$

BUBL P Calculations Figure 14.1 shows an iteration scheme to be implemented by computer. Input consists of the given values, T and $\{x_i\}$, and the parameters for evaluation of $\{P_i^{\text{sat}}\}$, $\{\gamma_i\}$, and $\{\Phi_i\}$. Because the values of $\{y_i\}$ required for calculation of Φ_i are not yet known, set $\Phi_i = 1$. Each P_i^{sat} is evaluated at the given T by Eq. (14.3) and values of γ_i come from an activity-coefficient correlation. Equations (14.10) and (14.8) yield P and $\{y_i\}$. Equation (14.6) then provides $\{\Phi_i\}$; substitution in Eq. (14.10) provides a new value for P. Iteration proceeds until δP, the change in P from one iteration to the next, is less than some tolerance ε, thus converging on final values for P and $\{y_i\}$.

DEW P Calculations Figure 14.2 shows a calculation scheme with input: T, $\{y_i\}$, and appropriate parameters. Neither $\{\Phi_i\}$ nor $\{\gamma_i\}$ can be evaluated initially, and all values are set equal to unity. Equation (14.3) yields $\{P_i^{\text{sat}}\}$, and Eqs. (14.11) and (14.9) are solved for P and $\{x_i\}$. Evaluation of $\{\gamma_i\}$ and substitution into Eq. (14.11) gives an improved value of P from which to determine $\{\Phi_i\}$ by Eq. (14.6). The inner iteration loop then converges on interim values for $\{x_i\}$ and $\{\gamma_i\}$. Because the calculated values of x_i are not constrained to sum

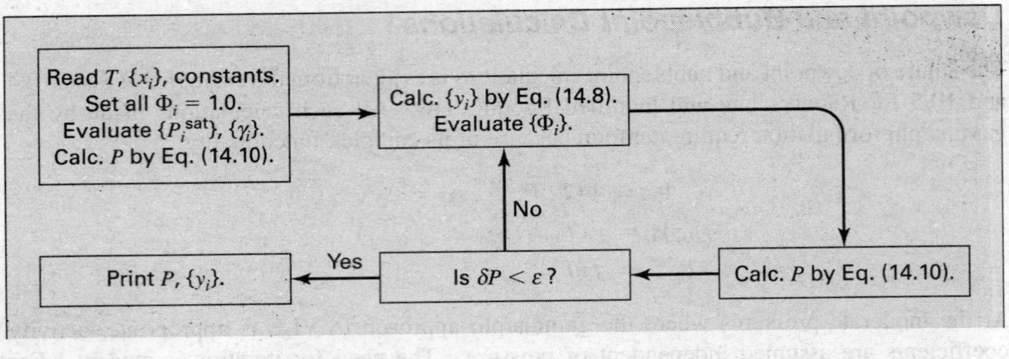

Figure 14.1: Block diagram for the calculation *BUBL P*

to unity, the set is normalized by setting $x_i = x_i / \sum_i x_i$. Subsequent recalculation of P by Eq. (14.11) leads to the outer loop and iteration to convergence on final values for P and $\{x_i\}$.

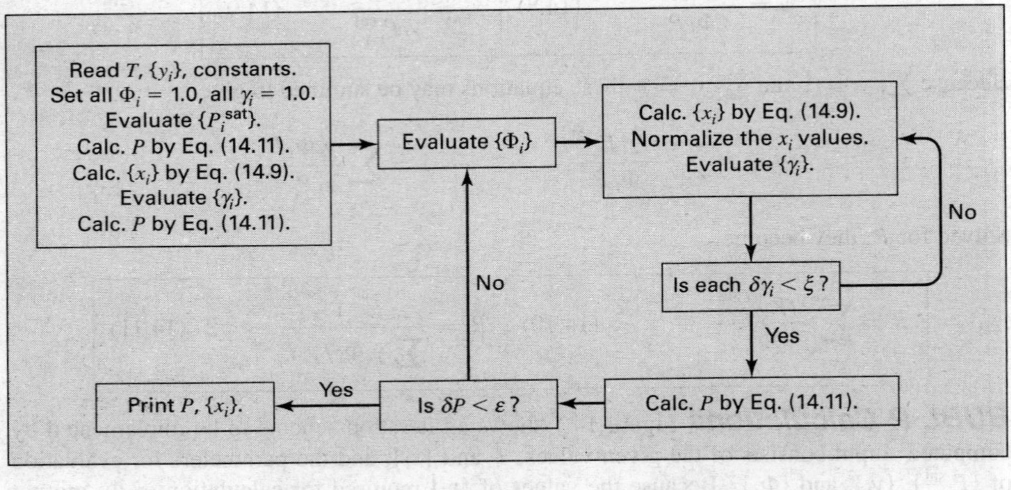

Figure 14.2: Block diagram for the calculation *DEW P*

In *BUBL P* and *DEW P* calculations, temperature is given, allowing immediate and final calculation of $\{P_i^{sat}\}$. This is not the case for procedures *BUBL T* and *DEW T*, where the temperature is unknown. Because iteration is controlled by T, an initial estimate is required. Depending on whether $\{x_i\}$ or $\{y_i\}$ is known, it is given by

$$T = \sum_i x_i T_i^{sat} \qquad \text{or} \qquad T = \sum_i y_i T_i^{sat}$$

where
$$T_i^{sat} = \frac{B_i}{A_i - \ln P} - C_i \tag{14.12}$$

Although individual vapor pressures are strong functions of temperature, vapor-pressure *ratios* are not, and calculations are facilitated by their introduction. Multiplying the right sides of Eqs. (14.10) and (14.11) by P_j^{sat} (outside the summation), dividing by P_j^{sat} (inside the summation), and solving for the P_j^{sat} appearing outside the summation gives the two results

$$P_j^{\text{sat}} = \frac{P}{\sum_i (x_i \gamma_i / \Phi_i)(P_i^{\text{sat}}/P_j^{\text{sat}})} \tag{14.13}$$

$$P_j^{\text{sat}} = P \sum_i \frac{y_i \Phi_i}{\gamma_i} \left(\frac{P_j^{\text{sat}}}{P_i^{\text{sat}}} \right) \tag{14.14}$$

The summations are over all species including j, which is an *arbitrarily selected species*. Once P_j^{sat} is known, the corresponding value of T is found from Eq. (14.3), written as

$$T = \frac{B_j}{A_j - \ln P_j^{\text{sat}}} - C_j \tag{14.15}$$

BUBL T Calculations Figure 14.3 shows an iterative scheme with input, P, $\{x_i\}$, and parameters. In the absence of T and $\{y_i\}$ values, set $\Phi_i = 1$. The simple iteration scheme that follows is clear from the figure.

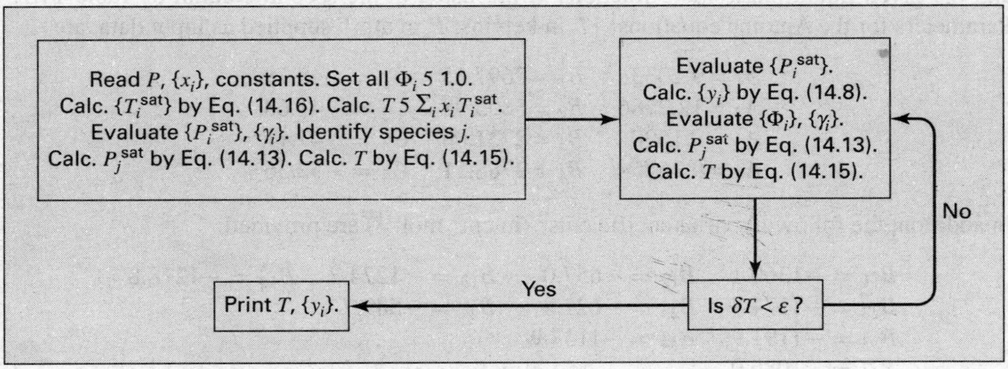

Figure 14.3: Block diagram for the calculation *BUBL T*

DEW T Calculations Here, neither T nor $\{x_i\}$ is known. The iteration scheme is shown in detail by Fig. 14.4. As in the *DEW P* procedure, the set $\{x_i\}$ calculated within the inner loop is not constrained to sum to unity, and is therefore normalized by setting $x_i = x_i / \sum_i x_i$.

Dewpoint and bubblepoint calculations are readily made with software packages such as Mathcad® and Maple®, in which iteration is an integral part of an equation-solving routine. Calculations for multicomponent systems made either with the iteration schemes detailed here or with software packages are readily carried out by computer.

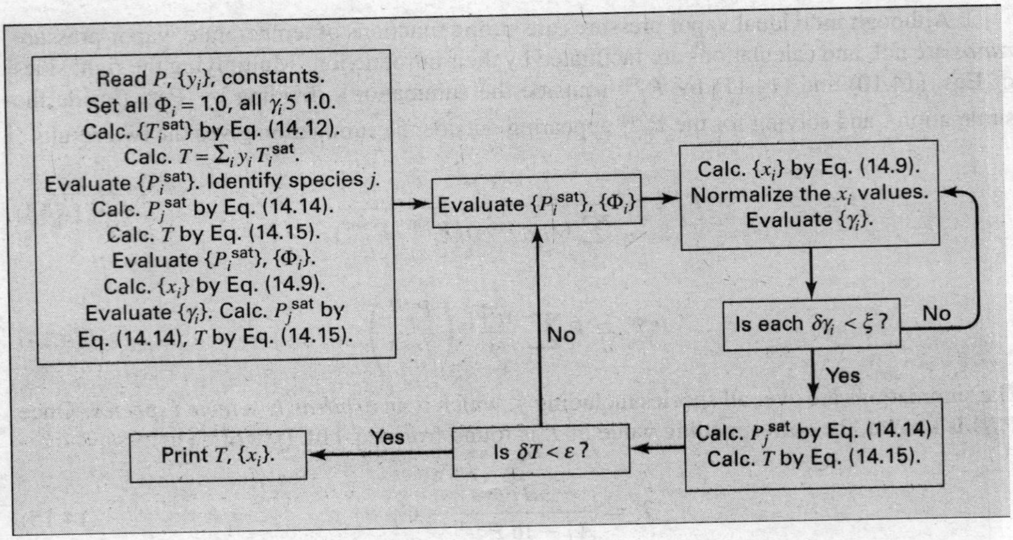

Figure 14.4: Block diagram for the calculation *DEW T*

The results for a complete *BUBL T* calculation are shown in Table 14.1 for the system n-hexane(1)/ethanol(2)/methylcyclopentane(3)/benzene(4). The given pressure P is 1 atm, and the given liquid-phase mole fractions x_i are listed in the second column of Table 14.1. Parameters for the Antoine equations[1] [T in kelvins, P in atm], supplied as input data, are

$$\begin{array}{lll} A_1 = 9.2033 & B_1 = 2697.55 & C_1 = -48.78 \\ A_2 = 12.2786 & B_2 = 3803.98 & C_2 = -41.68 \\ A_3 = 9.1690 & B_3 = 2731.00 & C_3 = -47.11 \\ A_4 = 9.2675 & B_4 = 2788.51 & C_4 = -52.36 \end{array}$$

In addition, the following virial coefficients[2] (in $cm^3\ mol^{-1}$) are provided:

$$\begin{array}{llll} B_{11} = -1360.1 & B_{12} = -657.0 & B_{13} = -1274.2 & B_{14} = -1218.8 \\ B_{22} = -1174.7 & B_{23} = -621.8 & B_{24} = -589.7 & \\ B_{33} = -1191.9 & B_{34} = -1137.9 & & \\ B_{44} = -1086.9 & & & \end{array}$$

Finally, input information includes parameters for the UNIFAC method (App. H). The calculated values of T and the vapor-phase mole fractions y_i compare favorably with experimental values.[3] Also listed in Table 14.1 are final computed values of P_i^{sat}, Φ_i, and γ_i.

[1] R. C. Reid, J. M. Prausnitz, and T. K. Sherwood, *The Properties of Gases and Liquids*, 3d ed., app. A, McGraw-Hill, New York, 1977.

[2] From the correlation of J. G. Hayden and J. P. O'Connell, *Ind. Eng. Chem. Proc. Des. Dev.*, vol. 14, pp. 209–216, 1975.

[3] J. E. Sinor and J. H. Weber, *J. Chem. Eng. Data*, vol. 5, pp. 243–247, 1960.

Table 14.1: System: *n*-Hexane/Ethanol/Methylcyclopentane(MCP)/Benzene

BUBL T calculations at 1 atm.

Species k	x_i	y_i(calc)	y_i(exp)	P_i^{sat}/atm	Φ_i	γ_i
n-Hexane(1)	0.162	0.139	0.140	0.797	0.993	1.073
Ethanol(2)	0.068	0.279	0.274	0.498	0.999	8.241
MCP(3)	0.656	0.500	0.503	0.725	0.990	1.042
Benzene(4)	0.114	0.082	0.083	0.547	0.983	1.289

T(calc) = 334.82 K (61.67°C) T(exp) = 334.85 K (61.5°C) Iterations = 4

The *BUBL T* calculations for which results are given in Table 14.1 are for a pressure of 1 atm, a pressure for which vapor phases are often assumed to be ideal gases and for which Φ_i is unity for each species. Indeed, these values here lie between 0.98 and 1.00. This illustrates the fact that at pressures of 1 bar and less, the assumption of ideal gases usually introduces little error. The additional assumption of liquid-phase ideality ($\gamma_i = 1$), on the other hand, is justified only infrequently. We note that γ_i for ethanol in Table 14.1 is greater than 8.

Values of parameters for the Margules, van Laar, Wilson, NRTL, and UNIQUAC equations are given for many binary pairs by Gmehling et al.[4] in a summary collection of the world's published VLE data for low to moderate pressures. These values are based on reduction of experimental data through application of modified Raoult's law, Eq. (10.5). On the other hand, data reduction for determination of parameters in the UNIFAC method (App. H) does not include the ideal-gas assumption, and is carried out with Eq. (14.1).

Flash Calculations

The treatment of flash calculations in Sec. 10.6 led to calculations based on Raoult's law and K-value correlations. Use of the gamma/phi formulation of VLE makes the calculations somewhat more complex, but the primary equation is unchanged:

$$y_i = \frac{z_i K_i}{1 + \mathcal{V}(K_i - 1)} \qquad (i = 1, 2, \ldots, N) \tag{10.16}$$

With $x_i = y_i / K_i$, an alternative equation is

$$x_i = \frac{z_i}{1 + \mathcal{V}(K_i - 1)} \qquad (i = 1, 2, \ldots, N) \tag{14.16}$$

Because both sets of mole fractions must sum to unity, $\sum_i x_i = \sum_i y_i = 1$. Thus, if we sum Eq. (10.16) over all species and subtract unity from this sum, the difference F_y is zero:

$$F_y = \sum_i \frac{z_i K_i}{1 + \mathcal{V}(K_i - 1)} - 1 = 0 \tag{14.17}$$

[4]J. Gmehling, U. Onken, and W. Arlt, *Vapor-Liquid Equilibrium Data Collection*, Chemistry Data Series, vol. I, parts 1–8, DECHEMA, Frankfurt/Main, 1977–1990.

Similar treatment of Eq. (14.16) yields the difference F_x, which is also zero:

$$F_x = \sum_i \frac{z_i}{1 + \mathcal{V}(K_i - 1)} - 1 = 0 \tag{14.18}$$

Solution to a P, T-flash problem is accomplished when a value of $\mathcal{V}$ is found that makes *either* function F_y *or* F_x equal to zero for known T, P, and overall composition. However, a more convenient function for a *general* solution procedure[5] is the difference $F_y - F_x = F$:

$$F = \sum_i \frac{z_i(K_i - 1)}{1 + \mathcal{V}(K_i - 1)} = 0 \tag{14.19}$$

The advantage of this function is apparent from its derivative

$$\frac{dF}{d\mathcal{V}} = -\sum_i \frac{z_i(K_i - 1)^2}{[1 + \mathcal{V}(K_i - 1)]^2} \tag{14.20}$$

Because $dF/d\mathcal{V}$ is always negative, the F vs. $\mathcal{V}$ relation is monotonic, and this makes Newton's method (App. I), a rapidly converging iteration procedure, well suited to solution for $\mathcal{V}$. Equation (I.1) for the nth iteration here becomes:

$$F + \left(\frac{dF}{d\mathcal{V}}\right) \Delta\mathcal{V} = 0 \tag{14.21}$$

where $\Delta\mathcal{V} \equiv \mathcal{V}_{n+1} - \mathcal{V}_n$, and F and $(dF/d\mathcal{V})$ are found by Eqs. (14.19) and (14.20). In these equations the K-values come from Eq. (14.1), written

$$K_i = \frac{y_i}{x_i} = \frac{\gamma_i P_i^{\text{sat}}}{\Phi_i P} \qquad (i = 1, 2, \ldots, N) \tag{14.22}$$

where Φ_i is given by Eq. (14.2). The K-values contain all of the thermodynamic information, and are related in a complex way to T, P, $\{y_i\}$, and $\{x_i\}$. Because solution is for $\{y_i\}$ and $\{x_i\}$, the P, T-flash calculation inevitably requires iteration.

A general solution scheme is shown by the block diagram of Fig. 14.5. The given information is read and stored. Because it is not known in advance whether the system of stated composition at the stated T and P is in fact a mixture of saturated liquid and saturated vapor and not entirely liquid or entirely vapor, preliminary calculations are made to establish the nature of the system. At the given T and overall composition, the system exists as a superheated vapor if its pressure is less than the dewpoint pressure P_{dew}. On the other hand, it exists as a subcooled liquid if its pressure is greater than the bubblepoint pressure P_{bubl}. Only for pressures between P_{dew} and P_{bubl} is the system an equilibrium mixture of vapor and liquid. We therefore determine P_{dew} by a *DEW P* calculation (Fig. 14.2) at the given T and for $\{y_i\} = \{z_i\}$, and P_{bubl} by a *BUBL P* calculation (Fig. 14.1) at the given T and for $\{x_i\} = \{z_i\}$. The P, T-flash calculation is performed only if the given pressure P lies between P_{dew} and P_{bubl}. If this is the case, we make use of the results of the preliminary *DEW P* and *BUBL P* calculations to

[5]H. H. Rachford, Jr., and J. D. Rice, *J. Petrol. Technol.*, vol. 4(10), sec. 1, p. 19 and sec. 2, p. 3, October, 1952.

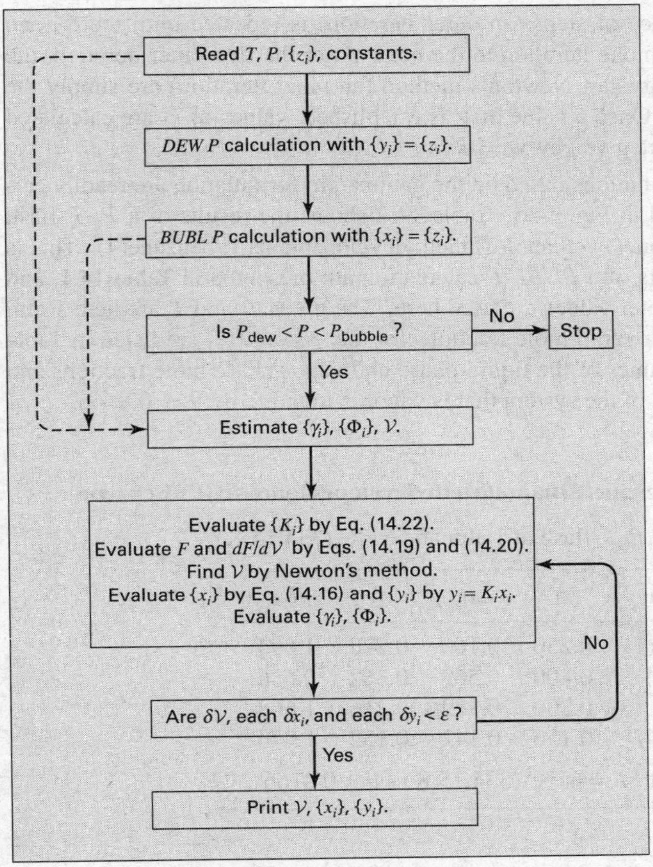

Figure 14.5: Block diagram for a P,T-flash calculation

provide initial estimates of $\{\gamma_i\}$, $\{\hat{\phi}_i\}$, and $\mathcal{V}$. For the dewpoint, $\mathcal{V} = 1$, with calculated values of P_{dew}, $\gamma_{i,\text{dew}}$, and $\hat{\phi}_{i,\text{dew}}$; for the bubblepoint, $\mathcal{V} = 0$, with calculated values of P_{bubl}, $\gamma_{i,\text{bubl}}$, and $\hat{\phi}_{i,\text{bubl}}$. The simplest procedure is to interpolate between dewpoint and bubblepoint values in relation to the location of P between P_{dew} and P_{bubl}:

$$\frac{\gamma_i - \gamma_{i,\text{dew}}}{\gamma_{i,\text{bubl}} - \gamma_{i,\text{dew}}} = \frac{\hat{\phi}_i - \hat{\phi}_{i,\text{dew}}}{\hat{\phi}_{i,\text{bubl}} - \hat{\phi}_{i,\text{dew}}} = \frac{P - P_{\text{dew}}}{P_{\text{bubl}} - P_{\text{dew}}}$$

and
$$\frac{\mathcal{V} - 1}{0 - 1} = \frac{P - P_{\text{dew}}}{P_{\text{bubl}} - P_{\text{dew}}} \quad \text{or} \quad \mathcal{V} = \frac{P_{\text{bubl}} - P}{P_{\text{bubl}} - P_{\text{dew}}}$$

With these initial values of the γ_i and $\hat{\phi}_i$, initial values of the K_i can be calculated by Eq. (14.22). The P_i^{sat} and ϕ_i^{sat} values are already available from the preliminary *DEW P* and *BUBL P* calculations. Equations (14.19) and (14.20) now provide starting values of F and $dF/d\mathcal{V}$ for Newton's method as represented by Eq. (14.21). Repeated application of this equation leads to the value of $\mathcal{V}$ for which Eq. (14.19) is satisfied for the present estimates of $\{K_i\}$. The remaining calculations serve to provide new estimates of $\{\gamma_i\}$ and $\{\Phi_i\}$ from which to reevaluate $\{K_i\}$. This sequence of steps (an outer iteration) is repeated until there is no significant change in results from one iteration to the next. After the first outer iteration, the values of $\mathcal{V}$ and $(dF/d\mathcal{V})$ used to start Newton's method (an inner iteration) are simply the most recently calculated values. Once a value of $\mathcal{V}$ is established, values of x_i are calculated by Eq. (14.16) and values of y_i are given by $y_i = K_i x_i$.

Multicomponent flash calculations based on the gamma/phi formulation are readily carried out by computer as outlined in Fig. 14.5. Table 14.2 shows the results of a P, T-flash calculation for the system n-hexane(1)/ethanol(2)/methylcyclopentane(3)/benzene(4). This is the same system for which results of a *BUBL T* calculation are presented in Table 14.1, and the same correlations and parameter values are used here. The given P and T are here 1 atm and 61°C (334.15 K). The given overall mole fractions for the system $\{z_i\}$ are listed in Table 14.2 along with the calculated values of the liquid-phase and vapor-phase mole fractions and the K-values. The molar fraction of the system that is vapor is found to be $\mathcal{V} = 0.8166$.

Table 14.2: System: *n*-Hexane/Ethanol/Methylcyclopentane(MCP)/Benzene

Calculation of P,T-flash at 1 atm and 61°C (334.15 K).

Species(i)	z_i	x_i	y_i	K_i
n-Hexane(1)	0.250	0.160	0.270	1.694
Ethanol(2)	0.400	0.569	0.362	0.636
MCP(3)	0.200	0.129	0.216	1.668
Benzene(4)	0.150	0.142	0.152	1.070

$P = 1$ atm $T = 61°C$ (334.15 K) $\mathcal{V} = 0.8166$

Solute (1)/Solvent (2) Systems

The gamma/phi approach to VLE calculations, based on Eq. (14.1), presumes knowledge of the vapor pressure of each species at the temperature of interest. Situations do arise however where a species is either unstable at the system temperature or is *supercritical*, i.e., the system temperature exceeds its critical temperature. Therefore its vapor pressure cannot be measured, and its fugacity f_1 as a pure liquid at the system temperature cannot be calculated by Eq. (11.44).

Consider a binary system wherein species 1, designated the solute, cannot exist as a pure liquid at the system temperature. Although Eqs. (14.1) and (14.2) can be applied to species 2, designated the solvent, they are not applicable to the solute, and an alternative approach is required. Figure 14.6 shows a typical plot of the liquid-phase fugacity of the solute $\hat{f}_1$ vs. its mole fraction x_1 at constant temperature. This figure differs from Fig. 12.3 in that the curve representing $\hat{f}_1$ does not extend all the way to $x_1 = 1$. Thus the location of f_1, the liquid-phase fugacity of pure species 1, is not established, and the line representing the Lewis/Randall rule cannot be drawn. The tangent line at the origin, representing Henry's law (Sec. 12.1), provides alternative information. Recall that the slope of the tangent line is Henry's constant, defined by Eq. (12.2). Thus,

$$\mathcal{H}_1 \equiv \lim_{x_1 \to 0} \frac{\hat{f}_1}{x_1} \tag{14.23}$$

Henry's constant is a strong function of temperature, but only weakly dependent on pressure. Note, however, that the definition of $\mathcal{H}_1$ at temperature T presumes the pressure is the equilibrium value at $x_1 \to 0$, i.e., the vapor pressure of the pure solvent P_2^{sat}.

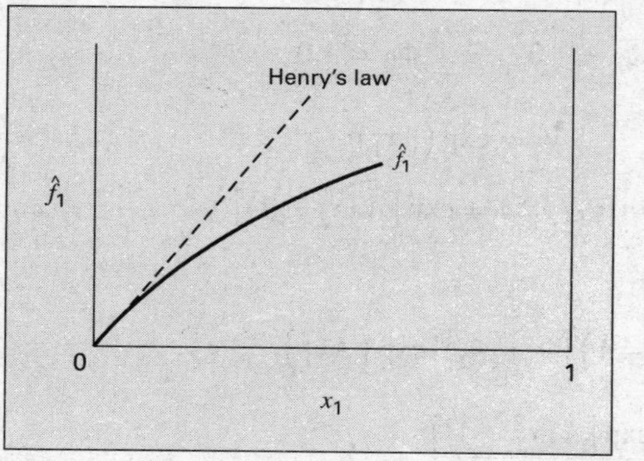

Figure 14.6: Solute fugacity $\hat{f}_1$ vs. x_1.

The activity coefficient of the solute is related to its fugacity by Eq. (11.90), which may be written:

$$\frac{\hat{f}_1}{x_1} = \gamma_1 f_1 \tag{14.24}$$

Combining this with Eq. (14.23) yields:

$$\mathcal{H}_1 = \gamma_1^{\infty} f_1$$

where γ_1^{∞} represents the infinite-dilution value of the activity coefficient of the solute. Because both $\mathcal{H}_1$ and γ_1^{∞} are evaluated at P_2^{sat}, this pressure also applies to f_1. However, the effect of P on a liquid-phase fugacity, given by a Poynting factor, is very small, and for practical purposes may usually be neglected. Elimination of f_1 from Eq. (14.24) gives on rearrangement:

$$\hat{f}_1 = x_1 \frac{\gamma_1}{\gamma_1^{\infty}} \mathcal{H}_1 \tag{14.25}$$

For vapor/liquid equilibrium,

$$\hat{f}_1 = \hat{f}_1^l = \hat{f}_1^v = y_1 P \hat{\phi}_1$$

where the final term comes from Eq. (11.52). Combining the two expressions for $\hat{f}_1$ gives, after rearrangement:

$$y_1 = \frac{x_1(\gamma_1/\gamma_1^{\infty})\mathcal{H}_1}{\hat{\phi}_1 P} \tag{14.26}$$

For the solute, this equation takes the place of Eqs. (14.1) and (14.2). For species 2, the solvent, Eq. (14.8) becomes

$$y_2 = \frac{x_2 \gamma_2 P_2^{sat}}{\Phi_2 P} \tag{14.27}$$

Because $y_1 + y_2 = 1$, a *BUBL P* calculation for a binary system is based on the equation:

$$P = \frac{x_1 (\gamma_1/\gamma_1^\infty) \mathcal{H}_1}{\hat{\phi}_1} + \frac{x_2 \gamma_2 P_2^{sat}}{\Phi_2} \qquad (14.28)$$

The same correlation that provides for the evaluation of γ_1 also allows evaluation of γ_1^∞.

As a simple example, consider a system for which

$$\frac{G^E}{RT} = A x_1 x_2 \qquad \hat{\phi}_1 = 1.0 \qquad \Phi_2 = 1.0$$

By Eqs. (12.15), $\gamma_1 = \exp(A x_2^2) \qquad \gamma_2 = \exp(A x_1^2)$

Whence, $\gamma_1^\infty = \exp(A)$ and $(\gamma_1/\gamma_1^\infty) = \exp\left[A(x_2^2 - 1)\right]$

Equation (14.28) here becomes:

$$P = x_1 \mathcal{H}_1 \exp\left[A\left(x_2^2 - 1\right)\right] + x_2 P_2^{sat} \exp\left(A x_1^2\right)$$

and by Eq. (14.26), $y_1 = \dfrac{x_1 \mathcal{H}_1 \exp\left[A(x_2^2 - 1)\right]}{P}$

For comparison, if P_1^{sat} were known, the formulation would be

$$P = x_1 P_1^{sat} \exp\left(A x_2^2\right) + x_2 P_2^{sat} \exp\left(A x_1^2\right) \qquad y_1 = \frac{x_1 P_1^{sat} \exp(A x_2^2)}{P}$$

The difference in the input data for the two formulations is that Henry's constant for species 1 is required in the former case whereas the vapor pressure of species 1 appears in the latter.

There remains the problem of finding Henry's constant from the available VLE data. For equilibrium,

$$\hat{f}_1 = \hat{f}_1^l = \hat{f}_1^v = y_1 P \hat{\phi}_1$$

Division by x_1 gives $\dfrac{\hat{f}_1}{x_1} = P \hat{\phi}_1 \dfrac{y_1}{x_1}$

Henry's constant is defined as the limit as $x_1 \to 0$ of the ratio on the left; therefore,

$$\mathcal{H}_1 = P_2^{sat} \hat{\phi}_1^\infty \lim_{x_1 \to 0} \frac{y_1}{x_1}$$

The limiting value of y_1/x_1 can be found by plotting y_1/x_1 vs. x_1 and extrapolating to zero.

14.2 VLE FROM CUBIC EQUATIONS OF STATE

As shown in Sec. 11.6, phases at the same T and P are in equilibrium when the fugacity of each species is the same in all phases. For VLE, this requirement is written:

$$\hat{f}_i^v = \hat{f}_i^l \qquad (i = 1, 2, \ldots, N) \tag{11.48}$$

An alternative form results from introduction of the fugacity coefficient, defined by Eq. (11.52):

$$y_i P \hat{\phi}_i^v = x_i P \hat{\phi}_i^l$$

or

$$\boxed{y_i \hat{\phi}_i^v = x_i \hat{\phi}_i^l \qquad (i = 1, 2, \ldots, N)} \tag{14.29}$$

Vapor Pressures for a Pure Species

Although vapor pressures for a pure species P_i^{sat} are subject to experimental measurement, it is also true that vapor pressures are implicit in a cubic equation of state. Indeed, the simplest application of equations of state for VLE calculations is to find the vapor pressure of a pure species at given temperature T.

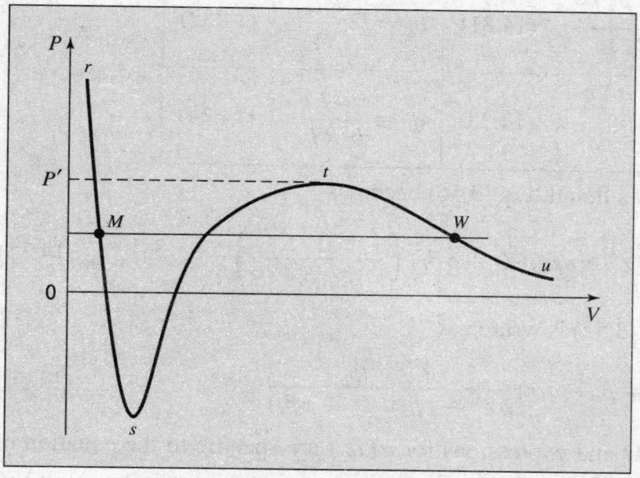

Figure 14.7: Isotherm for $T < T_c$ on PV diagram for a pure fluid

The subcritical PV isotherm of Fig. 3.11 labeled $T_2 < T_c$ is reproduced here as Fig. 14.7. As generated by a cubic equation of state, it consists of three segments. The very steep segment on the left (rs) is characteristic of liquids; in the limit as $P \to \infty$, the molar volume V approaches the constant b [Eq. 3.42]. The segment on the right (tu) with gentle downward slope is characteristic of vapors; in the limit as $P \to 0$ molar volume V approaches infinity. The middle segment (st), containing both a minimum (note here that $P < 0$) and a maximum, provides a smooth transition from liquid to vapor, but has no physical meaning. The actual transition from liquid to vapor occurs at the vapor pressure along a horizontal line, such as connects points M and W.

For pure species i, Eq. (14.29) reduces to Eq. (11.41), $\phi_i^v = \phi_i^l$, which may be written as

$$\ln \phi_i^l - \ln \phi_i^v = 0 \tag{14.30}$$

The fugacity coefficient of a pure liquid or vapor is a function of its temperature and pressure. For a *saturated* liquid or vapor, the equilibrium pressure is P_i^{sat}. Therefore Eq. (14.30) implicitly expresses the functional relation,

$$g(T, P_i^{\text{sat}}) = 0 \qquad \text{or} \qquad P_i^{\text{sat}} = f(T)$$

An isotherm generated by a cubic equation of state, as represented in Fig. 14.7, has three volume roots for a specific pressure between $P = 0$ and $P = P'$. The smallest root lies on the left line segment, and is a liquid-like volume, e.g., at point M. The largest root lies on the right line segment, and is a vapor-like volume, e.g., at point W. If these points lie at the vapor pressure, then M represents *saturated* liquid, W represents *saturated* vapor, and they exist in phase equilibrium. The root lying on the middle line segment has no physical significance.

Two widely used cubic equations of state, developed specifically for VLE calculations, are the Soave/Redlich/Kwong (SRK) equation[6] and the Peng/Robinson (PR) equation.[7] Both are special cases of Eq. (3.52) for a vapor phase and Eq. (3.56) for a liquid phase. Equation-of-state parameters are independent of phase, and in accord with Eqs. ((3.45), (3.46), (3.50), and (3.51) are given by

$a_i(T) = \Psi \dfrac{\alpha(T_{r_i}) R^2 T_{c_i}^2}{P_{c_i}}$ (14.31)	$b_i = \Omega \dfrac{RT_{c_i}}{P_{c_i}}$ (14.32)
$\beta_i \equiv \dfrac{b_i P}{RT}$ (14.33)	$q_i \equiv \dfrac{a_i(T)}{b_i RT}$ (14.34)

Written for pure species i as a liquid, Eq. (3.56) becomes

$$Z_i^l = \beta_i + (Z_i^l + \epsilon\beta_i)(Z_i^l + \sigma\beta_i)\left(\frac{1 + \beta_i - Z_i^l}{q_i\beta_i}\right) \tag{14.35}$$

For pure species i as a vapor, Eq. (3.52) is written as

$$Z_i^v = 1 + \beta_i - q_i\beta_i \frac{Z_i^v - \beta_i}{(Z_i^v + \epsilon\beta_i)(Z_i^v + \sigma\beta_i)} \tag{14.36}$$

The pure numbers ϵ, σ, Ψ, and Ω and expressions for $\alpha(T_{r_i})$ are specific to the equation of state, and are given in Table 3.1 (p. 98).

As shown in Sec. 11.5, and applicable to both vapor and liquid phases:

$$\ln\phi_i = Z_i - 1 - \ln(Z_i - \beta_i) - q_i I_i \tag{11.37}$$

Values for $\ln\phi_i$ are therefore implied by each of the equations of state considered here. In Eq. (11.37), q_i is given by Eq. (14.34), and I_i, by Eq. (6.65b). For given T and P, the liquid-phase value Z_i^l at point M of Fig. 14.7 is found by solution of Eq. (14.35). The vapor-phase value Z_i^v at point W comes from Eq. (14.36). Values for $\ln\phi_i^l$ and $\ln\phi_i^v$ are then found by Eq. (11.37). If they satisfy Eq. (14.30), then P is the vapor pressure P_i^{sat} at temperature T, and M and W represent the states of saturated liquid and vapor implied by the equation of state. If Eq. (14.30) is not satisfied, P_i^{sat} is found by trial, by iteration, or by the solve routine of a software package. The eight equations solved for eight unknowns are listed in Table 14.3.

[6]G. Soave, *Chem. Eng. Sci.*, vol. 27, pp. 1197–1203, 1972.

[7]D.-Y. Peng and D. B. Robinson, *Ind. Eng. Chem. Fundam.*, vol. 15, pp. 59–64, 1976.

Table 14.3: Equations for Calculating Vapor Pressures

The unknowns are: P_i^{sat}, β_i, Z_i^l, Z_i^v, I_i^l, I_i^v, $\ln \phi_i^l$, and $\ln \phi_i^v$

$$\beta_i \equiv \frac{b_i P_i^{\text{sat}}}{RT}$$

$$Z_i^l = \beta_i + (Z_i^l + \epsilon\,\beta_i)(Z_i^l + \sigma\beta_i)\left(\frac{1 + \beta_i - Z_i^l}{q_i\,\beta_i}\right)$$

$$Z_i^v = 1 + \beta_i - q_i\,\beta_i \frac{Z_i^v - \beta_i}{(Z_i^v + \epsilon\,\beta_i)(Z_i^v + \sigma\beta_i)}$$

$$I_i^l = \frac{1}{\sigma - \epsilon} \ln \frac{Z_i^l + \sigma\beta_i}{Z_i^l + \epsilon\,\beta_i} \qquad I_i^v = \frac{1}{\sigma - \epsilon} \ln \frac{Z_i^v + \sigma\beta_i}{Z_i^v + \epsilon\,\beta_i}$$

$$\ln \phi_i^l = Z_i^l - 1 - \ln(Z_i^l - \beta_i) - q_i\,I_i^l$$

$$\ln \phi_i^v = Z_i^v - 1 - \ln(Z_i^v - \beta_i) - q_i\,I_i^v$$

$$\ln \phi_i^v = \ln \phi_i^l$$

The calculation of pure-species vapor pressures as just described may be reversed to allow evaluation of an equation-of-state parameter from a known vapor-pressure P_i^{sat} at temperature T. Thus, Eq. (11.37) may be written for each phase of pure-species i and combined in accord with Eq. (14.30). Solving the resulting expression for q_i yields:

$$q_i = \frac{Z_i^v - Z_i^l + \ln \dfrac{Z_i^l - \beta_i}{Z_i^v - \beta_i}}{I_i^v - I_i^l} \tag{14.37}$$

where $\beta_i \equiv b_i P_i^{\text{sat}}/RT$. For the PR and SRK equations, I_i is given by Eq. (6.65b) written for pure species i:

$$I_i = \frac{1}{\sigma - \epsilon} \ln \frac{Z_i + \sigma\beta_i}{Z_i + \epsilon\beta_i}$$

This equation yields I_i^l with Z_i^l from Eq. (14.35), and I_i^v with Z_i^v from Eq. (14.36). However, the equations for Z_i^l and Z_i^v contain q_i, the quantity sought. Thus, an iterative procedure is indicated, with an initial value of q_i from a generalized correlation as given by Eqs. (14.31), (14.32), and (14.34).

Mixture VLE

The fundamental assumption when an equation of state is written for mixtures is that it has exactly the same form as when written for pure species. Thus for mixtures Eqs. (14.35) and

(14.36), written without subscripts, become

Liquid $$Z^l = \beta^l + (Z^l + \epsilon\beta^l)(Z^l + \sigma\beta^l)\left(\frac{1 + \beta^l - Z^l}{q^l\beta^l}\right) \tag{14.38}$$

Vapor $$Z^v = 1 + \beta^v - q^v\beta^v \frac{Z^v - \beta^v}{(Z^v + \epsilon\beta^v)(Z^v + \sigma\beta^v)} \tag{14.39}$$

Here, β^l, β^v, q^l, and q^v are for mixtures, with definitions:

$$\beta^p \equiv \frac{b^p P}{RT} \qquad (p = l, v) \tag{14.40}$$

$$q^p \equiv \frac{a^p}{b^p RT} \qquad (p = l, v) \tag{14.41}$$

The complication is that *mixture* parameters a^p and b^p, and therefore β^p and q^p, are *functions of composition*. Systems in vapor/liquid equilibrium consist in general of two phases with different compositions. The PV isotherms generated by an equation of state for these two fixed compositions are represented in Fig. 14.8 by two similar lines: the solid line for the liquid-phase composition and the dashed line for the vapor-phase composition. They are displaced from one another because the equation-of-state parameters are different for the two compositions. However, each line includes three *segments* as described in connection with the isotherm of Fig. 14.7. Thus, we distinguish between the *composition* which characterizes a complete line, and the *phases*, all of the same composition, which are associated with the segments of an isotherm.

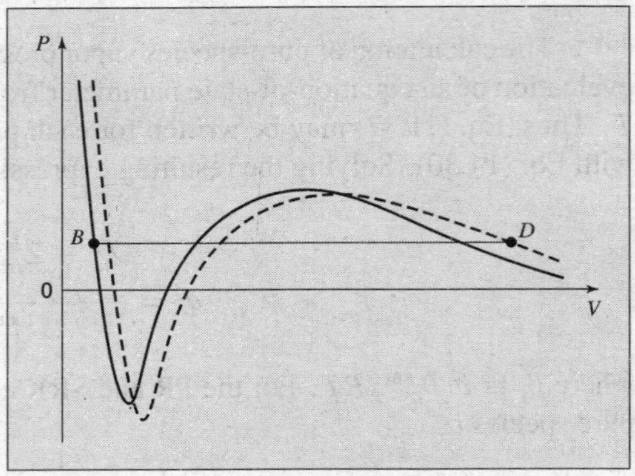

Figure 14.8: Two PV isotherms at the same T for mixtures. The solid line is for a liquid-phase composition; the dashed line is for a vapor-phase composition. Point B represents a bubblepoint with the liquid-phase composition; Point D represent a dewpoint with the vapor-phase composition. When these points lie at the same P (as shown) they represent phases in equilibrium.

Each line contains a bubblepoint on its left segment representing *saturated* liquid, and a dewpoint of the same composition on its right segment representing *saturated* vapor[8]. Because these points for a given line are for the same composition, they do not represent phases in equilibrium and do not lie at the same pressure. (See Fig. 10.3, where for a given constant-composition loop and a given T saturated liquid and saturated vapor are at different pressures.)

For a *BUBL P* calculation, the temperature and the liquid composition are known, and this fixes the location of the PV isotherm for the composition of the liquid phase (solid line).

[8]Note that bubblepoint B and dewpoint D in Fig. 14.8 are on *different* lines.

The *BUBL P* calculation then finds the composition for a second (dashed) line that contains a dewpoint D on its vapor segment that lies at the pressure of the bubblepoint B on the liquid segment of the solid line. This pressure is then the phase-equilibrium pressure and the composition for the dashed line is that of the equilibrium vapor. This equilibrium condition is shown by Fig. 14.8, where bubblepoint B and dewpoint D lie at the same P on isotherms for the same T but representing the different compositions of two phases in equilibrium.

Because no established theory prescribes the form of the composition dependence of the equation-of-state parameters, empirical *mixing rules* have been proposed to relate mixture parameters to pure-species parameters. The simplest realistic expressions are a linear mixing rule for parameter b and a quadratic mixing rule for parameter a:

$$b = \sum_i x_i b_i \quad (14.42) \qquad a = \sum_i \sum_j x_i x_j a_{ij} \quad (14.43)$$

with $a_{ij} = a_{ji}$. The general mole-fraction variable x_i is used here because application is to both liquid and vapor mixtures. The a_{ij} are of two types: pure-species parameters (like subscripts) and interaction parameters (unlike subscripts). Parameter b_i is for pure species i. The interaction parameter a_{ij} is often evaluated from pure-species parameters by *combining rules*, e.g., a geometric-mean rule:

$$a_{ij} = (a_i a_j)^{1/2} \qquad (14.44)$$

These equations, known as van der Waals prescriptions, provide for the evaluation of mixture parameters solely from parameters for the pure constituent species. Although they are satisfactory only for mixtures comprised of simple and chemically similar molecules, they allow straight-forward calculations that illustrate how complex VLE problems may be solved.

Also useful for application of equations of state to mixtures are *partial* equation-of-state parameters, defined by

$$\bar{a}_i \equiv \left[\frac{\partial(na)}{\partial n_i}\right]_{T,n_j} \quad (14.45) \qquad \bar{b}_i \equiv \left[\frac{\partial(nb)}{\partial n_i}\right]_{T,n_j} \quad (14.46) \qquad \bar{q}_i \equiv \left[\frac{\partial(nq)}{\partial n_i}\right]_{T,n_j} \quad (14.47)$$

Because equation-of-state parameters are, at most, functions of temperature and composition, these definitions are in accord with Eq. (11.7). They are general equations, valid regardless of the particular mixing or combining rules adopted for the composition dependence of mixture parameters.

Values of $\hat{\phi}_i^l$ and $\hat{\phi}_i^v$ are implicit in an equation of state, and with Eq. (14.29) allow calculation of *mixture* VLE. The same basic principle applies as for pure-species VLE, but the calculations are more complex. With $\hat{\phi}_i^l$ a function of T, P, and $\{x_i\}$, and $\hat{\phi}_i^v$ a function of T, P, and $\{y_i\}$, Eq. (14.29) represents N relations among the $2N$ variables: T, P, $(N-1)$ x_is and $(N-1)$ y_is. Thus, specification of N of these variables, usually either T or P *and* either the liquid- or vapor-phase composition, allows solution for the remaining N variables by *BUBL P*, *DEW P*, *BUBL T*, and *DEW T* calculations.

Cubic equations of state give Z as a function of the independent variables T and ρ (or V). Use of such an equation in VLE calculations therefore requires $\hat{\phi}_i$ to be given by an equation suited to these variables. The derivation of such an equation starts with Eq. (11.56), written for a mixture with V^R replaced by Eq. (6.40)

$$d\left(\frac{nG^R}{RT}\right) = \frac{n(Z-1)}{P}dP - \frac{nH^R}{RT^2}dT + \sum_i \ln\hat{\phi}_i\, dn_i$$

Division by dn_i and restriction to constant T, $n/\rho(=nV)$, and n_j $(j \neq i)$ leads to

$$\ln\hat{\phi}_i = \left[\frac{\partial(nG^R/RT)}{\partial n_i}\right]_{T,n/\rho,n_j} - \frac{n(Z-1)}{P}\left(\frac{\partial P}{\partial n_i}\right)_{T,n/\rho,n_j} \tag{14.48}$$

For simplicity of notation, the partial derivatives in the following development are written without subscripts, and are understood to be at constant T, $n/\rho(=nV)$, and n_j. Thus, with $P = (nZ)RT/(n/\rho)$,

$$\frac{\partial P}{\partial n_i} = \frac{RT}{n/\rho}\frac{\partial(nZ)}{\partial n_i} = \frac{P}{nZ}\frac{\partial(nZ)}{\partial n_i} \tag{14.49}$$

Combination of Eqs. (14.48) and (14.49) yields

$$\ln\hat{\phi}_i = \frac{\partial(nG^R/RT)}{\partial n_i} - \left(\frac{Z-1}{Z}\right)\frac{\partial(nZ)}{\partial n_i} = \frac{\partial(nG^R/RT)}{\partial n_i} - \frac{\partial(nZ)}{\partial n_i} + \frac{1}{Z}\left(n\frac{\partial Z}{\partial n_i} + Z\right)$$

Equation (6.66a), written for the mixture and multiplied by n, is differentiated to give the first term on the right:

$$\frac{nG^R}{RT} = nZ - n - n\ln(1-\rho b)Z - (nq)I$$

$$\frac{\partial(nG^R/RT)}{\partial n_i} = \frac{\partial(nZ)}{\partial n_i} - 1 - \ln(1-\rho b)Z - n\left[\frac{\partial\ln(1-\rho b)}{\partial n_i} + \frac{\partial\ln Z}{\partial n_i}\right] - nq\frac{\partial I}{\partial n_i} - I\bar{q}_i$$

where use has been made of Eq. (14.47). The equation for $\ln\hat{\phi}_i$ now becomes

$$\ln\hat{\phi}_i = \frac{\partial(nZ)}{\partial n_i} - 1 - \ln(1-\rho b)Z - n\frac{\partial\ln(1-\rho b)}{\partial n_i}$$
$$- \frac{n}{Z}\frac{\partial Z}{\partial n_i} - nq\frac{\partial I}{\partial n_i} - I\bar{q}_i - \frac{\partial(nZ)}{\partial n_i} + \frac{1}{Z}\left(n\frac{\partial Z}{\partial n_i} + Z\right)$$

This reduces to: $\ln\hat{\phi}_i = \dfrac{n}{1-\rho b}\dfrac{\partial(\rho b)}{\partial n_i} - nq\dfrac{\partial I}{\partial n_i} - \ln(1-\rho b)Z - \bar{q}_i I$

All that remains is evaluation of the two partial derivatives. The first is

$$\frac{\partial(\rho b)}{\partial n_i} = \frac{\partial\left(\dfrac{nb}{n/\rho}\right)}{\partial n_i} = \frac{\rho}{n}\bar{b}_i$$

The second follows from differentiation of Eq. (6.65a). After algebraic reduction this yields

$$\frac{\partial I}{\partial n_i} = \frac{\partial(\rho b)}{\partial n_i}\,\frac{1}{(1+\sigma\rho b)(1+\epsilon\rho b)} = \frac{\bar{b}_i}{nb}\,\frac{\rho b}{(1+\sigma\rho b)(1+\epsilon\rho b)}$$

Substitution of these derivatives in the preceding equation for $\ln\hat{\phi}_i$ reduces it to

$$\ln\hat{\phi}_i = \frac{\bar{b}_i}{b}\left[\frac{\rho b}{1-\rho b} - q\frac{\rho b}{(1+\epsilon\rho b)(1+\sigma\rho b)}\right] - \ln[(1-\rho b)Z] - \bar{q}_i I$$

Reference to Eq. (6.64) shows that the term in square brackets is $Z-1$. Therefore,

$$\ln\hat{\phi}_i = \frac{\bar{b}_i}{b}(Z-1) - \ln[(1-\rho b)Z] - \bar{q}_i I$$

However, $\beta \equiv \dfrac{bP}{RT}$ and $Z \equiv \dfrac{P}{\rho RT}$; whence $\rho b = \dfrac{\beta}{Z}$.

Thus,

$$\ln\hat{\phi}_i = \frac{\bar{b}_i}{b}(Z-1) - \ln(Z-\beta) - \bar{q}_i I$$

Because experience has shown that Eq. (14.42) is an acceptable mixing rule for parameter b, it is here adopted as appropriate for present purposes. Whence,

$$nb = \sum_i n_i b_i$$

and

$$\bar{b}_i \equiv \left[\frac{\partial(nb)}{\partial n_i}\right]_{T,n_j} = \left[\frac{\partial(n_i b_i)}{\partial n_i}\right]_{T,n_j} + \sum_j \left[\frac{\partial(n_j b_j)}{\partial n_i}\right]_{T,n_j} = b_i$$

The equation for $\ln\hat{\phi}_i$ is therefore written as

$$\boxed{\ln\hat{\phi}_i = \frac{b_i}{b}(Z-1) - \ln(Z-\beta) - \bar{q}_i I} \tag{14.50}$$

where I is evaluated by Eq. (6.65b). Equation (11.37) is a special case for pure species i.

Application of Eq. (14.50) requires prior evaluation of Z at the conditions of interest by an equation of state. This may be accomplished for a liquid phase by solution of Eq. (14.38) and for a vapor phase by solution of Eq. (14.39).

Parameter q is defined in relation to parameters a and b by Eq. (14.41). The relation of partial parameter $\bar{q}_i$ to $\bar{a}_i$ and $\bar{b}_i$ is found by differentiation of this equation, written as

$$nq = \frac{n(na)}{RT(nb)}$$

Whence,

$$\bar{q}_i \equiv \left[\frac{\partial(nq)}{\partial n_i}\right]_{T,n_j} = q\left(1 + \frac{\bar{a}_i}{a} - \frac{\bar{b}_i}{b}\right) = q\left(1 + \frac{\bar{a}_i}{a} - \frac{b_i}{b}\right) \tag{14.51}$$

Any two of the three partial parameters form an independent pair, and any one of them can be found from the other two.[9]

[9]Because q, a, and b are not linearly related, $\bar{q}_i \neq \bar{a}_i/\bar{b}_i RT$.

Example 14.1

A vapor mixture of $N_2(1)$ and $CH_4(2)$ at 200 K and 30 bar contains 40 mole % N_2. Determine the fugacity coefficients of nitrogen and methane in the mixture by Eq. (14.50) and the Redlich/Kwong equation of state.

Solution

For the Redlich/Kwong equation, $\epsilon = 0$ and $\sigma = 1$, and Eq. (14.39) becomes

$$Z = 1 + \beta - q\beta \frac{Z - \beta}{Z(Z + \beta)} \qquad (A)$$

where β and q are given by Eqs. (14.40) and (14.41). Superscripts are here omitted, because all calculations are for a vapor phase. The mixing rules most commonly used with the Redlich/Kwong equation for parameters $a(T)$ and b are given by Eqs. (14.42) through (14.44). For a binary mixture they become

$$a = y_1^2 a_1 + 2y_1 y_2 \sqrt{a_1 a_2} + y_2^2 a_2 \qquad (B)$$

$$b = y_1 b_1 + y_2 b_2 \qquad (C)$$

In Eq. (B), a_1 and a_2 are pure-species parameters given by Eq. (14.31) written for the Redlich/Kwong equation:

$$a_i = (0.427\,48) \frac{T_{r_i}^{-1/2} (83.14)^2 \, T_{c_i}^2}{P_{c_i}} \text{ bar cm}^6 \text{ mol}^{-2} \qquad (D)$$

In Eq. (C), b_1 and b_2 are pure-species parameters, given by Eq. (14.32):

$$b_i = (0.086\,64) \frac{83.14\, T_{c_i}}{P_{c_i}} \text{ cm}^3 \text{ mol}^{-1} \qquad (E)$$

Critical constants for nitrogen and methane from Table B.1 and calculated values for b_i and a_i from Eqs. (D) and (E) are

	T_{c_i}/K	T_{r_i}	P_{c_i}/bar	b_i	$10^{-5} a_i$
$N_2(1)$	126.2	1.5848	34.00	26.737	10.995
$CH_4(2)$	190.6	1.0493	45.99	29.853	22.786

Mixture parameters by Eqs. (B), (C), and (14.41) are

$$a = 17.560 \times 10^5 \text{ bar cm}^6 \text{ mol}^{-2} \qquad b = 28.607 \text{ cm}^3 \text{ mol}^{-1} \qquad q = 3.6916$$

Equation (A) becomes

$$Z = 1 + \beta - 3.6916 \frac{\beta(Z - \beta)}{Z(Z + \beta)} \qquad \text{with} \qquad \beta = 0.051\,612$$

where β comes from Eq. (14.40). Iterative solution yields $Z = 0.853\,93$. Moreover, Eq. (6.65b) reduces to

$$I = \ln \frac{Z + \beta}{Z} = 0.058\,68$$

Application of Eq. (14.45) to Eq. (B) yields

$$\bar{a}_1 = \left[\frac{\partial(na)}{\partial n_1}\right]_{T,n_2} = 2y_1a_1 + 2y_2\sqrt{a_1a_2} - a$$

$$\bar{a}_2 = \left[\frac{\partial(na)}{\partial n_2}\right]_{T,n_1} = 2y_2a_2 + 2y_1\sqrt{a_1a_2} - a$$

By Eq. (14.46) applied to Eq. (C),

$$\bar{b}_1 = \left[\frac{\partial(nb)}{\partial n_1}\right]_{T,n_2} = b_1 \qquad \bar{b}_2 = \left[\frac{\partial(nb)}{\partial n_2}\right]_{T,n_1} = b_2$$

Whence, by Eq. (14.51),

$$\bar{q}_1 = q\left(\frac{2y_1a_1 + 2y_2\sqrt{a_1a_2}}{a} - \frac{b_1}{b}\right) \tag{F}$$

$$\bar{q}_2 = q\left(\frac{2y_2a_2 + 2y_1\sqrt{a_1a_2}}{a} - \frac{b_2}{b}\right) \tag{G}$$

Substitution of numerical values into these equations and into Eq. (14.50) leads to the following results:

	$\bar{q}_i$	$\ln \hat{\phi}_i$	$\hat{\phi}_i$
$N_2(1)$	2.391 94	−0.056 64	0.944 93
$CH_4(2)$	4.557 95	−0.199 66	0.819 01

The values of $\hat{\phi}_i$ agree reasonably well with those found in Ex. 11.7.

Equation (14.50) provides the means to evaluate $\hat{\phi}_i$, and is the basis for VLE calculations. A common procedure makes use of Eq. (14.29), rewritten as $y_i = K_i x_i$. Because $\sum_i y_i = 1$,

$$\sum_i K_i x_i = 1 \tag{14.52}$$

where K_i, the K-value, is given by

$$K_i = \frac{\hat{\phi}_i^l}{\hat{\phi}_i^v} \tag{14.53}$$

Thus for bubblepoint calculations, where the liquid-phase composition is known, the problem is to find the set of K-values that satisfies Eq. (14.52). A block diagram of a computer program for *BUBL P* calculations is shown by Fig. 14.9.

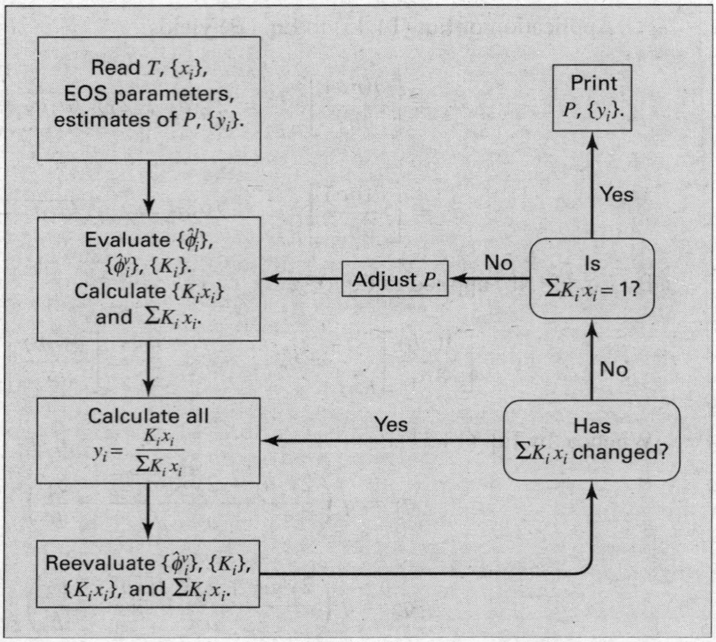

Figure 14.9: Block diagram for *BUBL P* calculation

Example 14.2

Develop the P-x-y diagram at 37.78°C (310.93 K) for the methane(1)/n-butane(2) binary system. Base calculations on the Soave/Redlich/Kwong equation with mixing rules given by Eqs. (14.42) through (14.44). Experimental data at this temperature for comparison are given by Sage et al.[10]

Solution

The procedure here is to do a *BUBL P* calculation for each experimental data point. Reference to Fig. 14.9 indicates that for each calculation estimated values of P and y_1 are required to initiate iteration. These estimates are here provided by the experimental data. Where no such data are available, several trials may be required to find values for which the iterative procedure of Fig. 14.9 converges.

Pure-species parameters a_i and b_i are found from Eqs. (14.31) and (14.32) with constants and an expression for $\alpha(T_r)$ from Table 3.1 (p. 98). For a temperature of 37.78°C (310.93 K) and with critical constants and ω_i from Table B.1, calculations provide the following pure-species values:

[10]B. H. Sage, B. L. Hicks, and W. N. Lacey, *Industrial and Engineering Chemistry*, vol. 32, pp. 1085–1092, 1940.

	T_{c_i}/K	T_{r_i}	ω_i	$\alpha(T_r)$	P_{c_i}/bar	b_i	$10^{-6}a_i$
CH_4(1)	190.6	1.6313	0.012	0.7425	45.99	29.853	1.7331
n-C_4H_{10}(2)	425.1	0.7314	0.200	1.2411	37.96	80.667	17.458

The units of b_i are cm^3 mol^{-1}, and for a_i, bar cm^6 mol^{-2}.

Note that the temperature of interest is greater than the critical temperature of methane. The P-x-y diagram will therefore be of the type shown by Fig. 10.2(a) for temperature T_b. The equations for $\alpha(T_r)$ given in Table 3.1 are based on vapor-pressure data, which extend only to the critical temperature. However, they may be applied to temperatures modestly above the critical temperature.

The mixing rules adopted here are the same as in Ex. 14.1, where Eqs. (B), (C), (F), and (G) give mixture parameters for the vapor phase. When applied to the liquid phase, x_i replaces y_i as the mole-fraction variable:

$$a^l = x_1^2 a_1 + 2x_1 x_2 \sqrt{a_1 a_2} + x_2^2 a_2 \qquad b^l = x_1 b_1 + x_2 b_2$$

$$\bar{q}_1^l = q^l \left(\frac{2x_1 a_1 + 2x_2\sqrt{a_1 a_2}}{a^l} - \frac{b_1}{b^l} \right) \qquad \bar{q}_2^l = q^l \left(\frac{2x_2 a_2 + 2x_1\sqrt{a_1 a_2}}{a^l} - \frac{b_2}{b^l} \right)$$

where q^l is given by Eq. (14.41).

For the SRK equation, $\epsilon = 0$ and $\sigma = 1$; Eqs. (14.38) and (14.39) reduce to

$$Z^l = \beta^l + Z^l(Z^l + \beta^l)\left(\frac{1 + \beta^l - Z^l}{q^l \beta^l}\right) \qquad Z^v = 1 + \beta^v - q^v \beta^v \frac{Z^v - \beta^v}{Z^v(Z^v + \beta^v)}$$

where β^l, β^v, q^l, and q^v are given by Eqs. (14.40) and (14.41). Each *BUBL P* calculation proceeds as indicated in Fig. 14.9. The first set of calculations is made for the assumed pressure. With the given liquid-phase composition and assumed vapor-phase composition, values for Z^l and Z^v are determined by the preceding equations, and fugacity coefficients $\hat{\phi}_i^l$ and $\hat{\phi}_i^v$ then follow from Eq. (14.50). Values of K_1 and K_2 come from Eq. (14.53). The constraint $y_1 + y_2 = 1$ has not been imposed, and Eq. (14.52) is unlikely to be satisfied. In this event, $K_1x_1 + K_2x_2 \neq 1$, and a new vapor composition for the next iteration is given by the normalizing equation

$$y_1 = \frac{K_1 x_1}{K_1 x_1 + K_2 x_2} \qquad \text{with} \qquad y_2 = 1 - y_1$$

This new vapor composition allows reevaluation of $\{\hat{\phi}_i^v\}$, $\{K_i\}$, and $\{K_i x_i\}$. If the sum $K_1x_1 + K_2x_2$ has changed, a new vapor composition is found and the sequence of calculations is repeated. Continued iteration leads to stable values of all quantities. If the sum $K_1x_1 + K_2x_2$ is not unity, the assumed pressure is incorrect, and must be adjusted according to some rational scheme. When $\sum_i K_i x_i > 1$, P is too low; when $\sum_i K_i x_i < 1$, P is too high. The entire iterative procedure is then repeated with a new pressure P. The last calculated values of y_i are used for the initial estimate of $\{y_i\}$. The process continues until $K_1x_1 + K_2x_2 = 1$.

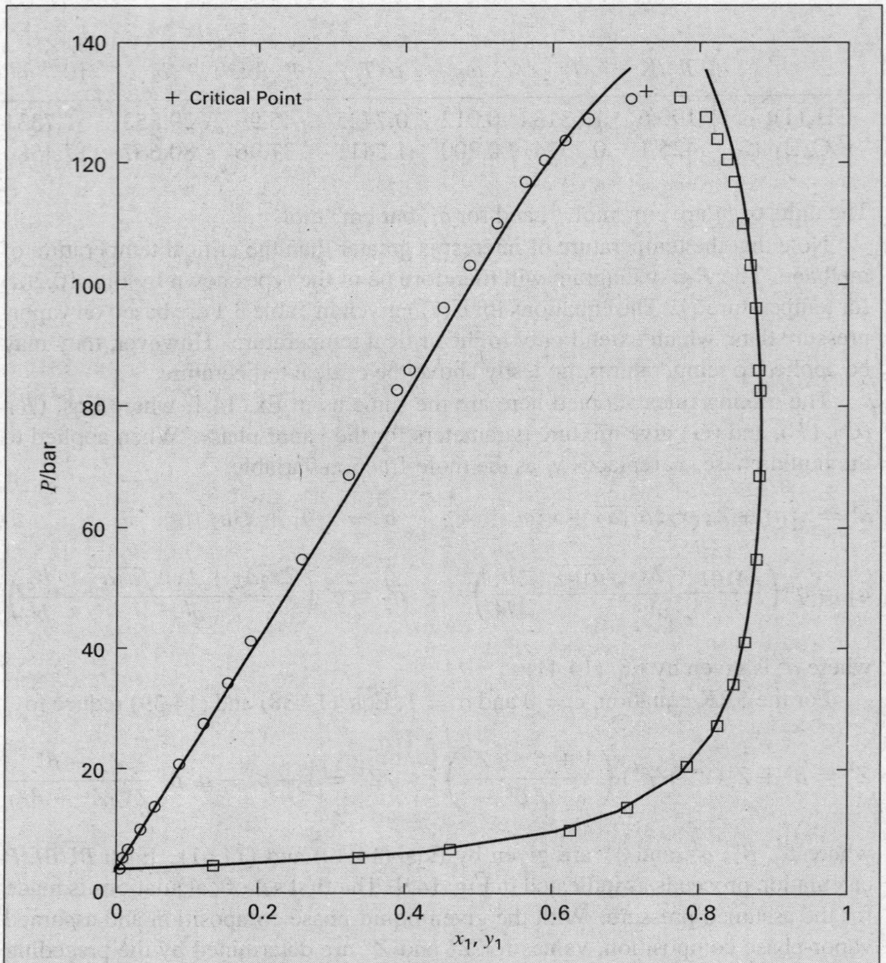

Figure 14.10: Pxy diagram at 37.78°C (310.93 K) for methane(1)/*n*-butane(2). Lines represent values from *BUBL P* calculations with the SRK equation; points are experimental values.

The results of all calculations are shown by the solid lines of Fig. 14.10. Experimental values appear as points. The root-mean-square percentage difference between experimental and calculated pressures is 3.9%, and the root-mean-square deviation between experimental and calculated y_1 values is 0.013. These results, based on the simple mixing rules of Eqs. (14.42) and (14.43), are representative for systems that exhibit modest and well-behaved deviations from ideal-solution behavior, e.g., to systems comprised of hydrocarbons and cryogenic fluids.

Summability Equation as a Mixing Rule

Although the linear mixing rule for b [Eq. (14.42)] is usually acceptable, the quadratic mixing rule for a [Eq. (14.43)] is often unsatisfactory. An alternative is a mixing rule for q that incorporates activity-coefficient data. Equation-of-state parameters are related to activity coefficients by the definitions of the activity coefficient and the fugacity coefficient:

$$\gamma_i \equiv \frac{\hat{f}_i}{x_i f_i} = \frac{\hat{f}_i / x_i P}{f_i / P} = \frac{\hat{\phi}_i}{\phi_i}$$

Whence,
$$\ln \gamma_i = \ln \hat{\phi}_i - \ln \phi_i \tag{14.54}$$

where γ_i, $\hat{\phi}_i$, and ϕ_i are all *liquid-phase properties evaluated at the same T and P*. Subtracting Eq. (11.37) from Eq. (14.50) in accord with this equation gives

$$\ln \gamma_i = \frac{b_i}{b}(Z-1) - Z_i + 1 - \ln \frac{(Z-\beta)}{(Z_i - \beta_i)} - \bar{q}_i I + q_i I_i$$

where symbols without subscripts are mixture properties. Solution for $\bar{q}_i$ yields:

$$\bar{q}_i = \frac{1}{I}\left[1 - Z_i + \frac{b_i}{b}(Z-1) - \ln \frac{(Z-\beta)}{(Z_i-\beta_i)} + q_i I_i - \ln \gamma_i\right] \tag{14.55}$$

For a pure species, this equation correctly reduces to the identity, $q_i \equiv q_i$. Because $\bar{q}_i$ is a partial property, the summability equation applies:

$$q = \sum_i x_i \bar{q}_i \tag{14.56}$$

Equations (14.55) and (14.56) together constitute a thermodynamically sound mixing rule for q.

Equations (14.55) and (14.56) apply to both liquid and vapor phases. For a liquid phase, application is direct, because the activity coefficients γ_i and the mixture properties b, Z, β, and I are for exactly the same phase. In Fig. 14.8, the solid line is for the composition of the *liquid* phase, and point B on this line lies on its *liquid* segment; there is here no confusion. Thus,

$$\bar{q}_i^l = \frac{1}{I^l}\left[1 - Z_i^l + \frac{b_i}{b^l}(Z^l - 1) - \ln \frac{(Z^l - \beta^l)}{(Z_i^l - \beta_i)} + q_i I_i^l - \ln \gamma_i\right] \tag{14.57}$$

and
$$q^l = \sum_i x_i \bar{q}_i^l \tag{14.58}$$

Application of Eq. (14.57) requires prior evaluation of Z_i^l and Z^l by Eqs. (14.35) and (14.38). These quantities are also required for evaluation of I_i^l and I^l by Eq. (6.65b). However, the equation of state contains q^l, evaluated from the $\bar{q}_i^l$ values through Eq. (14.58). Equations (14.57) and (14.58), together with Eq. (14.38) and the necessary auxiliary equations, must therefore be solved simultaneously for $\{Z_i^l\}$, Z^l, $\{I_i^l\}$, I^l, $\{\bar{q}_i^l\}$, and q^l. The results make possible the calculation of $\hat{\phi}_i^l$ values by Eq. (14.50).

In Fig. 14.8 the entire dashed line and its parameters $\bar{q}_i^v$ and q^v are for the *composition* of the vapor phase. However, its left segment represents a *liquid* with this composition. Because all properties in Eqs. 14.55 and 14.56 are *liquid*-phase properties, the activity coefficients are associated with this segment, and are values for a *liquid* phase with the *vapor* composition, denoted by the superscript l, v. Thus:

$$\bar{q}_i^v = \frac{1}{I^{l,v}}\left[1 - Z_i^l + \frac{b_i}{b^{l,v}}(Z^{l,v} - 1) - \ln\frac{(Z^{l,v} - \beta^{l,v})}{(Z_i^l - \beta_i)} + q_i I_i^l - \ln\gamma_i^{l,v}\right] \tag{14.59}$$

and

$$q^v = \sum_i y_i \bar{q}_i^v \tag{14.60}$$

These equations, together with Eq. (14.39) and the necessary auxiliary equations, must therefore be solved simultaneously for $\{Z_i^l\}$, $Z^{l,v}$, $\{I_i^l\}$, $I^{l,v}$, $\{\bar{q}_i^v\}$, and q^v, either by iteration or by the equation-solving feature of a software package. The results make possible calculation of $\hat{\phi}_i^v$ values by Eq. (14.50).

A choice must be made of an equation of state. Only the Soave/Redlich/Kwong and Peng/Robinson equations are treated here, and they usually give comparable results. A choice must also be made of a correlating equation for the liquid-phase composition dependence of $\ln\gamma_i$. The Wilson, NRTL, and UNIQUAC equations (Sec. 12.2) are of general applicability; for binary systems the Margules and van Laar equations may also be used. The equation selected depends on evidence of its suitability to the particular system treated.

The required input information includes not only the known values of T and $\{x_i\}$, but also estimates of P and $\{y_i\}$, the quantities to be evaluated. These estimates may be provided by preliminary calculations:

1. For the chosen equation of state (with appropriate values of Ω, Ψ, ϵ, and σ), for each species find values of b_i and q_i by Eqs. (14.32) and (14.34).
2. If the vapor pressure P_i^{sat} for species i at temperature T is known, determine a new value for q_i by iterative solution of Eq. (14.37) with Z_i and I_i for both liquid and vapor phases from Eqs. (14.35), (14.36), and (6.65b).
3. A reasonable estimate of P is given by the sum of known or estimated P_i^{sat} values, each weighted by its known liquid-phase mole fraction.
4. For each pure species i at the given T and estimated P, find *liquid*-phase values Z_i^l and I_i^l from Eqs. (14.35) and (6.65b).
5. For each pure species i at the given T and estimated P, find *vapor*-phase values Z_i^v and I_i^v from Eqs. (14.36) and (6.65b).
6. For each pure species i evaluate ϕ_i^l and ϕ_i^v by Eq. (11.37).
7. An initial estimate of the vapor-phase composition is based on the assumption that both the liquid and vapor phases are ideal solutions. Each fugacity coefficient is then given by $\hat{\phi}_i = \phi_i$, and Eq. (14.53) can be written ($K_i \equiv y_i/x_i$):

$$y_i = x_i \frac{\phi_i^l}{\phi_i^v}$$

Because these values are not constrained to sum to unity, they should be normalized to yield the initial estimate of vapor-phase composition.

The essential step in the iterative process of Fig. 14.9 is evaluation of $\{\hat{\phi}_i^l\}$ and $\{\hat{\phi}_i^v\}$ by Eq. (14.50). This is a complex iterative step, consisting of a number of parts. For a specific phase (liquid or vapor), application of Eq. (14.50) requires prior calculation of mixture properties Z, β, and I and partial properties $\bar{q}_i$. The mixture properties come from solution of the equation of state, Eq. (14.38) or (14.39), but this requires knowledge of q^l or q^v as calculated from $\bar{q}_i^l$ or $\bar{q}_i^v$ values by Eq. (14.58) or Eq. (14.60). Moreover, Eqs. (14.57) and (14.59) for $\bar{q}_i^l$ and $\bar{q}_i^v$ include the pure-species properties Z_i^l and q_i^l or Z_i^v and q_i^v, which must therefore be determined first. The sequence of calculations is as follows:

1. For each pure species at the current value of P (initial estimate or adjusted value) determine β_i by Eq. (14.33). Then for each pure species as a liquid at the current value of P determine Z_i^l and I_i^l by Eqs. (14.35) and (6.65b).

2. For the liquid mixture at known T and composition calculate $\{\ln \gamma_i\}$ (assumed independent of P). For this liquid mixture at the current value of P, determine Z^l, I^l, q^l, and $\{\bar{q}_i^l\}$ by iterative solution of Eqs. (14.38), (6.65b), (14.57), and (14.58). The process is implemented with an initial value, $q^l = \sum_i x_i q_i^l$. This allows solution of Eqs. (14.38) and (6.65b) for Z^l and I^l, which are used with Eq. (14.57) to yield values of $\bar{q}_i^l$. Equation (14.58) then provides a new value of q^l, and the process is repeated to convergence.

3. Evaluate the set $\{\hat{\phi}_i^l\}$ by Eq. (14.50). Values of Z^l, β^l, and I^l for the liquid mixture are known from the preceding item.

4. Repeat the calculations of item 2 for a *liquid* phase with the current *vapor*-phase composition (initial estimates or updated values) so as to determine q^v and $\{\bar{q}_i^v\}$ appropriate to the *vapor* phase. This requires iterative solution of Eqs. (14.38), (6.65b), (14.59), and (14.50) to evaluate $Z^{l,v}$, $I^{l,v}$, q^v and $\{\bar{q}_i^v\}$.

5. Determine *vapor*-phase-mixture values for Z^v, β^v, and I^v by Eqs. (14.39), (14.40), and (6.65b) at the current vapor composition.

6. Evaluate the set $\{\hat{\phi}_i^v\}$ by Eq. (14.50), with Z^v, β^v, and I^v for the vapor-phase mixture from the preceding item.

Values for $\{K_i\}$ now come from Eq. (14.53). These allow calculation of $\{K_i x_i\}$. The constraint $\sum_i y_i = 1$ has not yet been imposed; most likely $\sum_i K_i x_i \neq 1$, and Eq. (14.52) is therefore not satisfied. However, a new set of y_i values is given by the normalizing equation:

$$y_i = \frac{K_i x_i}{\sum\limits_i K_i x_i}$$

thus insuring that the y_i values for the next iteration do sum to unity.

This new set $\{y_i\}$ is used to reevaluate $\{\hat{\phi}_i^v\}$, $\{K_i\}$, and $\{K_i x_i\}$. If $\sum_i K_i x_i$ has changed, $\{y_i\}$ is again calculated and the sequence of calculations is repeated. Iteration leads to a stable value of $\sum_i K_i x_i$. If this sum is not unity, the assumed pressure is incorrect, and must be adjusted according to some rational scheme. When $\sum_i K_i x_i > 1$, P is too low; when $\sum_i K_i x_i < 1$, P is too high. The entire iterative procedure is then repeated with a new pressure P. The last calculated values of y_i are used for the initial estimate of $\{y_i\}$. The process continues until $\sum_i K_i x_i = 1$.

Extrapolation of Data to Higher Temperatures

A vast store of liquid-phase excess-property data for binary systems at temperatures near 30°C (303.15 K) and somewhat higher is available in the literature. Effective use of these data to extend G^E correlations to higher temperatures is critical to the procedure considered here. The key relations are Eq. (11.95), written as

$$d\left(\frac{G^E}{RT}\right) = -\frac{H^E}{RT^2} dT \qquad \text{(const } P, x\text{)}$$

and the excess-property analog of Eq. (2.21):

$$dH^E = C_P^E \, dT \qquad \text{(const } P, x\text{)}$$

Integration of the first of these equations from T_0 to T gives

$$\frac{G^E}{RT} = \left(\frac{G^E}{RT}\right)_{T_0} - \int_{T_0}^{T} \frac{H^E}{RT^2} dT \tag{14.61}$$

Similarly, the second equation may be integrated from T_1 to T:

$$H^E = H_1^E + \int_{T_1}^{T} C_P^E \, dT \tag{14.62}$$

In addition,

$$dC_P^E = \left(\frac{\partial C_P^E}{\partial T}\right)_{P,x} dT$$

Integration from T_2 to T yields:

$$C_P^E = C_{P_2}^E + \int_{T_2}^{T} \left(\frac{\partial C_P^E}{\partial T}\right)_{P,x} dT$$

Combining this equation with Eqs. (14.61) and (14.62) leads to

$$\frac{G^E}{RT} = \left(\frac{G^E}{RT}\right)_{T_0} - \left(\frac{H^E}{RT}\right)_{T_1} \left(\frac{T}{T_0} - 1\right) \frac{T_1}{T}$$

$$- \frac{C_{P_2}^E}{R} \left[\ln \frac{T}{T_0} - \left(\frac{T}{T_0} - 1\right) \frac{T_1}{T} \right] - J \tag{14.63}$$

where

$$J \equiv \int_{T_0}^{T} \frac{1}{RT^2} \int_{T_1}^{T} \int_{T_2}^{T} \left(\frac{\partial C_P^E}{\partial T}\right)_{P,x} dT \, dT \, dT$$

This general equation makes use of excess Gibbs-energy data at temperature T_0, excess enthalpy (heat of mixing) data at T_1, and excess heat-capacity data at T_2.

Evaluation of integral J requires information with respect to the temperature dependence of C_P^E. Because of the relative paucity of excess-heat-capacity data, the usual assumption is that this property is constant, independent of T. In this event, integral J is zero, and the closer T_0 and T_1 are to T, the less the influence of this assumption. When no information is available with respect to C_P^E, and excess enthalpy data are available at only a single temperature, the excess heat capacity must be assumed zero. In this case only the first two terms on the right side of Eq. (14.63) are retained, and it more rapidly becomes imprecise as T increases.

Because the parameters of 2-parameter correlations of G^E data are directly related to infinite-dilution values of the activity coefficients, our primary interest in Eq. (14.63) is its application to binary systems at infinite dilution of one of the constituent species. For this purpose, we divide Eq. (14.63) by the product x_1x_2. For C_P^E independent of T (and thus with $J = 0$), it then becomes

$$\frac{G^E}{x_1x_2RT} = \left(\frac{G^E}{x_1x_2RT}\right)_{T_0} - \left(\frac{H^E}{x_1x_2RT}\right)_{T_1}\left(\frac{T}{T_0} - 1\right)\frac{T_1}{T} - \frac{C_P^E}{x_1x_2R}\left[\ln\frac{T}{T_0} - \left(\frac{T}{T_0} - 1\right)\frac{T_1}{T}\right]$$

As shown in Sec. 12.1, $\left(\dfrac{G^E}{x_1x_2RT}\right)_{x_i=0} \equiv \ln\gamma_i^\infty$

The preceding equation applied at infinite dilution of species i may therefore be written as

$$\ln\gamma_i^\infty = (\ln\gamma_i^\infty)_{T_0} - \left(\frac{H^E}{x_1x_2RT}\right)_{T_1,x_i=0}\left(\frac{T}{T_0} - 1\right)\frac{T_1}{T} - \left(\frac{C_P^E}{x_1x_2R}\right)_{x_i=0}\left[\ln\frac{T}{T_0} - \left(\frac{T}{T_0} - 1\right)\frac{T_1}{T}\right] \tag{14.64}$$

Data for the ethanol(1)/water(2) binary system provide a specific illustration. At a base temperature T_0 of 90°C (363.15 K), the VLE data of Pemberton and Mash[11] yield accurate values for infinite-dilution activity coefficients:

$$(\ln\gamma_1^\infty)_{T_0} = 1.7720 \qquad \text{and} \qquad (\ln\gamma_2^\infty)_{T_0} = 0.9042$$

Correlation of the excess enthalpy data of J. A. Larkin[12] at 110°C (383.15 K) yields the values:

$$\left(\frac{H^E}{x_1x_2RT}\right)_{T_1,x_1=0} = -0.0598 \qquad \text{and} \qquad \left(\frac{H^E}{x_1x_2RT}\right)_{T_1,x_2=0} = 0.6735$$

[11]R. C. Pemberton and C. J. Mash, *Int. DATA Series, Ser. B*, vol. 1, p. 66, 1978.

[12]As reported in *Heats of Mixing Data Collection*, Chemistry Data Series, vol. III, part 1, pp. 457–459, DECHEMA, Frankfurt/Main, 1984.

Correlations of the excess enthalpy for the temperature range from 50 to 110°C (323.15 K to 383.15 K) lead to infinite-dilution values of C_P^E/x_1x_2R, which are nearly constant and equal to

$$\left(\frac{C_P^E}{x_1x_2R}\right)_{x_1=0} = 13.8 \quad \text{and} \quad \left(\frac{C_P^E}{x_1x_2R}\right)_{x_2=0} = 7.2$$

Equation (14.64) may be directly applied with these data to estimate $\ln \gamma_1^\infty$ and $\ln \gamma_2^\infty$ for temperatures greater than 90°C (363.15 K). The van Laar equations [Eqs. (12.17)] are appropriate here, with parameters directly related to the infinite-dilution activity coefficients:

$$A'_{12} = \ln \gamma_1^\infty \quad \text{and} \quad A'_{21} = \ln \gamma_2^\infty$$

These data allow prediction of VLE by an equation of state at 90°C (363.15 K) and at two higher temperatures, 150 to 200°C (423.15 K to 473.15 K), for which measured VLE data are given by Barr-David and Dodge.[13] Pemberton and Mash report pure-species vapor pressures at 90°C (363.15 K) for both ethanol and water, but the data of Barr-David and Dodge [at 150 to 200°C (423.15 K to 473.15 K)] do not include these values. They are therefore calculated from reliable correlations. Results of calculations based on the Peng/Robinson equation of state are given in Table 14.4. Shown for the three temperatures are values of the van Laar parameters A'_{12} and A'_{21}, the pure-species vapor pressures P_1^{sat} and P_2^{sat}, the equation of state parameters b_i and q_i, and root-mean-square (RMS) deviations between computed and experimental values for P and y_1.

Table 14.4: VLE Results for Ethanol(1)/Water(2)

t/T°C/K	A'_{12}	A'_{21}	P_1^{sat} bar	P_2^{sat} bar	q_1	q_2	RMS $\% \, \delta P$	RMS δy_1
90 (363.15)	1.7720	0.9042	1.5789	0.7012	12.0364	15.4551	0.29	*****
150 (423.15)	1.7356	0.7796	9.825	4.760	8.8905	12.2158	2.54	0.005
200 (473.15)	1.5204	0.6001	29.861	15.547	7.0268	10.2080	1.40	0.005

$b_1 = 54.0645 \qquad b_2 = 18.9772$

***** Vapor-phase compositions not measured.

The small value of RMS $\% \, \delta P$ shown for 90°C (363.15 K) indicates both the suitability of the van Laar equation for correlation of the VLE data and the capability of the equation of state to reproduce the data. A direct fit of these data with the van Laar equation by the gamma/phi procedure yields RMS $\% \, \delta P = 0.19$.[14] The results at 150 and 200°C (423.15 K to 473.15 K) are based only on vapor-pressure data for the pure species and on mixture data at lower temperatures. The quality of prediction is indicated by the P-x-y diagram of Fig. 14.11, which reflects the uncertainty of the data as well.

[13] F. H. Barr-David and B. F. Dodge, *J. Chem. Eng. Data*, vol. 4, pp. 107–121, 1959.

[14] As reported in *Vapor-Liquid Equilibrium Data Collection*, Chemistry Data Series, vol. 1, part 1a, p. 145, DECHEMA, Frankfurt/Main, 1981.

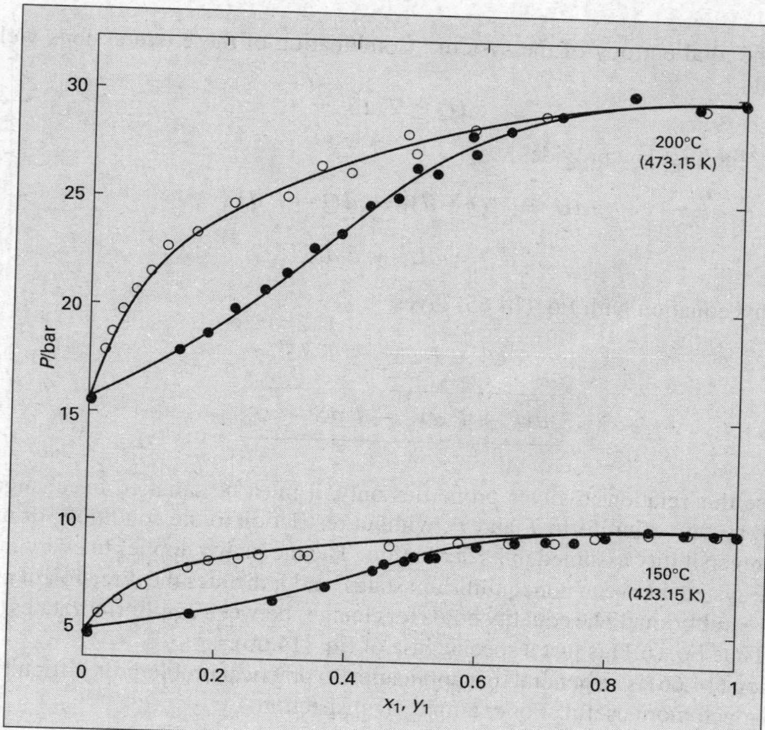

Figure 14.11: Pxy diagram for ethanol(1)/water(2). The lines represent predicted values; the points are experimental values

14.3 EQUILIBRIUM AND STABILITY

Consider a closed system containing an arbitrary number of species and comprised of an arbitrary number of phases in which the temperature and pressure are uniform (though not necessarily constant). The system is initially in a nonequilibrium state with respect to mass transfer between phases and chemical reaction. Changes which occur in the system are necessarily irreversible, and they take the system ever closer to an equilibrium state. We imagine that the system is placed in surroundings such that the system and surroundings are always in thermal and mechanical equilibrium. Heat exchange and expansion work are then accomplished reversibly. Under these circumstances the entropy change of the surroundings is

$$dS_{\text{surr}} = \frac{dQ_{\text{surr}}}{T_{\text{surr}}} = \frac{-dQ}{T}$$

The final term applies to the system, for which the heat transfer dQ has a sign opposite to that of dQ_{surr}, and the temperature of the system T replaces T_{surr}, because both must have the same value for reversible heat transfer. The second law requires

$$dS^t + dS_{\text{surr}} \geq 0$$

where S^t is the total entropy of the system. Combination of these expressions yields, upon rearrangement:

$$dQ \leq T\,dS^t \tag{14.65}$$

Application of the first law provides

$$dU^t = dQ + dW = dQ - P\,dV^t$$

or

$$dQ = dU^t + P\,dV^t$$

Combining this equation with Eq. (14.65) gives

$$dU^t + P\,dV^t \leq T\,dS^t$$

or

$$\boxed{dU^t + P\,dV^t - T\,dS^t \leq 0} \tag{14.66}$$

Because this relation involves properties only, it must be satisfied for changes in state of *any* closed system of uniform T and P, without restriction to the conditions of mechanical and thermal reversibility assumed in its derivation. The inequality applies to every incremental change of the system between nonequilibrium states, and it dictates the direction of change that leads toward equilibrium. The equality holds for changes between equilibrium states (reversible processes). Thus Eq. (6.1) is just a special case of Eq. (14.66).

Equation (14.66) is so general that application to practical problems is difficult; restricted versions are much more useful. For example, by inspection

$$(dU^t)_{S^t,V^t} \leq 0$$

where the subscripts specify properties held constant. Similarly, for processes that occur at constant U^t and V^t,

$$(dS^t)_{U^t,V^t} \geq 0$$

An *isolated* system is necessarily constrained to constant internal energy and volume, and for such a system it follows directly from the second law that the last equation is valid.

If a process is restricted to occur at constant T and P, then Eq. (14.66) may be written as

$$dU^t_{T,P} + d(PV^t)_{T,P} - d(TS^t)_{T,P} \leq 0$$

or

$$d(U^t + PV^t - TS^t)_{T,P} \leq 0$$

From the definition of the Gibbs energy [Eq. (6.3)],

$$G^t = H^t - TS^t = U^t + PV^t - TS^t$$

Therefore,

$$\boxed{(dG^t)_{T,P} \leq 0} \tag{14.67}$$

Of the possible specializations of Eq. (14.66), this is the most useful, because T and P, which are easily measured and controlled, are more logical as constants than are other pairs of variables, such as U^t and V^t.

Equation (14.67) indicates that all irreversible processes occurring at constant T and P proceed in such a direction as to cause a decrease in the Gibbs energy of the system. Therefore,

The equilibrium state of a closed system is that state for which the total Gibbs energy is a minimum with respect to all possible changes at the given *T* and *P*.

This criterion of equilibrium provides a general method for determination of equilibrium states. One writes an expression for G^t as a function of the numbers of moles (mole numbers) of the species in the several phases, and then finds the set of values for the mole numbers that minimizes G^t, subject to the constraints of mass conservation. This procedure can be applied to problems of phase, chemical-reaction, or combined phase and chemical-reaction equilibrium; it is most useful for complex equilibrium problems, and is illustrated for chemical-reaction equilibrium in Sec. 13.9.

At the equilibrium state differential variations can occur in the system at constant T and P without producing any change in G^t. This is the meaning of the equality in Eq. (14.67). Thus another form of this criterion of equilibrium is (See Fig. 13.1.):

$$\boxed{(dG^t)_{T,P} = 0} \tag{14.68}$$

To apply this equation, one develops an expression for dG^t as a function of the mole numbers of the species in the various phases, and sets it equal to zero. The resulting equation along with those representing the conservation of mass provide working equations for the solution of equilibrium problems. Equation (14.68) leads directly to Eq. (11.6) for phase equilibrium and it is applied to chemical-reaction equilibrium in Sec. 13.3.

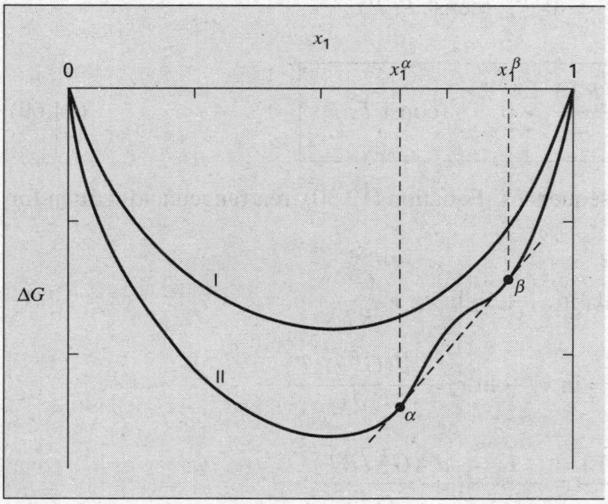

Figure 14.12: Gibbs-energy change of mixing. Curve I, complete miscibility; curve II, two phases between α and β

Equation (14.67) provides a criterion that must be satisfied by any single phase that is *stable* with respect to the alternative that it split into two phases. It requires that the Gibbs energy of an equilibrium state be the minimum value with respect to all possible changes at the given T and P. Thus, e.g., when mixing of two liquids occurs at constant T and P, the total Gibbs energy must decrease, because the mixed state must be the one of lower Gibbs energy with respect to the unmixed state. As a result,

$$G^t \equiv nG < \sum_i n_i G_i \qquad \text{from which} \qquad G < \sum_i x_i G_i$$

or

$$G - \sum_i x_i G_i < 0 \qquad (\text{const } T, P)$$

According to the definition of Eq. (12.29), the quantity on the left is the Gibbs energy change of mixing. Therefore, $\Delta G < 0$. Thus, as noted in Sec. 12.3, the Gibbs-energy change of mixing must always be negative, and a plot of G vs. x_1 for a binary system must appear as shown by one of the curves of Fig. 14.12. With respect to curve II, however, there is a further consideration. If, when mixing occurs, a system can achieve a lower value of the Gibbs energy by forming *two* phases than by forming a single phase, then the system splits into two phases. This is in fact the situation represented between points α and β on curve II of Fig. 14.12, because the straight dashed line connecting points α and β represents the G that would obtain for the range of states consisting of two phases of compositions x_1^α and x_1^β in various proportions. Thus the solid curve shown between points α and β cannot represent stable phases with respect to phase splitting. The equilibrium states between α and β consist of two phases.

These considerations lead to the following criterion of stability for a single-phase binary system for which $\Delta G \equiv G - x_1 G_1 - x_2 G_2$:

> **At constant temperature and pressure, ΔG and its first and second derivatives must be continuous functions of x_1, and the second derivative must everywhere be positive.**

Thus,

$$\frac{d^2 \Delta G}{dx_1^2} > 0 \qquad (\text{const } T, P)$$

and

$$\boxed{\frac{d^2(\Delta G/RT)}{dx_1^2} > 0 \qquad (\text{const } T, P)} \tag{14.69}$$

This requirement has a number of consequences. Equation (12.30), rearranged and written for a binary system, becomes

$$\frac{\Delta G}{RT} = x_1 \ln x_1 + x_2 \ln x_2 + \frac{G^E}{RT}$$

from which

$$\frac{d(\Delta G/RT)}{dx_1} = \ln x_1 - \ln x_2 + \frac{d(G^E/RT)}{dx_1}$$

and

$$\frac{d^2(\Delta G/RT)}{dx_1^2} = \frac{1}{x_1 x_2} + \frac{d^2(G^E/RT)}{dx_1^2}$$

Hence, equivalent to Eq. (14.69), stability requires

$$\boxed{\frac{d^2(G^E/RT)}{dx_1^2} > -\frac{1}{x_1 x_2} \qquad (\text{const } T, P)} \tag{14.70}$$

Further, for a binary mixture Eq. (12.6) is

$$\frac{G^E}{RT} = x_1 \ln \gamma_1 + x_2 \ln \gamma_2$$

and
$$\frac{d(G^E/RT)}{dx_1} = \ln \gamma_1 - \ln \gamma_2 + x_1 \frac{d \ln \gamma_1}{dx_1} + x_2 \frac{d \ln \gamma_2}{dx_1}$$

According to Eq. (12.7), the activity-coefficient form of the Gibbs/Duhem equation, the last two terms sum to zero; whence

$$\frac{d(G^E/RT)}{dx_1} = \ln \gamma_1 - \ln \gamma_2$$

A second differentiation and a second application of the Gibbs/Duhem equation gives

$$\frac{d^2(G^E/RT)}{dx_1^2} = \frac{d \ln \gamma_1}{dx_1} - \frac{d \ln \gamma_2}{dx_1} = \frac{1}{x_2} \frac{d \ln \gamma_1}{dx_1}$$

This equation in combination with Eq. (14.70) yields

$$\frac{d \ln \gamma_1}{dx_1} > -\frac{1}{x_1} \qquad \text{(const } T, P)$$

which is yet another condition for stability. It is equivalent to Eq. (14.69), from which it ultimately derives. Other stability criteria follow directly, e.g.,

$$\frac{d \hat{f}_1}{dx_1} > 0 \qquad \frac{d\mu_1}{dx_1} > 0 \qquad \text{(const } T, P)$$

The last three stability conditions can equally well be written for species 2; thus for *either* species in a binary mixture:

$$\frac{d \ln \gamma_i}{dx_i} > -\frac{1}{x_i} \qquad \text{(const } T, P) \tag{14.71}$$

$$\frac{d \hat{f}_i}{dx_i} > 0 \qquad \text{(const } T, P) \tag{14.72}$$

$$\frac{d\mu_i}{dx_i} > 0 \qquad \text{(const } T, P) \tag{14.73}$$

Example 14.3

The stability criteria apply to a *particular* phase. However, there is nothing to preclude their application to problems in phase equilibria, where the phase of interest (e.g., a liquid mixture) is in equilibrium with another phase (e.g., a vapor mixture). Consider binary isothermal vapor/liquid equilibria at pressures low enough that the vapor phase may be considered an ideal-gas mixture. What are the implications of liquid-phase stability to the features of isothermal *P-x-y* diagrams such as those in Fig. 10.8?

Solution

Focus initially on the *liquid* phase. By Eq. (14.72) applied to species 1,

$$\frac{d\hat{f}_1}{dx_1} = \hat{f}_1 \frac{d\ln\hat{f}_1}{dx_1} > 0$$

whence, because $\hat{f}_1$ cannot be negative,

$$\frac{d\ln\hat{f}_1}{dx_1} > 0$$

Similarly, with Eq. (14.72) applied to species 2 and $dx_2 = -dx_1$:

$$\frac{d\ln\hat{f}_2}{dx_1} < 0$$

Combination of the last two inequalities gives

$$\frac{d\ln\hat{f}_1}{dx_1} - \frac{d\ln\hat{f}_2}{dx_1} > 0 \qquad (\text{const } T, P) \qquad (A)$$

which is the basis for the first part of this analysis. Because $\hat{f}_i^v = y_i P$ for an ideal-gas mixture and because $\hat{f}_i^l = \hat{f}_i^v$ for VLE, the left side of Eq. (A) may be written:

$$\frac{d\ln\hat{f}_1}{dx_1} - \frac{d\ln\hat{f}_2}{dx_1} = \frac{d\ln y_1 P}{dx_1} - \frac{d\ln y_2 P}{dx_1} = \frac{d\ln y_1}{dx_1} - \frac{d\ln y_2}{dx_1}$$

$$= \frac{1}{y_1}\frac{dy_1}{dx_1} - \frac{1}{y_2}\frac{dy_2}{dx_1} = \frac{1}{y_1}\frac{dy_1}{dx_1} + \frac{1}{y_2}\frac{dy_1}{dx_1} = \frac{1}{y_1 y_2}\frac{dy_1}{dx_1}$$

Thus, Eq. (A) yields

$$\frac{dy_1}{dx_1} > 0 \qquad (B)$$

which is an essential feature of binary VLE. Note that, although P is not constant for isothermal VLE, Eq. (A) is still approximately valid, because its application is to the *liquid* phase, for which properties are insensitive to pressure.

The next part of this analysis draws on the fugacity form of the Gibbs/Duhem equation, Eq. (12.4), applied again to the *liquid* phase:

$$x_1 \frac{d\ln\hat{f}_1}{dx_1} + x_2 \frac{d\ln\hat{f}_2}{dx_1} = 0 \qquad (\text{const } T, P) \qquad (12.4)$$

Note again that the restriction here to constant P is of no significance, because of the insensitivity of liquid-phase properties to pressure. With $\hat{f}_i = y_i P$ for low-pressure VLE,

$$x_1 \frac{d\ln y_1 P}{dx_1} + x_2 \frac{d\ln y_2 P}{dx_1} = 0$$

Manipulations similar to those used to develop Eq. (B) yield

$$\frac{1}{P}\frac{dP}{dx_1} = \frac{(y_1 - x_1)}{y_1 y_2}\frac{dy_1}{dx_1} \qquad (C)$$

Because by Eq. (B) $dy_1/dx_1 > 0$, Eq. (C) asserts that the sign of dP/dx_1 is the same as the sign of the quantity $y_1 - x_1$.

The last part of this analysis is based on simple mathematics, according to which, at constant T,

$$\frac{dP}{dy_1} = \frac{dP/dx_1}{dy_1/dx_1} \qquad (D)$$

But by Eq. (B), $dy_1/dx_1 > 0$. Thus dP/dy_1 has the same sign as dP/dx_1.

In summary, the stability requirement implies the following for VLE in binary systems at constant temperature:

$$\frac{dy_1}{dx_1} > 0 \qquad \frac{dP}{dx_1},\ \frac{dP}{dy_1},\ \text{and } (y_1 - x_1) \text{ have the same sign}$$

At an azeotrope, where $y_1 = x_1$,

$$\frac{dP}{dx_1} = 0 \qquad \text{and} \qquad \frac{dP}{dy_1} = 0$$

Although derived for conditions of low pressure, these results are of general validity, as illustrated by the VLE data shown in Fig. 10.8.

14.4 LIQUID/LIQUID EQUILIBRIUM (LLE)

Many pairs of chemical species, were they to mix to form a single liquid phase in a certain composition range, would not satisfy the stability criterion of Eq. (14.69). Such systems therefore split in this composition range into two liquid phases of different compositions. If the phases are at thermodynamic equilibrium, the phenomenon is an example of *liquid/liquid equilibrium* (LLE), which is important for industrial operations such as solvent extraction.

The equilibrium criteria for LLE are the same as for VLE, namely, uniformity of T, P, and of the fugacity $\hat{f}_i$ for each chemical species throughout both phases. For LLE in a system of N species at uniform T and P, we denote the liquid phases by superscripts α and β, and write the equilibrium criteria as

$$\hat{f}_i^\alpha = \hat{f}_i^\beta \qquad (i = 1, 2, \ldots, N)$$

With the introduction of activity coefficients, this becomes

$$x_i^\alpha \gamma_i^\alpha f_i^\alpha = x_i^\beta \gamma_i^\beta f_i^\beta$$

If each pure species exists as liquid at the system temperature, $f_i^\alpha = f_i^\beta = f_i$; whence,

$$x_i^\alpha \gamma_i^\alpha = x_i^\beta \gamma_i^\beta \qquad (i = 1, 2, \ldots, N) \tag{14.74}$$

In Eq. (14.74), activity coefficients γ_i^α and γ_i^β derive from the *same function* G^E/RT; thus they are functionally identical, distinguished mathematically only by the mole fractions to which they apply. For a liquid/liquid system containing N chemical species

$$\gamma_i^\alpha = \gamma_i(x_1^\alpha, x_2^\alpha, \ldots, x_{N-1}^\alpha, T, P) \tag{14.75a}$$

$$\gamma_i^\beta = \gamma_i(x_1^\beta, x_2^\beta, \ldots, x_{N-1}^\beta, T, P) \tag{14.75b}$$

According to Eqs. (14.74) and (14.75), N equilibrium equations can be written in $2N$ intensive variables (T, P, and $N - 1$ independent mole fractions for each phase). Solution of the equilibrium equations for LLE therefore requires prior specification of numerical values for N of the intensive variables. This is in accord with the phase rule, Eq. (2.7), for which $F = 2 - \pi + N = 2 - 2 + N = N$. The same result is obtained for VLE with no special constraints on the equilibrium state.

In the general description of LLE, any number of species may be considered, and pressure may be a significant variable. We treat here a simpler (but important) special case, that of *binary* LLE either at constant pressure or at reduced temperatures low enough that the effect of pressure on the activity coefficients may be ignored. With but one independent mole fraction per phase, Eq. (14.74) gives

$$x_1^\alpha \gamma_1^\alpha = x_1^\beta \gamma_1^\beta \tag{14.76a}$$

$$(1 - x_1^\alpha)\gamma_2^\alpha = (1 - x_1^\beta)\gamma_2^\beta \tag{14.76b}$$

where

$$\gamma_i^\alpha = \gamma_i(x_1^\alpha, T) \tag{14.77a}$$

$$\gamma_i^\beta = \gamma_i(x_1^\beta, T) \tag{14.77b}$$

With two equations and three variables (x_1^α, x_1^β, and T), fixing one of the variables allows solution of Eqs. (14.76) for the remaining two. Because $\ln \gamma_i$, rather than γ_i, is a more natural thermodynamic function, application of Eqs. (14.76) often proceeds from the rearrangements:

$$\ln \frac{\gamma_1^\alpha}{\gamma_1^\beta} = \ln \frac{x_1^\beta}{x_1^\alpha} \tag{14.78a}$$

$$\ln \frac{\gamma_2^\alpha}{\gamma_2^\beta} = \ln \frac{1 - x_1^\beta}{1 - x_1^\alpha} \tag{14.78b}$$

For conditions of constant pressure, or when pressure effects are negligible, binary LLE is conveniently displayed on a *solubility diagram*, a plot of T vs. x_1. Figure 14.13 shows binary solubility diagrams of three types. The first, Fig. 14.13(*a*), shows curves (*binodal curves*) that define an "island." They represent the compositions of coexisting phases: curve UAL for the α phase (rich in species 2), and curve UBL for the β phase (rich in species 1). Equilibrium compositions x_1^α and x_1^β at a particular T are defined by the intersections of a horizontal *tie line* with the binodal curves. Temperature T_L is a lower *consolute temperature*, or lower *critical solution temperature* (LCST); temperature T_U is an upper *consolute temperature*, or upper

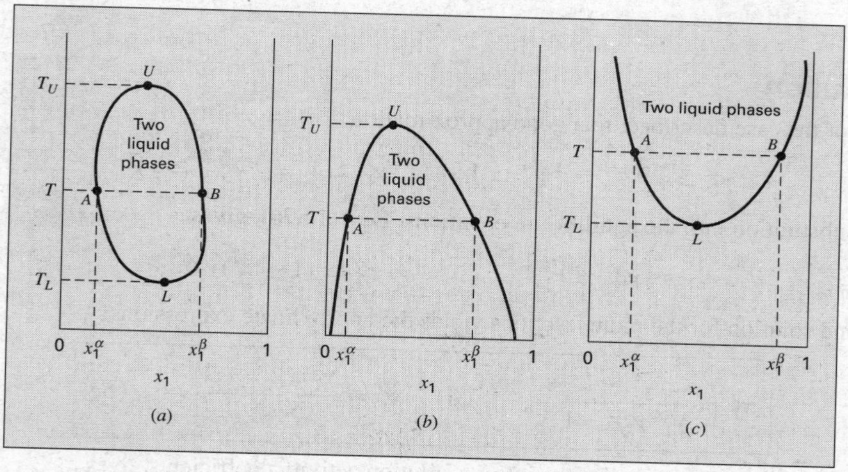

Figure 14.13: Three types of constant-pressure liquid/liquid solubility diagram

critical solution temperature (UCST). At temperatures between T_L and T_U, LLE is possible; for $T < T_L$ and $T > T_U$, a single liquid phase is obtained for the full range of compositions. The consolute points are limiting states of two-phase equilibrium for which all properties of the two equilibrium phases are identical.

Actually, the behavior shown on Fig. 14.13(a) is infrequently observed; the LLE binodal curves are often interrupted by curves for yet another phase transition. When they intersect the freezing curve, only a UCST exists [Fig. 14.13(b)]; when they intersect the VLE bubblepoint curve, only an LCST exists [Fig. 14.13(c)]; when they intersect both, no consolute point exists, and yet another behavior is observed.[15]

Thus it is apparent that real systems exhibit a diversity of LLE behavior. The thermodynamic basis for calculation or correlation of LLE is an expression for G^E/RT, from which activity coefficients are derived. The suitability of a particular expression is determined by its ability to accommodate the various features illustrated by Fig. 14.13. This is a *severe* test, because, unlike their role in low-pressure VLE where they represent corrections to Raoult's law, the activity coefficients here are the *only* thermodynamic contribution to an LLE calculation.

Example 14.4

Develop equations that apply to the limiting case of binary LLE for which the α phase is very dilute in species 1 and the β phase is very dilute in species 2.

[15]A comprehensive treatment of LLE is given by J. M. Sørensen, T. Magnussen, P. Rasmussen, and Aa. Fredenslund, *Fluid Phase Equilibria*, vol. 2, pp. 297–309, 1979; vol. 3, pp. 47–82, 1979; vol. 4, pp. 151–163, 1980. For a compilation of data see W. Arlt, M. E. A. Macedo, P. Rasmussen, and J. M. Sørensen, *Liquid-Liquid Equilibrium Data Collection*, Chemistry Data Series, vol. V, Parts 1–4, DECHEMA, Frankfurt/Main, 1979–1987.

Solution

For the case described, to a good approximation,

$$\gamma_1^\alpha \simeq \gamma_1^\infty \qquad \gamma_2^\alpha \simeq 1 \qquad \gamma_1^\beta \simeq 1 \qquad \gamma_2^\beta \simeq \gamma_2^\infty$$

Substitution into the equilibrium equations, Eqs. (14.76), gives:

$$x_1^\alpha \gamma_1^\infty \simeq x_1^\beta \qquad 1 - x_1^\alpha \simeq (1 - x_1^\beta)\gamma_2^\infty$$

and solution for the mole fractions yields the approximate expressions:

$$x_1^\alpha = \frac{\gamma_2^\infty - 1}{\gamma_1^\infty \gamma_2^\infty - 1} \quad (A) \qquad x_1^\beta = \frac{\gamma_1^\infty(\gamma_2^\infty - 1)}{\gamma_1^\infty \gamma_2^\infty - 1} \quad (B)$$

Alternatively, solution for the infinite-dilution activity coefficients gives

$$\gamma_1^\infty = \frac{x_1^\beta}{x_1^\alpha} \quad (C) \qquad \gamma_2^\infty = \frac{1 - x_1^\alpha}{1 - x_1^\beta} \quad (D)$$

Equations (A) and (B) provide order-of-magnitude estimates of equilibrium compositions from two-parameter expressions for G^E/RT, where γ_i^∞ is usually related to the parameters in a simple way. Equations (C) and (D) serve the opposite function; they provide simple explicit expressions for γ_i^∞ in relation to measurable equilibrium compositions. Equations (C) and (D) show that positive deviations from ideal-solution behavior promote LLE:

$$\gamma_1^\infty \simeq \frac{1}{x_1^\alpha} > 1 \qquad \text{and} \qquad \gamma_2^\infty \simeq \frac{1}{x_2^\beta} > 1$$

The extreme example of binary LLE is that of *complete immiscibility* of the two species. When $x_1^\alpha = x_2^\beta = 0$, γ_1^β and γ_2^α are unity, and Eqs. (14.76) therefore require

$$\gamma_1^\alpha = \gamma_2^\beta = \infty$$

Strictly speaking, probably no two liquids are completely immiscible. However, actual solubilities may be so small (e.g., for some hydrocarbon/water systems) that the idealizations $x_1^\alpha = x_2^\beta = 0$ provide suitable approximations for practical calculations (Ex. 14.9).

Example 14.5

The simplest expression for G^E/RT capable of predicting LLE is:

$$\frac{G^E}{RT} = A x_1 x_2 \qquad (A)$$

Derive the equations resulting from application of this equation to LLE.

Solution

The activity coefficients implied by the given equation are

$$\ln \gamma_1 = Ax_2^2 = A(1 - x_1)^2 \qquad \text{and} \qquad \ln \gamma_2 = Ax_1^2$$

Specializing these two expressions to the α and β phases and combining them with Eqs. (14.78) gives:

$$A\left[(1 - x_1^\alpha)^2 - (1 - x_1^\beta)^2\right] = \ln \frac{x_1^\beta}{x_1^\alpha} \qquad (B)$$

$$A\left[(x_1^\alpha)^2 - (x_1^\beta)^2\right] = \ln \frac{1 - x_1^\beta}{1 - x_1^\alpha} \qquad (C)$$

Given a value of parameter A, one finds equilibrium compositions x_1^α and x_1^β as the solution to Eqs. (B) and (C).

Solubility curves implied by Eq. (A) are symmetrical about $x_1 = 0.5$, because substitution of the relation,

$$x_1^\beta = 1 - x_1^\alpha \qquad (D)$$

into Eqs. (B) and (C) reduces them both to the *same* equation:

$$A(1 - 2x_1) = \ln \frac{1 - x_1}{x_1} \qquad (E)$$

When $A > 2$, this equation has three real roots: $x_1 = 1/2$, $x_1 = r$, and $x_1 = 1 - r$, where $0 < r < 1/2$. The latter two roots are the *equilibrium* compositions (x_1^α and x_1^β), whereas the first root is a trivial solution. For $A < 2$ only the trivial solution exists; the value $A = 2$ corresponds to a consolute point, where the three roots converge to the value 1/2. Table 14.5 shows values of A as calculated from Eq. (E) for various values of x_1^α ($= 1 - x_1^\beta$). Note particularly the sensitivity of x_1^α to small increases in A from its limiting value of 2.

The actual *shape* of a solubility curve is determined by the temperature dependence of G^E/RT. Assume the following T dependence of parameter A in Eq. (A):

$$A = \frac{a}{T} + b - c \ln T \qquad (F)$$

where a, b, and c are constants. By Eq. (11.95), this requires the excess enthalpy H^E to be linear in T, and the excess heat capacity C_P^E to be independent of T:

$$H^E = R(a + cT)x_1 x_2 \qquad (G)$$

$$C_P^E = \left(\frac{\partial H^E}{\partial T}\right)_{P,x} = Rcx_1x_2 \qquad (H)$$

The excess enthalpy and the temperature dependence of A are directly related.

Table 14.5: Liquid/liquid equilibrium compositions implied by Eq. (A)

A	x_1^α	A	x_1^α
2.0	0.5	2.4780	0.15
2.0067	0.45	2.7465	0.1
2.0273	0.4	3.2716	0.05
2.0635	0.35	4.6889	0.01
2.1182	0.3	5.3468	0.005
2.1972	0.25	6.9206	0.001
2.3105	0.2	7.6080	0.0005

From Eq. (F), $$\frac{dA}{dT} = -\frac{1}{T^2}(a + cT)$$

Combination of this equation with Eq. (G) yields

$$\frac{dA}{dT} = -\frac{H^E}{x_1 x_2 RT^2}$$

Thus dA/dT is negative for an endothermic system (positive H^E) and positive for an exothermic system (negative H^E). A negative value of dA/dT at a consolute point implies a UCST, because A decreases to 2.0 as T *increases*. Conversely, a positive value implies an LCST, because A decreases to 2.0 as T *decreases*. Hence a system described by Eqs. (A) and (F) exhibits a UCST if endothermic at the consolute point and an LCST if exothermic at the consolute point. Equation (F) written for a consolute point ($A = 2$) becomes

$$T \ln T = \frac{a}{c} - \left(\frac{2-b}{c}\right) T \tag{I}$$

Depending on the values of a, b, and c, this equation has zero, one, or two temperature roots.

Consider hypothetical binary systems described by Eqs. (A) and (F) and for which LLE obtains in the temperature range 250 to 450 K. Setting $c = 3.0$ makes the excess heat capacity positive, independent of T, for which by Eq. (H) the maximum value (at $x_1 = x_2 = 0.5$) is 6.24 J mol^{-1} K^{-1}. For the first case, let

$$A = \frac{-975}{T} + 22.4 - 3 \ln T$$

Here, Eq. (I) has two roots, corresponding to an LCST and a UCST:

$$T_L = 272.9 \qquad \text{and} \qquad T_U = 391.2 \text{ K}$$

Values of A are plotted vs. T in Fig. 14.14(a) and the solubility curve [from Eq. (E)] is shown by Fig. 14.14(b). This case— that of a closed solubility loop—

is of the type shown by Fig. 14.12(*a*). It requires that H^E *change sign* in the temperature interval for which LLE obtains.

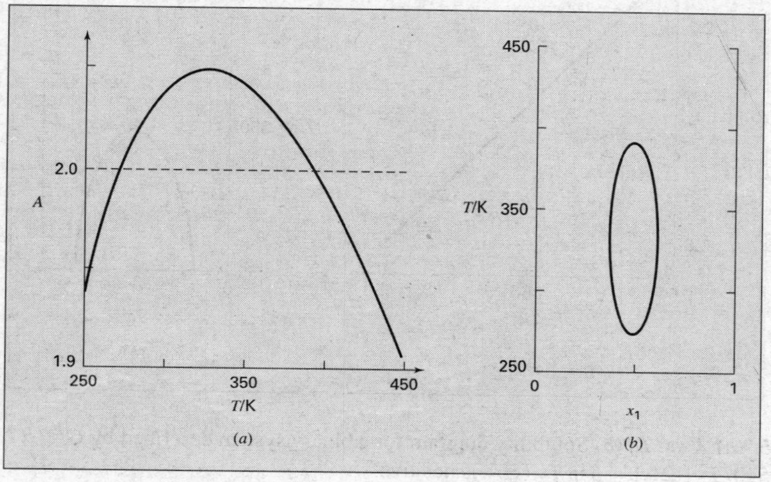

Figure 14.14: (*a*) A vs. T. (*b*) Solubility diagram for a binary system described by $G^E/RT = Ax_1x_2$ with $A = -975/T + 22.4 - 3\ln T$. ($H^E$ changes sign.)

As a second case, let

$$A = \frac{-540}{T} + 21.1 - 3\ln T$$

Here, Eq. (I) has only *one* root in the temperature range 250 to 450 K. It is a UCST, $T_U = 346.0$ K, because Eq. (G) yields positive H^E at this temperature. Values of A and the corresponding solubility curve are given by Fig. 14.15.

Finally, let

$$A = \frac{-1{,}500}{T} + 23.9 - 3\ln T$$

This case is similar to the second, there being only one T (339.7 K) that solves Eq. (I) for the temperature range considered. However, this is an LCST, because H^E is now negative. Values of A and the solubility curve are shown in Fig. 14.16.

Example 14.5 demonstrates in a "brute-force" way that LLE cannot be predicted by the expression $G^E/RT = Ax_1x_2$ for values of $A < 2$. If the goal is merely to determine under what conditions LLE can occur, but not to find the compositions of the coexisting phases, then one may instead invoke the stability criteria of Sec. 14.3, and determine under what conditions they are satisfied.

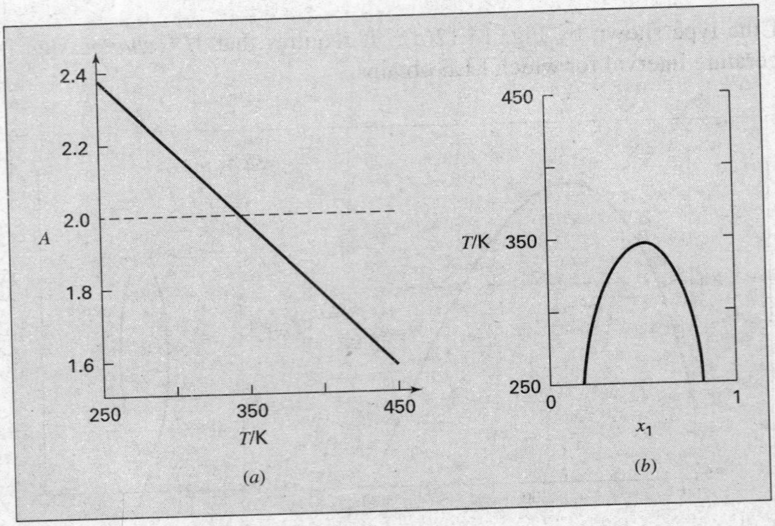

Figure 14.15: (a) A vs. T; (b) Solubility diagram for a binary system described by $G^E/RT = Ax_1x_2$ with $A = -540/T + 21.1 - 3\ln T$. ($H^E$ is positive.)

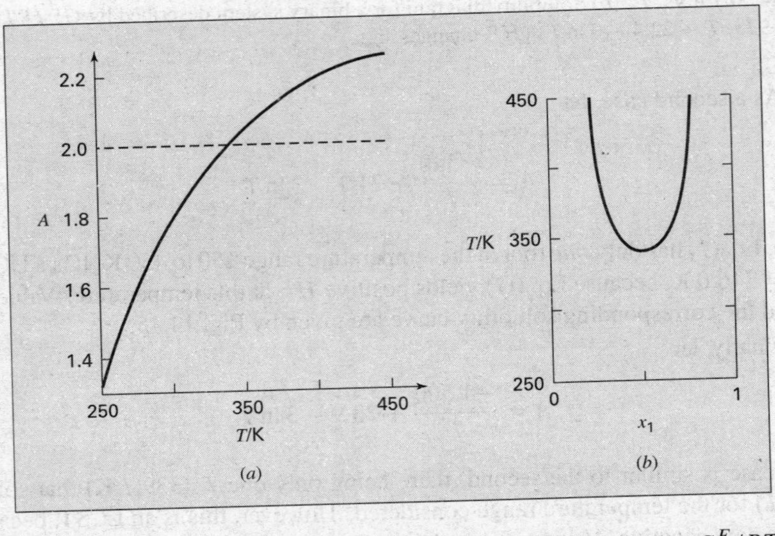

Figure 14.16: (a) A vs. T; (b) Solubility diagram for a binary system described by $G^E/RT = Ax_1x_2$ with $A = -1{,}500/T + 23.9 - 3\ln T$. ($H^E$ is negative.)

Example 14.6

If $G^E/RT = Ax_1x_2$ for a liquid phase, show by stability analysis that LLE is predicted for $A \geq 2$.

Solution

Application of inequality (14.70) requires evaluation of the derivative:

$$\frac{d^2(G^E/RT)}{dx_1^2} = \frac{d^2(Ax_1x_2)}{dx_1^2} = -2A$$

Thus, stability requires: $\quad 2A < \dfrac{1}{x_1x_2}$

When $x_1 = x_2 = 1/2$, the right side of this inequality has its minimum value of 4; thus $A < 2$ yields stability of single-phase mixtures over the entire composition range. Conversely, if $A > 2$, then binary mixtures described by $G^E/RT = Ax_1x_2$ form two liquid phases over some part of the composition range.

Example 14.7

Some expressions for G^E/RT are incapable of representing LLE. An example is the Wilson equation:

$$\frac{G^E}{RT} = -x_1 \ln(x_1 + x_2\Lambda_{12}) - x_2 \ln(x_2 + x_1\Lambda_{21}) \qquad (12.18)$$

Show that the stability criteria are satisfied for all values of Λ_{12}, Λ_{21}, and x_1.

Solution

An equivalent form of inequality (14.71) for species 1 is

$$\frac{d \ln(x_1\gamma_1)}{dx_1} > 0 \qquad (A)$$

For the Wilson equation, $\ln \gamma_1$ is given by Eq. (12.19a). Addition of $\ln x_1$ to both sides of that equation yields

$$\ln(x_1\gamma_1) = -\ln\left(1 + \frac{x_2}{x_1}\Lambda_{12}\right) + x_2\left(\frac{\Lambda_{12}}{x_1 + x_2\Lambda_{12}} - \frac{\Lambda_{21}}{x_2 + x_1\Lambda_{21}}\right)$$

from which: $$\frac{d \ln(x_1\gamma_1)}{dx_1} = \frac{x_2\Lambda_{12}^2}{x_1(x_1 + x_2\Lambda_{12})^2} + \frac{\Lambda_{21}^2}{(x_2 + x_1\Lambda_{21})^2}$$

All quantities on the right side of this equation are positive, and therefore Eq. (A) is satisfied for all x_1 and for all nonzero Λ_{12} and Λ_{21}.[16] Thus inequality (14.71) is always satisfied, and LLE cannot be represented by the Wilson equation.

[16]Both Λ_{12} and Λ_{21} are positive *definite*, because $\Lambda_{12} = \Lambda_{21} = 0$ yields infinite values for γ_1^∞ and γ_2^∞.

14.5 VAPOR/LIQUID/LIQUID EQUILIBRIUM (VLLE)

As noted in Sec. 14.4, the binodal curves representing LLE can intersect the VLE bubblepoint curve. This gives rise to the phenomenon of vapor/liquid/liquid equilibrium (VLLE). A binary system of two liquid phases and one vapor phase in equilibrium has (by the phase rule) but one degree of freedom. For a given pressure, the temperature and the compositions of all three phases are therefore fixed. On a temperature/composition diagram the points representing the states of the three phases in equilibrium fall on a horizontal line at T^*. In Fig. 14.17, points C and D represent the two liquid phases, and point E represents the vapor phase. If more of either species is added to a system whose overall composition lies between points C and D, and if the three-phase equilibrium pressure is maintained, the phase rule requires that the temperature and the compositions of the phases be unchanged. However, the relative amounts of the phases adjust themselves to reflect the change in overall composition of the system.

At temperatures above T^* in Fig. 14.17, the system may be a single liquid phase, two phases (liquid and vapor), or a single vapor phase, depending on the overall composition. In region α the system is a single liquid, rich in species 2; in region β it is a single liquid, rich in species 1. In region α–V, liquid and vapor are in equilibrium. The states of the individual phases fall on lines AC and AE. In region β–V, liquid and vapor phases, described by lines BD and BE, also exist at equilibrium. Finally, in the region designated V, the system is a single vapor phase. Below the three-phase temperature T^*, the system is entirely liquid, with features described in Sec. 14.4; this is the region of LLE.

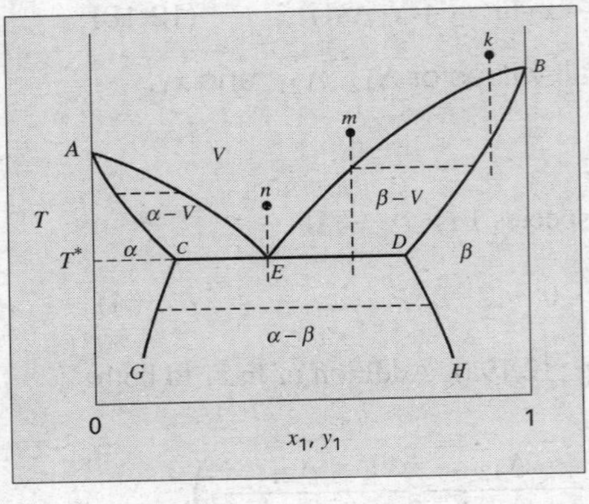

Figure 14.17: Txy diagram at constant P for a binary system exhibiting VLLE

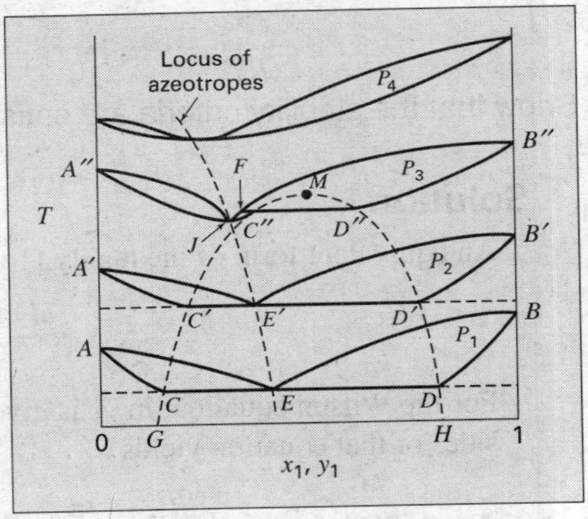

Figure 14.18: Txy diagram for several pressures

When a vapor is cooled at constant pressure, it follows a path represented on Fig. 14.17 by a vertical line. Several such lines are shown. If one starts at point k, the vapor first reaches its dewpoint at line BE and then its bubblepoint at line BD, where condensation into single liquid phase β is complete. This is the same process that takes place when the species are completely miscible. If one starts at point n, no condensation of the vapor occurs until temperature T^* is reached. Then condensation occurs entirely at this temperature, producing the two liquid phases represented by points C and D. If one starts at an intermediate point m, the process is a combination of the two just described. After the dewpoint is reached, the vapor, tracing a path along line BE, is in equilibrium with a liquid tracing a path along line BD. However, at temperature T^* the vapor phase is at point E. All remaining condensation therefore occurs at this temperature, producing the two liquids of points C and D.

Figure 14.17 is drawn for a single constant pressure; equilibrium phase compositions, and hence the locations of the lines, change with pressure, but the general nature of the diagram is the same over a range of pressures. For most systems the species become more soluble in one another as the temperature increases, as indicated by lines CG and DH of Fig. 14.17. If this diagram is drawn for successively higher pressures, the corresponding three-phase equilibrium temperatures increase, and lines CG and DH extend further and further until they meet at the liquid/liquid consolute point M, as shown by Fig. 14.18.

As the pressure increases, line CD becomes shorter and shorter (indicated in Fig. 14.18 by lines $C'D'$ and $C''D''$), until at point M it diminishes to a differential length. For still higher pressures (P_4) the temperature is above the critical-solution temperature, and there is but a single liquid phase. The diagram then represents two-phase VLE, and it has the form of Fig. 10.9(*d*), exhibiting a minimum-boiling azeotrope.

For an intermediate range of pressures, the vapor phase in equilibrium with the two liquid phases has a composition that does not lie between the compositions of the two liquids. This is illustrated in Fig. 14.18 by the curves for P_3, which terminate at A'' and B''. The vapor in equilibrium with the two liquids at C'' and D'' is at point F. In addition the system exhibits an azeotrope, as indicated at point J.

Not all systems behave as described in the preceding paragraphs. Sometimes the upper critical-solution temperature is never attained, because a vapor/liquid critical temperature is reached first. In other cases the liquid solubilities decrease with an increase in temperature. In this event a lower critical-solution temperature exists, unless solid phases appear first. There are also systems which exhibit both upper and lower critical-solution temperatures.[17]

Figure 14.19 is the phase diagram drawn at *constant* T corresponding to the constant-P diagram of Fig. 14.17. On it we identify the three-phase-equilibrium pressure as P^*, the three-phase-equilibrium vapor composition as y_1^*, and the compositions of the two liquid phases that contribute to the vapor/liquid/liquid equilibrium state as x_1^α and x_1^β. The phase boundaries separating the three liquid-phase regions are nearly vertical, because pressure has only a weak influence on liquid solubilities.

The compositions of the vapor and liquid phases in equilibrium for partially miscible systems are calculated in the same way as for miscible systems. In the regions where a single liquid is in equilibrium with its vapor, the general nature of Fig. 14.19 is not different in any essential way from that of Fig. 10.8(*d*). Because limited miscibility implies highly nonideal behavior, any general assumption of liquid-phase ideality is excluded. Even a combination of Henry's law, valid for a species at infinite dilution, and Raoult's law, valid for a species as it approaches purity, is not very useful, because each approximates actual behavior for only a very small composition range. Thus G^E is large, and its composition dependence is often not adequately represented by simple equations. Nevertheless, the NRTL and UNIQUAC equations and the UNIFAC method (App. H) provide suitable correlations for activity coefficients.

[17]For a comprehensive discussion of binary fluid-phase behavior, see J. S. Rowlinson and F. L. Swinton, *Liquids and Liquid Mixtures*, 3d ed., Butterworth Scientific, London, 1982.

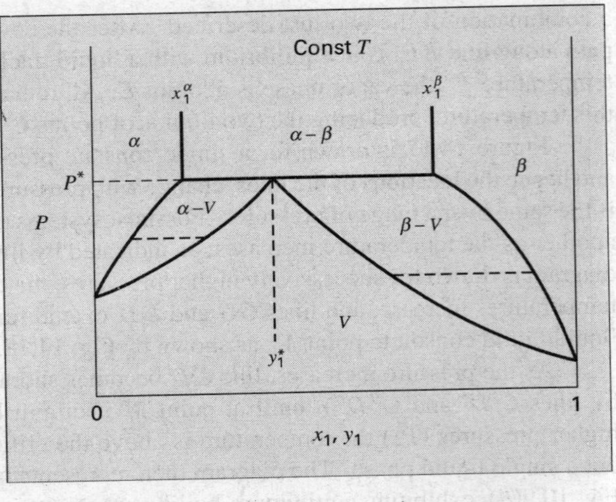

Figure 14.19: Pxy diagram at constant T for two partially miscible liquids

Example 14.8

Careful equilibrium measurements for the diethyl ether(1)/water(2) system at 35°C (308.15 K) have been reported.[18] Discuss the correlation and behavior of the phase-equilibrium data for this system.

Solution

The P-x-y behavior of this system is shown by Fig. 14.20, where the very rapid rise in pressure with increasing liquid-phase ether concentration in the dilute-ether region is apparent. The three-phase pressure, $P^* = 104.6$ kPa, is reached at an ether mole fraction of only 0.0117. Here, y_1 also increases very rapidly to its three-phase value of $y_1^* = 0.946$. In the dilute-water region, on the other hand, rates of change are quite small, as shown to an expanded scale in Fig. 14.20(b).

The curves in Fig. 14.20 provide an excellent correlation of the VLE data. They result from *BUBL P* calculations carried out as indicated in Fig. 14.1. The excess Gibbs energy and activity coefficients are here expressed as functions of liquid-phase composition by a 4-parameter modified Margules equation [see Eqs. (12.9) and (12.10)]:

$$\frac{G^E}{x_1 x_2 RT} = A_{21}x_1 + A_{12}x_2 - Q$$

$$\ln \gamma_1 = x_2^2\left[A_{12} + 2(A_{21} - A_{12})x_1 - Q - x_1\frac{dQ}{dx_1}\right]$$

$$\ln \gamma_2 = x_1^2\left[A_{21} + 2(A_{12} - A_{21})x_2 - Q + x_2\frac{dQ}{dx_1}\right]$$

[18] M. A. Villamañán, A. J. Allawi, and H. C. Van Ness, *J. Chem. Eng. Data*, vol. 29, pp. 431–435, 1984.

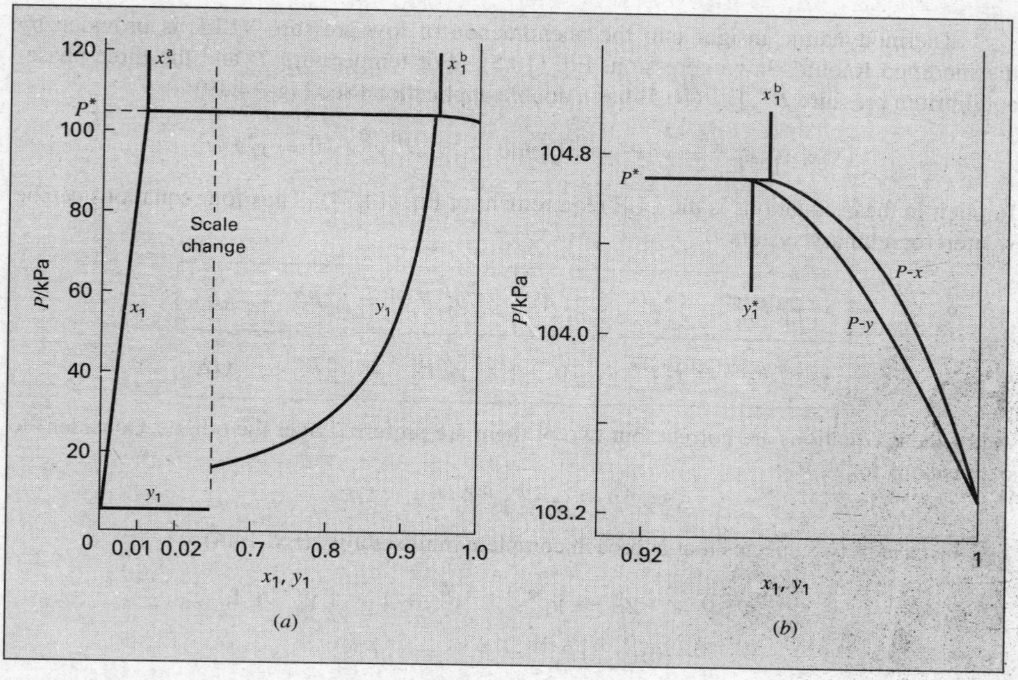

Figure 14.20: (*a*) Pxy diagram at 35°C (308.15 K) for diethyl ether(1)/water(2); (*b*) Detail of ether-rich region

$$Q = \frac{\alpha_{12}x_1\alpha_{21}x_2}{\alpha_{12}x_1 + \alpha_{21}x_2} \qquad \frac{dQ}{dx_1} = \frac{\alpha_{12}\alpha_{21}(\alpha_{21}x_2^2 - \alpha_{12}x_1^2)}{(\alpha_{12}x_1 + \alpha_{21}x_2)^2}$$

$$A_{21} = 3.356\,29 \qquad A_{12} = 4.624\,24 \qquad \alpha_{12} = 3.786\,08 \qquad \alpha_{21} = 1.817\,75$$

The *BUBL P* calculations also require values of Φ_1 and Φ_2, which come from Eqs. (14.7) with virial coefficients:

$$B_{11} = -996 \qquad B_{22} = -1245 \qquad B_{12} = -567 \text{ cm}^3 \text{ mol}^{-1}$$

In addition, the vapor pressures of the pure species at 35°C are

$$P_1^{\text{sat}} = 103.264 \qquad P_2^{\text{sat}} = 5.633 \text{ kPa}$$

The high degree of nonideality of the liquid phase is indicated by the values of the activity coefficients of the dilute species, which range for diethyl ether from $\gamma_1 = 81.8$ at $x_1^\alpha = 0.0117$ to $\gamma_1^\infty = 101.9$ at $x_1 = 0$ and for water from $\gamma_2 = 19.8$ at $x_1^\beta = 0.9500$ to $\gamma_2^\infty = 28.7$ at $x_1 = 1$.

Thermodynamic insight into the phenomenon of low-pressure VLLE is provided by the modified Raoult's-law expression, Eq. (10.5). For temperature T and the three-phase-equilibrium pressure P^*, Eq. (10.5) has a double application (See Fig. 14.19):

$$x_i^\alpha \gamma_i^\alpha P_i^{\text{sat}} = y_i^* P^* \quad \text{and} \quad x_i^\beta \gamma_i^\beta P_i^{\text{sat}} = y_i^* P^*$$

Implicit in these equations is the LLE requirement of Eq. (14.74). Thus four equations can be written for a binary system:

$x_1^\alpha \gamma_1^\alpha P_1^{\text{sat}} = y_1^* P^*$ (A)	$x_1^\beta \gamma_1^\beta P_1^{\text{sat}} = y_1^* P^*$ (B)
$x_2^\alpha \gamma_2^\alpha P_2^{\text{sat}} = y_2^* P^*$ (C)	$x_2^\beta \gamma_2^\beta P_2^{\text{sat}} = y_2^* P^*$ (D)

All of these equations are correct, but two of them are preferred over the others. Consider the expressions for $y_1^* P^*$:

$$x_1^\alpha \gamma_1^\alpha P_1^{\text{sat}} = x_1^\beta \gamma_1^\beta P_1^{\text{sat}} = y_1^* P^*$$

For the case of two species that approach complete immiscibility (Ex. 14.4),

$$x_1^\alpha \to 0 \qquad \gamma_1^\alpha \to \gamma_1^\infty \qquad x_1^\beta \to 1 \qquad \gamma_1^\beta \to 1$$

Thus,
$$(0)(\gamma_1^\infty)P_1^{\text{sat}} = P_1^{\text{sat}} = y_1^* P^*$$

This equation implies that $\gamma_1^\infty \to \infty$; a similar derivation shows that $\gamma_2^\infty \to \infty$. Thus Eqs. ($B$) and ($C$), which include neither γ_1^α nor γ_2^β, are chosen as the more useful expressions. They may be added to give the three-phase pressure:

$$P^* = x_1^\beta \gamma_1^\beta P_1^{\text{sat}} + x_2^\alpha \gamma_2^\alpha P_2^{\text{sat}} \tag{14.79}$$

In addition, the three-phase vapor composition is given by Eq. (B):

$$y_1^* = \frac{x_1^\beta \gamma_1^\beta P_1^{\text{sat}}}{P^*} \tag{14.80}$$

For the diethyl ether(1)/water(2) system at 35°C (Ex. 14.8), the correlation for G^E/RT provides the values:

$$\gamma_1^\beta = 1.0095 \qquad \gamma_2^\alpha = 1.0013$$

These allow calculation of P^* and y_1^* by Eqs. (14.79) and (14.80):

$$P^* = (0.9500)(1.0095)(103.264) + (0.9883)(1.0013)(5.633) = 104.6 \text{ kPa}$$

and
$$y_1^* = \frac{(0.9500)(1.0095)(103.264)}{104.6} = 0.946$$

Although no two liquids are totally immiscible, this condition is so closely approached in some instances that the assumption of complete immiscibility does not lead to apprecia-ble error. The phase characteristics of an immiscible system are illustrated by the temper-ature/composition diagram of Fig. 14.21(a). This diagram is a special case of Fig. 14.17

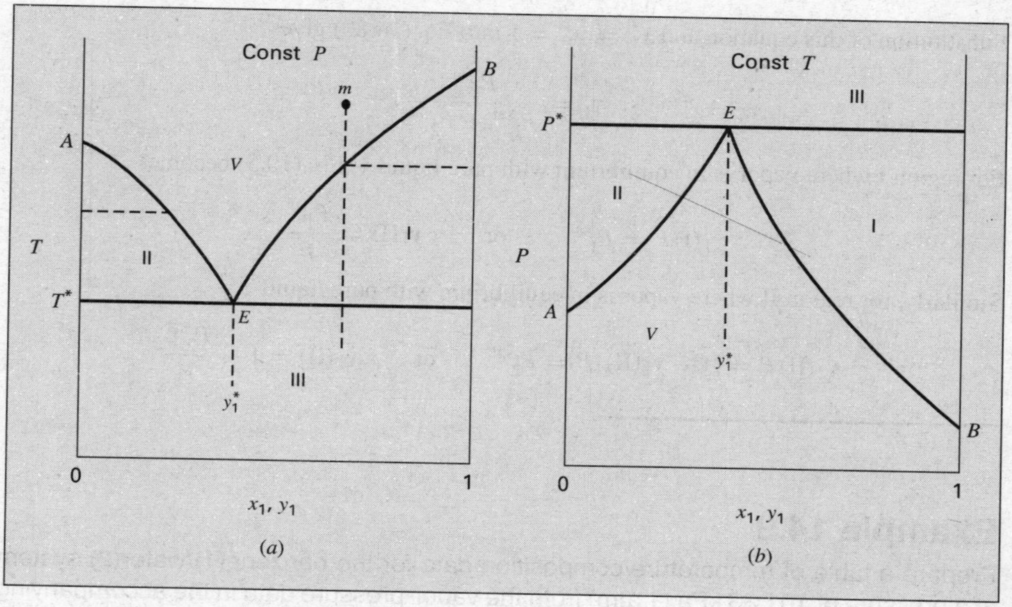

Figure 14.21: Binary system of immiscible liquids. (*a*) Txy diagram; (*b*) Pxy diagram

wherein phase α is pure species 2 and phase β is pure species 1. Thus lines ACG and BDH of Fig. 14.17 become in Fig. 14.21(*a*) vertical lines at $x_1 = 0$ and $x_1 = 1$.

In region I, vapor phases with compositions represented by line BE are in equilibrium with pure liquid 1. Similarly, in region II, vapor phases whose compositions lie along line AE are in equilibrium with pure liquid 2. Liquid/liquid equilibrium exists in region III, where the two phases are pure liquids 1 and 2. If one cools a vapor mixture starting at point m, the constant-composition path is represented by the vertical line shown in the figure. At the dewpoint, where this line crosses line BE, pure liquid 1 begins to condense. Further reduction in temperature toward T^* causes continued condensation of pure liquid 1; the vapor-phase composition progresses along line BE until it reaches point E. Here, the remaining vapor condenses at temperature T^*, producing two liquid phases, one of pure species 1 and the other of pure species 2. A similar process, carried out to the left of point E, is the same, except that pure liquid 2 condenses initially. The constant-temperature phase diagram for an immiscible system is represented by Fig. 14.21(*b*).

Numerical calculations for immiscible systems are particularly simple, because of the following identities:

$$x_2^\alpha = 1 \qquad \gamma_2^\alpha = 1 \qquad x_1^\beta = 1 \qquad \gamma_1^\beta = 1$$

The three-phase-equilibrium pressure P^* as given by Eq. (14.79) is therefore

$$P^* = P_1^{\text{sat}} + P_2^{\text{sat}}$$

Substitution of this equation and $x_1^\beta = \gamma_1^\beta = 1$ into Eq. (14.80) gives

$$y_1^* = \frac{P_1^{sat}}{P_1^{sat} + P_2^{sat}}$$

For region I where vapor is in equilibrium with pure liquid 1, Eq. (10.5) becomes

$$y_1(\text{I})P = P_1^{sat} \qquad \text{or} \qquad y_1(\text{I}) = \frac{P_1^{sat}}{P}$$

Similarly, for region II where vapor is in equilibrium with pure liquid 2,

$$y_2(\text{II})P = [1 - y_1(\text{II})]P = P_2^{sat} \qquad \text{or} \qquad y_1(\text{II}) = 1 - \frac{P_2^{sat}}{P}$$

Example 14.9

Prepare a table of temperature/composition data for the benzene(1)/water(2) system at a pressure of 101.33 kPa (1 atm) from the vapor-pressure data in the accompanying table.

Solution

Assume that benzene and water are completely immiscible as liquids. Then the three-phase equilibrium temperature t^* is estimated as

$$P(t^*) = P_1^{sat} + P_2^{sat} = 101.33 \text{ kPa}$$

t/T, °C/K	P_1^{sat}/kPa	P_2^{sat}/kPa	$P_1^{sat} + P_2^{sat}$
60/333.15	52.22	19.92	72.14
70/343.15	73.47	31.16	104.63
75/348.15	86.40	38.55	124.95
80/353.15	101.05	47.36	148.41
80.1/363.25	101.33	47.56	148.89
90/363.15	136.14	70.11	206.25
100.0/373.15	180.04	101.33	281.37

The last column of the preceding table of vapor pressures shows that t^* lies between 60 and 70°C, and interpolation yields $t^* = 69.0$°C (342.15 K). At this temperature, again by interpolation: $P_1^{sat}(t^*) = 71.31$ kPa. Thus,

$$y_1^* = \frac{P_1^{sat}}{P_1^{sat} + P_2^{sat}} = \frac{71.31}{101.33} = 0.704$$

For the two regions of vapor/liquid equilibrium,

$$y_1(\mathrm{I}) = \frac{P_1^{\mathrm{sat}}}{P} = \frac{P_1^{\mathrm{sat}}}{101.33}$$

and
$$y_1(\mathrm{II}) = 1 - \frac{P_2^{\mathrm{sat}}}{P} = 1 - \frac{P_2^{\mathrm{sat}}}{101.33}$$

Application of these equations for a number of temperatures gives the results summarized in the table that follows.

t/T, °C/K	y_1(II)	y_1(I)
100.0/373.15	0.000	…
90/363.15	0.308	…
80.1/353.25	0.531	1.000
80/353.15	0.533	0.997
75/348.15	0.620	0.853
70/343.15	0.693	0.725
69.0/342.15	0.704	0.704

14.6 SOLID/LIQUID EQUILIBRIUM (SLE)

Phase behavior involving the solid and liquid states is the basis for separation processes (e.g., crystallization) in chemical and materials engineering. Indeed, a wide variety of binary phase behavior is observed for systems exhibiting solid/solid, solid/liquid, and solid/solid/liquid equilibria. We develop here a rigorous formulation of solid/liquid equilibrium (SLE), and present as applications analyses of two limiting classes of behavior. Comprehensive treatments can be found elsewhere.[19]

The basis for representing SLE is

$$\hat{f}_i^l = \hat{f}_i^s \qquad (\text{all } i)$$

where uniformity of T and P is understood. As with LLE, each $\hat{f}_i$ is eliminated in favor of an activity coefficient. Thus,

$$x_i \gamma_i^l f_i^l = z_i \gamma_i^s f_i^s \qquad (\text{all } i)$$

where x_i and z_i are, respectively, the mole fractions of species i in the liquid and solid solutions. Equivalently,

$$x_i \gamma_i^l = z_i \gamma_i^s \psi_i \qquad (\text{all } i) \tag{14.81}$$

[19] See, e.g., R. T. DeHoff, *Thermodynamics in Materials Science*, chaps. 9 and 10, McGraw-Hill, New York, 1993. A data compilation is given by H. Knapp, M. Teller, and R. Langhorst, *Solid-Liquid Equilibrium Data Collection*, Chemistry Data Series, vol. VIII, DECHEMA, Frankfurt/Main, 1987.

where $$\psi_i \equiv f_i^s / f_i^l \tag{14.82}$$

The right side of this equation, defining ψ_i as the ratio of fugacities at the T and P of the system, may be written in expanded form:

$$\frac{f_i^s(T,P)}{f_i^l(T,P)} = \frac{f_i^s(T,P)}{f_i^s(T_{m_i},P)} \cdot \frac{f_i^s(T_{m_i},P)}{f_i^l(T_{m_i},P)} \cdot \frac{f_i^l(T_{m_i},P)}{f_i^l(T,P)}$$

where T_{m_i} is the melting temperature ("freezing point") of pure species i, i.e., the temperature at which pure-species SLE obtains. Thus the second ratio on the right side is *unity* because $f_i^l = f_i^s$ at the melting point of pure species i. Hence,

$$\psi_i = \frac{f_i^s(T,P)}{f_i^s(T_{m_i},P)} \cdot \frac{f_i^l(T_{m_i},P)}{f_i^l(T,P)} \tag{14.83}$$

According to Eq. (14.83), evaluation of ψ_i requires expressions for the effect of temperature on fugacity. By Eq. (11.33), with $\phi_i = f_i/P$,

$$\ln \frac{f_i}{P} = \frac{G_i^R}{RT} \qquad \ln f_i = \frac{G_i^R}{RT} + \ln P$$

Whence, $$\left(\frac{\partial \ln f_i}{\partial T}\right)_P = \left[\frac{\partial (G_i^R/RT)}{\partial T}\right]_P = -\frac{H_i^R}{RT^2}$$

where the second equality comes from Eq. (11.58). Integration of this equation for a *phase* from T_{m_i} to T gives

$$\frac{f_i(T,P)}{f_i(T_{m_i},P)} = \exp \int_{T_{m_i}}^{T} -\frac{H_i^R}{RT^2} dT \tag{14.84}$$

Equation (14.84) is applied separately to the solid and liquid phases. The resulting expressions are substituted into Eq. (14.83), which is then reduced by the identity

$$-(H_i^{R,s} - H_i^{R,l}) = -[(H_i^s - H_i^{ig}) - (H_i^l - H_i^{ig})] = H_i^l - H_i^s$$

This yields the exact expression:

$$\psi_i = \exp \int_{T_{m_i}}^{T} \frac{H_i^l - H_i^s}{RT^2} dT \tag{14.85}$$

Evaluation of the integral proceeds as follows:

$$H_i(T) = H_i(T_{m_i}) + \int_{T_{m_i}}^{T} C_{P_i}\, dT$$

and $$C_{P_i}(T) = C_{P_i}(T_{m_i}) + \int_{T_{m_i}}^{T} \left(\frac{\partial C_{P_i}}{\partial T}\right)_P dT$$

Hence, for a *phase*,

$$H_i(T) = H_i(T_{m_i}) + C_{P_i}(T_{m_i})(T - T_{m_i}) + \int_{T_{m_i}}^{T}\int_{T_{m_i}}^{T}\left(\frac{\partial C_{P_i}}{\partial T}\right)_P dT\,dT \tag{14.86}$$

Applying Eq. (14.86) separately to the solid and liquid phases and performing the integration required by Eq. (14.85) yields

$$\int_{T_{m_i}}^{T}\frac{H_i^l - H_i^s}{RT^2}dT = \frac{\Delta H_i^{sl}}{RT_{m_i}}\left(\frac{T - T_{m_i}}{T}\right) + \frac{\Delta C_{P_i}^{sl}}{R}\left[\ln\frac{T}{T_{m_i}} - \left(\frac{T - T_{m_i}}{T}\right)\right] + I \tag{14.87}$$

where integral I is defined by

$$I \equiv \int_{T_{m_i}}^{T}\frac{1}{RT^2}\int_{T_{m_i}}^{T}\int_{T_{m_i}}^{T}\left[\frac{\partial(C_{P_i}^l - C_{P_i}^s)}{\partial T}\right]_P dT\,dT\,dT$$

In Eq. (14.87), ΔH_i^{sl} is the enthalpy change of melting ("heat of fusion") and $\Delta C_{P_i}^{sl}$ is the heat-capacity change of melting. Both quantities are evaluated at the melting temperature T_{m_i}.

Equations (14.81), (14.85), and (14.87) provide a formal basis for solution of problems in solid/liquid equilibria. The full rigor of Eq. (14.87) is rarely maintained. For purposes of development, pressure has been carried through as a thermodynamic variable. However, its effect is rarely included in engineering applications. The triple integral represented by I is a second-order contribution, and is normally neglected. The heat-capacity change of melting can be significant, but is not always available; moreover, inclusion of the term involving $\Delta C_{P_i}^{sl}$ adds little to a qualitative understanding of SLE. With the assumptions that I and $\Delta C_{P_i}^{sl}$ are negligible, Eqs. (14.85) and (14.87) together yield:

$$\psi_i = \exp\frac{\Delta H_i^{sl}}{RT_{m_i}}\left(\frac{T - T_{m_i}}{T}\right) \tag{14.88}$$

With ψ_i given by Eq. (14.88), all that is required for formulating an SLE problem is a set of statements about the temperature and composition dependence of the activity coefficients γ_i^l and γ_i^s. In the general case, this requires algebraic expressions for $G^E(T, \text{composition})$ for both liquid and solid solutions. Consider two limiting special cases:

I. Assume ideal-solution behavior for both phases, i.e., let $\gamma_i^l = 1$ and $\gamma_i^s = 1$ for all T and compositions.

II. Assume ideal-solution behavior for the liquid phase ($\gamma_i^l = 1$), and complete immiscibility for all species in the solid state (i.e., set $z_i\gamma_i^s = 1$).

These two cases, restricted to binary systems, are considered in the following.

Case I

The two equilibrium equations which follow from Eq. (14.81) are

$$x_1 = z_1\psi_1 \qquad (14.89a) \qquad\qquad x_2 = z_2\psi_2 \qquad (14.89b)$$

where ψ_1 and ψ_2 are given by Eq. (14.88) with $i = 1, 2$. Because $x_2 = 1 - x_1$ and $z_2 = 1 - z_1$, Eqs. (14.89) can be solved to give x_1 and z_1 as explicit functions of the ψ_i s and thus of T:

$$x_1 = \frac{\psi_1(1-\psi_2)}{\psi_1 - \psi_2} \qquad (14.90) \qquad\qquad z_1 = \frac{1-\psi_2}{\psi_1 - \psi_2} \qquad (14.91)$$

with

$$\psi_1 = \exp\frac{\Delta H_1^{sl}}{RT_{m_1}}\left(\frac{T - T_{m_1}}{T}\right) \qquad (14.92a) \qquad\qquad \psi_2 = \exp\frac{\Delta H_2^{sl}}{RT_{m_2}}\left(\frac{T - T_{m_2}}{T}\right) \qquad (14.92b)$$

Inspection of these results verifies that $x_i = z_i = 1$ for $T = T_{m_i}$. Moreover, analysis shows that both x_i and z_i vary monotonically with T. Hence systems described by Eqs. (14.89) exhibit lens-shaped SLE diagrams, as shown on Fig. 14.22(a), where the upper line is the freezing curve and the lower line is the melting curve. The liquid-solution region lies above the freezing curve, and the solid-solution region lies below the melting curve. Examples of systems exhibiting diagrams of this type range from nitrogen/carbon monoxide at low temperature to copper/nickel at high temperature. Comparison of this figure with Fig. (10.12) suggests that Case I-SLE behavior is analogous to Raoult's-law behavior for VLE. Comparison of the assumptions leading to Eqs. (14.89) and (10.1) confirms the analogy. As with Raoult's law, Eq. (14.89) rarely describes the behavior of actual systems. However, it is an important limiting case, and serves as a standard against which observed SLE can be compared.

Case II

The two equilibrium equations resulting from Eq. (14.81) are here:

$$x_1 = \psi_1 \qquad (14.93) \qquad\qquad x_2 = \psi_2 \qquad (14.94)$$

where ψ_1 and ψ_2 are given as functions solely of temperature by Eqs. (14.92). Thus x_1 and x_2 are also solely functions of temperature, and Eqs. (14.93) and (14.94) can apply simultaneously only for the particular temperature where $\psi_1 + \psi_2 = 1$ and hence $x_1 + x_2 = 1$. This is the *eutectic temperature* T_e. Thus, three distinct equilibrium situations exist: one where Eq. (14.93) alone applies, one where Eq. (14.94) alone applies, and the special case where they apply together at T_e.

- Equation (14.93) alone applies. By this equation and Eq. (14.92a),

$$x_1 = \exp\frac{\Delta H_1^{sl}}{RT_{m_1}}\left(\frac{T - T_{m_1}}{T}\right) \qquad (14.95)$$

This equation is valid only from $T = T_{m_1}$, where $x_1 = 1$, to $T = T_e$, where $x_1 = x_{1e}$, the *eutectic composition*. (Note that $x_1 = 0$ only for $T = 0$.) Equation (14.95) therefore applies where a liquid solution is in equilibrium with pure species 1 as a solid phase. This is represented by region I on Fig. 14.22(*b*), where liquid solutions with compositions x_1 given by line BE are in equilibrium with pure solid 1.

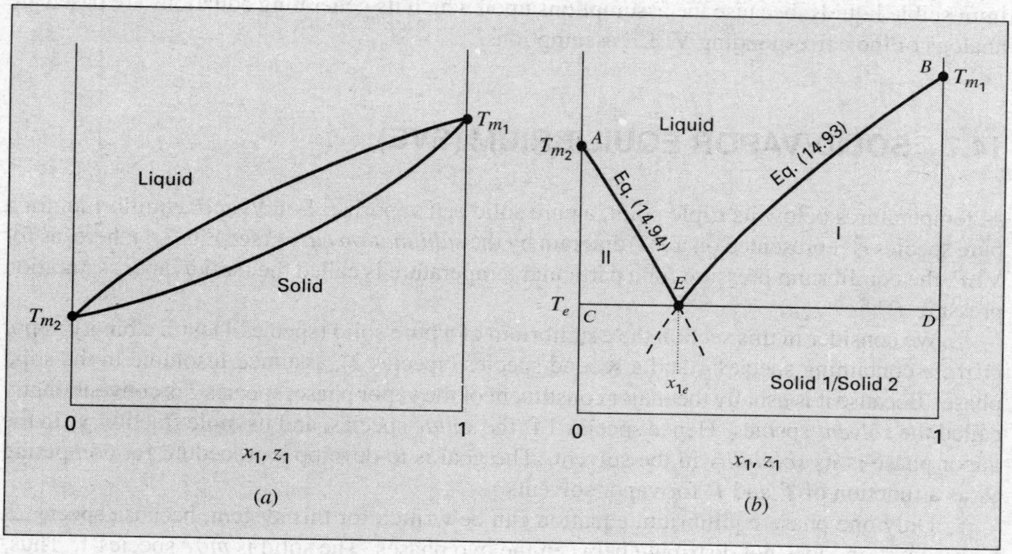

Figure 14.22: Txz diagrams (*a*) Case I, ideal liquid and solid solutions (*b*) Case II, ideal liquid solution; immiscible solids

- Equation (14.94) alone applies. By this equation and Eq. (14.92b), with $x_2 = 1 - x_1$:

$$x_1 = 1 - \exp\frac{\Delta H_2^{sl}}{RT_{m_2}}\left(\frac{T - T_{m_2}}{T}\right) \tag{14.96}$$

This equation is valid only from $T = T_{m_2}$, where $x_1 = 0$, to $T = T_e$, where $x_1 = x_{1e}$, the eutectic composition. Equation (14.96) therefore applies where a liquid solution is in equilibrium with pure species 2 as a solid phase. This is represented by region II on Fig. 14.22(*b*), where liquid solutions with compositions x_1 given by line AE are in equilibrium with pure solid 2.

- Equations (14.93) and (14.94) apply simultaneously, and are set equal because they must both give the eutectic composition x_{1e}. The resulting expression,

$$\exp\frac{\Delta H_1^{sl}}{RT_{m_1}}\left(\frac{T - T_{m_1}}{T}\right) = 1 - \exp\frac{\Delta H_2^{sl}}{RT_{m_2}}\left(\frac{T - T_{m_2}}{T}\right) \tag{14.97}$$

is satisfied for the single temperature $T = T_e$. Substitution of T_e into either Eq. (14.95) or (14.96) yields the eutectic composition. Coordinates T_e and x_{1e} define a *eutectic state*, a special state of three-phase equilibrium, lying along line CED on Fig. 14.22(*b*), for which liquid of composition x_{1e} coexists with pure solid 1 and pure solid 2. This is a state of solid/solid/liquid equilibrium. At temperatures below T_e the two pure immiscible solids coexist.

Figure 14.22(*b*), the phase diagram for Case II, is an exact analog of Fig. 14.21(*a*) for immiscible liquids, because the assumptions upon which its generating equations are based are analogs of the corresponding VLLE assumptions.

14.7 SOLID/VAPOR EQUILIBRIUM (SVE)

At temperatures below its triple point, a pure solid can vaporize. Solid/vapor equilibrium for a pure species is represented on a PT diagram by the *sublimation curve* (see Fig. 3.1); here, as for VLE, the equilibrium pressure for a particular temperature is called the (solid/vapor) saturation pressure P^{sat}.

We consider in this section the equilibrium of a pure solid (species 1) with a binary vapor *mixture* containing species 1 and a second species (species 2), assumed insoluble in the solid phase. Because it is usually the major constituent of the vapor phase, species 2 is conventionally called the *solvent* species. Hence species 1 is the *solute* species, and its mole fraction y_1 in the vapor phase is its *solubility* in the solvent. The goal is to develop a procedure for computing y_1 as a function of T and P for vapor solvents.

Only one phase-equilibrium equation can be written for this system, because species 2, by assumption, does not distribute between the two phases. The solid is *pure* species 1. Thus,

$$f_1^s = \hat{f}_1^v$$

Equation (11.44) for a pure liquid is, with minor change of notation, appropriate here:

$$f_1^s = \phi_1^{sat} P_1^{sat} \exp \frac{V_1^s(P - P_1^{sat})}{RT}$$

where P_1^{sat} is the solid/vapor saturation pressure at temperature T and V_1^s is the molar volume of the solid. For the vapor phase, by Eq. (11.52),

$$\hat{f}_1^v = y_1 \hat{\phi}_1 P$$

Combining the three preceding equations and solving for y_1 gives

$$y_1 = \frac{P_1^{sat}}{P} F_1 \tag{14.98}$$

where

$$F_1 \equiv \frac{\phi_1^{sat}}{\hat{\phi}_1} \exp \frac{V_1^s(P - P_1^{sat})}{RT} \tag{14.99}$$

Function F_1 reflects vapor-phase nonidealities through ϕ_1^{sat} and $\hat{\phi}_1$ and the effect of pressure on the fugacity of the solid through the exponential Poynting factor. For sufficiently low pressures, both effects are negligible, in which case $F_1 \approx 1$ and $y_1 \approx P_1^{sat}/P$. At moderate and high pressures, vapor-phase nonidealities become important, and for very high pressures even the Poynting factor cannot be ignored. Because F_1 is generally observed to be greater than unity, it is sometimes called an "enhancement factor," because according to Eq. (14.98) it leads to a solid solubility *greater* than would obtain in the absence of these pressure-induced effects.

Estimation of Solid Solubility at High Pressure

Solubilities at temperatures and pressures above the critical values of the solvent have important applications for supercritical separation processes. Examples are extraction of caffeine from coffee beans and separation of asphaltenes from heavy petroleum fractions. For a typical solid/vapor equilibrium (SVE) problem, the solid/vapor saturation pressure P_1^{sat} is very small, and the *saturated* vapor is for practical purposes an ideal gas. Hence ϕ_1^{sat} for pure solute vapor at this pressure is close to unity. Moreover, except for very low values of the system pressure P, the solid solubility y_1 is small, and $\hat{\phi}_1$ can be approximated by $\hat{\phi}_1^{\infty}$, the vapor-phase fugacity coefficient of the solute at infinite dilution. Finally, because P_1^{sat} is very small, the pressure difference $P - P_1^{sat}$ in the Poynting factor is nearly equal to P at any pressure where this factor is important. With these usually reasonable approximations, Eq. (14.99) reduces to

$$F_1 = \frac{1}{\hat{\phi}_1^{\infty}} \exp \frac{PV_1^s}{RT} \tag{14.100}$$

an expression suitable for engineering applications. In this equation, P_1^{sat} and V_1^s are pure-species properties, found in a handbook or estimated from a suitable correlation. Quantity $\hat{\phi}_1^{\infty}$, on the other hand, must be computed from a PVT equation of state— one suitable for vapor mixtures at high pressures.

Cubic equations of state, such as the Soave/Redlich/Kwong (SRK) and Peng/Robinson (PR) equations, are usually satisfactory for this kind of calculation. Equation (14.50) for $\hat{\phi}_i$, developed in Sec. 14.2, is applicable here, but with a slightly modified combining rule for interaction parameter a_{ij} used in calculation of $\bar{q}_i$. Thus, Eq. (14.44) is replaced by

$$a_{ij} = (1 - l_{ij})(a_i a_j)^{1/2} \tag{14.101}$$

The additional binary interaction parameter l_{ij} must be found for each ij pair ($i \neq j$) from experimental data. By convention, $l_{ij} = l_{ji}$ and $l_{ii} = l_{jj} = 0$.

Partial parameter $\bar{a}_i$ is found by application of Eq. (14.45) with a from Eq. (14.43):

$$\bar{a}_i = -a + 2\sum_j y_j a_{ji}$$

Substitution of this expression into Eq. (14.51) yields

$$\bar{q}_i = q\left(\frac{2\sum_j y_j a_{ji}}{a} - \frac{b_i}{b}\right) \tag{14.102}$$

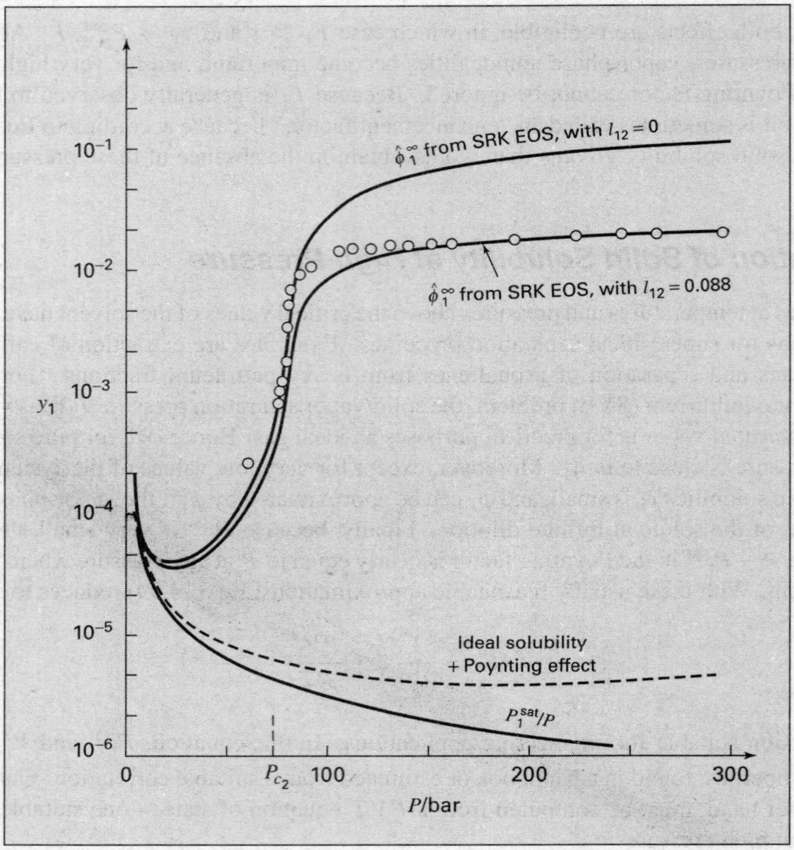

Figure 14.23: Solubility of naphthalene(1) in carbon dioxide(2) at 35°C (308.15 K). Circles are data. Curves are computed from Eqs. (14.98) and (14.100) under various assumptions.

where b and q are given by Eqs. (14.42) and (14.41).

For species 1 at infinite dilution in a binary system, the "mixture" is pure species 2. In this event, Eqs. (14.50), (14.101), and (14.102) yield an expression for $\hat{\phi}_1^\infty$:

$$\ln \hat{\phi}_1^\infty = \frac{b_1}{b_2}(Z_2 - 1) - \ln(Z_2 - \beta_2) - q_2 \left[2(1 - l_{12}) \left(\frac{a_1}{a_2} \right)^{1/2} - \frac{b_1}{b_2} \right] I_2 \tag{14.103}$$

where by Eq. (6.65b), $$I_2 = \frac{1}{\sigma - \epsilon} \ln \frac{Z_2 + \sigma\beta_2}{Z_2 + \epsilon\beta_2}$$

Equation (14.103) is used in conjunction with Eqs. (14.33) and (14.36), which provide values of β_2 and Z_2 corresponding to a particular T and P.

As an example, consider the calculation of the solubility of naphthalene(1) in carbon dioxide(2) at 35°C (308.15 K) and pressures up to 300 bar. Strictly, this is not solid/*vapor* equilibrium, because the critical temperature of CO_2 is 31.1°C. However, the development of this section remains valid.

The basis is Eq. (14.100), with $\hat{\phi}_1^\infty$ determined from Eq. (14.103) written for the SRK equation of state. For solid naphthalene at 35°C (308.15 K),

$$P_1^{\text{sat}} = 2.9 \times 10^{-4} \text{ bar} \qquad \text{and} \qquad V_1^s = 125 \text{ cm}^3 \text{ mol}^{-1}$$

Equations (14.103) and (14.36) reduce to the SRK expressions on assignment of the values $\sigma = 1$ and $\epsilon = 0$. Evaluation of parameters a_1, a_2, b_1, and b_2 requires values for T_c, P_c, and ω, which are found in App. B. Thus Eqs. (14.31) and (14.32) give

$$a_1 = 7.299 \times 10^7 \text{ bar cm}^6 \text{ mol}^{-2} \qquad b_1 = 133.1 \text{ cm}^3 \text{ mol}^{-1}$$

$$a_2 = 3.664 \times 10^6 \text{ bar cm}^6 \text{ mol}^{-2} \qquad b_2 = 29.68 \text{ cm}^3 \text{ mol}^{-1}$$

By Eq. (14.34),

$$q_2 = \frac{a_2}{b_2 RT} = 4.819$$

With these values, Eqs. (14.103), (14.33), and (14.36) become

$$\ln \hat{\phi}_1^\infty = 4.485(Z_2 - 1) - \ln(Z_2 - \beta_2) + [21.61 - 43.02(1 - l_{12})] \ln \frac{Z_2 + \beta_2}{Z_2} \qquad (A)$$

$$\beta_2 = 1.1585 \times 10^{-3} P \qquad (P/\text{bar}) \qquad (B)$$

$$Z_2 = 1 + \beta_2 - 4.819\beta_2 \frac{Z_2 - \beta_2}{Z_2(Z_2 + \beta_2)} \qquad (C)$$

To find $\hat{\phi}_1^\infty$ for a given l_{12} and P, one first evaluates β_2 by Eq. (*B*) and solves Eq. (*C*) for Z_2. Substitution of these values into Eq. (*A*) gives $\hat{\phi}_1^\infty$. For example, for $P = 200$ bar and $l_{12} = 0$, Eq. (*B*) gives $\beta_2 = 0.2317$ and solution of Eq. (*C*) yields $Z_2 = 0.4426$. By Eq. (*A*), $\hat{\phi}_1^\infty = 4.74 \times 10^{-5}$. This small value leads by Eq. (14.100) to a large enhancement factor F_1.

Tsekhanskaya et al.[20] report solubility data for naphthalene in carbon dioxide at 35°C (308.15 K) and high pressures, given as circles on Fig. 14.23. The sharp increase in solubility as the pressure approaches the critical value (73.83 bar for CO_2) is typical of supercritical systems. Shown for comparison are the results of calculations based on Eqs. (14.98) and (14.100), under various assumptions. The lowest curve shows the "ideal solubility" P_1^{sat}/P, for which the enhancement factor F_1 is unity. The dashed curve incorporates the Poynting effect, which is significant at the higher pressures. The topmost curve includes the Poynting effect as well as $\hat{\phi}_1^\infty$, estimated from Eq. (14.103) with SRK constants and with $l_{12} = 0$; this purely predictive result captures the general trends of the data, but overestimates the solubility at the higher pressures. *Correlation* of the data requires a nonzero value for the interaction parameter; the value $l_{12} = 0.088$ produces the semi-quantitative representation shown on Fig. 14.23 as the second curve from the top.

[20] Y. V. Tsekhanskaya, M. B. Iomtev, and E. V. Mushkina, *Russian J. Phys. Chem.*, vol. 38, pp. 1173–1176, 1964.

14.8 EQUILIBRIUM ADSORPTION OF GASES ON SOLIDS

The process by which certain porous solids bind large numbers of molecules to their surfaces is known as adsorption. Not only does it serve as a separation process, but it is also a vital part of catalytic-reaction processes. As a separation process, adsorption is used most often for removal of low-concentration impurities and pollutants from fluid streams. It is also the basis for chromatography. In surface-catalyzed reactions, the initial step is adsorption of reactant species; the final step is the reverse process, desorption of product species. Because most industrially important reactions are catalytic, adsorption plays a fundamental role in reaction engineering.

The nature of the adsorbing surface is the determining factor in adsorption. The molecular characterization of solid surfaces is not yet fully developed; however, current knowledge allows a helpful description. To be useful as an *adsorbent*, a solid must present a large surface area per unit mass (up to 1500 m^2 per gram). This can only be achieved with porous solids such as activated carbon, silica gels, aluminas, and zeolites, which contain many cavities or pores with diameters as small as a fraction of a nanometer. Surfaces of such solids are necessarily irregular at the molecular level, and they contain *sites* of particular attraction for adsorbing molecules. If the sites are close together, the adsorbed molecules may interact with one another; if they are sufficiently dispersed, the adsorbed molecules may interact only with the sites. Depending upon the strength of the forces binding them to the sites, these *adsorbate* molecules may be mobile or fixed in position. The relatively weak electrostatic, induction, and dispersion forces discussed in Sec. 16.1 favor mobility and result in *physical adsorption*. On the other hand, much stronger quasichemical forces can act to fix molecules to the surface, promoting *chemisorption*. Although adsorption may be classified in several ways, the usual distinction is between physical adsorption and chemisorption. Based on the strength of the binding forces, this division is observed experimentally in the magnitudes of the heat of adsorption.

In the adsorption of gases, the number of molecules attracted to a solid surface depends on conditions in the gas phase. For very low pressures, relatively few molecules are adsorbed, and only a fraction of the solid surface is covered. As the gas pressure increases at a given temperature, surface coverage increases. When all sites become occupied, the adsorbed molecules are said to form a *monolayer*. Further increase in pressure promotes *multilayer* adsorption. It is also possible for multilayer adsorption to occur on one part of a porous surface when vacant sites still remain on another part.

The complexities of solid surfaces and our inability to characterize exactly their interactions with adsorbed molecules limits our understanding of the adsorption process. It does not, however, prevent development of an exact thermodynamic description of adsorption equilibrium, applicable alike to physical adsorption and chemisorption and equally to monolayer and multilayer adsorption. The thermodynamic framework is independent of any *particular* theoretical or empirical description of material behavior. However, in application such a description is essential, and meaningful results require appropriate models of behavior.

The thermodynamic treatment of gas/adsorbate equilibrium is in many respects analogous to that of vapor/liquid equilibrium. However, the definition of a system to which the equations of thermodynamics apply presents a problem. The force field of the solid adsorbent influences properties in the adjacent gas phase, but its effect decreases rapidly with distance.

Thus the properties of the gas change rapidly in the immediate neighborhood of the solid surface, but they do not change abruptly. A region of change exists which contains gradients in the properties of the gas, but the distance into the gas phase that the solid makes its influence felt cannot be precisely established.

This problem is circumvented by a construct devised by J. W. Gibbs. Imagine that the gas-phase properties extend unchanged up to the solid surface. Differences between the actual and the unchanged properties can then be attributed to a mathematical surface, treated as a two-dimensional phase with its own thermodynamic properties. This provides not only a precisely defined surface phase to account for the singularities of the interfacial region, but it also extracts them from the three-dimensional gas phase so that it too may be treated precisely. The solid, despite the influence of its force field, is presumed inert and not otherwise to participate in the gas/adsorbate equilibrium. Thus for purposes of thermodynamic analysis the adsorbate is treated as a two-dimensional phase, inherently an *open* system because it is in equilibrium with the gas phase.

The fundamental property relation for an open PVT system is given by Eq. (11.2):

$$d(nG) = (nV)dP - (nS)dT + \sum_i \mu_i \, dn_i$$

An analogous equation may be written for a two-dimensional phase. The only difference is that pressure and molar volume are not in this case appropriate variables. Pressure is replaced by the *spreading pressure* Π, and the molar volume by the *molar area* a:

$$d(nG) = (na)d\Pi - (nS)dT + \sum_i \mu_i \, dn_i \tag{14.104}$$

This equation is written on the basis of a unit mass, usually a gram or a kilogram, of solid adsorbent. Thus n is the *specific* amount adsorbed, i.e., the number of moles of adsorbate *per unit mass of adsorbent*. Moreover, area A is defined as the specific surface area, i.e., the area *per unit mass of adsorbent*, a quantity characteristic of a particular adsorbent. The molar area, $a \equiv A/n$, is the surface area per mole of adsorbate.

The spreading pressure is the two-dimensional analog of pressure, having units of force per unit length, akin to surface tension. It can be pictured as the force in the plane of the surface that must be exerted perpendicular to each unit length of edge to keep the surface from spreading, i.e., to keep it in mechanical equilibrium. It is not subject to direct experimental measurement, and must be calculated, significantly complicating the treatment of adsorbed-phase equilibrium.

Because the spreading pressure adds an extra variable, the number of degrees of freedom for gas/adsorbate equilibrium is given by an altered version of the phase rule. For gas/adsorbate equilibrium, $\pi = 2$; therefore,

$$F = N - \pi + 3 = N - 2 + 3 = N + 1$$

Thus for adsorption of a pure species,

$$F = 1 + 1 = 2$$

and two phase-rule variables, e.g., T and P or T and n, must be fixed independently to establish an equilibrium state. Note that the inert solid phase is counted neither as a phase nor as a species.

Recall the summability relation for the Gibbs energy, which follows from Eqs. (11.8) and (11.12):

$$nG = \sum_i n_i \mu_i$$

Differentiation gives $$d(nG) = \sum_i \mu_i \, dn_i + \sum_i n_i \, d\mu_i$$

Comparison with Eq. (14.104) shows:

$$(nS)dT - (na)d\Pi + \sum_i n_i \, d\mu_i = 0$$

or $$S \, dT - a \, d\Pi + \sum_i x_i \, d\mu_i = 0$$

This is the Gibbs/Duhem equation for the adsorbate. Restricting it to constant temperature produces the *Gibbs adsorption isotherm*:

$$-a \, d\Pi + \sum_i x_i \, d\mu_i = 0 \qquad (\text{const } T) \tag{14.105}$$

The condition of equilibrium between adsorbate and gas presumes the same temperature for the two phases and requires

$$\mu_i = \mu_i^g$$

where μ_i^g represents the gas-phase chemical potential. For a change in equilibrium conditions,

$$d\mu_i = d\mu_i^g$$

If the gas phase is an *ideal gas* (the usual assumption), then differentiation of Eq. (11.29) at constant temperature yields:

$$d\mu_i^g = RT \, d \ln y_i P$$

Combining the last two equations with the Gibbs adsorption isotherm gives

$$-\frac{a}{RT} d\Pi + d \ln P + \sum_i x_i \, d \ln y_i = 0 \qquad (\text{const } T) \tag{14.106}$$

where x_i and y_i represent adsorbate and gas-phase mole fractions respectively.

Pure-Gas Adsorption

Basic to the experimental study of pure-gas adsorption are measurements at constant temperature of n, the moles of gas adsorbed, as a function of P, the pressure in the gas phase. Each set of data represents an *adsorption isotherm* for the pure gas on a particular solid adsorbent. Available data are summarized by Valenzuela and Myers.[21] The correlation of such data requires an analytical relation between n and P, and such a relation should be consistent with Eq. (14.106).

[21] D. P. Valenzuela and A. L. Myers, *Adsorption Equilibrium Data Handbook*, Prentice Hall, Englewood Cliffs, NJ, 1989.

Written for a pure chemical species, this equation becomes

$$\frac{a}{RT}d\Pi = d\ln P \qquad \text{(const } T\text{)} \tag{14.107}$$

The compressibility-factor analog for an adsorbate is defined by the equation:

$$z \equiv \frac{\Pi a}{RT} \tag{14.108}$$

Differentiation at constant T yields

$$dz = \frac{\Pi}{RT}da + \frac{a}{RT}d\Pi$$

Replace the last term by Eq. (14.107) and eliminate Π/RT in favor of z/a in accord with Eq. (14.108) to yield:

$$-d\ln P = z\frac{da}{a} - dz$$

Substituting $a = A/n$ and $da = -A\,dn/n^2$ gives

$$-d\ln P = -z\frac{dn}{n} - dz$$

Adding dn/n to both sides of this equation and rearranging,

$$d\ln\frac{n}{P} = (1-z)\frac{dn}{n} - dz$$

Integration from $P = 0$ (where $n = 0$ and $z = 1$) to $P = P$ and $n = n$ yields

$$\ln\frac{n}{P} - \ln\lim_{P\to 0}\frac{n}{P} = \int_0^n (1-z)\frac{dn}{n} + 1 - z$$

The limiting value of n/P as $n \to 0$ and $P \to 0$ must be found by extrapolation of experimental data. Applying l'Hôpital's rule to this limit gives

$$\lim_{P\to 0}\frac{n}{P} = \lim_{P\to 0}\frac{dn}{dP} \equiv k$$

Thus k is defined as the limiting slope of an isotherm as $P \to 0$, and is known as Henry's constant for adsorption. It is a function of temperature only for a given adsorbent and adsorbate, and is characteristic of the specific interaction between a particular adsorbent and a particular adsorbate.

The preceding equation may therefore be written as

$$\ln\frac{n}{kP} = \int_0^n (1-z)\frac{dn}{n} + 1 - z$$

or

$$n = kP\exp\left[\int_0^n (1-z)\frac{dn}{n} + 1 - z\right] \tag{14.109}$$

This general relation between n, the moles adsorbed, and P, the gas-phase pressure, includes z, the adsorbate compressibility factor, which may be represented by an equation of state for the adsorbate. The simplest such equation is the ideal-gas analog, $z = 1$, and in this case Eq. (14.109) yields $n = kP$, which is Henry's law for adsorption.

An equation of state known as the ideal-lattice-gas equation[22] has been developed specifically for an adsorbate:

$$z = -\frac{m}{n}\ln\left(1 - \frac{n}{m}\right)$$

where m is a constant. This equation is based on the presumptions that the surface of the adsorbent is a two-dimensional lattice of energetically equivalent sites, each of which may bind an adsorbate molecule, and that the bound molecules do not interact with each other. The validity of this model is therefore limited to no more than monolayer coverage. Substitution of this equation into Eq. (14.109) and integration leads to the *Langmuir isotherm*:[23]

$$n = \left(\frac{m-n}{m}\right)kP$$

Solution for n yields

$$n = \frac{mP}{\frac{m}{k} + P} \tag{14.110}$$

Alternatively,

$$n = \frac{kbP}{b + P} \tag{14.111}$$

where $b \equiv m/k$, and k is Henry's constant. Note that when $P \to 0$, n/P properly approaches k. At the other extreme, where $P \to \infty$, n approaches m, the *saturation* value of the specific amount absorbed, representing full monolayer coverage.

Based on the same assumptions as for the ideal-lattice-gas equation, Langmuir in 1918 derived Eq. (14.110) by noting that at equilibrium the rate of adsorption and the rate of desorption of gas molecules must be the same.[24] For monolayer adsorption, the number of sites may be divided into the fraction occupied θ and the fraction vacant $1 - \theta$. By definition,

$$\theta \equiv \frac{n}{m} \qquad \text{and} \qquad 1 - \theta = \frac{m-n}{m}$$

where m is the value of n for full monolayer coverage. For the assumed conditions, the rate of adsorption is proportional to the rate at which molecules strike the surface, which in turn is proportional to both the pressure and the fraction $1 - \theta$ of unoccupied surface sites. The rate of desorption is proportional to the occupied fraction θ of sites. Equating the two rates gives

$$\kappa P\frac{m-n}{m} = \kappa'\frac{n}{m}$$

[22] See, e.g., T. L. Hill, *An Introduction to Statistical Mechanics*, sec. 7-1, Addison-Wesley, Reading, MA, 1960.

[23] Irving Langmuir (1881–1957), the second American to receive the Nobel Prize in chemistry, awarded for his contributions in the field of surface chemistry.

[24] I. Langmuir, *J. Am. Chem. Soc.*, vol. 40, p. 1361, 1918.

where κ and κ' are proportionality (rate) constants. Solving for n and rearranging yields:

$$n = \frac{\kappa m P}{\kappa P + \kappa'} = \frac{mP}{\dfrac{1}{K} + P}$$

where $K \equiv \kappa/\kappa'$, the ratio of the forward and reverse adsorption rate constants, is the conventional adsorption equilibrium constant. The second equality in this equation is equivalent to Eq. (14.110), and indicates that the adsorption equilibrium constant is equal to Henry's constant divided by m, i.e., $K = k/m$.

Because the assumptions upon which it is based are fulfilled at low surface coverage, the Langmuir isotherm is always valid as $\theta \to 0$ and as $n \to 0$. Even though these assumptions become unrealistic at higher surface coverage, the Langmuir isotherm may provide an approximate overall fit to n vs. P data; however, it does not lead to reasonable values for m.

Substituting $a = A/n$ in Eq. (14.107) gives

$$\frac{A\, d\Pi}{RT} = n\, d \ln P$$

Integration at constant temperature from $P = 0$ (where $\Pi = 0$) to $P = P$ and $\Pi = \Pi$ yields

$$\frac{\Pi A}{RT} = \int_0^P \frac{n}{P} dP \tag{14.112}$$

This equation provides the *only* means for evaluation of spreading pressure. The integration may be carried out numerically or graphically with experimental data, or the data may be fit to an equation for an isotherm. For example, if the integrand n/P is given by Eq. (14.111), the Langmuir isotherm, then

$$\frac{\Pi A}{RT} = kb \ln \frac{P + b}{b} \tag{14.113}$$

an equation valid for $n \to 0$.

No equation of state is known that leads to an adsorption isotherm which in general fits experimental data over the entire range of n from zero to full monolayer coverage. Isotherms that find practical use are often 3-parameter empirical extensions of the Langmuir isotherm. An example is the Toth equation:[25]

$$n = \frac{mP}{(b + P^t)^{1/t}} \tag{14.114}$$

which reduces to the Langmuir equation for $t = 1$. When the integrand of Eq. (14.112) is expressed by the Toth equation and most other 3-parameter equations, its integration requires numerical methods. Moreover, the empirical element of such equations often introduces a singularity that makes them behave improperly in the limit as $P \to 0$. Thus for the Toth equation ($t < 1$) the second derivative d^2n/dP^2 approaches $-\infty$ in this limit, making values of Henry's constant as calculated by this equation too large. Nevertheless, the Toth equation finds frequent practical use as an adsorption isotherm. However, it is not always suitable, and

[25]Valenzuela and Myers, *op. cit.*

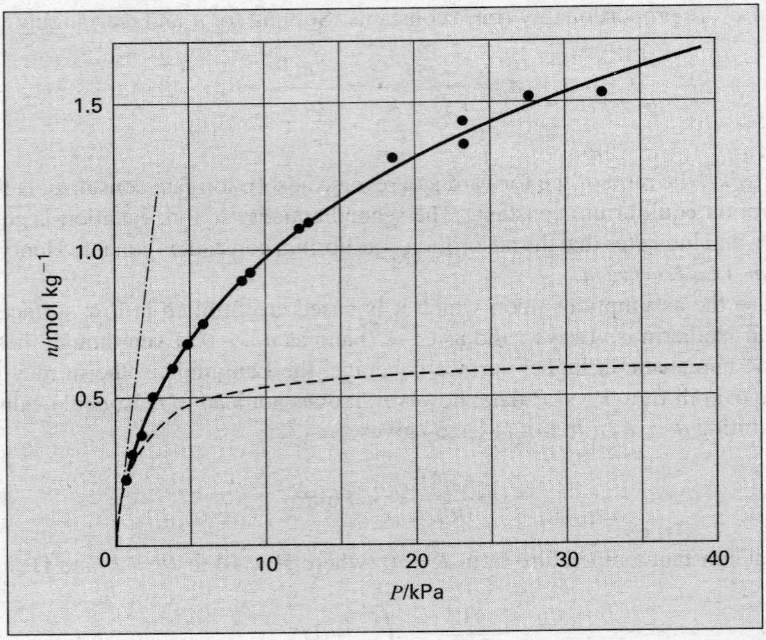

Figure 14.24: Adsorption isotherm for ethylene on a carbon molecular sieve at 50°C (323.15 K)
Legend: ● experimental data; — ● — ● — ● Henry's law; ———— Toth equation; — — — Langmuir equation $n \to 0$.

a number of other adsorption isotherms are in use, as discussed by Suzuki.[26] Among them, the Freundlich equation,

$$\theta = \frac{n}{m} = \alpha P^{1/\beta} \qquad (\beta > 1) \tag{14.115}$$

is a 2-parameter (α and β) isotherm that often successfully correlates experimental data for low and intermediate values of θ.

Example 14.10

Nakahara et al.[27] report data for ethylene adsorbed on a carbon molecular sieve ($A = 650\ \mathrm{m^2\ g^{-1}}$) at 50°C (323.15 K). The data, shown as filled circles on Fig. 14.24, consist of pairs of values (n, P), where n is moles of adsorbate per kg of adsorbent and P is the equilibrium gas pressure in kPa. Trends shown by the data are typical for physical

[26] M. Suzuki, *Adsorption Engineering*, pp. 35–51, Elsevier, Amsterdam, 1990.

[27] T. Nakahara, M. Hirata, and H. Mori, *J. Chem. Eng. Data*, vol. 27, pp. 317–320, 1982.

adsorption on a heterogeneous adsorbent at low-to-moderate surface coverage. Use these data to illustrate numerically the concepts developed for pure-gas adsorption.

Solution

The solid line on Fig. 14.24 represents a curve-fit to the data by Eq. (14.114), the Toth equation, with parameter values as reported by Valenzuela and Myers (*loc. cit.*):

$$m = 4.7087 \qquad b = 2.1941 \qquad t = 0.3984$$

These imply an apparent value of Henry's constant:

$$k(\text{Toth}) = \lim_{P \to 0} \frac{n}{P} = \frac{m}{b^{1/t}} = 0.6551 \text{ mol kg}^{-1} \text{ kPa}^{-1}$$

Although the overall quality of the fit is excellent, the value of Henry's constant is too large, as we will show.

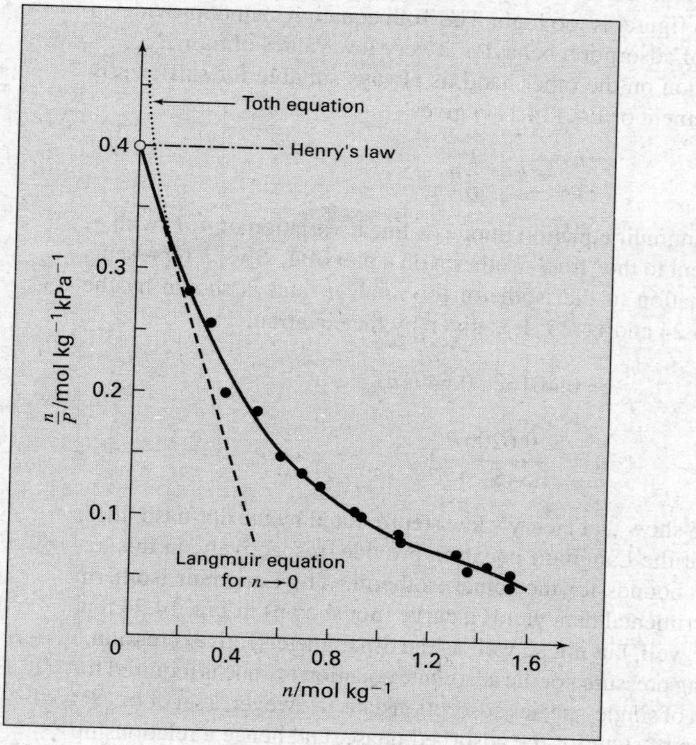

Figure 14.25: Plot of n/P vs. n for ethylene on a carbon molecular sieve at 50°C (323.15 K)

● experimental data;
——— cubic polynomial fit of n/P vs. n;
— — — Langmuir equation for $n \to 0$;
—•—•— Henry's law;
••••• Toth equation for small n

Extraction of Henry's constant from an adsorption isotherm is facilitated when n/P (rather than n) is considered the dependent variable and n (rather than P) the independent variable. The data plotted in this form are shown by Fig. 14.25. On this plot, Henry's constant is the extrapolated intercept:

$$k = \lim_{P\to 0} \frac{n}{P} = \lim_{n\to 0} \frac{n}{P}$$

where the second equality follows from the first because $n \to 0$ as $P \to 0$. Evaluation of the intercept (and hence of k) is done in this case by fitting all of the n/P data by a cubic polynomial in n:

$$\frac{n}{P} = C_0 + C_1 n + C_2 n^2 + C_3 n^3$$

The evaluated parameters are

$$C_0 = 0.4016 \qquad C_1 = -0.6471 \qquad C_2 = -0.4567 \qquad C_3 = -0.1200$$

Whence, $\quad k = C_0 = 0.4016 \text{ mol kg}^{-1} \text{ kPa}^{-1}$

Representation of n/P by the cubic polynomial appears as the solid curve on Fig. 14.25, and the extrapolated intercept ($C_0 = k = 0.4016$) is indicated by an open circle. For comparison, the dotted line is the low-n portion of the n/P curve given by the Toth equation. Here it is apparent that the extrapolated intercept k(Toth), off-scale on this figure, is too high. The Toth equation cannot provide an accurate representation of adsorption behavior at very low values of n or P.

The Langmuir equation on the other hand, is always suitable for sufficiently small n or P. Rearrangement of Eq. (14.111) gives

$$\frac{n}{P} = k - \frac{1}{b}n$$

which shows that the Langmuir equation implies a linear variation of n/P with n. Hence the limiting tangent to the "true" isotherm on a plot of n/P vs. n represents the Langmuir approximation to the isotherm for small n, and is shown by the dashed lines on Figs. 14.24 and 14.25. It is given by the equation:

$$\frac{n}{P} = 0.4016 - 0.6471n$$

or, equivalently, by $\quad n = \dfrac{0.6206P}{1.5454 + P}$

Figures 14.24 and 14.25 show that Henry's law (represented by the dot-dash lines) and the limiting form of the Langmuir equation provide, respectively, in this example upper and lower bounds for the actual isotherm. The Langmuir isotherm when fit to *all* the experimental data yields a curve (not shown) in Fig. 14.24 that fits the data reasonably well, but not so well as the 3-parameter Toth expression.

Neither the spreading pressure nor the adsorbate equation of state is required for an empirical correlation of single-species adsorption data. However, a set of $(n,\ P)$ data *implies* an equation of state for the adsorbed phase, and hence a relationship between the spreading pressure Π and the moles adsorbed. By Eq. (14.112),

$$\frac{\Pi A}{RT} = \int_0^P \frac{n}{P} dP = \int_0^n \frac{n}{P}\frac{dP}{dn} dn$$

Equation (14.108) may be written as

$$z = \frac{\Pi A}{nRT}$$

Whence,
$$z = \frac{1}{n}\int_0^P \frac{n}{P}\,dP = \frac{1}{n}\int_0^n \frac{n}{P}\frac{dP}{dn}\,dn$$

Finding numerical values for z and Π depends on evaluation of the integral:

$$I \equiv \int_0^P \frac{n}{P}\,dP = \int_0^n \frac{n}{P}\frac{dP}{dn}\,dn$$

Choice of the form depends on whether P or n is the independent variable. The Toth equation gives the integrand n/P as a function of P, and therefore

$$I\,(\text{Toth}) = \int_0^P \frac{m\,dP}{(b + P^t)^{1/t}}$$

The cubic polynomial gives n/P as a function of n; whence,

$$I\,(\text{cubic}) = \int_0^n \left(\frac{C_0 - C_2 n^2 - 2C_3 n^3}{C_0 + C_1 n + C_2 n^2 + C_3 n^3} \right) dn$$

These two expressions permit numerical determination of $z(n)$ and $\Pi(n)$ as a result of correlations presented in this example. Thus, for $n = 1$ mol kg^{-1} and $A = 650$ m^2 g^{-1}, both the Toth and cubic-polynomial equations yield $z = 1.69$. From this result,

$$\Pi = \frac{nRT}{A}z = \frac{1 \text{ mol kg}^{-1} \times 83.14 \text{ cm}^3 \text{ bar mol}^{-1} \text{ K}^{-1} \times 323.15 \text{ K}}{650\,000 \text{ m}^2 \text{ kg}^{-1}}$$

$$\times\, 1.69 \times 10^{-6} \text{ m}^3 \text{ cm}^{-3} \times 10^5 \text{ N m}^{-2} \text{ bar}^{-1}$$

$$= 6.99 \times 10^{-3} \text{ N m}^{-1} \equiv 6.99 \text{ mN m}^{-1} \equiv 6.99 \text{ dyn cm}^{-1}$$

The adsorptive capacity of an adsorbent depends directly on its specific surface area A, but determination of these large values is not a trivial matter. The means is provided by the adsorption process itself. The basic idea is to measure the quantity of a gas adsorbed at full monolayer coverage and to multiply the number of molecules adsorbed by the area occupied by a single molecule. Two difficulties attend this procedure. First is the problem of detecting the point of full monolayer coverage. Second, one finds that with different gases as adsorbates different area values result. The latter problem is circumvented by the adoption of nitrogen as a standard adsorbate. The procedure is to make measurements of the (physical) adsorption of N_2 at its normal boiling point (−195.8°C or 77.35 K) for pressures up to its vapor pressure of 1 atm. The result is a curve the first part of which is like that in Fig. 14.24. When monolayer coverage is nearly complete, multilayer adsorption begins, and the curve changes direction, with

n increasing ever more rapidly with pressure. Finally, as the pressure approaches 1(atm), the vapor pressure of the N_2 adsorbate, the curve becomes nearly vertical because of condensation in the pores of the adsorbent. The problem is to identify the point on the curve that represents full monolayer coverage. The usual procedure is to fit the Brunauer/Emmett/Teller (BET) equation, a 2-parameter extension of the Langmuir isotherm to multilayer adsorption, to the n vs. P data. From this, one can determine a value for m.[28] Once m is known, multiplication by Avogadro's number and by the area occupied by one adsorbed N_2 molecule (16.2 Å^2) yields the surface area. The method has its uncertainties, particularly for molecular sieves where the pores may contain unadsorbed molecules. Nevertheless, it is a useful and widely used tool for characterizing and comparing adsorption capacities.

Heat of Adsorption

The Clapeyron equation, derived in Sec. 6.4 for the latent heat of phase transition of pure chemical species, is also applicable to pure-gas adsorption equilibrium. Here, however, the two-phase equilibrium pressure depends not only on temperature, but on surface coverage or the amount adsorbed. Thus the analogous equation for adsorption is written

$$\left(\frac{\partial P}{\partial T}\right)_n = \frac{\Delta H^{av}}{T\,\Delta V^{av}} \tag{14.116}$$

where subscript n signifies that the derivative is taken at constant amount adsorbed. Superscript av denotes a property change of *desorption*, i.e., the difference between the vapor-phase and the adsorbed-phase property. The quantity $\Delta H^{av} \equiv H^v - H^a$ is defined as the *isosteric heat of adsorption*, and is usually a positive quantity.[29] The heat of adsorption is a useful indication of the strength of the forces binding adsorbed molecules to the surface of the adsorbent, and its magnitude can therefore often be used to distinguish between physical adsorption and chemisorption.

The dependence of heats of adsorption on surface coverage has its basis in the energetic heterogeneity of most solid surfaces. The first sites on a surface to be occupied are those which attract adsorbate molecules most strongly and with the greatest release of energy. Thus the heat of adsorption decreases with surface coverage. Once all sites are occupied and multilayer adsorption begins, the dominant forces become those between adsorbate molecules, and for subcritical species the decreasing heat of adsorption approaches the heat of vaporization.

Assumed in the derivation of the Langmuir isotherm is the energetic equivalence of all adsorption sites, implying that the heat of adsorption is independent of surface coverage. This explains in part the inability of the Langmuir isotherm to provide a close fit to most experimental data over a wide range of surface coverage. The Freundlich isotherm, Eq. (14.115), implies a logarithmic decrease in the heat of adsorption with surface coverage.

As in the development of the Clausius/Clapeyron equation (Example 6.5), if for low pressures one assumes that the gas phase is ideal and that the adsorbate is of negligible volume

[28] J. M. Smith, *Chemical Kinetics*, 3d ed., sec. 8-1, McGraw-Hill, New York, 1981.

[29] Other heats of adsorption, defined differently, are also in use. However, the isosteric heat is the most common, and is the one needed for energy balances on adsorption columns.

compared with the gas-phase volume, Eq. (14.116) becomes:

$$\left(\frac{\partial \ln P}{\partial T}\right)_n = \frac{\Delta H^{av}}{RT^2} \qquad (14.117)$$

Application of this equation requires the measurement of isotherms, such as the one at 50°C in Fig. 14.24, at several temperatures. Cross plotting yields sets of P vs. T relations at constant n, from which values for the partial derivative of Eq. (14.117) can be obtained. For chemisorption, ΔH^{av} values usually range from 60 to 170 kJ mol^{-1}. For physical adsorption, they are smaller. For example, measured values at very low coverage for the physical adsorption of nitrogen and n-butane on 5A zeolite are 18.0 and 43.1 kJ mol^{-1}, respectively.[30]

Mixed-Gas Adsorption

Mixed-gas adsorption is treated similarly to the gamma/phi formulation of VLE (Sec. 14.1). With a gas-phase property denoted by superscript g, Eqs. (11.31) and (11.46), which define fugacity, are rewritten:

$$G_i^g = \Gamma_i^g(T) + RT \ln f_i^g \qquad (14.118) \qquad \mu_i^g = \Gamma_i^g(T) + RT \ln \hat{f}_i^g \qquad (14.119)$$

Note as a result of Eqs. (11.32) and (11.53) that

$$\lim_{P\to 0} \frac{f_i^g}{P} = 1 \qquad \text{and} \qquad \lim_{P\to 0} \frac{\hat{f}_i^g}{y_i P} = 1$$

For the adsorbate analogous equations are

$$G_i = \Gamma_i(T) + RT \ln f_i \qquad (14.120) \qquad \mu_i = \Gamma_i(T) + RT \ln \hat{f}_i \qquad (14.121)$$

with

$$\lim_{\Pi\to 0} \frac{f_i}{\Pi} = 1 \qquad \text{and} \qquad \lim_{\Pi\to 0} \frac{\hat{f}_i}{x_i \Pi} = 1$$

The Gibbs energies as given by Eqs. (14.118) and (14.120) may be equated for pure-gas/adsorbate equilibrium:

$$\Gamma_i^g(T) + RT \ln f_i^g = \Gamma_i(T) + RT \ln f_i$$

Rearrangement gives

$$\frac{f_i}{f_i^g} = \exp\left[\frac{\Gamma_i^g(T) - \Gamma_i(T)}{RT}\right] \equiv F_i(T) \qquad (14.122)$$

The limiting value of f_i/f_i^g as both P and Π approach zero can be used to evaluate $F_i(T)$:

$$\lim_{\substack{P\to 0\\ \Pi\to 0}} \frac{f_i}{f_i^g} = \lim_{\substack{P\to 0\\ \Pi\to 0}} \frac{\Pi}{P} = \lim_{\substack{n_i\to 0\\ P\to 0}} \frac{n_i}{P} \lim_{\substack{\Pi\to 0\\ n_i\to 0}} \frac{\Pi}{n_i}$$

[30] N. Hashimoto and J. M. Smith, *Ind. Eng. Chem. Fund.*, vol. 12, p. 353, 1973.

The first limit of the last member is Henry's constant k_i; the second limit is evaluated from Eq. (14.108), written $\Pi/n_i = z_i RT/A$; thus,

$$\lim_{\substack{\Pi\to 0 \\ n_i\to 0}} \frac{\Pi}{n_i} = \frac{RT}{A}$$

In combination with Eq. (14.122) these equations give

$$F_i(T) = \frac{k_i RT}{A} \qquad (14.123) \qquad\qquad f_i = \frac{k_i RT}{A} f_i^g \qquad (14.124)$$

Similarly, equating Eqs. (14.119) and (14.121) yields

$$\Gamma_i^g(T) + RT \ln \hat{f}_i^g = \Gamma_i(T) + RT \ln \hat{f}_i$$

from which $$\frac{\hat{f}_i}{\hat{f}_i^g} = \exp\left[\frac{\Gamma_i^g(T) - \Gamma_i(T)}{RT}\right] \equiv F_i(T)$$

Then by Eq. (14.123), $$\hat{f}_i = \frac{k_i RT}{A}\hat{f}_i^g \tag{14.125}$$

These equations show that equality of fugacities is not a proper criterion for gas/adsorbate equilibrium. This is also evident from the fact that the units of gas-phase fugacities are those of pressure, while the units of adsorbate fugacities are those of spreading pressure. In most applications the fugacities appear as ratios, and the factor $k_i RT/A$ cancels. Nevertheless it is instructive to note that equality of chemical potentials, not fugacities, is the fundamental criterion of phase equilibrium.

An activity coefficient for the constituent species of a mixed-gas adsorbate is defined by the equation:

$$\gamma_i \equiv \frac{\hat{f}_i}{x_i f_i^\circ}$$

where $\hat{f}_i$ and f_i° are evaluated at the same T and *spreading pressure* Π. The degree sign (°) denotes values for the equilibrium adsorption of *pure i* at the spreading pressure of the *mixture*. Substitution for the fugacities by Eqs. (14.124) and (14.125) gives

$$\gamma_i = \frac{\hat{f}_i^g(P)}{x_i f_i^g(P_i^\circ)}$$

The fugacities are evaluated at the pressures indicated in parentheses, where P is the equilibrium mixed-gas pressure and P_i° is the equilibrium pure-gas pressure that produces the same spreading pressure. If the gas-phase fugacities are eliminated in favor of fugacity coefficients [Eqs. (11.34) and (11.52)], then

$$\gamma_i = \frac{y_i \hat{\phi}_i P}{x_i \phi_i P_i^\circ}$$

or

$$y_i \hat{\phi}_i P = x_i \phi_i P_i^\circ \gamma_i \tag{14.126}$$

The usual assumption is that the gas phase is ideal; the fugacity coefficients are then unity:

$$y_i P = x_i P_i^\circ \gamma_i \tag{14.127}$$

These equations provide the means for calculation of activity coefficients from mixed-gas adsorption data. Alternatively, if γ_i values can be predicted, they allow calculation of adsorbate composition. In particular, if the mixed-gas adsorbate forms an ideal solution, then $\gamma_i = 1$, and the resulting equation is the adsorption analog of Raoult's law:

$$y_i P = x_i P_i^\circ \tag{14.128}$$

This equation is always valid as $P \to 0$ and within the pressure range for which Henry's law is a suitable approximation.

Equation (14.112) is applicable not only for pure-gas adsorption but also for adsorption of a constant-composition gas mixture. Applied where Henry's law is valid, it yields

$$\frac{\Pi A}{RT} = kP \tag{14.129}$$

where k is the mixed-gas Henry's constant. For adsorption of pure species i at the same spreading pressure, this becomes

$$\frac{\Pi A}{RT} = k_i P_i^\circ$$

Combining these two equations with Eq. (14.128) gives

$$y_i k_i = x_i k$$

Summing over all i,

$$k = \sum_i y_i k_i \tag{14.130}$$

Eliminating k between these two equations yields

$$x_i = \frac{y_i k_i}{\sum_i y_i k_i} \tag{14.131}$$

This simple equation, requiring only data for pure-gas adsorption, provides adsorbate compositions in the limit as $P \to 0$.

For an ideal adsorbed solution, in analogy with Eq. (11.81) for volumes,

$$a = \sum_i x_i a_i^\circ$$

where a is the molar area for the mixed-gas adsorbate and a_i° is the molar area of the pure-gas adsorbate at the same temperature and spreading pressure. Because $a = A/n$ and $a_i^\circ = A/n_i^\circ$, this equation may be written as

$$\frac{1}{n} = \sum_i \frac{x_i}{n_i^\circ}$$

or
$$n = \frac{1}{\sum_i (x_i / n_i^\circ)} \tag{14.132}$$

where n is the specific amount of mixed-gas adsorbate and n_i° is the specific amount of pure-i adsorbate at the same spreading pressure. The amount of species i in the *mixed-gas* adsorbate is of course $n_i = x_i n$.

The prediction of mixed-gas adsorption equilibria by *ideal-adsorbed-solution theory*[31] is based on Eqs. (14.128) and (14.132). The following is a brief outline of the procedure. Because there are $N + 1$ degrees of freedom, both T and P, as well as the gas-phase composition, must be specified. Solution is for the adsorbate composition and the specific amount adsorbed. Adsorption isotherms for *each pure species* must be known over the pressure range from zero to the value that produces the spreading pressure of the mixed-gas adsorbate. For purposes of illustration we assume Eq. (14.111), the Langmuir isotherm, to apply for each pure species, writing it:

$$n_i^\circ = \frac{k_i b_i P_i^\circ}{b_i + P_i^\circ} \tag{A}$$

The inverse of Eq. (14.113) provides an expression for P_i°, which yields values of P_i° corresponding to the spreading pressure of the mixed-gas adsorbate:

$$P_i^\circ = b_i \left(\exp \frac{\psi}{k_i b_i} - 1 \right) \tag{B}$$

where
$$\psi \equiv \frac{\Pi A}{RT}$$

The following steps then constitute a solution procedure:

- An initial estimate of ψ is found from the Henry's-law equations. Combining the definition of ψ with Eqs. (14.129) and (14.130) yields
$$\psi = P \sum_i y_i k_i$$
- With this estimate of ψ, calculate P_i° for each species i by Eq. (B) and n_i° for each species i by Eq. (A).
- One can show that the error in ψ is approximated by
$$\delta\psi = \frac{P \sum_i \dfrac{y_i}{P_i^\circ} - 1}{P \sum_i \dfrac{y_i}{P_i^\circ n_i^\circ}}$$
  Moreover, the approximation becomes increasingly exact as $\delta\psi$ decreases. If $\delta\psi$ is smaller than some preset tolerance (say $\delta\psi < \psi \times 10^{-7}$), the calculation goes to the

[31] A. L. Myers and J. M. Prausnitz, *AIChE J.*, vol. 11, pp. 121–127, 1965; D. P. Valenzuela and A. L. Myers, *op. cit.*

final step; if not, a new value, $\psi = \psi + \delta\psi$, is determined, and the calculation returns to the preceding step.

- Calculate x_i for each species i by Eq. (14.128):

$$x_i = \frac{y_i P}{P_i^\circ}$$

Calculate the specific amount absorbed by Eq. (14.132).

Use of the Langmuir isotherm has made this computational scheme appear quite simple, because direct solution for P_i° (step 2) is possible. However, most equations for the adsorption isotherm are less tractable, and this calculation must be done numerically. This significantly increases the computational task, but does not alter the general procedure.

Predictions of adsorption equilibria by ideal-adsorbed-solution theory are usually satisfactory when the specific amount adsorbed is less than a third of the saturation value for monolayer coverage. At higher adsorbed amounts, appreciable negative deviations from ideality are promoted by differences in size of the adsorbate molecules and by adsorbent heterogeneity. One must then have recourse to Eq. (14.127). The difficulty is in obtaining values of the activity coefficients, which are strong functions of both spreading pressure and temperature. This is in contrast to activity coefficients for liquid phases, which for most applications are insensitive to pressure. This topic is treated by Talu et al.[32]

14.9 OSMOTIC EQUILIBRIUM AND OSMOTIC PRESSURE

Most of the earth's water resides in the oceans, as seawater. For some regions, this is the ultimate source of fresh water for public and commercial use. Conversion of seawater to fresh water requires the separation of more-or-less pure water from an aqueous solution containing dissolved solute species. About 65% of such conversion is currently done by distillation schemes. But another 30% is effected by *reverse osmosis*. Central to an understanding of osmotic separations are the concepts of osmotic equilibrium and osmotic pressure, the topics of this section.

Consider the idealized physical situation represented by Fig. 14.26. A chamber is divided into two compartments by a rigid semipermeable partition. The left compartment contains a binary solute(1)/solvent(2) liquid mixture, and the right contains pure solvent; the partition is permeable to solvent species 2 only. Temperature is uniform and constant throughout, but moveable pistons permit independent adjustment of the pressures in the two compartments.

Suppose that pressure is the same in the two compartments: $P' = P$. This implies inequality of the fugacity $\hat{f}_2$ of the only distributed species (the solvent), for by Eq. (14.72),

$$\frac{d\hat{f}_2}{dx_2} > 0 \qquad \text{(const } T, P)$$

meaning that $\quad \hat{f}_2(T, P' = P, x_2 < 1) < \hat{f}_2(T, P, x_2 = 1) \equiv f_2(T, P)$

[32]O. Talu, J. Li, and A. L. Myers, *Adsorption*, vol. 1, pp. 103–112, 1995.

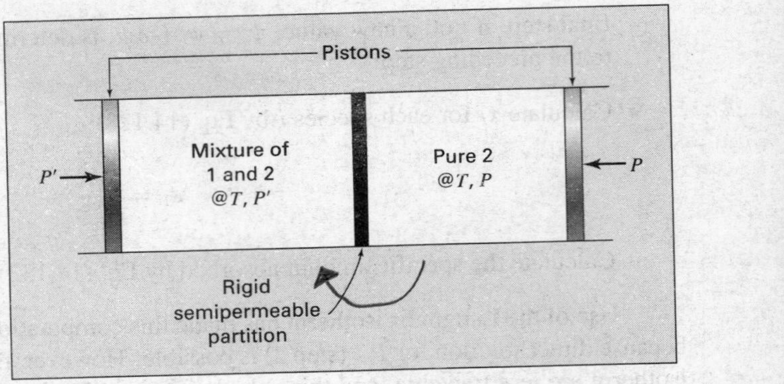

Figure 14.26: Idealized osmotic system

Thus, if $P' = P$, the solvent fugacity is smaller in the left compartment than in the right. The difference in solvent fugacities represents a driving force for mass transfer, and solvent diffuses through the partition, from right to left.

Equilibrium is established when pressure P' is increased to an appropriate value P^*, such that

$$\hat{f}_2(T, P' = P^*, x_2 < 1) = f_2(T, P)$$

The pressure difference, $\Pi \equiv P^* - P$, is the *osmotic pressure* of the solution, defined implicitly through the equilibrium equation for species 2, which in abbreviated form is

$$\hat{f}_2(P + \Pi, x_2) = f_2(P) \tag{14.133}$$

Equation (14.133) is a basis for developing explicit expressions for osmotic pressure Π. Development is facilitated by the identity:

$$\hat{f}_2(P + \Pi, x_2) \equiv f_2(P) \cdot \frac{\hat{f}_2(P, x_2)}{f_2(P)} \cdot \frac{\hat{f}_2(P + \Pi, x_2)}{\hat{f}_2(P, x_2)} \tag{14.134}$$

The first ratio on the right is, by Eq. (11.90),

$$\frac{\hat{f}_2(P, x_2)}{f_2(P)} = x_2 \gamma_2$$

where γ_2 is the activity coefficient of solvent in the mixture at pressure P. The second ratio is a *Poynting factor*, representing here a pressure effect on the fugacity of a species in solution. An expression for this factor is readily found from Eq. (11.46):

$$\left(\frac{\partial \ln \hat{f}_i}{\partial P}\right)_{T,x} = \frac{1}{RT}\left(\frac{\partial \mu_i}{\partial P}\right)_{T,x}$$

By Eqs. (11.18) and (11.8),
$$\left(\frac{\partial \mu_i}{\partial P}\right)_{T,x} = \bar{V}_i$$

Thus, for solvent species 2,
$$\left(\frac{\partial \ln \hat{f}_2}{\partial P}\right)_{T,x} = \frac{\bar{V}_2}{RT}$$

Whence,
$$\frac{\hat{f}_2(P+\Pi, x_2)}{\hat{f}_2(P, x_2)} = \exp \int_P^{P+\Pi} \frac{\bar{V}_2}{RT} dP$$

Equation (14.134) therefore becomes

$$\hat{f}_2(P+\Pi, x_2) = x_2\gamma_2 f_2(P) \exp \int_P^{P+\Pi} \frac{\bar{V}_2}{RT} dP$$

Combination with Eq. (14.133) yields

$$x_2\gamma_2 \exp \int_P^{P+\Pi} \frac{\bar{V}_2}{RT} dP = 1$$

or
$$\boxed{\int_P^{P+\Pi} \frac{\bar{V}_2}{RT} dP = -\ln(x_2\gamma_2)} \tag{14.135}$$

Equation (14.135) is exact; working expressions for Π follow by rational approximation.

If we ignore the effect of pressure on $\bar{V}_2$, the integral becomes $\Pi \bar{V}_2/RT$. Solution for Π then yields

$$\Pi = -\frac{RT}{\bar{V}_2} \ln(x_2\gamma_2) \tag{14.136}$$

If in addition the solution is sufficiently dilute in solute 1,

$$\bar{V}_2 \approx V_2 \qquad \gamma_2 \approx 1 \qquad \text{and} \qquad \ln(x_2\gamma_2) \approx \ln(1-x_1) \approx -x_1$$

With these approximations, Eq. (14.136) becomes

$$\Pi = \frac{x_1 RT}{V_2} \tag{14.137}$$

Equation (14.137) is the celebrated van't Hoff equation.[33]

Equation (14.135) is valid when species 1 is a nonelectrolyte. If the solute is a strong (completely dissociated) electrolyte containing m ions, then the right side is

$$-\ln(x_2^m \gamma_2)$$

and the van't Hoff equation becomes

$$\Pi = \frac{m x_1 RT}{V_2}$$

Osmotic pressure can be quite large, even for very dilute solutions. Consider an aqueous solution containing mole fraction $x_1 = 0.001$ of a nonelectrolyte solute species at 25°C (298.15 K). Then

$$\Pi = 0.001 \times \frac{1}{18.02\ \text{cm}^3} \frac{\text{mol}}{} \times 82.06 \frac{\text{cm}^3\ \text{atm}}{\text{mol K}} \times 298.15\ \text{K} = 1.36\ \text{atm}$$

[33] Jacobus Henricus van't Hoff (1852–1911), Dutch chemist who won the first Nobel prize for chemistry in 1901.

With reference to Fig. 14.26, this means that for a pure solvent pressure $P = 1$ atm, the pressure P' on the solution must be 2.36 atm to prevent diffusion of solvent from right to left, i.e., to establish *osmotic equilibrium*.[34] Pressures P' greater than this value make

$$\hat{f}_2(P', x_2) > f_2(P)$$

and a driving force exists for transfer of water (solvent) from left to right. This observation serves as motivation for the process called *reverse osmosis*, wherein a solvent (commonly water) is separated from a solution by application of sufficient pressure to provide the driving force necessary for solvent transfer through a membrane which for practical purposes is permeable only to the solvent. The minimum pressure difference (solution pressure vs. pure-solvent pressure) is just the osmotic pressure Π.

In practice, pressure differences significantly greater than Π are used to effect osmotic separations. For example, seawater has an osmotic pressure of about 25 bar, but working pressures of 50 to 80 bar are employed to enhance the rate of recovery of fresh water. A feature of such separations is that they require mechanical power only, for pumping the solution to an appropriate pressure level. This contrasts with distillation schemes, where steam is the usual source of energy. A brief overview of reverse osmosis is given by Perry and Green.[35]

PROBLEMS

14.1. The excess Gibbs energy for the system chloroform(1)/ethanol(2) at 55°C (328.15 K) is well represented by the Margules equation, written as

$$G^E/RT = (1.42\,x_1 + 0.59\,x_2)x_1x_2$$

The vapor pressures of chloroform and ethanol at 55°C (328.15 K) are:

$$P_1^{sat} = 82.37 \text{ kPa} \qquad P_2^{sat} = 37.31 \text{ kPa}$$

(*a*) Assuming the validity of Eq. (10.5), make *BUBL P* calculations at 55°C (328.15 K) for liquid-phase mole fractions of 0.25, 0.50, and 0.75.

(*b*) For comparison, repeat the calculations using Eqs. (14.1) and (14.2) with virial coefficients:

$$B_{11} = -963 \text{ cm}^3 \text{ mol}^{-1} \qquad B_{22} = -1{,}523 \text{ cm}^3 \text{ mol}^{-1} \qquad B_{12} = 52 \text{ cm}^3 \text{ mol}$$

14.2. Find expressions for $\hat{\phi}_1$ and $\hat{\phi}_2$ for a binary gas mixture described by Eq. (3.40). The mixing rule for B is given by Eq. (11.62). The mixing rule for C is given by the general equation:

$$C = \sum_i \sum_j \sum_k y_i y_j y_k C_{ijk}$$

[34]Note that, unlike conventional phase equilibrium, pressures are *unequal* for osmotic equilibrium, owing to the special constraints imposed by the rigid semipermeable partition.

[35]R. H. Perry and D. Green, *Perry's Chemical Engineers' Handbook*, 7th ed., pp. 22-37—22-42 and 22-48—22.56, McGraw-Hill, New York, 1997.

where Cs with the same subscripts, regardless of order, are equal. For a binary mixture, this becomes:

$$C = y_1^3 C_{111} + 3y_1^2 y_2 C_{112} + 3y_1 y_2^2 C_{122} + y_2^3 C_{222}$$

14.3. A system formed of methane(1) and a light oil(2) at 200 K and 30 bar consists of a vapor phase containing 95 mole % methane and a liquid phase containing oil and dissolved methane. The fugacity of the methane is given by Henry's law, and at the temperature of interest Henry's constant is $\mathcal{H}_1 = 200$ bar. Stating any assumptions, estimate the equilibrium mole fraction of methane in the liquid phase. The second virial coefficient of pure methane at 200 K is -105 cm^3 mol^{-1}.

14.4. Assume that the last three data points (including the value of P_1^{sat}) of Table 12.1, p. 431, cannot be measured. Nevertheless, a correlation based on the remaining data points is required. Assuming the validity of Eq. (10.5), Eq. (14.28) may be written as

$$P = x_1(\gamma_1/\gamma_1^\infty)\mathcal{H}_1 + x_2\gamma_2 P_2^{\text{sat}}$$

Data reduction may be based on Barker's method, i.e., minimizing the sum of squares of the residuals between the experimental values of P and the values predicted by this equation (see Ex. 12.1). Assume that the activity coefficients can be adequately represented by the Margules equation.

(*a*) Show that $\ln(\gamma_1/\gamma_1^\infty) = x_2^2[A_{12} + 2(A_{21} - A_{12})x_1] - A_{12}$.
(*b*) Find a value for Henry's constant $\mathcal{H}_1$.
(*c*) Determine values for parameters A_{12} and A_{21} by Barker's method.
(*d*) Find values for δy_1 for the data points.

How could the regression be done so as to minimize the sum of squares of the residuals in G^E/RT, thus including the y_1 values in the data-reduction process?

14.5. Assume that the first three data points (including the value of P_2^{sat}) of Table 12.1, p. 431, cannot be measured. Nevertheless, a correlation based on the remaining data points is required. Assuming the validity of Eq. (10.5), Eq. (14.28) may be written as

$$P = x_1\gamma_1 P_1^{\text{sat}} + x_2(\gamma_2/\gamma_2^\infty)\mathcal{H}_2$$

Data reduction may be based on Barker's method, i.e., minimizing the sum of squares of the residuals between the experimental values of P and the values predicted by this equation (see Ex. 12.1). Assume that the activity coefficients can be adequately represented by the Margules equation.

(*a*) Show that: $\ln(\gamma_2/\gamma_2^\infty) = x_1^2[A_{21} + 2(A_{12} - A_{21})x_2] - A_{21}$.
(*b*) Find a value for Henry's constant $\mathcal{H}_2$.
(*c*) Determine values for parameters A_{12} and A_{21} by Barker's method.
(*d*) Find values for δy_1 for the data points.

How could the regression be done so as to minimize the sum of squares of the residuals in G^E/RT, thus including the y_1 values in the data-reduction process?

14.6. Work Pb. 14.4 with the data set of Table 12.3, p. 439.

14.7. Work Pb. 14.5 with the data set of Table 12.3, p. 439.

14.8. Use Eq. (14.1) to *reduce* one of the isothermal data sets identified below, and compare the result with that obtained by application of Eq. (10.5). Recall that *reduction* means developing a numerical expression for G^E/RT as a function of composition.

(*a*) Methylethylketone(1)/toluene(2) at 50°C (323.15 K): Table 12.1, p. 431.
(*b*) Acetone(1)/methanol(2) at 55°C (328.15 K): Pb. 12.3, p. 470.
(*c*) Methyl *tert*-butyl ether(1)/dichloromethane(2) at 35°C (308.15 K): Pb. 12.6, p. 471.
(*d*) Acetonitrile(1)/benzene(2) at 45°C (318.15 K): Pb. 12.9, p. 472.

Second-virial-coefficient data are as follows:

	Part (*a*)	Part (*b*)	Part (*c*)	Part (*d*)
B_{11}	−1840	−1440	−2060	−4500
B_{22}	−1800	−1150	−860	−1300
B_{12}	−1150	−1040	−790	−1000

14.9. For one of the substances listed below determine P^{sat}/bar from the Redlich/Kwong equation at two temperatures: $T = T_n$ (the normal boiling point), and $T = 0.85T_c$. For the second temperature, compare your result with a value from the literature (e.g., *Perry's Chemical Engineers' Handbook*). Discuss your results.

(*a*) Acetylene (*b*) Argon (*c*) Benzene (*d*) *n*-Butane (*e*) Carbon monoxide
(*f*) *n*-Decane (*g*) Ethylene (*h*) *n*-Heptane (*i*) Methane (*j*) Nitrogen

14.10. Work Pb. 14.9 for one of the following:

(*a*) The Soave/Redlich/Kwong equation (*b*) The Peng/Robinson equation

14.11. Departures from Raoult's law are primarily from liquid-phase nonidealities ($\gamma_i \neq 1$). But vapor-phase nonidealities ($\hat{\phi}_i \neq 1$) also contribute. Consider the special case where the liquid phase is an ideal solution, and the vapor phase a nonideal gas mixture described by Eq. (3.38). Show that departures from Raoult's law at constant temperature are likely to be *negative*. State clearly any assumptions and approximations.

14.12. Determine a numerical value for the acentric factor ω implied by

(*a*) The van der Waals equation (*b*) The Redlich/Kwong equation

14.13. Starting with Eq. (14.71), derive the stability criteria of Eqs. (14.72) and (14.73).

14.14. An absolute upper bound on G^E for stability of an equimolar binary mixture is $G^E = RT \ln 2$. Develop this result. What is the corresponding bound for an equimolar mixture containing N species?

14.15. A binary liquid system exhibits LLE at 25°C (298.15 K). Determine from each of the following sets of miscibility data estimates for parameters A_{12} and A_{21} in the Margules equation at 25°C (298.15 K):

$$(a)\ x_1^\alpha = 0.10,\ x_1^\beta = 0.90;\ (b)\ x_1^\alpha = 0.20,\ x_1^\beta = 0.90;\ (c)\ x_1^\alpha = 0.10,\ x_1^\beta = 0.80.$$

14.16. Work Pb. 14.15 for the van Laar equation.

14.17. Consider a binary vapor-phase mixture described by Eqs. (3.38) and (11.62). Under what (highly unlikely) conditions would one expect the mixture to split into two immiscible vapor phases?

14.18. Figures 14.14, 14.15, and 14.16 are based on Eqs. (A) and (F) of Ex. 14.5 with C_P^E assumed *positive* and given by $C_P^E/R = 3\,x_1 x_2$. Graph the corresponding figures for the following cases, in which C_P^E is assumed *negative*:

$$(a)\ A = \frac{975}{T} - 18.4 + 3 \ln T$$

$$(b)\ A = \frac{540}{T} - 17.1 + 3 \ln T$$

$$(c)\ A = \frac{1{,}500}{T} - 19.9 + 3 \ln T$$

14.19. It has been suggested that a value for G^E of at least 0.5 RT is required for liquid/liquid phase splitting in a binary system. Offer some justification for this statement.

14.20. Pure liquid species 2 and 3 are for practical purposes immiscible in one another. Liquid species 1 is soluble in both liquid 2 and liquid 3. One mole each of liquids 1, 2, and 3 are shaken together to form an equilibrium mixture of two liquid phases: an α-phase containing species 1 and 2, and a β-phase containing species 1 and 3. What are the mole fractions of species 1 in the α and β phases, if at the temperature of the experiment, the excess Gibbs energies of the phases are given by

$$\frac{(G^E)^\alpha}{RT} = 0.4\,x_1^\alpha x_2^\alpha \qquad \text{and} \qquad \frac{(G^E)^\beta}{RT} = 0.8\,x_1^\beta x_3^\beta$$

14.21. It is demonstrated in Ex. 14.7 that the Wilson equation for G^E is incapable of representing LLE. Show that the simple modification of Wilson's equation given by:

$$G^E/RT = -C[x_1 \ln(x_1 + x_2\Lambda_{12}) + x_2 \ln(x_2 + x_1\Lambda_{21})]$$

can represent LLE. Here, C is a constant.

14.22. Vapor sulfur hexafluoride SF_6 at pressures of about 1600 kPa is used as a dielectric in large primary circuit breakers for electric transmission systems. As liquids, SF_6 and H_2O are essentially immiscible, and it is therefore necessary to specify a low enough moisture content in the vapor SF_6 so that if condensation occurs in cold weather a liquid-water phase will not form first in the system. For a preliminary determination, assume the vapor phase an ideal gas and prepare the phase diagram [Fig. 14.21(*a*)] for $H_2O(1)/SF_6(2)$ at 1600 kPa in the composition range up to 1000 parts per million of water (mole basis). The following approximate equations for vapor pressure are adequate:

$$\ln P_1^{sat}/\text{kPa} = 19.1478 - \frac{5363.70}{T/\text{K}} \qquad \ln P_2^{sat}/\text{kPa} = 14.6511 - \frac{2048.97}{T/\text{K}}$$

14.23. In Ex. 14.4 a plausibility argument was developed from the LLE *equilibrium* equations to demonstrate that positive deviations from ideal-solution behavior are conducive to liquid/liquid phase splitting.

(*a*) Use one of the binary stability criteria to reach this same conclusion.

(*b*) Is it possible *in principle* for a system exhibiting negative deviations from ideality to form two liquid phases?

14.24. Toluene(1) and water(2) are essentially immiscible as liquids. Determine the dew-point temperatures and the compositions of the first drops of liquid formed when vapor mixtures of these species with mole fractions $z_1 = 0.2$ and $z_1 = 0.7$ are cooled at the constant pressure of 101.33 kPa. What is the bubble-point temperature and the composition of the last drop of vapor in each case? See Table B.2, App. B, for vapor-pressure equations.

14.25. *n*-Heptane(1) and water(2) are essentially immiscible as liquids. A vapor mixture containing 65 mole % water at 100°C (373.15 K) and 101.33 kPa is cooled slowly at constant pressure until condensation is complete. Construct a plot for the process showing temperature vs. the equilibrium mole fraction of heptane in the residual vapor. See Table B.2, App. B, for vapor-pressure equations.

14.26. Consider a binary system of species 1 and 2 in which the liquid phase exhibits partial miscibility. In the regions of miscibility, the excess Gibbs energy at a particular temperature is expressed by the equation

$$G^E/RT = 2.25\, x_1 x_2$$

In addition, the vapor pressures of the pure species are

$$P_1^{sat} = 75 \text{ kPa} \qquad \text{and} \qquad P_2^{sat} = 110 \text{ kPa}$$

Making the usual assumptions for low-pressure VLE, prepare a P-x-y diagram for this system at the given temperature.

14.27. The system water(1)/*n*-pentane(2)/*n*-heptane(3) exists as a vapor at 101.33 kPa and 100°C (373.15 K) with mole fractions $z_1 = 0.45$, $z_2 = 0.30$, $z_3 = 0.25$. The system is slowly cooled at constant pressure until it is completely condensed into a water phase and a hydrocarbon phase. Assuming that the two liquid phases are immiscible, that the vapor phase is an ideal gas, and that the hydrocarbons obey Raoult's law, determine:

(*a*) The dew-point temperature of the mixture and composition of the first condensate.
(*b*) The temperature at which the second liquid phase appears and its initial composition.
(*c*) The bubble-point temperature and the composition of the last bubble of vapor.

See Table B.2, App. B, for vapor-pressure equations.

14.28. Work the preceding problem for mole fractions $z_1 = 0.32$, $z_2 = 0.45$, $z_3 = 0.23$.

14.29. The Case I behavior for SLE (Sec. 14.6) has an analog for VLE. Develop the analogy.

14.30. An assertion with respect to Case II behavior for SLE (Sec. 14.6) was that the condition $z_i \gamma_i^s = 1$ corresponds to complete immiscibility for all species in the solid state. Prove this.

14.31. Use results of Sec. 14.6 to develop the following (approximate) rules of thumb:

(*a*) The solubility of a solid in a liquid solvent increases with increasing T.
(*b*) The solubility of a solid in a liquid solvent is independent of the identity of the solvent species.
(*c*) Of two solids with roughly the same heat of fusion, that solid with the lower melting point is the more soluble in a given liquid solvent at a given T.
(*d*) Of two solids with similar melting points, that solid with the smaller heat of fusion is the more soluble in a given liquid solvent at a given T.

14.32. Estimate the solubility of naphthalene(1) in carbon dioxide(2) at a temperature of 80°C (353.15 K) at pressures up to 300 bar. Use the procedure described in Sec. 14.7, with $l_{12} = 0.088$. Compare the results with those shown by Fig. 14.23. Discuss any differences. $P_1^{sat} = 0.0102$ bar at 80°C (353.15 K).

14.33. Estimate the solubility of naphthalene(1) in nitrogen(2) at a temperature of 35°C (308.15 K) at pressures up to 300 bar. Use the procedure described in Sec. 14.7, with $l_{12} = 0$. Compare the results with those shown by Fig. 14.23 for the naphthalene/CO_2 system at 35°C (308.15 K) with $l_{12} = 0$. Discuss any differences.

14.34. The qualitative features of SVE at high pressures shown by Fig. 14.23 are determined by the equation of state for the gas. To what extent can these features be represented by the two-term virial equation in pressure, Eq. (3.38)?

14.35. The UNILAN equation for pure-species adsorption is

$$n = \frac{m}{2s} \ln\left(\frac{c + Pe^{s}}{c + Pe^{-s}}\right)$$

where m, s, and c are positive empirical constants.

(*a*) Show that the UNILAN equation reduces to the Langmuir isotherm for $s = 0$. (*Hint*: Apply l'Hôpital's rule.)

(*b*) Show that Henry's constant k for the UNILAN equation is

$$k(\text{UNILAN}) = \frac{m}{cs} \sinh s$$

(*c*) Examine the *detailed* behavior of the UNILAN equation at zero pressure ($P \to 0$, $n \to 0$).

14.36. In Ex. 14.10, Henry's constant for adsorption k, identified as the intercept on a plot of n/P vs. n, was found from a polynomial curve-fit of n/P vs. n. An alternative procedure is based on a plot of $\ln(P/n)$ vs. n. Suppose that the adsorbate equation of state is a power series in n: $z = 1 + Bn + Cn^2 + \cdots$. Show how from a plot (or a polynomial curve-fit) of $\ln(P/n)$ vs. n one can extract values of k and B. [*Hint*: Start with Eq. (14.109).]

14.37. It was assumed in the development of Eq. (14.109) that the gas phase is *ideal*, with $Z = 1$. Suppose for a *real* gas phase that $Z = Z(T, P)$. Determine the analogous expression to Eq. (14.109) appropriate for a real (nonideal) gas phase. [*Hint*: Start with Eq. (14.105).]

14.38. Use results reported in Ex. 14.10 to prepare plots of Π vs. n and z vs. n for ethylene adsorbed on a carbon molecular sieve. Discuss the plots.

14.39. Suppose that the adsorbate equation of state is given by $z = (1 - bn)^{-1}$, where b is a constant. Find the implied adsorption isotherm, and show under what conditions it reduces to the Langmuir isotherm.

14.40. Suppose that the adsorbate equation of state is given by $z = 1 + \beta n$, where β is a function of T only. Find the implied adsorption isotherm, and show under what conditions it reduces to the Langmuir isotherm.

14.41. Derive the result given in the third step of the procedure for predicting adsorption equilibria by ideal-adsorbed-solution theory at the end of Sec. 14.8.

14.42. Consider a ternary system comprising solute species 1 and a mixed solvent (species 2 and 3). Assume that

$$\frac{G^E}{RT} = A_{12}x_1x_2 + A_{13}x_1x_3 + A_{23}x_2x_3$$

Show that Henry's constant $\mathcal{H}_1$ for species 1 in the mixed solvent is related to Henry's constants $\mathcal{H}_{1,2}$ and $\mathcal{H}_{1,3}$ for species 1 in the pure solvents by

$$\ln \mathcal{H}_1 = x_2' \ln \mathcal{H}_{1,2} + x_3' \ln \mathcal{H}_{1,3} - A_{23} x_2' x_3'$$

Here x_2' and x_3' are solute-free mole fractions:

$$x_2' \equiv \frac{x_2}{x_2 + x_3} \qquad x_3' \equiv \frac{x_3}{x_2 + x_3}$$

14.43. It is possible in principle for a binary liquid system to show more than one region of LLE for a particular temperature. For example, the solubility diagram might have two side-by-side "islands" of partial miscibility separated by a homogeneous phase. What would the ΔG vs. x_1 diagram at constant T look like for this case? Suggestion: See Fig. 14.12 for a mixture showing *normal* LLE behavior.

14.44. With $\bar{V}_2 = V_2$, Eq. (14.136) for the osmotic pressure may be represented as a power series in x_1:

$$\frac{\Pi V_2}{x_1 RT} = 1 + \mathcal{B} x_1 + \mathcal{C} x_1^2 + \cdots$$

Reminiscent of Eqs. (3.11) and (3.12), this series is called an *osmotic virial expansion*. Show that the second osmotic virial coefficient $\mathcal{B}$ is

$$\mathcal{B} = \frac{1}{2}\left[1 - \left(\frac{d^2 \ln \gamma_2}{dx_1^2}\right)_{x_1=0}\right]$$

What is $\mathcal{B}$ for an ideal solution? What is $\mathcal{B}$ if $G^E = A x_1 x_2$?

14.45. A liquid-process feed stream F contains 99 mole % of species 1 and 1 mole % of impurity, species 2. The impurity level is to be reduced to 0.1 mole % by contacting the feed stream with a stream S of pure liquid solvent, species 3, in a mixer/settler. Species 1 and 3 are essentially immiscible. Owing to "good chemistry," it is expected that species 2 will selectively concentrate in the solvent phase.

(*a*) With the equations given below, determine the required solvent-to-feed ratio n_S/n_F.
(*b*) What is mole fraction x_2 of impurity in the solvent phase leaving the mixer/settler?
(*c*) What is "good" about the chemistry here? With respect to liquid-phase nonidealities, what would be "bad" chemistry for the proposed operation?

Given: $G_{12}^E/RT = 1.5\, x_1 x_2 \qquad G_{23}^E/RT = -0.8\, x_2 x_3$

14.46. At 25°C (298.15 K) the solubility of *n*-hexane in water is 2 ppm (molar basis), and the solubility of water in *n*-hexane is 520 ppm. Estimate the activity coefficients for the two species in the two phases.

14.47. A binary liquid mixture is only partially miscible at 298 K. If the mixture is to be made homogeneous by increasing the temperature, what must be the sign of H^E?

14.48. The relative volatility α_{12} is commonly used in applicationas involving binary VLE. In particular (see Ex. 10.3), it serves as a basis for assessing the possibility of binary azeotropy.

(*a*) Develop an expression for α_{12} based on Eqs. (14.1) and (14.2).

(*b*) Specialize the expression to the composition limits $x_1 = y_1 = 0$ and $x_1 = y_1 = 1$. Compare with the result obtained from modified Raoult's law, Eq. (10.5). The difference between the results reflects the effects of vapor-phase nonidealities.

(*c*) Further specialize the results of part (*b*) to the case where the vapor phase is an ideal solution of real gases.

14.49. Although isothermal VLE data are preferred for extraction of activity coefficients, a large body of good isobaric data exists in the literature. For a binary isobaric T-x_1-y_1 data set, one can extract point values of γ_i via Eq. (14.1):

$$\gamma_i(x, T_k) = \frac{y_i \Phi_i(T_k, P, y) P}{x_i P_i^{\text{sat}}(T_k)}$$

Here, the variable list for γ_i recognizes a primary dependence on x and T; pressure dependence is normally negligible. The notation T_k emphasizes that temperature varies with data point across the composition range, and the calculated activity coefficients are at different temperatures. However, the usual goal of VLE data reduction and correlation is to develop an appropriate expression for G^E/RT at a single temperature T. A procedure is needed to *correct* each activity coefficient to such a T chosen near the average for the data set. If a correlation for $H^E(x)$ is available at or near this T, show that the values of γ_i corrected to T can be estimated by the expression:

$$\gamma_i(x, T) = \gamma_i(x, T_k) \exp\left[\frac{-\bar{H}_i^E}{RT}\left(\frac{T}{T_k} - 1\right)\right]$$

14.50. What are the relative contributions of the various terms in the gamma/phi expression for VLE? One way to address the question is through calculation of the activity coefficients for a single binary VLE data point via Eq. (14.1):

$$\gamma_i = \underbrace{\frac{y_i P}{x_i P_i^{\text{sat}}}}_{\text{(A)}} \cdot \underbrace{\frac{\hat{\phi}_i}{\phi_i^{\text{sat}}}}_{\text{(B)}} \cdot \underbrace{\frac{f_i^{\text{sat}}}{f_i}}_{\text{(C)}}$$

Term (A) is the value that would follow from modified Raoult's law; term (B) accounts for vapor-phase nonidealities; term (C) is the Poynting factor [see Eq. (11.44)]. Use the single-point data below for the butanenitrile(1)/benzene(2) system at 45°C (318.15 K) to evaluate all terms for $i = 1$ and $i = 2$. Discuss the results.

VLE Data: $P = 0.20941$ bar, $x_1 = 0.4819$, $y_1 = 0.1813$

Ancillary data: $P_1^{\text{sat}} = 0.07287$ bar, $P_2^{\text{sat}} = 0.29871$ bar

$$B_{11} = -7\,993 \text{ cm}^3 \text{ mol}^{-1},\ B_{22} = -1\,247 \text{ cm}^3 \text{ mol}^{-1},$$
$$B_{12} = -2\,089 \text{ cm}^3 \text{ mol}^{-1},\ V_1^l = 90 \text{ cm}^3 \text{ mol}^{-1},\ V_2^l = 92 \text{ cm}^3 \text{ mol}^{-1}$$

14.51. The *spinodal curve* for a binary liquid system is the locus of states for which

$$\frac{d^2(\Delta G/RT)}{dx_1^2} = 0 \qquad \text{(const } T, P\text{)}$$

Thus it separates regions of stability from instability with respect to liquid/liquid phase splitting. For a given T, there are normally two spinodal compositions (if any). They are the same at a consolute temperature. On curve II of Fig. 14.12 they are a pair of compositions between x_1^α and x_1^β, corresponding to zero curvature.

Suppose a liquid mixture is described by the symmetrical equation

$$\frac{G^E}{RT} = A(T)x_1x_2$$

(*a*) Find an expression for the spinodal compositions as a function of $A(T)$.

(*b*) Assume that $A(T)$ is the expression used to generate Fig. 14.15. Plot on a single graph the solubility curve and the spinodal curve. Discuss.

14.52. Two special models of liquid-solution behavior are the *regular solution*, for which $S^E = 0$ everywhere, and the *athermal solution*, for which $H^E = 0$ everywhere.

(*a*) Ignoring the P-dependence of G^E, show that for a regular solution,

$$\frac{G^E}{RT} = \frac{F_R(x)}{RT}$$

(*b*) Ignoring the P-dependence of G^E, show that for an athermal solution,

$$\frac{G^E}{RT} = F_A(x)$$

(*c*) Suppose that G^E/RT is described by the symmetrical equation

$$\frac{G^E}{RT} = A(T)x_1x_2$$

From parts (*a*) and (*b*), we conclude that

$$\frac{G^E}{RT} = \frac{\alpha}{RT}x_1x_2 \quad \text{(regular)} \qquad (A)$$

$$\frac{G^E}{RT} = \beta x_1x_2 \quad \text{(athermal)} \qquad (B)$$

where α and β are *constants*. What are the implications of Eqs. (A) and (B) with respect to the shapes of predicted solubility diagrams for LLE? Find from Eq. (A) an expression for the consolute temperature, and show that it must be an *upper* consolute temperature.

Suggestion: See Ex. 14.5 for numerical guidance.

14.53. Many fluids could be used as solvent species for supercritical separation processes (Sec. 14.7). But the two most popular choices seem to be carbon dioxide and water. Why? Discuss the pros and cons of using CO_2 vs. H_2O as a supercritical solvent.

14.54. Generate P-x_1-y_1 diagrams at 100°C (373.15 K) for one of the systems identified below. Base activity coefficients on the Wilson equation, Eqs. (12.19). Use two procedures: (i) modified Raoult's law, Eq. (10.5), and (ii) the gamma/phi approach, Eq. (14.1), with Φ_i given by Eq. (14.2). Plot the results for both procedures on the same graph. Compare and discuss them.

Data sources: For P_i^{sat} use Table B.2. For vapor-phase nonidealities, use material from Chap. 3; assume that the vapor phase is an (approximately) ideal solution. Estimated parameters for the Wilson equation are given for each system.

(*a*) Benzene(1)/Carbon tetrachloride(2): $\Lambda_{12} = 1.0372$, $\Lambda_{21} = 0.8637$
(*b*) Benzene(1)/Cyclohexane(2): $\Lambda_{12} = 1.0773$, $\Lambda_{21} = 0.7100$
(*c*) Benzene(1)/*n*-Heptane(2): $\Lambda_{12} = 1.2908$, $\Lambda_{21} = 0.5011$
(*d*) Benzene(1)/*n*-Hexane(2): $\Lambda_{12} = 1.3684$, $\Lambda_{21} = 0.4530$
(*e*) Carbon tetrachloride(1)/Cyclohexane(2): $\Lambda_{12} = 1.1619$, $\Lambda_{21} = 0.7757$
(*f*) Carbon tetrachloride(1)/*n*-Heptane(2): $\Lambda_{12} = 1.5410$, $\Lambda_{21} = 0.5197$
(*g*) Carbon tetrachloride(1)/*n*-Hexane(2): $\Lambda_{12} = 1.2839$, $\Lambda_{21} = 0.6011$
(*h*) Cyclohexane(1)/*n*-Heptane(2): $\Lambda_{12} = 1.2996$, $\Lambda_{21} = 0.7046$
(*i*) Cyclohexane(1)/*n*-Hexane(2): $\Lambda_{12} = 1.4187$, $\Lambda_{21} = 0.5901$

Chapter 15

Thermodynamic Analysis of Processes

The purpose of this chapter is to present a procedure for the analysis of practical processes from the thermodynamic point of view. It is an extension of the *ideal work* and *lost work* concepts presented in Secs. 5.8 and 5.9.

Real irreversible processes are amenable to thermodynamic analysis. The goal of such an analysis is to determine how efficiently energy is used or produced and to show quantitatively the effect of inefficiencies in each step of a process. The cost of energy is of concern in any manufacturing operation, and the first step in any attempt to reduce energy requirements is to determine where and to what extent energy is wasted through process irreversibilities. The treatment here is limited to steady-state flow processes, because of their predominance in industrial practice.

15.1 THERMODYNAMIC ANALYSIS OF STEADY-STATE FLOW PROCESSES

Many processes consist of a number of steps, and lost-work calculations are then made for each step separately. By Eq. (5.34),

$$\dot{W}_{\text{lost}} = T_\sigma \dot{S}_G$$

For a single surroundings temperature T_σ, summing over the steps of a process gives

$$\sum \dot{W}_{\text{lost}} = T_\sigma \sum \dot{S}_G$$

Dividing the former equation by the latter yields

$$\frac{\dot{W}_{\text{lost}}}{\sum \dot{W}_{\text{lost}}} = \frac{\dot{S}_G}{\sum \dot{S}_G}$$

Thus an analysis of the lost work, made by calculation of the fraction that each individual lost-work term represents of the total, is the same as an analysis of the rate of entropy generation, made by expressing each individual entropy-generation term as a fraction of the sum of all entropy-generation terms. Recall that all terms in these equations are positive (p. 182).

An alternative to the lost-work or entropy-generation analysis is a work analysis. For this, Eq. (5.31) becomes

$$\sum \dot{W}_{\text{lost}} = \dot{W}_s - \dot{W}_{\text{ideal}} \tag{15.1}$$

For a work-requiring process, all of these work quantities are positive and $\dot{W}_s > \dot{W}_{\text{ideal}}$. The preceding equation is then written as

$$\boxed{\dot{W}_s = \dot{W}_{\text{ideal}} + \sum \dot{W}_{\text{lost}}} \tag{15.2}$$

A work analysis expresses each individual work term on the right as a fraction of $\dot{W}_s$.

For a work-producing process, $\dot{W}_s$ and $\dot{W}_{\text{ideal}}$ are negative, and $|\dot{W}_{\text{ideal}}| > |\dot{W}_s|$. Equation (15.1) is therefore best written as

$$\boxed{|\dot{W}_{\text{ideal}}| = |\dot{W}_s| + \sum \dot{W}_{\text{lost}}} \tag{15.3}$$

A work analysis expresses each individual work term on the right as a fraction of $|\dot{W}_{\text{ideal}}|$. Such an analysis cannot be carried out if a process is so inefficient that $\dot{W}_{\text{ideal}}$ is negative, indicating that the process should produce work, but $\dot{W}_s$ is positive, indicating that the process in fact requires work. A lost-work or entropy-generation analysis is always possible.

Example 15.1

The operating conditions of a practical steam power plant are described in Ex. 8.1, parts (*b*) and (*c*). In addition, steam is generated in a furnace/boiler unit where methane is burned completely to CO_2 and H_2O with 25% excess air. The flue gas leaving the furnace has a temperature of 460 K, and t_σ/T_σ = 25°C (298.15 K). Make a thermodynamic analysis of the power plant.

Solution

A flow diagram of the power plant is shown in Fig. 15.1. The conditions and properties for key points in the steam cycle, taken from Ex. 8.1, are listed as follows:

Point	State of steam	t/°C (T/K)	P/kPa	H/kJ kg^{-1}	S/kJ kg^{-1}K^{-1}
1	Subcooled liquid	45.83 (318.98)	8600	203.4	0.6580
2	Superheated vapor	500.00 (773.15)	8600	3391.6	6.6858
3	Wet vapor, $x = 0.9378$	45.83 (318.98)	10	2436.0	7.6846
4	Saturated liquid	45.83 (318.98)	10	191.8	0.6493

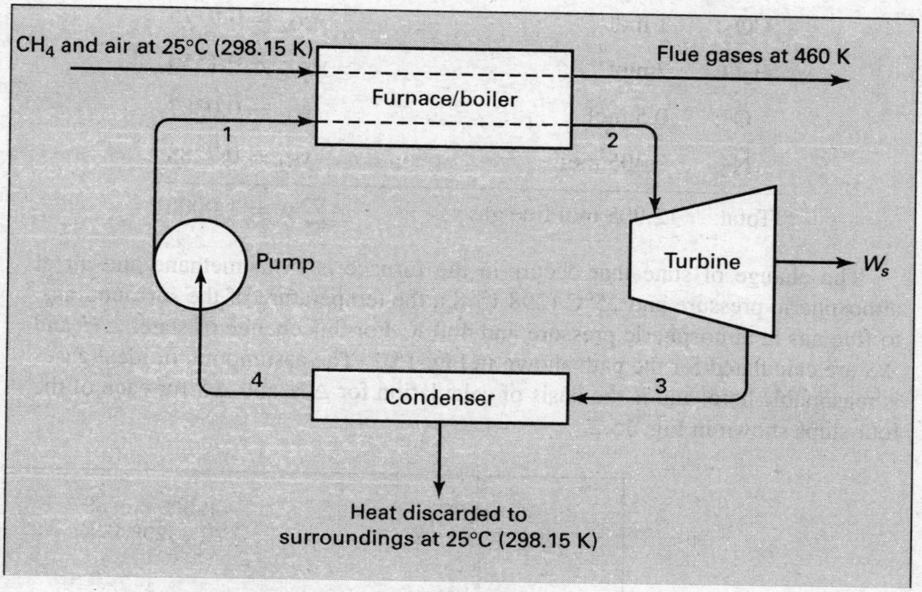

Figure 15.1: Power cycle of Ex. 15.1

Since the steam undergoes a cyclic process, the only changes that need be considered for calculation of the ideal work are those of the gases passing through the furnace. The reaction occurring is

$$CH_4 + 2O_2 \rightarrow CO_2 + 2H_2O$$

For this reaction, data from Table C.4 give

$$\Delta H^\circ_{298} = -393\,509 + (2)(-241\,818) - (-74\,520) = -802\,625 \text{ J}$$

$$\Delta G^\circ_{298} = -394\,359 + (2)(-228\,572) - (-50\,460) = -801\,043 \text{ J}$$

Whence, $$\Delta S^\circ_{298} = \frac{\Delta H^\circ_{298} - \Delta G^\circ_{298}}{298.15} = -5.306 \text{ J K}^{-1}$$

On the basis of 1 mol of methane burned with 25% excess air, the air entering the furnace contains

O_2: (2)(1.25) = 2.5 mol

N_2: (2.5)(79/21) = 9.405 mol

Total: 11.905 mol air

After complete combustion of the methane, the flue gas contains

CO_2:	1 mol	$y_{CO_2} = 0.0775$
H_2O:	2 mol	$y_{H_2O} = 0.1550$
O_2:	0.5 mol	$y_{O_2} = 0.0387$
N_2:	9.405 mol	$y_{N_2} = 0.7288$
Total:	12.905 mol flue gas	$\sum y_i = 1.0000$

The change of state that occurs in the furnace is from methane and air at atmospheric pressure and 25°C (298.15 K), the temperature of the surroundings, to flue gas at atmospheric pressure and 460 K. For this change of state, ΔH and ΔS are calculated for the path shown in Fig. 15.2. The assumption of ideal gases is reasonable here, and is the basis of calculation for ΔH and ΔS for each of the four steps shown in Fig. 15.2.

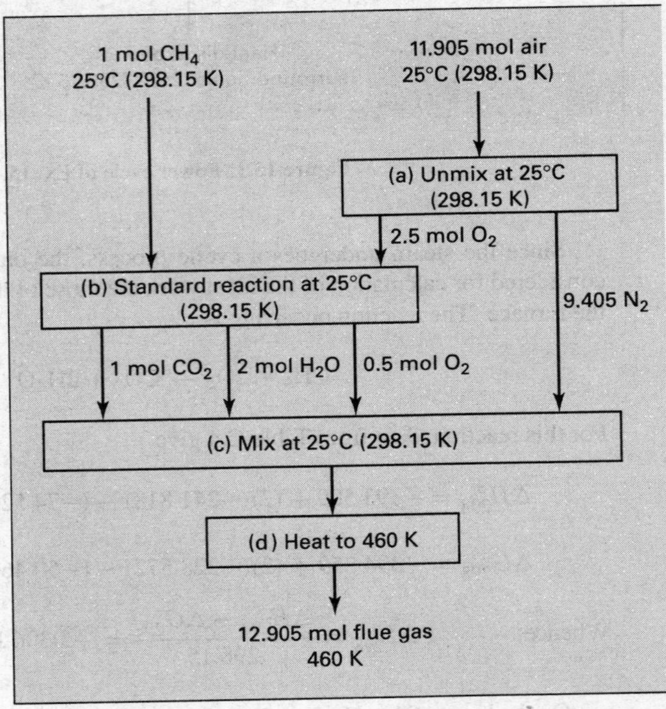

Figure 15.2: Calculation path for combustion process of Ex. 15.1

Step a For *unmixing* the entering air, Eqs. (12.37) and (12.35) with changes of sign give:

$$\Delta H_a = 0$$

$$\Delta S_a = nR \sum_i y_i \ln y_i$$

$$= (11.905)(8.314)(0.21 \ln 0.21 + 0.79 \ln 0.79) = -50.870 \text{ J K}^{-1}$$

Step b For the standard reaction at 25°C (298.15 K),

$$\Delta H_b = \Delta H^\circ_{298} = -802\,625 \text{ J} \qquad \Delta S_b = \Delta S^\circ_{298} = -5.306 \text{ J K}^{-1}$$

Step c For *mixing* to form the flue gas,

$$\Delta H_c = 0$$

$$\begin{aligned}\Delta S_c &= -nR\sum_i y_i \ln y_i\\ &= -(12.905)(8.314)(0.0775 \ln 0.0775 + 0.1550 \ln 0.1550\\ &\qquad + 0.0387 \ln 0.0387 + 0.7288 \ln 0.7288) = 90.510 \text{ J K}^{-1}\end{aligned}$$

Step d For the heating step, the mean heat capacities between 25°C (298.15 K) and 460 K are calculated by Eqs. (4.8) and (5.17) with data from Table C.1. The results in J mol^{-1} K^{-1} are summarized as follows:

	$\langle C_P \rangle_H$	$\langle C_P \rangle_S$
CO_2	41.649	41.377
H_2O	34.153	34.106
N_2	29.381	29.360
O_2	30.473	30.405

Each individual heat capacity is multiplied by the number of moles of that species in the flue gas, and the products are summed over all species. This gives total mean heat capacities for the 12.905 mol of mixture:

$$\langle C^t_P \rangle_H = 401.520 \qquad \text{and} \qquad \langle C^t_P \rangle_S = 400.922 \text{ J K}^{-1}$$

Then,

$$\Delta H_d = \langle C^t_P \rangle_H (T_2 - T_1) = (401.520)(460 - 298.15) = 64\,986 \text{ J}$$

$$\Delta S_d = \langle C^t_P \rangle_S \ln \frac{T_2}{T_1} = 400.922 \ln \frac{460}{298.15} = 173.852 \text{ J K}^{-1}$$

For the total process on the basis of 1 mol CH_4 burned,

$$\Delta H = \sum \Delta H_i = 0 - 802\,625 + 0 + 64\,986 = -737\,639 \text{ J}$$

$$\Delta S = \sum \Delta S_i = -50.870 - 5.306 + 90.510 + 173.852 = 208.186 \text{ J K}^{-1}$$

Thus, $\qquad \Delta H = -737.64 \text{ kJ} \qquad \Delta S = 0.2082 \text{ kJ K}^{-1}$

The steam rate found in Ex. 8.1 is $\dot{m} = 84.75$ kg s^{-1}. An energy balance for the furnace/boiler unit, where heat is transferred from the combustion gases to the steam, allows calculation of the entering methane rate $\dot{n}_{CH_4}$:

$$(84.75)(3{,}391.6 - 203.4) + \dot{n}_{CH_4}(-737.64) = 0$$

whence $\dot{n}_{CH_4} = 366.30 \text{ mol s}^{-1}$

The ideal work for the process, given by Eq. (5.26):

$$\dot{W}_{ideal} = 366.30[-737.64 - (298.15)(0.2082)] = -292.94 \times 10^3 \text{ kJ s}^{-1}$$

or

$$\dot{W}_{ideal} = -292.94 \times 10^3 \text{ kW}$$

The rate of entropy generation in each of the four units of the power plant is calculated by Eq. (5.22), and the lost work is then given by Eq. (5.34).

- ***Furnace/boiler*** We have assumed no heat transfer from the furnace/boiler to the surroundings; therefore $\dot{Q} = 0$. The term $\Delta(S\dot{m})_{fs}$ is simply the sum of the entropy changes of the two streams multiplied by their rates:

$$\dot{S}_G = (366.30)(0.2082) + (84.75)(6.6858 - 0.6580) = 587.12 \text{ kJ s}^{-1} \text{ K}^{-1}$$

or

$$\dot{S}_G = 587.12 \text{ kW K}^{-1}$$

and

$$\dot{W}_{lost} = T_\sigma \dot{S}_G = (298.15)(587.12) = 175.05 \times 10^3 \text{ kW}$$

- ***Turbine*** For adiabatic operation,

$$\dot{S}_G = (84.75)(7.6846 - 6.6858) = 84.65 \text{ kW K}^{-1}$$

and

$$\dot{W}_{lost} = (298.15)(84.65) = 25.24 \times 10^3 \text{ kW}$$

- ***Condenser*** The condenser transfers heat from the condensing steam to the surroundings at 25°C (298.15 K) in an amount determined in Ex. 8.1:

$$\dot{Q}(\text{condenser}) = -190.2 \times 10^3 \text{ kJ s}^{-1}$$

Thus

$$\dot{S}_G = (84.75)(0.6493 - 7.6846) + \frac{190{,}200}{298.15} = 41.69 \text{ kW K}^{-1}$$

and

$$\dot{W}_{lost} = (298.15)(41.69) = 12.32 \times 10^3 \text{ kW}$$

- ***Pump*** Since the pump operates adiabatically,

$$\dot{S}_G = (84.75)(0.6580 - 0.6493) = 0.74 \text{ kW K}^{-1}$$

and

$$\dot{W}_{lost} = 0.22 \times 10^3 \text{ kW}$$

The entropy-generation analysis is:

	kW K^{-1}	Percent of $\sum \dot{S}_G$
$\dot{S}_G$(furnace/boiler)	587.12	82.2
$\dot{S}_G$(turbine)	84.65	11.9
$\dot{S}_G$(condenser)	41.69	5.8
$\dot{S}_G$(pump)	0.74	0.1
$\sum \dot{S}_G$	714.20	100.0

A work analysis is carried out in accord with Eq. (15.3):

$$|\dot{W}_{\text{ideal}}| = |\dot{W}_s| + \sum \dot{W}_{\text{lost}}$$

The results of this analysis are

	kW	Percent of $|\dot{W}_{\text{ideal}}|$
$|\dot{W}_s|$ (from Ex. 8.1)	80.00×10^3	$27.3(=\eta_t)$
$\dot{W}_{\text{lost}}$(furnace/boiler)	175.05×10^3	59.8
$\dot{W}_{\text{lost}}$(turbine)	25.24×10^3	8.6
$\dot{W}_{\text{lost}}$(condenser)	12.43×10^3	4.2
$\dot{W}_{\text{lost}}$(pump)	0.22×10^3	0.1
$|\dot{W}_{\text{ideal}}|$	292.94×10^3	100.0

The thermodynamic efficiency of the power plant is 27.3%, and the major source of inefficiency is the furnace/boiler. The combustion process itself accounts for most of the entropy generation in this unit, and the remainder is the result of heat transfer across finite temperature differences.

Example 15.2

Methane is liquefied in a simple Linde system, as shown in Fig. 15.3. The methane enters the compressor at 1 bar and 300 K, and after compression to 60 bar is cooled back to 300 K. The product is saturated liquid methane at 1 bar. The unliquefied methane, also at 1 bar, is returned through a heat exchanger where it is heated to 295 K by the high-pressure methane. A heat leak into the heat exchanger of 5 kJ is assumed for each kilogram of methane entering the compressor. Heat leaks to other parts of the liquefier are assumed negligible. Make a thermodynamic analysis of the process for a surroundings temperature of T_σ = 300 K.

Solution

Methane compression from 1 to 60 bar is assumed to be carried out in a three-stage machine with inter- and after-cooling to 300 K and a compressor efficiency of 75%. The actual work of this compression is estimated as 1000 kJ per kilogram of methane. The fraction of the methane that is liquefied z is calculated by an energy balance:

$$H_4 z + H_6(1 - z) - H_2 = Q$$

where Q is the heat leak from the surroundings. Solution for z gives

$$z = \frac{H_6 - H_2 - Q}{H_6 - H_4} = \frac{1188.9 - 1140.0 - 5}{1188.9 - 285.4} = 0.0486$$

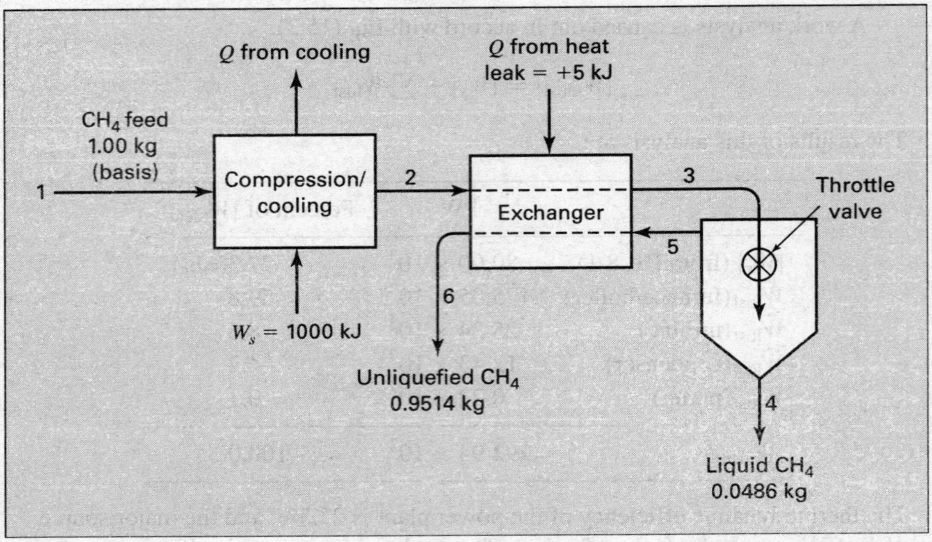

Figure 15.3: Linde liquefaction system for Ex. 15.2

This result may be compared with the value of 0.0541 obtained in Ex. 9.3 for the same operating conditions, but no heat leak.

The properties at the various key points of the process, given in the accompanying table, are either available as data or are calculated by standard methods. Data are from Perry and Green.[1] The basis of all calculations is 1 kg of methane entering the process, and all rates are expressed on this basis.

Point	State of the CH_4	T/K	P/bar	H/kJ kg^{-1}	S/kJ kg^{-1}K^{-1}
1	Superheated vapor	300.0	1	1199.8	11.629
2	Superheated vapor	300.0	60	1140.0	9.359
3	Superheated vapor	207.1	60	772.0	7.798
4	Saturated liquid	111.5	1	285.4	4.962
5	Saturated vapor	111.5	1	796.9	9.523
6	Superheated vapor	295.0	1	1188.9	11.589

The ideal work depends on the overall changes in the methane passing through the liquefier. Application of Eq. (5.25) gives

$$\dot{W}_{\text{ideal}} = \Delta(H\dot{m})_{\text{fs}} - T_\sigma \Delta(S\dot{m})_{\text{fs}}$$

$$= [(0.0486)(285.4) + (0.9514)(1188.9) - 1199.8]$$

$$- (300)[(0.0486)(4.962) + (0.9514)(11.589) - 11.629] = 53.8 \text{ kJ}$$

[1]R. H. Perry and D. Green, *Perry's Chemical Engineers' Handbook*, 7th ed., pp. 2-251 and 2-253, McGraw-Hill, New York, 1997.

The rate of entropy generation and the lost work for each of the individual steps of the process are calculated by Eqs. (5.33) and (5.34).

- ***Compression/cooling*** Heat transfer for this step is given by an energy balance:

$$\dot{Q} = \Delta H - \dot{W}_s = (H_2 - H_1) - \dot{W}_s$$

$$= (1140.0 - 1199.8) - 1000 = -1059.8 \text{ kJ}$$

Then,
$$\dot{S}_G = S_2 - S_1 - \frac{\dot{Q}}{T_\sigma}$$

$$= 9.359 - 11.629 + \frac{1059.8}{300} = 1.2627 \text{ kJ kg}^{-1} \text{ K}^{-1}$$

$$\dot{W}_{\text{lost}} = (300)(1.2627) = 378.8 \text{ kJ kg}^{-1}$$

- ***Exchanger*** With $\dot{Q}$ equal to the heat leak,

$$\dot{S}_G = (S_6 - S_5)(1 - z) + (S_3 - S_2)(1) - \frac{\dot{Q}}{T_\sigma}$$

Then,
$$\dot{S}_G = (11.589 - 9.523)(0.9514) + (7.798 - 9.359) - \frac{5}{300}$$

$$= 0.3879 \text{ kJ kg}^{-1} \text{ K}^{-1}$$

$$\dot{W}_{\text{lost}} = (300)(0.3879) = 116.4 \text{ kJ kg}^{-1}$$

- ***Throttle*** For adiabatic operation of the throttle and separator,

$$\dot{S}_G = S_4 z + S_5(1 - z) - S_3$$

$$= (4.962)(0.0486) + (9.523)(0.9514) - 7.798$$

$$= 1.5033 \text{ kJ kg}^{-1} \text{ K}^{-1}$$

$$\dot{W}_{\text{lost}} = (300)(1.5033) = 451.0 \text{ kJ kg}^{-1}$$

The entropy-generation analysis is

	kJ kg^{-1} K^{-1}	Percent of $\sum \dot{S}_G$
$\dot{S}_G$(compression/cooling)	1.2627	40.0
$\dot{S}_G$(exchanger)	0.3879	12.3
$\dot{S}_G$(throttle)	1.5033	47.7
$\sum \dot{S}_G$	3.1539	100.0

The work analysis, based on Eq. (15.2), is

	kW kg^{-1}	Percent of $\dot{W}_s$
$\dot{W}_{ideal}$	53.8	5.4(=η_t)
$\dot{W}_{lost}$(compression/cooling)	378.8	37.9
$\dot{W}_{lost}$(exchanger)	116.4	11.6
$\dot{W}_{lost}$(throttle)	451.0	45.1
$\dot{W}_s$	1,000.0	100.0

The largest loss occurs in the throttling step. Replacing this highly irreversible process by a turbine results in a considerable increase in efficiency.

From the standpoint of energy conservation, the thermodynamic efficiency of a process should be as high as possible, and the entropy generation or lost work as low as possible. The final design depends largely on economic considerations, and the cost of energy is an important factor. The thermodynamic analysis of a specific process shows the locations of the major inefficiencies, and hence the pieces of equipment or steps in the process that could be altered or replaced to advantage. However, this sort of analysis gives no hint as to the nature of the changes that might be made. It merely shows that the present design is wasteful of energy and that there is room for improvement. One function of the chemical engineer is to try to devise a better process and to use ingenuity to keep operating costs, as well as capital expenditures, low. Each newly devised process may, of course, be analyzed to determine what improvement has been made.

PROBLEMS

15.1. A plant takes in water at 21°C (294.15 K), cools it to 0°C (273.15 K), and freezes it at this temperature, producing 0.45 kg s^{-1} of ice. Heat rejection is at 21°C (294.15 K). The heat of fusion of water is 333.4 kJ kg^{-1}.

(*a*) What is $\dot{W}_{ideal}$ for the process?

(*b*) What is the power requirement of a single Carnot heat pump operating between 0°C (273.15 K) and 21°C (294.15 K)? What is the thermodynamic efficiency of this process? What is its irreversible feature?

(*c*) What is the power requirement if an ideal tetrafluoroethane vapor-compression refrigeration cycle is used? *Ideal* here implies isentropic compression, infinite cooling-water rate in the condenser, and minimum heat-transfer driving forces in evaporator and condenser of −18°C (255.15 K). What is the thermodynamic efficiency of this process? What are its irreversible features?

(*d*) What is the power requirement of a tetrafluoroethane vapor-compression cycle for which the compressor efficiency is 75%, the minimum temperature differences in evaporator and condenser are 4.5°C (4.5 K); and the temperature rise of the cooling water in the condenser is 11°C (11 K)? Make a thermodynamic analysis of this process.

15.2. Consider a steady-flow process in which the following gas-phase reaction takes place: $CO + \frac{1}{2}O_2 \rightarrow CO_2$. The surroundings are at 300 K.

(*a*) What is W_{ideal} when the reactants enter the process as pure carbon monoxide and air containing the stoichiometric amount of oxygen, both at 25°C (298.15 K) and 1 bar, and the products of complete combustion leave the process at the same conditions?

(*b*) The overall process is exactly the same as in (*a*), but the CO is here burned in an adiabatic reactor at 1 bar. What is W_{ideal} for the process of cooling the flue gases to 25°C (298.15 K)? What is the irreversible feature of the overall process? What is its thermodynamic efficiency? What has increased in entropy, and by how much?

15.3. A plant has saturated steam available at 2700 kPa, but there is little use for this steam. Rather, steam at 1000 kPa is required. Also available is saturated steam at 275 kPa. A suggestion is that the 275 kPa steam be compressed to 1000 kPa, using the work of expanding of the 2700 kPa steam to 1000 kPa. The two streams at 1000 kPa would then be mixed. Determine the rates at which steam at each initial pressure must be supplied to provide enough steam at 1000 kPa so that upon condensation to saturated liquid heat in the amount of 300 kJ s^{-1} is released,

(*a*) If the process is carried out in a completely reversible manner.

(*b*) If the higher-pressure steam expands in a turbine of 78% efficiency and the lower-pressure steam is compressed in a machine of 75% efficiency. Make a thermodynamic analysis of this process.

15.4. Make a thermodynamic analysis of the refrigeration cycle of Ex. 9.1(*b*).

15.5. Make a thermodynamic analysis of the refrigeration cycle described in one of the parts of Pb. 9.9. Assume that the refrigeration effect maintains a heat reservoir at a temperature 5°C (5 K) above the evaporation temperature and that T_σ is 5°C (5 K) below the condensation temperature.

15.6. Make a thermodynamic analysis of the refrigeration cycle described in the first paragraph of Pb. 9.12. Assume that the refrigeration effect maintains a heat reservoir at a temperature 5°C (5 K) above the evaporation temperature and that T_σ is 5°C (5 K) below the condensation temperature.

15.7. A colloidal solution enters a single-effect evaporator at 100°C (373.15 K). Water is vaporized from the solution, producing a more concentrated solution and 0.5 kg s^{-1} of steam at 100°C (373.15 K). This steam is compressed and sent to the heating coils of the evaporator to supply the heat required for its operation. For a minimum heat-transfer driving force across the evaporator coils of 10°C (10 K), for a compressor efficiency of 75%, and for adiabatic operation, what is the state of the steam leaving the heating coils of the evaporator? For a surroundings temperature of 300 K, make a thermodynamic analysis of the process.

15.8. Make a thermodynamic analysis of the process described in Pb. 8.8. $T_\sigma = 27°C$ (300.15 K).

15.9. Make a thermodynamic analysis of the process described in Ex. 9.3. $T_\sigma = 295$ K.

Chapter 16

Introduction to Molecular Thermodynamics

Classical thermodynamics is a deductive science, in which the general features of macroscopic-system behavior follow from a few laws and postulates. However, the practical application of thermodynamics requires values for the properties of individual chemical species and their mixtures. These may be presented either as numerical data (e.g., the steam tables for water) or as correlating equations (e.g., a PVT equation of state and expressions for the temperature dependence of ideal-gas heat capacities).

The usual source of property values is experiment. For example, the ideal-gas equation of state evolved as a statement of observed volumetric behavior of gases at low pressures. Similarly, the rule of thumb that $C_P \approx 29$ J mol^{-1} K^{-1} for diatomic gases at normal temperatures is based on experimental observation. However, macroscopic experiments provide no insight into why substances exhibit their observed property values. The basis for insight is a microscopic view of matter.

A central dogma of modern physics is that matter is *particulate*. The quest for the ultimate elementary particles is still in progress, but for engineering purposes we may adopt the following picture: ordinary matter consists of molecules; molecules consist of atoms; and atoms consist of a positively charged nucleus (comprising neutrons and protons), surrounded by negatively charged electrons. Atoms and molecules with equal numbers of electrons and protons have no net charge and are neutral.

16.1 MOLECULAR THEORY OF FLUIDS

Molecules are small and light: typical linear dimensions are 10^{-10} to 10^{-8} m, and typical masses are 10^{-27} to 10^{-25} kg. Hence the number of molecules in a macroscopic system is enormous. For example, one mole of matter contains 6.022×10^{23} molecules (Avogadro's number). Because of these features— smallness, lightness, and numerical abundance— the proper description of behavior at the molecular level and its extrapolation to a macroscopic scale require the special methods of quantum mechanics and statistical mechanics. We pursue neither of these topics here. Instead, we present material useful for relating molecular concepts to observed thermodynamic properties.

Intermolecular Forces and the Pair-Potential Function

As noted in Sec. 3.3, an ideal gas is characterized by the absence of molecular interactions; nevertheless, it still possesses internal energy. This energy is associated with the individual molecules, and results from their motion. Real gases and other fluids are comprised of molecules that have not only the energy of individual molecules, but also energy that is shared among them because of intermolecular forces. This *intermolecular potential energy* is associated with *collections* of molecules, and is the form of energy that reflects the existence of such forces. Well established is the fact that two molecules attract each other when they are far apart and repel one another when close together. Electromagnetic in origin, intermolecular forces represent interactions among the charge distributions of neighboring molecules.

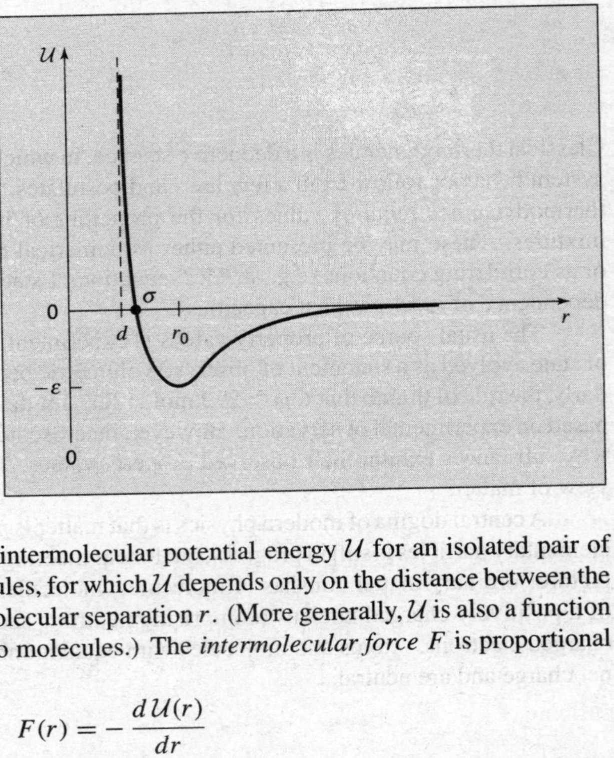

Figure 16.1: The intermolecular potential energy $\mathcal{U}$ for a pair of structureless, neutral molecules (Not to scale)

Figure 16.1 is a sketch of the intermolecular potential energy $\mathcal{U}$ for an isolated pair of spherically symmetric neutral molecules, for which $\mathcal{U}$ depends only on the distance between the molecular centers, i.e., on the intermolecular separation r. (More generally, $\mathcal{U}$ is also a function of the relative orientations of the two molecules.) The *intermolecular force* F is proportional to the r-derivative of $\mathcal{U}$:

$$F(r) = -\frac{d\,\mathcal{U}(r)}{dr}$$

By convention, a positive F represents an intermolecular repulsion, and a negative F an intermolecular attraction. Hence (Fig. 16.1) molecules repel each other at small separations, and attract each other at modest-to-large separations.

An algebraic expression for the *pair-potential function* $\mathcal{U}$ is one of the tools of the trade of the molecular scientist or engineer. The methods of statistical mechanics provide for its relation to both thermodynamic and transport properties. Shown in Fig. 16.1 are specific values for $\mathcal{U}$ and r that may appear as species-dependent parameters in a pair-potential function.

The *hard-core diameter* d is a measure of the center-to-center separation for which $\mathcal{U}$, and hence F, becomes infinite. It is not subject to precise determination, but plays the role of a modeling parameter in some expressions for $\mathcal{U}$. The *collision diameter* σ is defined as the separation for which $\mathcal{U} = 0$. The *equilibrium separation* r_0 is the separation for which $\mathcal{U}$ attains its minimum value of $-\epsilon$. At $r = r_0$, the net intermolecular force is zero. Quantity ϵ is called the *well depth*. For a particular class of chemical species (e.g., noble gases, or cyclic alkanes), each of these special quantities increases with increasing molecular size. Typical ranges of values for σ and ϵ are $\sigma \approx 3$ to 8×10^{-10} m and $\epsilon \approx 0.1$ to 1.0×10^{-20} J. Commonly, r_0 is about 10 to 15% greater than σ.

Scores of expressions have been proposed for $\mathcal{U}$.[1] All are essentially empirical, although their functional forms often have some basis in theory. The most widely used is the *Lennard-Jones* (LJ) *12/6 pair-potential function*:

$$\mathcal{U}(\mathrm{LJ}) = 4\epsilon\left[\left(\frac{\sigma}{r}\right)^{12} - \left(\frac{\sigma}{r}\right)^{6}\right] \tag{16.1}$$

Equation (16.1) provides semiquantitative representations of thermodynamic and transport properties for nonpolar substances of relatively simple molecular structure. In Eq. (16.1), the r^{-12} term is supposed to represent bimolecular repulsions, and the r^{-6} term bimolecular attractions. Although the attraction term has significant theoretical justification, the r^{-12} dependence for repulsions is chosen primarily for mathematical convenience. Table 16.1 shows some values of the dimensionless potential energy $\mathcal{U}/\epsilon$ as a function of the dimensionless separation r/σ, as implied by Eq. (16.1). Clearly, the effects of intermolecular forces are significant only over a modest range of separations. Although they operate over an infinite range ($\mathcal{U}$ and F together approach zero only in the limit as $r \to \infty$), both $\mathcal{U}$ and F for neutral molecular pairs are numerically negligible for separations greater than about 10 molecular diameters.

Contributions to the Intermolecular Potential Energy[2]

The *origins* of intermolecular forces stem from the essential concept that *a molecule is a distribution of charges*: a collection of positively charged nuclei, surrounded by a cloud of negatively charged electrons. Intermolecular repulsions at sufficiently small separations therefore result from the overlap of electron clouds of interacting molecules, giving rise to a Coulombic repulsion. At still smaller separations the positively charged nuclei "see" each other, again promoting repulsion.

The origins of intermolecular attractions are less obvious, and several mechanisms can contribute. First, consider the electrostatic interaction of two rigid charge distributions A and B. By Coulomb's law, the electrostatic potential energy of interaction $\mathcal{U}(\mathrm{el})$ is

$$\mathcal{U}(\mathrm{el}) = \frac{1}{4\pi\epsilon_0}\sum_i^A\sum_j^B \frac{q_i q_j}{r_{ij}} \tag{16.2}$$

[1]For a compilation of expressions for $\mathcal{U}$ see G. C. Maitland, M. Rigby, E. B. Smith, and W. A. Wakeham, *Intermolecular Forces: Their Origin and Determination*, app. 1, Clarendon Press, Oxford, 1981.

[2]A comprehensive discussion of these contributions to $\mathcal{U}(r)$ is given by J. O. Hirschfelder, C. F. Curtiss, and R. B. Bird, *Molecular Theory of Gases and Liquids*, pp. 25–30, 209, 983–1020, John Wiley and Sons, New York, 1954.

Table 16.1: Bimolecular Potential Energy as a Function of Separation for the Lennard-Jones 12/6 Potential.

r/σ	$\mathcal{U}/\epsilon$	r/σ	$\mathcal{U}/\epsilon$
0.0000	∞	1.0267	−0.5
0.6279	1000	1.1225	−1
0.7521	100	1.8413	−0.1
0.8797	10	2.7133	−0.01
0.9691	1	3.9841	−0.001
1.0000	0	∞	0

Here, q_i is a charge in distribution A, q_j is a charge in distribution B, and r_{ij} is the separation between charges q_i and q_j. Quantity ϵ_0 is the *electric permittivity of vacuum*, a physical constant[3] equal to 8.85419×10^{-12} C V^{-1} m^{-1}. (The unit of electric charge is the coulomb C, and the unit of electric potential difference is the volt V.) The sums are taken over all charges in the distributions.

Equation (16.2) is exact, but awkward to use as it stands. Application is facilitated when the charge separation r_{ij} is replaced by the center-of-mass separation r of the two distributions. Statistical averaging of contributions from all orientations of charge distribution yields the following approximate expression for $\mathcal{U}$(el) for two neutral rigid charge distributions:[4]

$$\mathcal{U}(\text{el}) = -\frac{2}{3}\frac{\mu_A^2\mu_B^2}{kT(4\pi\epsilon_0)^2}\frac{1}{r^6} \qquad (16.3)$$

Quantity k is *Boltzmann's constant*, equal to 1.381×10^{-23} J K^{-1}; μ_A and μ_B are the permanent *dipole moments* for charge distributions A and B associated with the molecules. This contribution to the pair-potential function vanishes only when one of the permanent dipole moments is zero. The averaging procedure which leads to Eq. (16.3) produces several remarkable results:

- Even though the distributions are electrically neutral, there is a net *attraction* between them.
- The dependence of $\mathcal{U}$(el) on charge-distribution orientation becomes on averaging an r^{-6} dependence.
- As given by Eq. (16.3) $\mathcal{U}$(el) varies with T^{-1}. Hence the magnitude of the permanent-dipole interaction decreases with increasing temperature.

Equation (16.3) is the simplest example of a direct electrostatic potential for two neutral molecules; here, the dipole moment emerges as an important physical property. Dipole

[3]Unrelated to the well depth ϵ of Fig. 16.1.

[4]This result is only valid for modest dipole moments. For a discussion, see T. M. Reed and K. E. Gubbins, *Applied Statistical Mechanics*, sec. 5-7, McGraw-Hill, New York, 1973.

moments are measures of the net separation of charge within a molecule. For a spherically symmetric neutral charge distribution (e.g., an atom of argon), μ is zero. For a molecule in which charge $+|q|$ is separated from charge $-|q|$ by distance l, the dipole moment is $\mu = |q|\,l$. Hence μ has dimensions of charge × length; its SI unit is the coulomb(C)·meter(m). However, values are usually reported in *debyes* (D); 1 D = 3.3357×10^{-30} C m. A molecule with a nonzero dipole moment is called *polar*. Water (μ = 1.9 D), acetone (μ = 2.9 D), and acetonitrile (μ = 4.0 D) are strongly polar molecules. Carbon monoxide (μ = 0.1 D), propylene (μ = 0.4 D), and toluene (μ = 0.4 D) are slightly polar. Carbon dioxide, neon, nitrogen, and n-octane are nonpolar (μ = 0).

The dipole moments just discussed are *permanent* dipole moments, intrinsic properties of a molecule. A net separation of charge may also be *induced* in any molecule by application of an external electric field. The *induced dipole moment* μ(ind) so created is approximately proportional to the strength of the applied field. Thus, for molecule A, $\mu_A(\text{ind}) = \alpha_A E$, where E is the applied field strength and α_A is the *polarizability* of A. If the source of the electric field is a permanent dipole in a neighboring molecule B, then the contribution to $\mathcal{U}$ from the permanent dipole/induced dipole interaction is

$$\mathcal{U} = -\frac{\mu_B^2 \alpha_A}{(4\pi\epsilon_0)^2}\frac{1}{r^6}$$

If molecules A and B are both polar (μ_A, $\mu_B \neq 0$), then the complete expression for the potential energy of induction $\mathcal{U}$(ind) is[5]

$$\mathcal{U}(\text{ind}) = -\frac{(\mu_A^2 \alpha_B + \mu_B^2 \alpha_A)}{(4\pi\epsilon_0)^2}\frac{1}{r^6} \tag{16.4}$$

The polarizability α, like the permanent dipole moment μ, is an intrinsic property of a molecule. SI units for α are C m^2 V^{-1}, but values are usually reported for the quantity $\hat{\alpha} \equiv \alpha/4\pi\epsilon_0$, in cm^3. The volumetric units for $\hat{\alpha}$ suggest a possible connection between polarizability and molecular volume. Typically, $\hat{\alpha}$ increases with molecular volume: very roughly, $\hat{\alpha} \approx 0.05\,\sigma^3$, where σ is the molecular collision diameter. Hence $\hat{\alpha}$ normally falls in the range of about 1 to 25×10^{-24} cm^3.

The two types of dipole (and dipole moment) so far discussed, *permanent* and *induced*, can both be rationalized and treated by the methods of classical electrostatics, and both produce a contribution to $\mathcal{U}$ proportional to r^{-6}. There is yet a third kind of dipole, an *instantaneous dipole*, whose calculation requires the methods of quantum mechanics. However, its existence can be rationalized on semi-classical grounds. If we picture a molecule A as nuclei with orbiting (i.e., *moving*) electrons, then we can imagine that a snapshot might show an instantaneous but temporary net separation of molecular charge. This is manifested as an instantaneous dipole, which induces a dipole in a neighboring molecule B. Interaction of the dipoles results in the intermolecular *dispersion force*, with corresponding dispersion potential $\mathcal{U}$(disp) given for large separations as

$$\mathcal{U}(\text{disp}) = -\frac{3}{2}\left(\frac{I_A I_B}{I_A + I_B}\right)\frac{\alpha_A \alpha_B}{(4\pi\epsilon_0)^2}\frac{1}{r^6} \tag{16.5}$$

[5] See Reed and Gubbins, *op. cit.*

Here, I is the *first ionization potential*, the energy required to remove one electron from a neutral molecule. Typically, I is of magnitude 1 to 4×10^{-18} J. All molecules possess nonzero ionization potentials and polarizabilities; hence all molecular pairs experience the dispersion interaction.

The dispersion potential $\mathcal{U}(\text{disp})$, like $\mathcal{U}(\text{el})$ and $\mathcal{U}(\text{ind})$, varies as r^{-6}. When molecules A and B are identical, these three special results lend justification for the r^{-6} attraction term in empirical intermolecular potential functions such as the Lennard-Jones 12/6 potential, Eq. (16.1). For identical molecules A and B, $\mu_A = \mu_B = \mu$, and Eqs. (16.3), (16.4), and (16.5) produce the expressions:

$$\mathcal{U}(\text{el}) = -\frac{2}{3}\frac{\mu^4}{kT(4\pi\epsilon_0)^2}\frac{1}{r^6} \tag{16.6}$$

$$\mathcal{U}(\text{ind}) = -\frac{2\mu^2\alpha}{(4\pi\epsilon_0)^2}\frac{1}{r^6} \tag{16.7}$$

$$\mathcal{U}(\text{disp}) = -\frac{3}{4}\frac{\alpha^2 I}{(4\pi\epsilon_0)^2}\frac{1}{r^6} \tag{16.8}$$

These equations provide estimates of the contributions of direct-electrostatic, induction, and dispersion forces to the intermolecular potential for pairs of identical molecules. Thus, if

$$\mathcal{U}(\text{long range}) = -\frac{C_6}{r^6}$$

then

$$C_6 = \frac{1}{(4\pi\epsilon_0)^2}\left(\frac{2}{3}\frac{\mu^4}{kT} + 2\mu^2\alpha + \frac{3}{4}\alpha^2 I\right) \tag{16.9}$$

Quantity C_6 is a measure of the strength of long-range intermolecular attractions. Fractional contributions of the three mechanisms to long-range forces are

$$f(\text{el}) = \mathcal{U}(\text{el})/\Sigma \qquad f(\text{ind}) = \mathcal{U}(\text{ind})/\Sigma \qquad f(\text{disp}) = \mathcal{U}(\text{disp})/\Sigma$$

where

$$\Sigma \equiv \mathcal{U}(\text{el}) + \mathcal{U}(\text{ind}) + \mathcal{U}(\text{disp})$$

and the $\mathcal{U}$'s are given by Eqs. (16.6), (16.7), and (16.8).

Values of C_6 calculated by Eq. (16.9) and the fractional contributions made by electrostatic, induction, and dispersion interactions to $\mathcal{U}$ are summarized in Table 16.2 for 15 polar substances, illustrating concepts just developed. Also shown are values of μ, $\hat{\alpha}$, and I for each species, and, in the last column, the ratio of the direct electrostatic to dispersion contributions:

$$\frac{f(\text{el})}{f(\text{disp})} = \frac{\mathcal{U}(\text{el})}{\mathcal{U}(\text{disp})} = \frac{8}{9}\frac{\mu^4}{\alpha^2 IkT}$$

The dimensionless ratio $f(\text{el})/f(\text{disp})$ is a measure of the effective polarity of a species. Note the following:

- In all cases, the *magnitude* of the dispersion interaction is substantial, even when $f(\text{disp})$ is small. These interactions can rarely be ignored.

Table 16.2: Long-range Attractions for Polar Molecules at 298 K

Compound	μ/D	$\alpha/10^{-24}$ cm^3	$I/10^{-18}$ J	$C_6/10^{-78}$ J m^6	f(el)	f(ind)	f(disp)	f(el)/f(disp)
CO	0.1	2.0	2.2	6.6	2.45×10^{-5}	0.001	0.999	2.45×10^{-5}
C_3H_6	0.4	6.0	1.6	43.4	9.55×10^{-4}	0.004	0.995	9.60×10^{-4}
$C_6H_5CH_3$	0.4	12.3	1.4	1593	2.60×10^{-4}	0.003	0.997	2.61×10^{-4}
HI	0.5	5.5	1.7	38.9	0.003	0.007	0.990	0.0026
HBr	0.8	3.6	1.9	19.6	0.034	0.024	0.942	0.0359
$CHCl_3$	1.0	9.0	1.8	112.8	0.014	0.016	0.970	0.0148
HCl	1.1	2.6	2.1	13.7	0.174	0.046	0.780	0.223
$(C_2H_5)_2O$	1.2	8.7	1.5	910	0.037	0.028	0.935	0.0394
NH_3	1.5	2.4	1.6	16.2	0.506	0.067	0.427	1.19
HF	1.9	0.8	2.5	22.9	0.922	0.025	0.053	17.6
H_2O	1.9	1.5	2.0	25.6	0.826	0.042	0.132	6.26
C_5H_5N	2.5	9.4	1.5	174.4	0.363	0.067	0.570	0.637
$(CH_3)_2CO$	2.9	6.4	1.6	174.5	0.656	0.062	0.282	2.33
HCN	3.2	2.6	2.2	186.3	0.912	0.029	0.059	15.2
CH_3CN	4.0	4.5	2.0	459.5	0.903	0.031	0.066	13.7

- The fractional contribution $f(\text{ind})$ of induction interactions is generally small, never exceeding about 7%.
- Contributions from permanent dipoles at near-ambient temperatures, through $\mathcal{U}(\text{el})$ and $\mathcal{U}(\text{ind})$, are small (less than about 5% of the total) for values of μ less than 1 D. Hence substances such as propylene (C_3H_6) and toluene ($C_6H_5CH_3$) are commonly classified as nonpolar, even though they have significant dipole moments.

16.2 SECOND VIRIAL COEFFICIENTS FROM POTENTIAL FUNCTIONS

The molar volume of a fluid depends on the behavior of its constituent molecules, and is therefore influenced by intermolecular forces. Thus a gas becomes more dense as the attractive forces between molecules become stronger. The reference point is an ideal gas, for which the intermolecular forces are zero. The nature and strength of these forces in an actual gas therefore determine the departure of its molar volume from that of an ideal gas.

In the virial equation as given by Eq. (3.12), the first term on the right is unity, and by itself provides the ideal-gas value for Z. The remaining terms provide corrections to the ideal-gas value, and of these the term B/V is the most important. As the two-body-interaction term, it is evidently related to the pair-potential function discussed in the preceding section. For spherically symmetric intermolecular force fields, statistical mechanics provides an exact expression relating the second virial coefficient B to the pair-potential function $\mathcal{U}(r)$[6]

$$B = -2\pi N_A \int_0^\infty \left(e^{-\mathcal{U}(r)/kT} - 1\right) r^2\, dr \tag{16.10}$$

Quantity N_A is Avogadro's number, and $k = R/N_A$ is Boltzmann's constant. By assumption, $\mathcal{U}(r)$ depends only on the intermolecular separation r between pairs of molecules. Given an expression for the pair-potential function $\mathcal{U}(r)$, one determines $B(T)$ by evaluation of the integral in Eq. (16.10). For realistic potential functions (Fig. 16.1), the integration must generally be done numerically or by series techniques. However, for *rectilinear* potential functions— those in which $\mathcal{U}(r)$ is defined by a collection of straight-line segments— one can obtain closed-form analytical expressions for $B(T)$.

The simplest realistic rectilinear potential function is the *square-well potential* $\mathcal{U}(\text{sw})$, shown in Fig. 16.2. It consists of four segments, producing the following piecewise contributions to $\mathcal{U}$:

$$\left.\begin{array}{lll} \mathcal{U}(\text{sw}) = \infty & \text{for} & r \le d \\ \mathcal{U}(\text{sw}) = -\epsilon & \text{for} & d \le r \le l \cdot d \\ \mathcal{U}(\text{sw}) = 0 & \text{for} & l \cdot d \le r \end{array}\right\} \tag{16.11}$$

Here, $d = \sigma$, and the hard-core and collision diameters are identical; ϵ is the well depth; and l is a constant which defines the width of the well. Comparison of Fig. 16.2 with Fig. 16.1 shows that $\mathcal{U}(\text{sw})$ mimics many of the features of the "true" intermolecular potential energy, for which repulsions prevail for sufficiently small separations, and attractions dominate for intermediate separations. For sufficiently large separations, $\mathcal{U}$ becomes negligible.

[6] D. A. McQuarrie, *Statistical Mechanics*, p. 228, Harper and Row, New York, 1976.

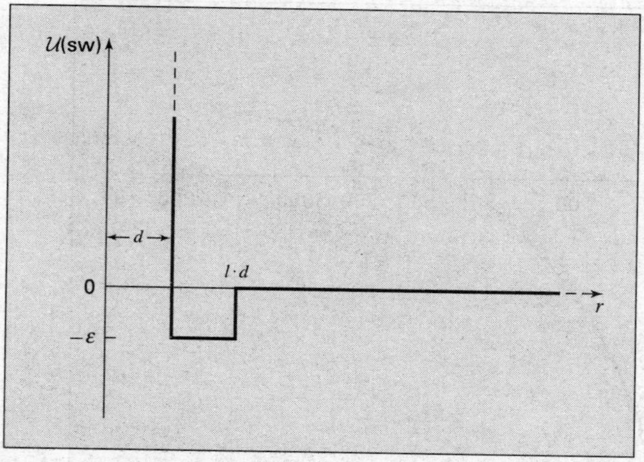

Figure 16.2: The square-well potential $\mathcal{U}$(sw) for a pair of molecules

With $\mathcal{U}$(sw) given by Eq. (16.11), evaluation of B by Eq. (16.10) is a straightforward exercise in integration. The result is

$$B(\text{sw}) = \frac{2}{3}\pi N_A d^3 \left[1 - (l^3 - 1)\left(e^{\epsilon/kT} - 1\right)\right] \tag{16.12}$$

where the first term in the square brackets (i.e., 1) arises from the repulsion part of the potential and the remaining term from the attraction part. Equation (16.12) therefore provides the following insights into the behavior of the second virial coefficient:

- The sign and magnitude of B are determined by the relative contributions of attractions and repulsions.
- At low temperatures, attractions dominate, producing negative values of B. The stronger the attractions (as determined by the magnitudes of ϵ and l), the more negative is B at fixed T.
- At high temperatures, repulsions dominate, producing positive values of B. In the (hypothetical) limit of infinite temperature, B approaches the value:

$$\lim_{T\to\infty} B(\text{sw}) = \frac{2}{3}\pi N_A d^3 = 4v_m$$

  where v_m is the volume occupied by a mole of hard spheres of diameter d.
- At the *Boyle temperature* T_B, the contributions of attractions are exactly balanced by those of repulsions, and B is zero. For the square-well potential, according to Eq. (16.12),

$$T_B(\text{sw}) = \frac{\epsilon/k}{\ln\left(\dfrac{l^3}{l^3 - 1}\right)}$$

  Hence, the stronger the attractions, the higher is the Boyle temperature.

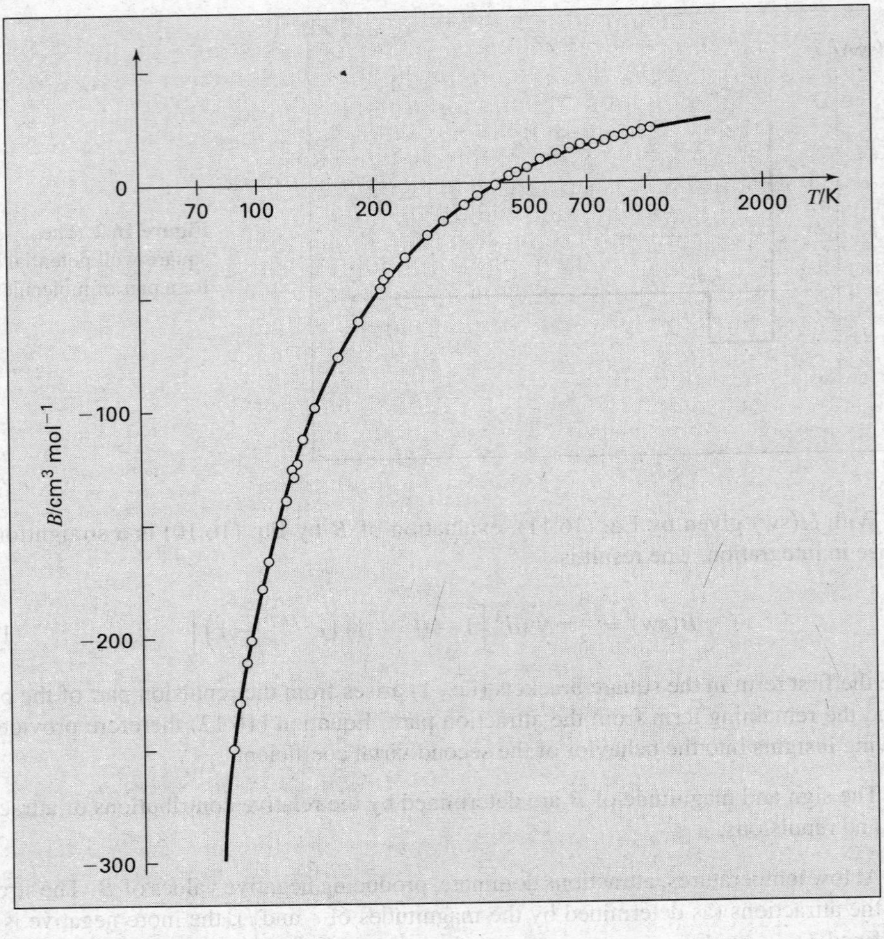

Figure 16.3: Second virial coefficients for argon by the square-well potential. Circles are data; curve is given by Eq. (16.12)

Although Eq. (16.12) is based on an intermolecular potential function that is in detail unrealistic, it nevertheless often provides an excellent fit of second-virial-coefficient data. An example is provided by argon, for which reliable data for B are available over a wide temperature range, from about 85 to 1000 K.[7] The correlation of these data by Eq. (16.12) as shown in Fig. 16.3 results from the parameter values $\epsilon/k = 95.2$ K, $l = 1.69$, and $d = 3.07 \times 10^{-8}$ cm. This empirical success depends at least in part on the availability of three adjustable parameters, and is no more than a limited validation of the square-well potential. Use of this potential does illustrate by a very simple calculation how the second virial coefficient (and hence the volume of a gas) may be related to molecular parameters.

[7] J. H. Dymond and E. B. Smith, *The Virial Coefficients of Pure Gases and Mixtures*, pp. 1–10, Clarendon Press, Oxford, 1980.

Such calculations carried out for more-realistic potential functions, though of greater complexity, also lead to values for molecular parameters. For example, experimental volumetric data for many gases have been regressed to yield values of σ and ϵ for the Lennard-Jones potential [Eq. (16.1)]. Values from several potential functions are given by R. L. Rowley.[8] This is an essential source of values, because theory does not provide the means for their prediction. One must remember, however, that potential functions are empirical *models*, and as such are approximations. The deficiency of a model is reflected by the values of the molecular parameters regressed from the model, and they must therefore be regarded as *effective* values of the parameters. Different effective values result from the use of different potential functions.

Since transport properties, such as viscosity and diffusivity, are also related to these same potential functions, data for the transport properties, particularly viscosity, are also used to provide values for ϵ and σ. Note, however, that any deficiency in the potential function influences the calculation of values in different ways, and the same molecular parameters obtained from different data sources are rarely in exact agreement.

16.3 INTERNAL ENERGY OF IDEAL GASES: MICROSCOPIC VIEW

Thermodynamic properties such as internal energy and enthalpy are manifestations on a gross scale of the positions, motions, and interactions of the countless molecules comprising a macroscopic system. The two theories that relate the behavior of molecules to macroscopic properties are *kinetic theory* and *statistical mechanics*. These theories together represent a very large body of extra-thermodynamic knowledge, well beyond the scope of this text. Our purpose here is to indicate in a very elementary fashion how the energy associated with the individual molecules of an ideal gas relates to the macroscopic internal energy of the ideal-gas state.

A fundamental postulate of quantum theory is that energy is quantized, that energy on the microscopic scale comes in very small discrete units. Thus a macroscopic system has associated with it an enormous number of quanta of energy, which sum to determine its energy level. Quantum theory specifies that the set of energy levels "allowed" to a closed system is determined by its volume. This does not mean that fixing the volume of a system fixes its energy; it just determines the discrete set of energy levels permitted to it. When a system is isolated (constrained from exchanging either mass or energy with its surroundings), it exists at one of the energy levels allowed to it. Each energy level of a system has associated with it a number of *quantum states*. This number g is known as the *degeneracy* of the level. Although an isolated system exists at a particular energy level, it passes over time through all of the g quantum states characterized by this same energy.

A large number of quantum states is accessible to a system of given volume in equilibrium with surroundings at fixed temperature. From the thermodynamic point of view, fixing T and V establishes the state of the system, including its internal energy. However, macroscopic equilibrium does not imply a static situation on the microscopic scale. The ceaseless motion of

[8]R. L. Rowley, *Statistical Mechanics for Thermophysical Property Calculations*, app. 5, PTR Prentice Hall, Englewood Cliffs, NJ, 1994.

the molecules and their collisions with the walls of the container result in exchanges of energy with the surroundings, which cause momentary fluctuations in the energy of the system. Thus the internal energy of thermodynamics is an average over the discrete set of energy levels of the allowed quantum states. Statistical mechanics provides the means for arriving at the proper average value.

The fundamental postulate of statistical mechanics for a system of given volume in equilibrium with surroundings at fixed temperature is that the probability of a quantum state depends only on its energy, and all quantum states with the same energy have the same probability. A value for the thermodynamic internal energy is found as the average of the energies of the accessible quantum states, each weighted by its probability. The quantity of fundamental importance to come out of this procedure is the *partition function*[9]

$$\mathcal{Z} = \sum_i g_i e^{-E_i/kT} \tag{16.13}$$

where E_i is the energy of level i, g_i is the degeneracy of the level, and k is Boltzmann's constant. This quantity is a state function, from which all thermodynamic properties may be found once it is known as a function of T and V. In particular, the internal energy is given by:

$$U = kT^2 \left(\frac{\partial \ln \mathcal{Z}}{\partial T} \right)_V \tag{16.14}$$

Equations (16.13) and (16.14) are written for the total energy of a macroscopic system. The problem of their application is greatly simplified for ideal gases, which (because of the absence of molecular interactions) do not possess intermolecular potential energy. The internal energy of ideal gases is therefore associated with individual molecules, and results from translation and rotation of each molecule as a whole and from rotations and vibrations internal to the molecule. Energy is also associated with the electrons and nuclei of atoms. For ideal gases all of these forms of energy are usually treated as separable, and this allows the partition function to be factored and written as a product of partition functions, each of which relates to a particular form of molecular energy. It suffices for present purposes to treat the translational kinetic energy as separable from all other contributions. These other contributions together constitute the *intramolecular energy* of a molecule, and they depend on *molecular structure*. We therefore write:

$$\mathcal{Z} = \frac{\mathcal{Z}_{\text{translation}} \mathcal{Z}_{\text{intramolecular}}}{N!}$$

whence

$$\ln \mathcal{Z} = \ln \mathcal{Z}_{\text{translation}} + \ln \mathcal{Z}_{\text{intramolecular}} - \ln N! \tag{16.15}$$

In these equations the quantity $N!$ arises because in the summation process the molecules are treated as distinguishable from one another, whereas in fact they are indistinguishable. The translational contribution comes from kinetic theory, whereas the intramolecular contributions derive from quantum mechanics, with the quantized energy levels determined from appropriate spectroscopic measurements.

[9]The name implies a sum over states partitioned according to energy levels, and the symbol comes from the German word, *Zustandssumme*, sum-over-states. The other commonly used symbol is Q, which is used in this book to represent heat.

For one mole of an ideal gas, the equation for the translational partition function is[10]

$$\mathcal{Z}_{\text{translation}} = V^{N_A}\left(\frac{2\pi mkT}{h^2}\right)^{(3/2)N_A}$$

where N_A = Avogadro's number; m = mass of the molecule; and h = Planck's constant. In logarithmic form this becomes:

$$\ln \mathcal{Z}_{\text{translation}} = N_A \ln V + \frac{3}{2} N_A \ln \frac{2\pi mkT}{h^2}$$

Substitution into Eq. (16.15) gives:

$$\ln \mathcal{Z} = N_A \ln V + \frac{3}{2} N_A \ln \frac{2\pi mkT}{h^2} - \ln N_A! + \ln \mathcal{Z}_{\text{intramolecular}} \tag{16.16}$$

where $\mathcal{Z}_{\text{intramolecular}}$ is evaluated by equations of the form of Eq. (16.13).

Differentiation of Eq. (16.16) with respect to temperature at constant V (and N_A) yields:

$$\left(\frac{\partial \ln \mathcal{Z}}{\partial T}\right)_V = \frac{3}{2}\frac{N_A}{T} + \left(\frac{\partial \ln \mathcal{Z}_{\text{intramolecular}}}{\partial T}\right)_V$$

whence by Eq. (16.14) applied to the ideal-gas state,

$$U^{ig} = \frac{3}{2} N_A kT + kT^2 \left(\frac{\partial \ln \mathcal{Z}_{\text{intramolecular}}}{\partial T}\right)_V$$

Representing the final term by $\mathcal{F}(T)$ and noting that $N_A k = R$ reduces this to:

$$U^{ig} = \frac{3}{2} RT + \mathcal{F}(T) \tag{16.17}$$

where R is the universal gas constant. Since $H^{ig} = U^{ig} + RT$,

$$H^{ig} = \frac{5}{2} RT + \mathcal{F}(T)$$

In view of Eq. (2.20),

$$C_P^{ig} \equiv \left(\frac{\partial H^{ig}}{\partial T}\right)_P = \frac{5}{2} R + \left(\frac{\partial \mathcal{F}(T)}{\partial T}\right)_P \tag{16.18}$$

The molecules of an ideal *monatomic* gas have no energy of rotation or vibration, and $\mathcal{F}(T)$ in Eq. (16.18) is therefore zero except at high temperatures where electronic energy contributions become important. Thus in Fig. 4.1 the value of C_P^{ig}/R for argon is constant at a value of 5/2. For diatomic and polyatomic gases, $\mathcal{F}(T)$ in Eq. (16.18) contributes importantly at all temperatures of practical importance. The contribution becomes larger the more complex the molecule and increases monotonically with temperature, as is evident from the curves shown in Fig. 4.1 for N_2, H_2O, and CO_2.

[10] D. A. McQuarrie, *Statistical Mechanics*, pp. 81–82, Harper & Row, New York, 1976.

16.4 THERMODYNAMIC PROPERTIES AND STATISTICAL MECHANICS

The equations of statistical mechanics are derived by application of Eq. (5.41) to a large number of macroscopically identical systems (an ensemble) in all of their many allowed quantum states. The entropy S as given by Eq. (5.42) is then a statistical average value for the ensemble.[11] Ultimately, the result is an equation for the entropy:

$$S = k \ln \mathcal{Z} + \frac{U}{T} \tag{16.19}$$

where $\mathcal{Z}$ is the partition function, given by Eq. (16.13), and U is the internal energy as given by Eq. (16.14).

For an ideal gas, combination of Eqs. (16.16) and (16.17) with Eq. (16.19) yields

$$S^{ig} = kN_A \ln V + \frac{3}{2} kN_A \ln \frac{2\pi mkT}{h^2} - k \ln N_A! + \ln \mathcal{Z}_{\text{intramolecular}} + \frac{3}{2} R + \frac{\mathcal{F}(T)}{T}$$

According to Stirling's formula $\ln N_A! = N_A \ln N_A - N_A$; also $kN_A = R$. Making these substitutions gives:

$$S^{ig} = R \ln V + \frac{3}{2} R \ln \frac{2\pi mkT}{h^2} - R \ln N_A + R + \ln \mathcal{Z}_{\text{intramolecular}} + \frac{3}{2} R + \frac{\mathcal{F}(T)}{T}$$

Upon rearrangement, this may be written as

$$S^{ig} = R \ln \left[\left(\frac{2\pi mkT}{h^2} \right)^{3/2} \frac{Ve^{5/2}}{N_A} \right] + \ln \mathcal{Z}_{\text{intramolecular}} + \frac{\mathcal{F}(T)}{T} \tag{16.20}$$

Equation (16.20) for the molar entropy of an ideal gas allows calculation of absolute entropies for the ideal-gas state. The data required for evaluation of the last two terms on the right are the bond distances and bond angles in the molecules, and the vibration frequencies associated with the various bonds, as determined from spectroscopic data. The procedure has been very successful in the evaluation of ideal-gas entropies for molecules whose atomic structures are known.

Both the classical and statistical equations [Eqs. (5.40) and (16.20)] yield absolute values of entropy. As is evident from Table 16.3,[12] good agreement between the statistical calculations and those based on calorimetric data is obtained. Results such as these provide impressive evidence for the validity of statistical mechanics and quantum theory. In some instances results based on Eq. (16.20) are considered more reliable because of uncertainties in heat-capacity data or about the crystallinity of the substance near absolute zero. Absolute entropies provide

[11] This mathematical development is lengthy but not unduly difficult. An elementary treatment is given by H. C. Van Ness, *Understanding Thermodynamics*, chap. 7, McGraw-Hill, New York, 1969; Dover, New York, 1983. Much more comprehensive are D. A. McQuarrie, *Statistical Mechanics*, Harper & Row, New York, 1976, and R. L. Rowley, *Statistical Mechanics for Thermophysical Property Calculations*, PTR Prentice Hall, Englewood Cliffs, NJ, 1994.

[12] From D. A. McQuarrie, *op. cit.*, p. 138.

Table 16.3: Absolute Entropies, Ideal-Gas State at 25°C (298.15 K) and 1 atm

	S^{ig}/J mol^{-1} K^{-1}	
	Eq. (5.40)	Eq. (16.20)
CO_2	213.4	213.8
NH_3	192.5	192.9
NO_2	240.6	240.6
CH_4	186.2	186.2
CH_3Cl	234.3	233.5
C_6H_6	269.5	269.9

much of the data base for calculation of the equilibrium conversions of chemical reactions, as discussed in Chap. 13.

The fundamental property relation most intimately connected with statistical mechanics is Eq. (6.9), which expresses the differential of the Helmholtz energy as a function of its canonical variables T and V:

$$dA = -P\,dV - S\,dT \tag{6.9}$$

We remarked in connection with Eq. (16.13) that the partition function $\mathcal{Z}$ is a state function from which all thermodynamic properties may be found once it is known as a function of T and V. Its relation to the Helmholtz energy follows from Eq. (16.19), which may be written as

$$U - TS = -kT \ln \mathcal{Z}$$

Reference to Eq. (6.2) shows that the left side of this equation is by definition the Helmholtz energy A. Therefore,

$$\boxed{A = -kT \ln \mathcal{Z}} \tag{16.21}$$

This equation provides a direct link between thermodynamics and statistical mechanics. Since $R = kN_A$, where N_A is Avogadro's number, Eq. (16.21) may be expressed alternatively as

$$\frac{A}{RT} = -\frac{\ln \mathcal{Z}}{N_A}$$

Equations (6.37) through (6.39) for the Gibbs energy have as their counterparts analogous equations for the Helmholtz energy. Derived from Eqs. (6.9) and (6.2), they are

$$d\left(\frac{A}{RT}\right) = -\frac{P}{RT}dV - \frac{U}{RT^2}dT \tag{16.22}$$

$$\frac{P}{RT} = -\left[\frac{\partial(A/RT)}{\partial V}\right]_T \tag{16.23}$$

$$\frac{U}{RT} = -T\left[\frac{\partial(A/RT)}{\partial T}\right]_V \tag{16.24}$$

The remaining properties come from defining equations:

$$\frac{S}{R} = \frac{U}{RT} - \frac{A}{RT} \qquad \frac{H}{RT} = \frac{U}{RT} + \frac{PV}{RT}$$

Note that Eq. (16.14) follows immediately from Eqs. (16.24) and (16.21).

Thus, when we know how A/RT (or $\ln \mathcal{Z}$) is related to its canonical variables, T and V, we can evaluate all other thermodynamic properties by simple mathematical operations. The Helmholtz energy and therefore the partition function serve as *generating functions* for the other thermodynamic properties, and implicitly represent complete property information.

Although a powerful tool for the estimation of thermodynamic properties, the application of statistical mechanics requires an enormous number of computations. Making the connection between the microscopic states of matter and its manifest macroscopic properties is best accomplished by molecular simulation, carried out numerically with high-speed computers. In Monte Carlo techniques the generation of a very large number of microscopic replicas of a system containing on the order of one hundred molecules serves to create an ensemble from which by appropriate statistics the partition function of Eq. (16.13) can be deduced. The intermolecular potential-energy function is key to the accurate prediction of the thermodynamic properties of real fluids, and this is a continuing area of research. Molecular simulation is a subject unto itself, and is treated in detail elsewhere.[13]

Fluids for which the intermolecular potential energy $\mathcal{U}(r)$ is given by the Lennard-Jones equation (Sec. 16.1) are said (as a class) to be *conformal*. More generally, fluids for which $\mathcal{U}(r)$ is of the same functional form comprise a conformal class. It is a property of conformal fluids that they obey the two-parameter theorem of corresponding states as stated in Sec. 3.5. Thus different classes of conformal fluids, distinguished by different functional forms of $\mathcal{U}(r)$, obey different corresponding-states correlations. The purpose of the acentric factor in Pitzer-type correlations (such as Lee/Kesler) is therefore to differentiate between classes of non-polar conformal fluids, primarily on the basis of molecular asymmetry. These classes then obey the three-parameter theorem of corresponding states. An extended set of Lee/Kesler correlations[14] incorporates a fourth parameter to characterize classes of *polar* conformal fluids. Thus an even larger collection of conformal classes of fluids obeys a four-parameter theorem of corresponding states.

16.5 HYDROGEN BONDING AND CHARGE-TRANSFER COMPLEXING

The intermolecular potential is dominated at small separations by repulsions, and at large separations by attractions varying approximately as r^{-6} (Sec. 16.1). These interactions are called "physical," because their origins are explained on the presumption that interacting species preserve their identities. For some systems another class of interactions, called "quasichemical,"

[13] R. L. Rowley, *Statistical Mechanics for Thermophysical Property Calculations*, PTR Prentice Hall, Englewood Cliffs, NJ, 1994. Both Monte Carlo and molecular-dynamics simulations, which have a different basis, are considered.

[14] R. L. Rowley, *Statistical Mechanics for Thermophysical Property Calculations*, sec. 11.5 and app. 11, PTR Prentice Hall, Englewood Cliffs, NJ, 1994.

Table 16.4: Pauling Electronegativity $\mathcal{X}_P$ for Some Nonmetallic Elements

Element	$\mathcal{X}_P$	Element	$\mathcal{X}_P$
F	4.0	I	2.5
O	3.5	C	2.5
N	3.0	S	2.5
Cl	3.0	Se	2.4
Br	2.8	H	2.1

operates primarily at intermediate separations, i.e., at $r \approx r_0$ (Fig. 16.1). As the name suggests, quasichemical forces are manifested as strong attractive interactions, in which participating species combine to form new chemical entities. We describe below two important classes of quasichemical interactions: hydrogen bonding and charge-transfer complexing.

Essential to a discussion of hydrogen bonding is the concept of *electronegativity*. According to valence-bond theory, the atoms which combine to form a molecule share electrons. If the bonded atoms are identical (e.g., the Cl atoms in a Cl_2 molecule), the bonding electrons are shared equally between the atoms. However, if the atoms are different (e.g., the H and Cl atoms of HCl), the shared electrons are generally attracted more strongly by one of the atoms (Cl in the case of HCl), and this atom is said to be *more electronegative* than the other. Thus, electronegativity is a measure of the relative ability of an atom in a molecule to attract electrons to itself.

The notion of electronegativity was introduced in 1932 by Pauling;[15] he was the first of several to propose a quantitative scale for its expression. Based largely on thermochemical data, Pauling's electronegativity $\mathcal{X}_P$ assumes values between about 0.7 and 4.0 for those elements known to participate in compound formation. Metallic elements have values less than about 2.0; nonmetals, values greater than about 2.0. Table 16.4 shows Pauling electronegativities for ten nonmetallic elements. Of these, fluorine is the most electronegative ($\mathcal{X}_P = 4.0$), and hydrogen, the least ($\mathcal{X}_P = 2.1$).

An intermolecular hydrogen bond forms between a hydrogen-donor molecule (conventionally represented as A-H) and an electron-rich acceptor site (conventionally denoted by the letter B). Entity A is an atom (possibly attached to other atoms), which is more electronegative than hydrogen. Hydrogen-acceptor site B may be an atom more electronegative than hydrogen; the site may also be a double or triple bond, or it may be an aromatic hydrocarbon ring. The hydrogen-bonded complex is conventionally represented as A-H $\cdots$ B, where the three dots denote the hydrogen bond.

Examples of strong hydrogen donors include hydrogen fluoride (HF), water (HOH), hydrogen peroxide (HOOH), alcohols (ROH), carboxylic acids (RCOOH), ammonia (H_2NH), primary amines (RNH_2), and secondary amines (R_2NH). In each of these molecules, one or more hydrogen atoms is attached to an atom of a highly electronegative element (F, O, or N; Table 16.4). The halogen acids HCl, HBr, and HI are also hydrogen donors, as are a few species containing the C-H bond. However, the difference in electronegativity between carbon

[15] Linus Pauling (1901–1994), American chemist and (twice) Nobel laureate.

and hydrogen is not large (Table 16.4), and the ability of the H in C-H to function as a donor hydrogen seems possible only when the carbon atom is itself attached to highly electronegative atoms or electron-rich sites. Verified examples of C-H hydrogen donors thus include chloroform (Cl_3CH), dichloromethane (Cl_2CH_2), and hydrogen cyanide (NCH).

The highly electronegative elements F, O, and N serve as atomic hydrogen-acceptor sites. Hence HF, HOH, HOOH, ROH, RCOOH, H_2NH, R_2NH and NCH are hydrogen acceptors. But so are aldehydes (ROCH), ketones (ROCR), ethers (ROR), esters (ROCOR), and tertiary amines (R_3N), species which have no active hydrogens.

The phenomenon of hydrogen bonding is easily rationalized. The H in donor species A-H is electron deficient because of the higher electronegativity of A. Hence the H is attracted to the electron-rich acceptor site B. Unfortunately, such a simple electrostatic picture is unable to account quantitatively for some important features of the hydrogen bond.[16] As a result, an algebraic contribution cannot generally be ascribed to the intermolecular potential function $\mathcal{U}(r)$ for hydrogen-bonding interactions. Nevertheless, we can by example indicate the kinds of intermolecular pairs for which hydrogen-bonding interactions are important. Convenience here suggests division of hydrogen-bonding interactions into two classes: *association* and *solvation*.

Association is an attractive interaction between molecules *of the same kind*. In the context of hydrogen bonding, an associating species must have both an active hydrogen and a hydrogen-acceptor site. Examples include water (the O is an acceptor site), ammonia (with N the acceptor site), alcohols, primary and secondary amines, and carboxylic acids. Hydrogen bonding by association is often reflected dramatically in the properties (e.g., boiling points, heats of vaporization, and viscosities) of the pure species.

Table 16.5: Hydrogen-bonding Interactions among Pairs of Species

$\mathcal{D}$ = nonassociating H-donor; $\mathcal{A}$ = nonassociating H-acceptor; $\mathcal{AD}$ = associating species

	$\mathcal{D}(1)$	$\mathcal{A}(1)$	$\mathcal{AD}(1)$
$\mathcal{D}(2)$	No H-bonding	$\mathcal{D}(2)\cdots\mathcal{A}(1)$	$\mathcal{D}(2)\cdots\mathcal{AD}(1)$ $\mathcal{AD}(1)\cdots\mathcal{AD}(1)$
$\mathcal{A}(2)$	$\mathcal{D}(1)\cdots\mathcal{A}(2)$	No H-bonding	$\mathcal{AD}(1)\cdots\mathcal{A}(2)$ $\mathcal{AD}(1)\cdots\mathcal{AD}(1)$
$\mathcal{AD}(2)$	$\mathcal{D}(1)\cdots\mathcal{AD}(2)$ $\mathcal{AD}(2)\cdots\mathcal{AD}(2)$	$\mathcal{AD}(2)\cdots\mathcal{A}(1)$ $\mathcal{AD}(2)\cdots\mathcal{AD}(2)$	$\mathcal{AD}(1)\cdots\mathcal{AD}(2)$ $\mathcal{AD}(2)\cdots\mathcal{AD}(1)$ $\mathcal{AD}(1)\cdots\mathcal{AD}(1)$ $\mathcal{AD}(2)\cdots\mathcal{AD}(2)$

Solvation is an attractive interaction between *unlike* molecular species. With respect to hydrogen bonding, solvation occurs between a species that is a hydrogen donor and another species that is a hydrogen acceptor. In "pure" solvation, neither species associates; an example is the acetone/chloroform system, in which chloroform is (only) a hydrogen donor and acetone

[16]See, e.g., J. E. Huheey, *Inorganic Chemistry*, 3d ed., pp. 268–272, Harper & Row, New York, 1983.

(only) a hydrogen acceptor. However, solvation may occur between two associators (e.g., ethanol and water), between an associator and a hydrogen donor (e.g., ethanol and chloroform), and between an associator and a hydrogen acceptor (e.g., ethanol and acetone).

Table 16.5 suggests the types of hydrogen-bonding interactions that can occur between molecules of various kinds. Here, $\mathcal{D}$ denotes a nonassociating hydrogen-donor species (e.g., Cl_3CH or Br_3CH), $\mathcal{A}$ is a nonassociating hydrogen acceptor [e.g., $(CH_3)_2CO$ or $(C_2H_5)_2O$], and $\mathcal{AD}$ is a species that can associate by hydrogen bonding [e.g., CH_3OH or $(C_2H_5)_2NH$]. Mixtures containing two different associating species offer the richest variety of opportunities for hydrogen bonding. For example, in a binary mixture of ammonia(1) and water(2), hydrogen-bonded dimers may be formed in four ways: two by solvation, two by association:

```
 H     H               H
 N-H···O         HO-H···NH
 H     H               H

 H     H               H
 N-H···NH        HO-H···O
 H     H               H
```

Compelling experimental evidence exists for quasichemical interactions between certain non-hydrogen-donor polar compounds (e.g., pyridine, ketones, and aldehydes) and aromatic hydrocarbons (e.g., benzene). In these cases, the polar compounds have no active hydrogens, and hence the interaction cannot be hydrogen bonding. Nevertheless, a complex appears to be formed. Mulliken[17] gave the name *electron donor-acceptor complex* to these and other such entities; they are more commonly called *charge-transfer complexes*. Proper explanation of charge-transfer complexing requires use of concepts from molecular orbital theory, which we cannot develop here. Additionally, because of the apparent near-ubiquity of charge-transfer phenomena, and of the widely varying strengths of the interactions, it is often difficult to *predict* when they will make significant contributions to intermolecular forces. Mulliken and Person (*loc. cit.*) offer guidance, but most engineers would view the invocation of charge-transfer complexing as a helpful explanatory, rather than a predictive, exercise. Its role is clearest for the kinds of systems mentioned at the beginning of this paragraph.

16.6 BEHAVIOR OF EXCESS PROPERTIES

As suggested by Fig. 11.4, the principal excess properties (G^E, H^E, and S^E) can exhibit a variety of combinations of signs. The signs and relative magnitudes of these quantities are useful for qualitative engineering purposes and for elucidating the molecular phenomena which are the basis for observed solution behavior. Abbott et al.[18] have organized $G^E/H^E/S^E$

[17] R. S. Mulliken and W. B. Person, *Molecular Complexes: A Lecture and Reprint Volume*, Wiley-Interscience, New York, 1969.

[18] M. M. Abbott, J. P. O'Connell, and Twenty Rensselaer Students, *Chem. Eng. Educ.*, vol. 28, pp. 18–23 and 77, 1994.

data for about 400 binary liquid mixtures in a visual scheme which permits identification of patterns, trends, and norms of behavior with respect to *mixture type*. In what follows, we describe the basis for the scheme, and present a few important generalizations which follow from examination of representative data.

Excess properties for liquid mixtures depend primarily on temperature and composition; therefore comparison of data for different mixtures is best done at *fixed* T and x. Since many M^E data are available at near-ambient temperatures, $t(T)$ is chosen as 25°C (298.15 K). Because extreme values for M^E often occur near equimolar composition; we fix $x_1 = x_2 = 0.5$.

Division of Eq. (11.86) by RT puts it into dimensionless form:

$$\frac{G^E}{RT} = \frac{H^E}{RT} - \frac{S^E}{R} \tag{16.25}$$

The six possible combinations of sign for the three excess properties are enumerated in Table 16.6. Each combination defines a region on the diagram of Fig. 16.4, which shows G^E/RT vs. H^E/RT in skeleton form.

Table 16.6: Definition of Regions on the G^E/RT vs. H^E/RT Diagram

Region	Sign G^E	Sign H^E	Sign S^E
I	+	+	+
II	+	+	−
III	+	−	−
IV	−	−	−
V	−	−	+
VI	−	+	+

Along the diagonal line on Fig. 16.4, $S^E = 0$. In regions to the right of the diagonal (V, VI, and I), S^E is positive; for regions to the left of the diagonal (II, III, and IV), S^E is negative. Lines of constant nonzero S^E are parallel to the diagonal.

Convenience in modeling and rationalizing the behavior of G^E suggests a focus on *enthalpic* (energetic) and *entropic* contributions, a separation suggested by Eqs. (11.86) and (16.25). According to these equations, G^E can be positive *or* negative if H^E and S^E have the same sign. If H^E and S^E are positive and if G^E is also positive, then $H^E > TS^E$ and "enthalpy dominates"; If H^E and S^E are positive and G^E is negative, then $TS^E > H^E$ and "entropy dominates". Similar reasoning applies when both H^E and S^E are negative, leading to the identification of Regions I and IV on Fig. 16.4 as regions of *enthalpy domination*, and of Regions III and VI as regions of *entropy domination*. The notions of enthalpy and entropy domination can be helpful for explaining the molecular origins of observed mixture-property behavior.

Abbott et al. classify binary organic and aqueous/organic mixtures by a simple scheme based on hydrogen-bonding concepts (Sec. 16.5). A pure species is categorized as nonpolar ("NP": e.g., benzene, carbon tetrachloride, or *n*-heptane); polar but nonassociating ("NA": e.g., acetone, chloroform, or diethylether); or polar and associating ("AS": e.g., acetic acid, ethanol, or water). With these categories for pure species, there are then six binary mixture types: NP/NP (e.g., benzene/*n*-heptane); NA/NP [e.g., chloroform/*n*-heptane, Fig. 11.4(*a*)]; AS/NP [e.g., ethanol/*n*-heptane, Fig. 11.4(*d*)]; NA/NA [e.g., acetone/chloroform, Fig. 11.4(*c*)]; AS/NA [e.g., ethanol/chloroform, Fig. 11.4(*e*)]; and AS/AS [e.g., ethanol/water, Fig. 11.4(*f*)].

Figure 16.5 is a G^E/RT vs. H^E/RT plot of data for 135 different binary mixtures at 298 K, with systems distinguished according to the NP/NA/AS classification scheme. For clarity, we mainly omit data for which the three principal excess properties are very small. The figure appears chaotic at first glance, but on inspection important patterns emerge. We list here a few; statistics, where given, apply to the full data set analyzed by Abbott et al.

- About 85% of all mixtures exhibit positive G^E *or* positive H^E (Regions I, II, III, and VI); about 70% have positive G^E *and* positive H^E (Regions I and II). Thus positive G^E and positive H^E are the "norms".

- About 60% of all mixtures fall in Regions I and IV, with only about 15% in Regions III and VI. Thus the enthalpy is more likely to dominate solution behavior than is the entropy.

- NP/NP mixtures (the open circles on Fig. 16.5) tend to concentrate in Regions I and VI: for such mixtures, H^E and S^E are normally positive. When G^E is positive (enthalpy domination), G^E/RT rarely exceeds about 0.2. If G^E is negative (entropy domination), G^E/RT is rarely less than −0.2.

- NA/NP mixtures (the filled circles) usually fall in Region I, with occasional significant excursions into Region II. Thus, G^E and H^E are positive, as is (normally) S^E. Both G^E and H^E can be large.

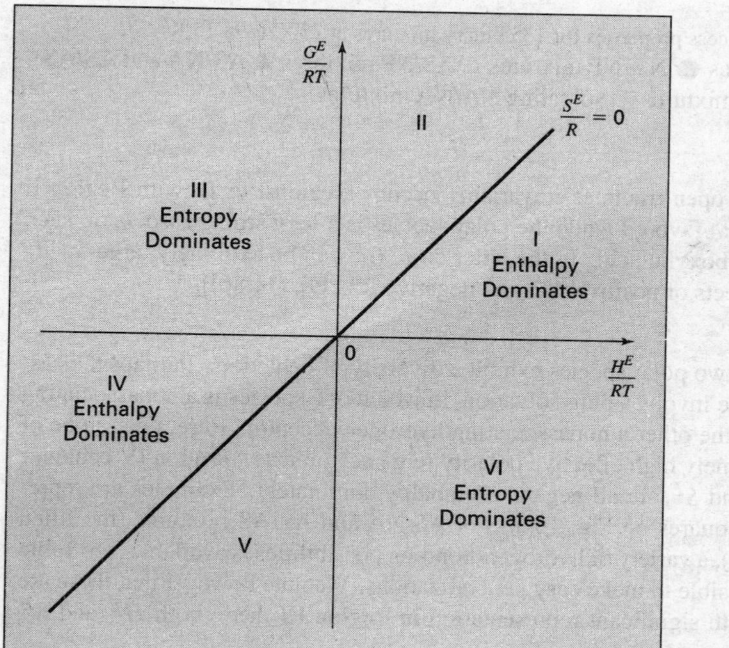

Figure 16.4: Diagram of G^E/RT vs. H^E/RT in skeleton form

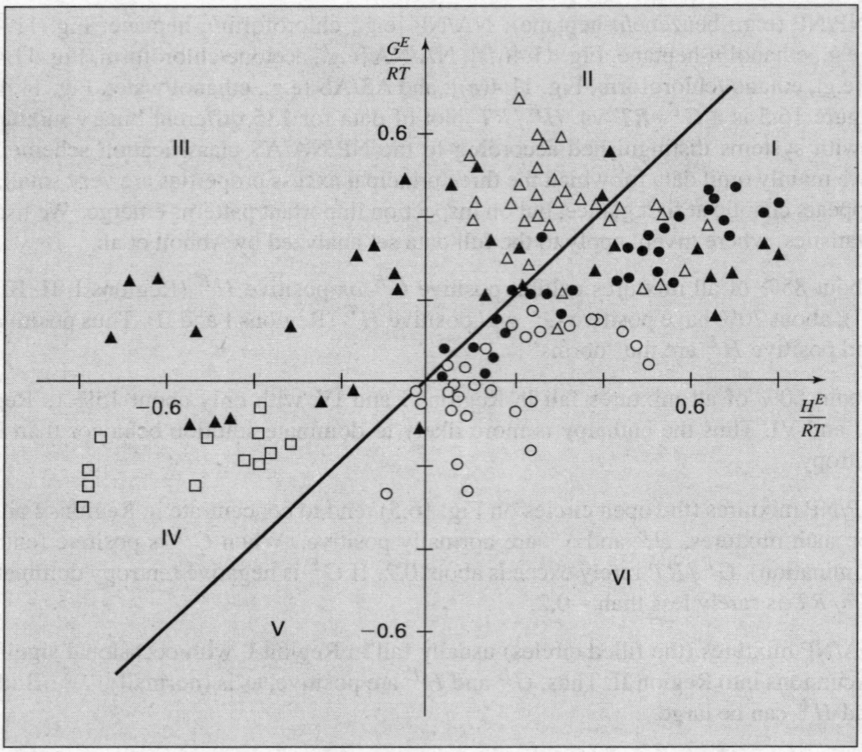

Figure 16.5: Equimolar excess properties for 135 binary mixtures at 25°C (298.15 K)
Legend: ○ NP/NP mixtures ● NA/NP mixtures △ AS/NP mixtures ▲ AS/NA and AS/AS mixtures □ solvating NA/NA mixtures

- AS/NP mixtures (the open triangles) invariably occupy Region I or II, with Region II behavior (negative S^E) favored when the polar species is a very strong associator, such as an alcohol or a carboxylic acid. In the latter case, G^E can be extremely large owing to the reinforcing effects of positive H^E and negative S^E [Eq. (11.86)].

- Mixtures containing two polar species exhibit a diversity of behaviors. Perhaps the easiest class to categorize involves pure solvation, in which one species is a nonassociating hydrogen donor and the other a nonassociating hydrogen acceptor. Here, unless one of the species has extremely high effective polarity (e.g., acetonitrile), Region IV behavior obtains: G^E, H^E, and S^E are all negative (enthalpy dominates). Examples are represented by the open squares on Fig. 16.5. For AS/NA and AS/AS mixtures (the filled triangles on Fig. 16.5), a variety of hydrogen-bonding possibilities is available (see Table 16.5), and it is impossible to make easy generalizations. We note however that these are the mixture types with significant representation in Region III; here, both H^E and S^E are negative, but entropy dominates.

16.7 MOLECULAR BASIS FOR MIXTURE BEHAVIOR

The relations between excess properties and property changes of mixing (Sec. 12.3) facilitate discussion of the molecular phenomena which give rise to observed excess-property behavior. An essential connection is provided by Eq. (12.33), which asserts the identity of H^E and ΔH. Thus we focus on the *mixing process* (and hence on ΔH) for explaining the behavior of H^E.

The sign and magnitude of ΔH roughly reflect differences in the strengths of intermolecular attractions between pairs of unlike species on the one hand, and pairs of like species on the other. In the standard mixing process (Fig. 12.10) interactions between like species are disrupted, and interactions between unlike species are promoted. If the unlike attractions are *weaker* than the average of those between species of the same kind, then in the mixing process more energy is required to break like attractions than is made available by formation of unlike attractions. In this case $\Delta H (= H^E)$ is positive, i.e., the mixing process is endothermic. If the unlike attractions are *stronger*, then ΔH is negative, and the mixing process is exothermic.

In Secs. 16.1 and 16.5 we identify intermolecular attractive interactions of four kinds: dispersion, induction, direct electrostatic, and quasichemical. A summary list of important points follows:

- Of the four attractive interactions, the dispersion force is always present. It dominates when interacting molecules are nonpolar or slightly polar. (See Table 16.2 and the accompanying discussion.)

- The induction force requires that at least one of the interacting species be polar. It is normally the weakest of the "physical" intermolecular attractive forces (Table 16.2).

- For neutral molecules, the simplest and normally the strongest direct electrostatic force is that operating between two permanent dipoles. This force can dominate "physical" attractive interactions if the molecules have high effective polarity, i.e., if they are small and have large permanent dipoles.

- Quasichemical forces, when present, can be the strongest of the four attractive interactions. However, their existence requires special chemical make-up of the interacting molecules. Hydrogen bonding is the most important interaction of this type, although charge-transfer complexing can play a major role in some kinds of systems.

Excess Enthalpy

With these notions in mind, we offer some rationalizations of the observed signs and magnitudes of $H^E (= \Delta H)$ for binary liquid mixtures of the kinds discussed in Sec. 16.6.

• *H^E of NP/NP Mixtures*

Here, dispersion forces are usually the only significant attractive intermolecular forces. Thus H^E reflects energetic effects associated with disruption of dispersion interactions between like species, and simultaneous promotion of dispersion interaction between unlike species. Molecular theory[19] suggests that dispersion forces between unlike species are weaker than the average

[19]See, e.g., J. M. Prausnitz, R. N. Lichtenthaler, and E. G. de Azevedo, *Molecular Thermodynamics of Fluid-Phase Equilibria*, 2d ed., sec. 4.4, Prentice Hall, Englewood Cliffs, NJ, 1986.

of dispersion forces between like species. (This is the molecular basis of the "like prefers like" rule of elementary chemistry.) Here, then, one expects H^E to be positive. This is what is usually observed for NP/NP mixtures (Fig. 16.5).

• H^E *of NA/NP Mixtures*

For this class of mixtures, interactions between molecules of like species are *different in kind* for the two species. In particular, two molecules of the polar species experience a direct-electrostatic interaction and a (usually weak) induction interaction, in addition to the usual dispersion interaction; here, the attractive forces are stronger than would be observed for a nonpolar species of similar size and geometry. Interaction between unlike species, on the other hand, involves only the dispersion and (weak) induction forces. One therefore expects H^E to be positive, only more so than for otherwise similar NP/NP mixtures. Experiment bears this out, on average (Fig. 16.5).

• H^E *of AS/NP Mixtures*

As for NP/NP and NA/NP mixtures, one expects positive H^E; this is what Fig. 16.5 shows. However, H^E is often observed to be only modest in magnitude, frequently less than H^E for otherwise similar NA/NP mixtures. The reason for this is the unusual strength of the like interactions for the associating polar species. Here, hydrogen-bonded complexes for the polar species can persist in solution up to rather high dilution, thus mitigating the otherwise very large positive values of H^E expected from simple disruption/promotion arguments.

• H^E *of Solvating NA/NA Mixtures*

These mixtures are the major occupants of Region IV in Fig. 16.5. Since neither species associates by hydrogen bonding, attractions between like species result from dispersion, induction, and dipole/dipole interactions. The same kinds of interaction obtain for unlike molecules, but in addition there is superposed a strong attraction owing to the formation of a hydrogen-bonded solvation complex. The net effect is a negative value for H^E; the system is exothermic.

• H^E *of AS/NA and AS/AS Mixtures*

All four types of attractive interaction occur between unlike species, and for at least one of the pure species. Thus the sign and magnitude of H^E reflect a balance between competing effects of dipole/dipole interactions, association, and solvation. Qualitative prediction of enthalpic behavior is difficult, except by analogy. Figure 16.5 suggests the diversity of behavior observed for such mixtures.

Excess Entropy

The excess entropy is related to ΔS through Eqs. (12.38) and (12.35). Thus,

$$S^E = \Delta S - \Delta S^{id} \tag{16.26}$$

where

$$\Delta S^{id} = -R \sum_i x_i \ln x_i \tag{12.35}$$

An ideal solution is one comprising molecules of identical size and shape, and for which intermolecular forces are the same for all molecular pairs, whether like or unlike. For such a hypothetical solution, the entropy change of mixing, given by Eq. (12.35), is always positive.

In a real mixture, molecules of different species have different sizes and/or shapes, and the intrinsic strengths of molecular interactions are different for different molecular pairs. As a result, ΔS for a real mixture may be greater or less than ΔS^{id}, and by Eq. (16.26), S^E may be positive or negative. The behavior of S^E is most conveniently rationalized by separate consideration of *size/shape* effects on the one hand and *structural* effects on the other. (The word "structure" refers to the order brought about at the molecular level by intermolecular forces.)

Pure size/shape effects result in a ΔS greater than ΔS^{id}, and hence provide a positive contribution to S^E. Prausnitz et al.[20] discuss the relative roles of size and shape, and give references to the relevant literature. If size effects alone are considered, an approximate upper bound to this contribution to S^E is given by the *Flory-Huggins equation*:

$$S^E = -R \sum_i x_i \ln \frac{\Phi_i}{x_i} \qquad \text{where} \qquad \Phi_i \equiv \frac{x_i V_i}{\sum_j x_j V_j}$$

Here, Φ_i is the apparent volume fraction, and V_i is molar volume of the pure species.

Structural contributions to ΔS (hence to S^E) reflect primarily the relative strengths of competing intermolecular attractions. Consider the mixing of a nonassociating polar species (e.g., acetone) with a nonpolar species (e.g., *n*-hexane). Energetically, the net result of the mixing process is determined primarily by the energy associated with disruption of dipole/dipole interactions, as discussed earlier with respect to H^E for NA/NP mixtures. With respect to entropy, this is a *structure-breaking* process wherein molecular aggregates promoted by a strong dipole/dipole interaction are *broken up* by mixing.

Consider instead the mixing of two nonassociating polar species, one a hydrogen donor and the other a hydrogen acceptor [e.g., chloroform/acetone, Fig. 11.4(*c*)]. Energetically, the net result of the mixing process is determined primarily by the energy associated with formation of a solvation complex, as discussed earlier regarding H^E for solvating NA/NA mixtures. This is a *structure-making* process, wherein molecular aggregates promoted by a strong quasichemical interaction are *formed* on mixing.

Structure breaking implies a positive contribution to S^E ($\Delta S > \Delta S^{id}$), and structure making a negative contribution to S^E ($\Delta S < \Delta S^{id}$). When used in conjunction with size/shape arguments, these simple notions help to explain observed signs for S^E. By way of example, we consider again binary liquid mixtures of the kinds discussed in Sec. 16.6.

- *S^E of NP/NP Mixtures*

In the absence of significant size/shape effects, S^E is usually positive, owing to the relative weakness of unlike vs. like intermolecular attractions. Thus structure breaking on mixing is a stronger effect than structure making. However, the enthalpy contribution to G^E often dominates, and Region I behavior obtains. For mixtures of species of significantly different size (e.g., *n*-hexane/*n*-hexadecane), positive size/shape contributions can reinforce structural effects, producing values of S^E large enough for entropy to dominate; G^E is then negative and Region VI behavior is observed.

[20] J. M. Prausnitz, R. N. Lichtenthaler, and E. G. de Azevedo, *op. cit.*, sec. 7.4.

• S^E *of NA/NP Mixtures*

As already noted, the mixing process here primarily involves structure breaking (positive contributions to S^E). Size/shape effects can have an augmenting influence to produce substantial positive S^E. However, H^E often is also large, and enthalpy usually dominates (Region I).

• S^E *of AS/NP Mixtures*

Mixing nominally promotes a structure-*breaking* disruption of hydrogen-bonded complexes of the associating species. However, the persistence of these complexes in solution up to rather high dilution can greatly reduce this positive contribution to S^E, leading to negative values of S^E over much of the composition range. This effect is observed for mixtures of strong associators (e.g., alcohols and carboxylic acids) with hydrocarbons. An example is the ethanol/*n*-heptane system of Fig 11.4(*d*), which shows Region II behavior.

• S^E *of Solvating NA/NA Mixtures*

As noted in earlier discussion, this is predominately a structure-*making* situation, and S^E is negative. However, H^E is also negative (and large), whence enthalpy usually dominates, making G^E negative (Region IV).

• S^E *of AS/NA and AS/AS Mixtures*

The complexities discussed with respect to H^E also apply to S^E; structure-breaking and structure-making effects compete to provide a variety of sign combinations and a range of magnitudes for S^E.

16.8 VLE BY MOLECULAR SIMULATION

In Secs. 16.2, 16.3, and 16.4 we describe how macroscopic thermodynamic properties, such as internal energy, entropy, and the Helmholtz energy are connected to properties of individual molecules and their assemblies. These connections are exploited quantitatively through computer simulation of collections of molecules.[21] This approach has also been applied directly to VLE, primarily to pure species and to binary and simple ternary mixtures. Descriptions of assumptions, methods, and calculational procedures are given by Panagiotopoulos[22] and in an extended review by Gubbins.[23] Their extensive bibliographies are a guide to relevant literature.

The method requires suitable intermolecular potential energy functions $\mathcal{U}(r)$ and solution of the equations of statistical mechanics for the assemblies of molecules. As mentioned in Sec. 16.1, potential energy functions are as yet primarily empirical. Except for the simplest

[21] M. P. Allen and D. J. Tildesley, *Computer Simulation of Liquids*, Clarendon Press, Oxford, 1989; D. Frenkel and B. Smit, *Understanding Molecular Simulations: From Algorithms to Applications*, Academic Press, San Diego, 1996.

[22] A. Z. Panagiotopoulos, *Molecular Simulation*, vol. 9, pp. 1–23, 1992.

[23] K. E. Gubbins, "Applications of Molecular Theory to Phase Equilibrium Predictions" in *Models for Thermodynamic and Phase Equilibrium Calculations*, S. I. Sandler, ed., pp. 507–600, Marcel Dekker, Inc., New York, 1994.

molecules, $\mathcal{U}(r)$ cannot be predicted by *ab initio*[24] calculations, because of still-inadequate computer speed. Therefore, semi-empirical functions based on quantum-mechanical theory and experimental data are employed.

Two procedures are used for the very large number of computer calculations required to treat molecular assemblies. The first, proposed by Panagiotopoulos,[25] is called the direct Gibbs-ensemble Monte Carlo method. One considers two separate phases, each represented by a finite number of molecules contained in a simulation box. Both are at the same specified temperature but are of different initial densities and compositions. The idea is to implement a sequence of perturbations which gradually bring these two phases into equilibrium. This ultimately insures internal equilibrium for each phase separately, equality of pressures between the two phases, and equality of the chemical potentials for each species in the two phases. The perturbations ("moves") designed to bring about these conditions of equilibrium are therefore:

1. Random displacement of molecules within each box. These are the usual moves of Monte Carlo simulation, insuring internal equilibrium and generating the ensemble upon which the partition function is based, thus leading to a set of thermodynamic properties for the molecules of each box.

2. Random equal and opposite volume changes in the two boxes. These moves alter the pressures in the boxes and ultimately bring about their equality. As the pressures change, the ongoing Monte Carlo simulations in the boxes generate evolving thermodynamic properties.

3. Random transfer of molecules between the two boxes. These moves alter compositions and chemical potentials μ_i of the species in the boxes, ultimately bringing about equality of the chemical potentials for each species in the two boxes. These moves also contribute to the evolution of the thermodynamic properties of the molecules in the boxes.

Moves may be accepted or rejected on the basis of certain probabilities that insure progression on average to states of lower Gibbs energy for the two boxes considered together. Phase equilibrium obtains at the state of minimum total Gibbs energy.

A limitation of the Gibbs-ensemble Monte Carlo method is that the successful transfer of molecules between phases (item 3) becomes difficult (improbable) for dense fluids, leading to excessive calculation time. In this event, a second, more indirect, procedure can be employed. The idea here is to calculate the chemical potentials of the species in each box for a range of states. Equilibrium compositions are then identified as those states having the same temperature, pressure, and chemical potential for each species in the two boxes. Much more computation is needed by this procedure than for the direct procedure, except where the molecular-transfer step becomes difficult. For high-density fluids and for solids, the indirect procedure is preferred.

Molecular simulation is not a routine method for VLE calculations nor does it substitute for experimental data. At present, it is most useful for extrapolating to conditions not accessible by other means.

[24]Meaning: from the beginning, i.e., from first principles.

[25]A. Z. Panagiotopoulos, *Molecular Physics*, vol. 61, pp. 813–826, 1987.

The Gibbs-ensemble procedure has also been employed to estimate adsorption isotherms for simple systems. The approach is illustrated[26] by calculations for a straight cylindrical pore where both fluid/fluid and fluid/adsorbent molecular interactions can be represented by the Lennard-Jones potential-energy function [Eq. (16.1)]. Simulation calculations have also been made for isotherms of methane and ethane adsorbed on a model carbonaceous slit pore.[27] Isosteric heats of adsorption have also been calculated.[28]

PROBLEMS

16.1. The following rectilinear potential is an augmentation of the square-well potential [See Eq. (16.11)]:

$$\begin{aligned} \mathcal{U} &= \infty \quad &&\text{for} \quad r \leq d \\ \mathcal{U} &= \xi \quad &&\text{for} \quad d \leq r \leq k \cdot d \\ \mathcal{U} &= -\epsilon \quad &&\text{for} \quad k \cdot d \leq r \leq l \cdot d \\ \mathcal{U} &= 0 \quad &&\text{for} \quad l \cdot d \leq r \end{aligned}$$

Here, quantities k, l, ξ, and ϵ are positive constants, with $k < l$. Draw a sketch of this potential, and find an algebraic expression for the second virial coefficient $B(T)$. Demonstrate that $B(T)$ for this model can exhibit a *maximum* with respect to T.

16.2. Table 16.2 applies for *like* molecular pairs. Prepare a similar table for all *unlike* molecular pairs comprising species from the following: methane, *n*-heptane, chloroform, acetone, and acetonitrile. Discuss the result. Data in addition to values that appear in Table 16.2: For methane, $\mu = 0$, $\hat{\alpha} = 2.6 \times 10^{-24}$ cm^3, $I = 2.1 \times 10^{-18}$ J. For *n*-heptane, $\mu = 0$, $\hat{\alpha} = 13.6 \times 10^{-24}$ cm^3, $I = 1.7 \times 10^{-18}$ J.

16.3. The heat of mixing (or heat of solution) is *negative* for the systems represented on Figs. 12.14, 12.17, and 12.19. Offer molecular explanations of *why* this is so.

16.4. Naive numerology suggests that there should be $2^3 = 8$ possible combinations of sign for G^E, H^E, and S^E. Table 16.6 shows only *six*. Why?

[26]A. Z. Panagiotopoulos, *Molecular Physics*, vol. 62, pp. 701–719, 1987.

[27]R. F. Cracknell and David Nicholson, *Adsorption*, vol. 1, p. 7, 1995.

[28]R. F. Cracknell, D. Nicholson, and N. Quirke, *Molecular Simulation*, vol. 13, p. 161, 1994.

16.5. Listed below are excess-enthalpy data at 25°C (298.15 K) for two series of equimolar binary liquid mixtures. Explain why the mixture containing benzene is the "outlier" in each series.

Series	Mixture	H^E/J mol^{-1}
A	CH_2Cl_2/benzene	−18.
	/cyclohexane	1188.
	/*n*-hexane	1311.
B	acetone/benzene	144.
	/cyclohexane	1574.
	/*n*-hexane	1555.

16.6. What *signs* would you expect to observe for G^E, H^E, and S^E for equimolar liquid solutions of the following pairs of species at 298 K? Explain your answers.

(*a*) Acetone/cyclohexane
(*b*) Acetone/dichloromethane
(*c*) Aniline/cyclohexane
(*d*) Benzene/carbon disulfide
(*e*) Benzene/*n*-hexane
(*f*) Chloroform/1,4-dioxane
(*g*) Chloroform/*n*-hexane
(*h*) Ethanol/*n*-nonane

16.7. The quantity $\delta_{ij} \equiv 2B_{ij} - B_{ii} - B_{jj}$ plays a role in the thermodynamics of gas mixtures at low pressures: see, e.g., Eq. (14.4) for $\hat{\phi}_i$. This quantity can be positive or negative, depending on the chemical nature of species i and j. For what kinds of molecular pairs would one expect δ_{ij} to be

(*a*) Positive? (*b*) Negative? (*c*) Essentially zero?

16.8. Table 10.1 includes Henry's constants for three C2 hydrocarbon gases dissolved in water at 25°C (298.15 K). Explain the observed trend, viz.,

$$\mathcal{H}_{\text{ethane}} > \mathcal{H}_{\text{ethylene}} > \mathcal{H}_{\text{acetylene}}$$

16.9. Interpreting entropy as a qualitative measure of the "structure" or "order" of a phase, suggest why the latent heats ΔH^{sl}, ΔH^{lv}, and ΔH^{sv} are positive.

16.10. Determine from Eq. (16.20) numerical values of the absolute entropies in the ideal-gas state at 1 bar and 25°C (298.15 K) for Argon, Krypton, and Xenon. Compare with values from the NIST Chemistry WebBook.

Reminder: h (Planck's constant) = 6.626×10^{-34} J s
k (Boltzmann's constant = 1.381×10^{-23} J K^{-1}
N_A (Avogadro's number = 6.023×10^{23} mol^{-1}

16.11. The heat of vaporization at the normal boiling point is an approximate measure of the strength of intermolecular forces in the liquid phase. Why? The compounds methane and water have similar molar masses and similar values of T_{r_n}. Yet for methane $\Delta H_n^{lv} = 8.17$ kJ mol^{-1}, and for water $\Delta H_n^{lv} = 40.66$ kJ mol^{-1}. Explain the large difference.

16.12. The molar heat capacity of a liquid is normally greater than its vapor-phase heat capacity at modest pressure and the same temperature. Why?

16.13. Use classical arguments to estimate the average separation (in m) between ideal-gas particles at 300 K and 1 bar. Discuss.

Appendix A

Conversion Factors and Values of the Gas Constant

Because standard reference books contain data in diverse units, we include Tables A.1 and A.2 to aid the conversion of values from one set of units to another. Those units having no connection with the SI system are enclosed in parentheses. The following definitions are noted:

(ft) ≡ U.S. defined foot ≡ 3.048×10^{-1} m
(in) ≡ U.S. defined inch ≡ 2.54×10^{-2} m
(gal) ≡ U.S. liquid gallon ≡ $231(\text{in})^3$
(lb_m) ≡ U.S. defined pound *mass* (avoirdupois)
≡ $4.535\,9237 \times 10^{-1}$ kg
(lb_f) ≡ force to accelerate $1(\text{lb}_\text{m})$ by $32.1740(\text{ft})\ \text{s}^{-2}$
atm ≡ standard atmospheric pressure ≡ 101 325 Pa
(psia) ≡ pounds *force* per square inch absolute pressure
torr ≡ pressure exerted by 1 mm mercury at 0°C and standard gravity
(cal) ≡ thermochemical calorie
(Btu) ≡ international steam table British thermal unit
(lb mole) ≡ mass in pounds *mass* with numerical value equal to the molar mass
(R) ≡ absolute temperature in Rankines

The conversion factors of Table A.1 are referred to a single basic or derived unit of the SI system. Conversions between other pairs of units for a given quantity are made as in the following example:

$$1 \text{ bar} = 0.986\,923 \text{ atm} = 750.061 \text{ Torr}$$

thus

$$1\text{atm} = \frac{750.061}{0.986\,923} = 760.00 \text{ Torr}$$

Table A.1: Conversion Factors

Quantity	Conversion
Length	1 m = 100 cm
	= 3.280 84 (ft) = 39.3701 (in)
Mass	1 kg = 10^3 g
	= 2.204 62 (lb_m)
Force	1 N = 1 kg m s^{-2}
	= 10^5 (dyne)
	= 0.224 809 (lb_f)
Pressure	1 bar = 10^5 kg m^{-1} s^{-2} = 10^5 N m^{-2}
	= 10^5 Pa = 10^2 kPa
	= 10^6 dyne cm^{-2}
	= 0.986 923 atm
	= 14.5038 psia
	= 750.061 Torr
Volume	1 m^3 = 10^6 cm^3 = 10^3 liters
	= 35.3147 $(ft)^3$
	= 264.172 (gal)
Density	1 g cm^{-3} = 10^3 kg m^{-3}
	= 62.4278 (lb_m) $(ft)^{-3}$
Energy	1 J = 1 kg m^2 s^{-2} = 1 N m
	= 1 m^3 Pa = 10^{-5} m^3 bar = 10 cm^3 bar
	= 9.869 23 cm^3 atm
	= 10^7 (dyne) cm = 10^7 (erg)
	= 0.239 006 (cal)
	= 5.121 97 × 10^{-3} $(ft)^3$(psia) = 0.737 562 (ft) (lb_f)
	= 9.478 31 × 10^{-4} (Btu) = 2.777 78 × 10^{-7} kWh
Power	1 kW = 10^3 W = 10^3 kg m^2 s^{-3} = 10^3 J s^{-1}
	= 239.006 (cal) s^{-1}
	= 737.562 (ft)(lb_f) s^{-1}
	= 0.947 831 (Btu) s^{-1}
	= 1.341 02 (hp)

Table A.2: Values of the Universal Gas Constant

R = 8.314 J mol^{-1} K^{-1} = 8.314 m^3 Pa mol^{-1} K^{-1}
= 83.14 cm^3 bar mol^{-1} K^{-1} = 8314 cm^3 kPa mol^{-1} K^{-1}
= 82.06 cm^3atm mol^{-1} K^{-1} = 62356 cm^3 Torr mol^{-1} K^{-1}
= 1.987 (cal) mol^{-1} K^{-1} = 1.986 (Btu)(lb mole)$^{-1}$(°R)$^{-1}$
= 0.7302 $(ft)^3$atm(lb mol)$^{-1}$(R)$^{-1}$ = 10.73 $(ft)^3$(psia)(lb mol)$^{-1}$(°R)$^{-1}$
= 1545 (ft)(lb_f)(lb mol)$^{-1}$(°R)$^{-1}$

Appendix B

Properties of Pure Species

Table B.1 Characteristic Properties of Pure Species

Listed here for various chemical species are values for the molar mass (molecular weight), acentric factor ω, critical temperature T_c, critical pressure P_c, critical compressibility factor Z_c, critical molar volume V_c, and normal boiling point T_n. Abstracted from Project 801, DIPPR®, Design Institute for Physical Property Data of the American Institute of Chemical Engineers, they are reproduced with permission. The full data compilation is published by T. E. Daubert, R. P. Danner, H. M. Sibul, and C. C. Stebbins, *Physical and Thermodynamic Properties of Pure Chemicals: Data Compilation*, Taylor & Francis, Bristol, PA, 1,405 chemicals, extant 1995. Included are values for 26 physical constants and regressed values of parameters in equations for the temperature dependence of 13 thermodynamic and transport properties.

Electronic versions by the same authors include

- *DIPPR® Data Compilation of Pure Compound Properties*, ASCII Files, National Institute of Science and Technology, Standard Reference Data, Gaithersburg, MD, 1458 chemicals, extant 1995.
- *DIPPR® Data Compilation, Student DIPPR Database*, PC-DOS Version, National Institute of Science and Technology, Standard Reference Data, Gaithersburg, MD, 100 common chemicals for teaching purposes, 1995.

Table B.2 Constants for the Antoine Equation for Vapor Pressures of Pure Species

Table B.1: Characteristic Properties of Pure Species

	Molar mass	ω	T_c/K	P_c/bar	Z_c	V_c $cm^3\ mol^{-1}$	T_n/K
Methane	16.043	0.012	190.6	45.99	0.286	98.6	111.4
Ethane	30.070	0.100	305.3	48.72	0.279	145.5	184.6
Propane	44.097	0.152	369.8	42.48	0.276	200.0	231.1
n-Butane	58.123	0.200	425.1	37.96	0.274	255.	272.7
n-Pentane	72.150	0.252	469.7	33.70	0.270	313.	309.2
n-Hexane	86.177	0.301	507.6	30.25	0.266	371.	341.9
n-Heptane	100.204	0.350	540.2	27.40	0.261	428.	371.6
n-Octane	114.231	0.400	568.7	24.90	0.256	486.	398.8
n-Nonane	128.258	0.444	594.6	22.90	0.252	544.	424.0
n-Decane	142.285	0.492	617.7	21.10	0.247	600.	447.3
Isobutane	58.123	0.181	408.1	36.48	0.282	262.7	261.4
Isooctane	114.231	0.302	544.0	25.68	0.266	468.	372.4
Cyclopentane	70.134	0.196	511.8	45.02	0.273	258.	322.4
Cyclohexane	84.161	0.210	553.6	40.73	0.273	308.	353.9
Methylcyclopentane	84.161	0.230	532.8	37.85	0.272	319.	345.0
Methylcyclohexane	98.188	0.235	572.2	34.71	0.269	368.	374.1
Ethylene	28.054	0.087	282.3	50.40	0.281	131.	169.4
Propylene	42.081	0.140	365.6	46.65	0.289	188.4	225.5
1-Butene	56.108	0.191	420.0	40.43	0.277	239.3	266.9
cis-2-Butene	56.108	0.205	435.6	42.43	0.273	233.8	276.9
trans-2-Butene	56.108	0.218	428.6	41.00	0.275	237.7	274.0
1-Hexene	84.161	0.280	504.0	31.40	0.265	354.	336.3
Isobutylene	56.108	0.194	417.9	40.00	0.275	238.9	266.3
1,3-Butadiene	54.092	0.190	425.2	42.77	0.267	220.4	268.7
Cyclohexene	82.145	0.212	560.4	43.50	0.272	291.	356.1
Acetylene	26.038	0.187	308.3	61.39	0.271	113.	189.4
Benzene	78.114	0.210	562.2	48.98	0.271	259.	353.2
Toluene	92.141	0.262	591.8	41.06	0.264	316.	383.8
Ethylbenzene	106.167	0.303	617.2	36.06	0.263	374.	409.4
Cumene	120.194	0.326	631.1	32.09	0.261	427.	425.6
o-Xylene	106.167	0.310	630.3	37.34	0.263	369.	417.6
m-Xylene	106.167	0.326	617.1	35.36	0.259	376.	412.3
p-Xylene	106.167	0.322	616.2	35.11	0.260	379.	411.5
Styrene	104.152	0.297	636.0	38.40	0.256	352.	418.3
Naphthalene	128.174	0.302	748.4	40.51	0.269	413.	491.2
Biphenyl	154.211	0.365	789.3	38.50	0.295	502.	528.2
Formaldehyde	30.026	0.282	408.0	65.90	0.223	115.	254.1
Acetaldehyde	44.053	0.291	466.0	55.50	0.221	154.	294.0
Methyl acetate	74.079	0.331	506.6	47.50	0.257	228.	330.1
Ethyl acetate	88.106	0.366	523.3	38.80	0.255	286.	350.2
Acetone	58.080	0.307	508.2	47.01	0.233	209.	329.4
Methyl ethyl ketone	72.107	0.323	535.5	41.50	0.249	267.	352.8
Diethyl ether	74.123	0.281	466.7	36.40	0.263	280.	307.6
Methyl *t*-butyl ether	88.150	0.266	497.1	34.30	0.273	329.	328.4

Table B.1 (Continued)

	Molar mass	ω	T_c/K	P_c/bar	Z_c	V_c cm^3 mol^{-1}	T_n/K
Methanol	32.042	0.564	512.6	80.97	0.224	118.	337.9
Ethanol	46.069	0.645	513.9	61.48	0.240	167.	351.4
1-Propanol	60.096	0.622	536.8	51.75	0.254	219.	370.4
1-Butanol	74.123	0.594	563.1	44.23	0.260	275.	390.8
1-Hexanol	102.177	0.579	611.4	35.10	0.263	381.	430.6
2-Propanol	60.096	0.668	508.3	47.62	0.248	220.	355.4
Phenol	94.113	0.444	694.3	61.30	0.243	229.	455.0
Ethylene glycol	62.068	0.487	719.7	77.00	0.246	191.0	470.5
Acetic acid	60.053	0.467	592.0	57.86	0.211	179.7	391.1
n-Butyric acid	88.106	0.681	615.7	40.64	0.232	291.7	436.4
Benzoic acid	122.123	0.603	751.0	44.70	0.246	344.	522.4
Acetonitrile	41.053	0.338	545.5	48.30	0.184	173.	354.8
Methylamine	31.057	0.281	430.1	74.60	0.321	154.	266.8
Ethylamine	45.084	0.285	456.2	56.20	0.307	207.	289.7
Nitromethane	61.040	0.348	588.2	63.10	0.223	173.	374.4
Carbon tetrachloride	153.822	0.193	556.4	45.60	0.272	276.	349.8
Chloroform	119.377	0.222	536.4	54.72	0.293	239.	334.3
Dichloromethane	84.932	0.199	510.0	60.80	0.265	185.	312.9
Methyl chloride	50.488	0.153	416.3	66.80	0.276	143.	249.1
Ethyl chloride	64.514	0.190	460.4	52.70	0.275	200.	285.4
Chlorobenzene	112.558	0.250	632.4	45.20	0.265	308.	404.9
Tetrafluoroethane	102.030	0.327	374.2	40.60	0.258	198.0	247.1
Argon	39.948	0.000	150.9	48.98	0.291	74.6	87.3
Krypton	83.800	0.000	209.4	55.02	0.288	91.2	119.8
Xenon	131.30	0.000	289.7	58.40	0.286	118.0	165.0
Helium 4	4.003	−0.390	5.2	2.28	0.302	57.3	4.2
Hydrogen	2.016	−0.216	33.19	13.13	0.305	64.1	20.4
Oxygen	31.999	0.022	154.6	50.43	0.288	73.4	90.2
Nitrogen	28.014	0.038	126.2	34.00	0.289	89.2	77.3
Air†	28.851	0.035	132.2	37.45	0.289	84.8	
Chlorine	70.905	0.069	417.2	77.10	0.265	124.	239.1
Carbon monoxide	28.010	0.048	132.9	34.99	0.299	93.4	81.7
Carbon dioxide	44.010	0.224	304.2	73.83	0.274	94.0	
Carbon disulfide	76.143	0.111	552.0	79.00	0.275	160.	319.4
Hydrogen sulfide	34.082	0.094	373.5	89.63	0.284	98.5	212.8
Sulfur dioxide	64.065	0.245	430.8	78.84	0.269	122.	263.1
Sulfur trioxide	80.064	0.424	490.9	82.10	0.255	127.	317.9
Nitric oxide (NO)	30.006	0.583	180.2	64.80	0.251	58.0	121.4
Nitrous oxide (N_2O)	44.013	0.141	309.6	72.45	0.274	97.4	184.7
Hydrogen chloride	36.461	0.132	324.7	83.10	0.249	81.	188.2
Hydrogen cyanide	27.026	0.410	456.7	53.90	0.197	139.	298.9
Water	18.015	0.345	647.1	220.55	0.229	55.9	373.2
Ammonia	17.031	0.253	405.7	112.80	0.242	72.5	239.7
Nitric acid	63.013	0.714	520.0	68.90	0.231	145.	356.2
Sulfuric acid	98.080	...	924.0	64.00	0.147	177.	610.0

†Pseudoparameters for $y_{N_2} = 0.79$ and $y_{O_2} = 0.21$. See Eqs. (6.97)–(6.99).

Table B.2: Constants for the Antoine Equation for Vapor Pressures of Pure Species

$$\ln P^{\text{sat}}/\text{kPa} = A - [B/(T/\text{K} + C)]$$

Latent heat of vaporization at the normal boiling point (ΔH_n) and normal boiling point (T_n)

Name	Formula	Parameters for Antoine Equation A**	B	C	Temperange Range K From	To	ΔH_n kJ/mol	T_n K
Acetone	C_3H_6O	14.3145	2756.22	−45.090	247.15	350.15	29.10	329.35
Acetic acid	$C_2H_4O_2$	15.0717	3580.80	−48.500	297.15	415.15	23.70	391.05
Acetonitrile*	C_2H_3N	14.8950	3413.10	−22.627	246.15	354.15	30.19	354.75
Benzene	C_6H_6	13.7819	2726.81	−55.578	279.15	377.15	30.72	353.15
iso-Butane	C_4H_{10}	13.8254	2181.79	−24.280	190.15	280.15	21.30	261.25
n-Butane	C_4H_{10}	13.6608	2154.70	−34.361	200.15	292.15	22.44	272.65
1-Butanol	$C_4H_{10}O$	15.3144	3212.43	−90.411	310.15	411.15	43.29	390.75
2-Butanol*	$C_4H_{10}O$	15.1989	3026.03	−86.650	298.15	393.15	40.75	372.65
iso-Butanol	$C_4H_{10}O$	14.6047	2740.95	−106.480	303.15	401.15	41.82	380.95
tert-Butanol	$C_4H_{10}O$	14.8445	2658.29	−95.500	283.15	374.15	39.07	355.45
Carbon tetrachloride	CCl_4	14.0572	2914.23	−41.002	259.15	374.15	29.82	349.75
Chlorobenzene	C_6H_5Cl	13.8635	3174.78	−61.450	302.15	432.15	35.19	404.85
1-Chlorobutane	C_4H_9Cl	13.7965	2723.73	−54.885	256.15	352.15	30.39	351.65
Chloroform	$CHCl_3$	13.7324	2548.74	−54.598	250.15	357.15	29.24	334.25
Cyclohexane	C_6H_{12}	13.6568	2723.44	−52.532	282.15	378.15	29.97	353.85
Cyclopentane	C_5H_{10}	13.9727	2653.90	−38.640	238.15	344.15	27.30	322.35
n-Decane	$C_{10}H_{22}$	13.9748	3442.76	−79.292	338.15	476.15	38.75	447.25
Dichloromethane	CH_2Cl_2	13.9891	2463.93	−49.910	235.15	333.15	28.06	312.85
Diethyl ether	$C_4H_{10}O$	14.0735	2511.29	−41.950	230.15	328.15	26.52	307.55
1,4-Dioxane	$C_4H_8O_2$	15.0967	3579.78	−32.813	293.15	378.15	34.16	374.45
n-Eicosane	$C_{20}H_{42}$	144,575	4680.46	−141.050	481.15	652.15	57.49	616.75
Ethanol	C_2H_6O	16.8958	3795.17	−42.232	276.15	369.15	38.56	351.35
Ethylbenzene	C_8H_{10}	13.9726	3259.93	−60.850	306.15	436.15	35.57	409.35
Ethylene glycol*	$C_2H_6O_2$	15.7567	4187.46	−94.500	373.15	495.15	50.73	470.45
n-Heptane	C_7H_{16}	13.8622	2910.26	−56.718	277.15	396.15	31.77	371.55
n-Hexane	C_6H_{14}	13.8193	2696.04	−48.833	254.15	365.15	28.85	341.85
Methanol	CH_4O	16.5785	3638.27	−33.650	262.15	356.15	35.21	337.85
Methyl acetate	$C_3H_6O_2$	14.2456	2662.78	−53.460	250.15	351.15	30.32	330.05
Methyl ethyl ketone	C_4H_8O	14.1334	2838.24	−54.460	265.15	376.15	31.30	352.75
Nitromethane*	CH_3NO_2	14.7513	3331.70	−45.550	329.15	419.15	33.99	374.35
n-Nonane	C_9H_{20}	13.9854	3311.19	−70.456	319.15	451.15	36.91	423.95
iso-Octane	C_8H_{18}	13.6703	2896.31	−52.383	275.15	398.15	30.79	372.35
n-Octane	C_8H_{18}	13.9346	3123.13	−63.515	299.15	425.15	34.41	398.75
n-Pentane	C_5H_{12}	13.7667	2451.88	−41.136	228.15	331.15	25.79	309.15
Phenol	C_6H_6O	14.4387	3507.80	−97.750	353.15	481.15	46.18	454.95
1-Propanol	C_3H_8O	16.1154	3483.67	−67.343	293.15	389.15	41.44	370.35
2-Propanol	C_3H_8O	16.6796	3640.20	−53.540	281.15	373.15	39.85	355.35
Toluene	C_7H_8	13.9320	3056.96	−55.525	286.15	409.15	33.18	383.75
Water	H_2O	16.3872	3885.70	−42.980	273.15	473.15	40.66	373.15
o-Xylene	C_8H_{10}	14.0415	3358.79	−61.109	313.15	445.15	36.24	417.55
m-Xylene	C_8H_{10}	14.1387	3381.81	−57.030	308.15	439.15	35.66	412.25
p-Xylene	C_8H_{10}	14.0579	3331.45	−58.523	308.15	439.15	35.67	411.45

Based primarily on data presented by B. E. Poling, J. M. Prausnitz and J. P. O'Connell, *The Properties of Gases and Liquids*, 5th ed., App. A, McGraw-Hill, New York, 2001.

*Antoine parameters adapted from Gmehling et al. See footnote 2, p. 791.

**Antoine parameters A are adjusted to reproduce the listed values of T_n.

Appendix C

Heat Capacities and Property Changes of Formation

Table C.1: Heat Capacities of Gases in the Ideal-Gas State[†]

Constants in equation $C_P^{ig}/R = A + BT + CT^2 + DT^{-2}$ T (kelvins) from 298.15 K to T_{max}

Chemical species		T_{max}	$C_{P_{298}}^{ig}/R$	A	$10^3\ B$	$10^6\ C$	$10^{-5}\ D$
Paraffins:							
Methane	CH_4	1500	4.217	1.702	9.081	−2.164	
Ethane	C_2H_6	1500	6.369	1.131	19.225	−5.561	
Propane	C_3H_8	1500	9.011	1.213	28.785	−8.824	
n-Butane	C_4H_{10}	1500	11.928	1.935	36.915	−11.402	
iso-Butane	C_4H_{10}	1500	11.901	1.677	37.853	−11.945	
n-Pentane	C_5H_{12}	1500	14.731	2.464	45.351	−14.111	
n-Hexane	C_6H_{14}	1500	17.550	3.025	53.722	−16.791	
n-Heptane	C_7H_{16}	1500	20.361	3.570	62.127	−19.486	
n-Octane	C_8H_{18}	1500	23.174	4.108	70.567	−22.208	
1-Alkenes:							
Ethylene	C_2H_4	1500	5.325	1.424	14.394	−4.392	
Propylene	C_3H_6	1500	7.792	1.637	22.706	−6.915	
1-Butene	C_4H_8	1500	10.520	1.967	31.630	−9.873	
1-Pentene	C_5H_{10}	1500	13.437	2.691	39.753	−12.447	
1-Hexene	C_6H_{12}	1500	16.240	3.220	48.189	−15.157	
1-Heptene	C_7H_{14}	1500	19.053	3.768	56.588	−17.847	
1-Octene	C_8H_{16}	1500	21.868	4.324	64.960	−20.521	
Miscellaneous organics:							
Acetaldehyde	C_2H_4O	1000	6.506	1.693	17.978	−6.158	
Acetylene	C_2H_2	1500	5.253	6.132	1.952	......	−1.299
Benzene	C_6H_6	1500	10.259	−0.206	39.064	−13.301	
1,3-Butadiene	C_4H_6	1500	10.720	2.734	26.786	−8.882	
Cyclohexane	C_6H_{12}	1500	13.121	−3.876	63.249	−20.928	
Ethanol	C_2H_6O	1500	8.948	3.518	20.001	−6.002	
Ethylbenzene	C_8H_{10}	1500	15.993	1.124	55.380	−18.476	
Ethylene oxide	C_2H_4O	1000	5.784	−0.385	23.463	−9.296	
Formaldehyde	CH_2O	1500	4.191	2.264	7.022	−1.877	
Methanol	CH_4O	1500	5.547	2.211	12.216	−3.450	
Styrene	C_8H_8	1500	15.534	2.050	50.192	−16.662	
Toluene	C_7H_8	1500	12.922	0.290	47.052	−15.716	
Miscellaneous inorganics:							
Air		2000	3.509	3.355	0.575	......	−0.016
Ammonia	NH_3	1800	4.269	3.578	3.020	......	−0.186
Bromine	Br_2	3000	4.337	4.493	0.056	......	−0.154
Carbon monoxide	CO	2500	3.507	3.376	0.557	......	−0.031
Carbon dioxide	CO_2	2000	4.467	5.457	1.045	......	−1.157
Carbon disulfide	CS_2	1800	5.532	6.311	0.805	......	−0.906
Chlorine	Cl_2	3000	4.082	4.442	0.089	......	−0.344
Hydrogen	H_2	3000	3.468	3.249	0.422	......	0.083
Hydrogen sulfide	H_2S	2300	4.114	3.931	1.490	......	−0.232
Hydrogen chloride	HCl	2000	3.512	3.156	0.623	......	0.151
Hydrogen cyanide	HCN	2500	4.326	4.736	1.359	......	−0.725
Nitrogen	N_2	2000	3.502	3.280	0.593	......	0.040
Nitrous oxide	N_2O	2000	4.646	5.328	1.214	......	−0.928
Nitric oxide	NO	2000	3.590	3.387	0.629	......	0.014
Nitrogen dioxide	NO_2	2000	4.447	4.982	1.195	......	−0.792
Dinitrogen tetroxide	N_2O_4	2000	9.198	11.660	2.257	......	−2.787
Oxygen	O_2	2000	3.535	3.639	0.506	......	−0.227
Sulfur dioxide	SO_2	2000	4.796	5.699	0.801	......	−1.015
Sulfur trioxide	SO_3	2000	6.094	8.060	1.056	......	−2.028
Water	H_2O	2000	4.038	3.470	1.450	......	0.121

[†] Selected from H. M. Spencer, *Ind. Eng. Chem.*, vol. 40, pp. 2152–2154, 1948; K. K. Kelley, *U.S. Bur. Mines Bull. 584*, 1960; L. B. Pankratz, *U.S. Bur. Mines Bull. 672*, 1982.

Table C.2: Heat Capacities of Solids[†]

Constants for the equation $C_P/R = A + BT + DT^{-2}$
T (kelvins) from 298.15 K to T_{max}

Chemical species	T_{max}	$C_{P_{298}}/R$	A	$10^3\ B$	$10^{-5}\ D$
CaO	2000	5.058	6.104	0.443	−1.047
$CaCO_3$	1200	9.848	12.572	2.637	−3.120
$Ca(OH)_2$	700	11.217	9.597	5.435	
CaC_2	720	7.508	8.254	1.429	−1.042
$CaCl_2$	1055	8.762	8.646	1.530	−0.302
C (graphite)	2000	1.026	1.771	0.771	−0.867
Cu	1357	2.959	2.677	0.815	0.035
CuO	1400	5.087	5.780	0.973	−0.874
Fe (α)	1043	3.005	−0.111	6.111	1.150
Fe_2O_3	960	12.480	11.812	9.697	−1.976
Fe_3O_4	850	18.138	9.594	27.112	0.409
FeS	411	6.573	2.612	13.286	
I_2	386.8	6.929	6.481	1.502	
LiCl	800	5.778	5.257	2.476	−0.193
NH_4Cl	458	10.741	5.939	16.105	
Na	371	3.386	1.988	4.688	
NaCl	1073	6.111	5.526	1.963	
NaOH	566	7.177	0.121	16.316	1.948
$NaHCO_3$	400	10.539	5.128	18.148	
S (rhombic)	368.3	3.748	4.114	−1.728	−0.783
SiO_2 (quartz)	847	5.345	4.871	5.365	−1.001

[†]Selected from K. K. Kelley, *U.S. Bur. Mines Bull. 584*, 1960; L. B. Pankratz, *U.S. Bur. Mines Bull. 672*, 1982.

Table C.3: Heat Capacities of Liquids[†]

Constants for the equation $C_P/R = A + BT + CT^2$
T from 273.15 K to 373.15 K

Chemical species	$C_{P_{298}}/R$	A	$10^3\ B$	$10^6\ C$
Ammonia	9.718	22.626	−100.75	192.71
Aniline	23.070	15.819	29.03	−15.80
Benzene	16.157	−0.747	67.96	−37.78
1,3-Butadiene	14.779	22.711	−87.96	205.79
Carbon tetrachloride	15.751	21.155	−48.28	101.14
Chlorobenzene	18.240	11.278	32.86	−31.90
Chloroform	13.806	19.215	−42.89	83.01
Cyclohexane	18.737	−9.048	141.38	−161.62
Ethanol	13.444	33.866	−172.60	349.17
Ethylene oxide	10.590	21.039	−86.41	172.28
Methanol	9.798	13.431	−51.28	131.13
n-Propanol	16.921	41.653	−210.32	427.20
Sulfur trioxide	30.408	−2.930	137.08	−84.73
Toluene	18.611	15.133	6.79	16.35
Water	9.069	8.712	1.25	−0.18

[†]Based on correlations presented by J. W. Miller, Jr., G. R. Schorr, and C. L. Yaws, *Chem. Eng.*, vol. 83(23), p. 129, 1976.

Table C.4: Standard Enthalpies and Gibbs Energies of Formation at 298.15 K†

Joules per mole of the substance formed

Chemical species		State (Note 2)	$\Delta H^\circ_{f_{298}}$ (Note 1)	$\Delta G^\circ_{f_{298}}$ (Note 1)
Paraffins:				
Methane	CH_4	(*g*)	−74 520	−50 460
Ethane	C_2H_6	(*g*)	−83 820	−31 855
Propane	C_3H_8	(*g*)	−104 680	−24 290
n-Butane	C_4H_{10}	(*g*)	−125 790	−16 570
n-Pentane	C_5H_{12}	(*g*)	−146 760	−8 650
n-Hexane	C_6H_{14}	(*g*)	−166 920	150
n-Heptane	C_7H_{16}	(*g*)	−187 780	8 260
n-Octane	C_8H_{18}	(*g*)	−208 750	16 260
1-Alkenes:				
Ethylene	C_2H_4	(*g*)	52 510	68 460
Propylene	C_3H_6	(*g*)	19 710	62 205
1-Butene	C_4H_8	(*g*)	−540	70 340
1-Pentene	C_5H_{10}	(*g*)	−21 280	78 410
1-Hexene	C_6H_{12}	(*g*)	−41 950	86 830
1-Heptene	C_7H_{14}	(*g*)	−62 760	
Miscellaneous organics:				
Acetaldehyde	C_2H_4O	(*g*)	−166 190	−128 860
Acetic acid	$C_2H_4O_2$	(*l*)	−484 500	−389 900
Acetylene	C_2H_2	(*g*)	227 480	209 970
Benzene	C_6H_6	(*g*)	82 930	129 665
Benzene	C_6H_6	(*l*)	49 080	124 520
1,3-Butadiene	C_4H_6	(*g*)	109 240	149 795
Cyclohexane	C_6H_{12}	(*g*)	−123 140	31 920
Cyclohexane	C_6H_{12}	(*l*)	−156 230	26 850
1,2-Ethanediol	$C_2H_6O_2$	(*l*)	−454 800	−323 080
Ethanol	C_2H_6O	(*g*)	−235 100	−168 490
Ethanol	C_2H_6O	(*l*)	−277 690	−174 780
Ethylbenzene	C_8H_{10}	(*g*)	29 920	130 890
Ethylene oxide	C_2H_4O	(*g*)	−52 630	−13 010
Formaldehyde	CH_2O	(*g*)	−108 570	−102 530
Methanol	CH_4O	(*g*)	−200 660	−161 960
Methanol	CH_4O	(*l*)	−238 660	−166 270
Methylcyclohexane	C_7H_{14}	(*g*)	−154 770	27 480
Methylcyclohexane	C_7H_{14}	(*l*)	−190 160	20 560
Styrene	C_8H_8	(*g*)	147 360	213 900
Toluene	C_7H_8	(*g*)	50 170	122 050
Toluene	C_7H_8	(*l*)	12 180	113 630

Table C.4 (Continued)

Chemical species		State (Note 2)	$\Delta H^\circ_{f_{298}}$ (Note 1)	$\Delta G^\circ_{f_{298}}$ (Note 1)
Miscellaneous inorganics:				
Ammonia	NH_3	(*g*)	−46 110	−16 450
Ammonia	NH_3	(*aq*)		−26 500
Calcium carbide	CaC_2	(*s*)	−59 800	−64 900
Calcium carbonate	$CaCO_3$	(*s*)	−1206 920	−1 128 790
Calcium chloride	$CaCl_2$	(*s*)	−795 800	−748 100
Calcium chloride	$CaCl_2$	(*aq*)		−8 101 900
Calcium chloride	$CaCl_2{\cdot}6H_2O$	(*s*)	−2607 900	
Calcium hydroxide	$Ca(OH)_2$	(*s*)	−986 090	−898 490
Calcium hydroxide	$Ca(OH)_2$	(*aq*)		−868 070
Calcium oxide	CaO	(*s*)	−635 090	−604 030
Carbon dioxide	CO_2	(*g*)	−393 509	−394 359
Carbon monoxide	CO	(*g*)	−110 525	−137 169
Hydrochloric acid	HCl	(*g*)	−92 307	−95 299
Hydrogen cyanide	HCN	(*g*)	135 100	124 700
Hydrogen sulfide	H_2S	(*g*)	−20 630	−33 560
Iron oxide	FeO	(*s*)	−272 000	
Iron oxide (hematite)	Fe_2O_3	(*s*)	−824 200	−742 200
Iron oxide (magnetite)	Fe_3O_4	(*s*)	−1118 400	−1 015 400
Iron sulfide (pyrite)	FeS_2	(*s*)	−178 200	−166 900
Lithium chloride	$LiCl$	(*s*)	−408 610	
Lithium chloride	$LiCl{\cdot}H_2O$	(*s*)	−712 580	
Lithium chloride	$LiCl{\cdot}2H_2O$	(*s*)	−1012 650	
Lithium chloride	$LiCl{\cdot}3H_2O$	(*s*)	−1311 300	
Nitric acid	HNO_3	(*l*)	−174 100	−80 710
Nitric acid	HNO_3	(*aq*)		−111 250
Nitrogen oxides	NO	(*g*)	90 250	86 550
	NO_2	(*g*)	33 180	51 310
	N_2O	(*g*)	82 050	104 200
	N_2O_4	(*g*)	9 160	97 540
Sodium carbonate	Na_2CO_3	(*s*)	−1130 680	−1 044 440
Sodium carbonate	$Na_2CO_3{\cdot}10H_2O$	(*s*)	−4081 320	
Sodium chloride	$NaCl$	(*s*)	−411 153	−384 138
Sodium chloride	$NaCl$	(*aq*)		−393 133
Sodium hydroxide	$NaOH$	(*s*)	−425 609	−379 494
Sodium hydroxide	$NaOH$	(*aq*)		−419 150
Sulfur dioxide	SO_2	(*g*)	−296 830	−300 194
Sulfur trioxide	SO_3	(*g*)	−395 720	−371 060
Sulfur trioxide	SO_3	(*l*)	−441 040	
Sulfuric acid	H_2SO_4	(*l*)	−813 989	−690 003
Sulfuric acid	H_2SO_4	(*aq*)		−744 530
Water	H_2O	(*g*)	−241 818	−228 572
Water	H_2O	(*l*)	−285 830	−237 129

†From *TRC Thermodynamic Tables—Hydrocarbons*, Thermodynamics Research Center, Texas A & M Univ. System, College Station, TX; "The NBS Tables of Chemical Thermodynamic Properties," *J. Phys. and Chem. Reference Data*, vol. 11, supp. 2, 1982.

Notes

1. The standard property changes of formation $\Delta H^\circ_{f_{298}}$ and $\Delta G^\circ_{f_{298}}$ are the changes occurring when 1 mol of the listed compound is formed from its elements with each substance in its standard state at 25°C (298.15 K).

2. Standard states: (*a*) Gases (*g*): pure ideal gas at 1 bar and 25°C (298.15 K). (*b*) Liquids (*l*) and solids (*s*): pure substance at 1 bar and 25°C (298.15 K). (*c*) Solutes in aqueous solution (*aq*): Hypothetical ideal 1-molal solution of solute in water at 1 bar and 25°C (298.15 K).

Appendix D

Representative Computer Programs

D.1 DEFINED FUNCTIONS

By Eq. (4.8),

$$\text{MCPH} \equiv \frac{\langle C_P \rangle_H}{R} = A + \frac{B}{2} T_0(\tau + 1) + \frac{C}{3} T_0^2(\tau^2 + \tau + 1) + \frac{D}{\tau T_0^2}$$

from which,

$$\text{ICPH} \equiv \int_{T_0}^{T} \frac{C_P}{R} dT = \text{MCPH} * (T - T_0)$$

By Eq. (5.17),

$$\text{MCPS} \equiv \frac{\langle C_P^{ig} \rangle_S}{R} = A + \left[BT_0 + \left(CT_0^2 + \frac{D}{\tau^2 T_0^2} \right) \left(\frac{\tau + 1}{2} \right) \right] \left(\frac{\tau - 1}{\ln \tau} \right)$$

from which

$$\text{ICPS} \equiv \int_{T_0}^{T} \frac{C_P^{ig}}{R} \frac{dT}{T} = \text{MCPS} * \ln \tau$$

where

$$\tau \equiv \frac{T}{T_0}$$

Maple®

```
tau:=(T0,T)->T/T0:
H2:=(T0,T,B)->(B/2)*T0*(tau(T0,T)+1):
H3:=(T0,T,C)->(C/3)*T0^2*(1+tau(T0,T)*(1+tau(T0,T))):
H4:=(T0,T,D)->D/(tau(T0,T)*T0^2):
S2:=(T0,T,C,D)->C*T0^2+D/(tau(T0,T)*tau(T0,T)*T0*T0):
S3:=(T0,T)->(tau(T0,T)+1)/2:
S4:=(T0,T)->(tau(T0,T)-1)/ln(tau(T0,T)):

MCPH:=(T0,T,A,B,C,D)->A+H2(T0,T,B)+H3(T0,T,C)+H4(T0,T,D):
ICPH:=(T0,T,A,B,C,D)->MCPH(T0,T,A,B,C,D)*(T-T0):
MCPS:=(T0,T,A,B,C,D)->A+(B*T0+S2(T0,T,C,D)*S3(T0,T))*S4(T0,T):
ICPS:=(T0,T,A,B,C,D)->MCPS(T0,T,A,B,C,D)*ln(tau(T0,T)):
```

Mathcad®

$$\tau(T_0,T):=\frac{T}{T_0}$$

$$H_2(T_0,T,B):=\frac{B}{2}\cdot T_0\cdot(\tau(T_0,T)+1)$$

$$H_3(T_0,T,C):=\frac{C}{3}\cdot T_0^2\cdot(\tau(T_0,T)^2+\tau(T_0,T)+1)$$

$$H_4(T_0,T,D):=\frac{D}{\tau(T_0,T)}\cdot T_0^2$$

$$S_2(T_0,T,C,D):=C\cdot T_0^2+\frac{D}{\tau(T_0,T)^2\cdot T_0^2}$$

$$S_3(T_0,T):=\frac{\tau(T_0,T)+1}{2}$$

$$S_4(T_0,T):=\frac{\tau(T_0,T)-1}{\ln(\tau(T_0,T))}$$

$$MCPH(T_0,T,A,B,C,D):=A+H_2(T_0,T,B)+H_3(T_0,T,C)+H_4(T_0,T,D)$$

$$ICPH(T_0,T,A,B,C,D):=MCPH(T_0,T,A,B,C,D)\cdot(T-T_0)$$

$$MCPS(T_0,T,A,B,C,D):=A+(B\cdot T_0+S_2(T_0,T,C,D)\cdot S_3(T_0,T))\cdot S_4(T_0,T)$$

$$ICPS(T_0,T,A,B,C,D):=MCPS(T_0,T,A,B,C,D)\cdot\ln(\tau(T_0,T))$$

By Eqs. (6.87) and (6.88),

$$\text{HRB} \equiv \frac{H^R}{RT_c} = P_r\left[B^0 - T_r\frac{dB^0}{dT_r} + \omega\left(B^1 - T_r\frac{dB^1}{dT_r}\right)\right]$$

and

$$\text{SRB} \equiv \frac{S^R}{R} = -P_r\left(\frac{dB^0}{dT_r} + \omega\frac{dB^1}{dT_r}\right)$$

By Eq. (11.68),

$$\text{PHIB} \equiv \phi = \exp\left[\frac{P_r}{T_r}(B^0 + \omega B^1)\right]$$

Maple®

```
B0:=(TR)- >0.083-0.422/TR^1.6:
DB0:=(TR)- >0.675/TR^2.6:
B1:=(TR)- >0.139-0.172/TR^4.2:
DB1:=(TR)- >0.722/TR^5.2:
HRB:=(TR,PR,omega)- >PR*(B0(TR)-TR*DB0(TR)+omega*(B1(TR)
    -TR*DB1(TR))):
SRB:=(TR,PR,omega)- >-PR*(DB0(TR)+omega*DB1(TR)):
PHIB:=(TR,PR,omega)- >exp((PR/TR)*(B0(TR)+omega*B1(TR))):
```

Mathcad®

$B_0(T_r) := 0.083 - \frac{0.422}{T_r^{1.6}}$

$DB_0(T_r) := \frac{0.675}{T_r^{2.6}}$

$B_1(T_r) := 0.139 - \frac{0.172}{T_r^{4.2}}$

$DB_1(T_r) := \frac{0.722}{T_r^{5.2}}$

$HRB(T_r, P_r, \omega) := P_r \cdot (B_0(T_r) - T_r \cdot DB_0(T_r) + \omega \cdot (B_1(T_r) - T_r \cdot DB_1(T_r)))$

$SRB(T_r, P_r, \omega) := -P_r \cdot (DB_0(T_r) + \omega \cdot DB_1(T_r))$

$PHIB(T_r, P_r, \omega) := \exp\left[\frac{P_r}{T_r} \cdot (B_0(T_r) + \omega \cdot B_1(T_r))\right]$

D.2 SOLUTION OF EXAMPLE PROBLEMS BY MATHCAD®

Example 3.9 — Molar volumes by the Redlich/Kwong equation

(a) Saturated vapor

Given: $q:=6.6048$ $\beta:=0.026214$

Initial guess: $Z:=1$

Solve block: GIVEN $Z=1+\beta-q\cdot\beta\,\dfrac{Z-\beta}{Z\cdot(Z+\beta)}$

$\text{FIND}(Z)=0.8305$

(b) Saturated liquid

Initial guess: $Z:=\beta$

Solve block: GIVEN $Z=\beta+Z\cdot(Z+\beta)\cdot\left(\dfrac{1+\beta-Z}{q\cdot\beta}\right)$

$\text{FIND}(Z)=0.04331$

Example 10.3 — Dewpoint and bubblepoint calculations

The problem formulation is the same for parts (*a*) through (*d*):

Antoine vapor-pressure equations

$A1:=16.59158$ $A2:=14.25326$

$B1:=3643.31$ $B2:=2665.54$

$C1:=-33.424$ $C2:=-53.424$

$P1(T):=\exp\left(A1-\dfrac{B1}{T-C1}\right)$ $P2(T):=\exp\left(A2-\dfrac{B2}{T-C2}\right)$

Expressions for activity coefficients

$A(T):=2.771-0.00523\cdot T$

$\gamma 1(T,x1):=\exp\left[A(T)\cdot(1-x1)^2\right]$ $\gamma 2(T,x1):=\exp\left[A(T)\cdot x1^2\right]$

(a) *BUBL P* Calculation

Given: $T:=318.15$ $x1:=0.25$ $x2:=1-x1$

$P:=x1\cdot\gamma 1(T,x1)\cdot P1(T)+x2\cdot\gamma 2(T,x1)\cdot P2(T)$ $y1:=\dfrac{x1\cdot\gamma 1(T,x1)\cdot P1(T)}{P}$

Calculated results: $P=73.5$ $y1=0.282$

(b) *DEW P* Calculation

Given: T:=318.15 y1:=0.60 y2:=1-y1

Initial guesses: P:=50 x1:=0.8

Solve block: GIVEN

$$P=\frac{1}{\dfrac{y1}{\gamma 1(T,x1)\cdot P1(T)}+\dfrac{y2}{\gamma 2(T,x1)\cdot P2(T)}} \qquad x1=\frac{y1\cdot P}{\gamma 1(T,x1)\cdot P1(T)}$$

$$\text{FIND}(x1,P)=\begin{pmatrix}0.817\\62.894\end{pmatrix}$$

(c) *BUBL T* Calculation

Given: P:=101.33 x1:=0.85 x2:=1-x1

$$\alpha(T):=\frac{P1(T)}{P2(T)}$$

Initial guesses: T:=300 y1:=0.7

Solve block: GIVEN

$$P1(T)=\frac{P}{x1\cdot\gamma 1(T,x1)+\dfrac{x2\cdot\gamma 2(T,x1)}{\alpha(T)}} \qquad y1=\frac{x1\cdot\gamma 1(T,x1)\cdot P1(T)}{P}$$

$$\text{FIND}(y1,T)=\begin{pmatrix}0.670\\331.20\end{pmatrix}$$

(d) *DEW T* Calculation

Given: P:=101.33 y1:=0.40 y2:=1-y1

Initial guesses: T:=300 x1:=0.5

Solve block: GIVEN

$$P1(T)=P\cdot\left(\frac{y1}{\gamma 1(T,x1)}+\frac{y2\cdot\alpha(T)}{\gamma 2(T,x1)}\right) \qquad T=\frac{B1}{A1+\ln(P1(T))}+C1$$

$$x1=\frac{y1\cdot P}{\gamma 1(T,x1)\cdot P1(T)} \qquad \text{FIND}(x1,T)=\begin{pmatrix}0.460\\326.70\end{pmatrix}$$

Example 13.13 — Solution of two reaction-equilibrium equations

Given: $K_a := 1.758$ $K_b := 2.561$

Initial guesses: $\varepsilon_a := 0.1$ $\varepsilon_b := 0.7$

Solve block: GIVEN $0.5 \geq \varepsilon_a \geq -0.5$ $0 \leq \varepsilon_b \leq 1$

$$K_a = \frac{(2 \cdot \varepsilon_a + \varepsilon_b)^2}{(0.5 - \varepsilon_a) \cdot (3.38 + \varepsilon_a + \varepsilon_b)} \cdot 20 \qquad K_b = \frac{\varepsilon_b (2 \cdot \varepsilon_a + \varepsilon_b)}{(1 - \varepsilon_a) \cdot (3.38 + \varepsilon_a + \varepsilon_b)} \cdot 20$$

$$\text{FIND}(\varepsilon_a, \varepsilon_b) = \begin{pmatrix} -0.0506 \\ 0.5336 \end{pmatrix}$$

Example 13.14 — Reaction equilibrium by minimizing the Gibbs energy

In the following, define: $\Lambda_i \equiv \lambda_i / RT$ and RT$\equiv R \times T = 8314$

Definition: $RT \equiv 8314$

Initial guesses: $\Lambda_C := 1$ $\Lambda_H := 1$ $\Lambda_O := 1$ $n := 1$

$y_{CH4} := 0.01$ $y_{H2O} := 0.01$ $y_{CO} := 0.01$ $y_{CO2} := 0.01$ $y_{H2} := 0.96$

Solve block: GIVEN

$$y_{CH4} + y_{CO} + y_{CO2} = \frac{2}{n} \qquad 4 \cdot y_{CH4} + 2 \cdot y_{H2O} + 2 \cdot y_{H2} = \frac{14}{n}$$

$$y_{H2O} + y_{CO} + 2 \cdot y_{CO2} = \frac{3}{n} \qquad y_{CH4} + y_{H2O} + y_{CO} + y_{CO2} + y_{H2} = 1$$

$$\frac{19720}{RT} + \ln(y_{CH4}) + \Lambda_C + 4 \cdot \Lambda_H = 0 \qquad -\frac{192420}{RT} + \ln(y_{H2O}) + 2 \cdot \Lambda_H + \Lambda_O = 0$$

$$-\frac{200240}{RT} + \ln(y_{CO}) + \Lambda_C + \Lambda_O = 0 \qquad -\frac{395790}{RT} + \ln(y_{CO2}) + \Lambda_C + 2 \cdot \Lambda_O = 0$$

$$\ln(y_{H2}) + 2 \cdot \Lambda_H = 0$$

$0 \leq y_{CH4} \leq 1$ $0 \leq y_{H2O} \leq 1$ $0 \leq y_{CO} \leq 1$ $0 \leq y_{CO2} \leq 1$ $0 \leq y_{H2} \leq 1$

$$\text{FIND}(y_{CH4}, y_{H2O}, y_{CO}, y_{CO2}, y_{H2}, \Lambda_C, \Lambda_H, \Lambda_O, n) = \begin{pmatrix} 0.0196 \\ 0.0980 \\ 0.1743 \\ 0.0371 \\ 0.6711 \\ 0.7635 \\ 0.1994 \\ 25.068 \\ 8.6608 \end{pmatrix}$$

Appendix E

The Lee/Kesler Generalized-correlation Tables

The Lee/Kesler tables are adapted and published by permission from "A Generalized Thermodynamic Correlation Based on Three-Parameter Corresponding States," by Byung Ik Lee and Michael G. Kesler, *AIChE J.*, **21**, 510–527 (1975). The numbers printed in italic type are liquid-phase properties.

TABLES **PAGE**

Table E.1: Values of Z^0

P_r = / T_r	0.0100	0.0500	0.1000	0.2000	0.4000	0.6000	0.8000	1.0000
0.30	*0.0029*	*0.0145*	*0.0290*	*0.0579*	*0.1158*	*0.1737*	*0.2315*	0.2892
0.35	*0.0026*	*0.0130*	*0.0261*	*0.0522*	*0.1043*	*0.1564*	*0.2084*	0.2604
0.40	*0.0024*	*0.0119*	*0.0239*	*0.0477*	*0.0953*	*0.1429*	*0.1904*	0.2379
0.45	*0.0022*	*0.0110*	*0.0221*	*0.0442*	*0.0882*	*0.1322*	*0.1762*	0.2200
0.50	*0.0021*	*0.0103*	*0.0207*	*0.0413*	*0.0825*	*0.1236*	*0.1647*	0.2056
0.55	0.9804	*0.0098*	*0.0195*	*0.0390*	*0.0778*	*0.1166*	*0.1553*	0.1939
0.60	0.9849	*0.0093*	*0.0186*	*0.0371*	*0.0741*	*0.1109*	*0.1476*	0.1842
0.65	0.9881	0.9377	*0.0178*	*0.0356*	*0.0710*	*0.1063*	*0.1415*	0.1765
0.70	0.9904	0.9504	0.8958	*0.0344*	*0.0687*	*0.1027*	*0.1366*	0.1703
0.75	0.9922	0.9598	0.9165	*0.0336*	*0.0670*	*0.1001*	*0.1330*	0.1656
0.80	0.9935	0.9669	0.9319	0.8539	*0.0661*	*0.0985*	*0.1307*	0.1626
0.85	0.9946	0.9725	0.9436	0.8810	*0.0661*	*0.0983*	*0.1301*	0.1614
0.90	0.9954	0.9768	0.9528	0.9015	0.7800	*0.1006*	*0.1321*	0.1630
0.93	0.9959	0.9790	0.9573	0.9115	0.8059	0.6635	*0.1359*	0.1664
0.95	0.9961	0.9803	0.9600	0.9174	0.8206	0.6967	*0.1410*	0.1705
0.97	0.9963	0.9815	0.9625	0.9227	0.8338	0.7240	0.5580	0.1779
0.98	0.9965	0.9821	0.9637	0.9253	0.8398	0.7360	0.5887	0.1844
0.99	0.9966	0.9826	0.9648	0.9277	0.8455	0.7471	0.6138	0.1959
1.00	0.9967	0.9832	0.9659	0.9300	0.8509	0.7574	0.6355	0.2901
1.01	0.9968	0.9837	0.9669	0.9322	0.8561	0.7671	0.6542	0.4648
1.02	0.9969	0.9842	0.9679	0.9343	0.8610	0.7761	0.6710	0.5146
1.05	0.9971	0.9855	0.9707	0.9401	0.8743	0.8002	0.7130	0.6026
1.10	0.9975	0.9874	0.9747	0.9485	0.8930	0.8323	0.7649	0.6880
1.15	0.9978	0.9891	0.9780	0.9554	0.9081	0.8576	0.8032	0.7443
1.20	0.9981	0.9904	0.9808	0.9611	0.9205	0.8779	0.8330	0.7858
1.30	0.9985	0.9926	0.9852	0.9702	0.9396	0.9083	0.8764	0.8438
1.40	0.9988	0.9942	0.9884	0.9768	0.9534	0.9298	0.9062	0.8827
1.50	0.9991	0.9954	0.9909	0.9818	0.9636	0.9456	0.9278	0.9103
1.60	0.9993	0.9964	0.9928	0.9856	0.9714	0.9575	0.9439	0.9308
1.70	0.9994	0.9971	0.9943	0.9886	0.9775	0.9667	0.9563	0.9463
1.80	0.9995	0.9977	0.9955	0.9910	0.9823	0.9739	0.9659	0.9583
1.90	0.9996	0.9982	0.9964	0.9929	0.9861	0.9796	0.9735	0.9678
2.00	0.9997	0.9986	0.9972	0.9944	0.9892	0.9842	0.9796	0.9754
2.20	0.9998	0.9992	0.9983	0.9967	0.9937	0.9910	0.9886	0.9865
2.40	0.9999	0.9996	0.9991	0.9983	0.9969	0.9957	0.9948	0.9941
2.60	1.0000	0.9998	0.9997	0.9994	0.9991	0.9990	0.9990	0.9993
2.80	1.0000	1.0000	1.0001	1.0002	1.0007	1.0013	1.0021	1.0031
3.00	1.0000	1.0002	1.0004	1.0008	1.0018	1.0030	1.0043	1.0057
3.50	1.0001	1.0004	1.0008	1.0017	1.0035	1.0055	1.0075	1.0097
4.00	1.0001	1.0005	1.0010	1.0021	1.0043	1.0066	1.0090	1.0115

Table E.2: Values of Z^1

$P_r =$	0.0100	0.0500	0.1000	0.2000	0.4000	0.6000	0.8000	1.0000
T_r								
0.30	*−0.0008*	*−0.0040*	*−0.0081*	*−0.0161*	*−0.0323*	*−0.0484*	*−0.0645*	−0.0806
0.35	*−0.0009*	*−0.0046*	*−0.0093*	*−0.0185*	*−0.0370*	*−0.0554*	*−0.0738*	−0.0921
0.40	*−0.0010*	*−0.0048*	*−0.0095*	*−0.0190*	*−0.0380*	*−0.0570*	*−0.0758*	−0.0946
0.45	*−0.0009*	*−0.0047*	*−0.0094*	*−0.0187*	*−0.0374*	*−0.0560*	*−0.0745*	−0.0929
0.50	*−0.0009*	*−0.0045*	*−0.0090*	*−0.0181*	*−0.0360*	*−0.0539*	*−0.0716*	−0.0893
0.55	−0.0314	*−0.0043*	*−0.0086*	*−0.0172*	*−0.0343*	*−0.0513*	*−0.0682*	−0.0849
0.60	−0.0205	*−0.0041*	*−0.0082*	*−0.0164*	*−0.0326*	*−0.0487*	*−0.0646*	−0.0803
0.65	−0.0137	−0.0772	*−0.0078*	*−0.0156*	*−0.0309*	*−0.0461*	*−0.0611*	−0.0759
0.70	−0.0093	−0.0507	−0.1161	*−0.0148*	*−0.0294*	*−0.0438*	*−0.0579*	−0.0718
0.75	−0.0064	−0.0339	−0.0744	*−0.0143*	*−0.0282*	*−0.0417*	*−0.0550*	−0.0681
0.80	−0.0044	−0.0228	−0.0487	−0.1160	*−0.0272*	*−0.0401*	*−0.0526*	−0.0648
0.85	−0.0029	−0.0152	−0.0319	−0.0715	*−0.0268*	*−0.0391*	*−0.0509*	−0.0622
0.90	−0.0019	−0.0099	−0.0205	−0.0442	−0.1118	*−0.0396*	*−0.0503*	−0.0604
0.93	−0.0015	−0.0075	−0.0154	−0.0326	−0.0763	−0.1662	*−0.0514*	−0.0602
0.95	−0.0012	−0.0062	−0.0126	−0.0262	−0.0589	−0.1110	*−0.0540*	−0.0607
0.97	−0.0010	−0.0050	−0.0101	−0.0208	−0.0450	−0.0770	−0.1647	−0.0623
0.98	−0.0009	−0.0044	−0.0090	−0.0184	−0.0390	−0.0641	−0.1100	−0.0641
0.99	−0.0008	−0.0039	−0.0079	−0.0161	−0.0335	−0.0531	−0.0796	−0.0680
1.00	−0.0007	−0.0034	−0.0069	−0.0140	−0.0285	−0.0435	−0.0588	−0.0879
1.01	−0.0006	−0.0030	−0.0060	−0.0120	−0.0240	−0.0351	−0.0429	−0.0223
1.02	−0.0005	−0.0026	−0.0051	−0.0102	−0.0198	−0.0277	−0.0303	−0.0062
1.05	−0.0003	−0.0015	−0.0029	−0.0054	−0.0092	−0.0097	−0.0032	0.0220
1.10	0.0000	0.0000	0.0001	0.0007	0.0038	0.0106	0.0236	0.0476
1.15	0.0002	0.0011	0.0023	0.0052	0.0127	0.0237	0.0396	0.0625
1.20	0.0004	0.0019	0.0039	0.0084	0.0190	0.0326	0.0499	0.0719
1.30	0.0006	0.0030	0.0061	0.0125	0.0267	0.0429	0.0612	0.0819
1.40	0.0007	0.0036	0.0072	0.0147	0.0306	0.0477	0.0661	0.0857
1.50	0.0008	0.0039	0.0078	0.0158	0.0323	0.0497	0.0677	0.0864
1.60	0.0008	0.0040	0.0080	0.0162	0.0330	0.0501	0.0677	0.0855
1.70	0.0008	0.0040	0.0081	0.0163	0.0329	0.0497	0.0667	0.0838
1.80	0.0008	0.0040	0.0081	0.0162	0.0325	0.0488	0.0652	0.0814
1.90	0.0008	0.0040	0.0079	0.0159	0.0318	0.0477	0.0635	0.0792
2.00	0.0008	0.0039	0.0078	0.0155	0.0310	0.0464	0.0617	0.0767
2.20	0.0007	0.0037	0.0074	0.0147	0.0293	0.0437	0.0579	0.0719
2.40	0.0007	0.0035	0.0070	0.0139	0.0276	0.0411	0.0544	0.0675
2.60	0.0007	0.0033	0.0066	0.0131	0.0260	0.0387	0.0512	0.0634
2.80	0.0006	0.0031	0.0062	0.0124	0.0245	0.0365	0.0483	0.0598
3.00	0.0006	0.0029	0.0059	0.0117	0.0232	0.0345	0.0456	0.0565
3.50	0.0005	0.0026	0.0052	0.0103	0.0204	0.0303	0.0401	0.0497
4.00	0.0005	0.0023	0.0046	0.0091	0.0182	0.0270	0.0357	0.0443

Table E.3: Values of Z^0

$P_r =$	1.0000	1.2000	1.5000	2.0000	3.0000	5.0000	7.0000	10.000
T_r								
0.30	0.2892	0.3479	0.4335	0.5775	0.8648	1.4366	2.0048	2.8507
0.35	0.2604	0.3123	0.3901	0.5195	0.7775	1.2902	1.7987	2.5539
0.40	0.2379	0.2853	0.3563	0.4744	0.7095	1.1758	1.6373	2.3211
0.45	0.2200	0.2638	0.3294	0.4384	0.6551	1.0841	1.5077	2.1338
0.50	0.2056	0.2465	0.3077	0.4092	0.6110	1.0094	1.4017	1.9801
0.55	0.1939	0.2323	0.2899	0.3853	0.5747	0.9475	1.3137	1.8520
0.60	0.1842	0.2207	0.2753	0.3657	0.5446	0.8959	1.2398	1.7440
0.65	0.1765	0.2113	0.2634	0.3495	0.5197	0.8526	1.1773	1.6519
0.70	0.1703	0.2038	0.2538	0.3364	0.4991	0.8161	1.1341	1.5729
0.75	0.1656	0.1981	0.2464	0.3260	0.4823	0.7854	1.0787	1.5047
0.80	0.1626	0.1942	0.2411	0.3182	0.4690	0.7598	1.0400	1.4456
0.85	0.1614	0.1924	0.2382	0.3132	0.4591	0.7388	1.0071	1.3943
0.90	0.1630	0.1935	0.2383	0.3114	0.4527	0.7220	0.9793	1.3496
0.93	0.1664	0.1963	0.2405	0.3122	0.4507	0.7138	0.9648	1.3257
0.95	0.1705	0.1998	0.2432	0.3138	0.4501	0.7092	0.9561	1.3108
0.97	0.1779	0.2055	0.2474	0.3164	0.4504	0.7052	0.9480	1.2968
0.98	0.1844	0.2097	0.2503	0.3182	0.4508	0.7035	0.9442	1.2901
0.99	0.1959	0.2154	0.2538	0.3204	0.4514	0.7018	0.9406	1.2835
1.00	0.2901	0.2237	0.2583	0.3229	0.4522	0.7004	0.9372	1.2772
1.01	0.4648	0.2370	0.2640	0.3260	0.4533	0.6991	0.9339	1.2710
1.02	0.5146	0.2629	0.2715	0.3297	0.4547	0.6980	0.9307	1.2650
1.05	0.6026	0.4437	0.3131	0.3452	0.4604	0.6956	0.9222	1.2481
1.10	0.6880	0.5984	0.4580	0.3953	0.4770	0.6950	0.9110	1.2232
1.15	0.7443	0.6803	0.5798	0.4760	0.5042	0.6987	0.9033	1.2021
1.20	0.7858	0.7363	0.6605	0.5605	0.5425	0.7069	0.8990	1.1844
1.30	0.8438	0.8111	0.7624	0.6908	0.6344	0.7358	0.8998	1.1580
1.40	0.8827	0.8595	0.8256	0.7753	0.7202	0.7761	0.9112	1.1419
1.50	0.9103	0.8933	0.8689	0.8328	0.7887	0.8200	0.9297	1.1339
1.60	0.9308	0.9180	0.9000	0.8738	0.8410	0.8617	0.9518	1.1320
1.70	0.9463	0.9367	0.9234	0.9043	0.8809	0.8984	0.9745	1.1343
1.80	0.9583	0.9511	0.9413	0.9275	0.9118	0.9297	0.9961	1.1391
1.90	0.9678	0.9624	0.9552	0.9456	0.9359	0.9557	1.0157	1.1452
2.00	0.9754	0.9715	0.9664	0.9599	0.9550	0.9772	1.0328	1.1516
2.20	0.9856	0.9847	0.9826	0.9806	0.9827	1.0094	1.0600	1.1635
2.40	0.9941	0.9936	0.9935	0.9945	1.0011	1.0313	1.0793	1.1728
2.60	0.9993	0.9998	1.0010	1.0040	1.0137	1.0463	1.0926	1.1792
2.80	1.0031	1.0042	1.0063	1.0106	1.0223	1.0565	1.1016	1.1830
3.00	1.0057	1.0074	1.0101	1.0153	1.0284	1.0635	1.1075	1.1848
3.50	1.0097	1.0120	1.0156	1.0221	1.0368	1.0723	1.1138	1.1834
4.00	1.0115	1.0140	1.0179	1.0249	1.0401	1.0747	1.1136	1.1773

Table E.4: Values of Z^1

P_r =	1.0000	1.2000	1.5000	2.0000	3.0000	5.0000	7.0000	10.000
T_r								
0.30	−0.0806	−0.0966	−0.1207	−0.1608	−0.2407	−0.3996	−0.5572	−0.7915
0.35	−0.0921	−0.1105	−0.1379	−0.1834	−0.2738	−0.4523	−0.6279	−0.8863
0.40	−0.0946	−0.1134	−0.1414	−0.1879	−0.2799	−0.4603	−0.6365	−0.8936
0.45	−0.0929	−0.1113	−0.1387	−0.1840	−0.2734	−0.4475	−0.6162	−0.8608
0.50	−0.0893	−0.1069	−0.1330	−0.1762	−0.2611	−0.4253	−0.5831	−0.8099
0.55	−0.0849	−0.1015	−0.1263	−0.1669	−0.2465	−0.3991	−0.5446	−0.7521
0.60	−0.0803	−0.0960	−0.1192	−0.1572	−0.2312	−0.3718	−0.5047	−0.6928
0.65	−0.0759	−0.0906	−0.1122	−0.1476	−0.2160	−0.3447	−0.4653	−0.6346
0.70	−0.0718	−0.0855	−0.1057	−0.1385	−0.2013	−0.3184	−0.4270	−0.5785
0.75	−0.0681	−0.0808	−0.0996	−0.1298	−0.1872	−0.2929	−0.3901	−0.5250
0.80	−0.0648	−0.0767	−0.0940	−0.1217	−0.1736	−0.2682	−0.3545	−0.4740
0.85	−0.0622	−0.0731	−0.0888	−0.1138	−0.1602	−0.2439	−0.3201	−0.4254
0.90	−0.0604	−0.0701	−0.0840	−0.1059	−0.1463	−0.2195	−0.2862	−0.3788
0.93	−0.0602	−0.0687	−0.0810	−0.1007	−0.1374	−0.2045	−0.2661	−0.3516
0.95	−0.0607	−0.0678	−0.0788	−0.0967	−0.1310	−0.1943	−0.2526	−0.3339
0.97	−0.0623	−0.0669	−0.0759	−0.0921	−0.1240	−0.1837	−0.2391	−0.3163
0.98	−0.0641	−0.0661	−0.0740	−0.0893	−0.1202	−0.1783	−0.2322	−0.3075
0.99	−0.0680	−0.0646	−0.0715	−0.0861	−0.1162	−0.1728	−0.2254	−0.2989
1.00	−0.0879	−0.0609	−0.0678	−0.0824	−0.1118	−0.1672	−0.2185	−0.2902
1.01	−0.0223	−0.0473	−0.0621	−0.0778	−0.1072	−0.1615	−0.2116	−0.2816
1.02	−0.0062	−0.0227	−0.0524	−0.0722	−0.1021	−0.1556	−0.2047	−0.2731
1.05	0.0220	0.1059	0.0451	−0.0432	−0.0838	−0.1370	−0.1835	−0.2476
1.10	0.0476	0.0897	0.1630	0.0698	−0.0373	−0.1021	−0.1469	−0.2056
1.15	0.0625	0.0943	0.1548	0.1667	0.0332	−0.0611	−0.1084	−0.1642
1.20	0.0719	0.0991	0.1477	0.1990	0.1095	−0.0141	−0.0678	−0.1231
1.30	0.0819	0.1048	0.1420	0.1991	0.2079	0.0875	0.0176	−0.0423
1.40	0.0857	0.1063	0.1383	0.1894	0.2397	0.1737	0.1008	0.0350
1.50	0.0854	0.1055	0.1345	0.1806	0.2433	0.2309	0.1717	0.1058
1.60	0.0855	0.1035	0.1303	0.1729	0.2381	0.2631	0.2255	0.1673
1.70	0.0838	0.1008	0.1259	0.1658	0.2305	0.2788	0.2628	0.2179
1.80	0.0816	0.0978	0.1216	0.1593	0.2224	0.2846	0.2871	0.2576
1.90	0.0792	0.0947	0.1173	0.1532	0.2144	0.2848	0.3017	0.2876
2.00	0.0767	0.0916	0.1133	0.1476	0.2069	0.2819	0.3097	0.3096
2.20	0.0719	0.0857	0.1057	0.1374	0.1932	0.2720	0.3135	0.3355
2.40	0.0675	0.0803	0.0989	0.1285	0.1812	0.2602	0.3089	0.3459
2.60	0.0634	0.0754	0.0929	0.1207	0.1706	0.2484	0.3009	0.3475
2.80	0.0598	0.0711	0.0876	0.1138	0.1613	0.2372	0.2915	0.3443
3.00	0.0535	0.0672	0.0828	0.1076	0.1529	0.2268	0.2817	0.3385
3.50	0.0497	0.0591	0.0728	0.0949	0.1356	0.2042	0.2584	0.3194
4.00	0.0443	0.0527	0.0651	0.0849	0.1219	0.1857	0.2378	0.2994

Table E.5: Values of $(H^R)^0/RT_c$

$P_r =$ / T_r	0.0100	0.0500	0.1000	0.2000	0.4000	0.6000	0.8000	1.0000
0.30	−6.045	−6.043	−6.040	−6.034	−6.022	−6.011	−5.999	−5.987
0.35	−5.906	−5.904	−5.901	−5.895	−5.882	−5.870	−5.858	−5.845
0.40	−5.763	−5.761	−5.757	−5.751	−5.738	−5.726	−5.713	−5.700
0.45	−5.615	−5.612	−5.609	−5.603	−5.590	−5.577	−5.564	−5.551
0.50	−5.465	−5.463	−5.459	−5.453	−5.440	−5.427	−5.414	−5.401
0.55	−0.032	−5.312	−5.309	−5.303	−5.290	−5.278	−5.265	−5.252
0.60	−0.027	−5.162	−5.159	−5.153	−5.141	−5.129	−5.116	−5.104
0.65	−0.023	−0.118	−5.008	−5.002	−4.991	−4.980	−4.968	−4.956
0.70	−0.020	−0.101	−0.213	−4.848	−4.838	−4.828	−4.818	−4.808
0.75	−0.017	−0.088	−0.183	−4.687	−4.679	−4.672	−4.664	−4.655
0.80	−0.015	−0.078	−0.160	−0.345	−4.507	−4.504	−4.499	−4.494
0.85	−0.014	−0.069	−0.141	−0.300	−4.309	−4.313	−4.316	−4.316
0.90	−0.012	−0.062	−0.126	−0.264	−0.596	−4.074	−4.094	−4.108
0.93	−0.011	−0.058	−0.118	−0.246	−0.545	−0.960	−3.920	−3.953
0.95	−0.011	−0.056	−0.113	−0.235	−0.516	−0.885	−3.763	−3.825
0.97	−0.011	−0.054	−0.109	−0.225	−0.490	−0.824	−1.356	−3.658
0.98	−0.010	−0.053	−0.107	−0.221	−0.478	−0.797	−1.273	−3.544
0.99	−0.010	−0.052	−0.105	−0.216	−0.466	−0.773	−1.206	−3.376
1.00	−0.010	−0.051	−0.103	−0.212	−0.455	−0.750	−1.151	−2.584
1.01	−0.010	−0.050	−0.101	−0.208	−0.445	−0.721	−1.102	−1.796
1.02	−0.010	−0.049	−0.099	−0.203	−0.434	−0.708	−1.060	−1.627
1.05	−0.009	−0.046	−0.094	−0.192	−0.407	−0.654	−0.955	−1.359
1.10	−0.008	−0.042	−0.086	−0.175	−0.367	−0.581	−0.827	−1.120
1.15	−0.008	−0.039	−0.079	−0.160	−0.334	−0.523	−0.732	−0.968
1.20	−0.007	−0.036	−0.073	−0.148	−0.305	−0.474	−0.657	−0.857
1.30	−0.006	−0.031	−0.063	−0.127	−0.259	−0.399	−0.545	−0.698
1.40	−0.005	−0.027	−0.055	−0.110	−0.224	−0.341	−0.463	−0.588
1.50	−0.005	−0.024	−0.048	−0.097	−0.196	−0.297	−0.400	−0.505
1.60	−0.004	−0.021	−0.043	−0.086	−0.173	−0.261	−0.350	−0.440
1.70	−0.004	−0.019	−0.038	−0.076	−0.153	−0.231	−0.309	−0.387
1.80	−0.003	−0.017	−0.034	−0.068	−0.137	−0.206	−0.275	−0.344
1.90	−0.003	−0.015	−0.031	−0.062	−0.123	−0.185	−0.246	−0.307
2.00	−0.003	−0.014	−0.028	−0.056	−0.111	−0.167	−0.222	−0.276
2.20	−0.002	−0.012	−0.023	−0.046	−0.092	−0.137	−0.182	−0.226
2.40	−0.002	−0.010	−0.019	−0.038	−0.076	−0.114	−0.150	−0.187
2.60	−0.002	−0.008	−0.016	−0.032	−0.064	−0.095	−0.125	−0.155
2.80	−0.001	−0.007	−0.014	−0.027	−0.054	−0.080	−0.105	−0.130
3.00	−0.001	−0.006	−0.011	−0.023	−0.045	−0.067	−0.088	−0.109
3.50	−0.001	−0.004	−0.007	−0.015	−0.029	−0.043	−0.056	−0.069
4.00	−0.000	−0.002	−0.005	−0.009	−0.017	−0.026	−0.033	−0.041

Table E.6: Values of $(H^R)^1/RT_c$

P_r =	0.0100	0.0500	0.1000	0.2000	0.4000	0.6000	0.8000	1.0000
T_r								
0.30	*−11.098*	*−11.096*	*−11.095*	*−11.091*	*−11.083*	*−11.076*	*−11.069*	−11.062
0.35	*−10.656*	*−10.655*	*−10.654*	*−10.653*	*−10.650*	*−10.646*	*−10.643*	−10.640
0.40	*−10.121*	*−10.121*	*−10.121*	*−10.120*	*−10.121*	*−10.121*	*−10.121*	−10.121
0.45	*−9.515*	*−9.515*	*−9.516*	*−9.517*	*−9.519*	*−9.521*	*−9.523*	−9.525
0.50	*−8.868*	*−8.869*	*−8.870*	*−8.872*	*−8.876*	*−8.880*	*−8.884*	−8.888
0.55	−0.080	*−8.211*	*−8.212*	*−8.215*	*−8.221*	*−8.226*	*−8.232*	−8.238
0.60	−0.059	*−7.568*	*−7.570*	*−7.573*	*−7.579*	*−7.585*	*−7.591*	−7.596
0.65	−0.045	−0.247	*−6.949*	*−6.952*	*−6.959*	*−6.966*	*−6.973*	−6.980
0.70	−0.034	−0.185	−0.415	*−6.360*	*−6.367*	*−6.373*	*−6.381*	−6.388
0.75	−0.027	−0.142	−0.306	*−5.796*	*−5.802*	*−5.809*	*−5.816*	−5.824
0.80	−0.021	−0.110	−0.234	−0.542	*−5.266*	*−5.271*	*−5.278*	−5.285
0.85	−0.017	−0.087	−0.182	−0.401	*−4.753*	*−4.754*	*−4.758*	−4.763
0.90	−0.014	−0.070	−0.144	−0.308	−0.751	*−4.254*	*−4.248*	−4.249
0.93	−0.012	−0.061	−0.126	−0.265	−0.612	−1.236	*−3.942*	−3.934
0.95	−0.011	−0.056	−0.115	−0.241	−0.542	−0.994	*−3.737*	−3.712
0.97	−0.010	−0.052	−0.105	−0.219	−0.483	−0.837	−1.616	−3.470
0.98	−0.010	−0.050	−0.101	−0.209	−0.457	−0.776	−1.324	−3.332
0.99	−0.009	−0.048	−0.097	−0.200	−0.433	−0.722	−1.154	−3.164
1.00	−0.009	−0.046	−0.093	−0.191	−0.410	−0.675	−1.034	−2.471
1.01	−0.009	−0.044	−0.089	−0.183	−0.389	−0.632	−0.940	−1.375
1.02	−0.008	−0.042	−0.085	−0.175	−0.370	−0.594	−0.863	−1.180
1.05	−0.007	−0.037	−0.075	−0.153	−0.318	−0.498	−0.691	−0.877
1.10	−0.006	−0.030	−0.061	−0.123	−0.251	−0.381	−0.507	−0.617
1.15	−0.005	−0.025	−0.050	−0.099	−0.199	−0.296	−0.385	−0.459
1.20	−0.004	−0.020	−0.040	−0.080	−0.158	−0.232	−0.297	−0.349
1.30	−0.003	−0.013	−0.026	−0.052	−0.100	−0.142	−0.177	−0.203
1.40	−0.002	−0.008	−0.016	−0.032	−0.060	−0.083	−0.100	−0.111
1.50	−0.001	−0.005	−0.009	−0.018	−0.032	−0.042	−0.048	−0.049
1.60	−0.000	−0.002	−0.004	−0.007	−0.012	−0.013	−0.011	−0.005
1.70	−0.000	−0.000	−0.000	−0.000	0.003	0.009	0.017	0.027
1.80	0.000	0.001	0.003	0.006	0.015	0.025	0.037	0.051
1.90	0.001	0.003	0.005	0.011	0.023	0.037	0.053	0.070
2.00	0.001	0.003	0.007	0.015	0.030	0.047	0.065	0.085
2.20	0.001	0.005	0.010	0.020	0.040	0.062	0.083	0.106
2.40	0.001	0.006	0.012	0.023	0.047	0.071	0.095	0.120
2.60	0.001	0.006	0.013	0.026	0.052	0.078	0.104	0.130
2.80	0.001	0.007	0.014	0.028	0.055	0.082	0.110	0.137
3.00	0.001	0.007	0.014	0.029	0.058	0.086	0.114	0.142
3.50	0.002	0.008	0.016	0.031	0.062	0.092	0.122	0.152
4.00	0.002	0.008	0.016	0.032	0.064	0.096	0.127	0.158

Table E.7: Values of $(H^R)^0/RT_c$

$P_r =$	1.0000	1.2000	1.5000	2.0000	3.0000	5.0000	7.0000	10.000
T_r								
0.30	−5.987	−5.975	−5.957	−5.927	−5.868	−5.748	−5.628	−5.446
0.35	−5.845	−5.833	−5.814	−5.783	−5.721	−5.595	−5.469	−5.278
0.40	−5.700	−5.687	−5.668	−5.636	−5.572	−5.442	−5.311	−5.113
0.45	−5.551	−5.538	−5.519	−5.486	−5.421	−5.288	−5.154	−5.950
0.50	−5.401	−5.388	−5.369	−5.336	−5.279	−5.135	−4.999	−4.791
0.55	−5.252	−5.239	−5.220	−5.187	−5.121	−4.986	−4.849	−4.638
0.60	−5.104	−5.091	−5.073	−5.041	−4.976	−4.842	−4.794	−4.492
0.65	−4.956	−4.949	−4.927	−4.896	−4.833	−4.702	−4.565	−4.353
0.70	−4.808	−4.797	−4.781	−4.752	−4.693	−4.566	−4.432	−4.221
0.75	−4.655	−4.646	−4.632	−4.607	−4.554	−4.434	−4.393	−4.095
0.80	−4.494	−4.488	−4.478	−4.459	−4.413	−4.303	−4.178	−3.974
0.85	−4.316	−4.316	−4.312	−4.302	−4.269	−4.173	−4.056	−3.857
0.90	−4.108	−4.118	−4.127	−4.132	−4.119	−4.043	−3.935	−3.744
0.93	−3.953	−3.976	−4.000	−4.020	−4.024	−3.963	−3.863	−3.678
0.95	−3.825	−3.865	−3.904	−3.940	−3.958	−3.910	−3.815	−3.634
0.97	−3.658	−3.732	−3.796	−3.853	−3.890	−3.856	−3.767	−3.591
0.98	−3.544	−3.652	−3.736	−3.806	−3.854	−3.829	−3.743	−3.569
0.99	−3.376	−3.558	−3.670	−3.758	−3.818	−3.801	−3.719	−3.548
1.00	−2.584	−3.441	−3.598	−3.706	−3.782	−3.774	−3.695	−3.526
1.01	−1.796	−3.283	−3.516	−3.652	−3.744	−3.746	−3.671	−3.505
1.02	−1.627	−3.039	−3.422	−3.595	−3.705	−3.718	−3.647	−3.484
1.05	−1.359	−2.034	−3.030	−3.398	−3.583	−3.632	−3.575	−3.420
1.10	−1.120	−1.487	−2.203	−2.965	−3.353	−3.484	−3.453	−3.315
1.15	−0.968	−1.239	−1.719	−2.479	−3.091	−3.329	−3.329	−3.211
1.20	−0.857	−1.076	−1.443	−2.079	−2.801	−3.166	−3.202	−3.107
1.30	−0.698	−0.860	−1.116	−1.560	−2.274	−2.825	−2.942	−2.899
1.40	−0.588	−0.716	−0.915	−1.253	−1.857	−2.486	−2.679	−2.692
1.50	−0.505	−0.611	−0.774	−1.046	−1.549	−2.175	−2.421	−2.486
1.60	−0.440	−0.531	−0.667	−0.894	−1.318	−1.904	−2.177	−2.285
1.70	−0.387	−0.446	−0.583	−0.777	−1.139	−1.672	−1.953	−2.091
1.80	−0.344	−0.413	−0.515	−0.683	−0.996	−1.476	−1.751	−1.908
1.90	−0.307	−0.368	−0.458	−0.606	−0.880	−1.309	−1.571	−1.736
2.00	−0.276	−0.330	−0.411	−0.541	−0.782	−1.167	−1.411	−1.577
2.20	−0.226	−0.269	−0.334	−0.437	−0.629	−0.937	−1.143	−1.295
2.40	−0.187	−0.222	−0.275	−0.359	−0.513	−0.761	−0.929	−1.058
2.60	−0.155	−0.185	−0.228	−0.297	−0.422	−0.621	−0.756	−0.858
2.80	−0.130	−0.154	−0.190	−0.246	−0.348	−0.508	−0.614	−0.689
3.00	−0.109	−0.129	−0.159	−0.205	−0.288	−0.415	−0.495	−0.545
3.50	−0.069	−0.081	−0.099	−0.127	−0.174	−0.239	−0.270	−0.264
4.00	−0.041	−0.048	−0.058	−0.072	−0.095	−0.116	−0.110	−0.061

Table E.8: Values of $(H^R)^1/RT_c$

$P_r =$	1.0000	1.2000	1.5000	2.0000	3.0000	5.0000	7.0000	10.000
T_r								
0.30	−11.062	−11.055	−11.044	−11.027	−10.992	−10.935	−10.872	−10.781
0.35	−10.640	−10.637	−10.632	−10.624	−10.609	−10.581	−10.554	−10.529
0.40	−10.121	−10.121	−10.121	−10.122	−10.123	−10.128	−10.135	−10.150
0.45	−9.525	−9.527	−9.531	−9.537	−9.549	−9.576	−9.611	−9.663
0.50	−8.888	−8.892	−8.899	−8.909	−8.932	−8.978	−9.030	−9.111
0.55	−8.238	−8.243	−8.252	−8.267	−8.298	−8.360	−8.425	−8.531
0.60	−7.596	−7.603	−7.614	−7.632	−7.669	−7.745	−7.824	−7.950
0.65	−6.980	−6.987	−6.997	−7.017	−7.059	−7.147	−7.239	−7.381
0.70	−6.388	−6.395	−6.407	−6.429	−6.475	−6.574	−6.677	−6.837
0.75	−5.824	−5.832	−5.845	−5.868	−5.918	−6.027	−6.142	−6.318
0.80	−5.285	−5.293	−5.306	−5.330	−5.385	−5.506	−5.632	−5.824
0.85	−4.763	−4.771	−4.784	−4.810	−4.872	−5.000	−5.149	−5.358
0.90	−4.249	−4.255	−4.268	−4.298	−4.371	−4.530	−4.688	−4.916
0.93	−3.934	−3.937	−3.951	−3.987	−4.073	−4.251	−4.422	−4.662
0.95	−3.712	−3.713	−3.730	−3.773	−3.873	−4.068	−4.248	−4.497
0.97	−3.470	−3.467	−3.492	−3.551	−3.670	−3.885	−4.077	−4.336
0.98	−3.332	−3.327	−3.363	−3.434	−3.568	−3.795	−3.992	−4.257
0.99	−3.164	−3.164	−3.223	−3.313	−3.464	−3.705	−3.909	−4.178
1.00	−2.471	−2.952	−3.065	−3.186	−3.358	−3.615	−3.825	−4.100
1.01	−1.375	−2.595	−2.880	−3.051	−3.251	−3.525	−3.742	−4.023
1.02	−1.180	−1.723	−2.650	−2.906	−3.142	−3.435	−3.661	−3.947
1.05	−0.877	−0.878	−1.496	−2.381	−2.800	−3.167	−3.418	−3.722
1.10	−0.617	−0.673	−0.617	−1.261	−2.167	−2.720	−3.023	−3.362
1.15	−0.459	−0.503	−0.487	−0.604	−1.497	−2.275	−2.641	−3.019
1.20	−0.349	−0.381	−0.381	−0.361	−0.934	−1.840	−2.273	−2.692
1.30	−0.203	−0.218	−0.218	−0.178	−0.300	−1.066	−1.592	−2.086
1.40	−0.111	−0.115	−0.128	−0.070	−0.044	−0.504	−1.012	−1.547
1.50	−0.049	−0.046	−0.032	0.008	0.078	−0.142	−0.556	−1.080
1.60	−0.005	0.004	0.023	0.065	0.151	0.082	−0.217	−0.689
1.70	0.027	0.040	0.063	0.109	0.202	0.223	0.028	−0.369
1.80	0.051	0.067	0.094	0.143	0.241	0.317	0.203	−0.112
1.90	0.070	0.088	0.117	0.169	0.271	0.381	0.330	0.092
2.00	0.085	0.105	0.136	0.190	0.295	0.428	0.424	0.255
2.20	0.106	0.128	0.163	0.221	0.331	0.493	0.551	0.489
2.40	0.120	0.144	0.181	0.242	0.356	0.535	0.631	0.645
2.60	0.130	0.156	0.194	0.257	0.376	0.567	0.687	0.754
2.80	0.137	0.164	0.204	0.269	0.391	0.591	0.729	0.836
3.00	0.142	0.170	0.211	0.278	0.403	0.611	0.763	0.899
3.50	0.152	0.181	0.224	0.294	0.425	0.650	0.827	1.015
4.00	0.158	0.188	0.233	0.306	0.442	0.680	0.874	1.097

Table E.9: Values of $(S^R)^0/R$

$P_r =$ T_r	0.0100	0.0500	0.1000	0.2000	0.4000	0.6000	0.8000	1.0000
0.30	−11.614	−10.008	−9.319	−8.635	−7.961	−7.574	−7.304	−7.099
0.35	−11.185	−9.579	−8.890	−8.205	−7.529	−7.140	−6.869	−6.663
0.40	−10.802	−9.196	−8.506	−7.821	−7.144	−6.755	−6.483	−6.275
0.45	−10.453	−8.847	−8.157	−7.472	−6.794	−6.404	−6.132	−5.924
0.50	−10.137	−8.531	−7.841	−7.156	−6.479	−6.089	−5.816	−5.608
0.55	−0.038	−8.245	−7.555	−6.870	−6.193	−5.803	−5.531	−5.324
0.60	−0.029	−7.983	−7.294	−6.610	−5.933	−5.544	−5.273	−5.066
0.65	−0.023	−0.122	−7.052	−6.368	−5.694	−5.306	−5.036	−4.830
0.70	−0.018	−0.096	−0.206	−6.140	−5.467	−5.082	−4.814	−4.610
0.75	−0.015	−0.078	−0.164	−5.917	−5.248	−4.866	−4.600	−4.399
0.80	−0.013	−0.064	−0.134	−0.294	−5.026	−4.694	−4.388	−4.191
0.85	−0.011	−0.054	−0.111	−0.239	−4.785	−4.418	−4.166	−3.976
0.90	−0.009	−0.046	−0.094	−0.199	−0.463	−4.145	−3.912	−3.738
0.93	−0.008	−0.042	−0.085	−0.179	−0.408	−0.750	−3.723	−3.569
0.95	−0.008	−0.039	−0.080	−0.168	−0.377	−0.671	−3.556	−3.433
0.97	−0.007	−0.037	−0.075	−0.157	−0.350	−0.607	−1.056	−3.259
0.98	−0.007	−0.036	−0.073	−0.153	−0.337	−0.580	−0.971	−3.142
0.99	−0.007	−0.035	−0.071	−0.148	−0.326	−0.555	−0.903	−2.972
1.00	−0.007	−0.034	−0.069	−0.144	−0.315	−0.532	−0.847	−2.178
1.01	−0.007	−0.033	−0.067	−0.139	−0.304	−0.510	−0.799	−1.391
1.02	−0.006	−0.032	−0.065	−0.135	−0.294	−0.491	−0.757	−1.225
1.05	−0.006	−0.030	−0.060	−0.124	−0.267	−0.439	−0.656	−0.965
1.10	−0.005	−0.026	−0.053	−0.108	−0.230	−0.371	−0.537	−0.742
1.15	−0.005	−0.023	−0.047	−0.096	−0.201	−0.319	−0.452	−0.607
1.20	−0.004	−0.021	−0.042	−0.085	−0.177	−0.277	−0.389	−0.512
1.30	−0.003	−0.017	−0.033	−0.068	−0.140	−0.217	−0.298	−0.385
1.40	−0.003	−0.014	−0.027	−0.056	−0.114	−0.174	−0.237	−0.303
1.50	−0.002	−0.011	−0.023	−0.046	−0.094	−0.143	−0.194	−0.246
1.60	−0.002	−0.010	−0.019	−0.039	−0.079	−0.120	−0.162	−0.204
1.70	−0.002	−0.008	−0.017	−0.033	−0.067	−0.102	−0.137	−0.172
1.80	−0.001	−0.007	−0.014	−0.029	−0.058	−0.088	−0.117	−0.147
1.90	−0.001	−0.006	−0.013	−0.025	−0.051	−0.076	−0.102	−0.127
2.00	−0.001	−0.006	−0.011	−0.022	−0.044	−0.067	−0.089	−0.111
2.20	−0.001	−0.004	−0.009	−0.018	−0.035	−0.053	−0.070	−0.087
2.40	−0.001	−0.004	−0.007	−0.014	−0.028	−0.042	−0.056	−0.070
2.60	−0.001	−0.003	−0.006	−0.012	−0.023	−0.035	−0.046	−0.058
2.80	−0.000	−0.002	−0.005	−0.010	−0.020	−0.029	−0.039	−0.048
3.00	−0.000	−0.002	−0.004	−0.008	−0.017	−0.025	−0.033	−0.041
3.50	−0.000	−0.001	−0.003	−0.006	−0.012	−0.017	−0.023	−0.029
4.00	−0.000	−0.001	−0.002	−0.004	−0.009	−0.013	−0.017	−0.021

Table E.10: Values of $(S^R)^1/R$

$P_r =$	0.0100	0.0500	0.1000	0.2000	0.4000	0.6000	0.8000	1.0000
T_r								
0.30	*−16.782*	*−16.774*	*−16.764*	*−16.744*	*−16.705*	*−16.665*	*−16.626*	−16.586
0.35	*−15.413*	*−15.408*	*−15.401*	*−15.387*	*−15.359*	*−15.333*	*−15.305*	−15.278
0.40	*−13.990*	*−13.986*	*−13.981*	*−13.972*	*−13.953*	*−13.934*	*−13.915*	−13.896
0.45	*−12.564*	*−12.561*	*−12.558*	*−12.551*	*−12.537*	*−12.523*	*−12.509*	−12.496
0.50	*−11.202*	*−11.200*	*−11.197*	*−11.092*	*−11.082*	*−11.172*	*−11.162*	−11.153
0.55	−0.115	*−9.948*	*−9.946*	*−9.942*	*−9.935*	*−9.928*	*−9.921*	−9.914
0.60	−0.078	*−8.828*	*−8.826*	*−8.823*	*−8.817*	*−8.811*	*−8.806*	−8.799
0.65	−0.055	−0.309	*−7.832*	*−7.829*	*−7.824*	*−7.819*	*−7.815*	−7.510
0.70	−0.040	−0.216	−0.491	*−6.951*	*−6.945*	*−6.941*	*−6.937*	−6.933
0.75	−0.029	−0.156	−0.340	*−6.173*	*−6.167*	*−6.162*	*−6.158*	−6.155
0.80	−0.022	−0.116	−0.246	−0.578	*−5.475*	*−5.468*	*−5.462*	−5.458
0.85	−0.017	−0.088	−0.183	−0.400	*−4.853*	*−4.841*	*−4.832*	−4.826
0.90	−0.013	−0.068	−0.140	−0.301	−0.744	*−4.269*	*−4.249*	−4.238
0.93	−0.011	−0.058	−0.120	−0.254	−0.593	−1.219	*−3.914*	−3.894
0.95	−0.010	−0.053	−0.109	−0.228	−0.517	−0.961	*−3.697*	−3.658
0.97	−0.010	−0.048	−0.099	−0.206	−0.456	−0.797	−1.570	−3.406
0.98	−0.009	−0.046	−0.094	−0.196	−0.429	−0.734	−1.270	−3.264
0.99	−0.009	−0.044	−0.090	−0.186	−0.405	−0.680	−1.098	−3.093
1.00	−0.008	−0.042	−0.086	−0.177	−0.382	−0.632	−0.977	−2.399
1.01	−0.008	−0.040	−0.082	−0.169	−0.361	−0.590	−0.883	−1.306
1.02	−0.008	−0.039	−0.078	−0.161	−0.342	−0.552	−0.807	−1.113
1.05	−0.007	−0.034	−0.069	−0.140	−0.292	−0.460	−0.642	−0.820
1.10	−0.005	−0.028	−0.055	−0.112	−0.229	−0.350	−0.470	−0.577
1.15	−0.005	−0.023	−0.045	−0.091	−0.183	−0.275	−0.361	−0.437
1.20	−0.004	−0.019	−0.037	−0.075	−0.149	−0.220	−0.286	−0.343
1.30	−0.003	−0.013	−0.026	−0.052	−0.102	−0.148	−0.190	−0.226
1.40	−0.002	−0.010	−0.019	−0.037	−0.072	−0.104	−0.133	−0.158
1.50	−0.001	−0.007	−0.014	−0.027	−0.053	−0.076	−0.097	−0.115
1.60	−0.001	−0.005	−0.011	−0.021	−0.040	−0.057	−0.073	−0.086
1.70	−0.001	−0.004	−0.008	−0.016	−0.031	−0.044	−0.056	−0.067
1.80	−0.001	−0.003	−0.006	−0.013	−0.024	−0.035	−0.044	−0.053
1.90	−0.001	−0.003	−0.005	−0.010	−0.019	−0.028	−0.036	−0.043
2.00	−0.000	−0.002	−0.004	−0.008	−0.016	−0.023	−0.029	−0.035
2.20	−0.000	−0.001	−0.003	−0.006	−0.011	−0.016	−0.021	−0.025
2.40	−0.000	−0.001	−0.002	−0.004	−0.008	−0.012	−0.015	−0.019
2.60	−0.000	−0.001	−0.002	−0.003	−0.006	−0.009	−0.012	−0.015
2.80	−0.000	−0.001	−0.001	−0.003	−0.005	−0.008	−0.010	−0.012
3.00	−0.000	−0.001	−0.001	−0.002	−0.004	−0.006	−0.008	−0.010
3.50	−0.000	−0.000	−0.001	−0.001	−0.003	−0.004	−0.006	−0.007
4.00	−0.000	−0.000	−0.001	−0.001	−0.002	−0.003	−0.005	−0.006

Table E.11: Values of $(S^R)^0/R$

$P_r =$ T_r	1.0000	1.2000	1.5000	2.0000	3.0000	5.0000	7.0000	10.000
0.30	−7.099	−6.935	−6.740	−6.497	−6.180	−5.847	−5.683	−5.578
0.35	−6.663	−6.497	−6.299	−6.052	−5.728	−5.376	−5.194	−5.060
0.40	−6.275	−6.109	−5.909	−5.660	−5.330	−4.967	−4.772	−4.619
0.45	−5.924	−5.757	−5.557	−5.306	−4.974	−4.603	−4.401	−4.234
0.50	−5.608	−5.441	−5.240	−4.989	−4.656	−4.282	−4.074	−3.899
0.55	−5.324	−5.157	−4.956	−4.706	−4.373	−3.998	−3.788	−3.607
0.60	−5.066	−4.900	−4.700	−4.451	−4.120	−3.747	−3.537	−3.353
0.65	−4.830	−4.665	−4.467	−4.220	−3.892	−3.523	−3.315	−3.131
0.70	−4.610	−4.446	−4.250	−4.007	−3.684	−3.322	−3.117	−2.935
0.75	−4.399	−4.238	−4.045	−3.807	−3.491	−3.138	−2.939	−2.761
0.80	−4.191	−4.034	−3.846	−3.615	−3.310	−2.970	−2.777	−2.605
0.85	−3.976	−3.825	−3.646	−3.425	−3.135	−2.812	−2.629	−2.463
0.90	−3.738	−3.599	−3.434	−3.231	−2.964	−2.663	−2.491	−2.334
0.93	−3.569	−3.444	−3.295	−3.108	−2.860	−2.577	−2.412	−2.262
0.95	−3.433	−3.326	−3.193	−3.023	−2.790	−2.520	−2.362	−2.215
0.97	−3.259	−3.188	−3.081	−2.932	−2.719	−2.463	−2.312	−2.170
0.98	−3.142	−3.106	−3.019	−2.884	−2.682	−2.436	−2.287	−2.148
0.99	−2.972	−3.010	−2.953	−2.835	−2.646	−2.408	−2.263	−2.126
1.00	−2.178	−2.893	−2.879	−2.784	−2.609	−2.380	−2.239	−2.105
1.01	−1.391	−2.736	−2.798	−2.730	−2.571	−2.352	−2.215	−2.083
1.02	−1.225	−2.495	−2.706	−2.673	−2.533	−2.325	−2.191	−2.062
1.05	−0.965	−1.523	−2.328	−2.483	−2.415	−2.242	−2.121	−2.001
1.10	−0.742	−1.012	−1.557	−2.081	−2.202	−2.104	−2.007	−1.903
1.15	−0.607	−0.790	−1.126	−1.649	−1.968	−1.966	−1.897	−1.810
1.20	−0.512	−0.651	−0.890	−1.308	−1.727	−1.827	−1.789	−1.722
1.30	−0.385	−0.478	−0.628	−0.891	−1.299	−1.554	−1.581	−1.556
1.40	−0.303	−0.375	−0.478	−0.663	−0.990	−1.303	−1.386	−1.402
1.50	−0.246	−0.299	−0.381	−0.520	−0.777	−1.088	−1.208	−1.260
1.60	−0.204	−0.247	−0.312	−0.421	−0.628	−0.913	−1.050	−1.130
1.70	−0.172	−0.208	−0.261	−0.350	−0.519	−0.773	−0.915	−1.013
1.80	−0.147	−0.177	−0.222	−0.296	−0.438	−0.661	−0.799	−0.908
1.90	−0.127	−0.153	−0.191	−0.255	−0.375	−0.570	−0.702	−0.815
2.00	−0.111	−0.134	−0.167	−0.221	−0.625	−0.497	−0.620	−0.733
2.20	−0.087	−0.105	−0.130	−0.172	−0.251	−0.388	−0.492	−0.599
2.40	−0.070	−0.084	−0.104	−0.138	−0.201	−0.311	−0.399	−0.496
2.60	−0.058	−0.069	−0.086	−0.113	−0.164	−0.255	−0.329	−0.416
2.80	−0.048	−0.058	−0.072	−0.094	−0.137	−0.213	−0.277	−0.353
3.00	−0.041	−0.049	−0.061	−0.080	−0.116	−0.181	−0.236	−0.303
3.50	−0.029	−0.034	−0.042	−0.056	−0.081	−0.126	−0.166	−0.216
4.00	−0.021	−0.025	−0.031	−0.041	−0.059	−0.093	−0.123	−0.162

Table E.12: Values of $(S^R)^1/R$

T_r \ $P_r =$	1.0000	1.2000	1.5000	2.0000	3.0000	5.0000	7.0000	10.000
0.30	−16.586	−16.547	−16.488	−16.390	−16.195	−15.837	−15.468	−14.925
0.35	−15.278	−15.251	−15.211	−15.144	−15.011	−14.751	−14.496	−14.153
0.40	−13.896	−13.877	−13.849	−13.803	−13.714	−13.541	−13.376	−13.144
0.45	−12.496	−12.482	−12.462	−12.430	−12.367	−12.248	−12.145	−11.999
0.50	−11.153	−11.143	−11.129	−11.107	−11.063	−10.985	−10.920	−10.836
0.55	−9.914	−9.907	−9.897	−9.882	−9.853	−9.806	−9.769	−9.732
0.60	−8.799	−8.794	−8.787	−8.777	−8.760	−8.736	−8.723	−8.720
0.65	−7.810	−7.807	−7.801	−7.794	−7.784	−7.779	−7.785	−7.811
0.70	−6.933	−6.930	−6.926	−6.922	−6.919	−6.929	−6.952	−7.002
0.75	−6.155	−6.152	−6.149	−6.147	−6.149	−6.174	−6.213	−6.285
0.80	−5.458	−5.455	−5.453	−5.452	−5.461	−5.501	−5.555	−5.648
0.85	−4.826	−4.822	−4.820	−4.822	−4.839	−4.898	−4.969	−5.082
0.90	−4.238	−4.232	−4.230	−4.236	−4.267	−4.351	−4.442	−4.578
0.93	−3.894	−3.885	−3.884	−3.896	−3.941	−4.046	−4.151	−4.300
0.95	−3.658	−3.647	−3.648	−3.669	−3.728	−3.851	−3.966	−4.125
0.97	−3.406	−3.391	−3.401	−3.437	−3.517	−3.661	−3.788	−3.957
0.98	−3.264	−3.247	−3.268	−3.318	−3.412	−3.569	−3.701	−3.875
0.99	−3.093	−3.082	−3.126	−3.195	−3.306	−3.477	−3.616	−3.796
1.00	−2.399	−2.868	−2.967	−3.067	−3.200	−3.387	−3.532	−3.717
1.01	−1.306	−2.513	−2.784	−2.933	−3.094	−3.297	−3.450	−3.640
1.02	−1.113	−1.655	−2.557	−2.790	−2.986	−3.209	−3.369	−3.565
1.05	−0.820	−0.831	−1.443	−2.283	−2.655	−2.949	−3.134	−3.348
1.10	−0.577	−0.640	−0.618	−1.241	−2.067	−2.534	−2.767	−3.013
1.15	−0.437	−0.489	−0.502	−0.654	−1.471	−2.138	−2.428	−2.708
1.20	−0.343	−0.385	−0.412	−0.447	−0.991	−1.767	−2.115	−2.430
1.30	−0.226	−0.254	−0.282	−0.300	−0.481	−1.147	−1.569	−1.944
1.40	−0.158	−0.178	−0.200	−0.220	−0.290	−0.730	−1.138	−1.544
1.50	−0.115	−0.130	−0.147	−0.166	−0.206	−0.479	−0.823	−1.222
1.60	−0.086	−0.098	−0.112	−0.129	−0.159	−0.334	−0.604	−0.969
1.70	−0.067	−0.076	−0.087	−0.102	−0.127	−0.248	−0.456	−0.775
1.80	−0.053	−0.060	−0.070	−0.083	−0.105	−0.195	−0.355	−0.628
1.90	−0.043	−0.049	−0.057	−0.069	−0.089	−0.160	−0.286	−0.518
2.00	−0.035	−0.040	−0.048	−0.058	−0.077	−0.136	−0.238	−0.434
2.20	−0.025	−0.029	−0.035	−0.043	−0.060	−0.105	−0.178	−0.322
2.40	−0.019	−0.022	−0.027	−0.034	−0.048	−0.086	−0.143	−0.254
2.60	−0.015	−0.018	−0.021	−0.028	−0.041	−0.074	−0.120	−0.210
2.80	−0.012	−0.014	−0.018	−0.023	−0.025	−0.065	−0.104	−0.180
3.00	−0.010	−0.012	−0.015	−0.020	−0.031	−0.058	−0.093	−0.158
3.50	−0.007	−0.009	−0.011	−0.015	−0.024	−0.046	−0.073	−0.122
4.00	−0.006	−0.007	−0.009	−0.012	−0.020	−0.038	−0.060	−0.100

Table E.13: Values of ϕ^0

$P_r =$ / T_r	0.0100	0.0500	0.1000	0.2000	0.4000	0.6000	0.8000	1.0000
0.30	*0.0002*	*0.0000*	*0.0000*	*0.0000*	*0.0000*	*0.0000*	*0.0000*	0.0000
0.35	*0.0034*	*0.0007*	*0.0003*	*0.0002*	*0.0001*	*0.0001*	*0.0001*	0.0000
0.40	*0.0272*	*0.0055*	*0.0028*	*0.0014*	*0.0007*	*0.0005*	*0.0004*	0.0003
0.45	*0.1321*	*0.0266*	*0.0135*	*0.0069*	*0.0036*	*0.0025*	*0.0020*	0.0016
0.50	*0.4529*	*0.0912*	*0.0461*	*0.0235*	*0.0122*	*0.0085*	*0.0067*	0.0055
0.55	0.9817	*0.2432*	*0.1227*	*0.0625*	*0.0325*	*0.0225*	*0.0176*	0.0146
0.60	0.9840	*0.5383*	*0.2716*	*0.1384*	*0.0718*	*0.0497*	*0.0386*	0.0321
0.65	0.9886	0.9419	*0.5212*	*0.2655*	*0.1374*	*0.0948*	*0.0738*	0.0611
0.70	0.9908	0.9528	0.9057	*0.4560*	*0.2360*	*0.1626*	*0.1262*	0.1045
0.75	0.9931	0.9616	0.9226	*0.7178*	*0.3715*	*0.2559*	*0.1982*	0.1641
0.80	0.9931	0.9683	0.9354	0.8730	*0.5445*	*0.3750*	*0.2904*	0.2404
0.85	0.9954	0.9727	0.9462	0.8933	*0.7534*	*0.5188*	*0.4018*	0.3319
0.90	0.9954	0.9772	0.9550	0.9099	0.8204	*0.6823*	*0.5297*	0.4375
0.93	0.9954	0.9795	0.9594	0.9183	0.8375	0.7551	*0.6109*	0.5058
0.95	0.9954	0.9817	0.9616	0.9226	0.8472	0.7709	*0.6668*	0.5521
0.97	0.9954	0.9817	0.9638	0.9268	0.8570	0.7852	0.7112	0.5984
0.98	0.9954	0.9817	0.9638	0.9290	0.8610	0.7925	0.7211	0.6223
0.99	0.9977	0.9840	0.9661	0.9311	0.8650	0.7980	0.7295	0.6442
1.00	0.9977	0.9840	0.9661	0.9333	0.8690	0.8035	0.7379	0.6668
1.01	0.9977	0.9840	0.9683	0.9354	0.8730	0.8110	0.7464	0.6792
1.02	0.9977	0.9840	0.9683	0.9376	0.8770	0.8166	0.7551	0.6902
1.05	0.9977	0.9863	0.9705	0.9441	0.8872	0.8318	0.7762	0.7194
1.10	0.9977	0.9886	0.9750	0.9506	0.9016	0.8531	0.8072	0.7586
1.15	0.9977	0.9886	0.9795	0.9572	0.9141	0.8730	0.8318	0.7907
1.20	0.9977	0.9908	0.9817	0.9616	0.9247	0.8892	0.8531	0.8166
1.30	0.9977	0.9931	0.9863	0.9705	0.9419	0.9141	0.8872	0.8590
1.40	0.9977	0.9931	0.9886	0.9772	0.9550	0.9333	0.9120	0.8892
1.50	1.0000	0.9954	0.9908	0.9817	0.9638	0.9462	0.9290	0.9141
1.60	1.0000	0.9954	0.9931	0.9863	0.9727	0.9572	0.9441	0.9311
1.70	1.0000	0.9977	0.9954	0.9886	0.9772	0.9661	0.9550	0.9462
1.80	1.0000	0.9977	0.9954	0.9908	0.9817	0.9727	0.9661	0.9572
1.90	1.0000	0.9977	0.9954	0.9931	0.9863	0.9795	0.9727	0.9661
2.00	1.0000	0.9977	0.9977	0.9954	0.9886	0.9840	0.9795	0.9727
2.20	1.0000	1.0000	0.9977	0.9977	0.9931	0.9908	0.9886	0.9840
2.40	1.0000	1.0000	1.0000	0.9977	0.9977	0.9954	0.9931	0.9931
2.60	1.0000	1.0000	1.0000	1.0000	1.0000	0.9977	0.9977	0.9977
2.80	1.0000	1.0000	1.0000	1.0000	1.0000	1.0000	1.0023	1.0023
3.00	1.0000	1.0000	1.0000	1.0000	1.0023	1.0023	1.0046	1.0046
3.50	1.0000	1.0000	1.0000	1.0023	1.0023	1.0046	1.0069	1.0093
4.00	1.0000	1.0000	1.0000	1.0023	1.0046	1.0069	1.0093	1.0116

Table E.14: Values of ϕ^1

$P_r =$ / T_r	0.0100	0.0500	0.1000	0.2000	0.4000	0.6000	0.8000	1.0000
0.30	*0.0000*	*0.0000*	*0.0000*	*0.0000*	*0.0000*	*0.0000*	*0.0000*	0.0000
0.35	*0.0000*	*0.0000*	*0.0000*	*0.0000*	*0.0000*	*0.0000*	*0.0000*	0.0000
0.40	*0.0000*	*0.0000*	*0.0000*	*0.0000*	*0.0000*	*0.0000*	*0.0000*	0.0000
0.45	*0.0002*	*0.0002*	*0.0002*	*0.0002*	*0.0002*	*0.0002*	*0.0002*	0.0002
0.50	*0.0014*	*0.0014*	*0.0014*	*0.0014*	*0.0014*	*0.0014*	*0.0013*	0.0013
0.55	0.9705	*0.0069*	*0.0068*	*0.0068*	*0.0066*	*0.0065*	*0.0064*	0.0063
0.60	0.9795	*0.0227*	*0.0226*	*0.0223*	*0.0220*	*0.0216*	*0.0213*	0.0210
0.65	0.9863	0.9311	*0.0572*	*0.0568*	*0.0559*	*0.0551*	*0.0543*	0.0535
0.70	0.9908	0.9528	0.9036	*0.1182*	*0.1163*	*0.1147*	*0.1131*	0.1116
0.75	0.9931	0.9683	0.9332	*0.2112*	*0.2078*	*0.2050*	*0.2022*	0.1994
0.80	0.9954	0.9772	0.9550	0.9057	*0.3302*	*0.3257*	*0.3212*	0.3168
0.85	0.9977	0.9863	0.9705	0.9375	*0.4774*	*0.4708*	*0.4654*	0.4590
0.90	0.9977	0.9908	0.9795	0.9594	0.9141	*0.6323*	*0.6250*	0.6165
0.93	0.9977	0.9931	0.9840	0.9705	0.9354	0.8953	*0.7227*	0.7144
0.95	0.9977	0.9931	0.9885	0.9750	0.9484	0.9183	*0.7888*	0.7797
0.97	1.0000	0.9954	0.9908	0.9795	0.9594	0.9354	0.9078	0.8413
0.98	1.0000	0.9954	0.9908	0.9817	0.9638	0.9440	0.9225	0.8729
0.99	1.0000	0.9954	0.9931	0.9840	0.9683	0.9528	0.9332	0.9036
1.00	1.0000	0.9977	0.9931	0.9863	0.9727	0.9594	0.9440	0.9311
1.01	1.0000	0.9977	0.9931	0.9885	0.9772	0.9638	0.9528	0.9462
1.02	1.0000	0.9977	0.9954	0.9908	0.9795	0.9705	0.9616	0.9572
1.05	1.0000	0.9977	0.9977	0.9954	0.9885	0.9863	0.9840	0.9840
1.10	1.0000	1.0000	1.0000	1.0000	1.0023	1.0046	1.0093	1.0163
1.15	1.0000	1.0000	1.0023	1.0046	1.0116	1.0186	1.0257	1.0375
1.20	1.0000	1.0023	1.0046	1.0069	1.0163	1.0280	1.0399	1.0544
1.30	1.0000	1.0023	1.0069	1.0116	1.0257	1.0399	1.0544	1.0716
1.40	1.0000	1.0046	1.0069	1.0139	1.0304	1.0471	1.0642	1.0815
1.50	1.0000	1.0046	1.0069	1.0163	1.0328	1.0496	1.0666	1.0865
1.60	1.0000	1.0046	1.0069	1.0163	1.0328	1.0496	1.0691	1.0865
1.70	1.0000	1.0046	1.0093	1.0163	1.0328	1.0496	1.0691	1.0865
1.80	1.0000	1.0046	1.0069	1.0163	1.0328	1.0496	1.0666	1.0840
1.90	1.0000	1.0046	1.0069	1.0163	1.0328	1.0496	1.0666	1.0815
2.00	1.0000	1.0046	1.0069	1.0163	1.0304	1.0471	1.0642	1.0815
2.20	1.0000	1.0046	1.0069	1.0139	1.0304	1.0447	1.0593	1.0765
2.40	1.0000	1.0046	1.0069	1.0139	1.0280	1.0423	1.0568	1.0716
2.60	1.0000	1.0023	1.0069	1.0139	1.0257	1.0399	1.0544	1.0666
2.80	1.0000	1.0023	1.0069	1.0116	1.0257	1.0375	1.0496	1.0642
3.00	1.0000	1.0023	1.0069	1.0116	1.0233	1.0352	1.0471	1.0593
3.50	1.0000	1.0023	1.0046	1.0023	1.0209	1.0304	1.0423	1.0520
4.00	1.0000	1.0023	1.0046	1.0093	1.0186	1.0280	1.0375	1.0471

Table E.15: Values of ϕ^0

$P_r =$ T_r	1.0000	1.2000	1.5000	2.0000	3.0000	5.0000	7.0000	10.000
0.30	0.0000	0.0000	0.0000	0.0000	0.0000	0.0000	0.0000	0.0000
0.35	0.0000	0.0000	0.0000	0.0000	0.0000	0.0000	0.0000	0.0000
0.40	0.0003	0.0003	0.0003	0.0002	0.0002	0.0002	0.0002	0.0003
0.45	0.0016	0.0014	0.0012	0.0010	0.0008	0.0008	0.0009	0.0012
0.50	0.0055	0.0048	0.0041	0.0034	0.0028	0.0025	0.0027	0.0034
0.55	0.0146	0.0127	0.0107	0.0089	0.0072	0.0063	0.0066	0.0080
0.60	0.0321	0.0277	0.0234	0.0193	0.0154	0.0132	0.0135	0.0160
0.65	0.0611	0.0527	0.0445	0.0364	0.0289	0.0244	0.0245	0.0282
0.70	0.1045	0.0902	0.0759	0.0619	0.0488	0.0406	0.0402	0.0453
0.75	0.1641	0.1413	0.1188	0.0966	0.0757	0.0625	0.0610	0.0673
0.80	0.2404	0.2065	0.1738	0.1409	0.1102	0.0899	0.0867	0.0942
0.85	0.3319	0.2858	0.2399	0.1945	0.1517	0.1227	0.1175	0.1256
0.90	0.4375	0.3767	0.3162	0.2564	0.1995	0.1607	0.1524	0.1611
0.93	0.5058	0.4355	0.3656	0.2972	0.2307	0.1854	0.1754	0.1841
0.95	0.5521	0.4764	0.3999	0.3251	0.2523	0.2028	0.1910	0.2000
0.97	0.5984	0.5164	0.4345	0.3532	0.2748	0.2203	0.2075	0.2163
0.98	0.6223	0.5370	0.4529	0.3681	0.2864	0.2296	0.2158	0.2244
0.99	0.6442	0.5572	0.4699	0.3828	0.2978	0.2388	0.2244	0.2328
1.00	0.6668	0.5781	0.4875	0.3972	0.3097	0.2483	0.2328	0.2415
1.01	0.6792	0.5970	0.5047	0.4121	0.3214	0.2576	0.2415	0.2500
1.02	0.6902	0.6166	0.5224	0.4266	0.3334	0.2673	0.2506	0.2582
1.05	0.7194	0.6607	0.5728	0.4710	0.3690	0.2958	0.2773	0.2844
1.10	0.7586	0.7112	0.6412	0.5408	0.4285	0.3451	0.3228	0.3296
1.15	0.7907	0.7499	0.6918	0.6026	0.4875	0.3954	0.3690	0.3750
1.20	0.8166	0.7834	0.7328	0.6546	0.5420	0.4446	0.4150	0.4198
1.30	0.8590	0.8318	0.7943	0.7345	0.6383	0.5383	0.5058	0.5093
1.40	0.8892	0.8690	0.8395	0.7925	0.7145	0.6237	0.5902	0.5943
1.50	0.9141	0.8974	0.8730	0.8375	0.7745	0.6966	0.6668	0.6714
1.60	0.9311	0.9183	0.8995	0.8710	0.8222	0.7586	0.7328	0.7430
1.70	0.9462	0.9354	0.9204	0.8995	0.8610	0.8091	0.7907	0.8054
1.80	0.9572	0.9484	0.9376	0.9204	0.8913	0.8531	0.8414	0.8590
1.90	0.9661	0.9594	0.9506	0.9376	0.9162	0.8872	0.8831	0.9057
2.00	0.9727	0.9683	0.9616	0.9528	0.9354	0.9183	0.9183	0.9462
2.20	0.9840	0.9817	0.9795	0.9727	0.9661	0.9616	0.9727	1.0093
2.40	0.9931	0.9908	0.9908	0.9886	0.9863	0.9931	1.0116	1.0568
2.60	0.9977	0.9977	0.9977	0.9977	1.0023	1.0162	1.0399	1.0889
2.80	1.0023	1.0023	1.0046	1.0069	1.0116	1.0328	1.0593	1.1117
3.00	1.0046	1.0069	1.0069	1.0116	1.0209	1.0423	1.0740	1.1298
3.50	1.0093	1.0116	1.0139	1.0186	1.0304	1.0593	1.0914	1.1508
4.00	1.0116	1.0139	1.0162	1.0233	1.0375	1.0666	1.0990	1.1588

Table E.16: Values of ϕ^1

$P_r =$ / T_r	1.0000	1.2000	1.5000	2.0000	3.0000	5.0000	7.0000	10.000
0.30	0.0000	0.0000	0.0000	0.0000	0.0000	0.0000	0.0000	0.0000
0.35	0.0000	0.0000	0.0000	0.0000	0.0000	0.0000	0.0000	0.0000
0.40	0.0000	0.0000	0.0000	0.0000	0.0000	0.0000	0.0000	0.0000
0.45	0.0002	0.0002	0.0002	0.0002	0.0001	0.0001	0.0001	0.0001
0.50	0.0013	0.0013	0.0013	0.0012	0.0011	0.0009	0.0008	0.0006
0.55	0.0063	0.0062	0.0061	0.0058	0.0053	0.0045	0.0039	0.0031
0.60	0.0210	0.0207	0.0202	0.0194	0.0179	0.0154	0.0133	0.0108
0.65	0.0536	0.0527	0.0516	0.0497	0.0461	0.0401	0.0350	0.0289
0.70	0.1117	0.1102	0.1079	0.1040	0.0970	0.0851	0.0752	0.0629
0.75	0.1995	0.1972	0.1932	0.1871	0.1754	0.1552	0.1387	0.1178
0.80	0.3170	0.3133	0.3076	0.2978	0.2812	0.2512	0.2265	0.1954
0.85	0.4592	0.4539	0.4457	0.4325	0.4093	0.3698	0.3365	0.2951
0.90	0.6166	0.6095	0.5998	0.5834	0.5546	0.5058	0.4645	0.4130
0.93	0.7145	0.7063	0.6950	0.6761	0.6457	0.5916	0.5470	0.4898
0.95	0.7798	0.7691	0.7568	0.7379	0.7063	0.6501	0.6026	0.5432
0.97	0.8414	0.8318	0.8185	0.7998	0.7656	0.7096	0.6607	0.5984
0.98	0.8730	0.8630	0.8492	0.8298	0.7962	0.7379	0.6887	0.6266
0.99	0.9036	0.8913	0.8790	0.8590	0.8241	0.7674	0.7178	0.6546
1.00	0.9311	0.9204	0.9078	0.8872	0.8531	0.7962	0.7464	0.6823
1.01	0.9462	0.9462	0.9333	0.9162	0.8831	0.8241	0.7745	0.7096
1.02	0.9572	0.9661	0.9594	0.9419	0.9099	0.8531	0.8035	0.7379
1.05	0.9840	0.9954	1.0186	1.0162	0.9886	0.9354	0.8872	0.8222
1.10	1.0162	1.0280	1.0593	1.0990	1.1015	1.0617	1.0186	0.9572
1.15	1.0375	1.0520	1.0814	1.1376	1.1858	1.1722	1.1403	1.0864
1.20	1.0544	1.0691	1.0990	1.1588	1.2388	1.2647	1.2474	1.2050
1.30	1.0715	1.0914	1.1194	1.1776	1.2853	1.3868	1.4125	1.4061
1.40	1.0814	1.0990	1.1298	1.1858	1.2942	1.4488	1.5171	1.5524
1.50	1.0864	1.1041	1.1350	1.1858	1.2942	1.4689	1.5740	1.6520
1.60	1.0864	1.1041	1.1350	1.1858	1.2883	1.4689	1.5996	1.7140
1.70	1.0864	1.1041	1.1324	1.1803	1.2794	1.4622	1.6033	1.7458
1.80	1.0839	1.1015	1.1298	1.1749	1.2706	1.4488	1.5959	1.7620
1.90	1.0814	1.0990	1.1272	1.1695	1.2618	1.4355	1.5849	1.7620
2.00	1.0814	1.0965	1.1220	1.1641	1.2503	1.4191	1.5704	1.7539
2.20	1.0765	1.0914	1.1143	1.1535	1.2331	1.3900	1.5346	1.7219
2.40	1.0715	1.0864	1.1066	1.1429	1.2190	1.3614	1.4997	1.6866
2.60	1.0666	1.0814	1.1015	1.1350	1.2023	1.3397	1.4689	1.6482
2.80	1.0641	1.0765	1.0940	1.1272	1.1912	1.3183	1.4388	1.6144
3.00	1.0593	1.0715	1.0889	1.1194	1.1803	1.3002	1.4158	1.5813
3.50	1.0520	1.0617	1.0789	1.1041	1.1561	1.2618	1.3614	1.5101
4.00	1.0471	1.0544	1.0691	1.0914	1.1403	1.2303	1.3213	1.4555

Appendix F

Steam Tables

F.1 INTERPOLATION

When a value is required from a table at conditions which lie between listed values, interpolation is necessary. If M, the quantity sought, is a function of a single independent variable X and if linear interpolation is appropriate, as in the tables for saturated steam, then a direct proportionality exists between corresponding differences in M and in X. When M, the value at X, is intermediate between two given values, M_1 at X_1 and M_2 at X_2, then

$$M = \left(\frac{X_2 - X}{X_2 - X_1}\right) M_1 + \left(\frac{X - X_1}{X_2 - X_1}\right) M_2 \tag{F.1}$$

For example, the enthalpy of saturated vapor steam at 140.8°C is intermediate between the following values taken from Table F.1:

t	H
$t_1 = 140°\text{C}$	$H_1 = 2733.1\ \text{kJ kg}^{-1}$
$t = 140.8°\text{C}$	$H = ?$
$t_2 = 142°\text{C}$	$H_2 = 2735.6\ \text{kJ kg}^{-1}$

Substitution of values into Eq. (F.1) with $M = H$ and $t = X$ yields

$$H = \frac{1.2}{2}(2733.1) + \frac{0.8}{2}(2735.6) = 2734.1\ \text{kJ kg}$$

When M is a function of two independent variables X and Y and if linear interpolation is appropriate, as in the tables for superheated steam, then double linear interpolation is required. Data for quantity M at values of the independent variables X and Y adjacent to the given values are represented as follows:

	X_1	X	X_2
Y_1	$M_{1,1}$		$M_{1,2}$
Y		$M = ?$	
Y_2	$M_{2,1}$		$M_{2,2}$

Double linear interpolation between the given values of M is represented by

$$M = \left[\left(\frac{X_2 - X}{X_2 - X_1}\right) M_{1,1} + \left(\frac{X - X_1}{X_2 - X_1}\right) M_{1,2}\right] \frac{Y_2 - Y}{Y_2 - Y_1}$$

$$+ \left[\left(\frac{X_2 - X}{X_2 - X_1}\right) M_{2,1} + \left(\frac{X - X_1}{X_2 - X_1}\right) M_{2,2}\right] \frac{Y - Y_1}{Y_2 - Y_1} \quad \text{(F.2)}$$

Example F.1

From data in the steam tables, find the

(*a*) specific volume of superheated steam at 816 kPa and 512°C (785.15 K)

(*b*) temperature and specific entropy of superheated steam at P = 2950 kPa and H = 3150.6 kJ kg^{-1}

Solution

(*a*) The following table shows specific volumes from Table F.2 for superheated steam at conditions adjacent to those specified:

P/kPa	t = 500°C	t = 512°C	t = 550°C
800	443.17		472.49
816		V = ?	
825	429.65		458.10

Substitution of values in Eq. (F.2) with $M = V$, $X = t$, and $Y = P$ yields

$$V = \left[\frac{38}{50}(443.17) + \frac{12}{50}(472.49)\right]\frac{9}{25}$$

$$+ \left[\frac{38}{50}(429.65) + \frac{12}{50}(458.10)\right]\frac{16}{25} = 441.42 \text{ cm}^3 \text{ g}^{-1}$$

(*b*) The following table shows enthalpy data from Table F.2 for superheated steam at conditions adjacent to those specified:

P/kPa	t_1 = 350°C	t = ?	t_2 = 375°C
2900	3119.7		3177.4
2950	H_{t_1}	H = 3150.6	H_{t_2}
3000	3117.5		3175.6

Here, use of Eq. (F.2) is not convenient. Rather, for $P = 2950$ kPa, interpolate linearly at $t_1 = 350°$C for H_{t_1} and at $t_2 = 375°$C for H_{t_2}, applying Eq. (F.1) twice, first at t_1 and second at t_2, with $M = H$ and $X = P$:

$$H_{t_1} = \frac{50}{100}(3119.7) + \frac{50}{100}(3117.5) = 3118.6$$

$$H_{t_2} = \frac{50}{100}(3177.4) + \frac{50}{100}(3175.6) = 3176.5$$

A third linear interpolation between these values with $M = t$ and $X = H$ in Eq. (F.1) yields:

$$t = \frac{3176.5 - 3150.6}{3176.5 - 3118.6}(350) + \frac{3150.6 - 3118.6}{3176.5 - 3118.6}(375) = 363.82°\text{C}$$

Given this temperature, a table of entropy values can now be constructed:

P/kPa	$t = 350°$C	$t = 363.82°$C	$t = 375°$C
2900	6.7654		6.8563
2950		$S = ?$	
3000	6.7471		6.8385

Application of Eq. (6.75) with $M = S$, $X = t$, and $Y = P$ yields:

$$S = \left[\frac{11.18}{25}(6.7654) + \frac{13.82}{25}(6.8563)\right]\frac{50}{100}$$

$$+ \left[\frac{11.18}{25}(6.7471) + \frac{13.82}{25}(6.8385)\right]\frac{50}{100} = 6.8066 \text{ kJ mol}^{-1}$$

STEAM TABLES

Table F.1 Properties of Saturated Steam, SI Units

Table F.2 Properties of Superheated Steam, SI Units

All tables are generated by computer from programs[1] based on "The 1976 International Formulation Committee Formulation for Industrial Use: A Formulation of the Thermodynamic Properties of Ordinary Water Substance," as published in the *ASME Steam Tables*, 4th ed., App. I, pp. 11–29, The Am. Soc. Mech. Engrs., New York, 1979. These tables served as a world-wide standard for 30 years, and are entirely adequate for instructional purposes. However, they have been replaced by the "International Association for the Properties of Water and Steam Formulation 1997 for the Thermodynamic Properties of Water and Steam for Industrial Use." These and other newer tables are discussed by A. H. Harvey and W. T. Parry, "Keep Your Steam Tables up to Date," *Chemical Engineering Progress*, vol. 95, no. 11, p. 45, Nov., 1999.

[1]We gratefully acknowledge the contributions of Professor Charles Muckenfuss, of Debra L. Sauke, and of Eugene N. Dorsi, whose efforts produced the computer programs from which these tables derive.

Table F.1: Saturated Steam, SI Units

V = SPECIFIC VOLUME $cm^3\ g^{-1}$

U = SPECIFIC INTERNAL ENERGY $kJ\ kg^{-1}$

H = SPECIFIC ENTHALPY $kJ\ kg^{-1}$

S = SPECIFIC ENTROPY $kJ\ kg^{-1}\ K^{-1}$

			SPECIFIC VOLUME V			INTERNAL ENERGY U			ENTHALPY H			ENTROPY S		
t °C	T K	P kPa	sat. liq.	evap.	sat. vap.	sat. liq.	evap.	sat. vap.	sat. liq.	evap.	sat. vap.	sat. liq.	evap.	sat. vap.
0	273.15	0.611	1.000	206300.	206300.	-0.04	2375.7	2375.6	-0.04	2501.7	2501.6	0.0000	9.1578	9.1578
0.01	273.16	0.611	1.000	206200.	206200.	0.00	2375.6	2375.6	0.00	2501.6	2501.6	0.0000	9.1575	9.1575
1	274.15	0.657	1.000	192600.	192600.	4.17	2372.7	2376.9	4.17	2499.2	2503.4	0.0153	9.1158	9.1311
2	275.15	0.705	1.000	179900.	179900.	8.39	2369.9	2378.3	8.39	2496.8	2505.2	0.0306	9.0741	9.1047
3	276.15	0.757	1.000	168200.	168200.	12.60	2367.1	2379.7	12.60	2494.5	2507.1	0.0459	9.0326	9.0785
4	277.15	0.813	1.000	157300.	157300.	16.80	2364.3	2381.1	16.80	2492.1	2508.9	0.0611	8.9915	9.0526
5	278.15	0.872	1.000	147200.	147200.	21.01	2361.4	2382.4	21.01	2489.7	2510.7	0.0762	8.9507	9.0269
6	279.15	0.935	1.000	137800.	137800.	25.21	2358.6	2383.8	25.21	2487.4	2512.6	0.0913	8.9102	9.0014
7	280.15	1.001	1.000	129100.	129100.	29.41	2355.8	2385.2	29.41	2485.0	2514.4	0.1063	8.8699	8.9762
8	281.15	1.072	1.000	121000.	121000.	33.60	2353.0	2386.6	33.60	2482.6	2516.2	0.1213	8.8300	8.9513
9	282.15	1.147	1.000	113400.	113400.	37.80	2350.1	2387.9	37.80	2480.3	2518.1	0.1362	8.7903	8.9265
10	283.15	1.227	1.000	106400.	106400.	41.99	2347.3	2389.3	41.99	2477.9	2519.9	0.1510	8.7510	8.9020
11	284.15	1.312	1.000	99910.	99910.	46.18	2344.5	2390.7	46.19	2475.5	2521.7	0.1658	8.7119	8.8776
12	285.15	1.401	1.000	93830.	93840.	50.38	2341.7	2392.1	50.38	2473.2	2523.6	0.1805	8.6731	8.8536
13	286.15	1.497	1.001	88180.	88180.	54.56	2338.9	2393.4	54.57	2470.8	2525.4	0.1952	8.6345	8.8297
14	287.15	1.597	1.001	82900.	82900.	58.75	2336.1	2394.8	58.75	2468.5	2527.2	0.2098	8.5963	8.8060
15	288.15	1.704	1.001	77980.	77980.	62.94	2333.2	2396.2	62.94	2466.1	2529.1	0.2243	8.5582	8.7826
16	289.15	1.817	1.001	73380.	73380.	67.12	2330.4	2397.6	67.13	2463.8	2530.9	0.2388	8.5205	8.7593
17	290.15	1.936	1.001	69090.	69090.	71.31	2327.6	2398.9	71.31	2461.4	2532.7	0.2533	8.4830	8.7363
18	291.15	2.062	1.001	65090.	65090.	75.49	2324.8	2400.3	75.50	2459.0	2534.5	0.2677	8.4458	8.7135
19	292.15	2.196	1.002	61340.	61340.	79.68	2322.0	2401.7	79.68	2456.7	2536.4	0.2820	8.4088	8.6908
20	293.15	2.337	1.002	57840.	57840.	83.86	2319.2	2403.0	83.86	2454.3	2538.2	0.2963	8.3721	8.6684
21	294.15	2.485	1.002	54560.	54560.	88.04	2316.4	2404.4	88.04	2452.0	2540.0	0.3105	8.3356	8.6462
22	295.15	2.642	1.002	51490.	51490.	92.22	2313.6	2405.8	92.23	2449.6	2541.8	0.3247	8.2994	8.6241
23	296.15	2.808	1.002	48620.	48620.	96.40	2310.7	2407.1	96.41	2447.2	2543.6	0.3389	8.2634	8.6023
24	297.15	2.982	1.003	45920.	45930.	100.6	2307.9	2408.5	100.6	2444.9	2545.5	0.3530	8.2277	8.5806
25	298.15	3.166	1.003	43400.	43400.	104.8	2305.1	2409.9	104.8	2442.5	2547.3	0.3670	8.1922	8.5592
26	299.15	3.360	1.003	41030.	41030.	108.9	2302.3	2411.2	108.9	2440.2	2549.1	0.3810	8.1569	8.5379
27	300.15	3.564	1.003	38810.	38810.	113.1	2299.5	2412.6	113.1	2437.8	2550.9	0.3949	8.1218	8.5168
28	301.15	3.778	1.004	36730.	36730.	117.3	2296.7	2414.0	117.3	2435.4	2552.7	0.4088	8.0870	8.4959
29	302.15	4.004	1.004	34770.	34770.	121.5	2293.8	2415.3	121.5	2433.1	2554.5	0.4227	8.0524	8.4751

30	303.15	4.241	1.004	32930.	32930.	125.7	2291.0	2416.7	125.7	2430.7	2556.4	0.4365	8.0180	8.4546
31	304.15	4.491	1.005	31200.	31200.	129.8	2288.2	2418.0	129.8	2428.3	2558.2	0.4503	7.9839	8.4342
32	305.15	4.753	1.005	29570.	29570.	134.0	2285.4	2419.4	134.0	2425.9	2560.0	0.4640	7.9500	8.4140
33	306.15	5.029	1.005	28040.	28040.	138.2	2282.6	2420.8	138.2	2423.6	2561.8	0.4777	7.9163	8.3939
34	307.15	5.318	1.006	26600.	26600.	142.4	2279.7	2422.1	142.4	2421.2	2563.6	0.4913	7.8828	8.3740
35	308.15	5.622	1.006	25240.	25240.	146.6	2276.9	2423.5	146.6	2418.8	2565.4	0.5049	7.8495	8.3543
36	309.15	5.940	1.006	23970.	23970.	150.7	2274.1	2424.8	150.7	2416.4	2567.2	0.5184	7.8164	8.3348
37	310.15	6.274	1.007	22760.	22760.	154.9	2271.3	2426.2	154.9	2414.1	2569.0	0.5319	7.7835	8.3154
38	311.15	6.624	1.007	21630.	21630.	159.1	2268.4	2427.5	159.1	2411.7	2570.8	0.5453	7.7509	8.2962
39	312.15	6.991	1.007	20560.	20560.	163.3	2265.6	2428.9	163.3	2409.3	2572.6	0.5588	7.7184	8.2772
40	313.15	7.375	1.008	19550.	19550.	167.4	2262.8	2430.2	167.5	2406.9	2574.4	0.5721	7.6861	8.2583
41	314.15	7.777	1.008	18590.	18590.	171.6	2259.9	2431.6	171.6	2404.5	2576.2	0.5854	7.6541	8.2395
42	315.15	8.198	1.009	17690.	17690.	175.8	2257.1	2432.9	175.8	2402.1	2577.9	0.5987	7.6222	8.2209
43	316.15	8.639	1.009	16840.	16840.	180.0	2254.3	2434.2	180.0	2399.7	2579.7	0.6120	7.5905	8.2025
44	317.15	9.100	1.009	16040.	16040.	184.2	2251.4	2435.6	184.2	2397.3	2581.5	0.6252	7.5590	8.1842
45	318.15	9.582	1.010	15280.	15280.	188.3	2248.6	2436.9	188.4	2394.9	2583.3	0.6383	7.5277	8.1661
46	319.15	10.09	1.010	14560.	14560.	192.5	2245.7	2438.3	192.5	2392.5	2585.1	0.6514	7.4966	8.1481
47	320.15	10.61	1.011	13880.	13880.	196.7	2242.9	2439.6	196.7	2390.1	2586.9	0.6645	7.4657	8.1302
48	321.15	11.16	1.011	13230.	13230.	200.9	2240.0	2440.9	200.9	2387.7	2588.6	0.6776	7.4350	8.1125
49	322.15	11.74	1.012	12620.	12620.	205.1	2237.2	2442.3	205.1	2385.3	2590.4	0.6906	7.4044	8.0950
50	323.15	12.34	1.012	12040.	12050.	209.2	2234.3	2443.6	209.3	2382.9	2592.2	0.7035	7.3741	8.0776
51	324.15	12.96	1.013	11500.	11500.	213.4	2231.5	2444.9	213.4	2380.5	2593.9	0.7164	7.3439	8.0603
52	325.15	13.61	1.013	10980.	10980.	217.6	2228.6	2446.2	217.6	2378.1	2595.7	0.7293	7.3138	8.0432
53	326.15	14.29	1.014	10490.	10490.	221.8	2225.8	2447.6	221.8	2375.7	2597.5	0.7422	7.2840	8.0262
54	327.15	15.00	1.014	10020.	10020.	226.0	2222.9	2448.9	226.0	2373.2	2599.2	0.7550	7.2543	8.0093
55	328.15	15.74	1.015	9577.9	9578.9	230.2	2220.0	2450.2	230.2	2370.8	2601.0	0.7677	7.2248	7.9925
56	329.15	16.51	1.015	9157.7	9158.7	234.3	2217.2	2451.5	234.4	2368.4	2602.7	0.7804	7.1955	7.9759
57	330.15	17.31	1.016	8758.7	8759.8	238.5	2214.3	2452.8	238.5	2365.9	2604.5	0.7931	7.1663	7.9595
58	331.15	18.15	1.016	8379.8	8380.8	242.7	2211.4	2454.1	242.7	2363.5	2606.2	0.8058	7.1373	7.9431
59	332.15	19.02	1.017	8019.7	8020.8	246.9	2208.6	2455.4	246.9	2361.1	2608.0	0.8184	7.1085	7.9269
60	333.15	19.92	1.017	7677.5	7678.5	251.1	2205.7	2456.8	251.1	2358.6	2609.7	0.8310	7.0798	7.9108
61	334.15	20.86	1.018	7352.1	7353.2	255.3	2202.8	2458.1	255.3	2356.2	2611.4	0.8435	7.0513	7.8948
62	335.15	21.84	1.018	7042.7	7043.7	259.4	2199.9	2459.4	259.5	2353.7	2613.2	0.8560	7.0230	7.8790
63	336.15	22.86	1.019	6748.2	6749.3	263.6	2197.0	2460.7	263.6	2351.3	2614.9	0.8685	6.9948	7.8633
64	337.15	23.91	1.019	6468.0	6469.0	267.8	2194.1	2462.0	267.8	2348.8	2616.6	0.8809	6.9667	7.8477
65	338.15	25.01	1.020	6201.3	6202.3	272.0	2191.2	2463.2	272.0	2346.3	2618.4	0.8933	6.9388	7.8322
66	339.15	26.15	1.020	5947.2	5948.2	276.2	2188.3	2464.5	276.2	2343.9	2620.1	0.9057	6.9111	7.8168
67	340.15	27.33	1.021	5705.2	5706.2	280.4	2185.4	2465.8	280.4	2341.4	2621.8	0.9180	6.8835	7.8015
68	341.15	28.56	1.022	5474.6	5475.6	284.6	2182.5	2467.1	284.6	2338.9	2623.5	0.9303	6.8561	7.7864
69	342.15	29.84	1.022	5254.8	5255.8	288.8	2179.6	2468.4	288.8	2336.4	2625.2	0.9426	6.8288	7.7714
70	343.15	31.16	1.023	5045.2	5046.3	292.9	2176.7	2469.7	293.0	2334.0	2626.9	0.9548	6.8017	7.7565
71	344.15	32.53	1.023	4845.4	4846.4	297.1	2173.8	2470.9	297.2	2331.5	2628.6	0.9670	6.7747	7.7417
72	345.15	33.96	1.024	4654.7	4655.7	301.3	2170.9	2472.2	301.4	2329.0	2630.3	0.9792	6.7478	7.7270
73	346.15	35.43	1.025	4472.7	4473.7	305.5	2168.0	2473.5	305.5	2326.5	2632.0	0.9913	6.7211	7.7124
74	347.15	36.96	1.025	4299.0	4300.0	309.7	2165.1	2474.8	309.7	2324.0	2633.7	1.0034	6.6945	7.6979

Table F.1. Saturated Steam, SI Units (Continued)

			SPECIFIC VOLUME V			INTERNAL ENERGY U			ENTHALPY H			ENTROPY S		
t °C	T K	P kPa	sat. liq.	evap.	sat. vap.	sat. liq.	evap.	sat. vap.	sat. liq.	evap.	sat. vap.	sat. liq.	evap.	sat. vap.
75	348.15	38.55	1.026	4133.1	4134.1	313.9	2162.1	2476.0	313.9	2321.5	2635.4	1.0154	6.6681	7.6835
76	349.15	40.19	1.027	3974.6	3975.7	318.1	2159.2	2477.3	318.1	2318.9	2637.1	1.0275	6.6418	7.6693
77	350.15	41.89	1.027	3823.3	3824.3	322.3	2156.3	2478.5	322.3	2316.4	2638.7	1.0395	6.6156	7.6551
78	351.15	43.65	1.028	3678.6	3679.6	326.5	2153.3	2479.8	326.5	2313.9	2640.4	1.0514	6.5896	7.6410
79	352.15	45.47	1.029	3540.3	3541.3	330.7	2150.4	2481.1	330.7	2311.4	2642.1	1.0634	6.5637	7.6271
80	353.15	47.36	1.029	3408.1	3409.1	334.9	2147.4	2482.3	334.9	2308.8	2643.8	1.0753	6.5380	7.6132
81	354.15	49.31	1.030	3281.6	3282.6	339.1	2144.5	2483.5	339.1	2306.3	2645.4	1.0871	6.5123	7.5995
82	355.15	51.33	1.031	3160.6	3161.6	343.3	2141.5	2484.8	343.3	2303.8	2647.1	1.0990	6.4868	7.5858
83	356.15	53.42	1.031	3044.8	3045.8	347.5	2138.6	2486.0	347.5	2301.2	2648.7	1.1108	6.4615	7.5722
84	357.15	55.57	1.032	2933.9	2935.0	351.7	2135.6	2487.3	351.7	2298.6	2650.4	1.1225	6.4362	7.5587
85	358.15	57.80	1.033	2827.8	2828.8	355.9	2132.6	2488.5	355.9	2296.1	2652.0	1.1343	6.4111	7.5454
86	359.15	60.11	1.033	2726.1	2727.2	360.1	2129.7	2489.7	360.1	2293.5	2653.6	1.1460	6.3861	7.5321
87	360.15	62.49	1.034	2628.8	2629.8	364.3	2126.7	2490.9	364.3	2290.9	2655.3	1.1577	6.3612	7.5189
88	361.15	64.95	1.035	2535.4	2536.5	368.5	2123.7	2492.2	368.5	2288.4	2656.9	1.1693	6.3365	7.5058
89	362.15	67.49	1.035	2446.0	2447.0	372.7	2120.7	2493.4	372.7	2285.8	2658.5	1.1809	6.3119	7.4928
90	363.15	70.11	1.036	2360.3	2361.3	376.9	2117.7	2494.6	376.9	2283.2	2660.1	1.1925	6.2873	7.4799
91	364.15	72.81	1.037	2278.0	2279.1	381.1	2114.7	2495.8	381.1	2280.6	2661.7	1.2041	6.2629	7.4670
92	365.15	75.61	1.038	2199.2	2200.2	385.3	2111.7	2497.0	385.4	2278.0	2663.4	1.2156	6.2387	7.4543
93	366.15	78.49	1.038	2123.5	2124.5	389.5	2108.7	2498.2	389.6	2275.4	2665.0	1.2271	6.2145	7.4416
94	367.15	81.46	1.039	2050.9	2051.9	393.7	2105.7	2499.4	393.8	2272.8	2666.6	1.2386	6.1905	7.4291
95	368.15	84.53	1.040	1981.2	1982.2	397.9	2102.7	2500.6	398.0	2270.2	2668.1	1.2501	6.1665	7.4166
96	369.15	87.69	1.041	1914.3	1915.3	402.1	2099.7	2501.8	402.2	2267.5	2669.7	1.2615	6.1427	7.4042
97	370.15	90.94	1.041	1850.0	1851.0	406.3	2096.6	2503.0	406.4	2264.9	2671.3	1.2729	6.1190	7.3919
98	371.15	94.30	1.042	1788.3	1789.3	410.5	2093.6	2504.1	410.6	2262.2	2672.9	1.2842	6.0954	7.3796
99	372.15	97.76	1.043	1729.0	1730.0	414.7	2090.6	2505.3	414.8	2259.6	2674.4	1.2956	6.0719	7.3675
100	373.15	101.33	1.044	1672.0	1673.0	419.0	2087.5	2506.5	419.1	2256.9	2676.0	1.3069	6.0485	7.3554
102	375.15	108.78	1.045	1564.5	1565.5	427.4	2081.4	2508.8	427.5	2251.6	2679.1	1.3294	6.0021	7.3315
104	377.15	116.68	1.047	1465.1	1466.2	435.8	2075.3	2511.1	435.9	2246.3	2682.2	1.3518	5.9560	7.3078
106	379.15	125.04	1.049	1373.1	1374.2	444.3	2069.2	2513.4	444.4	2240.9	2685.3	1.3742	5.9104	7.2845
108	381.15	133.90	1.050	1287.9	1288.9	452.7	2063.0	2515.7	452.9	2235.4	2688.3	1.3964	5.8651	7.2615
110	383.15	143.27	1.052	1208.9	1209.9	461.2	2056.8	2518.0	461.3	2230.0	2691.3	1.4185	5.8203	7.2388
112	385.15	153.16	1.054	1135.6	1136.6	469.6	2050.6	2520.2	469.8	2224.5	2694.3	1.4405	5.7758	7.2164
114	387.15	163.62	1.055	1067.5	1068.5	478.1	2044.3	2522.4	478.3	2219.0	2697.2	1.4624	5.7318	7.1942
116	389.15	174.65	1.057	1004.2	1005.2	486.6	2038.1	2524.6	486.7	2213.4	2700.2	1.4842	5.6881	7.1723
118	391.15	186.28	1.059	945.3	946.3	495.0	2031.8	2526.8	495.2	2207.9	2703.1	1.5060	5.6447	7.1507
120	393.15	198.54	1.061	890.5	891.5	503.5	2025.4	2529.0	503.7	2202.2	2706.0	1.5276	5.6017	7.1293
122	395.15	211.45	1.062	839.4	840.5	512.0	2019.1	2531.1	512.2	2196.6	2708.8	1.5491	5.5590	7.1082
124	397.15	225.04	1.064	791.8	792.8	520.5	2012.7	2533.2	520.7	2190.9	2711.6	1.5706	5.5167	7.0873
126	399.15	239.33	1.066	747.3	748.4	529.0	2006.3	2535.3	529.2	2185.2	2714.4	1.5919	5.4747	7.0666
128	401.15	254.35	1.068	705.8	706.9	537.5	1999.9	2537.4	537.8	2179.4	2717.2	1.6132	5.4330	7.0462

130	403.15	270.13	1.070	667.1	668.1	546.0	1993.4	2539.4	546.3	2173.6	2719.9	1.6344	5.3917	7.0261
132	405.15	286.70	1.072	630.8	631.9	554.5	1986.9	2541.4	554.8	2167.8	2722.6	1.6555	5.3507	7.0061
134	407.15	304.07	1.074	596.9	598.0	563.1	1980.4	2543.4	563.4	2161.9	2725.3	1.6765	5.3099	6.9864
136	409.15	322.29	1.076	565.1	566.2	571.6	1973.8	2545.4	572.0	2155.9	2727.9	1.6974	5.2695	6.9669
138	411.15	341.38	1.078	535.3	536.4	580.2	1967.2	2547.4	580.5	2150.0	2730.5	1.7182	5.2293	6.9475
140	413.15	361.38	1.080	507.4	508.5	588.7	1960.6	2549.3	589.1	2144.0	2733.1	1.7390	5.1894	6.9284
142	415.15	382.31	1.082	481.2	482.3	597.3	1953.9	2551.2	597.7	2137.9	2735.6	1.7597	5.1499	6.9095
144	417.15	404.20	1.084	456.6	457.7	605.9	1947.2	2553.1	606.3	2131.8	2738.1	1.7803	5.1105	6.8908
146	419.15	427.09	1.086	433.5	434.6	614.4	1940.5	2554.9	614.9	2125.7	2740.6	1.8008	5.0715	6.8723
148	421.15	451.01	1.089	411.8	412.9	623.0	1933.7	2556.8	623.5	2119.5	2743.0	1.8213	5.0327	6.8539
150	423.15	476.00	1.091	391.4	392.4	631.6	1926.9	2558.6	632.1	2113.2	2745.4	1.8416	4.9941	6.8358
152	425.15	502.08	1.093	372.1	373.2	640.2	1920.1	2560.3	640.8	2106.9	2747.7	1.8619	4.9558	6.8178
154	427.15	529.29	1.095	354.0	355.1	648.9	1913.2	2562.1	649.4	2100.6	2750.0	1.8822	4.9178	6.8000
156	429.15	557.67	1.098	336.9	338.0	657.5	1906.3	2563.8	658.1	2094.2	2752.3	1.9023	4.8800	6.7823
158	431.15	587.25	1.100	320.8	321.9	666.1	1899.3	2565.5	666.8	2087.7	2754.5	1.9224	4.8424	6.7648
160	433.15	618.06	1.102	305.7	306.8	674.8	1892.3	2567.1	675.5	2081.3	2756.7	1.9425	4.8050	6.7475
162	435.15	650.16	1.105	291.3	292.4	683.5	1885.3	2568.8	684.2	2074.7	2758.9	1.9624	4.7679	6.7303
164	437.15	683.56	1.107	277.8	278.9	692.1	1878.2	2570.4	692.9	2068.1	2761.0	1.9823	4.7309	6.7133
166	439.15	718.31	1.109	265.0	266.1	700.8	1871.1	2571.9	701.6	2061.4	2763.1	2.0022	4.6942	6.6964
168	441.15	754.45	1.112	252.9	254.0	709.5	1863.9	2573.4	710.4	2054.7	2765.1	2.0219	4.6577	6.6796
170	443.15	792.02	1.114	241.4	242.6	718.2	1856.7	2574.9	719.1	2047.9	2767.1	2.0416	4.6214	6.6630
172	445.15	831.06	1.117	230.6	231.7	727.0	1849.5	2576.4	727.9	2041.1	2769.0	2.0613	4.5853	6.6465
174	447.15	871.60	1.120	220.3	221.5	735.7	1842.2	2577.8	736.7	2034.2	2770.9	2.0809	4.5493	6.6302
176	449.15	913.68	1.122	210.6	211.7	744.4	1834.8	2579.3	745.5	2027.3	2772.7	2.1004	4.5136	6.6140
178	451.15	957.36	1.125	201.4	202.5	753.2	1827.4	2580.6	754.3	2020.2	2774.5	2.1199	4.4780	6.5979
180	453.15	1002.7	1.128	192.7	193.8	762.0	1820.0	2581.9	763.1	2013.1	2776.3	2.1393	4.4426	6.5819
182	455.15	1049.6	1.130	184.4	185.5	770.8	1812.5	2583.2	772.0	2006.0	2778.0	2.1587	4.4074	6.5660
184	457.15	1098.3	1.133	176.5	177.6	779.6	1804.9	2584.5	780.8	1998.8	2779.6	2.1780	4.3723	6.5503
186	459.15	1148.8	1.136	169.0	170.2	788.4	1797.3	2585.7	789.7	1991.5	2781.2	2.1972	4.3374	6.5346
188	461.15	1201.0	1.139	161.9	163.1	797.2	1789.7	2586.9	798.6	1984.2	2782.8	2.2164	4.3026	6.5191
190	463.15	1255.1	1.142	155.2	156.3	806.1	1782.0	2588.1	807.5	1976.7	2784.3	2.2356	4.2680	6.5036
192	465.15	1311.1	1.144	148.8	149.9	814.9	1774.2	2589.2	816.5	1969.3	2785.7	2.2547	4.2336	6.4883
194	467.15	1369.0	1.147	142.6	143.8	823.8	1766.4	2590.2	825.4	1961.7	2787.1	2.2738	4.1993	6.4730
196	469.15	1428.9	1.150	136.8	138.0	832.7	1758.6	2591.3	834.4	1954.1	2788.4	2.2928	4.1651	6.4578
198	471.15	1490.9	1.153	131.3	132.4	841.6	1750.6	2592.3	843.4	1946.4	2789.7	2.3117	4.1310	6.4428
200	473.15	1554.9	1.156	126.0	127.2	850.6	1742.6	2593.2	852.4	1938.6	2790.9	2.3307	4.0971	6.4278
202	475.15	1621.0	1.160	121.0	122.1	859.5	1734.6	2594.1	861.4	1930.7	2792.1	2.3495	4.0633	6.4128
204	477.15	1689.3	1.163	116.2	117.3	868.5	1726.5	2595.0	870.5	1922.8	2793.2	2.3684	4.0296	6.3980
206	479.15	1759.8	1.166	111.6	112.8	877.5	1718.3	2595.8	879.5	1914.7	2794.3	2.3872	3.9961	6.3832
208	481.15	1832.6	1.169	107.2	108.4	886.5	1710.1	2596.6	888.6	1906.6	2795.3	2.4059	3.9626	6.3686
210	483.15	1907.7	1.173	103.1	104.2	895.5	1701.8	2597.3	897.7	1898.5	2796.2	2.4247	3.9293	6.3539
212	485.15	1985.2	1.176	99.09	100.26	904.5	1693.5	2598.0	906.9	1890.2	2797.1	2.4434	3.8960	6.3394
214	487.15	2065.1	1.179	95.28	96.46	913.6	1685.1	2598.7	916.0	1881.8	2797.9	2.4620	3.8629	6.3249
216	489.15	2147.5	1.183	91.65	92.83	922.7	1676.6	2599.3	925.2	1873.4	2798.6	2.4806	3.8298	6.3104
218	491.15	2232.4	1.186	88.17	89.36	931.8	1668.0	2599.8	934.4	1864.9	2799.3	2.4992	3.7968	6.2960

Table F.1. Saturated Steam, SI Units (Continued)

			SPECIFIC VOLUME V			INTERNAL ENERGY U			ENTHALPY H			ENTROPY S		
t °C	T K	P kPa	sat. liq.	evap.	sat. vap.	sat. liq.	evap.	sat. vap.	sat. liq.	evap.	sat. vap.	sat. liq.	evap.	sat. vap.
220	493.15	2319.8	1.190	84.85	86.04	940.9	1659.4	2600.3	943.7	1856.2	2799.9	2.5178	3.7639	6.2817
222	495.15	2409.9	1.194	81.67	82.86	950.1	1650.7	2600.8	952.9	1847.5	2800.5	2.5363	3.7311	6.2674
224	497.15	2502.7	1.197	78.62	79.82	959.2	1642.0	2601.2	962.2	1838.7	2800.9	2.5548	3.6984	6.2532
226	499.15	2598.2	1.201	75.71	76.91	968.4	1633.1	2601.5	971.5	1829.8	2801.4	2.5733	3.6657	6.2390
228	501.15	2696.5	1.205	72.92	74.12	977.6	1624.2	2601.8	980.9	1820.8	2801.7	2.5917	3.6331	6.2249
230	503.15	2797.6	1.209	70.24	71.45	986.9	1615.2	2602.1	990.3	1811.7	2802.0	2.6102	3.6006	6.2107
232	505.15	2901.6	1.213	67.68	68.89	996.2	1606.1	2602.3	999.7	1802.5	2802.2	2.6286	3.5681	6.1967
234	507.15	3008.6	1.217	65.22	66.43	1005.4	1597.0	2602.4	1009.1	1793.2	2802.3	2.6470	3.5356	6.1826
236	509.15	3118.6	1.221	62.86	64.08	1014.8	1587.7	2602.5	1018.6	1783.8	2802.3	2.6653	3.5033	6.1686
238	511.15	3231.7	1.225	60.60	61.82	1024.1	1578.4	2602.5	1028.1	1774.2	2802.3	2.6837	3.4709	6.1546
240	513.15	3347.8	1.229	58.43	59.65	1033.5	1569.0	2602.5	1037.6	1764.6	2802.2	2.7020	3.4386	6.1406
242	515.15	3467.2	1.233	56.34	57.57	1042.9	1559.5	2602.4	1047.2	1754.9	2802.0	2.7203	3.4063	6.1266
244	517.15	3589.8	1.238	54.34	55.58	1052.3	1549.9	2602.2	1056.8	1745.0	2801.8	2.7386	3.3740	6.1127
246	519.15	3715.7	1.242	52.41	53.66	1061.8	1540.2	2602.0	1066.4	1735.0	2801.4	2.7569	3.3418	6.0987
248	521.15	3844.9	1.247	50.56	51.81	1071.3	1530.5	2601.8	1076.1	1724.9	2801.0	2.7752	3.3096	6.0848
250	523.15	3977.6	1.251	48.79	50.04	1080.8	1520.6	2601.4	1085.8	1714.7	2800.4	2.7935	3.2773	6.0708
252	525.15	4113.7	1.256	47.08	48.33	1090.4	1510.6	2601.0	1095.5	1704.3	2799.8	2.8118	3.2451	6.0569
254	527.15	4253.4	1.261	45.43	46.69	1100.0	1500.5	2600.5	1105.3	1693.8	2799.1	2.8300	3.2129	6.0429
256	529.15	4396.7	1.266	43.85	45.11	1109.6	1490.4	2600.0	1115.2	1683.2	2798.3	2.8483	3.1807	6.0290
258	531.15	4543.7	1.271	42.33	43.60	1119.3	1480.1	2599.3	1125.0	1672.4	2797.4	2.8666	3.1484	6.0150
260	533.15	4694.3	1.276	40.86	42.13	1129.0	1469.7	2598.6	1134.9	1661.5	2796.4	2.8848	3.1161	6.0010
262	535.15	4848.8	1.281	39.44	40.73	1138.7	1459.2	2597.8	1144.9	1650.4	2795.3	2.9031	3.0838	5.9869
264	537.15	5007.1	1.286	38.08	39.37	1148.5	1448.5	2597.0	1154.9	1639.2	2794.1	2.9214	3.0515	5.9729
266	539.15	5169.3	1.291	36.77	38.06	1158.3	1437.8	2596.1	1165.0	1627.8	2792.8	2.9397	3.0191	5.9588
268	541.15	5335.5	1.297	35.51	36.80	1168.2	1426.9	2595.0	1175.1	1616.3	2791.4	2.9580	2.9866	5.9446
270	543.15	5505.8	1.303	34.29	35.59	1178.1	1415.9	2593.9	1185.2	1604.6	2789.9	2.9763	2.9541	5.9304
272	545.15	5680.2	1.308	33.11	34.42	1188.0	1404.7	2592.7	1195.4	1592.8	2788.2	2.9947	2.9215	5.9162
274	547.15	5858.7	1.314	31.97	33.29	1198.0	1393.4	2591.4	1205.7	1580.8	2786.5	3.0131	2.8889	5.9019
276	549.15	6041.5	1.320	30.88	32.20	1208.0	1382.0	2590.1	1216.0	1568.5	2784.6	3.0314	2.8561	5.8876
278	551.15	6228.7	1.326	29.82	31.14	1218.1	1370.4	2588.6	1226.4	1556.2	2782.6	3.0499	2.8233	5.8731
280	553.15	6420.2	1.332	28.79	30.13	1228.3	1358.7	2587.0	1236.8	1543.6	2780.4	3.0683	2.7903	5.8586
282	555.15	6616.1	1.339	27.81	29.14	1238.5	1346.8	2585.3	1247.3	1530.8	2778.1	3.0868	2.7573	5.8440
284	557.15	6816.6	1.345	26.85	28.20	1248.7	1334.8	2583.5	1257.9	1517.8	2775.7	3.1053	2.7241	5.8294
286	559.15	7021.8	1.352	25.93	27.28	1259.0	1322.6	2581.6	1268.5	1504.6	2773.2	3.1238	2.6908	5.8146
288	561.15	7231.5	1.359	25.03	26.39	1269.4	1310.2	2579.6	1279.2	1491.2	2770.5	3.1424	2.6573	5.7997
290	563.15	7446.1	1.366	24.17	25.54	1279.8	1297.7	2577.5	1290.0	1477.6	2767.6	3.1611	2.6237	5.7848
292	565.15	7665.4	1.373	23.33	24.71	1290.3	1284.9	2575.3	1300.9	1463.8	2764.6	3.1798	2.5899	5.7697
294	567.15	7889.7	1.381	22.52	23.90	1300.9	1272.0	2572.9	1311.8	1449.7	2761.5	3.1985	2.5560	5.7545
296	569.15	8118.9	1.388	21.74	23.13	1311.5	1258.9	2570.4	1322.8	1435.4	2758.2	3.2173	2.5218	5.7392
298	571.15	8353.2	1.396	20.98	22.38	1322.2	1245.6	2567.8	1333.9	1420.8	2754.7	3.2362	2.4875	5.7237

300	573.15	8592.7	1.404	20.24	21.65	1333.0	1232.0	2565.0	1345.1	1406.0	2751.0	3.2552	2.4529	5.7081
302	575.15	8837.4	1.412	19.53	20.94	1343.8	1218.3	2562.1	1356.3	1390.9	2747.2	3.2742	2.4182	5.6924
304	577.15	9087.3	1.421	18.84	20.26	1354.8	1204.3	2559.1	1367.7	1375.5	2743.2	3.2933	2.3832	5.6765
306	579.15	9342.7	1.430	18.17	19.60	1365.8	1190.1	2555.9	1379.1	1359.8	2739.0	3.3125	2.3479	5.6604
308	581.15	9603.6	1.439	17.52	18.96	1376.9	1175.6	2552.5	1390.7	1343.9	2734.6	3.3318	2.3124	5.6442
310	583.15	9870.0	1.448	16.89	18.33	1388.1	1161.0	2549.1	1402.4	1327.6	2730.0	3.3512	2.2766	5.6278
312	585.15	10142.1	1.458	16.27	17.73	1399.4	1146.0	2545.4	1414.2	1311.0	2725.2	3.3707	2.2404	5.6111
314	587.15	10420.0	1.468	15.68	17.14	1410.8	1130.8	2541.6	1426.1	1294.1	2720.2	3.3903	2.2040	5.5943
316	589.15	10703.	1.478	15.09	16.57	1422.3	1115.2	2537.5	1438.1	1276.8	2714.9	3.4101	2.1672	5.5772
318	591.15	10993.4	1.488	14.53	16.02	1433.9	1099.4	2533.3	1450.3	1259.1	2709.4	3.4300	2.1300	5.5599
320	593.15	11289.1	1.500	13.98	15.48	1445.7	1083.2	2528.9	1462.6	1241.1	2703.7	3.4500	2.0923	5.5423
322	595.15	11591.0	1.511	13.44	14.96	1457.5	1066.7	2524.3	1475.1	1222.6	2697.6	3.4702	2.0542	5.5244
324	597.15	11899.2	1.523	12.92	14.45	1469.5	1049.9	2519.4	1487.7	1203.6	2691.3	3.4906	2.0156	5.5062
326	599.15	12213.7	1.535	12.41	13.95	1481.7	1032.6	2514.3	1500.4	1184.2	2684.6	3.5111	1.9764	5.4876
328	601.15	12534.8	1.548	11.91	13.46	1494.0	1014.8	2508.8	1513.4	1164.2	2677.6	3.5319	1.9367	5.4685
330	603.15	12862.5	1.561	11.43	12.99	1506.4	996.7	2503.1	1526.5	1143.6	2670.2	3.5528	1.8962	5.4490
332	605.15	13197.0	1.575	10.95	12.53	1519.1	978.0	2497.0	1539.9	1122.5	2662.3	3.5740	1.8550	5.4290
334	607.15	13538.3	1.590	10.49	12.08	1531.9	958.7	2490.6	1553.4	1100.7	2654.1	3.5955	1.8129	5.4084
336	609.15	13886.7	1.606	10.03	11.63	1544.9	938.9	2483.7	1567.2	1078.1	2645.3	3.6172	1.7700	5.3872
338	611.15	14242.3	1.622	9.58	11.20	1558.1	918.4	2476.4	1581.2	1054.8	2636.0	3.6392	1.7261	5.3653
340	613.15	14605.2	1.639	9.14	10.78	1571.5	897.2	2468.7	1595.5	1030.7	2626.2	3.6616	1.6811	5.3427
342	615.15	14975.5	1.657	8.71	10.37	1585.2	875.2	2460.5	1610.0	1005.7	2615.7	3.6844	1.6350	5.3194
344	617.15	15353.5	1.676	8.286	9.962	1599.2	852.5	2451.7	1624.9	979.7	2604.7	3.7075	1.5877	5.2952
346	619.15	15739.3	1.696	7.870	9.566	1613.5	828.9	2442.4	1640.2	952.8	2593.0	3.7311	1.5391	5.2702
348	621.15	16133.1	1.718	7.461	9.178	1628.1	804.5	2432.6	1655.8	924.8	2580.7	3.7553	1.4891	5.2444
350	623.15	16535.1	1.741	7.058	8.799	1643.0	779.2	2422.2	1671.8	895.9	2567.7	3.7801	1.4375	5.2177
352	625.15	16945.5	1.766	6.654	8.420	1659.4	751.5	2410.8	1689.3	864.2	2553.5	3.8071	1.3822	5.1893
354	627.15	17364.4	1.794	6.252	8.045	1676.3	722.4	2398.7	1707.5	830.9	2538.4	3.8349	1.3247	5.1596
356	629.15	17792.2	1.824	5.850	7.674	1693.4	692.2	2385.6	1725.9	796.2	2522.1	3.8629	1.2654	5.1283
358	631.15	18229.0	1.858	5.448	7.306	1710.8	660.5	2371.4	1744.7	759.9	2504.6	3.8915	1.2037	5.0953
360	633.15	18675.1	1.896	5.044	6.940	1728.8	627.1	2355.8	1764.2	721.3	2485.4	3.9210	1.1390	5.0600
361	634.15	18901.7	1.917	4.840	6.757	1738.0	609.5	2347.5	1774.2	701.0	2475.2	3.9362	1.1052	5.0414
362	635.15	19130.7	1.939	4.634	6.573	1747.5	591.2	2338.7	1784.6	679.8	2464.4	3.9518	1.0702	5.0220
363	636.15	19362.1	1.963	4.425	6.388	1757.3	572.1	2329.3	1795.3	657.8	2453.0	3.9679	1.0338	5.0017
364	637.15	19596.1	1.988	4.213	6.201	1767.4	552.0	2319.4	1806.4	634.6	2440.9	3.9846	0.9958	4.9804
365	638.15	19832.6	2.016	3.996	6.012	1778.0	530.8	2308.8	1818.0	610.0	2428.0	4.0021	0.9558	4.9579
366	639.15	20071.6	2.046	3.772	5.819	1789.1	508.2	2297.3	1830.2	583.9	2414.1	4.0205	0.9134	4.9339
367	640.15	20313.2	2.080	3.540	5.621	1801.0	483.8	2284.8	1843.2	555.7	2399.0	4.0401	0.8680	4.9081
368	641.15	20557.5	2.118	3.298	5.416	1813.8	457.3	2271.1	1857.3	525.1	2382.4	4.0613	0.8189	4.8801
369	642.15	20804.4	2.162	3.039	5.201	1827.8	427.9	2255.7	1872.8	491.1	2363.9	4.0846	0.7647	4.8492
370	643.15	21054.0	2.214	2.759	4.973	1843.6	394.5	2238.1	1890.2	452.6	2342.8	4.1108	0.7036	4.8144
371	644.15	21306.4	2.278	2.446	4.723	1862.0	355.3	2217.3	1910.5	407.4	2317.9	4.1414	0.6324	4.7738
372	645.15	21561.6	2.364	2.075	4.439	1884.6	306.6	2191.2	1935.6	351.4	2287.0	4.1794	0.5446	4.7240
373	646.15	21819.7	2.496	1.588	4.084	1916.0	238.9	2154.9	1970.5	273.5	2244.0	4.2325	0.4233	4.6559
374	647.15	22080.5	2.843	0.623	3.466	1983.9	95.7	2079.7	2046.7	109.5	2156.2	4.3493	0.1692	4.5185
374.15	647.30	22120.0	3.170	0.000	3.170	2037.3	0.0	2037.3	2107.4	0.0	2107.4	4.4429	0.0000	4.4429

Table F.2: Superheated Steam, SI Units

P/kPa t^{sat}/T^{sat} (°C/K)		sat. liq.	sat. vap.	75 (348.15)	100 (373.15)	125 (398.15)	150 (423.15)	175 (448.15)	200 (473.15)	225 (498.15)	250 (523.15)
				TEMPERATURE: t °C (TEMPERATURE: T kelvins)							
	V	1.000	129200.	160640.	172180.	183720.	195270.	206810.	218350.	229890.	241430.
1	U	29.334	2385.2	2480.8	2516.4	2552.3	2588.5	2624.9	2661.7	2698.8	2736.3
(6.98/280.13)	H	29.335	2514.4	2641.5	2688.6	2736.0	2783.7	2831.7	2880.1	2928.7	2977.7
	S	0.1060	8.9767	9.3828	9.5136	9.6365	9.7527	9.8629	9.9679	10.0681	10.1641
	V	1.010	14670.	16030.	17190.	18350.	19510.	20660.	21820.	22980.	24130.
10	U	191.822	2438.0	2479.7	2515.6	2551.6	2588.0	2624.5	2661.4	2698.6	2736.1
(45.83/318.98)	H	191.832	2584.8	2640.0	2687.5	2735.2	2783.1	2831.2	2879.6	2928.4	2977.4
	S	0.6493	8.1511	8.3168	8.4486	8.5722	8.6888	8.7994	8.9045	9.0049	9.1010
	V	1.017	7649.8	8000.0	8584.7	9167.1	9748.0	10320.	10900.	11480.	12060.
20	U	251.432	2456.9	2478.4	2514.6	2550.9	2587.4	2624.1	2661.0	2698.3	2735.8
(60.09/333.24)	H	251.453	2609.9	2638.4	2686.3	2734.2	2782.3	2830.6	2879.2	2928.0	2977.1
	S	0.8321	7.9094	7.9933	8.1261	8.2504	8.3676	8.4785	8.5839	8.6844	8.7806
	V	1.022	5229.3	5322.0	5714.4	6104.6	6493.2	6880.8	7267.5	7653.8	8039.7
30	U	289.271	2468.6	2477.1	2513.6	2550.2	2586.8	2623.6	2660.7	2698.0	2735.6
(69.12/342.27)	H	289.302	2625.4	2636.8	2685.1	2733.3	2781.6	2830.0	2878.7	2927.6	2976.8
	S	0.9441	7.7695	7.8024	7.9363	8.0614	8.1791	8.2903	8.3960	8.4967	8.5930
	V	1.027	3993.4	....	4279.2	4573.3	4865.8	5157.2	5447.8	5738.0	6027.7
40	U	317.609	2477.1	....	2512.6	2549.4	2586.2	2623.2	2660.3	2697.7	2735.4
(75.89/349.04)	H	317.650	2636.9	....	2683.8	2732.3	2780.9	2829.5	2878.2	2927.2	2976.5
	S	1.0261	7.6709	....	7.8009	7.9268	8.0450	8.1566	8.2624	8.3633	8.4598
	V	1.030	3240.2	....	3418.1	3654.5	3889.3	4123.0	4356.0	4588.5	4820.5
50	U	340.513	2484.0	....	2511.7	2548.6	2585.6	2622.7	2659.9	2697.4	2735.1
(81.35/354.50)	H	340.564	2646.0	....	2682.6	2731.4	2780.1	2828.9	2877.7	2926.8	2976.1
	S	1.0912	7.5947	....	7.6953	7.8219	7.9406	8.0526	8.1587	8.2598	8.3564
	V	1.037	2216.9	....	2269.8	2429.4	2587.3	2744.2	2900.2	3055.8	3210.9
75	U	384.374	2496.7	....	2509.2	2546.7	2584.2	2621.6	2659.0	2696.7	2734.5
(91.79/364.94)	H	384.451	2663.0	....	2679.4	2728.9	2778.2	2827.4	2876.6	2925.8	2975.3
	S	1.2131	7.4570	....	7.5014	7.6300	7.7500	7.8629	7.9697	8.0712	8.1681
	V	1.043	1693.7	....	1695.5	1816.7	1936.3	2054.7	2172.3	2289.4	2406.1
100	U	417.406	2506.1	....	2506.6	2544.8	2582.7	2620.4	2658.1	2695.9	2733.9
(99.63/372.78)	H	417.511	2675.4	....	2676.2	2726.5	2776.3	2825.9	2875.4	2924.9	2974.5
	S	1.3027	7.3598	....	7.3618	7.4923	7.6137	7.7275	7.8349	7.9369	8.0342

	V	1.044	1673.0	....	1673.0	1792.7	1910.7	2027.7	2143.8	2259.3	2374.5
101.325	U	418.959	2506.5	....	2506.5	2544.7	2582.6	2620.4	2658.1	2695.9	2733.9
(100.00/373.15)	H	419.064	2676.0	....	2676.0	2726.4	2776.2	2825.8	2875.3	2924.8	2974.5
	S	1.3069	7.3554	....	7.3554	7.4860	7.6075	7.7213	7.8288	7.9308	8.0280
	V	1.049	1374.6	....	....	1449.1	1545.6	1641.0	1735.6	1829.6	1923.2
125	U	444.224	2513.4	....	....	2542.9	2581.2	2619.3	2657.2	2695.2	2733.3
(105.99/379.14)	H	444.356	2685.2	....	....	2724.0	2774.4	2824.4	2874.2	2923.9	2973.7
	S	1.3740	7.2847	....	....	7.3844	7.5072	7.6219	7.7300	7.8324	7.9300
	V	1.053	1159.0	....	....	1204.0	1285.2	1365.2	1444.4	1523.0	1601.3
150	U	466.968	2519.5	....	....	2540.9	2579.7	2618.1	2656.3	2694.4	2732.7
(111.37/384.52)	H	467.126	2693.4	....	....	2721.5	2772.5	2822.9	2872.9	2922.9	2972.9
	S	1.4336	7.2234	....	....	7.2953	7.4194	7.5352	7.6439	7.7468	7.8447
	V	1.057	1003.34	....	....	1028.8	1099.1	1168.2	1236.4	1304.1	1371.3
175	U	486.815	2524.7	....	....	2538.9	2578.2	2616.9	2655.3	2693.7	2732.1
(116.06/389.21)	H	487.000	2700.3	....	....	2719.0	2770.5	2821.3	2871.7	2921.9	2972.0
	S	1.4849	7.1716	....	....	7.2191	7.3447	7.4614	7.5708	7.6741	7.7724
	V	1.061	885.44	....	....	897.47	959.54	1020.4	1080.4	1139.8	1198.9
200	U	504.489	2529.2	....	....	2536.9	2576.6	2615.7	2654.4	2692.9	2731.4
(120.23/393.38)	H	504.701	2706.3	....	....	2716.4	2768.5	2819.8	2870.5	2920.9	2971.2
	S	1.5301	7.1268	....	....	7.1523	7.2794	7.3971	7.5072	7.6110	7.7096
	V	1.064	792.97	....	....	795.25	850.97	905.44	959.06	1012.1	1064.7
225	U	520.465	2533.2	....	....	2534.8	2575.1	2614.5	2653.5	2692.2	2730.8
(123.99/397.14)	H	520.705	2711.6	....	....	2713.8	2766.5	2818.2	2869.3	2919.9	2970.4
	S	1.5705	7.0873	....	....	7.0928	7.2213	7.3400	7.4508	7.5551	7.6540
	V	1.068	718.44	....	....	....	764.09	813.47	861.98	909.91	957.41
250	U	535.077	2536.8	....	....	....	2573.5	2613.3	2652.5	2691.4	2730.2
(127.43/400.58)	H	535.343	2716.4	....	....	....	2764.5	2816.7	2868.0	2918.9	2969.6
	S	1.6071	7.0520	....	....	....	7.1689	7.2886	7.4001	7.5050	7.6042
	V	1.071	657.04	....	....	....	693.00	738.21	782.55	826.29	869.61
275	U	548.564	2540.0	....	....	....	2571.9	2612.1	2651.6	2690.7	2729.6
(130.60/403.75)	H	548.858	2720.7	....	....	....	2762.5	2815.1	2866.8	2917.9	2968.7
	S	1.6407	7.0201	....	....	....	7.1211	7.2419	7.3541	7.4594	7.5590
	V	1.073	605.56	....	....	....	633.74	675.49	716.35	756.60	796.44
300	U	561.107	2543.0	....	....	....	2570.3	2610.8	2650.6	2689.9	2729.0
(133.54/406.69)	H	561.429	2724.7	....	....	....	2760.4	2813.5	2865.5	2916.9	2967.9
	S	1.6716	6.9909	....	....	....	7.0771	7.1990	7.3119	7.4177	7.5176

Table F.2. Superheated Steam, SI Units (Continued)

P/kPa t^{sat}/T^{sat} (°C/K)		sat. liq.	sat. vap.	300 (573.15)	350 (623.15)	400 (673.15)	450 (723.15)	500 (773.15)	550 (823.15)	600 (873.15)	650 (923.15)
				TEMPERATURE: t °C (TEMPERATURE: T kelvins)							
1 (6.98/280.13)	V	1.000	129200.	264500.	287580.	310660.	333730.	356810.	379880.	402960.	426040.
	U	29.334	2385.2	2812.3	2889.9	2969.1	3049.9	3132.4	3216.7	3302.6	3390.3
	H	29.335	2514.4	3076.8	3177.5	3279.7	3383.6	3489.2	3596.5	3705.6	3816.4
	S	0.1060	8.9767	10.3450	10.5133	10.6711	10.8200	10.9612	11.0957	11.2243	11.3476
10 (45.83/318.98)	V	1.010	14670.	26440.	28750.	31060.	33370.	35670.	37980.	40290.	42600.
	U	191.822	2438.0	2812.2	2889.8	2969.0	3049.8	3132.3	3216.6	3302.6	3390.3
	H	191.832	2584.8	3076.6	3177.3	3279.6	3383.5	3489.1	3596.5	3705.5	3816.3
	S	0.6493	8.1511	9.2820	9.4504	9.6083	9.7572	9.8984	10.0329	10.1616	10.2849
20 (60.09/333.24)	V	1.017	7649.8	13210.	14370.	15520.	16680.	17830.	18990.	20140.	21300.
	U	251.432	2456.9	2812.0	2889.6	2968.9	3049.7	3132.3	3216.5	3302.5	3390.2
	H	251.453	2609.9	3076.4	3177.1	3279.4	3383.4	3489.0	3596.4	3705.4	3816.2
	S	0.8321	7.9094	8.9618	9.1303	9.2882	9.4372	9.5784	9.7130	9.8416	9.9650
30 (69.12/342.27)	V	1.022	5229.3	8810.8	9581.2	10350.	11120.	11890.	12660.	13430.	14190.
	U	289.271	2468.6	2811.8	2889.5	2968.7	3049.6	3132.2	3216.5	3302.5	3390.2
	H	289.302	2625.4	3076.1	3176.9	3279.3	3383.3	3488.9	3596.3	3705.4	3816.2
	S	0.9441	7.7695	8.7744	8.9430	9.1010	9.2499	9.3912	9.5257	9.6544	9.7778
40 (75.89/349.04)	V	1.027	3993.4	6606.5	7184.6	7762.5	8340.1	8917.6	9494.9	10070.	10640.
	U	317.609	2477.1	2811.6	2889.4	2968.6	3049.5	3132.1	3216.4	3302.4	3390.1
	H	317.650	2636.9	3075.9	3176.8	3279.1	3383.1	3488.8	3596.2	3705.3	3816.1
	S	1.0261	7.6709	8.6413	8.8100	8.9680	9.1170	9.2583	9.3929	9.5216	9.6450
50 (81.35/354.50)	V	1.030	3240.2	5283.9	5746.7	6209.1	6671.4	7133.5	7595.5	8057.4	8519.2
	U	340.513	2484.0	2811.5	2889.2	2968.5	3049.4	3132.0	3216.3	3302.3	3390.1
	H	340.564	2646.0	3075.7	3176.6	3279.0	3383.0	3488.7	3596.1	3705.2	3816.0
	S	1.0912	7.5947	8.5380	8.7068	8.8649	9.0139	9.1552	9.2898	9.4185	9.5419
75 (91.79/364.94)	V	1.037	2216.9	3520.5	3829.4	4138.0	4446.4	4754.7	5062.8	5370.9	5678.9
	U	384.374	2496.7	2811.0	2888.9	2968.2	3049.2	3131.8	3216.1	3302.2	3389.9
	H	384.451	2663.0	3075.1	3176.1	3278.6	3382.7	3488.4	3595.8	3705.0	3815.9
	S	1.2131	7.4570	8.3502	8.5191	8.6773	8.8265	8.9678	9.1025	9.2312	9.3546
100 (99.63/372.78)	V	1.043	1693.7	2638.7	2870.8	3102.5	3334.0	3565.3	3796.5	4027.7	4258.8
	U	417.406	2506.1	2810.6	2888.6	2968.0	3049.0	3131.6	3216.0	3302.0	3389.8
	H	417.511	2675.4	3074.5	3175.6	3278.2	3382.4	3488.1	3595.6	3704.8	3815.7
	S	1.3027	7.3598	8.2166	8.3858	8.5442	8.6934	8.8348	8.9695	9.0982	9.2217

	V	1.044	1673.0	2604.2	2833.2	3061.9	3290.3	3518.7	3746.9	3975.0	4203.1
101.325	U	418.959	2506.5	2810.6	2888.5	2968.0	3048.9	3131.6	3215.9	3302.0	3389.8
(100.00/373.15)	H	419.064	2676.0	3074.4	3175.6	3278.2	3382.3	3488.1	3595.6	3704.8	3815.7
	S	1.3069	7.3554	8.2105	8.3797	8.5381	8.6873	8.8287	8.9634	9.0922	9.2156
	V	1.049	1374.6	2109.7	2295.6	2481.2	2666.5	2851.7	3036.8	3221.8	3406.7
125	U	444.224	2513.4	2810.2	2888.2	2967.7	3048.7	3131.4	3215.8	3301.9	3389.7
(105.99/379.14)	H	444.356	2685.2	3073.9	3175.2	3277.8	3382.0	3487.9	3595.4	3704.6	3815.5
	S	1.3740	7.2847	8.1129	8.2823	8.4408	8.5901	8.7316	8.8663	8.9951	9.1186
	V	1.053	1159.0	1757.0	1912.2	2066.9	2221.5	2375.9	2530.2	2684.5	2838.6
150	U	466.968	2519.5	2809.7	2887.9	2967.4	3048.5	3131.2	3215.6	3301.7	3389.5
(111.37/384.52)	H	467.126	2693.4	3073.3	3174.7	3277.5	3381.7	3487.6	3595.1	3704.4	3815.3
	S	1.4336	7.2234	8.0280	8.1976	8.3562	8.5056	8.6472	8.7819	8.9108	9.0343
	V	1.057	1003.34	1505.1	1638.3	1771.1	1903.7	2036.1	2168.4	2300.7	2432.9
175	U	486.815	2524.7	2809.3	2887.5	2967.1	3048.3	3131.0	3215.4	3301.6	3389.4
(116.06/389.21)	H	487.000	2700.3	3072.7	3174.2	3277.1	3381.4	3487.3	3594.9	3704.2	3815.1
	S	1.4849	7.1716	7.9561	8.1259	8.2847	8.4341	8.5758	8.7106	8.8394	8.9630
	V	1.061	885.44	1316.2	1432.8	1549.2	1665.3	1781.2	1897.1	2012.9	2128.6
200	U	504.489	2529.2	2808.8	2887.2	2966.9	3048.0	3130.8	3215.3	3301.4	3389.2
(120.23/393.38)	H	504.701	2706.3	3072.1	3173.8	3276.7	3381.1	3487.0	3594.7	3704.0	3815.0
	S	1.5301	7.1268	7.8937	8.0638	8.2226	8.3722	8.5139	8.6487	8.7776	8.9012
	V	1.064	792.97	1169.2	1273.1	1376.6	1479.9	1583.0	1686.0	1789.0	1891.9
225	U	520.465	2533.2	2808.4	2886.9	2966.6	3047.8	3130.6	3215.1	3301.2	3389.1
(123.99/397.14)	H	520.705	2711.6	3071.5	3173.3	3276.3	3380.8	3486.8	3594.4	3703.8	3814.8
	S	1.5705	7.0873	7.8385	8.0088	8.1679	8.3175	8.4593	8.5942	8.7231	8.8467
	V	1.068	718.44	1051.6	1145.2	1238.5	1331.5	1424.4	1517.2	1609.9	1702.5
250	U	535.077	2536.8	2808.0	2886.5	2966.3	3047.6	3130.4	3214.9	3301.1	3389.0
(127.43/400.58)	H	535.343	2716.4	3070.9	3172.8	3275.9	3380.4	3486.5	3594.2	3703.6	3814.6
	S	1.6071	7.0520	7.7891	7.9597	8.1188	8.2686	8.4104	8.5453	8.6743	8.7980
	V	1.071	657.04	955.45	1040.7	1125.5	1210.2	1294.7	1379.0	1463.3	1547.6
275	U	548.564	2540.0	2807.5	2886.2	2966.0	3047.3	3130.2	3214.7	3300.9	3388.8
(130.60/403.75)	H	548.858	2720.7	3070.3	3172.4	3275.5	3380.1	3486.2	3594.0	3703.4	3814.4
	S	1.6407	7.0201	7.7444	7.9151	8.0744	8.2243	8.3661	8.5011	8.6301	8.7538
	V	1.073	605.56	875.29	953.52	1031.4	1109.0	1186.5	1263.9	1341.2	1418.5
300	U	561.107	2543.0	2807.1	2885.8	2965.8	3047.1	3130.0	3214.5	3300.8	3388.7
(133.54/406.69)	H	561.429	2724.7	3069.7	3171.9	3275.2	3379.8	3486.0	3593.7	3703.2	3814.2
	S	1.6716	6.9909	7.7034	7.8744	8.0338	8.1838	8.3257	8.4608	8.5898	8.7135

Table F.2. Superheated Steam, SI Units (Continued)

P/kPa t^{sat}/T^{sat} (°C/K)		sat. liq.	sat. vap.	150 (423.15)	175 (448.15)	200 (473.15)	220 (493.15)	240 (513.15)	260 (533.15)	280 (553.15)	300 (573.15)
				TEMPERATURE: t °C (TEMPERATURE: T kelvins)							
	V	1.076	561.75	583.58	622.41	660.33	690.22	719.81	749.18	778.39	807.47
325	U	572.847	2545.7	2568.7	2609.6	2649.6	2681.2	2712.7	2744.0	2775.3	2806.6
(136.29/409.44)	H	573.197	2728.3	2758.4	2811.9	2864.2	2905.6	2946.6	2987.5	3028.2	3069.0
	S	1.7004	6.9640	7.0363	7.1592	7.2729	7.3585	7.4400	7.5181	7.5933	7.6657
	V	1.079	524.00	540.58	576.90	612.31	640.18	667.75	695.09	722.27	749.33
350	U	583.892	2548.2	2567.1	2608.3	2648.6	2680.4	2712.0	2743.4	2774.8	2806.2
(138.87/412.02)	H	584.270	2731.6	2756.3	2810.3	2863.0	2904.5	2945.7	2986.7	3027.6	3068.4
	S	1.7273	6.9392	6.9982	7.1222	7.2366	7.3226	7.4045	7.4828	7.5581	7.6307
	V	1.081	491.13	503.29	537.46	570.69	596.81	622.62	648.22	673.64	698.94
375	U	594.332	2550.6	2565.4	2607.1	2647.7	2679.6	2711.3	2742.8	2774.3	2805.7
(141.31/414.46)	H	594.737	2734.7	2754.1	2808.6	2861.7	2903.4	2944.8	2985.9	3026.9	3067.8
	S	1.7526	6.9160	6.9624	7.0875	7.2027	7.2891	7.3713	7.4499	7.5254	7.5981
	V	1.084	462.22	470.66	502.93	534.26	558.85	583.14	607.20	631.09	654.85
400	U	604.237	2552.7	2563.7	2605.8	2646.7	2678.8	2710.6	2742.2	2773.7	2805.3
(143.62/416.77)	H	604.670	2737.6	2752.0	2807.0	2860.4	2902.3	2943.9	2985.1	3026.2	3067.2
	S	1.7764	6.8943	6.9285	7.0548	7.1708	7.2576	7.3402	7.4190	7.4947	7.5675
	V	1.086	436.61	441.85	472.47	502.12	525.36	548.30	571.01	593.54	615.95
425	U	613.667	2554.8	2562.0	2604.5	2645.7	2678.0	2709.9	2741.6	2773.2	2804.8
(145.82/418.97)	H	614.128	2740.3	2749.8	2805.3	2859.1	2901.2	2942.9	2984.3	3025.5	3066.6
	S	1.7990	6.8739	6.8965	7.0239	7.1407	7.2280	7.3108	7.3899	7.4657	7.5388
	V	1.088	413.75	416.24	445.38	473.55	495.59	517.33	538.83	560.17	581.37
450	U	622.672	2556.7	2560.3	2603.2	2644.7	2677.1	2709.2	2741.0	2772.7	2804.4
(147.92/421.07)	H	623.162	2742.9	2747.7	2803.7	2857.8	2900.2	2942.0	2983.5	3024.8	3066.0
	S	1.8204	6.8547	6.8660	6.9946	7.1121	7.1999	7.2831	7.3624	7.4384	7.5116
	V	1.091	393.22	393.31	421.14	447.97	468.95	489.62	510.05	530.30	550.43
475	U	631.294	2558.5	2558.6	2601.9	2643.7	2676.3	2708.5	2740.4	2772.2	2803.9
(149.92/423.07)	H	631.812	2745.3	2745.5	2802.0	2856.5	2899.1	2941.1	2982.7	3024.1	3065.4
	S	1.8408	6.8365	6.8369	6.9667	7.0850	7.1732	7.2567	7.3363	7.4125	7.4858
	V	1.093	374.68	....	399.31	424.96	444.97	464.67	484.14	503.43	522.58
500	U	639.569	2560.2	....	2600.6	2642.7	2675.5	2707.8	2739.8	2771.7	2803.5
(151.84/424.99)	H	640.116	2747.5	....	2800.3	2855.1	2898.0	2940.1	2981.9	3023.4	3064.8
	S	1.8604	6.8192	....	6.9400	7.0592	7.1478	7.2317	7.3115	7.3879	7.4614

525 (153.69/426.84)	*V*	1.095	357.84	....	379.56	404.13	423.28	442.11	460.70	479.11	497.38
	U	647.528	2561.8	....	2599.3	2641.6	2674.6	2707.1	2739.2	2771.2	2803.0
	H	648.103	2749.7	....	2798.6	2853.8	2896.8	2939.2	2981.1	3022.7	3064.1
	S	1.8790	6.8027	....	6.9145	7.0345	7.1236	7.2078	7.2879	7.3645	7.4381
550 (155.47/428.62)	*V*	1.097	342.48	....	361.60	385.19	403.55	421.59	439.38	457.00	474.48
	U	655.199	2563.3	....	2598.0	2640.6	2673.8	2706.4	2738.6	2770.6	2802.6
	H	655.802	2751.7	....	2796.8	2852.5	2895.7	2938.3	2980.3	3022.0	3063.5
	S	1.8970	6.7870	....	6.8900	7.0108	7.1004	7.1849	7.2653	7.3421	7.4158
575 (157.18/430.33)	*V*	1.099	328.41	....	345.20	367.90	385.54	402.85	419.92	436.81	453.56
	U	662.603	2564.8	....	2596.6	2639.6	2672.9	2705.7	2738.0	2770.1	2802.1
	H	663.235	2753.6	....	2795.1	2851.1	2894.6	2937.3	2979.5	3021.3	3062.9
	S	1.9142	6.7720	....	6.8664	6.9880	7.0781	7.1630	7.2436	7.3206	7.3945
600 (158.84/431.99)	*V*	1.101	315.47	....	330.16	352.04	369.03	385.68	402.08	418.31	434.39
	U	669.762	2566.2	....	2595.3	2638.5	2672.1	2705.0	2737.4	2769.6	2801.6
	H	670.423	2755.5	....	2793.3	2849.7	2893.5	2936.4	2978.7	3020.6	3062.3
	S	1.9308	6.7575	....	6.8437	6.9662	7.0567	7.1419	7.2228	7.3000	7.3740
625 (160.44/433.59)	*V*	1.103	303.54	....	316.31	337.45	353.83	369.87	385.67	401.28	416.75
	U	676.695	2567.5	....	2593.9	2637.5	2671.2	2704.2	2736.8	2769.1	2801.2
	H	677.384	2757.2	....	2791.6	2848.4	2892.3	2935.4	2977.8	3019.9	3061.7
	S	1.9469	6.7437	....	6.8217	6.9451	7.0361	7.1217	7.2028	7.2802	7.3544
650 (161.99/435.14)	*V*	1.105	292.49	....	303.53	323.98	339.80	355.29	370.52	385.56	400.47
	U	683.417	2568.7	....	2592.5	2636.4	2670.3	2703.5	2736.2	2768.5	2800.7
	H	684.135	2758.9	....	2789.8	2847.0	2891.2	2934.4	2977.0	3019.2	3061.0
	S	1.9623	6.7304	....	6.8004	6.9247	7.0162	7.1021	7.1835	7.2611	7.3355
675 (163.49/436.64)	*V*	1.106	282.23	....	291.69	311.51	326.81	341.78	356.49	371.01	385.39
	U	689.943	2570.0	....	2591.1	2635.4	2669.5	2702.8	2735.6	2768.0	2800.3
	H	690.689	2760.5	....	2788.0	2845.6	2890.1	2933.5	2976.2	3018.5	3060.4
	S	1.9773	6.7176	....	6.7798	6.9050	6.9970	7.0833	7.1650	7.2428	7.3173
700 (164.96/438.11)	*V*	1.108	272.68	....	280.69	299.92	314.75	329.23	343.46	357.50	371.39
	U	696.285	2571.1	....	2589.7	2634.3	2668.6	2702.1	2735.0	2767.5	2799.8
	H	697.061	2762.0	....	2786.2	2844.2	2888.9	2932.5	2975.4	3017.7	3059.8
	S	1.9918	6.7052	....	6.7598	6.8859	6.9784	7.0651	7.1470	7.2250	7.2997
725 (166.38/439.53)	*V*	1.110	263.77	....	270.45	289.13	303.51	317.55	331.33	344.92	358.36
	U	702.457	2572.2	....	2588.3	2633.2	2667.7	2701.3	2734.3	2767.0	2799.3
	H	703.261	2763.4	....	2784.4	2842.8	2887.7	2931.5	2974.6	3017.0	3059.1
	S	2.0059	6.6932	....	6.7404	6.8673	6.9604	7.0474	7.1296	7.2078	7.2827

Table F.2. Superheated Steam, SI Units (Continued)

P/kPa t^{sat}/T^{sat} (°C/K)		sat. liq.	sat. vap.	325 (598.15)	350 (623.15)	400 (673.15)	450 (723.15)	500 (773.15)	550 (823.15)	600 (873.15)	650 (923.15)
				TEMPERATURE: t °C (TEMPERATURE: T kelvins)							
325 (136.29/409.44)	V	1.076	561.75	843.68	879.78	951.73	1023.5	1095.0	1166.5	1237.9	1309.2
	U	572.847	2545.7	2845.9	2885.5	2965.5	3046.9	3129.8	3214.4	3300.6	3388.6
	H	573.197	2728.3	3120.1	3171.4	3274.8	3379.5	3485.7	3593.5	3702.9	3814.1
	S	1.7004	6.9640	7.7530	7.8369	7.9965	8.1465	8.2885	8.4236	8.5527	8.6764
350 (138.87/412.02)	V	1.079	524.00	783.01	816.57	883.45	950.11	1016.6	1083.0	1149.3	1215.6
	U	583.892	2548.2	2845.6	2885.1	2965.2	3046.6	3129.6	3214.2	3300.5	3388.4
	H	584.270	2731.6	3119.6	3170.9	3274.4	3379.2	3485.4	3593.3	3702.7	3813.9
	S	1.7273	6.9392	7.7181	7.8022	7.9619	8.1120	8.2540	8.3892	8.5183	8.6421
375 (141.31/414.46)	V	1.081	491.13	730.42	761.79	824.28	886.54	948.66	1010.7	1072.6	1134.5
	U	594.332	2550.6	2845.2	2884.8	2964.9	3046.4	3129.4	3214.0	3300.3	3388.3
	H	594.737	2734.7	3119.1	3170.5	3274.0	3378.8	3485.1	3593.0	3702.5	3813.7
	S	1.7526	6.9160	7.6856	7.7698	7.9296	8.0798	8.2219	8.3571	8.4863	8.6101
400 (143.62/416.77)	V	1.084	462.22	684.41	713.85	772.50	830.92	889.19	947.35	1005.4	1063.4
	U	604.237	2552.7	2844.8	2884.5	2964.6	3046.2	3129.2	3213.8	3300.2	3388.2
	H	604.670	2737.6	3118.5	3170.0	3273.6	3378.5	3484.9	3592.8	3702.3	3813.5
	S	1.7764	6.8943	7.6552	7.7395	7.8994	8.0497	8.1919	8.3271	8.4563	8.5802
425 (145.82/418.97)	V	1.086	436.61	643.81	671.56	726.81	781.84	836.72	891.49	946.17	1000.8
	U	613.667	2554.8	2844.4	2884.1	2964.4	3045.9	3129.0	3213.7	3300.0	3388.0
	H	614.128	2740.3	3118.0	3169.5	3273.3	3378.2	3484.6	3592.5	3702.1	3813.4
	S	1.7990	6.8739	7.6265	7.7109	7.8710	8.0214	8.1636	8.2989	8.4282	8.5520
450 (147.92/421.07)	V	1.088	413.75	607.73	633.97	686.20	738.21	790.07	841.83	893.50	945.10
	U	622.672	2556.7	2844.0	2883.8	2964.1	3045.7	3128.8	3213.5	3299.8	3387.9
	H	623.162	2742.9	3117.5	3169.1	3272.9	3377.9	3484.3	3592.3	3701.9	3813.2
	S	1.8204	6.8547	7.5995	7.6840	7.8442	7.9947	8.1370	8.2723	8.4016	8.5255
475 (149.92/423.07)	V	1.091	393.22	575.44	600.33	649.87	699.18	748.34	797.40	846.37	895.27
	U	631.294	2558.5	2843.6	2883.4	2963.8	3045.4	3128.6	3213.3	3299.7	3387.7
	H	631.812	2745.3	3116.9	3168.6	3272.5	3377.6	3484.0	3592.1	3701.7	3813.0
	S	1.8408	6.8365	7.5739	7.6585	7.8189	7.9694	8.1118	8.2472	8.3765	8.5004
500 (151.84/424.99)	V	1.093	374.68	546.38	570.05	617.16	664.05	710.78	757.41	803.95	850.42
	U	639.569	2560.2	2843.2	2883.1	2963.5	3045.2	3128.4	3213.1	3299.5	3387.6
	H	640.116	2747.5	3116.4	3168.1	3272.1	3377.2	3483.8	3591.8	3701.5	3812.8
	S	1.8604	6.8192	7.5496	7.6343	7.7948	7.9454	8.0879	8.2233	8.3526	8.4766

525 (153.69/426.84)	*V*	1.095	357.84	520.08	542.66	587.58	632.26	676.80	721.23	765.57	809.85
	U	647.528	2561.8	2842.8	2882.7	2963.2	3045.0	3128.2	3213.0	3299.4	3387.5
	H	648.103	2749.7	3115.9	3167.6	3271.7	3376.9	3483.5	3591.6	3701.3	3812.6
	S	1.8790	6.8027	7.5264	7.6112	7.7719	7.9226	8.0651	8.2006	8.3299	8.4539
550 (155.47/428.62)	*V*	1.097	342.48	496.18	517.76	560.68	603.37	645.91	688.34	730.68	772.96
	U	655.199	2563.3	2842.4	2882.4	2963.0	3044.7	3128.0	3212.8	3299.2	3387.3
	H	655.802	2751.7	3115.3	3167.2	3271.3	3376.6	3483.2	3591.4	3701.1	3812.5
	S	1.8970	6.7870	7.5043	7.5892	7.7500	7.9008	8.0433	8.1789	8.3083	8.4323
575 (157.18/430.33)	*V*	1.099	328.41	474.36	495.03	536.12	576.98	617.70	658.30	698.83	739.28
	U	662.603	2564.8	2842.0	2882.1	2962.7	3044.5	3127.8	3212.6	3299.1	3387.2
	H	663.235	2753.6	3114.8	3166.7	3271.0	3376.3	3482.9	3591.1	3700.9	3812.3
	S	1.9142	6.7720	7.4831	7.5681	7.7290	7.8799	8.0226	8.1581	8.2876	8.4116
600 (158.84/431.99)	*V*	1.101	315.47	454.35	474.19	513.61	552.80	591.84	630.78	669.63	708.41
	U	669.762	2566.2	2841.6	2881.7	2962.4	3044.3	3127.6	3212.4	3298.9	3387.1
	H	670.423	2755.5	3114.3	3166.2	3270.6	3376.0	3482.7	3590.9	3700.7	3812.1
	S	1.9308	6.7575	7.4628	7.5479	7.7090	7.8600	8.0027	8.1383	8.2678	8.3919
625 (160.44/433.59)	*V*	1.103	303.54	435.94	455.01	492.89	530.55	568.05	605.45	642.76	680.01
	U	676.695	2567.5	2841.2	2881.4	2962.1	3044.0	3127.4	3212.2	3298.8	3386.9
	H	677.384	2757.2	3113.7	3165.7	3270.2	3375.6	3482.4	3590.7	3700.5	3811.9
	S	1.9469	6.7437	7.4433	7.5285	7.6897	7.8408	7.9836	8.1192	8.2488	8.3729
650 (161.99/435.14)	*V*	1.105	292.49	418.95	437.31	473.78	510.01	546.10	582.07	617.96	653.79
	U	683.417	2568.7	2840.9	2881.0	2961.8	3043.8	3127.2	3212.1	3298.6	3386.8
	H	684.135	2758.9	3113.2	3165.3	3269.8	3375.3	3482.1	3590.4	3700.3	3811.8
	S	1.9623	6.7304	7.4245	7.5099	7.6712	7.8224	7.9652	8.1009	8.2305	8.3546
675 (163.49/436.64)	*V*	1.106	282.23	403.22	420.92	456.07	491.00	525.77	560.43	595.00	629.51
	U	689.943	2570.0	2840.5	2880.7	2961.6	3043.6	3127.0	3211.9	3298.5	3386.7
	H	690.689	2760.5	3112.6	3164.8	3269.4	3375.0	3481.8	3590.2	3700.1	3811.6
	S	1.9773	6.7176	7.4064	7.4919	7.6534	7.8046	7.9475	8.0833	8.2129	8.3371
700 (164.96/438.11)	*V*	1.108	272.68	388.61	405.71	439.64	473.34	506.89	540.33	573.68	606.97
	U	696.285	2571.1	2840.1	2880.3	2961.3	3043.3	3126.8	3211.7	3298.3	3386.5
	H	697.061	2762.0	3112.1	3164.3	3269.0	3374.7	3481.6	3589.9	3699.9	3811.4
	S	1.9918	6.7052	7.3890	7.4745	7.6362	7.7875	7.9305	8.0663	8.1959	8.3201
725 (166.38/439.53)	*V*	1.110	263.77	375.01	391.54	424.33	456.90	489.31	521.61	553.83	585.99
	U	702.457	2572.2	2839.7	2880.0	2961.0	3043.1	3126.6	3211.5	3298.1	3386.4
	H	703.261	2763.4	3111.5	3163.8	3268.7	3374.3	3481.3	3589.7	3699.7	3811.2
	S	2.0059	6.6932	7.3721	7.4578	7.6196	7.7710	7.9140	8.0499	8.1796	8.3038

Table F.2. Superheated Steam, SI Units (Continued)

P/kPa t^{sat}/T^{sat} (°C/K)		sat. liq.	sat. vap.	TEMPERATURE: t °C (TEMPERATURE: T kelvins) 175 (448.15)	200 (473.15)	220 (493.15)	240 (513.15)	260 (533.15)	280 (553.15)	300 (573.15)	325 (598.15)
750	V	1.112	255.43	260.88	279.05	293.03	306.65	320.01	333.17	346.19	362.32
(167.76/440.91)	U	708.467	2573.3	2586.9	2632.1	2666.8	2700.6	2733.7	2766.4	2798.9	2839.3
	H	709.301	2764.8	2782.5	2841.4	2886.6	2930.6	2973.7	3016.3	3058.5	3111.0
	S	2.0195	6.6817	6.7215	6.8494	6.9429	7.0303	7.1128	7.1912	7.2662	7.3558
775	V	1.113	247.61	251.93	269.63	283.22	296.45	309.41	322.19	334.81	350.44
(169.10/442.25)	U	714.326	2574.3	2585.4	2631.0	2665.9	2699.8	2733.1	2765.9	2798.4	2838.9
	H	715.189	2766.2	2780.7	2840.0	2885.4	2929.6	2972.9	3015.6	3057.9	3110.5
	S	2.0328	6.6705	6.7031	6.8319	6.9259	7.0137	7.0965	7.1751	7.2502	7.3400
800	V	1.115	240.26	243.53	260.79	274.02	286.88	299.48	311.89	324.14	339.31
(170.41/443.56)	U	720.043	2575.3	2584.0	2629.9	2665.0	2699.1	2732.5	2765.4	2797.9	2838.5
	H	720.935	2767.5	2778.8	2838.6	2884.2	2928.6	2972.1	3014.9	3057.3	3109.9
	S	2.0457	6.6596	6.6851	6.8148	6.9094	6.9976	7.0807	7.1595	7.2348	7.3247
825	V	1.117	233.34	235.64	252.48	265.37	277.90	290.15	302.21	314.12	328.85
(171.69/444.84)	U	725.625	2576.2	2582.5	2628.8	2664.1	2698.4	2731.8	2764.8	2797.5	2838.1
	H	726.547	2768.7	2776.9	2837.1	2883.1	2927.6	2971.2	3014.1	3056.6	3109.4
	S	2.0583	6.6491	6.6675	6.7982	6.8933	6.9819	7.0653	7.1443	7.2197	7.3098
850	V	1.118	226.81	228.21	244.66	257.24	269.44	281.37	293.10	304.68	319.00
(172.94/446.09)	U	731.080	2577.1	2581.1	2627.7	2663.2	2697.6	2731.2	2764.3	2797.0	2837.7
	H	732.031	2769.9	2775.1	2835.7	2881.9	2926.6	2970.4	3013.4	3056.0	3108.8
	S	2.0705	6.6388	6.6504	6.7820	6.8777	6.9666	7.0503	7.1295	7.2051	7.2954
875	V	1.120	220.65	221.20	237.29	249.56	261.46	273.09	284.51	295.79	309.72
(174.16/447.31)	U	736.415	2578.0	2579.6	2626.6	2662.3	2696.8	2730.6	2763.7	2796.5	2837.3
	H	737.394	2771.0	2773.1	2834.2	2880.7	2925.6	2969.5	3012.7	3055.3	3108.3
	S	2.0825	6.6289	6.6336	6.7662	6.8624	6.9518	7.0357	7.1152	7.1909	7.2813
900	V	1.121	214.81	....	230.32	242.31	253.93	265.27	276.40	287.39	300.96
(175.36/448.51)	U	741.635	2578.8	....	2625.5	2661.4	2696.1	2729.9	2763.2	2796.1	2836.9
	H	742.644	2772.1	....	2832.7	2879.5	2924.6	2968.7	3012.0	3054.7	3107.7
	S	2.0941	6.6192	....	6.7508	6.8475	6.9373	7.0215	7.1012	7.1771	7.2676
925	V	1.123	209.28	....	223.73	235.46	246.80	257.87	268.73	279.44	292.66
(176.53/449.68)	U	746.746	2579.6	....	2624.3	2660.5	2695.3	2729.3	2762.6	2795.6	2836.5
	H	747.784	2773.2	....	2831.3	2878.3	2923.6	2967.8	3011.2	3054.1	3107.2
	S	2.1055	6.6097	....	6.7357	6.8329	6.9231	7.0076	7.0875	7.1636	7.2543

950 (177.67/450.82)	V	1.124	204.03	....	217.48	228.96	240.05	250.86	261.46	271.91	284.81
	U	751.754	2580.4	....	2623.2	2659.5	2694.6	2728.7	2762.1	2795.1	2836.0
	H	752.822	2774.2	....	2829.8	2877.0	2922.6	2967.0	3010.5	3053.4	3106.6
	S	2.1166	6.6005	....	6.7209	6.8187	6.9093	6.9941	7.0742	7.1505	7.2413
975 (178.79/451.94)	V	1.126	199.04	....	211.55	222.79	233.64	244.20	254.56	264.76	277.35
	U	756.663	2581.1	....	2622.0	2658.6	2693.8	2728.0	2761.5	2794.6	2835.6
	H	757.761	2775.2	....	2828.3	2875.8	2921.6	2966.1	3009.7	3052.8	3106.1
	S	2.1275	6.5916	....	6.7064	6.8048	6.8958	6.9809	7.0612	7.1377	7.2286
1000 (179.88/453.03)	V	1.127	194.29	....	205.92	216.93	227.55	237.89	248.01	257.98	270.27
	U	761.478	2581.9	....	2620.9	2657.7	2693.0	2727.4	2761.0	2794.2	2835.2
	H	762.605	2776.2	....	2826.8	2874.6	2920.6	2965.2	3009.0	3052.1	3105.5
	S	2.1382	6.5828	....	6.6922	6.7911	6.8825	6.9680	7.0485	7.1251	7.2163
1050 (182.02/455.17)	V	1.130	185.45	....	195.45	206.04	216.24	226.15	235.84	245.37	257.12
	U	770.843	2583.3	....	2618.5	2655.8	2691.5	2726.1	2759.9	2793.2	2834.4
	H	772.029	2778.0	....	2823.8	2872.1	2918.5	2963.5	3007.5	3050.8	3104.4
	S	2.1588	6.5659	....	6.6645	6.7647	6.8569	6.9430	7.0240	7.1009	7.1924
1100 (184.07/457.22)	V	1.133	177.38	....	185.92	196.14	205.96	215.47	224.77	233.91	245.16
	U	779.878	2584.5	....	2616.2	2653.9	2689.9	2724.7	2758.8	2792.2	2833.6
	H	781.124	2779.7	....	2820.7	2869.6	2916.4	2961.8	3006.0	3049.6	3103.3
	S	2.1786	6.5497	....	6.6379	6.7392	6.8323	6.9190	7.0005	7.0778	7.1695
1150 (186.05/459.20)	V	1.136	169.99	....	177.22	187.10	196.56	205.73	214.67	223.44	234.25
	U	788.611	2585.8	....	2613.8	2651.9	2688.3	2723.4	2757.7	2791.3	2832.8
	H	789.917	2781.3	....	2817.6	2867.1	2914.4	2960.0	3004.5	3048.2	3102.2
	S	2.1977	6.5342	....	6.6122	6.7147	6.8086	6.8959	6.9779	7.0556	7.1476
1200 (187.96/461.11)	V	1.139	163.20	....	169.23	178.80	187.95	196.79	205.40	213.85	224.24
	U	797.064	2586.9	....	2611.3	2650.0	2686.7	2722.1	2756.5	2790.3	2832.0
	H	798.430	2782.7	....	2814.4	2864.5	2912.2	2958.2	3003.0	3046.9	3101.0
	S	2.2161	6.5194	....	6.5872	6.6909	6.7858	6.8738	6.9562	7.0342	7.1266
1250 (189.81/462.96)	V	1.141	156.93	....	161.88	171.17	180.02	138.56	196.88	205.02	215.03
	U	805.259	2588.0	....	2608.9	2648.0	2685.1	2720.8	2755.4	2789.3	2831.1
	H	806.685	2784.1	....	2811.2	2861.9	2910.1	2956.5	3001.5	3045.6	3099.9
	S	2.2338	6.5050	....	6.5630	6.6680	6.7637	6.8523	6.9353	7.0136	7.1064
1300 (191.61/464.76)	V	1.144	151.13	....	155.09	164.11	172.70	180.97	189.01	196.87	206.53
	U	813.213	2589.0	....	2606.4	2646.0	2683.5	2719.4	2754.3	2788.4	2830.3
	H	814.700	2785.4	....	2808.0	2859.3	2908.0	2954.7	3000.0	3044.3	3098.8
	S	2.2510	6.4913	....	6.5394	6.6457	6.7424	6.8316	6.9151	6.9938	7.0869

Table F.2. Superheated Steam, SI Units (Continued)

P/kPa t^{sat}/T^{sat} (°C/K)		sat. liq.	sat. vap.	TEMPERATURE: t °C (TEMPERATURE: T kelvins) 350 (623.15)	375 (648.15)	400 (673.15)	450 (723.15)	500 (773.15)	550 (833.15)	600 (873.15)	650 (923.15)
750	V	1.112	255.43	378.31	394.22	410.05	441.55	472.90	504.15	535.30	566.40
(167.76/440.91)	U	708.467	2573.3	2879.6	2920.1	2960.7	3042.9	3126.3	3211.4	3298.0	3386.2
	H	709.301	2764.8	3163.4	3215.7	3268.3	3374.0	3481.0	3589.5	3699.5	3811.0
	S	2.0195	6.6817	7.4416	7.5240	7.6035	7.7550	7.8981	8.0340	8.1637	8.2880
775	V	1.113	247.61	365.94	381.35	396.69	427.20	457.56	487.81	517.97	548.07
(169.10/442.25)	U	714.326	2574.3	2879.3	2919.8	2960.4	3042.6	3126.1	3211.2	3297.8	3386.1
	H	715.189	2766.2	3162.9	3215.3	3267.9	3373.7	3480.8	3589.2	3699.3	3810.9
	S	2.0328	6.6705	7.4259	7.5084	7.5880	7.7396	7.8827	8.0187	8.1484	8.2727
800	V	1.115	240.26	354.34	369.29	384.16	413.74	443.17	472.49	501.72	530.89
(170.41/443.56)	U	720.043	2575.3	2878.9	2919.5	2960.2	3042.4	3125.9	3211.0	3297.7	3386.0
	H	720.935	2767.5	3162.4	3214.9	3267.5	3373.4	3480.5	3589.0	3699.1	3810.7
	S	2.0457	6.6596	7.4107	7.4932	7.5729	7.7246	7.8678	8.0038	8.1336	8.2579
825	V	1.117	233.34	343.45	357.96	372.39	401.10	429.65	458.10	486.46	514.76
(171.69/444.84)	U	725.625	2576.2	2878.6	2919.1	2959.9	3042.2	3125.7	3210.8	3297.5	3385.8
	H	726.547	2768.7	3161.9	3214.5	3267.1	3373.1	3480.2	3588.8	3698.8	3810.5
	S	2.0583	6.6491	7.3959	7.4786	7.5583	7.7101	7.8533	7.9894	8.1192	8.2436
850	V	1.118	226.81	333.20	347.29	361.31	389.20	416.93	444.56	472.09	499.57
(172.94/446.09)	U	731.080	2577.1	2878.2	2918.8	2959.6	3041.9	3125.5	3210.7	3297.4	3385.7
	H	732.031	2769.9	3161.4	3214.0	3266.7	3372.7	3479.9	3588.5	3698.6	3810.3
	S	2.0705	6.6388	7.3815	7.4643	7.5441	7.6960	7.8393	7.9754	8.1053	8.2296
875	V	1.120	220.65	323.53	337.24	350.87	377.98	404.94	431.79	458.55	485.25
(174.16/447.31)	U	736.415	2578.0	2877.9	2918.5	2959.3	3041.7	3125.3	3210.5	3297.2	3385.6
	H	737.394	2771.0	3161.0	3213.6	3266.3	3372.4	3479.7	3588.3	3698.4	3810.2
	S	2.0825	6.6289	7.3676	7.4504	7.5303	7.6823	7.8257	7.9618	8.0917	8.2161
900	V	1.121	214.81	314.40	327.74	341.01	367.39	393.61	419.73	445.76	471.72
(175.36/448.51)	U	741.635	2578.8	2877.5	2918.2	2959.0	3041.4	3125.1	3210.3	3297.1	3385.4
	H	742.644	2772.1	3160.5	3213.2	3266.0	3372.1	3479.4	3588.1	3698.2	3810.0
	S	2.0941	6.6192	7.3540	7.4370	7.5169	7.6689	7.8124	7.9486	8.0785	8.2030
925	V	1.123	209.28	305.76	318.75	331.68	357.36	382.90	408.32	433.66	458.93
(176.53/449.68)	U	746.746	2579.6	2877.2	2917.9	2958.8	3041.2	3124.9	3210.1	3296.9	3385.3
	H	747.784	2773.2	3160.0	3212.7	3265.6	3371.8	3479.1	3587.8	3698.0	3809.8
	S	2.1055	6.6097	7.3408	7.4238	7.5038	7.6560	7.7995	7.9357	8.0657	8.1902

950 (177.67/450.82)	*V*	1.124	204.03	297.57	310.24	322.84	347.87	372.74	397.51	422.19	446.81
	U	751.754	2580.4	2876.8	2917.6	2958.5	3041.0	3124.7	3209.9	3296.7	3385.1
	H	752.822	2774.2	3159.5	3212.3	3265.2	3371.5	3478.8	3587.6	3697.8	3809.6
	S	2.1166	6.6005	7.3279	7.4110	7.4911	7.6433	7.7869	7.9232	8.0532	8.1777
975 (178.79/451.94)	*V*	1.126	199.04	289.81	302.17	314.45	338.86	363.11	387.26	411.32	435.31
	U	756.663	2581.1	2876.5	2917.3	2958.2	3040.7	3124.5	3209.8	3296.6	3385.0
	H	757.761	2775.2	3159.0	3211.9	3264.8	3371.1	3478.6	3587.3	3697.6	3809.4
	S	2.1275	6.5916	7.3154	7.3986	7.4787	7.6310	7.7747	7.9110	8.0410	8.1656
1000 (179.88/453.03)	*V*	1.127	194.29	282.43	294.50	306.49	330.30	353.96	377.52	400.98	424.38
	U	761.478	2581.9	2876.1	2917.0	2957.9	3040.5	3124.3	3209.6	3296.4	3384.9
	H	762.605	2776.2	3158.5	3211.5	3264.4	3370.8	3478.3	3587.1	3697.4	3809.3
	S	2.1382	6.5828	7.3031	7.3864	7.4665	7.6190	7.7627	7.8991	8.0292	8.1537
1050 (182.02/455.17)	*V*	1.130	185.45	268.74	280.25	291.69	314.41	336.97	359.43	381.79	404.10
	U	770.843	2583.3	2875.4	2916.3	2957.4	3040.0	3123.9	3209.2	3296.1	3384.6
	H	772.029	2778.0	3157.6	3210.6	3263.6	3370.2	3477.7	3586.6	3697.0	3808.9
	S	2.1588	6.5659	7.2795	7.3629	7.4432	7.5958	7.7397	7.8762	8.0063	8.1309
1100 (184.07/457.22)	*V*	1.133	177.38	256.28	267.30	278.24	299.96	321.53	342.98	364.35	385.65
	U	779.878	2584.5	2874.7	2915.7	2956.8	3039.6	3123.5	3208.9	3295.8	3384.3
	H	781.124	2779.7	3156.6	3209.7	3262.9	3369.5	3477.2	3586.2	3696.6	3808.5
	S	2.1786	6.5497	7.2569	7.3405	7.4209	7.5737	7.7177	7.8543	7.9845	8.1092
1150 (186.05/459.20)	*V*	1.136	169.99	244.91	255.47	265.96	286.77	307.42	327.97	348.42	368.81
	U	788.611	2585.8	2874.0	2915.1	2956.2	3039.1	3123.1	3208.5	3295.5	3384.1
	H	789.917	2781.3	3155.6	3208.9	3262.1	3368.9	3476.6	3585.7	3696.2	3808.2
	S	2.1977	6.5342	7.2352	7.3190	7.3995	7.5525	7.6966	7.8333	7.9636	8.0883
1200 (187.96/461.11)	*V*	1.139	163.20	234.49	244.63	254.70	274.68	294.50	314.20	333.82	353.38
	U	797.064	2586.9	2873.3	2914.4	2955.7	3038.6	3122.7	3208.2	3295.2	3383.8
	H	798.430	2782.7	3154.6	3208.0	3261.3	3368.2	3476.1	3585.2	3695.8	3807.8
	S	2.2161	6.5194	7.2144	7.2983	7.3790	7.5323	7.6765	7.8132	7.9436	8.0684
1250 (189.81/462.96)	*V*	1.141	156.93	224.90	234.66	244.35	263.55	282.60	301.54	320.39	339.18
	U	805.259	2588.0	2872.5	2913.8	2955.1	3038.1	3122.3	3207.8	3294.9	3383.5
	H	806.685	2784.1	3153.7	3207.1	3260.5	3367.6	3475.5	3584.7	3695.4	3807.5
	S	2.2338	6.5050	7.1944	7.2785	7.3593	7.5128	7.6571	7.7940	7.9244	8.0493
1300 (191.61/464.76)	*V*	1.144	151.13	216.05	225.46	234.79	253.28	271.62	289.85	307.99	326.07
	U	813.213	2589.0	2871.8	2913.2	2954.5	3037.7	3121.9	3207.5	3294.6	3383.2
	H	814.700	2785.4	3152.7	3206.3	3259.7	3366.9	3475.0	3584.3	3695.0	3807.1
	S	2.2510	6.4913	7.1751	7.2594	7.3404	7.4940	7.6385	7.7754	7.9060	8.0309

Table F.2. Superheated Steam, SI Units (Continued)

P/kPa t^{sat}/T^{sat} (°C/K)		sat. liq.	sat. vap.	TEMPERATURE: t °C (TEMPERATURE: T kelvins) 200 (473.15)	225 (498.15)	250 (523.15)	275 (548.15)	300 (573.15)	325 (598.15)	350 (623.15)	375 (648.15)
1350	V	1.146	145.74	148.79	159.70	169.96	179.79	189.33	198.66	207.85	216.93
(193.35/466.50)	U	820.944	2589.9	2603.9	2653.6	2700.1	2744.4	2787.4	2829.5	2871.1	2912.5
	H	822.491	2786.6	2804.7	2869.2	2929.5	2987.1	3043.0	3097.7	3151.7	3205.4
	S	2.2676	6.4780	6.5165	6.6493	6.7675	6.8750	6.9746	7.0681	7.1566	7.2410
1400	V	1.149	140.72	142.94	153.57	163.55	173.08	182.32	191.35	200.24	209.02
(195.04/468.19)	U	828.465	2590.8	2601.3	2651.7	2698.6	2743.2	2786.4	2828.6	2870.4	2911.9
	H	830.074	2787.8	2801.4	2866.7	2927.6	2985.5	3041.6	3096.5	3150.7	3204.5
	S	2.2837	6.4651	6.4941	6.6285	6.7477	6.8560	6.9561	7.0499	7.1386	7.2233
1450	V	1.151	136.04	137.48	147.86	157.57	166.83	175.79	184.54	193.15	201.65
(196.69/469.84)	U	835.791	2591.6	2598.7	2649.7	2697.1	2742.0	2785.4	2827.8	2869.7	2911.3
	H	837.460	2788.9	2798.1	2864.1	2925.5	2983.9	3040.3	3095.4	3149.7	3203.6
	S	2.2993	6.4526	6.4722	6.6082	6.7286	6.8376	6.9381	7.0322	7.1212	7.2061
1500	V	1.154	131.66	132.38	142.53	151.99	161.00	169.70	178.19	186.53	194.77
(198.29/471.44)	U	842.933	2592.4	2596.1	2647.7	2695.5	2740.8	2784.4	2826.9	2868.9	2910.6
	H	844.663	2789.9	2794.7	2861.5	2923.5	2982.3	3038.9	3094.2	3148.7	3202.8
	S	2.3145	6.4406	6.4508	6.5885	6.7099	6.8196	6.9207	7.0152	7.1044	7.1894
1550	V	1.156	127.55	127.61	137.54	146.77	155.54	164.00	172.25	180.34	188.33
(199.85/473.00)	U	849.901	2593.2	2593.5	2645.8	2694.0	2739.5	2783.4	2826.1	2868.2	2910.0
	H	851.694	2790.8	2791.3	2858.9	2921.5	2980.6	3037.6	3093.1	3147.7	3201.9
	S	2.3292	6.4289	6.4298	6.5692	6.6917	6.8022	6.9038	6.9986	7.0881	7.1733
1600	V	1.159	123.69	....	132.85	141.87	150.42	158.66	166.68	174.54	182.30
(201.37/474.52)	U	856.707	2593.8	....	2643.7	2692.4	2738.3	2782.4	2825.2	2867.5	2909.3
	H	858.561	2791.7	....	2856.3	2919.4	2979.0	3036.2	3091.9	3146.7	3201.0
	S	2.3436	6.4175	....	6.5503	6.6740	6.7852	6.8873	6.9825	7.0723	7.1577
1650	V	1.161	120.05	....	128.45	137.27	145.61	153.64	161.44	169.09	176.63
(202.86/476.01)	U	863.359	2594.5	....	2641.7	2690.9	2737.1	2781.3	2824.4	2866.7	2908.7
	H	865.275	2792.6	....	2853.6	2917.4	2977.3	3034.8	3090.8	3145.7	3200.1
	S	2.3576	6.4065	....	6.5319	6.6567	6.7687	6.8713	6.9669	7.0569	7.1425
1700	V	1.163	116.62	....	124.31	132.94	141.09	148.91	156.51	163.96	171.30
(204.31/477.46)	U	869.866	2595.1	....	2639.6	2689.3	2735.8	2780.3	2823.5	2866.0	2908.0
	H	871.843	2793.4	....	2851.0	2915.3	2975.6	3033.5	3089.6	3144.7	3199.2
	S	2.3713	6.3957	....	6.5138	6.6398	6.7526	6.8557	6.9516	7.0419	7.1277

1750 (205.72/478.87)	*V*	1.166	113.38	....	120.39	128.85	136.82	144.45	151.87	159.12	166.27
	U	876.234	2595.7	....	2637.6	2687.7	2734.5	2779.3	2822.7	2865.3	2907.4
	H	878.274	2794.1	....	2848.2	2913.2	2974.0	3032.1	3088.4	3143.7	3198.4
	S	2.3846	6.3853	....	6.4961	6.6233	6.7368	6.8405	6.9368	7.0273	7.1133
1800 (207.11/480.26)	*V*	1.168	110.32	....	116.69	124.99	132.78	140.24	147.48	154.55	161.51
	U	882.472	2596.3	....	2635.5	2686.1	2733.3	2778.2	2821.8	2864.5	2906.7
	H	884.574	2794.8	....	2845.5	2911.0	2972.3	3030.7	3087.3	3142.7	3197.5
	S	2.3976	6.3751	....	6.4787	6.6071	6.7214	6.8257	6.9223	7.0131	7.0993
1850 (208.47/481.62)	*V*	1.170	107.41	....	113.19	121.33	128.96	136.26	143.33	150.23	157.02
	U	888.585	2596.8	....	2633.3	2684.4	2732.0	2777.2	2820.9	2863.8	2906.1
	H	890.750	2795.5	....	2842.8	2908.9	2970.6	3029.3	3086.1	3141.7	3196.6
	S	2.4103	6.3651	....	6.4616	6.5912	6.7064	6.8112	6.9082	6.9993	7.0856
1900 (209.80/482.95)	*V*	1.172	104.65	....	109.87	117.87	125.35	132.49	139.39	146.14	152.76
	U	894.580	2597.3	....	2631.2	2682.8	2730.7	2776.2	2820.1	2863.0	2905.4
	H	896.807	2796.1	....	2840.0	2906.7	2968.8	3027.9	3084.9	3140.7	3195.7
	S	2.4228	6.3554	....	6.4448	6.5757	6.6917	6.7970	6.8944	6.9857	7.0723
1950 (211.10/484.25)	*V*	1.174	102.031	....	106.72	114.58	121.91	128.90	135.66	142.25	148.72
	U	900.461	2597.7	....	2629.0	2681.1	2729.4	2775.1	2819.2	2862.3	2904.8
	H	902.752	2796.7	....	2837.1	2904.6	2967.1	3026.5	3083.7	3139.7	3194.8
	S	2.4349	6.3459	....	6.4283	6.5604	6.6772	6.7831	6.8809	6.9725	7.0593
2000 (212.37/485.52)	*V*	1.177	99.536	....	103.72	111.45	118.65	125.50	132.11	138.56	144.89
	U	906.236	2598.2	....	2626.9	2679.5	2728.1	2774.0	2818.3	2861.5	2904.1
	H	908.589	2797.2	....	2834.3	2902.4	2965.4	3025.0	3082.5	3138.6	3193.9
	S	2.4469	6.3366	....	6.4120	6.5454	6.6631	6.7696	6.8677	6.9596	7.0466
2100 (214.85/488.00)	*V*	1.181	94.890	....	98.147	105.64	112.59	119.18	125.53	131.70	137.76
	U	917.479	2598.9	....	2622.4	2676.1	2725.4	2771.9	2816.5	2860.0	2902.8
	H	919.959	2798.2	....	2828.5	2897.9	2961.9	3022.2	3080.1	3136.6	3192.1
	S	2.4700	6.3187	....	6.3802	6.5162	6.6356	6.7432	6.8422	6.9347	7.0220
2200 (217.24/490.39)	*V*	1.185	90.652	....	93.067	100.35	107.07	113.43	119.53	125.47	131.28
	U	928.346	2599.6	....	2617.9	2672.7	2722.7	2769.7	2814.7	2858.5	2901.5
	H	930.953	2799.1	....	2822.7	2893.4	2958.3	3019.3	3077.7	3134.5	3190.3
	S	2.4922	6.3015	....	6.3492	6.4879	6.6091	6.7179	6.8177	6.9107	6.9985
2300 (219.55/492.70)	*V*	1.189	86.769	....	88.420	95.513	102.03	108.18	114.06	119.77	125.36
	U	938.866	2600.2	....	2613.3	2669.2	2720.0	2767.6	2812.9	2857.0	2900.2
	H	941.601	2799.8	....	2816.7	2888.9	2954.7	3016.4	3075.3	3132.4	3188.5
	S	2.5136	6.2849	....	6.3190	6.4605	6.5835	6.6935	6.7941	6.8877	6.9759

Table F.2. Superheated Steam, SI Units (Continued)

P/kPa t^{sat}/T^{sat} (°C/K)		sat. liq.	sat. vap.	400 (673.15)	425 (698.15)	450 (723.15)	475 (748.15)	500 (773.15)	550 (823.15)	600 (873.15)	650 (923.15)
				TEMPERATURE: t °C (TEMPERATURE: T kelvins)							
1350 (193.35/466.50)	V	1.146	145.74	225.94	234.88	243.78	252.63	261.46	279.03	296.51	313.93
	U	820.944	2589.9	2953.9	2995.5	3037.2	3079.2	3121.5	3207.1	3294.3	3383.0
	H	822.491	2786.6	3259.0	3312.6	3366.3	3420.2	3474.4	3583.8	3694.5	3806.8
	S	2.2676	6.4780	7.3221	7.4003	7.4759	7.5493	7.6205	7.7576	7.8882	8.0132
1400 (195.04/468.19)	V	1.149	140.72	217.72	226.35	234.95	243.50	252.02	268.98	285.85	302.66
	U	828.465	2590.8	2953.4	2994.9	3036.7	3078.7	3121.1	3206.8	3293.9	3382.7
	H	830.074	2787.8	3258.2	3311.8	3365.6	3419.6	3473.9	3583.3	3694.1	3806.4
	S	2.2837	6.4651	7.3045	7.3828	7.4585	7.5319	7.6032	7.7404	7.8710	7.9961
1450 (196.69/469.84)	V	1.151	136.04	210.06	218.42	226.72	234.99	243.23	259.62	275.93	292.16
	U	835.791	2591.6	2952.8	2994.4	3036.2	3078.3	3120.7	3206.4	3293.6	3382.4
	H	837.460	2788.9	3257.4	3311.1	3365.0	3419.0	3473.3	3582.9	3693.7	3806.1
	S	2.2993	6.4526	7.2874	7.3658	7.4416	7.5151	7.5865	7.7237	7.8545	7.9796
1500 (198.29/471.44)	V	1.154	131.66	202.92	211.01	219.05	227.06	235.03	250.89	266.66	282.37
	U	842.933	2592.4	2952.2	2993.9	3035.8	3077.9	3120.3	3206.0	3293.3	3382.1
	H	844.663	2789.9	3256.6	3310.4	3364.3	3418.4	3472.8	3582.4	3693.3	3805.7
	S	2.3145	6.4406	7.2709	7.3494	7.4253	7.4989	7.5703	7.7077	7.8385	7.9636
1550 (199.85/473.00)	V	1.156	127.55	196.24	204.08	211.87	219.63	227.35	242.72	258.00	273.21
	U	849.901	2593.2	2951.7	2993.4	3035.3	3077.4	3119.8	3205.7	3293.0	3381.9
	H	851.694	2790.8	3255.8	3309.7	3363.7	3417.8	3472.2	3581.9	3692.9	3805.3
	S	2.3292	6.4289	7.2550	7.3336	7.4095	7.4832	7.5547	7.6921	7.8230	7.9482
1600 (201.37/474.52)	V	1.159	123.69	189.97	197.58	205.15	212.67	220.16	235.06	249.87	264.62
	U	856.707	2593.8	2951.1	2992.9	3034.8	3077.0	3119.4	3205.3	3292.7	3381.6
	H	858.561	2791.7	3255.0	3309.0	3363.0	3417.2	3471.7	3581.4	3692.5	3805.0
	S	2.3436	6.4175	7.2394	7.3182	7.3942	7.4679	7.5395	7.6770	7.8080	7.9333
1650 (202.86/476.01)	V	1.161	120.05	184.09	191.48	198.82	206.13	213.40	227.86	242.24	256.55
	U	863.359	2594.5	2950.5	2992.3	3034.3	3076.5	3119.0	3205.0	3292.4	3381.3
	H	865.275	2792.6	3254.2	3308.3	3362.4	3416.7	3471.1	3581.0	3692.1	3804.6
	S	2.3576	6.4065	7.2244	7.3032	7.3794	7.4531	7.5248	7.6624	7.7934	7.9188
1700 (204.31/477.46)	V	1.163	116.62	178.55	185.74	192.87	199.97	207.04	221.09	235.06	248.96
	U	869.866	2595.1	2949.9	2991.8	3033.9	3076.1	3118.6	3204.6	3292.1	3381.0
	H	871.843	2793.4	3253.5	3307.6	3361.7	3416.1	3470.6	3580.5	3691.7	3804.3
	S	2.3713	6.3957	7.2098	7.2887	7.3649	7.4388	7.5105	7.6482	7.7793	7.9047

1750 (205.72/478.87)	*V*	1.166	113.38	173.32	180.32	187.26	194.17	201.04	214.71	228.28	241.80
	U	876.234	2595.7	2949.3	2991.3	3033.4	3075.7	3118.2	3204.3	3291.8	3380.8
	H	878.274	2794.1	3252.7	3306.9	3361.1	3415.5	3470.0	3580.0	3691.3	3803.9
	S	2.3846	6.3853	7.1955	7.2746	7.3509	7.4248	7.4965	7.6344	7.7656	7.8910
1800 (207.11/480.26)	*V*	1.168	110.32	168.39	175.20	181.97	188.69	195.38	208.68	221.89	235.03
	U	882.472	2596.3	2948.8	2990.8	3032.9	3075.2	3117.8	3203.9	3291.5	3380.5
	H	884.574	2794.8	3251.9	3306.1	3360.4	3414.9	3469.5	3579.5	3690.9	3803.6
	S	2.3976	6.3751	7.1816	7.2608	7.3372	7.4112	7.4830	7.6209	7.7522	7.8777
1850 (208.47/481.62)	*V*	1.170	107.41	163.73	170.37	176.96	183.50	190.02	202.97	215.84	228.64
	U	888.585	2596.8	2948.2	2990.3	3032.4	3074.8	3117.4	3203.6	3291.1	3380.2
	H	890.750	2795.5	3251.1	3305.4	3359.8	3414.3	3468.9	3579.1	3690.4	3803.2
	S	2.4103	6.3651	7.1681	7.2474	7.3239	7.3980	7.4698	7.6079	7.7392	7.8648
1900 (209.80/482.95)	*V*	1.172	104.65	159.30	165.78	172.21	178.59	184.94	197.57	210.11	222.58
	U	894.580	2597.3	2947.6	2989.7	3031.9	3074.3	3117.0	3203.2	3290.8	3380.0
	H	896.807	2796.1	3250.3	3304.7	3359.1	3413.7	3468.4	3578.6	3690.0	3802.8
	S	2.4228	6.3554	7.1550	7.2344	7.3109	7.3851	7.4570	7.5951	7.7265	7.8522
1950 (211.10/484.25)	*V*	1.174	102.031	155.11	161.43	167.70	173.93	180.13	192.44	204.67	216.83
	U	900.461	2597.7	2947.0	2989.2	3031.5	3073.9	3116.6	3202.9	3290.5	3379.7
	H	902.752	2796.7	3249.5	3304.0	3358.5	3413.1	3467.8	3578.1	3689.6	3802.5
	S	2.4349	6.3459	7.1421	7.2216	7.2983	7.3725	7.4445	7.5827	7.7142	7.8399
2000 (212.37/485.52)	*V*	1.177	99.536	151.13	157.30	163.42	169.51	175.55	187.57	199.50	211.36
	U	906.236	2598.2	2946.4	2988.7	3031.0	3073.5	3116.2	3202.5	3290.2	3379.4
	H	908.589	2797.2	3248.7	3303.3	3357.8	3412.5	3467.3	3577.6	3689.2	3802.1
	S	2.4469	6.3366	7.1296	7.2092	7.2859	7.3602	7.4323	7.5706	7.7022	7.8279
2100 (214.85/488.00)	*V*	1.181	94.890	143.73	149.63	155.48	161.28	167.06	178.53	189.91	201.22
	U	917.479	2598.9	2945.3	2987.6	3030.0	3072.6	3115.3	3201.8	3289.6	3378.9
	H	919.959	2798.2	3247.1	3301.8	3356.5	3411.3	3466.2	3576.7	3688.4	3801.4
	S	2.4700	6.3187	7.1053	7.1851	7.2621	7.3365	7.4087	7.5472	7.6789	7.8048
2200 (217.24/490.39)	*V*	1.185	90.652	137.00	142.65	148.25	153.81	159.34	170.30	181.19	192.00
	U	928.346	2599.6	2944.1	2986.6	3029.1	3071.7	3114.5	3201.1	3289.0	3378.3
	H	930.953	2799.1	3245.5	3300.4	3355.2	3410.1	3465.1	3575.7	3687.6	3800.7
	S	2.4922	6.3015	7.0821	7.1621	7.2393	7.3139	7.3862	7.5249	7.6568	7.7827
2300 (219.55/492.70)	*V*	1.189	86.769	130.85	136.28	141.65	146.99	152.28	162.80	173.22	183.58
	U	938.866	2600.2	2942.9	2985.5	3028.1	3070.8	3113.7	3200.4	3288.3	3377.8
	H	941.601	2799.8	3243.9	3299.0	3353.9	3408.9	3464.0	3574.8	3686.7	3800.0
	S	2.5136	6.2849	7.0598	7.1401	7.2174	7.2922	7.3646	7.5035	7.6355	7.7616

Table F.2. Superheated Steam, SI Units (Continued)

P/kPa t^{sat}/T^{sat} (°C/K)		sat. liq.	sat. vap.	TEMPERATURE: t °C (TEMPERATURE: T kelvins) 225 (498.15)	250 (523.15)	275 (548.15)	300 (573.15)	325 (598.15)	350 (623.15)	375 (648.15)	400 (673.15)
	V	1.193	83.199	84.149	91.075	97.411	103.36	109.05	114.55	119.93	125.22
2400	U	949.066	2600.7	2608.6	2665.6	2717.3	2765.4	2811.1	2855.4	2898.8	2941.7
(221.78/494.93)	H	951.929	2800.4	2810.6	2884.2	2951.1	3013.4	3072.8	3130.4	3186.7	3242.3
	S	2.5343	6.2690	6.2894	6.4338	6.5586	6.6699	6.7714	6.8656	6.9542	7.0384
	V	1.197	79.905	80.210	86.985	93.154	98.925	104.43	109.75	114.94	120.04
2500	U	958.969	2601.2	2603.8	2662.0	2714.5	2763.1	2809.3	2853.9	2897.5	2940.6
(223.94/497.09)	H	961.962	2800.9	2804.3	2879.5	2947.4	3010.4	3070.4	3128.2	3184.8	3240.7
	S	2.5543	6.2536	6.2604	6.4077	6.5345	6.6470	6.7494	6.8442	6.9333	7.0178
	V	1.201	76.856	....	83.205	89.220	94.830	100.17	105.32	110.33	115.26
2600	U	968.597	2601.5	....	2658.4	2711.7	2760.9	2807.4	2852.3	2896.1	2939.4
(226.04/499.19)	H	971.720	2801.4	....	2874.7	2943.6	3007.4	3067.9	3126.1	3183.0	3239.0
	S	2.5736	6.2387	....	6.3823	6.5110	6.6249	6.7281	6.8236	6.9131	6.9979
	V	1.205	74.025	....	79.698	85.575	91.036	96.218	101.21	106.07	110.83
2700	U	977.968	2601.8	....	2654.7	2708.8	2758.6	2805.6	2850.7	2894.8	2938.2
(228.07/501.22)	H	981.222	2801.7	....	2869.9	2939.8	3004.4	3065.4	3124.0	3181.2	3237.4
	S	2.5924	6.2244	....	6.3575	6.4882	6.6034	6.7075	6.8036	6.8935	6.9787
	V	1.209	71.389	....	76.437	82.187	87.510	92.550	97.395	102.10	106.71
2800	U	987.100	2602.1	....	2650.9	2705.9	2756.3	2803.7	2849.2	2893.4	2937.0
(230.05/503.20)	H	990.485	2802.0	....	2864.9	2936.0	3001.3	3062.8	3121.9	3179.3	3235.8
	S	2.6106	6.2104	....	6.3331	6.4659	6.5824	6.6875	6.7842	6.8746	6.9601
	V	1.213	68.928	....	73.395	79.029	84.226	89.133	93.843	98.414	102.88
2900	U	996.008	2602.3	....	2647.1	2702.9	2754.0	2801.8	2847.6	2892.0	2935.8
(231.97/505.12)	H	999.524	2802.2	....	2859.9	2932.1	2998.2	3060.3	3119.7	3177.4	3234.1
	S	2.6283	6.1969	....	6.3092	6.4441	6.5621	6.6681	6.7654	6.8563	6.9421
	V	1.216	66.626	....	70.551	76.078	81.159	85.943	90.526	94.969	99.310
3000	U	1004.7	2602.4	....	2643.2	2700.0	2751.6	2799.9	2846.0	2890.7	2934.6
(233.84/506.99)	H	1008.4	2802.3	....	2854.8	2928.2	2995.1	3057.7	3117.5	3175.6	3232.5
	S	2.6455	6.1837	....	6.2857	6.4228	6.5422	6.6491	6.7471	6.8385	6.9246
	V	1.220	64.467	....	67.885	73.315	78.287	82.958	87.423	91.745	95.965
3100	U	1013.2	2602.5	....	2639.2	2697.0	2749.2	2797.9	2844.3	2889.3	2933.4
(235.67/508.82)	H	1017.0	2802.3	....	2849.6	2924.2	2991.9	3055.1	3115.4	3173.7	3230.8
	S	2.6623	6.1709	....	6.2626	6.4019	6.5227	6.6307	6.7294	6.8212	6.9077

	V	1.224	62.439	....	65.380	70.721	75.593	80.158	84.513	88.723	92.829
3200	U	1021.5	2602.5	....	2635.2	2693.9	2746.8	2796.0	2842.7	2887.9	2932.1
(237.45/510.60)	H	1025.4	2802.3	....	2844.4	2920.2	2988.7	3052.5	3113.2	3171.8	3229.2
	S	2.6786	6.1585	....	6.2398	6.3815	6.5037	6.6127	6.7120	6.8043	6.8912
	V	1.227	60.529	....	63.021	68.282	73.061	77.526	81.778	85.883	89.883
3300	U	1029.7	2602.5	....	2631.1	2690.8	2744.4	2794.0	2841.1	2886.5	2930.9
(239.18/512.33)	H	1033.7	2802.3	....	2839.0	2916.1	2985.5	3049.9	3110.9	3169.9	3227.5
	S	2.6945	6.1463	....	6.2173	6.3614	6.4851	6.5951	6.6952	6.7879	6.8752
	V	1.231	58.728	....	60.796	65.982	70.675	75.048	79.204	83.210	87.110
3400	U	1037.6	2602.5	....	2626.9	2687.7	2741.9	2792.0	2839.4	2885.1	2929.7
(240.88/514.03)	H	1041.8	2802.1	....	2833.6	2912.0	2982.2	3047.2	3108.7	3168.0	3225.9
	S	2.7101	6.1344	....	6.1951	6.3416	6.4669	6.5779	6.6787	6.7719	6.8595
	V	1.235	57.025	....	58.693	63.812	68.424	72.710	76.776	80.689	84.494
3500	U	1045.4	2602.4	....	2622.7	2684.5	2739.5	2790.0	2837.8	2883.7	2928.4
(242.54/515.69)	H	1049.8	2802.0	....	2828.1	2907.8	2979.0	3044.5	3106.5	3166.1	3224.2
	S	2.7253	6.1228	....	6.1732	6.3221	6.4491	6.5611	6.6626	6.7563	6.8443
	V	1.238	55.415	....	56.702	61.759	66.297	70.501	74.482	78.308	82.024
3600	U	1053.1	2602.2	....	2618.4	2681.3	2737.0	2788.0	2836.1	2882.3	2927.2
(244.16/517.31)	H	1057.6	2801.7	....	2822.5	2903.6	2975.6	3041.8	3104.2	3164.2	3222.5
	S	2.7401	6.1115	....	6.1514	6.3030	6.4315	6.5446	6.6468	6.7411	6.8294
	V	1.242	53.888	....	54.812	59.814	64.282	68.410	72.311	76.055	79.687
3700	U	1060.6	2602.1	....	2614.0	2678.0	2734.4	2786.0	2834.4	2880.8	2926.0
(245.75/518.90)	H	1065.2	2801.4	....	2816.8	2899.3	2972.3	3039.1	3102.0	3162.2	3220.8
	S	2.7547	6.1004	....	6.1299	6.2841	6.4143	6.5284	6.6314	6.7262	6.8149
	V	1.245	52.438	....	53.017	57.968	62.372	66.429	70.254	73.920	77.473
3800	U	1068.0	2601.9	....	2609.5	2674.7	2731.9	2783.9	2832.7	2879.4	2924.7
(247.31/520.46)	H	1072.7	2801.1	....	2811.0	2895.0	2968.9	3036.4	3099.7	3160.3	3219.1
	S	2.7689	6.0896	....	6.1085	6.2654	6.3973	6.5126	6.6163	6.7117	6.8007
	V	1.249	51.061	....	51.308	56.215	60.558	64.547	68.302	71.894	75.372
3900	U	1075.3	2601.6	....	2605.0	2671.4	2729.3	2781.9	2831.0	2877.9	2923.5
(248.84/521.99)	H	1080.1	2800.8	....	2805.1	2890.6	2965.5	3033.6	3097.4	3158.3	3217.4
	S	2.7828	6.0789	....	6.0872	6.2470	6.3806	6.4970	6.6015	6.6974	6.7868
	V	1.252	49.749	....	....	54.546	58.833	62.759	66.446	69.969	73.376
4000	U	1082.4	2601.3	....	....	2668.0	2726.7	2779.8	2829.3	2876.5	2922.2
(250.33/523.48)	H	1087.4	2800.3	....	....	2886.1	2962.0	3030.8	3095.1	3156.4	3215.7
	S	2.7965	6.0685	....	....	6.2288	6.3642	6.4817	6.5870	6.6834	6.7733

Table F.2. Superheated Steam, SI Units (Continued)

P/kPa t^{sat}/T^{sat} (°C/K)		sat. liq.	sat. vap.	TEMPERATURE: t °C (TEMPERATURE: T kelvins) 425 (698.15)	450 (723.15)	475 (748.15)	500 (773.15)	525 (798.15)	550 (823.15)	600 (873.15)	650 (923.15)
	V	1.193	83.199	130.44	135.61	140.73	145.82	150.88	155.91	165.92	175.86
2400	U	949.066	2600.7	2984.5	3027.1	3069.9	3112.9	3156.1	3199.6	3287.7	3377.2
(221.78/494.93)	H	951.929	2800.4	3297.5	3352.6	3407.7	3462.9	3518.2	3573.8	3685.9	3799.3
	S	2.5343	6.2690	7.1189	7.1964	7.2713	7.3439	7.4144	7.4830	7.6152	7.7414
	V	1.197	79.905	125.07	130.04	134.97	139.87	144.74	149.58	159.21	168.76
2500	U	958.969	2601.2	2983.4	3026.2	3069.0	3112.1	3155.4	3198.9	3287.1	3376.7
(223.94/497.09)	H	961.962	2800.9	3296.1	3351.3	3406.5	3461.7	3517.2	3572.9	3685.1	3798.6
	S	2.5543	6.2536	7.0986	7.1763	7.2513	7.3240	7.3946	7.4633	7.5956	7.7220
	V	1.201	76.856	120.11	124.91	129.66	134.38	139.07	143.74	153.01	162.21
2600	U	968.597	2601.5	2982.3	3025.2	3068.1	3111.2	3154.6	3198.2	3286.5	3376.1
(226.04/499.19)	H	971.720	2801.4	3294.6	3349.9	3405.3	3460.6	3516.2	3571.9	3684.3	3797.9
	S	2.5736	6.2387	7.0789	7.1568	7.2320	7.3048	7.3755	7.4443	7.5768	7.7033
	V	1.205	74.025	115.52	120.15	124.74	129.30	133.82	138.33	147.27	156.14
2700	U	977.968	2601.8	2981.2	3024.2	3067.2	3110.4	3153.8	3197.5	3285.8	3375.6
(228.07/501.22)	H	981.222	2801.7	3293.1	3348.6	3404.0	3459.5	3515.2	3571.0	3683.5	3797.1
	S	2.5924	6.2244	7.0600	7.1381	7.2134	7.2863	7.3571	7.4260	7.5587	7.6853
	V	1.209	71.389	111.25	115.74	120.17	124.58	128.95	133.30	141.94	150.50
2800	U	987.100	2602.1	2980.2	3023.2	3066.3	3109.6	3153.1	3196.8	3285.2	3375.0
(230.05/503.20)	H	990.485	2802.0	3291.7	3347.3	3402.8	3458.4	3514.1	3570.0	3682.6	3796.4
	S	2.6106	6.2104	7.0416	7.1199	7.1954	7.2685	7.3394	7.4084	7.5412	7.6679
	V	1.213	68.928	107.28	111.62	115.92	120.18	124.42	128.62	136.97	145.26
2900	U	996.008	2602.3	2979.1	3022.3	3065.5	3108.8	3152.3	3196.1	3284.6	3374.5
(231.97/505.12)	H	999.524	2802.2	3290.2	3346.0	3401.6	3457.3	3513.1	3569.1	3681.8	3795.7
	S	2.6283	6.1969	7.0239	7.1024	7.1780	7.2512	7.3222	7.3913	7.5243	7.6511
	V	1.216	66.626	103.58	107.79	111.95	116.08	120.18	124.26	132.34	140.36
3000	U	1004.7	2602.4	2978.0	3021.3	3064.6	3107.9	3151.5	3195.4	3284.0	3373.9
(233.84/506.99)	H	1008.4	2802.3	3288.7	3344.6	3400.4	3456.2	3512.1	3568.1	3681.0	3795.0
	S	2.6455	6.1837	7.0067	7.0854	7.1612	7.2345	7.3056	7.3748	7.5079	7.6349
	V	1.220	64.467	100.11	104.20	108.24	112.24	116.22	120.17	128.01	135.78
3100	U	1013.2	2602.5	2976.9	3020.3	3063.7	3107.1	3150.8	3194.7	3283.3	3373.4
(235.67/508.82)	H	1017.0	2802.3	3287.3	3343.3	3399.2	3455.1	3511.0	3567.2	3680.2	3794.3
	S	2.6623	6.1709	6.9900	7.0689	7.1448	7.2183	7.2895	7.3588	7.4920	7.6191

3200	V	1.224	62.439	96.859	100.83	104.76	108.65	112.51	116.34	123.95	131.48
(237.45/510.60)	U	1021.5	2602.5	2975.9	3019.3	3062.8	3106.3	3150.0	3193.9	3282.7	3372.8
	H	1025.4	2802.3	3285.8	3342.0	3398.0	3454.0	3510.0	3566.2	3679.3	3793.6
	S	2.6786	6.1585	6.9738	7.0528	7.1290	7.2026	7.2739	7.3433	7.4767	7.6039
3300	V	1.227	60.529	93.805	97.668	101.49	105.27	109.02	112.74	120.13	127.45
(239.18/512.33)	U	1029.7	2602.5	2974.8	3018.3	3061.9	3105.5	3149.2	3193.2	3282.1	3372.3
	H	1033.7	2802.3	3284.3	3340.6	3396.8	3452.8	3509.0	3565.3	3678.5	3792.9
	S	2.6945	6.1463	6.9580	7.0373	7.1136	7.1873	7.2588	7.3282	7.4618	7.5891
3400	V	1.231	58.728	90.930	94.692	98.408	102.09	105.74	109.36	116.54	123.65
(240.88/514.03)	U	1037.6	2602.5	2973.7	3017.4	3061.0	3104.6	3148.4	3192.5	3281.5	3371.7
	H	1041.8	2802.1	3282.8	3339.3	3395.5	3451.7	3507.9	3564.3	3677.7	3792.1
	S	2.7101	6.1344	6.9426	7.0221	7.0986	7.1724	7.2440	7.3136	7.4473	7.5747
3500	V	1.235	57.025	88.220	91.886	95.505	99.088	102.64	106.17	113.15	120.07
(242.54/515.69)	U	1045.4	2602.4	2972.6	3016.4	3060.1	3103.8	3147.7	3191.8	3280.8	3371.2
	H	1049.8	2802.0	3281.3	3338.0	3394.3	3450.6	3506.9	3563.4	3676.9	3791.4
	S	2.7253	6.1228	6.9277	7.0074	7.0840	7.1580	7.2297	7.2993	7.4332	7.5607
3600	V	1.238	55.415	85.660	89.236	92.764	96.255	99.716	103.15	109.96	116.69
(244.16/517.31)	U	1053.1	2602.2	2971.5	3015.4	3059.2	3103.0	3146.9	3191.1	3280.2	3370.6
	H	1057.6	2801.7	3279.8	3336.6	3393.1	3449.5	3505.9	3562.4	3676.1	3790.7
	S	2.7401	6.1115	6.9131	6.9930	7.0698	7.1439	7.2157	7.2854	7.4195	7.5471
3700	V	1.242	53.888	83.238	86.728	90.171	93.576	96.950	100.30	106.93	113.49
(245.75/518.90)	U	1060.6	2602.1	2970.4	3014.4	3058.2	3102.1	3146.1	3190.4	3279.6	3370.1
	H	1065.2	2801.4	3278.4	3335.3	3391.9	3448.4	3504.9	3561.5	3675.2	3790.0
	S	2.7547	6.1004	6.8989	6.9790	7.0559	7.1302	7.2021	7.2719	7.4061	7.5339
3800	V	1.245	52.438	80.944	84.353	87.714	91.038	94.330	97.596	104.06	110.46
(247.31/520.46)	U	1068.0	2601.9	2969.3	3013.4	3057.3	3101.3	3145.4	3189.6	3279.0	3369.5
	H	1072.7	2801.1	3276.8	3333.9	3390.7	3447.2	3503.8	3560.5	3674.4	3789.3
	S	2.7689	6.0896	6.8849	6.9653	7.0424	7.1168	7.1888	7.2587	7.3931	7.5210
3900	V	1.249	51.061	78.767	82.099	85.383	88.629	91.844	95.033	101.35	107.59
(248.84/521.99)	U	1075.3	2601.6	2968.2	3012.4	3056.4	3100.5	3144.6	3188.9	3278.3	3369.0
	H	1080.1	2800.8	3275.3	3332.6	3389.4	3446.1	3502.8	3559.5	3673.6	3788.6
	S	2.7828	6.0789	6.8713	6.9519	7.0292	7.1037	7.1759	7.2459	7.3804	7.5084
4000	V	1.252	49.749	76.698	79.958	83.169	86.341	89.483	92.598	98.763	104.86
(250.33/523.48)	U	1082.4	2601.3	2967.0	3011.4	3055.5	3099.6	3143.8	3188.2	3277.7	3368.4
	H	1087.4	2800.3	3273.8	3331.2	3388.2	3445.0	3501.7	3558.6	3672.8	3787.9
	S	2.7965	6.0685	6.8581	6.9388	7.0163	7.0909	7.1632	7.2333	7.3680	7.4961

Table F.2. Superheated Steam, SI Units (Continued)

P/kPa t^{sat}/T^{sat} (°C/K)		sat. liq.	sat. vap.	TEMPERATURE: t °C (TEMPERATURE: T kelvins) 260 (533.15)	275 (548.15)	300 (573.15)	325 (598.15)	350 (623.15)	375 (648.15)	400 (673.15)	425 (698.15)
	V	1.256	48.500	50.150	52.955	57.191	61.057	64.680	68.137	71.476	74.730
4100	U	1089.4	2601.0	2624.6	2664.5	2724.0	2777.7	2827.6	2875.0	2920.9	2965.9
(251.80/524.95)	H	1094.6	2799.9	2830.3	2881.6	2958.5	3028.0	3092.8	3154.4	3214.0	3272.3
	S	2.8099	6.0583	6.1157	6.2107	6.3480	6.4667	6.5727	6.6697	6.7600	6.8450
	V	1.259	47.307	48.654	51.438	55.625	59.435	62.998	66.392	69.667	72.856
4200	U	1096.3	2600.7	2620.4	2661.0	2721.4	2775.6	2825.8	2873.6	2919.7	2964.8
(253.24/526.39)	H	1101.6	2799.4	2824.8	2877.1	2955.0	3025.2	3090.4	3152.4	3212.3	3270.8
	S	2.8231	6.0482	6.0962	6.1929	6.3320	6.4519	6.5587	6.6563	6.7469	6.8323
	V	1.262	46.168	47.223	49.988	54.130	57.887	61.393	64.728	67.942	71.069
4300	U	1103.1	2600.3	2616.2	2657.5	2718.7	2773.4	2824.1	2872.1	2918.4	2963.7
(254.66/527.81)	H	1108.5	2798.9	2819.2	2872.4	2951.4	3022.3	3088.1	3150.4	3210.5	3269.3
	S	2.8360	6.0383	6.0768	6.1752	6.3162	6.4373	6.5450	6.6431	6.7341	6.8198
	V	1.266	45.079	45.853	48.601	52.702	56.409	59.861	63.139	66.295	69.363
4400	U	1109.8	2599.9	2611.8	2653.9	2716.0	2771.3	2822.3	2870.6	2917.1	2962.5
(256.05/529.20)	H	1115.4	2798.3	2813.6	2867.8	2947.8	3019.5	3085.7	3148.4	3208.8	3267.7
	S	2.8487	6.0286	6.0575	6.1577	6.3006	6.4230	6.5315	6.6301	6.7216	6.8076
	V	1.269	44.037	44.540	47.273	51.336	54.996	58.396	61.620	64.721	67.732
4500	U	1116.4	2599.5	2607.4	2650.3	2713.2	2769.1	2820.5	2869.1	2915.8	2961.4
(257.41/530.56)	H	1122.1	2797.7	2807.9	2863.0	2944.2	3016.6	3083.3	3146.4	3207.1	3266.2
	S	2.8612	6.0191	6.0382	6.1403	6.2852	6.4088	6.5182	6.6174	6.7093	6.7955
	V	1.272	43.038	43.278	46.000	50.027	53.643	56.994	60.167	63.215	66.172
4600	U	1122.9	2599.1	2602.9	2646.6	2710.4	2766.9	2818.7	2867.6	2914.5	2960.3
(258.75/531.90)	H	1128.8	2797.0	2802.0	2858.2	2940.5	3013.7	3080.9	3144.4	3205.3	3264.7
	S	2.8735	6.0097	6.0190	6.1230	6.2700	6.3949	6.5050	6.6049	6.6972	6.7838
	V	1.276	42.081	....	44.778	48.772	52.346	55.651	58.775	61.773	64.679
4700	U	1129.3	2598.6	....	2642.9	2707.6	2764.7	2816.9	2866.1	2913.2	2959.1
(260.07/533.22)	H	1135.3	2796.4	....	2853.3	2936.8	3010.7	3078.5	3142.3	3203.6	3263.1
	S	2.8855	6.0004	....	6.1058	6.2549	6.3811	6.4921	6.5926	6.6853	6.7722
	V	1.279	41.161	....	43.604	47.569	51.103	54.364	57.441	60.390	63.247
4800	U	1135.6	2598.1	....	2639.1	2704.8	2762.5	2815.1	2864.6	2911.9	2958.0
(261.37/534.52)	H	1141.8	2795.7	....	2848.4	2933.1	3007.8	3076.1	3140.3	3201.8	3261.6
	S	2.8974	5.9913	....	6.0887	6.2399	6.3675	6.4794	6.5805	6.6736	6.7608

4900 (262.65/535.80)	V	1.282	40.278	....	42.475	46.412	49.909	53.128	56.161	59.064	61.874
	U	1141.9	2597.6	....	2635.2	2701.9	2760.2	2813.3	2863.0	2910.6	2956.9
	H	1148.2	2794.9	....	2843.3	2929.3	3004.8	3073.6	3138.2	3200.0	3260.0
	S	2.9091	5.9823	....	6.0717	6.2252	6.3541	6.4669	6.5685	6.6621	6.7496
5000 (263.91/537.06)	V	1.286	39.429	....	41.388	45.301	48.762	51.941	54.932	57.791	60.555
	U	1148.0	2597.0	....	2631.3	2699.0	2758.0	2811.5	2861.5	2909.3	2955.7
	H	1154.5	2794.2	....	2838.2	2925.5	3001.8	3071.2	3136.2	3198.3	3258.5
	S	2.9206	5.9735	....	6.0547	6.2105	6.3408	6.4545	6.5568	6.6508	6.7386
5100 (265.15/538.30)	V	1.289	38.611	....	40.340	44.231	47.660	50.801	53.750	56.567	59.288
	U	1154.1	2596.5	....	2627.3	2696.1	2755.7	2809.6	2860.0	2908.0	2954.5
	H	1160.7	2793.4	....	2833.1	2921.7	2998.7	3068.7	3134.1	3196.5	3256.9
	S	2.9319	5.9648	....	6.0378	6.1960	6.3277	6.4423	6.5452	6.6396	6.7278
5200 (266.37/539.52)	V	1.292	37.824	....	39.330	43.201	46.599	49.703	52.614	55.390	58.070
	U	1160.1	2595.9	....	2623.3	2693.1	2753.4	2807.8	2858.4	2906.7	2953.4
	H	1166.8	2792.6	....	2827.8	2917.8	2995.7	3066.2	3132.0	3194.7	3255.4
	S	2.9431	5.9561	....	6.0210	6.1815	6.3147	6.4302	6.5338	6.6287	6.7172
5300 (267.58/540.73)	V	1.296	37.066	....	38.354	42.209	45.577	48.647	51.520	54.257	56.897
	U	1166.1	2595.3	....	2619.2	2690.1	2751.0	2805.9	2856.9	2905.3	2952.2
	H	1172.9	2791.7	....	2822.5	2913.8	2992.6	3063.7	3129.9	3192.9	3253.8
	S	2.9541	5.9476	....	6.0041	6.1672	6.3018	6.4183	6.5225	6.6179	6.7067
5400 (268.76/541.91)	V	1.299	36.334	....	37.411	41.251	44.591	47.628	50.466	53.166	55.768
	U	1171.9	2594.6	....	2615.0	2687.1	2748.7	2804.0	2855.3	2904.0	2951.1
	H	1178.9	2790.8	....	2817.0	2909.8	2989.5	3061.2	3127.8	3191.1	3252.2
	S	2.9650	5.9392	....	5.9873	6.1530	6.2891	6.4066	6.5114	6.6072	6.6963
5500 (269.93/543.08)	V	1.302	35.628	....	36.499	40.327	43.641	46.647	49.450	52.115	54.679
	U	1177.7	2594.0	....	2610.8	2684.0	2746.3	2802.1	2853.7	2902.7	2949.9
	H	1184.9	2789.9	....	2811.5	2905.8	2986.4	3058.7	3125.7	3189.3	3250.6
	S	2.9757	5.9309	....	5.9705	6.1388	6.2765	6.3949	6.5004	6.5967	6.6862
5600 (271.09/544.24)	V	1.306	34.946	....	35.617	39.434	42.724	45.700	48.470	51.100	53.630
	U	1183.5	2593.3	....	2606.5	2680.9	2744.0	2800.2	2852.1	2901.3	2948.7
	H	1190.8	2789.0	....	2805.9	2901.7	2983.2	3056.1	3123.6	3187.5	3249.0
	S	2.9863	5.9227	....	5.9537	6.1248	6.2640	6.3834	6.4896	6.5863	6.6761
5700 (272.22/545.37)	V	1.309	34.288	....	34.761	38.571	41.838	44.785	47.525	50.121	52.617
	U	1189.1	2592.6	....	2602.1	2677.8	2741.6	2798.3	2850.5	2899.9	2947.5
	H	1196.6	2788.0	....	2800.2	2897.6	2980.0	3053.5	3121.4	3185.6	3247.5
	S	2.9968	5.9146	....	5.9369	6.1108	6.2516	6.3720	6.4789	6.5761	6.6663

Table F.2. Superheated Steam, SI Units (Continued)

P/kPa t^{sat}/T^{sat} (°C/K)		sat. liq.	sat. vap.	TEMPERATURE: t °C (TEMPERATURE: T kelvins) 450 (723.15)	475 (748.15)	500 (773.15)	525 (798.15)	550 (823.15)	575 (848.15)	600 (873.15)	650 (923.15)
	V	1.256	48.500	77.921	81.062	84.165	87.236	90.281	93.303	96.306	102.26
4100	U	1089.4	2601.0	3010.4	3054.6	3098.8	3143.0	3187.5	3232.1	3277.1	3367.9
(251.80/524.95)	H	1094.6	2799.9	3329.9	3387.0	3443.9	3500.7	3557.6	3614.7	3671.9	3787.1
	S	2.8099	6.0583	6.9260	7.0037	7.0785	7.1508	7.2210	7.2893	7.3558	7.4842
	V	1.259	47.307	75.981	79.056	82.092	85.097	88.075	91.030	93.966	99.787
4200	U	1096.3	2600.7	3009.4	3053.7	3097.9	3142.3	3186.8	3231.5	3276.5	3367.3
(253.24/526.39)	H	1101.6	2799.4	3328.5	3385.7	3442.7	3499.7	3556.7	3613.8	3671.1	3786.4
	S	2.8231	6.0482	6.9135	6.9913	7.0662	7.1387	7.2090	7.2774	7.3440	7.4724
	V	1.262	46.168	74.131	77.143	80.116	83.057	85.971	88.863	91.735	97.428
4300	U	1103.1	2600.3	3008.4	3052.8	3097.1	3141.5	3186.0	3230.8	3275.8	3366.8
(254.66/527.81)	H	1108.5	2798.9	3327.1	3384.5	3441.6	3498.6	3555.7	3612.9	3670.3	3785.7
	S	2.8360	6.0383	6.9012	6.9792	7.0543	7.1269	7.1973	7.2658	7.3324	7.4610
	V	1.266	45.079	72.365	75.317	78.229	81.110	83.963	86.794	89.605	95.177
4400	U	1109.8	2599.9	3007.4	3051.9	3096.3	3140.7	3185.3	3230.1	3275.2	3366.2
(256.05/529.20)	H	1115.4	2798.3	3325.8	3383.3	3440.5	3497.6	3554.7	3612.0	3669.5	3785.0
	S	2.8487	6.0286	6.8892	6.9674	7.0426	7.1153	7.1858	7.2544	7.3211	7.4498
	V	1.269	44.037	70.677	73.572	76.427	79.249	82.044	84.817	87.570	93.025
4500	U	1116.4	2599.5	3006.3	3050.9	3095.4	3139.9	3184.6	3229.5	3274.6	3365.7
(257.41/530.56)	H	1122.1	2797.7	3324.4	3382.0	3439.3	3496.6	3553.8	3611.1	3668.6	3784.3
	S	2.8612	6.0191	6.8774	6.9558	7.0311	7.1040	7.1746	7.2432	7.3100	7.4388
	V	1.272	43.038	69.063	71.903	74.702	77.469	80.209	82.926	85.623	90.967
4600	U	1122.9	2599.1	3005.3	3050.0	3094.6	3139.2	3183.9	3228.8	3273.9	3365.1
(258.75/531.90)	H	1128.8	2797.0	3323.0	3380.8	3438.2	3495.5	3552.8	3610.2	3667.8	3783.6
	S	2.8735	6.0097	6.8659	6.9444	7.0199	7.0928	7.1636	7.2323	7.2991	7.4281
	V	1.276	42.081	67.517	70.304	73.051	75.765	78.452	81.116	83.760	88.997
4700	U	1129.3	2598.6	3004.3	3049.1	3093.7	3138.4	3183.1	3228.1	3273.3	3364.6
(260.07/533.22)	H	1135.3	2796.4	3321.6	3379.5	3437.1	3494.5	3551.9	3609.3	3667.0	3782.9
	S	2.8855	6.0004	6.8545	6.9332	7.0089	7.0819	7.1527	7.2215	7.2885	7.4176
	V	1.279	41.161	66.036	68.773	71.469	74.132	76.768	79.381	81.973	87.109
4800	U	1135.6	2598.1	3003.3	3048.2	3092.9	3137.6	3182.4	3227.4	3272.7	3364.0
(261.37/534.52)	H	1141.8	2795.7	3320.3	3378.3	3435.9	3493.4	3550.9	3608.5	3666.2	3782.1
	S	2.8974	5.9913	6.8434	6.9223	6.9981	7.0712	7.1422	7.2110	7.2781	7.4072

	V	1.282	40.278	64.615	67.303	69.951	72.565	75.152	77.716	80.260	85.298
4900	U	1141.9	2597.6	3002.3	3047.2	3092.0	3136.8	3181.7	3226.8	3272.0	3363.5
(262.65/535.80)	H	1148.2	2794.9	3318.9	3377.0	3434.8	3492.4	3549.9	3607.6	3665.3	3781.4
	S	2.9091	5.9823	6.8324	6.9115	6.9874	7.0607	7.1318	7.2007	7.2678	7.3971
	V	1.286	39.429	63.250	65.893	68.494	71.061	73.602	76.119	78.616	83.559
5000	U	1148.0	2597.0	3001.2	3046.3	3091.2	3136.0	3181.0	3226.1	3271.4	3362.9
(263.91/537.06)	H	1154.5	2794.2	3317.5	3375.8	3433.7	3491.3	3549.0	3606.7	3664.5	3780.7
	S	2.9206	5.9735	6.8217	6.9009	6.9770	7.0504	7.1215	7.1906	7.2578	7.3872
	V	1.289	38.611	61.940	64.537	67.094	69.616	72.112	74.584	77.035	81.888
5100	U	1154.1	2596.5	3000.2	3045.4	3090.3	3135.3	3180.2	3225.4	3270.8	3362.4
(265.15/538.30)	H	1160.7	2793.4	3316.1	3374.5	3432.5	3490.3	3548.0	3605.8	3663.7	3780.0
	S	2.9319	5.9648	6.8111	6.8905	6.9668	7.0403	7.1115	7.1807	7.2479	7.3775
	V	1.292	37.824	60.679	63.234	65.747	68.227	70.679	73.108	75.516	80.282
5200	U	1160.1	2595.9	2999.2	3044.5	3089.5	3134.5	3179.5	3224.7	3270.2	3361.8
(266.37/539.52)	H	1166.8	2792.6	3314.7	3373.3	3431.4	3489.3	3547.1	3604.9	3662.8	3779.3
	S	2.9431	5.9561	6.8007	6.8803	6.9567	7.0304	7.1017	7.1709	7.2382	7.3679
	V	1.296	37.066	59.466	61.980	64.452	66.890	69.300	71.687	74.054	78.736
5300	U	1166.1	2595.3	2998.2	3043.5	3088.6	3133.7	3178.8	3224.1	3269.5	3361.3
(267.58/540.73)	H	1172.9	2791.7	3313.3	3372.0	3430.2	3488.2	3546.1	3604.0	3662.0	3778.6
	S	2.9541	5.9476	6.7905	6.8703	6.9468	7.0206	7.0920	7.1613	7.2287	7.3585
	V	1.299	36.334	58.297	60.772	63.204	65.603	67.973	70.320	72.646	77.248
5400	U	1171.9	2594.6	2997.1	3042.6	3087.8	3132.9	3178.1	3223.4	3268.9	3360.7
(268.76/541.91)	H	1178.9	2790.8	3311.9	3370.8	3429.1	3487.2	3545.1	3603.1	3661.2	3777.8
	S	2.9650	5.9392	6.7804	6.8604	6.9371	7.0110	7.0825	7.1519	7.2194	7.3493
	V	1.302	35.628	57.171	59.608	62.002	64.362	66.694	69.002	71.289	75.814
5500	U	1177.7	2594.0	2996.1	3041.7	3086.9	3132.1	3177.3	3222.7	3268.3	3360.2
(269.93/543.08)	H	1184.9	2789.9	3310.5	3369.5	3427.9	3486.1	3544.2	3602.2	3660.4	3777.1
	S	2.9757	5.9309	6.7705	6.8507	6.9275	7.0015	7.0731	7.1426	7.2102	7.3402
	V	1.306	34.946	56.085	58.486	60.843	63.165	65.460	67.731	69.981	74.431
5600	U	1183.5	2593.3	2995.0	3040.7	3086.1	3131.3	3176.6	3222.0	3267.6	3359.6
(271.09/544.24)	H	1190.8	2789.0	3309.1	3368.2	3426.8	3485.1	3543.2	3601.3	3659.5	3776.4
	S	2.9863	5.9227	6.7607	6.8411	6.9181	6.9922	7.0639	7.1335	7.2011	7.3313
	V	1.309	34.288	55.038	57.403	59.724	62.011	64.270	66.504	68.719	73.096
5700	U	1189.1	2592.6	2994.0	3039.8	3085.2	3130.5	3175.9	3221.3	3267.0	3359.1
(272.22/545.37)	H	1196.6	2788.0	3307.7	3367.0	3425.6	3484.0	3542.2	3600.4	3658.7	3775.7
	S	2.9968	5.9146	6.7511	6.8316	6.9088	6.9831	7.0549	7.1245	7.1923	7.3226

Table F.2. Superheated Steam, SI Units (Continued)

P/kPa t^{sat}/T^{sat} (°C/K)		sat. liq.	sat. vap.	280 (553.15)	290 (563.15)	300 (573.15)	325 (598.15)	350 (623.15)	375 (648.15)	400 (673.15)	425 (698.15)
				TEMPERATURE: t °C (TEMPERATURE: T kelvins)							
	V	1.312	33.651	34.756	36.301	37.736	40.982	43.902	46.611	49.176	51.638
5800	U	1194.7	2591.9	2614.4	2645.7	2674.6	2739.1	2796.3	2848.9	2898.6	2946.4
(273.35/546.50)	H	1202.3	2787.0	2816.0	2856.3	2893.5	2976.8	3051.0	3119.3	3183.8	3245.9
	S	3.0071	5.9066	5.9592	6.0314	6.0969	6.2393	6.3608	6.4683	6.5660	6.6565
	V	1.315	33.034	33.953	35.497	36.928	40.154	43.048	45.728	48.262	50.693
5900	U	1200.3	2591.1	2610.2	2642.1	2671.4	2736.7	2794.4	2847.3	2897.2	2945.2
(274.46/547.61)	H	1208.0	2786.0	2810.5	2851.5	2889.3	2973.6	3048.4	3117.1	3182.0	3244.3
	S	3.0172	5.8986	5.9431	6.0166	6.0830	6.2272	6.3496	6.4578	6.5560	6.6469
	V	1.319	32.438	33.173	34.718	36.145	39.353	42.222	44.874	47.379	49.779
6000	U	1205.8	2590.4	2605.9	2638.4	2668.1	2734.2	2792.4	2845.7	2895.8	2944.0
(275.55/548.70)	H	1213.7	2785.0	2804.9	2846.7	2885.0	2970.4	3045.8	3115.0	3180.1	3242.6
	S	3.0273	5.8908	5.9270	6.0017	6.0692	6.2151	6.3386	6.4475	6.5462	6.6374
	V	1.322	31.860	32.415	33.962	35.386	38.577	41.422	44.048	46.524	48.895
6100	U	1211.2	2589.6	2601.5	2634.6	2664.8	2731.7	2790.4	2844.1	2894.5	2942.8
(276.63/549.78)	H	1219.3	2783.9	2799.3	2841.8	2880.7	2967.1	3043.1	3112.8	3178.3	3241.0
	S	3.0372	5.8830	5.9108	5.9869	6.0555	6.2031	6.3277	6.4373	6.5364	6.6280
	V	1.325	31.300	31.679	33.227	34.650	37.825	40.648	43.248	45.697	48.039
6200	U	1216.6	2588.8	2597.1	2630.8	2661.5	2729.2	2788.5	2842.4	2893.1	2941.6
(277.70/550.85)	H	1224.8	2782.9	2793.5	2836.8	2876.3	2963.8	3040.5	3110.6	3176.4	3239.4
	S	3.0471	5.8753	5.8946	5.9721	6.0418	6.1911	6.3168	6.4272	6.5268	6.6188
	V	1.328	30.757	30.962	32.514	33.935	37.097	39.898	42.473	44.895	47.210
6300	U	1221.9	2588.0	2592.6	2626.9	2658.1	2726.7	2786.5	2840.8	2891.7	2940.4
(278.75/551.90)	H	1230.3	2781.8	2787.6	2831.7	2871.9	2960.4	3037.8	3108.4	3174.5	3237.8
	S	3.0568	5.8677	5.8783	5.9573	6.0281	6.1793	6.3061	6.4172	6.5173	6.6096
	V	1.332	30.230	30.265	31.821	33.241	36.390	39.170	41.722	44.119	46.407
6400	U	1227.2	2587.2	2587.9	2623.0	2654.7	2724.2	2784.4	2839.1	2890.3	2939.2
(279.79/552.94)	H	1235.7	2780.6	2781.6	2826.6	2867.5	2957.1	3035.1	3106.2	3172.7	3236.2
	S	3.0664	5.8601	5.8619	5.9425	6.0144	6.1675	6.2955	6.4072	6.5079	6.6006
	V	1.335	29.719	....	31.146	32.567	35.704	38.465	40.994	43.366	45.629
6500	U	1232.5	2586.3	....	2619.0	2651.2	2721.6	2782.4	2837.5	2888.9	2938.0
(280.82/553.97)	H	1241.1	2779.5	....	2821.4	2862.9	2953.7	3032.4	3103.9	3170.8	3234.5
	S	3.0759	5.8527	....	5.9277	6.0008	6.1558	6.2849	6.3974	6.4986	6.5917

6600 (281.84/554.99)	V	1.338	29.223	....	30.490	31.911	35.038	37.781	40.287	42.636	44.874
	U	1237.6	2585.5	....	2614.9	2647.7	2719.0	2780.4	2835.8	2887.5	2936.7
	H	1246.5	2778.3	....	2816.1	2858.4	2950.2	3029.7	3101.7	3168.9	3232.9
	S	3.0853	5.8452	....	5.9129	5.9872	6.1442	6.2744	6.3877	6.4894	6.5828
6700 (282.84/555.99)	V	1.342	28.741	....	29.850	31.273	34.391	37.116	39.601	41.927	44.141
	U	1242.8	2584.6	....	2610.8	2644.2	2716.4	2778.3	2834.1	2886.1	2935.5
	H	1251.8	2777.1	....	2810.8	2853.7	2946.8	3027.0	3099.5	3167.0	3231.3
	S	3.0946	5.8379	....	5.8980	5.9736	6.1326	6.2640	6.3781	6.4803	6.5741
6800 (283.84/556.99)	V	1.345	28.272	....	29.226	30.652	33.762	36.470	38.935	41.239	43.430
	U	1247.9	2583.7	....	2606.6	2640.6	2713.7	2776.2	2832.4	2884.7	2934.3
	H	1257.0	2775.9	....	2805.3	2849.0	2943.3	3024.2	3097.2	3165.1	3229.6
	S	3.1038	5.8306	....	5.8830	5.9599	6.1211	6.2537	6.3686	6.4713	6.5655
7000 (285.79/558.94)	V	1.351	27.373	....	28.024	29.457	32.556	35.233	37.660	39.922	42.068
	U	1258.0	2581.8	....	2597.9	2633.2	2708.4	2772.1	2829.0	2881.8	2931.8
	H	1267.4	2773.5	....	2794.1	2839.4	2936.3	3018.7	3092.7	3161.2	3226.3
	S	3.1219	5.8162	....	5.8530	5.9327	6.0982	6.2333	6.3497	6.4536	6.5485
7200 (287.70/560.85)	V	1.358	26.522	....	26.878	28.321	31.413	34.063	36.454	38.676	40.781
	U	1267.9	2579.9	....	2589.0	2625.6	2702.9	2767.8	2825.6	2878.9	2929.4
	H	1277.6	2770.9	....	2782.5	2829.5	2929.1	3013.1	3088.1	3157.4	3223.0
	S	3.1397	5.8020	....	5.8226	5.9054	6.0755	6.2132	6.3312	6.4362	6.5319
7400 (289.57/562.72)	V	1.364	25.715	....	25.781	27.238	30.328	32.954	35.312	37.497	39.564
	U	1277.6	2578.0	....	2579.7	2617.8	2697.3	2763.5	2822.1	2876.0	2926.9
	H	1287.7	2768.3	....	2770.5	2819.3	2921.8	3007.4	3083.4	3153.5	3219.6
	S	3.1571	5.7880	....	5.7919	5.8779	6.0530	6.1933	6.3130	6.4190	6.5156
7600 (291.41/564.56)	V	1.371	24.949	....	....	26.204	29.297	31.901	34.229	36.380	38.409
	U	1287.2	2575.9	....	....	2609.7	2691.7	2759.2	2818.6	2873.1	2924.3
	H	1297.6	2765.5	....	....	2808.8	2914.3	3001.6	3078.7	3149.6	3216.3
	S	3.1742	5.7742	....	....	5.8503	6.0306	6.1737	6.2950	6.4022	6.4996
7800 (293.21/566.36)	V	1.378	24.220	....	....	25.214	28.315	30.900	33.200	35.319	37.314
	U	1296.7	2573.8	....	....	2601.3	2685.9	2754.8	2815.1	2870.1	2921.8
	H	1307.4	2762.8	....	....	2798.0	2906.7	2995.8	3074.0	3145.6	3212.9
	S	3.1911	5.7605	....	....	5.8224	6.0082	6.1542	6.2773	6.3857	6.4839
8000 (294.97/568.12)	V	1.384	23.525	....	....	24.264	27.378	29.948	32.222	34.310	36.273
	U	1306.0	2571.7	....	....	2592.7	2679.9	2750.3	2811.5	2867.1	2919.3
	H	1317.1	2759.9	....	....	2786.8	2899.0	2989.9	3069.2	3141.6	3209.5
	S	3.2076	5.7471	....	....	5.7942	5.9860	6.1349	6.2599	6.3694	6.4684

Table F.2. Superheated Steam, SI Units (Continued)

P/kPa t^{sat}/T^{sat} (°C/K)		sat. liq.	sat. vap.	450 (723.15)	475 (748.15)	500 (773.15)	525 (798.15)	550 (823.15)	575 (848.15)	600 (873.15)	650 (923.15)
				TEMPERATURE: t °C (TEMPERATURE: T kelvins)							
	V	1.312	33.651	54.026	56.357	58.644	60.896	63.120	65.320	67.500	71.807
5800	U	1194.7	2591.9	2992.9	3038.8	3084.4	3129.8	3175.2	3220.7	3266.4	3358.5
(273.35/546.50)	H	1202.3	2787.0	3306.3	3365.7	3424.5	3483.0	3541.2	3599.5	3657.9	3775.0
	S	3.0071	5.9066	6.7416	6.8223	6.8996	6.9740	7.0460	7.1157	7.1835	7.3139
	V	1.315	33.034	53.048	55.346	57.600	59.819	62.010	64.176	66.322	70.563
5900	U	1200.3	2591.1	2991.9	3037.9	3083.5	3129.0	3174.4	3220.0	3265.7	3357.9
(274.46/547.61)	H	1208.0	2786.0	3304.9	3364.4	3423.3	3481.9	3540.3	3598.6	3657.0	3774.3
	S	3.0172	5.8986	6.7322	6.8132	6.8906	6.9652	7.0372	7.1070	7.1749	7.3054
	V	1.319	32.438	52.103	54.369	56.592	58.778	60.937	63.071	65.184	69.359
6000	U	1205.8	2590.4	2990.8	3036.9	3082.6	3128.2	3173.7	3219.3	3265.1	3357.4
(275.55/548.70)	H	1213.7	2785.0	3303.5	3363.2	3422.2	3480.8	3539.3	3597.7	3656.2	3773.5
	S	3.0273	5.8908	6.7230	6.8041	6.8818	6.9564	7.0285	7.0985	7.1664	7.2971
	V	1.322	31.860	51.189	53.424	55.616	57.771	59.898	62.001	64.083	68.196
6100	U	1211.2	2589.6	2989.8	3036.0	3081.8	3127.4	3173.0	3218.6	3264.5	3356.8
(276.63/549.78)	H	1219.3	2783.9	3302.0	3361.9	3421.0	3479.8	3538.3	3596.8	3655.4	3772.8
	S	3.0372	5.8830	6.7139	6.7952	6.8730	6.9478	7.0200	7.0900	7.1581	7.2889
	V	1.325	31.300	50.304	52.510	54.671	56.797	58.894	60.966	63.018	67.069
6200	U	1216.6	2588.8	2988.7	3035.0	3080.9	3126.6	3172.2	3218.0	3263.8	3356.3
(277.70/550.85)	H	1224.8	2782.9	3300.6	3360.6	3419.9	3478.7	3537.4	3595.9	3654.5	3772.1
	S	3.0471	5.8753	6.7049	6.7864	6.8644	6.9393	7.0116	7.0817	7.1498	7.2808
	V	1.328	30.757	49.447	51.624	53.757	55.853	57.921	59.964	61.986	65.979
6300	U	1221.9	2588.0	2987.7	3034.1	3080.1	3125.8	3171.5	3217.3	3263.2	3355.7
(278.75/551.90)	H	1230.3	2781.8	3299.2	3359.3	3418.7	3477.7	3536.4	3595.0	3653.7	3771.4
	S	3.0568	5.8677	6.6960	6.7778	6.8559	6.9309	7.0034	7.0735	7.1417	7.2728
	V	1.332	30.230	48.617	50.767	52.871	54.939	56.978	58.993	60.987	64.922
6400	U	1227.2	2587.2	2986.6	3033.1	3079.2	3125.0	3170.8	3216.6	3262.6	3355.2
(279.79/552.94)	H	1235.7	2780.6	3297.7	3358.0	3417.6	3476.6	3535.4	3594.1	3652.9	3770.7
	S	3.0664	5.8601	6.6872	6.7692	6.8475	6.9226	6.9952	7.0655	7.1337	7.2649
	V	1.335	29.719	47.812	49.935	52.012	54.053	56.065	58.052	60.018	63.898
6500	U	1232.5	2586.3	2985.5	3032.2	3078.3	3124.2	3170.0	3215.9	3261.9	3354.6
(280.82/553.97)	H	1241.1	2779.5	3296.3	3356.8	3416.4	3475.6	3534.4	3593.2	3652.1	3770.0
	S	3.0759	5.8527	6.6786	6.7608	6.8392	6.9145	6.9871	7.0575	7.1258	7.2572

6600 (281.84/554.99)	V	1.338	29.223	47.031	49.129	51.180	53.194	55.179	57.139	59.079	62.905
	U	1237.6	2585.5	2984.5	3031.2	3077.4	3123.4	3169.3	3215.2	3261.3	3354.1
	H	1246.5	2778.3	3294.9	3355.5	3415.2	3474.5	3533.5	3592.3	3651.2	3769.2
	S	3.0853	5.8452	6.6700	6.7524	6.8310	6.9064	6.9792	7.0497	7.1181	7.2495
6700 (282.84/555.99)	V	1.342	28.741	46.274	48.346	50.372	52.361	54.320	56.254	58.168	61.942
	U	1242.8	2584.6	2983.4	3030.3	3076.6	3122.6	3168.6	3214.5	3260.7	3353.5
	H	1251.8	2777.1	3293.4	3354.2	3414.1	3473.4	3532.5	3591.4	3650.4	3768.5
	S	3.0946	5.8379	6.6616	6.7442	6.8229	6.8985	6.9714	7.0419	7.1104	7.2420
6800 (283.84/556.99)	V	1.345	28.272	45.539	47.587	49.588	51.552	53.486	55.395	57.283	61.007
	U	1247.9	2583.7	2982.3	3029.3	3075.7	3121.8	3167.8	3213.9	3260.0	3353.0
	H	1257.0	2775.9	3292.0	3352.9	3412.9	3472.4	3531.5	3590.5	3649.6	3767.8
	S	3.1038	5.8306	6.6532	6.7361	6.8150	6.8907	6.9636	7.0343	7.1028	7.2345
7000 (285.79/558.94)	V	1.351	27.373	44.131	46.133	48.086	50.003	51.889	53.750	55.590	59.217
	U	1258.0	2581.8	2980.1	3027.4	3074.0	3120.2	3166.3	3212.5	3258.8	3351.9
	H	1267.4	2773.5	3289.1	3350.3	3410.6	3470.2	3529.6	3588.7	3647.9	3766.4
	S	3.1219	5.8162	6.6368	6.7201	6.7993	6.8753	6.9485	7.0193	7.0880	7.2200
7200 (287.70/560.85)	V	1.358	26.522	42.802	44.759	46.668	48.540	50.381	52.197	53.991	57.527
	U	1267.9	2579.9	2978.0	3025.4	3072.2	3118.6	3164.9	3211.1	3257.5	3350.7
	H	1277.6	2770.9	3286.1	3347.7	3408.2	3468.1	3527.6	3586.9	3646.2	3764.9
	S	3.1397	5.8020	6.6208	6.7044	6.7840	6.8602	6.9337	7.0047	7.0735	7.2058
7400 (289.57/562.72)	V	1.364	25.715	41.544	43.460	45.327	47.156	48.954	50.727	52.478	55.928
	U	1277.6	2578.0	2975.8	3023.5	3070.4	3117.0	3163.4	3209.8	3256.2	3349.6
	H	1287.7	2768.3	3283.2	3345.1	3405.9	3466.0	3525.7	3585.1	3644.5	3763.5
	S	3.1571	5.7880	6.6050	6.6892	6.7691	6.8456	6.9192	6.9904	7.0594	7.1919
7600 (291.41/564.56)	V	1.371	24.949	40.351	42.228	44.056	45.845	47.603	49.335	51.045	54.413
	U	1287.2	2575.9	2973.6	3021.5	3068.7	3115.4	3161.9	3208.4	3254.9	3348.5
	H	1297.6	2765.5	3280.3	3342.5	3403.5	3463.8	3523.7	3583.3	3642.9	3762.1
	S	3.1742	5.7742	6.5896	6.6742	6.7545	6.8312	6.9051	6.9765	7.0457	7.1784
7800 (293.21/566.36)	V	1.378	24.220	39.220	41.060	42.850	44.601	46.320	48.014	49.686	52.976
	U	1296.7	2573.8	2971.4	3019.6	3066.9	3113.8	3160.4	3207.0	3253.7	3347.4
	H	1307.4	2762.8	3277.3	3339.8	3401.1	3461.7	3521.7	3581.5	3641.2	3760.6
	S	3.1911	5.7605	6.5745	6.6596	6.7402	6.8172	6.8913	6.9629	7.0322	7.1652
8000 (294.97/568.12)	V	1.384	23.525	38.145	39.950	41.704	43.419	45.102	46.759	48.394	51.611
	U	1306.0	2571.7	2969.2	3017.6	3065.1	3112.2	3158.9	3205.6	3252.4	3346.3
	H	1317.1	2759.9	3274.3	3337.2	3398.8	3459.5	3519.7	3579.7	3639.5	3759.2
	S	3.2076	5.7471	6.5597	6.6452	6.7262	6.8035	6.8778	6.9496	7.0191	7.1523

Table F.2. Superheated Steam, SI Units (Continued)

P/kPa t^{sat}/T^{sat} (°C/K)		sat. liq.	sat. vap.	TEMPERATURE: t °C (TEMPERATURE: T kelvins) 300 (573.15)	320 (593.15)	340 (613.15)	360 (633.15)	380 (653.15)	400 (673.15)	425 (698.15)	450 (723.15)
8200	V	1.391	22.863	23.350	25.916	28.064	29.968	31.715	33.350	35.282	37.121
(296.70/569.85)	U	1315.2	2569.5	2583.7	2657.7	2718.5	2771.5	2819.5	2864.1	2916.7	2966.9
	H	1326.6	2757.0	2775.2	2870.2	2948.6	3017.2	3079.5	3137.6	3206.0	3271.3
	S	3.2239	5.7338	5.7656	5.9288	6.0588	6.1689	6.2659	6.3534	6.4532	6.5452
8400	V	1.398	22.231	22.469	25.058	27.203	29.094	30.821	32.435	34.337	36.147
(298.39/571.54)	U	1324.3	2567.2	2574.4	2651.1	2713.4	2767.3	2816.0	2861.1	2914.1	2964.7
	H	1336.1	2754.0	2763.1	2861.6	2941.9	3011.7	3074.8	3133.5	3202.6	3268.3
	S	3.2399	5.7207	5.7366	5.9056	6.0388	6.1509	6.2491	6.3376	6.4383	6.5309
8600	V	1.404	21.627	....	24.236	26.380	28.258	29.968	31.561	33.437	35.217
(300.06/573.21)	U	1333.3	2564.9	....	2644.3	2708.1	2763.1	2812.4	2858.0	2911.5	2962.4
	H	1345.4	2750.9	....	2852.7	2935.0	3006.1	3070.1	3129.4	3199.1	3265.3
	S	3.2557	5.7076	....	5.8823	6.0189	6.1330	6.2326	6.3220	6.4236	6.5168
8800	V	1.411	21.049	....	23.446	25.592	27.459	29.153	30.727	32.576	34.329
(301.70/574.85)	U	1342.2	2562.6	....	2637.3	2702.8	2758.8	2808.8	2854.9	2908.9	2960.1
	H	1354.6	2747.8	....	2843.6	2928.0	3000.4	3065.3	3125.3	3195.6	3262.2
	S	3.2713	5.6948	....	5.8590	5.9990	6.1152	6.2162	6.3067	6.4092	6.5030
9000	V	1.418	20.495	....	22.685	24.836	26.694	28.372	29.929	31.754	33.480
(303.31/576.46)	U	1351.0	2560.1	....	2630.1	2697.4	2754.4	2805.2	2851.8	2906.3	2957.8
	H	1363.7	2744.6	....	2834.3	2920.9	2994.7	3060.5	3121.2	3192.0	3259.2
	S	3.2867	5.6820	....	5.8355	5.9792	6.0976	6.2000	6.2915	6.3949	6.4894
9200	V	1.425	19.964	....	21.952	24.110	25.961	27.625	29.165	30.966	32.668
(304.89/578.04)	U	1359.7	2557.7	....	2622.7	2691.9	2750.0	2801.5	2848.7	2903.6	2955.5
	H	1372.8	2741.3	....	2824.7	2913.7	2988.9	3055.7	3117.0	3188.5	3256.1
	S	3.3018	5.6694	....	5.8118	5.9594	6.0801	6.1840	6.2765	6.3808	6.4760
9400	V	1.432	19.455	....	21.245	23.412	25.257	26.909	28.433	30.212	31.891
(306.44/579.59)	U	1368.2	2555.2	....	2615.1	2686.3	2745.6	2797.8	2845.5	2900.9	2953.2
	H	1381.7	2738.0	....	2814.8	2906.3	2983.0	3050.7	3112.8	3184.9	3253.0
	S	3.3168	5.6568	....	5.7879	5.9397	6.0627	6.1681	6.2617	6.3669	6.4628
9600	V	1.439	18.965	....	20.561	22.740	24.581	26.221	27.731	29.489	31.145
(307.97/581.12)	U	1376.7	2552.6	....	2607.3	2680.5	2741.0	2794.1	2842.3	2898.2	2950.9
	H	1390.6	2734.7	....	2804.7	2898.8	2977.0	3045.8	3108.5	3181.3	3249.9
	S	3.3315	5.6444	....	5.7637	5.9199	6.0454	6.1524	6.2470	6.3532	6.4498

9800	V	1.446	18.494	....	19.899	22.093	23.931	25.561	27.056	28.795	30.429
	U	1385.2	2550.0	....	2599.2	2674.7	2736.4	2790.3	2839.1	2895.5	2948.6
(309.48/582.63)	H	1399.3	2731.2	....	2794.3	2891.2	2971.0	3040.8	3104.2	3177.7	3246.8
	S	3.3461	5.6321	....	5.7393	5.9001	6.0282	6.1368	6.2325	6.3397	6.4369
10000	V	1.453	18.041	....	19.256	21.468	23.305	24.926	26.408	28.128	29.742
	U	1393.5	2547.3	....	2590.9	2668.7	2731.8	2786.4	2835.8	2892.8	2946.2
(310.96/584.11)	H	1408.0	2727.7	....	2783.5	2883.4	2964.8	3035.7	3099.9	3174.1	3243.6
	S	3.3605	5.6198	....	5.7145	5.8803	6.0110	6.1213	6.2182	6.3264	6.4243
10200	V	1.460	17.605	....	18.632	20.865	22.702	24.315	25.785	27.487	29.081
	U	1401.8	2544.6	....	2582.3	2662.6	2727.0	2782.6	2832.6	2890.0	2943.9
(312.42/585.57)	H	1416.7	2724.2	....	2772.3	2875.4	2958.6	3030.6	3095.6	3170.4	3240.5
	S	3.3748	5.6076	....	5.6894	5.8604	5.9940	6.1059	6.2040	6.3131	6.4118
10400	V	1.467	17.184	....	18.024	20.282	22.121	23.726	25.185	26.870	28.446
	U	1410.0	2541.8	....	2573.4	2656.3	2722.2	2778.7	2829.3	2887.3	2941.5
(313.86/587.01)	H	1425.2	2720.6	....	2760.8	2867.2	2952.3	3025.4	3091.2	3166.7	3237.3
	S	3.3889	5.5955	....	5.6638	5.8404	5.9769	6.0907	6.1899	6.3001	6.3994
10600	V	1.474	16.778	....	17.432	19.717	21.560	23.159	24.607	26.276	27.834
	U	1418.1	2539.0	....	2564.1	2649.9	2717.4	2774.7	2825.9	2884.5	2939.1
(315.27/588.42)	H	1433.7	2716.9	....	2748.9	2858.9	2945.9	3020.2	3086.8	3163.0	3234.1
	S	3.4029	5.5835	....	5.6376	5.8203	5.9599	6.0755	6.1759	6.2872	6.3872
10800	V	1.481	16.385	....	16.852	19.170	21.018	22.612	24.050	25.703	27.245
	U	1426.2	2536.2	....	2554.5	2643.4	2712.4	2770.7	2822.6	2881.7	2936.7
(316.67/589.82)	H	1442.2	2713.1	....	2736.5	2850.4	2939.4	3014.9	3082.3	3159.3	3230.9
	S	3.4167	5.5715	....	5.6109	5.8000	5.9429	6.0604	6.1621	6.2744	6.3752
11000	V	1.489	16.006	....	16.285	18.639	20.494	22.083	23.512	25.151	26.676
	U	1434.2	2533.2	....	2544.4	2636.7	2707.4	2766.7	2819.2	2878.9	2934.3
(318.05/591.20)	H	1450.6	2709.3	....	2723.5	2841.7	2932.8	3009.6	3077.8	3155.5	3227.7
	S	3.4304	5.5595	....	5.5835	5.7797	5.9259	6.0454	6.1483	6.2617	6.3633
11200	V	1.496	15.639	....	15.726	18.124	19.987	21.573	22.993	24.619	26.128
	U	1442.1	2530.3	....	2533.8	2629.8	2702.2	2762.6	2815.8	2876.0	2931.8
(319.40/592.55)	H	1458.9	2705.4	....	2710.0	2832.8	2926.1	3004.2	3073.3	3151.7	3224.5
	S	3.4440	5.5476	....	5.5553	5.7591	5.9090	6.0305	6.1347	6.2491	6.3515
11400	V	1.504	15.284	....	....	17.622	19.495	21.079	22.492	24.104	25.599
	U	1450.0	2527.2	....	....	2622.7	2697.0	2758.4	2812.3	2873.1	2929.4
(320.74/593.89)	H	1467.2	2701.5	....	....	2823.6	2919.3	2998.7	3068.7	3147.9	3221.2
	S	3.4575	5.5357	....	....	5.7383	5.8920	6.0156	6.1211	6.2367	6.3399

Table F.2. Superheated Steam, SI Units (Continued)

P/kPa t^{sat}/T^{sat} (°C/K)		sat. liq.	sat. vap.	TEMPERATURE: t °C (TEMPERATURE: T kelvins) 475 (748.15)	500 (773.15)	525 (798.15)	550 (823.15)	575 (848.15)	600 (873.15)	625 (898.15)	650 (923.15)
8200	V	1.391	22.863	38.893	40.614	42.295	43.943	45.566	47.166	48.747	50.313
(296.70/569.85)	U	1315.2	2569.5	3015.6	3063.3	3110.5	3157.4	3204.3	3251.1	3298.1	3345.2
	H	1326.6	2757.0	3334.5	3396.4	3457.3	3517.8	3577.9	3637.9	3697.8	3757.7
	S	3.2239	5.7338	6.6311	6.7124	6.7900	6.8646	6.9365	7.0062	7.0739	7.1397
8400	V	1.398	22.231	37.887	39.576	41.224	42.839	44.429	45.996	47.544	49.076
(298.39/571.54)	U	1324.3	2567.2	3013.6	3061.6	3108.9	3155.9	3202.9	3249.8	3296.9	3344.1
	H	1336.1	2754.0	3331.9	3394.0	3455.2	3515.8	3576.1	3636.2	3696.2	3756.3
	S	3.2399	5.7207	6.6173	6.6990	6.7769	6.8516	6.9238	6.9936	7.0614	7.1274
8600	V	1.404	21.627	36.928	38.586	40.202	41.787	43.345	44.880	46.397	47.897
(300.06/573.21)	U	1333.3	2564.9	3011.6	3059.8	3107.3	3154.4	3201.5	3248.5	3295.7	3342.9
	H	1345.4	2750.9	3329.2	3391.6	3453.0	3513.8	3574.3	3634.5	3694.7	3754.9
	S	3.2557	5.7076	6.6037	6.6858	6.7639	6.8390	6.9113	6.9813	7.0492	7.1153
8800	V	1.411	21.049	36.011	37.640	39.228	40.782	42.310	43.815	45.301	46.771
(301.70/574.85)	U	1342.2	2562.6	3009.6	3058.0	3105.6	3152.9	3200.1	3247.2	3294.5	3341.8
	H	1354.6	2747.8	3326.5	3389.2	3450.8	3511.8	3572.4	3632.8	3693.1	3753.4
	S	3.2713	5.6948	6.5904	6.6728	6.7513	6.8265	6.8990	6.9692	7.0373	7.1035
9000	V	1.418	20.495	35.136	36.737	38.296	39.822	41.321	42.798	44.255	45.695
(303.31/576.46)	U	1351.0	2560.1	3007.6	3056.1	3104.0	3151.4	3198.7	3246.0	3293.3	3340.7
	H	1363.7	2744.6	3323.8	3386.8	3448.7	3509.8	3570.6	3631.1	3691.6	3752.0
	S	3.2867	5.6820	6.5773	6.6600	6.7388	6.8143	6.8870	6.9574	7.0256	7.0919
9200	V	1.425	19.964	34.298	35.872	37.405	38.904	40.375	41.824	43.254	44.667
(304.89/578.04)	U	1359.7	2557.7	3005.6	3054.3	3102.3	3149.9	3197.3	3244.7	3292.1	3339.6
	H	1372.8	2741.3	3321.1	3384.4	3446.5	3507.8	3568.8	3629.5	3690.0	3750.5
	S	3.3018	5.6694	6.5644	6.6475	6.7266	6.8023	6.8752	6.9457	7.0141	7.0806
9400	V	1.432	19.455	33.495	35.045	36.552	38.024	39.470	40.892	42.295	43.682
(306.44/579.59)	U	1368.2	2555.2	3003.5	3052.5	3100.7	3148.4	3195.9	3243.4	3290.9	3338.5
	H	1381.7	2738.0	3318.4	3381.9	3444.3	3505.9	3566.9	3627.8	3688.4	3749.1
	S	3.3168	5.6568	6.5517	6.6352	6.7146	6.7906	6.8637	6.9343	7.0029	7.0695
9600	V	1.439	18.965	32.726	34.252	35.734	37.182	38.602	39.999	41.377	42.738
(307.97/581.12)	U	1376.7	2552.6	3001.5	3050.7	3099.0	3146.9	3194.5	3242.1	3289.7	3337.4
	H	1390.6	2734.7	3315.6	3379.5	3442.1	3503.9	3565.1	3626.1	3686.9	3747.6
	S	3.3315	5.6444	6.5392	6.6231	6.7028	6.7790	6.8523	6.9231	6.9918	7.0585

9800 (309.48/582.63)	V	1.446	18.494	31.988	33.491	34.949	36.373	37.769	39.142	40.496	41.832
	U	1385.2	2550.0	2999.4	3048.8	3097.4	3145.4	3193.1	3240.8	3288.5	3336.2
	H	1399.3	2731.2	3312.9	3377.0	3439.9	3501.9	3563.3	3624.4	3685.3	3746.2
	S	3.3461	5.6321	6.5268	6.6112	6.6912	6.7676	6.8411	6.9121	6.9810	7.0478
10000 (310.96/584.11)	V	1.453	18.041	31.280	32.760	34.196	35.597	36.970	38.320	39.650	40.963
	U	1393.5	2547.3	2997.4	3047.0	3095.7	3143.9	3191.7	3239.5	3287.3	3335.1
	H	1408.0	2727.7	3310.1	3374.6	3437.7	3499.8	3561.4	3622.7	3683.8	3744.7
	S	3.3605	5.6198	6.5147	6.5994	6.6797	6.7564	6.8302	6.9013	6.9703	7.0373
10200 (312.42/585.57)	V	1.460	17.605	30.599	32.058	33.472	34.851	36.202	37.530	38.837	40.128
	U	1401.8	2544.6	2995.3	3045.2	3094.0	3142.3	3190.3	3238.2	3286.1	3334.0
	H	1416.7	2724.2	3307.4	3372.1	3435.5	3497.8	3559.6	3621.0	3682.2	3743.3
	S	3.3748	5.6076	6.5027	6.5879	6.6685	6.7454	6.8194	6.8907	6.9598	7.0269
10400 (313.86/587.01)	V	1.467	17.184	29.943	31.382	32.776	34.134	35.464	36.770	38.056	39.325
	U	1410.0	2541.8	2993.2	3043.3	3092.4	3140.8	3188.9	3236.9	3284.8	3332.9
	H	1425.2	2720.6	3304.6	3369.7	3433.2	3495.8	3557.8	3619.3	3680.6	3741.8
	S	3.3889	5.5955	6.4909	6.5765	6.6574	6.7346	6.8087	6.8803	6.9495	7.0167
10600 (315.27/588.42)	V	1.474	16.778	29.313	30.732	32.106	33.444	34.753	36.039	37.304	38.552
	U	1418.1	2539.0	2991.1	3041.4	3090.7	3139.3	3187.5	3235.6	3283.6	3331.7
	H	1433.7	2716.9	3301.8	3367.2	3431.0	3493.8	3555.9	3617.6	3679.1	3740.4
	S	3.4029	5.5835	6.4793	6.5652	6.6465	6.7239	6.7983	6.8700	6.9394	7.0067
10800 (316.67/589.92)	V	1.481	16.385	28.706	30.106	31.461	32.779	34.069	35.335	36.580	37.808
	U	1426.2	2536.2	2989.0	3039.6	3089.0	3137.8	3186.1	3234.3	3282.4	3330.6
	H	1442.2	2713.1	3299.0	3364.7	3428.8	3491.8	3554.1	3615.9	3677.5	3738.9
	S	3.4167	5.5715	6.4678	6.5542	6.6357	6.7134	6.7880	6.8599	6.9294	6.9969
11000 (318.05/591.20)	V	1.489	16.006	28.120	29.503	30.839	32.139	33.410	34.656	35.882	37.091
	U	1434.2	2533.2	2986.9	3037.7	3087.3	3136.2	3184.7	3233.0	3281.2	3329.5
	H	1450.6	2709.3	3296.2	3362.2	3426.5	3489.7	3552.2	3614.2	3675.9	3737.5
	S	3.4304	5.5595	6.4564	6.5432	6.6251	6.7031	6.7779	6.8499	6.9196	6.9872
11200 (319.40/592.55)	V	1.496	15.639	27.555	28.921	30.240	31.521	32.774	34.002	35.210	36.400
	U	1442.1	2530.3	2984.8	3035.8	3085.6	3134.7	3183.3	3231.7	3280.0	3328.4
	H	1458.9	2705.4	3293.4	3359.7	3424.3	3487.7	3550.4	3612.5	3674.4	3736.0
	S	3.4440	5.5476	6.4452	6.5324	6.6147	6.6929	6.7679	6.8401	6.9099	6.9777
11400 (320.74/593.89)	V	1.504	15.284	27.010	28.359	29.661	30.925	32.160	33.370	34.560	35.733
	U	1450.0	2527.2	2982.6	3033.9	3083.9	3133.1	3181.9	3230.4	3278.8	3327.2
	H	1467.2	2701.5	3290.5	3357.2	3422.1	3485.7	3548.5	3610.8	3672.8	3734.6
	S	3.4575	5.5357	6.4341	6.5218	6.6043	6.6828	6.7580	6.8304	6.9004	6.9683

Temperature values correspond to ITS-68 temperature scale.

Appendix G

Thermodynamic Diagrams

Figure G.1 Methane

Figure G.2 1,1,1,2-tetrafluoroethane (HFC-134a)

Extensive tables of data for 1,1,1,2-tetrafluoroethane, refrigerant (HFC-134a), can be accessed through the URL:

http://www.dupont.com/suva/na/usa/literature/thermoprop/index.html

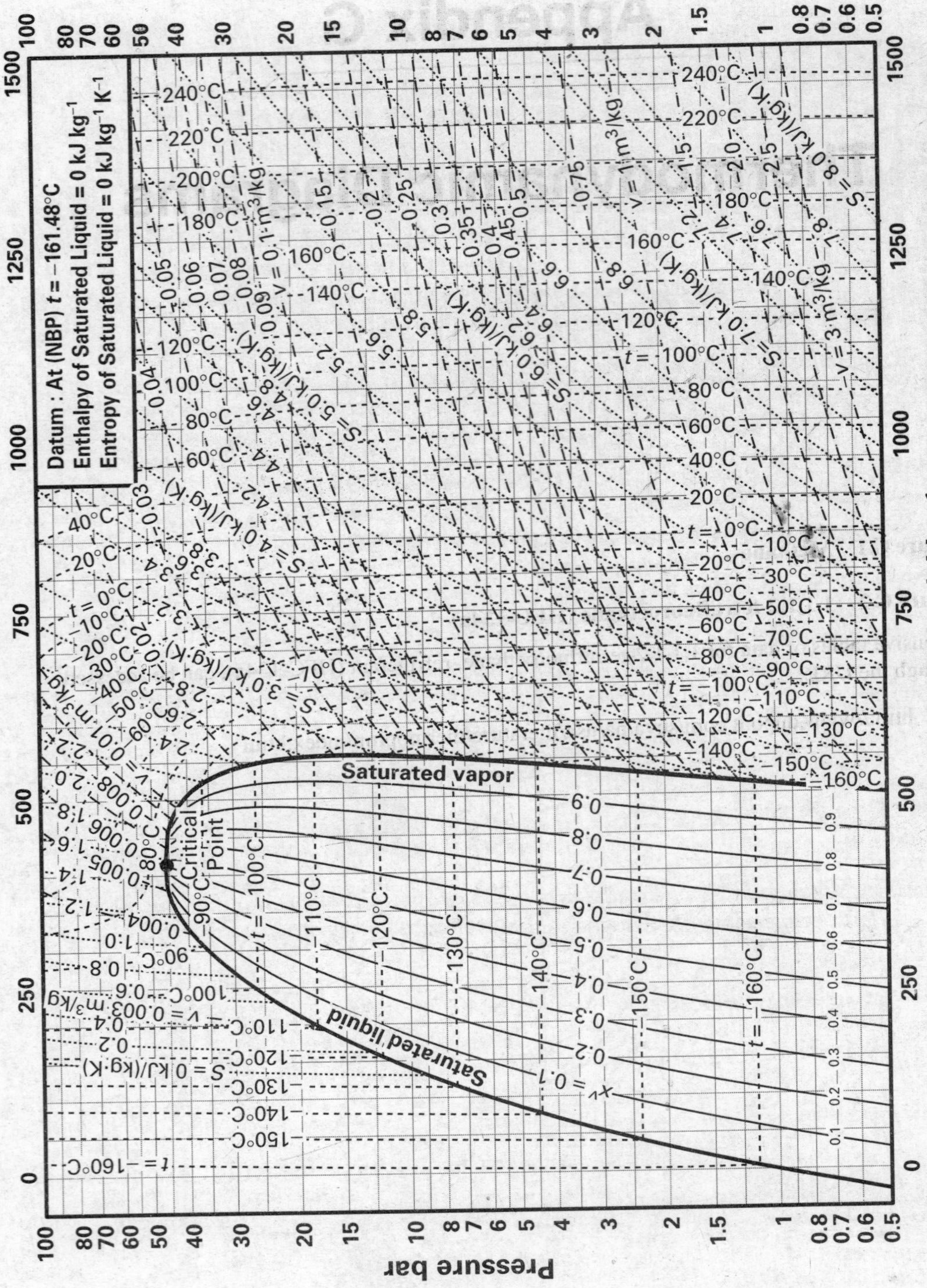

Figure G.1: *PH* diagram for methane. Drawn with the help of REFPROP Ver. 8, National Institute of Standards and Technology, USA, 2007.

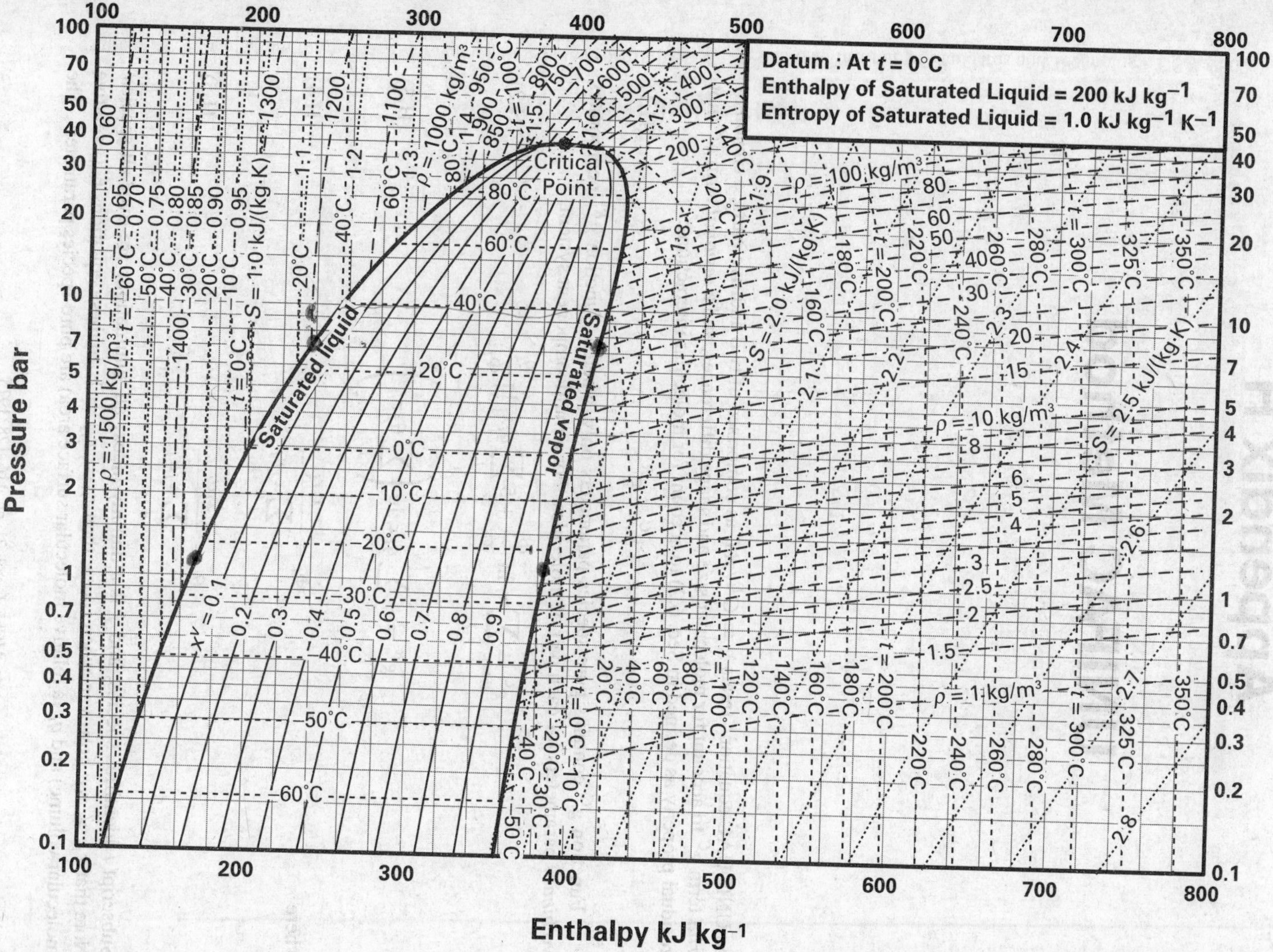

Figure G.2: *PH* diagram for tetrafluoroethane (HFC-134a). Drawn with the help of REFPROP Ver. 8, National Institute of Standards and Technology, USA, 2007.

Appendix H

UNIFAC Method

The UNIQUAC equation[1] treats $g \equiv G^E/RT$ as comprised of two additive parts, a *combinatorial* term g^C to account for molecular size and shape differences, and a *residual* term g^R (not a residual property as defined in Sec. 6.2) to account for molecular interactions:

$$g \equiv g^C + g^R \tag{H.1}$$

Function g^C contains pure-species parameters only, whereas function g^R incorporates two *binary* parameters for each pair of molecules. For a multicomponent system,

$$g^C = \sum_i x_i \ln \frac{\Phi_i}{x_i} + 5 \sum_i q_i x_i \ln \frac{\theta_i}{\Phi_i} \tag{H.2}$$

$$g^R = -\sum_i q_i x_i \ln \left(\sum_j \theta_j \tau_{ji} \right) \tag{H.3}$$

where

$$\Phi_i \equiv \frac{x_i r_i}{\sum_j x_j r_j} \tag{H.4}$$

$$\theta_i \equiv \frac{x_i q_i}{\sum_j x_j q_j} \tag{H.5}$$

Subscript i identifies species, and j is a dummy index; all summations are over all species. Note that $\tau_{ji} \neq \tau_{ij}$; however, when $i = j$, then $\tau_{ii} = \tau_{jj} = 1$. In these equations r_i (a relative molecular volume) and q_i (a relative molecular surface area) are pure-species parameters. The

[1] D. S. Abrams and J. M. Prausnitz, *AIChE J.*, vol. 21, pp. 116–128, 1975.

influence of temperature on g enters through the interaction parameters τ_{ji} of Eq. (H.3), which are temperature dependent:

$$\tau_{ji} = \exp \frac{-(u_{ji} - u_{ii})}{RT} \tag{H.6}$$

Parameters for the UNIQUAC equation are therefore values of $(u_{ji} - u_{ii})$.

An expression for $\ln \gamma_i$ is found by application of Eq. (11.96) to the UNIQUAC equation for g [Eqs. (H.1) through (H.3)]. The result is given by the following equations:

$$\ln \gamma_i = \ln \gamma_i^C + \ln \gamma_i^R \tag{H.7}$$

$$\ln \gamma_i^C = 1 - J_i + \ln J_i - 5q_i \left(1 - \frac{J_i}{L_i} + \ln \frac{J_i}{L_i}\right) \tag{H.8}$$

$$\ln \gamma_i^R = q_i \left(1 - \ln s_i - \sum_j \theta_j \frac{\tau_{ij}}{s_j}\right) \tag{H.9}$$

where in addition to Eqs. (H.5) and (H.6),

$$J_i = \frac{r_i}{\sum_j r_j x_j} \tag{H.10}$$

$$L_i = \frac{q_i}{\sum_j q_j x_j} \tag{H.11}$$

$$s_i = \sum_l \theta_l \tau_{li} \tag{H.12}$$

Again subscript i identifies species, and j and l are dummy indices. All summations are over all species, and $\tau_{ij} = 1$ for $i = j$. Values for the parameters $(u_{ij} - u_{jj})$ are found by regression of binary VLE data, and are given by Gmehling et al.[2]

The UNIFAC method for estimation of activity coefficients[3] depends on the concept that a liquid mixture may be considered a solution of the structural units from which the molecules are formed rather than a solution of the molecules themselves. These structural units are called ***subgroups***, and a few of them are listed in the second column of Table H.1. A number, designated k, identifies each subgroup. The relative volume R_k and relative surface area Q_k are properties of the subgroups, and values are listed in columns 4 and 5 of Table H.1. Also shown (columns 6 and 7) are examples of molecular species and their constituent subgroups. When it is possible to construct a molecule from more than one set of subgroups, the set containing the least number of *different* subgroups is the correct set. The great advantage of the UNIFAC method is that a

[2]J. Gmehling, U. Onken, and W. Arlt, *Vapor-Liquid Equilibrium Data Collection*, Chemistry Data Series, vol. I, parts 1–8, DECHEMA, Frankfurt/Main, 1974-1990.

[3]Aa. Fredenslund, R. L. Jones, and J. M. Prausnitz, *AIChE J.*, vol. 21, pp. 1086–1099, 1975.

Table H.1: UNIFAC–VLE Subgroup Parameters[†]

Main group	Subgroup	k	R_k	Q_k	Examples of molecules and their constituent groups	
1 "CH_2"	CH_3	1	0.9011	0.848	n-Butane:	$2CH_3, 2CH_2$
	CH_2	2	0.6744	0.540	Isobutane:	$3CH_3, 1CH$
	CH	3	0.4469	0.228	2,2-Dimethyl	
	C	4	0.2195	0.000	propane:	$4CH_3, 1C$
3 "ACH" (AC = aromatic carbon)	ACH	10	0.5313	0.400	Benzene:	6ACH
4 "$ACCH_2$"	$ACCH_3$	12	1.2663	0.968	Toluene:	$5ACH, 1ACCH_3$
	$ACCH_2$	13	1.0396	0.660	Ethylbenzene:	$1CH_3, 5ACH, 1ACCH_2$
5 "OH"	OH	15	1.0000	1.200	Ethanol:	$1CH_3, 1CH_2, 1OH$
7 "H_2O"	H_2O	17	0.9200	1.400	Water:	$1H_2O$
9 "CH_2CO"	CH_3CO	19	1.6724	1.488	Acetone:	$1CH_3CO, 1CH_3$
	CH_2CO	20	1.4457	1.180	3-Pentanone:	$2CH_3, 1CH_2CO, 1CH_2$
13 "CH_2O"	CH_3O	25	1.1450	1.088	Dimethyl ether:	$1CH_3, 1CH_3O$
	CH_2O	26	0.9183	0.780	Diethyl ether:	$2CH_3, 1CH_2, 1CH_2O$
	CH–O	27	0.6908	0.468	Diisopropyl ether:	$4CH_3, 1CH, 1CH{-}O$
15 "CNH"	CH_3NH	32	1.4337	1.244	Dimethylamine:	$1CH_3, 1CH_3NH$
	CH_2NH	33	1.2070	0.936	Diethylamine:	$2CH_3, 1CH_2, 1CH_2NH$
	CHNH	34	0.9795	0.624	Diisopropylamine:	$4CH_3, 1CH, 1CHNH$
19 "CCN"	CH_3CN	41	1.8701	1.724	Acetonitrile:	$1CH_3CN$
	CH_2CN	42	1.6434	1.416	Propionitrile:	$1CH_3, 1CH_2CN$

[†]H. K. Hansen, P. Rasmussen, Aa. Fredenslund, M. Schiller, and J. Gmehling, *IEC Research*, vol. 30, pp. 2352–2355, 1991.

relatively small number of subgroups combine to form a very large number of molecules.

Activity coefficients depend not only on the subgroup properties R_k and Q_k, but also on interactions between subgroups. Here, similar subgroups are assigned to a main group, as shown in the first two columns of Table H.1. The designations of main groups, such as "CH_2", "ACH", etc., are descriptive only. All subgroups belonging to the same main group are considered identical with respect to group interactions. Therefore parameters characterizing group interactions are identified with pairs of *main* groups. Parameter values a_{mk} for a few such pairs are given in Table H.2.

The UNIFAC method is based on the UNIQUAC equation, for which the activity coefficients are given by Eq. (H.7). When applied to a solution of groups, Eqs. (H.8) and (H.9) are written:

$$\ln \gamma_i^C = 1 - J_i + \ln J_i - 5q_i \left(1 - \frac{J_i}{L_i} + \ln \frac{J_i}{L_i}\right) \tag{H.13}$$

Table H.2: UNIFAC–VLE Interaction Parameters, a_{mk}, in kelvins[†]

	1	3	4	5	7	9	13	15	19
1 CH_2	0.00	61.13	76.50	986.50	1,318.00	476.40	251.50	255.70	597.00
3 ACH	−11.12	0.00	167.00	636.10	903.80	25.77	32.14	122.80	212.50
4 $ACCH_2$	−69.70	−146.80	0.00	803.20	5,695.00	−52.10	213.10	−49.29	6,096.00
5 OH	156.40	89.60	25.82	0.00	353.50	84.00	28.06	42.70	6.712
7 H_2O	300.00	362.30	377.60	−229.10	0.00	−195.40	540.50	168.00	112.60
9 CH_2CO	26.76	140.10	365.80	164.50	472.50	0.00	−103.60	−174.20	481.70
13 CH_2O	83.36	52.13	65.69	237.70	−314.70	191.10	0.00	251.50	−18.51
15 CNH	65.33	−22.31	223.00	−150.00	−448.20	394.60	−56.08	0.00	147.10
19 CCN	24.82	−22.97	−138.40	185.40	242.80	−287.50	38.81	−108.50	0.00

[†]H. K. Hansen, P. Rasmussen, Aa. Fredenslund, M. Schiller, and J. Gmehling, *IEC Research*, vol. 30, pp. 2352–2355, 1991.

$$\ln \gamma_i^R = q_i \left[1 - \sum_k \left(\theta_k \frac{\beta_{ik}}{s_k} - e_{ki} \ln \frac{\beta_{ik}}{s_k} \right) \right] \tag{H.14}$$

The quantities J_i and L_i are still given by Eqs. (H.10) and (H.11). In addition, the following definitions apply:

$$r_i = \sum_k \nu_k^{(i)} R_k \tag{H.15}$$

$$q_i = \sum_k \nu_k^{(i)} Q_k \tag{H.16}$$

$$e_{ki} = \frac{\nu_k^{(i)} Q_k}{q_i} \tag{H.17}$$

$$\beta_{ik} = \sum_m e_{mi} \tau_{mk} \tag{H.18}$$

$$\theta_k = \frac{\sum_i x_i q_i e_{ki}}{\sum_j x_j q_j} \tag{H.19}$$

$$s_k = \sum_m \theta_m \tau_{mk} \tag{H.20}$$

$$\tau_{mk} = \exp \frac{-a_{mk}}{T} \tag{H.21}$$

Subscript i identifies species, and j is a dummy index running over all species. Subscript k identifies subgroups, and m is a dummy index running over all subgroups. The quantity $\nu_k^{(i)}$ is the number of subgroups of type k in a molecule of species i. Values of the subgroup parameters R_k and Q_k and of the group interaction parameters a_{mk} come from tabulations in the literature. Tables H.1 and H.2 show a few parameter values; the number designations of the complete tables are retained.[4]

The equations for the UNIFAC method are presented here in a form convenient for computer programming. In the following example we run through a set of hand calculations to demonstrate their application.

Example H.1

For the binary system diethylamine(1)/n-heptane(2) at 35°C (308.15 K), find γ_1 and γ_2 when $x_1 = 0.4$ and $x_2 = 0.6$.

[4]H. K. Hansen, P. Rasmussen, Aa. Fredenslund, M. Schiller, and J. Gmehling, *IEC Research*, vol. 30, pp. 2352–2355, 1991.

Solution

The subgroups involved are indicated by the chemical formulas:

$$CH_3\text{–}CH_2NH\text{–}CH_2\text{–}CH_3(1)/CH_3\text{–}(CH_2)_5\text{–}CH_3(2)$$

The following table shows the subgroups, their identification numbers k, values of parameters R_k and Q_k (from Table H.1), and the numbers of each subgroup in each molecule:

	k	R_k	Q_k	$\nu_k^{(1)}$	$\nu_k^{(2)}$
CH_3	1	0.9011	0.848	2	2
CH_2	2	0.6744	0.540	1	5
CH_2NH	33	1.2070	0.936	1	0

By Eq. (H.15),

$$r_1 = (2)(0.9011) + (1)(0.6744) + (1)(1.2070) = 3.6836$$

Similarly, $\quad r_2 = (2)(0.9011) + (5)(0.6744) = 5.1742$

In like manner, by Eq. (H.16),

$$q_1 = 3.1720 \qquad \text{and} \qquad q_2 = 4.3960$$

The r_i and q_i values are molecular properties, independent of composition. Substituting known values into Eq. (H.17) generates the following table for e_{ki}:

	e_{ki}	
k	$i = 1$	$i = 2$
1	0.5347	0.3858
2	0.1702	0.6142
33	0.2951	0.0000

The following interaction parameters are found from Table H.2:

$$a_{1,1} = a_{1,2} = a_{2,1} = a_{2,2} = a_{33,33} = 0 \text{ K}$$

$$a_{1,33} = a_{2,33} = 255.7 \text{ K}$$

$$a_{33,1} = a_{33,2} = 65.33 \text{ K}$$

Substitution of these values into Eq. (H.21) with $T = 308.15$ K gives

$$\tau_{1,1} = \tau_{1,2} = \tau_{2,1} = \tau_{2,2} = \tau_{33,33} = 1$$

$$\tau_{1,33} = \tau_{2,33} = 0.4361$$

$$\tau_{33,1} = \tau_{33,2} = 0.8090$$

Application of Eq. (H.18) leads to the values of β_{ik} in the following table:

	β_{ik}		
i	$k = 1$	$k = 2$	k = 33
1	0.9436	0.9436	0.6024
2	1.0000	1.0000	0.4360

Substitution of these results into Eq. (H.19) yields

$$\theta_1 = 0.4342 \qquad \theta_2 = 0.4700 \qquad \theta_{33} = 0.0958$$

and by Eq. (H.20),

$$s_1 = 0.9817 \qquad s_2 = 0.9817 \qquad s_{33} = 0.4901$$

The activity coefficients may now be calculated. By Eq. (H.13),

$$\ln \gamma_1^C = -0.0213 \qquad \text{and} \qquad \ln \gamma_2^C = -0.0076$$

and by Eq. (H.14),

$$\ln \gamma_1^R = 0.1463 \qquad \text{and} \qquad \ln \gamma_2^R = 0.0537$$

Finally, Eq. (H.7) gives:

$$\gamma_1 = 1.133 \qquad \text{and} \qquad \gamma_2 = 1.047$$

Appendix I

Newton's Method

Newton's method is a procedure for the numerical solution of algebraic equations, applicable to any number M of such equations expressed as functions of M variables.

Consider first a single equation $f(X) = 0$, in which $f(X)$ is a function of the single variable X. Our purpose is to find a root of this equation, i.e., the value of X for which the function is zero. A simple function is illustrated in Fig. I.1; it exhibits a single root at the point where the curve crosses the X-axis. When it is not possible to solve directly for the root,[1] a numerical procedure, such as Newton's method, is employed.

[1]For example, when $e^X + X^2 + 10 = 0$.

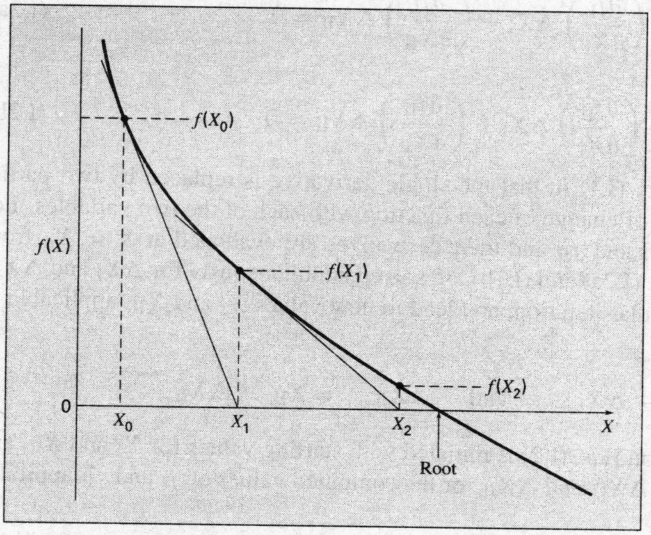

Figure I.1: Newton's method applied to a single function

The application of Newton's method is illustrated in Fig. I.1. In the neighborhood of an arbitrary value $X = X_0$ the function $f(X)$ can be approximated by the tangent line drawn at $X = X_0$. The equation of the tangent line is given by the linear relation:

$$g(X) = f(X_0) + \left[\frac{d\,f(X)}{dX}\right]_{X=X_0} (X - X_0)$$

where $g(X)$ is the value of the ordinate at X, as shown in Fig. I.1. The root of this equation is found by setting $g(X) = 0$ and solving for X; as indicated in Fig. I.1, the value is X_1. Since the actual function is not linear, this is not the root of $f(X)$. However, it lies closer to the root than does the starting value X_0. The function $f(X)$ is now approximated by a second line, drawn tangent to the curve at $X = X_1$, and the procedure is repeated, leading to a root for this linear approximation at X_2, a value still closer to the root of $f(X)$. This root can be approached as closely as desired by continued successive linear approximation of the original function. The general formula for iteration is:

$$f(X_n) + \left[\frac{d\,f(X)}{dX}\right]_{X=X_n} \Delta X_n = 0 \tag{I.1}$$

where

$$\Delta X_n \equiv X_{n+1} - X_n \qquad \text{or} \qquad X_{n+1} = X_n + \Delta X_n$$

Equation (I.1), written for successive iterations ($n = 0, 1, 2, \ldots$), produces successive values of ΔX_n and successive values of $f(X_n)$. The process starts with an initial value X_0 and continues until either ΔX_n or $f(X_n)$ approaches zero to within a preset tolerance.

Newton's method is readily extended to the solution of simultaneous equations. For the case of two equations in two unknowns, let $f_{\rm I} \equiv f_{\rm I}(X_{\rm I}, X_{\rm II})$ and $f_{\rm II} \equiv f_{\rm II}(X_{\rm I}, X_{\rm II})$ represent two functions, the values of which depend on the two variables $X_{\rm I}$ and $X_{\rm II}$. Our purpose is to find the values of $X_{\rm I}$ and $X_{\rm II}$ for which both functions are zero. In analogy to Eq. (I.1), we write:

$$f_{\rm I} + \left(\frac{\partial f_{\rm I}}{\partial X_{\rm I}}\right) \Delta X_{\rm I} + \left(\frac{\partial f_{\rm I}}{\partial X_{\rm II}}\right) \Delta X_{\rm II} = 0 \tag{I.2a}$$

$$f_{\rm II} + \left(\frac{\partial f_{\rm II}}{\partial X_{\rm I}}\right) \Delta X_{\rm I} + \left(\frac{\partial f_{\rm II}}{\partial X_{\rm II}}\right) \Delta X_{\rm II} = 0 \tag{I.2b}$$

These equations differ from Eq. (I.1) in that the single derivative is replaced by two partial derivatives, reflecting the rates of change of each function with each of the two variables. For iteration n the two functions $f_{\rm I}$ and $f_{\rm II}$ and their derivatives are evaluated at $X = X_n$ from the given expressions, and Eqs. (I.2a) and (I.2b) are solved simultaneously for $\Delta X_{\rm I}$ and $\Delta X_{\rm II}$. These are specific to the particular iteration, and lead to new values $X_{\rm I}$ and $X_{\rm II}$, applicable to the next iteration:

$$X_{{\rm I}_{n+1}} = X_{{\rm I}_n} + \Delta X_{{\rm I}_n} \qquad \text{and} \qquad X_{{\rm II}_{n+1}} = X_{{\rm II}_n} + \Delta X_{{\rm II}_n}$$

The iterative procedure based on Eqs. (I.2) is initiated with starting values for $X_{\rm I}$ and $X_{\rm II}$, and continues until the increments $\Delta X_{{\rm I}_n}$ and $\Delta X_{{\rm II}_n}$ or the computed values of $f_{\rm I}$ and $f_{\rm II}$ approach zero.

Equations (I.2) can be generalized to apply to a system of M equations in M unknowns; the result for each iteration is

$$f_K + \sum_{J=\mathrm{I}}^{M} \left(\frac{\partial f_K}{\partial X_J}\right) \Delta X_J = 0 \qquad (K = \mathrm{I},\ \mathrm{II},\ \ldots,\ M) \tag{I.3}$$

with

$$X_{J_{n+1}} = X_{J_n} + \Delta X_{J_n} \qquad (J = \mathrm{I},\ \mathrm{II},\ \ldots,\ M)$$

Newton's method is well suited to application in multireaction equilibria. As an illustration, we solve Eqs. (A) and (B) of Ex. 13.13 for the case of $T = 1{,}000$ K. From these equations with values given there for K_a and K_b at 1,000 K and with $P/P^\circ = 20$, we find the functions:

$$f_a = 4.0879\,\varepsilon_a^2 + \varepsilon_b^2 + 4.0879\,\varepsilon_a\varepsilon_b + 0.2532\,\varepsilon_a - 0.0439\,\varepsilon_b - 0.1486 \tag{A}$$

and

$$f_b = 1.12805\,\varepsilon_b^2 + 2.12805\,\varepsilon_a\varepsilon_b - 0.12805\,\varepsilon_a + 0.3048\,\varepsilon_b - 0.4328 \tag{B}$$

Equations (I.2) are written here as:

$$f_a + \left(\frac{\partial f_a}{\partial \varepsilon_a}\right) \Delta\varepsilon_a + \left(\frac{\partial f_a}{\partial \varepsilon_b}\right) \Delta\varepsilon_b = 0 \tag{C}$$

$$f_b + \left(\frac{\partial f_b}{\partial \varepsilon_a}\right) \Delta\varepsilon_a + \left(\frac{\partial f_b}{\partial \varepsilon_b}\right) \Delta\varepsilon_b = 0 \tag{D}$$

The solution procedure is initiated with a choice of starting values for ε_a and ε_b. Numerical values are obtained for f_a and f_b and for their derivatives from Eqs. (A) and (B). Substitution of these values in Eqs. (C) and (D) yields two linear equations which are readily solved for the unknowns $\Delta\varepsilon_a$ and $\Delta\varepsilon_b$. These yield new values of ε_a and ε_b with which to carry out a second iteration. The process continues until $\Delta\varepsilon_a$ and $\Delta\varepsilon_b$ or f_a and f_b approach zero.

Setting $\varepsilon_a = 0.1$ and $\varepsilon_b = 0.7$ as starting values,[2] we find initial values of f_a and f_b and their derivatives from Eqs. (A) and (B):

$$f_a = 0.6630 \qquad \left(\frac{\partial f_a}{\partial \varepsilon_a}\right) = 3.9230 \qquad \left(\frac{\partial f_a}{\partial \varepsilon_b}\right) = 1.7648$$

$$f_b = 0.4695 \qquad \left(\frac{\partial f_b}{\partial \varepsilon_a}\right) = 1.3616 \qquad \left(\frac{\partial f_b}{\partial \varepsilon_b}\right) = 2.0956$$

These values are substituted in Eqs. (C) and (D) to yield

$$0.6630 + 3.9230\,\Delta\varepsilon_a + 1.7648\,\Delta\varepsilon_b = 0$$

$$0.4695 + 1.3616\,\Delta\varepsilon_a + 2.0956\,\Delta\varepsilon_b = 0$$

The values of the increments that satisfy these equations are

$$\Delta\varepsilon_a = -0.0962 \qquad \text{and} \qquad \Delta\varepsilon_b = -0.1614$$

[2]These are well within the limits, $-0.5 \le \varepsilon_a \le 0.5$ and $0 \le \varepsilon_b \le 1.0$, noted in Ex. 13.13.

from which,

$$\varepsilon_a = 0.1 - 0.0962 = 0.0038 \qquad \text{and} \qquad \varepsilon_b = 0.7 - 0.1614 = 0.5386$$

These values are the basis for a second iteration, and the process continues, yielding results as follows:

n	ε_a	ε_b	$\Delta\varepsilon_a$	$\Delta\varepsilon_b$
0	0.1000	0.7000	−0.0962	−0.1614
1	0.0038	0.5386	−0.0472	−0.0094
2	−0.0434	0.5292	−0.0071	0.0043
3	−0.0505	0.5335	−0.0001	0.0001
4	−0.0506	0.5336	0.0000	0.0000

Convergence is clearly rapid. Moreover, any reasonable starting values lead to convergence on the same answers.

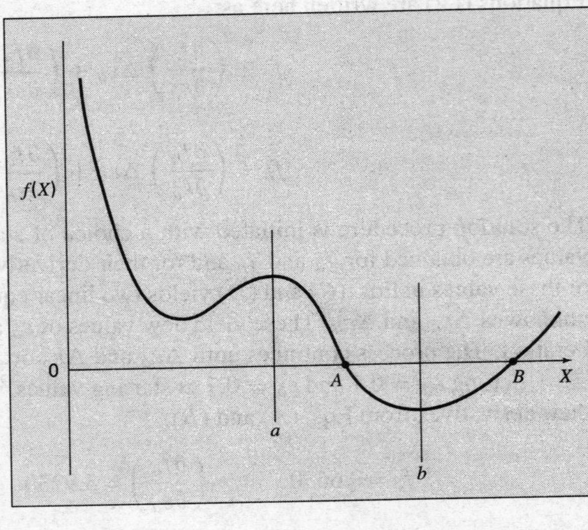

Figure I.2: Finding the roots of a function showing extrema

Convergence problems can arise with Newton's method when one or more of the functions exhibit extrema. This is illustrated for the case of a single equation in Fig. I.2. The function has two roots, at points A and B. If Newton's method is applied with a starting value of X smaller than a, a very small range of X values produces convergence on each root, but for most values it does not converge, and neither root is found. With a starting value of X between a and b, it converges on root A only if the value is sufficiently close to A. With a starting value of X to the right of b, it converges on root B. In cases such as this, a proper starting value can be found by trial, or by graphing the function to determine its behavior.

Appendix J

Answers for Problems

CHAPTER 1

1.4 $t = -40$

1.5 mass = 384.4 kg

1.6 mass = 454.3 kg

1.7 $P_{abs} = 176.808$ kPa

1.9 $h = 302.3$ m

1.10 g (Mars) = 0.01 m K kg^{-1}

1.11 P (Denver) = 0.823 atm
P (Denver) = 0.834 bar

1.12 $M = 113.498$ lb$_m$
$F_{(moon)} = 18.767$ lbf

1.13 cost$_{total}$ = 43.829 dollars y^{-1}

1.14 (*a*) $F = 1.909 \times 10^4$ N
(*b*) $P_{abs} = 110.054$ kPa
(*c*) $W = 15.848$ kJ
$\Delta E_p = 1.222$ kJ

1.16 $E_K = 1000$ kJ
$W = 1000$ kJ

1.17 $\dot{m} = 0.488$ kg s^{-1}

1.20 (*a*) cost of coal = 0.95 GJ^{-1}
cost of gasoline = 14.28 GJ^{-1}
cost of electricity = 27.778 GJ^{-1}

1.22 $A = 13.421$
$B = 2.29 \times 10^3$
$C = -69.053$
$t_n/T_n = 56°\text{C}/329.15$ K

1.23 (*a*) $C_2 = 0.3976$ dollars L^{-1}
(*b*) $i = 5.51\%$

CHAPTER 2

2.1 (*a*) $W = 1.715$ kJ
(*b*) $\Delta U_{total} = 1.715$ kJ
(*c*) $t_2/T_2 = 20°\text{C}/293.15$ K
(*d*) $Q = -1.715$ kJ
(*e*) Total change in internal energy of universe = 0

2.2 (*a*) $W = 1.715$ kJ
(*b*) $\Delta U = 1.429$ kJ
(*c*) $t_2/T_2 = 20°\text{C}/293.15$ K
(*d*) $Q = -1.715$ kJ

2.4 $\dot{Q} = 0.137$ kW

2.5 $Q_{12} = 5.8$ kJ
$\Delta Ut_{34} = -500$ J
$\Delta Ut_{23} = -4000$ J
$W_{23} = -200$ J

$W_{12341} = -1400$ J
$W_{41} = 4.5$ kJ
$Q_{41} = 200$ J

2.11 $\Delta\tau = 0.929$ h

2.12 $W = -19.5$ kJ
$Q = -12$ kJ

2.13 $t_2/T_2 = 27.78°C/300.93$ K

2.15 (*a*) $\Delta U_t = 4.18$ kJ
(*b*) $\Delta z = 426.531$ m
(*c*) $u = 91.433$ m s^{-1}

2.17 $\dot{W} = 7.697 \times 10^3$ kW

2.18 (*a*) $H_1 = 763.131$ kJ kg^{-1}
(*b*) $\Delta U = 2022.4$ kJ kg^{-1}
$\Delta H = 2275.8$ kJ kg^{-1}

2.22 (*a*) $u_2 = 0.5$ m s^{-1}
(*b*) $\Delta E_K = -1.875$ J kg^{-1}

2.23 $t_3/T_3 = 43.24°C/316.39$ K

2.25 $\Delta t = 0.019°C$
$\Delta t = 0.023°C$
$\Delta t = 0.023°C$

2.26 $\dot{Q} = -9.904$ kW

2.27 $T_2/t_2 = 320.57$ K/47.42°C

2.28 $Q = 2411.6$ kJ kg^{-1}

2.29 $u_2 = 578.36$ m s^{-1}
$D_2 = 1.493$ cm

2.30 (*a*) $Q = 13.728$ kJ
$Q = 11\,014$ kJ with vessel mass
(*b*) $Q = -18.62$ kJ

2.31 (*a*) $Q = 4914$ kJ
$Q = 11\,989$ kJ with vessel mass
(*b*) $Q = -8145$ kJ

2.33 $\dot{W} = 14.08$ kW

2.34 $\dot{Q} = -67\,573$ kJ h^{-1} $= -18.77$ kW

2.36 $W = -172.61$ kJ
$\Delta H = 17.4$ kJ mol^{-1}
$Q = 602.08$ kJ
$\Delta U = 12.41$ kJ mol^{-1}

2.37 $\Delta U = 0.831$ kJ mol^{-1}
$\Delta H = 1.164$ kJ mol^{-1}

2.39 (*a*) $\dot{m} = 0.313$ kg s^{-1}
(*b*) $\dot{m} = 1.956$ kg s^{-1}
(*c*) $\dot{m} = 1.565$ kg s^{-1}
(*d*) $\dot{m} = 9.778$ kg s^{-1}
(*a*) $\Delta P/\Delta L = -0.632$ kPa m^{-1}
(*b*) $\Delta P/\Delta L = -0.206$ kPa m^{-1}
(*c*) $\Delta P/\Delta L = -11.254$ kPa m^{-1}
(*d*) $\Delta P/\Delta L = -3.88$ kPa m^{-1}

2.42 Cost = 799 924 dollars

CHAPTER 3

3.1 $P_2 = 226.2$ bar

3.4 $W = 0.516$ J gm^{-1}

3.5 $W = 0.471$ atm m^3

3.6 $\Delta V_{\text{total}} = 7.638 \times 10^{-5}$ m^3
$W = -7.638$ J
$Q = 84$ kJ
$\Delta H_{\text{total}} = 84$ kJ
$\Delta U_{\text{total}} = 83.99$ kJ

3.8 (*a*) $\Delta U = -10.91$ kJ mol^{-1}
$\Delta H = -15.28$ kJ mol^{-1}
(*b*) $W = -10.37$ kJ mol^{-1}
(*c*) $\Delta U = -5.586$ kJ mol^{-1}
$\Delta H = -7.821$ kJ mol^{-1}

3.9 (*b*) Step 41: $P_2 = 3$ bar $T_2 = 600$ K
Step 12: $P_3 = 2$ bar $T_3 = 400$ K
(*c*) Step 41: $Q = 0$ J mol^{-1}
$\Delta U = 0$ J mol^{-1}
$\Delta H = 0$ J mol^{-1}
$W_2 = -6.006$ kJ mol^{-1}
Step 23: $Q = -4.157$ kJ mol^{-1}
$\Delta U = -4.157$ kJ mol^{-1}
$\Delta H = -5.82$ kJ mol^{-1}
$W = 0$ J mol^{-1}

Step 34: $Q = -616$ J mol^{-1}
$\Delta U = -440$ J mol^{-1}
$\Delta H = -616$ J mol^{-1}
$W = 176$ J mol^{-1}

3.10 (*a*) $W = 2982$ kJ
(*b*) $W = 5106$ kJ
(*c*) $W = 7635$ kJ
(*d*) $W = 13\,200$ kJ
(*e*) $W = 1100$ kJ

3.17 (*a*) $t_2/T_2 = 100$°C/373.15 K
(*b*) $W = 878.9$ kJ

3.18 (*a*) $\Delta U_{12} = 3.679$ kJ mol^{-1}
$\Delta H_{12} = 5.15$ kJ mol^{-1}
$W_{12} = 3.679$ kJ mol^{-1}
$\Delta U_{23} = -3.679$ kJ mol^{-1}
$W_{23} = 1.471$ kJ mol^{-1}
$W_{31} = -4.056$ kJ mol^{-1}
$Q_{31} = 4.056$ kJ mol^{-1}
For the complete cycle:
$Q = -1.094$ kJ mol^{-1}
$W = 1.094$ kJ mol^{-1}

(*b*) $W_{12} = 4.598$ kJ mol^{-1}
$Q_{12} = -0.92$ kJ mol^{-1}
$W_{23} = 1.839$ kJ mol^{-1}
$Q_{23} = -5.518$ kJ mol^{-1}
$W_{31} = -3.245$ kJ mol^{-1}
$Q_{31} = 3.245$ kJ mol^{-1}
For the complete cycle:
$Q = -3.192$ kJ mol^{-1}
$W = 3.192$ kJ mol^{-1}

3.19 (*a*) $T_2 = 600$ K $\quad P_2 = 200$ kPa
$W = -1609$ kJ
(*b*) $T_2 = 208.96$ K $\quad P_2 = 69.65$ kPa
$W = -994.4$ kJ
(*c*) $W = -400$ kJ
$T_2 = 442.71$ K
$P_2 = 147.57$ kPa

3.20 $W = -2.502$ kJ mol^{-1}
$Q = 0.424$ kJ mol^{-1}
$\Delta H = -2.91$ kJ mol^{-1}
$\Delta U = -2.079$ kJ mol^{-1}

3.21 $t_2/T_2 = 148.8$°C/421.95 K

3.22

	For $C_P = (7/2)$ R and $C_V = (5/2)$ R	For $C_P = (5/2)$ R $C_V = (3/2)$ R
	$\Delta U = 2.079$	1.247 kJ mol^{-1}
	$\Delta H = 2.91$	2.079 kJ mol^{-1}
(*a*)	$W = 6.762$	6.762 kJ mol^{-1}
	$Q = -4.684$	-5.515 kJ mol^{-1}
(*b*)	$W = 6.886$	6.886 kJ mol^{-1}
	$Q = -4.808$	-5.639 kJ mol^{-1}
(*c*)	$W = 4.972$	4.972 kJ mol^{-1}
	$Q = -2.894$	-3.725 kJ mol^{-1}

3.23 $\Delta U = 1.871$ kJ mol^{-1}
$\Delta H = 2.619$ kJ mol^{-1} $W = 5.608$ kJ mol^{-1}
$Q = -3.737$ kJ mol^{-1}

3.24 $P = 2.279$ bar

3.25 $V_B = 3750.3$ cm^3

3.26 (*a*) $T_B = 319.75$ K
$T_A = 430.25$ K
$q = 3.118$ kJ mol^{-1}
(*b*) $T_B = 319.02$ K
$P_2 = 1.24$ atm
$q = 2.993$ kJ mol^{-1}
(*c*) $P_2 = 1.323$ atm
$T_A = 469$ K
$q = 4.032$ kJ mol^{-1}
(*d*) $P_2 = 1.241$ atm
$T_B = 319.06$ K
$T_A = 425.28$ K

3.30 (*a*) $W = 12.62$ kJ mol^{-1}
(*b*) $W = 12.596$ kJ mol^{-1}

3.32

(*a*)	$V = 1919$ cm^3 mol^{-1}	$Z = 0.929$
(*b*)	$V = 1924$ cm^3 mol^{-1}	$Z = 0.932$
(*c*)	$V = 1916.5$ cm^3 mol^{-1}	$Z = 0.928$
(*d*)	$V = 1918$ cm^3 mol^{-1}	$Z = 0.928$
(*e*)	$V = 1900.6$ cm^3 mol^{-1}	$Z = 0.92$

3.33

(*a*)	$V = 1625$ cm^3 mol^{-1}	$Z = 0.907$
(*b*)	$V = 1634$ cm^3 mol^{-1}	$Z = 0.912$
(*c*)	$V = 1622.7$ cm^3 mol^{-1}	$Z = 0.906$
(*d*)	$V = 1624.8$ cm^3 mol^{-1}	$Z = 0.907$
(*e*)	$V = 1605.5$ cm^3 mol^{-1}	$Z = 0.896$

3.34

(*a*)	$V = 1722$ cm^3 mol^{-1}	$Z = 0.893$
(*b*)	$V = 1734$ cm^3 mol^{-1}	$Z = 0.899$
(*c*)	$V = 1714.1$ cm^3 mol^{-1}	$Z = 0.888$
(*d*)	$V = 1726.9$ cm^3 mol^{-1}	$Z = 0.895$
(*e*)	$V = 1701.5$ cm^3 mol^{-1}	$Z = 0.882$

3.35 (*a*) $V = 2250 \text{ cm}^3 \text{ mol}^{-1}$ $Z = 0.931$
(*b*) $V = 2268 \text{ cm}^3 \text{ mol}^{-1}$ $Z = 0.939$
(*c*) $V = 2252 \text{ cm}^3 \text{ mol}^{-1}$

3.37 (*b*) Up to $P = 100$ bar

3.38 (*a*) For propane:
Redlich / Kwong EOS:
$V^v = 1499.2 \text{ cm}^3 \text{ mol}^{-1}$
$V^l = 108.1 \text{ cm}^3 \text{ mol}^{-1}$
Pitzer correlation:
$V^v = 1538 \text{ cm}^3 \text{ mol}^{-1}$
Rackett equation:
$V^l = 94.17 \text{ cm}^3 \text{ mol}^{-1}$

3.39 (*a*) For propane:
SRK EOS:
$V^v = 1480.7 \text{ cm}^3 \text{ mol}^{-1}$
$V^l = 104.7 \text{ cm}^3 \text{ mol}^{-1}$

3.40 (*a*) For propane:
Peng / Robinson EOS:
$V^v = 1454.5 \text{ cm}^3 \text{ mol}^{-1}$
$V^l = 92.2 \text{ cm}^3 \text{ mol}^{-1}$

3.41 (*a*) $V^l = 0.421 \text{ m}^3$
(*b*) $m = 60.898$ kg

3.42 $V_2 = 3.046 \times 10^3 \text{ cm}^3 \text{ mol}^{-1}$

3.43 $V = 989 \text{ cm}^3 \text{ mol}^{-1}$
$V^{id} = 1044 \text{ cm}^3 \text{ mol}^{-1}$

3.44 $m^l = 127.594$ kg
$m^v = 2.341$ kg

3.45 $m^v = 98.213$ kg

3.46 (*a*) $m_{\text{ethane}} = 49.64$ kg
(*b*) $t/T = 118.5°\text{C}/391.65$ K

3.47 $P = 79.73$ bar

3.48 $P = 9920$ kPa

3.49 $P_2 = 42.68$ bar

3.50 $P = 10.863$ bar

3.51 $P = 450.1$ bar

3.52 $V_2 = 2.519 \text{ cm}^3 \text{ g}^{-1}$

3.53 $\rho_2 = 0.532 \text{ g cm}^{-3}$

3.54 $\rho = 0.629 \text{ g cm}^{-3}$

3.55 $\Delta V = 2589 \text{ cm}^3 \text{ mol}^{-1}$

3.58 $V_{\text{tank}} = 0.1574 \text{ m}^3$

3.59 $Z = 0.823$-Pitzer correlation
$Z = 0.791$-RK EOS

3.61 (*a*) $q_2 = 0.182 \text{ Mm}^3\text{d}^{-1}$
(*b*) $n_1 = 6.944 \text{ kmol h}^{-1}$
(*c*) $u = 8.111 \text{ m s}^{-1}$

3.62 The equation of the line is:
$Z_c = 0.291 - 0.091\omega$

3.65 (*a*) For reversible cycle:
Step 1 → 2 Adiabatic compression:
$\Delta U_{12} = 3.618 \text{ kJ mol}^{-1}$
$\Delta H_{12} = 5.065 \text{ kJ mol}^{-1}$
$Q_{12} = 0 \text{ kJ mol}^{-1}$
$W_{12} = 3.618 \text{ kJ mol}^{-1}$
Step 2 → 3 Isobaric cooling
$\Delta U_{23} = -3.618 \text{ kJ mol}^{-1}$
$\Delta H_{23} = -5.065 \text{ kJ mol}^{-1}$
$Q_{23} = -5.065 \text{ kJ mol}^{-1}$
$W_{23} = 1.447 \text{ kJ mol}^{-1}$
Step 3 → 1 Isothermal expansion
$\Delta U_{31} = 0 \text{ kJ mol}^{-1}$
$\Delta H_{31} = 0 \text{ kJ mol}^{-1}$
$Q_{31} = 3.99 \text{ kJ mol}^{-1}$
$W_{31} = -3.99 \text{ kJ mol}^{-1}$
$Q_{\text{cycle}} = -1.076 \text{ kJ mol}^{-1}$
$W_{\text{cycle}} = 1.076 \text{ kJ mol}^{-1}$
(*b*) For irreversible cycle:
Step 1 → 2 Adiabatic compression
$W_{12} = 4.522 \text{ kJ mol}^{-1}$
$Q_{12} = -0.904 \text{ kJ mol}^{-1}$
Step 2 → 3 Isobaric cooling
$W_{23} = 1.809 \text{ kJ mol}^{-1}$
$Q_{23} = -5.427 \text{ kJ mol}^{-1}$
Step 3 → 1 Isothermal expansion
$W_{31} = -3.192 \text{ kJ mol}^{-1}$
$Q_{31} = 3.192 \text{ kJ mol}^{-1}$
$Q_{\text{cycle}} = -3.14 \text{ kJ mol}^{-1}$
$W_{\text{cycle}} = 3.14 \text{ kJ mol}^{-1}$

3.67 (*a*) $B = -128.42$ cm^3 mol^{-1} at 300°C (573.15 K)
(*b*) $B = -105.899$ cm^3 mol^{-1} at 350°C (623.15 K)
(*c*) $B = -89.902$ cm^3 mol^{-1} at 400°C (673.15 K)

3.70 $\hat{B} = -0.332$
$B^0 = -0.339$

3.71 $V = 86.1$ cm^3 mol^{-1}

3.72 (b) $P = 197.8$ bar

3.73 (*a*) $V_t = 2.379 \times 10^7$ m^3 - very high
(*b*) $V_t = 75.133$ m^3

Spherical tank with $D = 5.235$ m

CHAPTER 4

4.1 (*a*) $Q = 470.073$ kJ
(*b*) $Q = 1.942$ MJ

4.2 (*a*) $T = 1374.5$ K
(*b*) $T = 1413.8$ K
(*c*) $T = 1202.8$ K

4.3 $Q = 3.469$ kJ

4.4 $Q = 9.4315$ MJ

4.7 $C_p = 56.95$ J mol^{-1} K^{-1}

4.9 (*a*) $\Delta H_n = 30.108$ kJ mol^{-1} for acetone
(*b*) $\Delta H_2 = 26.448$ kJ mol^{-1} for *n*-pentane
$= 31.533$ kJ mol^{-1} for *n*-hexane
$= 33.571$ kJ mol^{-1} for benzene
$= 32.816$ kJ mol^{-1} for cyclohexane

4.10 $\Delta H = 209.45$ kJ kg^{-1} at -5°C (268.15 K)
$= 199.61$ kJ kg^{-1} at 0°C (273.15 K)
$= 188.5$ kJ kg^{-1} at 5°C (278.15 K)
$= 176.8$ kJ kg^{-1} at 10°C (283.15 K)
$= 162.5$ kJ kg^{-1} at 15°C (288.15 K)

4.11 (*a*) $\Delta H_n = \begin{pmatrix} 245 \\ 1055.2 \\ 193.2 \end{pmatrix}$ J g^{-1}

(*b*) $\Delta H_n = \begin{pmatrix} 247.7 \\ 1195.3 \\ 192.3 \end{pmatrix}$ J g^{-1}

4.12 $\Delta H_{calc} = 29.662$ kJ mol^{-1} for acetone

4.13 $B = -1369.5$ cm^3 mol^{-1}

4.14 (*a*) $Q = 1.372$ MW
(*b*) $Q = 1.536$ MW
(*c*) $Q = 1.822$ MW

4.15 $x = 0.498$

4.16 (*a*) $\Delta H_{298} = 220.8$ kJ mol^{-1} for acetylene
(*b*) $= 88.5$ kJ mol^{-1} for 1, 3-butadiene
(*c*) $= -12.3$ kJ mol^{-1} for ethylbenzene
(*d*) $= -196.8$ kJ mol^{-1} for *n*-hexane
(*e*) $= 103.9$ kJ mol^{-1} for styrene

4.17 $Q = 6477.5$ J mol^{-1}
$P_2 = 11.45$ bar

4.18 $\Delta H_{298} = -4058.91$ kJ
$\Delta H_{298} = -3770.01$ kJ

4.19 (*a*) $T = 2533.5$ K
(*b*) $T = 2198.6$ K
(*c*) $T = 1950.9$ K
(*d*) $T = 1609.2$ K
(*e*) $T = 2282.5$ K

4.20 $\Delta H_{298} = -3535.76$ kJ

4.21 (*a*) $\Delta H_{298} = -92.22$ kJ

4.22 (*a*) $\Delta H_{873} = -109.8$ kJ

4.23 $\Delta H_T = -5.871 + 4.181 \times 10^{-3}$
$T - 0.661 \times 10^{-5}/T$

4.24 Revenue $= 7.947 \times 10^5$ dollars d^{-1}

4.25 (*a*) $\Delta H_c = -921.714$ kJ mol^{-1}
(*b*) $\Delta H_c = -946.194$ kJ mol^{-1}
(*c*) $\Delta H_c = -932.875$ kJ mol^{-1}

4.26 $\Delta H_{298} = -333.509$ kJ mol^{-1}

4.28 $\Delta H_{298} = -6748.436$ kJ mol^{-1}

4.29 $Q = -70.612$ kJ
$Q = -766.677$ kJ

4.30 $T = 978.9$ K

4.31 $Q = -115.653$ kJ

4.32 $Q = 54.881$ kJ

4.33 $T = 542.2$ K

4.34 $\Delta H_{773} = -12\,679$ J mol^{-1}

4.35 $Q = -9470$ J

4.36 4.288 kg H_2O/kg oil burnt

4.37 $Q = 30.124$ kJ

4.38 $Q = -13.229$ kJ

4.39 Flue gas to air = 5.221
mole % CO = 34.054
mole % N_2 = 65.946

4.40 $\dot{q} = 0.407$ m^3 sec^{-1}

4.41 $Q = 38.896$ kJ

4.42 (*a*) $\dot{q} = 0.943$ m^3 s^{-1}
(*b*) $\dot{q} = 0.7707$ m^3 s^{-1}

4.43 (*a*) $\dot{Q} = -25.967$ kW
(*b*) $\dot{Q} = -17.3216$ kW

4.44 Heating cost = 0.0317 dollars MJ^{-1}

4.45 (*a*) $Q = 26.12$ kJ mol^{-1} for acetylene

4.46 (*a*) $t/T = 562.25$°C/835.4 K for acetylene

4.47 (*a*) $y = 0.637$
(*b*) $y = 0.245$
(*c*) $y = 0.512$

4.48 (*a*) $\dot{m}_s/\dot{n}_a = 0.011$ kg mol^{-1}
(*b*) $\dot{m}_s/\dot{n}_a = 5.03 \times 10^{-3}$ kg mol^{-1}

4.50 (*a*) $\Delta H_R^\circ = -2801.634$ kJ mol^{-1}
(*b*) mass_glucose = 0.549 kg
(*c*) CO_2 produced = 2.216×10^8 kg kg^{-1}

4.51 (*a*) $\Delta H_c^\circ = -825.096$ kJ mol^{-1}
(*b*) $Q = -529.889$ kJ mol^{-1}

CHAPTER 5

5.2 $\dot{W} = 148.78$ kW
$\dot{Q}_C = 101.22$ kW

5.3 (*a*) $\dot{Q}_H = 1.583 \times 10^5$ kW
$\dot{Q}_C = 6.333 \times 10^4$ kW
(*b*) $\dot{Q}_H = 2.714 \times 10^5$ kW
$\dot{Q}_C = 1.764 \times 10^5$ kW

5.4 (*a*) $\eta = 0.282$
(*b*) $T_H = 833.66$ K

5.7 $\dot{W} = 5.336 \times 10^6$ kW
$\dot{Q}_H = 8.538 \times 10^6$ kW

5.8 (*a*) $\Delta S_{res} = -1.121$ kJ kg^{-1} K^{-1}
$\Delta S_{total} = 0.184$ kJ kg^{-1} K^{-1}
(*b*) $\Delta S_{total} = 0.097$ kJ kg^{-1} K^{-1}

5.9 (*a*) $\Delta S = 20.794$ J K^{-1}
(*b*) $\Delta S_{total} = 10.794$ J K^{-1}

5.10 (*a*) $\Delta S_A = 8.726$ J mol^{-1} K^{-1}
$\Delta S_B = -6.577$ J mol^{-1} K^{-1}
(*b*) $\Delta S_{total} = 2.149$ J mol^{-1} K^{-1}
(*c*) $\Delta S_A = 8.726$ J mol^{-1} K^{-1}
$\Delta S_B = -8.512$ J mol^{-1} K^{-1}
$\Delta S_{total} = 0.214$ J mol^{-1} K^{-1}

5.16 $W = -2280$ J mol^{-1}
$Q_\sigma = 3540$ J mol^{-1}
$\Delta S_{reservoir} = 11.8$ J mol^{-1} K^{-1}

5.17 $\tau = 2.5$

5.18 (*a*) $\Delta H = 4.365 \times 10^3$ J mol^{-1}
$\Delta S = -1.582$ J mol^{-1} K^{-1}
(*b*) $\Delta H = 5.82$ kJ mol^{-1}
$\Delta S = 1.484$ J mol^{-1} K^{-1}
(*c*) $\Delta H = -3.118$ kJ mol^{-1}
$\Delta S = 4.953$ J mol^{-1} K^{-1}
(*d*) $\Delta H = -3.741$ kJ mol^{-1}
$\Delta S = 2.618$ J mol^{-1} K^{-1}
(*e*) $\Delta H = -6.651$ kJ mol^{-1}
$\Delta S = -3.607$ J mol^{-1} K^{-1}

5.19 $\eta = 0.591$

5.21 $\Delta S = 2.914 \text{ J mol}^{-1} \text{ K}^{-1}$

5.25 $\eta = 0.068$

5.26 $\Delta S = -7.944 \text{ J mol}^{-1} \text{ K}^{-1}$
$\Delta S_{\text{res}} = 13.96 \text{ J mol}^{-1} \text{ K}^{-1}$
$\Delta S_{\text{total}} = 6.02 \text{ J mol}^{-1} \text{ K}^{-1}$

5.27 (*a*) $\Delta S = 536.1 \text{ J K}^{-1}$
(*b*) $\Delta S = 2018.7 \text{ J K}^{-1}$

5.28 (*a*) $\Delta S = 900.86 \text{ J K}^{-1}$
(*b*) $\Delta S = 2657.5 \text{ J K}^{-1}$
(*c*) $\Delta S = 1.2436 \times 10^6 \text{ J K}^{-1}$

5.29 $\Delta S_{\text{total}} = 12.97 \text{ J mol}^{-1} \text{ K}^{-1}$

5.30 $\Delta S_{\text{total}} = 3.42 \text{ J mol}^{-1} \text{ K}^{-1}$
Process is impossible.

5.33 $\dot{W} = 951.6 \text{ kW}$

5.34 $\dot{S}_G = 0.457 \text{ W K}^{-1}$

5.35 $\dot{S}_G = 8.333 \text{ W K}^{-1}$

5.38 (*a*) $T_2 = 298.15 \text{ K}$
(*b*) $\Delta S = 17.628 \text{ J mol}^{-1} \text{ K}^{-1}$
(*c*) $\dot{S}_G = 48.966 \text{ W K}^{-1}$
(*d*) $W = 5.168 \times 10^3 \text{ J mol}^{-1}$

5.39 $W_s = -3753.8 \text{ J}$
$W_{\text{ideal}} = -5163 \text{ J}$
$W_{\text{lost}} = 1409.3 \text{ J}$
$S_G = 4.698 \text{ J K}^{-1}$

5.41 $\dot{S}_G = 0.468 \text{ W K}^{-1}$
$\dot{W}_{\text{lost}} = 140.344 \text{ kW}$

5.42 Since $\eta_{\text{actual}} > \eta_{\text{max}}$,
the process is impossible.

5.43 (*a*) $S_G = 0.27 \text{ kJ K}^{-1}$
(*b*) $W_{\text{lost}} = 81.039 \text{ kJ}$

5.44 (*a*) $\eta_{\text{max}} = 0.502$
$\dot{Q}_C = 745.297 \text{ MW}$
(*b*) $\dot{Q}_C = 1.742 \times 10^3 \text{ MW}$
$\Delta T = 2.522 \text{ K}$

5.46 $S_G = 0.013 \text{ kJ mol}^{-1} \text{ K}^{-1}$

5.47 $\dot{W}_{\text{ideal}} = 1.952 \text{ kW}$

5.48 (*a*) $W_{\text{lost}} = 14.8 \text{ kJ mol}^{-1}$
(*b*) $W_{\text{ideal(min)}} = -6.866 \text{ kJ mol}^{-1}$
(*c*) $W_{\text{ideal}} = -21.686 \text{ kJ mol}^{-1}$

5.49 $W_{\text{lost}} = 33.803 \text{ kJ mol}^{-1}$
$W_{\text{HE}} = 33.803 \text{ kJ mol}^{-1}$

CHAPTER 6

6.7 $\Delta S = -2.661 \text{ J kg}^{-1} \text{ K}^{-1}$
$\Delta H = 551.7 \text{ J kg}^{-1}$

6.8 $\Delta S = 0.733 \text{ J mol}^{-1} \text{ K}^{-1}$
$\Delta T = -0.768 \text{ K}$

6.9 $\Delta H = 134.6 \text{ kJ kg}^{-1}$
$\Delta U = -5.93 \text{ kJ kg}^{-1}$
$\Delta S = -0.036\,36 \text{ kJ kg}^{-1} \text{ K}^{-1}$
$Q = -10.84 \text{ kJ kg}^{-1}$
$W = 4.91 \text{ kJ kg}^{-1}$

6.10 $P_2 = 205.75 \text{ bar}$

6.14 (*a*) For acetylene: RK EOS
$Z = 0.695$
$H^R = -2.302 \text{ kJ mol}^{-1}$
$S^R = -5.461 \text{ J mol}^{-1} \text{ K}^{-1}$

6.15 (*a*) For acetylene: SRK EOS
$Z = 0.691$
$H^R = -2.695 \text{ kJ mol}^{-1}$
$S^R = -6.412 \text{ J mol}^{-1} \text{ K}^{-1}$

6.16 (*a*) For acetylene: PR EOS
$Z = 0.667$
$H^R = -2.655 \text{ kJ mol}^{-1}$
$S^R = -6.41 \text{ J mol}^{-1} \text{ K}^{-1}$

(*a*) For acetylene: Lee-Kesler Correlation
$Z = 0.669$
$H^R = -2.916 \text{ kJ mol}^{-1}$
$S^R = -7.405 \text{ J mol}^{-1} \text{ K}^{-1}$

6.17 (*a*) $\Delta S = 100.34$ J mol^{-1} K^{-1}
(*b*) $\Delta S = 102.14$ J mol^{-1} K^{-1}

6.20 $x = 0.076$
$\Delta S = 1.0347 \times 10^{-3}$ J g^{-1} K^{-1}

6.21 $\Delta S = 0.4135$ kJ kg^{-1} K^{-1}

6.22 $H_{\text{total}} = 80\,173.5$ kJ
$S_{\text{total}} = 192.145$ kJ K^{-1}

6.23 $H = 789.495$ J g^{-1} $S = 2.198$ J g^{-1} K^{-1}

6.24 $H_{\text{total}} = 1606.9$ kJ

6.25 $x = 0.552$ $H = 1991$ J g^{-1}
$S = 4.599$ J g^{-1} K^{-1}

6.26 $m^l = 377.72$ g
$V^l = 379.23$ cm^3

6.27 $x = 0.953$

6.28 $\Delta S = 1.268$ J g^{-1} K^{-1}
$\Delta S = 1.302$ J g^{-1} K^{-1}

6.29 $\Delta S = 1.2497$ J g^{-1} K^{-1}

6.30 $H_2 = 2599.6$ J g^{-1}

6.31 $x_{\text{water}} = 0.031$ at 25°C (298.15 K)
$x_{\text{water}} = 0.122$ at 50°C (323.15 K)

6.32 $Q = 1221.8$ J g^{-1}

6.33 $Q = -869.9$ kJ

6.34 $Q = 41\,860.5$ kJ

6.35 $Q = -271.15$ kJ

6.36 (*a*) $Q = 392.29$ kJ
$W = -365.89$ kJ
(*b*) $W = -262.527$ kJ

6.37 $Q = 949.52$ kJ

6.38 $Q = 401.317$ J g^{-1}
$W = -280.034$ J g^{-1}

6.39 $Q = -775.66$ kJ $W = 667.66$ kJ

6.40 (*a*) $\Delta H = -600.1$ J g^{-1}
$\Delta S = 0.115$ J g^{-1} K^{-1}
(*b*) $\Delta H^{\text{ig}} = -620.6$ J g^{-1}
$\Delta S^{\text{ig}} = 0.0605$ J g^{-1} K^{-1}
(*c*) $\Delta H = -593.95$ J g^{-1}
$\Delta S = 0.078$ J g^{-1} K^{-1}

6.41 $\eta = 0.1675$

6.42 $\eta = 0.1946$

6.43 (*a*) $P_2 = 572.83$ kPa
(*b*) $P_2 = 250.16$ kPa

6.44 (*a*) $\Delta T = 346.79$ K
(*b*) $W = 4760$ kW

6.45 $\eta = 0.681$

6.46 $\eta = 0.78$

6.47 Based on Steam Tables:
$V^R = -10.96$ cm^3 g^{-1}
$H^R = -72.4$ J g^{-1}
$S^R = -0.11$ J g^{-1} K^{-1}
Based on virial-coefficient correlation:
$V^R = -9.33$ cm^3 g^{-1}
$H^R = -53.4$ J g^{-1}
$S^R = -0.077$ J g^{-1} K^{-1}

6.48 (*a*) $G^l = -206.06$ J g^{-1}
$G^v = -206.01$ J g^{-1}
(*b*) $\Delta H^{lv}/T = 4.445$ J g^{-1} K^{-1}
$\Delta S^{lv} = 4.445$ J g^{-1} K^{-1}
(*c*) $V^R = -14.785$ cm^3 g^{-1}
$H^R = -64.9$ J g^{-1}
$S^R = -0.1126$ J g^{-1} K^{-1}
(*d*) $\Delta S^{lv} = 4.44$ J g^{-1} K^{-1}
$V^R = -11.93$ cm^3 g^{-1}
$H^R = -43.18$ J g^{-1}
$S^R = -0.069$ J g^{-1} K^{-1}

6.49 (*a*) $G^l = -208.89$ J g^{-1}
$G^v = -208.84$ J g^{-1}
(*b*) $\Delta H^{lv}/T = 4.421$ J g^{-1} K^{-1}
$\Delta S^{lv} = 4.4213$ J g^{-1} K^{-1}
(*c*) $V^R = -1.361 \times 10^{-3}$ m^3 kg^{-1}
$H^R = -66.3$ J g^{-1} K^{-1}
$S^R = -0.1143$ J g^{-1} K^{-1}
(*d*) $V^R = -0.0118$ m^3 kg^{-1}
$H^R = -44.26$ J g^{-1}
$S^R = -0.0703$ J g^{-1} K^{-1}

6.50 $V = 184.2$ cm^3 mol^{-1}
$\Delta H = 6734.9$ J mol^{-1}
$\Delta S = -15.9$ J mol^{-1} K^{-1}

6.51 $\Delta H = -1431.3$ J mol^{-1}
$\Delta S = -25.287$ J mol^{-1} K^{-1}

6.52 $x = 0.136$

6.53 $V^v = 1182.2$ cm^3 mol^{-1}
$H^v = 6315.9$ J mol^{-1}
$S^v = -1.624$ J mol^{-1} K^{-1}
$V^l = 109.89$ cm^3 mol^{-1}
$H^l = -7687.4$ J mol^{-1}
$S^l = -38.475$ J mol^{-1} K^{-1}

6.54 $V = 1590.1$ cm^3 mol^{-1}
$H^v = 7427.4$ J mol^{-1}
$S^v = 4.197$ J mol^{-1} K^{-1}
$V^l = 123.86$ cm^3 mol^{-1}
$H^l = -7867.8$ J mol^{-1}
$S^l = -37.141$ J mol^{-1} K^{-1}

6.55 $V = 45.5$ m^3

6.56 $T_f = 363.27$ K
$\Delta S = 28.048$ J mol^{-1} K^{-1}

6.57 $T_f = 408.91$ K
$\Delta S = 24.699$ J mol^{-1} K^{-1}

6.58 $\Delta H = -801.9$ J mol^{-1}
$\Delta S = -20.639$ J mol^{-1} K^{-1}

6.59 $\Delta H = 7407.3$ J mol^{-1}
$\Delta S = 1.828$ J mol^{-1} K^{-1}

6.60 $T_f = 302.71$ K
$\Delta S = 22.36$ J mol^{-1} K^{-1}

6.61 (*a*) Ideal gas equation:
$T_f = 308.19$ K
$W = -11\,852$ J mol^{-1}
(*b*) Virial-coefficient correlation:
$T_f = 303.11$ K
$W = -11\,567$ J mol^{-1}

6.62 (*a*) Ideal Gas law:
$T = 367.59$ K
$W = -8735$ J mol^{-1}
(*b*) Virial coefficient correlation:
$T = 362.73$ K
$W = -8476$ J mol^{-1}

6.63 $T = 381.43$ K
$W = 5680$ J mol^{-1}

6.64 $W_{ideal} = -1224.3$ J g^{-1}

6.65 Frac = 0.4058

6.66 $\dot{S}_G = 21.19$ kW K^{-1}
$\dot{W}_{lost} = 6356.9$ kW

6.67 $\dot{W} = 42.77$ kW

6.68 $T' = 409.79$ K

6.69 $S_G = 1.25 \times 10^{-3}$ J g^{-1} K^{-1}

6.70 steam vented, $m_s = 25.11$ kg

6.71 $t_2/T_2 = 362.46$°C/635.61 K
$\Delta m = 137.43$ kg

6.72 $Q = 832\,534$ kJ

6.73 $m_{vap} = 13.821$ kg

6.74 $m_{steam} = 4.855 \times 10^3$ kg

6.75

Pressure kPa	m_{steam} kg
1	5.77×10^{-3}
100	0.577
200	1.155
300	1.733
400	2.311

6.76 $Q = 5159$ kJ

6.77 $\dot{m}_{steam} = 0.484$ kg s^{-1}
$\dot{m}_{water} = 4.516$ kg s^{-1}

6.78 $\dot{m}_{water} = 1.89$ kg s^{-1}
$\dot{S}_G = 1.973$ kW k^{-1}

6.79 $\dot{m}_{water} = 3.241$ kg s^{-1}
$\dot{S}_G = 3.508$ kW K^{-1}

6.80 $T = 542.857$ K
$P = 4.319$ bar

6.81 $\dot{m}_{steam} = 1.961$ kg s^{-1}
$\dot{S}_G = 4.194$ kW K^{-1}

6.85 D = 2.964 cm

6.86 (*a*) 1, 3-Butadiene:
Virial coefficient correlation:
$V^R = -200.647$ cm^3 mol^{-1}
$H^R = -1.377$ kJ mol^{-1}
$S^R = -1.952$ J mol^{-1} K^{-1}

(*b*) Carbon dioxide:
Lee/Kesler correlation:
$V^R = -48.289\ \text{cm}^3\ \text{mol}^{-1}$
$H^R = -5.21\ \text{kJ mol}^{-1}$
$S^R = -10.207\ \text{J mol}^{-1}\ \text{K}^{-1}$

6.88 (*a*) Benzene/cyclohexane:
$Z = 0.68$
$H^R = -6.920\ \text{kJ mol}^{-1}$
$S^R = -8.213\ \text{J mol}^{-1}\ \text{K}^{-1}$

6.94 $\omega = 0.344$

6.95 $\omega = 0.326$

6.100 (*a*) $\Delta H^{lv} = 30.802\ \text{kJ mol}^{-1}$ for benzene

6.102 (*a*) $\omega = 0.224$
(*b*) $T_n = 185.3\ \text{K}$

CHAPTER 7

7.1 $\Delta T = -52.45\ \text{K}$

7.4 $u_2 = 565.2\ \text{m s}^{-1}$
$A_2 = 7.05\ \text{cm}^2$

7.5 $P_{\min} = 431.78\ \text{kPa}$
$A_{(P_{\min})} = 7.021\ \text{cm}^2$

7.9 $\dot{m}_S = 1.081\ \text{kg s}^{-1}$
$x = 0.966$

7.10 $S_{G,\text{total}} = 0.1633\ \text{J g}^{-1}\ \text{K}^{-1}$

7.11 $\Delta T = -167.05\ \text{K}$

7.12 $W_{\text{lost}} = 0.413\ \text{J g}^{-1}$

7.13 (*a*) Carbon dioxide:
RK EOS:
$T_2 = 279.97\ \text{K}$
$\Delta S = 31.545\ \text{J mol}^{-1}\ \text{K}^{-1}$

7.14 (*a*) Carbon dioxide:
SRK EOS:
$T_2 = 272.76\ \text{K}$
$\Delta S = 31.565\ \text{J mol}^{-1}\ \text{K}^{-1}$

7.15 (*a*) Carbon dioxide:
PR EOS:
$T_2 = 269.74\ \text{K}$
$\Delta S = 31.2\ \text{J mol}^{-1}\ \text{K}^{-1}$

7.18 $\dot{m}_S = 4.103\ \text{kg s}^{-1}$
$\eta = 0.819$

7.19

	H_2 J g^{-1}	S_2 J g^{-1} K^{-1}	$\dot{W}$ kW
(a)	2423.9	7.3808	−68 030
(b)	2535.9	7.6873	−87 653
(c)	2467.8	7.7842	−87 672
(d)	2471.4	7.1022	−44 836
(e)	2543.4	6.7127	−12 900
(f)	2400.2	7.4366	−65 333
(g)	2459.5	7.3202	−35 048

7.20 $T_0 = 762.42\ \text{K}$

7.21 $W_S = -11\,728\ \text{J mol}^{-1}$
$T_2 = 856.64\ \text{K}$

7.22 $\dot{W} = -4665.6\ \text{kW}$
$T = 457.8\ \text{K}$

7.23 (*a*) $\dot{Q} = -12.92\ \text{kW}$
(*b*) $\dot{W} = -394.2\ \text{kW}$

7.24 $W = -7.326\ \text{kJ mol}^{-1}$
$T = 519.9\ \text{K}$

7.25 η
(*a*) 0.7
(*b*) 0.803
(*c*) 0.649
(*d*) 0.748
(*e*) 0.699

7.26 $\dot{W} = 594.716\ \text{kW}$
$\eta = 0.576$
$\dot{S}_G = 1.126\ \text{kW K}^{-1}$

7.27 $x_H = 0.924$
$x_S = 0.925$

7.29 $\Delta T = 0.044°\text{C}$

7.30

	T K	$\dot{W}$ kW
(a)	497.97	– 1554
(b)	492.63	– 819
(c)	525.14	– 1326
(d)	529.34	– 590
(e)	516.28	– 1653

7.31 $\eta_t = 0.761$
$\dot{S}_G = 58.949$ kW K^{-1}
$\dot{W}_{lost} = 17\,685$ kW

7.32 (a) $\dot{W} = -135.65$ kW
(b) $\eta_t = 0.4316$
(c) $\dot{S}_G = 0.4534$ kW K^{-1} for boiler
$\dot{S}_G = 0.156$ kW K^{-1} for turbine
(d)

	$\dot{W}_{lost}$ kW	Fraction of total $\dot{W}$
Boiler	132.914	0.4229
Turbine	45.731	0.1455

7.34 $H_2 = 3154.6$ kJ kg^{-1}
$S_2 := 7.4586\cdot$J g^{-1} K^{-1}
$\dot{W} = 1173.4$ kW

7.35

	$\dot{W}$ kW	T K
(a)	523	474.68
(b)	474	511.58
(c)	962	518.66
(d)	226	524.3
(e)	1205	479.01
(f)	932	476.79

7.36 $T = 447.47$ K
$\Delta S = 2.347$ J mol^{-1} K^{-1}

7.37 $\dot{W} = 1205.2$ kW
$T = 327.15$ K

7.38 $\dot{W} = 2228.4$ kW
$T = 351.18$ K

7.39 $S_G = 3.2012$ J mol^{-1} K
$W_{ideal} = 4349.8$ J mol^{-1}
$W_{lost} = 938.4$ J mol^{-1}
$\eta_t = 0.823$

7.42 (a) $N = 3.743$
(b) $\dot{W}_r = 87.944$ kW
(c) $\dot{Q}_r = -87.944$ kW
(d) $\dot{m}_{cw} = 1.052$ kg s^{-1}

7.44 η
(a) 0.675
(b) 0.698
(c) 0.793
(d) 0.636
(e) 0.75

7.45 $\dot{W}$ kW
(a) 50.82
(b) 213.12
(c) 101.29
(d) 62.5
(e) 514.21

7.48 $W_{ideal} = 8.87$ J g^{-1}
$\eta_t = 0.767$
$S_G = 9 \times 10^{-3}$ J g^{-1} K^{-1}
$W_{lost} = 2.7$ J g^{-1}

7.53 $W_S = 0.053$ kJ mol^{-1}
$Q = 51.1$ kJ mol^{-1}

7.54 $W_S = 6.834$ kJ mol^{-1}
$Q = 44.393$ kJ mol^{-1}

7.57 $C_{compressor} = 307\,452$ dollars
$C_{motor} = 32\,572$ dollars

7.59 (a) $T_2 = 365.47$ K
$\Delta S = 22.128$ J mol^{-1} K^{-1}
(b) $T_2 = 268.54$ K
$\Delta S = 7.77$ J mol^{-1} K^{-1}
$P = -3.147$ kJ mol^{-1}

7.60 (b) $x = 0.643$

CHAPTER 8

8.1 $\eta_{turbine} = 0.805$
$\eta_{cycle} = 0.311$

8.2 (*a*) $P_1 = 3.533$ $P_2 = 3.533$
$P_3 = 1616.0$ $P_4 = 1616.0$
All pressures in kPa
(*b*) $x_3 = 0.741$ $x_4 = 0.241$ kW
(*c*) $\dot{Q}_{12} = 1.931 \times 10^3$ kW
(*d*) $\dot{Q}_{34} = -1.22 \times 10^3$ kW
(*e*) $\dot{W}_{23} = -873.222$ kW
$\dot{W}_{41} = 161.617$ kW
(*f*) $\eta = 0.368$

8.3

	Steam rate $\dot{m}$ kg s^{-1}	Boilerduty $\dot{Q}_H$ kW
(*a*)	70.43	240 705
(*b*)	108.64	355 111
(*c*)	62.13	213 277
(*d*)	67.29	205 061
(*e*)	78.95	240 592

	Condenser duty $\dot{Q}_C$ kW	Thermal efficiency η
(*a*)	160 705	0.332
(*b*)	255 111	0.282
(*c*)	143 277	0.328
(*d*)	155 061	0.244
(*e*)	60 591	0.246

8.4

Steam temp. K	Quality of exhaust steam x	Thermal efficiency η
723.15	0.914	0.297
823.15	0.959	0.314
923.15	0.999	0.332

8.5

Steam pressure kPa	Quality of exhaust steam x	Thermal efficiency η
5 000	0.925	0.359
7 000	0.895	0.375
10 000	0.873	0.386

8.6 $\eta_{overall} = 0.8202$
Intermediate $P = 765.16$ kPa
$t/T = 366.6°\text{C}/639.75$ K

8.7 mass fraction of steam extracted = 0.130 28
$\eta = 0.2861$

8.8 mass fraction of steam extracted
1st BFW heater = 0.115 63
2nd BFW heater = 0.099 71
$\eta = 0.3265$

8.9 $\dot{m} = 119.59$ mol s^{-1}
$\dot{Q}_C = -4360$ kW
$\dot{Q}_H = 5360$ kW $\eta = 0.187$

8.10 (*a*) $\dot{W} = 5834$ kW
$\dot{Q}_C = -27\,553$ kW
$\dot{Q}_H = 33\,387$ kW
$\eta = 0.175$
(*b*) Turbin $\eta = 0.8$
$\dot{W} = 4475$ kW
$\dot{Q}_C = -28\,805$ kW
$\dot{Q}_H = 33\,280$ kW
$\eta = 0.134$

8.12 $r_c = 3.157$
$r_e = 2.841$

8.13

Compression ratio r_c	Efficiency η
3	0.248
5	0.341
7	0.396
9	0.434

8.16 $u_E = 843.4$ m s^{-1}
$P_D = 3.589$ bar

8.17

T_C K	η_a mol mol^{-1}	T_D K	W Jmol^{-1}
1000	57.638	343.12	-7.364×10^5
1200	37.48	343.12	-7.365×10^5
1500	24.07	598.94	-5.7519×10^5

8.18 Cost of electricity = 0.05 cents kW h^{-1}

8.19 $n_{CH_4} = 0.201$ mol kJ^{-1}

8.20 (*a*) $\eta_{Carnot} = 0.07$
(*b*) $\eta_{actual} = 0.028$
(*c*) Possible working fluids: ammonia, *n*-butane and propane

CHAPTER 9

9.2 Cost = 267.183 dollars y^{-1}

9.4 (*a*) $P_1 := 9.6315$ $P_2 := 9.6315$
$P_3 := 1.8524$ $P_4 := 1.8524$
All pressures are in bar.
(*b*) $x_3 = 0.971$ $x_4 = 0.3027$
(*c*) $Q_{43} = 138.60$ kJ
(*d*) $Q_{21} = -165.12$ kJ
(*e*) $W_{21} = 0$ $W_{43} = 0$
$W_{32} = 33.1$ kJ/kg
$W_{14} = 6.59$ kJ/kg
(*f*) $\omega = 5.228$

9.7 For Carnot engine
$Q_H = 7.448$ kW
For actual engine
$Q_H = 20.689$ kW

9.8 (*a*) $\omega = 2.667$
(*b*) $Q_H = 5.5$ kW
(*c*) $t_C/T_C = -45.4°C/227.75$ K

9.9

	$\dot{m}$ kg s^{-1}	$\dot{Q}_H$ kW	$\dot{W}$ kW
(*a*)	3.938	− 716.8	83.76
(*b*)	3.355	− 617.6	90.11
(*c*)	2.737	− 509.3	87.26
(*d*)	2.102	− 397.0	80.51
(*e*)	1.431	− 274.5	63.32

	ω_{actual}	ω_{Carnot}
(*a*)	7.557	9.72
(*b*)	5.854	7.828
(*c*)	4.836	6.696
(*d*)	3.931	5.67
(*e*)	3.332	5.003

9.10 $\dot{m} = 0.507$ kg s^{-1}
$\dot{Q}_H = -1404$ kW
$\dot{W} = 204$ kW
$\omega = 5.881$
$\omega_{Carnot} = 9.238$

9.11 (*a*) $\dot{m} = 0.0362$ kg s^{-1}
(*b*) $\dot{m} = 0.034\,52$ kg s^{-1}
(*c*) $\dot{m} = 0.0286$ kg s^{-1}
(*d*) $\omega_a = 3.582$
$\omega_b = 3.760$
$\omega_c = 3.873$

9.12 $\dot{W} = 423.03$ kW

9.13

Condensation temperature K	ω Isentropic compression	ω Compressor $\eta = 0.75$
60	8.328	6.246
80	5.517	4.138
100	4.011	3.008

9.14 $t_C/T_C = -4.21°C/268.94$ K
$t_H/T_H = -49.42°C/322.57$ K

9.15 methane liquefied = 0.17 (fraction)

9.16 methane liquefied = 0.351 (fraction)

9.17 $\dot{W} = 19.979$ kW for combination unit
$\dot{W} = 24.016$ kW for conventional heater

9.18 $\omega_{overall} = 1.497$
$\omega_{Carnot} = 2.210$

9.22 $Q_H = 2.025$ kW

9.23 $\dot{n} = 9.258$ mol s^{-1}

CHAPTER 10

10.1 (*a*) $y_1 = 0.545$ $P = 109.303$ kPa
(*b*) $x_1 = 0.169$ $P = 92.156$ kPa
(*c*) $y_1 = 0.542$ $T = 376.46$ K
(*d*) $x_1 = 0.173$ $T = 382.28$ K
(*e*) $x_1 = 0.282$ $y_1 = 0.484$
(*f*) $\mathcal{V} = 0.238$ $\mathcal{L} = 0.762$
(*g*) Both are non-polar and similar in size and shape.

10.3 (*a*) $x_1 = 0.5$ $y_1 = 0.89$

10.4

t(°C)/T(K)	y_1 for $x_1 = 0.5$
65/338.15	0.88
75/348.15	0.871
85/358.15	0.862
95/368.15	0.853

10.7

	t(°C)/T(K)	P·kPa
(*a*)	134.1/407.25	207.46
(*b*)	111.88/385.03	118.72
(*c*)	91.44/364.59	66.38
(*d*)	72.43/345.58	36.02

Information on composition of feed is required to calculate relative amounts of liquid and vapor phases.

10.9 (*a*) $\mathcal{V} = 0.836$

$$x = \begin{pmatrix} 0.142 \\ 0.306 \\ 0.552 \end{pmatrix} \quad y = \begin{pmatrix} 0.371 \\ 0.339 \\ 0.29 \end{pmatrix}$$

(*b*) $\mathcal{V} = 0.575$

$$x = \begin{pmatrix} 0.188 \\ 0.334 \\ 0.478 \end{pmatrix} \quad y = \begin{pmatrix} 0.441 \\ 0.333 \\ 0.226 \end{pmatrix}$$

(*c*) $\mathcal{V} = 0.352$

$$x = \begin{pmatrix} 0.238 \\ 0.345 \\ 0.417 \end{pmatrix} \quad y = \begin{pmatrix} 0.508 \\ 0.312 \\ 0.18 \end{pmatrix}$$

(*d*) $\mathcal{V} = 0.146$

$$x = \begin{pmatrix} 0.293 \\ 0.342 \\ 0.366 \end{pmatrix} \quad y = \begin{pmatrix} 0.572 \\ 0.284 \\ 0.144 \end{pmatrix}$$

10.11

	x_1	y_1	$\mathcal{V}$	$\mathcal{R}$
(*a*)	0.644	0.705	0.656	0.705
(*b*)	0.285	0.678	0.547	0.741
(*c*)	0.183	0.320	0.487	0.624
(*d*)	0.340	0.682	0.469	0.639

10.13 $x_1 = 4.502 \times 10^{-3}$ $y_1 = 0.9$

10.16 (*a*) $P_{\text{bubl}} = 56.745$ kPa to
$P_{\text{dew}} = 43.864$ kPa
Pressure range for 2 phases is from P_{dew} to P_{bubble}.
(*b*) $P(x_1, x_2) = 51.892$ kPa $\mathcal{V} = 0.379$
(*c*) $\alpha_{12.0} = 0.862$ $\alpha_{12.1} = 0.226$
Since α is less than 1, no azeotrope forms.

10.17 (*a*) $P_{\text{bubl}} = 47.971$ kPa $y_1 = 0.196$
(*b*) $P_{\text{dew}} = 42.191$ kPa $x_1 = 0.0104$
(*c*) $x_1 = y_1 = 0.857$ at $P = 81.366$ kPa

10.18 $P = 90.104$ kPa $y_1 = 0.701$

10.19 (*a*) $0.6013 \leq z_1 \leq 0.65$
(*b*) $y_1 = 0.6013$ $P = 1.671$ kPa
(*c*) $x_1 = y_1 = 0.592$ at $P = 1.673$ bar

10.20 $t/T = 59.53°\text{C}/302.68$ K
$y_1 = 0.307$

10.22 $T = 376.453$ K
$P = 0.137$ bar

10.25 (*a*) $P = 1525$ kPa
$y_{CH_4} = 0.515$
$y_{C_2H_4} = 0.325$
(*b*) $P = 1300$ kPa
$x_{CH_4} = 0.089$
$x_{C_2H_4} = 0.357$
(*c*) $T = 222.65$ K
$y_{CH_4} = 0.570$
$y_{C_2H_4} = 0.240$
(*d*) $T = 230.35$ K
$y_{CH_4} = 0.085$
$y_{C_2H_4} = 0.486$

10.26 (*a*) $P = 14.5$ bar
$y_{C_2H_6} = 0.382$
$y_{C_3H_8} = 0.296$
$y_{i\text{-}C_4H_{10}} = 0.216$
(*b*) $P = 13.50$ bar
$x_{C_2H_6} = 0.129$
$x_{C_3H_8} = 0.167$
$x_{i\text{-}C_4H_{10}} = 0.208$
(*c*) $T = 335.15$ K
$y_{C_2H_6} = 0.511$
$y_{C_3H_8} = 0.189$
$y_{i\text{-}C_4H_{10}} = 0.176$
(*d*) $T = 338.15$ K
$x_{C_2H_6} = 0.112$
$x_{C_3H_8} = 0.200$
$x_{i\text{-}C_4H_{10}} = 0.200$

10.27 $\mathcal{L} = 0.145$ $\mathcal{V} = 0.855$
$x_{CH_4} = 0.575$ $y_{CH_4} = 0.058$
$x_{C_2H_6} = 0.108$ $y_{C_2H_6} = 0.052$
$x_{C_3H_8} = 0.187$ $y_{C_3H_8} = 0.275$
$x_{C_4H_{10}} = 0.129$ $y_{C_4H_{10}} = 0.616$

10.28 $\mathcal{L} = 0.346$ $\mathcal{V} = 0.654$
$x_{C_4H_{10}} = 0.25$ $y_{C_4H_{10}} = 0.633$

10.29 $\mathcal{L} = 0.61$ $\mathcal{V} = 0.39$

$x_{C_5H_{12}} = 0.168$ $y_{C_5H_{12}} = 0.378$

$x_{C_6H_{14}} = 0.450$ $y_{C_6H_{14}} = 0.450$

10.30 $P = 8.30$ bar

$x_{C_2H_6} = 0.047$ $y_{C_2H_6} = 0.219$

$x_{C_3H_8} = 0.255$ $y_{C_3H_8} = 0.699$

10.31 $P = 300$ kPa

$x_{C_2H_6} = 0.004$ $y_{C_2H_6} = 0.034$

$x_{C_3H_8} = 0.037$ $y_{C_3H_8} = 0.101$

$x_{n\text{-}C_4H_{10}} = 0.464$ $y_{n\text{-}C_4H_{10}} = 0.740$

10.32 $P = 18.5$ kPa

$x_{CH_4} = 0.129$ $y_{CH_4} = 0.800$

$x_{C_2H_6} = 0.103$ $y_{C_2H_6} = 0.092$

$x_{C_3H_8} = 0.373$ $y_{C_3H_8} = 0.086$

10.33 $T = 288.65$ K

$x_{n\text{-}C_4H_{10}} = 0.66$ $y_{n\text{-}C_4H_{10}} = 0.89$

10.34 $P = 7.93$ bar

$x_{CH_4} = 0.092$ $y_{CH_4} = 0.772$

10.35 (*a*) $\mathcal{H}_i = \dfrac{1}{\mathcal{M}_s \cdot k_i}$

(*b*) $\mathcal{H}_i = 1633$ bar

10.36 (*a*) $P_{\text{bubl}} = 0.573$ atm

$P_{\text{dew}} = 0.478$ atm

(*b*) t/T(bubble) = 46.32°C (319.47 K)

t/T(dew) = 51.24°C (324.39 K)

10.37 (*a*) $x_1 = 0.252$ $y_1 = 0.458$

at $P = 75$ kPa and $T = 363.15$ K

(*b*) Equilibrium does not exist and air leak is a strong cause.

10.38 $\dot{Q} = -19.865$ kW

10.39 $P = 1.27$ bar

10.40 (*a*) $y_{H_2O,\ \text{vap}} = 0.308$

$y_{SO_2} = 0.692$

(*b*) $\dot{n}_{\text{vap}} = 14.461$ kmol h^{-1}

$\dot{n}_{H_2O,\ \text{liq}} = 5.539$ kmol h^{-1}

10.41 (*a*) $y_{H_2O} = 0.0158$

(*b*) $p_{H_2O} = 1.606$ kPa

(*c*) t/T(dew) = 10°C/283.15 K

10.42 $\dot{m}_{H_2O} = 10.074$ kg h^{-1}

10.43 The Bancroft Point of Systems

Components		t/T	P
1	2	°C/K	kPa
Benzene	Cyclohexane	52.3/325.45	39.6
2-Butanol	Water	87.7/360.85	64.2
Acctonitrile	Ethanol	65.8/338.95	60.6

CHAPTER 11

11.1 $\Delta S = 204.885$ J K^{-1}

11.2 $\Delta S = 38.27$ J K^{-1}

11.3 $\Delta \dot{S} = 1411$ W K^{-1}

11.4 $W_{\text{ideal}} = -2484$ J mol^{-1}

11.5 W = 25 638 J mol^{-1}

11.16 Fugacity and fugacity coefficient agree well upto 200 bar when tabulated values are compared with those calculated with the generalized correlation.

11.17 $f = 217.14$ bar

$G^R/RT = -0.323$

11.18 (*a*) $f = 18.76$ bar

(*b*) $f = 73.169$ bar

11.19 (*a*) $f = 11.78$ bar

(*b*) $f = 20.29$ bar

11.21 $\dfrac{f}{f^{\text{sat}}} = 1.084$

11.22 (*a*) $\dfrac{f_2}{f_1} = 0.0377$

(*b*) $\dfrac{f_2}{f_1} = 0.0536$

11.23 (*a*) $f = 2.445$ bar

(*b*) $f = 3.326$ bar

(*c*) $f = 1.801$ bar

11.25

	Eq. (11.63)	Ideal solution behaviour
$\hat{f}_1$	10.053 bar	9.978 bar
$\hat{f}_2$	17.059 bar	17.022 bar
$\hat{\phi}_1$	0.957	0.95
$\hat{\phi}_2$	0.875	0.873

11.27

	Eq. (11.64)	Ideal solution behaviour
$\hat{f}_1$	7.491 bar	7.182 bar
$\hat{f}_2$	13.254 bar	13.251 bar
$\hat{f}_3$	9.764 bar	9.569 bar
$\hat{\phi}_1$	1.019	0.977
$\hat{\phi}_2$	0.881	0.88
$\hat{\phi}_3$	0.775	0.759

11.28 (*a*) $\ln \gamma_1 = -1.8 + 2\cdot x_1 + 1.4\cdot x_1^2 - 1.6\cdot x_1^3$

$\ln \gamma_2 = -x_1^2 - 1.6\cdot x_1^3$

(*b*) $\dfrac{G^E}{RT} = x_1\cdot\left(-1.8 + 2\cdot x_1 + 1.4\cdot x_1^2 - 1.6\cdot x_1^3\right) + (1 - x_1)\cdot\left(-x_1^2 - 1.6\cdot x_1^3\right)$

(*c*) $x_1\cdot\dfrac{d(\ln \gamma_1)}{dx_1} = 2\cdot x_1 + 2.8\cdot x_1^2 - 4.8\cdot x_1^3$

$x_2\cdot\dfrac{d(\ln \gamma_1)}{dx_1} = (1 - x_1)\cdot\left(-2\cdot x_1 - 4.8\cdot x_1^2\right)$

$x_1\dfrac{d(\ln \gamma_1)}{dx_1} + x_2\dfrac{d(\ln \gamma_2)}{dx_1} = 0$

This satisfies Gibbs/Duhem equation.

(*d*) $\left[\dfrac{d(\ln \gamma_1)}{dx_1}\right]_{x_1=1} = 0$

$\left[\dfrac{d(\ln \gamma_2)}{dx_1}\right]_{x_1=0} = 0$

(*e*) $\ln \gamma_1^\infty = -1.8$

$\ln \gamma_2^\infty = -2.6$

11.32 (*a*) $a = 3.448 \cdot 10^3$

$b = 3.202 \cdot 10^3$

$c = 244.615$

(*b*) $x_1 = 0.353$

$V^E_{max} = 536.294 \times 10^{-3}\ \text{cm}^3\ \text{mol}^{-1}$

11.33 $Z = 0.965$

$H^R = -348.037\ \text{J mol}^{-1}$

$S^R = -0.71\ \text{J mol}^{-1}\ \text{K}^{-1}$

11.36 (*a*) $a = -539.653$

$b = -1011$

$c = 913.122$

(*b*) $x_1 = 0.512$

$H^E_{min} = -204.401\ \text{J mol}^{-1}$

11.37 (*a*) $V = 15\,694\ \text{cm}^3\ \text{mol}^{-1}$

$H^R = -344.051\ \text{J mol}^{-1}$

$S^R = -0.727\ \text{J mol}^{-1}\ \text{K}^{-1}$

$G^R = -101.7\ \text{J mol}^{-1}$

(*b*) $V = 15\,694\ \text{cm}^3\ \text{mol}^{-1}$

$H^R = -450.322\ \text{J mol}^{-1}$

$S^R = -1.006\ \text{J mol}^{-1}\ \text{K}^{-1}$

$G^R = -125.1\ \text{J mol}^{-1}$

(*c*) $V = 24\,255\ \text{cm}^3\ \text{mol}^{-1}$

$H^R = -175.666\ \text{J mol}^{-1}$

$S^R = -0.41\ \text{J mol}^{-1}\ \text{K}^{-1}$

$G^R = -53.3\ \text{J mol}^{-1}$

(*d*) $V = 80\,972\ \text{cm}^3\ \text{mol}^{-1}$

$H^R = -36.48\ \text{J mol}^{-1}$

$S^R = -0.097\ \text{J mol}^{-1}\ \text{K}^{-1}$

$G^R = -8.1\ \text{J mol}^{-1}$

(*e*) $V = 56\,991\ \text{cm}^3\ \text{mol}^{-1}$

$H^R = -277.96\ \text{J mol}^{-1}$

$S^R = -0.647\ \text{J mol}^{-1}\ \text{K}^{-1}$

$G^R = -85.2\ \text{J mol}^{-1}$

11.38 RK EOS:

	ϕ	f bar
(a)	0.930	13.944
(b)	0.744	74.352
(c)	0.749	29.952
(d)	0.896	31.362
(e)	0.730	36.504
(f)	0.900	8.998
(g)	0.890	22.264
(h)	0.850	63.743

11.39 SRK EOS:

	ϕ	f bar
(a)	0.931	13.965
(b)	0.748	74.753
(c)	0.781	30.050
(d)	0.903	31.618
(e)	0.733	36.660
(f)	0.902	9.018
(g)	0.891	22.274
(h)	0.869	65.155

11.40 PR EOS

	ϕ	f bar	ϕ by Virial EOS
(a)	0.923	13.842	0.932
(b)	0.711	71.113	0.745
(c)	0.730	29.197	0.746
(d)	0.890	31.142	0.904
(e)	0.709	35.465	0.731
(f)	0.891	8.910	0.903
(g)	0.876	21.895	0.895
(h)	0.832	62.363	0.862

11.43 (*a*) $\dot{Q} = 0$
(*b*) $\Delta \dot{S}_t = 8.82$ W K^{-1}

11.44 (*a*) $\dot{n}_{air} = 31.646$ mol s^{-1}
$\dot{n}_{O_2} = 18.354$ mol s^{-1}
(*b*) $\dot{Q} = 0$
(*c*) $\dot{S}_G = 152.919$ W K^{-1}

11.50 $H^E_{298} = 901.242$ J mol^{-1}
$G^E_{298} = 522.394$ J mol^{-1}
$T \cdot S^E_{298} = 378.848$ J mol^{-1}

CHAPTER 12

12.1 (*a*) $A_{12} = 0.683$ $A_{21} = 0.475$
(*b*) $A'_{12} = 0.705$ $A'_{21} = 0.485$
(*c*) $\Lambda_{12} = 0.476$
$\Lambda_{21} = 1.026$
(*d*) $A_{12} = 0.758$
$A_{21} = 0.435$
(*e*) $A'_{12} = 0.83$
$A'_{21} = 0.468$
(*f*) $\Lambda_{12} = 0.348$
$\Lambda_{21} = 1.198$

12.3 (*a*) $A_{12} = 0.708$ $A_{12} = 0.69$
(*b*) $A'_{12} = 0.693$ $A'_{21} = 0.686$
(*c*) $\Lambda_{12} = 0.71$
$\Lambda_{21} = 0.681$
(*d*) $A_{12} = 0.644$
$A_{21} = 0.672$
(*e*) $A'_{12} = 0.644$
$A'_{21} = 0.672$
(*f*) $\Lambda_{12} = 0.732$
$\Lambda_{21} = 0.663$

12.6 (*a*) $A_{12} = -0.336$
$A_{21} = -0.535$
$C = 0.195$
(*d*) Consistency test shows that correlated data and experimental data match well.
(*e*) $A_{12} = -0.364$
$A_{21} = -0.521$
$C = 0.23$

12.8 (*b*) $\Lambda_{12} = 0.286$ $\Lambda_{21} = 0.534$
(*c*) High degree of consistency

12.9 (*a*) $A_{12} = 1.128$
$A_{21} = 1.155$
$C = 0.53$
(*d*) High degree of consistency
(*e*) $A_{12} = 1.114$
$A_{21} = 1.098$
$C = 0.387$

12.16 For 1-propanol(1) and water (2):
(*a*) $P_{bubl} = 31.33$ kPa
$y_1 = 0.413$
$y_2 = 0.587$
(*b*) $P_{dew} = 27.79$ kPa
$x_1 = 0.042$
$x_2 = 0.958$
(*c*) $x_1 = 0.08$ $x_2 = 0.92$
$y_1 = 0.351$ $y_2 = 0.649$
$\mathcal{V} = 0.813$
(*d*) $P^{az} = 31.511$ kPa
$x_1 = y_1 = 0.4386$

12.17 For 1-propanol(1) and water(2):
(*a*) $P_{bubl} = 31.05$ kPa
$y_1 = 0.395$
$y_2 = 0.605$
(*b*) $P_{dew} = 27.81$ kPa
$x_1 = 0.037$
$x_2 = 0.963$
(*c*) $x_1 = 0.06$ $x_2 = 0.94$
$y_1 = 0.345$ $y_2 = 0.655$
$\mathcal{V} = 0.843$
(*d*) $P^{az} = 31.18$ kPa
$x_1 = y_1 = 0.4187$

12.18 For 1-propanol(1)-water(2):

(*a*) $T_{bubl} = 361.1$ K
$y_1 = 0.418$
$y_2 = 0.582$

(*b*) $T_{dew} = 364.28$ K
$x_1 = 0.048$
$x_2 = 0.952$

(*c*) $x_1 = 0.0$ $x_2 = 0.91$
$y_1 = 0.35$ $y_2 = 0.65$
$\mathcal{V} = 0.807$

(*d*) $T_{az} = 360.88$ K
$x_1 = y_1 = 0.4546$

12.19 For 1-propanol(1)-water(2):

(*a*) $T_{bubl} = 360.84$ K
$y_1 = 0.415$
$y_2 = 0.585$

(*b*) $T_{dew} = 364.27$ K
$x_1 = 0.042$
$x_2 = 0.958$

(*c*) $x_1 = 0.069$
$x_2 = 0.931$
$y_1 = 0.352$
$y_2 = 0.648$
$\mathcal{V} = 0.816$

(*d*) $T_{az} = 360.68$ K
$x_1 = y_1 = 0.4461$

12.20 (*a*) $y_1 = 0.527$
$y_2 = 0.367$
$y_3 = 0.106$
$P_{bubl} = 117.1$ kPa

(*b*) $x_1 = 0.035$
$x_2 = 0.19$
$x_3 = 0.775$
$P_{dew} = 69.14$ kPa

(*c*) $x_1 = 0.109$ $y_1 = 0.391$
$x_2 = 0.345$ $y_2 = 0.345$
$x_3 = 0.546$ $y_3 = 0.183$
$\mathcal{V} = 0.677$

12.21 (*a*) $y_1 = 0.525$
$y_2 = 0.37$
$y_3 = 0.105$
$P_{bubl} = 115.3$ kPa

(*b*) $x_1 = 0.038$
$x_2 = 0.192$
$x_3 = 0.77$
$P_{dew} = 68.9$ kPa

(*c*) $x_1 = 0.118$ $y_1 = 0.391$
$x_2 = 0.347$ $y_2 = 0.426$
$x_3 = 0.534$ $y_3 = 0.183$
$\mathcal{V} = 0.667$

12.22 (*a*) $y_1 = 0.536$
$y_2 = 0.361$
$y_3 = 0.102$
$T_{bubl} = 334.08$ K

(*b*) $x_1 = 0.043$
$x_2 = 0.204$
$x_3 = 0.753$
$T_{dew} = 347.4$ K

(*c*) $x_1 = 0.125$ $y_1 = 0.536$
$x_2 = 0.170$ $y_2 = 0.241$
$x_3 = 0.705$ $y_3 = 0.223$
$\mathcal{V} = 0.426$

12.23 (*a*) $y_1 = 0.533$
$y_2 = 0.365$
$y_3 = 0.102$
$T_{bubl} = 334.6$ K

(*b*) $x_1 = 0.046$
$x_2 = 0.205$
$x_3 = 0.749$
$T_{dew} = 347.5$ K

(*c*) $x_1 = 0.133$ $y_1 = 0.537$
$x_2 = 0.173$ $y_2 = 0.238$
$x_3 = 0.694$ $y_3 = 0.225$
$\mathcal{V} = 0.414$

12.26 $\bar{V}_1 = 190.28$ cm^3 mol^{-1}
$\bar{V}_2 = 49.68$ cm^3 mol^{-1}

12.27 $V_{total} = 2243$ cm^3 with $\Delta\mathcal{V}$
$V_{total} = 2250$ cm^3 as ideal solution

12.28 $\Delta H = -53.55$ J mol^{-1}

12.29 $\Delta H = -39.2$ kJ

12.30 $Q = -14\,213$ kJ

12.31 $x_{LiCl} = 0.087$ mole fraction

12.32 $\Delta H = -646.905$ J

12.33 (*a*) $\Delta H = -5.1$ kJ
(*b*) $\Delta H = -0.949$ kJ
(*c*) $\Delta H = -1.472$ kJ
(*d*) $\Delta H = -2.22$ kJ
(*e*) $\Delta H = -0.561$ kJ
(*f*) $\Delta H = -0.403$ kJ

12.34 $\dot{Q} = 1830$ kW

12.35 $Q = 19.488$ kJ

12.36 $x_{LiCl} = 0.1012$ mole fraction

12.38 $Q = -63.72$ kJ

12.39 $t/T = 16.3°C/289.45$ K

12.43 $Q = -39\ 653$ kJ

12.44 $H^E = -309$ kJ kg^{-1}

12.45 (*a*) $Q = 42\ 157$ kJ
(*b*) $t/T = 74°C/347.15$ K

12.46 $Q = 21\ 670$ kJ s^{-1}

12.47 $H = -381.7$ kJ kg^{-1}

12.48 $Q = -215.4$ kJ kg^{-1}

12.49 $t/T = 48°C/321.15$ K

12.50 $m_s = 54.4$ kg
$x_2 = 0.37$ mass fraction

12.51 $m_s = 0.048$ kg
$x_2 = 0.429$ mass fraction

12.52 $t/T = 68°C/341.15$ K

12.53 $\Delta H = -239.4$ kJ kg^{-1}

12.54 $t/T = 120°C/393.15$ K

12.55 $Q = -80\ 573$ kJ

12.56 $\Delta H = -326.6$ kJ kg^{-1}
$\bar{H}_1 = -316$ kJ kg^{-1}
$\bar{H}_2 = -239$ kJ kg^{-1}

12.57 $m_{CW} = 0.354$ kg

12.58 (*a*) $Q = -11\ 607$ kJ
(*b*) $t/T = 37°C/310.15$ K

12.59 $Q = -62\ 187$ J

12.60 $Q = -14\ 049$ J

12.61 Since heat of mixing is high (exothermic), for safe mixing, water is added to acid.

12.62 $H^E = x_1x_2\left[-735.28 - 824.518x_1 + 195.199x_1^2 - 914.579x_1^3\right]$

12.64 (*a*) $\dot{m}_{CW} = 5400$ kg h^{-1}
(*b*) $\dot{Q} = -48\ 600$ kJ h^{-1}
Since $\dot{Q}$ is negative, heat is removed.
(*c*) $t/T = 74°C/347.15$ K

12.65 % Loss of organic = 15.744%

12.69 From Wilson equation:
$\ln \gamma_1^\infty = 0.613$ $\ln \gamma_2^\infty = 0.603$
From Fig. 12.9(b):
$\ln \gamma_1^\infty = 0.62$ $\ln \gamma_2^\infty = 0.61$
From NRTL equation:
$\ln \gamma_1^\infty = 0.611$ $\ln \gamma_2^\infty = 0.600$

12.71 (*a*) $y_1 = 0.743$ $P = 160.148$ kPa
(*b*) $\alpha_{12}^0 = 3.612$ $\alpha_{12}^1 = 1.175$
Since α_{12} is >1, azeotrope is not possible.

12.72 (*a*) $y_1 = 0.554$
(*b*) $P = 110.228$ kPa
(*c*) $\alpha_{12}^0 = 3.201$ $\alpha_{12}^1 = 0.826$
Since α_{12} can be unity, azeotrope is likely.

CHAPTER 13

13.4 $\varepsilon_e = 0.453\ 08$ at 1000 K

13.5 (*a*) $\varepsilon_e = 0.502$ at 1100 K
(*b*) $\varepsilon_e = 0.539\ 88$ at 1200 K
(*c*) $\varepsilon_e = 0.570\ 88$ at 1300 K

13.6 Using equilibrium constants:

Temp. K	ε
1000	0.4531
1100	0.5021
1200	0.5399
1300	0.5709

13.11 $y_{HCl} = 0.3508$ $y_{O_2} = 0.0397$
$y_{H_2O} = 0.3048$ $y_{Cl_2} = 0.3048$

13.12 $y_{N_2} = 0.4715$ $y_{C_2H_4} = 0.4715$
$y_{HCN} = 0.057$
No effect of increase in pressure

13.13 At $P = 3$ bar
$y_{CH_3CHO} = 0.108$ $y_{H_2} = 0.4053$
$y_{C_2H_5OH} = 0.4867$
At $P = 1$ bar
$y_{CH_3CHO} = 0.1968$ $y_{H_2} = 0.4645$
$y_{C_2H_5OH} = 0.3387$

13.14 $y_{C_6H_5CHCH_2} = 0.2794$
$y_{H_2} = 0.5196$ $y_{C_6H_5C_2H_5} = 0.201$

13.15 $Q = -14\,314$ J mol^{-1}

13.16 (*a*) $\varepsilon = 0.777$
(*b*) $T = 646.8$ K

13.17 $y_{C_2H_6} = 0.0899$ $y_{C_2H_4} = 0.4551$
$y_{H_2} = 0.4551$ on dry basis

13.18 (*a*) $y_{C_2H_5CHCH_2} = 0.0186$
$y_{H_2O} = 0.7814$
(*b*) $y_{steam} = 0.8682$ in feed

13.19 (*a*) $y_{C_4H_{10}} = 0.023$ $y_{H_2O} = 0.617$
(*b*) $y_{steam} = 0.812$ in feed

13.20 (*a*) $y_{NH_3} = 0.9349$
(*b*) $T = 399.5$ K
(*c*) $T = 577.6$ K
(*d*) $T = 568.6$ K

13.21 (*a*) $y_{CH_3OH} = 0.9291$
(*b*) $T = 364.47$ K
(*c*) $T = 516.48$ K
(*d*) $T = 528.7$ K

13.22 $T = 1151.83$ K

13.23 $T = 623.97$ K

13.25 $y_{NO} = 7.307 \times 10^{-12}$ or $7 \cdot 10^{-6}$ ppm

13.26 $\varepsilon = 8824$
$T = 949.23$ K

13.27 (*a*) $\varepsilon = 0.7173$
$y_{CH_4} = 0.1646$ $y_{H_2} = 0.8354$
(*b*) $\varepsilon = 0.7893$ $y_{H_2} = 0.5659$
$y_{CH_4} = 0.0756$ $y_{N_2} = 0.3585$

13.28 (1) $y_{NO} = 3.75 \times 10^{-3}$
(2) $y_{NO_2} = 4.104 \times 10^{-5}$

13.29 Percent conversion = 76.67

13.30 (*a*) $y_{N_2O_4} = 0.4241$
(*b*) $Q = 17\,021$ J mol^{-1}

13.31 $x_A = 0.3955$
$x_A = 0.4005$ as ideal solution

13.32 (*a*) No
(*b*) No
(*c*) molar ratio of steam/water gas = 4.1
(*d*) No

13.33 $y_{H_2} = 0.6606$ $y_{CO} = 0.0528$
$y_{CO_2} = 0.0539$ $y_{CH_3OH} = 0.1555$
$y_{H_2O} = 0.0116$ $y_{N_2} = 0.0655$

13.34 (*a*) No
(*b*) No
(*c*) moles H_2/moles CO ≈ 3.0
(*d*) moles H_2/moles CO = 3.638
(*e*) Add CO_2 in feed
(*f*) No

13.37 $y_{CH_4} = 0.0196$ $y_{H_2O} = 0.098$
$y_{CO} = 0.1743$ $y_{CO_2} = 0.0371$
$y_{H_2} = 0.6711$

13.39 $K = 6.018 \times 10^{12}$

13.41 (*a*) $\dot{n} = 52.632$ kmol h^{-1}
$y_C = 0.8$ $y_D = 0.05$
(*b*) $\dot{n}_A = 12$ kmol h^{-1}
$\dot{n}_B = 10$ kmol h^{-1}
$\dot{n}_C = 26$ kmol h^{-1}
$\dot{n}_D = 2$ kmol h^{-1}
(*c*) $\dot{n}_A = 50$ kmol h^{-1}
$\dot{n}_B = 25$ kmol h^{-1}
$\dot{n}_C = 37.5$ kmol h^{-1}
$\dot{n}_D = 12.5$ kmol h^{-1}
(*d*) $\dot{n}_A = 4$ kmol h^{-1} $y_A = 0.05$
$\dot{n}_B = 24$ kmol h^{-1} $y_B = 0.3$
$\dot{n}_C = 20$ kmol h^{-1} $y_C = 0.25$
$\dot{n}_D = 16$ kmol h^{-1} $y_D = 0.2$
$\dot{n}_E = 16$ kmol h^{-1} $y_E = 0.2$

13.45 (*a*) $K_{298} = 29.366$
(*b*) $K_{400} = 0.263$
(*c*) $y_{C_2H_4} = 0.447$ $y_{H_2O} = 0.447$
$y_{C_2H_5OH} = 0.105$
(*d*) Due to decrease in pressure to 1 bar, reaction will shift to left.

13.46 $\Delta G^{o}_{f298} = -105.432$ kJ mol^{-1}

13.48

$T =$	750 K	1000 K	1250 K
$y_{C_3H_8}$	0.0130	4.7×10^{-4}	6×10^{-5}
$y_{C_3H_6}$	0.0132	0.034	0.0593
y_{H_2}	0.0132	0.034	0.0593
$y_{C_2H_4}$	0.4803	0.4658	0.4407
y_{CH_4}	0.4803	0.4658	0.4407

13.49 (*a*) $y_{n\text{-}C_4H_{10}} = 0.664$
$y_{i\text{-}C_4H_{10}} = 0.336$
(*b*) $y_{n\text{-}C_4H_{10}} = 0.661$
$y_{i\text{-}C_4H_{10}} = 0.339$
Both results are nearly same. Gas phase reaction is preferred.

CHAPTER 14

14.1 (*a*) Validity of Eq. (10.5):

x_1	P_{bubl} kPa	y_1
0.25	64.533	0.562
0.50	80.357	0.731
0.75	85.701	0.808

virial coefficients:

x_1	P_{bubl} kPa	y_1
0.25	63.757	0.558
0.50	79.621	0.733
0.75	85.140	0.812

14.3 $x_1 = 0.118$

14.4 (*b*) $\mathcal{H}_1 = 51.337$ bar
$A_{12} = 0.348$
$A_{21} = 0.178$

14.5 (*b*) $\mathcal{H}_2 = 14.87$ bar
$A_{12} = 0.469$
$A_{21} = 0.279$

14.6 (*b*) $\mathcal{H}_2 = 32.065$ bar
$A_{12} = -0.731$
$A_{21} = -1.187$

14.7 (*b*) $\mathcal{H}_2 = 3.969$ bar
$A_{12} = -0.679$
$A_{21} = -1.367$

14.8 (*a*)

	Eq. (10.5)	Eq. (14.1)
A_{12}	0.374	0.379
A_{21}	0.197	0.216

14.9 RK EOS:
(*a*) For acetylene
$T_n = 189.4$ K $P^{sat} = 1.60$ bar
$T = 262.1$ K $P^{sat} = 20.27$ bar

14.10 (*a*) SRK EOS:
For acetylene
$T_n = 189.4$ K $P^{sat} = 1.073$ bar
$T = 262.1$ K $P^{sat} = 20.016$ bar
(*b*) PR EOS:
For acetylene
$T_n = 189.4$ K $P^{sat} = 1.090$ bar
$T = 262.1$ K $P^{sat} = 19.768$ bar

14.12 (*a*) $\omega = -0.302$ van der Waals equation
(*b*) $\omega = 0.058$ RK EOS

14.15 (*a*) $A_{21} = 2.747$ $A_{12} = 2.747$
(*b*) $A_{12} = 2.148$ $A_{21} = 2.781$
(*c*) $A_{12} = 2.781$ $A_{21} = 2.148$

14.16 (*a*) $A'_{12} = 2.747$ $A'_{21} = 2.747$
(*b*) $A'_{12} = 2.199$ $A'_{21} = 2.81$
(*c*) $A'_{12} = 2.81$ $A'_{21} = 2.199$

14.18 (*a*) UCST = 272.93 K
LCST = 391.21 K
(*b*) LCST = 346 K
(*c*) UCST = 339.66 K

14.20 $x_1^{\alpha} = 0.371$ $x_1^{\beta} = 0.291$

14.24

z_1	t_{dew}/T_{dew}
0.2	93.86°C/367.01 K
0.7	98.49°C/371.64 K

14.26 $x_1^{\alpha} = 0.224$ $x_1^{\beta} = 0.776$ $y_1^* = 0.405$

14.27 (*a*) $t_{dew}/T_{dew} = 66.60$°C/339.75 K
$x_2^{\alpha} = 0.294$ $x_3^{\alpha} = 0.706$
(*b*) $t_{dew}/T_{dew} = 68.44$°C/341.59 K
$x_2^{\alpha} = 0.1446$ $x_3^{\alpha} = 0.8554$
(*c*) $t_{bubl}/T_{bubl} = 48.11$°C/321.26 K
$y_2 = 0.81$ $y_3 = 0.078$

14.28 (*a*) $t_{\text{dew}}/T_{\text{dew}} = 65.12°\text{C}/338.27\ \text{K}$
$x_2^\alpha = 0.314 \quad x_3^\alpha = 0.686$
(*b*) $t_{\text{dew}}/T_{\text{dew}} = 64.3°\text{C}/337.45\ \text{K}$
$x_2^\alpha = 0.662 \quad x_3^\alpha = 0.338$
(*c*) $t_{\text{bubl}}/T_{\text{bubl}} = 43.94°\text{C}/317.09\ \text{K}$
$y_2 = 0.861 \quad y_3 = 0.049$

14.45 (*a*) $n_S/n_F = 0.9112$
(*b*) $x_2^\beta = 0.009\ 79$
(*c*) Good chemistry means species 2 and 3 like each other.

14.46 $y_1^\alpha = 1.923 \times 10^3$
$y_1^\beta = 4.997 \times 10^5$

14.50 Term-A : $A_1 = 1.081$
$A_2 = 1.108$
Term-B : $B_1 = 0.986$
$B_2 = 1.006$
Term-C : $C_1 = C_2 = 1$

14.51 (*a*) $x_1 = \dfrac{1+\sqrt{1-\frac{2}{A(T)}}}{2}$
$x_2 = \dfrac{1-\sqrt{1-\frac{2}{A(T)}}}{2}$

CHAPTER 15

15.2 (*a*) $\dot{W}_{\text{ideal}} = 14.5\ \text{kW}$
(*b*) $\dot{W}_{\text{Carnot}} = 16.198\ \text{kW}$
(*c*) $\dot{W} = 18.5\ \text{kW} \quad \eta = 0.784$
(*d*) $\dot{W} = 51.14\ \text{kW} \quad \eta = 0.284$
$\dot{W}_{\text{lost,compressor}} = 926\ \text{kW}$

15.2 (*a*) $\dot{W}_{\text{ideal}} = -259\ \text{kJ}$
(*b*) $\dot{W}_{\text{ideal.cooling}} = -208\ 904\ \text{J}$
$\eta_t = 0.8078 \quad \Delta S_\sigma = 246.93\ \text{J K}^{-1}$
Combustion reaction is irreversible.

15.3 (*a*) $\dot{m}_{\text{s}(2700)} = 0.086\ \text{kg s}^{-1}$
$\dot{m}_{\text{s}(275)} = 0.064\ \text{kg s}^{-1}$
(*b*) $\dot{m}_{\text{s}(2700)} = 0.106\ 08\ \text{kg s}^{-1}$
$\dot{m}_{\text{s}(275)} = 0.042\ 74\ \text{kg s}^{-1}$
(*c*) $\dot{W}_{\text{lost.turb}} = 2.9034\ \text{kW}\ (48.28\%)$
$\dot{W}_{\text{lost.comp.}} = 2.054\ \text{kW}\ (34.16\%)$
$\dot{W}_{\text{lost.mixing}} = 1.0561\ \text{kW}\ (17.56\%)$

15.4 $\dot{W}_{\text{ideal}} = 4.488\ \text{kW}\ (47.56\%)$
$\dot{W}_{\text{lost,comp.}} = 1.652\ \text{kW}\ (17.66\%)$
$\dot{W}_{\text{lost,throttle}} = 1.350\ \text{kW}\ (14.43\%)$
$\dot{W}_{\text{lost,evap.}} = 8.896\ \text{kW}\ (9.58\%)$
$\dot{W}_{\text{lost,cond.}} = 1.007\ \text{kW}\ (10.77\%)$

15.5

	(a)	(b)	(c)	(d)	(e)
$\dot{W}_{\text{ideal}}$ kW	51.170	55.495	53.326	48.377	48.377
$\dot{W}_{\text{lost,comp.}}$ kW	41.006	44.015	42.509	41.797	34.137
$\dot{W}_{\text{lost,cond.}}$ kW	35.446	40.916	41.080	41.897	34.668
$\dot{W}_{\text{lost,throttle}}$ kW	9.499	11.842	12.076	12.613	10.944
$\dot{W}_{\text{lost,evap.}}$ kW	41.006	44.015	42.509	41.797	34.137

15.6 $\dot{W}_{\text{ideal}} = 174.765\ \text{kW}\ (43.50\%)$
$\dot{W}_{\text{lost,comp.}} = 57.489\ \text{kW}\ (14.31\%)$
$\dot{W}_{\text{lost,cond.}} = 92.175\ \text{kW}\ (22.94\%)$
$\dot{W}_{\text{lost,throttle}} = 10.565\ \text{kW}\ (2.63\%)$
$\dot{W}_{\text{lost,evap.}} = 46.275\ \text{kW}\ (11.52\%)$
$\dot{W}_{\text{lost,exch.}} = 20.491\ \text{kW}\ (5.10\%)$

15.7 $\dot{W}_{\text{ideal}} = 8.606\ \text{kW}$
$\dot{W}_{\text{lost.evap.}} = 24.651\ \text{kW}$
$\dot{W}_{\text{lost.comp.}} = 7.41\ \text{kW}$

15.8 $\dot{Q} = 2879\ \text{kJ}$
$\dot{W}_{\text{ideal}} = 1796.9\ \text{kJ}$

15.9

	Work analysis	Entropy generation	
	kJ kg^{-1}	kJ kg^{-1}	K^{-1}
$\lvert\dot{W}_{\text{out}}\rvert$	53.20	–	–
$\dot{W}_{\text{lost,exch.1}}$	13.02	$S_{\text{G,exch.1}}$	0.044
$\dot{W}_{\text{lost,exch.2}}$	92.24	$S_{\text{G,exch.2}}$	0.313
$\dot{W}_{\text{lost,expan.}}$	46.24	$S_{\text{G,expan.}}$	0.157
$\dot{W}_{\text{lost,throttle}}$	284.30	$S_{\text{G,throttle}}$	0.964

CHAPTER 16

16.10 (*a*) For agron:

$S_G^{id} = 154.84 \text{ J mol}^{-1} \text{ K}^{-1}$ calcd.

$= 154.84 \text{ J mol}^{-1} \text{ K}^{-1}$ NIST

(*b*) For krypton:

$S_G^{id} = 164.08 \text{ J mol}^{-1} \text{ K}^{-1}$ calcd.

$= 164.05 \text{ J mol}^{-1} \text{ K}^{-1}$ NIST

(*c*) $S_G^{id} = 164.08 \text{ J mol}^{-1} \text{ K}^{-1}$ calcd.

$= 169.68 \text{ J mol}^{-1} \text{ K}^{-1}$ NIST

Name Index

Subject Index